978 07 12 11 3441

D1810908

# MANAGEMENT ACCOUNTANCY

# MANAGEMENT ACCOUNTANCY

*by*

## J. BATTY

D.Comm.(SA), M.Com.(Dunelm), A.C.W.A.,
M.I.O.M., M.B.I.M.

*THIRD EDITION*

MACDONALD AND EVANS LTD.
8 JOHN STREET, LONDON, W.C.1
1970

*First Published February 1963*
*Reprinted December 1963*
*Reprinted May 1965*
*Reprinted March 1966*
*Second Edition, July 1966*
*Reprinted December 1966*
*Reprinted August 1967*
*Third Edition, January 1970*
*Reprinted October 1970*
*Reprinted February 1971*

©

MACDONALD & EVANS LTD
1970
SBN 7121 1344 4

*By the same author:*

STANDARD COSTING
INDUSTRIAL ADMINISTRATION AND MANAGEMENT
CORPORATE PLANNING AND BUDGETARY CONTROL
MANAGERIAL STANDARD COSTING

*Printed in Great Britain by Richard Clay (The Chaucer Press), Ltd.,*
*Bungay, Suffolk*

# PREFACE TO THE FIRST EDITION

MANAGEMENT accountancy is now a wide and diverse subject. It is the blending together into a coherent whole, financial accounting, cost accounting and all aspects of financial management. The complexities which exist in this age of large scale production make *personal* supervision and calculation of profit or loss on each transaction quite impossible. More and more dependence must inevitably be placed upon information accumulated by accountants, not only for seeing what has happened, but also to predetermine *what should* happen.

Because of management's reliance upon accounting information the correct training of accountants is of vital importance. Information collected and presented to management should be in the form most suitable for solving particular problems while ensuring long-term stability and maximum profitability. From these needs management accountancy has grown.

This subject is no longer in its infancy, but neither has it reached complete maturity. Moreover, there is no universal agreement on what matters should come within the field of management accountancy. For this book the subject has been interpreted in the widest sense and includes the *procedures* for raising capital as well as reporting to shareholders—these procedures are sometimes referred to as "financial management."

One of the major problems in a work of this type is to select, and to give adequate coverage of, the topics which come within the subject. In this task I have obtained guidance from the syllabuses on management accountancy and financial management issued by a number of accountancy bodies. These are the Association of Certified and Corporate Accountants, the Institute of Chartered Accountants in England and Wales, the Institute of Cost and Works Accountants and the Society of Commercial Accountants. Past examination questions set by these bodies are included at the end of each chapter.

When answering questions on management accountancy, students should appreciate that quite often there is no *one*, perfect solution. Management accountancy is not an exact science; accountants are trained to be as objective as possible, but many facts are capable of being interpreted in many ways. Quite often the major problem facing the management accountant is to reduce the number of alternative interpretations to a minimum and to put these in a form which will assist management to the maximum possible extent.

Much of the work covered formed the basis of lectures given to students of accountancy and management. The book is intended primarily for students who are preparing for the final examinations of the accountancy bodies mentioned earlier, in the subjects of management accounting, advanced cost accounting, and financial management. However, students of management, and university students in their final year who are studying accountancy as a special subject, should find much of interest in the contents. Because of the subject's practical slant practising managers and accountants should find there is much to help them in their work of planning, controlling, and making decisions. In fact, to add to the practical value of the book the appendices include a list of the members of the Accepting Houses Committee and Issuing Houses Association, a specimen Offer for Sale, the Stock Exchange Requirements for quotations, prospectuses and accounts, and Notes on Amalgamations of British Businesses.

As indicated in previous paragraphs, the topics covered in this book are diverse. Indeed, the field is so wide that, without the assistance and guidance from others, the writing of this work would have been impossible. A list of persons, professional bodies, and companies who aided me in my research is given on page ix. My grateful thanks are offered to all of them. In addition, I would like to acknowledge the assistance given by my former colleagues at the Medway College of Technology. In particular, I would like to mention D. L. Houldridge, M.A., F.L.A., the librarian who went to great lengths to obtain research material and G. L. Brownlee, B.Sc.(Econ), A.A.C.C.A., who gave me the benefit of his experience and knowledge, particularly in connection with the problems on financial management. My wife played an indispensable part in getting the book completed and was responsible for the preparation of the typescript.

*January 1963*                                                J. BATTY

## PREFACE TO THE THIRD EDITION

VARIOUS developments have taken place since the second edition, and in so far as they affect management accountancy these have been incorporated into the text. The *Companies Act, 1967*, has made some modifications in the requirements for company reports issued to shareholders, and these have now been covered in the text. There are now two Acts— the 1948 and 1967— so any reference to the legal aspects of companies has been summarised to the "provisions of the Companies Acts," this indicating that one or both Acts contain the relevant sections.

In view of the importance of a sound depreciation policy a new chapter has been added on this subject. In addition, extra examination questions have been included in the book.

The introduction of Corporation Tax and Capital Gains Tax, which affected the financing of companies, was taken account of in the second edition. The main provisions have now been fully incorporated into the text, and, as before, I have had the guidance of Mr. J. Ellinson, B.Sc. (Econ.), A.C.A. The detailed provisions have not been included, but the Bibliography contains titles of books for further reading.

Case studies, although no longer regarded as the *only* method of teaching Management, are invaluable for seminars and discussions. Therefore additional summarised cases have been included in the chapter introduced in the previous edition.

I am extremely grateful to companies, government departments and other organisations for the assistance they give in helping to keep the text up to date. The assistance given by my colleagues at the Robert Gordon's Institute of Technology is also acknowledged—in particular John Kellock, C.A., and Renwick St. C. C. Daniel, M.A., F.C.W.A., gave their views and advice on some of the procedures as well as assisting with the reading of proofs. J. S. Adler, B.Com., prepared the Case Study entitled *Organisation and Corporate Planning*. Honeywell Ltd. kindly supplied information on Management Information Systems. I am indebted to L. P. N. McMonnies, C.A., of the Institute of Chartered Accountants of Scotland for permission to quote from an article on depreciation which appeared in *The Accountants Magazine*. Further acknowledgements will be found on pages ix and x.

*November 1969*                                                    J. BATTY

# ACKNOWLEDGMENTS

In a comprehensive work of this type an author must depend upon the generosity of others, directly or indirectly, for up-to-date information on the subject being covered. The principal sources from which I have obtained information and/or assistance are gratefully acknowledged below:

The following for permission to reproduce sections from their published accounts:

British Oxygen Company Limited.

Fisons Limited.

Tube Investments Limited.

Imperial Tobacco Company Limited.

Carreras Limited.

Federation of British Industries and the National Institute of Economic and Social Research for permission to quote from their book *Industrial Research in Manufacturing Industry, 1959–60.*

Midland Bank for information on services offered by the banks.

Council of the Stock Exchange for details of Stock Exchange Requirements.

J. Henry Schroder and Co., Ltd., for permission to reproduce the *Offer for Sale* of shares in Anderson, Boyes & Co., Ltd.

Finance Corporation for Industry Ltd., and Industrial and Commercial Finance Corporation Ltd., for details of methods of financing industry.

Board of Trade—financial aid.

Philips Electrical Company for permission to quote from the *Annual Report 1960.*

Centre for Inter-firm Comparison for details of the operation of the centre.

Society of Investment Analysts for permission to quote from their publication, *Compiling and Presenting Company Reports.*

Issuing Houses Association for permission to quote from *Notes on Amalgamations of British Businesses*, a paper which deals with the question of take-over bids.

International Computers and Tabulators Ltd., and the Owen Organisation for details of the procedures followed when installing a computer.

Credit Insurance Association Ltd., for information on credit insurance.

Export Credits Guarantee Department for details of the operations of that department.

Accepting Houses Association for details relating to accepting houses.

ix

London Trade Protection Association for details of the functioning of their organisation.

Association of Certified and Corporate Accountants for permission to reproduce past examination questions and for guidance obtained from their publications, including *The Accountant's Journal*, especially on the subjects of internal auditing and capital employed.

Institute of Chartered Accountants in England and Wales for permission to reproduce past examination papers and to quote from their *Recommendations*. In addition, permission was given by the Editor of *The Accountant* to refer to articles in that journal.

Institute of Cost and Works Accountants for permission to reproduce past examination papers and to quote from *The Cost Accountant*.

Society of Commercial Accountants for permission to reproduce past examination papers.

*The Manager:* Journal of the British Institute of Management, for permission to quote from Articles.

*Business:* Journal for Management for permission to quote from an article.

*Accountancy* for guidance on matters of principle in the field of management accountancy.

*The Daily Telegraph* for information on take-over dealings.

H. W. G. Kendall, Costing Secretary to the British Federation of Master Printers for permission to draw on an article entitled, "The B.F.M.P. Management Ratios Scheme," which appeared in *The Cost Accountant* for November, 1961.

Messrs. Ableway, Cox, Cuming, Giles, and Wardle, former colleagues at the Medway College of Technology, who assisted with the checking of the typescript and proofs.

Alan Stokes of Gillingham, Kent, who was responsible for the artwork necessary for reproduction of the break-even and profit charts.

# CONTENTS

CONTENTS

# LIST OF ILLUSTRATIONS

xv

CHAPTER 1

# INTRODUCTION

## DEFINITION; PROCESSES OF MANAGEMENT

MANAGEMENT Accountancy is the term used to describe the accounting methods, systems, and techniques which, coupled with special knowledge and ability, assist management in its task of maximising profits or minimising losses.

*Accountancy* is used instead of the narrower description *accounting*. This is quite deliberate, to indicate that the subject under review is *wide* in its sphere and application, and is not limited merely to the use of recognised principles in the *recording of information*. Management accountancy draws on many other fields of knowledge, all of which affect business efficiency.

The accounting methods, systems, and techniques are those designed to meet the specific needs of the business concerned. They should collect and record the information in the manner most suitable for assisting management in its work.

Reference is made to "special knowledge." This covers the use made of the principles and practice of Management, Economics, Law, Statistical Method, Psychology and related subjects. The management accountant has to be able to apply his knowledge of these subjects to the field of accountancy.

A clear understanding of the processes of management is essential. The relationship of each to the management accountancy functions should also be understood. There are seven major processes involved in managing:

1. *Forecasting* ⎫ deciding what should be done; *i.e.* determining policy
⎬ and formulating plans to achieve the desired ob-
2. *Planning* ⎭ jectives.

Management accountancy is able to make a valuable contribution to these processes. Sales, production, cash, and related forecasts (*see* page 53) can assist management in determining policy and making plans. Alternative courses of action can be converted into terms of costs, prices, revenues, and profits. The plan which is likely to result in the target profit can be chosen. The advisability of obtaining fresh funds will also come from the information supplied by the management accountant (Chapter 8). When making decisions management may be guided by accounting data: marginal costing and other techniques can all be utilised as a tool of management (Chapter 10). All this adds up to corporate planning and strategy, which are meaningless without management accountancy.

3. *Organising*—establishing a framework in which responsibilities are defined and lines of authority are laid down.

The total profit obtained, expressed as a percentage on capital employed, should show the effectiveness of the organisation used. However, management accountancy goes further than this in establishing a sound organisation. With its emphasis upon budget and cost centres and the location and controlling of responsibilities and costs there should emerge a more efficient business structure. Moreover, the examination of systems and procedures to make them efficient before a standard costing system can be installed can result in great benefits. The work of internal audit and organisation and methods departments can also bring increased efficiency. Keeping methods and procedures under constant review makes workers and management alert to possible improvements.

4. *Motivating*—establishing sound leadership and getting the most out of employees through a high standard of morale and co-operation.

A sound management system, backed with adequate communications, makes better managers. This, in turn, should lead to greater confidence in leadership with more effective motivation.

5. *Co-ordinating*—weaving together the segments of a business into a coherent whole in such a way that all parts operate at the most efficient level and produce maximum profit.

Production and sales must go hand-in-hand; financial resources should be adequate to meet planned requirements; material purchases should be related to current needs; planned capital expenditure and future expansion have to be co-ordinated. These are only a few examples; there are others. The essential co-ordination can come through budgetary control (*see* Chapter 3) which is an integral part of management accountancy.

6. *Controlling*—the systematic appraisal of results to ensure that actual and planned operations coincide or, if there are any deviations, the carrying out of corrective action.

Great emphasis is placed upon the control function. This is natural, because without control there can be no adherence to the plans. Management accountancy plays a principal role in controlling performances and costs. Detailed control is obtained through standard costing (*see* Chapter 2), whereas functional and departmental control comes from the operation of budgets (*see* Chapter 3). These systems incorporate the extensive use of departmental operating statements, and thereby bring about effective communication and control.

System design to cover material, labour, and overhead control comes within the scope of the management accountancy system.

Measurement of the overall effectiveness of the policies, plans, and management is provided by the Profit and Loss Account and Balance Sheet. These, too, impose a control through the shareholders, creditors, and public at large. The shareholders expect adequate dividends; creditors expect to be repaid, and the public are customers and potential investors. Decisions made by any of these groups can affect the present and future operations of a company. It must depend upon them to some extent for finance or revenue from sales. The published final accounts may be the only ambassador representing a company to a particular shareholder, creditor, or other party. For this reason alone it seems very desirable that the preparation and publication of final accounts should be just as much a part of the management accountancy function as *internal* control.

7. *Communicating*—transmitting instructions and information within the organisation and to outside customers, suppliers, and others.

Management accountancy plays an important part in the communication process. Operating results may be incorporated into reports and statements. Costs of processes and jobs emerge from the costing systems. Shareholders, creditors, and the general public are kept informed through the medium of the published accounts. Simplified accounts and balance sheets can be issued to employees to show them what measure of success is being achieved.

Information is vital to all levels of management; without it there is likely to be stagnation. The manager who is making a decision normally wants to be sure that his knowledge is complete. This is possible only through the effective presentation and interpretation of the accountancy information and its use in appropriate circumstances. Recognition of the importance of communication is stressed by the development of Management Information Systems in many companies.

These definitions of the management processes have been kept as brief as possible. Nevertheless, they should show how management accountancy and the management functions are very much related. Indeed, it is possible to go further and say that management accountancy is an integral part of business management. In all phases of the latter decisions have to be made and, although these necessarily involve intuition, experience, and judgment, all these processes are assisted in a material fashion by facts relating to costs, prices, and the economic environment.

The management accountant draws on the subject of Economics for guidance on how prices and interest rates are determined; why finance is difficult or relatively simple to obtain, and why other phenomena behave in a certain way: in short, for information on the mechanism of the economy. Determination of optimum output, the fact that capital invested has to be used in the most effective manner and the concept of maintaining capital intact in real terms, are all aspects which have received beneficial contributions from economists. There is no doubt that many more benefits can emerge from the co-operation of accountants and economists, particularly when the latter are employed in industry on forecasting sales and other trends.

The legal aspects of business are also a part of the management accountancy framework. There must be compliance with statutory requirements so far as they affect business decisions. The raising of finance is affected by the *Companies Acts*, 1948 and 1967, and the regulations of the Stock Exchange. What form the published accounts should take is also dictated by the Companies Acts, as is also the question of the duties of the external auditor. So far as the objectives of a company are concerned, no action should be taken which is *ultra vires* of the Memorandum or Articles of Association.

Full use should be made of the techniques of statistical method. Graphs, charts, and pictorial representation all assist in making information clearer and easier to assimilate. The fact that information should be edited to suit the needs of each specific problem has long since been recognised in the theory of statistical method and is one of the major principles of management accountancy. Division of overhead costs into their fixed and variable elements is accomplished by the use of regression charts and the application of least squares, both of which belong to the field of statistical method. The separation of costs in this way is an indispensable part of a system of marginal costing. Operational research, the collection of data and their application to solving business problems, owes much of its modern state to the work of statisticians.* Again, use is made of this technique—often in a simplified form—in management accountancy.

Psychology enters into the processes of control, communication, and motivation. The control being exercised is not purely of costs, but rather of the *actions* of people who are responsible for costs. This fact is often overlooked, with a resultant deterioration in worker–management relationships. Cost control is necessarily a human problem, and the most suitable methods of presenting the facts should be employed so that antagonism is avoided.

## FRAMEWORK OF MANAGEMENT ACCOUNTANCY

In the previous section the use made of various disciplines within the framework of management accountancy is outlined. These subjects, together with the techniques of Cost Accounting, Financial Accounting, and Budgetary Control, form the structure of management accountancy.

* The reference here is to the mathematical techniques employed. Engineers and cost accountants have used the basic idea of collecting data and then employing them as an aid in making decisions for many years. The birth of a *new* discipline has occurred principally because of the growth of linear programming and other techniques which have been aided by the development and use of computers in industry.

What is essential is the total *integration* of systems, procedures, form designing, and related matters into a complete, co-ordinated system.

Information is collected and recorded for many purposes. A common practice is to separate the different purposes into distinct groups in such a way that each is dealt with by different departments. Financial accounting is the responsibility of one person, cost accounting the responsibility of another, and statistical method under the direction of someone else. Each works within a narrow field, producing the facts and figures that policy decrees he should produce. Often the same information is recorded two or three times in some slightly different form. Financial accountants think in terms of personal accounts, real accounts and nominal accounts. (The latter meaning that the records are classified according to the type of expense; *e.g.* rent account, lighting account, insurance account, and so on.) On the other hand, cost accountants, because of their own problems and the methods of dealing with them, use a different classification. The emphasis is on the tracing of responsibility for costs, and this favours the analysis of costs according to their nature; in particular, whether they are direct or indirect costs (*see* Chapter 2).

Specialisation, with its resultant benefits, has tended to bring about this separation of work into what appear to be different categories. Unless carried too far, there is nothing wrong with this specialisation. What should be recognised is the need to improve the control and co-ordination of the different sections dealing with management information. All the management accountancy functions should operate within an integrated system, avoiding unnecessary duplication of effort. Only then can it be said that a business is truly employing management accountancy in its fullest sense.

There should be appreciation of the fact that management accountancy is more than a collection of procedures into a complete system. There must be acceptance by top management of all the principles involved. Furthermore, the backing of this same management is essential; if difficulties are experienced in installation or operation, then the necessary authority should be equal to the responsibilities involved. There is nothing new in this principle. Management theory recognises that authority and responsibility should run together.

The accountant himself has to get away from the idea that his task involves the recording of *historical* costs and nothing more. Historical costs are essential for showing what expenditure has been incurred, but by themselves they do not reveal the state of efficiency. Standards of performance which reflect the expected state of efficiency are essential; these can be employed for comparing with actual performances. This is the basis of standard costing and budgetary control systems.

There should be recognition that accounting data can be useful to people other than accountants. This will mean modification and adaptation of some of the older ideas on accountancy. Too much emphasis upon "balancing the books" without trying to make full use of the figures for improving efficiency is a common failure of an accounting system. The management accountant has to use imagination and resourcefulness to produce information which informs and is useful. What is more, this information should be ready at the time when it is likely to be of maximum value. This does not mean that *all* figures should be available immediately—the cost of achieving this end would tend to be prohibitive. The purpose in mind, and therefore the value of the information, should have a direct bearing upon the speed with which details are produced.

### PRINCIPAL SYSTEMS AND TECHNIQUES

There are many financial and cost accounting systems contained in the management accountancy framework. These are covered in some detail in subsequent chapters. Here a summary is given:

### 1. *Financial Policy and Accounting*

Financial policy determines how a business is to be financed, whether by Equity or Preference Share capital, and the extent to which reliance is to be placed upon long-term or short-term borrowing. In addition, the credit and discount policies to be followed have to be determined.

Public companies have a duty to publish accounts which comply with the requirements of the Companies Acts. These are intended primarily to safeguard creditors and shareholders.

### 2. *Historical Cost Accounting*

Historical cost accounting is so called because it concerns itself with the recording of actual costs on or after the date when these are incurred. There are two basic costing systems—job costing and process costing. Actual costs are an essential part of the most modern Standard Costing system, but by themselves they are of very limited value.

### 3. *Standard Costing*

Standard Costing is a technique which uses predetermined standard costs and controls through variances. It is the most effective method available for controlling performances and costs.

### 4. *Marginal Costing*

The most important feature of Marginal Costing is the division of costs into those which are marginal (variable) and those which are fixed. The latter are not apportioned to cost centres or products as under an orthodox costing system; instead, they are charged against sales revenues within the period in which they are incurred. This division of the costs and their application in an appropriate manner is extremely useful in showing management the effect of decisions, particularly those connected with short-term utilisation of production capacity.

## 5. *Budgetary Control*

Budgetary Control shows policy and plans in financial terms, thereby establishing responsibilities by means of budgets, and co-ordinating and controlling through the budget committee and suitably drafted departmental operating statements and reports (*see* Chapter 3).

## 6. *Decision Accounting*

The comparison of alternative courses of action may be facilitated by the use of cost data. The latter may be collected as part of a routine or to deal with a special problem when it arises (an *ad hoc* investigation). Strictly speaking, this is not a separate system. It calls upon all other systems to produce information which indicates to management the project likely to maximise profit or minimise loss. Decisions on capital expenditure, whether to make or buy, what price to charge, whether to subcontract, and other important matters, may all be assisted by the employment of accounting information. A few words on the role of decision-making are very appropriate at this stage.

One of the most important functions of top management is to make decisions. Irrespective of the method employed, decision-making implies a choice from a number of alternatives. In fact, there are two basic selections. First, there is the selection of the particular field in which the final decision is to be made: if production is to be increased, then the labour force may be enlarged or new machines may be introduced; if sales are to be expanded, then the initial choice is between employing more salesmen or intensifying the advertising or other sales publicity. Once an initial selection has been made, the second choice must follow; if machinery is to be purchased the question is: what type of machinery?

The comparison of alternatives may be done deliberately, in which case, to reduce uncertainty to a minimum, the use of figures is essential. How each alternative may affect output, costs or other important factors, and finally profit, has to be determined.

Another approach to decision-making is by the trial-and-error method. A decision is made intuitively and plans are put into operation. After a time, when the effects of a decision are becoming known, action may be necessary to improve the situation. So the procedure goes on: a trial is made and, if there is an apparent error, corrective action is taken. Intuition may again be used to decide the necessity for further action. When dealing with complex issues—commonplace in a large company—there are only a few men who can emerge successfully from the use of intuitive methods alone. Some men are able to analyse a situation, and know which way to go in order to improve the position. However, at times this can be rather like driving a car on a dark road without the aid of lights; one wrong move and the outcome can be serious. Without facts and figures relating to the problem in hand there is great danger that an important fact may be omitted from the reasoning, with disastrous results.

When making decisions, management should consider the risks involved, and if the extent of the risks is calculable, the advisability of insurance coverage should be considered. The accountant is in the best position to assess whether insurance should be obtained.

### 7. Control Accounting

Again this is not strictly a separate accounting system. Standard costing and budgetary control have within them their own control mechanisms—variance analysis, reports and statements, and the stimulation of action.

In addition, there is the control afforded by internal check, internal audit, statutory audit, and organisation and methods work.

It is in this field that the management accountant has scope to display ingenuity in the analysis, interpretation, and presentation of information to all levels of management.

### 8. Revaluation Accounting

Revaluation or replacement value accounting is concerned with ensuring that capital is maintained intact in real terms and profit is calculated with this fact in mind.

### 9. Management Information Systems

With the introduction of electronic data processing and computer systems there has been considerable development in thought on Management Information Systems. These integrate all sub-systems within the individual business so that information is available on all aspects of planning, co-ordination and control. Much more has to be done before fully comprehensive systems are available which begin with the defining of company objectives and go on to give detailed plans and then likely consequences. Subsequently, control is exercised through a systematic approach which incorporates "feedback" and responsive action from managers.

Within the framework of management accountancy these nine functions should operate in an integrated fashion. In the exercise of his duties the management accountant will operate and co-ordinate each aspect, being guided in the way matters are dealt with by the principles which have been developed by the accountancy profession. These principles are known as accountancy conventions.

## CONVENTIONS OF MANAGEMENT ACCOUNTANCY

Over the years many conventions of accounting have been developed. These relate to both financial and cost accounting. Here they are all taken together as the "rules of the game" of management accountancy.

They are the foundation stones upon which any accounting system should be built; in addition, they are the guide-posts to sound practice. If the management accountant ignores these conventions he fails in his duties; his work will tend to be less effective and he will certainly be out of step with his profession. For convenience the conventions are summarised as follows:

1. Accounting concerns itself with the *affairs of the business.*

This means that the accountant is concerned with recording the transactions relating to the business and not to persons as individuals.

2. Costs and revenues should be *matched* as far as possible.

This is not easy to follow. How are advertising costs to be matched against sales revenues? What proportion of fixed assets (depreciation) should be written off each year? These and other questions have to be answered satisfactorily; otherwise the calculation of profit is unrealistic and not as accurate as it should be. There can be no absolute accuracy: the arbitrary division of the life of a business into accounting years makes approximation inevitable. The management accountant has to endeavour to match costs and revenues in the best possible manner and thereby avoid a serious mis-statement of profit.

3. The calculation of profit should *allow* for all possible *losses* and *disregard* any unrealised *gains.*

This rule generally means that profit is shown at a lower rather than a higher figure. This tendency to adopt the most conservative attitude means that there is no danger of more profit than that really earned being taken out of the business as dividends. Moreover, the *rate* of profit on capital employed tends to be lower, and management is not beguiled into thinking that efficiency is on a higher plane than is really the case.

4. Only profits which have been actually *realised* are recognised (linked with 3).

Put in other words, only when a sale has been completed can it be said that a profit has been earned. If goods have not been sold there can be no profit. Any stocks held should not be valued at a figure which is greater than cost or other acceptable valuation (*see* Chapter 25, "Stock Valuation"). However, an important exception is maturing stocks, such as wine, timber, whisky, and other commodities which have to be held for a number of years before being sold. Another variation from the general rule is where there is a large contract or job which takes many years to complete. In both cases it may be permissible to anticipate a profit for each year. As is usual though, there will be conservatism displayed in estimating the figure. Two-thirds of the expected figure may be taken, thereby making due allowance for any possible fall in value of the stocks or the contract.

5. *Consistency* in methods procedures and principles employed.

There are at least two good reasons why consistency is essential. The first is that management is concerned with seeing the state of efficiency and trend of results. If methods are changed there will be difficulty experienced in deciding what the comparisons of results, from period to period, really mean. In fact, if methods are changed too frequently, or if a *single* change is made of an important method, the results shown before and after the change may be quite incapable of being validly compared. The second reason, linked with the first, is the need to calculate profit in a manner which shows the true operating results of the accounting year. Changing a basis of accounting is one way of "window dressing" the profit. Thus, for example, a change in the method of valuing work-in-progress or raw materials has the effect of varying the method of calculating the profit.

Consistency is also essential for the normal day-by-day control through departmental managers. If methods are changed too frequently there can be no faith in the results obtained. Any deviations from normal efficiency are unlikely to be given the attention they deserve. Departmental managers, foremen, and others may tend to regard the figures as a reflection of the accountant's manipulative talents, rather than showing the true state of affairs.

6. In cost accounting only the *normal* costs should be treated as the costs of producing, selling, and distributing.

This means that expenditure has to be divided into: (*a*) normal costs, and (*b*) abnormal or exceptional costs. The latter are written off to Costing Profit and Loss Account. Examples are: the costs of idle facilities due to a recession; loss due to obsolescence where this is unusual; loss incurred due to holding stocks of materials when there is a drastic fall in prices.

The purpose of this convention is to show costs of products which reflect normal, realistic conditions. In this way the efficiency of producing and selling is portrayed in the product costs.

7. The accounting records are kept as *objective* as possible.

This rule also applies to accounting reports and statements. Both the records and the reports should be based on objective facts and evidence and not affected by personal, biased opinions. The management accountant should ensure that the figures recorded and presented to management are free from prejudice and can be interpreted correctly without undue difficulty.

In addition to the conventions given above, which are accepted generally throughout the accountancy profession, the following additional conventions are now regarded as an essential part of management accountancy. Not all these enjoy *general* acceptance, but there seems no doubt that this condition is not far away.

8. Accounting information, records, reports, statements, and other evidence of past, present, or future results should be designed and compiled to meet the needs of the particular business and/or specific problem.

This implies a certain flexibility of system. When a particular problem is to be solved the system should be capable of producing the relevant data. If necessary, there must be departure from double-entry principles. Accounting and operational-research principles should be linked together. Information should be accumulated and then presented to solve problems. The accounting information should be modified and adapted to meet *each need* whenever possible. However, it is important to remember that if this principle is carried too far the cost of the management accountancy system may become excessive. It is partly for this reason that a systematic, rather than an *ad hoc* method, is used for accumulating costing data.

9. The "principle of exception" is followed when presenting information to management.

This assumes that plans are *predetermined* and then actual results are compared with expected results. If there are no deviations there is no necessity to report. When there are variations from predetermined plans management is *informed* precisely of what is going wrong. In this way, the information presented to management is kept to the minimum, yet at the same time all important facts are being revealed. What is more, management has less to read and study and, therefore, should have more time to take action.

10. Costs are best controlled at the points at which they are incurred—"Control-at-source accounting."

Recognition of this convention is acknowledged through the preparation of departmental operating statements and the design of costing systems which control individual workers, material issues, and the usage of services. The inculcation of cost consciousness is also an essential part of this convention.

11. A profit cannot be said to be earned unless capital is *maintained intact in real terms.*

This convention recognises that the monetary unit is not stable. Attempts to overcome the effects of changes in the value of money have been made via revaluation accounting, but as yet there is no *general* acceptance of the theory. However, there is strong evidence that more and more accountants are modifying their views to meet the dynamic state of business and the economy.

To some extent the reluctance to accept complete revaluation accounting principles is no doubt due to the convention which decrees objectivity ((7) above). Historical costs are the costs that have actually been incurred; they are *fact*, not conjecture. Revaluation accounting (discussed in Chapter 27) introduces estimates and opinions and—so the argument runs—is undesirable. There is no denying these facts. However, management accountancy must meet the needs of the times: if there is inflation, it cannot be ignored. Management cannot afford to ignore *any* conditions which affect the profit-earning capacity of the business. In other words, the accounting system must serve management, and if a convention threatens to shackle progress, then it should be modified.

12. Return on capital employed is used as the criterion for measuring the efficiency of the business. For this purpose the capital employed should be calculated by reference to current replacement values (*see* Chapter 27).

13. Management accounting systems and related forms should be used only as long as they serve a useful purpose.

14. There should be *integration* of all management information, so that fullest use is made of the facts available and, at the same time, the accounting service should be provided at minimum cost.

15. Overhead costs should be apportioned to cost centres and recovered by products on the *basis of benefits received for fixed costs or responsibilities incurred for variable costs.* The method or methods selected should bring about the desired result of recovering the overheads in the most equitable manner. However, this is subject to what is stated on this matter in Chapter 10 on Marginal Costing.

16. Management accountancy should endeavour to show whether or not the resources of the business are being utilised in the most effective manner (*see* Chapter 15, "Return on Capital Employed," p. 381).

17. When tracing responsibility a clear distinction should be made between those costs which are controllable and those which are uncontrollable by the management of the business or department concerned.

18. Management accountancy should seek to anticipate problems and prevent them. There should be a *forward-looking approach*, and actual costs should be employed only as measures of achievements realised. This principle recognises the importance of budgetary control and standard costing.

19. The *most appropriate means* of accumulating, recording, and presenting the accountancy information should be selected.

This normally implies that mechanisation should be adopted as much as possible. It does *not* mean that every business should employ a computer. The machines selected should be of a size and type that can economically be employed by the particular concern to deal with its own problems. If there is insufficient work for a computer, then clearly this should not be acquired.

20. *Personal contact* with departmental managers, foremen, and others cannot be replaced entirely by reports and statements.

This convention recognises once more that cost control involves people. Furthermore, planning, co-ordination, motivation, and communication are all improved by maintaining personal contact. Quite often this essential condition is secured through budget, cost reduction, and other committees. Obviously, though, because of the time-consuming aspect of attending committees, the number of these has to be kept to reasonable dimensions. Accordingly, personal contact with production, sales, and other functional personnel by means other than committees will be essential. Works accountants, cost accountants, and cost clerks should all participate in this liaison: it should not be left simply to the chief management accountant.

## ORGANISATION FOR MANAGEMENT ACCOUNTANCY

The organisation of the management accountancy system should be designed for the particular business. It should be capable of providing the information required for all levels of management in order to achieve maximum efficiency.

A typical Organisation Chart for a large organisation is shown below (Fig. 1). This illustrates the principles involved in achieving the necessary control and co-ordination of all functions through the Chief Management Accountant. In practice, many variations will be found. Furthermore, if a company is divisionalised, having factories in different locations, an extension of the chart would be necessary to show how each division fits into the general pattern. Possibly the necessary link would come through a works accountant being located within each division.

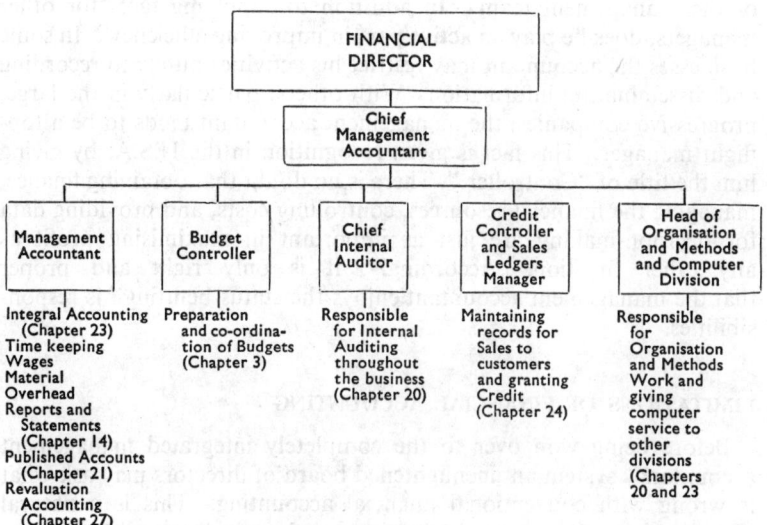

FIG. 1.—*Organisation for Management Accountancy*

## THE MANAGEMENT ACCOUNTANT'S RESPONSIBILITY

In discussions on management accountancy a question which often arises is the management accountant's responsibility for decisions made on the basis of accounting information. If a wrong decision is made, who is responsible—the manager to whom the information was supplied and who made the particular decision *or* the accountant?

The answer to this question depends upon the circumstances. If the management accountant supplies facts which are as accurate as possible and are presented in a manner which allows proper interpretation, then he cannot be held responsible for any error of judgment. On the other hand, if the information is inaccurate, biased, and misleading, then the blame for a wrong decision may rest on the shoulders of the accountant.

Another matter which has received attention is whether or not the management accountant is a manager. Why this question should be raised is hard to imagine. The same question could be posed in respect of any functional executive, whether he is a production engineer, purchasing officer, sales manager, or other responsible official. A functional executive is necessarily the manager of his own department. He controls the work of others and is responsible for a particular function.

Whether the management accountant is a manager in the wider sense depends upon his status within the organisation. Does he take part in planning operations and decision-making? Is he an important member of the management team? In addition to supplying facts for other managers, does he play an active part in improving efficiency? In some businesses the accountant may restrict his activities purely to recording and disseminating information. With others, particularly in the large, progressive companies, the management accountant tends to be a top-flight manager. This fact is given recognition in the U.S.A. by giving him the title of "Controller." There is no doubt that obtaining finance, managing the financial resources, controlling costs, and providing data for decision-making are just as important in maximising profit as any other function. Accordingly, it is only right and proper that the management accountant enjoys the status befitting his responsibilities.

## LIMITATIONS OF FINANCIAL ACCOUNTING

Before being won over to the completely integrated management accountancy system an unenlightened board of directors may ask what is wrong with conventional financial accounting. This is a natural response from those who do not have a clear understanding of what financial accounting seeks to achieve. For this reason an outline of its broad functions and limitations is advisable.

Financial accounting records business transactions in a manner which allows the values of assets and liabilities to be ascertained. In addition, expenses and revenues are accumulated and from time to time, normally at least once a year, the profit or loss is calculated.

Generally the *actual* cost expended in obtaining a service, commodity, material, or asset is the one used for recording the transactions. The effects of changes in prices of services, commodities, and materials, whether to be purchased in the future or already acquired, are largely ignored. The view normally taken is that amounts spent or to be spent are recorded, but the effects of spending at one time rather than another, or the problem of the maintenance of the assets in terms of equivalent purchasing power, are matters of conjecture and cannot, therefore, be recorded. There is no doubt that a sum of money spent is an indisputable fact which cannot be changed. However, to assume that the historical values reflect the true position for all times is to ignore changes in conditions and the value of money. The business, and the economy in which it operates, is dynamic in nature, and this fact should be recognised by the accountant.

So far as the needs of management are concerned, legal requirements, including those relating to taxation, have tended to cloud the issue. Protection of creditors and shareholders and calculation of profit figures acceptable to the Commissioners of Inland Revenue have tended to be the criteria used for determining the correct methods to employ for recording and drafting accounts. The annual Profit and Loss Account and Balance Sheet have been an end in themselves, even though the story they tell is already out of date and is past history. For managerial purposes the static picture is of limited value. It is an accepted principle that the past is often of little or no guide to the future; yet the latter is the main concern of management, and therefore some aid, other than the conventional financial accounts, is essential.

The financial accounts portray a broad, overall picture of events that have taken place over a period of time—usually a year. Attempts have been made to overcome the disadvantage of the time lag by more frequent presentation, such as once a month. This is a step in the right direction, but all too often the actual presentation is delayed two or three weeks after the month-end, so that, once more, the facts are very much out of date.

Even when presented promptly, the conventional financial accounts cannot do more than show the overall result of a period's trading. The cost of each product or job cannot be obtained from the accounts. Neither is it possible to see the cost of operating each producing and service cost centre. The effectiveness of cost control, storekeeping, material utilisation, and labour employment are other important facts which are not revealed.

Information on alternative courses of action, so vital for assisting in formulating plans and making decisions, must come from cost accounting and analysis. Management *has* to be concerned with detail, with plans and their achievement. The financial accounts will not show what part of the plan is going wrong or, possibly, that it *is* going wrong.

In the following chapters, outlines of the many modern techniques of management accountancy are given.

B

## EXAMINATION QUESTIONS

1. The Productivity Report *Management Accounting* included the following recommendation:

"That top management should make use of standards of performance and of accounting control techniques to enable it to decentralise responsibility, and that all standards of performance should be agreed with those who are to work to them."

Explain the steps you would take, as cost accountant in a large factory, to implement this recommendation. (*I.C.W.A.*)

2. Explain the term "Management Accounting" and state what you understand to be its main objectives. (*S.C.A.*)

3. A management accounting system is not restricted to the large organisation. Outline the steps you would take in installing such a system in a small business.

*Note:* In this context small can be taken as employing less than 100 people. (*A.C.C.A.*)

4. One of the criticisms frequently levelled at industrial management is that although control systems are introduced into manufacturing units, these controls are rarely integrated with one another. If one accepts that the main controls required are of output, its quality and cost, what contributions would you, as management accountant, make towards integration of cost control techniques with production control and quality control? (*I.C.W.A.*)

5. A manufacturing company is operating a system of cost-finding for products. What changes are necessary to establish a comprehensive system of budgetary control and standard costing? (*I.C.W.A.*)

# CHAPTER 2

## OUTLINE OF COST ACCOUNTING

As the previous chapter shows, a major part of management accountancy is concerned with cost accounting. This is hardly surprising; the classification, collection, and analysis of costs, principal features of cost accounting, are essential to management planning and control. The installation of appropriate systems for controlling the purchase and use of materials, the effective utilisation of labour, and obtaining and using services are also part of the field of cost accounting.* Another function is obviously the ascertainment of costs of jobs, products, processes, cost centres, and other divisions of a business. In addition, the predetermination of costs (standard costing and budgetary control†); and the analysis and arrangement of costs in a manner suitable for aiding management to make decisions or for cost control are all aspects which are dealt with by the cost accountant. In short, cost accounting is a wide and diverse field of activity.

It is possible to distinguish between two techniques of recording costs and approaching costing problems. There is *historical costing*, which is concerned with recording actual costs when or after such costs have been incurred. Actual costs are an essential part of any costing system, but because they portray only what has happened and not what *should have happened*, by themselves they are not a realistic means of measuring efficiency. Instead they are used whenever possible in conjunction with the second principal technique—*standard costing*, which is dealt with later in this chapter. The distinction between historical costing and predetermined costing is extremely important, because only when job costing is being employed, when jobs are entirely non-repetitive, will a modern system be based purely on historical costs. If standard costing is not a practical proposition, then the control of costs may come through budgetary control (introduced in Chapter 3).

## COSTING SYSTEMS

### JOB COSTING

Job costing is mentioned in the previous paragraph. It is the system of costing used when non-standard jobs are made to customers' specifications. Contractors, general engineering factories, shipbuilders, and

---

* In a large company part of this function may be performed by an Organisation and Methods Department.

† Budgetary control is very much a part of the cost accountant's work, but there seems to be a convention followed which treats it as a subject which is separate from cost accounting. Since costs are classified in the same manner as in cost accounting, there seems no logical reason for its treatment as an entirely distinct technique or system. Management accountancy recognises the vital inter-relationship which should exist between budgetary control and cost accounting.

furniture manufacturers are just a few of the many businesses which employ job costing. Because each order is different, all costs incurred on an individual job are booked to a cost sheet reserved for that job (Fig. 2).

## JOB COST SHEET

**Description** ..........................　　**Job No.** ...........................

..............................................

**Date Commenced** ..................　　**Date Completed** ..............

| Date | Ref. | Details | Material £ | Labour £ | Overhead £ |
|------|------|---------|------------|----------|------------|
|      |      |         |            |          |            |
|      |      |         |            |          |            |
|      |      |         |            |          |            |
|      |      |         |            |          |            |

*Summary*　　　　　　　　　　£
　　Material ...　　...　　...　　　　Customer ...........................
　　Labour ...　　...　　...
　　Overhead　　...　　...　　　　...........................................

　　Total Factory Cost　...　　　　Price Obtained　　... £
　　*Add* Selling and
　　　　　Distribution ...　　　　Profit/Loss　...　　... £
　　*Add* Administration ...

　　　　　　　£

FIG. 2.—*Job Cost Sheet*

Very briefly, the procedures involved in job costing may be as follows:

　　1. An enquiry is received from a customer.

　　2. The costs expected to be involved for the job in question are estimated. These form the basis of the price quoted.

　　3. If a firm order is received for the job, a production order is completed.

4. Once a job has been commenced the tracing of the following costs is essential—

(a) Direct material costs—authorised and traced by Material Requisitions.

(b) Direct labour costs—controlled and traced by the use of Job Clock Cards.

(c) Factory overhead costs—absorbed by the use of pre-determined, normal overhead rates.*

(d) Selling, distribution, and administration costs are added to total factory costs, possibly on the basis of a standard percentage.

5. A Cost Ledger or Integrated Ledger as described in Chapter 23 is maintained.

6. As each job is completed, the total cost and price obtained are compared and the profit earned or loss incurred is ascertained.

Various summaries or abstracts are employed to classify and analyse the costs for posting to Cost Sheets, Stores Ledger, and the Cost or Integrated Ledger. Reference is made to using predetermined overhead rates. These allow Job Cost Sheets to be completed as early as possible, thereby allowing management to see what has happened in terms of profitability as early as possible. In addition, they tend to eliminate wide fluctuations in the overhead rate. Unfortunately, these benefits are offset to some extent by the inevitable emergence of under- or over-absorption of overhead costs. These have to be disposed of via the Profit and Loss Account or by adjustment of Work-in-progress, Cost of Sales and Finished Goods Accounts. Sometimes supplementary overhead rates are employed as a means of adjusting a large under- or over-absorption of overhead costs.

Because of the nature of special-order industries, it will be essential to employ special-order (job) costing. However, if elements of jobs are repetitive and capable of being standardised the predetermination of Standard Costs for such elements becomes possible and advisable. This allows a higher standard of efficiency to be achieved, and cost control is greatly facilitated. When each job is entirely different, cost control† *in detail* is difficult to carry out, and therefore the fullest use should be made of the wider form of control afforded by a budgetary control system.

There is no doubt that job costing in its pure form can be expensive to operate in terms of accounting and clerical costs. If it has to be employed the fullest use should be made in the production control system of the labour and machine times accumulated. Moreover, in the

---

* These are not to be confused with Standard Overhead Costs. Predetermined overhead costs for job costs are based on an estimate of what *actual* costs *will be*. Standard Costing attempts to show what they *should be* for clearly defined conditions and circumstances.

† What is meant by "cost control" is covered in Chapter 14.

large concern there will be a necessity to introduce a suitable form of machine accounting, which should be linked with appropriate control systems for material, labour, and overhead costs. Obviously, in the absence of predetermined standard costs there will be no suitable measures against which to compare the actual performances, and this fact has to be appreciated from the start. There will be no previous actual costs, because each job is quite different; there should be the estimated costs obtained to calculate a price for the quotation and, while these will tend to contain inefficiencies, provided they have been carefully compiled they are clearly better than nothing. Although comparison of actual and estimated costs does not permit adequate control, it should allow a form of profit control for each individual job. Management can see what gain or loss results from each order obtained. The control may be facilitated by incorporating marginal costing (defined in Chapter 10) into the job costing system.

## PROCESS COSTING

Process costing is the second principal method of cost accounting. It is generally employed when a standard product is being made which involves a number of distinct processes performed in a definite sequence. In oil refining, chemical manufacture, paper making, flour milling, and cement manufacturing, as well as many other industries, this method is used. The object is to trace and record costs for each distinct stage. Here the concern is not with finding the costs for individual units as in job costing, but with obtaining the average cost per unit for each accounting period. Often by-products or joint products are produced and these have to be considered when calculating the average cost per unit.

The total time spent and materials used on each process, as well as services such as power, light, and heating, are all charged. For this purpose a Process Cost Sheet may be employed (Fig. 3).

The Process Cost Sheet is a summary of all operations for the month. The current operating charges are entered on the sheet showing:

1. The transfer cost from the previous operation.
2. The costs incurred by each operation showing material, labour, and overhead in separate columns.

This separation of transfer costs and conversion cost is extremely important, for the charges incurred by a department are its measure of efficiency. These are the responsibility of the head of the department, so it is readily apparent what has been incurred within that department and the cost is not distorted by charging costs in previous processes.

The sheet can be used as a basis for:

(a) Closing entries at the end of each month.
(b) Operating statements, without need to look up the ledger accounts.

**PROCESS COST SHEET**

Accounting Period ........................

| Date | Ref. | Mat. | Labour | O/head | Cost Centre No. 1 | | | Cost Centre No. 2 | | |
|------|------|------|--------|--------|------|------|--------|------|------|--------|
| | | | | | Mat. | Lab. | O/head | Mat. | Lab. | O/head |
| | | | | | | | | | | |
| | | | | | | | | | | |

| Summary | | | | Production | |
|---------|---|---|---|------------|---|
| Dept. No. 1 | £ | £ | | No. of Units | |
| Materials | xxx | | | | |
| Labour | xxx | | | Cost per Unit | £ |
| Overhead | xxx | xxx | | | |
| | | | | | |
| Dept. No. 2 | | | | | |
| Materials | xxx | | | | |
| Labour | xxx | | | | |
| Overhead | xxx | xxx | | | |
| | | £xxx | | | |

FIG. 3.—*Process Cost Sheet*

Within the Cost Ledger an account is kept for each process. The direct material, direct labour, and factory overhead costs are transferred from the Process Cost Sheet. These are debited to the process account, and then any completed units are credited to cover the transfer to the next process. The balance on the account represents the work-in-progress at the end of the period, which, of course, becomes the opening balance for the *next* period. An example of a process account is as follows:

*Process Account I*

| | £ | | £ |
|---|---|---|---|
| To Direct material | 400 | By Transfer to | |
| „ Direct labour | 300 | Process II | 1,100 |
| „ Factory overhead | 600 | „ Balance c/d | 200 |
| | £1,300 | | £1,300 |
| To Balance b/d | £200 | | |

The units involved in each process may also be shown.

Because of the repetitive, standardised nature of the processes, units produced, and conditions, it is possible to employ standard costing to its fullest extent. Calculation and analysis of cost variances allows costs to be controlled, and the yield variances show the efficiency obtained in converting the raw materials to the finished product.

## HYBRID COSTING SYSTEMS

Many costing systems do not fall neatly into the category of either job costing or process costing. Often systems use some features of both main costing systems. Many engineering companies use *batch costing*, which treats each batch of components as a job and then finds the average cost of a single unit. Another variation is *multiple costing*, used when many different finished products are made. Many components are made which are subsequently assembled into the completed article, which may be cycles, cars, or other products of a complex nature. Costs have to be ascertained for operations, processes, units, and jobs, building together until the total cost is found.

Different names may be used to describe either process costing or job costing. Thus, for example, *unit costing* is the name given to the system where there is a natural unit, such as a sack of flour, a hundredweight of cement, or a barrel of beer. *Operation costing* is a variation of unit costing, and is used when production is carried out on a large scale, popularly known as mass production. *Operating costing* is the term applied to describe the system used to find the cost of performing a service such as transport, gas, or electricity. These are all variations of process costing. *Contract* or *terminal costing* is the name given to job costing employed by builders and constructional engineers.

All these methods ascertain the actual cost. In addition, as indicated earlier, there may be superimposed on a particular system standard costing and/or marginal costing, both of which are special techniques.

## THE CLASSIFICATION OF COSTS

Production involves the use of materials, which are changed in form by workers to produce a commodity, or to render services. Use is also made of buildings, machinery, and equipment. Payments have to be made to obtain these things, and these are classified, according to the nature of the item or service received, as "material cost," "labour cost," and "expense."

A principal function of costing is the allocation or apportionment of expenditure to cost centres or to products. Where possible and practicable, because of the desirability to "attach" responsibility, a particular payment should be "allocated" (*i.e.* charged in total, or *pro rata* on the total, according to *actual* usage, or benefit received by a product) instead of being "apportioned" (*i.e.* charged in total or *pro rata* on the total, according to *estimated* usage or benefit received by a product).

To achieve this aim, the elements of cost—material, labour, and expense—are subdivided into "direct" and "indirect" costs. Thus there are:

1. Direct materials.          4. Indirect materials.
2. Direct labour.            5. Indirect labour.
3. Direct expense.           6. Indirect expense.

The first three together are the prime costs of production; the other three are the overheads.

The general rule for determining which costs are direct and which are indirect is to be found by considering whether or not the materials, services, or other benefit obtained by incurring a cost can be traced *directly* to a specific product, or job or batch of products. If direct responsibility for a cost can be traced there is a direct cost; if otherwise there is an indirect cost. The leather which goes to make a batch of shoes can be traced to that batch, as can the labour which carries out the conversion of the leather into the shoes; they are, therefore, direct costs. The wages paid to the maintenance worker who carries out repairs and keeps the machinery running which, say, cuts out the uppers for the shoes cannot be traced directly to any specific batch of shoes and is therefore an indirect cost.

The general rule is not always followed in determining which are direct and which are indirect costs. Sometimes the tracing of direct costs would not be justified; for example, where a number of similar products which are assembled from a variety of components are being manufactured, the small standard items, such as screws and small nuts and bolts, would rarely justify being treated as direct material costs. Instead, the expenditure involved would be treated as indirect material costs and taken to overheads. As will be shown later, the absorption of overheads is, necessarily, on some arbitrary basis, so it follows, from this, that refinements relating to direct costs can hardly be justified when only small items are involved.

ILLUSTRATION OF PRINCIPLE

*A.B. Manufacturing Co.*
*Summary of Costs for 1 Month*
*Machine; Part No. 600–30.*

|     |                                                           | £      |
|-----|-----------------------------------------------------------|--------|
| (a) | Direct material used                                      | 5,000  |
| (b) | Direct labour                                             | 8,000  |
| (c) | Overhead costs                                            | 7,000  |
| (d) | Direct materials (sundry items: screws, small nuts and bolts, etc.) | 25 |
|     |                                                           | £20,025 |

Number of machines produced: 200.

The amount for (a) will be traced to each individual machine produced. In other words, each will be charged with a figure of around £25; some will incur a small amount less and some a small amount more than the £25, but the £5000 will be fully allocated to the 200 machines.

A similar procedure will be followed for (b), a charge of around £40 being made to each machine, depending upon the exact time spent on each.

The overheads will be apportioned on some suitable basis; for example, according to the number of hours operated by either workers or machines used in production. Thus, the £7000 will be divided by the total number of hours for the month, to obtain an hourly rate. Such rate is multiplied by the hours taken to produce each separate machine, thus arriving at the overhead cost for each machine.

The balance of £25 could be treated as follows:

(i) Trace the sundry direct materials consumed by each machine produced and charge them accordingly, or

(ii) Treat the £25 as overheads and apply a proportionately increased rate.

The latter treatment will involve very little extra work, since the £25 will simply be added to the £7000, thus automatically increasing the hourly rate, i.e. £7025 is divided by the number of hours worked in the period.

If method (i) is adopted the documents used to issue the sundry materials will have to be priced and extended; a process involving much clerical work and therefore expense; all to show that the direct costs are increased by approximately £0.125 per machine produced. Some idea of the number of items involved can be obtained by reflecting on the fact that many screws and similar small items often cost only a small fraction of a penny. If the number of small items on each machine produced is multiplied by the number of machines, the total number of items becomes very large indeed.

This illustration is upon simple lines, and flaws in the analysis can no doubt be found. Why, it may be asked, go to all the trouble of tracing any costs to specific products when all that is needed to give a total machine cost or machine's share of each element of cost, is to divide the total of £20,025 (or £5000, £8000, £7025) by 200. The answer to this question is that, in practice, the machines would be produced "piecemeal" and there would be work-in-progress, both at the beginning and at the end of the month; at no time would there simply be a figure of, say, 200 machines produced, with no machines in the process of being completed. Thus, the only way to produce reasonably accurate costs is to trace each cost to the particular machine at the time it is incurred. A further practical point to remember is that, usually, more than one type of machine will be manufactured; a necessity when a reasonably wide market is to be supplied. The possible limitations of the illustration should therefore be borne in mind; the principle illustrated, however, will still apply, irrespective of the circumstances, whether a large variety or small variety of products is being made or work-in-progress does exist.

The cardinal points to remember in determining whether a direct cost should be treated as an indirect cost are, first, the significance of the amounts involved in relation to total prime cost and, secondly, the purposes for which the costs are likely to be required. In connection with the latter, if the management feel that the value of the data accumulated justifies the extra expense of tracing sundry, direct costs to products, then this will be done; otherwise they will be treated as indirect costs.

## DIRECT MATERIAL

All material which can be allocated to a product or batch of products is direct material. Such material thus becomes an essential part of the product.

The word "material" is used in a wide sense to include both raw materials, part-finished components or sub-assemblies, and finished components or sub-assemblies. In all these cases, looking at the problem from the point of view of the *present* operation, the material or part being converted or assembled is the "raw material" of that operation.

In the price of the direct material can be included all costs incurred in connection with procuring that material, provided such costs can be traced to a specific lot of material and to nothing else. When a price is quoted "delivered," the carriage to the buyer's place of business being met by the seller, the price of each lot of material includes an amount to cover the average carriage charge: such charge is automatically included in the costs of the materials in the Stores Ledger. When the material is booked out to jobs, the direct material cost thus covers the carriage charge. To be logical, it follows that the carriage paid by the *buyer*, when the seller's quotation is "ex works," should also be added to the cost of the materials and charged to products. This provision also applies to other similar charges incurred in connection with direct materials. Examples are freight charges, dock dues, import duties, and any special charge or tax on the material concerned.

From a theoretical standpoint, it can be argued that all cost incurred in purchasing and storing materials right up to the time they are required should be included in the direct material cost, and thus allocated to a product when an issue is made. Not only the invoice price but also the costs of the Purchasing Department, freight and carriage inward, and the costs of the Receiving Department and Stores could be charged to arrive at the direct material cost. In practice, the tracing of each cost to the appropriate batch of material presents numerous difficulties, and only when the cost incurred by a particular batch of material is *obvious* can accuracy be obtained. To include the *obvious* charges and no others is to introduce an inconsistency which is undesirable; to include *all* extra charges incurred, over and above the invoice price, may mean that the direct material cost is, in some cases, overstated. By treating the extra charges as general overheads, this difficulty could be overcome, but very often the total amounts involved in relation to direct material costs are fairly substantial, and general overhead is not usually absorbed—charged to products—on a basis which is directly related to the cost of direct material. Thus, to obtain reasonable accuracy the extra charges should be absorbed in a more equitable manner. At the same time, to keep clerical costs to a minimum, detailed analysis should be avoided whenever possible.

One way of accomplishing this purpose is to absorb the costs incurred on a basis of material costs obtained from invoices. While this will charge some materials with freight when none has been incurred by them, and will ignore the different characteristics of the material involved, the method should give reasonable results with the minimum of clerical work.

ILLUSTRATION OF PRINCIPLE

|  | £ |
|---|---|
| Invoice cost of materials | 45,000 |
| Carriage and freight inward | 1,000 |
| Receiving Department and Stores | 2,500 |
| Purchasing Department | 1,000 |

The total supplementary costs are £4500 and direct material cost £45,000. To absorb the £4500, 10% will be added to the direct material cost of all jobs completed. Thus, if £100 is the direct material cost of Job No. 34, £10 will be added to cover the supplementary costs. Any costs not absorbed would be attributable to, and therefore could legitimately be added to, the stock of materials held at the end of the accounting period. When the costs are estimated—which is quite usual—the £4500 may be under- or over-absorbed.

Because of the effect of stock valuation on profit and the necessity to produce accurate costs, the problem of valuing issues of direct material is extremely important. If the issues are undervalued actual production is not being charged with a high enough cost; if issues are overvalued jobs are being shown as costing more than they have actually cost. The values of the materials left—the period-end stocks—will be overvalued when issues are undervalued and undervalued when issues are overvalued. Over-valuation of *closing* stock only in a particular period means that profit is overstated in that period; undervaluation has the opposite effect. Moreover, the definition of profit—the excess of receipts in a period over expenditure in a period—implies the correct "matching" of revenue and expenditure. This is done when material procurement costs are correctly treated. If all supplementary costs relating to materials are charged as expenditure in the period when they are incurred, then very rarely will revenue and expense be truly matched and stocks valued correctly. It is admitted that, after the first year, provided the methods adopted are followed consistently, the errors will, to some extent, tend to cancel each other out. Nevertheless, the aim should be to achieve reasonable accuracy, for only then can the fullest and best use be made of accounting information.

## DIRECT LABOUR

The employees in a factory or other place where manufacturing is carried out are called "labour," and those employees who actually work upon, or are directly connected with, the conversion of the direct material in its various stages of manufacture to the finished product are known as "direct labour." The indispensable requirement is that the benefit obtained by the cost incurred can, without doubt, be traced to a particular product or batch of products. The payments made to direct labour are "direct wages."

The words "directly connected with the conversion" are used to include in the definition chargehands, supervisors, or foremen, who are normally indirect labour, but who are sometimes, in practice, treated as direct labour. Thus, the chargehand who supervises the men working on a particular process, and no other, could have his wages treated as direct wages, even though not actually working upon the conversion. The unit cost for the process would automatically be increased when the chargehand's wage was included in the total direct labour cost.

Where job costing or a modified form of job costing (*e.g.* batch costing) is adopted, the question as to the workers to be treated as direct labour, and therefore to book "on" and "off" jobs, will arise. So far as the operators working, say, at the machines which convert the direct materials or the men who assemble the components are concerned, there is normally no difficulty. The problem is a little more difficult with working-chargehands, working-foremen, setters, or similar workers. If a man supervises for part of the time is he to book "on" and "off" jobs or not? From a practical point of view the answer seems to depend upon the nature of the supervisor's duties; clearly if he starts upon a job, then breaks off to supervise, recommencing the job later, the booking "on" and "off" may become rather onerous, and great care would have to be taken by the man to ensure that the booking is done at the exact time of starting or finishing the particular job. Where the supervisor breaks off the job to deal with some production difficulty he will tend to regard that difficulty as being more important than the timing of the job he has left. To enable meaningful costs to be compiled, accuracy of timing jobs is essential; furthermore, haphazard methods of timing jobs will make comparisons quite invalid. Costs based on inaccurate times are no better, and may be worse, than reasonable estimates.

If the supervisor is actually supervising, and not working on jobs for most of his attendance time, there may be no case for treating him as direct labour; if he works for more than 50% of his total time he could record the time spent on jobs, the wages for such time being treated as direct wages and the balance as indirect wages. These suggestions, however, can only be taken as a guide, since a decision will have to be taken in the light of particular circumstances.

## DIRECT EXPENSE

Any costs, other than direct material and direct labour costs, the incurring of which results in a benefit which can be traced to a particular product or batch of products are "direct expenses." The naming of a number of these expenses will clarify the definition.

The cost relating to patterns or drawings produced for a specific job may be treated as the direct expense of such a job, provided one of two conditions is satisfied. The first is that the patterns or drawings are totally consumed on the job; the second is that, though the patterns or drawings can be used again, there is no reasonable expectation that they will be used again.

Any additional payment for overtime (overtime premiums) may be treated as the direct expense of a particular job, provided that when the order was taken overtime working was anticipated, the overtime premium thus being expected. Overtime premiums arising from a request by the customer for overtime on a job to be worked can also be treated as a direct expense, provided the customer is to pay the extra cost. When the overtime premiums relate to general overtime; that is, overtime to meet normal production commitments, then the extra cost is usually treated as an overhead expense. Reference to the "benefit rule" will show why this is so.

Tools or equipment used for a specific job, and no other, may have their costs of purchase or hire charged to that job as direct expense.

Any costs incurred on experiments in connection with a specific job, and no other, could be treated in a similar manner. However, where benefit to the future is likely to accrue the costs may be capitalised and charged to the jobs receiving the benefit.

## INDIRECT COSTS (OVERHEADS)

When cost incurring results in a benefit which cannot be directly traced to, and therefore charged to, a product or batch of products, such costs are indirect costs. The cost accountant calls these "overheads."

Direct costs will be found only in a producing department; that is, a department in which a product is actually manufactured. Overheads will arise in all departments. For the purpose of assigning responsibility a factory or works is usually divided into sections which represent the principal functions: viz. "production," "research and development," "selling," "distribution," and "administration." In addition to assigning responsibility, the purpose is the tracing of costs to the appropriate section.

## INDIRECT PRODUCTION COSTS (PRODUCTION OR FACTORY OVERHEAD)

Indirect production costs are divided according to the elements of cost—materials, labour, and expense.

All service department* costs are indirect costs. A service department is a department directly connected with production yet not actually producing a product; from the cost accountant's point of view it is therefore a department which has no costs which can be associated directly with a product. The Plant Maintenance Department is a typical example. The head of this department is charged with the responsibility of ensuring that all machinery and equipment used in production is regularly oiled and maintained and, in addition, he attends to other related matters. Not only the producing departments but also other service departments rely upon the efficient operation of the Maintenance Department.

All materials consumed by a service department are indirect materials, and all workers employed in a service department are indirect labour. Payments made for lighting, heating, and insurance, on behalf of a service department, are indirect expenses.

A list of service departments usually found in a general engineering factory should make the definition clearer:

| Name of Service Department | Principal Functions |
|---|---|
| Tool-room | The manufacture and repair of jigs, fixtures, and small tools |
| Inspection | The inspection of raw materials, components, and finished products |
| Internal Transport | The transporting *within* the factory of materials, equipment, and other items |
| Receiving and Stores | The receiving of raw materials and other items from outside suppliers and the correct storage of these once they have been entered on a Goods Received Note or Sheet and the Stores Bin Card |
| Works Canteen | The preparation of meals and refreshments for the employees of the production departments |

* The description "department" is used here to describe a particular division of a business. The terms "cost centre" and "budget centre" used later generally have the same meaning.

| First Aid and Welfare | The rendering of first aid and assistance with personnel problems: generally ensuring the well-being of employees |
| Works Office (*Note.* Normal Office comes under *Administration*) | Dealing with all clerical matters that must be carried out in the production departments |

In the producing departments, which are all departments where certain costs can be directly traced to a specific product or batch of products, all workers not actually engaged upon the conversion of the direct material are *indirect labour*. The payments made to these workers are indirect wages, and the materials they use are indirect materials. Taken from a general engineering factory, the following are examples of producing departments and indirect labour:

*Producing Departments*

Machine Shop
Welding Shop
Assembly Shop
Finishing Shop
Paint and Spray Shop

*Indirect Labour*

Supervisors, foremen, and chargehands
Machine setters
General workers
Apprentices and Trainees

If any of these workers should be connected with a particular process, or actually work on the conversion of direct materials to the finished product, they may be treated as direct labour.

## INDIRECT MATERIAL AND EXPENSE

Indirect material consists of "consumables" such as cotton waste, machine oil, and various small items consumed by the producing departments. Direct materials, such as screws and small nuts and bolts, can, if of insignificant value in relation to prime cost, be treated as indirect material, thus obviating the need for costly analysis of the costs of these items (*see under* "Direct Material," pages 25–27).

The balance of indirect costs is expenses incurred by the producing departments, which include heating, lighting, rent, rates, and insurance costs, and depreciation.

From the above will be seen that all indirect expenditure incurred by a business in connection with the actual manufacture of a product is indirect production cost or factory overhead. The remainder of the functional sections' costs are, of course, excluded from the term. Since all costs incurred by the remainder of the functional sections are necessarily "indirect," the term "expense" or "overhead" is normally used to denote such costs. Thus, the term "selling expense" or "selling overhead" is used to describe all selling costs.

## RESEARCH AND DEVELOPMENT COSTS

All costs incurred in connection with research into the improvement and development of products, or methods, are research costs.

When the research results in a tangible benefit which can be developed, from that point onwards to the stage when a prototype is ready for formal production, or when a plan is ready for adoption, all expenditures incurred are development costs.

In practice, there may be difficulty in distinguishing between these two types of cost (*see* Chapter 5).

## SELLING COSTS

All efforts in increasing sales, and retaining custom once obtained, result in selling costs (*see* Chapter 5).

## DISTRIBUTION COSTS

Once products are manufactured there are costs incurred for packing and transporting to customers. Storage and transport costs are the principal expenses involved (*see* Chapter 5).

## ADMINISTRATION COSTS

All management expenses *not* falling under the above headings of production, research and development, selling and distribution are grouped together to form administration costs (*see* Chapter 5).

All indirect costs have to be recorded, classified, and finally apportioned to products. They are normally recorded in a manner which shows the department and, later, the product responsible for the cost incurred.

## ALLOCATION OF DIRECT COSTS

All direct costs of manufacture are allocated to products or jobs by the most appropriate method available. Provision of suitable systems is an indispensable part of tracing direct costs to products; some of the most important features of systems relating to materials and labour are outlined below.

*Material Control**

Cost accounting recognises the need to control the ordering, storage, issue, and usage of materials. This is done through properly designed procedures which use appropriate forms. Attention is paid to the following aspects:

1. Requisitioning purchases.
2. Ordering by the Purchasing Department.
3. Receiving of materials.
4. Issuing of materials.
5. Payment for materials purchased.

The diagram on page 33 (Fig. 4) shows the link between forms and procedures employed.

Records maintained are Bin Cards, Stores Ledger, and a Stores Control Account in the Cost or Integrated Ledger. These have to be reconciled at reasonably frequent intervals.

The need to keep records on a *perpetual inventory* basis is a generally recognised principle. This is a method which uses planned procedures and specially designed records to show, at any time, the stock in hand, both as to quantity and value, for each item of material or each component. In addition, *continuous stock-taking* should be employed, stock auditors checking a few times a year each item of stock held. In this way the records and physical stocks can be kept in a reasonable state of agreement, and any discrepancies can be brought to light so that management can, if necessary, take corrective action.

Particular attention should be paid to the pricing of materials and its related problem, the valuation of stocks. This matter is so important that a separate chapter is devoted to covering the principal aspects involved (Chapter 25).

*Labour Control*

Because there is a direct transfer of cash between a business and its employees, it is not surprising that labour-control systems have received a considerable amount of attention from cost accountants.

In many industries labour cost is a very large proportion of total cost. The accounting system should not only record what has been paid in wages but should also provide information which allows effective control of labour cost. An employee is engaged for the service he is able to to give a business; cost accounting must make a full disclosure of how that service is being utilised.

---

* For examples of forms employed see *Standard Costing*, by J. Batty (Macdonald & Evans, 1966), hereafter referred to as *Standard Costing*.

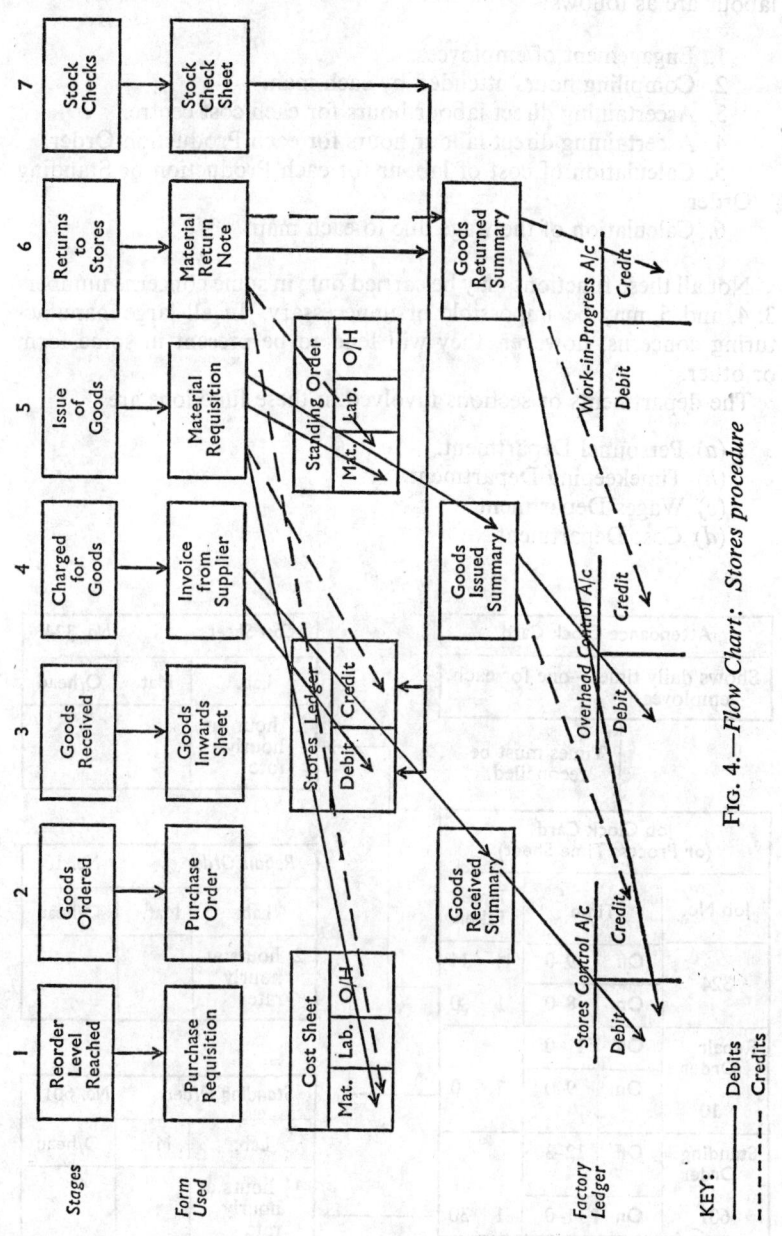

FIG. 4.—*Flow Chart: Stores procedure*

The principal functions necessary for recording and accounting for labour are as follows:

1. Engagement of employees.
2. Compiling hours attended by each man.
3. Ascertaining direct labour hours for each cost centre.
4. Ascertaining direct labour hours for each Production Order.
5. Calculation of cost of labour for each Production or Standing Order.
6. Calculation of the wage due to each man.

Not all these functions may be carried out; in some concerns numbers 3, 4, and 5, may be impossible or unnecessary. In all large manufacturing concerns, however, they will tend to be present in some form or other.

The departments or sections involved in these functions are:

(*a*) Personnel Department.
(*b*) Timekeeping Department.
(*c*) Wages Department.
(*d*) Cost Department.

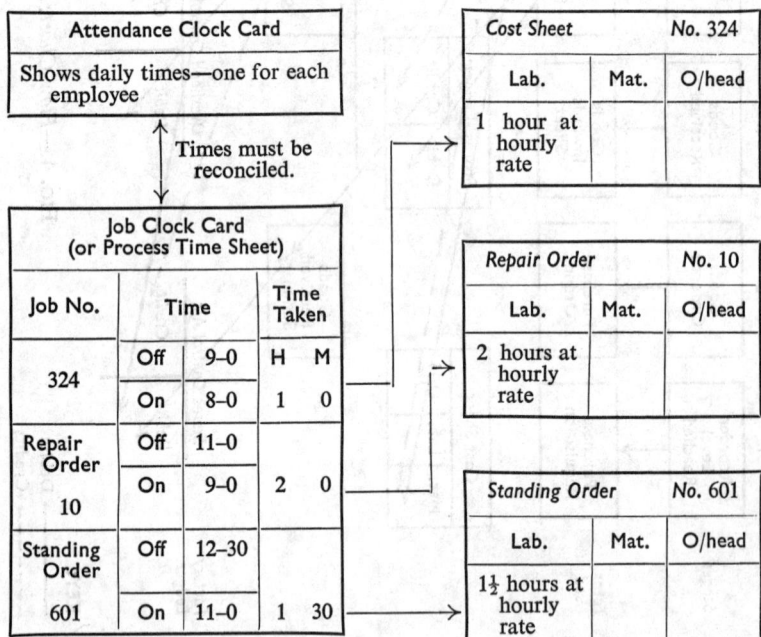

FIG. 5.—*Labour Control procedures* (*tracing labour costs*)

In addition, other departments, such as the Work Study Department, are affected.

Whenever possible and practicable mechanical time recorders should be employed for recording both attendance time and effective time on jobs or processes. Moreover, these times should be reconciled for each employee.

The procedures followed for tracing labour costs are shown in Fig. 5. It will be seen from the Job Clock Card that the charge may be to a production order, a repair order, or a standing order. The first two are self-explanatory, the third is the account which represents indirect labour, *i.e.* an overhead account. Another possible charge not shown on the diagram is an item of capital expenditure; that is, work by a company's own labour in installing or making a fixed asset.

## Cost Control

The control of material, labour, and overhead costs is dealt with in some detail in Chapter 14. As shown in that chapter, effective cost control means predetermination of costs and, subsequently, comparison of predetermined and actual costs, so that remedial action can be taken at the point at which the costs are incurred.

## PROCEDURES

### FACTORY OVERHEAD COSTS

The factory overhead costs are usually apportioned to individual departments of production. This practice of departmentalisation is essential in all cases where it is necessary to trace responsibility for costs. The justification can be summarised as follows:

1. The total costs incurred by both Service and Producing Departments can be ascertained. This is essential for cost control.

2. An overhead rate can be calculated for each Department or Cost Centre. An average rate for the whole factory is very rarely acceptable for the differing conditions normally found. Overhead responsibility will vary between departments: some may have expensive machinery, others have very little machinery, *e.g.* a Machine Shop and an Assembly Department.

3. Departmental idle capacity can be measured much more easily.

Apart from these reasons is the fact that departmental Profit and Loss Account preparation is greatly facilitated. Also decisions regarding the continuance of a department (when fixed cost will be excluded from the calculation) or the reasonableness of expenses incurred can be made.

To achieve these aims the cost accountant must clearly define the "cost centres" of a factory before going on to accumulate and attempt to control costs relating to such centres. A "cost centre" is a department, or equipment, or a person, or a group of persons in respect of which costs are accumulated and over which cost control can be exercised. When the costs ascertained relate only to a person or persons, then the cost centre is a "personal cost centre," otherwise it is an "impersonal cost centre."

The physical layout of the factory and the cost centres very often coincide, but such relationship is not essential; there may be one department which covers a particular function, but this may be divided into a number of cost centres. A single operation being performed by men and machines could be a cost centre.

Methods of apportioning factory overhead costs to cost centres are covered in the next section. Whenever possible a direct charge should be made to the appropriate cost centre. The remaining overhead costs have to be apportioned to both service and producing cost centres. The service charges are then transferred to producing cost centres, so that all costs are absorbed into the products or jobs. Examples of the procedures can be seen from the Overhead Apportionment Sheet opposite (Fig. 6) and the diagram given on page 228 (Fig. 30). In connection with the latter, a comparison with the procedure for marginal costing is possible by referring to Figure 31 on page 229.

## APPORTIONING FACTORY OVERHEADS

The principal methods used for apportioning factory overhead costs are as follows:

1. Square or cubic footage.
2. Capital values.
3. Number of employees.
4. Employees' wages.
5. Kilowatt-hour capacity.
6. Radiators; number or area.
7. Departmental direct charges.

### Square or Cubic Footage

Building service and land costs can be apportioned on this basis. Thus, occupancy costs, such as depreciation on buildings, building repairs, heating, fire insurance on buildings, and the upkeep of the grounds, can be charged to departments according to the square or cubic footage enjoyed by each department.

The method is generally satisfactory, but there may be some unfairness where some departments occupy preferential positions. Space in a certain part of a building, say, on the first floor, may be more valuable than in other parts. Some departments may have higher ceilings than others, and this fact may mean that a larger cubic volume is included.

Corridors and stairways may complicate matters, but this difficulty may be overcome in one of two ways. They may be excluded from the

## OVERHEAD APPORTIONMENT SHEET

| Factory Overhead Cost | Service Cost Centres | | | Producing Cost Centres | | |
| --- | --- | --- | --- | --- | --- | --- |
| | General Expenses | Maint. | Stores | 1 | 2 | 3 |
| | £ | £ | £ | £ | £ | £ |
| Clerical | | | | | | |
| Idle Time | | | | | | |
| Materials | | | | | | |
| Labour | | | | | | |
| Inspection | | | | | | |
| Supervision— General | | | | | | |
| Supervision— Departmental | | | | | | |
| Rent | | | | | | |
| Rates | | | | | | |
| Depreciation | | | | | | |
| | | | | | | |
| General Expenses— Apportioned | | | | | | |
| Transfers between Service Cost Centres | | | | | | |
| Maintenance Apportioned | | | | | | |
| Stores Apportioned | | | | | | |
| Total Charges to Producing Cost Centres | | | | | | |

FIG. 6.—*Example of Overhead Apportionment Sheet*

NOTES

1. In practice there will probably be many more service cost centres.
2. The transfer between service cost centres is carried out to arrive at the total cost of each after usage by other service cost centres has been considered. Not all accountants agree with this procedure on the grounds that the exercise does not assist cost control.
3. It will be seen that the service charges are transferred to producing cost centres so that the total involved can be absorbed by the products. This topic is covered later in this Chapter. The apportionment should be based on actual, estimated or standard usage of the service by the producing cost centres.

total area, but their costs included in the total costs; this automatically takes care of the apportionment. Alternatively, the cost of the corridors and stairways may be apportioned on the basis of the number of employees in each department.

## Capital Values

Depreciation of equipment and machinery, and insurance and repairs on machinery, may be apportioned on this basis.

Insurance is probably more accurately apportioned on the insurance values of the individual assets, and a better basis for repairs is by direct charge to each department, the amount calculated by reference to time sheets.

## Number of Employees

Canteen and first-aid costs may be apportioned according to the number of employees in each department. In the case of canteen costs this basis may not be very accurate, for not all employees may use the canteen. Those workers on the lowest rates of pay may be concentrated in certain departments; these workers may find canteen meals too expensive and adopt some other means, such as bringing their own lunches. If meals are free, apportionment according to the number of employees in a department should give reasonable results. Otherwise, unless the view that the charge should be shared according to service offered to departments (even though not used!) is adopted, the fairer basis is according to the number of employees actually using the canteen.

Supervision costs may be apportioned on the basis of number of employees or on a basis of the time spent in each department by the supervisor. The latter method is preferred when a supervisor has to give more attention to some workers than to others. The time spent in each department can be obtained for a limited period and an average basis determined for use in the future.

Cost accounting and statistical costs, especially those connected with timekeeping, may be equitably apportioned according to the number of employees in each department. In many cases the number of forms, statements, or reports, or even the number of entries, may provide a better basis.

Where the number of tools supplied and repaired by the Tool-room is approximately the same for each worker, then the number of employees in a department should be a reasonable basis for charging Tool-room costs to other departments. Often an estimate of a department's usage is more accurate. This can be obtained by keeping a schedule of tools made and tools repaired, and detailing the time spent on each and materials used, and the department to which each tool is sent.

*Employees' Wages*

Employers' liability insurance may be charged according to the total wages paid to the employees in each department. National Insurance and related contributions paid by the employer may also be dealt with in this way unless workers of different ages and sexes work in the same department, when an analysis of actual payments made is much better. The reason for this is obviously the various rates payable: there is a rate for male and a rate for female, and these are further varied according to age.

*Kilowatt-hour Capacity*

The lighting costs when lamps are of a different size may be apportioned on this basis.

*Number of Radiators or Sizes of Radiators*

Heating costs may be apportioned on this basis and reasonable results obtained. The method is suitable where temperatures differ greatly between departments or where heating losses vary widely. Where uniform heat has to be supplied under similar conditions in each department, the square or cubic footage basis will suffice.

*Direct Charges to Departments*

Bases are ascertained by study of time sheets, departmental meters, requisition, or other records. Thus, machinery maintenance and repairs may be traced by the use of time sheets and material requisitions. Indirect labour cost, such as supervision, may also use this basis. When the number of employees does not provide a suitable basis the tool-room cost can also be charged in this way. When timekeeping and wages calculations are not proportionate to the number of employees—say, where different methods of payment are in force, piece-work in one department, time rates in another—a direct charge, where possible, will be more accurate. Power, light, water, and steam, when directly metered, are also apportioned by this method.

**METHODS OF ABSORBING OVERHEADS**

*Introduction*

When only one product is being produced a uniform charge for overhead may be possible. Total overhead cost for the factory or department is divided by the number of units to arrive at an absorption rate per unit of production. This method is unsuitable for Job Costing, and only in certain cases suitable for Process Costing.

Where a number of different commodities is being manufactured, some means must be found to charge each commodity with a fair and reasonable share of the overhead cost. There is one of two factors to consider, depending upon whether an overhead is fixed or variable. Wherever possible, fixed costs are charged on a basis of relative benefit, and variable costs are charged according to responsibility. A method which covers both bases should be the aim. The modern approach is to assign responsibility and relative benefit by reference to the time spent on each job or unit of production. The direct-labour hour rate and machine hour rate methods are typical examples. In most cases the recognition of time absorbed, it should be noticed, will refer only to departmental times; the tracing of responsibility or receipt of benefit may be achieved at the time departmentalisation of expenses is carried out. Thus, the relative benefits received by each department from the rent of the factory may be determined by comparing the space occupied: the appropriate charge could then be made to each department. If a department occupies one-quarter of total floor space, then it benefits accordingly and is charged with a quarter of the rent.

One method of apportioning overhead to products may not be suitable for general application even in the same factory or department. One department may employ highly specialised, expensive machinery when the machine hour basis will be the obvious choice; another may have no machine work, so a direct-labour hour basis will be appropriate.

The rates used to absorb overhead may be based upon Actual Expenditure or Normal (estimated) Expenditure. The latter is probably more usual under Job Order Costing, but can also be used with a Process Costing System. With actual overhead there is a time lag before the rate can be calculated; the normal overhead rate avoids the necessity of waiting for overhead costs to be accumulated. The most important methods used to apportion overhead to products are as follows:

1. *Material Cost Percentage Rate*

The formula is as follows:

$$\frac{\text{Factory overhead for period}}{\text{Direct material cost for period}} \times \frac{100}{1} = \frac{\text{Percentage of direct}}{\text{material cost}}$$

If for a particular department direct material cost for a month is £8000 and factory overhead for the same month is £4000, then:

$$\frac{£4000}{8000} \times \frac{100}{1} = 50\%$$

Thus if Job No. 22 has a direct material cost of £20, then £10 will be added for overhead.

In very few cases will overhead benefits or responsibilities vary in direct proportion to materials used. Where different types of materials go into a product, results which are nothing more than ludicrous may emerge. In the manufacture of industrial instruments a great variety of materials is used, including gold and platinum wire. Any instruments not requiring the incorporation of rare metals will obviously fare better than the others on the question of incurring overhead costs. The costs obtained will tend to be quite inaccurate. For this reason the method has limited use: an example where it may be used is in the production of bulk materials; *e.g.* cement, sugar, paint.

## 2. *Wages Percentage Rate*

A formula for determining the Wages Percentage Rate is:

$$\frac{\text{Factory overhead for period}}{\text{Direct labour cost for period}} \times \frac{100}{1} = \frac{\text{Percentage of direct}}{\text{labour cost}}$$

*Example.* Dept. "X"

Factory overhead for month    =    £2000
Direct labour cost for month    =    £6000
Job No. 36 Direct Labour Cost    =    £30

$$\frac{£2000}{£6000} \times \frac{100}{1} = 33\tfrac{1}{3}\%$$

The overhead cost for Job No. 36 will be £10.

For some overhead costs, this method will give reasonable results; with others, there is little relation between direct labour and the overhead cost incurred. The lower-paid worker may occupy the same floor space as the higher-paid worker, yet the latter's products may be charged with more rent, rates, depreciation, and other space costs. This inaccuracy may be mitigated if the higher wage is due to greater efficiency, for then more units per period will be produced by the higher-paid worker. When, in a department, expensive machines are used by some workers and others use hand tools, unfair overhead charges will be made; this is also the case when workers vary in ability—some working at an average rate, whereas others work at high speed.

The method is easy to apply, and reaches its highest degree of efficiency when there is uniformity in wage-rates, skill of workers, equipment used, and work performed. When standard costing is used the Wages Percentage Rate may be employed with advantage.

## 3. *Prime Cost Percentage Rate*

The appropriate formula is:

$$\frac{\text{Factory overhead for period}}{\text{Prime cost for period}} \times \frac{100}{1} = \frac{\text{Percentage of prime}}{\text{cost}}$$

(*Note.* Direct expense is usually omitted from the calculation because it appears only in certain cases.)

This is similar to Methods (1) and (2). Instead of taking a percentage on direct material or direct labour, the two are taken together and applied to each job. Thus, if the prime cost of Job No. 40 is £50 and the percentage of prime cost to factory overhead is 50%, then £25 will be added for overheads.

Because, like the other two methods, the time element is ignored, the weaknesses of those methods also apply to the Prime Cost Method.

Recognition of the importance of time is shown in both the Direct-labour Hour Method and the Machine Hour Method. Time is the most important element in the incurring of overhead, and it is for this reason that methods which consider the productive time taken are the most equitable.

## 4. *Labour-hour Rate*

A formula for calculating the labour rate is:

$$\frac{\text{Factory overhead for period}}{\text{Direct labour hours for period}} = \text{Direct-labour hour rate}$$

Factory overhead would be applied to jobs by multiplying the number of direct labour hours on a job by the direct-labour hour rate. Thus if the total of factory overhead costs is £2000 and the number of direct labour hours is 10,000, then the direct-labour hour rate $= \frac{£2000}{10,000} = £0\cdot20$.

If a job takes 20 hours, then the overhead applied will be £4.

A disadvantage of the method sometimes alleged is the fact that additional clerical records are necessary. These should show:

(*a*) The number of direct labour hours spent on each Production Order or Job.

(*b*) The total number of direct labour hours worked by the employees in each producing department.

However, this information should, strictly speaking, be kept so as to control costs; moreover, the information may be required for production control. Thus, where full use is made of the information the disadvantage becomes an advantage.

The method is suitable from the point of view of cost control where the wages percentage rate is suitable; *i.e.* where uniformity of rates, workers, conditions, etc., is present. Where there is a predominance of machinery, however, the Machine Hour Rate Method is more suitable.

## 5. *Machine Hour Rate*

Again a formula can be employed; viz.:

$$\frac{\text{Factory overhead for period}}{\text{Machine hours for period}} = \text{Machine hour rate}$$

This formula should be applied for each machine or group of similar machines. The latter avoids having too many rates and, accordingly, keeps clerical costs to a minimum.

The procedure followed for calculating the Machine Hour Rate is to treat each machine or group of similar machines as a cost centre. Apportioning overhead costs to cost centres is dealt with earlier in this chapter. In the case of a machine cost centre the following costs would be apportioned to the individual machine (or appropriate group):

(a) *Operating expenses*, such as depreciation, insurance, maintenance, power, and lighting.

(b) *General overhead expenses* not included in (a).

(c) *Cost of floor space occupied*—rent or depreciation of building and other occupancy costs not included in (a).

All these are added together and then divided by the machine hours to give a rate per hour. Products made on the machine are then charged at the hourly rate on the basis of machining time involved.

There is no doubt that the recognition of the machine as a vital factor in the apportionment and absorption of factory overhead costs can lead to greater accuracy. In the modern age of mechanisation and automation the factory overheads resulting from the use of machinery are far in excess of costs from other sources, and it is only right and proper that this fact should be considered.

When calculating the machine hour rate great care should be taken to avoid *excessive* refinements which would complicate the procedures and lead to high clerical costs.

## Conclusion on Methods

The methods which would normally be employed are as follows:

Wages Percentage Rate.
Labour Hour Rate.
Machine Hour Rate.

No method can give absolute accuracy, but carefully compiled and used in appropriate circumstances, one or more of these three should provide acceptable results. However, this matter is taken further in Chapter 10 on Marginal Costing.

## ABSORPTION OF OTHER OVERHEAD COSTS

The absorption of factory overhead costs is covered above. This section is concerned with the principles involved in absorbing the remaining overhead costs.

## Research and Development Costs

Research and development costs may be absorbed on one or more of the following bases:

1. Treat in the same way as fixed assets, writing a proportion off each year, *i.e.* as depreciation. This can be included in the factory overhead costs.

2. In appropriate circumstances treat as a *direct expense* and charge to jobs or products involved; *i.e.*, when traceable to the job and attributable to no other.

3. Write off to Profit and Loss Account in the period in which the expense is incurred. The products may be charged with an appropriate amount. Alternatively, any research expenditure which does not result in tangible benefits may simply be written off without any charge being made to individual jobs or products.

There is no general agreement on which method to employ. The circumstances should be allowed to determine the choice.

### Selling and Distribution Costs

Selling and distribution costs are normally written off to Cost of Sales Account in the period in which they are incurred. This is logical, because these costs arise from the sales in a period, and it would be quite wrong to defer the writing off to a future period. Advertising costs are a possible exception.

For effective control it is usual to apportion costs to sales areas, thus extending the principle of establishing cost centres to the areas of sales and distribution. Thus, for example, sales salaries may be recovered on the basis of a direct charge. On the other hand, general advertising costs may be apportioned according to actual or estimated potential advertising. If advertising costs in one year are expected to result in benefits in future years the total cost is capitalised, a proportion being written off each year.

Analysis of selling and distribution costs is subdivided according to sales areas, salesmen, sizes of orders, methods of selling and delivery, and products or jobs. In the latter case the absorption may be based on a percentage calculated by reference to factory cost or gross profit or selling price. Alternatively, a rate per product may be charged. Whether such apportionment to individual jobs or products is worthwhile is a debatable point on which different accountants hold opposing points of view. In any case, it will be difficult to obtain a reasonable standard of accuracy.

### Administration Costs

Administration costs may be treated as period costs, being written off to Profit and Loss Account in the period in which they are incurred. Alternatively, they may be divided between work-in-progress (production) and cost of sales (selling). A further possible procedure is to treat the *total* administration costs as a charge to production. Charges to products or jobs may be made on the same bases shown above for selling and distribution costs.

When administrative functions are centralised an attempt is often made to charge the costs to area factories or branches. This may be done on the basis of turnover, total cost, or the total number of employees in each area.

## STANDARD COSTING *

### DEFINITION OF STANDARD COSTING

"Standard Costing is a system of cost accounting which makes use of pre-determined Standard Costs relating to each element of cost—labour, material and overhead—for each line of product manufactured or service supplied. Actual Costs incurred are compared with the Standard Costs as the work proceeds, the differences between the two being known as "variances"; these are analysed by "reasons" so that inefficiencies may be quickly brought to the notice of the persons responsible for them, and appropriate action may be taken."

It will be seen that the following processes are involved:

1. Predetermination of Standard Costs.
2. Recording of Actual Costs.
3. Comparison of Actual Costs and Standard Costs.
4. Obtaining the Cost Variances.
5. Reporting to management so that *action* can be taken.

The action is the most important part of cost control, and it is obviously very important for this to be the *correct* action. This is a topic which is dealt with in Chapter 14 on Control.

The most important factor to remember is that Standard Costs reflect what the costs *should be* for stated conditions and volume of output. If these change, then the Standard Costs must also change. Fortunately, the flexible budget allows Standard Costs to be set for a number of different levels of output.

There are three main types of Standard Cost distinguishable by reference to the conditions or circumstances taken as a basis for their development. These are as follows:

1. *Ideal Standard Costs*—these assume that 100% efficiency will be obtained by men, machines, and other factors affecting production and selling. Since this state of efficiency is rarely achieved it follows that Ideal Standard Costs are not used very often although they could be for a specific plant in appropriate circumstances.

2. *Expected Standard Costs*—which reflect the highest state of efficiency which may be expected in the *actual* conditions prevailing within the particular plant.

Both (1) and (2) relate to present-day conditions and are therefore termed *Current Standard Costs*.

3. *Basic Standard Costs*—these may be based on either ideal or expected conditions. The difference between Current Standards and Basic Standards is that the latter remain in force for a number of years,

* For further details of this topic reference should be made to *Standard Costing*.

whereas the former are normally revised once a year. Basic Standard Costs are useful for showing statistical trends in prices or wage-rates and operate in rather a similar fashion to the Cost of Living Price Index.

## SETTING STANDARD COSTS

Very briefly the most favoured methods for setting Standard Costs are as follows:

1. *Direct Materials*—A Standard Material Specification is compiled, and by reference to size, weight, or other measure the standard quantity of material is determined. Due allowance should be made for normal waste or cutting losses.

The standard price is determined by the purchasing agent and accountant after due attention has been paid to possible increases or reductions in prices within the future period for which the standards are being set.

2. *Direct Labour*—For setting standard times it is advisable to employ Work Study. This means that there should be close co-operation between the cost accountants and work study engineers.

Work study consists of two distinct but related functions:

(a) Motion Study—the technique of studying work with a view to selecting the best combination of operations, eliminating any which are unnecessary.

(b) Time Study or Work Measurement—determining the work to be done and the time required.

The principal stages involved are as follows:

(i) Selecting the best method of performing each operation and the tools to use.

(ii) Recording each operation and making this standard practice.

(iii) Determining how long an average worker should take to carry out each operation.

(iv) Training each operator to carry out the work in the prescribed manner.

The wage-rates should be set after all work has been graded into different categories. Future trends have to be estimated before the standard rates can be set.

3. *Overhead Costs*—The procedures described for budgeting costs when a budgetary control system is being employed also apply to setting Standard Costs. This is so for *all* overhead costs, whether they are production, selling, distribution, research, development, or administration.

This statement should not be construed to mean that where there is a Standard Costing system there is always a Budgetary Control system, and vice versa. However, in this book it is assumed that where it is possible to operate Standard Costing, then quite rightly and logically the management accountant will also employ budgetary control, thus obtaining the benefits of a fully integrated and co-ordinated system. As noticed earlier in this chapter, when job costing is employed it may not always be possible to use Standard Costs.

When budgeting costs it is essential to divide each type of expense into those which are fixed and those which are variable. In addition, there will be a need to determine and define quite clearly what volume of output is to be regarded as 100% capacity. The latter requirement is an essential prerequisite of *all* budgeting or costing systems.

*Definitions of Capacity*

There is a number of definitions of "capacity," and these may be summarised as follows:

(a) *Maximum Theoretical Capacity*. This assumes that the plant will operate without any loss in time for the stipulated possible number of hours, *e.g.* 8 hours per day.

(b) *Normal Capacity to Manufacture*. All *normal* time losses due to breakdowns, setting-up machines, or other reasons are deducted from the maximum theoretical capacity ((a) above).

(c) *Normal Capacity to Manufacture and Sell*. This capacity makes due allowance for the fact that there will be trade recessions. Accordingly, the normal capacity to manufacture ((b) above) is reduced by an appropriate figure to allow for idle time due to not being able to obtain sufficient sales. A number of years may be considered and an average capacity calculated for use in each individual year.

(d) *Short-period Capacity to Sell*. Each year is taken in isolation and the available sales capacity is taken as the basis for calculating the capacity. If there is no sales problem it is clear that the normal capacity to manufacture and the short-period capacity to sell will coincide.

*Capacity to Adopt*

There are differences of opinion on which capacity to adopt. The normal capacity to manufacture is generally appropriate when sales remain reasonably constant, and the short-period capacity to sell may be used when sales fluctuate from one year to another.

The importance of defining the capacity cannot be overemphasised. Unless managers clearly understand the number of standard hours, the number of units, the value of sales, or other measure being employed, there can be no effective control of performances or overhead costs.

## ADVANTAGES OF STANDARD COSTING

By adopting carefully compiled Standard Costs the weaknesses of an historical costing system, which records only Actual Costs when the transactions have been finalised, are overcome. The following are the advantages to be gained from the use of Standard Costs:

1. Standard Costs are a yardstick against which Actual Costs can be

c

compared. The alternative is to compare Actual Costs for one period with Actual Costs of another period. To be able to assume that Actual Costs can be used as a basis of comparison the following questions would have to be answered:

(a) Which accounting period can be taken as the base period?

(b) Assuming the first question can be answered satisfactorily, how many previous Actual Costs should be compared with the cost being investigated?

(c) If a number of Actual Costs is necessary, should they be averaged and, if so, which is the most suitable average to adopt—the arithmetic mean, median, mode, or other average?

(d) If there is no great difference between the previous Actual Cost and the present Actual Cost, can it be assumed that the latter is as low as it could have been, and that there are no inefficiencies?

These, and similar questions, should be answered before comparing Actual Costs with Actual Costs. Unfortunately no satisfactory answer is possible to the majority of such questions; it is for this reason that Standard Costs are essential.

2. The analysis of variances as part of the ordinary accounting routine ensures that regular checks are made upon expenditure incurred. Deviations from the predetermined standards of performance can quickly be localised and, taking advantage of the "principle of exception," management can concentrate upon matters which are not proceeding according to plan.

3. The clerical work associated with costing is usually reduced and yet much more useful information is made available to management. Under the older types of costing systems voluminous records, many of which were of little value, were kept. Often information would be recorded just in case it was needed. The reduction in time and effort needed for costing arises, chiefly, from the following:

(a) Reduction in the cost of report preparation. Less time is required, which in turn allows prompter presentation, thus enhancing the value of the reports.

(b) Some records can be kept in terms of quantities only, sterling values being omitted. This is of special importance for Stores or Stock Ledgers; pricing of requisitions is simplified, and the balancing is in quantities only. The total Standard Cost can be obtained by multiplying the quantity of each type of material or component by the appropriate standard price per unit. The ratio between Actual and Standard Cost can be used for converting total Standard Cost to total average Actual Cost.

Preliminary work may, of course, be very great, but once the Standards have been developed, they can be used until amendment becomes necessary.

4. Interpretation of management reports is made easier and there is

a reduction in the time taken to study these reports. All matters requiring attention are readily apparent, for superfluous details are not shown; management thus need not be troubled with unimportant matters.

5. Provided the Standards are constantly being studied with a view to improvement, control over costs is greatly facilitated. Moreover, if prompt action is taken on the lines indicated by the study it should be possible to reduce costs. Cost control and cost reduction are probably the most important aims of any costing system, and Standard Costing gives due recognition to this fact.

6. Setting Standards requires a detailed study of all manufacturing, administrative, selling, and distribution functions so that they may be made efficient. This fact alone usually results in improved methods being adopted, with resultant lower costs. Cost centres are established, lines of authority are defined, and responsibilities for costs are clearly assigned to supervisors and workers. In carrying out this preliminary work it is possible to eliminate inefficiencies and generally improve all aspects of making the product and reaching the consumer. Thus, for example, the setting of Standards for labour may require the use of work study with consequent benefits.

7. Production and price policies can be formulated with certainty before production takes place. Standards set along objective lines are to be preferred for this purpose, for Actual Costs may include excessive usage of material, abnormal labour times, or an inequitable charge for overhead. In competitive industries there can be no provision, in price, for the costs of inefficiency.

8. Once the Standard Costs have been compiled they can be used as a basis for other gains, such as the provision of an incentive scheme of payment for employees.

## EXAMINATION QUESTIONS

1. When Standard Costing is used it has been found that the Actual sales figures differ from the Standard sales figures.

What consequences would arise? How would you report, explaining the reasons for the variances? (*I.C.W.A.*)

2. In many manufacturing companies, overhead is divided between:

   (*a*) production overhead;
   (*b*) administration overhead;
   (*c*) selling and distribution overhead.

Explain why such a division is made and how such costs differ. In the light of your explanation, suggest methods by which each class of overhead should be absorbed in the product cost. (*I.C.W.A.*)

3. What are the essential factors in the presentation of costing results to Management? (*S.C.A.*)

4. Increased mechanisation and automation adds to the importance of control of indirect costs. Discuss this statement. (*S.C.A.*)

5. The allotment of overheads and their absorption by individual products often presents difficulties to the cost accountant.

Discuss this point in relation to a manufacturing concern which produces a variety of products with different classes of labour and where each class of overhead (factory, administration, and selling) includes elements of fixed, variable, and semi-variable expenses.                    (I.C.W.A.)

6. A business expanding rapidly uses historical costing methods. Towards the end of a year the reconciliation of cost and financial accounts reveals considerable differences between overheads incurred and overheads absorbed in production. It is suggested that the differences would not have occurred if a standard costing system had been used.

Give your views on this suggestion, indicate the type of difference likely to have arisen, and show how the differences would have been avoided and/or indicated in standard costing.                    (I.C.W.A.)

7. In a certain business it has been the custom to absorb administration costs as a percentage of production costs. A customer buys otherwise identical products in different materials, one cheap, one expensive, and complains about the difference in the prices quoted, which he contends should amount to the difference in material price only.   Give fully your views on the problem.
                    (I.C.W.A.)

8. "Standard costing is always accompanied by a system of budgeting, but budgetary control may be operated in businesses where standard costing would be impracticable."

Discuss this statement, and indicate the method and use of budgetary control systems in the type of business mentioned in the latter part of the quotation.                    (I.C.W.A.)

9. A manufacturer produces standard lines, but also takes in work of a non-standard character.   In preparing a system of standard costs, show how you would deal with the special work, bearing in mind that the cost and financial accounts are agreed.                    (I.C.W.A.)

10. As cost accountant you are asked to advise a company on the best method of absorbing overheads and to compute the rate or rates to be applied. No cost accounts have been kept, but estimates have been prepared for jobs undertaken on the following basis:

Estimated materials and direct wages, plus 150% on direct wages for factory overheads, plus 15% on factory cost for all other overheads. To this figure a further 15% is added for profit.

The accounts for the year show the following figures:

|  | | | | | | £ |
|---|---|---|---|---|---|---|
| Direct material | ... | ... | ... | ... | ... | 21,000 |
| Factory overheads | ... | ... | ... | ... | ... | 27,500 |
| Selling overheads | ... | ... | ... | ... | ... | 3,000 |
| Sales  ... | ... | ... | ... | ... | ... | 75,000 |
| Direct wages ... | ... | ... | ... | ... | ... | 18,500 |
| Administration overheads | ... | ... | ... | ... | 5,000 |
| Distribution overheads | ... | ... | ... | ... | 1,500 |
| Net loss | ... | ... | ... | ... | ... | 1,500 |

There are two production departments and the overhead rates for the departments vary considerably.

(a) Summarise your computation and observations.
(b) State what advice you would give to the management.
(c) Suggest lines on which further investigation should proceed.
                    (I.C.W.A.)

11. You are employed by a manufacturing organisation where direct material costs average 75% of total cost. In spite of this, most attention in recent years has been given to the study of direct and indirect labour in the search for cost improvements. Attention is now to be turned to raw materials and component parts. State the possible fields of investigation into material costs and indicate briefly the approach you would propose to secure cost improvements. *(I.C.W.A.)*

12. What do you understand by the term ideal standard?

Do you consider that an ideal standard is a satisfactory measure of performance? *(I.C.W.A.)*

13. State what are the factors relative to quality which affects costs, and describe a costing system which will give management a control of these.

*(I.C.W.A.)*

14. What information would be required to set a standard manufacturing cost for a completely new machine which an engineering company is to make for sale? From where would this information be obtained?

Present your answer in brief numbered paragraphs. *(I.C.W.A.)*

15. It is the consultant's contention that your business needs to employ a system of standard marginal costing, and that there is no more effective way to get real value from a costing system than to use this approach. He claims that if one can calculate the standard marginal cost of each product, then one has a satisfactory basis for control, and for determination of product profitability.

State what you consider to be the benefits and disadvantages which are likely to come from such a system, and demonstrate two effective applications of the technique. *(I.C.W.A.)*

16. (*a*) In the accounting treatment of research and development expenditure, there are two main classified groups which are equally applicable to all costs. What are these two main groups?

(*b*) Into which of the two groups would you place the following costs in each case, and for what reasons?

    (i) Creation of new lines:
    (ii) Development, or improvement, of existing lines;
    (iii) Purchase of patents;
    (iv) Patent litigation expense.

(*c*) What considerations would influence you in deciding whether to charge the cost of research work to a customer when the work has been undertaken at his request? *(I.C.W.A.)*

17. A company employing 120 workpeople and producing specialist grey-iron castings is expanding rapidly. Its turnover three years ago was £220,000 in the year, and last year was £400,000. The directors have set their sights on an increase to a turnover figure of £1,000,000 per annum in a further two years.

The business is a profitable one. Whereas three years ago net profit before tax was £30,000, last year it was £76,000. The average total capital employed last year was £200,000.

The managing director of the company is concerned about the lack of cost information and costing routines. He is particularly interested to know what sorts of faults there could be in cost-estimating procedures for selling price fixing. Although the constituent parts of prime costs are scientifically estimated, that is, the metal cost, the sand cost, and the direct operating labour cost, his worry is on the subject of overhead absorption. All the overhead of the business is, in fact, absorbed on the basis of time spent in one operation, moulding. This is only one operation of a possible ten operations on any casting. However, the argument used by the consultant who recommended this method of overhead absorption was that moulding capacity was the limiting factor and therefore was a suitable basis.

(a) What are your thoughts about this particular method of overhead absorption?

(b) How would you like to see such a small business developing its overhead costing activities? (I.C.W.A.)

## CHAPTER 3

## BUDGETARY CONTROL

### INTRODUCTION

BUDGETARY Control is a system which uses budgets as a means of planning and controlling all aspects of producing and/or selling commodities or services.

Preplanning is a cardinal feature of Budgetary Control. The overall plan is represented in the Master Budget. Each segment of the Master Budget is covered by a functional budget. There is therefore a series of budgets all co-ordinated together into the plan of action. Behind each budget are the actions of people, their performances and the costs they incur. All are measured in financial terms, but the physical efforts and quantities involved should not be overlooked.

The preplanning covers broad policy as well as day-to-day planning. What is to be produced and what profit and return on investments are expected to be obtained are examples of matters to be covered. The daily activities are scheduled and go to make up the weekly, quarterly, and yearly budgets. Standard hours, direct material content, and expense are all shown in the work schedules and therefore, in summary form, in the budgets. The entire process of preparing the budgets is known as "budgeting."

Great care has to be taken to ensure that all budgets are co-ordinated. This is not always easy; in fact, it may be quite a difficult matter. Maximum profitability will be the aim, provided this is consistent with the achievement of long-term growth and stability. Unfortunately, it is not always easy to achieve, profit earning being affected by a variety of factors. Prices and costs are two important considerations, but there are others which are discussed in subsequent chapters.

Restrictions imposed on demand, on the volume of production, or on any other aspect which affect profit maximisation are known as "limiting factors." Unless due attention is paid to any limiting factors which may be present, the necessary co-ordination will not be achieved. If, for example, the plant capacity is capable of producing 10,000 units of a certain product and yet the sales organisation is capable of selling 15,000 units—which will maximise profit—then a policy decision will have to be made on whether to expand production or restrict the sales force. Co-ordination means viewing the system as a whole and dovetailing all parts together. This in itself is one of the greatest advantages of Budgetary Control. Harmony is sought from the very beginning, and an effort is made to ensure that this harmony continues throughout the period covered by the budgets. If *one* factor predominates to such an extent that all budgets are influenced by it this is known as the "principal budget factor."* Finance available may limit the extent of all activities: therefore this will then be the principal budget factor.

Control follows the planning and co-ordination. Deviations from the predetermined plans are brought to light by comparing actual and budgeted performances and costs. Subsequently the differences between the actual and budgeted figures—the variances—are analysed. The action taken on the variances is possibly the most important part of the control mechanism; this has to be taken quickly, at the right time, and in the correct place. Accounting ratios may also aid control. Ideal ratios can be established, and these are used as guides to what is expected in the future. The actual ratios show what progress has been made by comparing the ideal and actual ratios.

Great emphasis is placed upon the location of responsibilities. Recognition that performances and costs can be traced to employees—managers, supervisors, and workers—is an integral part of Budgetary Control. Clearly distinguishing between "controllable" and "uncontrollable" costs aids the tracing of responsibilities. The controllable costs are those which can be traced to a particular person or group of persons: they are influenced by internal factors. Direct material costs are made up of two parts, the prices paid and the quantities used. Similarly, direct wages are formed of wage-rates and hours worked. Although not an invariable rule, it may be stated that the usage of materials and the hours worked for a given volume of work are controllable. Accordingly, as will be explained later, variances analysis attempts to isolate any controllable deviations from the budgeted costs. From what has been said, the reader will appreciate that uncontrollable costs are outside the control of employees, and are therefore affected only by external factors. Again, this is not a rigid formula. Material prices and wage-rates are usually influenced by economic conditions. However, material prices arise from contracts entered into by the Purchasing Agent. If he makes a bad contract, then clearly the cost moves from the uncontrollable to the controllable category. Fixed overhead costs are incurred as part of policy. Managers who can change policy can therefore control these costs. Employees who are below the ranks of policy-making management cannot control fixed overhead costs. On the other hand, the *variable overhead* costs are generally controllable by the rank and file. These are general observations. When compiling the detailed, written procedures—the Budget Manual—due emphasis must be given to defining terms and showing how variances are to be isolated and analysed. The idiosyncrasies of the particular business have to be ascertained, and the system evolved should be suitable to cover all likely requirements.†

* Also known as "governing factor" and "key factor."
† Chapter 20 covers System Design.

## BUDGET CENTRES

Efficient control requires that due recognition must be given to the fact that costs are best controlled at the point at which they are incurred. Thus, for example, in the case of production costs the point of control will be at supervisor and operator level. Suitable areas of control have to be selected. These should not be too large. Management theorists have long since recognised that the "span of control" should be limited. This concept must necessarily apply here; there cannot be one organisation for "management planning" and another for budgetary control. The areas selected should comply with the natural responsibilities of supervisors and executives. Such areas are known as "budget centres" or, alternatively, as "cost centres." A budget which relates to a budget centre is referred to as a "departmental budget."

In addition to departmental budgets it will also be necessary to have functional budgets. The conventional division of a business into the functions of production, selling and distribution, administration, and research and development is followed. A separate budget is normally prepared to summarise the performances and costs for each function. The departmental budgets are naturally an integral part of the functional budget. The budget for, say, the Machine Shop is clearly a departmental budget, yet, because this budget relates to *production*, the figures must also be summarised in the functional budget for production.

Throughout any system of budgetary control it is usual to follow the well-known management law, the "principle of exception."* Management is given information on matters which are *not* proceeding according to the plans as represented by the budgets. Where budgeted and actual figures agree, then no action is required; accordingly, management is not given facts and figures. Only the exceptions are reported upon, so that corrective action may be taken.

## PROCEDURES FOLLOWED

The procedures followed in designing and operating a Budgetary Control system will necessarily vary from one business to another. However, a general pattern can be established, and this is summarised overleaf. In addition, a diagram is given which also illustrates the procedures (Fig. 7).

Where further explanation and examples are considered necessary these are given in subsequent chapters.

* This management law is sometimes described as the "principle of exceptions." There is no difference in meaning.

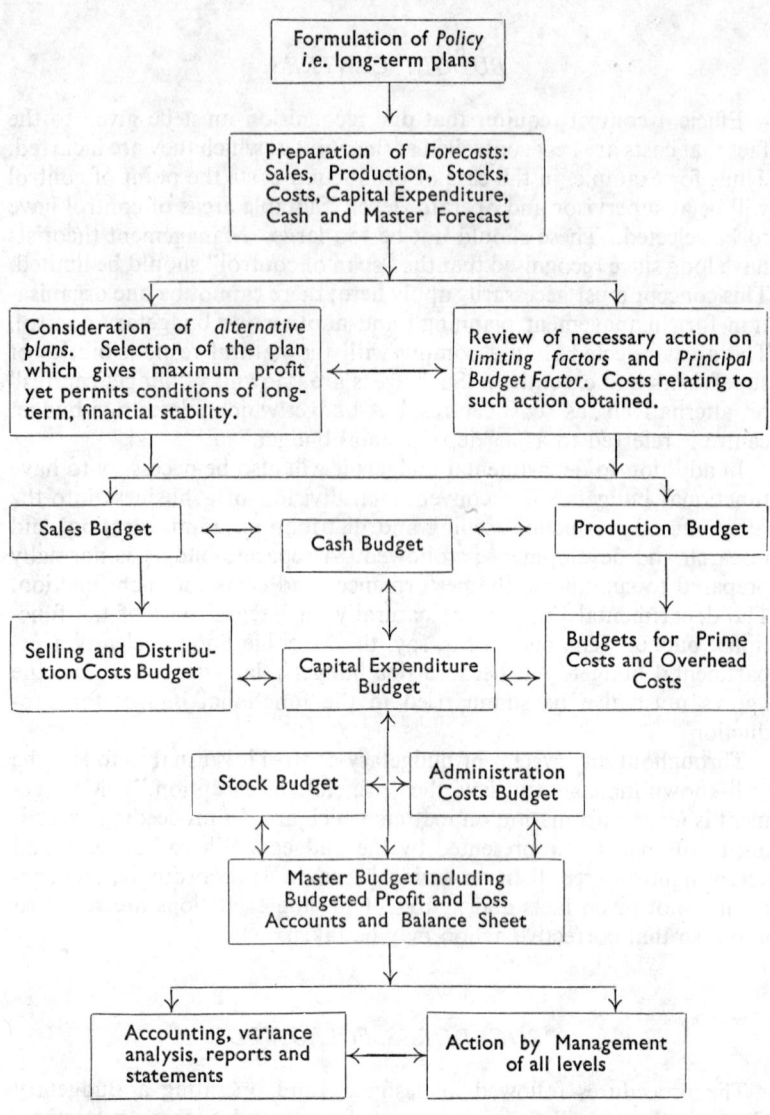

FIG. 7.—*Budgetary Control: diagram of procedure*

NOTES

1. Only the functional breakdown has been shown. A budget will be required for each budget centre within each functional division.

2. Quite often the sales forecast will be the first step in budgeting. However, this will not necessarily be the case. In some businesses production capacity will be the principal budget factor and, therefore, the production forecast will be the starting-point.

## SUMMARY OF PROCEDURES

1. *Forecasts* are made to cover the following:

    (a) Sales.
    (b) Production.
    (c) Stocks.
    (d) Costs—
        (i) Production.
        (ii) Selling and Distribution.
        (iii) Administration.
        (iv) Research and Development.
    (e) Cash.
    (f) Credit—Debtors and Creditors.
    (g) Purchasing.
    (h) Capital Expenditure.
    (i) Master Forecast—
        (i) Profit and Loss Forecast.
        (ii) Balance Sheet Forecast.

These will show physical quantities and monetary values. Details may be shown on work sheets or schedules. The forecasts are therefore summaries. The figures shown represent probabilities—probable sales, probable production, and probable costs.

2. *Alternative combinations of forecasts* are compared. The principal budget factor, if any, and limiting factors are noted, and the actions needed to overcome these are considered. Having due regard to the necessary actions and their likely cost, the combination of forecasts which appears to represent the most efficient overall plan, and therefore is likely to maximise profits, is selected.

Only when the largest-profit combination of forecasts has been selected can the forecasts be regarded as being finalised and therefore in the nature of budgets. In other words, the forecasts represent *possible* plans. They become budgets only when they are co-ordinated and are part of an overall plan—one which should maximise profits.

3. *Budgets* are prepared to cover precisely the same items as listed in (1) (a) to (i) above.

From this time the segments of business activity become integrated into a complete plan. They are joined together in a manner which is expected to maximise profits. The co-ordination and control, just as essential as the planning, are also brought into operation.

Some writers also include within the scope of budgetary control the making of broad plans and the statement of objectives. This, of course, is policy-making, which is essential to any business, whether or not Budgetary Control is used. The author believes that policy-making should as far as possible be an integral part of Budgetary Control. Plans should be made within the framework afforded by policy: recognition that the latter exists can obviously lead to better planning and therefore budgeting. There is no doubt that the management accountant should be aware that a sound policy is essential for any business; moreover, he should know that policy may have to be amended with changes in circumstances, and he should be able to supply the data necessary for reaching management decisions. The optimum output and the most profitable sales mixture are typical examples of where the management accountant can give assistance and guidance.

4. *The necessary organisation* is set up for dealing with the detailed procedures. An appropriate accounting system with accounts suitably classified, and a mechanism for analysing variances and for reporting upon them so that action may be taken should all be dealt with. Comparisons of budgeted and actual figures have to take place regularly and continuously.

## BUDGET PERIOD AND CONTROL PERIODS

The period covered by a budget is known as the "budget period." The length of the budget period depends upon the nature of the plan being made. Some forecasts can be made for a relatively long period—up to ten years or even longer in exceptional circumstances. Others can safely cover a few months only. Irrespective of the type of budget, the longer the period covered, generally speaking, the less reliable will be the figures obtained. Obviously this will not always be the case. Short-period budgets of sales may turn out to be incorrect, and yet it is possible for a long-period budget of sales to be correct simply because the fluctuations experienced in different periods are averaged out when a number of years is considered.

Because of the convention of dividing business activity into yearly periods, it is natural that budgets are prepared for a period, a division, or a multiple, of a year. Sales, production, and related costs often cover one year; if uncertainty is great, then a six-monthly, or even a quarterly period, may be necessary. This will be so where there is great economic uncertainty or the products are dictated by changes in fashion or other reasons which make demand unpredictable. In the case of cash a company which has regular inflows and outflows of cash may be able to have a budget period of one year. On the other hand, if difficulties are being experienced or purchases and/or sales are seasonal, so that the cash flows are irregular, then a very short budget period may be essential.

Long-term forecasts, and therefore long-term budget periods, may be possible and necessary for capital expenditure; that is, expenditure on fixed assets. Here, however, the reader has to watch the terminology. If the capital expenditure forecast—in effect the probable expansion programme—covers five years, then theoretically the budget period could involve five years. In practice, since the longest budget period is normally a year, it is usual to restrict the budget period for capital expenditure to a year. The longer-term *forecast* is still essential, but the necessary co-ordination through budgeting is carried out annually.

There cannot—except perhaps for the very stable type of business—be rigid rules formulated on what length of time should be covered by the budget period. Much depends upon external economic conditions and internal circumstances. As these change, then so may the ideal length of the budget period. The greater the uncertainty, the shorter should be the projection into the future, and therefore the shorter should be the length of the budget period. Even when the budget period has been "settled," the position should be carefully watched.

For *control purposes* the budget period is divided into shorter periods. For obvious reasons these are known as "control periods." The frequency with which comparisons of results are made and the appropriate reporting is carried out is dictated by the control periods. A calendar month, or a month of four weeks, is often taken, with the latter receiving much greater support, for the simple reason that the possible number of days is the same for each four-weekly period, and therefore the comparisons made from one period to another are much more useful. This means that there are thirteen periods in each financial year.

Even the four-weekly period does not produce ideal results. The number of possible working days, having regard to holidays, will not be the same for each control period. Accordingly, any comparisons of one period with another must necessarily be vitiated to some extent. Some accountants advocate the use of a control period which is based on the average of the available *working* days. The net total working days are divided by twelve to give the length of the control period.

The control period can be adjusted to allow for differences in the number of working days from one period to another. However, many accountants favour the selection of control periods which do not require figures to be adjusted. The calculation of calendar variances is a form of adjustment. The under- or over-absorption of fixed costs caused by working fewer or more days than budgeted form the basis of the calendar variance.

Although the division of a year into twelve or thirteen control periods gives the most usual frequency for controlling performances and costs, it is by no means the only division which is adopted. Quarterly, weekly, daily, and other periods may also be used. In any one business there will be used a combination of periods of different lengths. Some costs may best be controlled daily, others weekly, and yet others monthly. Those controlled daily may also be watched in total, both weekly and four-weekly. Performances will also require to be controlled at different intervals of time. Production and sales figures may have to be watched daily, weekly, four-weekly, quarterly, and finally, yearly. Direct labour and material costs—particularly hours and material usage—are often best watched day-by-day. The latter will probably involve the use of standard costing. Overhead costs may be controlled each four-weekly period. The most useful control periods should be selected and used.

## BENEFITS FROM BUDGETARY CONTROL

Many benefits to be derived from Budgetary Control arise from the fact that policy, plans, and action are co-ordinated, integrated, and controlled. All personnel, from the Managing Director to the most junior supervisor, know the part they have to play to achieve the targets set. Whether boom or recession conditions are being encountered, the best results are likely to be obtained when there is a clear plan of action and there is guiding control through the Budget Controller. Alternative courses of action are considered before selecting the one which is likely to maximise profit. The policy-making and planning covers not only the present but also the future. Each year's operations are planned with the previous results in mind and yet with an eye to the future. Once the monetary effects of present plans are known, the forecasting and drafting of future plans become much simpler and more straightforward.

Measurement of performances—production targets, sales quotas, and other targets—are achieved automatically as part of the system. Costs are also controlled. The comparison of actual and budgeted costs and actual and budgeted physical quantities (*e.g.* hours or units of material) allows the control to be exercised. In the dynamic system there will not only be control: there will also be positive efforts made to improve on the targets and costs. Greater efforts may be stimulated through the use of incentive payments based on output and sales quotas. Cost reduction can be brought about by incentive payments, by special cost reduction campaigns, or by the simple everyday control that can come through the instilling of cost consciousness into the rank and file.

Under suitable conditions Standard Costing* and Budgetary Control may go hand-in-hand. The two can harmonise and make the planning and control more effective. Detailed analysis and control made possible through Standard Costing and the overall co-ordination and control of Budgetary Control dovetail to make the almost ideal system. Absolute perfection is impossible to achieve, but this should not act as a deterrent against trying to obtain a system which is sound, effective, and flexible enough to encounter all circumstances and conditions. The well-organised and managed systems which combines Standard Costing and Budgetary Control is likely to give the most satisfactory results, and therefore will allow target profits to be achieved.

The necessary examination of the organisation structure and the study of how costs behave and are incurred usually result in improved efficiency. Weaknesses that exist become apparent, and action to eliminate them can be taken. Thus, many advantages may accrue even *before* a Budgetary Control system has actually been installed.

Budgeting follows sound management principles. Delegation of responsibilities is given positive recognition. In most organisations there

* *See* Chapter 2.

is at least one manager who finds it very difficult to delegate responsibilities. Instead he does as much as possible himself, often working on
routine matters when he should be spending his time on more important
things. The overall result would be loss of efficiency. Budgetary Control
reduces the possibility of this danger.

The cost variances reveal any weaknesses that exist. Moreover, they
reveal the *nature* of each weakness. The prime cost variances will show
the efficiency achieved in the employment of workers and the usage of
materials. The overhead variances can show the extent of plant utilisation, the efficiency achieved for the actual production, and the care
exercised in spending on overheads. Variance analysis and management
reporting can together reveal the state of progress. Any necessary action
can be taken quickly and in time to minimise losses. Changes in sales
mixture, in amounts produced, price increases or reductions, and any
other necessary steps can be made without delay.

Because of the high degree of control which is exercised throughout
the whole system, it follows that the most effective use is made of the
productive resources. Furthermore, since costs are kept to a minimum
and performances are maximised, this will normally mean that the
financial resources will be used most advantageously. The cash budget
will show how much can be spent and, provided the budget figures
materialise, excessive spending cannot take place. If the budget figures
are not achieved, then management is able to take action—once more
avoiding the danger of overspending.

Results should be viewed objectively with the minimum amount of
personal prejudice. This in itself is a great advantage. Personnel are
likely to respond willingly and try to achieve the targets set. They will
tend to meet the needs of the system and to co-operate with each other
towards the stated objectives and, finally, planned profit.*

Budgetary Control is no longer regarded as an expensive luxury which
is within the reach of only a few large, profitable companies. There is
now general agreement among enlightened managements that Budgetary
Control is essential. Moreover, the very existence of a suitable control
system may make all the difference between stagnation and expansion.
The later chapters, dealing with obtaining finance, show that banks and
other financial institutions require details of past results and future
plans. Budgetary Control can show that plans *do* exist and, furthermore, will indicate the expected profitability of the plans. Without
budgets there would be great difficulty in convincing a would-be lender
that the loan is reasonably secure. There should be evidence that a
reasonable profit can be earned, so that all money used can be paid an
adequate return. The chapter on capital employed covers this aspect.

Not every Budgetary Control system gives all the advantages outlined
in this section. Some systems are more efficient than others: managers

* Management theorists will possibly recognise that this is an application of the
"law of the situation."

and employees who operate systems also vary in efficiency. Inevitably, therefore, different results and benefits will accrue from each system. Moreover, there may be problems.

The forecasting and budgeting are by no means easy matters. Absolute accuracy is impossible, but, nevertheless, a high standard has to be sought. If the targets set are hopelessly inaccurate, then the system concerned is likely to be of very limited value. Personnel must have faith and confidence; these require that the plans made are realistic targets which have been established after *all* pertinent facts have been considered. If the budgeted figures are not related to reality, then there is little purpose served by using them.

A major problem which must arise is the defining of responsibilities. Quite often there is overlapping of duties. Sometimes costs are incurred jointly by a number of departments. These and other difficulties have to be faced and resolved. As far as possible, a system should permit putting the appropriate responsibilities squarely on the shoulders of the person responsible. At times this may not be simple. Nevertheless, for Budgetary Control to operate efficiently the problem has to be overcome.

Care should be taken to ensure that a Budgetary Control system does not become so rigid that it loses its usefulness. Increased efficiency should be the aim, but this will not be forthcoming if the system will not permit plans to be changed. Budgetary Control should be an aid to management; it cannot replace management nor make decisions. The system should be flexible enough to allow the implementation of any decisions that are made. Yet if too much flexibility is permitted there may be some loss of control and co-ordination may be more difficult to accomplish. Moreover, arguments can be advanced *against* changing plans too often: if they are made carefully in the first place frequent revision should be unnecessary. Clearly the answer is a compromise. Frequent revision of budgets should be avoided; in fact, any changes should be permitted only when significant changes in conditions and circumstances have taken place.

Another factor which should not be overlooked is the cost of installing and operating a Budgetary Control system. From time to time attempts have been made to fix a percentage for comparing the total cost of the accounting function with the direct labour cost or with the value of sales. However, it should be realised that no hard-and-fast rules can be established. Much depends upon the size and the nature of the activities of the individual business. Nevertheless, much can be done to keep these costs within reasonable limits. It may be possible to obtain comparative costs through a trade association or from other businesses. Articles in accountancy journals often give guidance on the practical aspects of operating a Budgetary Control system. Obviously, the employment of qualified men and women who understand budgeting is essential to minimise costs. Mechanisation of the accounting function may also help. In short, the principles observed in Budgetary Control are also applied to keep down the costs of operating a system of Budgetary Control.

A possible shortcoming of Budgetary Control—as indeed of any control system—is that too much dependence may be placed upon it by management. This tends to be especially so when a system is first introduced. Possibly this is due to some extent to lack of instruction on the part of the Budget Controller and his staff on the purpose of Budgetary Control. The scope and *limitations* should be explained before the system is brought into operation. In particular, it should be explained that a wrongly made decision will still be wrongly made, even though Budgetary Control is being operated. Budgetary Control will bring to light the fact that a mistake has been made and will allow corrective action to be taken within a reasonable time. Even so, a certain loss will be incurred, although obviously less than when no Budgetary Control system is used.

## DETERMINATION OF POLICY

Every business should have a definite policy. The location of the business; the determination of the best size of the business unit, and optimum level of output and the prices to charge are examples of policy matters. In addition, it will be necessary to determine and state: the expected return on capital employed; the methods of production and distribution; the normal capacity and the bases for recovering overhead costs; the most profitable sales mixture, and the methods to be adopted to obtain the necessary finance.

These and many other policy decisions should be made *before* tackling the intricate work of compiling budgets. The reason is not difficult to understand. Budgetary Control should be an all-embracing concept, backed by the highest levels of management. Decisions made by directors and others affect plans, and therefore the budgets. Accordingly, as stated, the policy that has been determined must be fully understood by the Budget Controller and his staff before any attempt is made to carry out the budgeting.

## ASSIGNING RESPONSIBILITIES

The executive responsible for drafting the budget may be known as the Budget Director, the Budget Controller, the Budget Officer, the Budget Accountant, or by some other suitable name. Irrespective of the title used, the holder of the post should be a capable administrator with a sound knowledge of *all* aspects of the business concerned and should, of course, be an expert on budgeting, costing, and industrial accounting. Above all, he should be a diplomat who is capable of obtaining all the necessary data for forecasting and budgeting without conflict, and yet is firm enough to control and co-ordinate efficiency through operation of the Budgetary Control system.

The Budget Controller is not a back-room boy who is remote from the everyday activities which go on within the business. He is part of a team; often a leader, often an adviser. Without top-management backing and co-operation from functional and line management he cannot do his work efficiently. Each member of the team has to play his part—concerted effort is absolutely essential.

In the large organisation it will clearly be an impossible task to keep in touch with every person connected with administration, production, and selling. Instead, the necessary co-ordination is maintained through a Budget Committee. The Budget Controller is usually the committee secretary. Along with fellow executives—normally one from each functional division of the business—and a chairman (*e.g.* General Manager), he forms the Budget Committee. A typical committee may be formed of a Production Engineer, a Sales Executive, a Purchasing Officer, the Chief Accountant, the Budget Controller (who may also be the Chief Accountant), and the General Manager or Managing Director, who acts as chairman. Some businesses prefer a larger committee, but this is a matter of choice. There is no doubt that a very large committee can become unwieldy and relatively unproductive.

The Committee's functions are obviously far-reaching. Once the Board of Directors has determined policy, it is up to the Committee to put the objectives into practical terms and ensure that they are carried out efficiently. The Budget Controller will be concerned with planning the procedures and putting them into written form. The Committee ensures that the plans made, the operation of the system, and, above all, the co-ordination and control are a *joint* effort.

Forecasts and budgets are received and discussed by the Committee. Managers concerned with each individual forecast or budget are often invited to explain points which arise from that forecast or budget. Later, when the plans have been put into operation, *i.e.*, when the forecasts become budgets, periodic results are usually discussed in the same way by the Committee and the responsible manager. One company known by the author operates a system in which departmental operating statements are sent to departmental managers within a stated time after the end of each four-weekly period. The managers are given two full days to study the statements, and then each one is called in turn to discuss variances and any incidental matters which arise from the statement. The facts revealed are acted upon, so there is thus a policy of continuous improvement. All important matters are reviewed quickly yet thoroughly. Under normal circumstances all aspects can be covered in one afternoon.

Special problems may also be considered by the Budget Committee. Measures to be taken regarding an unexpected increase in certain costs or a falling off in sales are examples. In addition, the Committee may also act in the capacity of Capital Expenditure Projects Committee. Here the main function will be to decide which projects are the most urgent and which can be purchased in a future budget period. The finance available as well as the urgency will have to be considered, and information on the cash position will be required from the Budget Controller himself.

The responsibilities for setting budgeted costs and performances and later for controlling have to be clearly understood and stated. The precise responsibilities of a particular executive; *e.g.* the Production Engineer, will vary from one business to another. Nevertheless, the following list should act as a guide:

RESPONSIBILITY FOR BUDGETS AND CONTROL

| *Executive* | *Budget and area of control* |
|---|---|
| Budget Controller | Administration Budget* |
| | Cash Budget† |
| | Capital Budget† |
| | Master Budget† |

The Budget Controller will usually be directly responsible for collecting the facts and ensuring that all necessary steps are taken to compile the budgets stated. *In addition*, he will take all the necessary steps to ensure that all executives understand the part they have to play in setting up the budgets. Once the information has been collected and has been sifted by the Budget Controller's department and has been examined by the Budget Committee, the Controller arranges for the interim and final budgets to be drafted. Successful launching of the system and its continued operation also come within the responsibility of the Budget Controller. He will provide all the facts needed for co-ordination and control, but he cannot *himself* ensure that co-ordination and control become realities and not merely plans. All executives, supervisors, and even the rank and file workers can contribute towards these achievements.

| Buyer (or Purchasing Agent) | Purchasing Budget |
|---|---|

In conjunction with the budget controller or accountant the Buyer establishes standard prices. Quantities of materials and supplies have to be estimated by the Production Engineer, the Works (Maintenance) Engineer, and other departmental heads; the Buyer integrates the information and supplies it to the budget controller so that the Purchasing Budget can be prepared.

| Departmental Managers or Foremen | Departmental Budgets |
|---|---|

Each departmental manager is consulted by the budget controller and by the Budget Committee. In this way he is able to understand the nature of his budget and, because he takes part in its preparation, can accept it as a target which is capable of attainment.

* Often the responsibility of the Office or Administrative Manager.
† Often dealt with by the Accountant.

Distribution Manager                Distribution Budget

This assumes that a separate distribution budget is compiled. This will cover all distribution costs—transport and storage costs and certain packing costs. Sometimes distribution costs are dealt with along with selling costs and included in the Selling Costs Budget. They then become the responsibility of the Sales Manager, although, in this case, there may still be a Distribution Manager, who reports to the Sales Manager.

Research Engineer,
Research Chemist,          } Research and Development
or Development Engineer       Budget

Sales Manager                 Sales Budget

## TIME ELEMENT IN BUDGETING

Earlier in this chapter the budget period and control period were defined. There are other times to be considered in budgeting.

If Budgetary Control has never been employed before, then careful study of the organisation and methodical preplanning will be essential. The time involved in this preliminary work will vary from one business to another. The size of the business, the complexity of production and distribution, and, perhaps most important, the accounting and costing organisation that already exists all affect the time involved. If a sound costing system is already being operated, then, since this is essential for effective budgeting, the time involved for introducing a system of Budgetary Control will tend to be greatly reduced.

For the medium- and large-size business it is unlikely that any soundly conceived and planned scheme could be drafted and introduced under less than six months. In some cases a period of twelve or even eighteen months may be essential. Whether the system is introduced by a company's own staff or by outside consultants may affect the time involved.

When the Budgetary Control system has been brought into operation there will be the necessity to revise the plans, and therefore budgets, normally once a year. When demand is subject to fluctuations a six-monthly or even more frequent revision may be necessary. Each revision has to be planned. Dead-line dates should be issued to all concerned. Information has to be collected, the forecasts and budgets have to be drafted and approved by the Budget Committee. One company with which the author is familiar requires all budgets to be completed for the first week in November. They are then approved by the Budget Committee and brought into operation on January 1st. Setting the final date only will clearly be inadequate; successful operation of the system will require that *each stage* is scheduled and timetabled and a strict watch is observed on the keeping of the times. Any falling behind schedule should be observed by the Budget Controller and the necessary steps should be taken to overcome the delay.

## THE BUDGET MANUAL

The Budget Manual is the schedule, document, or booklet which shows, in written form, the budgeting organisation and procedures.

A manual should be well written, indexed, and divided into distinct sections, so that each departmental manager can be issued with the section appropriate to his work and responsibilities. The loose-leaf type of manual facilitates division into sections and easy distribution to the persons affected.

Some of the most important matters covered in a Budget Manual are summarised below:

1. *Introduction* and brief explanation of the principles of Budgetary Control, including its objectives and the benefits to be derived from its use.

2. *Responsibilities*: functional and departmental (budget centres).

Organisation charts may be useful in supplementing the descriptions. The titles of executives, foremen, and supervisors would be stated, along with a full and comprehensive explanation of the duties of each. Functions covered would include those connected with preparing the budgets as well as the duties related to operating the system.

3. *Authority*. Management theorists have long since recognised that responsibility and authority must go together. The statements of responsibilities will normally also cover the authority given to each manager. Special attention should be given to explaining the routines to be followed for obtaining the necessary approval of budgets, vouchers, and all other forms and documents which authorise the spending of money. The authority for granting approval should be clearly stated. Whether one, two, or more signatures are to be required on each document should be clearly indicated. Approval will also be required for the introduction of new forms.

4. *Timetables* for all stages of budgeting.

5. *Reports* and statements to be employed. Specimen forms, number of copies to be used, the purpose of each form, and the budget centres involved should all be stated. Precisely why and when each form or statement would be used would be covered. No new forms should be allowed to be introduced without prior consent of the authority named under (3) above—normally this authority will be the Budget Committee.

6. *Budget periods* and control periods should be defined, the length of each being stated.

7. *The procedures to be followed* throughout the system. Many of these procedures will be covered in connection with responsibilities under (2) above. Those not so covered or those that are of a general nature may be included under a separate heading.

8. *The accounts classification* to be employed.

**ADVANTAGES OF BUDGET MANUAL**

There are many advantages attaching to the use of a well-prepared Budget Manual. Just imagine attempting to build a modern house without using plans—the result would be chaos and, accordingly, nobody should attempt to work without careful planning. The operations of the modern business are far more complex than building a house; moreover, much more money is involved.

The overall, co-ordinated plan provided through Budgetary Control shows all personnel what part each manager is expected to play in maximising profit. There is no "passing of the buck"; everyone knows what are his responsibilities.

Problems and difficulties which inevitably arise from the operation of any complex system can be settled quickly and easily from the Budget Manual. Matters which cannot be settled from the manual may be dealt with by the budget controller or the full Budget Committee.

New employees, particularly at managerial level, can be introduced to the company's methods and procedures quite easily through the Budget Manual.

Through the Budget Manual, methods and procedures become standardised. Furthermore, by the careful selection of these methods and the forms which go with them, the *very best* methods should emerge. The employment of organisation and methods experts is not excluded from a Budgetary Control system. This practice would simply ensure that more attention is paid to studying and selecting the most efficient methods and procedures. These would then be incorporated into the Budget Manual.

The fact that all personnel are following the same carefully drafted instructions should mean concerted effort. The action of one manager is not cancelled by the action of another: they are aware of the path that each has to follow. There is synchronisation of all efforts, and the objectives should be achieved with the minimum of friction.

Finally, there is the very important advantage that a manual, well conceived and arranged, should help to persuade all levels of management that Budgetary Control is worthwhile and essential. In other words, management is "sold" the idea of Budgetary Control through the Budgetary Control system, and therefore the Budget Manual.

## *PREPARATION OF FORECASTS AND BUDGETS*

The executives responsible for preparing the forecasts and budgets were shown in an earlier section—"Assigning Responsibilities." The principal methods used for forecasting the figures to be used in the budgets are summarised below. In many cases two or more methods will be employed; one can be used to check the reasonableness of the figures obtained by the other method. Sometimes an average may produce the best results.

The methods employed are as follows:

## 1. *Executive Opinion*

Each functional executive may prepare the forecast for which he is responsible. The Sales Manager prepares the sales forecast, the Production Manager the production forecast and so on: the managers and their responsibilities were outlined earlier. In practice, this method varies in accuracy from one business to another. Much depends upon the business records and other information available for estimating the necessary figures. The optimism (or pessimism) of the particular executive also influences the accuracy of the forecast. Personal prejudice or bias will also affect the position.

A modification of this method is to combine the opinions of all functional executives. All ideas are pooled and discussed and, finally, a forecast which is acceptable to all concerned is adopted. In appropriate circumstances there is no doubt that quite good results can be obtained. Preparation of the sales forecast may be effected quite successfully by this method. The market may be studied daily through newspapers, journals, and trade periodicals. If trends are observed, along with significant occurrences which affect sales, then realistic figures may be obtained. Quite often statistical analysis based on historical facts may not show the *future* trend: executive opinion may assess the future more accurately, especially when unusual or abnormal occurrences show themselves. Judgment, experience, and sound opinions are then the qualities which help to arrive at more accurate figures. This method is sometimes referred to as a "jury of executive opinion."

There is no doubt that the method is easy to apply and can be employed, even though statistical records are not maintained. Moreover, a balanced, co-ordinated approach is made to the problem of forecasting. On the other hand, there are disadvantages. The method cannot be regarded as "scientific"; it is based on opinions which may lack the high degree of objectivity which is essential for all sound forecasting. One group of executives may arrive at entirely different figures from those estimated by another group. The strength of individuals forming the group will be reflected in the forecast made. One man may force his opinions on the others, so that the forecast becomes, in effect, that man's forecast and not the forecast of the group. A further possible disadvantage is the fact that the responsibilities of individuals are not easily defined, and therefore control may be very difficult to accomplish. Thus, for example, if an overall sales forecast is made, who is to say what part of the forecast is the responsibility of individual salesmen? Only by establishing sales quotas—which usually means keeping records—can individual responsibility be settled.

There is no doubt that the method can be useful. However, because of its limitations, it may be advisable to use the method in conjunction with one or more of the other methods outlined below.

## 2. *Opinions of Workers, Foremen, and Executives*

Just as control of costs and performances is achieved best at the point at which they are incurred or carried out, so often the forecasting of costs or performances is best accomplished at the same point. The forecast is built "stone by stone" from the bottom upwards. The opinions of all personnel concerned with the particular forecast are brought together, analysed, scrutinised, amended where necessary at each stage, and finally approved by the responsible executive.

The idea can be utilised in all functional divisions. Opinions of workers and foremen can be obtained on standard quantities of materials, standard hours, and overhead expenditure. On the sales side, each salesman and branch manager can estimate his own contribution to sales and his expected costs. These estimates are then scrutinised by someone who has a sound knowledge of the market. Discussions may then take place and adjustments be made.

There is no doubt that this method has much to offer in sales forecasting, where conditions being considered are usually far from standardised. On the other hand, efficient production generally calls for standardisation of methods and materials, so that the application of scientific method and statistical method is simpler and generally more accurate. Work study, technical estimates, and statistical analyses can all be employed together to finalise the output and related costs forecasts.

This method has many followers. One of its principal advantages is the fact that all personnel concerned with the activities represented in the budget take part in its compilation. This should lead to more confidence in all aspects of Budgetary Control; greater co-operation should result. Furthermore, the assigning of responsibilities is greatly facilitated. In connection with selling, sales quotas can be established for individual salesmen and sales areas. The fact that experts, who are in close contact with everyday problems, assist with the preparation of the forecast will tend to mean greater accuracy.

There are disadvantages. Knowledge of a particular function may not be enough for accurate forecasting. A salesman may be an expert on a particular sales territory, but accurate sales forecasting needs more than consideration of each salesman's quota. The general economic situation and cyclical, seasonal, or sporadic trade fluctuations, present or expected, all affect the total forecast. Therefore, if this method is adopted, careful appraisal of the situation as a whole by a responsible manager or committee will be essential. A further possible failing is the time absorbed by the estimating and compiling of records. The personnel engaged on a function may not be able to spare the time without neglecting the work on which they are normally employed. In the large company forecasting is likely to be a fairly lengthy process; any attempts to take short cuts may reduce any possibility of obtaining realistic figures. The presence of biased opinions may affect the validity of the forecasts. If the individual targets are to be used as the basis for incentive payments, then clearly a person who is asked to set his own target may err on the side which is likely to give him financial benefits. This could obviously be a further disadvantage.

Like the method which relies on executive opinion only, this method may be very useful, provided it is utilised with a full knowledge of its limitations. It is possibly in the field of selling that it is likely to be of the greatest value. The supplementing of opinions with past performance results or statistical analyses is likely to enhance its value. For products that have not been sold previously the method has obvious limitations: market research will give much better results.

## 3. *Market Research and Other Statistical Techniques*

Market research is concerned with finding out where demand exists, when it exists, and at what price. The principal object is to ascertain what quantities of products should be produced for profit to be maximised. All facts likely to be useful are collected and analysed, and from them a forecast is made.

Some methods make extensive use of *past* performance records. These are adjusted to allow for expected, *future* trends—the past is projected into the future. Many companies, whenever possible, adopt a policy of continuous expansion; they believe that production facilities should be increased and then, if necessary, any additional demand should be created. Accordingly, the output forecast is based on the capacity of all assets. The sales forecast is compiled in a similar manner; in fact the two coincide.

Statistical analysis can assist in very many phases of budgeting. Data can be collected, analysed, and used to make management decisions—a technique known as operational research. Statistical techniques can assist in arriving at optimum stock levels and for dividing overhead costs into their fixed and variable elements. These and many similar methods can be invaluable. They are not affected by personal prejudice or bias, so the necessary degree of objectivity is achieved. However, care should be taken to ensure that the conditions which existed in the period to which the collected data refers are the same as those conditions which are to operate over the budget period. Unfortunately, this is not an easy matter to determine. The personal opinions of experienced executives may be extremely useful here; significant facts which are not revealed by statistics may invalidate any conclusions which have been reached.

The uncertainty of the future emphasises once more the need to utilise more than one forecasting method. Statistical and accounting information should be used as much as possible, but, at the same time, responsible managers should be called upon to exercise what should be one of their functions—the exercise of managerial initiative, discretion, and judgment.

## FORM BUDGETS TAKE

The form each forecast and, therefore, budget will take is shown in subsequent chapters. There is no standardised form, for each business develops its own particular requirements. Nevertheless, the general principles operate for practically all concerns, and therefore the illustrations given can be adapted to meet most needs.

As shown earlier in this chapter, the forecasts are made first, and later, when the most profitable levels of operations have been determined, these are converted into budgets and become part of the co-ordinated plan.

### EXAMINATION QUESTIONS

1. Discuss the advantages you would expect to result from the introduction of a system of budgetary control into a small factory producing a variety of products. Detail the difficulties you are likely to encounter in setting up and operating such a system. (S.C.A.)

2. Write a critical survey of a budgetary control system with particular reference to (a) the various types of budgets and (b) changing production and sales levels. (A.C.C.A.)

3. (a) Who should participate, and what part should each play, in setting standards?

   (b) For a mechanised process requiring a group of differently graded operatives tabulate possible reasons for deviations from the labour standard. Show how these deviations are differently treated when setting the standard according to whether (i) perfect, or (ii) attainable performance is the aim. (I.C.W.A.)

4. What do you understand by a flexible budget?
What degree of flexibility applies to the following:

   (a) shop supplies
   (b) indirect labour
   (c) repairs to plant and machinery
   (d) electrical power?

Write a short note on each of the above, relative to

   (i) a short period of 1–3 months
   (ii) a long period of 12 months. (I.C.W.A.)

5. What are the essential differences between budgeting and forecasting? Illustrate their relationship by examples from one or more industries.
(I.C.W.A.)

6. A business expanding rapidly uses historical costing methods. Towards the end of a year the reconciliation of cost and financial accounts reveals considerable differences between overheads incurred and overheads absorbed in production. It is suggested that the differences would not have occurred if a standard costing system had been used.

Give your views on this suggestion, indicate the type of difference likely to have arisen, and show how the differences would have been avoided and/or indicated in standard costing. (*I.C.W.A.*)

7. "These budgets for tomorrow never work out just as planned. Conditions always change. So why bother to make them?"

Enumerate the points which you would make, briefly, when confronted by the argument expressed in the above quotation. (*I.C.W.A.*)

8. How does budgetary control facilitate the delegation of authority and yet act as an instrument of co-ordination? (*I.C.W.A.*)

9. Outline an adequate but simple system of *cost control* for a small jobbing factory employing, say, twelve people. Give your recommendations.

(*I.C.W.A.*)

10. Do you consider that a system of standard costs could be useful to a concern specialising in the manufacture of non-standard components to customers' individual specifications? Owing to the special nature of the components, repeat orders very rarely occur.

Give your views, with reasons. (*I.C.W.A.*)

11. (*a*) State three main control objectives which a manufacturing organisation seeks to attain by budgeting.

(*b*) Set out the four main factors which need to be considered in the budgeted plan for profit, and outline briefly the points to be taken into account for each of those factors.

(*c*) List in broad terms the items of information which you would present to management when summarising results, showing any ratios you regard as appropriate. (*I.C.W.A.*)

12. The AB Holding Company controls over twenty subsidiary companies engaged in various industries. The companies are run on autonomous lines and some of them themselves have their own subsidiary companies. It has been decided by the holding company to set a target return on capital employed for all of its subsidiaries, and so that each of the subsidiaries will start off in a similar situation it has been decided that the assets of each company shall be revalued as at 1st October, 1969. Discuss the problems which will arise in both carrying-out this revaluation and also in establishing the desired target rate of return. (*A.C.C.A.*)

# CHAPTER 4

## SALES AND PRODUCTION FORECASTS

### INTRODUCTION

FOR many types of business the sales forecast is the commencement of budgeting. The quantity of the company's products which can be sold may be the principal budget factor, and therefore it is around this that the system revolves. When the demand is assured, so that selling is principally a matter of producing as much as possible* at the right price, then the production or output forecast is the most important aspect; it also becomes the sales forecast.

### THE SALES FORECAST

The sales forecast is concerned with probable sales—physical quantities and values—for a future budget period. The choice of method to employ for forecasting sales is influenced by a number of factors. The nature of the product, the methods of distribution, the size of the business, and the degree of competition which exists are some of the considerations. Generally speaking, companies will obtain the best results from a combination of the methods given below. These are also considered in the previous chapter.

#### OPINIONS OF SALESMEN AND SALES MANAGERS

Salesmen, Branch Managers, Area Managers, and the Sales Director all contribute to the sales forecast. The procedures followed will vary from one business to another, but a possible plan may take the following form:

1. Each salesman is issued with past performance figures for each product sold. These figures are shown on a Forecast Statement drawn up in columnar form. A column is left blank for the salesman to insert his estimated figures. If preferred, four blank columns may be shown—one for each quarter.

An effort should be made to keep the work of each salesman down to a minimum. There would be no justification in asking for estimates on entirely new products which had not been marketed before. Nor is there much to be gained by asking for precise details of all sundry items which in total contribute only a small percentage to the grand total sales value. A better plan is to limit the enquiry to the principal lines to be sold and have a round figure for sundries. An example of the statement is shown in Fig. 8.

* Chapter 13 covers the problems connected with ascertaining optimum output.

Additional information may also be supplied; *e.g.* quantities of units sold *each* year for the past three years. If management wishes to ascertain the probable effect of changes in the price of each line, then two or three possible prices may be given and an estimate of sales at each price may be required. A limited time should be given for the completion and return of the forecasts. It is difficult to formulate general rules, but usually a period of two weeks will be adequate for a salesman to provide the necessary information.

| X.Y. Co. Ltd. | | | |
|---|---|---|---|
| Sales Forecast For Year Ending.................... | | | |
| Sales Area .......................... | | Salesman .......................... | |
| Product | Estimate for Year (Units) | Units Sold | |
| | | Last Year | Average for Last 3 Years |
| A at Standard Price £......... | | 5,000 | 4,500 |
| B ,, ,, ,, £......... | | 8,000 | 7,000 |
| C ,, ,, ,, £......... | | 4,000 | 6,000 |
| D ,, ,, ,, £......... | | 10,000 | 9,000 |
| Sundries (value) | | £2,000 | £1,500 |

FIG. 8.—*Specimen Sales Forecast* (*salesman*)

2. Branch Managers and Area Managers are asked to submit their *own* forecasts of sales.

A good plan is to instruct the managers to work quite independently of the salesmen. Reconciliation of the salesmen's and Branch Manager's forecasts, and then the Area Manager's forecasts, can take place after they have all been compiled. Where there is a difference between the salesmen's and managers' figures, then a compromise has to be adopted. If, for example, there are twelve salesmen attached to a particular branch and the total number of units per the salesmen is shown as 30,000 units of product "A," whereas the branch manager's forecast states 34,000 units, then a simple solution may be to take 32,000.

3. A summary of probable sales is supplied to the Sales Director. This is generally analysed by products, areas, and sales territories.

The work involved in summarising the figures may be carried out by the statistical section responsible for such work.

4. Standard prices are established. This task should be carried out jointly by the Sales Director, the Budget Controller, and other

accounting executives. The prices may be approved by the Budget Committee.

At this stage any influences which are likely to affect the sales forecast should be considered. A change in policy may affect the sales forecast, and therefore a suitable modification may be necessary. There may be other limiting factors, and these should also be taken into account. If statistical analyses are available these should be studied and compared with the forecasts with a view to possible amendment.

5. Having regard to the optimum level of operations, the sales mixture which is likely to maximise profit is selected.

The rate of return on each product has to be predetermined. The sales mixture selected becomes the *standard* sales mixture, and any deviation from this will subsequently be revealed by the sales mixture variance.

6. The sales forecast is evaluated. This involves multiplying quantities by standard prices. Once the forecast has been finalised—and this will include modifications for limiting factors—it becomes the sales budget.

## NON-STANDARD PRODUCTION

An estimate of probable sales in terms of physical units is only possible when homogeneous units are produced. Pairs of shoes, sacks of flour, gallons of paint, and hundredweights of chemicals are all examples where physical units can be forecasted. There are many other possible examples.

When jobs produced or contracts completed are different from each other, being built to customers' specifications, then a forecast in terms of physical units would be meaningless. Moreover, because standard units are not being produced, it generally means that a precise estimate of what customers will be requiring in the future is extremely difficult to produce.

If a company has a full order book extending into the future the problem of forecasting will clearly be much simplified. In all cases the forecast should be thought of in terms of pounds sterling. The expected *sales value* of the machines to be produced, the castings to be made, or any other special products can be shown on the forecast. Salesmen's and manager's opinions can be useful in determining the value of expected sales, but, at the same time, considerable use should be made of market research and statistical techniques.

## MARKET RESEARCH AND STATISTICAL TECHNIQUES

Sales forecasting involves the determination of future demand. Unless a company is in a monopolistic position, its management can expect only a proportion of the total demand which exists for a particular product. The part salesmen and managers can play is discussed in the preceding section. This section is concerned with the use which can be made of statistical data.

The necessary facts and figures may be collected in a variety of ways. In the small business very few records may be maintained. On the other hand, the medium to large concern may have a special statistical department. Sometimes an outside specialist may be employed to collect and analyse the relevant data. Many large companies now employ economists, who concern themselves with trade trends and inter-firm comparisons. Field workers may be employed to collect information on possible sales. In the realm of consumer goods, questions may be asked on a door-to-door basis or by stopping potential consumers in the streets. Extensive use can be made of financial and trade journals, as well as those issued by trade associations and Government Departments. The whole process—whether using internal or external records or other means—is known as "market research." On the detailed working there are many excellent books to which reference can be made.

Information on past sales, irrespective of how collected, is a guide to possible future sales. It is not an *absolute* guide, but rather an indication of probabilities. Conditions change, and therefore any estimates must consider what conditions are expected to exist during the budget period. Unusual or abnormal occurrences that have taken place in the past, such as an acute shortage of material or labour, the incidence of war, or an unusually "tense situation" in international relations between two or more countries, may have affected sales. The extent of the influence exerted has to be estimated when forecasting future sales.

Besides past occurrences, present and future developments should be considered. A growth in population, a rise in average incomes or the incomes of particular classes, immigration or emigration, and other social changes may affect possible sales. The growth of competition, a change in the cost of basic materials, imposition of purchase tax, or a change in tariff regulations may also affect the position. Even the control of money and credit by a "credit squeeze," or a government decision to enter into a "common market," must play its part in influencing the sales figures. Above all, the optimism or pessimism of government, businessmen, and consumers must affect possible sales. When there is optimism people will invest and consumers will buy; accordingly, industry prospers, increases its profits, and expands. If there is pessimism, stagnation and possibly decline are almost inevitable.

Study of the factors mentioned in previous paragraphs in this section should show to what extent past sales can be taken as a guide to the future. The total demand for a product may have increased or diminished. Careful analysis of all relevant facts should show what can actually be expected.

Demand is not the only factor which has to be considered. Careful study of the aspects which are likely to affect possible sales will be essential. Even if a large demand exists for a product, the individual business may not be able to market the full quantity. The limiting factors, defined earlier, may impose restrictions. There may be a shortage of finance, with the result that any necessary expansion is impossible. Alternatively, a shortage of suitable workers or of a basic raw material may limit the volume of production. It is possible that the optimum level of operations (discussed in Chapter 13) has been reached, so that any further increase in production will increase costs quite excessively. Even if the required volume of *production* is feasible, the selling, promotion, and advertising costs necessary for obtaining additional sales may be out of all proportion to the extra revenue.

When considering the volume of sales which can be expected to accrue to a particular business in a future budget period an attempt is usually made to establish significant relationships. An increase in the average incomes of wage-earners may normally be followed by a fractional increase in sales of a particular product. There may be a definite correlation between orders received in a certain month and orders received for the full budget period. Often the orders being received by *other* industries may be of significance. A planned increase in the number of building projects being undertaken by building contractors may be an indication that there is to be an increase in the demand for raw materials, such as bricks, cement, and other building materials. Often the sales of one product go hand in hand with the sales of a product made by another industry. The sales of cars will tend to influence the sale of car radios, safety belts, and similar accessories. Even competing products cannot be disregarded. The introduction of man-made fibres has replaced, to a large extent, many natural products. Nylon has largely replaced silk, and plastics have tended to supersede metals; these are well-known examples, there are many others. Above all, the supremacy of the consumer should not be overlooked; his preferences change, and the sales forecast should reflect this fact.

Market research and related techniques may not provide the cheapest method of obtaining data on future sales. This fact should not be overlooked when selecting the method to employ.

## COMBINATION OF METHODS

As already indicated, in practice a combination of methods will be employed. Much depends upon the nature of the business, the products involved, and the methods of selling and distribution. For some concerns forecasting may be relatively simple and cover a full year; with others, due to uncertainty, a quarterly forecast may be the most reasonable solution. The methods employed should be the most appropriate to the needs of the business.

## THE FORM OF THE SALES FORECAST

The form that the sales forecast, and therefore the sales budget, may take is shown in the illustration (Fig. 9). In practice, many variations may be found.

An annual sales forecast is illustrated. In order to show responsibilities the forecast is divided into sales areas. Quarterly figures are illustrated: a further subdivision to show four-weekly details may be included on the forecast; alternatively, the breakdown may be carried out on separate work sheets. A further analysis into sales quotas, showing the responsibilities of individual salesmen, can also be covered on work sheets.

**ANNUAL SALES FORECAST**

Year ending.......................................

| | Last Year | Total Year | First Quarter | Second Quarter | Third Quarter | Fourth Quarter |
|---|---|---|---|---|---|---|
| *Southern Area* | | | | | | |
| UNITS of: | | | | | | |
| Product A | 10,000 | 11,000 | 3,000 | 5,000 | 1,000 | 2,000 |
| Product B | 12,000 | 13,200 | 4,000 | 4,000 | 3,000 | 2,200 |
| Product C | 6,000 | 6,600 | 1,000 | 2,000 | 2,000 | 1,600 |
| | | | | | | |
| *Northern Area* | | | | | | |
| UNITS OF: | | | | | | |
| Product A | 4,000 | 4,400 | 1,000 | 1,000 | 1,000 | 1,400 |
| Product B | 16,000 | 17,600 | 5,000 | 4,000 | 4,000 | 4,600 |
| Product C | 10,000 | 11,000 | 3,000 | 4,000 | 2,000 | 2,000 |
| | | | | | | |
| *Southern Area* | | | | | | |
| VALUE of: | £ | £ | £ | £ | £ | £ |
| Std. Price | | | | | | |
| Product A £0·5 | 5,000 | 5,500 | 1,500 | 2,500 | 500 | 1,000 |
| Product B £1·0 | 12,000 | 13,200 | 4,000 | 4,000 | 3,000 | 2,200 |
| Product C £0·1 | 600 | 660 | 100 | 200 | 200 | 160 |
| | 17,600 | 19,360 | 5,600 | 6,700 | 3,700 | 3,360 |
| | | | | | | |
| *Northern Area* | | | | | | |
| VALUE of: | £ | £ | £ | £ | £ | £ |
| Std. Price | | | | | | |
| Product A £0·5 | 2,000 | 2,200 | 500 | 500 | 500 | 700 |
| Product B £1·0 | 16,000 | 17,600 | 5,000 | 4,000 | 4,000 | 4,600 |
| Product C £0·1 | 1,000 | 1,100 | 300 | 400 | 200 | 200 |
| | 19,000 | 20,900 | 5,800 | 4,900 | 4,700 | 5,500 |
| | | | | | | |
| *Grand Totals* £ | 36,600 | 40,260 | 11,400 | 11,600 | 8,400 | 8,860 |

FIG. 9.—*Specimen Annual Sales Forecast*

D

In the example both physical units and standard values are shown. The fact that, for companies producing to customers' specifications, physical units cannot be forecast has already been noticed. For such companies sales values only will be shown. Some writers on Budgetary Control describe the initial forecast containing physical units only (or sales value only) as the "sales estimate," thus distinguishing it from the completed sales forecast or budget.

A useful addition to the forecast is a summary which shows the annual totals of physical units and values. Sometimes the cost of sales and budgeted profits on each product are also shown on the sales forecast, but many accountants prefer to include these on the budgeted Profit and Loss Statement.

If the standard-hour concept is used—and this will be essential for jobbing production—the "sales value" may be determined by reference to the cost elements plus the normal margin of profit as determined by the Board of Directors or other top management. A good starting-point may be the output forecast. Following this can come the forecasts of primary and overhead costs for the level of output shown in the output forecast. The costs expected to be incurred can be augmented by the profit percentage to arrive at forecasted sales. If different divisions or departments earn different rates of profit, then a breakdown for each division will be essential. The form the forecast should take should present no problem. Forecasts of costs, explained in a later section, should be summarised and then the rate of profit added to arrive at the sales values.

## PRODUCTION OR OUTPUT FORECAST

The production or output forecast is concerned with estimating the probable output of each product in the forthcoming budget period. Where standard products are made the problem is one of deciding how many units of each product can be made by the machines, equipment, and other production facilities. Alternatively, output may be shown in tons or, for non-standard work, in terms of "standard hours." The standard-hour concept is used frequently, both in Standard Costing and budgeting. It refers to the amount of work that can be performed in one hour. Since, in businesses producing to customers' specifications, each job produced will be different, the only common measure available is time to be spent on producing—hence the use of the standard hour.

Which should come first, the sales forecast or output forecast, is difficult to determine. Much depends upon the nature of the business; the variety of products, the complexity of production, and the nature of the selling problem all affect the decision. In some circumstances it will be essential to forecast what products can be sold and then attempt to produce them with the facilities that are available, bearing in mind that costs have to be kept at a minimum. When selling presents no great problem the output forecast may be the starting-point. Attention should be paid to producing the largest volume compatible with maximising profit and achieving long-term financial stability.

If there are any differences between the sales forecast and the output forecast figures, whether in volume or product mixture, then these may be reconciled by the Budget Committee.

For many businesses a single forecast of production (or sales) may be of very limited value. A number of forecasts may be necessary to arrive at the one which reveals the most profitable output. Co-ordination of the sales potential and production capacity is essential at all times. Accordingly, there is much to be said for preparing a number of "sets" of sales and production forecasts. The combination of the two forecasts which show the best results should be the one adopted.

When standardised products are made, along mass-production lines, it should be possible to set standard times for each. The number of units which can be produced involves a relatively simple calculation. The hours available can be divided by the standard time or times. If only one product is to be made and the standard time is one hour each, then a production capacity of 10,000 hours should produce 10,000 units. If a variety of products is to be made the problem is more complex; nevertheless, the same principle applies. Factories concerned with batch production can use similar procedures. The Production Planning Department will calculate the times involved in each department or process, and these enable an estimate of production volume to be made.

The need to hold stocks complicates the procedure. A corollary of this is the necessity to keep stocks of finished goods in quantities which enable customers' requirements to be met quickly and yet are the minimum levels.

The matter does not end there. Minimum stock holding may not be compatible with full employment of production facilities and labour. Accordingly, management has to determine which is more important: minimising the cost of holding stocks or minimising the costs of production by maintaining a high level of output. When sales tend to be seasonal the problem has to be faced without delay. Is production to be maintained at a stable level, or are stocks to be minimised?

On the side of a steady level of production are a number of advantages. The detailed planning of production is much easier; labour turnover is kept to a minimum, with consequent improved personnel relations; investment in plant can be kept to a minimum, thereby keeping fixed costs as low as possible, and overtime is also kept to a low level. There is no doubt that many of these factors, especially those connected with labour turnover, are of special importance in a period of full employment, when difficulties are experienced in obtaining the necessary man-power.

Nevertheless, the possible disadvantages should not be overlooked. The higher the level of production, the greater will be the stocks carried in the slack periods. Increased storage space, with resultant increases in the costs of storekeeping, including insurance premiums, as well as a greater possibility of obsolescence and the danger of loss on a falling market, are all matters which have to be considered and compared with the possible advantages.

The nature of the product must have a definite bearing on the solving of the problem. If it is of a staple character with little possibility of becoming unpopular through changes of fashion, or obsolete due to technical advancement, then stabilised production—and seasonal stock levels—may be a sound policy. When there is danger of obsolescence, price reductions, or similar risks, these have to be considered in the light of the benefits of stabilised production, and a decision on what line to follow has to be made.

## IMPORTANCE OF PRODUCTION FORECAST

The production forecast and, later, the production budget is an essential part of the budgetary control system. Without it there can be no co-ordination of the sales and production efforts. The Sales Department may like to sell a certain variety of products, whereas the Production Department may not be in a position to produce that variety in the quantities suggested. Only by studying both aspects can a workable plan be made.

From the production forecast and related schedules it will be possible to work out labour, material, and service requirements for both the producing departments and service departments. The fact that formal recognition is being given to calculating the requirements should mean that nothing is overlooked. If there are any problems to resolve in obtaining the information, then these should become quite apparent well in advance, allowing any necessary action to be taken in good time.

This action may also include arranging for a sub-contractor to carry out part of the work. Additional business may be dealt with by an outside contractor until such times as the firm's own plant can be expanded. If there is some doubt as to the permanency of the additional volume of work then entering into subcontracts may be the best solution.

The stock position must also be clarified before the production forecast can be compiled. How much stock of work-in-progress at different stages of production and what quantities of finished goods should be carried have to be determined before the forecast is made. The importance of the decision made—whether to carry minimum stocks *or* aim at stabilised production—is covered in other sections in this chapter.

From the production forecast and related cost forecasts emerges the forecasted cost of sales. This can be used to ascertain the profitability of each line produced. If necessary, action can be taken to eliminate unprofitable lines and possibly substitute more profitable products. This once more emphasises the desire to maximise profit: a fact to be remembered throughout Budgetary Control.

Underlying all activities is the necessity to spend money. Whether expansion or any other proposed measure on the production side can be taken depends very much upon anticipated cash flow, both incoming from sales and outgoing from expenditure. The production forecast indicates what the cash requirements of production are likely to be and materially assists the compiling of the cash forecast.

## PRODUCTION FORECASTS ILLUSTRATED

The production or output forecast will be compiled from material specifications, time schedules, and other records, all of which have to be carefully built up by production engineers, draughtsmen, work-study engineers, and other production personnel. Particular attention has to be paid to ensuring that work flows through the factory at an even rate without doubling back in its tracks and without causing bottlenecks. In short, the largest possible volume of output should be the aim.

| PRODUCTION FORECAST Quarter: from...................... to ........................... | | | |
|---|---|---|---|
| Product | Budget Centre Producing X | Budget Centre Producing Y | Budget Centre Producing Z |
| A B C | Units 4000 9000 4000 | Units 4000 — 4000 | Units 4000 9000 — |

FIG. 10.—*Specimen Production Forecast*

NOTES

Where units are shown this indicates the forecast of work to be carried out in the budget centre indicated. Thus, for example, "4000" in column "X" in respect of product "A" indicates that material, labour and other requirements will be needed for operations to be covered in that centre. The same applies in columns "Y" and "Z." It should be noted that these are the same units as in column "X."

In the case of product "B" it will be apparent that no operations are involved in budget centre "Y"; this is also the case for product "C" in centre "Z."

When there are no stocks the problem of forecasting is simplified. A simple production forecast in terms of units may take the form shown above (Fig. 10). This assumes that standard products are made. For the majority of businesses the assumption that no stocks exist is clearly an oversimplification. Accordingly, the forecasts shown later in this section are likely to apply.

## INTRODUCING STOCKS INTO FORECASTS

When finished stocks have to be carried the questions already discussed above—whether minimum stocks *or* stabilised production are to be the aim—have to be determined. These clearly affect the compiling of the forecast. An example of a production forecast with minimum stocks is shown in Fig. 11, whereas varying stock levels and, therefore, stabilised production are illustrated in Fig. 12. Obviously the principles involved in drafting the forecast are the same in both cases. However, there is a very important difference. The management policy behind the forecasts will produce different results, which will affect long-term prospects and profit.

| PRODUCTION FORECAST (or STOCK FORECAST) Quarter: from.................. to .................... | | | | | |
|---|---|---|---|---|---|
| Product | Month | Opening Stock | Production for Month | Sales | Closing Stock |
| | | Units | Units | Units | Units |
| A | Jan. | 250 | 1200 | 1200 | 250 |
| A | Feb. | 250 | 1500 | 1500 | 250 |
| A | March | 250 | 1050 | 1050 | 250 |

FIG. 11.—*Specimen Production Forecast (or Stock Forecast)*

NOTES

1. Management has determined that a stock level of 250 should not be exceeded. It is felt that, due to the uncertainty of future demand for product "A," the stock should be kept to the minimum figure which is compatible with meeting any unexpected orders which may come along.

2. The fact that production is to fluctuate means that the labour force may have to be increased—or reduced, from one month to another. This presents problems which may be overcome by the employment of casual workers. Naturally, in some industries where skilled work is predominant, there may be difficulty in carrying out such a policy.

3. This forecast may be used for showing expected output and stocks. Therefore it serves a dual purpose.

4. The forecast has been shortened deliberately. Only product "A" has been shown. The complete forecast would show all products.

5. A quarter has been taken and broken down into monthly control periods. A longer period of a year would be necessary to reconcile with the sales forecast.

## FORECASTS FOR PRODUCTION COSTS

There are three* forecasts for production costs, and these are as follows:

1. Direct Material Forecast.
2. Direct Labour Forecast.
3. Factory Overhead Forecast.

* A fourth possibility is a "Direct Expense Forecast." However, direct expense could be included in the Direct Material Forecast.

These are explained below. The examples given have been kept quite simple. In practice, they may be more complex; nevertheless, the same principles still apply.

| | | | PRODUCTION FORECAST (OR STOCK FORECAST) | | |
| | | | Quarter: from................ | | |
| | | | to................... | | |
| Product | Month | Opening Stock | Production for Month | Sales | Closing Stock Units |
|---|---|---|---|---|---|
| | | Units | Units | Units | Units |
| A | Jan. | 250 | 1250 | 1200 | 300 |
| A | Feb. | 300 | 1250 | 1500 | 50 |
| A | March | 50 | 1250 | 1050 | 250 |

FIG. 12.—*Specimen Production Forecast (or Stock Forecast)*

NOTES

1. Again only part of the forecast is shown, but this should be quite adequate to illustrate the principles involved.

2. The rate of production is maintained at a steady level throughout the year, thus enjoying the advantages of stabilised production.

## DIRECT MATERIAL* FORECAST

Before commencing the preparation of the material forecast it is a sound plan to set up procedures for ensuring that only the correct quality of materials is to be purchased. Standardisation of all features —sizes, qualities, colours, and other aspects—ensures that the most suitable materials are used at minimum cost.

When standardised products are manufactured, along mass-production or batch production lines, preparation of a standard material specification is the first step. This is a detailed analysis of the materials required to make each product. When determining the standard quantities it is usual to allow for normal wastage and for cutting or "parting off." Production personnel will be concerned with assessing the quantities from past records, test runs, or technical estimates based on weight content or other factor.

The standard prices of materials should be fixed by the Purchasing Agent, who collaborates with the Accountant or Budget Controller. These prices will be used to evaluate the standard material specifications which are summarised on schedules before the final figures are transferred to departmental forecasts for materials.

---

* Direct material becomes part of the product being produced for sale. However, if its cost is quite small a material may be treated as indirect, even though it is strictly direct material (*see* Chapter 2).

An example of a departmental forecast is shown below (Fig. 13). All departmental forecasts will be taken together and summarised to form the material forecast.

When job production is in operation the task of estimating raw-material requirements is far from easy. The usual method is to refer to

## DEPARTMENTAL FORECAST FOR MATERIALS
### Department X

Period: from ..........................

to...............................

| Product and Quantities | Material Code | Standard Quantity | Standard Price | Values | Totals |
|---|---|---|---|---|---|
| | | Units | £ | £ | £ |
| A. 4000 units | | | | | |
| B. 9000 units | | | | | |
| C. 4000 units | | | | | |
| | | | | | £ |

FIG. 13.—*Specimen Departmental Forecast for Materials*

NOTES

1. The material code and standard quantities for the actual production (*e.g.* 4000 units for product "A") would be entered in the second and third columns.

2. The standard prices are determined and entered in the fourth column and then the product of standard quantities and prices is entered in the "value column." Sub-totals are extended into the final column.

3. The concern is with direct materials.

the sales forecast, to past years' production figures, and to the normal direct material content of output. The main types of materials used should receive attention. The quantities of each of these are evaluated by the use of standard prices. A total allowance can be made to cover sundry direct materials.

With due attention and care quite good results should emerge. In some cases a departmental breakdown for standard lines should improve accuracy.

## DIRECT LABOUR FORECAST

Once the preliminary classification of labour into its principal grades has been carried out, the labour requirements needed for each product can be estimated. The operations involved are listed, and then standard times are set.

The standard times are preferably established by use of work study. Alternatively, they may be set by reference to past performance records.

Calculation of the total number of hours now takes place. The hours are then converted into labour requirements. The labour needs for each department are entered on a departmental labour forecast. This is illustrated below (Fig. 14).

### DEPARTMENTAL LABOUR FORECAST

**Budget Centre X**    **Period:** from ...................... to..........................

**Output:** 4000 units 'A'
9000 units 'B'  } 34,000 standard hours.
4000 units 'C'

| Employees | Number | Hours | Standard Rate | Direct Labour Cost | Total |
|---|---|---|---|---|---|
| | | | £ | £ | £ |
| *Male*<br>Skilled<br>Semi-skilled<br>Unskilled | | | | | |
| *Female*<br>Skilled<br>Semi-skilled<br>Unskilled | | | | | |
| *Juniors*<br>Male<br>Female | | | | £ | |

FIG. 14.—*Specimen Departmental Labour Forecast*

NOTES

1. The headings and rulings given may be varied to suit particular requirements.
2. Each department's requirements are covered in the same way—one departmental forecast for each. All these forecasts are summarised on a direct labour forecast summary.

These remarks apply principally to standard product lines. For companies who are concerned with job or special order production a different procedure will be necessary. When order books cover a substantial part of the budget period it will be possible to forecast labour requirements from the estimates prepared to arrive at the costs and prices. Alternatively, if orders have not been received the direct labour requirements can be estimated by applying a percentage—based on past experience—to the total value of the sales forecast.

The preparation of the forecast is in three main stages. The first is the calculation of the man-power required for each department. The different grades of labour, male and female, and the numbers involved would be ascertained and listed for each department.

The second stage is the setting of standard wage-rates. Much depends upon the system of payment as to the procedure followed. All factors, local and national, which affect wage-rates have to be analysed. If time rates are in operation in the company, then the object should be to assess the future trend for the budget period and set the standard rate accordingly. If there is a wages agreement which covers the future budget period, then the rate can be taken from that agreement. When piece-rates are used the calculation of the labour cost will be made by reference to the standard rate per piece and the forecasted output. When bonuses are paid these have to be estimated in relation to output and included as part of the standard rate or as part of the factory overhead cost. The former method may be preferred, because it tends to show quite clearly the total direct labour cost.

The third stage is the bringing together of the number of each grade and the appropriate standard wage-rate on the departmental labour forecast, at the same time showing the direct labour cost.

## FACTORY OVERHEAD FORECAST

The factory overhead costs have to be predetermined for producing centres and service centres. Careful analysis of costs into those which are "variable" and those which are "fixed" is essential before any attempt is made to forecast the costs. All indirect costs likely to be incurred by the factory departments have to be covered. Indirect labour, material, sundry supplies, rent, depreciation, insurance, clerical costs, supervision, repairs and maintenance, overtime premiums, and idle time costs are all examples, provided they relate to the factory and not to one of the other functions.

A good deal of planning, careful study, and determination of the behaviour of different types of costs will be essential. One of the most important tasks is to determine the relation which exists between each type of overhead cost and some factor which exists within the business. Some costs vary directly with volume of output; a 10% increase in output results in a similar increase in some overhead costs. Others may increase or reduce with changes in direct labour cost or direct material cost. These remarks apply to variable overhead costs.

Work study may be useful for fixing allowances for indirect labour costs. Routine work of a standardised nature may be thought of in terms of "work units": square yards of sweeping, pointing or other work; points to grease or oil; hundredweights of coal, ash, or other material regularly moved. These are all examples of where a standard time can be set for each work unit. Making due allowance for rest periods, it should be possible to work back and calculate the number of sweepers, painters, maintenance workers, and other indirect workers who are to be engaged on routine work of the nature described.

Unfortunately not all indirect labour can be thought of in terms of work units. Much of the work is of a varied, heterogeneous nature. Often there is no standardised pattern either in the way the work is performed or when it is performed. Repairs and maintenance work often occur intermittently. Planned, preventive maintenance can introduce a balancing influence on the work load, but, even then, there is still the unexpected, unpredictable breakdown which makes the forecasting of costs very difficult.

Maintenance labour costs will tend to vary with changes in the volume of output. An increase in the volume will tend to bring about a related increase in the labour cost. This applies to the long-run tendency; in the short period a reduction in output may mean that major overhauls can now be tackled, so that maintenance labour costs increase substantially.

The age and condition of plant and machinery and the intensity of use are very important factors in determining the cost of maintenance, both for materials and labour. New machines tend to be more reliable—naturally so—and, furthermore, the maintenance problem is often made simpler by the use of special "non-grease" bearings or other labour-saving devices. On the other hand, generally speaking, the older machines have to be maintained constantly.

A useful device for forecasting the number of indirect workers within a department for different levels of activity is a flexible estimate for indirect labour. The use of this estimate presupposes that there is a definite relationship between the number of direct workers and the number of indirect workers. Production personnel and accountants can collaborate in the determination of the relationship which exists. From past experience and careful study it should be possible to ascertain the increase in *indirect* work of a particular type which is likely to follow from an increase in the volume of output. The increase in indirect work can be converted into terms of man-power, and thereby the estimate is built up. An example is given in Fig. 15.

Fixed overhead costs will tend to vary over a *wide* range of output. However, within certain limits the fixed costs remain constant, and therefore within the short period, for all practical purposes, the costs are

## FLEXIBLE ESTIMATE FOR INDIRECT LABOUR

### Department X

| | Numbers of Direct Workers | | | | |
| --- | --- | --- | --- | --- | --- |
| | Up to 50 | 51–70 | 71–90 | 91–110 | 111–130 |
| Foremen | 1 | 1 | 1 | 2 | 2 |
| Chargehands | 7 | 8 | 9 | 10 | 11 |
| Shop Clerks | 1 | 1 | 2 | 2 | 3 |
| Setters | 2 | 3 | 4 | 5 | 6 |
| General Workers | 4 | 4 | 4 | 5 | 5 |
| Internal Transport Workers | 4 | 4 | 4 | 6 | 6 |

FIG. 15.—*Example of a Flexible Estimate for Indirect Labour*

NOTES

1. Instead of using the number of direct workers it may be possible to take standard hours for each level of activity. Obviously the same results should be obtained.

2. The figures given are shown only for the purpose of illustration. The number of foremen, chargehands or other indirect employees will vary very much with the type of work being undertaken. Some work involves little or no supervision; other kinds, of an intricate nature, may need a large staff of supervisors.

3. The principle may be extended to cover an estimate of other costs besides those relating to indirect labour. Depreciation may be regarded as being related to machine hours worked. Therefore, the possible levels of activity in machine hours could replace the number of direct workers to estimate the depreciation charge.

"fixed." The great difficulty is to predetermine *how much* each type of cost will vary when there is a significant change in the volume of output. Past experience, with allowances for changes in conditions, is likely to be the foundation for most fixed overhead costs. Many are controllable by top management, and for this reason are known as "policy costs." Most of them are incurred on a time basis, so this at least introduces a constant factor into the problem of predetermination of fixed costs.

The preparation of flexible estimates is, of course, the commencement of flexible budgeting, which is absolutely essential for controlling costs. More details of this topic are given later in this chapter.

When considering sundry supplies and other indirect materials, past experience can again be invaluable. Naturally, care must be taken to reflect any changes in conditions and material prices. In this way the past is brought into line with likely events in the future. Careful analysis of material requisitions covering the issue of indirect materials over, say, the previous year may be a good guide. Related to output the appropriate budget allowances can be determined.

## PREPARATION OF THE BUDGET

An understanding of terms used in forecasting and budgeting is essential before proceeding to the drawing up of the budget. Essentially there are only two types of budget. There is the fixed budget and the flexible budget. The former shows one volume of output and related costs. The flexible budget portrays a number of possible outputs and different cost structures. Since it is very unlikely that the volume selected in the forecast and budget will be the one obtained in practice, the flexible budget is the only one which can enable costs to be controlled effectively.

| FLEXIBLE BUDGET OF MANUFACTURING OVERHEAD COSTS | | | | | | | | |
|---|---|---|---|---|---|---|---|---|
| Month January | | | | | | | | Dept. A.B. |
| Overhead Cost Description | Bases for calculating Total Cost | | Output in Percentages | | | | | |
| | Fixed | Variable | 90% | 95% | 100% | 105% | 110% | 115% |
| | £ | Per Std. hr. £ | £ | £ | £ | £ | £ | £ |
| *Variable Costs:* | | | | | | | | |
| Spoilage | | 0·050 | 450 | 475 | 500 | 525 | 550 | 575 |
| Indirect Materials | | 0·100 | 900 | 950 | 1,000 | 1,050 | 1,100 | 1,150 |
| *Semi-Variable Costs:* | | | | | | | | |
| Indirect Labour | 500 | 0·250 | 2,750 | 2,875 | 3,000 | 3,125 | 3,250 | 3,375 |
| Power and Light | 400 | 0·100 | 1,300 | 1,350 | 1,400 | 1,450 | 1,500 | 1,550 |
| Heat and Water | 200 | 0·100 | 1,100 | 1,150 | 1,200 | 1,250 | 1,300 | 1,350 |
| Insurance on Stocks | 150 | 0·025 | 375 | 388 | 400 | 413 | 425 | 438 |
| Repairs and Maintenance | 600 | 0·250 | 2,850 | 2,975 | 3,100 | 3,225 | 3,350 | 3,475 |
| *Fixed Costs:* | | | | | | | | |
| Supervision | 1000 | | 1,000 | 1,000 | 1,000 | 1,000 | 1,000 | 1,000 |
| Depreciation | 4000 | | 4,000 | 4,000 | 4,000 | 4,000 | 4,000 | 4,000 |
| Rent Charges | 1500 | | 1,500 | 1,500 | 1,500 | 1,500 | 1,500 | 1,500 |
| Other Space Charges | 900 | | 900 | 900 | 900 | 900 | 900 | 900 |
| | | | £17,125 | £17,563 | £18,000 | £18,438 | £18,875 | £19,313 |
| Rate per Standard Hour | | | £1·90 | £1·85 | £1·80 | £1·76 | £1·72 | £1·68 |

FIG. 16.—*Example of a Flexible Budget of Manufacturing Overhead Costs*

NOTES

1. The figures used are purely hypothetical; they are taken to the nearest £1.
2. Output may be stated in terms of:

(a) Percentages, when it is quite usual to state what "100%" represents (*e.g.* as in example, 10,000 standard hours or, say, 10,000 units of Product "X").
(b) Units of Output.
(c) Sales Values.
(d) Standard Hours.

3. The semi-variable costs will have been separated into their fixed and variable elements by one of the methods covered in Chapter 10.
4. Comparison with the budget shown in the section on Selling Costs may be made with advantage.
5. Costs for any output which is not an exact multiple of 5% may be found by interpolation.
6. The charge "per hour" is used for simplicity—in practice, for many costs, it would be unrealistic.

In practice, it will be necessary to use both types of budget. The budgeted level of operations which forms part of the co-ordinated budget plan will have to act as the foundation of the budgetary control system. All personnel will aim at the targets set and, provided deviations are not too wide, the plans are taken to be operating satisfactorily. Even if this is so, control is still essential. This is where the flexible budget comes in; it is the only practical way of controlling factory overhead costs (considered further in Chapter 14).

An example of a flexible budget (or forecast) is given in Fig. 16. One of the main problems is to classify the overhead costs into variable and fixed. This is not altogether an easy matter, especially when the costs are of a semi-variable nature. Each one has to be separated into its fixed and variable elements. Regression or scattergraph charts may be used. The costs are plotted on a chart in relation to output and a line is drawn through the points to show the variability of the costs. An alternative method is the use of the statistical technique known as "least squares" (see Chapter 10, "Marginal Costing").

### EXAMINATION QUESTIONS

1. Having prepared a scheme of Budgetary Control, you are asked by the Management to submit a short tabulated report stating how you propose to ensure effectiveness of the scheme. Prepare such a report. (*I.C.W.A.*)

2. "Costs are best controlled by the use of Standard Marginal Costing, together with Budgetary Control for Fixed Overheads." Discuss this statement. (*I.C.W.A.*)

3. Outline a budget procedure suitable for a company manufacturing a product in seasonal demand, and having two main selling seasons a year. Production is restricted between seasons to a level sufficient to maintain minimum stocks only, extra personnel being engaged at peak periods to cope with seasonal demand. (*I.C.W.A.*)

4. Production costs of a factory for a year are as follows:

|  | £ |
|---|---|
| Direct Wages ... ... ... ... ... ... ... | 40,000 |
| Direct Materials ... ... ... ... ... ... | 60,000 |
| Fixed Production Overheads ... ... ... ... | 20,000 |
| Variable Production Overheads ... ... ... ... | 30,000 |

During the forthcoming year it is anticipated that:

(*a*) The average rate for remuneration of direct labour will fall from £0·166 per hour to £0·156 per hour;

(*b*) Production efficiency will be unchanged;

(*c*) Direct labour hours will increase by 33⅓ per cent.;

(*d*) The purchase price per unit of direct materials and of the other materials and services included amongst overheads will remain unchanged.

Draw up a Budget and compute a factory overhead rate, the overheads being absorbed on a direct wages basis. (*S.C.A.*)

5. The accounts for a manufacturing company for a year are as follows:

|  |  | £ |
|---|---|---|
| Direct materials ... ... ... ... ... | ... | 175,000 |
| Direct wages ... ... ... ... ... ... | ... | 100,000 |
| Variable factory overheads ... ... ... ... | ... | 100,000 |
| Fixed factory overheads ... ... ... ... | ... | 100,000 |
| Other variable costs ... ... ... ... ... | ... | 80,000 |
| Other fixed costs ... ... ... ... ... | ... | 80,000 |
| Profit ... ... ... ... ... ... ... | ... | 115,000 |
| Sales ... ... ... ... ... ... ... | ... | 750,000 |

Two products, A and B, are manufactured, and during the year output and costs were as follows:

|  | A | B |
|---|---|---|
| Output (units) ... ... | 200,000 | 100,000 |
| Selling price (each) ... ... | £2·00 | £3·50 |
| Direct materials (each) ... | £0·50 | £0·75 |
| Direct wages (each) ... ... | £0·25 | £0·50 |

Factory overheads are absorbed as a percentage on direct wages; other overheads, half fixed, half variable, have been computed to amount to 10s. per unit for product A and £0·60 per unit for product B.

During the coming year it is expected that demand for product A will fall by 25%, and for product B by 50%: it is decided to manufacture a further product C, the costs, etc., for which are estimated as follows:

| Output (units) ... ... | 200,000 |
|---|---|
| Selling price (each) ... ... | £1·750 |
| Direct materials (each) ... | £0·375 |
| Direct wages (each) ... ... | £0·250 |

It is anticipated that the other variable costs per unit will be the same as for product A.

Compile a budget to present to management, showing the current position, and the anticipated results for the coming year. (*I.C.W.A.*)

6. Outline the steps necessary for the preparation of a detailed man-power estimate which would be of value in preparing a labour budget.

Compile a man-power estimate for a production department showing the break-down to cost centres of the various grades of labour required.

(*I.C.W.A.*)

7. What difficulties would you expect to find in the compilation of a flexible budget?

Give sufficient detail to justify any assumptions you make. How would such a budget be used? (*I.C.W.A.*)

8. Briefly define the following:

(a) Works Budget.
(b) Material Control.
(c) Overtime Premium.
(d) Fixed Cost.
(e) Stock Control. (*S.C.A.*)

9. A manufacturing company produces four main lines of standard products. The following is an analysis of its trading account for the year ended 31st May, .... :

| Product | Sales (units) | Sales value | Material cost | Labour cost | Variable expenses | Margin |
|---|---|---|---|---|---|---|
| | | £ | £ | £ | £ | £ |
| A | 4,000 | 3,200 | 800 | 800 | 600 | 1,000 |
| B | 5,000 | 5,000 | 1,500 | 1,250 | 1,000 | 1,250 |
| C | 10,000 | 12,500 | 8,400 | 1,600 | 1,300 | 1,200 |
| D | 3,000 | 7,500 | 1,800 | 2,900 | 2,300 | 500 |
| | | £28,200 | £12,500 | £6,550 | £5,200 | £3,950 |

Deduct: Fixed expenses    ...    ...    ...    ...    4,200

Net loss for year    ...    ...    ...    ...    ...    £250

The sales department have produced a sales budget for the following year ending 31st May, ...., as under:

| Product | Units | Value (£) |
|---|---|---|
| A | 3,000 | 2,500 |
| B | 6,000 | 5,500 |
| C | 12,500 | 15,000 |
| D | 4,000 | 10,000 |
| | | £33,000 |

In advising the Board whether or not to accept the sales budget as a basis of operations for the year ahead, what points would you consider and what further information would you require?      (I.C.W.A.)

CHAPTER 5

## MISCELLANEOUS BUDGETS

IN the previous two chapters many of the budgets to be found in a Budgetary Control system are given. Other budgets are discussed in later chapters, the most important of these relating to cash and capital expenditure.

A summary of the matters covered in this chapter is given below:

1. Selling and Distribution Costs Budgets.
2. Advertising Costs Budget.
3. Administration Costs Budget.
4. Research and Development Costs Budget.
5. Purchasing Budget.
6. Service Departments' Budgets.
7. Fixed Costs Budget.
8. Master Budget.

The control aspect is dealt with in Chapter 14.

### SELLING AND DISTRIBUTION COSTS

Selling and distribution are essential aspects of the profit-earning functions. Indeed, it is true to say that in many businesses selling and distribution are just as important as production. Unfortunately, in many instances the predetermination of the costs involved is extremely difficult. Control, covered in Chapter 14, is often more difficult still.

#### SELLING COSTS BUDGET

Selling costs are spent in order to maintain and increase the level of sales. All expenses connected with advertising, sales promotion, sales office, salesmen, and credit and collection are generally grouped together and are the responsibility of the Sales Manager.

Division of the selling costs into the following is advisable:

1. Variable Costs.
2. Fixed Costs.

Any semi-variable costs should be separated into variable and fixed elements. This action should make predetermination of costs much easier. However, even when this is done, the task may be far from easy. Often heavy expenditure has to be incurred at a time when the volume of sales is falling off. Sometimes intensive sales and promotion effort is called for in one year, but the benefits are expected to accrue over a number of years.

A.B. & Co. Ltd., Flexible Budget—Selling Costs. Year Ending December 31st, 19...

| Functional Cost | Fixed Variable Semi-Variable | Fixed element | Variable element per Std. Unit | Possible Sales Volumes (in £000s) and Related Costs | | | | | |
|---|---|---|---|---|---|---|---|---|---|
| | | | | £600 | £620 | £640 | £660 | £680 | £700 |
| | | £ | | £ | £ | £ | £ | £ | £ |
| *Variable and Semi-Variable Costs:* | | | | | | | | | |
| Salesmen's Salaries | S.V. | 14,000 | 1% on sales | 20,000 | 20,200 | 20,400 | 20,600 | 20,800 | 21,000 |
| Salesmen's Commissions | V. | — | 2% ,, | 12,000 | 12,400 | 12,800 | 13,200 | 13,600 | 14,000 |
| Salesmen's Telephones | S.V. | 200 | ½% ,, | 3,200 | 3,300 | 3,400 | 3,500 | 3,600 | 3,700 |
| Salesmen's Travelling | S.V. | 3,500 | 1% ,, | 9,500 | 9,700 | 9,900 | 10,100 | 10,300 | 10,500 |
| Salesmen's Stationery | V. | — | ¼% ,, | 1,500 | 1,550 | 1,600 | 1,650 | 1,700 | 1,750 |
| Salesmen's Postages | V. | — | ¼% ,, | 1,500 | 1,550 | 1,600 | 1,650 | 1,700 | 1,750 |
| Bad Debts | V. | — | ½% ,, | 3,000 | 3,100 | 3,200 | 3,300 | 3,400 | 3,500 |
| | | | | 50,700 | 51,800 | 52,900 | 54,000 | 55,100 | 56,200 |
| | | | *Source of information* | | | | | | |
| *Fixed Costs:* | | | | | | | | | |
| Sales Administration Salaries | F. | 8,000 | No. of employees | 8,000 | 8,000 | 8,000 | 8,000 | 8,000 | 8,000 |
| Rent of Sales Office | F. | 10,000 | Contract | 10,000 | 10,000 | 10,000 | 10,000 | 10,000 | 10,000 |
| Rent of Show Rooms | F. | 5,000 | Contract | 5,000 | 5,000 | 5,000 | 5,000 | 5,000 | 5,000 |
| Depreciation of Equipment | F. | 2,000 | 5% on Cap. values | 2,000 | 2,000 | 2,000 | 2,000 | 2,000 | 2,000 |
| Insurance | F. | 1,500 | Insurance Policy | 1,500 | 1,500 | 1,500 | 1,500 | 1,500 | 1,500 |
| Administration Costs—Sales Office | F. | 1,000 | Estimate Past Records | 1,000 | 1,000 | 1,000 | 1,000 | 1,000 | 1,000 |
| Advertising | F. | 12,000 | Contract Adv. Agency | 12,000 | 12,000 | 12,000 | 12,000 | 12,000 | 12,000 |
| | | | | £90,200 | £91,300 | £92,400 | £93,500 | £94,600 | £95,700 |
| Standard Selling Cost per £100 of Sales | | | | £15·03 | £14·7258 | £14·4375 | £14·166 | £13·9118 | £13·671 |

FIG. 17.—Example of a Flexible Budget: selling costs (for Notes see opposite page)

NOTES ON FIG. 17

1. The figures used are not intended to show what the various classes of cost are likely to be, but to illustrate the principles involved; *i.e.* the figures are purely hypothetical.

2. By statistical analysis of past records—salesmen's reports, expense sheets, salary sheets and other records—and after making adjustments for present conditions, the variable cost percentages, in relation to Sales Volume, have been calculated.

3. The bases for calculation of the variable element may be approached in a different way. Alternative bases are as follows:

| Functional cost | Alternative bases |
|---|---|
| Salesmen's Salaries | Fixed sum per salesman or salesman day or per call |
| „ Commission | Units sold |
| „ Telephones | Per customer |
| „ Travelling | Rate per mile |
| „ Meals and Hotel | Sum per day |
| „ Stationery | Fixed sum per salesman |
| „ Postage | Fixed sum per salesman or per customer |
| Advertising | When regarded as Variable Cost—number of catalogues and/or percentage on sales |

The division into Fixed and Variable is, of course, arbitrary. Much depends upon the basis used for computing the payment. Thus, as indicated, advertising costs may be fixed or variable. Similarly, the salaries of salesmen may be entirely fixed. Often costs are "fixed" over a certain range of physical sales and then "vary" when a certain stage is reached. Salesmen's salaries may be £20,000 for any sales volume between 450,000 and 550,000 units of product, but from 551,000 to 660,000 units the cost may be fixed at £22,000.

4. Sales Volumes are shown in monetary values. In some cases physical units would also be shown, *e.g.* when homogeneous units are sold.

5. A Flexible Budget would also be prepared to cover Distribution Costs, although these, for some concerns, would be adequately covered by inclusion in the one budget with Selling Costs.

6. For effective control the figures should be broken down further to show the costs relating to each territory, sales department, commodity, methods of sale, methods of delivery (distribution costs), sizes of orders, and salesmen. Obviously, not all enterprises will require the same detailed analysis; the nature of the business and the type of selling organisation will determine how much detail will be necessary. Generally speaking, however, the more complex the business—multiplicity of products, sales offices, showrooms, and so on—the more important is the need for analysis. Standard Unit Costs would also be used to measure the efficiency achieved. The Actual Unit Cost incurred for a particular operation, such as travelling, will be compared with the predetermined Standard Unit Cost and any significant differences investigated.

7. The costs relating to a volume of sales which fall between two of the volumes shown on the Budget may be obtained by interpolation. The fixed costs will of course remain the same irrespective of volume.

8. The principles illustrated apply to all types of budget. Students are expected to be able to draft budgets, not just understand them, so practise in drafting is advised.

Nevertheless, there is generally some relationship between volume of sales and selling costs. When budgeting selling costs it will be necessary to understand the nature of each type. The Sales Manager should collaborate with the Budget Controller in determining how much should be spent in order to achieve the desired volume of sales.

Sometimes a fixed budget is employed, but since this shows only one possible volume of output and relevant costs, it is of limited value when sales fluctuate. Since the latter is quite usual, most businesses prefer to use a flexible budget, one which gives a range of volumes of sales and related costs.

An important fact to remember is that *future* as well as current conditions should be considered when budgeting the costs. Past experience is often used as a guide, but it can be no more than a guide. The future trends of sales, including possible changes in conditions (*e.g.* changes in competition), have to be considered when predetermining costs.

The fixed costs predetermination should not present any great problem. They are incurred as a result of the policy followed and the organisation in existence. Provided there is no change in policy or organisation, and prices or rates remain the same, then the fixed costs should remain at the same level. Accordingly, budgeting of these costs should not prove difficult. Variable costs are not as straightforward. They are generally predetermined as a percentage on sales. However, as is shown by Note 3 on page 97, there are alternative bases which may be employed.

In the flexible budget the advertising costs are shown as being of a fixed nature. They could be partially variable and, in fact, when a separate advertising budget is prepared (*see* page 104) the total figure from that budget would be transferred to the Selling Costs Budget.

Examples of which costs are fixed, variable, or semi-variable are shown in the illustration of the flexible budget.

## DISTRIBUTION COSTS BUDGET

Distribution is the group of activities concerned with ensuring that the finished products reach the consumer. There are two basic categories of cost: (*a*) transport costs; (*b*) storage and warehousing costs.

In both cases there will be fixed and variable costs, and therefore a classification into these divisions will be essential.

Fixed costs should present no great problem. Many of these are determined by agreement or contract. Any change in policy should be reflected in the budget for distribution costs.

Variable costs have to be considered by nature of expense. In addition, the use made of outside transport facilities will be a very important factor. Different forms of transport may incur different rates per mile. Whether the goods are to be despatched from a factory warehouse to customer, or from a depot to customer, or from some other source will affect the charges incurred for transport.

## EXAMPLE OF FLEXIBLE BUDGET

An illustration of a flexible budget for distribution costs is shown in Fig. 18. Figures have not been included, but basically the compilation is the same as for selling costs. Therefore it is possible to see how the

| PRO-FORMA DISTRIBUTION COSTS BUDGET | | | | | | | | |
|---|---|---|---|---|---|---|---|---|
| A. B. & Co. Ltd., Flexible Budget for Year Ending December 31st, 19... | | | | | | | | |
| | Fixed Variable Semi-Variable | Fixed | Variable rate per standard unit | Possible Sales Volumes and Related Costs | | | | |
| | | | | £ | £ | £ | £ | £ |
| *TRANSPORT COSTS* | | | | | | | | |
| Outside Transport | | | | | | | | |
| Road | V | | (Tariff rates | | | | | |
| Rail | V | | from outside | | | | | |
| Air | V | | organisations) | | | | | |
| Ship | V | | | | | | | |
| Own Transport: | | | | | | | | |
| *Vehicle Costs* | | | | | | | | |
| Standing Costs { Administration Licences and Insurance | SV F | | | | | | | |
| Crew's Wages | V | | | | | | | |
| National Insurance | F | | | | | | | |
| Employers Liab. Insurance | F | | | | | | | |
| Depreciation | SV | | | | | | | |
| Running Costs { Fuel | V | | | | | | | |
| Oil | V | | | | | | | |
| Tyres | V | | | | | | | |
| Repairs and Maintenance | SV | | | | | | | |
| *STORAGE AND WAREHOUSING COSTS* | | | | | | | | |
| Salaries: Management and Clerical | F | | | | | | | |
| Depreciation of Equipment | SV | | | | | | | |
| Power and Light | SV | | | | | | | |
| Rent of Warehouse | F | | | | | | | |
| Repairs and Maintenance | SV | | | | | | | |
| Wages | F | | | | | | | |
| Stationery | SV | | | | | | | |
| Insurance | F | | | | | | | |
| | £ | | | | | | | |

FIG. 18.—*Pro-forma Distribution Costs Budget*

figures are computed by reference to the Selling Costs Budget (Fig. 17) and the notes relating thereto given on page 97. It will be seen that certain costs are variable, whereas others are fixed or semi-variable. The latter are made up of fixed and variable elements. The fixed charge plus a rate per standard unit is used to calculate the total for each possible level of output. Many of the costs may be predetermined on the basis of a rate per mile. However, in connection with transport running costs, it is important to notice that a standard rate per mile for *all* vehicles may not be a practical proposition. The usage of petrol or diesel oil and the rate of wear and tear of vehicle and tyres are influenced by the conditions under which a vehicle operates and the way it is handled. As everyone knows, even the age of a vehicle can have a considerable influence on its running costs. If some vehicles operate on long journeys, whereas others are restricted to short runs, this too can affect running costs.

Ideally each vehicle should be considered separately, and a standard rate per mile for each type of expense should be calculated after considering all relevant facts.

The distribution costs may be incorporated into a budget which covers both selling and distribution costs.

## ADVERTISING COSTS BUDGET

Advertising costs may be the direct responsibility of the sales manager or of the advertising manager. Irrespective of the executive who is given the task of controlling the advertising function there will be a need for the following:

1. Determine the best method or methods of advertising for the business concerned.

2. Fix the total amount to be spent on advertising in the budget period—usually one year. This amount is known as the advertising appropriation.

3. Co-ordinate the sales function and advertising. There would be little point in having an intensive advertising campaign unless sufficient products were available in shops or other channels of distribution to meet the increased demand.

4. Control the expenditure within the limits laid down and also attempt to measure the *effectiveness* of advertising.

The most appropriate methods of advertising will be determined by reference to the product, the channels of distribution, the methods of selling, and the type of consumer being served. Advertising is expected to maintain and increase sales, and the choice of methods should be influenced by this fact.

Advertising may also affect production costs. A larger volume of output should mean lower production costs per unit; these result from the economies of large-scale production and the fact that fixed overhead costs are apportioned over a larger number of products.

Some companies have to advertise more than others; this is inevitable because of different types of products being made. For this reason it is difficult to state how much advertising expenditure is reasonable. What is clear is that *total* expenditure has now reached gigantic proportions,* and there is no doubt that the Advertising Manager, Sales Manager and Management Accountant within each organisation should exert all possible skill in ensuring that maximum benefits are obtained from the advertising appropriation. There is always a danger that advertising, in a fiercely competitive field, may become a monster which a company finds impossible to feed adequately from its financial resources.

## FIXING THE ADVERTISING APPROPRIATION

Predetermination of advertising costs is an essential part of control. Different methods are available for assessing how much should be spent on advertising each year. This sum is then divided among the different advertising media. A summary of these methods is as follows:

1. A percentage based on the total sales value of the budget period *or* on the profit expected.

The percentage to use may be determined by reference to past experience and previous years' records. If it is found that on average a figure representing 5% of total sales is spent on advertising, then this same percentage may be used for fixing the advertising appropriation for the current year. This method assumes that the conditions which prevailed in previous years will also exist in the year for which the budget is being prepared. In fact, the degree of competition may be quite different; a number of new products may be in the process of being introduced; there may be a policy of trying to obtain a more general acceptance of a trade-mark or brand name. These and other relevant matters should influence the total amount to be spent on advertising in the particular year.

2. Method (1) above, adjusted to allow for expected changes in conditions as reflected in the budgets for the forthcoming budget period.

3. An amount based on the approximate expenditure being incurred by competitors.

This method is based on the principle that anything competitors can do we can do just as well or better. If a competitor is spending £10,000 a year, then there is an obligation to spend just as much.

There is little doubt that this method is employed, but since actual expenditure by competitors is unknown until it has been incurred, it is clearly of limited value for budgeting, which is essentially *predetermination* of costs. Moreover, if this method is to be followed to its fullest

---

* No exact figures are available, but the total cost for all advertising media in this country is in the region of £500 million representing approximately 2% of net national income.

extent, control will be very difficult to apply, because, in effect, the control is being exercised by the whims of competitors.

4. A sum per product based on the selling price.

The selling price of each product sold is assumed to contain a definite sum for advertising. Accordingly, the number of products of each type (the sales mix) in the budget will determine the advertising appropriation.

Sometimes the amount for advertising is based on the *previous* period's sales of each type of product. If 1000 units of product "A" were sold, then the advertising appropriation for the future budget period would be 1000 times the fixed sum per unit. This version assumes that the same volume of sales will be obtained, which, of course, does not necessarily follow.

5. An amount based on what a company is able to afford; *i.e.* on what cash is expected to be free for advertising.

This is an arbitrary method, but is likely to be used combined with one of the other methods explained. Much of what goes on in a business is determined by what a company can afford, and while this method cannot be said to be scientific, it is at least practical. What should not be forgotten is the fact that when a business is experiencing a recession, and therefore the directors feel they cannot afford certain expenditure, this may be the time when advertising is essential.

6. The amount of advertising by the appropriate media required to sell the planned volume of output, bearing in mind any seasonal variations in sales and warehousing facilities available.

Goods have to be sold as quickly as possible. This may only be possible by advertising and other sales promotion. The Sales Manager and Advertising Manager have to determine how much effort and cost are required to sell the desired volume at the appropriate times. If warehousing is limited, then advertising or other selling devices should be planned so that excessive accumulation of stocks of finished goods is avoided. Past records and the experience of salesmen, advertising men, and managers may be employed to determine the advertising appropriation amount.

In theory, advertising expenditure should be incurred so long as there is an increase in sales, and therefore gross profit. In practice, the point at which advertising can be said to be "unproductive" is very difficult to determine. The matching of costs and benefits is a vital part of budgeting, but is not an easy task. It can be done, although generally this is often along broad lines matching total cost with total sales.

## PREPARATION OF THE ADVERTISING BUDGET

An advertising budget co-ordinated with all other budgets, and particularly the Sales Budget, is an essential part of a Budgetary Control system. Preparation of the Advertising Budget and carrying out the plan it represents should not be regarded merely as an exercise on paper; this would not be Budgetary Control. The whole process should permit contact to be maintained, and regular discussions to be held, with all sales and advertising personnel. The budget gives formal expression to what is expected to occur in the budget period.

The form the budget will take must necessarily vary from one business to another. Some companies may plan and arrange all the advertising, whereas others may rely to a large extent upon an advertising agency. Another possible variation will be the number and type of advertising media employed and the number of products involved. These and other differences must inevitably affect the preparation of the budget.

One possible approach is to analyse the advertising appropriation on the basis of advertising media: an example of this is given in Fig. 19. The expenses shown in the budget are not intended to portray a complete list of all possible types. Again, these will vary from one business to another. When costs are incurred jointly by the different media an equitable apportionment may be necessary. Thus, for example, the salaries of clerks in the Advertising Office may be apportioned on the basis of *time spent* by the clerks on planning and arranging the different forms of advertising.

An alternative form of Advertising Budget is given in Fig. 20. This analyses the expenditure by products, the cost of the different media being divided to show expenditure expected to be incurred on each line.

Sometimes the budget shows the expenditure to be incurred on the basis of sales areas. Another variation is analysis according to the month or quarter in which the appropriation is to be spent. If advertising is carried out more intensively in some parts of the year than in others, then it is only logical to show the different sums to be spent in the periods concerned. This allows the advertising to be done at the most appropriate times, and then later on enables a more realistic and effective control to be exercised. Actual expenditure for a busy period is compared with the budgeted expenditure for the same busy period, so that reasonably accurate conclusions can be reached.

## *ADMINISTRATION COSTS BUDGET*

Administration costs are all management, administrative, and office expenses which do not specifically relate to production, selling and distribution, research and development, or capital expenditure.

An example of an Administration Costs Budget is given in

ADVERTISING BUDGET (advertising media)

For Year Ending........................

| Expense | Total £ | National Newspaper £ | Local Newspaper £ | Magazines and Journals £ | Outdoor £ | Television £ | Cinema £ | Catalogues £ | Exhibitions £ | Samples and Gifts £ | Miscel-laneous £ |
|---|---|---|---|---|---|---|---|---|---|---|---|
| Salaries | | | | | | | | | | | |
| Rent—Advertising Office | | | | | | | | | | | |
| Rates—Advertising Office | | | | | | | | | | | |
| Travelling Expenses—Advertising | | | | | | | | | | | |
| Lighting and Heating | | | | | | | | | | | |
| Payments to Agencies, Newspapers or other "suppliers" | | | | | | | | | | | |
| | £ | | | | | | | | | | |

FIG. 19.—*Specimen Advertising Budget: advertising media*

ADVERTISING BUDGET (Products)

For Year Ending........................

| Expense | Total £ | Product "R" £ | Product "S" £ | Product "T" £ | Product "U" £ | Product "V" £ | Product "W" £ |
|---|---|---|---|---|---|---|---|
| National Newspapers | | | | | | | |
| Local Newspapers | | | | | | | |
| Magazines and Journals | | | | | | | |
| Outdoor (hoardings, bills) | | | | | | | |
| Television | | | | | | | |
| Cinema | | | | | | | |
| Catalogues | | | | | | | |
| Exhibitions | | | | | | | |
| Samples and Gifts | | | | | | | |
| Miscellaneous | | | | | | | |
| | £ | | | | | | |

FIG. 20.—*Specimen Advertising Budget: products*

Fig. 21. All the expenses relate to the administrative function, and therefore the budget should serve as an illustration of costs.

Careful setting of each type of expense is essential. Without reasonable accuracy there can be no control. Many of the costs will be of a fixed nature, and therefore predetermination should present no great problem. The salaries of executives, accountants, lawyers, clerks, machine operators, systems analysts, and others should be reasonably constant over the budget period.

## ADMINISTRATION COSTS BUDGET
### for Year Ending..................

| | Total £ | Accounts £ | Buying £ | Costing £ | Pricing £ |
|---|---|---|---|---|---|
| Audit Fees | | | | | |
| Bank Charges | | | | | |
| Cleaning Costs | | | | | |
| Depreciation | | | | | |
| Directors' Fees | | | | | |
| Donations | | | | | |
| Insurance: Cash in Transit Credit | | | | | |
| Legal Costs | | | | | |
| Postages | | | | | |
| Printing and Stationery | | | | | |
| Rates and Taxes | | | | | |
| Rent | | | | | |
| Salaries | | | | | |
| Supplies (Sundry) | | | | | |
| Telephones | | | | | |
| Travelling Expenses | | | | | |

FIG. 21.—*Specimen Administration Costs Budget*

The same principle will apply for professional services, such as auditing and bank charges. Rates, taxes, and rent also come into the category of fixed costs.

Some costs are of a semi-variable nature. They contain a fixed element and a variable element, with the result that, as the volume of output increases, there is a tendency for the particular cost to increase, although not in direct proportion to output. Clerical salaries, stationery, travelling costs, depreciation of office machinery, and sundry supplies may all come within this category. How the fixed and variable elements may be separated so as to show the extent of the variability with changes in output is given on page 237.

When work is standardised a guide to budgeted costs may be obtained by considering the number of work units which should be produced by the average clerk, typist, or machine operator. Typical work units are: invoices, delivery notes, letters, statements, and other forms or documents which are of a uniform character, each unit being similar to the next. Thus, for example, if a business has to produce 200 invoices per day, then, provided these involve on average the same amount of work each day, there should be no difficulty experienced in predetermining the number of invoice typists, the amount of stationery, and other facilities. In turn, these can be converted to budgeted costs.

A very important aspect of predetermining administration costs is to make sure that all administrative functions are carried out as efficiently as possible. All systems and methods should result in lowest cost. Organisation and methods specialists may be employed with advantage; where there is no Organisation and Methods Department the Cost Accountant or Budget Controller may carry out any necessary investigations and improvements.

## RESEARCH AND DEVELOPMENT COSTS BUDGET

Research costs are incurred in order to develop and/or improve products and methods. When research results in a definite benefit which has commercial possibilities the development function commences. Accordingly, from that point development costs are incurred. Once formal production begins, the relevant costs are production costs. Unfortunately, it is not always easy to determine when one stage ends and the other begins. For this reason the research and development costs may be included together, no attempt being made to show them separately.

These costs may or may not produce a worthwhile new product or method; the outcome is uncertain. Yet in many industries, research and development play a vital part in maintaining a business as a leader in its own particular field. In many spheres, a business would not even be able to remain competitive unless it continued to develop new styles or products. The reader has only to look at the new or improved products which have emerged in the last few years from the fields of aircraft, plastics, electronics, chemicals, motor vehicles, and office machinery; these are only a few of the many examples which may be taken from industry.

The problems involved in predetermining, authorising, and controlling research and development costs are similar to those encountered for capital expenditure covered in Chapters 18 and 19. However, there is a difference: research and development together form the very first stage of the production process (they are sometimes called "pre-production costs"). Indeed, many research projects may never even reach the point at which they can be regarded as being part of any beneficial process because they produce *nothing*. When capital expenditure is being considered there is generally something tangible to be produced which will increase revenues and profits. A feature of expenditure on research and development is the uncertainty of any benefits resulting from it. Obviously, a business must incur this expenditure, but it should be kept within reasonable limits, and a satisfactory percentage of projects should produce tangible results.

## ALLOCATION OF EXPENDITURE

There are many possible methods of allocating expenditure for research and development. This allocation is essential, for in this way a limit is placed on the amount that can be spent in the budget period. Possible methods are as follows:

1. A percentage based on total sales value. This may be an acceptable basis provided the profit margin remains the same from one year to another. The percentage may be based on the previous year's sales *or* the budgeted sales.

2. A percentage based on net profit.

3. A total amount determined by reference to past expenditure and future plans and policy. If a company has been spending £10,000 a year on research and development, but a 20% increase in output is being planned, then the directors may decide to spend 20% more on research and development, making a total of £12,000.

4. A sum determined by reference to expected cash resources in the budget period in question. In other words, the basis is "how much can we afford?"

5. All factors affecting the importance of research are studied before allocating an appropriate amount. The general economic situation, the degree of competition, the policy being followed, the demand for existing products, and the need to reduce costs are all factors which may be considered in deciding whether or not research and development should be given top priority or some lower status.

There is no doubt that each of these methods has its place in appropriate circumstances. However, all are arbitrary, and therefore should not be regarded as providing an easy solution as to the amount a company can afford. Oddly enough, when a company is doing extremely well it can afford to spend large sums on research and development, yet it may have no need to introduce new products. On the other hand, when trade is poor a new product may provide the answer and overcome a temporary recession. This fact should be remembered when planning the expenditure. On the whole, it is probably better to have a stable programme rather than one which fluctuates from year to year. Certainly the provision of laboratories and other research buildings and the employment of suitable research and development staff are made much simpler by having a programme which is not varied too much from year to year. Moreover, a *consistent*, rather than sporadic, approach to solving problems is the one likely to produce results. Clearly, though, the organisation of research and development activities will be influenced very much by the type of business concerned.

## CLASSIFICATION OF RESEARCH

Research functions may be classified as follows:

1. *Pure or Basic Research.* This is also known as "fundamental research." It involves carrying out experiments or doing some other work which increases knowledge in a particular field, but without aiming to produce a specific result or benefit. In other words, the research is general in nature and there is great difficulty in foreseeing the possible outcome of the effort. Some valuable facts may emerge, but there is no way of telling what these will be.

2. *Applied Research.* Applied research aims at producing a definite result. Known facts and techniques are employed, along with experimental methods, with a view to producing a new or improved product, process, or method.

The distinction is important, because the pure research, although vital for long-term prosperity, may not improve profit prospects in the near future. When a business depends to a large extent upon technical progress and innovation for earning profit there will be a vital need for applied research. At the same time, ideas may be necessary, and these can come from pure research. Put another way, both applied and pure research are essential. What is important is the *correct balance* between the two, the extra revenue from the applied research covering the pure research.

## AUTHORISATION OF RESEARCH EXPENDITURE

The authorisation of expenditure should receive attention. As noted earlier, this can follow the lines laid down in Chapters 18 and 19 on capital expenditure. A possible procedure may be as follows:

1. Fix an annual expenditure for pure research. This expenditure would be detailed and then included in a research and development budget.
2. Determine what projects are worthwhile and how much is to be spent on each during the year (applied research).

As indicated, there is a need to keep a good balance between pure research and applied research. How much should be spent on pure research is difficult to determine. However, profit being earned and cash available will have a definite influence upon the decision. The person in charge of research should have a good idea as to how much should be spent to produce a steady flow of basic information.

On the question of applied research the answer to what is a reasonable amount to be spent on each project seems to rest on obtaining a fair return on the money being spent. In other words, each project should at least pay for itself and, if possible, show a profit. The latter is very desirable, and should be large enough to cover any projects which turn out to be of little or no value.

Attempts have been made to use scientific formulae to assess the profitability of research projects. These are based on the assumption that each project should yield a reasonable rate of profit.

Whether formulae can be employed to *advantage* will be questioned by many accountants. A good deal of information is required to calculate the answer. Often this information is not available and is extremely difficult to estimate. Nevertheless, in suitable conditions this approach has definite possibilities. Certainly some attempt should be made to ascertain whether or not research expenditure is worthwhile. On evidence available there is a marked lack of any realistic attempt in practice to select the most suitable projects, to assess the profitability of such projects or the final outcome of each project.

Authorisation of research projects can be accomplished by the use of suitably designed sanction forms. An example of a pro-forma Research Project Sanction is given in Fig. 22. The procedures which may be followed for drafting forms and submitting them to the Committee are described in Chapter 19 on Control of Capital Expenditure.

**DRAWING UP THE BUDGET**

The research and development unit can be treated as a budget centre and a budget compiled for it. Costs involved are really no different from those incurred by other centres. There will be the salaries and wages of research workers and technicians. Depreciation of buildings and plant and machinery and other overhead costs, such as lighting, heating, and maintenance costs, will also be incurred. Many of these costs will be of a fixed nature. In addition, there will be variable costs, of which sundry materials and hourly paid wages are examples.

There is no definite volume of output to produce, and therefore the predetermination of what the costs should be is difficult. As shown earlier, under "Allocation of Expenditure," there is no scientific method of calculating the amount to be spent each year. It should be based on what the company can afford and what is necessary to maintain the desired profit level. A company must keep its place within the industry, and if this involves spending £X, then that sum should be included and detailed in the budget.

## PURCHASING BUDGET

As the name implies, the Purchasing Budget is concerned with purchases for the budget period. Different interpretations are given as to what is meant by a purchasing budget in terms of *content*. Sometimes only the purchase of materials is included. In other cases all purchases are incorporated into the budget. These would include those for both direct and indirect materials, fixed assets, and services such as electricity and gas.

---

Proposal No. .......................

Date of Proposal .................

## RESEARCH PROJECT SANCTION

To: *Research Expenditure Committee/General Manager\**

---

Application is submitted for authority to incur the following research/development\* expenditure:

1. Project (give full details)

2. Costs Involved

Total £

3. Reasons for Project

4. Timing of Costs (*i.e.* when costs are to be incurred)

5. Benefits Expected (show expected cost savings or increase in revenues)

6. Miscellaneous—any other relevant information

(Note: all figures to be supported by detailed schedules.)

Research Expenditure Committee APPROVAL/REJECTION \*

Date........................          Reasons for Rejection (if applicable)

...................................................

\* Delete where appropriate.

---

FIG. 22.—*Pro-forma Research Project Sanction*

In effect, the Purchasing Budget represents the purchasing plans for the period in question. When all items, both goods and services, are included in the Purchasing Budget it is, in effect, a summary of a number of other budgets; *i.e.* Material Budget, Factory Overhead Budget, Selling Costs Budget, and so on.

The object of a Purchasing Budget is to formulate a plan which will allow all the necessary materials and other items to be obtained at minimum cost. The purchase of the most economical size of order; obtaining trade or quantity discounts; ensuring that there is always adequate stock on hand and yet capital tied-up in stock is kept to a minimum, should all receive attention. In short, the most economical purchasing programme which gives the service required should be the aim.

### PREPARING THE PURCHASING BUDGET

The requirements for each main type of cost are listed in the Purchasing Budget. Many variations of this budget will be found in practice. A system of Budgetary Control could exist without a Purchasing Budget. As noted earlier, it is a summary of other budgets. Accordingly, it could be argued that, since costs should be controlled at the point at which they are incurred, there is no justification for preparing a Purchasing Budget which deals with costs for a number of departments. While there is some truth in this statement, it should be remembered that in many businesses the skill of the purchasing agent is an essential part of efficient management. Accordingly, for this reason it seems advisable to include a Purchasing Budget within the framework of the system.

The pro-forma example given (Fig. 23) may be varied to suit particular needs. The columns for "units" and "unit price" refer to materials and material prices. Instead of showing detail of this nature on the budget itself, many accountants would prefer to show it on separate working sheets. The volumes of output given presuppose that a flexible budget is to be employed. Whether this will be the case depends upon the system in use. Thus, for example, if fixed budgets have been prepared for direct materials and other relevant budgets, then the Purchasing Budget could also show *one* output and appropriate costs.

Different forms of control system for ordering, and therefore purchasing, materials are possible. The most usual are:

1. Following a system of using maximum, minimum, and re-order levels. When the latter point is reached a Purchase Requisition is initiated by the storekeeper or departmental head.

2. By schedule. This method may be employed when large-scale production methods are employed. The ordering is based on the production programme and, as far as possible, the aim is to obtain materials so that they flow from the supplier to the production line, thereby keeping stocks to an absolute minimum. Ideally there should be no stocks of production materials. With this method particular attention should be paid to planning the timing of purchases.

With both methods there will be need to analyse material requirements. Reference to Material Specifications will be essential.

A monthly control of purchases may be obtained through using an alternative form of Purchasing Budget (Fig. 24). This includes only the direct materials required for production.

E

**PURCHASING BUDGET**

**For 6 Months Ending...............**

| | Units | Unit Price | Volume of Output | | | | |
|---|---|---|---|---|---|---|---|
| | | | Units* | Units | Units | Units | Units |
| | | | £ | £ | £ | £ | £ |
| Direct Materials (these would be shown under broad headings) | | | | | | | |
| Indirect Materials (classified by departments using the materials or by broad headings of types of materials) | | | | | | | |
| Overhead Costs (other than indirect material and labour) Factory Selling and Distribution Administration Fixed Assets | | | | | | | |
| £ | | | | | | | |

\* Refers to products. It may be expressed as standard hours.

FIG. 23.—*Pro-forma Purchasing Budget*

For both budgets a six-monthly period has been taken. It could be a shorter or longer period to suit the particular circumstances.

### SERVICE DEPARTMENTS' BUDGETS

Control of the costs of each service department should be one of the aims of a Budgetary Control system. Obviously, cost incurred should be reasonable having regard to the service being supplied. There are different ways of dealing with service departments' costs: they may be treated in the following manner:

(a) include the service costs in the user producing departments and do not prepare a budget for each service department, *or*

(b) include the budgeted service costs in the user producing departments and also prepare a separate budget for each service department.

The second procedure is the one recommended. Even here, though, there are at least two variations possible. The service costs can be shown in the producing departments' budgets on the basis of *estimated* usage in the budgeted period; alternatively, the service *available* can be

| | | | 1<br>Production<br>Requirements | 2<br>Stock<br>at end<br>of month | 3<br>Opening<br>Stock | 4<br>To be<br>purchased<br>(1+2−3) |
|---|---|---|---|---|---|---|
| | Units | Unit<br>Cost | | | | |
| January<br>Material A<br>„ B<br>„ C<br>„ D<br>„ E<br>February (detailed as above)<br>March (detailed as above)<br>April (detailed as above)<br>May (detailed as above)<br>June (detailed as above) | | | | | | |

PURCHASING BUDGET

For 6 Months Ending...............

FIG. 24.—*Alternative form of Purchasing Budget*

shown in the appropriate producing department's budget. The latter charges each producing department with the cost of the service it could use, and therefore recovers the full cost through the producing departments.

An example of a service department's budget is explained below, the department concerned being Maintenance.

MAINTENANCE COSTS BUDGET

The Maintenance Department is an essential part of any industrial business. It plays a vital role in ensuring that lost time is kept to a minimum. Even so, there is still a need to control the costs involved. Budgetary Control can supply the means of controlling the service and the cost, but the task is not easy.

An understanding of the nature of maintenance work is essential. Basically there are two types:

1. Preventive maintenance, which is planned maintenance carried out at regular intervals with the object of preventing breakdowns.

The times required for each routine maintenance task can be set by the Work Study Department. The standard times can then be transformed into standard labour costs by application of the appropriate wage-rates. Material costs should also be capable of being budgeted without great difficulty.

2. Emergency repair work. This work cannot be predetermined. By its very nature there is no way of telling how many repairs will arise and how serious they will be.

There should be some emergency repairs, otherwise it is likely that too much is being spent on preventive maintenance. Avoidance of all repairs is possible, provided enough is spent on preventive maintenance. However, this is not likely to result in minimum costs and minimum inconvenience. The correct balance between preventive maintenance and emergency repairs should be obtained. If the latter become excessive there should be an improvement made in the preventive maintenance programme.

When planning maintenance, and therefore budgeting costs, it should be remembered that often when activity is low the maintenance costs may be at a high level. This will be so because a good Maintenance Engineer plans his work in a manner which keeps interference with production down to a minimum. When plant is slack large maintenance jobs can be carried out.

Co-operation between the Maintenance Engineer and the Budget Controller is an essential part of preparing and operating a Maintenance Budget. The engineer should participate in drawing up the budget and understand that the object is to give a better service at the lowest cost.

Particular attention should be paid to ensuring that the true cost of maintenance is shown. Any work done on fixed assets, either making or installing them, should be segregated from the normal maintenance costs. In fact, strictly speaking, this expenditure on fixed assets should appear in the Capital Expenditure Budget. When controlling maintenance, attention should be paid to hours lost due to breakdowns as well as to the cost of providing the service.

A simple example of a Maintenance Budget is given in Fig. 25. This will be varied to meet the needs of the particular business.

The division of costs into those relating to (a) preventive maintenance and (b) emergency repairs, follows the procedure adopted by the Maintenance Engineer, and therefore makes the budget as realistic as possible. The general costs could be divided between the two types of maintenance.

Many more costs could be included in the budget; thus, for example, costs relating to the provision of steam and power. However, they may be better included in separate budgets.

## FIXED COSTS BUDGET

Fixed costs, are those which tend to remain constant irrespective of the volume of output. They are often called "policy costs" or "period costs." The latter name arises because most of the fixed costs are incurred on a time basis, so much per week, month, year, or other period.

---

### MAINTENANCE COSTS BUDGET

**For Year Ending.............................**

Total Labour Hours Budgeted............

£

*Preventive Maintenance*
    Electricians
    Fitters
    General Workers
    Materials
    Sundry Supplies

*Emergency Repairs*
    Electricians
    Fitters
    General Workers
    Materials
    Sundry Supplies

*General Costs*
    Rent of Department
    Depreciation of Equipment
    Heating and Lighting

£

---

Fig. 25.—*Specimen Maintenance Costs Budget*

Because fixed costs are determined by policy, some accountants advocate that they should be included in a separate Fixed Costs Budget and not in the functional budgets, such as Production and Selling Costs Budgets. It is argued that such costs are uncontrollable by functional and departmental heads, and therefore no purpose is served by showing them in each functional budget as part of the costs which come within the responsibility of the appropriate manager.

Not all accountants follow this procedure. They prefer to show the complete story within each budget.

If a separate Fixed Costs Budget is to be used it may follow the lines indicated in the example given below (Fig. 26). The total fixed costs for each main function are shown. The breakdown could be given on separate schedules, the number of the schedule being shown in the final column of the budget.

| | Hours | | Budget to Capacity % | Total Cost | Details Schedule No. |
|---|---|---|---|---|---|
| | Capacity | Budgeted | | | |
| Factory Selling Distribution Administration Research and Development | | | | £ | |

**FIXED COSTS BUDGET**
**For Year Ending........................**

FIG. 26.—*Example of a Fixed Costs Budget*

## THE MASTER BUDGET

There are differences of opinion on what is meant by a "master budget." It is generally regarded as a summary budget which incorporates all other principal budgets. Disagreement exists on the *form* the summary should take.

Some accountants regard the budgeted Profit and Loss Account and Balance Sheet as the Master Budget. The Profit and Loss Account shows the expected profit or loss for the budget period, whereas the Balance Sheet or Position Statement* summarises capital, liabilities, and assets. An example of a budgeted Profit and Loss Account is given in Fig. 27. A budgeted Balance Sheet can be drafted along the lines shown on pages 538–539 in the chapter which deals with company accounts. Obviously budgeted figures would replace actual figures.

An alternative definition, which is much wider than the first, includes the information from all functional budgets. In this case the Master Budget portrays the *overall plan* for the budget period. Information normally shown in this budget is as follows:

* A preference has been shown in recent times, especially in the U.S.A., for the title "Position Statement" on the grounds that this is more appropriate than "Balance Sheet."

1. Sales.    2. Production.
3. Costs—(a) Direct Labour.
          (b) Direct Material.
          (c) Selling Costs.
          (d) Distribution Costs.
          (e) Administration Costs.
4. Profit.    5. Accounting ratios.    6. Profit appropriations.

| | BUDGETED PROFIT AND LOSS ACCOUNT<br>For the Year Ending...................... | | | |
|---|---|---|---|---|
| | This Year | | Last Year | |
| | Product A | Product B | Product A | Product B |
| | £ | £ | £ | £ |
| I. SALES | | | | |
| Manufacturing Costs: | | | | |
| Direct Labour<br>Direct Material<br>Factory Overhead<br>*Add* Opening Stock | | | | |
| *Less* Closing Stock | | | | |
| 2. COST OF GOODS SOLD | £ | £ | £ | £ |
| 3. Gross Profit (I less item 2) | | | | |
| 4. Selling and Distribution Costs<br>5. Administration Costs | | | | |
| 6. NET PROFIT (3 less items 4 and 5) | £ | £ | £ | £ |

FIG. 27.—*Typical Budgeted Profit and Loss Account*

Before being put into operation the Master Budget will require the approval of the Budget Committee. Possibly a number of Master Budgets will have to be drafted before the final one is agreed upon.

A useful device for presenting the most important facts in the Master Budget is a special form of break-even chart. Examples are given on page 272 (Figs. 43 and 44).

## MASTER BUDGET

### For the Year Ending....................

Normal Capacity ..................................... standard hours (100%)

Capacity Budgeted ............................... standard hours

| | Budgeted Figures | | |
|---|---|---|---|
| | Product A £ | Product B £ | Total £ |
| I. SALES | | | |
| Manufacturing Costs: Direct Labour Direct Material Factory Overhead *Add* Opening Stock *Less* Closing Stock | | | |
| 2. COST OF GOODS SOLD | £ | £ | £ |
| 3. Gross Profit (I less item 2) | | | |
| 4. Selling and Distribution Costs 5. Administration Costs | | | |
| 6. NET PROFIT (3 less items 4 and 5) | £ | £ | £ |
| 7. Fixed Assets 8. Current Assets | | | |
| 9. CAPITAL EMPLOYED | £ | £ | £ |
| 10. Ratio of Profit to Capital Employed 11. Ratio of Sales to Capital Employed 12. Current Ratio 13. Quick Ratio | | | |
| 14. PROFIT APPROPRIATIONS 15. Net Profit (6 above) *Less* Dividends Transfer to General Reserve Transfer to Asset Replacement Reserve Taxation | £ | £ | £ |
| 16. TOTAL APPROPRIATIONS | £ | £ | £ |
| 17. PROFIT AND LOSS BALANCE (15 less item 16) | £ | £ | £ |

FIG. 28.—*Specimen Master Budget*

The example of a Master Budget (Fig. 28) may be varied to meet the needs of the particular business. Here the period covered is one year, but this may be shorter when the budget period is shorter. Some accountants may prefer to show more details of Balance Sheet items; in particular, the nature of the finance for capital employed; *i.e.* whether Ordinary Share capital, Preference Share capital, or Debentures. Additional accounting ratios may be included in the Master Budget. Details of all the principal ratios are given in Chapter 16.

## EXAMINATION QUESTIONS

1. As Chief Accountant you are asked by the Chief Executive of your Company to comment on a request for authority to expend £120,000 on advertising during 1954 put forward by the General Manager of a Department concerned with the marketing of products to the consumer market. The figures put forward in support of the proposed Advertising Programme, are as under:

| | "Wonder" Toothpaste | | | "The Different" Denture Powder | | | "Wonder" Face Cream | | |
|---|---|---|---|---|---|---|---|---|---|
| | Sales £ | Profit £ | Advtg. £ | Sales £ | Profit £ | Advtg. £ | Sales £ | Profit £ | Advtg. £ |
| 1949 ... | 800,000 | 100,000 | 75,000 | — | — | — | 300,000 | 100,000 | — |
| 1950 ... | 900,000 | 125,000 | 75,000 | — | — | — | 280,000 | 85,000 | — |
| 1951 ... | 700,000 | 60,000 | 90,000 | 5,000 | *5,000* | 10,000 | 210,000 | 35,000 | — |
| 1952 ... | 850,000 | 115,000 | 100,000 | 40,000 | *1,000* | 10,000 | 200,000 | 30,000 | — |
| 1953 ... | 875,000 | 120,000 | 75,000 | 75,000 | 100 | 15,000 | 180,000 | 15,000 | — |
| Budget, 1954 ... | 1,000,000 | 145,000 | 100,000 | 125,000 | 12,000 | 20,000 | 150,000 | *5,000* | — |

*Note.* "Profits" are shown before charging Advertising expenditure. "Losses" (indicated by figures in italics) likewise.

Assume that the "Wonder" trade-mark has been established over a number of years and that "The Different" Denture Powder was introduced in 1951, to take up spare production facilities. Advise the Chief Executive what further information, if any, he should call for from the General Manager before a final decision is made.                    (*I.C.W.A.*)

2. "Company objectives should be reflected in the master budget." Explain this statement.

3. How may the levels of expenditure be governed, short of fixing amounts arbitrarily, in respect of the costs of administration? Your answer should embody ideas likely to assist the various officials in controlling those costs for which they are responsible.                    (*I.C.W.A.*)

4. Administration costs have been defined as the cost of formulating policy which is not directly related to other functions of the business.

Prepare a schedule of administration costs for a company with many departments, employing a large sales force. State on what bases you would make any appropriate apportionments.                    (*I.C.W.A.*)

5. In connection with Budgetary Control, enumerate and describe briefly the usual subsidiary budgets which make up the master budget.    (*S.C.A.*)

6. State the basic factors which must be taken into account in building up an Administration Budget. To the best of your ability show also further considerations which would have a bearing on the building up of this Budget.
(S.C.A.)

7. Explain the different uses of:

(a) standard costs,    (b) flexible budgets,
(c) fixed expense budgets,

with particular reference to the control of costs.      (I.C.W.A.)

8. The classification of all overhead expenditure in a manufacturing business of medium size has formerly been by nature of expense only. This has been for cost finding purposes, where an overall rate of overhead absorption, based upon direct wages, has been used. You are about to introduce (a) more precise product costing, and (b) budgetary control procedures.

Explain how you would approach the problems of overhead classification, allocation, apportionment and absorption, bearing in mind that the cost centres for overhead absorption are not necessarily the same as the centres of budget responsibility.      (I.C.W.A.)

9. Draw up a budget of service department costs, using your own figures.
(I.C.W.A.)

10. Discuss how you would deal with the following problems associated with the establishment of a flexible budgetary control system in the service departments of a manufacturing company.

(a) When the activity of the transport department increases, it may be due to heavier demands being made on it by the user departments or due to bad planning on the part of the transport department manager. How would you differentiate between the two?

(b) When a departmental foreman prepares a requisition for supplies he has no information on the prices of the articles he requires. He is, nevertheless, expected to keep his cost of supplies within a monetary allowance. What, if anything, should be done about this?

(c) For those items of supplies bought from outside suppliers there is usually a considerable time-lag between the date of the requisition and the eventual receipt of the invoice. How, in such circumstances, can detailed control over suppliers' costs be achieved?

(d) Repair costs appear to fall into two main categories—those of a fairly regular maintenance nature, and those consisting of major repairs to buildings and machinery which are undertaken to top management decision. How should one control repair costs in these circumstances?    (A.C.C.A.)

11. You are asking the works engineer to produce a maintenance costs budget for the first time. Prepare the outline, with expense headings, of such a budget, and indicate the sources of all the relevant data required for its construction.      (I.C.W.A.)

12. (a) "Budgets and standards may be set on different bases of achievement." Explain this statement. Which basis do you recommend and why? Is your opinion affected by the use of flexible budgetary control?

(b) A business can be affected by external conditions resulting in marked changes in the level of output or sales; raw material prices or selling prices may sometimes move substantially away from the budgeted prices. If substantial variances are constantly occurring, what action, if any, would you take regarding the budgets themselves? State your reasons.    (I.C.W.A.)

13. What factors would you consider when preparing a budget of plant and machinery maintenance? Describe how the expenses included in this budget would be controlled by management and absorbed in the costs. (*I.C.W.A.*)

14. You are required to assist in the formation of a forecast for plant and machinery maintenance expenditure. Enumerate the factors you would consider, stating your sources of information. (*I.C.W.A.*)

15. You are employed in a seasonal trade, where the volume of sales has been declining in recent years. This decline has been met by increased advertising on television, in journals and the national press, and by increased expenditure on presentation and packaging of the domestic consumer products.

The advertising expenditure is planned to occur in those periods immediately before seasonal events such as Christmas, Easter and Whitsuntide, whereas the presentation and packaging expenditure is more or less directly variable with sales at all times.

State how you would propose to exercise control over these costs, and how you would absorb them in periodic accounts. (*I.C.W.A.*)

16. In considering generally the subject of product cost improvement, how should plant maintenance arrangements be surveyed and controlled?
(*I.C.W.A.*)

17. Under present day conditions, it is often found to be extremely difficult to maintain standards of cost without frequent adjustments. State the main causes and give your views as to the remedies which could be applied.
(*I.C.W.A.*)

18. Selling costs can be expressed (*a*) by nature of cost or (*b*) by function. Give the general headings of an analysis by the latter method and against each heading state the cost unit (for some headings alternatives should be given) by which such costs can be controlled. (*I.C.W.A.*)

19. Outline the considerations that would guide you in fixing a budget for a given period for:

(*a*) research expenditure;     (*b*) selling expenditure.

(*I.C.W.A.*)

20. P. Products Limited maintains a research department which until now has been relatively small, operating on a cost budget of approximately £10,000 per annum. This represents 1 % of total cost. There is to be a considerable extension of research activities during the budget year commencing on 1 August, 1967 and research projects already under consideration are of the following types:

(*a*) two projects for the development of new products;
(*b*) one project for the improvement of a product already being manufactured, where the emphasis is on both functional aspects and cost reduction;
(*c*) three projects for the improvement of manufacturing methods.

The industrial engineer of the company, who is responsible for the research department along with all other engineering activities, expects to increase annual spending on research up to a total of £50,000. He is asking you, as the management accountant, to present your ideas on the cost ascertainment and cost control arrangements which should be applied to this function. Set out your ideas in the form of a report to the industrial engineer.

(*A.C.C.A.*)

21. Advertising costs often represent one of the largest single areas of marketing cost in any business.

Explain the ways in which you might trace and allocate advertising costs so as to enable measurement. Then specify possible means of control, dealing specifically with the ways in which budgeting principles might be applied.

(*I.C.W.A.*)

22. In a manufacturing business, some of the civil maintenance and plant maintenance is executed by the company's own maintenance team, while some is sub-contracted.

On such maintenance costs, what do you see as:

    (*a*) the problems of budgeting; and
    (*b*) the necessary features of cost reporting?     (*I.C.W.A.*)

23. A manufacturing company plans to make a profit of £40,000 in a year.

In compiling the budget for this year the following points are taken into consideration:

    (*a*) Labour is the principal budget factor (or the limiting factor) and is estimated at 160,000 hours of direct labour for the year.
    (*b*) Standard labour hour rates average £0·40 per hour.
    (*c*) Variable overhead rates average £0·30 per direct labour hour.
    (*d*) Fixed overheads are expected to total £70,000.

Owing to the wide variety of products, material content varies considerably, and may range between 40 and 60% of sales.

Prepare figures to show the expected sales, costs and profits, if materials average 40, 50 or 60% respectively of sales.

What contribution per labour hour is necessary to achieve the desired profit of £40,000?     (*I.C.W.A.*)

24. A manufacturing process on a continuous operation achieves an output of 4 tons per hour valued at £10 per ton. Process wages cost £5 per hour and raw material £2 per ton of product. Regular maintenance amounts to £100 per week.

Breakdowns averaging 25 hours per week occur due to mechanical faults which cost £1000 to repair. These could be reduced or eliminated if additional maintenance on the following scale were undertaken:

| Breakdown hours per week ... | 0 | 5 | 10 | 15 | 20 |
|---|---|---|---|---|---|
| | £ | £ | £ | £ | £ |
| Maintenance costs ... ... | 3200 | 1600 | 800 | 400 | 200 |
| Repair costs ... ... ... | 0 | 300 | 400 | 600 | 800 |

Process labour during stoppages can be used elsewhere up to 10 hours per week.

Tabulate the information provided to show:

(a) the optimum amount of maintenance to undertake each week;

(b) the additional revenue obtainable at that level compared with the present situation.    (I.C.W.A.)

25. Your company manufactures two products A and B. A forecast of the number of units to be sold in the first seven months of 1968 is given below:

|  | | | | Product A | Product B |
|---|---|---|---|---|---|
| January ... | ... | ... | ... | 1000 | 2800 |
| February... | ... | ... | ... | 1200 | 2800 |
| March | ... | ... | ... | 1600 | 2400 |
| April | ... | ... | ... | 2000 | 2000 |
| May | ... | ... | ... | 2400 | 1600 |
| June | ... | ... | ... | 2400 | 1600 |
| July | ... | ... | ... | 2000 | 1800 |

It is anticipated that:

(i) there will be no work-in-progress at the end of any month;

(ii) finished units equal to half the sales for the next month will be in stock at the end of each month (including December 1967).

Budgeted production and production costs for the year ending 31st December, 1968, are as follows:

|  | | | | Product A | Product B |
|---|---|---|---|---|---|
| Production (units) | ... | ... | ... | 22,000 | 24,000 |
|  | | | | £ | £ |
| Direct materials per unit | ... | ... | | 12·5 | 19·0 |
| Direct wages per unit ... | ... | ... | | 4·5 | 7·0 |
| Total factory overhead apportioned to each type of product | ... | ... | | 66,000 | 96,000 |

Prepare for the six months period ending 30th June, 1968, a production budget for each month and a summarised production cost budget.

(I.C.W.A.)

26. A small company making a single standard product, produces accounts for a costing period as follows:

|  | | | | £ |
|---|---|---|---|---|
| Direct materials | ... | ... | ... | 396 |
| Direct wages ... | ... | ... | ... | 596 |
| Variable overheads | ... | ... | ... | 970 |
| Fixed overheads | ... | ... | ... | 520 |
| Profit ... | ... | ... | ... | 488 |
| Sales ... | ... | ... | ... | 2970 |

The original budget was in respect of 1000 units per period, but during this period only 960 units were produced and sold.

Standard direct wage rate is £0·30 per hour and standard variable overhead rate is £0·50 per hour.

Cost variances during the period are as follows:

|                              | Gains | Losses |
|------------------------------|-------|--------|
|                              | £     | £      |
| Material price ... ... ...   | —     | 4      |
| Material usage ... ... ...   | —     | 8      |
| Wages rate ... ... ...       | 10    | —      |
| Labour efficiency ... ...    | —     | 30     |
| Variable overhead price ...  | 40    | —      |
| Variable overhead efficiency ... | — | 50   |
| Fixed overhead cost ... ...  | —     | 20     |
| Sales price ... ... ...      | 90    | —      |

From this information prepare for the period the original budget and budgeted cost of actual sales, and prepare a statement showing all standards in respect of the product. (*I.C.W.A.*)

27. An organisation manufacturing kitchen-ware with a range of 120 products sells to the wholesale and retail channels of distribution, to several large chain stores and to mail order houses. The selling and distribution costs of each of these channels is different, as is the discount which has to be offered on a gross list price. Cost control in the factory is exercised by means of standard product costs, and within these standard costs there is a clear division between the variable and fixed costs.

Tabulate the costing and cost control routines which you would apply to selling and distribution activities in these circumstances. (*A.C.C.A.*)

CHAPTER 6

## FINANCIAL PLANNING

### INTRODUCTION

AN adequate balance and flow of cash is essential. At all times a business must be able to meet its commitments. More than this; a business cannot afford to stand still. In any competitive field it will be essential to effect improvements, to introduce new products, and to expand. Experience has shown that a business does not remain static; there is a tendency to go forward or backward, but not to stagnate. If expansion is to take place, then there must be adequate financial resources.

### FINANCIAL REQUIREMENTS

Generally speaking, the same principles may be followed whether the business concerned is well established or just being started. There may be more difficulty experienced in obtaining the necessary finance in the latter case and, because there may be no past experience available as a guide to requirements, the amount of cash needed may be difficult to forecast.

The finance required will be influenced by the following:

1. Fixed assets necessary for producing and distributing the products; plant, machinery, and equipment are examples.
2. Raw materials, piece-parts, and miscellaneous supplies to be purchased, and wages and other expenses which have to be paid.

In other chapters management decisions relating to fixed assets and optimum stock levels are discussed. The chapter on capital budgeting will also be of interest when considering the problems of cash requirements.

#### FIXED OR PERMANENT CAPITAL

All fixed assets, intangible assets (such as goodwill, patents, and trade marks) investments and other assets which are retained permanently in the business are purchased from funds which may be regarded as the fixed or permanent capital.

These assets earn profit by being employed within the business. Year by year the charge for their use is made by including depreciation in the annual accounts. Occasionally they may be sold, but usually the object of the sale will be to improve the overall effectiveness of the total assets being employed, and not directly to earn a profit. If an asset becomes out of date, obsolete, or badly worn, then it loses its attractiveness as an investment, and therefore may be sold.

The number of assets and their cost will not be the same for all types of business. In steel-making, flour milling, oil refining, paper making, and chemical manufacturing the fixed capital needed is very great. On the other hand, when no manufacturing is involved, such as when retailing or wholesaling only is carried on, the fixed capital will be relatively small. The precise requirements will be detailed in the Capital Budget.

If a business is new there will be a time lag between its date of commencement and the earning of revenue. There will be a further lag before money is coming in faster than it has to be paid out. This early period will have to be financed, and there is much to be said for including the amount needed in the estimate of fixed capital requirements. If dependence is placed entirely upon short-term borrowing to cover the gap, then difficulties may be experienced if the lender curbs the rate of borrowing at a time when money is most needed.

A further consideration is uncertainty in the cash forecast. Inevitably there will be a margin of error, the size of which will depend upon the nature of the new venture. A buffer stock of cash or its equivalent will thus be essential. Again, this should preferably come from fixed capital. A wrong time to have to borrow is when difficulties are being experienced; if money *can* be obtained the price to be paid may be exorbitant. In any event, management should not risk the possibility of being short of cash at a crucial time. Idle cash earns nothing, but in the early stages of development it is better to have idle cash than have no cash at all. Later, when experience shows more precisely the needs of the business, the reserve for contingencies may be reduced. An arrangement with a bank or other financial institution which allows borrowing on overdraft or loans to be made, if and when required, may overcome the problem of keeping too large a cash balance. However, the arrangement should be made before an emergency arises, not afterwards. Preplanning is an essential feature of all efficient management; financial management is no exception.

### CIRCULATING AND WORKING CAPITAL

Assets purchased with permanent capital described above are kept in the business for the purpose of earning profit. However, in addition to these, there are assets which are not normally retained for longer than one year. Indeed, they will usually change their forms, time and time again, during the course of a year. These are known as current assets, and the money used to purchase them is circulating or floating capital. Raw materials are purchased, wages and expenses are incurred, and then the products manufactured are sold. If for cash, then the cash in hand or at bank will be increased. If sold on credit, the debtors' balance will increase. Eventually all the sales will bring in cash, which is then used to meet cash expenses and wages and to pay off creditors.

Sometimes the *total* of the current assets is described as the "working capital." However, it is more usual and correct to limit this description to the difference between current assets and current liabilities. Current assets by themselves give no true indication of a concern's financial position. If current liabilities exceed current assets, then the working capital is clearly a negative quantity. It should be noted that some authorities prefer to use the term "net working capital" to describe the difference between current assets and current liabilities. A more realistic approach to financial requirements may be obtained by considering working-capital needs rather than total current assets.

The period of credit allowed will clearly influence the volume of cash needed at any time. If long periods of credit are allowed to customers this policy will have its effect on the cash position, and this is especially so if similar credit facilities are not offered by suppliers. An extension of the period normally allowed—say from one month to two months—may have serious effects upon the cash holdings. If the object is to increase sales and the extension of the credit period *is* successful in accomplishing this aim, then the cash position may deteriorate still further. Increased sales will probably mean added expenditure on raw materials and labour, and yet the receipts from this extra business may not be forthcoming for a considerable period of time. The time lag brought about by the production and sales cycles as well as the period of credit all contribute to the delay.

The production and sales cycles are important factors in the determination of the working capital needed. Generally speaking, the longer the periods, the larger will be the working capital requirements. When considering the initial needs full recognition must be given to the non-earning period involved. Closely linked with the sales cycle is seasonality. If sales are obtained at certain seasons only, and the rest of the year the stocks are built up, then the cash requirements in the slack period may call for special measures.

Whether permanent or short-term finance should cover a company's working-capital needs depends to some extent upon the state of the market for funds. Availability and cost of borrowing should be considered. Another important consideration is the length of the production and sales cycles already mentioned in the previous paragraph. Some authorities take the view that a long cycle may be covered by temporary funds, whereas when the production cycle is short and the turnover is rapid the smaller amount of working capital is better provided out of the fixed capital. However, in the author's opinion, when a business is first started it would appear prudent policy to cover normal cash requirements by permanent capital for the full extent of the material, labour, and overhead requirements until earnings flow into the business.

Once this happens, the revenue from sales should take care of future needs. If normal credit facilities are extended to the business, then it should be able to meet its commitments without borrowing. Obviously, however, there can be no hard-and-fast rule on this matter.

In favour of borrowing it can be stated that a high degree of flexibility is introduced into the financial structure. The permanent capital can provide the normal requirements, and the short-term funds from borrowing can meet any unusual or unexpected need. Another advantage is that borrowing allows fixed capital to be kept to a minimum. Since return on capital employed is usually regarded as the measure of success, it follows that, provided the interest payable is reasonable, a more favourable result may be shown by short-term borrowing. A "reasonable" rate of interest implies that borrowing is a temporary measure and not a permanent solution. If working capital is met from regular borrowing the cost is likely to be excessive. For this reason, since the rate of interest payable will be influenced by the risks involved, it follows that interest paid for a year will tend to cancel out any profit earned on the borrowed money. Admittedly, a business may be in a position where extraordinary profit may be earned, so that a surplus may still be available over and above the interest payable. However, such extraordinary profit accrues only to a few, and any planning is better if based on normal, conservative estimates. From these observations it can be seen that *temporary* shortages of cash may be overcome by short-term borrowing; in fact, seasonal sales or seasonal purchases may necessitate the use of this device. This is especially so when expansion begins to absorb all available cash. The additional amount of cash required to meet the seasonal needs may then be borrowed. The remarks made earlier still apply. If the expansion is likely to be permanent, then it is a wiser policy to plough back profits or to obtain additional fixed capital or a long-term loan.

Stock turnover and the sales cycle are very much a part of each other. On an average, stock may turn over, say, six times a year; put another way, the average sales cycle is two months. Increased turnover means greater profits, and less working capital is needed relative to sales.

Reference has already been made to the importance of the period of credit allowed or received. If business can be obtained which is on a cash basis, then the problem of financing may be reduced to minor proportions. Large orders from, say, departmental or multiple stores, and payable on delivery, may be worthwhile, even though the profit margin is reduced.

Internal factors can also influence the amount of cash needed or available. A reduction in costs, an increase in prices* (provided there is no loss in the number of units sold), or a general improvement in the routing of work-in-progress can all improve the working capital posi-

* This assumes that the business can exert an influence on costs and prices. Obviously there will be external factors which also affect these.

tion. If investments in stocks of materials and work-in-progress can be reduced, then clearly the cash situation is not the only aspect to benefit. The taking or giving of cash discounts may also have an important bearing on the flow of cash. Similarly, the amount of tax payable will affect the position.

The dividend policy followed by the Board of Directors of a company will have an important effect upon the cash available. In some companies a steady expansion may allow a consistent dividend policy to be followed; a rate of dividend which varies very little from year to year may be paid. This has the advantage of giving the appearance of stability and encourages investment from members of the public who look for a regular income. The rate of earning and expansion may not go hand in hand. With the new business the calls upon cash may often be in excess of the inflow of cash. In some fields of enterprise trade may fluctuate from year to year, and investment in assets—fixed and current—may also have to be varied. The dividend policy may be influenced by this irregular rate of spending; if cash has to be conserved, then dividends may be reduced or not paid at all. If the ploughed-back profits eventually bring higher returns in the form of capital appreciation and dividends, then the enlightened shareholder may be quite content. However, if dividend limitations are such that the rate of dividend is permanently pegged at an unreasonably low figure, then the future prospects of obtaining permanent capital may be seriously affected. This fact should be borne in mind when considering a dividend "freeze"; the shareholders, however remote, are still the owners of a company, and should be treated fairly at all times.

The taxation laws in operation at a particular time may also affect dividend policy. Since its introduction under the Finance Act, 1965, companies are liable for corporation tax on all profits. No allowance is made for dividends paid and this fact tends to have an effect on the amount distributed. Retention of profits which the Act encourages naturally leads to a more stringent dividend policy. There is a partial exception to this general guide in the case of "close companies," *i.e.* those controlled by five or fewer "participators." Capital gearing is also likely to be affected, and this topic is covered under the sections which deal with capital structures. For further particulars and detailed provisions the reader is advised to consult a specialist book on Corporation Tax. (*See* the Bibliography, page 865.)

Recognition that the real capital, in terms of the physical assets used, should be maintained before it can be said that a profit has been earned is important. The charging of costs, including depreciation, is often based on historical costs; yet, in times of rising prices, this means that profits are overstated. This may lead to excessive spending and too generous dividend payments. Moreover, the fact that replacements and replenishments of fixed and current assets are costing more and therefore draining cash resources more quickly is often overlooked. If prices are rising at a fast rate, then the cash forecast should try to estimate the rate of change and incorporate it into costs and sales values. Only by considering future trends can a realistic forecast be obtained.

## RELATIONSHIPS: FIXED AND WORKING CAPITAL

Relationships exist between the fixed and working capital. Inadequate working capital may mean that the fixed assets purchased from permanent capital cannot be utilised effectively. Shortage of materials or labour may mean that machines can be used for only part of the available time. On the other hand, if efficient use is not being made of current assets and working capital is excessive it may be impossible to expand or even maintain fixed assets. An abnormally high number of indirect workers in relation to direct workers; lack of control over labour performances; inefficient storekeeping and the carrying of excessive stocks of raw materials and finished goods; delays in the flow of work-in-progress and a general lack of purpose and co-ordination in the methods and systems used—all mean that working capital is too high. Because working-capital requirements are excessive there may be no resources left for fixed assets. If the low state of efficiency persists the position may become aggravated still further. Assets wear out or become very costly to operate and profits are depleted, thereby making even the maintenance of adequate working capital quite a problem.

### IMPORTANCE OF WORKING CAPITAL

Without adequate working capital there can be no progress. A business must go forward; it must expand and assert itself in a competitive world. If expansion takes place without the firm being able to cover its commitments, then overtrading will be the result. Available working capital is stretched to capacity until, finally, bankruptcy or liquidation are forced upon the business.

The length of the production and sales cycles will play an important part in the overtrading process. If short, and the period of credit is not excessive, then money from sales will help to replenish working capital. However, the longer the total period from the buying of the raw materials to the receipt of the cash from sales, the more likely is overtrading. In the process of expansion extra materials are purchased, more workers are engaged, and additional expenses are incurred, and this process continues over a period of time. If extra finance has not been provided, then overtrading will be inevitable.

Even if the disastrous liquidation or bankruptcy does not occur the goodwill of the business may be damaged. Lack of confidence in the financial ability of a business may mean restriction of credit from suppliers. If this occurs, then production curtailment takes the place of expansion, profits are reduced, and cash resources are affected still further. If money is borrowed now the price may be high: possibly control of the business will pass from the shareholders to debenture holders or other creditors.

The taking of cash discounts will also be affected by a shortage of funds. Some suppliers encourage prompt payment by the offer of a discount. It is interesting to notice here that some accountants regard the cash discount as a charge made by the seller for the loan of the cash value of the goods he has sold. The taking of the discount, they argue, is not the earning of a profit, but rather the avoidance of a cost. If £1 discount can be deducted from a £20 invoice, then the actual price is really £19, the £1 representing the charge made by the supplier for the use of his £19. More will be said on this subject in the chapter on Credit Control.

The importance of expansion has already been noted. Innovation is regarded by many economists and accountants as the mainspring of profit earning. There is no doubt that this is true for many industries. If new ideas, products, methods, and techniques are not germinated and brought into existence a business will fail to keep its place in competition. Innovation implies, among other things, research, sound organisation, and the willingness to undertake risks. Without adequate cash there can be no progress. Research and development would be at a standstill and the essential innovation would fail to appear. When technological development is essential an appropriation of cash should be made to meet expected requirements for normal research and development. In addition, there should be a surplus of cash to cover any contingencies. The purchase of another company or a new process or product may be possible only by having available the necessary cash resources. A falling off in sales may be overcome by having sufficient working capital to launch a publicity and sales campaign. Advertising can overcome sales resistance and, if necessary, even create a demand for a new product.

Clearly, however, the surplus should not be excessive; if cash is not being made to work it is not contributing to profit. Some companies overcome this difficulty by investing in securities which can be realised at short notice without loss of capital. These are explained below.

## WORKING CAPITAL RATIOS

The kind of information which is revealed by a Balance Sheet can be very useful for ascertaining whether or not the working capital is adequate. Ratios can be calculated and, although *ideal* ratios are difficult to establish, those predetermined and/or ascertained from actual figures can be extremely useful. Chapter 16 deals with typical ratios.

## INVESTMENT OF SURPLUS FUNDS

All cash available in the business should be used as effectively as possible. If there is a surplus, over and above requirements for *current* production and selling, efforts should be made to invest the funds in the most suitable manner. There are many factors to consider before investing surplus funds outside the existing business; in particular, there must be a clear understanding on whether the available cash is free for investment for a long period of indefinite duration or for a short period. The surplus can then be considered in terms of two principal types of investment:

1. *Permanent or Long-term Investments.* If the business wishes to extend its activities or to have some form of "hedge" against fluctuations in trade, then a permanent form of investment may be appropriate. It does not necessarily mean that a large sum is invested at one particular time; instead, regular annual transfers may be made, building up an investment to a large amount over a number of years. In some cases there may be a specific purpose behind the investments, such as the replacement of assets or the redemption of debentures (these are examples of "sinking funds"). The forms the investments may take are covered below.

2. *Temporary or Short-term Investments.* Short-term investments may be a profitable outlet for surplus funds which are expected to be used within the business in a reasonably short period. There may be uncertainty regarding precisely *when* the surplus funds will be used, but due to the nature of the company's activities, it is very desirable for the cash to be retained in a fairly liquid form, thus making immediate conversion possible.

### TYPES OF PERMANENT INVESTMENTS

The principal types of permanent investment are covered below. This summary is not exhaustive, but should indicate the possible long-term uses for surplus funds. When selecting the most appropriate investments the following factors should be considered:

(*a*) Does the investment benefit, or is it likely to benefit, the long-term profitability of the business?

(*b*) Is there adequate income?

(*c*) Is purchasing power likely to be preserved? (If prices are rising, then an investment will tend to lose its value, although this loss may be offset by a super-normal income or a growth in the value of the investment due to future profit expectations.)

(*d*) Is the risk reasonable? (Investments which appear to present excessive risks may be better avoided.)

(*e*) If the business is a limited company the investment must not be *ultra vires* of the Memorandum and Articles of Association.

There may be other considerations. The important point to remember is that the investment should be worthwhile and in the best interests of the business. The investment of money outside should not be allowed to cloud the real issues involved—that of producing and selling commodities or services. If money can be employed more profitably in the business, then there should be a good reason before considering external investment. There may be instances where *internal* expansion of the existing facilities may be advisable. For this reason, both internal and external investments are considered.

## Expansion of Existing Facilities

The expansion of existing facilities may take one of a number of forms. New factories, plant, machinery, and other fixed assets may be purchased to introduce new products, to utilise by-products, or to increase the volume of existing products. The profitability of capital expenditure is discussed in Chapter 18. Other possibilities are the introduction of a two- or three-shift system or the working of overtime, although, in actual fact, the latter may be an uneconomical proposition over a long period.

## External Investment

There are many types of external investment. One method is the acquiring of other businesses, either by normal amalgamation or by the take-over bid, which is discussed in Chapter 22.

A second method is investment by the purchase of Debentures, and Preference and Ordinary shares. In the latter case the number of shares purchased need not constitute a controlling interest. The important point is that the company in which investment is made should be a sound proposition. The products being made, the volume of sales, profit margins, and the relation of total profit to capital employed should all be considered. The size of the company, its financial stability, and the status of the directors are also important. The requirements of the Council of the Stock Exchange and the Companies Acts, are a good guide to what information should be studied before investing in a company. Chapter 16 dealing with accounting ratios is very pertinent to this matter.

If Preference shares or Debentures are to be purchased, then attention should be paid to earnings cover and capital cover. Dividend and interest should be covered at least three times by available earnings; moreover, this income should have been consistent over, say, the past five years. Irregular and intermittent income earning is an undesirable sign, indicating instability. As regards capital cover, many accountants believe that Preference share cover should be at least three times, whereas Debentures should be covered at least twice.* These remarks

* Chapter 7 dealing with Unsecured Notes and Mortgage Debentures, page 167, is relevant.

are generalisations, and are written at a time when earnings tend to be fairly high; when times are less favourable a smaller earnings cover may be an acceptable criterion.

When Ordinary shares are to form the basis of the investment there should still be favourable earnings, with dividends covered at least two and a half times. The principal advantage of Ordinary shares over other types of investment is the possibility of growth in market values, thereby compensating for any possible falling off in purchasing power of money and the reduction in the value of the original investment. In addition, there *may* be a higher rate of dividend than that paid on Preference shares or the interest paid on Debentures. However, this is not always the case; experience has shown that Ordinary share values can rise to such an extent that dividend yields are extremely low and yet, due to a high Bank Rate, the percentage rate on Preference shares and Debentures can reach quite high levels.

Because of the high rate of return available on Preference shares and Debentures, they have naturally become very acceptable investments. If the earnings on Ordinary shares are 3% and yet 6% can be obtained on the fixed-income investment, then the margin of 3% may be regarded as being quite adequate to cover any loss in the value of the original investment due to the fall in the value of money. Sometimes a *conversion privilege* may be an important feature of Preference shares or Debentures.

The shares need not necessarily be purchased, but instead an investment may be made in a unit trust, thus avoiding the necessity of having to manage the investments. Moreover, there is a wide range of securities represented in the trust's funds, and this helps to spread the risks.

Gilt-edged securities should not be overlooked. Dated stock may enable a capital profit to be earned within a few years and give a reasonable rate of interest in the meantime. The securities of Commonwealth countries and certain foreign countries may also be good investments. Loans to local authorities come under a similar category.

A very reasonable income may be obtainable from investing in finance companies and in building societies. However, these, like Preference shares and Debentures, rely on the income for offsetting changes in the value of money. Care must be taken in selecting the finance companies and building societies: membership of the Finance Houses Association or the Building Societies Association may be a very good recommendation, although, of course, finance companies and building societies which are not members of these associations may still be quite reasonable risks.

If investments are held for capital gains rather than income, then it must be borne in mind that, when sold, they will attract Capital Gains Tax at the standard rate, plus surtax in the case of an individual. How this is computed for companies should be ascertained from a book which gives the current law and rates.

Some of the investments given may also be suitable as short-term investments, and are therefore considered below.

## TEMPORARY OR SHORT-TERM INVESTMENT

With short-term investments it is essential to ensure that there is no danger of a loss being incurred by having to sell the investment at very short notice.

For ease of reference the principal forms of investment are summarised as follows:

1. *Bank Deposits.* Bank deposits with the London clearing banks are a very convenient form of investment. In England the rate of interest payable is normally 2% below Bank Rate, and is credited to the deposit account periodically (*e.g.* each half-year). Seven days' notice of withdrawal is generally required, although, in practice, immediate withdrawal may be permitted.

2. *Deposits with Merchant Banks and Branches of Foreign Banks.* The rates of interest and withdrawal terms on deposits with merchant banks and branches of foreign banks may be similar to those given by the ten London clearing banks. However, this may not always be the case; some of them may give higher rates. Much depends upon the size of the deposit and the period of time involved; if longer than seven days' notice of withdrawal is agreed upon, then a higher rate of interest may be payable.

3. *Deposits with Discount Houses.* The discount houses, which provide a service by discounting bills of exchange, will accept deposits at terms which are fixed by the London Discount Market Association. Deposits may be accepted with the right of immediate withdrawal (sight deposits) at a rate of interest which is 2% below Bank Rate, or with the right to withdraw at seven days' notice at a rate which is $1\frac{3}{4}$% below Bank Rate: *i.e.* $\frac{1}{4}$% more than the sight deposit.

4. *Local Authority Loans.* Loans to local authorities may be for a number of years or for part of a year. In the latter case the rate of interest payable tends to be below Bank Rate, whereas for a number of years the rate is above Bank Rate.* For the very short-term loans two days' notice of withdrawal may be possible. In other cases the loan is usually for a fixed term.

The Radcliffe Report has stressed that the creditworthiness of local authorities is of the highest order, and therefore it follows that the lender should have no qualms regarding the risk involved.

Loans for more than one year are covered by mortage deed executed under seal. The stamp duty of $\frac{1}{4}$% is payable by the local authority. Loans for less than one year are unsecured, and therefore do not attract stamp duty. The unsecured loans are obviously very appropriate to

* This refers to the fixing of the rate at the time of lending. It does not vary with the Bank Rate.

temporary lending, whereas the secured loans are more of a permanent investment.

5. *Lending to Finance Companies.* Money lent is used principally to finance hire-purchase transactions. For this reason the risk tends to be high, and great care should be taken to ensure that the finance company selected is financially sound. Membership of the Finance Houses Association or the Industrial Bankers Association is a definite recommendation. A sound plan is to make sure that the amount to be lent does not exceed, say, 5% of the *total* amount being borrowed by the finance company. Another safeguard is to ensure that there is a reasonable relationship between capital and reserves *and* total borrowings. The Industrial Bankers Association in their rules suggest that total borrowing should be limited to five times the capital and reserves for smaller companies and seven times for larger companies, *i.e.* for those with a share capital of more than £200,000.

The rate of interest payable by finance companies varies from one to another. Moreover, the rate is very much influenced by the withdrawal period, which may be either three months or six months. There is a tendency for the rate to fluctuate with changes in Bank Rate, although this is not an invariable rule.

There is no doubt that, provided a finance company of good standing is selected, investments of this nature can be quite profitable.

6. *Loans to Building Societies.* Building societies accept loans from companies, but generally at less-favourable terms than those given to individuals. This is due to a tax concession given to the building societies in respect of the tax deducted at source from individuals.

Because of the lower rate of interest the building societies are not an exceptionally attractive investment; in fact, loans to finance houses and local authorities will tend to earn more. Furthermore, a building society tends to limit the total sum it will accept from one source to a maximum of around £25,000.

7. *Tax Reserve Certificates.* Tax reserve certificates provide a means of using funds which have to be conserved for the payment of taxes (not P.A.Y.E.). The rate of interest payable on certificates held is varied from time to time, any changes being published in the *London Gazette*.

The terms of each series of tax reserve certificates are contained in the Prospectus, which applies to the current series issued by the Treasury. Subscriptions must be for amounts of £5 or multiples thereof, and payment in full at par must accompany an application form. The certificates may be obtained through a bank.

When certificates are tendered in payment of tax the interest due is added to the face value of the certificates and goes towards paying the tax due. The certificates may be held for an indefinite period, but no interest is earned after they are two years old.

If repayment of the investment is desired, then the certificate may be cashed—the repayment will be made within ten days. However, repayment cannot be made until after two months from the date of the issue of the certificates.

When the value of certificates tendered, plus the interest thereon, exceeds the tax due a balance certificate will be issued for £5 or more; if the balance is less than £5, then the amount will be returned by cheque. In the case of the latter no interest will be allowed.

8. *Gilt-edged Securities.* Gilt-edged securities with a few years to go before maturity may be suitable investments. Care should be taken to ensure that any securities purchased do not have to be sold prematurely, with a danger of losing part of the capital sum. Obviously the shorter the period before maturity, the less danger there will be of a loss in value. Carefully selected, this investment can offer a very good return in capital and income.

9. *Tendering for Treasury Bills.* Treasury bills are issued via the Bank of England. Every Friday tenders are invited for the bills, which are issued in different denominations, the minimum being £5000. London banks, discount houses, and brokers are permitted to offer tenders for a minimum amount of £50,000.

Companies cannot make direct tenders, but must go through a bank or broker. The amount tendered per cent is published each week in the financial columns of newspapers. The most common maturity date falls 91 days after issue. A bank or broker may tender, say, £98·85 per cent. The difference of £1·15 per cent represents discount, which, of course, is the amount to be earned by lending to the Government.

This survey of possible forms of investment has been kept as brief as possible, and because they change so often, the precise rates of dividend or interest have been omitted. Information on the various rates can be obtained quite easily from the prospective borrower or from newspapers and professional journals.

## FINANCING VIA BUDGETARY CONTROL

Only by co-ordinating all functions of a business can maximum profit be earned. Some idea of cash requirements can be obtained by considering the expected receipts and payments for a period, but this cannot really be called "planning." The latter should include a survey of long-term trends, the general economic situation now and in the future, and the relation to each other of production, selling, research and development, and administration. A change in one function may affect the others and, accordingly, will tend to affect the cash position. Budgetary Control enables the necessary dovetailing to be obtained and control to be exercised over each part.

There are two essential stages:

1. *Cash forecasting*, which is the estimating of cash receipts and payments for a future period before any necessary adjustments have been made.

2. *Cash budgeting*, which is the estimating of cash receipts and payments for a future period, *after* due consideration has been given to expected conditions and the overall budget plan.

The "adjustments" which may be necessary before the Cash Budget is compiled are: action to obtain any necessary cash, or to invest any amount which is in excess of current requirements, and to bring the working-capital forecast into line with the desirable accounting ratios as previously determined by reference to the nature of the business and the general economic situation (*see* Chapter 16, "Accounting Ratios"). Only then can any attempt be made to prepare the Cash Budget. At all times it must be remembered that the business is intending to make a profit which is as substantial as possible. If money to be spent cannot be justified directly or indirectly in terms of earning profit, then an alternative choice should be selected. The importance of long-term trends and possibilities is once more emphasised. Management cannot expect *immediate* returns on all investments, but, in the long run, any outlay should pay, or be expected to pay, for itself. Turning to justification in an indirect manner, it can be said that research and development expenditure cannot usually be justified by profits which are attributable to it and no other cause; the provision of food and refreshments at or below cost, and the maintenance of gardens or similar facilities, are examples of where direct profit earning is not the main consideration. However, in these cases benefits accruing from the expenditure are considered worthwhile, either because they will eventually lead to profit or because the provision of the facilities increases prestige and improves conditions of work, and therefore tends towards obtaining more co-operation and team spirit.

### PLANNING THE FORECAST

Basically the line of approach is the same whether considering a new or existing business. If it is a new venture, then there will be increased uncertainty and possibly more difficulty in showing justification for expenditure in terms of expected profits. Not only will the internal management have to be convinced but also possibly shareholders or other investors. For this reason therefore a modest start may be advisable. Once the idea shows promise expansion can follow.

Postponing the methods of acquiring the finance for later consideration, the procedure for forecasting cash may be summarised as follows:

*For a New Business.* The various forecasts relating to sales, output, expenditure on fixed assets, expenditure on materials, and other requirements must be studied. The cash available from the proprietor's own resources should be compared with total requirements. The cash which has to be found will be the difference between the two figures. If provision has been made to cover the difference, then full details can be shown on the cash forecast; alternatively, if there is a problem in finding adequate cash, then the deficit should be shown to indicate that action is necessary to obtain that amount. It may be that adequate cash cannot be obtained, in which case all forecasts and, later, budgets will have to be brought into line with available resources.

*For an Established Business.* Expected receipts from cash sales, debtors, and miscellaneous sources, and the estimated expenditure which will be necessary to run the business at the level planned have to be forecast. If the expansion of operations is within reasonable limits there may be no need to obtain funds from external sources; any additional working capital and fixed-asset improvement or replacement can come from profits retained in the business. Generally, the problem of cash forecasting for the established unit should be simpler than for the new business. To begin with, the balance of cash is brought forward, and then the size of the payments and receipts will be governed by the existing framework of the production and sales facilities.

*Period Covered*

Convention usually requires that the Cash Forecast covers a year, a number of years, or part of a year. The success of any business is normally measured at the end of each financial year, so adherence to a yearly forecast to cover cash is inevitable. With the new business especially a longer period may be covered. If a modest start is made and the venture comes up to, or exceeds, expectations, then it will usually be inevitable for expansion to take place. This fact must be faced by preparation of a long-term forecast. Cash needed for extension of plant, for advertising, and expansion of the labour force, as well as other needs, should be estimated and plans made for obtaining the necessary finance. Anticipation is the key word in successful cash forecasting; only by studying future needs and possible sources to match these needs can the correct amount of cash be obtained in the form desired, whether this be by the issue of shares, debentures, or by loan or overdraft. Selecting the time which is psychologically correct is important to any kind of financing operation; the issue of shares or debentures or borrowing can be affected favourably by careful planning and action at the right moment—when investors are willing to invest. Political or economic unrest, a possible change of government, or a recession in a major industry may have adverse effects upon the willingness of the public or financial institutions to take on responsibilities which are of an uncertain nature. The credit policy of the Government, its direct control and its indirect control, through the Bank of England, the commercial banks, and other financial institutions, can also have its effect upon the availability of long-term and short-term finance.

A shorter-term forecast to cover a quarter or four-weekly period will be advisable when financial difficulties are being experienced. Seasonal variations in sales and purchases may also require short-period forecasting. Even if there is no real shortage of cash from month to month, it is generally advisable to analyse receipts and payments into quarterly, four-weekly, or even weekly periods; budgeting implies control, and this must be accomplished at regular, short intervals. If attempted on a yearly basis any danger signs may not be detected early enough to take the action necessary to regulate spending or obtain additional funds. Furthermore, there may be instances where the yearly position may be satisfactory, and yet from one control period to another temporary shortages of cash may be expected to occur. Seasonal sales and purchases have already been noted; the payment of yearly bonuses or holiday pay will also tend to make an extra claim upon the liquid resources.

### THE FORECASTS ILLUSTRATED

Below are shown two questions and suggested solutions. If these are followed through carefully the application of the principles, already explained, should be made clear.

There are three basic methods of forecasting cash. The best known is that which considers expected payments and receipts for a period. Because short periods, such as a week, month, or quarter, are considered, this *payments-and-receipts method* gives the best results. Any seasonal or intermittent fluctuations in receipts or payments can be seen and corrective action can be taken. For viewing the final position after the planned operations have been carried out for a quarter, six months, a year, or longer time—it may be useful to use the *Balance Sheet Cash Forecast* or the *Profits Cash Forecast method*. Certainly these methods may be useful as a means of checking the accuracy of the final balance shown by the payments-and-receipts cash forecast.

**QUESTION** to illustrate a new venture.

R. Jones, L. Barton, and R. Marshall have developed a new idea to the point where it is now a sound commercial proposition. The work, hitherto, has been done part-time, but now the time has come to produce and sell the product on a full-time basis. For technical reasons the minimum size of plant is such that an outlay of £30,000 is needed, being made up of £12,000 for a freehold factory and £18,000 for plant and machinery. A limited company is to be formed from January 1st, 19..., when production will begin.

Other relevant information is as follows:

1. *Costs*

Prime cost is estimated at £2 per unit, being £1 direct labour and £1 direct material. Factory and administration overhead cost for each month is estimated to be £1000.* In *addition*, a publicity campaign which is to be launched from February 1st is to cost £1000 the first month and then £200 for each subsequent month. Selling and distribution costs should amount to £1500 per month, again commencing February 1st.

Preliminary and legal costs have been estimated at £4000; these are payable in cash. At this stage there are a number of unknown factors; so a reserve of cash amounting to £4000 is to be provided.

### 2. Sales

These have been estimated as follows:

| | |
|---|---|
| January 19... | 2000 units |
| February 19... | 3000 units |
| March to December 19... | 4000 units per month. |

The selling price has been fixed at £5 per unit.

### 3. Stocks

Raw materials costing £6000 are to be purchased for the initial stock, and this is to be maintained at that level. A stock of finished goods is also to be kept, amounting to 500 units. Work-in-progress at the end of each period, when full production is reached, will be valued at approximately £2000.

### 4. Terms of Purchase and Sale

Materials purchased are to be paid for within one month. Twenty per cent of sales will be for cash and the balance receivable within one month. Approximately a quarter of these credit sales will be allowed a cash discount of 5%.

All overhead costs are payable within the month in which they are incurred. Provision has to be made for the cost of the stocks.

### 5. Cash Available

The cash available is as follows:

| | |
|---|---|
| Jones | £3,000 |
| Barton | £1,500 |
| Marshall | £15,000 |

All of which is to be used in the new company.

### 6. Requirements

You have been commissioned by Jones, Barton, and Marshall to advise on the cash forecasting and related matters. Assuming that the estimates made are acceptable to you, the following have to be prepared:

(a) Work sheets to show how the forecast has to be built up and the division into permanent and circulating capital.

(b) Initial Cash Forecast for six months to June 30th, 19..., divided to show working capital and permanent capital.

(c) Balance sheet at the end of June 19....

Finally, as part (d) of the question, you should comment on the closing cash balance. Will this affect your plans for obtaining the initial capital requirements?

---

\* A more realistic result may be obtained by separating the costs into "fixed" and "variable." The *variable* costs total can then be calculated by reference to the number of units to be produced.

## SUGGESTED SOLUTION

### (a) WORK SHEET

#### Permanent Capital Required

|  |  | £ |
|---|---|---|
| Freehold factory |  | 12,000 |
| Plant and machinery |  | 18,000 |
|  |  | 30,000 |
| Preliminary expenses and legal costs |  | 4,000 |
| Stocks: | £ |  |
| Raw materials | 6,000 |  |
| Work-in-progress | 2,000 |  |
| Finished goods (500 units at £2·25 each) | 1,125† |  |
|  |  | 9,125 |
| Working Capital: | £ |  |
| Reserve for January | 1,000* |  |
| Reserve for contingencies | 4,000 |  |
|  |  | 5,000 |
|  |  | £48,125 |

† Based on overhead costs of £1000 at a production capacity of 4000 units per month, which gives £0·25 per unit. In addition, £2 per unit for prime cost.

* Based on calculation shown below.

*Note.* In this computation the stocks are covered out of permanent capital. The work-in-progress valuation has to be taken as stated. Presumably it covers direct material and labour costs, but excludes overhead cost, because the latter is given as a total figure with no instructions regarding apportionments.

#### Circulating Capital: Payments and Receipts

#### Cash Payments

| Mnth. | Direct labour | | Direct material | | Factory and administrative overheads £ | Advertising overhead £ | Selling and distribution £ | Total cash £ |
|---|---|---|---|---|---|---|---|---|
|  | Units | Cost £ | Units | Cost £ |  |  |  |  |
| 19... |  |  |  |  |  |  |  |  |
| Jan. | 2,000 | 2,000 | — | — | 1,000 | — | — | 3,000 |
| Feb. | 3,000 | 3,000 | 2,000 | 2,000 | 1,000 | 1,000 | 1,500 | 8,500 |
| Mar. | 4,000 | 4,000 | 3,000 | 3,000 | 1,000 | 200 | 1,500 | 9,700 |
| April | 4,000 | 4,000 | 4,000 | 4,000 | 1,000 | 200 | 1,500 | 10,700 |
| May | 4,000 | 4,000 | 4,000 | 4,000 | 1,000 | 200 | 1,500 | 10,700 |
| June | 4,000 | 4,000 | 4,000 | 4,000 | 1,000 | 200 | 1,500 | 10,700 |
| £ |  | 21,000 |  | 17,000 | 6,000 | 1,800 | 7,500 | 53,300 |

|  |  |
|---|---|
| July Payment (Creditors) | 4,000 |
|  | £57,300 |

## Cash Receipts

| Month | Cash sales Units | Cash sales £5 each £ | Debtors Units | Debtors £ | Total £ | Cash discount £ | Net total £ |
|---|---|---|---|---|---|---|---|
| Jan. ... ... | 400 | 2,000 | — | — | 2,000 | — | 2,000 |
| Feb. ... ... | 600 | 3,000 | 1,600 | 8,000 | 11,000 | 100 | 10,900 |
| Mar. ... ... | 800 | 4,000 | 2,400 | 12,000 | 16,000 | 150 | 15,850 |
| April ... ... | 800 | 4,000 | 3,200 | 16,000 | 20,000 | 200 | 19,800 |
| May ... ... | 800 | 4,000 | 3,200 | 16,000 | 20,000 | 200 | 19,800 |
| June ... ... | 800 | 4,000 | 3,200 | 16,000 | 20,000 | 200 | 19,800 |
| £ | | 21,000 | | 68,000 | 89,000 | 850 | 88,150 |

July Receipt (Debtors) 15,800

£103,950

*Notes.* In January only the cash from cash sales will be received. In February there will be cash sales plus receipts from January debtors amounting to £8000. Cash discount in February is 5% of £2000.

If the factory overhead costs had been separated into "fixed" and "variable" elements, an additional column would have been required with an appropriate heading. The total variable cost would be obtained by multiplying the number of units by the unit rate. By definition the total fixed costs remain the same irrespective of the volume of output.

### (b) CASH FORECASTS

*Cash Forecast—Working Capital for Six Months to June 30th, 19...*

| | Totals £ | Jan. £ | Feb. £ | Mar. £ | April £ | May £ | June £ |
|---|---|---|---|---|---|---|---|
| | | | *Control periods* | | | | |
| RECEIPTS | | | | | | | |
| Opening balance ... | — | — | 1,000 Cr. | 1,400 | 7,550 | 16,650 | 25,750 |
| Cash sales ... | 21,000 | 2,000 | 3,000 | 4,000 | 4,000 | 4,000 | 4,000 |
| Debtors ... ... | 67,150 | — | 7,900 | 11,850 | 15,800 | 15,800 | 15,800 |
| | 88,150 | 2,000 | 9,900 | 17,250 | 27,350 | 36,450 | 45,550 |
| PAYMENTS | | | | | | | |
| Direct material ... | 17,000 | — | 2,000 | 3,000 | 4,000 | 4,000 | 4,000 |
| Direct labour ... | 21,000 | 2,000 | 3,000 | 4,000 | 4,000 | 4,000 | 4,000 |
| Factory and administration | 6,000 | 1,000 | 1,000 | 1,000 | 1,000 | 1,000 | 1,000 |
| Advertising ... | 1,800 | — | 1,000 | 200 | 200 | 200 | 200 |
| Selling and distribution ... | 7,500 | — | 1,500 | 1,500 | 1,500 | 1,500 | 1,500 |
| | 53,300 | 3,000 | 8,500 | 9,700 | 10,700 | 10,700 | 10,700 |
| £ | | 1,000 Cr. | 1,400 | 7,550 | 16,650 | 25,750 | 34,850 |

*Note.* From this forecast can be seen the month-by-month position. Provided estimates work out as expected, only January will have a cash deficit. This £1000 should be provided out of the initial permanent capital. The closing balances have to be calculated and then carried forward.

This forecast brings together the cash receipts and payments figures shown

F

in part (*a*) of the solution. A check on accuracy can be obtained from the total figures in part (*a*). Thus:

|  | £ |
|---|---|
| Expected receipts | 88,150 |
| Expected payments | 53,300 |
|  | **£34,850** |

This figure of £34,850 is the closing balance of cash at the end of June. When pressed for time and there is no specific request for work sheets, the student may omit those relating to receipts and payments and go, immediately, to the working-capital forecast.

### Cash Forecast—Permanent Capital

|  |  | £ |
|---|---|---|
| Permanent capital required |  | £48,125 |
| (Calculated in (*a*) above) |  |  |
| Cash available | £ |  |
| Jones | 3,000 |  |
| Barton | 1,500 |  |
| Marshall | 15,000 |  |
|  | ——— | 19,500 |
| Permanent capital deficit |  | £28,625 |

This deficit would have to be found by the issue of shares or by borrowing.

### (*c*) BALANCE SHEET

*Pro-forma Balance Sheet as at June 30th, 19...*

| | £ | | £ | £ |
|---|---|---|---|---|
| Share capital and/or | | *Fixed Assets* | | |
| loans | 48,125 | Freehold factory | 12,000 | |
| | | Plant and | | |
| | | machinery | 18,000 | |
| | | | ——— | 30,000 |
| Profit for period | 46,650 | *Current Assets* | | |
| (see below, Note 1) | | Stocks: | | |
| Sundry creditors | 4,000 | Raw materials | 6,000 | |
| | | Work-in-progress | 2,000 | |
| | | Finished goods | 1,125 | |
| | | | ——— | |
| | | | 9,125 | |
| | | Debtors | 15,800 | |
| | | Cash (see | 39,850 | |
| | | below, Note 2) | ——— | 64,775 |
| | | Preliminary | | |
| | | expenses | | 4,000 |
| | **£98,775** | | | **£98,775** |

*Note* (1)

### Calculation of Profit

|  |  | £ |
|---|---|---|
| Sales for period, including net Debtors | | 103,950 |
| *Less* Costs for period, including creditors | | 57,300 |
| Profit = | | £46,650 |

The value of the stocks has been omitted both from costs and sales.

*Note* (2)

### Calculation of Cash Balance

|  | £ |
|---|---|
| Balance per cash forecast working capital | 34,850 |
| *Add* Cash for January to cover deficit | 1,000 |
| *Add* Cash Reserve for contingencies | 4,000 |
| Cash Balance = | £39,850 |

### (*d*) CLOSING CASH BALANCE

The forecasted cash balance at the end of June is very substantial, and if turnover continues at the present rate this will improve even further. Whether this should be allowed to influence the plans for obtaining the initial capital will depend very much upon *future* plans. If expansion is envisaged, then cash will be needed to meet future commitments. Accordingly, it may be advisable to obtain the full amount of the balance of permanent capital by the issue of shares.

On the other hand, if it is expected that the cash is more than is needed for future expansion, and the co-directors wish to retain as much control as possible over the future of the business, then a short-term loan may be preferred. This can be repaid out of profits within, say, the first two to three years from commencement. However, care must be taken to obtain *all* facts before a decision is made. In the question there is no mention of dividends, directors' remuneration, taxation, or research and development. When these have been considered the cash and profit estimates may have to be modified.

*Note.* In practice an attempt would be made to cover a longer period than shown in the question given above. Long-term planning is essential.

**QUESTION** to illustrate an established venture.

The Balance Sheet of the A.B. Co. Ltd., as at December 31st, 19..., is as follows:

## Balance Sheet as at December 31st, 19...

| | £ | | £ | £ |
|---|---|---|---|---|
| *Share Capital* | | Goodwill at cost | 50,000 | |
| 80,000 Ordinary Shares | | Patents and trade-marks | 10,000 | |
| of £1 each fully paid | 80,000 | | | 60,000 |
| Capital Reserve | 30,000 | *Fixed Assets* | | |
| General Reserve | 50,000 | Freehold property at | | |
| Profit and Loss balance | 40,000 | cost | 60,000 | |
| | 200,000 | Plant and £ | | |
| Future taxation | 35,000 | machinery 40,000 | | |
| | | *Less* Depreci- | | |
| | | ation 10,000 | | |
| | | | 30,000 | |
| | | Motor Vehicles 80,000 | | |
| *Current Liabilities* | | *Less* Depreci- | | |
| £ | | ation 20,000 | | |
| Sundry creditors 50,000 | | | 60,000 | |
| Taxation 40,000 | | Fixtures | 20,000 | |
| Proposed | | | | 170,000 |
| dividend 8,000 | | *Current Assets* | | |
| | 98,000 | Stock | 40,000 | |
| | | Debtors | 35,000 | |
| | | Cash at bank | 28,000 | |
| | | | | 103,000 |
| | £333,000 | | | £333,000 |

### Data for next twelve months:

| | Quarter 1 | Quarter 2 | Quarter 3 | Quarter 4 |
|---|---|---|---|---|
| | £ | £ | £ | £ |
| Payments for purchases | 100,000 | 200,000 | 100,000 | 150,000 |
| Wages for direct labour | 50,000 | 60,000 | 40,000 | 55,000 |
| Wages for indirect labour | 20,000 | 23,000 | 18,000 | 21,000 |
| Management salaries | 20,000 | 20,000 | 20,000 | 20,000 |
| Cash sales | 60,000 | 70,000 | 50,000 | 80,000 |
| Payment from debtors | 280,000 | 300,000 | 270,000 | 150,000 |
| Capital expenditure (plant and machinery) | 50,000 | — | 20,000 | 10,000 |
| Interim dividend (does not include proposed dividend on Balance Sheet) | — | — | — | 12,000 |
| Debtors' closing balances | 30,000 | 20,000 | 25,000 | 28,000 |
| Creditors' closing balances | 15,000 | 50,000 | 30,000 | 40,000 |

Depreciation is to be charged at 10% on plant and machinery, including additions, and 20% on Motor Vehicles, both being calculated on the straight-line method.

Stock at the end of the year is expected to be valued at £50,000.
The figure for future taxation is expected to meet next year's requirements.
For the following year £40,000 is to be reserved.
A transfer of £10,000 is to be made to General Reserve.
Assume that last year's tax is to be paid and so are the dividends.
Required:

1. A cash forecast in the conventional manner showing the break-down into quarterly control periods.
2. A verification of the final figures by drafting two forecasts—(a) Balance Sheet cash forecast, and (b) Profits cash forecast.

## SUGGESTED SOLUTION

(1) CASH FORECAST

*Cash Forecast for Year Ending December 31st, 19...*

|  | Total | Control periods | | | |
|---|---|---|---|---|---|
|  |  | Quarter 1 | Quarter 2 | Quarter 3 | Quarter 4 |
|  | £ | £ | £ | £ | £ |
| Opening balances | 28,000 | 28,000 | 80,000 | 147,000 | 269,000 |
| RECEIPTS |  |  |  |  |  |
| Cash sales | 260,000 | 60,000 | 70,000 | 50,000 | 80,000 |
| Payments from debtors | 1,000,000 | 280,000 | 300,000 | 270,000 | 150,000 |
|  | 1,288,000 | 368,000 | 450,000 | 467,000 | 499,000 |
| PAYMENTS |  |  |  |  |  |
| Purchases | 550,000 | 100,000 | 200,000 | 100,000 | 150,000 |
| Wages: |  |  |  |  |  |
|   Direct labour | 205,000 | 50,000 | 60,000 | 40,000 | 55,000 |
|   Indirect labour | 82,000 | 20,000 | 23,000 | 18,000 | 21,000 |
| Management salaries | 80,000 | 20,000 | 20,000 | 20,000 | 20,000 |
| Capital expenditure | 80,000 | 50,000 | — | 20,000 | 10,000 |
| Dividends: |  |  |  |  |  |
|   Proposed last year | 8,000 | 8,000 |  |  |  |
|   Proposed this year | 12,000 |  |  |  | 12,000 |
| Taxation, last year | 40,000 | 40,000 |  |  |  |
|  | 1,057,000 | 288,000 | 303,000 | 198,000 | 268,000 |
| Closing balances £ | 231,000 | 80,000 | 147,000 | 269,000 | 231,000 |

## Note on Cash Forecast

The concern is with *cash* expected to be paid and received within the period. Creditors' and debtors' balances are not included; neither is depreciation or any provision or reserve not paid out in cash.

(2a) BALANCE SHEET CASH FORECAST

*Pro-forma Balance Sheet as at December 31st, 19...*

| | £ | | | £ | £ | £ |
|---|---|---|---|---|---|---|
| *Share Capital* | | | Goodwill at cost | 50,000 | | |
| 80,000 Ordinary Shares | | | Patents and Trademarks | 10,000 | | |
| of £1 each fully paid | 80,000 | | | | | 60,000 |
| Capital Reserve | 30,000 | | *Fixed Assets* | | | |
| General Reserve | 60,000 | | Freehold property | | 60,000 | |
| Profit and Loss balance | 306,000 | | Plant and | | | |
| (see Notes below) | ——— | | machinery | 120,000 | | |
| | 476,000 | | *Less* | | | |
| Future taxation | 40,000 | | Depreciation | 22,000 | | |
| | | | | | 98,000 | |
| | | | Motor Vehicles | 80,000 | | |
| | | | *Less* | | | |
| | | | Depreciation | 36,000 | | |
| | | | | | 44,000 | |
| | | | Fixtures | | 20,000 | |
| | | | | | | 222,000 |
| *Current Liabilities* | | | *Current Assets* | | | |
| Sundry creditors | 40,000 | | Stock | | 50,000 | |
| Taxation | 35,000 | | Debtors | | 28,000 | |
| | ——— | 75,000 | Cash at bank | | 231,000 | |
| | | | | | | 309,000 |
| | | £591,000 | | | | £591,000 |

*Notes on Balance Sheet Cash Forecast*

Capital reserves, Profit and Loss balance, and liabilities are forecast. Similarly, an estimate is made of the value of all the assets at the end of the period; that is, *all* the assets except cash. When all the assets (except cash), liabilities, and capital are projected on to a Balance Sheet the cash on hand will be the "balance" to be inserted on the assets side. On the other hand, if the figure to make the two sides agree has to be inserted on the liabilities side of the balance sheet, then the cash will be overdrawn; that is, an overdraft will have to be arranged or adjustments will have to be made before the final Cash Budget is drafted.

Care must be taken when calculating the expected Profit and Loss balance. If there has been a change in the creditors' balance and/or debtors' balance, then an adjustment will be necessary. Purchases, costs, provisions, and profit appropriations have to be deducted from the value of sales to arrive at the Profit and Loss balance. If a credit Profit and Loss balance exists from the previous year, then this must be added to arrive at the figure to be shown on the Balance Sheet. Any debit Profit and Loss balance brought forward would be deducted from the profit for the current year. The example given below should illustrate the principles involved.

*Calculation of Profit*

| | £ | £ |
|---|---|---|
| Sales | | 1,260,000 |
| *Less* Adjustment: reduction in debtors | | 7,000 |
| | | 1,253,000 |
| *Add* Closing stock | | 50,000 |
| | | 1,303,000 |
| *Less* Opening stock | | 40,000 |
| | | 1,263,000 |
| *Less* Costs including purchases | | 917,000 |
| | | 346,000 |
| *Add* Adjustment: reduction in creditors | | 10,000 |
| | | 356,000 |
| *Less* Depreciation: | | |
| Plant and machinery | 12,000 | |
| Motor vehicles | 16,000 | |
| | | 28,000 |
| Current Profit = | | 328,000 |
| *Less* Profit appropriations: | | |
| Dividends | 12,000 | |
| Reserve for tax | 40,000 | |
| General Reserve | 10,000 | |
| | | 62,000 |
| | | 266,000 |
| *Add* Profit brought forward | | 40,000 |
| Profit and Loss balance | | £306,000 |

Debtors at the end of the period have been reduced, which means that the sales figure has to be reduced. The reduction in creditors means that the purchases figure is £10,000 less than the cash payments total of £550,000.

(2*b*) PROFITS CASH FORECAST

| | £ | £ |
|---|---|---|
| Current profit (see Notes below) | | 328,000 |
| *Add* Depreciation for year | 28,000 | |
| „ Reduction in debtors | 7,000 | |
| | | 35,000 |
| | | 363,000 |
| *Less* Capital expenditure | 80,000 | |
| „ Reduction in creditors | 10,000 | |
| „ Increase in stock | 10,000 | |
| „ Dividends payable this | £ | |
| year | 8,000 | |
| | 12,000 | |
| | | 20,000 |
| Tax payable this year | | 40,000 |
| | | 160,000 |
| | | £203,000 |

When the opening balance of cash £28,000 is added the closing cash balance becomes £231,000.

### Notes on Profit Cash Forecast

The earning of profit brings cash into the business. If the business remained static, if there was no wearing out of assets or expansion, and if the balances for debtors, creditors, and stocks remained unchanged, then the total cash available for distribution would be equal to the profit earned. Because a business does *not* remain stationary—it is constantly changing its form—adjustments are essential. Moreover, if appropriations of profit are to be paid out in cash, then these must be deducted from the total profit earned. The depreciation charged in a year reduces the amount of profit available for distribution. Since no charge, in terms of cash, has been made for the depreciation in the year in question, the total cash available will be increased. Accordingly, the depreciation is added back to the profit earned. This, then, has the result of adjusting the cash to its actual figure.

## CONVERSION; CASH FORECAST TO CASH BUDGET

Study of the Cash Forecast may reveal that there is a shortage of cash. If the volumes of production and sales anticipated in the forecast are not to be adjusted, then more cash will have to be found, or measures will have to be taken which allow the available cash to go further.

The first fact to be established is whether the cash required should be obtained from permanent capital or short-term borrowing. A discussion of the sources of cash is to be found in the next chapter. These are external remedies.

There are internal remedies which may be applied within the business. Improvements in efficiency may bring about cost reductions. Changes in prices and discounts may help to speed up the inflow of cash. Salary and wage "freezes" and careful control over spending will also have beneficial effects.* The extension of the period of credit allowed by creditors and reduction of stocks carried can also improve the cash situation. Another possibility is buying assets on hire purchase; alternatively, they may be hired and a hire rental paid. A similar method can be adopted for property: sometimes buildings are sold and then a lease is obtained on them; at other times the business has never owned the property, but leases it instead of buying, thereby conserving cash resources.

If there is a very large surplus of cash, then steps may be taken to invest it by expansion; alternatively, external investments may be purchased. These are discussed earlier in the chapter.

The form of the Cash Budget will be the same as for the Cash Forecast. Any difference between the two is not in the layout and preparation, but in what the figures represent. The Cash Budget figures become part of the integrated budget plan. They become part of the Budgetary

---

* Assumes that these are possible without introducing more problems.

Control system. This will be so *after* any necessary adjustments to the Cash Forecast have been carried out, but not before.

## SOURCE AND APPLICATION OF FUNDS

An important statement is the Source and Application of Funds Statement (*see* Fig. 29). This may be used:

1. For internal control purposes so that cash planning is greatly facilitated.
2. For issue to shareholders as part of the published accounts.

### GROUP CASH FLOW STATEMENT
*Figures in italics represent deductions*

| | Year Ended 30th June, 1968 | Ten Years Ended 30th June, 1968 |
|---|---|---|
| CASH RECEIVED FROM: | £000 | £000 |
| Sources within the Company— | | |
| Profit retained in business | 898 | 7,933 |
| Depreciation retained | 3,712 | 22,925 |
| Increased tax retention | 2,123 | 1,150 |
| Sale of investments | 3.683 | 3,683 |
| Sources outside the Company— | | |
| Issue of new ordinary stock | — | 1,868 |
| Loans (*less* repayments), including minority interests | 473 | 19,405 |
| | 10,889 | 56,964 |
| CASH EXPENDED ON: | | |
| Buildings and plant (*less* investment grants) | 4,128 | 42,921 |
| Increased working capital | 2,029 | 10,999 |
| Interests in associated companies, and trade investments | *122* | 3,638 |
| Intangible assets | — | 5,137 |
| | 6,035 | 62,695 |
| Increase (*decrease*) in liquid resources | *4,854* | 5,731 |

FIG. 29.—*Source and Application of Funds Statement*
(*Reproduced by kind permission of Fisons Limited.*)

The calculations used for arriving at the actual or estimated cash balance are similar to those shown for the Balance Sheet Cash Forecast shown earlier in this chapter. A Source and Application of Funds Statement is closely related to the matter of working capital discussed in various parts of the book.

Important questions can be answered from the statement. These can assist in formulating policy as well as controlling the cash resources. The board of directors of a company act as trustees or stewards; they have to fulfil the social obligations of ensuring that employees, shareholders, and consumers are treated honestly and fairly.

The policy being followed can make all the difference to the success of a business. An astute and clever team of directors ensure that there is constant growth, yet there is no danger of the company outgrowing its financial strength. Typical questions on top management control are as follows:

1. *How much finance is coming from* (a) *external sources and* (b) *internal retentions*

This is an important matter which is discussed further on pages 161 to 178. From Fig. 29, which is taken from the Report and Accounts of Fisons Limited, it will be seen that profit and depreciation retained in the business amounts to around 45% of total cash received for the year ended 30th June, 1968. For the ten-year period a total of £32,008,000 was retained in the business.

Progressive companies usually retain a substantial proportion of funds in this way. However, no standard percentage can be given. Much depends upon the nature of the operations. A company which is spending very large sums on research and development and expanding at a very rapid rate will probably have to seek a larger proportion from external sources than a business which is static.

Another factor which should be considered is the profit being earned on total capital employed. From whatever source capital is obtained it should be capable of earning an adequate return: this should be certain when funds are obtained from external sources whether by issue of shares or debentures.

2. *How the funds are being employed*

There should be a reasonable balance between funds used for fixed assets *and* current assets. The former are kept in the business in order to earn profit; it is essential that they are maintained and expanded so that the earning power is extended.

Study of the illustration (Fig. 29) shows that £4,128,000 was spent on buildings and plant. Other figures also indicate a progressive policy— purchase of interests in associated companies and acquisition of intangible assets are sure signs of expansion.

3. *Whether depreciation is adequate for the type of business*

Depreciation is important for a number of reasons:

(*a*) enables a profit to be calculated which allows for the intensity of use of fixed assets;

(*b*) allows funds to be retained in the business;

(*c*) permits a constructive policy to be followed as regards the maintenance of capital in real terms (*see* Revaluation Accounting, Chapter 27);

(*d*) gives an indication of technological progress and change.

If fixed assets are written off in a relatively few years, then this may be a sign of rapid technological change. This could be a sign of very progressive management which follows a policy of employing the latest types of fixed assets. Alternatively, it may be a sign of rapid progress within the industry as a whole; this, in turn, may be an indication that fierce competition is being experienced. No conclusion can be reached until all the facts are known. The size and strength of the company within the industry will be very important.

In the example given the depreciation for the year is £3,712,000. In order to reach any conclusion it will be necessary to study the Statistical Record on page 404. It will be seen that the total amount invested in fixed assets (Land, Buildings, Plant and Equipment) is £44,316,000. On this basis the fixed assets could be regarded as having a life of around eleven years. However, closer analysis of the accounts may be necessary to see the life of the assets at different periods, thus allowing for fluctuations in technological development. The figures for year ended 30th June, 1968, have been adjusted for disposals and acquisitions.

## EXAMINATION QUESTIONS

1. Your company wishes to acquire adjoining factory premises at a cost of £60,000 to manufacture a new product. The present owner is prepared to take a mortgage on the property for one-half of the purchase price, carrying interest at 5% per annum.

The equipping of the factory with plant, machinery, tools, fittings, etc., is expected to cost £75,000.

The prime cost of the product is estimated at £10 per unit, being labour £6 and material £4, the latter being purchased on the usual trade terms for payment in the month following delivery.

Power, stores, tools, and other variable expenses are expected to cost £1·50 per unit.

Management, supervision, indirect labour, and all other fixed expenses, including mortgage interest, but excluding depreciation, are budgeted at £9,000 per month.

Selling and distribution expenses, apart from advertising, may be taken at £3,000 per month.

It is expected that an initial advertising campaign costing £15,000 will be required to establish a market for the product. In addition, normal advertising will cost about £1,000 per month.

The selling price is to be £17·5 per unit, and sales are estimated as follows:

| | |
|---|---|
| First month     ...    ...    ...    ...    ...    ... | 1,000 units |
| Second month   ...    ...    ...    ...    ...    ... | 2,000 „ |
| Third and subsequent months ...    ...    ...    ... | 3,000 „ |

10% of sales will be for cash, the remainder for settlement in the following month.

Stocks required at the commencement of trading are:

| | |
|---|---|
| Materials...    ...    ...    ...    ...    ...    ... | £20,000 |
| Finished goods   ...    ...    ...    ...    ...    ... | 1,000 units |

and these will require to be maintained.

The value of work in progress at full production is estimated at £5,000.

The patent rights for the new product will cost £15,000, and legal expenses for purchase of property £1,000.

A charge of £500 per month will be made against the factory for head office administration expenses.

Compute the amount of capital required to finance this project, and prepare a statement showing the expected earnings for the first and subsequent years.                                      (*I.C.W.A.*)

2. What is "Working Capital"? On the formation of a new business, what considerations are involved in estimating the amount of the required working capital?                                              (*S.C.A.*)

3. You are required to produce a *Cash Budget* for your Directors for the ensuing year. What information would you require and from what source would you obtain it for each of the following items:

(*a*) Fixed Assets—Plant and Machinery.
(*b*) Motor Vehicles.
(*c*) Sales Ledger Debtors.
(*d*) Bought Ledger Creditors.
(*e*) Taxation Payments.
(*f*) Long term large advertising campaign.

                                             (*I.C.W.A.*)

4. A company has £1 million cash available which it will not require for six months. State the various opportunities for investing this sum. Which one would you recommend and why?                            (*S.C.A.*)

5. A manufacturing company produces a number of standardised accessories for motor vehicles. Sales are composed of direct sales to motor manufacturers and sales ex stock from a number of depots owned by the company in various parts of the country. State the considerations which would guide you in planning the company's investment in stocks of raw materials and components, work in progress and finished stock.      (*I.C.W.A.*)

6. L and M, who are contemplating the purchase of a business, have consulted you and one point on which you are asked to advise them is the average

amount of working capital which would need to be employed in the first year's trading.

You are given the following estimates and instructed to add 10 per cent. to your computed figure to allow for contingencies.

|  | *Per Annum* £ |
|---|---|
| (1) Average amount locked up in stocks: | |
|     Stock of Finished Products and Work-in-progress  ... | 500 |
|     Stocks of Stores, Materials, etc.    ...   ...   ... | 800 |
| (2) Average credit given: | |
|     Home Sales—6 weeks' credit  ...   ...   ...   ... | 31,200 |
|     Export Sales—1½ weeks' credit ...   ...   ...   ... | 7,800 |
| (3) Lag in payment of expenses: | |
|     Wages—1½ weeks    ...   ...   ...   ...   ... | 26,000 |
|     Other Expenses (including Purchases)—4 weeks   ... | 9,600 |

Set out your calculation of the average amount of working capital required.

(*S.C.A.*)

7. Set out, in final summary form, a quarterly cash forecast, as necessary to a scheme of budgetary control. Insert illustrative figures for two months.

(*I.C.W.A.*)

8. The Liquidator of West Ltd. has offered to East Ltd. for £18,000, manufacturing plant which cost £50,000 in 1957 and is estimated to operate efficiently for a further 10 years and, for £4,500, stocks and work-in-progress.

If the offer is accepted the tenancy of the factory will be transferred to East Ltd., but not that of the office as that company's office will suffice.

You are given the following information of the last year's trading of West Ltd.

|  | £ | £ |
|---|---|---|
| Sales—average credit 2 calendar months   ...   ...   ... |  | 111,678 |
| Purchases—average credit 6½ weeks   ...   ...   ...   ... | 61,381 | |
| Wages—lag in payment, 1½ weeks   ...   ...   ... | 20,800 | |
| Factory Rent—payable quarterly in advance  ...   ...   ... | 2,392 | |
| Other Factory Expenses—average credit 1 calendar month  ... | 7,212 | |
| Depreciation of Plant   ...   ...   ...   ...   ...   ... | 2,500 | |
| Decrease of Stocks and Work-in-progress   ...   ...   ... | 2,219 | 96,504 |
| Gross Profit   ...   ...   ...   ...   ...   ... |  | 15,174 |
| Office Rent—payable quarterly in arrear   ...   ... | 1,260 | |
| Salaries—lag in payment ¼ week...   ...   ...   ... | 6,656 | |
| General Expenses—average credit 1 calendar month ... | 2,472 | |
| Managing Director's Salary—paid monthly in arrear ... | 3,000 | |
| Directors' Fees—paid quarterly in advance   ...   ... | 2,000 | 15,388 |
| Net Loss   ...   ...   ...   ...   ...   ...   ... |  | £214 |

You are instructed to assume:

(1) that sales would be maintained at the former level with no significant seasonal variations;

(2) that there would be savings of 4 per cent. of the cost of materials used and 2½ per cent. of the cost of wages;

(3) that the managing director would be appointed manager on the same terms, but directors' fees as well as office rent would be saved;

(4) that no profits would be withdrawn until they were surplus to working capital requirements; and

(5) that it would be necessary to increase immediately the stocks and work-in-progress offered by the Liquidator for £4,500 by further stock costing £4,000.

The Directors of East Ltd. are disposed to accept the offer, which remains open until 1st January, 1969, but before doing so wish to know the additional amount of money which the business would require for working capital.

You are required to set out your calculations of the additional money required for working capital:

(a) at the maximum during the year 1968, and

(b) at the end of that year.          (S.C.A.)

9. The summarised Balance Sheets of Clive, Ltd. on 31st March, 1967, and 31st March, 1968, were as follows:

| | 1967 £ | 1968 £ | | 1967 £ | 1968 £ |
|---|---|---|---|---|---|
| Share Capital— | | | Fixed Assets at cost | 19,500 | 35,500 |
| Ordinary Shares ... | 12,500 | 12,500 | Less Depreciation | 5,000 | 7,000 |
| Redeemable Preference Shares ... | 2,500 | | | 14,500 | 18,500 |
| | | | Shares in Associated | | |
| Capital Redemption | | | Company at cost | 1,250 | 1,250 |
| Reserve Fund ... | | 2,500 | | | |
| General Reserve ... | 3,000 | 3,500 | Loan to Associated | | |
| Profit and Loss | | | Company ... | | 1,250 |
| Account ... ... | 750 | 750 | Current Assets ... | 11,750 | 7,750 |
| Taxation— | | | | | |
| 1967–68 ... ... | 4,500 | | | | |
| 1968–69 ... ... | | 2,000 | | | |
| Current Liabilities ... | 4,250 | 7,500 | | | |
| | £27,500 | £28,750 | | £27,500 | £28,750 |

The final section of the Profit and Loss Account for the year to 31st March, 1968, was as follows:

| | £ | | £ |
|---|---|---|---|
| Taxation, 1968–69 ... ... | 2,000 | Balance brought forward ... | 750 |
| Balance carried forward ... | 3,750 | Net Profit for Year ... | 5,000 |
| | £5,750 | | £5,750 |

You are approached by certain shareholders of the Company, who are puzzled by the contrast between the two Balance Sheets in regard to working capital, and seek an explanation. They are unable to reconcile the adverse change in working capital with the fact that the Company made a substantial profit of £5000 in the year to 31st March, 1968. The profit, they suggest, should be reflected by an increase in working capital.

You are required to prepare an explanatory statement, for the benefit of these shareholders, showing, with figures, the cause of the change in the Company's position as regards working capital. (*S.C.A.*)

10. (*a*) A highly mechanised manufacturing company contemplates substantial expansion of output and will need increased stocks during a period of rising prices. You are asked, as management accountant, to comment on the future cash position, giving attention to liquidity, availability of cash, and additional finance. Present your comments briefly, point by point.

(*b*) Design a form upon which short-term information for periodic presentation to management may be summarised concerning cash forecast. Rulings, headings and accounts should be given, but no figures are required. (*I.C.W.A.*)

11. (*a*) What is the significance of cash budgeting for management purposes and why is the cash budget dependent on both the operating and the capital budgets?

(*b*) From the following information taken from the budget of the A.B. Co. Ltd. prepare a statement showing the average amount of working capital required by the company.

(i) Annual sales are estimated at 100,000 units at £1 per unit.

(ii) Production quantities coincide with sales and will be carried on evenly throughout the year and production cost is:

| | |
|---|---|
| Material | £0·500 per unit |
| Labour | £0·200 per unit |
| Expenses | £0·175 per unit |

(iii) Customers are given 60 days credit, and 50 days credit is taken from suppliers.

(iv) Forty days supply of raw materials and fifteen days supply of finished goods are kept.

(v) The production cycle is 20 days and all material is issued at the commencement of each production cycle.

(vi) A cash balance equivalent to one-third of the average other working capital requirements is kept for contingencies. (*A.C.C.A.*)

12. Budgetary control is often described as a system of "responsibility" accounting. Comment on this description indicating the problems which it presents to the management accountant. (*A.C.C.A.*)

13. A considerable increase in production and sales activity is planned in an organisation which manufactures a standard range of domestic consumer products. This increase will be provided partly by a more intensive use of existing premises and plant and equipment, and partly by extensions of premises and fixed assets.

The increase in activity is phased as follows:

Phase 1. Over the next twelve months, a 20% on present activity, stemming entirely from intensive expansion.

Phase 2. Over the second period of twelve months a further 25% increase on present activity, coming from an extension of capacity.

Detail what you see as the main problems of cost and working capital budgeting over the two-year period.          (*I.C.W.A.*)

14. A small private company, after several years of unprofitable trading, was taken over by a new management on the 31st December.

The accounts for the following year were as follows:

|  |  |  |  | £ |
|---|---|---|---|---:|
| Direct materials | ... | ... | | 78,000 |
| Direct wages ... | ... | ... | | 31,200 |
| Variable overheads | ... | ... | | 15,600 |
| Fixed overheads | ... | ... | | 30,000 |
| Profit ... | ... | ... | ... | 1,200 |
| Sales ... | ... | ... | ... | 156,000 |

The balance sheet as at the end of the first twelve months' trading was as follows:

| | £ | | | £ |
|---|---:|---|---|---:|
| Share capital ... | 40,000 | Fixed assets ... ... | 24,000 |
| Creditors ... ... | 19,000 | Stocks ... ... ... | 26,000 |
| Bank overdraft ... | 26,500 | Debtors ... ... ... | 26,000 |
| | | Profit and loss account... | 10,000 |
| | £86,000 | | £86,000 |

The budgeted sales for the second year of trading are as follows:

|  |  |  |  | £ |
|---|---|---|---|---:|
| 1st quarter | ... | ... | ... | 42,000 |
| 2nd „ | ... | ... | ... | 45,000 |
| 3rd „ | ... | ... | ... | 48,000 |
| 4th „ | ... | ... | ... | 51,000 |

It is anticipated that the ratios of material consumption, direct wages and variable overheads to sales are unlikely to change, that fixed overheads (incurred evenly during the year) will remain at £30,000 per annum, and that creditors can be held at three months direct material usage. Both stock and debtors can be maintained at two months sales.

Bank interest and depreciation, the latter at 10% per annum on fixed assets, are included in the overheads.

Prepare quarterly budgets for the second year of trading to indicate to management:

(*a*) whether the results are likely to be satisfactory; and
(*b*) whether overdraft facilities (which are normally limited to £25,000) are sufficient, or whether further capital must be introduced.

(*I.C.W.A.*)

## 15. XYZ Company Ltd.

### Summary Balance Sheet

| | End of Period I £ | End of Period II £ | | End of Period I £ | End of Period II £ |
|---|---|---|---|---|---|
| Share Capital: | | | Fixed Assets: | | |
| Ordinary Shares | 65,500 | 65,500 | Plant/Machinery | 75,760 | 94,040 |
| Preference Shares | 41,100 | 38,000 | Land/Buildings | 32,000 | 31,000 |
| Reserves: | | | Loose Tools ... | 840 | 760 |
| General ... ... | 6,000 | 8,000 | Goodwill/Patents | | |
| Unappropriated | | | Trade Marks | 12,000 | 9,000 |
| Profits ... | 121,000 | 124,799 | | 120,600 | 134,800 |
| Taxation ... ... | 13,000 | 13,600 | | | |
| Loans ... ... | 20,000 | 30,000 | Trade Investments | 9,400 | 10,600 |
| Current Liabilities: | | | Current Assets: | | |
| Taxation... ... | 14,200 | 17,994 | Stock ... ... | 172,789 | 150,372 |
| Dividends ... | 4,900 | 7,111 | Investments ... | 1,050 | 7,602 |
| Creditors ... | 34,600 | 40,987 | Debtors... ... | 30,250 | 48,147 |
| Bank Overdraft... | 15,500 | 18,770 | Bills Receivable | 1,206 | 3,079 |
| | 69,200 | 84,862 | Cash ... ... | 505 | 10,161 |
| | | | | 205,800 | 219,361 |
| | £335,800 | £364,761 | | £335,800 | £364,761 |

### Summary Profit and Loss Account for Period II

| | £ | £ | £ |
|---|---|---|---|
| Trading Profit (prior to deducting the undernoted items) | | | 64,684 |
| Depreciation Buildings ... ... ... ... ... | 1,000 | | |
| Depreciation Plant/Equipment ... ... ... ... | 15,120 | | |
| Depreciation Loose Tools ... ... ... ... | 360 | | |
| | | 16,480 | |
| Audit Fee ... ... ... ... ... ... ... | | 1,500 | |
| Directors' Remuneration Fees ... ... ... ... | 1,200 | | |
| Others ... ... ... ... ... ... ... | 9,400 | | |
| | | 10,600 | |
| Loan Interest ... ... ... ... ... ... | | 1,600 | |
| | | | 30,180 |
| Profit before taxation ... ... ... ... ... | | | 34,504 |
| Corporation Tax based on Profit for the Year ... ... | | | 13,600 |
| Net Profit for Year after Corporation Tax ... ... | | | 20,904 |
| Appropriations: | | | |
| Amount written off Goodwill ... ... ... ... | | 3,000 | |
| Transfer to General Reserve ... ... ... ... | | 2,000 | |
| Proposed Preference Dividend | | | |
| Less Income Tax ... ... ... ... ... | | 1,339 | |
| Proposed Ordinary Dividend | | | |
| Less Income Tax ... ... ... ... ... | | 5,772 | |
| Income Tax payable in respect of Dividends ... ... | | 4,994 | |
| | | | 17,105 |
| Unappropriated Profits brought forward ... ... ... | | | 3,799 |
| Unappropriated Profits carried forward ... ... ... | | | 121,000 |
| | | | £124,799 |

*Fixed Assets Schedules*

| | End of Period I | | | End of Period II | | |
|---|---|---|---|---|---|---|
| | Cost £ | Depre-ciation £ | Book Value £ | Cost £ | Depre-ciation £ | Book Value £ |
| Plant/Machinery ... | 101,560 | 25,800 | 75,760 | 126,560 | 32,520 | 94,040 |
| Land/Buildings ... | 35,000 | 3,000 | 32,000 | 35,000 | 4,000 | 31,000 |
| | £136,560 | £28,800 | 107,760 | £161,560 | £36,520 | 125,040 |
| Loose Tools... ... ... ... ... | | | 840 | | | 760 |
| Goodwill/Patents/Trade Marks ... ... | | | 12,000 | | | 9,000 |
| | | | £120,600 | | | £134,800 |

*Note.* During Period II plant and machinery was purchased at a cost of £35,200. Some old machinery was also sold for £2000. Any gain/loss on sale is included in the Trading Profit of £64,684.

From the above information prepare a statement accounting for the increase of £9656 in the cash position which has taken place during Period II. This statement should be accompanied by a report commenting on the position, and indicating what further information would be required before this statement could be used for predicting future cash movements.

*(A.C.C.A.)*

CHAPTER 7

## FINANCING THE BUSINESS

THE importance of adequate cash resources and the methods utilised for forecasting and budgeting cash requirements were covered earlier. This and the next two chapters are concerned with capital structures and the principal sources of capital required. For convenience, the sources will be divided according to the length of time the money is required. The permanent capital is covered first; next comes medium-term; and short-term capital is considered last. These descriptions may be given different meanings when considered by different people, so any discussion on them must be clear as to the definitions being used. Often medium-term capital is referred to as "short-term." Some forms of finance do not conveniently fit into either category, and these are considered separately.

## STAGES OF GROWTH

Generally speaking, the larger the business, the more complex the financial structure and the problems which may arise. An appreciation of the importance of the size of a business in relation to its financial needs is therefore essential. The methods of obtaining finance in the early stages of growth may not be appropriate when a business is well established; even if appropriate, there may be cheaper ways of financing. When profit prospects crystallise in a manner which indicates a good return on capital employed or to be employed, then the problems associated with attracting capital may diminish and, accordingly, the cost of borrowing may become cheaper.

The one-man business is the first stage of growth. Alternatively, or as a second stage, comes the partnership. In both these cases capital will normally come from the owner (or owners) of the business or from friends or relatives. Provided a good credit-standing can be established, this size of business will be able to meet its requirements by "living on credit." Purchases can be obtained one month and be paid for the following month, out of the proceeds of the sales. Any reasonable request for cash will probably be met by a bank loan or overdraft. Fixed assets may be acquired through hire purchase or, in the case of premises, by obtaining a lease. Careful spending, and the retention of as much profit as possible in the business, should enable growth to take place at a steady rate. At all times there must be an awareness of the danger of running short of cash. Attempts to expand at too fast a rate may have serious consequences, and yet a certain amount of growth is essential. Budgeting will enable control to be exercised; more important, it will show the maximum interest, hire purchase, or rental payments that can be made without running into difficulties.

Once the owners commence to employ others and the volume of trade is such that the capital employed is in terms of thousands of pounds, then serious thought has to be given to forming a private limited company. This not only gives the advantage of limited liability to shareholders but also paves the way for future development. The attraction of outside investment is generally easier when the business is in the form of a company. As will be shown later, specialist organisations, which enable capital to be obtained, are in existence, and these can be utilised. Continuity of the business may also be an important consideration. At law a company is a legal entity quite separate from the directors or owners, so there is less danger of the business ceasing to exist upon the death of a principal. This is a serious threat in the one-man business or partnership form of organisation. Linked with permanency of existence is the problem of finding death duties when an owner dies. Again the company form of organisation, because it allows outside investment to be obtained without losing control, is better than other forms of organisation.

When a company emerges from the stage of being "small" to the stage of being "medium" is difficult to define. In industries which require a large investment in fixed assets a company which has a capital of £500,000 may be regarded as small for that industry. However, speaking generally, the medium-size business may be regarded as being one with a capital of, say, £100,000–£1,000,000. It is at this stage, and particularly at the latter part of the scale, that outside investment may have to be attracted. Short-term borrowing and ploughed-back profits become inadequate to meet the normal requirements and, possibly, the fear of death duties becomes prominent.

The private company* cannot invite the public to subscribe for its shares or debentures, and since the number of shareholders, excluding past and present employees, is limited to fifty, the prospect of acquiring substantial capital may not be very bright. Conversion to a public company *may* be the answer to obtaining more capital. However, this does involve the loss of the status of "private company," and possibly means the sale of part of the equity capital to outsiders; a step which, to some owners of a business, would signify the first sign of loss of control or, at any rate, would indicate the possibility of interference in control. In actual fact, of course, if due care is exercised when drafting a scheme of financing, there should be no loss or interference in control. On the other hand, conversion to a public company means that the shares become marketable—being bought and sold quite easily—and therefore may be an attractive investment.

Loss of "private" status may not be valued to a great extent by the

* The reader can find the full definition of, and provisions relating to, a private company in the *Companies Acts, 1948* and *1967*, or a textbook on Company Law.

owners of a business, and yet a public issue may be impracticable. There is a minimum size of issue of shares below which the *cost* per pound sterling obtained becomes excessive. Many of the costs of "flotation," such as legal and printing expenses, are of a fixed nature, so the smaller the issue, the larger the cost per share. Another consideration is the status of the company trying to attract capital. Generally, the company attempting to make a small issue does not have a proven record of profit-earning, and therefore the costs of "selling" tend to be higher than when a company's capabilities are well known. In these circumstances the Industrial and Commercial Finance Corporation, the Board of Trade, or commercial banks may be able to assist with finance. Specialist organisations, such as finance houses, merchant bankers, investment trusts, and insurance companies, may also provide the means in the form of long-, medium-, or short-term funds. At a later stage a public issue of shares may become possible.

When a company has become well established it may make an approach to the public via an issuing house. On the other hand, if very favourably placed, in size and profitability, a company may be able to make a direct issue to the public.

These observations should indicate, in a general way, the different stages of growth. There can be no preconceived ideas on how a business should obtain its finance, so the suggestions put forward in the discussion should not be regarded as rigid rules, but rather as possibilities. More details of these are given in this and other chapters.

## PERMANENT CAPITAL*

Permanent or long-term capital provides the foundation and super-structure of the financial edifice. If inadequate, a business may have to limit its activities or, alternatively, may have to borrow short-term funds at high rates of interest. If a business is encountering difficulties there may be *no* short-term funds available; all financial institutions expect to see signs that a proposed loan is likely to be repaid; a falling off in trade is hardly likely to inspire confidence.

What form the capital structure should take in the case of a company is discussed below. The plans adopted by sole-traders and partnerships are generally influenced by the means available from the owners of the business, or from relatives and friends. Often, therefore, the arrange-ment is rather of a quasi-domestic nature, and may not be capable of being assessed in terms of what is the ideal capital structure. Mutual agreement between partners or other interested parties is often more

---

* The references to Company Law have been kept to a minimum. This subject has become so vast that any attempt to cover it adequately would have made this volume unmanageable. There are many excellent works on Company Law, and the reader is advised to study one of these on legal points which may arise in connection with the issue of shares or Debentures.

important than getting the correct balance between the different types of capital. Nevertheless, much of what is stated below, relating to loans and similar methods of obtaining finance, should be of value to the managers of any type of business organisation.

The issue of shares and debentures by a company is the principal method of obtaining long-term capital. Different types of shares exist, each having different characteristics and therefore possessing qualities of a varied nature. Investors will look at the risk, the expected yield, and the voting powers of each class of share. The company will want to obtain the finance at reasonable cost, and will want to take advantage of any concessions which affect taxation. These matters are discussed below under the heading "Capital Structure." Before considering which capital structure is likely to be the most efficient, a knowledge of each class of share and types of Debentures is essential.

## CLASSES OF SHARES

Broadly speaking, there are two classes of shares: Ordinary shares and Preference shares. Variations in the rights which these give exist to meet different requirements.

### Ordinary Shares

Ordinary shares normally form the backbone of the capital structure. Although they may be issued at a premium or at a discount, they do have a fixed nominal value, which is not changed unless there is a special reason. The Ordinary share capital is usually termed "equity capital."

Ordinary shareholders are entitled to a share of the surplus profits after the Debenture holders and/or Preference shareholders have received their fixed rate of interest or dividend. Sometimes the view is put forward that the whole of the profits, after payment of Preference dividends, should go to Ordinary shareholders, but this appears to be a purely theoretical concept and is not borne out by actual practice. The necessity to appropriate profits to reserves means that the surplus available to Ordinary shareholders is depleted. Clearly though, because of the risk involved in having to take second place to the Preference shareholders, a company will normally pay a higher rate of dividend than that paid in respect of the Preference shares: otherwise it would have great difficulty in attracting the necessary amount of capital. Any attempt to obtain finance by the issue of Ordinary shares should show that future expectations are quite attractive. The expected rate of earnings should be at least that obtainable elsewhere on capital which carries similar risks.

Ordinary shares usually carry with them a right to vote at company meetings. Since the Ordinary shareholders bear a heavy responsibility it seems only fair that they should have the power to vote. Non-voting Ordinary shares do exist. Sometimes they are issued in this form as a means of maintaining control of a company. If a scrip issue of non-voting Ordinary shares is made to existing shareholders, then, provided the voting shares do not change hands, there can be no transfer of control. This is likely to be the case when the majority holding is held by a particular family. In the family business there is always a danger that death duties will necessitate a sale of shares; if the non-voting shares are sold, control can still be maintained. The scrip issue is clearly a different proposition from the normal issue for cash. The possibility of future take-over bids, and therefore capital profits, may be absent if shares do not carry the right to vote. When considering the purchase of Ordinary shares of different companies, all showing approximately the same return, the investor is unlikely to be attracted to the non-voting shares. Why should he when he is expected to bear the ultimate risks? The least he can expect is to have some say, however small it may prove to be in practice, in developing the policy of the company.

The necessity for a company to show that a minimum rate of dividend can be expected, representing a fair reward for the risk involved, has already been mentioned. What is a "fair reward" will vary from time to time. When business confidence runs high investors may be persuaded to become shareholders without great difficulty. On the other hand, in a trade recession, no matter what tactics are used or promises made, a company may be extremely hard pushed to obtain any new finance. In between the two extremes—high and low confidence—the normal state of affairs should exist. Investors will expect to be shown that prospects are good and that a reasonable return can be earned even when the company is not working at full capacity. The "margin of safety" which exists (see page 256) will play an important role in determining the extent of profitable activity.

When dealing with the existing company and intending to issue further Ordinary shares, care must be taken not to prejudice the rights of present shareholders or to bring about a devaluation of their shares. If over-capitalisation occurs the return on total capital employed will be too small. In fact, if Debentures and Preference shares form a large part of the capital the Ordinary shareholders may find that earnings are never large enough to pay them a dividend. The fixed payments may take all the profits and never leave any surplus for distribution to Ordinary shareholders. This matter of being fair to existing shareholders is considered further under the section which deals with rights issues.

If Debentures or Preference shares form a large part of the company's capital then earnings will be restricted for Ordinary shareholders. This is made more acute by the fact that under the *Finance Act, 1965*, tax must be paid on Preference dividends which must be maintained net, thus leaving even less to be distributed to the Ordinary shareholders.

There is no one, standard type of Ordinary share. The rights to be enjoyed by the holders are as stated when the issue is made. The facts given above must therefore be taken as a general guide to the rights which are *normal* practice. Deferred or founders' shares are a type of Ordinary share, often of small nominal value, which entitle the holders—possibly company promoters or the vendors of the business—to surplus profits after the other Ordinary shares have received a certain fixed amount.

## Preference Shares

As the name "Preference shares" implies, the holders have prior claims, before Ordinary shareholders, to dividends and, possibly, in the event of liquidation, to repayment of capital. The rights do not extend to the Preference shareholders being given privileges before Debenture holders or other lenders. The latter are creditors, and therefore must be satisfied before there is any thought of payment of dividends.

Preference shares generally carry a right to a fixed rate of dividend and are described to show this fact on the company's Balance Sheet or other statements. This right may be carried forward from year to year; if a dividend is not paid in one year, then the right to it is carried forward to the next and subsequent years. These are "Cumulative Preference shares." On the other hand, if failure to declare a dividend in a particular year cancels the right to that year's dividend, then the shares are said to be "Non-cumulative." Sometimes Preference shareholders are given the right to a second dividend, when the shares are called "Participating." They may also be entitled to be paid back a part of capital upon liquidation.

The right for the company to redeem may also be a feature of a Preference share issue. Certainly this is something which must not be overlooked when preparing a capital structure. If the rate of dividend required to attract funds is particularly high, then a company may find that Redeemable Preference shares would be beneficial. When interest and therefore dividend rates fall a company may be able to redeem the old Preference shares from the proceeds of a new issue made on more advantageous terms. The Companies Acts stipulate certain conditions. Shares can be redeemed only if the Articles so provide. Moreover, they should be fully paid up, and either they must be replaced by a new issue of shares or, if redeemed out of profits, there must be an equivalent amount transferred to the Capital Redemption Reserve Fund.

A conversion privilege may be used as an attraction to investors. At some time in the future the Preference shareholders may be given a right to convert the shares held into Ordinary shares. From the company's standpoint it should be noted that the existence of this right is sometimes viewed as being an indication of lack of financial strength. The company, it is argued, is unable to obtain funds without offering some extra inducement. There may be some truth in this statement.

Care has to be exercised when fixing the price at which the conversion privilege can be exercised. There should be a gap between the present value of the Ordinary shares and the price which must be reached before the conversion can be made. Yet the closing of the gap must be a possibility, or the conversion privilege will not be taken seriously by potential investors. Normally a particular time is stated in which the privilege can be exercised. The overall time lag will enable the assets purchased from the proceeds of the issue to start earning sufficient to cover the total amount of capital in the form of Ordinary shares. If the price fixed and the time stated do not bring about a sufficient delay before conversion there is a danger that the value of the Ordinary shares will be reduced. This will come from the fact that earnings are insufficient to pay a fair return on *all* the Ordinary shares. A reduction in value may also be brought about by the price and time fixed for conversion not being synchronised. If the option to convert to Ordinary shares can be made at a price of £2, but, due to the time set for conversion being miscalculated, the existing Ordinary share prices rise to £3 before the right can be exercised, then the fact that the Preference shareholders are obtaining Ordinary shares at £2 will probably mean that the value of each share will fall below £3 once the conversion has been made.

In favour of a conversion option it can be said that, once the option has been exercised, the capital structure may be strengthened. This applies to both Debenture and Preference share issue options. A company which reduces its fixed charges may be able to offer more to its equity shareholders, both in dividends and capital appreciation.

Often Preference shares do not carry a voting right, but this is not an invariable rule. It is possible to divide any class of share into "A," "B," and subsequent divisions, some with voting rights and some without. However, as noted earlier, there appears to be a much stronger case for giving the Ordinary shareholders the right to control.

There are many accountants who regard Preference shares as a most unsatisfactory method of raising finance. In periods of high interest rates the Preference shareholders have to be paid as much, or possibly more, than the Ordinary shareholders; yet they are no better than Debentures. Unfortunately, some companies do not have the properties to back Debentures, or have the financial standing to issue unsecured notes. Holding companies, attempting to expand, may be forced to issue Preference shares instead of Debentures.

## LOAN CAPITAL—DEBENTURES

A Debenture is a document by which a company acknowledges a loan. The terms for repayment, the interest payable, and the charge, if any, on the company's assets, will be stipulated.

Debentures do not form part of the share capital, but are generally referred to as "loan capital." Debenture holders are not shareholders. If the Debenture provides for a charge on the company's assets, then the Debenture holder is a creditor with special privileges. When there is no charge conferred, then the lender is an ordinary, unsecured creditor.

There are different classes of Debentures. The naked Debenture is a bare promise to repay the loan and, until the loan is repaid, it states the interest payable. Another term used is "unsecured notes." The fact that these Debentures do not confer a charge means that only companies of very high standing can use this method of raising finance. Unsecured loan *stock** may be issued in units of, say, £100 each. The right to convert to Ordinary shares at a future date or series of dates is often a feature of unsecured notes. This privilege has been explained earlier in connection with Preference shares.

The issue of unsecured notes provides a convenient method for the large company to obtain finance at *reasonable rates of interest*. When earnings become adequate to enable shares to be a practical proposition, then these may be issued.

Debentures may confer a floating *or* a fixed charge on a company's assets. The floating charge does not attach to any specific asset, and therefore may allow the company to change the structure of the assets to meet changing conditions. A floating charge may crystallise when a company goes into liquidation, when a receiver is appointed, or when one of the conditions stated on the Debentures occurs. From a management point of view the preservation of control without possible interference from mortgage Debenture holders is clearly an advantage. The borrower, on the other hand, may not find the floating Debenture as attractive as the mortgage Debenture. The former allows a company to create mortgage Debentures which rank in priority next to the existing floating Debentures.

When a fixed charge is given on the company's assets the debentures are generally called "mortgage Debentures." When issued in a series and given a specific charge they are then covered by a trust deed. The latter vests the legal estate in trustees, who can take action if necessary to protect the Debenture holders' interests. Breach of one of the covenants contained in the trust deed would be grounds for this action, which may take the form of selling the assets charged.

Debentures may be issued to named persons and registered by the company, or they may be made payable to bearer. In the latter case the Debentures are negotiable instruments, so that they can be transferred with ease from one person to another. In addition to registration by the company it is necessary for *any charge* created by a company to be registered with the Registrar of Companies within twenty-one days. Obviously this provision will not apply to unsecured notes.

Debentures may be issued in perpetuity; alternatively, they may be issued as being redeemable at some future date.

There is no doubt that the issue of Debentures provides a convenient method of obtaining finance. If made at the appropriate time, when interest rates are not high, money may be obtained at reasonable cost.

* Debenture Stock is the company's borrowed money capitalised. It can be divided into fractional amounts.

Interest payable to Debenture holders is a charge against profits and is paid direct to the Commissioners of Inland Revenue, only the net amount being paid to Debenture holders. The *Finance Act, 1965,* stipulates that when dividends are payable to Preference shareholders the tax should be paid to the Commissioners of Inland Revenue at the standard rate on the amount distributed. This has the effect of making tax on Debenture interest a recipient's expense whereas, with Preference dividends, the tax is at the company's expense. In addition, a company has to pay Corporation Tax on profits which have *not* been reduced by the Preference dividends paid. This provision is likely to encourage companies to issue fewer Preference shares and more loan capital.

What type of Debentures to issue is a problem which must be settled. There can be no ready answer to this question. Much depends upon the standing of the company and the type of lender. Unsecured notes will be a possibility only to companies which command a very high credit rating. When a company is of moderate or weak standing, then the highest form of security may be demanded. If the borrowing is necessary to overcome financial difficulties the type of Debenture may be determined not by the company, but by the banker or other financial institution called in to give assistance. When the issue is to be made to the public an attempt has to be made to make the terms of the issue as attractive as possible; these will vary from time to time with market conditions. The latter *may* be quite apparent, but if there is any doubt a special investigation should be made. The importance of the timing of an issue must not be overlooked. Indeed, it is so vital that the advice of a broker or issuing house should be sought by any company which is not in the happy position of having its own specialists who are experts on the raising of loan capital.

The fact that companies do not obtain all the finance required by issuing Debentures is evidence that there are shortcomings in this method. If money is borrowed from a financial institution, then it is almost certain that conditions, which restrict a company's freedom of action, will be imposed. Clearly, this can be expected, for any lender must endeavour to safeguard himself. In particular, it will be usual for other types of borrowing to be restricted. If the borrowing is from the public, then the terms of the issue must be such as to make it attractive to investors, possibly giving a charge on assets. This may mean that the other sources of finance will view the company with less favour, and there may be some difficulty experienced in obtaining additional funds. More is said on the assessment of the correct proportion of loans to share capital in the section which deals with capital structures.

## DISCOUNTS AND PREMIUMS

Shares are often issued at a discount—at a figure less than nominal value—or at a premium—at a figure in excess of nominal value. Debentures may be issued at a discount; say, a £100 Debenture for £98.

The newly formed company cannot issue *shares* at a discount, because by law the issue at a discount must be of a class of shares already issued and must be in respect of a company which has been entitled to carry on business for at least one year. Permission of the Court must also have been given. These restrictions limit the usefulness of this method, so if a company's shares are quoted on the Stock Exchange at below par value it may be better to issue shares at a price (nominal value) which approximates to the actual market value of the shares already issued. The new issue could be given rights which are similar to those shares already in existence. In this way the shares being issued would be as attractive as shares at a discount and yet there would be no complying with special provisions before they could be issued; *e.g.*, nominal value of old shares £1, entitled to dividend of 5%: new shares of £0·50 each could be given a 10% dividend.

A company is free to issue Debentures at a discount at any time, because they do not form part of the share capital. However, care must be taken when designing any scheme of financing which gives the option for Debentures to be converted into fully paid shares. Clearly, there must be no infringement of the law relating to issue of shares at a discount.

No special legal requirements are needed for the issue of shares at a premium. The guiding factor should be the market value of the existing shares which carry similar rights to the proposed new issue. Expected future earnings will also influence the premium which may be charged. If the new issue is likely to water the capital to the extent that the percentage earnings on capital employed will be reduced, then this fact should be brought into the valuation, and therefore the price asked for each new share.

## STOCKS COMPARED WITH SHARES

For most practical purposes stocks and shares are the same. They can carry similar rights and are transferable in the same way. However, stock may be transferred in fractional amounts, whereas shares must always be dealt with in whole units. Stock cannot be issued partly paid, although this is possible with shares.

## *CAPITAL STRUCTURES*

A company should aim at a capital structure which allows it to take full advantage of the factors considered below.

### COST OF CAPITAL

Capital in the form of shares or Debentures has to be attracted and then maintained. The latter means that the interest payable in the case of a loan can be met or an adequate return can be paid on the share capital invested.

The total cost of maintaining loan and share capital should be kept to a minimum so it is necessary for alternative capital structures to be compared. Different proportions of share capital and loan capital will give different results. Loan capital from alternative sources or for different periods of time should be considered and, other things being equal, the one which results in minimum costs should be the one selected. Care should be taken to ensure that the terms of the cheapest loan do not impose restrictions which are onerous and limit the activity of the company to the extent that it cannot earn maximum profit.

Borrowing by means of a long-term loan will generally be more expensive than the short-term loan method. However, it should be remembered that the long-term loan gives security of tenure. With the overdraft or short-term bank loan there is always the danger that repayment will be demanded at very short notice.*

Interest on Debentures and dividends on Preference shares represent a fixed charge which a company must pay before dividends can be paid to Ordinary shareholders. In a trade recession a company may find that the fixed charges impose a heavy financial burden. It may be possible to defer paying Preference dividends, but non-payment of Debenture interest could be disastrous, possibly resulting in liquidation.

What has been stated here should be read in conjunction with the remarks made below on the other factors which are important when planning the capital structure. Cost of borrowing is an extremely important consideration, but it is not the only one—there are others which should not be overlooked.

The term "cost of capital" generally refers to the interest or dividend payable. However, it should not be forgotten that costs are also incurred in raising the capital. Share and Debenture issues, financing connected with property, and many other methods of raising capital do involve legal and publicity costs. On the other hand, short-term borrowing, hire purchase, acceptance credits, and discounting of bills of exchange may involve little or no legal and other charges, over and above the interest charge. This is not to suggest that short-term funds should be used as permanent capital. However, there may be cases where short-term finance will be quite adequate for the purpose in mind.

Many discussions centre around the cost of capital. Management decisions often depend upon the size of the rate at a particular time; *e.g.* when deciding whether to invest in fixed assets, the cost of capital serves as a guide to the rate to be used for the appropriate capital-expenditure decision techniques (*see* Chapter 18). In profit planning

---

* This danger was recognised in the Radcliffe Report. The Radcliffe Committee felt that small borrowers should be given an assurance that a loan would not be recalled without very good reason. Clearly, there are difficulties here. The bank manager has also a duty to his bank.

the cost of capital should be the starting point; this also applies when establishing the target profit for corporate planning and budgetary control. A table showing how the cost of capital can be calculated is shown below:

| Type of Capital | Capital Structure A | Cost % B | Weighted Average Cost % C = A × B |
|---|---|---|---|
| Equity shares (including reserves) ... ... ... | 0·50 | 10 | 5·0 |
| Preference shares ... ... | 0·30 | 8 | 2·4 |
| Loans ... ... ... ... | 0·20 | 6 | 1·2 |
| | 1·00 | | 8·6 |

The cost of capital is, therefore, 8·6%. From the table it will be seen that equity shareholders own 50% of the total capital, whereas Preference shareholders and long-term lenders have an investment of 30 and 20% respectively. When planning the ideal capital gearing the percentages can be varied until the desirable level is reached. The effect of *Corporation Tax legislation* would also have to be considered. Generally speaking the payment of interest receives more favourable treatment than the payment of dividends, and there is encouragement to retain profits in the business. For full details of the legal provisions readers are advised to study a book which deals with Corporation Tax.

### MAXIMUM CONTROL

Certain shares will have voting rights, and therefore through them control can be exercised. The correct balance between the voting capital—normally the equity capital—and the loan capital should be maintained, but the ideal ratio is difficult to determine. Some accountants may take the view that the *absence* of loans is a sign of great strength; others may argue that the *existence* of loans is an indication of growth, and therefore profitability.

From time to time writers on financial management have attempted to formulate general rules on the maximum amount of loan capital which should be employed by a business. This is a difficult task. Each business has different characteristics, and what is good for one may be quite different for another. Some of the factors which should be considered are as follows:

### 1. Fixed Assets Owned

If money is borrowed for a long period it will be usual for the lender to require some form of a security. Companies of high financial standing can borrow without giving security, but this fact cannot be construed as establishing a general rule that securities will not be required. Even when unsecured notes can be issued, there will be a limit to the amount that can be raised in this way.

There is no doubt that the value of fixed assets can be used as a guide to determining what is a reasonable amount to borrow. To ensure that a sound policy is being followed, the total amount borrowed should not exceed a reasonable proportion of the fixed-assets figure. Between one-third and one-half may be taken as an approximate guide. This then leaves a margin of safety and allows for any emergency borrowing that may be found necessary. It may also enable borrowing to be made at the lowest possible rates for the simple reason that the loan can be adequately secured. Whether historical costs or present replacement costs of fixed assets should be taken for the purpose of valuation is a matter on which there is no absolute agreement. The conservative approach dictates that historical costs should be used; on the other hand, it may seem illogical to advocate present replacement costs for cal-culating capital employed * (*see* Chapters 15 and 27) and yet say, for the purpose of borrowing, that the assets are not worth their present values. Clearly, the larger the proportion of Debentures to fixed assets the greater may be the danger of losing control to creditors.

## 2. *Earnings*

The question of earnings is considered more fully below. In connec-tion with Debentures and control it will be apparent that profit prospects will be of the utmost importance. Certainty is essential; there can be no hoping that Debenture holders will defer their rights because the company is experiencing difficulties. They may exercise the right to appoint a receiver, and then control will vanish. There cannot be any question of absolute certainty that profit will be earned, but some busi-nesses are more stable than others. This matter is very much related to the gearing of capital discussed later in this chapter. The stable com-pany may be able to have a very high gearing, whereas companies who experience fluctuations in trade have to have relatively low gearing.

Leaving the matter of Debentures and turning to Preference shares, it should be appreciated that, although *normally* there may be no voting rights attaching to Preference shares, such rights may arise from the terms of the issue.† If there is a large Preference share capital non-payment of Preference dividends for a stated period may give the

---

* Assumes a period of rising prices; *i.e.* present values are greater than previous values.

† The terms of issue often state that Preference shareholders shall receive notice to attend or to vote at meetings if dividend is six months in arrear or the meeting is for a special purpose which affects their rights, *e.g.* winding up of a company.

Preference shareholders control of the business. This emphasises once more that earnings should be adequate to cover all types of fixed charges, whether interest or dividends. This safeguarding of any shareholder can be expected from all companies whose directors wish to have the continued support of the public and the Stock Exchange.

## CAPITAL GEARING

The relation of Ordinary shares (equity capital) to Preference shares capital and loan capital is described as the "capital gearing." A highly geared capital is one which has a small proportion of equity capital, including any reserves or undistributed profits which may be regarded as being part of the interest of the Ordinary shareholders. If the larger proportion of total capital is made up of equity capital the capital is said to be "low geared."

From the point of view of freedom from interference—present or future—by Preference shareholders or Debenture holders, it is advisable to have a very large proportion of capital in Ordinary shares. Indeed, the larger, the better. The control aspect was covered earlier, so this matter requires no further explanation. However, when considering capital gearing there is also the question of an adequate return to *all* capital employed.

Only by acknowledging the fact that investors do have different outlooks can any capital structure planning be successful. Some investors will prefer a relatively small, regular income with little risk, whereas others will be willing to bear the major risks and receive high dividends. Only by dividing the capital into different categories will it be possible to meet these different requirements. Moreover, only in this way—by having fixed-interest or fixed-dividend capital—will the income be large enough to allow for adequate dividends to be paid to Ordinary shareholders and to bring about capital appreciation. However, the latter is subject to a Capital Gains Tax when shares are sold.

The necessity of retaining earnings in the business to cover expansion is a very important consideration. No soundly managed company distributes all its profits to shareholders. Even if this practice was a practical proposition the fluctuations in earnings of some companies, and therefore dividend payments, may introduce variations in the value of the equity shares to such an extent that a business would appear unstable. The modern tendency is to stabilise dividend payments around a certain percentage and then retain the balance in the business. Investors are then able to see that regular, fixed payments have been made, and this in itself tends to inspire confidence. Clearly, though, the dividend paid should be comparable with that obtainable elsewhere. If not there is a danger that the quoted price of the Ordinary shares will not represent the true value of the assets employed, and therefore there will always be a danger of a take-over bid (*see* Chapter 22).

The capital gearing adopted will obviously affect future prospects of obtaining finance. If the capital structure gearing is very high, then further loans or Preference share capital may be out of the question. On the other hand, an issue of Ordinary shares may be an attractive proposition to investors. However, care has to be taken to ensure that an issue of Ordinary shares will not weaken the control. A rights issue may overcome this problem. Alternatively, Preference shares or loan capital may be feasible, *provided* a conversion option is given in the terms of the issue. This matter was discussed earlier in this chapter.

Low gearing may mean that the Ordinary shareholders cannot be paid an adequate return. A highly geared capital, on the other hand, may mean that the Ordinary shares are a very speculative investment. When profits are substantial the large fixed interest or dividend can be paid, leaving the balance for payment as dividends on Ordinary shares and/or building up of the equity capital. Clearly the management must adopt a compromise, the nature of which will depend to a large degree on the nature of the business.

If a company manufactures food products with a stable demand, or is engaged in investing in property which it leases for fairly long periods, the profits may be large enough and consistent enough to allow a fairly highly geared capital to be employed. On the other hand, if trade is subject to unpredictable fluctuations which may result in substantial profits one year and very little the next, then a low-geared capital structure may be advisable. These are only generalisations and cannot be regarded as rigid, invariable rules. Much depends upon the finance available: different sources offer attractions which change in relative importance from one period to another. One source may offer cheaper finance than another at a particular time, but the position may be reversed a few months later. However, this fact will not be known at the time the finance is required. The incidence of tax may also be of extreme importance. Under the *Finance Act, 1965*, there is a distinct advantage taxwise, in having loan capital instead of Preference share capital.

Any scheme of capital structure must be tailored to fit into the framework which is provided by the earning potentiality. A business should plan a capital structure which it can afford. Also the fact that the structure can be changed with changed conditions should not be forgotten. Preference shares and Debentures may be redeemed, and if short-term capital is employed as a temporary expedient, this may be paid off and replaced by retained earnings. The capital structure most suitable for the newly created business is often different from that which should be employed when the company has become established and successful. The securities which can be offered and the confidence which is felt by the investing public or financial institutions all affect the types of capital available. Examples of the two extreme types of capital gearing are shown below. Following these are three examples of *actual* capital structures taken from the accounts of well-known companies.

G

The figures used have been adjusted slightly so that the significant relationships can more readily be observed.

|  | Low gearing £ | High gearing £ |
|---|---|---|
| Ordinary shares | 160,000 | 40,000 |
| Preference shares (6%) | 20,000 | 100,000 |
| Debentures (5%) | 20,000 | 60,000 |
|  | £200,000 | £200,000 |

This assumes that there are no capital or revenue reserves which relate to the interests of the Ordinary shareholders. If these are present, then they must be considered when deciding if the capital gearing is high or low. Thus, for example, if the capital structure shown above as being high had included reserves of £200,000, then the capital gearing would have tended towards being low. Some accountants include only the value of Preference shares and Ordinary shares in the gearing computation, but a true picture cannot be obtained unless loan capital and reserves are included.

From the example it will be seen that the fixed charges for the low-geared capital are £1200 + £1000, whereas the highly geared capital calls for £6000 + £3000. In the first case all profits after £2200 will be available for distribution to the holders of the Ordinary shares, whereas in the case of the highly geared capital £3000 must be met before Preference shareholders are paid a dividend and over £9000 + tax on £6000 Preference dividend must be available before Ordinary shareholders can receive any payment.

PRACTICAL ILLUSTRATIONS OF CAPITAL STRUCTURES

*Large Organisation in Electrical Engineering*

The company is engaged in the manufacture and sale of many types of machinery and equipment.

| Share capital: | £ |
|---|---|
| Preference shares | 5,000,000 |
| Ordinary shares | 40,000,000 |
| Reserves: | |
| Capital | 40,000,000 |
| Revenue | 40,000,000 |
|  | 125,000,000 |
| Mortgage Debenture stock | 25,000,000 |
|  | £150,000,000 |

From this can be seen that Debentures form a small part of total capital. As would be expected, the equity capital plus the reserves amount to most of the total capital. The current liabilities of this company amounted to more than £40,000,000, including a £3,000,000 bank overdraft. On the other hand, current assets came to a total approaching £145,000,000. Therefore, although the company may be said to be a large borrower, in relation to the size of capital employed the borrowing is relatively small.

*Large Organisation in Soap, Margarine, and Foodstuffs*

The parent company owns a number of companies which are engaged in the manufacture and sale of margarine, soap, foodstuffs, toilet preparations, and other products.

| | £ |
|---|---|
| Share capital: | |
| Preference shares | 80,000,000 |
| Ordinary shares | 80,000,000 |
| Reserves | 300,000,000 |
| | 460,000,000 |
| Loan capital (approximately 50% secured) | 40,000,000 |
| | £500,000,000 |

Again the Debentures form a relatively small part of total capital.

*Medium Organisation: Property Company*

| | £ |
|---|---|
| Share Capital: | |
| Preference shares | 200,000 |
| Ordinary shares | 350,000 |
| Reserves: | |
| Capital | 550,000 |
| Revenue | 150,000 |
| | 1,250,000 |
| Loan capital: mortgages and mortgage | |
| Debentures | 1,000,000 |
| | £2,250,000 |

In this case the total for loan capital and Preference shares is greater than the equity capital. Fixed assets amount to £2,150,000, so clearly the £1,000,000 is covered more than twice. Net rents from property amount to approximately £200,000. This is presumably a regular income, and the fact that approximately £50,000 has to be met each year before Ordinary shareholders can be paid a dividend is no serious problem. As will be appreciated, this is a company with a large proportion of fixed assets. Accordingly, the borrowing can be done at reasonable rates of interest because securities offered amply cover the loans. Moreover, the fairly substantial, regular income allows the fixed charges to be met without difficulty.

### Note on Practical Illustrations

The three examples given are typical of a large number of capital structures which were studied when the figures were selected. There is a tendency for companies to have neither very low nor very highly geared capital structures, but instead to seek a compromise. If uncertain about the type of structure to adopt for a particular kind of business, a guide may be obtained by referring to other companies' published accounts. A word of warning, though! A certain company may have an *unusual* structure simply because it has grown that way without proper planning; quite likely a more efficient capital gearing is possible. For this reason it may be advisable to study a *number* of companies' accounts. A typical gearing for that type of business may then be seen.

### EXAMINATION QUESTIONS

1. You are auditor of a limited company which has overdraft facilities to the extent of £50,000. This has been found to be adequate in the past but your clients now find that they are having difficulty in meeting their liabilities.

You abstract the following information from the books:

| Year to 31st March | Year 1 | Year 2 | Year 3 | Present |
|---|---|---|---|---|
| | £ | £ | £ | £ |
| Number of Units sold ... | 10,000 | 12,000 | 17,000 | 20,000 |
| | | | | |
| Sales ... ... ... ... | 200,000 | 240,000 | 425,000 | 500,000 |
| Purchases and Direct Labour Cost ... ... ... ... | 100,000 | 140,000 | 225,000 | 280,000 |
| Gross Profit ... ... ... | 100,000 | 100,000 | 200,000 | 220,000 |
| Overhead Expenses ... ... | 60,000 | 65,000 | 70,000 | 80,000 |
| Income Tax ... ... ... | 20,000 | 17,000 | 70,000 | 80,000 |
| | (80,000) | (82,000) | (140,000) | (160,000) |
| Net Profit ... ... ... | £20,000 | £18,000 | £60,000 | £60,000 |

| Year to 31st March | Year 1 | Year 2 | Year 3 | Present |
|---|---|---|---|---|
| Stock at 31st March in Units | 1,800 | 2,000 | 4,000 | 6,000 |
| | £ | £ | £ | £ |
| Fixed Assets at 31st March ... | 20,000 | 20,000 | 28,000 | 44,000 |
| Trade Debtors at 31st March | 17,000 | 22,000 | 60,000 | 80,000 |
| Trade Creditors at 31st March | 8,000 | 12,000 | 36,000 | 40,000 |
| Bank Overdraft ... ... | 15,000 | 20,000 | 46,000 | 52,500 |

You are asked to report to your client on the reasons why they are experiencing a shortage of capital and the steps which might be taken to improve the position. (*A.C.C.A.*)

2. A Company wishes to obtain further funds amounting to £160,000 for the extension of its factory (£120,000) and for the purchase of additional stock (£40,000). Suggest alternative methods by which the required amount of £160,000 could be raised and discuss the merits and demerits of each method. (*S.C.A.*)

3. Discuss the form of capital structure which you would favour for new companies undertaking each of the following:

(*a*) property owning;
(*b*) manufacture of plastic household kitchen equipment;
(*c*) owning aeroplanes for charter.

Set out your reasons for any variations in the capital structures and assume that each company is to have an issued capital of £1,000,000. (*I.C.W.A.*)

4. What do you understand by the expression "High Geared" and "Low Geared" used in connection with the capitalisation of a company? Illustrate your answer by examples. (*S.C.A.*)

5. A private company, of which you are the accountant, requires additional working capital and the directors ask you to submit a report containing suggestions for raising money under the two main headings of temporary and permanent capital. Describe what you understand by these two types of capital, give three examples of each and state the circumstances in which each example is to be recommended. (*S.C.A.*)

6. The XY Manufacturing Company Ltd. has been a public company since 1938, its 6% preference shares and its ordinary shares being quoted on a provincial stock exchange. The company has recently entered upon a major scheme to expand its production and trading, and it is estimated that this will involve expenditure on fixed assets over the next two years of £500,000, with a further £250,000 for additional working capital. The following are abridged balance sheets at 31st December, 19... and 31st December, a year later.

You are asked to write a report for the board outlining comprehensive proposals for bringing the company's issued capital more into line with the value of its net assets and for raising the additional capital required to finance the expansion scheme.

| | | This Year | Last Year |
|---|---|---|---|
| | | £ | £ |
| Capital: Authorised and issued, fully paid: | | | |
| 300,000 6% cum. pref. shares of £0·666 each ... ... | | 200,000 | 200,000 |
| 100,000 10% cum. 2nd pref. shares of £1 each ... ... | | 100,000 | 100,000 |
| 1,000,000 ord. shares of £0·20 each ... ... ... | | 200,000 | 200,000 |
| | | 500,000 | 500,000 |
| Capital Reserve: | | | |
| Share premiums ... ... | | 100,000 | 100,000 |

| Revenue Reserves: | £ | | £ | |
|---|---|---|---|---|
| Future taxation ... ... | 210,000 | | 200,000 | |
| General ... ... ... | 650,000 | | 550,000 | |
| Profit and loss account ... | 180,000 | 1,040,000 | 150,000 | 900,000 |
| | | £1,640,000 | | £1,500,000 |

| Fixed assets: | | £ | | £ |
|---|---|---|---|---|
| Freehold land, buildings, plant & equipment: at net book value at 31/12/47, less sales, plus additions since at cost... ... ... | | 920,000 | | 885,000 |
| Less: Depreciation ... | | 500,000 | | 410,000 |
| | | 420,000 | | 475,000 |

| Current assets: | £ | | £ | |
|---|---|---|---|---|
| Stocks & work in progress ... | 985,000 | | 860,000 | |
| Debtors ... ... ... | 692,000 | | 570,000 | |
| Cash at bank and in hand ... | 3,000 | | 25,000 | |
| | | 1,680,000 | | 1,455,000 |

| Less: Current liabilities: | £ | | £ | |
|---|---|---|---|---|
| Creditors ... ... ... | 177,250 | | 202,050 | |
| Bank overdraft ... ... | 44,800 | | — | |
| Dividends, less tax: | | | | |
| on 6% pref. shares ... | 3,450 | | 3,450 | |
| on 10% 2nd pref. shares ... | 5,750 | | 5,750 | |
| on ord. shares (final dividend of 25% making 40% for year) ... ... | 28,750 | | 28,750 | |
| Taxation ... ... ... | 200,000 | 460,000 | 190,000 | 430,000 |
| | | 1,220,000 | | 1,025,000 |
| | | £1,640,000 | | £1,500,000 |

*(I.C.W.A.)*

# CHAPTER 8

## OBTAINING PERMANENT CAPITAL

### INTRODUCTION

SHARES and Debentures may be issued to the public directly or via an issuing house. Any invitation to the public must be covered by the issue of a special document which must include, *inter alia*, the names of directors, capital required, past financial results, and the voting and dividend rights of each class of shares. This document is known as a "prospectus." The principal object is to show all the relevant facts which will allow interested investors to determine the future prospects of the company. The law lays down very stringent rules on what the prospectus or similar document must contain. Even so there are still criticisms made of the contents of prospectuses. Possibly one of the most serious criticisms is the valuation of assets at historical costs (discussed in Chapter 27).

Large companies can afford to employ their own legal and financial experts who are able to advise on all matters affecting the raising of capital. However, many companies are not in this position and must employ outside assistance and seek advice. An issuing house or broker will be the specialist normally called upon.

### ISSUING HOUSES*

An issuing house is an organisation which specialises in obtaining permanent capital for companies in the form of Debentures or shares. It bridges the gap between companies requiring finance and investors. Some of the most important functions of issuing houses are discussed below.

#### CONVERSION FROM PRIVATE TO PUBLIC COMPANY

A private company has certain advantages over a public company. The owners of the voting capital are able to manage their affairs without being influenced by press and public opinion.† The dividends paid or policy followed are their own concern; they are able to control at will. Often there is the fear that converting to a public company will increase the danger of a take-over bid; so private status may induce a feeling of security.

---

* A list of the members of the Issuing Houses Association is given in Appendix II, pp. 799–800.

† These remarks apply to the normal running of the company. Clearly, even a private company can suffer from outraged public opinion on a matter which affects the employees or consumers.

181

On the other hand the private company suffers from certain disadvantages. Put another way, the *public* company is able to obtain benefits which are not available to the private company. There is no doubt that these benefits are often greater than those obtainable from private status.

First there is the question of obtaining additional capital. Undoubtedly, the act of converting to a public company can provide the means of obtaining any extra capital needed and, what is more, if carefully planned this can be done without loss of control.

The fact that a company's shares are quoted on the Stock Exchange is a definite advantage. The shares are readily transferable and are, therefore, an attractive form of investment; provided, always, of course, that the company is operating successfully. In addition, there is also the free publicity given to companies by newspapers and professional journals.* New developments, dividend declarations, shares issues and all matters which affect the profitability of a company are all reported upon. That this fact may also be a disadvantage was noted earlier in this section. However, there is no doubt that the gains often outweigh the losses. If a company becomes a household name then it can generally rely upon its products being purchased.

The *Finance Act, 1965*, lays down that a "close company," that is a company under the control of five or fewer participators, must account for tax on a special basis. These provisions do not encourage the retention of profits. However, if 35% of the shares with voting powers are held by the public, and are officially quoted, the special provisions do not apply.

The "golden handshake," a device for compensating directors who are compulsorily retired upon a public company being merged with another, has now lost much of its attraction. There is a limit of £5000. Amounts over this figure are subject to income tax and surtax. For the owners of a private company there is still the "golden handshake" available by converting to a public company. Admittedly it takes a different form, but, nevertheless, the cash obtainable from selling a proportion of the capital can allow directors to benefit substantially and yet still retain the ownership.

The necessity to meet death duties should not be forgotten. The personal representatives of a deceased director of a private company may find that the valuation of the shares held takes a considerable time. Once the valuation has been agreed upon, the payment of the death duties may have a crippling effect upon the company. A Stock Exchange quotation simplifies the process of valuation and also enables a proportion of the shares to be sold without difficulty.

Advice on the procedure to follow to convert from a private to a

---

* The *Companies Act, 1967*, has abolished the status of *exempt private company* thereby requiring disclosure of information for such companies (*see* Chapter 21).

public company will be given by an issuing house. The Stock Exchange rules which have to be observed will be explained and then followed. The requirements of the Companies Acts will also have to be met. In order to make the operation run as smoothly as possible the company concerned will be expected to co-operate and supply all the necessary information.

## ISSUING HOUSE BACKING AND SERVICES

An issuing house has a reputation to maintain. Accordingly, it will be most careful in its enquiries to decide whether or not to lend its name to an issue. This fact has advantages to the companies who do receive issuing house backing. The goodwill of the issuing house is put at their disposal; this may make all the difference between success and failure.

### Capital Gearing Advice

The capital gearing most appropriate to the company will be determined. Advice on the most appropriate type of share or Debenture to issue and the price to charge may also be given. The appropriate rate of return for the type of security to be issued will be known by the issuing house. What the company can afford to pay in dividend and interest and the type of security can be "matched"; in this way the best financial structure can be obtained.

### Publicity and Marketing

Advertising is an art in itself. Great care must be taken in drafting advertisements. Securities have to be *sold*. Legal requirements have to be observed. Offers for sale and public issues have to be advertised in at least two newspapers three or more working days before the lists of applications are allowed to open. In addition to carrying out these functions the issuing house will also select the best time for making the issue and then make sure that the marketing is carried out effectively.

### Miscellaneous Services

An issuing house may give services other than those outlined above. A "placing" of shares may be handled: this function is explained later. In addition, it will give advice on all financial matters such as the best dividend policy to adopt, reconstructions, amalgamations and how best to deal with any problem connected with finance. Nevertheless, it should be remembered that the main function is the raising of new capital.

## ISSUING HOUSE REQUIREMENTS

The fact that an issuing house has to watch its reputation was noted earlier. Only by laying down a number of minimum requirements can the issuing house be satisfied that its goodwill is not impaired.

There must be evidence of an efficient and sound management. The organisation should be suitable for the type of business concerned; line and functional relationships will normally be necessary. Dependence upon one man is inadvisable. Furthermore, the correct delegation of authority and responsibility is essential for the continuity of any business. The keeping of correct books and records may be a sign of efficient management. Cost and financial accounting can reveal the rate of progress that has been made. The trend in unit costs; the rate of earnings in relation to capital employed, and accounting ratios, may all show the degree of efficiency that has been achieved.

Wide fluctuations in profits from one year to another, varying from low to high figures without any definite trend, are not favourable signs. An issuing house will normally expect to see a steady rate of growth in profits. In any case, investors will wish to see evidence of profits; otherwise the issue is unlikely to be a success. To satisfy the Stock Exchange the requirement has to be more precise than a general tendency for profits to increase. There must be publication of the last ten years' profit figures, plus an estimate to cover the following year.

There must also be evidence that the working capital is adequate. A company applying for a quotation, not previously having had a quotation, must include a statement from the directors (*see* Part A of Schedule II, para. R, which is part of Appendix IV in this book).

An additional requirement is that there must be a letter from the issuing house concerned (or a sponsoring broker), stating that "they have satisfied themselves that the statement as to the sufficiency of working capital has been made by the directors after due and careful enquiry."

The business should not be highly sensitive to trade fluctuations or be highly speculative. A sound sales organisation backed by the existence of at least a core of satisfied customers will generally be essential. There should not be absolute reliance upon a single large customer with the danger that, if his patronage disappears, the company is left in a critical position. Importance will be attached to the products being developed *now* and those to be developed in the future. In some types of business innovation plays an extremely important part in the maximisation of profit. Unless new products are constantly being developed the business may find itself in a very embarrassed state. These possible weaknesses and their attendant risks can be overcome by having management which is skilled, experienced, and progressive; once more emphasising that sound management is of the utmost importance.

The size of a company may affect its acceptability to an issuing house. There is no definite rule which excludes a company of a certain size being advised by an issuing house, but if below the size which allows an issue to be made at reasonable cost, the issuing house will probably suggest and arrange an introduction to a broker who would then act for the company. The volume of work involved does not vary very much with changes in the size of the issue. Accordingly, the *percentage* charge for expenses tends to be much higher for small issues.

The question of size was mentioned in an earlier chapter. There is no single factor which can be taken to determine whether a company can be regarded as small, medium, or large. Capital employed, measured in terms of net assets, may be a guide to size, but this is not an invariable criterion. For manufacturing companies the assets owned tend to be very important and a minimum valuation of £100,000 will probably be essential. However, for companies offering services, such as insurance broking, the value of assets will tend to be small. Here the guiding factor will be the likely market value of the shares. The size of the gross profit may also be used as a guide to minimum size; around £50,000* gross profit and/or £30,000 net profit is the level at which issuing houses will act for a company. This figure applies to London, but may be smaller for the provinces.

*Present* size is not the only consideration. Possible future growth is of the utmost importance. If the potentiality is there, some issuing houses will act on a company's behalf, bringing it along to the appropriate size, before acting in an issue.† There will, of course, be a limit to the time one issuing house can wait for a company to reach the minimum size. Generally speaking, there must be definite evidence that the required growth will take place within a reasonable time.

The actual size of the issue which will be undertaken by an issuing house is rather difficult to determine. Indeed, the position appears to vary from one issuing house to another. Some seem to be equipped to deal with small and medium size issues, whereas others are more able to give satisfaction to those issues which may be regarded as being medium or large. When speaking of "size" the concern is with the *actual* value of the shares and not the nominal value. Around £200,000 is the smallest issue which may be regarded as a practical and economic proposition. A market value of about £500,000 may be regarded as a medium size issue. The large issue involves £1,000,000 or more. These are guides only.

Generally speaking, there is a tendency for the issuing houses to accept the larger size issues and the brokers to deal with smaller issues. However, again there is difficulty in formulating any definite rules. At the time of writing this chapter there are press notices which advertise a number of new issues. Two of these are for shares valued at £750,000; one is being sponsored by a broker and the other by a very well-known issuing house. On the other hand, there are three issues being dealt with by brokers; two are around £200,000 each and one, on the Birmingham Stock Exchange, is for approximately £80,000. The latter figure would

---

* Quoted from *Business: Journal for Management*, May 1961.

† For example, by giving advice or assistance on obtaining the necessary finance by the most appropriate method.

be considered too small and, possibly uneconomical, for an issue in London. For a company to obtain a quotation on the Stock Exchange when no part of its capital is already quoted, there should be an expected market value of at least £250,000 for total capital and £100,000 for any one security for which quotation is sought.

## METHODS ADOPTED: CAPITAL ISSUES

The principal methods adopted for making capital issues are as follows:

1. Introductions.
2. Placings.
3. Offers for Sale.
4. Issue by Prospectus.
5. Issue by Tender.
6. Rights Issue (issue to existing shareholders).
7. Bonus Issue (not strictly a new issue, but a readjustment between reserves and capital).

These methods are outlined below.

### INTRODUCTIONS

An issuing house will act on behalf of the shareholders and make the necessary arrangements, through a stockbroker, to obtain a quotation for the shares. This process is known as an "introduction." It is not necessarily the basis for a public issue although, in actual fact, application for an introduction may be made to the Council of the Stock Exchange before a first public issue is made. A minimum of fifty shareholders is necessary before an introduction can be effected. Furthermore, a company must comply with the requirements of the Stock Exchange on this matter (*see* Appendix IV, p. 811). In order to make the introduction a practical proposition it will be necessary to make shares available to jobbers for dealings on the Stock Exchange. If part of the share or loan capital is already quoted then it may be desired to apply for a quotation for the new issue. This fact is usually stated across the top of the prospectus or "offer for sale." As already noted, the fact that shares are quoted on the Stock Exchange makes them a much more attractive investment than unquoted securities.

An introduction can take a similar form to a "placing," described below. The essential difference is that, with a placing, there is a contract between the company and a broker for the purchase of shares, whereas there is no such contract when there is an introduction. With the latter, a minimum number of shares may have to be made available, but only for the purpose of satisfying the Stock Exchange that the shares are held widely enough to promote dealings and to establish a fair price for the shares.

Existing shareholders can make the necessary shares available to the jobbers. If this is the case there is no "public issue" of shares and no prospectus is required. An advertisement which complies with the requirements laid down by the Council of the Stock Exchange is essential. When an application for a quotation is made in conjunction with a public issue, then the procedure is referred to as an "offer for sale," a "placing" or other appropriate description, but not as an "introduction."

The timing of the introduction may be arranged before an offer for sale. This may be the same as *after* a private placing, for often an offer for sale takes place subsequent to a placing.

The Council of the Stock Exchange have now stipulated that certain conditions must be satisfied before an adequate market can be said to exist. These are as shown below:

1. A company must have a minimum market value of £250,000;
2. There must be a minimum market value of £100,000 for any one security;
3. At least 35% of any class of issued equity capital, or securities convertible into equity capital, for which quotation is sought, must be in the hands of the public. In the case of very large issues the Council may be prepared to allow the distribution of a lower percentage;
4. At least 30% of any class of issued fixed income capital for which quotation is sought must be in the hands of the public.

## PLACINGS

A "placing," like an introduction, is usually appropriate when a private company converts to a public company. The amount involved in the issue is relatively small: possibly £250,000 will be the figure, but this is only an approximate guide; much depends upon the circumstances.

As the description implies, the shares are "placed" by an issuing house or broker with interested investors. The shares are purchased by the intermediary—issuing house or broker—at a stated price at or above par and then sold at a profit to institutional investors such as insurance companies. Alternatively, instead of buying the shares and then selling them, the issuing house or broker may simply act as the middleman, making full use of its connection and knowledge to place the shares with investors.

The Council of the Stock Exchange are reluctant to permit shares to be dealt in by means of a placing.* This attitude stems from a regard

* Applies principally to equity shares. Companies who wish to offer fixed interest securities may find a different attitude.

for public interest. The lack of publicity and the fact that the shares are not available on a free market means that investors who are able to participate in a placing may be in a position to obtain benefit from the capital appreciation which may take place after a quotation has been obtained for the shares. It follows, therefore, that a company must have a very sound reason for offering the shares by means of a placing: indeed, if the issue involved is large enough the company may be better advised to adopt one of the other methods described below; *e.g.* an "offer for sale."

An offer by an issuing house or brokers to clients generally, constitutes an invitation to offer to the public and, therefore, the notice of information which is advertised must comply with the requirements of both the provisions of the Companies Acts and the rules of the Stock Exchange shown in Appendix IV. Before any dealing can take place the Stock Exchange has to give its permission. A letter which states the reasons for desiring this method and also gives an outline of the contemplated marketing arrangements must be sent to the Secretary of the Share and Loan Department of the Stock Exchange.

Even with these requirements the expenses of issue tend to be much smaller than with the other methods. Advertising and other publicity is cut down to an absolute minimum and, therefore, so is the cost. Moreover, underwriting can be avoided.

### OFFERS FOR SALE*

Offers for sale are very similar to placings in that an issuing house or broker purchases the shares or Debentures and then issues them to investors. The latter, in the case of an offer for sale, is the public at large and not, as with a placing, selected clients.

The "offer for sale" which is issued by the issuing house or other holder must comply with the statutory requirements of the Companies Acts and the regulations of the Stock Exchange. The price paid for the securities by the issuing house should be stated in the "offer for sale" document or advertisement. A copy must also be delivered to the Registrar of Companies for registration.

There is no doubt that the offer for sale method has many advantages. From the public point-of-view there is an opportunity to apply for the shares being offered and, therefore, the method is fairer to investors generally. Considered from the company's viewpoint, the method enables a definite sum of money to be obtained—no more, no less. When seeking new finance it is often very important, in the interests of plans which have been made, that precisely the correct amount of money is available. Any shortage may mean that plans have to be changed or even abandoned. By adopting the offer for sale method the anxiety attaching to an issue is eliminated; the risks of failure are taken on by

---

* The concern is with obtaining funds for the company. Many offers for sale involve selling shares for *existing* shareholders and not the company.

the issuing house. The alternative is the issue by prospectus in conjunction with underwriting, a process which is described below.

Both the directors of the company issuing the shares and the directors of the issuing house are liable to pay compensation for damages which arise from untrue statements made in the offer. Accordingly, the issuing house will be very careful in its enquiries before agreeing to become a party to an offer for sale.

In Appendix III is shown an Offer for Sale Document. This covers the issue of 910,000 Ordinary shares in Anderson, Boyes and Co., Ltd. From the document can be seen that J. Henry Schroder and Co., Ltd., and Helbert, Wagg and Co., Ltd., major issuing houses, and subsidiaries of Schroders Ltd., dealt with the issue.

Page 801 gives general details regarding the offer for sale. This is followed by a letter to the Vendors of the shares being offered. In this case the Vendors are J. Henry Schroder and Co., Ltd. and Helbert, Wagg and Co., Ltd., a fact which is made clear on page 806. The letter in question gives all the details which are required by law and the Council of the Stock Exchange to be shown in a prospectus.

Pages 804–806 show an Accountants' Report from the auditors and accountants of Schroders Ltd. This, again, is a statutory requirement and, at the same time, complies with the requirements laid down by the Council of the Stock Exchange. In particular it should be noted that the profits for the past ten years are shown. This is in accordance with Stock Exchange Regulations: the *Companies Act, 1948,* specifies the shorter period of five years.

On the final part of the Offer for Sale are details of matters, not previously stated, which are of such a nature that they are likely to influence investors making a decision on whether or not to purchase the shares being offered. Contracts of a special nature, remuneration of directors, particulars of the Vendor, and the costs and expenses incidental to the Offer for Sale, are all given.

An Offer for Sale is to be regarded as a form of Prospectus and must therefore, comply with the requirements of the Companies Acts regarding a Prospectus. The Prospectus and Offer for Sale announcements thus follow a very similar pattern. In the case of a prospectus there will obviously be no "letter" to the Vendors of the shares, but the details shown in the letter in the example will still have to be listed. It should be remembered too that the object of an Offer for Sale or Prospectus is to *sell* shares, not merely to make details available to the public. Accordingly, as much information as possible should be given with the object of making the shares as attractive as possible.

## ISSUE BY PROSPECTUS

From the details given in the Offer for Sale Document illustrated it will be appreciated that the issue of shares or Debentures can be an extremely complicated procedure. For this reason companies nearly always seek the advice of an issuing house even though an issue could be made directly to the public without going through an intermediary.

The issuing house will deal with all matters connected with the issue. Subscription lists normally open and close on the same day, so the publicity has to be planned so that as many shares as possible—in fact, the total amount of the issue—are sold on the one day. Advertisements may have to appear in a large number of newspapers; the Stock Exchange states that a minimum of two papers should be used.

The subscription lists cannot be opened until the beginning of the third day following the issue of a Prospectus through the medium of the newspaper or by some other means. Thus, for example, the advertisements in the form of a Prospectus may appear in the newspapers on the 12th June announcing that the subscription lists are to open on the 15th June. The Stock Exchange will give its permission to deal only after the issue has been made, but normally, since the Stock Exchange will have been consulted well before this time, it will be extremely unusual for permission to be withheld. If for some reason there is a refusal and yet on the prospectus is stated that an application to deal on the Stock Exchange has been made, then all applicants are entitled to the return of their monies.

The requirements of the Council of the Stock Exchange in connection with a Prospectus are printed in Appendix IV. Details of the requirements of the Companies Acts can be obtained quite easily from the official acts published by H.M. Stationery Office or from a textbook on Company Law. For this reason a *detailed* explanation of the legal requirements is not included in this book. Some of the principal regulations prescribed by the Companies Acts are summarised below:

1. The Prospectus must be registered with the Registrar of Companies before it can be issued. At this time it must have been signed by directors and any expert (*e.g.* Accountant) who gives opinions on the Prospectus. To it should be attached a copy of any material contract; *i.e.* a contract of a special nature, *e.g.* Purchase of Property—full details have to be given.

2. The Prospectus should be dated and state on the face of it that a copy has been delivered to the Registrar.

The contents should include:

3. Full details regarding the directors including qualification shares, remuneration and any interest in the promotion of the company or property to be acquired.

4. Promoter's profits and amounts payable or paid for underwriting brokerage and commission in connection with the issue or other issue made in the past two years. Also details of preliminary expenses.

5. Details of capital required including amounts to be paid in cash.

6. Company's financial record for the past five years (*see* Auditors' Report below, 11 (*a*)).

7. Voting and other rights and dividend rates of each class of shares including full details of the rights of the holders of deferred shares.

8. Minimum subscription required to meet adequately the plans made, with special reference to property to be purchased, preliminary expenses and commission to be paid and working capital required.

9. The time of opening of the subscription lists and the amounts payable on application and allotment.

10. Details of any option to subscribe for shares or debentures.

11. The following reports are essential:

(*a*) Auditors' Report showing profits or losses for past five years and dividends paid. Assets and liabilities of the company at the last date to which the accounts of the company were made up should also be dealt with.

(*b*) Business Purchase Report when the intention is to purchase a business from the proceeds of the issue.

(*c*) Acquisition of Shares Report when the intention is to purchase shares and thus obtain a controlling interest in a company.

For both (*b*) and (*c*) the respective reports should show the profits or losses of the business or subsidiary for the past five years and the assets and liabilities at the last date to which the accounts were made up. The report should be prepared by named accountants who are qualified for appointment as auditors of a public company.

As already emphasised, the summary of the contents of the Prospectus given above should not be construed as stating the precise legal requirements.

A Prospectus which complies with the above provisions is required for *all* offers of shares to the public. An offer to existing shareholders (a rights issue) or existing Debenture holders is not a direct offer to the public and, therefore, no statutory form of Prospectus is required. However, great care must be exercised when attempting to invite an offer for shares. Even if a Prospectus is headed: "for private circulation only" it may still be an invitation to the public and, therefore, must comply with the Companies Acts.

## Underwriting

Underwriting is a form of insurance against the possibility that the public will not take up all the shares being issued. For the payment of an underwriting commission an issuing house will guarantee to subscribe for any shares not taken up by the public.

As already emphasised, the exact amount of capital may be needed to carry out the plans of development. In some cases, a loan or bank overdraft may have to be paid off from the proceeds of the issue. If, therefore, it is essential for the issue to be fully subscribed, underwriting will be advisable.

A common practice is to sub-underwrite with a large number of underwriters. Issuing houses may sub-underwrite for others—either issuing houses or brokers who are making an issue.

If a commission is paid to a broker for procuring underwriting this is known as overriding commission.

### ISSUE BY TENDER

When subscriptions by tender are invited the investors making the highest bids are issued with the shares. Obviously there should only be one price per share for *all* the shares issued. This will be the price which enables all the shares to be sold.

If a minimum price of £0·80 is fixed and the offer for sale invites tenders above this minimum price in multiples of £0·025 on to the £0·80, then if tenders are submitted with prices of £1·00, £0·90, £0·875, £0·850 and £0·80 the price selected will be determined by the quantities involved in the highest bids. If 300,000 shares are being issued and this number is covered by the tenders at prices ranging from £1·00 to £0·875 then the latter will be the price at which shares are issued.

There cannot be two prices for the same share. Moreover, by adopting the lowest price tendered,* those people who foolishly tender very high prices are safeguarded.

Water companies are required by law to invite tenders for their stock. Industrial companies are not in this position. Indeed, the Council of the Stock Exchange have been very reluctant to allow industrial shares to be issued by tender.

The object of an issue by tender is to eliminate the high profits obtainable by "stags" when an issue is made by an offer for sale or other method at a time when the demand for shares exceeds the supply. The "stags" apply for the shares, paying the amount due on application, then later sell the shares at a profit before the balance of the full price has to be paid. Naturally, if the full price must be paid on application the issue is not so attractive. With the tender method the market should determine what is a fair price; in turn, this price will represent current values and the possibility of "stags" making a quick profit will be eliminated. Dealings on the Stock Exchange will be carried out at around the price at which the issue is made.

The Council of the Stock Exchange gave its permission for an offer for sale involving 250,000 Ordinary shares of £0·25 each at a minimum price of £0·80 or at any higher price which is a multiple of £0·025 to be

---

* The reference is to the lowest price which will sell the *total* number of shares.

made on 16th June, 1961. The merchant bankers, Kleinwort Benson, used the method and the shares were in Parway Land and Investments Limited.

The issue met with considerable success and, in fact, was over-subscribed. Prices tendered ranged from £0·80 to £2·00, but the latter was an isolated and exceptionally high quotation. Of the 540 successful applicants only about one-fifth tendered prices over £1·00. The price at which the shares were issued was £0·875. Therefore, the price obtained was not excessive and, in fact, had been forecast in the financial columns of newspapers before the issue was made. Obtaining 540 successful applications also gave satisfaction for this could be construed as giving a "wide spread" to the issue.

There is no doubt that this first issue by tender received more pub-licity than the normal issue would. Any novel idea must inevitably be discussed and publicised to a great extent. Part of the success must, therefore, go to the extra publicity. The fact that, at the time of issue, property shares were in great demand should also be remembered. Further issues by tender have been made since the original version of this section was written. Although the method appears to be here to stay it cannot as yet be regarded as being one of the most popular means of raising capital.

### RIGHTS ISSUES AND BONUS ISSUES

An issuing house may give advice on the most appropriate terms for either a rights issue or a bonus issue of shares. These two aspects are covered later under the section dealing with Miscellaneous Topics.

## GENERAL PROCEDURES FOLLOWED

A company wishing to make an issue of shares or Debentures with the help of an issuing house may obtain an introduction through its bank, accountant, stockbroker or solicitor. Alternatively, a direct con-tact can be made. Many of the issuing houses make announcements from time to time in the financial press; e.g. The Financial Times; so the names and addresses can be obtained quite easily. Another method is to write to the Secretary of the Issuing Houses Association, 19 Fen-church Street, London, E.C.3.

Once contact has been made the issuing house will require to investi-gate the company's financial position. All enquiries are of a confidential nature. The issuing house is concerned only with making sure that the company is an acceptable client (see page 183). The Memorandum and Articles of Association will also be examined. If Debentures have been issued the issuing house will request sight of the Trust Deed; from this can be seen if the company's powers of raising money are restricted in any way.

If the issuing house agrees to act on behalf of the company the most appropriate method of raising the capital will be determined and the most advantageous terms to the company, which at the same time will give a reasonable chance of success, will be worked out.

Consultation will take place with officials of the Stock Exchange. A broker will also have to be employed. Great care has to be taken to ensure that all statements and documents are free of ambiguity before being submitted to the Share and Loan Department of the Stock Exchange. This department makes sure that the rules of the Stock Exchange are being observed and that present and future shareholders are being adequately protected in accordance with the terms of issue. In particular, full disclosure of all relevant facts to investors is expected.

Four copies of the prospectus must be lodged with the Share and Loan Department at least fourteen days before publication. Great emphasis is placed upon the integrity and standing of directors, secretary, auditors, bankers, issuing house and others concerned with the issue. Checks are made on the reputation of all concerned. The City of London Police and Scotland Yard may be asked to assist in these checks. Any special matters such as a clearance certificate for surtax direction or estate duty will also have to be dealt with.

There are no definite rules for the preparation and layout of the Auditors' or Accountants' Report which has to show the profits or losses for the preceding ten years. However, the Share and Loan Department of the Stock Exchange do make suggestions on this matter. The Memorandum issued by them is reproduced in Appendix V. It is suggested that the "written statement" (the Accountants' Report) should be divided into two sections—Section A and Section B—and each should deal with the items listed under the appropriate heading on the Memorandum. A letter from the accountants should be attached to the "written statement," showing that all necessary adjustments have been made. Other letters must also be submitted to the Share and Loan Department to confirm that stocks and work-in-progress have been properly valued throughout the period in question, that depreciation is adequate and if assets have been or are to be, revalued, that the effect of such revaluation has been taken into account.*

The enquiries which have to be made by the Stock Exchange will obviously take many days. Since the information submitted to the Stock Exchange will probably take a few weeks to collect and put into the correct form, it will be clear that the entire process, from the time of approaching an issuing house to the actual issue, may take many weeks. The correct timing of the issue is also important and, in some circumstances, may involve a delay until the market is "ready."

Because of the tremendous amount of work involved in connection with an issue the costs will tend to run into many thousands of pounds. There is the fee charged by the issuing house and also the fees of the company's own specialists such as accountants, auditors, and lawyers.

* This Memorandum is of great practical significance so careful study of Appendix V is advised.

There will also be legal, printing, and advertising costs. In addition there will be the charge made by the Stock Exchange for granting a quotation. Some of the costs such as underwriting and overriding commission, which may be included in the issuing house fee, and the Stock Exchange fee, tend to vary with the size of the issue, but many are of a fixed nature. Some idea of the costs involved can be obtained by looking at the Offer for Sale document shown in Appendix III. More than £1,000,000 was involved in that issue; it should be remembered that the cost can only be measured in relation to the size of the issue.

Provided at least the minimum subscription has been received allotments can be made. If there has been an overwhelming response to the issue the applications may be scaled down and moneys carried forward or returned. Alternatively, some applications may be rejected altogether. Generally speaking, the genuine investor—if he is distinguishable by his application—is given preferential treatment whereas the speculators (the "stags") have their money returned. However, this is not always possible for in the interests of economy of handling the holdings, the company may have to reject any application for a small number of shares.

## MISCELLANEOUS TOPICS

### RIGHTS ISSUES

A "rights issue" is an invitation to existing shareholders to subscribe for shares to be issued by a company. The shareholders are allowed to purchase the shares at the price stated and the number each shareholder is able to obtain is governed by his existing holding. If the rights issue is to be one Ordinary share for each Ordinary share held, then a shareholder holding one hundred Ordinary shares is able, if he chooses, to purchase a further one hundred.

The price fixed for the rights issue should be lower than the current market price of the shares being issued. There are two main reasons why this should be so. The first is that the members are able to benefit from the issue; this also acts as an encouragement for them to subscribe to the new issue. The second reason is based on the necessity to make the issue a success. If there is a danger of the value of the shares falling below the price asked by the company, especially during the subscription period, then it is unlikely that the shares will be taken up. For these reasons it is probably better to err on the side of under-pricing. Remember the issue is to existing members who, if they are holders of the equity capital, have a right to enjoy any advantages that may arise.

If there is a desire to preserve control of a company in the hands of the existing Ordinary shareholders, then the rights issue may achieve this aim.

In assessing the likely success of a rights issue regard must be had to the status of the existing shareholders. Generally speaking, it will be rather difficult to encourage a shareholder to take up more shares than he already possesses. Naturally, much depends upon the attractiveness of the shares as an investment. However, the smaller the issue in relation to existing share capital of the same class the more likely is the new issue to succeed. Admittedly, the shareholders may be able to renounce the letters of acceptance in favour of others; that is, transfer the shares at a profit without actually buying them, but there is also the question of the effect on the price of the shares after the new issue has been made. If the new issue is large in relation to the existing number of shares then the new price may prove to be relatively unattractive.

The fact that the price asked for the new shares will be below the price of the existing shares has already been noted. When the new issue has been made the new price of *all* the shares will tend to be somewhere between the two previous prices which existed. If 100,000 shares are in existence at a market price of £1·00 each and a further issue of 100,000 is made at £0·75 each then the new price will tend to settle at around £0·875 each. The latter is obtained by taking the two sums, £100,000 and £75,000, and dividing by the number of shares now in existence—200,000. The "profit" on each share may thus be taken at around £0·125 each. On the other hand, if the *new* issue is only 10,000 shares at £0·75 each then the new price will tend to be around £0·975 and will give a "profit" of £0·225 per share which is a much more attractive proposition.

These observations assume that the earning power will be in proportion to the issued share capital. That is to say an issue of a certain number of shares will result in an increase in profit which bears the same relation to the old profit as the number of new shares bears to the old share capital. If shares are increased by 25% then it is assumed that profit will also increase 25%. This fact will be reflected in the value of the shares, hence the adding together of the two values to obtain the new, average price. In actual practice, *eventually* the increased profit will often tend to represent a larger or smaller proportion than the increase in capital. However, when planning an issue the *immediate* effect on price is the important consideration. Clearly the profit forecasts made by a company may also affect the determination of the new price. If improved prospects are indicated and the shareholders and investing public have confidence in the forecast then the final price will tend to settle at a figure which shows the expected dividends as a reasonable return. This will probably be higher than the price obtained by dividing the total value by the number of shares explained earlier. Shareholders look for gains in the form of dividends or capital appreciation; these are the determinants of share prices.

That there is no rigid formula which may be adopted to decide the size of the new issue in relation to old share capital is shown by three rights issues which were announced on the same day:*

* Obviously the size is only of significance when considered along with capital issued before *and after* the bonus issue.

Biscuit company to make one-for-eight issue.

Timber company to make a one-for-two issue thereby raising £500,000.

Multiple stores to make an offer of one new share for every five held to raise £600,000.

Like any other method of raising capital, the rights issue is affected by the degree of confidence which exists at a particular time. For any issue to be successful there must be a high degree of confidence generally and there must be a similar confidence in the prospects of the company making the issue. Since optimism or pessimism varies from period to period it will be evident that the size of the new issue which would be successful will also differ from one period to another. Nevertheless, the remark already made, that the relatively small issue is likely to be more successful, still applies. If a company has plans for a large expansion then it may be better to carry this out in stages, obtaining the extra capital at suitable intervals of time. If this is not a practicable measure then the possibility of making an issue to existing shareholders without limiting the number of shares which may be purchased by each should be considered. Here an issuing house would be helpful. The possibility of all the shares not being taken up can be guarded against by getting an issuing house to underwrite.

A public issue which offers existing shareholders preferential treatment is a further possibility. In effect this is a combination of a public issue and a rights issue. Existing shareholders are given the first opportunity to buy the shares and any that are left may then be taken up by new investors.

The normal procedure adopted for a rights issue is to send a circular to shareholders. A provisional allotment letter may be sent to each member showing the number of shares and the price. He, or a person to whom he sells his right, will have to pay the amount due on application before the due date and then the shares are allotted to him. Publicity and advertisements essential with the normal public issue are thus avoided and the method tends to be very much cheaper than the other methods. However, the rules of the Stock Exchange must still be observed.

There is no doubt that issues to existing shareholders form a substantial part of total new capital obtained in any one year. This is due to a combination of a number of factors. There is the relative cheapness and simplicity of operation of the method. In addition, there is likely to be a shorter period needed for preparation, prior to making the issue.

## BONUS ISSUES

Making a bonus issue of shares means that shareholders are issued with shares out of the balances on reserve accounts. Other names adopted to describe a bonus issue are "capitalisation issue" and "scrip issue."

Normally a bonus issue is made to Ordinary shareholders, but if the new issue will affect the voting rights, giving Ordinary shareholders an advantage over Preference shareholders who are entitled to vote, there may be moral justification for adjusting the Preference voting rights. However, it may be that, relatively speaking, the rights are not affected between the two classes of shareholders so no action will be needed. There is, of course, the possibility that the position is covered in the Articles of Association, in which case the action to take will be guided by these.

The bonus issue brings the nominal value and the market value of the ordinary shares into line. If there are 20,000 £1 shares issued and these are quoted at £3 each then it is clear that at least part of the £40,000 difference will normally represent reserves, share premiums or other accumulated balances. If there are balances to the extent of £40,000 and a bonus issue of two shares for each held is made then the actual and nominal value of the capital is brought into line.

Generally speaking, the Ordinary shareholder is no better off from a bonus issue. If he was entitled to one-tenth of the voting rights and one-tenth of the dividend declared then this will still be the case after the bonus issue has been made. The bonus issue merely represents an adjustment to the capital and reserves. However, as will be appreciated, the precise way the market price of the shares will move depends very much upon the optimism of the market: this will be influenced by statements issued by the chairman of the company making the issue. The shareholder is issued with units of smaller value and these may be more convenient to him if he is considering selling some of his holding, but this cannot be said to represent a true advantage in terms of monetary gain.

Non-redeemable shares issued as a bonus are *not*, with certain exceptions, considered as "distribution" so that no tax is payable under the *Finance Act, 1965*. This is not the case with redeemable shares issued as a bonus; they must be treated as a "distribution."

From the points of view of the company, employees, shareholders, and investors there is no doubt that after a bonus issue has been made, the balance sheet is a much clearer representation of the facts. Any method or device which makes the statement of assets and liabilities much clearer to the professional man or layman has obviously much to commend it. After the issue the assets owned by the company and the capital owned by shareholders will be more in line. Moreover, the issue may have a "tidying up" effect.

Any justification of a bonus issue should be based on the earning capacity of the business. A reasonable rate of return should be forthcoming after the bonus issue; furthermore, there should be good prospects of the earnings being maintained. If not, the capital is said to be "watered"—a state of affairs which will tend to depress the value of the shares.

There is no doubt that the presence of reserves gives more flexibility to the capital structure. If a company encounters difficulties it will be much easier to adjust reserves rather than share capital. What is more, the stigma which attaches to a capital reduction scheme is avoided.

A rule of thumb which is sometimes put forward is that the value of permanent capital should not exceed the value of the fixed assets plus, possibly, part of the current assets. Much depends upon the type of business concerned so this "rule," like similar ones, must be treated with reserve. Certainly there is much to be said for all fixed assets and normal stock being covered by the permanent capital. Chapter 6 on Financial Planning will give guidance on this matter.

From the observations made it will be evident that there is no need, nor may it be desirable, to capitalise the total amount available from the General Reserve Account, the Profit and Loss Balance, Premium on Shares Account or other capital reserves. In the interests of safety and flexibility it may be better to maintain a balance on one of the reserve accounts. The need to keep the accounts and balance sheet as simple as possible precludes the leaving of a number of small balances on various reserve accounts. Any scheme for a bonus issue should aim as far as possible at simplifying the capital structure.

## EXAMINATION QUESTIONS

1. The following are the summarised Balance Sheets of Waterloo Trading Co. Ltd., as at 31st December, 1968 and 1969:

| | 1968 Dr. £ | 1968 Cr. £ | 1969 Dr. £ | 1969 Cr. £ |
|---|---|---|---|---|
| Fixed Assets at cost ... ... | 318,450 | | 389,000 | |
| Current Assets ... ... ... | 314,650 | | 295,450 | |
| Debenture Discount ... ... | 1,650 | | 1,500 | |
| Capital—Authorised and Issued: | | | | |
| Ordinary Shares ... ... | | 200,000 | | 200,000 |
| Preference Shares ... ... | | 25,000 | | 50,000 |
| Share Premium Account ... ... | | 75,000 | | 77,500 |
| Debentures repayable at par in 1978 | | 50,000 | | 50,000 |
| Current Liabilities ... ... ... | | 186,050 | | 146,700 |
| Provision for Depreciation ... | | 42,250 | | 49,300 |
| Provision for Doubtful Debts ... | | 2,100 | | 1,750 |
| Dividend paid for 1968 ... ... | | | 20,000 | |
| Balance on Profit and Loss Account from previous year ... ... | | 1,550 | | 54,350 |
| Net Profit for the year ... ... | | 52,800 | | 76,350 |
| | £634,750 | £634,750 | £705,950 | £705,950 |

(1) During the year 1969 machinery costing £12,500 (accumulated depreciation (£7,000)) was sold for £6,000.

(2) £25,000 Preference Share Capital was issued for cash during the year at a premium of £2,500.

(3) The net profit for 1969 is arrived at after crediting profit on sale of machinery and the reduction in the provision for doubtful debts and after writing off £150 debenture discount.

You are required to prepare (a) a statement showing the net increase in working capital during 1969, and (b) a statement showing the sources and application of working capital during that year. (S.C.A.)

2. A rights issue of ordinary stock is being considered by the directors of a company to provide additional working capital of £2,000,000, which will finance expansion and enable a bank overdraft of £1,000,000 to be repaid. You are asked to advise the directors on:

(a) The price at which the ordinary stock units should be issued, and

(b) The effect on the company's Profit and Loss Account of the proposed new issue.

You are also asked to make any additional recommendations or suggestions which you think necessary.

You have the following information about the company:

(i) The present capital structure is

|  | £ |
|---|---|
| 5% Preference Stock (£1·00 Units)... ... ... ... | 500,000 |
| Ordinary Stock (£0·50 Units) ... ... ... ... | 2,000,000 |
|  | £2,500,000 |

(ii) The net profits prior to tax have averaged £750,000 per year for the last five years and are expected to increase to £1,000,000 per year as a result of the expansion.

(iii) A dividend of 10 per cent. has been paid on the Ordinary Stock for each of the last five years.

(iv) The middle Stock Exchange quotation of the £0·50 Ordinary Stock Units is stable at around £1·00 and the £1·00 Preference Stock Units are quoted at par. (I.C.W.A.)

3. State, briefly, the steps to be taken (a) to obtain permission to deal in the shares of a company on the London Stock Exchange, and (b) to obtain an official quotation for such shares on the London Stock Exchange. Are the requirements similar for both (a) and (b)? (S.C.A.)

4. A private company is desirous of obtaining a stock exchange quotation. Detail:

(a) the likely reasons for seeking a quotation;

(b) the prior considerations;

(c) the methods of marketing available. (A.C.C.A.)

CHAPTER 9

# OBTAINING MEDIUM- AND SHORT-TERM CAPITAL

## *INTRODUCTION*

THE methods available for obtaining permanent capital have already been discussed. This chapter is concerned with giving the sources and methods of obtaining medium-term and short-term capital. There may be instances when this alternative capital is preferable; the permanent capital may be obtained at a more appropriate, future time.

Seasonal variations in spending or receiving of cash may make a bank overdraft appropriate. Alternatively, a company may not be of a size which permits a public issue of shares or Debentures to be made. A bank loan or assistance from the Industrial and Commercial Finance Corporation Limited may be appropriate. These are two examples only: there are others which were mentioned in earlier chapters. Some will be discussed below in connection with the different sources of finance. How appropriate each method will be depends upon the nature of the business concerned, its financial standing and problems and the conditions and circumstances which exist at the time the finance is required. It is quite impossible to formulate inflexible rules which can be used in all cases.

Generally speaking, "short-term capital" refers to finance which is required for no longer than one year. Medium-term capital is obtained for longer than one year, but not with the idea of its being permanent capital. The period involved may vary from one business to another. In this connection, the rate of growth will be very important and this does not tend to follow a definite pattern, but varies from one organisation to another. However, on the average it seems safe to assume that medium-term capital should not be obtained for longer than five years. Otherwise, what in effect is happening is that capital which should be regarded as being of a temporary nature is being treated as permanent capital. This may involve rather high interest or other charges and, at the same time, give the business a high degree of vulnerability; a credit squeeze or trade set-back may have disastrous consequences. Sometimes it is very difficult to distinguish between what is short-term and what is medium-term capital. For this reason, the division between the two, shown below, should be regarded as being rather arbitrary.

Another possible classification is based on the nature of the finance rather than the period involved. Permanent capital is that obtained for an indefinite period: it takes the form of shares or Debentures. On the other hand, some forms of financing, although possibly giving facilities for longer than five years, cannot be regarded as permanent capital simply because in the well-managed business the cheaper and more

201

acceptable, orthodox permanent capital will be sought as soon as it is convenient. For convenience, therefore, these methods will also be treated as medium-term capital.

## MEDIUM-TERM CAPITAL

The principal methods and sources of medium-term capital are as follows:

1. Loans—banks and other financial institutions.
2. Hire purchase and block discounting—finance companies.
3. Sale and lease back—property investment companies, insurance companies and similar institutional investors.
4. Mortgages—insurance companies.
5. Equipment Leasing—manufacturers, or organisations who specialise in leasing.

### LOANS

In the past, a convention that banks lent only on short-term was well established. There were exceptions to this general rule and, in fact, loans for longer terms than the accepted twelve months were permitted. Even here, with the exceptions, there was a danger that the loan would be called in at a time when the businessman could ill afford to make the repayment.

The Radcliffe Report stressed the need for banks to offer term loan facilities, especially to the small concern. Since this announcement banks have given more publicity to this aspect. A scheme which is operated by one of the large banks* and which is typical of similar schemes run by other banks is known as "term loans."

Term loans cater for the "small industrial and business units" and are "intended primarily for the purchase or improvement of plant, equipment, premises and other capital assets."† Clearly the loans are intended to fill the gap noticed by the Radcliffe Committee.

The size of the loan will depend upon individual requirements. However, there must obviously be a limit; the fact that the facility is intended primarily for the small business implies that this will be so. Normally the maximum figure which may be borrowed is £10,000, but a larger loan may be obtained in appropriate circumstances.

There is no possibility of the term loan being prematurely recalled. As noticed earlier, this was a danger which deterred businessmen from placing too much reliance on the orthodox bank loan. The duration of the term loan will vary according to the probable life of the asset to be purchased. If the latter is plant then the period of the loan may be, say, three to five years, whereas if property is to be purchased, the

---

* Midland Bank Limited.
† Quoted from leaflet explaining scheme issued by Midland Bank.

period may be ten years or more. In all cases the exact period is determined *before* the loan is made: the borrower thus knows where he stands.

Repayments are spread over the period of the loan. Each amount repaid will include a portion of the total loan plus an interest charge. This will be debited to the borrower's current account every six months. Obviously, any falling into arrears will usually allow the right to recall the balance of the loan immediately.

Term loans are not cheap. The reason for this is very obvious. Any loan which is to cover a period of years must inevitably carry greater risk than a loan which is made on a year-to-year basis. In fact, the longer the period the greater the risk is likely to be. At the time of writing, the rate of interest is 2% above Bank Rate with a minimum charge of 6%. This is on the full amount of the loan for the period of the loan; therefore, the *true* rate of interest, when it is considered that the balance is reduced at the end of each six months, will be much higher than 6%. Even so, this method compares quite favourably with any of the other methods described in this chapter.

The assets should earn sufficient to pay off the loan and interest and, at the same time, to allow a profit to be made. A discipline is enforced by the terms of the agreement. The businessman has a definite repayment to make at regular intervals. There is a great similarity to hire purchase, but term loans tend to be cheaper.

Quite often it may be necessary to provide security for the loan: this matter is discussed in connection with short-term loans and overdrafts covered later in this chapter. Banks are not the only sources of loans: other sources are mentioned in connection with mortgages dealt with on page 206.

## HIRE PURCHASE

Hire purchase is a method of obtaining goods *immediately* upon payment of a deposit, the balance of the price due being spread over a period of months or years. The hirer pays for the service by means of an interest and service charge. This has to be paid along with the purchase price over the period to which the hire purchase refers, usually by equal instalments.

The importance of hire purchase was recognised in the Radcliffe Report. There is no doubt that the method possesses many advantages, for without this facility many businesses would not have developed to the extent they have. Assets can be purchased quickly and easily and, therefore, help to increase the earning power of the business.

However, not all types of assets can be purchased through the medium of hire purchase. The finance companies have formulated a number of rules which are followed in determining the type of asset which is suitable for acquiring through hire purchase.

Assets should be capable of being identified without trouble. In particular, any goods which are to be the subject of hire purchase should not be component parts which go towards making a larger piece of plant or equipment; nor should they be spare parts which are difficult to identify. The reason for this stipulation that assets can be identified is presumably connected with being able to describe an article with certainty on the agreement. If this is done there cannot afterwards be much doubt as to which asset was the subject of the hiring.

One of the requirements is that the estimated, serviceable life of the asset should be greater than the period covered by the hire purchase agreement. Linked with the serviceable life and hire purchase period is the expected market value. It is desirable that the latter should, during the period of the hire purchase, always be greater than the amount owed under the hire purchase agreement.

If the fact that the market value is greater than the amount owing is to be of benefit to the finance company it follows that the asset concerned should be resaleable without trouble. Therefore, if an agreement is brought to an end, the asset can be taken back and sold without the hire purchase company incurring loss.

The final condition refers to the potential earning capacity of the asset. Because of the relatively short period over which the asset is hired and finally purchased—usually from two to five years—it is essential that the earning commences immediately and, what is more, because hire purchase interest charges tend to be high, that the rate of earning is quite substantial. The latter makes the purchase worthwhile and also enables the hire purchase instalments to be met on the due dates. The field of machinery and equipment which comes within the high earning category is quite wide. It includes machine tools, motor vehicles, earth-moving machines and equipment, cement mixers and similar machinery, and printing machines.

### Advantages of Hire Purchase

There is no doubt that hire purchase is a very convenient and quick method of obtaining finance. Moreover, there are no special legal requirements with resultant high costs. Legal documents do not have to comply with special requirements and this fact expedites procedures.*

Tax advantages may accrue. Investment and initial allowances may be claimed on the payments made each year and the normal wear and tear allowance may also be allowed for tax purposes.

The compulsory "saving" which is imposed under the hire purchase agreement can also be an advantage. Replacement and expansion can take place out of the earnings, present and future. Naturally there must be careful planning of the growth. In particular a watch must be kept on the total indebtedness—outgoings must be kept within limits which

* The *Hire Purchase Act, 1965*, governs hire purchase transactions. Any hire purchase transaction involving up to £2,000 is legally controlled.

are reasonable in relation to incomings. In short, the ease with which extra hire purchase can be obtained should not be allowed to induce the entering into excessive future commitments.

The assets being purchased are securities in themselves. Therefore, except for satisfying themselves on creditworthiness, the finance companies do not insist on some form of "collateral." This is clearly a definite advantage. Moreover, there will not usually be any need to seek permission from creditors. Linked with the absence of securities is the avoidance of having to register charges on assets, necessary with some forms of borrowing.

### Disadvantages of Hire Purchase

One of the most obvious disadvantages of hire purchase is that it tends to be a very expensive form of financing. A charge of between 7 and 10%, or even more, is quite usual and this is made on the total amount involved; *i.e.* the initial purchase price. The *effective* rate charged, on the balance outstanding, having regard to the fact that instalments are being paid regularly, will tend to be in the region of double the actual rate charged. A 10% per annum charge on the original sum will amount to an effective rate in the region of 20%—truly a very high cost!

A principal reason for the high charge is the need for the finance companies to cover past and future bad debts. Not only are they concerned with industrial hire purchase, but also with providing facilities for domestic appliances and equipment such as washing machines, refrigerators, sewing machines, and cars. Bad debts in respect of transactions involving all types of goods have to be covered in the charges made. Another factor in the high costs is the work involved in recording and collecting the payments under the hire purchase agreements. A further consideration is the servicing which is provided under some hire purchase agreements. The expenses of such servicing are often heavy and these must be covered in the charges added to the hire purchase price. However, it should be remembered that the right to servicing may be a feature of a guarantee or warranty supplied with the asset. If so, the charge for this will already be included in the purchase price, therefore, there can be no justification for inclusion of a further charge.

The second disadvantage of hire purchase is the fact that it provides finance for only a limited period, the length of which is dependent upon the life of the asset involved. However, this should not be stressed too much. If an asset is being purchased over a period of, say, three years, then the payments due can be covered in the budgets for that period. Once the payments have been made the asset *is* owned by the business so there is no need for finance for that *specific* purpose. In any case, if further assets are required, then a further hire purchase agreement can be entered into. Hire purchase is not strictly a method of obtaining finance, but rather a method of acquiring assets thereby avoiding the necessity to spend available cash on an outright purchase. Present liquid assets are, therefore, conserved.

*Block Discounting*

"Block discounting" is the term used to describe the discounting of rights under hire purchase agreements. A manufacturer or retailer may sell his goods on hire purchase, but instead of waiting for the customers to pay the instalments he may obtain the *present* value of the total sales from a finance house. When the instalments are paid they are then transferred to the finance house.

This method may carry great appeal to any supplier of goods who finds himself short of finance. Unfortunately the cost of discounting tends to reduce the profit margin considerably. Moreover, the manufacturer or retailer may be required to guarantee the hire purchase agreements sold to the finance house. The use of normal hire purchase facilities may be preferred to block discounting.

## SALE AND LEASE BACK

A company which owns valuable property and requires additional finance may sell it to a property investment company or, possibly, an insurance company. Simultaneously with the sale, a long-term lease is agreed upon, the former owner now becoming the lessee of the property at a stated rental.

Undoubtedly, the sale and lease back method has the advantage of making a substantial amount of cash available and, at the same time, *may* transfer the responsibility for repairs and maintenance to the new owner. Furthermore, the rental paid is a permitted charge against profits.

The danger of losing the property when the period of the lease expires can be eliminated by insisting upon a renewal option on reasonable terms. Clearly, however, although the sale and lease back method has been classified as "medium-term capital," if options are exercised the finance may become very long-term indeed.

If there is a need for a permanent increase in working capital, the method may be worthy of consideration. However, it should be remembered that the rental has to be met each year irrespective of the size of the profit. Therefore, for all practical purposes, there is a fixed charge rather similar to that payable on debentures or other loans. If a company encounters trade difficulties and is unable to meet the rental then the lessor may bring the agreement to an end and the company will then be without property which is absolutely essential to its continuance.

## MORTGAGES

Mortgage Debentures were explained in a previous chapter. Basically, the mortgages available from insurance companies, trust funds, banks or investment companies are the same as mortgage Debentures.

Money is borrowed and, as security, the company gives a charge or lien on its property. If the company fails to repay the interest due, the insurance company or other lender will be able to exercise its right under the mortgage deed and take possession of the property mortgaged.

The period covered by the mortgage is not standardised. Insurance and investment companies appear to prefer periods of twenty or more years, but not much in excess of twenty. Shorter periods may also be arranged.

There is no definite stipulation regarding the amount which can be borrowed under this method. Much depends upon the value of the property available. Obviously, the amount lent will not be to the full value of the property; in fact, generally the loan will not exceed two-thirds of a conservative estimate.

Repayment of the loan will be according to the terms previously determined when the agreement was entered into. Equal instalments of capital and interest is a common method. Alternatively a mortgage redemption insurance policy may be used for repayment of the capital.

It is true that the mortgage method has its uses. However, it does tend to be a fairly expensive method of borrowing. If a company is in a position to raise finance by issuing mortgage Debentures then this may be cheaper. Often a company is obliged to obtain a loan by the mortgage method when financial difficulties are being experienced. In these circumstances, high interest rates are demanded and, quite often onerous conditions are stipulated. A right to convert the loan to equity capital may also be a feature of the terms of the loan. There is no doubt that great care should be exercised and other possibilities should be considered before obtaining a mortgage with its possible restrictions and heavy burden of fixed interest charges. However, the latter can rate for tax relief.

## EQUIPMENT LEASING

Equipment leasing or hiring is a relatively new idea in Great Britain. No doubt the lead and inspiration comes from the United States of America where equipment leasing schemes have been in operation for many years.

Manufacturers requiring machinery and equipment of all types, provided they have a fairly long life, can approach a finance house who will then lease the fixed asset required for a term of years at an agreed rental. Alternatively, an approach may be made to a manufacturer of the asset required who may then make arrangements for it to be leased—usually through a finance house—or suggest an approach to a finance house which deals with leasing.

Leases for property have been employed for many years. Fundamentally there is no difference between the property lease and the equipment lease.

Leasing should not be confused with hire purchase. There is a
H

similarity in that regular payments have to be made under both methods. However, there is an important difference. With a hire purchase transaction the title to the asset eventually passes to the hirer. With a leasing contract this is not the case; the title remains vested in the lessor (the finance company).

The period covered by a contract for leasing or hiring may vary from one finance company to another. Much depends upon the type of equipment involved. The contract may cover, say, five years with an option for extension at a reduced rental or the right to terminate the agreement at the end of the five years. Up to five years appears to be a normal period. In connection with the period involved it should be noted that some people distinguish between "leasing" and "renting" by regarding the former as being all contracts which cover not less than five years.

### Advantages of Leasing

Many advantages are offered by the method of leasing. The asset hired should be able to earn a profit over and above the rental charge so the company involved stands to gain. Furthermore rentals can be charged against profits for tax purposes. Naturally, of course, the allowances which go with ownership—investment and wear and tear allowances—cannot be claimed by the lessee.

The use of the leasing method gives the benefit of conserving immediate financial resources. This may be particularly important when there has been a period of rising prices. A company wishing to replace a highly priced fixed asset may find itself facing difficulties. The lease overcomes the problem. A further advantage claimed for leasing is that no balance sheet entry is required. Additional claims are that obsolescence is avoided and so are heavy repair costs on badly worn assets. There is a good deal of truth in these assertions. However, much depends upon the conditions laid down in the agreement. The finance company will clearly wish to cover itself in the rental for obsolescence, the cost of the asset and any commitments forming part of the agreement. Accordingly, the alleged gains are simply what the lessee is already paying for in his rental.

### Possible Disadvantages of Leasing

The fixed charge in the form of a rental has to be paid whether a profit is earned or a loss is incurred. In times of difficult trading conditions, when there is a shortage of cash, there may be great difficulty in meeting the rental.

Not owning assets may limit a company's borrowing abilities. The assessment of creditworthiness is usually based on a company's Profit and Loss Account and Balance Sheet. With few fixed assets there is likely to be a "weak" balance sheet and a reluctance to lend by banks and other financial institutions.

The cost of the leasing may be a further deterrent. Investment in capital expenditure is at the best a very risky venture. Any finance company must necessarily cover the risks in the rental charged. Therefore, the costs will tend to be high.

## SHORT-TERM CAPITAL

Short-term capital is all capital obtained for not longer than one year. There are very many forms, the principal of which are summarised below:

1. Short-term lending by banks—overdrafts and loans.
2. Acceptance credits—accepting houses.
3. Credit facilities.

### SHORT-TERM LENDING BY BANKS

Lending by banks has tended to be restricted to short-term loans or overdrafts. This function is the one which will be described in this section. That banks now lend for long periods and also have interests in hire purchase companies should also be remembered: these functions are considered in the preceding section which deals with medium-term capital.

### Bank Overdrafts

When a bank grants overdraft facilities it means that a customer is allowed to overdraw his account by a stated amount. In other words, the bank agrees to honour cheques drawn on a current account which contains insufficient funds to meet such cheques.

One of the principal advantages of the overdraft form of borrowing is its flexibility. When a businessman requires extra funds he is able to draw on his account and when he receives payment from accounts or other sources the act of paying in the cheques or cash automatically reduces the amount overdrawn. Because interest is payable only on the actual daily balance of the overdraft it follows that this method tends to be cheaper than the loan method of borrowing.

From the point-of-view of certainty of tenure the bank overdraft has a weakness. Normally a borrower may be called upon to repay on demand the amount overdrawn. If the facility is withdrawn when most needed a business may find itself in difficulties. Fortunately, a bank manager will be quite anxious to maintain his lending at as high a level as possible, so a complete withdrawal of overdraft facilities is unlikely. If, due to a Government credit squeeze, overdrafts have to be reduced then it will usually be done in a manner which minimises the adverse effects. Even so, because of the "repayment on demand" aspect it is probably wiser to restrict overdraft borrowing to cover abnormal calls on cash which are of a seasonal or intermittent nature.

The security and cost aspects of bank overdrafts are discussed below.

### Bank Loans

The bank loan has tended to be on a year to year basis. These short-term loans are still available, but, in addition, long-term loans may also be obtained.

Interest on the loan is payable for the full period at the rate which has been agreed. Provisions for repayment of the principal and interest will be made in the agreement drawn up by the bank. Because the loan is for a definite period there is not the danger that it will be "called in." On the other hand, because the interest is payable for a full period the cost may be greater than when the overdraft method is used.

The general economic situation will tend to influence the method of borrowing. If times are uncertain and there is a constant danger of credit restrictions being imposed then the loan is possibly a better method than the overdraft. This statement assumes that extra money is required for a definite period; obviously, if the shortage is of a *temporary* nature the overdraft may be quite adequate.

### Conditions of Borrowing

There are no hard and fast rules as to who may borrow and under what conditions. All businesses tend to exhibit some difference in character and mode of operation so standardised rules may be difficult to apply. Moreover, personal opinions—those of the borrower and the bank manager—may influence a decision one way or the other. The general economic situation and the Government policy at any particular time will also affect the amount to be lent. These, and other influences, all react upon the availability of overdrafts and loans: therefore, they must be kept in mind when considering the possibility of augmenting working capital.

A bank manager expects to take risks, but he will naturally minimise these as much as possible. He does this by thorough investigation and assessment of the character of the borrower—in the case of a limited company, the directors.

The purpose of the loan or overdraft will be a principal consideration. A bank manager must satisfy himself that the money is to be used in the normal course of business and in a manner which will bring in sufficient cash to allow repayment. In banking terminology, the loan must be "self liquidating."

In addition to considering the purpose the bank manager will like to make an assessment of the overall position of the business. Examination of Balance Sheets and Profit and Loss Accounts for a number of years may be necessary. For the short-term bank loan or overdraft the object will be to assess whether or not there are sufficient current assets which, when sold, will allow repayment. The longer the period of the loan the more concerned he will be with assessing future earning power and valuation of fixed assets. Ideally he will want the business to go from strength to strength and pay off the loan without difficulty. However, he must also consider the possibility of business failure and, accordingly, he must value the business not only as a going concern, but also on the basis of a possible sale due to bankruptcy or liquidation. Piecemeal disposition of assets may mean a much lower realisable value than when the business is a going concern; this will be particularly so if there is a trade recession. Additional information may be required on particular assets or liabilities: the principal debtors; slow-moving stocks; unsecured creditors and details of any unusual commitments may be requested. The observations made in Chapter 16 on Accounting Ratios may be read with advantage at this point.

The amount of the money invested by the proprietors will also be considered. A loan—or overdraft—must not exceed the holdings of the shareholders. If it did there would be no margin of safety. Any lender tries to ensure that the assets owned by the borrower more than cover the amount of the loan.

Just in case the expectations of a business are not realised the bank manager will usually ask for some form of collateral security. This is a security provided under an agreement. The object is not to take the security, but rather to ensure that the main purpose of an agreement is carried out (*e.g.* repayment of loan) or, if there is a breach, to allow the banker to indemnify himself. A security is only used as a last resort, when the possibility of repayment has diminished to a very low state.

Many things can be offered as securities. Ideally they should comply with certain conditions. There should be no doubt regarding the validity of the title to the security. Moreover, the banker will want to have a first charge on assets; a second mortgage may be of doubtful value if there is an enforced liquidation. Stability in value is another important factor. The minimum value that can be expected from the security, *in all* circumstances, should be more than the amount of the loan or overdraft, thus providing a margin of safety. Finally, the possibility of having to transfer the security should not be forgotten; accordingly, the agreement entered into, and the type of security accepted, by a bank will be of the type that can be transferred to the bank without undue difficulty.

Not all securities possess to a high degree the desirable qualities described in the previous paragraph. Nevertheless, banks may still accept them; in such cases possibly the margin of safety may have to be larger. Normal securities are documents of title to goods, bills of exchange, assurance policies, and title deeds to buildings and land. In the case of a limited company the personal guarantees of directors may be requested. A mortgage on the fixed assets is another possibility. A floating charge on the assets allows the company to deal in assets in the normal course of business whereas a fixed or specific charge relates to definite fixed assets which cannot be sold without obtaining the prior consent of the mortgagee or Debenture holder (the bank). From a company's point-of-view the floating charge is clearly to be preferred.

## Cost of Borrowing from Banks

At the time of writing the cost of short-term borrowing from commercial banks is 1% above Bank Rate with a minimum of 5%. The Bank Rate is the rate of interest charged by the Bank of England for discounting first class bills of exchange. This rate varies with the policy followed by the Government and the Bank of England. When credit is being restricted the Bank Rate tends to be increased; when credit is being relaxed the Rate tends to be reduced. At times when money is scarce a businessman will, therefore, have to pay more to borrow. Since the scarcity will tend to be of a general nature many businesses will also be short of cash. Unfortunately, therefore, a management may find itself short of cash at a time when there is little cash available. If it is possible to obtain a loan or overdraft then this will tend to be at a high rate of interest. Clearly this is a definite indication of the need for cash budgeting; plans can then be made in good time to obtain any necessary cash.

### ACCEPTANCE CREDITS

For short-term finance, companies may make use of an acceptance credit. This involves opening an account with an accepting house, a merchant bank which specialises in acceptance credits. Once the acceptance house selected is satisfied of a company's creditworthiness it will issue a letter of credit which permits the borrower to draw for acceptance Bills of Exchange which are payable at three months after sight. By accepting the bills the accepting house gives them a first class status—hence the name "prime bank bills."

The prime bank bill can be discounted with one of the London discount houses at a rate of interest which is generally cheaper than that charged for bank loans or overdrafts. "Discounting" means simply selling the bill of exchange for its *present* value: the difference between the total value of the bill and the present value is the discount charge.

Companies may be allowed to arrange permanent facilities with an acceptance house, being allowed to draw bills as and when required. Such an arrangement is known as a "revolving credit."

Acceptance credits may have to be covered by the lodging of securities with the accepting houses. Bills of Exchange drawn on other traders, Stock Exchange securities or similar documents of title may be accepted as securities. Whether or not securities are required there must be evidence of a commercial transaction which will produce adequate funds to pay the accepting house the amount due a few days before the maturity of the Bill of Exchange. Normally, therefore, an accepting house will be meeting any bill accepted from funds already supplied by the borrower.

Acceptance credits can be useful for the buying or selling of goods, whether this is in domestic or foreign trade. The seasonal needs of a business may also be financed by acceptance credits. In these cases, as already stated, a self-liquidating transaction must be in evidence. Obviously, any difficulties which may arise in obtaining trade may affect the availability of cash. Generally speaking this remark also applies to other sources of short-term credit so this disadvantage must not be overstated.

In connection with acceptance credits an argument sometimes advanced is that the accepting houses are in a much better position to assess the worth of each proposition than are any other financial institutions such as banks. The precise significance of each transaction can be determined. Accordingly, if a credit squeeze is imposed by the Government there will be no need to restrict every proposition. A credit restriction is usually aimed at internal spending; exporting goods or importing raw materials which cannot be obtained otherwise may not be intended to be affected. The accepting houses, so the argument runs, are in a very favourable position to distinguish the essential from the non-essential transactions.

A list of the members of the Accepting Houses Committee is given in Appendix I, page 797.

## CREDIT FACILITIES

The normal credit arrangement between a company and its suppliers is a very important source of short-term finance. Terms vary from one business to another, but it is quite a normal practice to be able to obtain around one month's credit. Sometimes, for capital goods, a "credit sale" agreement may be possible. The buyer enters into an agreement to pay off the total amount due within a relatively short period; say, by equal instalments over nine months. This is rather similar to hire purchase, but possibly without the heavy burden of interest.

Special arrangements may be possible with some suppliers. Thus, for example, if there is a long production cycle the supplier of raw material may agree to wait for a number of months before being paid. Another special facility is the supplying of the material by a customer (known as "free issue materials") or the advancing of sufficient cash to purchase the material. Subsequently the advance is deducted from the price to be charged to the customer. These and similar arrangements may be quite valuable to the small business—without them such businesses may have great difficulty in accepting extra work.

The main objection to the use of credit facilities is the possible loss in cash discount. Some companies have very generous discounts for prompt cash payments. A discount of 5% on an account which will have to be paid within one month is a considerable percentage when calculated on a per annum basis.

Not to be forgotten is the fact that credit may have to be *allowed* as well as being received. This matter is so important that it is dealt with at some length in Chapter 24.

## SPECIALIST INSTITUTIONS

In addition to the banks, issuing houses, accepting houses, and related financial institutions which form the money market there are a number of financial institutions which cater for specific needs. Each of these institutions was established with a particular range of activities in mind.

A summary of the principal institutions is shown below. Reference should also be made to Chapter 24 on obtaining finance for exporting or expanding overseas (E.C.G.D.).

1. Finance Corporation for Industry Ltd. (F.C.I.).
2. Industrial and Commercial Finance Corporation Ltd. (I.C.F.C.).

These two are discussed in greater detail below.

3. Ship Mortgage Finance Co. Ltd.

As the name implies, the Ship Mortgage Finance Co. Ltd. is concerned with supplying finance for building ships in the United Kingdom.

4. Agricultural Mortgage Corporation Ltd.

The Agricultural Mortgage Corporation Ltd. specialises in advancing long-term loans to farmers. Any loan is covered by mortgages on land and buildings which exist in England and/or Wales. A period of up to sixty years may be covered by a loan.

Other institutions also exist, but they are chiefly concerned with serving a special purpose and are not available to industry generally.

### FINANCE CORPORATION FOR INDUSTRY LIMITED

The Finance Corporation for Industry Limited (F.C.I.) provides medium-term finance in the form of loan capital. The funds provided must exceed £200,000; any amount less than this is the concern of the Industrial and Commercial Finance Corporation Limited.

The Corporation does not supplant other financial institutions. If finance can be obtained through the money market by normal capital issues or borrowing, then a company must look to that source. Only when funds cannot be obtained on reasonable terms from the normal sources will the F.C.I. consider a proposal and only then if "the project appears to be important for the national economic interest." When the borrowing company is able to attract capital through normal channels it can then pay off the loan from F.C.I.

Each proposal submitted to the Corporation is considered on its merits. Some form of security may have to be lodged before the loan is made. There may also be a provision in the agreement for an option to purchase Ordinary shares: these may be sold by the Corporation when the company has become established.

Interest is normally payable at a rate which is linked with the Bank Rate. If the Bank Rate rises then so will the rate charged on the loan; a fall in the Bank Rate will mean a reduction in the loan rate. The full amount of the loan need not be taken at one time—advances can be obtained as and when required. Quite often capital development projects must be spread over a long period. The Corporation recognises this fact by enabling the borrower to take the money when needed. Flexibility is also aimed at for repayment of the loans. If a borrower finds that he can repay the loan earlier than expected then he can do so at any time although, naturally, the F.C.I. expects short notice of the borrower's intentions. In addition to the payment of interest a borrower will have to meet other costs, such as an engagement fee and other relatively small charges.

Because the Corporation is operated along normal commercial lines it is natural that a borrower is asked to prove his worthiness before a loan is granted. In addition to the possibility of providing securities there is the question of sound management, and its concomitant, profitability. There must also be evidence of integrity and good credit-standing. Of vital importance is the nature of the project and its likely contribution to the nation's economic growth.

Applications for assistance should in the first instance be limited to a broad, yet brief, outline of the nature and scope of the project. The money needed and how it is to be repaid should be stated and a copy of the final accounts should be submitted along with the application. If the Corporation is able to participate in the project it will request further details. The following list has been issued by the Corporation as a guide to the type of information which will be required:

1. *The Firm*

(i) History and nature of the business.

(ii) Present capital structure.

(iii) Capital raised during the last five years and the purpose for which it was needed. Method of raising, and names of stockbrokers or issuing houses concerned.

(iv) Names of principal shareholders, loan stockholders, or long-term creditors.

(v) Bankers and details of overdraft or other banking facilities.

(vi) Names of directors and details of their other interests and connections.

(vii) Names of senior executives; details of their functions and responsibilities, length of service with the Company and special qualifications.

(viii) Record of turnover and profits for the past ten years (or since incorporation).

(ix) Copies of audited accounts for the past five years (or since incorporation) with copies or summaries of appropriate tax computations.

(x) Specimens of routine accounting and costing information prepared for the Company's Board.

## 2. The Proposed Development

(i) The purpose of the scheme and description of its various parts. The date by which it should be completed.

(ii) Name of the person responsible for carrying the scheme through, note of his experience in this capacity.

(iii) Details of buildings, plant, machinery, and other fixed assets involved; their cost individually and in aggregate, and a note of the extent to which costs have been estimated; the amount of contingency provision.

(iv) Timetable for construction, delivery, and erection of fixed assets and the phasing of expenditure on them.

(v) Working capital required and the purpose for which it is to be used, e.g. stocks, work-in-progress, debtors, etc.

(vi) Estimated date of first operation and the extent of "running-in" or "start-up" time provided.

(vii) Estimated overall cash position (monthly or quarterly) during the period of construction, delivery or erection, and during the "running-in" period and subsequent first two years full operation.

(viii) Estimate of profits or losses during "running-in" period and first two years of full operation.

(ix) Selling prospects or market survey of home and export markets.

(x) Names of principal competitors.

(xi) Government Departments interested in the scheme.

## 3. The Finance Required

(i) Total new capital involved in the scheme.

(ii) Amount required from F.C.I., the period to be covered, and the proposed method of repayment.

(iii) Security offered.

(iv) Any sources additional to F.C.I. from which it is proposed to find any part of the new capital.

(v) Reasons why the amount required from F.C.I. cannot be found elsewhere with a note of the enquiries made.

Two copies of the Company's Memorandum and Articles of Association and any Trust Deed or other documents concerning loans outstanding at the date of the application should be sent with the above information.

### INDUSTRIAL AND COMMERCIAL FINANCE CORPORATION LIMITED

The name of the Industrial and Commercial Finance Corporation Limited is usually abbreviated to I.C.F.C. Although established with the approval of the Government it does not come under the control of the latter. In fact, the equity capital is owned by the Bank of England and joint stock banks.

Obtaining financial aid from the Corporation does not mean that a business will lose its independence; in fact, the I.C.F.C. believes that each concern should be allowed to control its own activities. However, this statement does not preclude the giving of advice; if customers encounter problems they may call on the I.C.F.C. experts and obtain the benefit of their knowledge and experience.

Like any other commercial undertaking the I.C.F.C. is in business to earn profits. It provides share or loan capital and for this service charges interest. The rate of interest will be determined by two factors: an assessment of the risk involved and the current market rates of interest. Once the rate has been determined it will apply for the entire period of the loan, but is payable only in respect of the balance of the loan which has not been paid back to I.C.F.C. On acceptance of a formal offer of finance, the customer becomes liable to a negotiation fee which is normally $1\frac{1}{2}\%$ on the first £50,000 and 1% on any excess over £50,000. He will also be expected to pay his *own* legal and printing costs and stamp duties— these can be expected with any business transaction of this nature and are no gain to the Corporation.

The I.C.F.C. provides permanent or long-term capital in the main for buildings and plant, but the provision of working capital is not ruled out where the need for this is more than short-term.

Amounts provided, whether in the form of secured or unsecured loans, preference or ordinary share capital, vary between £5000 and £300,000 on first application. Further applications may increase the Corporation's total investment to £500,000.

Generally speaking the Corporation specialises in giving assistance to the soundly-managed, small company. Possibly the private company whose management is capable of expanding the business, but is unable to do so without additional permanent capital, is the best example of the type of concern which can benefit from the facilities offered by the Corporation.

The flexible policy adopted recognises that not all businesses have the same needs. The loan may be repaid over a period which is agreeable to both the customer and the Corporation; between ten and twenty years is a usual period. Generally a customer is expected to repay by annual instalments: but, again, there is no hard and fast rule; different intervals may be agreed upon. Obviously, though, once an agreement has been finalised a customer will be expected to carry out its provisions.

In addition to the facilities described above, the I.C.F.C. provides plant, machinery, and other fixed assets either by leasing or by hire purchase. It also acts as an Issuing House in sponsoring public flotations for its customers. It also manages the Estate Duties Investment Trust Limited, a specialised body whose "primary object is to make possible the provision, actual or prospective, of the Estate Duty incident on the estates of shareholders in private companies whose holdings are large in relation to their total resources, especially in cases where continuity of control in the same family, or group of proprietors, is a major consideration."* The family can realise part of the interest and yet retain control.

I.C.F.C. also manage Ship Mortgage Finance Company Limited, a Company specialising in loans for British-built ships.

## GOVERNMENT FINANCIAL AID

The Board of Trade are in certain circumstances able to assist a company in the expansion of an existing business or in the planning of a new business *provided* the business concerned gives employment to workers in a selected area, which, for the time being, has been designated a development area by the Government. Generally speaking, the term indicates that there is a problem of present or impending unemployment within the area. A list of development areas may be obtained from the Secretary, The Board of Trade, Distribution of Industry Division, 1 Victoria Street, London, S.W.1.

Assistance available may be summarised as follows:

1. Provision of premises for rent or sale on deferred terms. This is not strictly the provision of finance. Obviously, though, finance is conserved and can be used for a purpose other than obtaining premises; *e.g.* purchase of machinery or materials.

2. If premises are to be built by the applicant then *part* of the cost may be met in the form of a building grant.

3. Loans for both permanent and working capital.

4. Grants to meet the abnormal expenditure involved in setting up business in a development area. These grants are very exceptional and are not payable unless unusual circumstances are present. For this reason they are not discussed further.

Each application for assistance under the headings (1) to (4) is taken on its merits. The following conditions will have to be complied with: (*a*) suitable and continuing employment will be provided by the undertaking; (*b*) the financial assistance is reasonable having regard to the expected extra jobs; (*c*) there are good prospects of the project being successful. Assistance under headings (3) and (4) and, in some cases (2), can only be offered in accordance with the recommendations of the independent Board of Trade Advisory Committee.

In the first instance an application for information should be sent to the Secretary of the Board of Trade at the address shown earlier. A set of booklets published under the collective title *Room to Expand* outlines the schemes and the procedures to follow.

The Board of Trade has considerable power over new developments by virtue of the fact that the siting of any proposed factory or extension which is to exceed 5000 square feet has to be approved. This is done

* Quotation from a Chairman's Report.

by the Board of Trade issuing an Industrial Development Certificate. Withholding of a Certificate can mean that a business is unable to proceed with its proposals. Obviously a way of overcoming the difficulty is to take the project to a development area, where it will normally receive approval.

The amount of the loan which will be made available depends upon the circumstances. The present value of a business including the proposed extension, or, in the case of a new business, the total expected value, will set a limit to the sum that can be obtained. New ventures are eligible for the loans. Provided a good case can be put forward the loan may be quite substantial.

The rate of interest charged on loans is quite reasonable and compares favourably with charges made for other possible methods. The rate is not higher than that currently charged to a first-class commercial borrower for a well-secured loan.

Repayment of the loan can be spread over a reasonable period—five to eight years is the average period. Exceptionally the payment of interest may be deferred for the first year or two.

Before a loan is made the Board of Trade will have to be satisfied as to the soundness of the proposition. Moreover, some form of security will be required. However, there is generally no interference in the management of the business, the only requirement being that the Advisory Committee's officials have regular access to the firm's books and records to check on its financial position and other matters.

On the matter of Government loans some interesting facts emerge from the *Local Employment Acts, 1960* to *1966*, Accounts 1967–68 (H.C., 1968–69, 109, published by H.M.S.O.). During the year ending 31st March, 1968, £8·5 million was paid out in loans and the total loans outstanding at that date was £68·9 million.

All applications for loan assistance are referred by the Board of Trade to the independent Board of Trade Advisory Committee (BOTAC), the address of whose Secretariat is 2 Bunhill Row, London, E.C.1. The officials of the Secretariat are always willing to discuss, even at a preliminary stage, the approach of BOTAC to loan applications. Basically, the criteria which BOTAC expect to find in a successful loan application are:

1. The applicant should have a reasonable stake in the project in the form of equity capital.
2. The project should not be unduly dependent on loan finance.
3. There should be satisfactory evidence of good management.
4. There must be good evidence about the market projects.
5. Trading accounts (for the past five years) should be satisfactory.
6. Forward trading estimates (for the next three years) should, given the assistance requested, show the ability to trade profitably while servicing all obligations.
7. There must be adequate security for the loan.

## AID FROM COMPANIES

A source of capital which is quite important is the provision of finance by another, quite unconnected company or group of companies. Instead of adopting one of the normal approaches of obtaining permanent capital a business may turn to a company which has surplus funds. Sometimes the initiative may come from a group of companies within an industry whose managements feel that they should give some assistance. Readers are advised to study details reported in national newspapers and accountancy journals.

Generally, the reason for seeking finance in this way is a shortage of funds coupled with unfavourable conditions for raising capital in the normal way. In appropriate circumstances the provision of funds by another company may be on more advantageous terms than those obtainable elsewhere, particularly if it is possible to give some benefit to the contributing company. Long-term contracts to purchase that company's products or to supply goods or services at attractive prices are examples of such benefit. There is no doubt that such agreements can be of value provided there is no danger of losing control. The company supplying finance may naturally wish to be represented on the board and it will also wish to take all reasonable steps to safeguard its investment.

One form of finance which is very worthy of mention is that offered by the industrial holding company. A very fine example is the Tilling organisation, generally referred to as "a family of firms." Companies are invited to apply for admission to the group and those who are selected can apparently take advantage of the financial and technical resources available and yet operate as separate units. The advantages of amalgamations are discussed in Chapter 22 which deals with that topic.

## PLOUGHED-BACK PROFITS

There is no doubt that ploughed-back profits, including depreciation provisions and reserves, are a major source of finance. The need to expand cannot be ignored and undoubtedly the cheapest form of finance for expansion comes from a company's own funds.

The main factors which will affect the size of the profits retained in the business are as follows:

1. Total profit earned.

2. Dividend policy followed.

The modern tendency is to stabilise the rate of dividend, thus paying approximately the same return each year on capital contributed. In fixing the rate of dividend which is reasonable, attention should be paid to (*a*) rate of interest available on a "risk-free investment" such as a bank deposit and (*b*) risk involved. The greater the risk the larger should be the rate of dividend. If the latter is maintained at too low a level there may be a danger of a take-over bid and, should retained profits be inadequate to meet the expansion needs, there may be great difficulty in attracting fresh capital.

3. Fixed assets employed—depreciation.

Depreciation is the normal reduction in the value of an asset through use and the effluxion of time. There is an absolute necessity to charge the correct proportion of a fixed asset—the sum "used up" —in each year's accounts (*see* Chapters 26 and 27).

In addition, there is the problem of replacing fixed assets. In times of rising prices, calculation of a realistic profit figure requires that capital is maintained intact by appropriating a suitable sum to reserve.

4. Nature of business.

Many businesses require large sums to be spent on research and development and/or selling and advertising. Others may be of the type which demands a constant growth by internal expansion—new factories and other fixed assets—or by absorbing other companies. This could be brought about by the need to diversify, to take advantage of large scale production, or by some other economic factor. Yet another possible type is the business, such as the private limited company, which cannot obtain capital funds from the public, but instead must depend upon retained profits or loans. Since the latter may be undesirable on the grounds of cost or fear of loss of control there will be no alternative except to plough back as much profit as possible.

5. Reserves earmarked for a specific purpose.

Reserves are retained profits accumulated over a period of time. They *exclude* (*a*) provisions which are amounts set aside to meet depreciation or a "known liability of which the amount cannot be determined with substantial accuracy"* and (*b*) amounts outstanding and unpaid (liabilities) which can be determined with substantial accuracy, *e.g.* rent and rates accrued due. The provisions and liabilities are a legitimate *charge against* profits whereas reserves are simply an *appropriation* of profit. Besides ploughing back profits to create a strong financial structure, essential to weather any trade depression, a company may earmark the retained profits for specific functions. The need to do this will tend to vary with the nature of the company, a matter dealt with briefly in the previous section. Some of the most usual reasons for reserves are as follows:

> (i) Replacement of fixed and current assets in times of rising prices, discussed in (3) above.
> (ii) Possibility of obsolescence of fixed assets.

---

* *Companies Act, 1948,* Eighth Schedule (para. 27.).

(iii) Dividend equalisation. Instead of paying a low dividend when there have been adverse trading conditions and a high dividend when profits are high a stabilising device—a dividend equalisation reserve—can be used. In prosperous years this equalisation reserve can be used for payment of a dividend in the lean years.

(iv) Redemption of loans such as Debentures or capital; *e.g.* redeemable preference shares.

(v) Future taxation.

In addition there may be reserves arising not from the transfer of profit, but from accounting transactions or adjustments; *e.g.* when a company is purchased and net assets exceed the price paid, then the difference should be regarded as a capital reserve. Another example arises from the revaluation of fixed assets, changing from historical costs to replacement costs. In this case the "profit" is treated as a capital reserve.* It is interesting to note that any capital reserve cannot be distributed in the form of dividends whereas revenue reserves can be so treated.

Some of the matters covered in (i) to (v) above involve the exercise of financial policy and management. Depending upon the views taken by the directors the amounts set aside may vary in size; one board may regard a certain figure for reserve as being prudent, whereas another would regard the same figure as being quite inadequate. Wherever judgment and opinions have a bearing on amounts to be set aside then there must inevitably be differences of opinion. When advising on this matter the management accountant must fully consider the current circumstances. Prudence must necessarily have an important influence on the advice tendered. However, there is more to it than this: the expected rate of expansion may require a very substantial ploughing back of profits and, even if such action means dividend restraint, it should still be followed. In the long term the shareholder should, of course, gain from the building up of reserves and general expansion.

When referring to Balance Sheets the student should appreciate that separate reserves may not be given for each item listed above. Instead, the only reserves which may be shown would be: Profit and Loss Account Balance; General Reserve, and Reserve for Tax Adjustments. Any dividing of the General Reserve could be shown in the books of account, although not on the Balance Sheet. However, it should be noted that separate headings to distinguish between Capital Reserves and Revenue Reserves are no longer essential.

* Eighth Schedule to *Companies Act, 1948*, defines capital reserve as follows: "the expression 'capital reserve' shall not include any amount regarded as free for distribution through the profit and loss account." Apparently this is construed as covering legal capital reserves; *e.g.* Share Premiums, as well as policy capital reserves.

## EXAMINATION QUESTIONS

1. Describe the various sources from which finance may be obtained by a company incorporated in the United Kingdom and indicate briefly the circumstances in which the use of each source would be appropriate.

*(I.C.W.A.)*

2. Your company is considering a further expansion of business in the near future which will necessitate finding additional capital over a period of several years. As controller you have to advise the board on possible sources of funds.

Write a short report and mention factors which might influence the decision as to which additional sources of capital should be sought. *(A.C.C.A.)*

3. Your company is about to commence a subsidiary business and has provided finance in respect of the acquisition of the necessary fixed assets and you are now required to advise the directors as to the additional amount which should be made available for working capital.

You are provided with the following estimates for the year 19... and you are informed that an overdraft limit of £1,500 has been arranged with the company's bankers.

| | Average period of credit | Estimate for 19... £ |
|---|---|---|
| Purchases of Materials ... ... ... | 6 weeks | 26,000 |
| Wages ... ... ... ... ... ... | 1½ weeks | 19,500 |
| Overheads— | | |
| Rent, etc. ... ... ... ... ... | 6 months | 1,000 |
| Directors' and Manager's Salaries ... | 1 month | 3,600 |
| Travelling and Office Salaries ... ... | 2 weeks | 4,550 |
| Travellers' Commission ... ... ... | 3 months | 2,000 |
| Other Overheads ... ... ... ... | 2 months | 6,000 |
| Sales—Cash ... ... ... ... ... | — | 1,400 |
| Credit ... ... ... ... ... | 7 weeks | 65,000 |
| Average amount of Stocks and Work-in-Progress ... ... ... ... ... | | 3,000 |
| Average amount of Undrawn Profits ... | | 3,100 |

Sales were made at an even rate over the year.

You are required to prepare from the above figures and information, a table for submission to your directors, giving an estimate of the average amount of working capital which they should provide. *(S.C.A.)*

4. A firm of transport hauliers wish to spend £100,000 on buying new heavy vehicles for their fleet. They have been offered leasing terms by one of the National leasing companies, but their Joint Stock Bank have offered to finance the acquisitions on a normal bank overdraft basis.

Advise the Directors what information is required to make the decision between leasing and purchase. *(A.C.C.A.)*

# CHAPTER 10

## MARGINAL COSTING

### INTRODUCTION

MARGINAL Costing* is a special *technique* which may be used in conjunction with costing *methods*—job or process—or with other techniques such as Standard Costing or Budgetary Control. The importance of the technique lies in the assistance it may give in solving managerial problems. Many of these are discussed in this and other chapters.

### DEFINITION AND USEFULNESS

There is some difficulty in defining in precise terms what is meant by "Marginal Costing." From enquiries made and guidance given in accountancy journals and textbooks it would appear that the number of businesses which follow Marginal Costing principles to the exclusion of all others is in the minority. On the other hand, there is general acceptance that separation of fixed and variable costs can assist materially in controlling costs and arriving at sound decisions. Therefore, it would seem that a large number of concerns do use one or more of the principles which form the basis of a complete system of Marginal Costing. Furthermore, quite often the employment of these principles is not construed as evidence that Marginal Costing is in existence. There is no reference to "marginal costs," but instead the equivalent term— variable costs—is employed. In other words, Marginal Costing is subordinate to some other method or technique such as Process Costing and/or Standard Costing. Whether Marginal Costing truly exists in these circumstances is a debatable point and conflicting views would probably be held by different accountants.

Bearing these possible differences of opinion in mind the best possible approach to defining Marginal Costing is to list the main features normally found in a complete system of Marginal Costing. If only some of the features or principles are present then there is *partial* Marginal Costing.

The technique of Marginal Costing involves two principal steps:

(*a*) Determination of marginal costs;

(*b*) Arrangement of these costs in the most suitable manner for showing the state of profitability and enabling management to reach conclusions which are conceived on a sound basis; *i.e.* on the true costs of carrying out the particular action.

* Also known as Direct Costing, Variable Costing, Out-of-pocket Costing Differential Costing, Incremental Costing.

*In addition*, there are certain features which are an essential part of a complete system of Marginal Costing. They are summarised here and explained in detail later in this and other chapters. Briefly then these features are as follows:

(*a*) The marginal (variable) costs are regarded as the costs of the products.*

(*b*) Stocks of work-in-progress and finished goods are valued on the basis of marginal costs.*

(*c*) Prices are based on marginal costs plus the contribution.

(*d*) A special form of Profit and Loss Account or statement is employed (Marginal Profit and Loss Account).

(*e*) Profit is calculated in a special way. Marginal costs are deducted from Sales Revenue to arrive at the "contribution" (defined below) which meets fixed costs, any surplus being profit.

(*f*) Break-even techniques and calculations which show the effect of increasing or reducing the volume of output or of changing the mixture or types of products are an integral part of the technique.

(*g*) The relative "profitability" of departments or products is usually based on a study of the contributions made available by each department or product.

These steps and features require further explanation. An understanding of what is meant by "marginal costs" is essential. There are two possible meanings. First, they may be regarded as prime costs plus variable overhead costs; *i.e. all* variable costs of whatever type they may be. The second definition gives a special meaning to these variable costs. However, in this connection it may be better to use the singular form—"marginal cost" (*not costs*). If a definite output is taken then the marginal cost is the amount (variable cost) by which total cost changes as a result of producing one unit more or one unit less. In this context "unit" may mean a single unit, 100, 1 gross, 1000 or some other convenient multiple. Accountants also use the terms "differential" and "incremental" to describe the addition to total cost due to increasing or reducing output.†

There is generally no great difficulty in ascertaining prime costs. Direct materials can be traced by means of material requisitions and direct wages by the use of job clock cards or time sheets. Variable overhead costs tend to vary with changes in output so there should be no problem in defining these. Generally the greatest difficulty is the

* Generally with the *exclusion* of variable selling and distribution costs.

† Here the concern is with marginal costing only. In Chapter 13—"Determination of Optimum Output"—the economist's and the accountant's approaches are compared. Study of the relevant paragraphs in that chapter may be appropriate at this stage.

separation of the variable element from semi-variable overhead costs. The latter vary with output, but in an irregular manner; this is because a proportion of the particular cost is of a fixed nature whereas the remainder is variable. The methods of separating these costs are covered later.

How the costs are to be arranged depends upon the problem to be solved, a matter which is illustrated in the chapter which gives problems and suggested solutions (*see* page 286). There is, however, a fundamental arrangement of the costs which is common to all marginal systems. Fixed costs are kept quite separate from the variable (marginal) costs. In the books of account and on accounting reports and statements this separation is an invariable procedure. When calculating profit the same principle is followed. The revenue from sales is taken and from it is deducted marginal costs leaving what is known as the "contribution." If many products are made then each earns its own contribution. All contributions are assumed to be channelled into a fund from which fixed costs are met, any surplus being, of course, the profit for the period under review.

The principal differences between orthodox or "total costs" costing* and Marginal Costing are shown in the flow diagrams given in Figs. 30 and 31. In the case of orthodox costing it will be seen that *all* overhead costs—variable and fixed—are apportioned first to cost centres and then to products. On the other hand, when Marginal Costing is used only the variable overhead costs are charged to products. In *all* systems the prime costs are assumed to relate to actual products and are, therefore, traceable and chargeable to such products. In the flow diagrams there are two producing centres, one service centre and three products. The costs are apportioned to all centres and then the service costs are transferred to producing centres: the latter is repeated in the second column of the diagrams to illustrate the procedures followed.

When Marginal Costing is used in its pure form there is no apportioning of fixed overhead costs to products. The justification for this is based on two facts: first, that fixed costs relate to a particular period of time and should, therefore, be charged to that period and to no other and, secondly, that there is no method which is capable of *accurately* apportioning fixed costs to products. There is no doubt that both reasons carry considerable weight and, therefore, may be adequate to justify the fullest possible use being made of Marginal Costing. However, not to be forgotten is the fact that variable overhead costs and, where unsuitable costing methods are employed, even prime costs, cannot be traced to products with any great accuracy. In all costing systems absolute accuracy is extremely difficult to achieve and, even if possible, may be too costly to justify its being obtained.

* Also known as "absorption costing," indicating that all costs are absorbed in the product costs.

## ADVANTAGES

Arising principally from the fact that fixed costs are not apportioned to products a number of advantages are claimed.* These are summarised below:

1. Marginal costs remain the same per unit of product irrespective of the volume of production.

When fixed costs are charged to products the unit cost varies from one month to another simply because the number of units produced is different; e.g. if in January a business produced 1000 units of a product with a total fixed overhead of £1000 and variable costs of £1·00 per unit, then the total unit cost is £2·00.

If in February, 2000 units are produced, the total fixed costs remaining the same, then the total *unit* cost is £1·50; with Marginal Costing the unit cost will remain at £1·00.

However, a fact which is often overlooked and yet is extremely important is that variable costs *do not* always remain constant per unit of output. Instead they may fluctuate from time to time for two principal reasons. In the first place there may be changes in the value of money. In a period of rising prices it is almost inevitable that material price and wage rates should increase and, therefore, cause marginal costs to increase. Secondly, the internal conditions under which the business is operating may also influence the variable costs. After a certain level of output has been reached increasing costs will tend to apply. These may arise from overtime working, shift work, and excessive depreciation and maintenance of plant and machinery.† In addition, abnormal increases in selling costs are not unknown: an attempt to push sales beyond a certain point may incur a disproportionate increase in such costs. Clearly, these observations qualify advantage (1) above. In certain circumstances they may in fact invalidate the argument for Marginal Costing, cancelling the advantage altogether.

For the advantage to be a valid one a particular point of time must be taken. If this is done, the conditions and circumstances will not have had an opportunity to change. The longer the period being considered the more likelihood is there of costs behaving in an "unusual" manner.

It should be appreciated that the unit costs will not change from one period to another if Standard Costing is employed, so Marginal Costing is not alone in enjoying stability of costs.

2. When predetermined overhead costs are used as is generally the case when job costing is employed, there is the complication of under or over-absorption of overhead costs. Marginal Costing avoids this.

Overhead costs may be absorbed on the basis of machine hours, direct labour hours, a percentage on direct labour cost or a percentage

---

* The advantages should not be taken at their face value without also considering the possible limitations.

† Covered in more detail in Chapter 13, "Determination of Optimum Output."

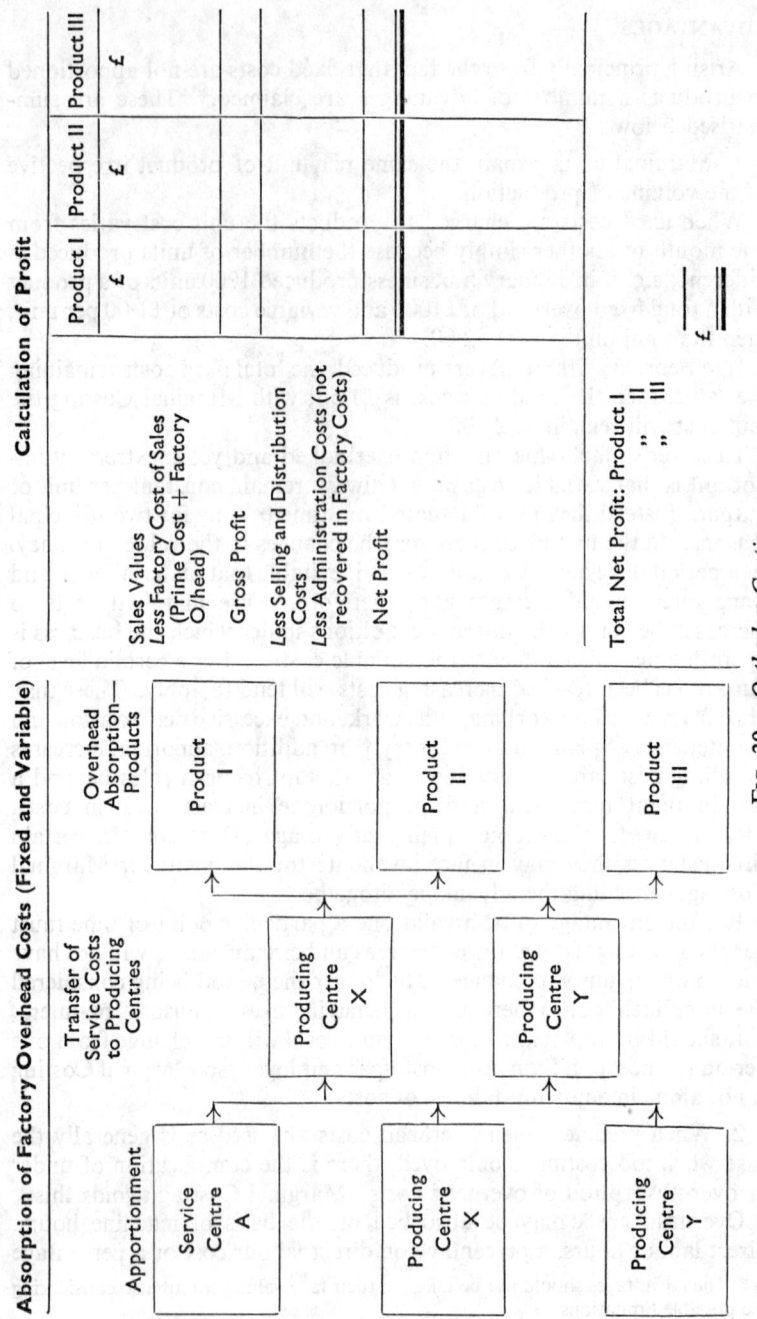

FIG. 30.—Orthodox Costing

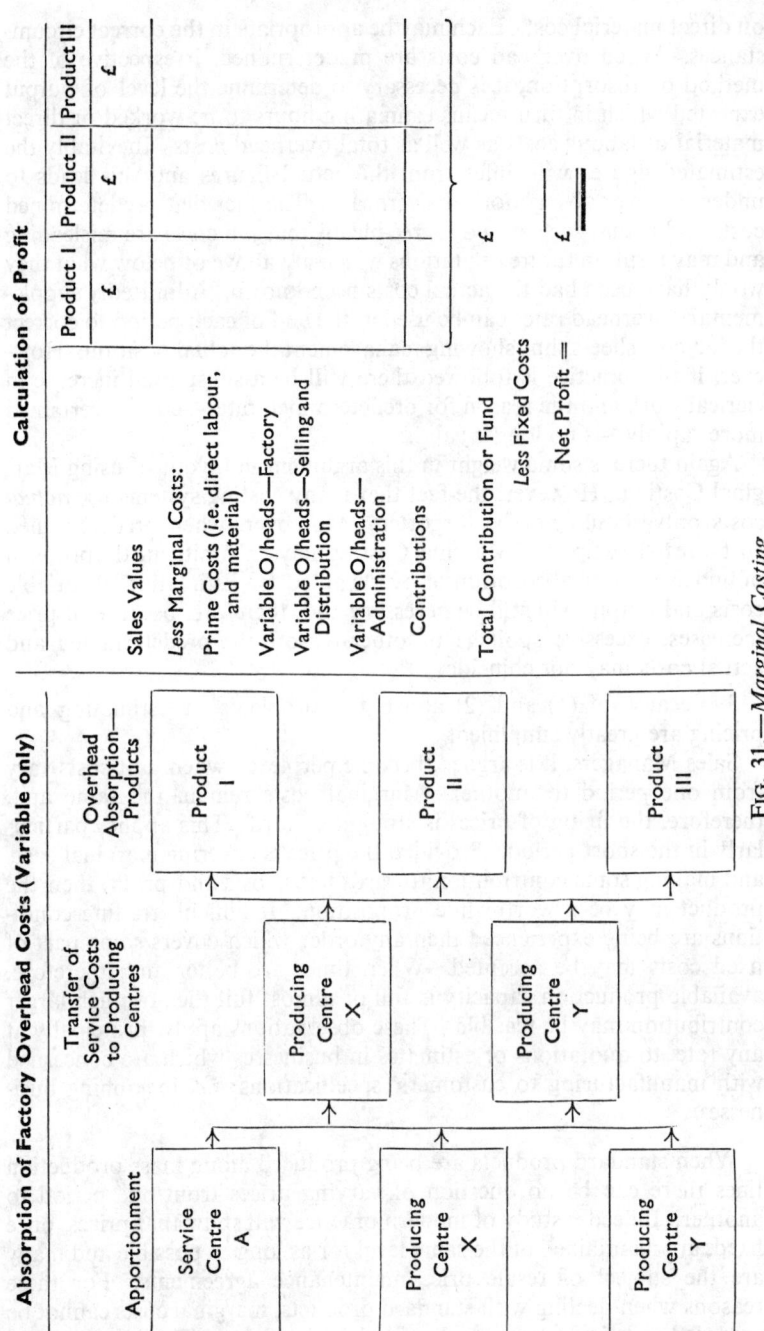

FIG. 31.—*Marginal Costing*

**Absorption of Factory Overhead Costs (Variable only)**

| Apportionment | Transfer of Service Costs to Producing Centres | Overhead Absorption— Products |
|---|---|---|
| Service Centre A | Producing Centre X | Product I |
| Producing Centre X | Producing Centre Y | Product II |
| Producing Centre Y | | Product III |

**Calculation of Profit**

| | Product I | Product II | Product III |
|---|---|---|---|
| | £ | £ | £ |
| Sales Values | | | |
| *Less* Marginal Costs: | | | |
| Prime Costs (*i.e.* direct labour, and material) | | | |
| Variable O/heads—Factory | | | |
| Variable O/heads—Selling and Distribution | | | |
| Variable O/heads—Administration | | | |
| Contributions | | | |

Total Contribution or Fund £

*Less* Fixed Costs £

Net Profit = £

on direct material cost. Each may be appropriate in the correct circumstances. When overhead costs are predetermined, irrespective of the method of absorption, it is necessary to determine the level of output expected which in turn means estimating hours to be worked or direct material or labour costs as well as total overhead costs. Inevitably the estimated figures will differ from the actual figures and this leads to under- or over-absorption of overheads. The fact that predetermined costs and actual costs do not agree means that job costs are misleading and may result in future quotations which are above or below what they would have been had the actual costs been known. Admittedly supplementary overhead rates can be used at the end of each period to correct the job cost sheets thus showing management the actual position. However, if this practice is followed there will be a substantial increase in clerical work and the reason for predetermined rates—costs ascertained more rapidly—is no longer valid.

Again there is some weight in this argument in favour of using Marginal Costing. However, the fact that many costing systems use *actual* costs only should not be forgotten. Moreover, when predetermined costs are to be employed Marginal Costing may only mitigate the problem of under- or over-absorption of overhead costs. Estimation of variable costs and output will still be necessary and, therefore, because of price increases, excessive spoilage or other reason, the predetermined and actual costs may not coincide.

3. Because of (1) and (2) above the problems of estimating and pricing are greatly simplified.

Sales Managers, it is argued, become perplexed when unit costs vary from one period to another. Marginal costs remain the same and, therefore, the fixing of prices is straightforward. This applies particularly in the short period. Provided the price is covering marginal costs and making some contribution towards fixed costs and profit, then the product may be a worthwhile proposition. If difficult trading conditions are being experienced then any order which covers some part of fixed costs may be accepted. When times are better and, therefore, available production capacity is full or almost full then a much larger contribution may be feasible. These observations apply, principally at any rate, to quotations or estimates in businesses which are concerned with manufacturing to customers' specifications; *i.e.* in jobbing businesses.

When standard products are being produced along mass production lines there can be no question of varying prices from one period to another. Indeed a study of modern practice will show that prices, once fixed, are maintained at the same level for as long as possible and many are the subject of resale price maintenance agreements. For these reasons when dealing with standard products, marginal costs cannot be regarded as being a very good guide in price fixing. The prices should be so fixed that they cover variable costs and fixed costs over a long period. Accordingly, consideration of total costs of products, not merely marginal costs, will be necessary. In actual fact, of course, for many standard products the fixed overhead is really charged to each cost centre or process and not to each separate individual product. Thus, for example, a certain process may produce 500 units per period. If there are thirteen periods in each accounting year then the total fixed overhead for the cost centre (the process) will be divided by thirteen and the amount allocated to the process; subsequently total cost for the period may be divided by the number of units to give an average unit cost. Naturally there may be small variations in the volume of output from one period to another. However, over a year a definite volume of output should be possible and the periodic average cost may be used as a guide to assessing the reasonableness of the price being charged or to be charged.

Even with jobbing production, marginal costs may only be a useful guide in the short term. Over the long period fixed costs as well as marginal costs have to be covered by the price charged for each job. Only by considering total costs will it be possible to see that an adequate profit is earned by each job.

In connection with using marginal (incremental) costs Mr. John C. Dewar in a letter in *The Cost Accountant** sums up the attitude of many accountants when he states:

"Whilst not denying that the incremental cost approach is useful when making the best of a bad deal, I would always look for a recovery of total cost plus fair profit. I am severely critical of the omission of fixed costs and sunk costs. In the one-man business producing one product all costs are attributable to the product and overhead costs are at a minimum; if the order book is suddenly cleared, the proprietor can do a bit of selling, or catch up on his accounting, machine overhaul, or tool making; if business continues bad he will then take steps to cut his overhead costs, accepting orders at lower prices to recoup those fixed costs he considers it policy to continue; sunk costs he can do nothing about, but at present he has no new outgoings on that score. Soon, however, even sunk cost figures; his rent is due next month and he badly needs a new drilling machine. He must decide whether there is a market at a price which will give him total cost recovery plus fair profit; there are a number of possibilities, *e.g.* increased production selling at lower price, change of product. But total cost is what figures in his decision, not incremental cost taking present fixed and sunk costs as static. In the highly specialised multi-product concern, the impact of fixed and sunk costs is much more serious and much more fluid.

The production of wealth arises through the application of human effort to existing resources. The measurement of product is the efforts applied and resources consumed. But wealth is only created if its value exceeds input of effort and resources; output sales value must exceed input costs: and here, input cost is the total current value of effort paid for over the production

* February 1961, Volume 39; No. 2.

cycle and resources consumed. Material lying in store and labour contracted for in advance are just as fixed or sunk as machine depreciation or rent; if total cost were to be discounted to incremental cost in this way then using incremental costs would lead to the wrong decisions and almost inevitably to the bankruptcy of the concern. Total cost must be recovered at the end of the day, and it is therefore vital to bring to management's attention the total cost; any decision which has the effect of recovering less than this cost means eventual loss and to avoid this loss management is bound to examine possible alternative courses—more profitable utilisation or cut-back. When considering changes in product-mix, increasing production or other proposals calculated to increase the output/input ratio, the total costs would be reassessed to cover the new situation; cost standards would then be updated."

4. Exclusion of fixed overhead cost from the cost of products means that work-in-progress and finished goods are valued much more realistically than when total costs are employed.

The fixed costs are incurred on a time basis and should, therefore, be written off within the period that they are incurred. Only by doing this—so the argument runs—can each accounting period be charged with the correct total cost and the true profit calculated.

Unfortunately, those who use these arguments in support of Marginal Costing tend to ignore the fact that many variable costs are also incurred on a time basis. Furthermore, products being made do consume time which is being paid for by fixed—as well as variable—costs. If fixed costs are not apportioned to products then the benefits being received by each are not given due recognition and a false impression may be created. Only by calculating total costs (it may be argued) will it be possible to see the relative costs and degrees of profitability of each product.

No doubt other related arguments could be used for and against employing Marginal Costing. It is more important to notice that the Marginal Costing basis of stock valuation may be appropriate in some circumstances, but not in others. In other words, the dogmatic approach to stock valuation is wrong: there is no *one* right way; each business has its own particular needs and whether these are best met by Marginal Costing is a question to be settled by the accountant concerned. On this matter guidance may be obtained from Recommendation No. 22 of the Institute of Chartered Accountants in England and Wales issued in November 1960. The *Duple Motor Bodies* case is also pertinent to the problem of stock valuation (a subject covered in Chapter 25).

Here it is very important to notice that with Marginal Costing there is a convention generally observed that permits only the variable costs relating to manufacture to appear in the valuation of stocks of work-in-progress and finished goods. In other words, selling costs and finance costs are not included in the valuations. Presumably this rule would also apply to administration costs although if part of these are regarded as relating to manufacture and are, therefore, charged to products (*i.e.*

work-in-progress account) then they would be included in the value of stocks. On the other hand, if administration costs are treated as fixed costs then they would be written off to Profit and Loss Account and would not appear in the value of stocks.

5. The effect on profit of producing a greater or smaller volume of output can be ascertained without great difficulty.

Break-even calculations and break-even charts are the most used techniques and these are explained later. There is no doubt that this advantage can be of great value to successful profit planning. However, there are possible disadvantages and limitations which are discussed at the same time as break-even techniques.

6. The division of costs into fixed and variable, facilitates cost control.

Flexible budgeting relies on clearly distinguishing between those costs which vary with changes in output and those which tend to remain constant irrespective of the volume of output. However, if the flexible budget and related notes shown on page 91 are studied it will be quite apparent that the classification of costs according to whether they are fixed or variable is not limited to when Marginal Costing is employed. When budgeting or Standard Costing is used it is quite usual to have this classification of costs.

The main reason why control is made easier is that recognition is given to the *nature* of the cost. Fixed costs more often than not arise from policy decisions—*e.g.* rent payable would come from deciding to obtain leasehold instead of freehold; managerial salaries would be based on salary policy and negotiation by top management—and for this reason are controllable only by the highest level of management. On the other hand, variable costs are incurred by all levels of management and by operators. The responsibility for variable costs can be traced with a substantial degree of certainty and this allows the necessary control to be exercised.

7. Reports to management are based on sales figures not production figures. Unless products are sold a plant does not earn profit; therefore it is better to make comparisons of efficiency on the basis of sales and related costs not affected by stocks.

Other possible advantages of Marginal Costing will become apparent from the descriptions of the techniques and calculations given later.

## POSSIBLE DISADVANTAGES

Besides the limitations and disadvantages explained in conjunction with the alleged advantages there are others which should also be noted. There is no doubt that Marginal Costing can be a very useful tool of management, but it must be used in the appropriate circumstances and with a full knowledge of its limitations.

Possible limitations additional to those outlined in the previous section are summarised below:

1. The effects of failing to achieve, or exceeding, the normal activity or volume of production are only illustrated in an indirect manner.

Standard Costing with its volume (capacity) variance may give much more information on this important matter.

2. Great emphasis is placed on the selling function, but the achievements of the manufacturing divisions are subordinated. Production as well as sales should be taken into consideration when viewing the state of efficiency.

3. The break-even techniques and charts used are subject to limitations which are often ignored when these techniques are being employed. This matter is covered in Chapter 11.

## DETERMINATION OF MARGINAL COSTS

Marginal costs, as defined earlier, are all variable costs incurred in production, selling and administration. These are the direct material costs, direct labour costs and, in addition, variable overhead costs—all tend to vary in direct relation to the volume of output.

Variable overhead costs are not always easy to discern. Examples of these are listed below: they should serve as a guide to the nature of variable costs. It should be remembered that many costs are semi-variable (or semi-fixed) and, therefore, the variable element from each of these has to be separated: examples of these are also given.

**VARIABLE OVERHEAD COSTS:**

| | |
|---|---|
| Indirect Labour. | Power and Light.* |
| Factory Supplies. | Insurance on Stocks.* |
| Overtime Premium. | Inspection.* |
| Lost Time. | Spoilage.* |
| Repairs and Maintenance.* | |

Fixed overhead costs are those costs which tend to remain the same in total irrespective of the volume of output. In actual fact there are very few costs which are truly fixed. There are many reasons why this may be so. The longer the period involved the more likely it is that price changes and policy changes will take place. These inevitably result in increases or reductions in fixed costs. If, for example, policy determines that a factory is to be extended then once this decision is implemented fixed costs are bound to increase by a certain amount and this is so no matter what volume of output is produced. For this reason it is not surprising that fixed costs are sometimes called "policy costs."

* These *may* be regarded as semi-variable overhead costs.

Because of the long period tendency for even fixed costs to display some variability, many writers have stated that in the long run *all* costs are variable. There is no doubt that this is true, but it should be remembered that the accountant who is compiling a budget or arranging cost data so as to aid management decisions is normally concerned with a short period—a particular day, week, month, quarter, or year. In addition, the short period variations in output are unlikely to be very wide and this again makes the definition of fixed costs much more realistic than would otherwise be possible.

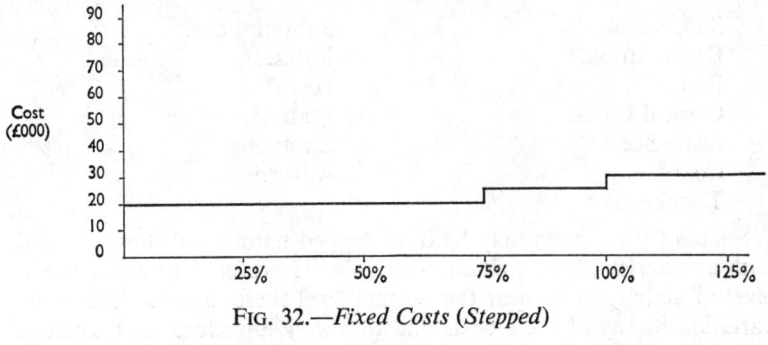

FIG. 32.—*Fixed Costs* (*Stepped*)

NOTE

The particular cost is fixed at £20,000 up to 75% activity, but over 75% the fixed costs are £25,000. The third step, above 100%, shows that costs increase to £30,000. It is important to notice that within each output range specified the total cost does not vary.

Even so, the possibility of variations in the volume of output should be recognised and it is with this view in mind that another term is sometimes used—"stepped costs." Within a well-defined range of output the costs are fixed but once a new range is reached the costs change. Thus, for example, one foreman and two supervisors may be able to deal with an output which represents 70 to 100% of normal capacity. On the other hand, from 101 to 105% one foreman and *three* supervisors may be necessary. Over each of these defined ranges of output the costs are of a fixed nature (*see* Fig. 32). Clerical costs may behave in a similar manner. When dealing with this type of cost great care has to be taken to determine the point at which the increase in costs is likely to take place. Unfortunately, there is no generally accepted definition of the terms being dealt with; sometimes these fixed costs which are of a stepped nature are called semi-variable costs. Definition of the latter is appropriate at this stage.

Semi-variable costs are hybrid costs; each is made up of a fixed element and a fully variable element. There is a tendency for the cost to vary with output, but the variation is irregular. This is to be expected because the fixed and variable elements are combined. However, when the two elements are separated it is usually possible to determine the degree of variability of the variable cost, *i.e.* at a rate per unit of output, per standard hour, machine hour, or other suitable basis. How this separation is accomplished is described later in this section. Before this is done a list of fixed overhead costs is given. Just as with the variable overheads the costs given are simply examples; the list is not intended to be exhaustive—different types of business tend to exhibit varying characteristics and, therefore, costs, so a complete coverage would take up a great deal of space.

### FIXED OVERHEAD COSTS:

| | |
|---|---|
| Supervision. | Subscriptions. |
| Depreciation.* | Rates. |
| Rent. | Heat.* |
| Clerical Costs. | Water.* |
| Insurance.* | Electricity.* |
| Coal.* | Advertising. |
| Telephones.* | |

Some of these costs may be of a stepped nature and those marked with an asterisk (*) may be semi-variable. However, for a well-defined level of activity at or near the normal level there may be little or no variation in any of these costs and they *may*, therefore, be treated as being entirely fixed.

### FLEXIBILITY OF DEFINITION

Marginal Costing may be an integral part of the accounting system. If this is so then it will be necessary—if valid comparisons are to be made and trends observed—for variable and fixed costs to be defined quite clearly. This implies a certain lack of flexibility of definition: in fact, if stock valuation and contribution and profit calculations are to be based on the figures, consistency is very desirable.

However, when considering management decisions a different approach may be necessary. This is the case even when Marginal Costing is not integrated into the accounting system, but, instead, is used as and when required for dealing with special problems. These are being referred to in accounting literature as *ad hoc* questions or problems and not, unnaturally, the collection and analysis of costs to answer the specific problem is known as an *ad hoc* investigation. In these circumstances a flexible approach is necessary in determining which costs are variable and which are fixed. For a particular problem certain variable costs may be quite fixed. Thus, for example, direct labour cost normally regarded as being of a variable nature may be quite fixed in particular circumstances. If a company has entered into a contract to guarantee employment to its workers for, say, three months, then if business is depressed to the point where there is little or no work being done due to lack of orders the direct labour cost becomes very much a fixed cost. Accordingly, if an order can be obtained which covers variable costs (other than direct labour) and makes some contribution towards fixed costs it could be worth accepting. Notice though that all variable costs as per the conventional definition are *not* being covered.

Examples need not be limited to trade recessions—although this does appear to be the time when Marginal Costing is used most frequently. If a business has a full order book acceptance of further business may result in overtime working, shift working, extension of plant or other extra costs. For the purpose of deciding whether or not to accept additional business, any resultant extra costs should possibly be regarded as variable costs even though they are normally of a fixed nature. The important point is that the variation in cost is brought about by the extra orders and, therefore, in this sense there is a variable cost which should be covered by the revenue to be received from additional sales. In this connection it is logical to consider whether the extra costs are attributable to one particular order or to a number and, if the latter, to what extent each order incurs responsibility for the costs.

### SEPARATION OF FIXED AND VARIABLE ELEMENTS

In order to determine the marginal (variable) costs any semi-variable costs must be separated into their fixed and variable elements. The variable proportion becomes part of the marginal costs.

One way of separating the fixed and variable elements is by what is known as the "high-low method." Past records are used to determine the appropriate cost at two different levels of activity. As with all the methods, each type of expense has to be considered separately.

A simple example is given below:

| Activity | Semi-Variable Cost |
|----------|--------------------|
|          | £                  |
| 100      | 400                |
| 80       | 380                |

Calculation of the fixed and variable elements involves consideration of the increase in activity and the increase in cost; *i.e.* 20 units increase for a £20 increase in cost. This shows a variable cost per unit of £1. The fixed proportion is clearly £300.

The fact that only two points of activity are taken usually implies that the past records are incapable of supplying further information—a disadvantage in itself for there is no way of checking the degree of accuracy obtained in the calculation. If, as the name of the method suggests, a truly low figure and a high figure are taken (this is not so in the example) then there is more chance of error occurring. Moreover, it is very unlikely that a business will normally operate at a capacity of, say, 10%—it would soon go out of existence if this happened for long. For these reasons there may be great difficulty in ascertaining the low figure.

Another possible failing is the assumption that a linear relationship exists with the variable costs; *i.e.* that each unit of output will incur the same variable cost. At different levels of activity this may not be the case. Furthermore, which two points will give the best results is difficult to determine. The levels 120 units and 30 units may give somewhat different results from the combination of 100 and 80 shown above. If the method is to be used—and this procedure cannot be recommended —it would appear to be better to take two points which are within the normal range of activity rather than two extremes neither of which is ever reached except in unusual circumstances.

The more accurate methods of separating the fixed and variable elements have already been covered in *Standard Costing* and the text is reproduced below:

    1. Regression or Scattergraph Charts, plotting a line by inspection.
    2. Least Squares with or without Regression Charts.

Flexible budgeting makes use of these techniques, any "gaps" being covered by interpolation or extrapolation.

For each type of semi-variable cost an attempt is made to show the correlation which exists between production and the incurring of expenditure. Neither charts nor least squares are perfect, for there are factors, other than volume of production, which may influence expenditure incurred. For example, in one month there may be an exceptionally long run of rejected parts, but, in another, very few. This and similar irregular occurrences can clearly negate any conclusions that may be reached from the figures determined by *any* method used for separating the fixed and variable cost elements.

### PROBLEM: SEPARATION OF FIXED AND VARIABLE ELEMENTS

| Past 6 months | Semi-variable cost (power) | Volume of production (units of output or standard hours) |
|---|---|---|
| | £ | |
| January | 2800 | 3000 |
| February | 2500 | 2800 |
| March | 3000 | 3200 |
| April | 2000 | 1800 |
| May | 2100 | 1900 |
| June | 3200 | 3500 |

**REGRESSION CHARTS**

The procedure for preparing a Regression Chart is enumerated below.

1. *On the horizontal axis of the chart, plot the volume of production or sales*

The figures used may be physical units or sterling values. Alternatively, activity may be expressed in terms of standard hours. Since the standard overhead rate is likely to be "so much per hour," the use of the budgeted number of the latter on the chart is likely to prove very useful.

## 2. On the vertical axis plot the overhead cost

The class intervals for both production data and costs will largely be determined by the size of the figures in the problem being solved. Thus, for example, when reasonably small sums are involved, the costs may be graduated in intervals of £50, i.e. £0–£50–£100, etc. When quite large figures are being dealt with, the scale may be, say £0–£200–£400–£600, etc. The object must be to keep the chart within reasonable dimensions and, at the same time, be able to use figures, when calculating the degree of correlation, which are small enough to be of value.

## 3. Produce cost and production or sales schedule

Obtain a schedule of figures of, say, the past six or twelve months, relating to:

(a) Overhead cost incurred each month.
(b) Production or sales for each month.

## 4. Plot the first point on the chart

Referring to the schedule in (3), take the overhead cost for the first month, say, January and find the appropriate point on the vertical axis on the chart. Similarly, take the production figure (units, sterling, or standard hours) for January and then "match" the cost and production figures on the chart, plotting a point where the two meet. An example of this is shown in Fig. 33. On the chart the £2800 and 3000 units are taken together and the point of meeting shown.

## 5. Plot subsequent points

Each month is dealt with as in (4) until all the points have been plotted.

## 6. Draw regression line

By inspection, draw a straight line through the points plotted, or through the mean of all points, with the same number of points, of equal distance from it, on each side of the line. When drawing the regression line any abnormal costs may be disregarded.

## 7. Establish fixed cost

The point where the regression line intersects the vertical axis is taken to be the amount of the fixed cost, i.e. approximately £850 in Fig. 33.

Clearly the slightest bias exhibited in drawing the line will make a difference of £100 in fixed cost. This fact is a serious objection to the method.

I

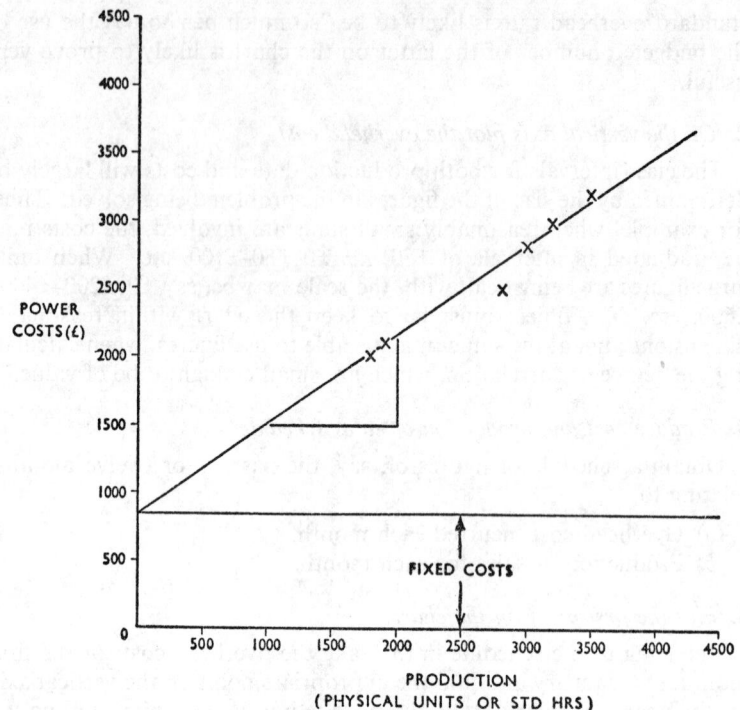

FIG. 33.—*Regression Chart*
*Separation of Fixed and Variable Elements*

This unit cost may be checked by noting that an increase of 4000 units will result in an increase in total variable cost of £2650, which is approximately £0·65 per unit.

No attempt has been made to obtain exactness. As indicated earlier, the variable unit cost can only be an approximation.

## USE OF CHART

The degree of correlation may now be seen. Referring to the horizontal axis, it will be possible to see the extent of an increase in variable costs which follows an increase in output. For example, on the chart an increase in output of 1000 units results in approximately £650, indicating that the variable cost per unit is £0·65 (*see* lines forming triangle).

### Solution

The Regression Chart shown indicates that each additional unit will result in a variable cost of approximately £0·65. For any activity the cost equation FC + (U × VC) will apply. FC = Fixed Cost, U = Units of Output or Standard Hours and VC = Variable Cost per unit. For an output of 1000 units the cost structure will therefore be £850 + (1000 × £0·65) = £850 + £650 = £1500, whereas for 2000 units the cost will be £850 + (2000 × £0·65) or £2150.

In the problem the volume of production has been shown as units of output *or* standard hours. Unless each unit of output has a standard time of one hour the two will obviously not coincide: normally one *or* the other will have to be used. In the example it has been assumed that they are the same, *i.e.* one unit takes one hour to produce.

The student should experiment by copying the chart on graph paper and by drawing, at slightly different angles, two or three regression lines. He will notice that variable cost per unit may be changed, within the range of a few shillings, simply by estimating differently the angle of the line. It is for this reason that the method of least squares, which is not affected by biased estimates, is adopted.

### LEAST SQUARES

The calculations necessary for obtaining an "average" by least squares are more involved than those required when Regression Charts are used. However, since they will normally be carried out once a year only, and a more objective result is obtained, this extra refinement may well be justified.

Below is an outline of the procedures for applying least squares. The figures used for the Regression Chart will be taken and then the two results can be compared. Needless to say, an explanation of the theory of least squares is beyond the scope of this book, the concern simply being with how the fixed and variable costs are estimated. The necessary calculations may be summarised thus:

| (1) Power cost ($y$) | (2) Production (units) ($x$) | (3) No. of units squared ($x^2$) | (4) (1) × (2) ($xy$) |
|---|---|---|---|
| £ | | | |
| 2,800 | 3,000 | 9,000,000 | 8,400,000 |
| 2,500 | 2,800 | 7,840,000 | 7,000,000 |
| 3,000 | 3,200 | 10,240,000 | 9,600,000 |
| 2,000 | 1,800 | 3,240,000 | 3,600,000 |
| 2,100 | 1,900 | 3,610,000 | 3,990,000 |
| 3,200 | 3,500 | 12,250,000 | 11,200,000 |
| 15,600 | 16,200 | 46,180,000 | 43,790,000 |

The steps involved are:

1. Calculate the monthly average output or activity $\left( i.e. \ \dfrac{\Sigma x}{N} \right)$.

2. Obtain the monthly average cost $\left( i.e. \ \dfrac{\Sigma y}{N} \right)$.

3. Square the number of units of production for each month and find the monthly average $\left( i.e.\ \dfrac{\sum x^2}{N} \right)$.

4. Multiply, for each month, units by costs and find the monthly average $\left( i.e.\ \dfrac{\sum xy}{N} \right)$.

The variable element may then be found by the formula:

$$VC = \frac{(4) - ((1) \times (2))}{(3) - (1)^2}$$

The fixed element formula is:

$$FC = (2) - (VC \times (1))$$

By reference to the table and omitting noughts it will be seen that the following relate to the above steps:

Step (1) $= \dfrac{162}{6} = 27.$

Step (2) $= \dfrac{156}{6} = 26.$

Step (3) The multiplication has already been done, so the final calculation is:

$$\frac{4618}{6} = 769 \cdot 7$$

Step (4) Again referring to the table it will be seen that the final figures are:

$$\frac{4379}{6} = 729 \cdot 8$$

The variable element is found, therefore, as shown below:

$$\frac{729 \cdot 8 - (27 \times 26)}{769 \cdot 7 - 27^2}$$

$$= \frac{729 \cdot 8 - 702}{769 \cdot 7 - 729} = \frac{27 \cdot 8}{40 \cdot 7}$$

$$= £0 \cdot 683 \text{ (approx.)}$$

Comparison with the result obtained by means of the Regression Chart will indicate that there is little difference in the two answers. A variable cost of between £0·650 and £0·675 per unit is obviously a good enough estimate.

## NOTE ON ACCURACY OF METHODS

The method of least squares is likely to give the most accurate separation of the fixed and variable elements in a semi-variable cost. Moreover, as already observed, the necessary objectivity is achieved.

Both the direct estimate and the use of a Regression Chart leave much to be desired. When a chart is used it is important to observe that, for a reasonably accurate estimate, it is essential for (1) all the plotted points to appear *on* the regression line, and (2) the conditions which operated in the past, from which the basic data have been taken, to operate in the future.

From these observations, it follows that the greater is the degree of scatter of the points from the estimating line and the more changed are actual conditions when compared with past conditions, then the less accurate will be the estimate.

## ACCOUNTING FOR MARGINAL COSTS

Accounting systems may be classified as follows:

1. Separate ledgers for (a) costing and (b) financial transactions.
In both cases the conventional double-entry system is followed. Periodically the costing profit has to be reconciled with the financial profit.

2. Integral accounting when both costing and financial ledgers are entered in the same set of books.

Irrespective of the type of system used to record the costing transactions the accounts classification will be affected by the normal method of costing—Job or Process. In both cases there will be control accounts for material, labour and overheads. The principal difference lies in the accounting for work-in-progress. In the case of Job Costing a separate cost sheet is kept for each job. These are subsidiary records the results of which are summarised in the books of account in a work-in-progress account. When Process Costing is appropriate, separate cost sheets are not required. Instead the cost for each separate process is debited to a Process Account. In the ledger there would be as many of these accounts as there are processes. Thus, for example, there may be separate accounts for preparation, mixing, baking, and packing. The costs relating to each of these are charged to the appropriate account and then subsequently transferred to the next process.

If Marginal Costing principles are to be incorporated into the accounting system the procedures outlined above will still be appropriate. However, there will be recognition of the nature of costs; these will be classified in a manner that will clearly bring to light (a) marginal costs and (b) fixed costs. If Standard Costing is employed then the variance analysis may show deviations from standard variable costs and standard fixed costs quite clearly. This is a subject which is covered in Chapters 2, 14 and 23.

The Profit and Loss Accounts or statements deserve special attention and it is to these that attention is now turned.

## PROFIT AND LOSS ACCOUNTS AND STATEMENTS

Those principles which affect the Profit and Loss Account are summarised below:

1. Fixed costs are written off in the period in which they are incurred.

This means that the fixed costs are charged against the sales made in a period: it is right—so the argument runs—that the fixed costs should be matched against the sales for the same period.

2. Stocks are valued on the basis of marginal (variable) costs.

Because of (1) and (2) there is no distortion of trading results. When fixed costs *are* included in stock valuations and stocks vary in size from one period to another then misleading profit figures may be shown by the profit and loss accounts of the different periods. An example of how profit figures may vary according to whether Marginal Costing or Total Costing is employed is given below.

3. Stocks of finished goods and work-in-progress can be excluded from the Profit and Loss Account altogether.

This is achieved by charging to Profit and Loss Account only marginal costs in respect of sales actually obtained during a period; *e.g.* month, quarter, or year.

4. No trading account is necessary.

This fact simplifies the preparation of final accounts. The need to divide costs between Trading Account and Profit and Loss Account is avoided.

*Against* using the marginal form of accounts it may be argued that:

1. Accounts issued to shareholders and the public are not generally in this form. Accordingly there is no justification for having another type of final accounts.

There is no doubt that convention dies hard. On the other hand, if marginal accounts inform management in a way that is clearer and more easily assimilated there can be no excuse for avoiding the use of these, even if some duplication is necessary.

2. Stocks tend to be undervalued. This argument brings up how stocks should be valued, a matter which is covered in Chapter 25.

3. Where the volume of production and stocks remain at approximately the same level, similar results will be shown in both the marginal accounts and the orthodox final accounts.

4. If Standard Costing is employed, involving total costs, the stocks will be valued at predetermined rates and not at rates which are at a certain level because of the actual volume of production.

Accordingly, stock valuations are just as consistent as under Marginal Costing. Moreover, the overhead volume variance shows the effectiveness of policy as regards making use of available production facilities.

5. When different parts of a business—factory, department, or cost centre—benefit in varying degrees from assets which incur fixed costs, the latter should be allocated or apportioned to these different parts or very misleading results may be shown.

Thus, for example, if a company has two departments, one which is heavily mechanised and another which is equipped only with benches and light equipment it will be quite apparent that the fixed cost for the heavily mechanised department will be much greater than for the other department. Any differences in the sizes of the departments (square or cubic feet) would also affect the position. For these reasons, apportionment of fixed costs is essential. The contribution by itself will not show how profitable each department is unless they are of similar size and similarly equipped.

This criticism also applies to the products made in the different departments. To be logical those being produced in a heavily mechanised department should earn a larger contribution.

A way of overcoming the difficulty is to fix beforehand the size of the contribution which is normal for each department or product. This implies apportionment of fixed costs so that there is a combination of Total Costing and Marginal Costing.

It will be appreciated, of course, that at any time departmental accounting is fraught with difficulties. If products pass through many departments there is the problem of determining the cost to be used for interdepartmental transactions. Presumably, if Marginal Costing is employed, the transfer cost would be marginal cost. Yet those departments which have heavy fixed costs may have comparatively low marginal costs; an automated plant produces cheaply because of low variable costs and a very large volume of output for absorbing fixed costs. In circumstances where the burden of fixed costs is not approximately the same from one department to another it is very unlikely that equitable results will be obtained by using marginal costs for interdepartmental pricing.

Reverting to the problem of showing the profitability of different departments it may be feasible to use a diluted form of Marginal Costing. That is to say the fixed costs could be allocated or apportioned to departments although not, of course, to products.

## EXAMPLES OF MARGINAL ACCOUNTS

Examples of Marginal Profit and Loss Accounts are shown in Fig. 34. These are not given in strict account form (*i.e.* debits and credits) and for this reason many accountants would prefer to call these Profit and Loss *Statements*. The explanations given in the previous section are

## MARGINAL PROFIT AND LOSS ACCOUNT
### For Quarter Ended.....................

| | £ | £ | £ |
|---|---|---|---|
| Sales (net) (100,000 units at £1 each) | | | 100,000 |
| Less Marginal Costs of Goods Sold | | | |
|     Direct Labour £0·10 per unit | 10,000 | | |
|     Direct Material £0·25 per unit | 25,000 | 35,000 | |
| | | | |
|     Variable Expenses: | | | |
|       Indirect Labour | 5,000 | | |
|       Factory Supplies | 1,000 | | |
|       Power and Light | 800 | | |
|       Insurance on Stocks | 200 | | |
|       Inspection | 700 | | |
|       Spoilage | 300 | | |
|       Repairs and Maintenance | 1,000 | 9,000 | 44,000 |
| | | | |
| CONTRIBUTION | | | 56,000 |
| Less Fixed Costs for Quarter | | | |
|     Supervision and Management | — | 7,000 | |
|     Depreciation | — | 3,000 | |
|     Rent and Rates | — | 600 | |
|     Clerical Costs | — | 1,000 | |
|     Insurance (National, and | | | |
|       Employers' Liability) | — | 600 | |
|     Coal | — | 400 | |
|     Telephones | — | 300 | |
|     Power and Light | — | 800 | |
|     Advertising | — | 1,000 | |
|     Subscriptions | — | 100 | |
|     Travelling Expenses | — | 1,000 | |
|     Stationery and Postage | — | 600 | |
|     Salesmen's Salaries | — | 3,000 | 19,400 |
| | | | |
| NET PROFIT (before tax) | | | £36,600 |

FIG. 34.—*An example of a Marginal Profit and Loss Account*

NOTES

1. The figures used are quite hypothetical. Particular notice should be taken of the fact that the variable costs relate to the 100,000 units sold irrespective of the volume of production.

2. Rates per unit are given for direct material and direct labour. Similar rates could have been given for other variable costs.

3. This Profit and Loss Account assumes very simplified conditions. There is no breakdown into departments and only one product.

4. Semi-variable costs can be seen by the fact that they are shown first under variable costs (the variable element) and then under fixed costs (the fixed element).

5. The use which may be made of the Marginal Profit and Loss Account in management decisions may be seen by referring to pages 287–297.

relevant to the form of these accounts. An alternative form of presenting the first part of the Profit and Loss Account shown is as follows:

|  |  | £ |
|---|---|---|
| Sales (net) |  | 100,000 |
| *Less Marginal Cost of Goods Sold:* |  |  |
|  | £ |  |
| Direct Labour | 10,000 |  |
| Purchases of Direct Material | 20,000 |  |
| Indirect Labour | 5,000 |  |
| Factory Supplies | 1,000 |  |
| Power and Light | 800 |  |
| Insurance on Stocks | 200 |  |
| Inspection | 700 |  |
| Spoilage | 300 |  |
| Repairs and Maintenance | 1,000 |  |
| Stock of Materials Adjustment: Reduction | 5,000 | 44,000 |
| CONTRIBUTION = |  | £56,000 |

## COMPARING MARGINAL AND ORTHODOX ACCOUNTS

The differences in stock valuation and in profit calculation shown by (*a*) Marginal Accounts and (*b*) Orthodox (total costs) Accounts, are illustrated below. A question and suggested solution are given.

QUESTION

Timms Ltd. manufacture a single product *Trinco*. The figures given below relate to the six months ended 30th June, 19... and to the following six months; *i.e.* ended 31st December, 19...

|  | *Six months to 30th June* | *Six months to 31st December* |
|---|---|---|
| Units of *Trinco*: |  |  |
| Produced | 30,000 | 8,000 |
| Sold | 15,000 | 23,000 |
| Variable Costs per unit | £1·00 each | £1·00 each |
| Fixed Costs | £25,000 | £25,000 |

*Normal Activity per annum:*

| Units of *Trinco* to be produced | 100,000 |
|---|---|
| Variable Costs | £1·00 per unit |
| Fixed Costs | £50,000 or £0·50 per unit |

The selling price of *Trinco* has been fixed at £2·50 per unit and this is the price that has been charged for the sales obtained. There was no stock of *Trinco* at 1st January.

You are required to show profit and loss accounts for use by management in (*a*) marginal form and (*b*) orthodox (total costs) form.

SUGGESTED SOLUTION

(a) *Marginal Profit and Loss Account of Timms Ltd., for Year Ended 31st December, 19...*

| | 6 Months to 30th June, 19... | 6 Months to 31st Dec., 19... |
|---|---|---|
| | £ | £ |
| Sales at £2·50 per unit | 37,500 | 57,500 |
| *Less* Variable Costs | 15,000 | 23,000 |
| Contribution | 22,500 | 34,500 |
| *Less* Fixed Costs | 25,000 | 25,000 |
| | £2,500 (loss) | £9,500 (profit) |
| Contribution Ratio* | 60% | 60% |

(b) *Profit and Loss Account (Total Costs Method) of Timms Ltd., for Year Ended 31st December, 19...*

| | 6 months to 30th June, 19... | 6 Months 31st Dec., 19... |
|---|---|---|
| | £ | £ |
| Sales at £2·50 per unit | 37,500 | 57,500 |
| Stocks: | | |
| *Add* Closing Stock 15,000 units at £1·50 per unit | 22,500 | — |
| | 60,000 | 57,500 |
| *Less* Opening Stock 15,000 units at £1·50 per unit | — | 22,500 |
| | 60,000 | 35,000 |
| *Less* Costs of Production | | |
| 30,000 at £1·50 per unit | 45,000 | |
| 8000 at £1·50 per unit | | 12,000 |
| | 15,000 | 23,000 |
| *Adjustment for Fixed Costs* | | |
| *Less* Under-absorption 20,000 units at £0·50 | 10,000 | |
| *Less* Under-absorption 42,000 units at £0·50 | | 21,000 |
| Profits | £5,000 | £2,000 |

* Calculation of the contribution is dealt with in Chapter 11, pages 254 and 258.

*Notes on Solution*

1. From the solution it is possible to criticise *both* forms of profit and loss account. Thus:

(*a*) Marginal Profit and Loss Account.

Whilst this shows what has been earned from sales during each period it does not show what has happened regarding production.

It shows that a loss of £2500 was incurred in the first six months. In actual fact from a production point of view this period was better than the second period. Although the latter shows a much improved position profit-wise, it is very clear that if production continues at the level achieved in the second period the company will soon find itself in the process of liquidation.

Clearly, the Marginal Profit and Loss Account would be improved by showing in note form at the foot of the account details of production and stocks for each period. A further improvement would be to show the effects of over- and under-capacity working—a fact illustrated by the over- and under-absorption of fixed overheads.

(*b*) Orthodox Profit and Loss Account.

The main criticism here is that the costs are the costs of production and not of sales.

Accountants who favour marginal costing valuation of stocks will also point out the error of including fixed costs amounting to £7500 in the stock and carrying this forward to the next period.

2. Six-monthly periods have been taken to illustrate the two approaches. These periods could have been full years or other length of time.

*Departmental Profit and Loss Accounts*

Whether to continue operating a particular department or to produce a particular product may be answered by the marginal form of Profit and Loss Account given in Chapter 12 which deals with problems associated with volume of output.

## EXAMINATION QUESTIONS

1. State what you understand by the technique of marginal costing and control. State its purposes and illustrate the manner in which it is used.

(*I.C.W.A.*)

2. Explain clearly what you understand by contribution in a cost accounting sense. How is it related to profit?

List three benefits that management can obtain from knowing the contribution from its units. (*I.C.W.A.*)

3. What considerations govern management in the fixing of selling prices when business is difficult to obtain and competition is keen? Discuss the statistics and graphs which you would prepare for the guidance of management at such a time. (*I.C.W.A.*)

4. The sales manager contends that costs should be based on maximum output as otherwise he cannot compete with more efficient competitors, while the works manager contends that they should be based on average output in past periods.

Give your views on these contentions, dealing particularly with:

(a) selling prices,

(b) significance of quantity variations as an indication of factory efficiency. (*I.C.W.A.*)

5. Discuss the practical disadvantages which may be experienced in basing the export prices of goods on a system of marginal costing. (*S.C.A.*)

6. It has been stated that for price fixing purposes, total costing cannot be compared for efficiency with the accuracy and clarity afforded by the marginal costing technique. Discuss the significance of this statement from the Cost Accountant's point of view. (*I.C.W.A.*)

7. State what you consider to be the advantages and disadvantages of the marginal cost method of costing as compared with other methods. (*I.C.A.*)

8. A company manufactures a product in three qualities of material. The value of the material used in these products is £2·00, £2·50 and £3·00 per unit. The direct labour cost remains constant at £0·50 per unit. The company absorbs overhead expenditure by:

(a) a percentage addition to the material content calculated to recover the fixed overheads on the budgeted output;

(b) a percentage addition to direct wages calculated to recover the variable overheads on the budgeted output.

Describe the effect of this method of absorption on the cost of the products, and state with reasons whether you consider it to be an equitable method in the circumstances. (*I.C.W.A.*)

9. Criticise the statement, "the more machinery employed, the more the manufacturer is at the mercy of the market." (*I.C.W.A.*)

10. Proponents of marginal costing argue that the only relevant costs are those which will be affected by the proposal under consideration. Discuss which costs will be considered as relevant and how such costs are computed. (*A.C.C.A.*)

11. A company manufacturing a single product produces accounts for the year 1965 as follows:

|  |  |  |  | £ |
|---|---|---|---|---|
| Direct materials | ... | ... | 80,000 |
| Direct wages ... | ... | ... | 40,000 |
| Variable overheads | ... | ... | 30,000 |
| Fixed overheads | ... | ... | 30,000 |
| Profit ... | ... | ... | ... | 20,000 |
| Sales ... | ... | ... | ... | 200,000 |

It is anticipated that sales will increase by 25% in respect of the year 1966, fixed overheads remaining unchanged.

During March 1966, management is considering the 1967 programme, in which year the sales manager anticipates sales of £300,000, the selling price of the product remaining unchanged.

Present methods can be continued, though the fixed expenses would increase to £40,000, and labour may be difficult to obtain.

Alternatively, a complete revision of the method of manufacture would reduce the cost of direct wages by 25% per unit of manufacture, but would increase variable overheads to 100% of direct wages, and would increase fixed overheads to £50,000 per annum.

Present figures to assist management in making a decision, and recommend a course of action based on your figures. *(I.C.W.A.)*

12. A foundry with 200 direct employees, each earning an average wage of £25 per week, produces 10,000 rough castings each four-week period.

The castings have a direct material cost of £4·50 each and an average sales value of £12 each. Details of the overhead are:

Production:

Variable: 75% of direct wages
Fixed: £144,000 per annum

Selling and Distribution:

Variable: 2½% of sales value
Fixed: £48,000 per annum

It is now proposed to machine the castings and this will increase the sales value by 50%. To do this both direct wages and fixed production overhead will be increased by 75%, while variable production overhead will be 80% of the increased wages. Variable selling and distribution overhead will increase to 5% of sales value while the fixed remains unchanged.

Prepare two comparative statements showing the present, and the future proposed cost and profit position as:

(*a*) a marginal cost and profit statement for the operation of a year of 52 working weeks:

(*b*) a cost and profit per unit by absorption cost method. (Calculations to one decimal place of £1.)

*(A.C.C.A.)*

CHAPTER 11

## BREAK-EVEN ANALYSIS

### *INTRODUCTION*

BREAK-EVEN analysis is very much an extension, or even a part of, Marginal Costing. Basically it is concerned with finding the point at which revenues and costs agree exactly—hence the term "break-even." The break-even point is, therefore, the volume of output at which neither a profit is made nor a loss is incurred.

As a result of calculating break-even points accountants have come to realise that many valuable facts, all essential for operating a business enterprise, can emerge from the exercise. Typical problems which may be solved by break-even analysis are as follows:

1. What volume of sales will be necessary to cover:
    (*a*) A reasonable return on capital employed.
    (*b*) Preference dividends.
    (*c*) Ordinary dividends.
    (*d*) Reserves.

2. To compare a number of companies by arranging probable earnings from each in order of magnitude.

3. Determination of the price of a product which will give the desired break-even point and profit.

4. Calculation of costs and revenues for all possible volumes of output thereby aiding in fixing budgeted sales.

5. Variable cost per unit can be calculated quite easily from a break-even chart.

6. The cash involved in obtaining a particular volume of output (Cash Break-even Chart considered later).

### *CALCULATION OF THE BREAK-EVEN POINT*

The break-even point may be found by use of the following formula:

$$\text{Break-even Point} = \frac{F}{1 - \frac{V}{P}}$$

When F = Fixed Costs.
    1 = A whole number (ONE)
    V = Variable Cost per unit (or total Variable Costs)*
    P = Selling price per unit (or total sales value may be substituted, symbol "S")

* By the definition given on page 225 variable costs and marginal costs are the same for most purposes.

252

An example will show how the formula is applied. Unit variable cost and selling price should be used together in the formula. Alternatively, these may be substituted by total variable cost and sales value.

QUESTION

The fixed costs for the year are £40,000. Variable cost per unit for the single product being made is £2.

Estimated sales for the period are valued at £100,000. The number of units involved coincides with the expected volume of output. Each unit sells at £10 each.

You are required to calculate the break-even point.

SUGGESTED SOLUTION

Using the formula the break-even point is:

$$\frac{£40,000}{1 - \dfrac{£2}{£10}} = \frac{£40,000}{1 - \dfrac{1}{5}}$$

$$= \frac{£40,000}{\dfrac{4}{5}} = \frac{£40,000 \times 5}{4}$$

$$= £50,000 \text{ Break-even Point.}$$

This calculation may be checked as follows:

| | |
|---|---|
| Fixed Costs | £40,000 |
| Variable Costs | |
| ⅕ of £50,000 (break-even point) | 10,000 |
| | £50,000 |

An alternative formula is given below:

$$\frac{F}{P - V} = \textit{Units} \text{ needed to break-even}$$

When F = Fixed Costs
     P = Selling Price
     V = Variable Cost *per Unit*

Solving the same problem the new formula gives the following:

$$\frac{40,000}{10 - 2} = \frac{40,000}{8} = 5000 \text{ units}$$

5000 units × £10 = £50,000.  Break-even Point.

When using the "units formula" care must be taken to ensure that the numerator and denominator are in the same units of value; *i.e.* pounds or shillings. Otherwise wrong conclusions may be drawn.

For example, if the variable cost per unit in the problem given above is £0·80 and not £2 the break-even point should be found as follows:

$$\frac{40,000}{10 - 0.8} = \frac{40,000}{9.2} = 4347.8 \text{ units}$$

4347·8 units × £10 = £43,478.

Again the calculation may be checked:

| | |
|---|---|
| Fixed Costs | £40,000 |
| Variable Costs | |
| $\frac{2}{25}$ of £43,478 | 3,478 |
| | £43,478 |

Note: The fraction $\frac{2}{25}$ is $\frac{0.8}{10}$ ; *i.e.* $\frac{8}{100}$

This is the ratio of the variable cost per unit to the selling price. For those who prefer to use decimals the decimal fraction would be 0·08 which multiplied by £43,478 gives £3,478.

## ADDITIONAL CALCULATIONS

Calculations which are additional to those given above for the break-even point are also a part of break-even analysis.

Using the problem given earlier a number of questions will be answered. It will be recalled that the principal facts are as follows:

| | |
|---|---|
| Fixed Costs | £40,000 |
| Variable Cost | £2 per unit |
| Selling Price | £10 per unit |
| Total Sales Value | £100,000 |

*Calculation of Profit for Different Turnovers*

It has been found that £80,000 will be the likely sales turnover for the next budget period. The costs and selling price remain the same.

Calculate the estimated contribution and profit.

*Formulae*

$$\text{Contribution} = S\left(1 - \frac{V}{P}\right)$$

When S = Sales turnover or Total Sales
     1 = One unit
     V = Variable Cost per unit
     P = Selling price per unit

Profit = C − F

     C = Contribution
     F = Fixed costs

For the problem, therefore, the necessary calculations are:

$$\text{Contribution} = £80,000 \ (1 - \tfrac{2}{10})$$
$$= £80,000 \ (1 - 0\cdot2)$$
$$= £80,000 \times 0\cdot8 \quad = \underline{\underline{£64,000}}$$

$$\text{Profit} = £64,000 - £40,000 = \underline{\underline{£24,000}}$$

The profit figures for both turnovers may be checked on the break-even chart shown on page 264 (Fig. 37).

*Calculation of Turnover for Desired Profit*

The importance of earning an adequate return on capital employed is stressed in Chapter 15 which deals with this matter. Once the profit target has been fixed it will be desirable to fix the turnover necessary to earn that profit. This may be done as follows:

$$\begin{array}{ll}
\text{Fixed Costs} & £40,000 \\
\text{Variable Cost} & £2 \text{ per unit} \\
\text{Selling Price} & £10 \text{ per unit}
\end{array}$$

A profit target of £30,000 has been budgeted. Calculate the turnover required.

A formula for determining the turnover necessary to earn a stated profit is shown below:

$$\begin{array}{c}
\text{Turnover} \\
\text{for stated} \\
\text{profit}
\end{array} = \dfrac{F + Pt}{1 - \dfrac{V}{P}}$$

$$\begin{array}{rl}
\text{When } F & = \text{ Fixed costs} \\
Pt & = \text{ Profit} \\
1 & = \text{ One unit} \\
V & = \text{ Variable Cost per unit} \\
P & = \text{ Selling Price}
\end{array}$$

This formula is the break-even point formula given earlier with the addition of the desired profit.

Using the formula the turnover required is calculated:

$$\dfrac{£40,000 + £30,000}{1 - \tfrac{2}{10}}$$

$$= \dfrac{£70,000}{1 - 0\cdot2}$$

$$= \dfrac{£70,000}{0\cdot8} = \underline{\underline{£87,500}} \quad \text{Turnover}$$

## RELATED TERMS AND TECHNIQUES

Many terms and techniques have been developed which now form part of break-even analysis. Before going on to explain break-even charts the most important of these terms are explained.

## CONTRIBUTION THEORY

The contribution theory is the term used to describe the relationships between variable cost and selling price which form the basis of the calculations given in the previous section. The use of the word "theory" may be regarded by many accountants as rather a grandiose description to give to the rules and procedures involved. In summary form these are:

1. The difference between selling price and variable cost per unit is the contribution.
2. If nothing is produced the loss involved will be the total fixed costs.
3. Variable cost *per unit* remains the same for different levels of output. (This is a "linear relationship").

Comparison with the description of Marginal Costing (page 224, Chapter 10) will show that the so-called contribution theory adds nothing new to what has already been said.

## MARGIN OF SAFETY

The "margin of safety" is the difference between the total sales and the sales figure at the break-even point. It may be expressed in monetary terms or as a percentage—the margin of safety in relation to total sales.

The size of the margin of safety is an extremely valuable guide to the strength of a business. If large, this means that there can be a substantial falling off in sales and yet a profit can still be made. On the other hand, if the margin is small any loss of sales may be a serious matter. These are general observations which will be qualified later.

How the margin of safety is calculated is shown below.

|  | Company A £ | Company B £ |
|---|---|---|
| Total Sales | 100,000 | 60,000 |
| Break-even Point | 50,000 | 50,000 |
| Margin of Safety | £50,000 | £10,000 |
| Margin of Safety as a percentage | 50% | $16\frac{2}{3}\%$ |

If the rate of profit earned on sales above the break-even point is the same for both companies then it is clear that Company A is in a much stronger position than the other company.

At the break-even point the following applies:

$$\text{Fixed Costs} + \text{Variable Cost} = \text{Sales Value}$$

Both sides of the equation agree exactly so that there is neither a profit nor a loss. The fixed costs are covered so it follows that once the break-even point has been reached only variable costs have to be deducted from all sales above that level (the margin of safety).

If the variable cost per £1 of sales differs between the companies being compared then the general rules stated above have to be used with caution.

To take another example, if the selling price is £10 and for one company the variable costs are £2 per unit, and for another company £5 per unit, and in each case the margin of safety is £40,000, can the two companies be said to be equally sound? Comparison of the profits shows which company is the better proposition.

|  | Company I | Company II |
|---|---|---|
|  | £ | £ |
| Margin of Safety | 40,000 | 40,000 |
| Variable Costs | 8,000 | 20,000 |
| Profit     = | £32,000 | £20,000 |

A 50% reduction in sales above break-even point would show the following results:

|  | Company I | Company II |
|---|---|---|
|  | £ | £ |
| Margin of Safety | 20,000 | 20,000 |
| Variable Costs | 4,000 | 10,000 |
| Profit     = | £16,000 | £10,000 |

If the margin of safety is unsatisfactory possible steps to rectify the matter are as shown below:

1. Increase the selling price.

For this to be possible the company must be in a very strong and favourable position, being able to influence the price charged. The demand must be inelastic otherwise the same quantity will not be sold.

2. Reduce fixed costs.
3. Reduce variable costs.

For both (2) and (3) a cost reduction committee may be formed and all possible steps taken to reduce the costs.

4. Substitution of the existing product or products by more profitable lines.
5. Increase the volume of output.

It should be appreciated that cost reductions do not come about automatically. Indeed, maintaining the same quality and yet reducing costs may be difficult, especially when the business concerned is already operating at a high level of efficiency.

### PROFIT/VOLUME RATIO

The profit/volume (P/V) ratio—often expressed as a percentage—is a *guide* to the profitability of a business. This ratio shows the relationship between the contribution and the value of sales. A more appropriate term might be the "contribution/sales ratio."

A formula for determining the profit/volume ratio is as follows:

$$\frac{S - V}{S} \times \frac{100}{1} \text{ which simplified is:}$$

$$\frac{C}{S} \times \frac{100}{1}$$

When S = Sales Value
V = Variable Costs (total)
C = Contribution

A simple example will show how the formula is applied:

Contribution        £80,000
Total sales         £100,000

$$\text{P/V Ratio} \quad = \quad \frac{£80,000 \times 100}{£100,000} = 80\%$$

As with other Marginal Costing techniques there is an assumption that costs can be separated into two definite groups—variable (marginal) costs and fixed cost. Moreover, so far as variable costs are concerned, a linear relationship is assumed.

A single P/V ratio should not be taken at face value. Oddly enough although "volume" appears in the term the actual volume of output or sales is not indicated in the ratio. In fact, it is possible to calculate the P/V ratio by comparing the contribution per product with the selling price per product. If the contribution is £8 and the selling price is £10 then the P/V is 80% just as in the previous example. Clearly, if in one period sales are £50,000 and in another £100,000, with no change in the P/V ratio, then the positions cannot be said to be equal. The P/V ratio should not be taken by itself; other relevant information should also be considered.

Some of the uses to which the P/V ratio can be put are shown below:

1. Determination of variable costs for any volume of sales. This is done by deducting the P/V ratio from 100 per cent and then, using the percentage, arriving at the total variable cost.

EXAMPLE

P/V Ratio = 20%
Company A turnover    £60,000
Company B turnover    £100,000

Calculate the variable costs for each company.

SOLUTION    Company A:
100% − 20%    = 80%
80% of £60,000    = £48,000    Variable Cost.

Company B:
80% of £100,000 = £80,000    Variable Cost.

2. Comparisons can be made by calculating the P/V ratio for each factor to be compared; viz.:

(a) Line of product.
(b) Sales area.
(c) Method of sale; e.g. sale through wholesalers or retailers.
(d) Individual factories.
(e) Separate companies.

EXAMPLE—LINE OF PRODUCT

The following products are made by a company. Variable costs and prices are shown alongside.

| Product | Prices | Variable Cost |
|---------|--------|---------------|
| X | £1 | £0·50 |
| Y | £2 | £1·50 |
| Z | £4 | £2·50 |

Show the P/V ratio for each line.

SOLUTION    Product

X  $\dfrac{0·50 \times 100}{1} = 50\%$

Y  $\dfrac{0·50 \times 100}{2} = 25\%$

Z  $\dfrac{1·50 \times 100}{4} = 37\frac{1}{2}\%$

3. Calculations of the desired volume of output, profit or other essential fact. It should be possible to see how these calculations are carried out from the "Additional Calculations" section, given earlier.

Management has to aim at increasing the P/V ratio. This may be done by reducing variable costs or by raising prices. If a composite P/V ratio (average ratio for a number of products) is being considered an effort should be made to improve the sales mixture by increasing the volume of the products with a high P/V ratio and reducing the volume of those products with a low P/V ratio.

However, just like the margin of safety, the P/V ratio should not be considered in isolation. In fact, the margin of safety, the P/V ratio, the volume of sales and the fixed costs should all be studied.

Earlier, in connection with budgeting, the principal budget factor and limiting factors were explained (Chapter 3, page 53). These factors, particularly the former, may also be important when considering, say, which products have the highest P/V ratio. The principal budget factor places a limit on the volume of output which can be achieved. Examples of limiting factors, the one which is the most important for the present being the principal budget factor, are given below:

| | |
|---|---|
| Shortage of labour. | Cash available. |
| Shortage of an essential raw material. | Inadequate sales |
| Plant capacity available. | capacity. |

A principal budget factor may be actual or potential. The object of assessing the principal budget factor is to "weight" the P/V ratios, thereby giving due recognition to special circumstances. Unfortunately, although theoretically the weighing of the P/V ratios appears sound, it may be very difficult to put the theory into practice. Thus, for example, giving due emphasis in concrete terms to lack of sales capacity when considering alternative courses of action may be extremely difficult. Nevertheless, weighting may be feasible in appropriate circumstances, examples of which are given below.

*Direct Labour as P.B.F.\**

| | Product X | Product Y |
|---|---|---|
| Selling Price | £1·50 | £2·50 |
| Variable Cost | £1·00 | £1·00 |
| Contribution | £0·50 | £1·50 |
| P/V Ratio | 33⅓% | 60% |

There is a shortage of skilled labour necessary for producing both products. Product X takes 1 hour to produce, whereas Product Y involves 4 hours.

If due weight is given to the fact that the hours involved for the products are different then the position may be shown as follows:

| | Product X | Product Y |
|---|---|---|
| Amended P/V Ratio | 33⅓% | 15% |
| Contribution per Direct Labour Hour = | £0·500 | £0·375 |

According to these amended figures Product X is more desirable than Product Y. The significant fact is the contribution per direct labour hour.

Clearly, this is an oversimplification. Among other things, the volume of sales for each product has to be considered. It can be argued that due weight is *already* being given to the differences in direct labour hours by the fact that for X the cost for 1 hour is being charged whereas for Y the cost for four hours is included in the variable costs.

* P.B.F. = Principal Budget Factor, Key Factor, Governing Factor or Limiting Factor.

*Direct Material as P.B.F.*

The principles explained in the preceding section are applied. Naturally, material quantities and/or prices are taken as the "weights."

*Machine Hours as P.B.F.*

The contribution may be expressed as a rate per machine hour.

More is said on this matter in Chapter 12 which deals with management problems and decisions.

## BREAK-EVEN CHARTS

A Break-even Chart is a chart or graph which portrays:

1. Likely profits or losses at different levels of output.

2. The relationship between marginal (variable) costs and fixed costs.

3. The margin of safety (explained in a previous section of this chapter, page 256).

4. The rate of growth of profit-earning for a suitable multiple of output; *e.g.* for each £100 of sales.

5. The break-even point; *i.e.* the point at which the total cost line and sales revenue line intersect, indicating that this is where neither a profit is earned nor a loss incurred.

6. On an appropriately designed chart the contribution and the P/V ratio may be shown.

### STAGES IN PREPARING BREAK-EVEN CHARTS

Break-even Charts are fairly simple to compile provided the elementary, basic principles are understood.

A chart has two sides which are known as "axes." The left-hand vertical side is the Y axis and the horizontal side at the bottom of the chart is the X axis.

On the Y axis it is usual to show costs and revenues whereas on the X axis one or more of the following factors may be employed:

> Volume of Sales (Units)
>     ,,    ,,    ,,    (Monetary: £s)
> Capacity shown in Percentage form (Sales)
> Volume of Production (Units*)
> Volume of Production (Monetary: £s)
> Capacity shown in Percentage form (Production)

Which of these factors to show on the chart should be influenced by the purpose of the chart; *i.e.* the information required for the problem(s) to be solved. However, it should be remembered that a profit is not earned until goods are sold. Accordingly, there is a strong case for using a sales basis; either units, monetary, or percentage of capacity. In

* These may be physical units, or standard hours.

many cases the production and sales figures may coincide. The monetary basis may be preferred because this shows directly the financial relationship between costs and sales.

Below are shown the three principal stages in compiling a Break-even Chart. As will be seen the first stage consists of a number of steps. The question given earlier to illustrate the calculation necessary to arrive at the break-even point is again used. The mathematical results should be compared with those given on the Break-even Chart.

### QUESTION

The fixed costs for the year are £40,000. Variable cost per unit for the single product being made is £2.

Estimated sales for the period are valued at £100,000. The number of units involved coincides with the expected volume of output. Each unit sells at £10.

You are required to draft a Break-even Chart. Show clearly on the chart the profit earned at a turnover of £80,000.

### SUGGESTED APPROACH

*Stage I*

The first stage involves drawing the axes on suitable graph paper, inserting the costs and sales values and then drafting the fixed cost line at the appropriate point on the chart; *i.e.* £40,000 on the Y axis.

All the steps involved can be seen from the Break-even Chart shown (Fig. 35).

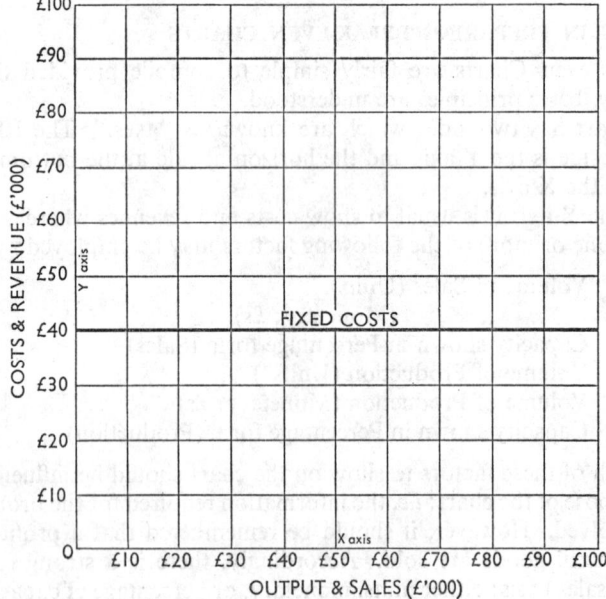

Fig. 35.—*Break-even Chart. Stage I*

*Stage II*

The total cost line is inserted above the fixed cost line. This is found as follows:

| Fixed Cost | £40,000 |
|---|---|
| Variable Cost | |
| 10,000 units at £2 each | £20,000 |
| Total Costs     = | £60,000 |

This is shown in Fig. 36.

*Stage III*

The sales revenue line is drawn commencing at zero and finishing at the £100,000 point on the chart.

From the completed Break-even Chart (Fig. 37) suitable descriptions are written on the chart to show what is portrayed; *e.g.* profit, loss, margin of safety, and so on.

It will be noticed that straight lines have been used to plot the points on the chart. This need not necessarily be so. Curved lines, stepped lines or even irregular lines may be used. It is true to say, however, that for simplicity it is more usual to use straight lines. Nevertheless, the imperfections which may exist when straight lines are used should not be overlooked. These are discussed in detail below.

## CRITICISMS OF THE SIMPLE BREAK-EVEN CHART*

The simple Break-even Chart which uses straight lines to portray costs and revenues is subject to a number of limitations. Some of the criticisms also apply to charts which use curved or irregular lines to plot costs and revenues. Accountants and managers who have to use Break-even Charts should be aware of the possible limitations which are summarised below:

1. The total cost line, representing the variable costs added to fixed costs, should not be shown as a straight line because, in actual fact, costs do not usually vary in direct proportion; *i.e.* the linear relationship assumed is not present. Each unit produced and sold will *not* necessarily incur the same variable cost; *e.g.* say, £1 per unit.

2. Because of (1), the assumption that maximum profit is earned at the maximum level of output is incorrect.

Instead of showing a linear function there should, in the period be an upward swing in the total cost line at the higher levels of output.

* For a very good critical analysis of this subject, see "Marginal Costing and Break-even Analysis" by Gerald H. Lawson, M.A. (Econ.), in *The Cost Accountant*; September, 1960.

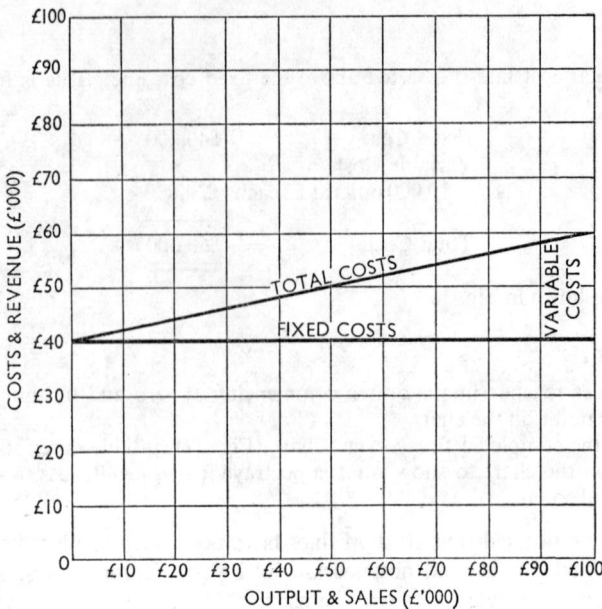

FIG. 36.—*Break-even Chart. Stage II*

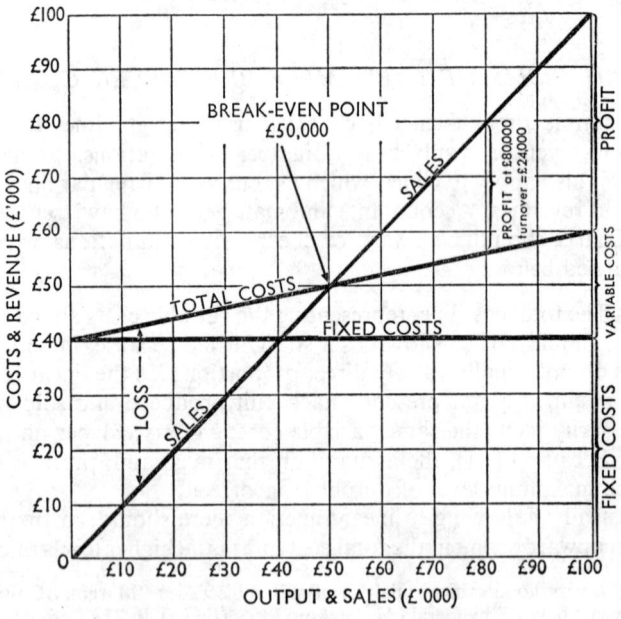

FIG. 37.—*Break-even Chart. Stage III*

This tends to be the case because overtime, shiftwork, week-end working, and the increased use of labour to augment machinery all may appear in the effort to squeeze more out of existing facilities. This is explained further in Chapter 13, "Determination of Optimum Output."

3. The straight line which represents sales revenue may also misrepresent the true facts.

The demand, for conditions shown on a conventional Break-even Chart, is assumed to be the same irrespective of the volume of output. In actual fact, demand may be affected by price charged and/or volume produced. Any increase in output may only be sold by reducing price which in turn would affect the sales revenue line.

4. The Break-even Chart presents a static picture. Yet the operations of a business are far from static. Changes take place all the time; accordingly, there is a danger that the Break-even Chart is out-of-date immediately it has been prepared.

However, the fact that Break-even Charts cover the past and the *future* should not be forgotten. If forecasting on a Break-even Chart can be criticised, because conditions change, then the same criticism can be levelled against all forms of forecasting and budgeting.

5. When a variety of products is produced problems arise which are additional to those described above. Some of these are as follows:

(*a*) Each possible product-mix will tend to incur different costs so any change in the product-mix will tend to invalidate the facts shown on a Break-even Chart.

A way of overcoming this problem would be to prepare a Break-even Chart for each possible product-mix.

(*b*) Volume of sales or production in terms of physical units will be meaningless.

This is quite true, but there is no compulsion to use units: sales values can be used instead.

(*c*) Many variable costs may be common to a number of products and if so there may be great difficulty in calculating the cost for each different product. Accordingly, it may be an impossible task even to determine the marginal cost, let alone to compile a Break-even Chart for each line of product. Instead, a chart which shows total costs will generally be the only possibility.

## CONTINUED USE OF BREAK-EVEN CHARTS

Despite the possible limitations of Break-even Charts they still continue to be used extensively for the following reasons:

1. Although accounting statements, such as profit and loss accounts, operating statements and comparative cost schedules can show the same information they cannot show it as effectively and

clearly as can a Break-even Chart. The latter shows the relationship between volume, costs, and profit.

2. There is no disputing that the use of straight lines introduces enormous assumptions on to the Break-even Chart. However, it should be remembered that generally a business will only be operating within a limited range of output. Within that narrow range the straight lines should tend to approximate to the actual position and, therefore, any error that may arise should not be large.

## DIFFERENT TYPES OF BREAK-EVEN CHART

A Break-even Chart should be in a form which is suitable for the particular problem under review. Some of the most common types of chart are given below.

### CONTRIBUTION BREAK-EVEN CHART (Fig. 38)

The contribution break-even point commences with the variable or marginal costs. These are plotted from zero operations and costs to the total variable cost at maximum output.

Fixed costs are represented by a line drawn above the variable cost line. Care has to be taken to ensure that the line slopes upwards from left to right; it is not a horizontal line.

The figures on the chart are the same as those used previously, viz.:

| | |
|---|---|
| Variable Cost | £2 per unit. |
| Fixed Costs | £40,000. |
| Sales at 100% capacity £100,000. | (10,000 units at £10 each) |

From the chart can be seen that the contribution at maximum capacity is £80,000. The contribution at different levels of activity can be seen quite easily from the chart.

### BREAK-EVEN CHART (SHOWING PROFIT APPROPRIATIONS) (Fig. 39)

The Break-even Chart, which shows profit appropriations, is the orthodox type with the additional information relating to how profit is divided. How this type of chart is compiled is shown by referring to the data given below:

Fixed Costs £20,000.
Variable Cost £2 per unit.
Debenture Interest not included in the fixed costs £10,000.
Preference Dividends £10,000.
Ordinary Dividends £20,000.
Sales 10,000 units at £10 each.

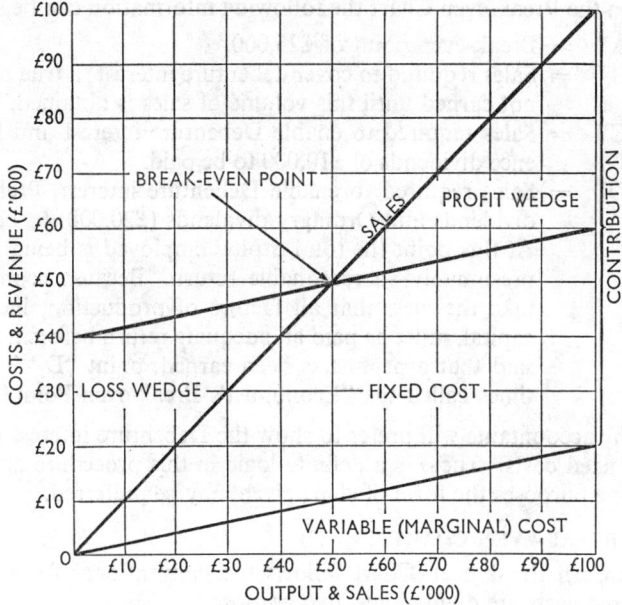

FIG. 38.—*Break-even Chart (showing contribution)*

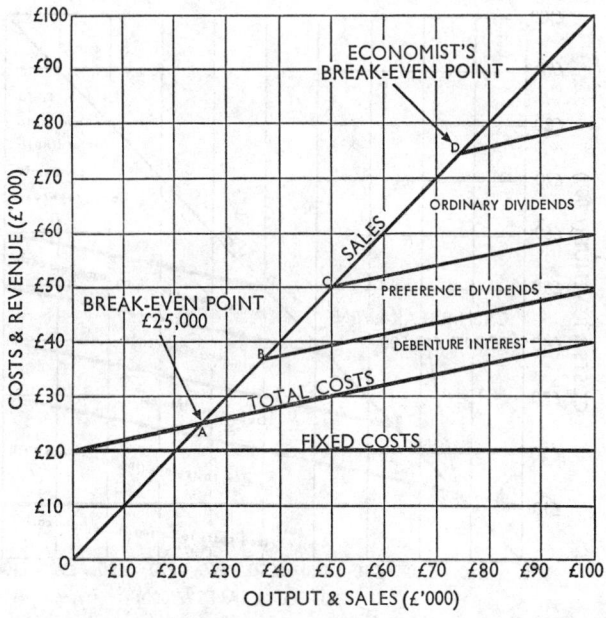

FIG. 39.—*Break-even Chart (showing profit appropriations)*

From the Break-even Chart the following information can be seen:

"A" = Break-even point of £25,000.

"B" = Sales required to cover debenture interest; a true profit is not earned until this volume of sales is obtained.

"C" = Sales required to enable Debenture interest and Preference dividends of £10,000 to be paid.

"D" = Sales required to enable Debenture interest, Preference dividends and Ordinary dividends (£20,000) to be paid. At this point the total capital employed is being paid—presumably—a reasonable return. Because economists take the view that all factors of production, including capital, must be paid an adequate return before it can be said that a profit has been earned, point "D" is sometimes called the "Economist's Break-even Point."

Many accountants will prefer to show the Debenture interest as part of the fixed costs. There is a definite logic in this procedure although for some purposes the form of chart given may be preferred.

### CASH BREAK-EVEN CHART (Fig. 40)

The Cash Break-even Chart follows the conventional form except that fixed costs are divided into two groups:

1. Fixed costs requiring immediate cash: *e.g.* rent, rates, insurance, salaries.

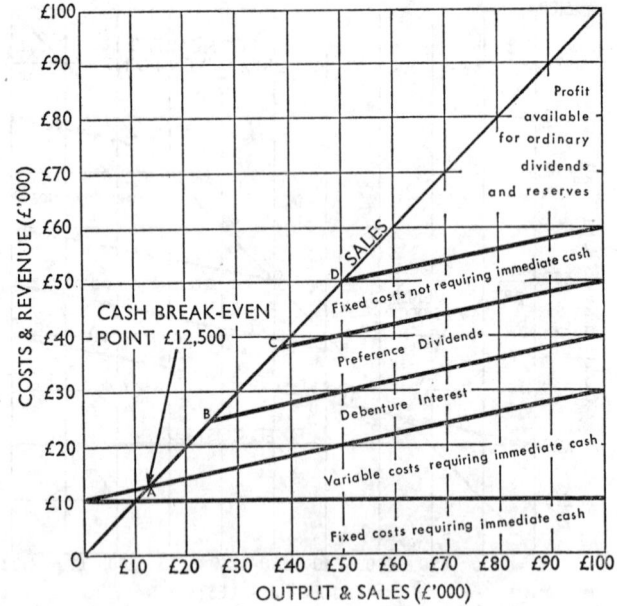

FIG. 40.—*Cash Break-even Chart*

"Immediate" means during the course of the period covered by the chart.

2. Fixed costs *not* requiring immediate cash; *e.g.* depreciation and other deferred expenses such as advertising and research and development expenditures, which have already been incurred and which refer to a number of years; also where a notional cost, such as reasonable rent when an asset is fully depreciated, is included in the annual fixed costs.

The former (1), is shown at the base of the Break-even Chart. On the other hand, the fixed costs not requiring immediate cash are shown last. In this way it is possible to see what cash is required to break-even (point "A"), to pay Debenture interest ("B") and to pay Preference dividends ("C"). The fixed costs already paid for are left until the end. Later, when fixed assets have to be replaced it will be necessary to increase the fixed costs requiring immediate cash. From what has been said, therefore, it should be apparent that strictly speaking, the fixed costs in the sense meant in this context will vary in total depending upon the cash to be spent within the period.

The variable costs are assumed to be payable in cash. If credit transactions are involved then their effect should be measured and the cash payments adjusted. How this is done is dealt with in schedule form in Chapter 6 which deals with cash forecasting.

Figures used in the chart are as follows:

Fixed Costs: Cash £10,000. Already paid £10,000.
Variable Cost £2 per unit. Preference dividends and Debenture interest £10,000 for each.
Sales 10,000 units of £10 each.

## CONTROL BREAK-EVEN CHART (Fig. 41)

The Control Break-even Chart is extremely useful for comparing budgeted and actual profits, break-even points and sales. The chart is based on the information shown below:

| | |
|---|---|
| Budgeted fixed costs | £15,000. |
| Budgeted variable costs | £12,000 for budgeted sales. |
| Budgeted sales | £40,000. |
| Actual fixed costs | £15,000. |
| Actual variable costs | £16,200. |
| Actual sales | £45,000. |

All this information is shown on the Break-even Chart. Significant facts brought to light by the chart are indicated on and below the chart. Special care should be taken to study the relation between sales and costs. The fact that a larger volume of sales has been obtained is obviously a mark in favour of the sales force. However, the budgeted cost for the increased sales should be £13,500, not £16,200. This apparently disproportionate increase in costs should be explained;

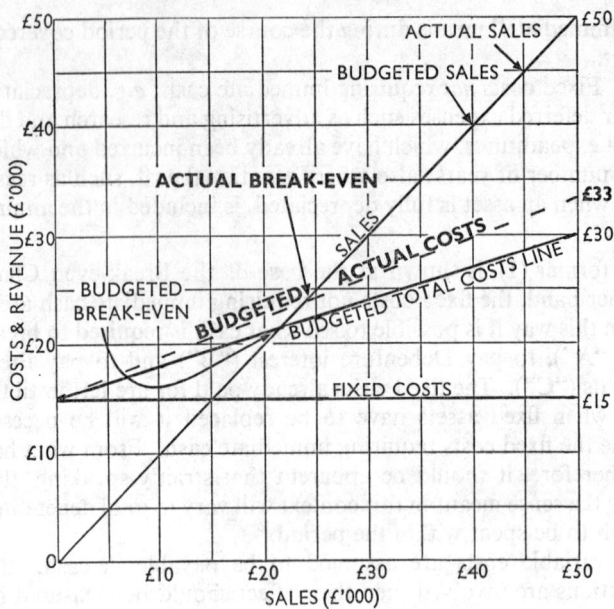

FIG. 41.—*Control Break-even Chart* (*comparing budgeted and actual profits*)

Notes: Profit for Budgeted Sales = £13,000

| | £ |
|---|---|
| Profit for Actual Sales: | |
| Budgeted Profit | 16,500 |
| —Actual Profit | 13,800 |
| Profit Variance | £2,700 |

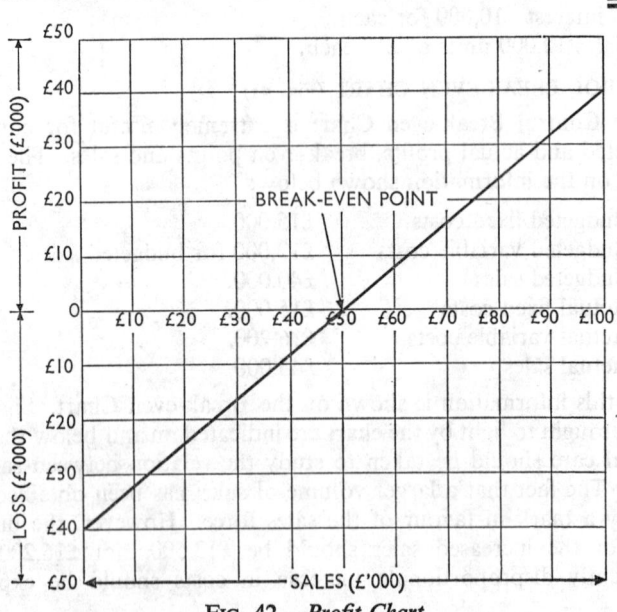

FIG. 42.—*Profit Chart*

Management will want to know why the additional costs were incurred. If Budgeting or Standard Costing is employed then an appropriate variance analysis should give the details required. Note carefully that variable costs are extended to cover sales of £50,000.

## PROFIT CHART (Fig. 42)

The Profit Chart is a special type of Break-even Chart. As implied by the name, the concern is with showing the profit and loss at different levels of sales.

How the Profit Chart is compiled should be clear from the example given on page 270. The horizontal line represents the volume of sales—in this case values are given, although percentages or units could also be shown. The two vertical lines represent profit and loss conditions. That part of the vertical lines which is above the horizontal line represents profit, whereas that below shows loss. At zero operations the total loss is the full amount of the fixed costs; *i.e.* £40,000.

The data relating to this particular chart are:

Fixed Costs £40,000.   Variable Cost £2 per unit.
Sales 10,000 units at a price of £10 each.

## PROFIT CHART FOR DIFFERENT PRICES (Fig. 43)

The effect on profit of charging different prices can be seen from the Profit Chart. There are three prices: £11, £10 and £8. Fixed costs are £40,000 and variable costs amount to £2 per unit. The sales are shown in units, the maximum being 10,000. Because different prices are being compared the use of units is essential. From the chart the three different break-even points can be seen. It will be seen that costs are shown below the horizontal line (representing a loss), whereas profit is above the line.

## ANALYSIS BREAK-EVEN CHART (Fig. 44)

The Analysis Break-even Chart is an extension of the conventional Break-even Chart given earlier.

Marginal (variable) costs are divided into the principal types of cost—direct labour, direct material, and the variable costs relating to factory, administration, selling, and distribution.

In addition, profit appropriations are shown. These include Taxation, Preference dividends, Ordinary dividends, and Reserves.

The figures used to compile the Break-even Chart are as follows:

Fixed costs          £10,000.
Variable costs       £30,000 divided into:
    direct labour                    £5,000
    direct material                  £4,000
    factory overheads                £6,000
    administration overheads         £5,000
    selling overheads                £5,000
    distribution overheads           £5,000

K

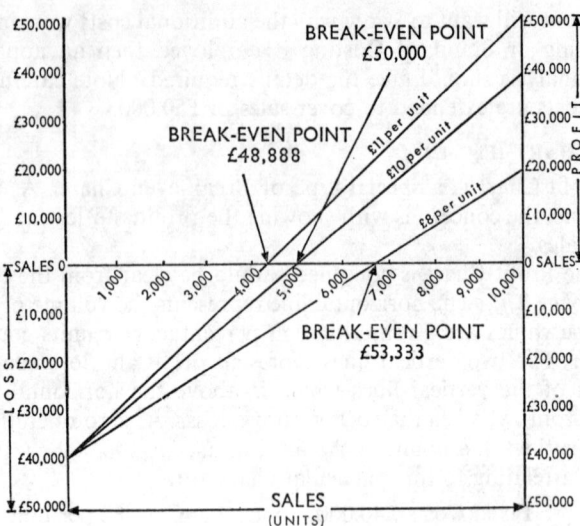

FIG. 43.—*Profit Chart* (*showing different prices*)

Note: Each break-even point may be checked by multiplying the price by the number of units at break-even point; *e.g.* £10 price × 5000 = £50,000 B.E.P.

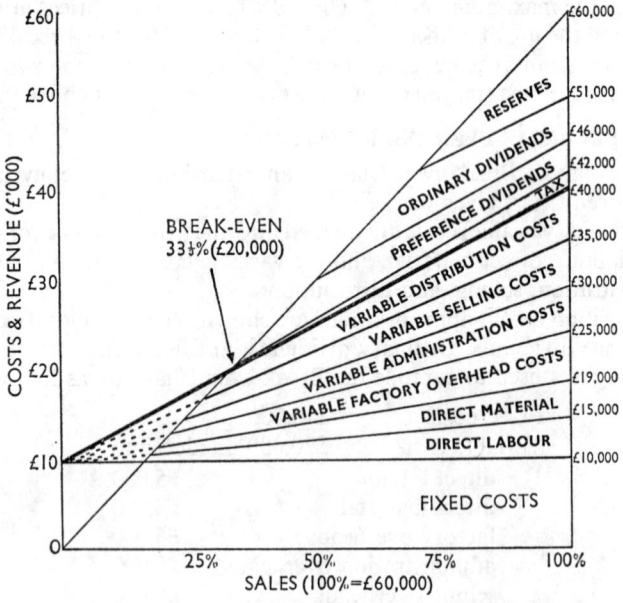

FIG. 44.—*Analysis Break-even Chart*

Taxation       £2,000 at maximum
output decreasing in direct proportion to reduction in profit.

Preference Dividends    £4,000
Ordinary Dividends     £5,000

All the figures are hypothetical and are not to be construed as
indicating possible relationships between the different costs and
appropriations.

The analysis Break-even Chart may be very useful for portraying the
major elements in a Master Budget employed as part of a budgetary
control system.

**BREAK-EVEN CHARTS FOR PRODUCTS (Figs. 45 and 46)**

Break-even Charts may be prepared to cover single products. If one
chart is used for each product the relative profitability of a number of
products may be seen from a series of charts as shown overleaf.

Four products are taken and compared as regards costs, sales, and
profits (Fig. 45). In the examples it has been assumed that the same
volume of sales is feasible for all products. If this is not so then clearly
the different potential sales volumes should be shown on the charts.
Many accountants may object to apportioning fixed costs to products
in the way suggested by the illustration. Instead they would prefer to
use the contribution Break-even Charts (Fig. 46).

The significant facts regarding relative profitability/"contributability"
are:

| Product | RANKING | | |
| | Profitability | Contribution | Break-even |
|---|---|---|---|
| R | 1 | 1 | 1 |
| S | 2 | 3 | 2 |
| T | 3 | 4 | 4 |
| U | 2 | 2 | 3 |

From the comparative data it is quite clear that Product R is given
the first order in the ranking. It is significant to notice that Product T
*does* contribute to fixed costs and, therefore, management should consider the matter very carefully before discontinuing the production and
sale of that product.

At this point a pertinent fact should perhaps be repeated. Some
writers have suggested that Break-even Charts are of limited value in
the multi-product business. Many variable costs are common to a
number of products and great difficulty is experienced in ascertaining
what proportion of common costs can fairly be attributed to a specific
product.

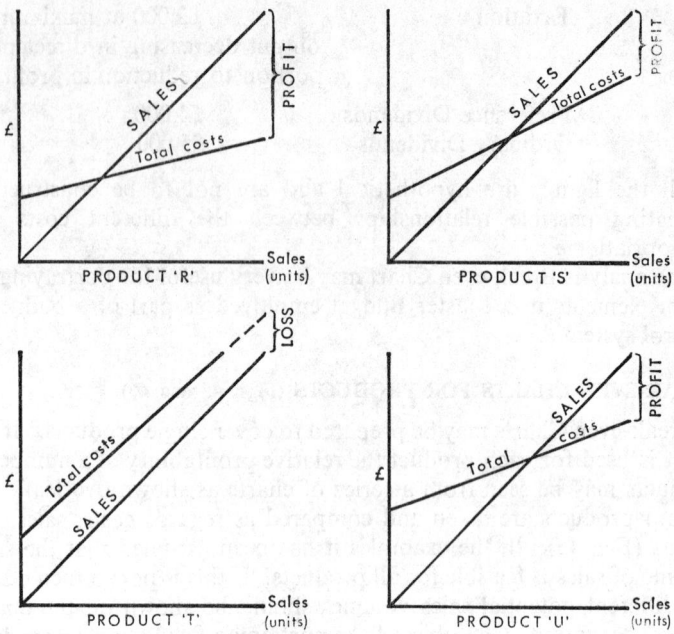

FIG. 45.—*Break-even Chart (for comparing product profitability)*

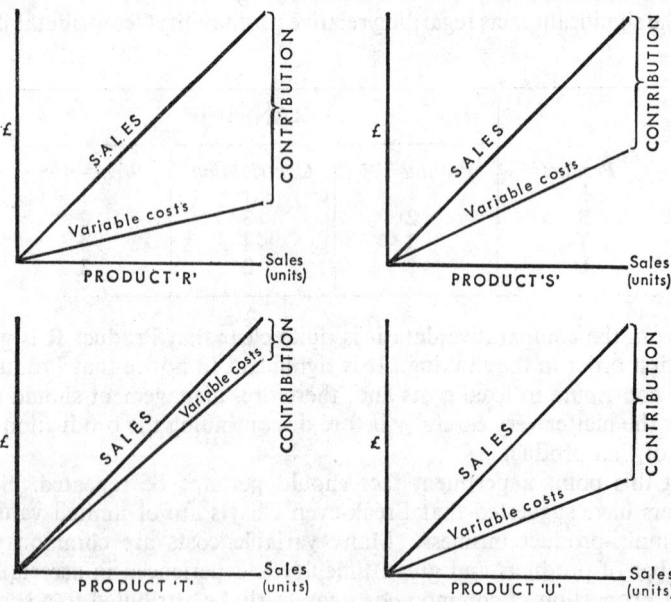

FIG. 46.—*Break-even Charts (for comparing product contributions)*

## BREAK-EVEN CHART FOR OPTIMUM OUTPUT (Fig. 47)

The Break-even Charts shown earlier had straight lines to portray costs and sales. The use of straight lines, with its attendant advantage of simplicity, can normally be justified for any ordinary break-even analysis. However, when determining optimum output—the one giving maximum profit—it should not be forgotten that sales may fall off and costs may increase after a certain volume of sales has been achieved. Saturation of existing demand accounts for the behaviour of sales whereas the law of increasing costs brings about the increase in costs (*see* Chapter 13, "Determination of Optimum Output").

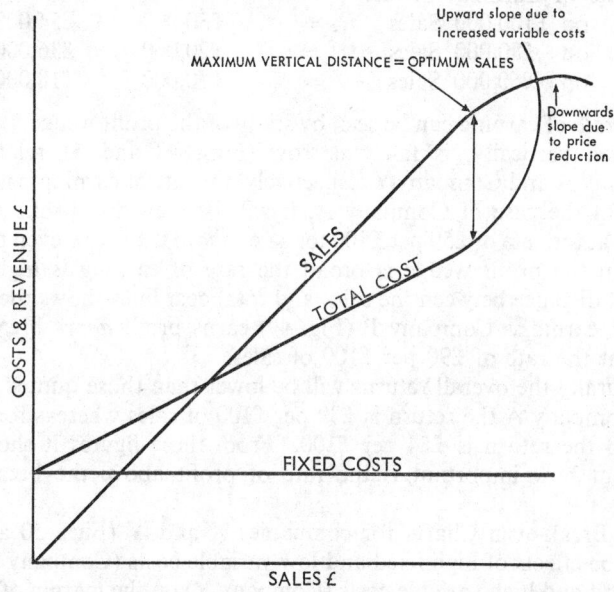

FIG. 47.—*Break-even Chart (showing optimum output)*

From the chart there are two points where the total cost line and sales line intersect. Technically, therefore, there are two break-even points although, clearly, the second—near the maximum output—is not a true break-even point.

Selection of the point which gives maximum profit involves the determination of the greatest vertical distance which exists between the sales and total cost lines. In the example given (Fig. 47) the optimum output is signified by the arrow. This is the point where marginal cost and marginal revenue agree.

If the reader has studied the examples given earlier in this chapter he should have no difficulty in compiling a Break-even Chart which shows optimum output.

## CHARTS TO SHOW MARGIN OF SAFETY (Figs. 48 to 51)

As noticed earlier, the difference between total sales—actual or potential—and sales at the break-even point is known as the margin of safety.

From the two charts (Figs. 48 and 49) the following facts emerge:

|  |  | Company A | Company B |
|---|---|---|---|
| Fixed Costs |  | £20,000 | £36,000 |
| Variable Costs |  | £50,000 | £10,000 |
| Margin of Safety |  | £60,000 | £60,000 |
| Rate of Earning: Profit: |  |  |  |
| on £100,000 Sales | = | £30,000 | £54,000 |
| on  £80,000 Sales | = | £20,000 | £36,000 |
| on  £60,000 Sales | = | £10,000 | £18,000 |

The *rate* of earning can be seen by study of the profit wedge.* If this, measured vertically, is fairly narrow (Figs. 48 and 51 relating to Company A and Company Y respectively) the rate of earning is not very high. In the case of Company A, it will be seen that profit is being earned at the rate of £50 per £100 for sales *above* the break-even point.

When the profit wedge is broad the rate of earning is high. The vertical distance between the sales and total cost lines shows the actual rate of earning. Company B (Fig. 49) earns profit *above* break-even point at the rate of £90 per £100 of sales.

Naturally the overall returns will be lower than those quoted above. For Company A the return is £30 per £100 of sales whereas for Company B the return is £54 per £100. From these figures it should be apparent how important is the rate of profit above the break-even point.

The Break-even Charts for companies X and Y (Figs. 50 and 51) show the effects of high fixed and low variable costs (Company X) and low fixed and high variable costs (Company Y) on the margin of safety. These are summarised below:

*High Fixed Costs: (Company X)*

1. A large volume of sales is necessary to reach break-even point. Accordingly, it takes a long time to achieve the break-even volume.

2. Once the break-even point has been covered by sales, the profit wedge tends to broaden quite rapidly; *i.e.* the rate of earning is high.

3. The margin of safety tends to be relatively small. For this reason Company X may be more speculative than Company Y. However, like all generalisations this "law" should be used with caution. Company X may be producing a product which has a regular demand unaffected

---

* The rate of earning is indicated by the angles of the total cost line and sales line above the break-even point taken in relation to each other. This relationship is sometimes referred to as the "angle of incidence" or, alternatively, the "profit path."

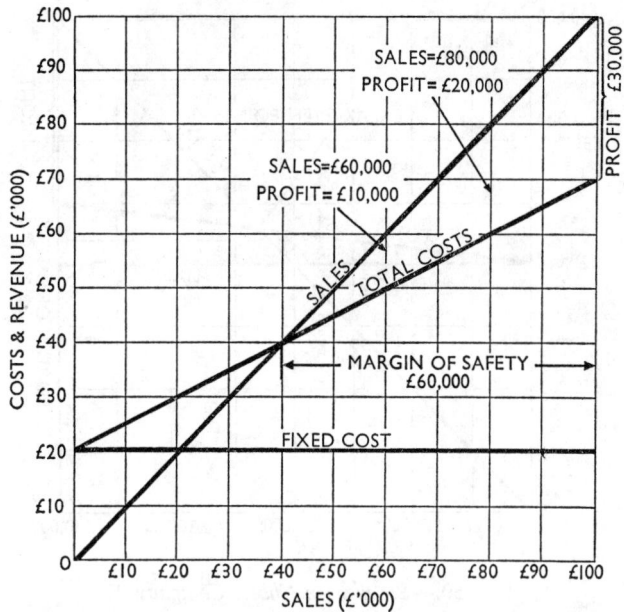

FIG. 48.—*Break-even Chart: Company A*

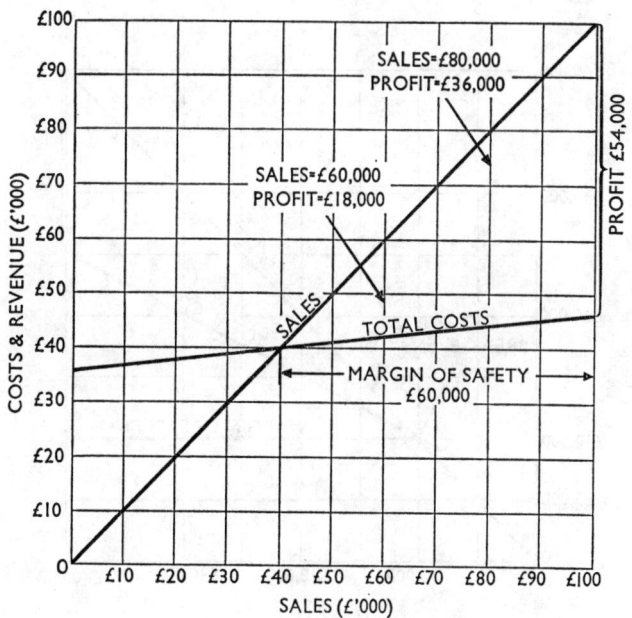

FIG. 49.—*Break-even Chart: Company B*

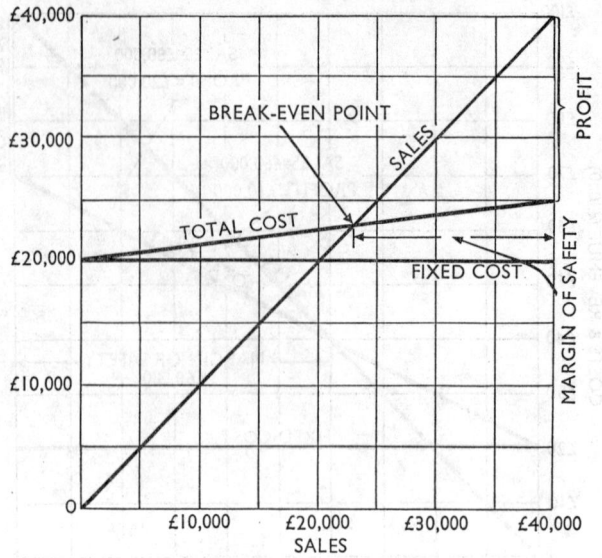

FIG. 50.—*Break-even Chart: Company X*

Note: High fixed costs and low variable costs which may be speculative, but is typical of modern, automated industry.

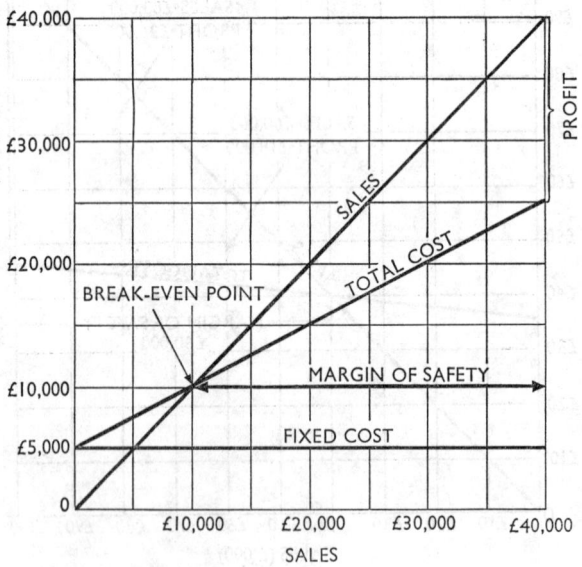

FIG. 51.—*Break-even Chart: Company Y*

by fashions or other changes whereas Y may be manufacturing a product whose demand is subject to fluctuations.

4. Because of (1) and (3) above, the importance of operating at the largest possible output consistent with maximum profit is very great.

*Low Fixed Costs: (Company Y)*

The company with low fixed costs and high variable costs (Company Y, Fig. 51) tends to exhibit characteristics which are opposite to those listed above. Comparison of the charts for X and Y should indicate why this is the case.

Because of tendencies outlined above, there should be no preconceived notions on which relationship (high fixed and low variable costs or vice versa) should be the aim. Costs should obviously be kept to a minimum and controlled. However, quite often the technical process dictates that fixed costs will be high. In turn, because of mechanisation, and possible automation, the variable costs can be kept quite low and this fact, backed by a large enough volume of output, ensures that large profits can be earned. Without the initial investment in fixed assets economical production may be impossible.

## EXAMINATION QUESTIONS

1. Illustrate on a Break-even Chart the effect of giving all employees an extra week's holiday per year. Assume that due to full employment numbers of employees cannot be increased. (*S.C.A.*)

2. Two businesses, North and South, sell the same type of product in the same type of market.

Their budgeted Profit and Loss Accounts for the year ended 31st March, 19.., are as follows:

|  | *North* | | *South* | |
|---|---|---|---|---|
|  | £ | £ | £ | £ |
| Sales ... ... ... ... ... |  | 75,000 |  | 75,000 |
| *Less* Variable Costs ... ... ... | 60,000 |  | 50,000 |  |
| Fixed Costs ... ... ... | 7,500 | 67,500 | 17,500 | 67,500 |
| Net Profit ... ... ... ... |  | £7,500 |  | £7,500 |

You are required to:

(*a*) Calculate the break-even points of each business.

(*b*) State, with reasons, which business is likely to earn greater profits in conditions of (i) heavy demand for the product, and (ii) low demand for the product. (*S.C.A.*)

3. (*a*) X Ltd. and Y Ltd. each anticipate sales turnover amounting to £2,500,000, 10% of which is expected to be profit if each achieves 100% of normal capacity. The variable costs are £1,350,000 for X Ltd., and £2,000,000 for Y Ltd.

Present the necessary details graphically on a single break-even chart, and determine therefrom the capacity at each of the break-even points.

(*b*) What observation can you make regarding the effect of increased or decreased business for each company in the future? (*I.C.W.A.*)

4. Explain what is meant by break-even analysis. Discuss the assumptions which underlie the technique, and its uses. (*I.C.W.A.*)

5. (*a*) Explain concisely what is meant by (i) idle capacity and (ii) excess capacity.

(*b*) Mention *three* possible ways in which production capacity may be expressed, and outline the circumstances in which each of the three may be used in practice, naming an industry to which each may apply. (*I.C.W.A.*)

6. A company makes two products which vary considerably in their material and direct labour content. Overheads are absorbed by the addition of 300% to direct wages. Profit is added as a 20% uplift to total cost.

Do you agree with this basis of fixing prices? If so, state your reasons. If you do not agree, what other basis would you suggest and why? Illustrate your answer with figures relating to two products. (*I.C.W.A.*)

7. The costs of a manufacturing organisation for a normal year are as follows:

|  | £ | £ |
|---|---|---|
| Direct materials ... ... ... |  | 17,452 |
| Direct wages |  |  |
| machine shop ... ... ... | 3,911 |  |
| process department ... ... | 1,104 |  |
| assembly ... ... ... | 5,007 |  |
|  |  | 10,022 |
| Works overheads |  |  |
| machine shop ... ... ... | 5,193 |  |
| process department ... ... | 1,678 |  |
| assembly ... ... ... | 1,507 |  |
|  |  | 8,378 |
| Administration overheads ... ... |  | 3,975 |
| Selling expenses ... ... ... ... |  | 4,983 |
| Distribution expenses ... ... ... |  | 4,306 |

The technical estimate for a job is as follows:

Materials ... 22 lbs. A at £0·15 per lb.
    14 lbs. B at £6·00 per cwt.
Labour—machine ... ... 7 hours at £0·20 per hour.
    process department 2 ,, at £0·15 ,, ,,
    assembly ... ... 9 ,, at £0·23 ,, ,,

Complete the cost estimate for the job, and, using a suitable layout, present the information to enable your sales manager to quote. (*I.C.W.A.*)

8. A manufacturing company with spare capacity proposes to increase its range of products in order to utilise its resources more fully. The fixed costs which amount to £57,500 are unlikely to be affected by the contemplated increase in output. Budgeted sales, now running at £245,000 per month, are to be increased so that the budgeted total will be £367,500 per month.

Expected figures for variable overhead per month, are as follows:

|  | Production £ | Selling and Distribution £ | Adminis- tration £ |
|---|---|---|---|
| Present scale of manufacture ... | 25,000 | 23,750 | 17,500 |
| Proposed future scale of manu- facture ... ... ... ... | 37,500 | 60,000 | 25,000 |

The direct material cost per month is expected to rise from a total of £27,500 to £42,500, and direct wages per month from a total of £42,500 to £75,000.

Using a marginal costing technique tabulate this data in the form in which you would present it to management to give assistance in reaching a decision upon the proposal. Add your recommendation to management.

(*I.C.W.A.*)

9. About 30% of an engineering company's output is sold on a "cost plus" basis in the home market. It is claimed that overseas selling expenses should be excluded when computing cost for price fixing in respect of this home trade.

Exports absorb about 40% of the total output.

What comments would you make on this claim? Give your reasons.

(*I.C.W.A.*)

10. A manufacturing business has drawn up a budget for the current year, the proportions of the expected costs, etc., being as follows:

|  | % |
|---|---|
| Direct materials ... ... ... ... ... ... ... | 34·0 |
| Direct wages ... ... ... ... ... ... ... | 22·0 |
| Variable factory overheads ... ... ... ... ... | 16·5 |
| Fixed factory overheads ... ... ... ... ... | 12·0 |
| Other variable costs ... ... ... ... ... ... | 5·5 |
| Other fixed costs... ... ... ... ... ... ... | 4·0 |
| Profit ... ... ... ... ... ... ... ... | 6·0 |
| Sales ... ... ... ... ... ... ... ... | 100·0 |

After six months working it becomes apparent that the volume of business anticipated will not be obtained, and management considers that a figure of approximately 75% of budgeted sales will be obtained, *i.e.*, £330,000 for the full year.

As cost accountant of this business, present information to management at this stage, which will enable decision to be made on matters of policy.

(*I.C.W.A.*)

11. The following figures for one month apply to a manufacturing company:

| Fixed cost ... ... ... ... ... ... | £15,000 |
|---|---|
| Variable cost for 100 units of output ... ... ... | £20,000 |
| Total ... ... | £35,000 |

(*i.e.*, £350 per unit)

These figures were adopted as a basis for budgeting and standard costing. In the first month of the budget period (March) 140 units were produced at an actual total cost of £46,000. In April, 80 units were produced at an actual total cost of £29,000. The fixed expense was valid for this output range.

On a "break-even" type of graph, plot the total cost line (0 to £35,000 for 100 units) and a further line representing the budget standard, for March output. Plot also the points representing:

(*a*) total actual cost for March; and (*b*) total actual cost for April.

Ascertain monthly volume variances from the graph. What other variances, and in what amounts, are ascertainable from the graph?

(*I.C.W.A.*)

12. The following figures apply to a manufacturing company:

|  |  |  |  |  |  | £ |
|---|---|---|---|---|---|---|
| Annual sales at 100% effective capacity | ... | ... | 1,200,000 |
| Fixed overhead ... | ... | ... | ... | ... | ... | 400,000 |
| Total variable costs | ... | ... | ... | ... | ... | 600,000 |

It is proposed to increase the capacity by the acquisition of 30% additional space and plant. One result will be to increase fixed overhead by £100,000 per annum.

Plot the foregoing on a single break-even chart, and determine from the chart at what capacity-utilisation the same profit as before will be produced after the extensions have been made. (*I.C.W.A.*)

13. It has been said that the statement "fluctuating overheads are those which vary with output" is an unjustifiable simplification.

How would you qualify the statement? How would your qualification affect your treatment of fluctuating overheads when compiling costs?

(*I.C.W.A.*)

14. A tool room in a general engineering factory:

(*a*) makes tools for sale
(*b*) makes new tools for use in the factory
(*c*) repairs tools for use in the factory.

What problems of cost ascertainment, allocation and apportionment arise, and how are these problems dealt with? (*I.C.W.A.*)

15. "The more highly mechanised a company becomes, the greater is the proportion of fixed cost." Discuss this statement. (*S.C.A.*)

16. The overheads incurred in a certain department are estimated to amount to 250 per cent. of direct wages, but at the end of a year's working you find that they have risen to 350 per cent. of direct wages. Explain what factors must be considered, and how they would be evaluated in assessing the significance of the variation. (*I.C.W.A.*)

17. "The more highly mechanised a company becomes, the more important sales volume becomes." Illustrate this on a "break-even" chart.

(*S.C.A.*)

18. Briefly define the following:

(*a*) Fixed Cost.
(*b*) Variable Cost.
(*c*) Oncost or Overhead Rate.
(*d*) Production Control.
(*e*) Stock Control. (*S.C.A.*)

19. The board of directors have called a meeting to discuss possible selling price changes. The proposal before the board is that a $7\frac{1}{2}\%$ reduction in selling price should be made.

The budget for the next twelve months discloses that estimated sales are 200,000 units at £4 each, variable costs are £2·50. per unit and fixed costs are £125,000 per annum. It is estimated that 260,000 units per annum could be produced with no further increase in fixed costs, or in variable costs per unit.

Write a brief report without using technical accounting language bringing out, from the facts given, the significant features of the proposal.

(A.C.C.A.)

20. In connection with its operations for the year ahead the XYZ Company, which makes four products A, B, C and D is contemplating price reductions to stimulate sales. Following are the relevant figures for the year 1967–1968:

Budgeted production and cost data

| Product | Output | Variable cost each £ | Product fixed cost £ |
|---|---|---|---|
| A | 2100 | 21·30 | 17,251·50 |
| B | 1300 | 19·00 | 12,505·00 |
| C | 1200 | 16·50 | 13,770·00 |
| D | 1200 | 15·00 | 11,827·50 |

Relevant budgeted sales data

| Product | At existing prices | | At suggested prices | |
|---|---|---|---|---|
| | Sales price each £ | Sales commission each £ | Sales price each £ | Sales commission each £ |
| A | 33 | 0·85 | 30 | 0·75 |
| B | 32 | 0·80 | 30 | 0·75 |
| C | 30 | 0·75 | 28 | 0·70 |
| D | 28 | 0·55 | 25 | 0·50 |

Tabulate figures, showing the steps in your calculations, to give:

(a) the sales quantity; and

(b) the sales value;

for each product at each of the two unit prices to absorb the fixed costs.

(I.C.W.A.)

21. The following sales figures for a year apply to a manufacturing company with three main product lines:

| Product | Sales quantity | Selling price £ |
|---|---|---|
| A | 650 | 1500 each |
| B | 580 | 1800 each |
| C | 700 | 1200 each |

The unit standard costs of the products are:

| Product | Material £ | Factory wages and variable overhead £ | Variable selling and distribution costs £ |
|---|---|---|---|
| A | 600 | 300 | 60 |
| B | 800 | 400 | 100 |
| C | 500 | 220 | 50 |

The variances for the year are summarised below:

|  | Product A £ | Product B £ | Product C £ |
|---|---|---|---|
| Factory wages and variable overhead | 10,000 (loss) | 12,000 (gain) | 3,000 (gain) |
| Material usage | 10,000 (gain) | 16,000 (loss) | 2,000 (gain) |
| Material price | 4,000 (loss) | 3,000 (loss) | 2,000 (loss) |

There are no variances in variable selling and distribution costs.

The fixed costs were budgeted at £200,000 for product A, £170,000 for product B, and £174,000 for product C. Favourable variances occurred of £27,000 (product A) and £10,000 (product C).

(a) From the foregoing details prepare a columnar income and expenditure statement to show individual product results and total results. Insert in the statement in total, and for each product, the following:

    (i) contributions at standard;
    (ii) contributions at actual;
    (iii) actual fixed costs;
    (iv) net operating profits or losses, and
    (v) express (i), (ii) and (iv) as percentages of the relevant sales values.

(b) What is the overall margin of safety for the year? (*I.C.W.A.*)

22. The following figures relate to a manufacturing company:

|  | £ | £ |
|---|---|---|
| Annual sales ... ... ... ... ... | | 700,000 |
| Direct material ... ... ... ... ... | 100,000 | |
| Direct wages ... ... ... ... ... | 150,000 | |
| Semi-variable overhead ... ... ... ... | 120,000 | |
| Fixed overhead ... ... ... ... ... | 80,000 | |
| Fixed administrative and selling cost ... ... | 40,000 | |
| Variable selling and distribution cost ... ... | 100,000 | |

Apart from the cost described as fixed overhead there is included in the semi-variable overhead figure a fixed element amounting to £50,000.

On a single graph display the cost-volume relationship for each category of cost, and also for the total costs.

Plot the sales line on the graph. What is the break-even point?

(*I.C.W.A.*)

23. A manufacturing company produces and sells three products X, Y and Z. From the accounts of the past year, the following information is available:

| Product | Selling price per unit £ | Profit volume ratio % | Percentage of total sales by units |
|---|---|---|---|
| X | 50·0 | 10 | 50 |
| Y | 37·5 | 20 | 40 |
| Z | 25·0 | 40 | 10 |
| Total fixed costs ... ... | £32,500 | | |

Management is concerned that the overall profit picture might be improved by selling a greater proportion of more profitable lines. After a full investigation it is found that the following sales mix should be possible in future.

|  Product |  |  | Percentage by units |
|---|---|---|---|
| X ... | ... | ... | 30 |
| Y ... | ... | ... | 50 |
| Z ... | ... | ... | 20 |

Present the following information to management:

(a) a break-even chart for the existing sales mix showing the combined units of sale in 1000 unit intervals up to a maximum of 7000 units;

(b) a profit-volume graph for both the existing and proposed sales mix over the same range as in (a) above.                (I.C.W.A.)

# CHAPTER 12

# MARGINAL COSTS AND MANAGEMENT DECISIONS

## *INTRODUCTION*

In the two chapters preceding this one, Marginal Costing and break-even analysis are covered. Here the concern is with management decisions and the value of costing information in arriving at conclusions which allow management to maximise profits or minimise losses.

Costing information cannot replace the exercise of initiative and judgment. Nevertheless, properly employed, it can assist in decision making by furnishing all possible facts. Armed with the latter the exercise of judgment should be made easier.

Possibly one of the main problems in decision making is to pre-determine the effect of a *present* decision on the long-term efficiency of the business. It is necessary to consider the goodwill of employees—extremely important in times of full employment—and consumers. A price change can affect both parties. If, because of a shortage of supply, the consumers can be made to pay a high price, the likely effects of "squeezing" as much as possible from them should be considered. Keeping the price as low as possible may give the best long-term benefits. Obviously there are difficulties in making general rules on this matter; each set of circumstances should be considered. The nature of the product, the type of customer and distribution outlet and other relevant information should be taken into account before a decision is made.

Some of the problems which may be simplified by the use of marginal costing techniques are listed below:

1. Profitability of Departments or Products (Marginal Profit and Loss Accounts).
2. Pricing of Products, particularly in the short period.
3. Suspending Activities, *i.e.* closing down.
4. Make or Buy Decisions.
5. Expand or Buy Decisions.
6. Comparing Machines and Hand Labour.
7. Profit Planning.

## *DEPARTMENTAL (OR PRODUCT) PROFIT AND LOSS ACCOUNTS*

The departmental (or product) profit and loss account in Marginal Costing form is very useful for determining whether or not a department should continue to operate or whether a product should be eliminated. In either case the decision can be determined by reference to the contribution made or loss incurred by the department or product.

An example of how a marginal profit and loss account is compiled is shown below. This is in the form of a question and suggested solution.

QUESTION

The Arnold Co. Ltd. has three departments each of which makes a different product. Cost and related data for the past year—not expected to change very much in the next year—are as follows:

|  | Department | | |
|---|---|---|---|
|  | A | B | C |
|  | £ | £ | £ |
| Sales Revenue ... ... ... ... | 80,000 | 40,000 | 60,000 |
| Marginal Costs: | | | |
| Direct Material ... ... ... | 10,000 | 5,000 | 10,000 |
| Direct Labour ... ... ... | 4,000 | 5,000 | 16,000 |
| Variable Overhead ... ... ... | 10,000 | 5,000 | 20,000 |
| Fixed Overhead Cost ... ... ... | 20,000 | 10,000 | 20,000 |
| Total Costs ... ... ... | £44,000 | 25,000 | 66,000 |

The manager in charge of Department C is very perturbed by the results. The product being made has an assured market and there is no other product which could be substituted for the product already being made. Prime and variable overhead costs (marginal costs) are down to a low level and there is little hope of these being reduced further.

You are required to present the information in the most suitable manner, indicating as far as possible whether or not Department C should be closed down.

SUGGESTED SOLUTION

The Marginal Costing approach to the Question is shown below.

*Marginal Profit and Loss Account of the Arnold Co. Ltd.*

| Department | Sales Value | Marginal Cost | Contribution | Loss |
|---|---|---|---|---|
|  | £ | £ | £ | |
| A | 80,000 | 24,000 | 56,000 | — |
| B | 40,000 | 15,000 | 25,000 | — |
| C | 60,000 | 46,000 | 14,000 | — |
|  | 180,000 | 85,000 | 95,000 | — |
|  | *Less* Total Fixed Costs | | 50,000 | |
|  | NET PROFIT = | | £45,000 | |

Department C makes a contribution of £14,000 towards fixed costs. If this department is eliminated altogether the following applies:

| Department | Sales Value | Marginal Cost | Contribution |
|---|---|---|---|
| | £ | £ | £ |
| A | 80,000 | 24,000 | 56,000 |
| B | 40,000 | 15,000 | 25,000 |
| | 120,000 | 39,000 | 81,000 |
| | *Less* Total Fixed Costs | | 50,000 |
| | NET PROFIT = | | £31,000 |

The profit is reduced by £14,000, the contribution made by Department C.

### Special Note on Method

The method of approach employed above assumes that fixed costs should not be allocated and/or apportioned to departments. However, in certain circumstances this may be quite illogical. If a department is entirely separate and self-contained it will incur its own fixed overhead costs which are traceable to that department and to no other. Accordingly, no amount of arguing is likely to convince management that fixed costs from a number of separate departments (or factories) should be lumped together in the manner suggested by the marginal costing approach. In these circumstances, each department should clearly cover its own fixed costs.

If all fixed costs cannot be traced to separate departments with certainty then, rather than put all fixed costs into a common pool, a different approach may give better results, viz.:

(a) Charge all fixed overhead costs which are incurred for a particular department to that department.

(b) Any fixed costs which are incurred on behalf of a number of departments go into a common pool.

This method (a) and (b) is likely to give more acceptable results than the pure form of Marginal Costing. This applies whether departments *or products* are being considered.

An example of a marginal profit and loss account with partial allocation of fixed overhead costs is shown below. To illustrate the principles the question given above is modified and a suggested solution is produced.

Using the information given in the question on page 287 relating to The Arnold Co. Ltd., and the following additional facts, you are required to prepare a modified form of marginal profit and loss statement.

| Department | Fixed Costs traceable to a particular department |
|:---:|:---:|
| | £ |
| A | 14,000 |
| B | 8,000 |
| C | 16,000 |

The balance of the fixed costs is common to all three departments.

SUGGESTED SOLUTION

### Marginal Profit and Loss Statement
### The Arnold Co. Ltd.

| Department | Sales Value | Marginal Cost | Contribution | Traceable Fixed Costs | Gain+ Loss− |
|:---:|:---:|:---:|:---:|:---:|:---:|
| | £ | £ | £ | £ | £ |
| A | 80,000 | 24,000 | 56,000 | 14,000 | 42,000+ |
| B | 40,000 | 15,000 | 25,000 | 8,000 | 17,000+ |
| C | 60,000 | 46,000 | 14,000 | 16,000 | 2,000− |
| | 180,000 | 85,000 | 95,000 | 38,000 | 57,000+ |

Less Fixed Costs not allocated to departments   12,000

NET PROFIT   =   £45,000

On the basis of this additional information relating to fixed costs it is quite clear that Department C is unprofitable. Accordingly, steps should be taken to try to put it on a more profitable basis. For example although the costs are apparently at a minimum, it may be possible by work study or other techniques to reduce them still further. Another possibility is the more effective utilisation of the capacity available in Department C. A larger volume of output of the existing product, or of a related product or by-product, should be considered.

If there is a principal budget factor or important limiting factor (defined on page 53) then this may also affect the position. The contribution obtainable from a department or product may have to be weighted in the manner discussed on pages 258 and 260 in connection with the Profit Volume Ratio.

### COMPARISON OF BUDGETED AND ACTUAL RESULTS

The fact that Marginal Costing principles may be followed within a Budgetary Control or Standard Costing system was noticed in the Chapter on Marginal Costing. The drafting of profit and loss accounts which compare budgeted (or standard) figures with actual figures should present no great problem.

In its simplest form the marginal profit and loss account or statement may be as shown in Fig. 52. This should be compared with those given on pages 246, 287 and 289.

| Department | Marginal Profit and Loss Account | | | | | |
| | Sales Values | | Marginal Costs | | Contributions | |
| | Budget | Actual | Budget | Actual | Budget | Actual |
|---|---|---|---|---|---|---|
| | £ | £ | £ | £ | £ | £ |
| | | | | | | |
| Less Fixed Costs | | | | | | |
| NET PROFIT | | | | £ | | £ |

FIG. 52.—*Simple Marginal Profit and Loss Account*

## PRICING OF PRODUCTS OR JOBS*

The Marginal Costing approach to the pricing of products or jobs is based on the formula:

$$\text{Sales Price} - \text{Marginal Cost} = \text{Contribution}$$

If the price obtainable makes a contribution towards fixed cost and profit the theory is that the products which make the largest contributions should be produced and sold first. A corollary to this is that in a trade recession any orders which cover marginal costs and some part of fixed costs should be accepted, thereby minimising losses.

Some accountants have gone further and suggested that in order to obtain additional business, over and above what is regarded as normal capacity, any jobs which cover more than marginal costs should be accepted. This is based on the assumption that fixed overhead costs will be absorbed by the products made as part of the normal capacity and, therefore, an additional product which makes any contribution—

* The Marginal Costing approach to pricing is examined in Chapter 10, page 230 and in Chapter 13, page 332.

no matter how little—is a worthwhile proposition. Other accountants have criticised this procedure as being dangerous and unsound. There is always the danger that the marginal or "out-of-pocket" business will take the place of the ordinary business and thereby reduce profits instead of increasing them.

The principles involved in arriving at a decision on whether or not a job is worthwhile are illustrated below:

QUESTION

Drake and Co. Ltd. is experiencing a difficult trading period and, as a result, is operating well below the normal capacity to produce and sell.

An enquiry has been received for 100 units of a product ("X") and the directors are very anxious to obtain the order. The costing information relating to X is as follows:

Direct Labour per unit: 2 hours at £0·25 per hour.
Direct Material Cost per unit: £0·50.
Overheads are recovered on the basis of £1·00 per direct labour hour for variable costs and £1·50 per direct labour hour for fixed costs.
Additional costs relate to special moulds which have to be purchased 1 per product at £0·10 each, and equipment costing £200. In both cases (moulds and equipment) there is no hope of the costs being recovered by other products.

Assuming that the order can be fitted into the existing capacity without difficulty you are required to calculate the *minimum price* which could be quoted.

SUGGESTED SOLUTION

*Statement of Marginal Costs for 100 Units of Product X*

|  | £ | £ |
|---|---:|---:|
| Direct Labour Cost: |  |  |
| 200 hours at £0·25 per hour |  | 50 |
| Direct Material Cost: |  |  |
| 100 Units at £0·50 per unit |  | 50 |
| Direct Expense: |  |  |
| 100 moulds at £0·10 each | 10 |  |
| Equipment | 200 |  |
|  |  | 210 |
| Variable Overhead Cost: |  |  |
| 200 hours at £1·00 per direct labour hour |  | 200 |
|  |  | £510 |

The marginal cost shown by the statement is £510, so this is the absolute minimum price. However, this does not allow for any contribution towards fixed costs. Accordingly, it may be advisable to quote a higher figure. How much should be added to the figure of £510 depends on the urgency of obtaining the order. Clearly, an attempt should be made to cover some part of fixed costs; *i.e.* to earn a contribution.

The fixed costs which should be added to marginal costs may be estimated by reference to the recovery rate for fixed overhead and the hours involved; *i.e.* £1·50 × 200 direct labour hours = £300. This is the minimum recovery at normal capacity operations. When difficult trading conditions are in existence a lower figure than £300 would be added to the marginal costs. If too much is allowed in the quotation for fixed costs there is a danger that the order will not be obtained.

## Note on Approach

The amount which should be added to marginal costs depends upon trade conditions. A standard procedure for pricing may take the following form:

| Percentage of Capacity Employed | Percentage of Fixed Costs to be added to Marginal Cost |
|---|---|
| 20 | 20 |
| 40 | 40 |
| 60 | 60 + % for Profit |
| 80 | 80 + % for Profit |
| 100 | 100 + % for Profit |

The percentages shown are quite hypothetical. However, they should indicate the principles involved. In this example no profit is earned when operating below 60 per cent of normal capacity. On the other hand, when capacity is being filled quite well, percentages would be added to cover fixed costs and the desired rate of profit. Naturally, in the long run, total production will have to be sold at a value which exceeds *all* costs, marginal and fixed. If losses are incurred too often over a long period then there is a danger that a business will go into liquidation.

## PRINCIPAL BUDGET FACTOR AND PRICE

Sometimes the principles outlined above are applied when goods are to be dumped in a foreign market at a price which is lower than the normal selling price. Provided the prices charged bring in some contribution, any additional units, over and above normal market requirements, can be dumped thereby increasing profit. Obviously the market in which dumping is to take place must be quite distinct and separate from the normal market where the bulk of the production is sold.

If there is a shortage of a basic raw material or a particular grade of labour then, when considering whether to accept one order *or* another or to go "all out" to try to get one order *or* another, the order which uses the smallest quantity of the material or needs the fewest number of hours of the particular labour may be the best one. This will be the case when the orders being considered make an equal contribution. The idea of the principal budget factor or limiting factor is explained in the previous chapter and below.

A shortage of a particular requirement may not be the only consideration. If materials have already been purchased, or if there is no wish to deplete the labour force, this may be regarded as a form of limiting factor. Orders which use a large quantity of materials from stock or which involve a large number of hours may be preferred. At all times it will be necessary to consider the capacity available and the possibility of filling that capacity at the present and for each future month.

If the principal budget factor or limiting factor is to be brought into the calculation of the price for an order or unit, this may be done by determining the contribution using the following formula:

$$\text{Contribution} = \frac{F + P}{PBF}* \; ;$$

when F   = Fixed overhead cost.
     P   = Profit.
     PBF = Principal Budget Factor.

This contribution is added to the marginal cost to indicate the price to charge.

An example of how the formula is applied is shown below.

QUESTION

A.B. Co. Ltd. has the following budget.

*BUDGET for Period to.................*

|  | Capacity | | |
|---|---|---|---|
|  | 80% | 100% | 120% |
|  | £ | £ | £ |
| *Fixed Costs* | | | |
| Factory Overheads | 8,000 | 8,000 | 15,000 |
| Selling and Distribution Costs | 2,000 | 2,000 | 6,000 |
| Administration Costs | 3,000 | 3,000 | 7,000 |
|  | £13,000 | £13,000 | £28,000 |
| *Variable or Marginal Costs* | | | |
| Direct Labour | 6,000 | 7,500 | 9,000 |
| Direct Material | 2,000 | 2,500 | 3,000 |
| Factory Overheads | 3,000 | 3,750 | 4,500 |
| Selling and Distribution | 2,000 | 2,500 | 3,000 |
| Administration | 4,000 | 5,000 | 6,000 |
|  | £17,000 | £21,250 | £25,500 |

* Based on the formula given in *A Report on Marginal Costing* by the Institute of Cost and Works Accountants.

100% capacity represents 30,000 standard hours; *i.e.* 8 hours per product. This is the same as the total direct labour hours. A number of products are made. Product "A" has variable costs as follows: Labour £2; Material £4; Factory overhead £3; Selling and Distribution Costs £2; and Administration Costs £4. You are required to calculate for "A":

(*a*) The price to charge at each level of output assuming there is no limiting factor:

(*b*) The price to charge:

    (i) if direct labour is in short supply.
    (ii) if direct material is in short supply.

(*c*) Total profit at the three levels of activity showing that total profit is the same irrespective of the method of pricing employed.

Profit is to be calculated at 50% of variable costs, *i.e.* marginal costs.

SUGGESTED SOLUTION

(*a*) *Price with No Principal Budget Factor*

*Schedule of Costs, etc. for Product A*

| | Capacity | | |
|---|---|---|---|
| | 80% | 100% | 120% |
| *Marginal Costs:* | £ | £ | £ |
| Direct Labour | 2 | 2 | 2 |
| Direct Material | 4 | 4 | 4 |
| Factory Overhead | 3 | 3 | 3 |
| Selling and Distribution | 2 | 2 | 2 |
| Administration | 4 | 4 | 4 |
| | £15 | £15 | £15 |
| *Add* Contribution Expected: Fixed Overhead Cost at rate per direct labour hour. (Note (1) below.) | 4·336 | 3·464 | 6·24* |
| Profit 50% of Marginal Cost | 7·500 | 7·500 | 7·50 |
| | £11·836 | £10·964 | £13·74 |
| Price at Capacity Shown | £26·836 | £25·964 | £28·74 |
| Prices to be charged (say) | £27 | £26 | £29 |

* Only taken to two figures after this decimal point.

(b) *Price with Principal Budget Factor*

*Schedule of Costs, etc. for Product A*

|  | Capacity | | |
|---|---|---|---|
|  | 80% | 100% | 120% |
|  | £ | £ | £ |
| Marginal Cost | 15 | 15 | 15 |
| Contribution with direct labour as P.B.F. (to nearest £1). (Note (2) below.) | 7 | 6 | 9 |
|  | £22 | £21 | £24 |
|  | £ | £ | £ |
| Marginal Cost | 15 | 15 | 15 |
| Contribution with direct material as P.B.F. (to nearest £1). (Note (3) below.) | 43 | 38 | 54 |
|  | £58 | £53 | £69 |

*Notes.*

1. The overhead rate per direct labour hour is found by dividing fixed overhead by the number of hours at each level of activity; viz.

$$80\%: \frac{£13,000}{24,000} = £0 \cdot 542$$

$$100\%: \frac{£13,000}{30,000} = £0 \cdot 433$$

$$120\%: \frac{£28,000}{36,000} = £0 \cdot 780$$

These rates are multiplied by the hours involved—eight in each case—to give the fixed cost per unit. This method combines marginal costing and total or absorption costing. It is useful to find out the desirable contribution even if this is not always obtained.

2. The contribution *per £1 of direct labour* is found by using the formula given earlier. For each of the levels of activity the following apply:

$$80\%: \frac{£13,000 + £8,500}{6000} = \frac{£21,500}{6000} = £3 \cdot 583$$

$$100\%: \frac{£13,000 + £10,625}{7500} = \frac{£23,625}{7500} = £3 \cdot 150$$

$$120\%: \frac{£28,000 + £12,750}{9000} = \frac{£40,750}{9000} = £4 \cdot 528$$

Each unit of A contains £2 of direct labour so the rates above are multiplied by 2 to arrive at the contribution.

3. The contribution *per £1 of direct material* is calculated as follows:

$$80\%: \quad \frac{£13,000 + £8,500}{2000} = \frac{£21,500}{2000} = £10\cdot75$$

$$100\%: \quad \frac{£13,000 + £10,625}{2500} = \frac{£23,625}{2500} = £9\cdot450$$

$$120\%: \quad \frac{£28,000 + £12,750}{3000} = \frac{£40,750}{3000} = £13\cdot583$$

The material cost is £4 per unit. Accordingly, the contribution is found by multiplying the rates above by 4.

(c) *Total Profit at the three levels*

*Statement of Profit*

|  | Capacity | | |
|---|---|---|---|
|  | 80% | 100% | 120% |
|  | £ | £ | £ |
| Marginal Costs | 17,000 | 21,250 | 25,500 |
| Total Profit 50% of Marginal Costs | 8,500 | 10,625 | 12,750 |
| Total Profit with no P.B.F. (as above) | £8,500 | £10,625 | £12,750 |
| Total Profit with direct labour as P.B.F.: (6000 × £3·583) — £13,000 | £8,500 | | |
| (7500 × £3·15) — £13,000 | | £10,625 | |
| (9000 × £4·528 (£4·5278)) — £28,000 | | | £12,750 |
| Total Profit with direct material as P.B.F. (2000 × £10·75) — £13,000 | £8,500 | | |
| (2500 × £9·45) — £13,000 | | £10,625 | |
| (3000 × £13·583) — £28,000 | | | £12,750 |

The total profit is clearly the same irrespective of the method of pricing adopted.

## Special Note on Use of Principal Budget Factor

Many accountants will question the usefulness of applying the principal budget factor or limiting factor in the way illustrated above. For example, is it probable that the selling prices shown when material is the principal budget factor are even likely to be a reality? They are more than double the figures shown when labour is the principal budget factor. If material is in short supply then the material price will reflect this fact.

A further weakness may be the very thing that the application of the principal budget factor tries to overcome, *i.e.*, exceptional circumstances or conditions. As these are constantly changing, a factor which is important one period may be relatively unimportant the next. Obviously there should be consistency in pricing, yet the financial interpretation of conditions via the principal budget factors is unlikely to achieve such consistency. This can be seen by comparing the examples given above.

The main value—if the technique is to be adopted at all—lies in comparing the profitability of different products. The contribution from each can be "weighted" to allow for the principal budget factor. If only one line of product is made no purpose is served by employing the technique.

## SUSPENDING ACTIVITIES

In a previous section of this chapter the problem of obtaining orders in a trade recession was mentioned. Here the analysis is taken further. If a sufficient volume of business cannot be obtained management may have to decide whether or not activities should be suspended altogether. This may take one of two forms:

1. Temporary suspension.
The factory, mill, or other type of works is closed down for the time being, but with a view to reopening in the future.
2. Permanent closing down of works.
Complete abandonment is a very drastic decision and will only be carried out in extreme circumstances.

These two forms are explained in more detail below.

### TEMPORARY SUSPENSION

Temporary suspension is essentially a short-term concept. The object is usually to cease operations until the trade recession has passed. Obviously the most important question is—when should operations be suspended?

The best way of answering this question is to rephrase it to ask—how long should operations be continued? The answer to this has already been suggested in an earlier section. If products are making a contribution* towards fixed costs then, generally speaking, production should continue. In other words, if prices exceed marginal (variable) costs, losses will tend to be minimised by continuing to operate.

However, it should be remembered that, strictly speaking, the contribution should be of a size which exceeds the *difference* between the following:

1. Fixed costs at normal operations.
2. Fixed costs when the plant is closed down.

* This term is defined in Chapter 10.

Certain fixed costs may be avoided by closing down. Thus, for example, a number of clerical, salesmen's and management salaries may be avoided. Moreover, the longer the period involved the larger is the total of avoidable costs likely to be. Practically all personnel may be discharged, boilers may be closed down, stocks of raw materials may be cleared and all repairs and maintenance can be suspended. These are likely cost *savings*, but it should not be forgotten that certain additional costs may have to be incurred in the act of closing down. Moreover, further costs will be necessary to reopen the factory.

The additional costs connected with closing down will vary according to the nature of the plant concerned. It may be necessary to dismantle certain machinery; other machines may have to be covered in oil or other protective material. Doors and windows may have to be boarded up and any grounds adjoining the factory may have to be fenced. Power supplies and other services will have to be disconnected.

When a factory is reopened the protective coverings on machines and other closing down modifications will have to be dealt with. In addition there will be preparation of machines, reordering of supplies and engagement and training of personnel. All these costs are part of the cost of suspending operations.

Costs alone cannot be used for determining whether or not a factory should be closed down. Other factors which may affect the decision are summarised below:

1. Interests of employees.

A business may prefer to continue operating even though sales revenues do not produce a large enough contribution to meet with the requirements explained above.

Much depends upon the relationships which exist between management and workers. If the latter have co-operated and have not indulged in unnecessary restrictive practices, *e.g.* unofficial strike actions, then management may prefer to maintain the goodwill that exists by keeping workers employed as long as possible.

2. Keeping the products before the public.

Even if no contributions are earned the directors of a company may decide that the products should continue to be manufactured and sold. If production ceases altogether then even the greatly diminished market may be lost so that the re-establishment of the products may be more difficult than ever. This is probably most important when products are sold under a trade mark or brand name. Generally a large expenditure on advertising is essential at any time, so the losses of continuing in these circumstances are really a form of sales publicity.

3. Danger of obsolescence of plant.

If special-purpose plant and machinery is being employed which is likely to become obsolete within a few years then any decision to close down should be taken only after the possible consequences of this action have been estimated. The cost involved will not be depreciation alone; there is also the possibility of having to write off a large asset loss due to obsolescence. An estimate of this cost should be included in the cost of closing down.

4. Special problems of the industry.

If any special difficulties are likely to arise as a result of closing down then these should be considered before making a final decision. An example of such a problem was shown at the Steel Company of Wales. Confronted with labour difficulties the company decided to face the consequences of suspending operations.* The tremendous problem which then had to be faced was the gradual closing down and cooling of the giant furnaces, an operation which had to be spread over many days. When the plant reopened the problem had to be faced in reverse— the restarting and raising to the correct temperature the blast furnaces.

No doubt other industries have similar problems which have to be considered when deciding whether or not to close down.

## TEMPORARY CLOSING DOWN

Keeping in mind that other matters besides costs may have to be taken into consideration when deciding whether or not to close down a plant, the reader is shown below how the costing information should be arranged. A question is given and this is followed by a suggested solution.

### QUESTION

Arkwells Ltd. is experiencing trading difficulties and, as a result, the directors are considering whether or not their single factory should be closed down until the recession has passed.

A flexible budget has been compiled which is as follows:

| | Fixed Costs | | Production Capacity (Fixed Costs + Variable Costs) | | | |
|---|---|---|---|---|---|---|
| | Close-down | Normal | 40% | 60% | 80% | 100% |
| | £ | £ | £ | £ | £ | £ |
| COSTS: | | | | | | |
| Factory overheads | 6,000 | 8,000 | 10,000 | 11,000 | 12,000 | 13,000 |
| Administration | 4,000 | 6,000 | 6,500 | 7,000 | 7,500 | 8,000 |
| Selling and distribution | 4,000 | 6,000 | 7,000 | 8,000 | 9,000 | 10,000 |
| Miscellaneous | 1,000 | 1,000 | 1,500 | 2,000 | 2,500 | 3,000 |
| Direct labour | — | — | 10,000 | 15,000 | 20,000 | 25,000 |
| Direct material | — | — | 12,000 | 18,000 | 24,000 | 32,000 |
| | £15,000 | £21,000 | £47,000 | £61,000 | £75,000 | £91,000 |

* A decision made on 11th October, 1961.

Additional information:

1. Present sales at 50% capacity are estimated at £30,000 per annum.
2. Estimated costs of closing down are £4500. In addition, maintenance of plant and machinery is expected to amount to £800 per annum.
3. Costs of reopening after being closed down would be approximately £2000 for overhauling machines and getting ready and £1400 for training of personnel.
4. Investigations made by a market research unit have indicated that sales should take an upward swing to around 70% capacity at prices which would produce revenue of £100,000 in approximately twelve months' time.

You are required to present the information in a manner which will show what decision should be taken—whether to close down for twelve months or remain open indefinitely.

SUGGESTED SOLUTION

*Arkwells Ltd.*
*Statement of Profit and Loss*
*for Expected Levels of Operations*

| Level of Operations | Sales | Marginal Costs | Contribution | Fixed Costs (F) Special Costs (S) | Gain (G) Loss (L) |
|---|---|---|---|---|---|
| % | £ | £ | £ | £ | £ |
| 0 | NIL | NIL | NIL | 15,000 (F) 8,700 (S) | 23,700 (L) |
| 50 | 30,000 | 33,000 | 3,000 − | 21,000 (F) | 24,000 (L) |
| 70 | 100,000 | 47,000 | 53,000 + | 21,000 (F) | 32,000 (G) |

*Summary of Special Costs of*
*Closing Down, etc. (Zero Operations)*
£

Closing Down, Costs        4,500
Maintenance of Plant, etc.   800
Cost of Reopening:
  Overhauling Machines 2,000
  Training of Personnel 1,400

£8,700

---

CONCLUSION: From the figures shown the best course of action would appear to be to close down. However, the difference in the loss at zero operations and the loss at 50% operations is only £300. Accordingly, it is a matter of indifference—on costs alone—as to whether or not the plant should be closed down. In fact, taking into consideration non-financial matters there may be a stronger case for continuing to operate.

The marginal (variable) costs are found as follows:

50% *Operations.* The variability of costs is shown by obtaining the difference between £61,000 and £47,000; *i.e.* £14,000. From this can be seen that the variable costs for a 10% increase in activity (from 40% to 50%) are

£7000. When the latter is added to £47,000 this gives the total cost for 50% operations; *i.e.* £54,000. The marginal cost is the difference between £54,000 and £21,000; *i.e.* £33,000.

70% *Operations.* Total cost is £68,000; therefore, the marginal costs are £47,000.

## An Alternative Approach

A modified approach to the problem of whether a plant should continue to operate or be closed down may be made via the technique of converting to present values as described in Chapter 18 on capital expenditure decisions. Expected payments and sales revenues may be converted to present values. This type of refinement may be justified when a factory may have to be closed down for a number of years. The alternative plans can be converted to present values thus allowing valid comparisons to be made.

## PERMANENT CLOSING DOWN

All investments should earn a reasonable rate of interest.* If a particular section of a business, such as a factory, is not earning sufficient to compensate for the risk involved then the project may be abandoned altogether.

The problem of whether to continue operating or to abandon altogether may be solved by comparing the value of revenues from:

1. Continued operations;
2. Complete close-down and sale of plant.

How these two may be compared is shown below in question and answer form. It should be appreciated from the start that many estimates are involved and, therefore, there may be inaccuracies. Moreover, the further into the future estimates have to cover the more danger there is of errors occurring.

### QUESTION

Raymonds Ltd. have a factory which manufactures a product whose sales have declined to £40,000 per annum. Special purpose machinery is employed to make the product and there is no hope of this being used for any other purpose. Nor is there any hope of stimulating demand of the existing product.

The estimated life of the factory plant is five years and sales should continue at the same level for the whole of this period. Total variable costs per annum for the expected sales are £20,000. Fixed costs per annum total £15,000 made up of £7000 depreciation and £8000 which requires outlay of cash.

If the factory is sold "lock, stock, and barrel" immediately, £30,000 may be obtained. On the other hand, if it is operated for five years approximately £4000 is the estimated residual value. A normal rate of return for the risk involved in the particular business is 5% and this may be regarded as the rate

* Chapter 18, "Return on Capital Employed," deals with management's obligation to earn an adequate return.

| Periods $n$ | 1% | 2% | 3% | 4% | 5% | 6% |
|---|---|---|---|---|---|---|
| 1 | 1·000 | 1·000 | 1·000 | 1·000 | 1·000 | 1·000 |
| 2 | 2·010 | 2·020 | 2·030 | 2·040 | 2·050 | 2·060 |
| 3 | 3·030 | 3·060 | 3·090 | 3·121 | 3·153 | 3·184 |
| 4 | 4·060 | 4·122 | 4·184 | 4·246 | 4·310 | 4·375 |
| 5 | 5·101 | 5·204 | 5·309 | 5·416 | 5·526 | 5·637 |
| 6 | 6·152 | 6·308 | 6·468 | 6·633 | 6·802 | 6·975 |
| 7 | 7·214 | 7·434 | 7·662 | 7·898 | 8·142 | 8·394 |
| 8 | 8·286 | 8·583 | 8·892 | 9·214 | 9·549 | 9·897 |
| 9 | 9·369 | 9·755 | 10·159 | 10·583 | 11·027 | 11·491 |
| 10 | 10·462 | 10·950 | 11·464 | 12·006 | 12·578 | 13·181 |
| 11 | 11·567 | 12·169 | 12·808 | 13·486 | 14·207 | 14·972 |
| 12 | 12·683 | 13·412 | 14·192 | 15·026 | 15·917 | 16·870 |
| 13 | 13·809 | 14·680 | 15·618 | 16·627 | 17·713 | 18·882 |
| 14 | 14·947 | 15·974 | 17·086 | 18·292 | 19·599 | 21·015 |
| 15 | 16·097 | 17·293 | 18·599 | 20·024 | 21·579 | 23·276 |
| 16 | 17·258 | 18·639 | 20·157 | 21·825 | 23·657 | 25·673 |
| 17 | 18·430 | 20·012 | 21·762 | 23·698 | 25·840 | 28·213 |
| 18 | 19·615 | 21·412 | 23·414 | 25·645 | 28·132 | 30·906 |
| 19 | 20·811 | 22·841 | 25·117 | 27·671 | 30·539 | 33·760 |
| 20 | 22·019 | 24·297 | 26·870 | 29·778 | 33·066 | 36·786 |
| 40 | 48·886 | 60·402 | 75·401 | 95·026 | 120·800 | 154·762 |

Fig. 53.—*Interest Table: future value of £1 per period*

$$S_n r = \frac{(1 + r)^n - 1}{r}$$

that could be earned if the factory is sold and the money transferred to another investment.

You are required to compare the two possibilities (*a*) if the factory continues to operate and (*b*) if the factory closes immediately.

SUGGESTED SOLUTION

(*a*) *Statement of Position if Factory Operates for Another Five Years*

|  | £ |
|---|---|
| Sales per annum | 40,000 |
| Marginal Costs per annum | 20,000 |
| Contribution | 20,000 |
| *Less* Fixed Costs which require funds | 8,000 |
| Net inflow of Cash | £12,000 |

The £12,000 is expected to be earned for five years. Therefore, taking interest at the rate of 5% per annum the future value of £12,000 per annum is as follows:

|  | £ |
|---|---|
| £12,000 × 5·526 | 66,312 |
| Residual value of Plant | 4,000 |
|  | £70,312 |

The figure of 5·526 may be obtained from future value interest tables, a section of which is given in Fig. 53. Alternatively, the total amount may be built up by adding on the 5% at the end of each period starting from the end of the second year, viz.:

|  |  | £ |
|---|---|---|
| Year 1 Earnings | | 12,000 |
| Year 2      „ | | 12,000 |
| | | 24,000 |
| 5% Interest on £12,000 | | 600 |
| | | 24,600 |
| Year 3 Earnings | | 12,000 |
| | | 36,600 |
| 5% Interest on £24,600 | | 1,230 |
| | | 37,830 |
| Year 4 Earnings | | 12,000 |
| | | 49,830 |
| 5% Interest on £37,830 | | 1,891·5 |
| | | 51,721·5 |
| Year 5 Earnings | | 12,000 |
| | | 63,721·5 |
| 5% Interest on £51,721·5 | | 2,586·0 (approx.) |
| Future value of £12,000 per annum for 5 years | | £66,307·5 |

The discrepancy in the two results could no doubt be overcome by using tables which employ above four figures. However, for all practical purposes the slight difference is not likely to be of any consequence.

(b) *Statement of Position if Factory Closes Down Immediately*

|  | £ |
|---|---|
| Immediate Sale of Plant | 30,000 |
| 5% Interest on £30,000 for 1 Year = £1500 | |
| For 5 years the future value is £1500 × 5·526 | 8,289 |
| | £38,389 |

On the cost data it is quite clear that the business should continue to operate.

In the solution it has been assumed that the earnings accrue at the *end* of each year. This is done for convenience. However, many accountants may prefer to assume that earnings accrue half yearly.

L

## MAKE OR BUY DECISIONS

Decisions on whether to make or buy a particular product or component may be aided by cost information. However, just as with other management decisions it is essential to appreciate that facts cannot replace judgment. Moreover, there are often important key factors other than costs which affect a decision. In the case of a make or buy decision some of the most important factors may be:

1. Plant capacity—in the case of an expanding business subcontracting may be the only feasible way of keeping up the necessary sales volume. This may also be the case when sales are of a seasonal nature.

2. Profit maximisation—in order to get long runs of the most profitable products it may be desirable to sub-contract the less profitable products.

3. Certain types of work may best be undertaken by outside specialist organisations; e.g. special finishes on components may be done better by a business specialising in that work.

4. Nature of the product or component—if other departments are dependent upon receiving regular supplies then it may be better to make the product. This is discussed below.

It is possible to distinguish between different sets of circumstances:

1. Capacity available to produce the product; i.e. there is a shortage of work; or

2. Capacity available but only to a limited extent; or

3. Capacity in short supply.

If capacity is in very short supply with the result that machine loading becomes a perpetual problem of keeping down a back-log of work, cost is clearly not the main consideration. Nevertheless, keeping costs to a minimum will still be important.

When there is a shortage of work then provided orders cover marginal costs and make some contribution towards fixed costs they should be made. In other words, provided facilities are available for making products which earn a contribution they should not be bought outside.

In circumstances where the products are competing for the available capacity then the method—buy or make—should be selected on the basis of minimum costs. If marginal costs of making are more than the price of obtaining from outside, then clearly purchasing ready-made is the best course.

An example of how a decision on costs may be reached is shown below:

QUESTION

Expansions Ltd. produce a variety of products and components. The following components with relevant manufacturing costs are under consideration for purchase outside:

| Part No. | Direct Material | Direct Labour | Variable Overhead | Fixed Cost | Bought out Price |
|---|---|---|---|---|---|
| | £ | £ | £ | £ | £ |
| 10–231 | 6 | 2 | 1 | 3 | 8 |
| 10–245 | 2 | 8 | 2 | 10 | 23 |
| 10–639 | 1 | 3 | 2 | 5 | 12 |

*Two* of these products are to be bought from an outside supplier at the prices indicated above. Select the parts which should be bought outside, indicating the reasons for the choice.

SUGGESTED SOLUTION

### Comparative Cost Schedule

| | Part No. | | |
|---|---|---|---|
| | 10–231 | 10–245 | 10–639 |
| | £ | £ | £ |
| 1. Marginal Cost | 9 | 12 | 6 |
| 2. Bought Out Price | 8 | 23 | 12 |
| 3. Difference (1 − 2) <br> (Saving (−): Increase (+)) | 1− | 11+ | 6+ |
| Order of Preference | 1 | 3 | 2 |

On a Marginal Costing basis it is clear that Part No. 10–245 should be produced, whereas the other two should be bought outside. This is based on the savings or increase in cost which could arise from buying outside. Any saving in cost will tend to increase the contribution from the part; a cost increase will have the opposite effect.

Not all accountants would agree with this approach. A different method is one which compares *total* cost and bought-out price. If this view is accepted a statement may be prepared as shown below.

### Comparative Cost Statement

| | Part No. | | |
|---|---|---|---|
| | 10–231 | 10–245 | 10–639 |
| | £ | £ | £ |
| 1. Variable Costs | 9 | 12 | 6 |
| 2. Fixed Costs | 3 | 10 | 5 |
| 3. Total Costs | 12 | 22 | 11 |
| 4. Bought Out Price | 8 | 23 | 12 |
| 5. Difference (3 − 4) | 4− | 1+ | 1+ |

In this case Part No. 10–231 should clearly be bought outside. However, so far as the other two parts are concerned on a total costs basis the position is not clear: each shows a cost increase, if bought out, of £1.

Another possible way of selecting the product to be manufactured is to consider the principal budget factor or limiting factor. If there is a shortage of direct material and both parts (10–245 and 10–639) use this same type of material then the one which uses most should be bought-out thus transferring the responsibility to the outside manufacturer; *i.e.* Part No. 10–245.

## EXPAND OR BUY?

If capacity is limited, an alternative to buying from outside is to expand by acquiring additional machinery. Whether or not this is feasible can be determined by one of the methods explained in Chapter 18. When making a comparison between (*a*) the bought-out price and (*b*) cost of producing by a new machine, some accountants would prefer to include interest as part of the cost, thereby acknowledging the size of the investment. This is not to say that interest is a true cost of production, but its inclusion may indicate what additional sacrifice is involved in the expansion. If the money needed to purchase the necessary fixed assets is, instead, invested in securities, it will earn a definite rate of interest.

## COMPARING MACHINES AND HAND LABOUR

Whether to employ a machine or to produce entirely by hand labour is a problem which may arise. Thus, for example, a new product may have been developed and management is faced with determining how best the production may be carried out. A variety of methods may be employed to reach a decision on which should be employed—machine or hand labour. Some of these are as follows:

1. Marginal Costing approach—the method which gives the largest contribution; *i.e.* the lowest marginal cost.

2. Total or absorption cost approach, when the total cost for the two alternatives per annum or other period, is compared. This may be actual costs only *or* actual costs plus a notional figure for interest on the capital invested.

The method of manufacture which gives the lowest cost will be the one to select.

3. Costs or cost savings may be converted to present values.

How far calculations should be accepted depends upon the circumstances and the data available. However, just as with the other problems entire reliance on costing information may be unwise.

Comparison of the two alternative methods of manufacture will generally be on the understanding that the prices obtained for the product are exactly the same whether made by machine or by hand. This may not always be the case. For a few products the hand finish may enable a higher price to be obtained. If so, the extra revenue should be taken into the calculations.

Another important factor may be the availability of finance. If this is not available to purchase machinery there may be no option except to employ hand labour.

The possibility of an increase in the number of units of the product should not be overlooked. A machine may be capable of producing, say, 10% more units without much difficulty.

Further considerations may be personnel policy (avoiding displacement of labour as much as possible) and the danger of obsolescence of the machine.

A question and possible solution now follows.

QUESTION

Planners Ltd. have developed a new product of which 10,000 units are to be produced each year. Details of costs are as follows:

|  | Machine £ | Hand Labour £ |
|---|---|---|
| Purchase Price of Machine | 20,000 | — |
| Direct Material | 5,000 per annum | 5,000 per annum |
| Direct Labour | 500 ,, ,, | 3,000 ,, ,, |
| Variable Overhead Cost | 2,000 ,, ,, | 1,000 ,, ,, |
| Fixed Overhead Cost (not including depreciation) | 1,500 ,, ,, | 1,000 ,, ,, |

The selling price of the products has been fixed at £3 each. If the machine is purchased it will have an estimated life of ten years with little or no residual value.

You are required to show the following:

(a) Marginal costs and contributions.
(b) "Total costs" including interest at 5%.

SUGGESTED SOLUTION

(a) Statement of Marginal Costs

|  |  | Machine £ | Hand Labour £ |
|---|---|---|---|
| Sales Values |  | 30,000 | 30,000 |
| Direct Material |  | 5,000 | 5,000 |
| Direct Labour |  | 500 | 3,000 |
| Variable Overhead Cost |  | 2,000 | 1,000 |
| Marginal Costs = | | 7,500 | 9,000 |
| Contribution |  | £22,500 | £21,000 |

Note. On this basis (the lower marginal cost and larger contribution) the machine is clearly preferable. In actual fact, of course, if quantities and prices are identical, there is no need to calculate the contribution.

*(b) Statement of Total Costs*

| | Machine £ | Hand Labour £ |
|---|---|---|
| Direct Material | 5,000 | 5,000 |
| Direct Labour | 500 | 3,000 |
| Variable Overhead Cost | 2,000 | 1,000 |
| Fixed Overhead Cost | 1,500 | 1,000 |
| Depreciation $\frac{1}{10}$ of £20,000 | 2,000 | — |
| | £11,000 | £10,000 |
| Interest at 5% | 550 | 500 |
| | £11,550 | £10,500 |

*Note.* In this case, the hand labour is the cheaper method. This illustrates a weakness of the Marginal Costing approach. Obviously the fixed costs have to be covered as they are incurred on the specific products. Accordingly, such fixed costs cannot really be ignored.

## SUBSTITUTING MACHINES FOR HAND LABOUR

If a machine is to take the place of labour then an alternative approach to this problem may be to convert the cost savings to present values. How this is done is indicated below.

### QUESTION

A company is contemplating using a machine instead of hand labour. The machine would cost £30,000, have a life of ten years and the residual value would be negligible. Operating costs are estimated at £20,000 per annum (excluding depreciation).

At the present time the work under review is performed by five workers and total costs amount to £40,000 per annum.

You are required to calculate whether the change is worthwhile, discounting any cost savings at a rate of 5% per annum.

### SUGGESTED SOLUTION

Statement of Costs

| | |
|---|---|
| Operating Costs: | |
| Hand Labour | £40,000 |
| Machine | 20,000 |
| Cost Savings | £20,000 |
| Present Value of Cost Savings for 10 years: | |
| £20,000 × 7·72173 | £154,435 |
| *Less* Total Depreciation | 30,000 |
| Net Cost Savings | £124,435 |

*Notes.* The figure of 7·72173 is obtained from tables which show the present value of £1 per period. (See Fig. 54.)

A more logical approach to the question of the depreciation may be to convert the amount to the value of the £30,000 in ten years' time. For this purpose it is usual to assume that only half the amount is invested, the balance being written off at an average rate of 50% over the *entire* life of the asset.

Interest on the investment has been ignored although some accountants would prefer to have it included.

A similar approach may be used when comparing the running costs of two machines. Clearly, though, in this case the inclusion of interest to reflect the difference in the size of the investments will be essential.

| Periods $n$ | 1% | 2% | 3% | 4% | 5% | 6% | 7% | 8% |
|---|---|---|---|---|---|---|---|---|
| 1 | 0·99010 | 0·98039 | 0·97087 | 0·96154 | 0·95238 | 0·94340 | 0·93458 | 0·92593 |
| 2 | 1·97040 | 1·94156 | 1·91347 | 1·88609 | 1·85941 | 1·83339 | 1·80802 | 1·78326 |
| 3 | 2·94099 | 2·88388 | 2·82861 | 2·77509 | 2·72325 | 2·67301 | 2·62432 | 2·57710 |
| 4 | 3·90197 | 3·80773 | 3·71710 | 3·62990 | 3·54595 | 3·46511 | 3·38721 | 3·31213 |
| 5 | 4·85343 | 4·71346 | 4·57971 | 4·45182 | 4·32948 | 4·21236 | 4·10020 | 3·99271 |
| 6 | 5·79548 | 5·60143 | 5·41719 | 5·24214 | 5·07569 | 4·91732 | 4·76654 | 4·62288 |
| 7 | 6·72819 | 6·47199 | 6·23008 | 6·00205 | 5·78637 | 5·58238 | 5·38929 | 5·20637 |
| 8 | 7·65168 | 7·32548 | 7·01969 | 6·73274 | 6·46321 | 6·20979 | 5·97130 | 5·74664 |
| 9 | 8·56602 | 8·16224 | 7·78611 | 7·43533 | 7·10782 | 6·80169 | 6·51523 | 6·24689 |
| 10 | 9·47130 | 8·98259 | 8·53020 | 8·11090 | 7·72173 | 7·36009 | 7·02358 | 6·71008 |
| 11 | 10·36763 | 9·78685 | 9·25262 | 8·76048 | 8·30641 | 7·88687 | 7·49867 | 7·13896 |
| 12 | 11·25508 | 10·57534 | 9·95400 | 9·38507 | 8·86325 | 8·38384 | 7·94269 | 7·53608 |
| 13 | 12·13374 | 11·34837 | 10·63496 | 9·98565 | 9·39357 | 8·85268 | 8·35765 | 7·90378 |
| 14 | 13·00370 | 12·10625 | 11·29607 | 10·56312 | 9·89864 | 9·29498 | 8·74547 | 8·24424 |
| 15 | 13·86505 | 12·84926 | 11·93794 | 11·11839 | 10·37966 | 9·71225 | 9·10791 | 8·55948 |
| 16 | 14·71787 | 13·57771 | 12·56110 | 11·65230 | 10·83777 | 10·10590 | 9·44665 | 8·85137 |
| 17 | 15·56225 | 14·29187 | 13·16612 | 12·16567 | 11·27407 | 10·47726 | 9·76322 | 9·12164 |
| 18 | 16·39827 | 14·99203 | 13·75351 | 12·65930 | 11·68959 | 10·82760 | 10·05909 | 9·37189 |
| 19 | 17·22601 | 15·67846 | 14·32380 | 13·13394 | 12·08532 | 11·15812 | 10·33560 | 9·60360 |
| 20 | 18·04555 | 16·35143 | 14·87747 | 13·59033 | 12·46221 | 11·46992 | 10·59401 | 9·81815 |
| 40 | 32·83469 | 27·35548 | 23·11477 | 19·79277 | 17·15909 | 15·04630 | 13·33171 | 11·92461 |

FIG. 54.—*Interest Table: present value of £1 per period*

$$A_n r = \frac{1 - (1 + r)^{-n}}{r}$$

## PROFIT PLANNING

A company should have clear objectives which are being pursued by all personnel. These objectives should come within the policy determined by the board of directors. Generally, with all commercial companies, profit is the principal motive and provides the necessary driving force. There is now recognition that this does not necessarily have to be *maximum* profit; indeed, a reasonable profit which gives assurance of permanency of the business is now regarded as the normal aim.

When dealing with the question of profit planning it is usual to consider:

1. The volume of output in terms of numbers of products or other units.
2. The variety to be produced (the product mix).
3. The costs to be incurred.
4. The prices to be charged.

The aim of profit planning should be to ensure an adequate return on capital employed (*see* Chapter 15) and financial stability. Both sides of the formula for calculating profit should be considered: this is as follows:

Revenue minus Costs = Profit

Any factor which changes one side or other, or both, should be included in the profit-planning calculations. Quite often there is no distinct factor, but rather a combination of factors. As some aspect is changed, this affects many others. It is the overall, *net* result which is required.

The management accountant may have to calculate figures for a number of alternative courses of action. From these the most appropriate can be selected. When budgetary control is employed the forecast showing the necessary characteristics in terms of profit and financial stability can become the basis of the sales forecast.

## UNDERSTANDING THE NATURE OF THE COSTS

The conventional breakdown of costs into variable, semi-variable and fixed is adequate for most purposes. However, some accountants prefer to take the analysis still further and distinguish between:

(1) Authorised Costs (Unavoidable Costs); and
(2) Policy Decision Costs (Avoidable Costs).

*Authorised costs* are those which have been sanctioned for a period by the board of directors and, therefore, can be spent provided the normal procedures for ordering are followed. Examples are: a contract for three years for the supply of a commodity; a lease on premises taken for a five-year period without any right to cancel or transfer; an advertising programme spread over four years.

These costs appear in all the functional divisions—manufacturing, selling and distribution, administration, and research and development. They are generally fixed in nature so that they are known in advance.

The *policy decision costs* require a management decision before they can be incurred. For the present, or a future period, they are avoidable in the sense that management can decide that they cannot be justified.

If there is an economy drive then costs which are avoidable are simply not authorised.

These costs differ from true variable costs in that they are not necessarily correlated to the volume of output. If they were variable costs then any avoidance would result in loss of output unless, of course, they were not essential in the first place. Examples of decisions which would incur policy decision costs are given below:

1. Employment of a public relations officer.
2. Increased advertising expenditure.
3. Launching of a scheme to award prizes.
4. Introduction of a medical service for all employees.
5. Extension of the pure or basic research facilities.
6. Employment of more development engineers.
7. Redundant employees being absorbed into service departments although they are not really essential.
8. Increase in a manager's salary.

It will be seen from these examples that the board of directors or senior management would be required to decide whether these costs should be incurred. In periods when profits are high there is a tendency for these costs to rise. Unfortunately, once sanctioned they can become part of the authorised costs and may be unavoidable when there is a trade depression. Managers should, therefore, consider the long-period effect as well as the short period when authorising expenditure of this type.

This is not to suggest that policy-decision costs are wrong. Many companies rely on new inventions and developments to earn profit. Without policy decisions being taken at the right time opportunities would be missed and so would the profits. However, there is certainly need to study these costs carefully before agreeing that they should be incurred. The questions which are relevant are:

1. If a policy decision cost is avoided is there likely to be any *adverse* effect upon sales or upon the long-term image of the business?
2. Can the business afford to finance the cost in question?

If the answer to question (1) is "*Yes*," then it may be necessary to obtain the finance. In appropriate circumstances such as, for example, when an advertising campaign is considered essential, the writing off of the expenditure may be carried out over a number of years.

When there is some uncertainty, regarding the answer to question (1) and there is no finance available, then it may be better to avoid the expenditure.

In these cases there has to be the exercise of judgment and a decision has to be made. The management accountant should ensure that the fullest possible knowledge is available on the relevant costs. Sometimes non-financial considerations will affect the decision; the laying off of employees, the dismissal of a manager, or the non-award of an expected increase in salary, can all have adverse effects on employee morale.

A simple example and suggested solution is given below. This serves to illustrate the importance of understanding how costs behave.

QUESTION

The Rule Co. Ltd. manufactures a measuring device which sells direct to customers at £3. The essential details relating to this product are as follows:

| | |
|---|---|
| Estimated sales for next year | 200,000 units |

Manufacturing Costs:

| | |
|---|---|
| Variable | £50,000 |
| Fixed (authorised) | £20,000 |
| Policy decision costs | £5,000 |

Administration Costs:

| | |
|---|---|
| Variable | £10,000 |
| Fixed (authorised) | £30,000 |
| Policy decision costs | £12,000 |

Selling and Distribution Costs:

| | |
|---|---|
| Variable | £40,000 |
| Fixed | £30,000 |
| Policy decision costs | £54,000 |

Analysis of the policy decision costs has revealed that the following could be avoided without detracting from policy:

| | |
|---|---|
| Manufacturing | £3,000 |
| Administration | £4,000 |
| Selling and Distribution | £40,000 |

If the £40,000 is dispensed with then it is estimated that 6000 units of sales will be lost for at least five years.

*Required:* a forecast to show the expected results for one year:

    (*a*) including all costs;

    (*b*) exclusion of the manufacturing and administration costs which can be avoided without any problems; and

    (*c*) exclusion of the manufacturing, administration, and selling and distribution costs which can be avoided.

SUGGESTED SOLUTION

A suggested solution is given below.

*The Rule Co. Ltd.*
*Forecast for the year ending* .................

|  | Course 1 | Course 2 | Course 3 |
|---|---|---|---|
| 1. Sales in units | 200,000 | 200,000 | 194,000 |
| 2. Standard Price | £3 | £3 | £3 |
| 3. Sales Revenue (1 × 2) | £600,000 | 600,000 | 582,000 |
| 4. Cost of Sales—Manufacturing: | | | |
| Variable | 50,000 | 50,000 | 48,500 |
| Fixed | 20,000 | 20,000 | 20,000 |
| Policy decision costs | 5,000 | 2,000 | 2,000 |
| 5. Non-Manufacturing Costs: | | | |
| Variable | 50,000 | 50,000 | 48,500 |
| Fixed | 60,000 | 60,000 | 60,000 |
| Policy decision costs | 66,000 | 62,000 | 22,000 |
| 6. Total Costs (4 + 5) | £251,000 | 244,000 | 201,000 |
| 7. Profits (3 − 6) | £349,000 | 356,000 | 381,000 |

### NOTES

(*a*) Courses of action:

   (1) includes all costs;
   (2) excludes £7000 avoidable costs;
   (3) excludes £47,000 avoidable costs.

(*b*) From the forecast it is indicated that Course 3 should be adopted. Profit increases by £32,000 for the year.

(*c*) If the avoidance of the £40,000 had led to a much larger reduction in the volume of sales, then the expenditure may have been worth while.

## EXAMINATION QUESTIONS

1. (*a*) Prepare from the following information, relating to a division of a manufacturing business, a four-weekly profit statement, and show in a convenient way any differences between the estimated costs and the actual costs. Use the "direct cost" method, *i.e.* do not allocate overhead cost.

Two products are made, X and Y, and each uses two materials, P and Q. At the beginning of the four weeks the following stocks were in hand:

| | | | | | |
|---|---|---|---|---|---|
| X | 12 units at £34 | ... | ... | ... | £408 |
| Y | 7 units at £48 | ... | ... | ... | £336 |

Materials:

| | | | | | |
|---|---|---|---|---|---|
| P | 87 tons at £5 ... | ... | ... | ... | £435 |
| Q | 53 tons at £12 ... | ... | ... | ... | £636 |

The planned specifications per unit of product are:

|                          |       |       |       | X        | Y        |
|--------------------------|-------|-------|-------|----------|----------|
| Direct Material P ...     | ...   | ...   | ...   | 3 tons   | 2 tons   |
| Direct Material Q ...     | ...   | ...   | ...   | 1 ton    | 2 tons   |
| Direct Labour Grade 1     | ...   | ...   | ...   | 35 hours |          |
| Direct Labour Grade 2     | ...   | ...   |       |          | 56 hours |

The estimated material prices are:

|     |     |     |     |               |
|-----|-----|-----|-----|---------------|
| P   | ... | ... | ... | £5 per ton    |
| Q   | ... | ... | ... | £12 per ton   |

The estimated labour rates are:

|         |     |     |                   |
|---------|-----|-----|-------------------|
| Grade 1 | ... | ... | £0·20 per hour    |
| Grade 2 | ... | ... | £0·25 per hour    |

The estimated manufacturing overhead expense for the four weeks was £174

During the period the following was recorded:

100 tons of P was purchased at £5 and 80 tons of Q at £12.
60 tons of P were issued for production of X.
32 tons of P were issued for production of Y.
20 tons of Q were issued for production of X.
32 tons of Q were issued for production of Y.
Grade 1 labour cost was £146 for 730 hours.
Grade 2 labour cost was £212 for 848 hours.
The overhead expense was £192.
Production of finished X was 20 units.
Production of finished Y was 16 units.
Sales of X were 24 at £40 each.
Sales of Y were 11 at £60 each.

There was no work-in-progress at the beginning or end of the period. Stocks of materials and finished goods are to be valued at direct cost based on the manufacturing specifications and the estimated prices and wage rates, not at actual cost.

(b) Write a brief note on the causes of the differences between actual and estimated costs in (a).                                    (A.C.C.A.)

2. Many companies apportion their selling costs to products as a percentage on realised price. It is argued that this means that a product with low material cost, a wide margin of profit, and an easy sales market is charged with, say, 10% on £1, whereas a product with very expensive materials, a very narrow profit margin, and a restricted and strongly competitive market is charged with, say, 10% on £5.

This is considered inequitable. What suggestions would you make?
(I.C.W.A.)

3. Assuming adequate facilities are available in either case, what considerations would guide you in deciding whether certain work should be done in your own factory or placed with outside contractors?     (I.C.W.A.)

4. "The three factors of price, cost and volume are fundamental to virtually every business activity, every business decision." Discuss this statement, explaining the inter-relation of the factors named.     (I.C.W.A.)

5. A small general engineering company has been offered a two-year contract to supply small articles of hardware in large quantities to a large retailing organisation. The customer would provide all designs and detailed

specifications.  The selling prices proposed would be fixed for the duration of the contract, and are estimated to yield a net profit of about 8% on the capital which would be employed on the contract work.  Acceptance would necessitate either increasing productive capacity by about 50% or abandoning half the present business.

Advise the board as to the economic advantages and disadvantages of accepting the proposed contract. (*I.C.W.A.*)

6. You are requested to consider the advisability of closing down one of two retail shops operated in a particular provincial town by your company which has a chain of such shops.  You are aware of the following facts:

(*a*) The trading account of the shop concerned for the past financial year is as follows:

### TRADING ACCOUNT
#### For year to 31st December, 19..

| | £ | £ |
|---|---:|---:|
| Sales ... ... ... ... ... ... | | 35,000 |
| Cost of goods sold: | | |
|   Stock at 1st January, 19.. ... ... | 7,000 | |
|   Purchases during year: | | |
|     Direct ... ... ... ... ... | 10,800 | |
|     From wholesale depot ... ... | 18,000 | |
| | 35,800 | |
|   *Less:* Stock at 31st December, 19.. ... | 7,300 | |
| | | 28,500 |
| Gross profit ... ... ... ... ... | | 6,500 |
| Expenses: | | |
|   Wages and national insurance ... ... | 5,000 | |
|   Carriage inwards ... ... ... | 300 | |
|   Warehouse delivery charges ... ... | 500 | |
|   Packing materials ... ... ... | 250 | |
|   Motor expenses ... ... ... ... | 350 | |
|   Rent, rates and insurances ... ... | 1,250 | |
|   Heating and lighting ... ... ... | 200 | |
|   Postages and telephone ... ... ... | 200 | |
|   Stationery ... ... ... ... | 225 | |
|   Repairs ... ... ... ... | 100 | |
|   Depreciation on motor van ... ... | 100 | |
|   Advertising ... ... ... ... | 500 | |
|   Head office expenses ... ... ... | 500 | |
| | | 9,475 |
| *Loss* for year ... ... ... ... | | £2,975 |

(*b*) Goods are bought partly direct by each shop and partly by bulk buying through a wholesale depot whose charge price to each shop for goods supplied is manufacturer's cost, plus 10%.

(*c*) The motor vehicle expenses are incurred in delivering goods to customers for the two shops, the total being allocated between the shops on turnover.

(*d*) The warehouse delivery charges are an allocation of the expenses of the fleet of delivery vans operated by the wholesale depot based on journeys run.

(*e*) One manager is in charge of the two shops, his salary of £1,500 per annum being allocated equally between them.

(*f*) It is estimated that at least 20% of the business done will be transferred to the remaining shop.

(*g*) The charge for advertising is an allocation from head office.

(*h*) The lease of the premises is expiring in the current year, and an increase in rent of £400 per annum is expected.

Draft a statement of your findings and indicate any other particulars or aspects of the matter to which you would direct attention.    (*I.C.W.A.*)

7. A chemical manufacturing company produces two products, C 100 and C 300. From the information given below you are required to produce the following statements relating to the ensuing year:

(*a*) A standard cost statement for 1,000 grams of each product.

(*b*) A profit forecast for the year in an appropriate form.

(*c*) A cash forecast for the year.

(*d*) The estimated closing balance sheet at the end of the year (estimated to the nearest £).

Supporting schedules showing clearly how these statements have been built up are to be supplied where appropriate.

Taxation may be ignored.

The direct cost method is to be used: that is to say, overhead expenses are not to be allocated to products and stocks are to be valued at prime cost.

The information is as follows:

Production specifications:

| | Batches of 1,000 grams | |
| --- | --- | --- |
| | C 100 | C 300 |
| Direct materials: | | |
| XY ... ... ... ... | 110 grams | 60 grams |
| DR ... ... ... ... | 900 grams | 1,000 grams |
| Cost of energy used ... ... | £4 | £5 |
| Direct labour time: | | |
| Process 1 ... ... ... | 1 hour | 1 hour 20 minutes |
| Process 2 ... ... ... | 30 minutes | 30 minutes |
| Standard material prices are: | | |
| XY ... ... ... ... | £0·10 per 10 grams | |
| DR ... ... ... ... | £0·15 per 10 grams | |
| Standard labour rates are: | | |
| Process 1 ... ... ... | £0·30 per hour | |
| Process 2 ... ... ... | £0·40 per hour | |

Budgeted manufacturing overheads for the ensuing year are £4,500, of which £600 is depreciation.

Budgeted sales for the year are:

| | C 100 | C 300 |
| --- | --- | --- |
| Batches of 1,000 grams... ... | 1,800 | 1,000 |
| Price per 1,000 grams ... ... | £24 | £26 |

Purchases of materials, and sales, are expected to be constant from month to month.

Planned stocks at year-end are:

| | | | | | |
|---|---|---|---|---|---|
| C 100 | ... | ... | ... | ... | 260 batches of 1,000 grams |
| C 300 | ... | ... | ... | ... | 135 batches of 1,000 grams |
| XY | ... | ... | ... | ... | 12,000 grams |
| DR | ... | ... | ... | ... | 125,000 grams |

General administrative overheads are budgeted at £3,800, of which £100 is depreciation.

Debtors and creditors at the end of the year are planned to represent one month's sales and purchases respectively. It may be assumed all other costs except depreciation are cash outlays.

The capital expenditure budget includes £2,200 for new equipment, to be spent in cash during the year.

The balance sheet at the beginning of the year is expected to be as follows:

| | £ | | £ | £ |
|---|---|---|---|---|
| Share capital | 50,000 | Equipment: | | |
| Profit and loss | 13,863 | Cost | 62,000 | |
| Creditors | 2,920 | Depreciation | 8,000 | |
| | | | | 54,000 |
| | | Stock* | 4,283 | |
| | | Debtors | 6,200 | |
| | | Cash | 2,300 | |
| | | | | 12,783 |
| | £66,783 | | | £66,783 |

*Details of the stock are as follows:

| | | | | |
|---|---|---|---|---|
| C 100 | 60 batches of 1,000 grams at £19·1 ... | ... | ... | 1,146 |
| C 300 | 35 batches of 1,000 grams at £21·2 ... | ... | ... | 742 |
| XY | 22,000 grams at £0·10 per 10 grams | ... | ... | 220 |
| DR | 145,000 grams at £0·15 per 10 grams | ... | ... | 2,175 |
| | | | | £4,283 |

There will be no opening or closing work-in-progress.        (*A.C.C.A.*)

8. A machine purchased new in 19.. for £10,000 is capable of producing at the rate of 25 units per hour. A later model of the same machine is now on the market costing £15,000 and capable of producing at the rate of 30 units per hour, and your Board is considering the desirability of replacing the existing machine by the newer model. Describe the various economic factors which may influence the decision, and indicate what information you would require in order to assess their importance.        (*I.C.W.A.*)

9. A company which manufactures small items of electrical equipment, mainly to standard designs, is extending its factory buildings and plant to increase its total capacity by one-third. The additional capacity is planned to come into use on 1st July, 19.., and is expected to be fully employed, partly on expanded production of existing products, partly on new products. Prepare an estimate of the additional working capital required to finance the expansion in trading, using assumed figures and indicating for each item the basis on which the estimate has been arrived at.        (*I.C.W.A.*)

10. (*a*) A manager has to decide whether to install a new, improved machine in place of an existing machine. The new machine would produce an identical product. The information prepared by the cost accountant is given below Prepare a statement to show whether, on the basis of these figures, the new machine should be bought and give your conclusions. Ignore interest.

|  | Old machine | Proposed New machine |
|---|---|---|
| Original cost ... ... ... ... ... | £6,000 | £16,000 |
| Book value now ... ... ... ... ... | £1,800 | — |
| Saleable value now ... ... ... ... | £720 | — |
| Current maintenance cost per annum ... | £1,000 | £200 |
| Annual depreciation being charged in the books | £600 | — |
| Expected life from present date ... ... | 3 years | 10 years |
| Annual output, units per annum ... ... | 12,000 | 16,000 |
| Material and operating costs per unit (excluding maintenance) ... ... ... ... | £0·30 | £0·25 |
| Sale price of product per unit: |  |  |
| For annual sales of 12,000 units ... ... | £0·60 | £0·60 |
| „ „ „ „ 16,000 „ ... ... | — | £0·50 |

(*b*) Explain how you would adjust the calculations under (*a*) to bring the interest factor into account. Actual calculations are not required.

(A.C.C.A.)

11. XY Ltd., an engineering company, has had one-third of its capacity idle for some time owing to lack of orders, and the number of employees has dropped to 240 from the normal level of about 300.

It is approached by a large manufacturing group, AB Ltd., which wishes to find a regular source of supply of specialised pieces of equipment required in connection with its experimental and development work. AB's orders would be of a miscellaneous character with little likelihood of repeat orders, and the volume of work might vary widely from one period to another. A quick delivery service is essential for AB's purpose.

In general, the work would call for a higher standard of precision than XY is accustomed to, and would necessitate the engagement of additional design, drawing-office and tool-room staff at an estimated cost of £15,000 per annum.

AB makes a proposition to XY on the following lines:

(*a*) XY to reserve one-third of its capacity for AB's orders in return for a fixed annual retaining fee.

(*b*) In addition to the retaining fee, XY to be paid for the cost of work carried out for AB with an allowance for profit of 10% of the capital actually employed on the orders.

(*c*) AB to have absolute priority for its orders over all other customers of XY in respect of the one-third capacity reserved to it, but XY to be permitted to use that capacity on work for other customers when not required for AB's work.

(*d*) The amount of the retaining fee and the precise definition of "cost" and "capital employed" to be matters for negotiation.

You are asked to prepare a report for the Board of XY, setting out the economic factors to be considered in negotiating with AB and suggesting an equitable basis for arriving at the amount of the retaining fee and for calculating the cost of AB's orders and the capital employed on them. (*I.C.W.A.*)

12. The profit and loss account for 19.. of the Palace Sound Co. Ltd. and its combined variance statements are shown below.

The Palace Sound Co. Ltd. comprises three factories which make the same types of product, though not always the same product mix, and has the same approximate production capacity. During 19.. Factory X ran at 90% volume and Factory Y at 80% volume.

In view of the poor performance of Factory Z consideration is being given to disposing of this factory. If this were done certain equipment (whose depreciation was £2,200) would be transferred from this factory equally to the other two. This would increase the productive capacity of each by 10% of the sales volume of Factory Z.

You are required to:

(a) Adjust the profit and loss account for factories X and Y to show an increase to full capacity AND the addition of 10% of the sales volume of Factory Z resulting from the transfer of equipment.

(b) In relation to each item indicate the assumption that you have made, and what additional information you would need to obtain a more reliable answer.

|  | Factory | | | |
|  | X | Y | Z | Total |
|  | £ | £ | £ | £ |
| Net Sales ... ... ... ... | 668,800 | 658,000 | 461,700 | 1,788,000 |
| Actual costs incurred: | | | | |
|   Materials ... ... ... | 355,100 | 356,400 | 274,200 | 985,700 |
|   Direct wages ... ... ... | 128,800 | 129,300 | 111,600 | 369,700 |
| Manufacturing expenses: | | | | |
|   Supervision ... ... ... | 12,800 | 13,100 | 11,100 | 37,000 |
|   Indirect factory wages ... | 11,200 | 11,000 | 10,900 | 33,100 |
|   Administration costs (A) ... | 4,600 | 4,500 | 3,600 | 12,700 |
|   Salaries (A) ... ... ... | 5,100 | 5,100 | 4,100 | 14,300 |
|   Carriage inwards ... ... | 3,500 | 4,600 | 2,900 | 11,000 |
|   Fuel, power and light ... | 21,500 | 18,200 | 17,500 | 57,200 |
|   Depreciation on machinery ... | 6,400 | 5,900 | 7,800 | 20,100 |
|   Depreciation on buildings ... | 4,400 | 7,800 | 5,900 | 18,100 |
|   Rent and rates ... ... | 4,600 | 4,100 | 3,800 | 12,500 |
|   Supplies ... ... ... | 12,800 | 8,900 | 13,600 | 35,300 |
|   General expenses ... ... | 1,200 | 900 | 800 | 2,900 |
|   Insurance ... ... ... | 1,600 | 1,400 | 1,300 | 4,300 |
| Total manufacturing expenses | £89,700 | 85,500 | 83,300 | 258,500 |
| Total costs ... ... ... | 573,600 | 571,200 | 469,100 | 1,613,900 |
| Increase/Decrease in: | | | | |
|   Work-in-progress (B) ... | (8,100) | (4,500) | (3,800) | (200) |
|   Finished goods (B) ... | (8,200) | (9,100) | (7,700) | (25,000) |
| Surplus ... ... ... ... | 573,500 | 557,600 | 457,600 | 1,588,700 |
|   Selling expenses ... ... | 26,500 | 26,300 | 18,500 | 71,300 |
| Profits before tax ... ... | £547,000 | 531,300 | 439,100 | 1,517,400 |

(A) = Apportioned to each factory. (B) = Standard cost values.

*Variance analysis for the year*    X      Y      Z

| Material cost variance ... | ... £25,400 | 23,200 | (9,200) |
|---|---|---|---|
| Wages variance ... | ... 4,200 | 1,600 | (11,200) |
| Overhead variance ... | ... (15,800) | (16,500) | (27,100) |

(*A.C.C.A.*)

13. A business is engaged in making a standard product. A summary of the Profit and Loss account prepared for April, 19.., was as follows:

|  | £ | £ |
|---|---|---|
| Sales: 648 units at £4 each   ... |  | 2,592 |
| Increase in stock during month: |  |  |
| 72 units valued at £2 each ... |  | 144 |
|  |  | £2,736 |
| Material used in manufacture... | 520 |  |
| Direct wages   ...   ...   ... | 640 |  |
| Other variable costs: |  |  |
| Manufacturing   ...   ... | 720 |  |
| Selling   ...   ...   ... | 185 |  |
| Administration   ...   ... | 63 |  |
| Fixed charges: |  |  |
| Manufacturing   ...   ... | 360 |  |
| Selling   ...   ...   ... | 297 |  |
| Administration   ...   ... | 243 | £3,028 |
| Net loss for the month   ... |  | £292 |

On investigation it was ascertained that:

(i) normal capacity of the works is 900 units per month;

(ii) during the month, due to faulty materials, 80 defective units were made and subsequently scrapped, and no part of the cost was recovered.

Making use of this additional information, redraft the Profit and Loss account bringing out clearly the causes of the unsatisfactory results for the month.          (*I.C.W.A.*)

14. The costs of a manufacturing company for a year are as follows:

|  | £ |
|---|---|
| Direct materials   ...   ...   ...   ... | ... 120,000 |
| Direct wages   ...   ...   ...   ... | ... 80,000 |
| Production overheads (variable) ...   ... | ... 60,000 |
|      ,,      ,,    (fixed)   ...   ... | ... 40,000 |
| Selling and distribution costs (variable)... | ... 20,000 |
|    ,,    ,,    ,,    ,,    (fixed)   ... | ... 40,000 |

During this period sales were as follows:

|  | £ |
|---|---|
| Main product   ...   ...   ...   ... | ... 340,000 |
| By-product A (8,000 units)   ...   ... | ... 40,000 |
| By-product B (5,000 units)   ...   ... | ... 20,000 |

It is discovered that a further process combining by-product B with some of by-product A, and adding further material, will yield a saleable product C. Investigation shows that if the 5,000 units of B are combined with 4,000 units of A, together with additional material costing £60,000, at an additional direct wages cost of £30,000, the production of C will give a sales value of £180,000.

Plant, machinery and facilities are available in the business to accommodate this extra work, but it is estimated that additional fixed expenses amounting to £12,000 will be incurred during a year if the additional process is carried out.

Present a report to management, making recommendations on the course of action you suggest.                                                     (*I.C.W.A.*)

15. Your directors are contemplating the purchase of a new machine to replace a machine which has been in operation in the factory for five years. From the following information prepare a statement for submission to the board showing the effect of the installation on costs and profits and comment on the results shown. Ignore interest.

|  | Old machine | New machine |
|---|---|---|
| Purchase price ... ... ... | £4,000 | £6,000 |
| Estimated life of machine ... | 10 years | 10 years |
| Machine running hours per annum... ... ... ... | 2,000 | 2,000 |
| Units produced per hour ... | 24 | 36 |
| Wages per running hour ... | £0·30 | £0·53 |
| Power per annum ... ... | £200 | £450 |
| Consumable stores per annum | £600 | £750 |
| All other charges per annum ... | £800 | £900 |
| Material cost per unit ... ... | £0·05 | £0·05 |
| Selling price per unit ... ... | £0·15 | £0·15 |

(*I.C.W.A.*)

16. A certain factory producing packaging material has a ten-year-old plant, depreciated by the *straight-line* method, to which the following details apply:

| | |
|---|---|
| Purchase price, including installation ... | £60,000. |
| Estimated total life ... ... ... ... | 20 years. |
| Residual value after 20 years ... ... ... | £10,000. |
| Output per minute ... ... ... ... | 200 units. |

An offer is received to supply new plant to the value of £95,000. The offer also proposes a part-exchange provision of £20,000 in respect of the existing plant. The output of the new plant is 400 units per minute. It has an estimated life of 15 years, and residual value of £10,000.

The annual costs, etc., are to be taken as follows:

|  | Existing plant £ | New plant £ |
|---|---|---|
| Repairs and maintenance | 2,000 | 2,500 |
| Sundry indirect materials | 12,000 | 15,000 |
| Power and steam service | 6,000 | 7,000 |
| Proportion of general fixed cost ... ... | 1,500 | 2,000 |
| Running hours ... ... | 2,500 | 2,500 |
| Wages of attendants ... | 2,500 | 3,500 |

The installation cost of the new plant will be £5,000. No change in the method of charging depreciation is proposed.

Disregarding direct material cost, which is constant to both, prepare a comparative cost schedule to show total, and marginal costs per 1,000 units of product produced by the new, and the existing, plant.          (*I.C.W.A.*)

17. A company has three factories making similar products. Business has fallen off. but in the opinion of management, this is only a temporary recession. It is suggested that one of the factories might be closed for a period of two to three years.

As cost accountant, detail the factors to be considered in arriving at a decision. What cost information is necessary to enable management to decide which factory to close?          (*I.C.W.A.*)

18. A company finds that costs of a certain product leave insufficient margin to meet competition in the open market. An examination of the records shows that the main reason for this is the excessive labour cost which has arisen from the difficulty of recruiting suitably trained labour in the area. Times occupied in certain operations are consistently greater than estimated and an abnormal amount of spoiled work and re-processing has resulted. Overheads are absorbed by a percentage addition to direct wages of 200%.

Using suitable figures, draft a report to the management. (*I.C.W.A.*)

19. Your directors have decided to commence the manufacture of a product, similar to those already manufactured, which will be sold in an entirely new market where the selling price must be kept to a minimum, possibly below total cost. How would you determine the selling price in such an instance?          (*I.C.W.A.*)

20. A manufacturing company concentrates its resources upon one single product which it sells to wholesale merchants at £4·80 per unit. The following details apply:

| Output (units) | 75,000 | 85,000 | 100,000 |
|---|---|---|---|
| | £ | £ | £ |
| Variable overhead cost ... ... | 40,000 | 48,000 | 55,000 |
| Variable selling and administrative | | | |
| expense ... ... ... ... | 15,000 | 17,500 | 22,000 |

Material costs £2 per unit, but quantity rebates of 10% and 15% apply to purchase contracts for 85,000 and 100,000 units respectively. Average wages cost is 10s. per unit. Fixed overhead is £70,000 (production); and £25,000 (selling and administrative).

In order to sell the whole output, selling price reductions of 5% and 10% are contemplated for the output levels of 85,000 and 100,000 units respectively.

An offer to purchase 10,000 units at £4 per unit has been received from abroad.

(*a*) Tabulate the necessary figures to show marginal costs and the increases in selling value for the three output levels, and indicate which of the three is most profitable.

(*b*) Prepare a simple statement to show profit or loss at each output level.

(*c*) Prepare a statement showing the effect upon net income if the offer from abroad is accepted, assuming that other prices will not be affected, and the output level indicated in your answer to (*a*) is adopted.          (*I.C.W.A.*)

21. Following a successful "take-over bid" for a similar factory to the one being operated, you are requested, as the management accountant, to compile comparative figures of income-cost-volume relationships for the two factories.

Design a suitable form for tabulating the figures. Provision should be made for last year's actual, and current year's estimated, figures. Classification of the data should be broadly drawn, using headings appropriate to income-cost-volume requirements. Provide also for appending, to the tabulation, percentages representing variations between current and last year; and also such ratio percentages as you consider useful. Actual figures are not required.                                                (*I.C.W.A.*)

22. A small company manufacturing components for the motor car industry consists of a light machine shop and an assembly department. In a normal year when sales amounted to £120,683, its costs were as follows:

|  | £ |
|---|---|
| Direct materials ... ... ... ... ... ... | 24,832 |
| Direct wages, machine shop ... ... ... ... | 16,694 |
| Direct wages, assembly ... ... ... ... ... | 8,090 |
| Factory overheads, machine shop ... ... ... ... | 31,742 |
| Factory overheads, assembly ... ... ... ... | 7,264 |
| Administration costs ... ... ... ... ... ... | 8,767 |
| Selling costs ... ... ... ... ... ... | 4,445 |
| Distribution costs ... ... ... ... ... ... | 6,427 |

Direct labour hours amounted to 67,284 in the machine shop and 40,073 in the assembly department.

It is the company's custom to absorb overheads as follows:

Factory overhead, machine shop at £0·48 per direct labour hour.
Factory overhead, assembly dept. at £0·18 per direct labour hour.
Administration, selling and distribution costs as $22\frac{1}{2}\%$ on production cost.

A certain component is made from 50 lbs. of steel strip costing £56 per ton and requires $3\frac{1}{2}$ hours of machine shop labour charged at £0·50 per hour, and $1\frac{3}{4}$ hours of assembly labour charged at £0·40 per hour. The customer is being charged a price of £12 each, and asks for quotations for exactly the same component (*a*) made in "free issue" material, and (*b*) made from brass strip requiring 50 lbs. per article at a cost of £0·13 per lb. Management asks for information to enable quotations to be made as required, and also to see whether the present selling price is reasonable.

Present figures as required.                                                (*I.C.W.A.*)

23. A factory consists of:

    (*a*) heavy machine shop;
    (*b*) light machine shop;
    (*c*) electro-plating department;
    (*d*) assembly department,

together with the usual service departments, administrative, selling and distributive organisation.

Owing to pressure of work which is regarded as likely to last for at least two years, the management is considering:

    (*a*) getting plating done outside or working overtime in the plating shop;
    (*b*) extending the heavy machine shop or working a night shift.

The other production departments have capacity to cope with the additional work.

Assuming a sound costing system to be in existence, explain how you would advise the management, to enable them to make decisions. (*I.C.W.A.*)

24. Costs presented to management should show clearly the efficiency of departments and the profitability of products.

Write notes indicating how this is done, with special reference to standard costing, marginal costing and budgetary control. (*I.C.W.A.*)

25. Using suitable figures, present a report to management, justifying the purchase of a very expensive machine requested and recommended by the Works Manager and other technical experts. You are to assume that a system of budgetary control is in operation. (*I.C.W.A.*)

26. A business manufactures three quite different types of product, for all of which a steadily increasing demand arises. Capital, space and technical knowledge are available for expansion of any one of the three.

Using suitable figures, present a report to management on the profitability of the three products, and advise regarding the expansion of the most suitable product as revealed by your figures. (*I.C.W.A.*)

27. The trading results of XYZ Manufacturers Ltd. for the year 19.. were as follows:

|  | £ | £ |
|---|---|---|
| Direct materials ... ... ... ... ... |  | 80,000 |
| Direct wages: |  |  |
|     Dept. A ... ... ... ... ... ... | 20,000 |  |
|     „ B ... ... ... ... ... ... | 31,500 |  |
|  |  | 51,500 |
| Variable overheads: |  |  |
|     Dept. A ... ... ... ... ... ... | 25,000 |  |
|     „ B ... ... ... ... ... ... | 63,000 |  |
|  |  | 88,000 |
| Fixed overheads ... ... ... ... ... |  | 77,250 |
| Total costs ... ... ... ... ... ... |  | 296,750 |
| Profit ... ... ... ... ... ... ... |  | 13,250 |
| Sales ... ... ... ... ... ... ... |  | £310,000 |

Three products are made, and details of costs, sales, etc., for the year are as follows:

|  | X | Y | Z |
|---|---|---|---|
| Sales (units) ... ... ... ... | 80,000 | 100,000 | 12,000 |
|  | £ | £ | £ |
| Selling price (per unit) ... ... | 1·25 | 1·20 | 7·50 |
| Costs (per unit): |  |  |  |
|     Direct materials ... ... ... | 0·25 | 0·50 | 0·83 |
| Direct wages: |  |  |  |
|     Dept. A ... ... ... ... | 0·10 | 0·10 | 0·17 |
|     „ B ... ... ... ... | 0·15 | 0·07 | 1·00 |

It is the company's practice to absorb departmental variable costs as a percentage on direct departmental wages, and the fixed expenses of the business on the basis of total wages.

The results for the year are regarded as unsatisfactory, and as a result of a conference between sales and general management, with the year's costs available to them, the following is suggested:

(a) As product X is unprofitable, its sales should be allowed to fall. It is anticipated that 60,000 units will be sold at £1·25 in the year 1960.

(b) Product Y can be sold by additional sales effort and sales in 1960 should increase by 50% at the same selling price as in the previous year.

(c) By reducing the price of product Z, on which high profits are made, to £6 per unit, sales should be increased by 50%.

Prepare a forecast of the probable results for the year 1960, assuming no variance in manufacturing efficiency, and no change in the total fixed expenses of the business, and make notes of any advice you would tender to management, based on your figures.       (*I.C.W.A.*)

28. A company making a single product has a factory in the South, and distributes its production through three depots situated in the South, Midlands and North.

It is estimated that during the coming year 100,000 units will be manufactured and sold at a price of £20 per unit, the sales being spread as follows:

| | |
|---|---|
| South ... ... | 70,000 units |
| Midlands ... | 20,000 „ |
| North ... ... | 10,000 „ |

Standard costs of production are:

| | |
|---|---|
| Direct materials ... ... | £4·80 per unit |
| Direct wages ... ... | £3·00 „ |
| Factory variable overheads | 140% on direct wages |
| Factory fixed overheads | £400,000 per annum |

The costs of selling and distribution incurred by the depots are estimated as follows:

| | | | |
|---|---|---|---|
| Fixed costs | ... | South ... | £80,000 per annum |
| „ | ... | Midlands ... | £50,000 „ |
| „ | ... | North ... | £30,000 „ |
| Variable costs | ... | South ... | 5% of sales value |
| „ | ... | Midlands ... | 8% „ |
| „ | ... | North ... | 10% „ |

From the budget for the business prepared from these figures, management is considering the desirability of closing the depots and selling organisations in the Midlands and/or North. If this is done it is expected that all sales in these areas will be lost, but that sales in the South will remain unaffected.

Prepare a budget for the business from the figures provided, indicating why management is thinking of closing the depots in the Midlands and/or North.

Present additional information to help management make a decision in regard to this problem, and make recommendations from your figures.

      (*I.C.W.A.*)

29. The board of directors have called a meeting to discuss possible selling price changes. The proposal before the board is that a $7\frac{1}{2}\%$ reduction in selling price should be made.

The budget for the next twelve months discloses that estimated sales are 200,000 units at £4 each, variable costs are £2·5 per unit and fixed costs are £125,000 per annum. It is estimated that 260,000 units per annum could be produced with no further increase in fixed costs, or in variable costs per unit.

Write a brief report without using technical accounting language bringing out, from the facts given, the significant features of the proposal. (*A.C.C.A.*)

30. It has been the practice to carry out a certain job on Machine "A". This job could be done on another type of machine (Machine "B"), which is at present installed in the factory, or on still another type of machine (Machine "C"), which would have to be bought. Neither Machine "A" nor Machine "B" is being used to capacity at the present time.

Using suitable figures submit a report to Management and make recommendations based on the figures used. (*I.C.W.A.*)

31. The annual flexible budget of a company is as follows:

| Production capacity ... | 40% £ | 60% £ | 80% £ | 100% £ |
|---|---|---|---|---|
| Costs: | | | | |
| Direct labour ... | 16,000 | 24,000 | 32,000 | 40,000 |
| Direct material ... | 12,000 | 18,000 | 24,000 | 30,000 |
| Production overhead | 11,400 | 12,600 | 13,800 | 15,000 |
| Administration over- | | | | |
| head ... ... | 5,800 | 6,200 | 6,600 | 7,000 |
| Selling and distribution | | | | |
| overhead ... ... | 6,200 | 6,800 | 7,400 | 8,000 |
| | £51,400 | £67,600 | £83,800 | £100,000 |

Owing to trading difficulties the company is operating at 50% capacity. Selling prices have had to be lowered to what the directors maintain is an uneconomic level, and they are considering whether or not their single factory should be closed down until the trade recession has passed.

A market research consultant has advised that in about twelve months' time there is every indication that sales will increase to about 75% of normal capacity and that the revenue to be produced in the second year will amount to £90,000. The present revenue from sales at 50% capacity would amount to only £49,500 for a complete year.

If the directors decide to close down the factory for a year it is estimated that:

(a) the present fixed costs would be reduced to £11,000 per annum;
(b) closing down costs (redundancy payments, etc.) would amount to £7,500;
(c) necessary maintenance of plant would cost £1,000 per annum;
(d) on reopening the factory, the cost of overhauling plant, training and engagement of new personnel would amount to £4,000.

Prepare a statement for the directors, presenting the information in such a way as to indicate whether or not it is desirable to close the factory.

(*I.C.W.A.*)

32. The monthly cost figures for production in a manufacturing company are:

|  |  | £ |
|---|---|---|
| Variable costs | ... ... ... | 120,000 |
| Fixed costs ... | ... ... ... | 35,000 |
| Total ... | ... ... ... | £155,000 |

The normal monthly sales figure is £200,000.
Actual sales figures for three separate months are:

| First month | Second month | Third month |
|---|---|---|
| £ | £ | £ |
| 200,000 | 165,000 | 235,000 |

Under a system of marginal costing stocks are valued as follows:

|  | First month | Second month | Third month |
|---|---|---|---|
|  | £ | £ | £ |
| Opening stock | 84,000 | 84,000 | 105,000 |
| Closing stock | 84,000 | 105,000 | 84,000 |

If the marginal costing technique were not used stocks would be valued as follows:

|  | First month | Second month | Third month |
|---|---|---|---|
|  | £ | £ | £ |
| Opening stock | 108,500 | 108,500 | 135,625 |
| Closing stock | 108,500 | 135,625 | 108,500 |

Prepare *two* tabulations, side by side, to summarise these results for *each* of the three months, basing one tabulation on marginal cost theory and the tabulation alongside on absorption cost theory.
Comment on the tabulations. *(I.C.W.A.)*

33. An engineering company receives an enquiry for the manufacture of certain products where the costs are estimated as follows, per product:

|  |  | £ |
|---|---|---|
| Direct materials | ... ... | 3·50 |
| Direct labour (5 hours) | ... | 2·25 |
| Direct expenses | ... ... | 0·25 |
| Variable overheads ... | ... | 1·50 |

The manufacture of these products will necessitate the provision of special tooling costing approximately £375. The sales manager, from his knowledge of the market, envisages a selling price of £10·625 per product. For an order to be considered profitable, it is necessary for it to yield a target contribution rate of £0·40 per labour hour.
Prepare a chart showing:

(a) the sales level at which a contribution to fixed costs commences;
(b) the sales level at which the contribution rate meets the target.

*(I.C.W.A.)*

34. Your company manufactures a range of electrical accessories to a catalogue price list. There are about 200 product items in all which can be varied if a customer so requests. It sells its products through several different distribution channels, each of which has its own particular distribution costs, while in each channel selling prices are subject to hard bargaining and negotiation.

The sales director has co-operated with you as the management accountant in developing the use of marginal analysis in the company. This is mainly because he has been called upon frequently to fix selling prices in a competitive situation. He has required on these occasions to know costs at different volumes of output and for batches of different sizes. He has also required a sound knowledge of cost facts when making decisions on minimum selling prices. The approach has worked reasonably well, but the applications of it have been *ad hoc* in character.

How could you now formalise the use of marginal costing so as to give the sales director regular and meaningful information?  (*I.C.W.A.*)

35. Your company operates a factory which is working at full machine capacity producing the total requirements of three component parts: A, B and C used in equal proportions in an assembly type product. Data concerning one unit of the product is as follows:

|  | Machine hours | Variable £ | Costs Fixed £ | Total £ |
|---|---|---|---|---|
| Component parts: |  |  |  |  |
| A ... ... ... | 5 | 24 | 8 | 32 |
| B ... ... ... | 8 | 30 | 10 | 40 |
| C ... ... ... | 10 | 30 | 30 | 60 |
| Assembly ... ... | — | 50 | 20 | 70 |
| Total ... ... | 23 | £134 | £68 | £202 |
| Selling price... ... |  |  |  | £250 |

In preparing a budget for the coming year an increase of sales and production is being considered. It is ascertained that the present machine capacity of the factory will be capable of producing the requirements of only two of the three component parts. No increase of machine capacity can be effected during the course of the next year although other facilities can be increased at very short notice.

In the circumstances it has been decided to consider purchasing supplies of one component part from outside suppliers and quotations have been received as follows:

| Part | Each £ |
|---|---|
| A ... ... ... | 34 |
| B ... ... ... | 44 |
| C ... ... ... | 52 |

The sales manager feels that the minimum increase on existing sales and production that should be considered is 50%, and that he could sell up to an increase of 80% provided the factory capacity is available.

You are required to prepare a report for management giving your recommendations as to which component part should be ordered from outside suppliers for the coming year if production is increased by 50%, and also if full factory capacity is utilised. (I.C.W.A.)

# CHAPTER 13

## DETERMINATION OF OPTIMUM OUTPUT

### *INTRODUCTION*

A BUSINESS produces and sells to make a profit—if possible the maximum profit. Clearly, for any product, there must be a demand which is large enough to allow the optimum level of operations to be achieved. Optimum level, in this connection, means that the volume of production is at the size which enables maximum efficiency and, therefore, maximum profit to be obtained.

### *PROBLEMS OF MANAGEMENT PLANNING*

There are four principal problems connected with maximisation of profit. Management has to select an acceptable product, determine the optimum output, understand the part it can play in fixing prices and establish methods of controlling costs and performances. These problems are outlined below; the management accountant must be able to appreciate what they are and how he can help to solve them.

#### THE ACCEPTABLE PRODUCT

Only by considering the needs of the consumer can management earn profit. Demand has to be estimated: the utility possessed by the product is the principal factor to consider. Management has the task of determining consumers' requirements. Products can then be developed which serve their functional needs and, at the same time, have some aesthetic appeal. Production and distribution must be carried out within the limits imposed by the prices which can be obtained: only by keeping costs within reasonable limits can satisfaction of the consumers' needs be assured.

The estimated demand for a product at a certain price, or at a number of different prices, is estimated by market research. Economists, statisticians and market research workers employ up-to-date techniques to provide all relevant data for reaching conclusions. The accountant then has the responsibility of determining the most profitable output, a matter which will now be discussed.

#### OPTIMUM OUTPUT

The determination of optimum output has received much attention from economists. There are two problems: minimisation of average unit cost and maximisation of sales revenue.

For each business unit, there is a point at which the volume of production will result in the lowest average unit cost. Before this point is

330

reached the cost per unit will tend to reduce with each increase in volume; after the point of minimum cost is reached each successive addition to output then tends to result in increased average unit cost. This tendency for costs to reduce, level out for a time, and then to increase may be shown diagrammatically (Fig. 55).

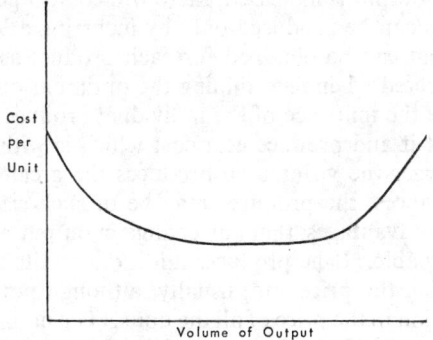

Cost per Unit

Volume of Output

FIG. 55.—*Relation of Unit Cost and Volume*

For a specific plant and assuming no change in policy, the same total fixed costs are incurred for a small volume of output as for a large volume. In the early stages of production, increases in volume mean that the fixed costs are apportioned over a larger number of units and, therefore, the average unit cost is smaller. However, after a time, variable costs per unit tend to increase more than the fixed costs per unit so that additional volume can only be produced at a higher average unit cost. Overtime and shift work, excessive depreciation of plant, machinery and other fixed assets, and the general falling off in efficiency which inevitably results from attempting to "squeeze" too much from existing facilities, all contribute to the increase in unit costs. Clearly, then, there is a limit to the volume of output which can be produced from existing plant, equipment, and personnel. For a time greater efficiency and, therefore, increased output may be obtained from new methods of production, improved layout of machines or better planning of the work-flow. However, improvements cannot be made indefinitely. Moreover, an important fact that should not be forgotten is that each improvement will have to be introduced into the existing pattern of production; the introduction itself will tend to increase costs and, if a stoppage or curtailment of output is caused, then the expense is inflated still further. With a factory which employs a large number of workers, a one-day stoppage can result in a loss of many thousands of pounds. The lesson is obvious; improvements should be made, but they should be of value and be capable of being fitted into the existing arrangements at a cost which is less than the value of the additional benefits to be received. If there is some doubt as to the benefits, then possibly the "improvement" should not be introduced; certainly frequent amendments, adjustments, and changes are not to be recommended for they bring about confusion and a lack of trust and confidence in the personnel who are to operate the systems. To reiterate, even improvements cannot hold back the inevitable increase in unit cost; once the change has been made the immediate impact may make a reduction in the cost per unit, but if output is increased, there will come a point when subsequent increases can be produced only by incurring a loss in efficiency.

The price that can be obtained for each product as well as its cost must be considered when determining the optimum output. Often the price is outside the influence of the individual producer and, therefore, he must accept it and produce at a cost which is within the limit laid down. The larger the volume he produces the greater the profit. In other circumstances, the producer may be of such size, or be in possession of such advantages, that any change in output will tend to affect the price obtainable. If he produces additional units they can be sold only by reducing the price and, usually, although not invariably, this means a reduction in the price of all the units. The nature of the product will play an important part in the relation of price and volume; generally, luxury or non-essential products have a fixed demand at a stated price; to increase that demand the price must be reduced. On the other hand, the price for staple, essential products may not react in the same way to changes in demand. Clearly, these remarks are generalisations. In practice, the actual product and its nature will be known; accordingly, the effect on price of an increase in volume *can* be estimated. The accountant must recognise the price-volume relationships and consider them when determining the most profitable output.

Economists have evolved a technique for determining optimum output. They say that the entrepreneur should produce to the point at which marginal cost and marginal revenue agree. The marginal cost is the difference in cost caused by producing one unit more or one unit less. If total cost for X output is £100 and total cost for X + 1 output is £102 then the marginal cost is £2. On the other hand, if the cost for X − 1 is £99 then the marginal cost is £1. The marginal revenue is the difference made to total revenue by selling one more unit. Until marginal cost and marginal revenue are equal the former is smaller than the latter and, therefore, each unit sold earns a margin of profit. Reference to the way costs behave with increases in output has already been made; because of the tendency after a certain point has been reached for costs to increase it follows that there will be a limit to the number of units that can be produced at a cost which is below the revenue obtained from the additional sales.

Here the concern must be with the accountant's approach to determining optimum output. Fortunately the method used is not very different from that outlined in the previous paragraph. However, marginal cost to the accountant does not necessarily have exactly the same meaning as that given by the economist. The direct labour and material costs together with variable overhead costs are the marginal costs; in other words, the total cost *less* fixed costs is the marginal cost. When the accountant speaks of marginal cost he does not necessarily mean the cost of the *additional* unit. If he wishes to denote the cost of this unit, he may refer to "differential cost." More usual though is the use of the term "variable costs" which are the costs which tend to vary with increases in output. Within a certain range each additional unit produced will incur the same variable cost. The larger the volume of output, the larger the total variable cost. On the other hand, fixed costs remain the same in total, irrespective of the volume of output. This difference in meaning is shown in the formula given below for determining optimum output.

A manufacturer does not generally consider the effect of producing and selling *one* more unit. Managers, including accountants, think in terms of multiples of 100, 1000, or even larger units. If extra business is required, then unless dealing with large and valuable contracts, management attempts to get orders for a large number of units. Quite often, the setting-up costs of machines, or other technical considerations, make the production of a certain minimum number of units essential. The difficulty and expense of compiling records to show the marginal cost of each single unit cannot normally be justified and this is another reason for the accountant taking compound multiples rather than unit multiples.

In accounting terminology the rule for determining optimum output may now be stated. *Production should be increased provided the variable cost\* arising from the increase in volume does not exceed the addition to sales revenue arising from the same increase in volume.* As already indicated, the increases in volume will tend to be thought of in terms of a number of units rather than a single product. For many purposes, consideration of the costs for each 5% of possible capacity may be quite adequate. However, there can be no hard and fast rule on this matter. Clearly, the degree of competition and the profit margin being earned will influence the decision. The fact that fixed costs may also be increased by an expansion of volume should not be overlooked. All too often additional business is secured on the theory that any increase in volume is beneficial, provided variable costs are covered and some margin of profit is obtained. If care is not taken this "extra business" fills part of the capacity needed to produce the normal volume which covers fixed costs. Therefore, fixed costs are not fully recovered. Another possibility is that the business has to expand its plant to meet all its commitments with the result that further fixed costs are incurred.

## COSTS AND SELLING PRICES

Many businessmen take the view that prices must be accepted because they are determined by market conditions and not by the costs of

---

\* The term "marginal cost" may be substituted for variable cost. Exponents of Marginal Costing will probably prefer this. (*See* page 224.)

producing. There is a good deal of truth in this line of thought, but it is not invariably true. Even if a particular business does not produce enough to influence price, and an increase in volume from that business makes very little difference to *total* supply, it does not follow that similar increases from *all* relatively small business units would not influence price. If all competing units succeed in increasing volume then the total supply would be much greater so that to sell every unit produced it would be necessary to reduce the price. This action would eliminate inefficient business units or would compel them to reduce costs so that they could sell within the new price. Briefly then, the lesson is that a single producer may not be able to influence price, but, collectively, all producers in an industry can affect price. Moreover, if production is to be continued at the same level then costs must be covered by the selling prices obtained. No business can continue to operate over a long period without making profits.

A business may be large enough to influence prices. Alternatively, it may be in possession of a unique product which allows advantageous terms to be obtained. The "uniqueness" may even be mythical, introduced by intensive advertising and publicity campaigns. Quite often the stimulating of demand has, as its main object, the increase of the production volume so that the cost of each unit can be reduced. Whether this reduction will be allowed to influence the price charged depends upon the policy of the particular business. An important fact, not to be forgotten, is that even when a product is branded or possesses some quality which makes it "different," there will generally be substitutes available. Accordingly, the businessman should study the prices paid for products which are in competition with his own, otherwise he may find difficulty in selling the desired volume. Furthermore, since competitors' prices may be based on costs, a position may arise where a producer will have to consider not only his own costs, but also, indirectly, the costs of his competitors.

The most important considerations of the cost-price relationships have already been noted by the author in *Standard Costing*. These are repeated below:

"From what has been said, some idea of the role of costs in pricing should have been obtained. Many people point out that, when it comes to selling, the price that rules is the best that can be obtained; in other words, the amount that will be paid by the customer. As will be shown in a moment, there is often much truth in this view. However, two very important facts should not be forgotten. The first is that, under normal conditions, the prices in an industry will tend to be based on the costs of the efficient concerns. Only by keeping costs low, and thus keeping its prices within reasonable dimensions, can a business hope to meet direct competition and competition from substitutes. The other important fact is connected with the possibility of external direction or control from government action. Public feeling against excessive prices or a routine probe by a government-sponsored commission of enquiry may indicate that prices are too high. The only way for a business to defend itself logically is to show that its prices and costs are related and that the former are not abnormally in excess of the latter. Some businesses do actually work on a small percentage added to cost; they depend on a very large volume of business to enable them to earn adequate profits. Clearly, any enquiry into the reasonableness of a price cannot ignore the cost.

Some difficulties of accepting cost as the sole basis for price fixing will now be enumerated.

1. Anticipated demand conditions may not be realised. If demand is underestimated prices will tend to rise; if it is overestimated, prices may not cover costs. In such circumstances, the Standard Costs will indicate the size of the profit earned or loss incurred by each line of product. The full consequences of the miscalculation, as affecting that particular business, will thus be fully appreciated.

2. Costs may be incurred on producing a commodity which turns out to be of no value and therefore cannot be sold except for scrap. This reason is linked with (1) above.

3. Many costs are determined by an estimate of the price that can be expected for a certain quality product.

The market is carefully studied and the price at which profits should be maximised is determined. Working backwards from the price, the quality of product which will give the desired volume of sales is estimated and then the product is made. In this way, so the argument runs, costs are determined by price. Thus, for example, if it was felt that a cheap family car would have a ready demand, a suitable price would be determined and then the cost would be worked out within the boundaries laid down by the price minus expected profit. A similar procedure may be followed in clothing and footwear industries.

Clearly, this reversal of the apparent normal order of things cannot be denied, but it is not as unusual as some people seem to believe. The very act of entering into the business of manufacturing and selling of commodities implies that, consciously or otherwise, the manufacturer decides he should be able to earn a profit. This assumption is based on expected cost and price, so although perhaps the selection of price as a first step may not be so obvious, the selection is, nevertheless, still present.

4. When products are produced jointly with each other the cost of each cannot be determined accurately.

Sometimes an apportionment of cost is made on the basis of sales values. There is thus a reliance on price, to determine how much cost a product will stand. Such a procedure cannot be regarded as sound costing practice; it is often done merely to arrive at a satisfactory cost-price relationship."

## METHODS OF CONTROL

Performances and costs have to be controlled within predetermined limits. Only by setting targets, measuring achievements and carrying out corrective action can profit be maximised. Responsibilities have to be defined and executives must be made aware of what these are; only

M

then can real control be exercised—at the point where the particular work is done and the costs are incurred.

Budgetary control, Standard Costing, special cost investigations and cost reduction campaigns, can all be used to exercise the necessary control. These techniques are covered in detail in other chapters.

## EXAMPLE OF PRINCIPLE: OPTIMUM OUTPUT

The determination of output has already been explained. To illustrate the principles involved a question and solutions are given below.

QUESTION

Optimists Ltd. produce an article which sells at £1·50 each, this being the price determined by market conditions and the industry as a whole. The accountant has prepared the following schedule:

| Production and Sales Units | Total Costs £ | Variable Costs £ | Fixed Costs £ |
|---|---|---|---|
| 0 | 2,000 | — | 2,000 |
| 4,000 | 6,000 | 4,000 | 2,000 |
| 4,500 | 6,500 | 4,500 | 2,000 |
| 5,000 | 7,000 | 5,000 | 2,000 |
| 5,500 | 7,500 | 5,500 | 2,000 |
| 6,000 | 8,100 | 6,100 | 2,000 |
| 6,500 | 8,700 | 6,700 | 2,000 |
| 7,000 | 9,400 | 7,400 | 2,000 |
| 7,500 | 10,300 | 8,300 | 2,000 |

You are required to estimate the most profitable output presenting all relevant facts in the form of a tabulation.

The volume of 7500 units is the absolute maximum number that can be produced with existing facilities.

SUGGESTED SOLUTION

*Table to Show Changes in Costs and Revenue*

| Sales Units | Variable Cost Increase for 500 units £ | Sales Increase for 500 units £ | Profit £ |
|---|---|---|---|
| 4,000 | ? | 750 | — |
| 4,500 | 500 | 750 | 250 |
| 5,000 | 500 | 750 | 500 |
| 5,500 | 500 | 750 | 750 |
| 6,000 | 600 | 750 | 900 |
| 6,500 | 600 | 750 | 1,050 |
| 7,000 | 700 | 750 | 1,100 |
| 7,500 | 900 | 750 | 950 |

Clearly 7000 or, possibly, between 7000 and 7500 is the most profitable volume. The optimum point is indicated by the figures being shown in rectangles.

*Observations on Optimum Output*

As shown earlier, costs per unit will tend to increase for a time, then reduce and, finally, start to increase once more. In the example given above, the variable cost per unit is shown to remain constant over a certain range and then to increase over the remaining range of output. For simplicity the initial increase and reduction per unit have been ignored. This simplifying assumption does not affect the validity of the conclusion that has been reached.

The *regularity* of cost increases is necessary for the theory outlined to operate. If there is an abnormal increase in one step of the volume range then unusual results may be shown by trying to match variable cost and the additional revenue arising from an increase in volume. There may be *two* points where the "matching" can be carried out, and yet there will not usually be two points which yield the same, maximum profit. Indeed, the rule followed does not require two points to be compared. In fact the significance of an unusual cost-revenue relationship may not be appreciated unless the full range of possible output and related data are known. An example of the effect of this irregularity is given below.

*Schedule of Output and Costs*

| Units | Total Costs £ | Variable Costs £ | Fixed Costs £ |
|---|---|---|---|
| 5,000 | 7,000 | 5,000 | 2,000 |
| 5,500 | 7,500 | 5,500 | 2,000 |
| 6,000 | 8,400 | 6,400 | 2,000 |
| 6,500 | 9,000 | 7,000 | 2,000 |
| 7,000 | 9,700 | 7,700 | 2,000 |
| 7,500 | 10,500 | 8,500 | 2,000 |

The related schedule would take the form shown below.

*Schedule to Show Changes in Costs and Revenue*

| Units | Variable Cost Increase for 500 units £ | Value of Sales £ | Sales Increase for 500 units £ | Profit £ |
|---|---|---|---|---|
| 5,000 | 500 | 7,500 | 750 | 500 |
| 5,500 | 500 | 8,250 | 750 | 750 |
| 6,000 | 900 | 9,000 | 750 | 600 |
| 6,500 | 600 | 9,750 | 750 | 750 |
| 7,000 | 700 | 10,500 | 750 | 800 |
| 7,500 | 800 | 11,250 | 750 | 750 |

Clearly there are two points at which the variable cost increase is less than the increase in revenue. If data up to and including 6000 units and no further were compiled then the most profitable output would be shown as 5500 units, or between 5500 and 6000 units. Fortunately such irregularities in costs may not occur although they are a possibility. When pioneering new territories selling costs may increase out of all proportion to extra sales initially and then level out once the first obstacles have been overcome. It is also feasible to suppose that in some industries the nature of the technical process may bring about a certain irregularity in the behaviour of the variable production costs. Accordingly, the possibility of abnormal changes in costs has to be considered when estimating the data required.

When estimating revenue and costs a high standard of accuracy may be difficult to achieve. In the example, the selling price does not vary with increases in the volume of sales, but this will not always be the case. When attempting to increase the sales of certain types of products a cost increase will be inevitable. When confronted with the problem of estimating costs the chief difficulty will be estimating the variable costs for each level of operations. Care will be necessary when separating the variable element from the semi-variable costs. The use of Regression Charts or the method of least-squares is likely to give the best results.

### Optimum Output and Imperfect Competition

A business may not be able to sell an unlimited quantity of a certain product without changing the price. A schedule of different levels of output would present a range of prices as well as a range of costs. Generally, the more to be sold the lower the price which can be obtained.

If, for a given output, management has to accept a reduced price then this will be for the total number of units. This assumes that price discrimination—charging different prices in different markets—is not practised. Observations on this matter are made later in this chapter. At this point, the important fact to remember is that with each addition in output there will be an increase in revenue, but there will be a "loss" in the revenue due to a reduction in the price of *all* the units.

When considering the effect on price the margin of profit and the cost structure of the business are extremely important. If, at a certain output, a business is working on a small profit margin then future increases in output may be impossible. Much depends upon whether costs can be reduced sufficiently to at least offset the loss in revenue due to the reduction in price. Provided additional machines and other facilities are not required, the fixed cost per unit will tend to reduce with increases in volume. If the business is in a phase where costs are reducing then a gain may also be expected from the change in variable cost per unit. The total profit earned is not only affected by the profit margin; there is also the volume sold. Many companies operate on a very narrow margin of profit on each product, but by selling a very large volume, are able to earn a substantial, total profit. The revenue from a *substantial* increase in volume may offset any falling off in profit due to a reduction in the profit margin.

When selecting the optimum output the "additional variable cost equals additional revenue" rule can still be followed. An example is given below.

*Example of Principle: Imperfect Competition*

QUESTION

Monopolists Ltd. produce a single commodity. Study of the market and matters affecting costs has allowed the relevant data to be estimated.

*Monopolists Ltd.: Prices and Costs*

| Production and Sales Units | Total Costs £ | Variable Costs £ | Fixed Costs £ | Price Obtainable |
|---|---|---|---|---|
| 0 | 500 | — | 500 | |
| 2000 | 2500 | 2000 | 500 | £1·25 |
| 3000 | 3500 | 3000 | 500 | £1·20 |
| 4000 | 4500 | 4000 | 500 | £1·15 |
| 5000 | 5600 | 5100 | 500 | £1·10 |
| 6000 | 6800 | 6300 | 500 | £1·00 |
| 7000 | 8000 | 7500 | 500 | £1·00 |
| 8000 | 9300 | 8800 | 500 | £0·80 |

You are required to determine the output which is likely to maximise profit showing your findings in the form of a tabulation.

SUGGESTED SOLUTION

*Table to Show Changes in Costs and Revenue*

| Sales Units | Variable Cost Increase for 1000 units £ | Value of Sales £ | Sales Increase for 1000 units £ | Profit (Sales Value minus Total cost) £ |
|---|---|---|---|---|
| 2000 | — | 2500 | — | — |
| 3000 | 1000 | 3600 | +1100 | + 100 |
| 4000 | 1000 | 4600 | +1000 | + 100 |
| 5000 | 1100 | 5500 | + 900 | − 100 |
| 6000 | 1200 | 6000 | + 500 | − 800 |
| 7000 | 1200 | 7000 | +1000 | −1000 |
| 8000 | 1300 | 6400 | − 600 | −2900 |

The level selected as the optimum output is 4000 units; at this point the *additional* revenue and cost agree. At 3000 units the profit is also £100, so that level could also have been selected as the optimum output. This is not to say that the volume of 4000 units should not be selected; indeed, the larger volume is normally to be preferred for this is likely to give greater stability.

*Irregularities in Price Trend*

In the previous example it was shown that, when determining optimum output, any irregular movements in costs may have important effects. Similarly an unusual price movement may require special treatment.

If the first part of the schedule shown earlier took the form shown below, the price at 4000 units being £1·20, then the "differences" in cost and revenue must be taken for an increase of 2000, and not 1000 units.

*Monopolists Ltd.: Prices and Costs*

| Production and Sales Units | Total Costs £ | Variable Costs £ | Fixed Costs £ | Price Obtainable |
|---|---|---|---|---|
| 0 | 500 | — | 500 | |
| 2000 | 2500 | 2000 | 500 | £1·25 |
| 3000 | 3500 | 3000 | 500 | £1·20 |
| 4000 | 4500 | 4000 | 500 | £1·20 |
| 5000 | 5600 | 5100 | 500 | £1·10 |
| 6000 | 6800 | 6300 | 500 | £1·00 |

The correct approach to this problem is shown below.

*Changes in Costs and Revenue*

| Sales Units | Variable Increase for 2000 units £ | Value of Sales £ | Sales Increase for 2000 units £ | Profit £ |
|---|---|---|---|---|
| 2000 | — | 2500 | — | NIL |
| 4000 | 2000 | 4800 | 2300 | + 300 |
| 6000 | 2300 | 6000 | 1200 | − 800 |

Clearly, 4000 units should be produced. At this point sales will be valued at £4800 and costs will amount to £4500, a profit of £300. If the units produced are considered in terms of multiples of 1000 units then the position would be shown as follows:

| Sales Units | Variable Cost Increase for 1000 units £ | Value of Sales £ | Sales Increase for 1000 units £ | Profit £ |
|---|---|---|---|---|
| 2000 | — | 2500 | | NIL |
| 3000 | 1000 | 3600 | +1100 | + 100 |
| 4000 | 1000 | 4800 | +1200 | + 300 |
| 5000 | 1100 | 5500 | + 700 | − 100 |
| 6000 | 1200 | 6000 | + 500 | − 800 |

In these circumstances the point where the increase in variable cost and the increase in sales revenue come nearest to agreement (£1000 and £1100) shows a profit of £100. Yet maximum profit is £300.

*Multiple Products*

If more than one product is made by a business it will be necessary to obtain estimates of costs and prices for each different level of output. In these circumstances there is the problem of apportioning fixed overhead costs which may be done with reasonable ease, but possibly not with great accuracy. Much depends upon the nature of the products and the plant and equipment used; sometimes apportionments can be relatively simple matters, other times rather complex. The justification for apportionments must be left to the individual accountant. On page 287 the reader will be able to see the application of marginal costing to the problem of whether or not to continue producing a certain product. The problem is, to some extent, related to the selection of optimum output. When more than one product is produced there is implied an allocation of the productive resources between the different lines produced. By varying the product mix (or mixture) a different profit may result.

## JOB PRODUCTION

When producing to customers' specifications whether on jobs produced in the factory, on building contracts or on any other type of special work, the producer has an advantage in that he is able to fix the price charged which will normally be based on cost with the addition of a margin of profit. Obviously there will be a limit to the price that can be charged because, if excessive, the customer will take his business elsewhere.

From the point of view of forecasting optimum output the apparent difficulty is the absence of standardised units which can be used to show the possible volumes. This problem can be solved by using "standard hours" or, in a limited number of cases, tonnage to be produced. The "standard hour" is the term used to describe the amount of work which should be produced in one hour. Unrelated types of work can be shown in terms of identical units—the time which should be taken. Each machine will be capable of producing a certain number of standard hours. The total standard hours can be determined by reference to the potential capacity of all the machines, equipment, and labour.

Where a business has fairly substantial order books the determination of optimum output should be no more difficult than when standard units are produced. In these circumstances it is feasible to suppose that a uniform rate of profit can be obtained on each standard hour produced. If this is the case the most profitable point, in terms of standard hours, can be ascertained by reference to the "differences" in costs and revenue. When the profit from a standard hour increment is equal to the increase in cost, then, at this point, profit should be maximised.

If a business is obliged to accept orders with different profit margins then the sales revenue for different levels of output (in standard hours) will have to be estimated. The marginal costing approach may be useful in these circumstances. Provided an order makes a contribution towards fixed cost and profit it may be accepted. However this is not strictly the determination of the optimum output, but rather the selection of profitable orders.

Instead of using standard hours the sales values may be preferred. Often the sales forecast in the co-ordinated budget plan for a job production concern is made in terms of pounds sterling. Costs are then estimated and the most profitable volume of business can then be selected.

## IMPORTANCE OF COST DATA

The cost and related data cannot be taken as conclusive evidence that a certain policy will be adopted. A businessman may follow a course which appears irrational at the particular time and yet he may believe he has a sound reason for the action taken. Figures cannot be a substitute for perception. They show possibilities or likely occurrences. When compiling decision data for optimum output, forecasts and estimates will be inevitable. The price or prices obtainable, the volume which can be produced and sold in a period, and the costs for different sizes of output have usually to be estimated. The Manager who makes the final decision must exercise his knowledge, experience, and judgment as well as consider the policy of the business. He can be helped by the accounting information, but he must also be aware of the limitations. Some data may be more accurate than others. The Management Accountant has a duty to ensure that the degree of reliability which can be attached to the information is known and is understood. However, provided the estimates are made carefully and with a full knowledge of all available information, even if not 100% accurate, they are likely to be of considerable value. Often they are the only guides available.

Selecting the optimum output is not a decision which can be made in isolation from all other factors. Indeed, to follow such a practice would be attempted business suicide. Profit earning cannot be attributed to any one factor. The size of the output alone cannot maximise profit; there must be the appropriate quality of the product at the right price; each division of the plant should operate smoothly; the sales force should be adequate to deal with volume being produced and, perhaps most important of all, there must be an efficient management. Without the latter the necessary efficiency, co-ordination, and control can become chaos and profits turn to losses. In relation to determining optimum output a number of important factors are linked with the policy of the business, the period of time being considered and the size and nature of the capital investment. They are all considered below.

## POLICY OF THE BUSINESS

A policy may be followed consciously with an awareness of a definite object in mind. There may be a formal plan to give employees the best working conditions or the customers the best possible service in a particular field. On the other hand, a certain policy may be followed because of expediency or necessity. Profit is earned by giving service to the consumer. Only by considering the effects of decisions on the goodwill of the consumer can a businessman hope to continue to earn maximum profit. Blindly following the maxim that price should be what the market can stand may not ensure the continuance of the customer's patronage.

Convention or custom may have its effect upon the policy followed. In certain industries greater value is given by changing the size of the product rather than changing the price. Manufacturers of sweets and chocolate appear to favour an increase in the number of sweets per packet or an increase in the size of the bar of chocolate rather than a reduction of price. Yet in some food industries price reductions are the accepted weapon of competitive warfare. This appears to be the case in the frozen foods industry; no doubt the growing popularity of the products of this relatively new industry brings about an increase in volume which allows economies to be obtained.

Price reductions should not be made regularly without considering the effect on the psychological reaction of the consumer. With some products, a price reduction may have the effect of checking sales; customers may hope for a further price reduction and, therefore, refrain from buying. Another important matter is the attitude of the potential consumer towards price. If a high quality product is alleged to meet the needs of a discerning part of the public, then a price reduction may tend to reduce, rather than increase, the volume of sales. In order to get the best quality the customer expects to pay a high price; a lower price may imply that the quality offered is not that desired by the customer.

The practice of price discrimination may have its effect upon the volume produced and price charged. Provided the market can be broken up into separate divisions, different prices may be charged. To attract orders for large quantities a special quantity discount may be allowed. Another device is to give a discount on the total quantity purchased in, say, a year. Alternatively, the channel of distribution may affect the price. Wholesalers may be allowed discounts so there are two sets of prices, one for wholesalers and one for retailers. Clearly, these practices can affect the validity of the accounting analysis. In effect the business is concerned not with one, but with two or more markets. The matching of the incremental cost and revenue can still be accomplished. Costs and revenue of each market can be compared or, alternatively, each increment to output can be considered on its own merits, an attempt being made to justify or reject the additional business along the lines followed in *Marginal Costing* (*see* page 291).

Management and, therefore, business generally, earns its keep by serving consumers. There is a certain social obligation to society as a whole. Price discrimination, output restrictions, and similar practices may be necessary to maximise profit. The dismissal of employees or the provision of sub-standard conditions of employment may also be defended as a means to an end-maximum profit. In some circumstances there is no doubt that manipulation of price or output is justifiable both ethically and financially. However, management has a duty to ensure that decisions made give service to consumer and employee as well as to profit. Businesses are not expected to be charitable institutions, but they are so much an essential part of everyday life that they should at least be fair and just. Only by following a policy that recognises these aims can management create and maintain commercial goodwill and, *in the long period*, maximum profit.

## PERIOD OF TIME

Decisions made for the short period—week, month, or year—affect the profitability in the long period—two, three, four, or longer number of years. Each long period is made up of a number of short periods. How long a period in terms of weeks, months, or years is covered by each "long period" cannot be stated with certainty. Some companies never forecast beyond five years and yet others, by the very nature and life expectancy of the plant and machinery used, must consider twenty years or even longer. Needless to say, the further into the future a forecast is made the more uncertain is its accuracy. That long-term forecasts must be made is now becoming generally recognised and no doubt, as techniques, experience, and knowledge develop, attempts will be made to cover longer and longer periods. This is one of the fields in which the management accountant can play an important part.

An important fact which must be recognised is the relation of the profit of the short period to that of the long period. The theory of matching incremental costs and revenues until the differences in cost and revenue approach agreement should ensure that profit is maximised. However, this is a case where theory and practice may not coincide. Maximisation of profit by the selection of optimum output in each short period may not lead to the largest total profit in the long period. The internal operations of the modern business are complex; the external influences which react upon the validity of decisions made are even more complex. Conditions and circumstances are for ever changing; this dynamic state requires a flexible theory, one which recognises both short period and long period profitability. The most important factors to be recognised are changes in consumers' preferences, in prices and in costs. All these matters are related.

The occurrences in one short period tend to react upon future periods.

If an extraordinarily high profit is earned in a period then there will be a tendency for production to be increased. The existing producers may expand and new businesses may also enter the field. If all estimates of demand, taken together, approximate to total demand, then the profit earned by each business will tend to reduce to a normal level for the type of business concerned. Should estimates be too optimistic the individual producer may have to reduce his prices, in extreme cases, to below cost. Unfortunately, optimism and pessimism do not appear to come in small doses and over- or under-estimating is a normal feature of a modern society. As stated earlier, these oscillations may result in a lower profit being earned. The position may be aggravated further by charging an excessive price in the period of short supply. In the section on policy, in this chapter, the importance of maintaining the goodwill of the consumer was noticed. Short period avariciousness may lead to long period ill-will and loss in revenue. The future as well as the present are important to profit earning capabilities.

From what has been said it will be clear that both long-term and short-term influences must be considered when determining optimum output. Only then can the desired degree of stability be achieved and profit maximisation be ensured for the long period. The techniques described can still be used, but, if dealing with the short period, the selection of price (where possible) and volume should be influenced by future as well as present expectations. A smaller revenue may be taken *now* to ensure a larger total revenue over a long period.

### SIZE OF CAPITAL INVESTMENT

Ideally profit should be maximised over the entire life of the business. The longevity of the joint stock company makes the expected life an unknown factor so, clearly, a shorter period will have to be taken as a guide to success.

Before an asset is purchased the expected benefits to be gained from the purchase should be estimated in terms of profitability. This in itself should involve consideration of output and selling prices. One asset may represent one segment of the complex mechanism which goes to make up the business unit so it may be extremely difficult to forecast *separately* each asset's contribution to profit. Moreover, assets are purchased at different dates and have different life expectancies. A compromise may, therefore, be necessary. The average life of a plant or group of assets may be taken as the period of time to be covered by the long period forecast. If the period is, say, ten years, then an attempt has to be made to maximise profit over that period.

### LIMITING FACTORS

The analysis described above assumes that any level of production can be selected. However, this may be quite unrealistic. In the short period variations in volume may be made within the limits imposed by the existing plant and machinery *provided* the necessary labour, materials and cash are available. If skilled workers are required they may be difficult to obtain or, if obtainable, they may have to be attracted by conditions and salaries which are better than those already in their possession. Similarly, difficulties may be experienced in varying the supply of an essential raw material; the delivery period may be quite long or the price for quick supplies may be excessive. Shortage of cash can be a very serious limiting factor; this in itself may prevent the employment of additional workers or the purchase of extra materials. For a time this difficulty may be overcome by obtaining extended credit from suppliers, but this is a very temporary remedy.

Shift or overtime working may allow expansion of output, but the cost of the additional output may be unduly high. Overtime or shift-work premiums will normally have to be paid and there will be a tendency for lighting costs to increase disproportionately. There may also be a greatly accelerated depreciation of plant and machinery. Mitigating this increase in costs will be the more effective spread of the fixed overhead costs: more units are produced so the fixed cost per unit will be reduced. However, this saving may not reduce the costs sufficiently to warrant overtime or shift work. Furthermore, there is not only the cost incidence to be considered. Administrative problems also multiply and planning and control become more difficult. These are possible disadvantages, but they should not be regarded as conclusive evidence that overtime or shift work should never be carried on. In some industries the extremely large investment involved and rapid technological development make the fullest utilisation absolutely essential. However, outside such industries, management may find that greater efficiency and lower costs result from the avoidance of overtime and shift work. As temporary measures they may be justifiable, but, for permanent increases in output, plant expansion may be a better procedure. Naturally in these circumstances the availability of finance will play an important part.

## EXAMINATION QUESTIONS

1. "The optimum level of inventory is that level at which the cost of carrying one more unit is exactly the same as the cost of not carrying it."

Discuss the meaning of this statement outlining the nature of the costs to which it refers. Give a brief outline of how you would use this idea as a foundation for planning future stock levels.  (*I.C.W.A.*)

2. In a manufacturing organisation, short runs are almost invariably more costly than long runs.

Using appropriate figures, prepare a report to management illustrating this fact, first indicating the nature of the industry and the size of the business.

(*I.C.W.A.*)

3. What do you understand by the *optimum production level* of a business? Outline the matters you would consider to determine the optimum of a small concern with which you are familiar. (*I.C.W.A.*)

4. The XYZ Company are considering whether or not to market a new product NP 456. A management meeting has been called to discuss possible selling prices which could be charged for this product. Prepare a report, in statement form, outlining the factors which you think should be taken into account before a final decision is reached. Your report should indicate the cost data which you would prepare and any additional information you would require in order that this data could be assembled.

N.B. Your answer should assume the following:

1. The market for NP 456 is not perfectly competitive although it is more competitive abroad than at home.

2. The capacity utilisation at the factory where NP 456 will be produced has been:

| | % |
|---|---|
| 1965 | 90 |
| 1966 | 92 |
| 1967 | 94 |
| 1968 | 90 |
| 1969 | 88 |
| 1970 | 84 (to date) |

3. NP 456 requires 2 units of machine time on a special machine and the time available on this is likely to be restricted because of competing demands of other products. Supplies of skilled labour have also presented problems in the past although this is not likely to arise in the case of NP 456.

4. The decision to produce and sell NP 456 will require an initial investment of £50,000 excluding any additional working capital requirements.

5. Although NP 456 is new it is similar in many respects to other products which the company markets and falls naturally into the company's product range. (*A.C.C.A.*)

5. A company manufactures radiograms to order and makes a profit of 30% of sales value. A study showed that making the sets in large batches in anticipation of future sales would save £150,000 in annual production costs.

This method was introduced but it was found that some sets were not sold in the current year. To encourage sales, an obsolescence discount of 5% of selling price was allowed in the second year and 10% in the third year. After the third year any sets remaining were immediately written off and sold as scrap at 10% of cost price.

Warehousing expense, including interest on capital, averaged 3% of selling price in the current year and 7% thereafter. Maintenance cost of sets while in the warehouse amounted to 1% of selling price in the current year, 2% in the second year and 7% in the third year.

The sales record given below relates to the production of a year when 1000 sets each of four different models were manufactured:

*Sales Record*

| Model | | A £ | B £ | C £ | D £ |
|---|---|---|---|---|---|
| Selling price (each) | ... | 80 | 100 | 120 | 150 |
| Sales: | | | | | |
| | | units | units | units | units |
| Current year | ... | 800 | 900 | 400 | 700 |
| Second year | ... | 100 | 50 | 200 | 150 |
| Third year ... | ... | 100 | — | 200 | 100 |

(*a*) Prepare a table showing the actual percentage of return achieved on sets sold in each year.

(*b*) Using the production and sales figures given above calculate:

(i) the percentage return made by each model;

(ii) the actual additional profit achieved by batch production.

(*A.C.C.A.*)

## CHAPTER 14

## CONTROL AND COMMUNICATION

As shown in Chapter 1, control and communication are vital and related management processes. Both should be incorporated into a management accountancy system.

### *WHAT IS CONTROL?*

Before control can be effective the following matters should receive attention:

1. All aspects of producing, selling, administration, and other functions should be examined and made as efficient as possible. Obviously, if management does not *commence* being efficient it cannot hope to achieve a high standard of control. The latter must operate within well-defined systems.

2. Plans should be made and all segments should be co-ordinated. This involves predetermination of performances and costs at the level of efficiency determined by (1) above.

3. Actual performances and costs are compared with predetermined performances and costs and any variances are isolated.

4. Variances are analysed—divided into their component parts and reasons found for their existence—so that management can take corrective action, thereby maintaining a state which will bring about what has been planned.

Control properly exercised should reduce business risks to a minimum and thereby ensure that planned profit and actual profit agree. Certain risks are an inevitable part of business operations: they cannot be eliminated altogether, but appropriate management decisions should overcome the risks, thus keeping their ill effects to a minimum. If necessary, certain risks can be *insured against*. In its widest sense, therefore, control is the overcoming of risks.

Budgetary Control and Standard Costing employ these principles. The former achieves the necessary co-ordination of plans and controls through departmental and functional budgets. Standard Costing provides a much more detailed control and is, therefore, particularly important for controlling production costs. In practice, whenever possible, the two techniques are generally combined so that there is a system of Standard Costing which employs co-ordinated budgets.

What is important to notice is that unless budgeted or standard performances and costs are carefully predetermined there can be no effective control. Only by ensuring that plans and standards are realistic

349

can the correct variance analysis be accomplished and, through this, the appropriate action be taken by management.

When costs are being controlled it is essential to distinguish between controllable and uncontrollable variances. The former are those which are the responsibility of a particular person or group of persons, whereas the latter are outside the control of someone employed within the business, being due to outside influences. A price increase of a raw material or the award of a wage increase may be uncontrollable costs and, therefore, uncontrollable variances. Costs should be controlled at the point at which they are incurred and the assigning of responsibilities for variances is, therefore, of the utmost importance.

Details of how control is accomplished are given later in this chapter.

## WHAT IS COMMUNICATION?

Basically the communication function means to *inform* management and employees of all the vital facts which affect the efficient running of the business. It also includes informing shareholders and the public through the medium of the published accounts (*see* Chapter 21). Suitably drafted reports and statements, where necessary incorporating charts, diagrams, and other statistical aids, should be a feature of a management accountancy system. It is possible to distinguish two types of information, and, therefore, two basic forms of report. There is the routine information produced at daily, weekly, monthly, quarterly or other suitable intervals to show deviations from the plans made: this is generally covered by *routine reports*. In addition, there is unusual or special information which is necessary to overcome a particular problem: a *special report* is prepared to cover this type of situation.

A number of fundamental principles have been formulated: these lay down the essentials of report preparation and presentation. In brief terms they are as follows:

1. Reports should be prepared to show expected achievements *before* these are carried out. Subsequently, reports will show what has happened.

Managers cannot be expected to carry out plans unless they are aware of what is involved.

2. All reports should serve a useful purpose and be in the form which best serves that purpose.

3. Information should be presented in a manner which is as unbiased as possible, not being affected by personal opinions.

4. Each report should be prepared for the purpose for which it is intended and not made so general as to cover all possible contingencies.

There is a tendency when designing reports and statements to try to include every significant and—all too often—every *insignificant* fact. The result may be that the important facts are obscured.

5. Scientific or technical language is best left out of reports.

This remark also applies to accounting terminology. Terms employed in accountancy may not be understood by foremen and supervisors so if they are used they should be explained.

6. The management law, the principle of exception, should be followed in compiling reports.

Matters not proceeding according to plan are reported upon; other factors are disregarded. Keeping facts to a minimum means that management requires less time to study the reports and, therefore, has more time for taking remedial action.

7. What *should* have happened and what *has* happened should be shown on the report.

This means showing *actual* performances and/or costs against the same budgeted or standard costing information.

8. Compile a schedule of the dates when the different routine reports should be prepared.

It is sometimes asserted that all reports should be presented *immediately*. Whilst this is partially true it is not the entire truth. If all reports are produced immediately the accounting costs may prove to be exorbitant. Obviously the *purpose* of the report should determine its urgency.

In appropriate circumstances speed may require a certain loss of accuracy. Some accountants advocate that speed is more important than 100% accuracy. Again there is a good deal of truth in this suggestion. However, the circumstances should dictate the level of accuracy required. There is always a danger that "approximations" will lead to the relaxing of accounting and management principles. A criticism sometimes levelled against accountants is that they are too engrossed in balancing the books to see the significance of the information they record. If there is any substance in this statement it is still no reason to err the other way and produce figures which may not enjoy the confidence of the managers using them. Clearly, if approximate figures are to be employed this should be in appropriate circumstances, and not be regarded as a rule to be applied generally.

9. In a special report any supporting figures or other details should be included in an appendix. This helps to keep down the main body of the report to a reasonable size which is more easily read and understood.

10. A report should have an appropriate title, clearly show the origin and persons for whom it is intended, and the units being dealt with, whether £s, tons or other measure, should be indicated quite clearly.

11. If a report is quite long or detailed then a synopsis should be prepared to cover all significant facts and conclusions. This rule will generally apply to special reports. The synopsis should precede the report thus introducing the reader to the subject matter by easy stages.

12. There should be a clear distinction made between controllable and uncontrollable costs.

Many accountants take the view that only controllable costs should be included in a departmental operating statement or report. However, much depends upon the circumstances. It may be advisable to show the uncontrollable costs as well, thereby giving a manager a complete story. He may not be able to control them, but at least he may appreciate any difficulties the business is facing if he is given the true facts.

These are provided as *guides* and not rigid rules of conduct. The main fact to remember is that each report should serve a useful purpose and be produced at a cost which is reasonable having regard to the possible benefits arising from the action taken on the basis of its contents.

## CO-ORDINATION OF CONTROL AND COMMUNICATION

A vital part of management accountancy is to ensure that the control and communication processes are fully co-ordinated. Business activities are in a constant state of motion; matters which are very urgent at one time may be of negligible importance at another. Yet there is a tendency once certain reports have been prepared for them to go on being prepared just as if the same sequence of events is going to take place over and over again. Admittedly there are certain procedures which follow a standardised pattern, but there is a tendency for conditions and circumstances to call for a change even in matters which appear to be of a stereotyped nature. Accordingly, it is very important to keep a close watch on the number and types of reports being prepared. The numbers should be kept within reasonable limits and should be providing information which is acted upon.

A careful watch should be maintained on the reports being prepared to ensure that there is no unnecessary duplicating. A quarterly or half-yearly review by the budget committee (*see* Chapter 3) may serve a very useful purpose. The members on this committee represent all major departments and, therefore, any study of the reports and elimination when necessary may be achieved with less friction than when the decision comes from a single person or department. All too often duplication of effort arises because each functional executive is jealously trying to safeguard and expand his own empire. He prefers to assign the duty of collecting information to a clerk in his own department. Yet quite likely the same information is being reported on by the Management Accountant or by some other department. Clearly if one report can cover the work of two then the duplication can be avoided. However, this remark is subject to the principle of report preparation listed (4 above); namely, that reports should not be made so general as to cover all possible contingencies. For this reason there is a limit to the number of purposes which a report can serve successfully.

One of the major problems of communication is ascertaining what information is really useful to management. Unfortunately, all too often managers do not know themselves what facts are essential for them to carry out their work in the most efficient fashion. Educating managers should, therefore, be a vital part of a company's personnel policy. Facilities for formal training in general management techniques and in the tools-of-management subjects are available at colleges of technology and universities. In the large company special short courses

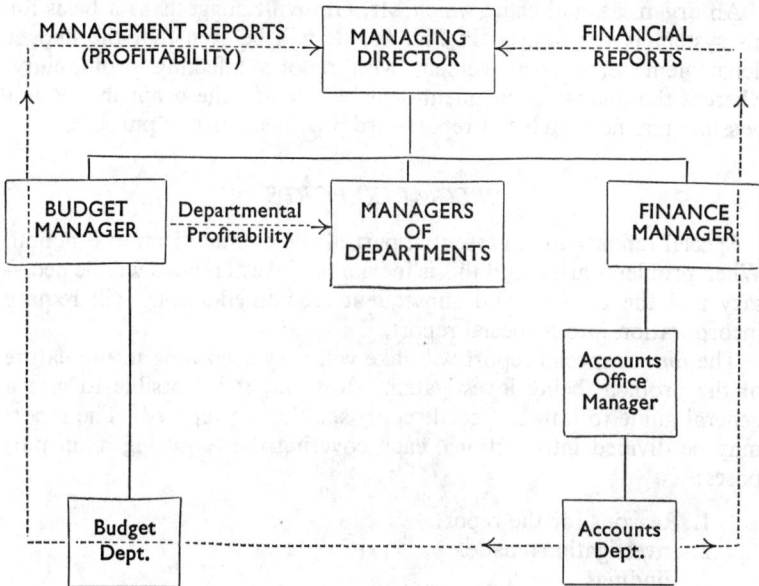

FIG. 56.—*Organisation Chart*

Showing the responsibility of both the budget and finance departments and feedback to managing director.

can also assist in training junior executives and foremen and supervisors. The Management Accountant can play a vital part in this important function. It is also imperative that the accounting staff concerned with Budgeting, Standard Costing and report writing are qualified men and women who have had the necessary training and practical experience to understand what *managing* means and what information is likely to be useful.

A criticism sometimes levelled against management accountancy is that it tends to ignore the fact that management is a dynamic process. Often variances are presented which purport to show that efficiency has increased or diminished, but there is no way of showing how the problems are to be overcome. The control system, it is alleged, is not an integrated part of the management processes. One writer* has suggested that a special department, dealing only with profit control, should be part of the organisation structure. In effect the work of the budgetary control section and the operational research section would be combined to keep management informed on the actual or estimated profitability of present or future decisions. In this way it is claimed that budgeting should become an indispensable aid to managing and earning maximum profit. There is great merit in the idea and it emphasises once more the need for a *complete* management accountancy system.

An organisational chart which Mr. Granville suggests as a basis for his system is reproduced in Fig. 56. It will be seen that the budget department serves management with reports affecting profitability, whereas the finance department deals with using the profit in the best possible manner: financial reports are provided for this purpose.

## SPECIAL REPORTS

Special reports are an essential part of the communication function. When problems arise, and this is inevitable, investigations will be necessary and the findings and subsequent recommendations will require incorporation into a special report.

The *form* a special report will take will vary according to the nature of the problem being investigated. However, it is possible to give a general guide to how a special report should be prepared. The report may be divided into sections, each covering the following main purposes:

1. Reasons for the report.
2. Investigations made.
3. Findings.
4. Conclusion and recommendations.

As noted earlier, detailed figures and diagrams should be included in an appendix. If, even after this action has been taken, the report is rather long then a synopsis should be prepared. Each report should be included in an indexed folder to facilitate easy filing when not in use.

### MATTERS TO BE COVERED

Many of the matters to be covered by special reports are dealt with in different parts of this book. Here a number of these are listed in order to illustrate the problems which may be dealt with. Whenever possible the effect on revenues, costs, or profits should be given in reports and, if alternative courses of action are suggested, the relative value of each should be stated in monetary terms.

* D. A. GRANVILLE in "A New Look at Profit Control," *The Manager*, March 1961. The chart shown (Fig. 56) is reproduced by kind permission of the Editor of *The Manager*.

Matters which may be covered by special reports are as follows:

1. Production delays when considerable time has been lost (an example is given below).
2. Machine breakdowns involving a large number of hours.
3. The effects of labour disputes.
4. Whether to make or buy components or products (*see* Chapter 12).
5. Whether to purchase or hire fixed assets.
6. Capital expenditure decision reports (*see* Chapters 18 and 19).
7. Minimum price to charge in a trade recession (*see* Chapter 12).
8. Whether to substitute machines for hand labour (*see* Chapter 12).
9. Cost reduction recommendations (this chapter).
10. The most appropriate method of obtaining new funds (*see* Chapters 6–9).
11. The best methods of investing cash which is surplus to present needs (*see* Chapter 6).
12. Special investigations into particular systems employed (*see* Chapter 20).
13. The feasibility of employing a computer (*see* Chapter 23).
14. Study of effect of idle capacity on the profitability of the business (*see* Chapters 10–13).
15. Effects of diversification or simplification of the product range.
16. Market research projects.
17. Study of the strength of competitors.
18. Closing down of departments or plant (*see* Chapter 12).
19. Costs of holding stocks of raw materials or finished goods.
20. Significant developments which arise from time to time, whether due to political action or other reason: *e.g.* a Government credit squeeze, entry into a common market, removal or introduction of tariffs on particular products, cancellation of important contracts by an overseas buyer.

These twenty examples of matters which may be covered by special reports should serve to illustrate the nature of these reports.

A pro-forma example of a special report is given below. This is along very simple lines and has been kept reasonably brief. In practice, detailed facts and figures relating to costs, revenues, or profits would be shown in the appendix which has been omitted from the example.

QUESTION

There has been a considerable delay in producing a major contract (X362) with a result that the customer has refused to accept delivery on the grounds that there has been a breach in the terms of the order. He was allowed to do this as the delivery date had been promised as quite certain.

Prepare a special report for the managing director suggesting what action should be taken in the future to avoid any recurrence and also showing the reasons for the delay. Make any assumptions necessary for a realistic report.

SOLUTION:

To: Managing Director                    Accountant's Department
                                          Date ........................

### Special Report on Contract X362

Following the cancellation of Contract X362 on the grounds of delay in delivery, investigations have been made to supply the information you requested, *i.e.* the reasons for the extended delay.

### Investigations

The procedure for processing orders and making delivery promises was examined, and it was found that delivery promises are being made on the basis of machine loading times calculated by reference to standard times for the operations involved. In actual fact, these standard times are quite inaccurate, being based on the best of previous *actual* times and not scientifically calculated by means of work study. The result is that actual machine loading is entirely different from what is shown by the standard times. The outcome has been the building up of a large back-log of work and an extension of all delivery dates. In addition, the work flow is inefficient. Large stocks of work-in-progress are kept on the shop floor with the result that the production volume is much less than it should be. Furthermore, the booking of times on jobs leaves much to be desired. There are no mechanical time recorders and as a consequence there is no proper planning of the issue of work. This appears to be left to the individual worker who is given work if he makes a request for it.

### Recommendations

1. The feasibility of employing a Work Study Engineer should be examined. Immediate correction of all standard times is essential as this use of incorrect times is creating production planning and costing problems.

2. A Progress Manager should be employed to be responsible for the efficient routing of all work through the factory.

3. Job Time Recorders should be installed and a system of control based on standard times should be brought into operation.

4. The work-in-progress on the shop floor should be inspected before any fresh orders are put into production.

### Conclusion

If the above recommendations are carried out there should be no difficulty in estimating delivery dates which *can be met*. In addition, the more accurate information based on standard times will tend to make control much more effective and the estimating of pricing much more reliable.

### Appendix

Details of the additional expenditure involved in the changes are shown in the attached supplementary statement.

                                          *I. Smith*
                                          Management Accountant

(*Special Note.* As indicated earlier, the appendix is not shown although in practice this would be essential.)

## ROUTINE REPORTS AND STATEMENTS

Some of the most important areas in which control has to be exercised are covered below. Coverage of all types of report is, of course, impossible. However, a number of examples are given and more may be seen in *Standard Costing* by the same author.

Usually the areas of control and, therefore, the reports are classified along the following lines:

1. General Management Reports.
2. Production Reports.
3. Sales Reports.
4. Distribution Reports.
5. Administration Reports.
6. Research and Development Reports.

Obviously the reports for general management may cover all the functions given (2) to (6) inclusive. However, these reports should be concerned with broad trends and not minute details. The latter will be the concern of departmental managers, foremen, and supervisors.

An important part of controlling and reporting is the calculation and presentation of variances and these are explained in the appropriate sections.

It is important to remember that each report should be designed to suit particular requirements. Accordingly, the examples given should only be regarded as guides to the type of information which may be useful to the management indicated. The knowledge of the individual should be considered. If he is not experienced in using and interpreting figures then more detail may be necessary.

Reports themselves do not provide the control. In fact, quite often the facts given are already history. However, they do give guidance and knowledge for the future and it is from here that the necessary action can be taken.

### RETURN ON CAPITAL EMPLOYED

The most significant measure for top management is the return on capital employed. This is explained in Chapter 15 and is discussed in other chapters. When budgetary control is employed this measure, expressed as a ratio, is generally included in the master budget.*

A number of reports are shown below. The first (Fig. 57) relates to the Principal Management Ratios. In addition to the return on Capital Employed Ratio are shown a number of other significant ratios. These are given for the purpose of illustration; others may be added to meet the needs of the particular business.

Sometimes a graph is used to show the expected return on capital. An example is given in Fig. 58. This covers three years: last year, this year, and next year. In the latter case, the *forecasted* profit is plotted.

A second form of statement is the General Operating Statement

* Chapter 5.

| Ratio | Calculation | Unit | Actual | Budgeted | Variance |
|---|---|---|---|---|---|
| **COMPARATIVE STATEMENT OF MANAGEMENT RATIOS** | | | | | |
| Period Ended ........................ | | | | | |
| | | | £ | £ | (+ or −) |
| Return on Capital Employed | Profit *before tax* / Gross Assets Employed | % | | | |
| Profit to Sales | Profit *before tax* / Sales | % | | | |
| Sales to Assets | Sales / Assets Employed | times | | | |
| Cost of Sales to Sales | Production Cost of Sales / Sales | % | | | |
| Current Ratio | Current Assets / Current Liabilities | times | | | |
| Sales to Stock | Sales at Cost / Stock at Cost | times | | | |

FIG. 57.—*Comparative Statement of Management Ratios*

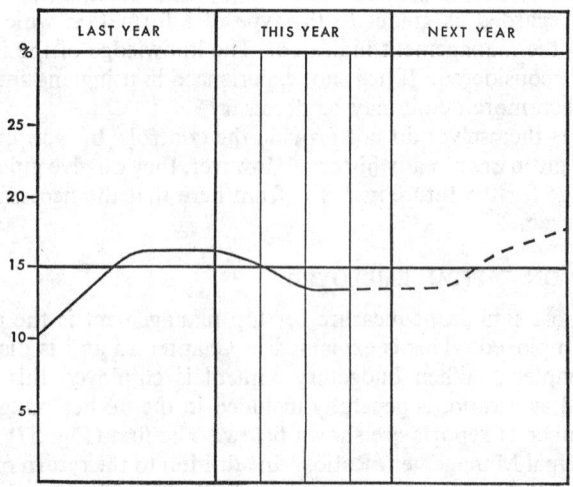

FIG. 58.—*Return on Capital Graph: year ending* 19..

NOTES

1. Expected return on capital employed is 15%, represented by the horizontal line.

2. Actual return on capital employed is represented by the thick black line ————

3. Forecasted return on capital employed is represented by the dashed line - - - - -

4. Capital employed is represented by gross assets valued at £.........

## GENERAL OPERATING STATEMENT ·
### Period Ended.................................

| | Revenues and Costs | | | |
|---|---|---|---|---|
| | Actual £ | Budget £ | Variance £ | % + or − |
| Sales | | | | |
| Factory Cost of Sales: £ Material Labour Overhead | | | | |
| Gross Profit £ | | | | |
| Selling Costs Distribution Costs Administration Costs | | | | |
| Total Overhead Costs £ (other than Factory) Net Trading Profit Other Income (Net) | | | | |
| Net Profit before Tax £ | | | | |
| Estimated Taxes | | | | |
| Net Profit after Tax £ | | | | |
| Return on Capital Employed: Before Tax After Tax | % % | % % | % % | |

Remarks ...........................................................................................

FIG. 59.—*Example of a General Operating Statement*

(Fig. 59). This gives an overall picture of operations. It is also known as a Profit and Loss Statement.

When a company has a number of divisions it may be advisable to prepare an Operating Statement for each division. This may follow the lines suggested by the Operating Statement for Division "X" (Fig. 60). Any costs which are not actually incurred by the division are shown separately on the grounds that these costs are not controllable. In the illustration unfavourable variances have been shown as one total: it is

---

### OPERATING STATEMENT FOR DIVISION "X"
#### Period Ended.................................

|  | £ | £ |
|---|---|---|
| Sales | | |
| *Less* Factory Cost of Sales | | |
| Unfavourable Variances | | |
| Selling and Distribution Costs | | |
| | | |
| Total Controllable Costs.... | | |
| Contribution from Division.... | | |
| *Less* Administration Costs of Head Office Apportioned | | |
| | | |
| Net Profit for Division "X" | £ | |

---

FIG. 60.—*Operating Statement for a division*

advisable to supplement the Operating Statement with a *detailed* analysis of all variances.

### WORKING TO FULL CAPACITY

Reference to the possible *capacities* of a business is made towards the end of Chapter 2. When budgeting for maximum profit the optimum size of output should be determined. This then becomes the foundation stone of all planning.

If for any reason plant is not employed fully there is a real danger that the expected profit will not be earned. Many businesses depend upon a very large volume of output to earn the desired level of profit, the principal reasons for this being a large total of fixed overheads and a relatively small rate of profit earned per £1 of sales.

All levels of management are concerned with ensuring that the capacity selected is achieved. To the general management this is of great significance. Not only will there be a loss of profit due to fewer sales, but there will also be a failure to recover fixed overhead costs in the costs of the products.

Management may be informed on what is happening through the calculation and analysis of the Overhead Volume Variance or, as it is also called, the Overhead Capacity Variance. If plant is idle due to a trade recession, machinery breakdowns, shortage of material or labour, power failures, inefficient planning or any other reasons, then management should be informed of this fact together with the effect on costs.

The Overhead Volume or Capacity Variance may be calculated by application of the following formula:

$$\left( \begin{array}{c} \text{Standard hours} \\ \text{for period} \end{array} - \begin{array}{c} \text{Actual hours} \\ \text{for period} \end{array} \right) \times \begin{array}{c} \text{Standard} \\ \text{Overhead Rate} \end{array}$$

If the normal capacity in a period is represented by a volume of output equal to 10,000 standard hours then any loss in this total will mean under-absorption of overhead costs. When calculating the Overhead Volume Variance, care should be taken to use the appropriate standard number of hours as shown in the budget; *i.e.* the total number of hours regarded as normal capacity.

When overhead costs are divided into (*a*) fixed and (*b*) variable, then the formula is modified slightly; the "Standard Overhead Rate" becomes the "standard rate for fixed overheads." The use of separate rates is advisable when a flexible budget is operated and there is a discrepancy between actual and budgeted activity. A simple example will serve to show the calculations involved.

PROBLEM

### SC Producing Department

Summary Flexible Budget for Month

| Total Hours | 5000 | 5200 | 5400 |
|---|---|---|---|
| Total Overhead Cost £7600 | | £7800 | £8000 |

Normal Capacity is 5200 hours. A single product "S" is made which should take 1 hour to produce.

In the period in question there were 5000 units of "S" produced and the overhead cost was £8000. Hours worked were 5100.

Show the most significant facts in a routine statement.

SUGGESTED SOLUTION

### Preliminary Note

The Overhead Volume or Capacity Variance has already been explained. In addition to this variance, management will want to know how the budgeted spending compares with the actual spending and, also, what level of efficiency has been achieved for the output produced. The former purpose is served by the Budget or Expenditure Variance whereas the latter is answered by calculation and analysis of the Overhead Efficiency Variance.

Calculation of the Budget Variance is fairly straightforward. It involves comparing the budgeted cost with the actual cost. When a fixed budget is employed it means simply the deduction of one figure from another. However, when a flexible budget is used—and this is advisable for control purposes—an adjustment is necessary to show the spending for the *actual* and not the budgeted level of activity. There is in effect a transfer to the Budget Variance from the Volume Variance shown by the fixed budget. How this is accomplished is shown below.

The Overhead Efficiency Variance is calculated by taking the difference between actual and standard hours and multiplying by the standard overhead rate (fixed and variable).

*Calculation of the Variances*

The difference between actual cost and standard cost for the actual output is known as the Overhead Cost Variance. The other three variances explained above are contained in the Overhead Cost Variance.

*Overhead Cost Variance*

| | |
|---|---|
| Actual Overhead Cost | £8000 |
| Standard Overhead Cost for Actual Output 5000 × £1·50 standard overhead rate | £7500 |
| | £500 (Unfavourable) |

*Overhead Budget Variance*

| | |
|---|---|
| Actual Overhead | £8000 |
| Overhead at Normal Capacity per the Budget | £7800 |
| | £200 (Unfavourable) |

This is when a *fixed* budget is employed. In actual fact only 5100 hours were worked so the budgeted cost should be taken as £7700 making a variance of £300 (Unfavourable).

*Overhead Efficiency Variance*

A formula may be used to calculate this variance:

$$\left(\begin{array}{c}\text{Actual} \\ \text{hours}\end{array} - \begin{array}{c}\text{Standard} \\ \text{hours}\end{array}\right) \times \begin{array}{c}\text{Standard} \\ \text{Overhead Rate}\end{array}$$

$$= (5100 - 5000)\ £1·50$$

$$= 100 \times £1·50 = £150 \text{ (Unfavourable)}$$

*Overhead Volume Variance*

With a *fixed* budget the calculation would be as follows:

$$\left(\begin{array}{c}\text{Standard hours} \\ \text{for period}\end{array} - \begin{array}{c}\text{Actual hours} \\ \text{for period}\end{array}\right) \times \begin{array}{c}\text{Standard} \\ \text{Overhead Rate}\end{array}$$

$$= (5200 - 5100)\ £1·50$$

$$= 100 \times £1·50 = £150 \text{ (Unfavourable)}$$

For a *flexible* budget the concern is with budgeted cost for the *actual* level of output: *i.e.* £7600.

Actual hours are 5100 which, multiplied by £1·50, gives £7650.

The variance is, therefore, £7650–£7600 which equals £50 (Unfavourable).

Another way to calculate the variance is to use a fixed overhead rate. From the budget can be seen that at a capacity of 5000 hours the total cost is £7600. An increase of 200 hours results in an increase of cost of £200. The latter is clearly the variable element so, therefore, the variable overhead rate is £1·00 per hour. It follows from this that the total fixed overhead cost is £2600 which, at normal capacity, is £0·50 per hour.

The Overhead Volume Variance for a flexible budget is, therefore, 100 hours × = £0·50 £50 (Unfavourable).

As explained earlier, there is a transfer made from the Volume Variance to the Budget Variance. It represents 100 hours at the variable overhead rate of £1·00.

The statement required by the question is given below. It is on this type of statement that the management accountant can employ original ideas to show the information in the best possible manner. The reasons for the variances would also be shown, thus allowing preventive action to be taken.

Department S.C.

STATEMENT OF OVERHEAD COSTS AND VARIANCES

Month..............................

*Budgeted Activity 5200 hours (normal capacity): 5200 units of "S".*

| | £ | £ |
|---|---|---|
| Actual Overhead Cost incurred | | 8000 |
| Standard Overhead Cost for Actual Output (5000 units) | | 7500 |
| We had *excess* spending | | £500 |

*Analysis of Excess Spending*
Budget Variance:

| | £ | £ |
|---|---|---|
| Actual expenditure | 8000 | |
| Budgeted expenditure for 5100 hours worked | 7700 | |
| | | 300 |
| Efficiency Variance: | | |
| Excess hours worked = 100 | | |
| Costing 100 × £1·00 variable overhead rate | | |
| 100 × £0·50 fixed overhead rate | | 150 |
| Volume Variance: | | |
| Loss in hours 100 × £0·50 fixed overhead rate | | 50 |
| | | £500 |

## EFFECT OF CAPACITY ON PROFIT

As shown in the previous section, one effect of not working to full capacity will be to underrecover the budgeted costs. In addition to this effect, there will also be a tendency for profit to be lost due to not selling as much as expected. Both general management and sales management will want to know how much profit is being lost and the reasons for the loss.

One of the principal reasons for loss of profit is failure to obtain an adequate volume of orders. A Sales Volume Variance may be calculated to show the result of this deficiency. A formula is as follows:

(Standard Volume — Actual Volume) × Standard Profit

The volume in each case refers to the number of units of products. If less than the standard volume is sold there is an unfavourable variance.

Another important factor is failure to obtain the standard price for each product. Again a variance can be calculated, this time the Sales Price Variance:

(Standard Price — Actual Price) × Actual Volume

The principal variances relating to volume and price can be further subdivided into sub-variances. The latter are the constituent parts of a quantity or price variance. Thus, for example, if the sales mixture is not the one budgeted then a Sales Mixture Sub-variance may be calculated, the difference between the actual and standard proportions being multiplied by the standard profit for each line of product. A Sales Allowance Sub-variance may also be calculated.

### SALES OPERATING STATEMENT

Period.....................................

| | Budgeted | | | Actual | | | Variance | Remarks |
|---|---|---|---|---|---|---|---|---|
| | Units | Price | Value | Units | Price | Value | | |
| Products: | | | | | | | | |
| A | | | | | | | | |
| B | | | | | | | | |
| C | | | | | | | | |
| | | | £ | | | £ | £ | |

Fig. 61.—*Specimen Sales Operating Statement*

Selling costs may be smaller or larger than budgeted and this fact can be shown by the Selling Costs Variance. This is simply the difference between actual and standard costs.

When these variances have been calculated detailed analysis is generally essential. Armed with the reasons for the variances, management can then take steps to prevent recurrence in the future control periods.

There are so many possible variations of statements affecting sales that it would be quite impossible to cover them all. Analysis by products, sales areas, salesmen, or other important factors may be shown on operating statements. Figure 61 shows a Sales Operating Statement which presents a broad picture of sales and total variances analysed by products. A further breakdown is given in the Variance Analysis Statement (Fig. 62). These statements may be prepared for each control period; *e.g.* once a month.

Selling costs should also be analysed so as to trace responsibility to salesmen, products, sales areas, and so on. A typical statement is given in Figure 63. This is intended to compare the budgeted and actual costs for the different advertising media analysed by products.

## OPERATING STATEMENTS FOR OTHER FUNCTIONS

Detailed statements should be prepared for administration, production, and research and development functions. Where necessary each type of expense—wages, salaries, materials, rates, insurance, and so on—can be shown and the difference between the budgeted and actual cost can be calculated. Each operating statement should be designed to meet the needs of the particular functional executive, so no hard and fast rules can be drawn up for their preparation. However, it is essential that they are as simple as possible and compare the budgeted and actual results for the appropriate control period. In addition they should seek to stimulate action on the part of the manager concerned.

## PRODUCTION VARIANCES

The principal factory *overhead* variances are explained in a previous section. In order to complete the story the variances relating to direct labour and direct material have to be defined.

Material Variances show whether more or less than the standard price has been paid for material (Material Price Variance) and whether a smaller or larger than standard quantity of material has been used (Material Usage Variance). The Labour Variances are similar, the concern being with labour rates (Labour Rate Variance) and labour hours (Labour Efficiency Variance).

Management will be very concerned to know why there have been variations from standard and statements can be prepared to show the reasons.

Formulae for calculating the variances are as follows:

*Material Price Variance:*

$$\left( \begin{matrix} \text{Actual} \\ \text{Price} \end{matrix} - \begin{matrix} \text{Standard} \\ \text{Price} \end{matrix} \right) \times \text{Actual Quantity.}$$

*Material Usage Variance:*

$$\left( \begin{matrix} \text{Actual} \\ \text{Quantity} \end{matrix} - \begin{matrix} \text{Standard} \\ \text{Quantity} \end{matrix} \right) \times \text{Standard Price.}$$

*Labour Rate Variance:*

$$\left( \begin{matrix} \text{Actual} \\ \text{Rate} \end{matrix} - \begin{matrix} \text{Standard} \\ \text{Rate} \end{matrix} \right) \times \text{Actual Hours.}$$

*Labour Efficiency Variance:*

$$\left( \begin{matrix} \text{Actual} \\ \text{Hours} \end{matrix} - \begin{matrix} \text{Standard} \\ \text{Hours} \end{matrix} \right) \times \text{Standard Rate.}$$

## VARIANCE ANALYSIS STATEMENT

Period................

| Sales Areas: | Product A | | | Product B | | | Product C | | |
|---|---|---|---|---|---|---|---|---|---|
| | Budget | Actual | Variance | Budget | Actual | Variance | Budget | Actual | Variance |
| South East | | | | | | | | | |
| South West | | | | | | | | | |
| North East | | | | | | | | | |
| North West | | | | | | | | | |
| Midlands | | | | | | | | | |
| Scotland | | | | | | | | | |
| £ | | | | | | | | | |

FIG. 62.—Specimen Variance Analysis Statement

## ADVERTISING OPERATING STATEMENT

Period................

| Advertising Media: | Product A | | | Product B | | | Product C | | |
|---|---|---|---|---|---|---|---|---|---|
| | Budget | Actual | Variance | Budget | Actual | Variance | Budget | Actual | Variance |
| Newspapers | | | | | | | | | |
| Television | | | | | | | | | |
| Catalogues and Leaflets | | | | | | | | | |
| Free Samples | | | | | | | | | |
| £ | | | | | | | | | |

FIG. 63.—Typical Advertising Operating Statement

The position of the actual price or actual quantity within the brackets assumes that the variance is unfavourable for each variance. (For detailed examples of variance calculations see *Standard Costing*.)

Just as with the overhead variances, analysis by reasons is essential. Both favourable and unfavourable variances should be investigated. Some companies adopt a method of dividing variances into "significant" and "insignificant." A percentage may be fixed to distinguish the significant variances from the others; *e.g.* 5% and above may call for immediate action. However, the arbitrary allocation of a percentage is only a rough guide and should not be relied upon solely. Totals as well as percentages should be considered.

In connection with the control of direct labour costs some accountants have suggested the use of ratios or indices. Two worthy of mention are:

1. Measured Work Performance Ratio or Index.
2. Attendance Time Performance Ratio or Index.

The first deals with showing the efficiency achieved by a worker or group of workers and compares standard and actual performances for a certain quantity of work. A formula for its calculation is as follows (SM = Standard Minutes):

$$\frac{\text{Measured Work Produced (SM)}}{\text{Time taken to Produce the Work}} \times \frac{100}{1}$$

The second measure indicates how efficient, on average, a worker or group of workers has been over a period of time. Again a formula is available for its calculation:

$$\frac{\text{Measured Work Produced (SM)}}{\text{Total Attendance Time}} \times \frac{100}{1}$$

| LABOUR EFFICIENCY REPORT | | | | | |
|---|---|---|---|---|---|
| Department............................ | | | | Date............ | |
| Clock No. | Name | "Standard Hours" Produced | Actual Hours Worked | % Efficiency Act. to Std. | Remarks |
| | | | | | |
| | | | | | |

FIG. 64.—*Simple Labour Efficiency Report*

N

Both are a guide to the efficiency being achieved. They should be backed with the necessary information for showing why the actual performances vary from standard.

A simple report for summarising the information is given in Fig. 64. This may be adapted to meet specific circumstances.

### DEPARTMENTAL OPERATING STATEMENTS

The fact that costs should be controlled at the point at which they are incurred is stressed earlier. Departmental managers, foremen, and supervisors may be given information regarding overheads on operating statements. An example is given in Fig. 65.

When preparing these statements care should be taken to ensure that the levels of activity—budgeted and actual—coincide. In the example (Fig. 64) it will be seen that the budgeted costs are for the actual hours. Put another way, if *actual* activity is 80% of normal activity then the budgeted costs should relate to 80%. This is the point of having a flexible budget.

### TIMING OF REPORTS AND STATEMENTS

A very important aspect of control is the timing of the reports and statements. Only presentation at the correct time and place will ensure that the most effective use is made of the information. It is usual to prepare a schedule to show the reports to be prepared, the managers to receive them and the dates when they should be presented. Only by having a systematic approach to report writing can maximum efficiency be realised.

## COST REDUCTION AND REVISION OF STANDARDS

Cost control implies the comparison of actual and standard costs and then taking action on any variances which have arisen. However, it is clear that, for control to be really effective, there should be a planned programme of cost reduction. A business may have no difficulty whatsoever in achieving standards set many years ago, but this is not true control.

There should be a programme of continuous improvement in cost standards. This may come as a natural part of the Budgetary Control and/or Standard Costing system. Alternatively, special cost reduction committees or investigators may be employed to deal with improving efficiency within a particular field. The work of the organisation and methods and internal audit departments should also bring about improvements and, therefore, cost reductions.

The question of employing special committees or investigators deserves mention. These can play a very important part in ensuring that profits are maximised. The principal advantage of this method is that the people concerned are given a definite assignment and positive results

## DEPARTMENTAL OPERATING STATEMENT

**Department AB**          **Period January 19...**

Activity { **Standard: 10,000 Standard Hours**
{ **Actual: 9,500 Hours**

| Overhead Cost | Actual | Budgeted for Actual Hours | Analysis of Variances | | | Remarks |
| --- | --- | --- | --- | --- | --- | --- |
| | | | Favour-able | Un-favour-able | Con-trol-lable | |
| | £ | £ | £ | £ | £ | |
| *Variable Costs:* | | | | | | |
| Spoilage | 480 | 475 | | 5 | 5 | |
| Indirect Materials | 975 | 950 | | 25 | | Uncontrollable price increase |
| *Semi-Variable Costs:* | | | | | | |
| Indirect Labour | 3,000 | 2,875 | | 125 | 125 | Investigate |
| Power and Light | 1,390 | 1,350 | | 40 | 40 | Investigate |
| Heat and Water | 1,100 | 1,150 | 50 | | 50 * | Investigate |
| Insurance on Stocks | 390 | 388 | | 2 | 2 | |
| Repairs and Maintenance | 2,900 | 2,975 | 75 | | 75 * | Repairs kept to a minimum this period. Major break-down X Dept. |
| *Fixed Costs:* | | | | | | |
| Supervision | 1,000 | 1,000 | — | — | — | |
| Depreciation | 4,000 | 4,000 | — | — | — | |
| Rent Charges | 1,500 | 1,500 | — | — | — | |
| Other Space Charges | 900 | 900 | — | — | — | |
| | £17,635 | £17,563 | £125 | £197 | £47 | |

\* Favourable Variance deducted to arrive at total "Controllable."

FIG. 65.—*Example of a Departmental Operating Statement*

NOTES

1. The budgeted costs refer to *actual* activity, thus making the Variance Analysis figures more realistic.

2. The Insurance on Stocks cost *may* be regarded as an uncontrollable cost, but in the illustration the variation between Standard and Actual is, in any event, too small to warrant any action being taken.

3. Whether or not any deviation from Standard warrants investigation depends upon its size in relation to the Standard Cost. In practice, the cost analyst will know, from experience, which items require attention. Some businesses fix a percentage (*e.g.* 10%); any deviations from Standard are converted to percentages, and those below the stated figure are ignored, whereas all others are investigated.

4. A further column may be added to show what action has been taken.

may, therefore, be expected. If a company is experiencing difficulties cost reductions may be the only answer. These may take the following forms:

1. A comprehensive survey of the range of products being produced. When cost reductions are essential, simplification of the product range may be considered. Thus, for example, instead of producing twenty different products the effect of limiting the number to, say, ten products may be considered. By this reduction in the range it may be possible to effect economies of larger scale production. Larger purchase quantities, longer production runs and other benefits may be possible.

Not only costs should be considered. The effect on profitability is extremely important: only the least profitable products should be eliminated.

2. Each function or department is systematically investigated. Important questions should be asked and answered.

EXAMPLES

*Purchasing*

(*a*) Are quotations being obtained before purchases are made?

(*b*) Is the material being inspected immediately it is received?

(*c*) When materials are rejected are they dealt with promptly?

(*d*) Is standardisation of parts, materials and quantities practised?

(*e*) Can the storage facilities be improved?

(*f*) Are receipts and issues from the Stores dealt with in the best manner?

*Direct Labour*

(*a*) Are the timekeeping systems effective?

(*b*) Is the fullest use being made of work study?

(*c*) Are tools and equipment properly maintained?

(*d*) Do the workers have any incentive to work fast?

(*e*) Is the routing of work efficient?

(*f*) Is the fullest use made of mechanical aids such as conveyors and internal transport?

(*g*) Are standard costs set for direct labour and are these realistic and representative of current conditions?

Other areas of control relating to production, selling, distribution, and research and development could be scrutinised in the same way.

When a committee is employed this may be formed of members from the principal functional divisions. There may be a Cost Accountant, a Production Engineer, a Work Study Engineer and a Sales Executive. However, no hard and fast rules can be laid down on what is an ideal committee. Much depends upon the problem being investigated. If this affects many divisions of the business then it is only logical to have representatives from each. Even so it is advisable to limit the number of committee members to a size which will allow fairly swift action to be taken. If too large, discussions and arguments on what should be done may be protracted with a resultant failure to get results.

Obviously cost reduction should not be left entirely to special cost investigators and committees. All executives, foremen, supervisors, and workers should be aware of the importance of improving on standards. Subsequently, any real improvements can be incorporated into the budgets.

Generally standard or budgeted costs should be revised once a year. However, if interim adjustments have to be made they need not be incorporated into the budgets. Instead the effect of the revision may be shown in a Revision Variance Account. This applies to either reduced or increased standards; the effect of the reduction or increase can be segregated into the special account.

## CONTROL THROUGH INSURANCE

The internal control aspect is covered earlier in this chapter. Here the concern is with a wider aspect of control—offsetting risks through the medium of insurance. Management has to decide which risks should be covered. A premium is then payable to an insurance company and, if the event covered by a policy occurs, a claim may be made.

A full explanation of all insurance is outside the scope of a book of this nature. Accordingly, for further details you are advised to refer to a textbook on insurance.

Credit insurance is described in Chapter 24. This covers both home insurance and export insurance. Some of the other important forms of insurance are summarised below:

1. *Fire Insurance*—covers loss of buildings and contents by fire.

2. *Consequential Loss Insurance* (also known as "Loss of Profits Insurance")—may cover *loss of profit* arising from interruption of the business due to damage caused by fire, lightning, and explosion of boilers or gas used for lighting or heating a building.

Standing charges which must continue to be paid and any increase in costs due to working under impoverished conditions may also be covered.

Any claim for loss of profits is calculated in relation to the loss of turnover of which it is a part. The indemnity period is decided at the time the insurance is arranged.

3. *Fidelity Guarantee Insurance*—covers possible loss brought about by dishonesty of employees, particularly those who are concerned with handling cash or valuables. Cashiers and salesmen are often the subject of a fidelity guarantee policy.

4. *Cash or Goods in Transit Insurance*—intended to cover loss of cash, while in charge of an employee, in the process of being taken from one place to another; *e.g.* from the office to the bank.

5. *Employers' Liability Insurance*—provides an indemnity against liability for injuries that may result from the negligence of the employer. However, the National Insurance Act covers normal injuries.

6. *Public Liability Insurance*—covers any claims which may be made by third parties for personal injury due to the negligence or carelessness of the employer or employees. Damage to property or food poisoning may also be covered by the policy.

7. *Engineering Insurance*—covers damage to boilers, engines, and electrical plant. Third party liability arising from explosion, flying fragments, or other specified reason may also be covered.

Other types are burglary, motor, marine, and aviation insurance, all terms which are self-explanatory.

## EXAMINATION QUESTIONS

1. A company which manufactured paints in wide variety up to the year 1939 was obliged, under war-time conditions, to concentrate its activities on a much narrower range and as a result achieved notable economies in production and other costs. Since the war, increasing competition in the paint industry has led the company to expand its range of paints considerably. Write a report for the Board pointing out the financial implications of this diversification of products and discussing the advantages of reversing the present policy and concentrating on a much smaller range.    (*I.C.W.A.*)

2. What is a loss of profits insurance?
State how a claim arising under such a policy is calculated and summarise the information required to formulate a claim.    (*I.C.W.A.*)

3. You are Chief Accountant of a general engineering company with 600 employees, manufacturing a variety of products, principally to customers' orders, but including a few standard lines. What information would you provide for the Sales Manager of the company to assist him to obtain sufficient profitable orders to keep the plant, labour and other resources employed at a satisfactory level?    (*I.C.W.A.*)

4. Design a summary operating statement for use with Standard Costing. Assume that there are two production departments, and provide also for:

(*a*) general works service;    (*b*) materials;
(*c*) head office expense.

Each production department has achieved less output than planned, and the level of performance is below standard.

Enter appropriate columnar figures reflecting the foregoing. Show also total variances, and analyse these in adjacent columns, one of which should be headed, "Works Controllable Variance." This last should be further analysed in a subsidiary tabulation.

Cost figures for each production and service department, and for materials, should be totals only.    (*I.C.W.A.*)

5. What is a departmental operating statement?
Prepare such a statement to indicate the efficiency of the use of each element of cost.    (*I.C.W.A.*)

6. Draw up a summary operating statement for a factory with four production departments, giving figures for activity, efficiency, Standard cost of output, Actual cost of output, and total variance. A variance analysis should be appended to the main statement, giving the composition of the total variance under the five main variance headings, of which works controllable variance is one. This last should be further analysed into the individual variances of which it is made up. (*I.C.W.A.*)

7. Draft a departmental operating statement for a factory using a flexible budgeting system (figures are not required). (*I.C.W.A.*)

8. What are the main difficulties likely to be encountered in the control of administration costs? Give your reasoned opinion as to the relative importance of the control of expenditure on administrative as distinct from manufacturing costs. (*I.C.W.A.*)

9. You are asked by the board of Chop & Change Ltd. to report on the financial aspects of their commercial policy. The company manufactures four main products and you are supplied with an analysis of sales, expenses and profit margins as shown below. You are informed that there is a steady demand for all four products but that market resistance to selling price increases is now strong and that further increases are considered to be impracticable for the time being. Raw materials are readily available, but prices have risen in the past three years. There is an acute shortage of labour of the kind employed by the company and for this reason about 20% of the productive capacity is at present idle. Write your report for the board.

Analysis of Sales, Expenses and Profit Margins
(*all figures in thousands*)

| Product | Sales (units) | Materials £ | Direct labour £ | Variable expense £ | Fixed expense £ | Net profit £ | Sales value £ |
|---|---|---|---|---|---|---|---|
| **1968** | | | | | | | |
| A | 54 | 10·0 | 2·0 | 1·8 | 3·0 | 1·2 | 18·0 |
| B | 48 | 6·0 | 2·0 | 1·8 | 2·0 | 0·2 | 12·0 |
| C | 60 | 4·0 | 4·0 | 3·4 | 2·5 | 1·1 | 15·0 |
| D | 45 | 2·0 | 5·0 | 4·0 | 2·5 | 1·5 | 15·0 |
| | | 22·0 | 13·0 | 11·0 | 10·0 | 4·0 | 60·0 |
| **1969** | | | | | | | |
| A | 72 | 15·6 | 3·2 | 3·0 | 4·1 | −0·6 | 25·3 |
| B | 42 | 5·6 | 1·7 | 1·6 | 1·7 | 0·1 | 10·7 |
| C | 45 | 3·6 | 3·1 | 2·6 | 1·9 | 0·6 | 11·8 |
| D | 50 | 2·3 | 6·0 | 4·6 | 2·8 | 1·5 | 17·2 |
| | | 27·1 | 14·0 | 11·8 | 10·5 | 1·6 | 65·0 |
| **1970** | | | | | | | |
| A | 48 | 11·6 | 2·3 | 2·2 | 3·2 | −1·0 | 18·3 |
| B | 28 | 4·0 | 1·1 | 1·2 | 1·4 | 0·1 | 7·8 |
| C | 50 | 4·3 | 3·5 | 3·1 | 2·5 | 0·8 | 14·2 |
| D | 60 | 3·0 | 8·1 | 6·0 | 3·9 | 0·7 | 21·7 |
| | | 22·9 | 15·0 | 12·5 | 11·0 | 0·6 | 62·0 |

(*I.C.W.A.*)

10. "For effective management, the Manager should receive only condensed, summarised, and invariably comparative reports."

Assuming agreement with this statement, design a form and add suitable figures to present a report to management upon departmental overhead variances. (*I.C.W.A.*)

11. "For planning, the manager wants information about the future; for control, about the past."

Comment on this statement, and indicate the type of information supplied by the cost accountant for these purposes. (*I.C.W.A.*)

12. What factors should be borne in mind when presenting labour cost reports to foremen? Illustrate with a specimen form and show how you would distinguish between:

    (*a*) the Actual labour efficiency of the section, and

    (*b*) the way in which the labour force has been planned, utilised, and supervised. (*I.C.W.A.*)

13. To what extent and with what object would you give statistical information as to Overheads to Works Managers and Foremen? (*I.C.W.A.*)

14. Outline how you would prepare a Cost Statement to show the Profit and Loss on trading in various salesmen's areas. (*I.C.W.A.*)

15. In a business in which information is regularly given to the Works Manager, draft a *special* report on *one* of the following:

    (*a*) scrap;         (*c*) machine utilisation;

    (*b*) lost time;      (*d*) controllable overtime.

16. State briefly the information the cost accountant should provide for the following:

    (*a*) chargehand;

    (*b*) foreman;

    (*c*) service department manager;

    (*d*) works manager;

    (*e*) managing director. (*I.C.W.A.*)

17. The following chart is for the use of the foreman. Enumerate its faults as a method of presentation of this information.

| TYPE No. 3412. | | Date presented: 5th July, 195.... | |
| --- | --- | --- | --- |
| PRODUCTION MADE GOOD, 994 | | | |
| MATERIAL LOSSES FOR MONTH ENDING 30th April, 1953 | | | |
| PROCESS 1<br>3·38% | PROCESS 2<br>14·56% | PROCESS 3<br>0·77% | PROCESS 4<br>6·65% |
| CAUSE A.   0·5%<br>  „   B.   0·4%<br>  „   C.   2·04%<br>  „   D.   0·25%<br>  „   E.   0·1% | CAUSE A. 0·65%<br>  „   B. 1·26%<br>  „   C. 1·79%<br>  „   D. 4·78%<br>  „   E. 1·87%<br>  „   F. 2·99%<br>  „   G. 0·31%<br>  „   H. 0·37%<br>  „   I.  0·13% | CAUSE A. 0·2%<br>  „   B. 0·32%<br>  „   C. 0·25% | CAUSE A. 4·28%<br>  „   B. 1·45%<br>  „   C. 0·71% |

(*I.C.W.A.*)

18. (a) The following data relates to the manufacture of a standard product. Prepare a standard cost statement suitable for management control purposes.

| | Budgeted figures | Actual figures |
|---|---|---|
| *Overheads:* Fixed ... ... ... | 2,250 | 2,400 |
| Semi-variable ... ... | 1,500 | 1,550 |
| Sales ... ... ... ... ... | 30,000 units | 29,100 units |
| Selling prices ... ... ... ... | £2 per unit | £2·25 per unit |
| Materials price per lb. ... ... ... | £0·08 | £0·10 |
| Usage of materials ... ... ... | 300,000 lbs. | 304,000 lbs. |
| Wages ... ... ... ... ... | 60,000 hours | 57,000 hours |
| Standard hourly wage rate ... ... | £0·25 hour | |
| Wages paid ... ... ... ... | | £14,350 |
| *Standard profit per Unit:* | | |
| Selling price... ... ... ... | | £2·00 |
| Materials 10 lbs. ... ... | £0·875 | |
| Wages 2 hours ... ... ... | £0·500 | |
| Overhead: Fixed ... ... | £0·075 | |
| Semi-variable ... | £0·050 | £1·50 |
| Standard profit ... | | £0·50 |

There is no closing or opening stock of materials or work in progress.

The normal number of working days for a four week period is twenty; in this particular period there were nineteen days only. Calculations to the nearest £.

(b) Write brief notes explaining the significance of the principal variances disclosed above. (A.C.C.A.)

19. It sometimes happens that a favourable variance from one standard is directly related to an adverse variance from another, e.g. the purchase of processed materials may cause an adverse material price variance but a favourable labour efficiency variance. Give *two* examples, other than the one given above, and explain how you would present and interpret the analysis of variances in such cases. (I.C.W.A.)

20. In a business manufacturing a wide range of products, a suggestion is made that production should be concentrated on a few standard lines. What are the advantages and disadvantages of following the suggested course of action, and what would be the probable effects upon production, administration, selling and distribution costs? (I.C.W.A.)

21. A manufacturing company, for whose output there is a seasonal demand, has figures showing sales for the current month and the sales during the year to date. In adjoining columns the comparative figures for previous years are given.

Suggest improvements, and indicate how you would present information in similar circumstances. (I.C.W.A.)

22. State briefly three uses which each of the following analyses of sales may have in contributing to the provision of planning and control information for management. Analysis by:

    (a) salesmen;        (c) product;
    (b) territory;        (d) unit price.

Suggest two additions to this list mentioning similarly three uses for each. (I.C.W.A.)

23. The following comparative statement of trading results has been prepared for presentation to your board. Reconstruct the statement on the basis of costs per productive man-hour. Productive man-hours worked were 106,209 in the first quarter and 115,305 in the second quarter. Comment upon any variation in the new statement. Show the factors which have accounted for the fall in profit and suggest the possible causes as indicated by your figures.

|                    |     | 1st quarter £ | 2nd quarter £ |
| ------------------ | --- | ------------- | ------------- |
| Direct wages   ... | ... | 21,729        | 24,376        |
| Direct material ... | ... | 15,326        | 15,575        |
| Other costs    ... | ... | 45,263        | 46,586        |
| Total costs    ... | ... | 82,318        | 86,537        |
| Sales   ...    ... | ... | 84,921        | 86,096        |
|                    |     | £2,603        | £441 (loss)   |

(I.C.W.A.)

24. As cost accountant to a medium sized engineering firm describe the type and contents of monthly report which you would submit to:

    (a) managing director;
    (b) production manager;
    (c) sales manager.    (I.C.W.A.)

25. On the assumption that the investigation and correction of unsatisfactory conditions revealed by variances are essential to the effective use of standard costing, briefly outline the assistance which the cost accountant should give to management to promote success.    (I.C.W.A.)

26. As cost accountant to a large manufacturing company you are instructed to supply periodical cost information to the:

    (a) general manager;        (b) works manager;
    (c) sales manager;         (d) maintenance manager.

Outline the main points of information on which emphasis should be placed in each case and prepare a draft of any one of these statements to illustrate the points you have made.    (I.C.W.A.)

27. It is found that reports to management on standard costs and budgetary control are not completed before the end of the month following the period under consideration. Apart from clerical inefficiency, state the probable causes for this delay and indicate how you would seek to reduce the time of preparation.    (I.C.W.A.)

28. As Cost Accountant in a business, you observe that although the volume of business in a certain department is increasing, productivity is decreasing.

Using suitable figures, present a report to the Works Manager drawing attention to the facts which have given rise to this situation.    (I.C.W.A.)

29. The actual sales exceed budgeted sales by 5% yet the actual profit is 10% less than budgeted profit. Analysis shows this to be due to variations in sales mix of products earning different rates of profit.

Draft a report presenting an explanation.    (I.C.W.A.)

30. Reports for top management may be broadly classified into two classes: routine, and special. Mention three distinctive examples of each class, briefly indicating the main points to be covered in each. (*I.C.W.A.*)

31. What is a departmental operating statement?

Prepare such a statement to indicate the efficiency of the use of each element of cost. (*I.C.W.A.*)

32. The following figures were extracted from a standard costing system:

(i) Budget, at normal capacity—
| | | |
|---|---|---|
| Fixed factory overhead | ... | £10,000 |
| Variable factory overhead | ... | £20,000 |
| Machine hours ... | ... | 20,000 |

(ii) Actual—
| | | |
|---|---|---|
| Total factory overhead | ... | £25,000 |
| Machine hours ... | ... | 15,000 |

(iii) Standard machine hours for actual
| | | | |
|---|---|---|---|
| output | ... | ... | ... | 14,000 |

From the above information, present a statement setting out:

(*a*) the cost of idle capacity;
(*b*) efficiency variance. (*I.C.W.A.*)

33. "Lack of turnover results in two losses; loss of profit due to sales being under budgeted level, and cost of under-utilisation of the factory."

Illustrate this contention by drawing up a form of cost statement, with suitable figures inserted, to present to management. (*I.C.W.A.*)

34. Your company manufactures five varieties of product, distributed nation-wide at fixed retail prices. Selling and distribution costs form a substantial part of total cost. Design a summarised statement to inform your Board of the monthly results of their operations. (*I.C.W.A.*)

35. In a business producing consumer goods subject to seasonal demand, list the items of information which should be given by:

(*a*) the Cost Accountant to the Sales Manager;
(*b*) the Sales Manager to the Cost Accountant.

Indicate against each item the suggested frequency of presentation. (*I.C.W.A.*)

36. Production of a certain product is by passing large batches through a series of operations. Inspection is carried out only after the final operation and this reveals an appreciable proportion of scrap units due to incorrect workmanship. It is suggested that inspection should consequently be carried out after certain intermediate operations.

As cost accountant, what information would you present to management to show whether intermediate inspection would prove economic, and if so at which stages it should be done? (*I.C.W.A.*)

37. Cost reduction is to be pursued by a company which seeks to improve its competitive pricing position by increased output from existing plant. Present profit before tax is 15% of sales value and 30% of the value of capital employed. Other working ratios are: gross margin 35%; margin of safety 43%; and turnover 2. The actual figures for the year are as follows:

|  | £ |
|---|---|
| Total sales value ... | 1,200,000 |
| Variable costs ... | 780,000 |
| Fixed costs ... ... | 240,000 |
| Capital employed ... | 600,000 |
| Break-even point ... | 684,000 |

The proposal is to reduce sales prices by 10% and add 20% to the output. No change in fixed costs is expected. Cost reduction is estimated to amount to £42,000.

Tabulate existing and expected figures including comparative ratios. State briefly whether you favour the proposals.     (*I.C.W.A.*)

38. Design a form suitable for the monthly presentation of figures for advertising expenditure where budgetary control operates, and several types of advertising are used. Insert specimen figures.     (*I.C.W.A.*)

39. Discuss the economic importance of plant utilisation in a highly mechanised factory. Draft a suitable form for reporting periodically to management upon plant utilisation.     (*I.C.W.A.*)

40. A commodity is to be sold at a predetermined price which is insufficient to recover full costs.

Prepare a statement for any item with which you are familiar, showing the effect of taking the order at this reduced price both from the point of view of absorption of overhead expenses and of the company's net profit.

    (*I.C.W.A.*)

41. In view of the uneconomic nature of short runs and the necessity during the present difficult period of maintaining high efficiency, lay out a statement using imaginary figures, which will indicate the varying costs of production runs.

Include in your answer the costs of set up, storage costs and clerical planning, in addition to the cost of material, labour and factory expense.

    (*I.C.W.A.*)

42. A company received steel in strip form from a nearby steel-mill. On a specialised machine, from one kind of steel strip, there are produced three products A, B and C. Product A a taken from the machine and further processed to make it available for sale at £1·25 each. The additional processing cost for product A is £176 per month. Products B and C are run through a dipping vat to make them heat-resistant. The dipping material costs are calculated at £0·075 per cubic foot of product. Product B will then sell at £1·80 each and product C at £3·00 each.

In the month of May, 19.., the costs of running the machine for the month were:

|  | £ |
|---|---|
| Materials ... ... ... ... | 2835 |
| Direct labour ... ... ... ... | 600 |
| Maintenance and depreciation ... | 435 |
|  | £3870 |

Production and sales for the month were: Product A 600 units, product B 800 units, and product C 1000 units, and this can be regarded as a typical product mix.

Product B has a volume of ½ cubic ft and product C of ¾ cubic ft.

The dipping vat is being depreciated at the rate of £24 per month. It requires six men for its operation at a total cost of £540 per month and necessitates other operating costs of £60 per month; these costs are regarded as fixed costs.

(a) Produce a cost statement for May 19.. assigning the joint costs to each product.

(b) Make your recommendations on the advisability of the company selling, on a long-run basis, product B undipped, at £1·70 each.

(*I.C.W.A.*)

43. Would you advocate the launching of a cost reduction programme as part of the preparatory work of budgeting? Write brief numbered paragraphs setting out the reasons for your answer. (*I.C.W.A.*)

44. (a) Define and in the form of a tabulation distinguish between:

    (i) cost control; and
    (ii) cost reduction.

(b) Explain how the use of "value analysis" can reduce costs.

(*I.C.W.A.*)

45. A company manufactures a product by passing raw materials through a series of processes.

Materials used consist of three basic materials as follows:

| Material | | | | | Standard price per ton £ |
|---|---|---|---|---|---|
| A | ... | ... | ... | 50% | 30 |
| B | ... | ... | ... | 30% | 50 |
| C | ... | ... | ... | 20% | 70 |

There is an expected (standard) loss of 12% in processing.

Standard costs are in operation, and during one month 90 batches of 10 tons are put into process.

Commencing stocks are:

| Material | | | | Tons |
|---|---|---|---|---|
| A | ... | ... | ... | 70 |
| B | ... | ... | ... | 20 |
| C | ... | ... | ... | 80 |

Purchases during the period are:

| Material | | | | Tons | Cost £ |
|---|---|---|---|---|---|
| A | ... | ... | ... | 400 | 12,500 |
| B | ... | ... | ... | 250 | 10,400 |
| C | ... | ... | ... | 200 | 14,750 |

Requisitions show that 900 tons have been issued, but divided as follows:

| Material | | | | Tons |
|---|---|---|---|---|
| A | ... | ... | ... | 460 |
| B | ... | ... | ... | 260 |
| C | ... | ... | ... | 180 |

Actual production amounts to 788 tons of finished product.
Stock-taking reveals the following stocks at the end of the period:

| Material | | | | Tons |
|---|---|---|---|---|
| A | ... | ... | ... | 5 |
| B | ... | ... | ... | 15 |
| C | ... | ... | ... | 85 |

Present figures to management, showing actual costs, standard costs, and all variances, assuming that there is no work in progress at the beginning and end of the period. *(I.C.W.A.)*

# CHAPTER 15

## RETURN ON CAPITAL EMPLOYED

### INTRODUCTION

THE principal motivating force in the normal commercial business is profit. Efficiency is measured by the amount of profit earned; the larger the profit the more efficient is the business considered. However, although movements in total profit *may* show changes in efficiency they will not show the *state* of efficiency. If two businesses each earn £10,000 profit can they be said to be operating at the same level of efficiency? Clearly, unless further information is made available there is no way of telling the true position. The principal question to be answered is—what is the size of the investment?

Assets brought together by a business for the purpose of producing and selling are an investment. The size of this must obviously affect the size of the profit earned. Other things being equal, an increase in the investment should be followed by an approximately proportionate increase in the total profit. Only by comparing profit with investment and expressing the result as a percentage can any relative movement in efficiency be seen. If the two businesses earning £10,000 each have equal asset investments then, provided the risks involved are also equal, they are considered to be equal in efficiency. This principle may not always be strictly true, but it contains enough truth to allow a very acceptable measure of efficiency to be established.

The term used to describe this measure is "rate of return on capital employed." This chapter is concerned with how this measure is applied and its usefulness. Unfortunately, there is no generally accepted definition of the two essential terms (1) Capital Employed and (2) Profit. These are considered below.

### CAPITAL EMPLOYED

"Capital employed" is used to describe the investment made in a business. As noticed earlier, there is no generally accepted definition of the term. Some accountants think of one thing, whereas others think of another. One definition may include certain assets and the other exclude them altogether. Another definition may consider ordinary share capital, thus measuring how much is actually invested by shareholders. The principal definitions are summarised below. Study of a Chairman's Report and Final Accounts will often show the definitions being adopted (*see* Chapter 21).

381

**DEFINITION**

Possible definitions of capital employed are as follows:

1. Gross Capital Employed.

This would include fixed assets and current assets. (Some accountants use the term "gross capital employed" even though current liabilities are *deducted*.)

2. Net Capital Employed.

Fixed assets and current assets are added together and then current liabilities are deducted.

3. Proprietors' Net Capital Employed.

This can be obtained from the assets side of the balance sheet. From total assets are deducted current liabilities, long-term borrowing (*e.g.* debentures) and any other "outside funds."

Alternatively, proprietors' net capital employed may be computed by taking paid up capital and adding to this any reserves which may rightly be regarded as belonging to shareholders. For the purpose of revealing the return on capital employed for each class of shareholder the capital may be divided into (*a*) Proprietors' Equity Net Capital Employed, (*b*) Proprietors' Preference Net Capital Employed.

In connection with the proprietors' net capital employed some accountants suggest that the appropriate term to use is "return on capital *contributed*." There are many other variations of the term. Obviously both gross capital employed and net capital employed may be obtained by considering paid-up share capital reserves and loan capital There appears to be a preference for using the "assets approach" and for this reason this is the one adopted in this book.* Certainly, by taking assets, the conversion of capital to replacement values is greatly facilitated. This is a subject which is considered later.

**CHOICE OF APPROPRIATE METHOD**

The choice of the most appropriate method is clearly very important. How is this to be determined? Possibly the most important consideration is the *purpose* for which the capital employed figure is to be used. If the purpose is to show shareholders what is being earned for them then the use of the proprietors' net capital employed (the capital contributed) appears to be the one to use. However, for measuring the effectiveness of a business—a reflection of the efficiency of internal management—the gross (or net) capital employed concept is likely to be the best method. Each method is considered in greater detail on following page.

* See, for example, *The Planning and Measurement of Profit* (page 15). Published by the Association of Certified and Corporate Accountants.

## NET CAPITAL OR GROSS CAPITAL

The principal difference between the two terms "net capital employed" and "gross capital employed" is in the treatment of current liabilities.

The "net capital employed" is the figure obtained by taking total assets *less* current liabilities. The "gross capital employed" takes all assets without considering current liabilities. Later it is shown that "total assets" may be an adjusted total.

Arguments put forward for using the gross capital employed may be summarised:

1. *All* funds available to management should be gainfully employed.

The needs of businesses vary. Some have a large proportion of fixed assets; others have few fixed assets, but have a very large investment in current assets such as stocks and debtors. Only by including all assets can a realistic figure be obtained.

2. Short-term liabilities, including creditors, are simply a form of capital.

The difference between share capital and credit obtained from suppliers is based on the period of time for which the money is obtained. Since it is a common practice for a company to have a certain total of creditors at all times then the distinction based on the time factor may be regarded as being artificial. A similar principle could be applied to all short-term borrowing including bank overdrafts.

3. A profit cannot be said to be earned unless total capital in real terms is maintained intact. (The meaning of this is shown in Chapter 27.)

The disadvantages of the gross capital concept and, therefore, the advantages of the net capital employed method may be summarised as shown below:

1. If creditors are included as capital then the debtors should be excluded from capital.

Creditors are a form of short-term borrowing. On the other hand, debtors are a form of short-term lending. If short-term borrowing is included then it is only logical to exclude debtors. Accordingly it can be argued that the gross capital method is inconsistent and illogical.

2. Current assets such as stocks of raw materials and work-in-progress generally include some unpaid accounts—the current liabilities. Accordingly, a true capital employed figure can be obtained only when creditors are deducted.

## ITEMS INCLUDED IN CAPITAL EMPLOYED

Below are observations on the assets and liabilities which enter into the capital employed computation.

### FIXED ASSETS

There is no doubt regarding the inclusion of fixed assets; whether machinery, buildings, equipment, motor vehicles, or other fixed assets they are all included in the computation. However, problems do arise; viz.:

### *Historical or Replacement Costs*

Should historical (actual) costs or replacement costs be used for valuing fixed assets?

There is no general agreement on which valuation should be used. However, it is true to say that there appears to be a strong body of opinion which favours the use of replacement costs. One major difficulty is determining replacement cost, a matter discussed in Chapter 27. *In favour* of replacement costs for computing capital employed the following arguments may be used:

1. Valid comparisons of capital employed by different manufacturing units or by different companies are only possible when fixed assets are valued on the same basis.

2. Use of replacement costs gives the *current* value of capital employed. A true measure of return on capital employed must necessarily consider earnings and costs at current values with capital employed at current values.

3. A convention of accounting is that a conservative estimate of results should be shown. Measuring return on capital employed (at replacement values) complies with this convention. The return will tend to be lower than when historical costs are used.

4. By converting to replacement costs, all fixed assets, irrespective of when purchased, are brought in line to the same basis of valuation.

5. Arising from the advantages listed above there is the fact that management is given a realistic return which does measure, from one period to another, changes in efficiency.

6. Shareholders can be supplied with the true economic facts and not merely with figures based on historical costs. Justification of dividend limitation or seeking fresh capital is simplified.

7. Due recognition is given to the fact that real capital in terms of effective assets should be maintained intact.

Arguments *against* using replacement costs, put forward by the supporters of historical-cost valuation, are as follows:

1. Ascertaining replacement costs is fraught with uncertainties and difficulties.
2. Profit calculated by reference to replacement costs will not be accepted for taxation purposes.
3. Accountants are concerned with showing what has actually happened, not what might have happened.

There is no doubt that (1) and (2) are substantially correct. However, the advantages from using replacement costs for many purposes outweigh the disadvantages. The third disadvantage cannot really be taken seriously. Any Management Accountant worthy of that title should concern himself with past, present, and future. On the whole, therefore, there seems to be a very strong case for converting fixed assets to replacement costs values.*

## Idle Assets

A further problem, connected with fixed assets, is what should be done with assets which are not being employed.

A convention of cost accounting on the treatment of idle assets may serve as a guide to what should be done. If assets and plant are idle due to abnormal or unusual events such as a trade recession, fire or obsolescence then it is usual to exclude the costs of those from the normal costs of production. The capital employed figure can be calculated with this convention in mind; all fixed assets not being used for the reasons indicated can be excluded. This is not to say that these idle assets should be ignored altogether; indeed management should be made very much aware of the effects of idle facilities. However, this can be done outside the normal calculation of the capital employed.

Standby plant and equipment essential to the *normal* running of a plant should *not*, of course, be excluded from the computation.

## Value of Assets

There appear to be at least two possible interpretations that can be placed on "value of assets"; these are as follows:

1. Written-down values after depreciation has been charged.
2. Gross value of assets without deducting depreciation.

---

* A Report on the Centre for Interfirm Comparison included: "It is becoming more and more clear that the 'top test' must be profit on capital employed, and this yardstick must be based on a measurement of real asset values in current monetary terms." (*See* page 445 for description of C.I.F.C.)

In both cases the value may be shown at historical costs or replacement costs.

There is no hard and fast rule regarding which valuation (1) or (2) above should be taken: arguments used in *favour* of gross values are as follows:

(*a*) All assets are taken at the same valuation—gross value—without being adjusted and possibly distorted by the use of different rates of depreciation for different assets.

(*b*) There is no danger that assets will be ignored because the costs have been recovered; *i.e.* they have been reduced to a nominal or zero figure.

Clearly, from a management point of view, this is a major advantage. A realistic guide to efficiency can be obtained only by taking current values of assets.

(*c*) Comparisons between one company and another are likely to be much more valuable when gross values are used. If net values are taken the fact that there are different rates of depreciation or the fact that the assets have different life spans will tend to vitiate any comparisons.

This advantage is likely to be realised when current replacement costs are employed.

(*d*) The rate of return will tend to be lower than when net values are taken.

A conservative attitude is deemed desirable in all accounting matters.

*Against* using the gross values of the assets the following arguments may be put forward:

(*a*) The assets are "used up" year by year and this fact can only be reflected by making use of the net figures after depreciation.

(*b*) The depreciation charge makes cash available which is then reinvested in some form. This may be in fixed or current assets.

For this reason it can be argued that the old asset, partially worn-out, should be relieved of the duty of earning an adequate return on the original cost.

There is no doubt that the arguments used for and against the use of gross values are quite sound. However, if current replacement values are used these may, to a large extent, overcome the problems normally connected with both the gross and net valuations. Much depends upon how the current replacement values are determined: if the method used tends to show *actual* current values of individual assets then book values—net or gross—tend to be immaterial.

## INTANGIBLE ASSETS

Under this heading are included commercial goodwill, patents, and trade marks.

A rule often followed with intangible assets is that they are written off as quickly as possible. This applies particularly to goodwill which normally appears on a balance sheet only when it has been purchased as, for example, when an established business is acquired. The value of the goodwill is usually based on a number of years' purchase of future super-profits; *i.e.* profit over and above normal yield for the type of business concerned. Since profits may vary from one period to another it follows that super-profits may be non-existent. In the years which have a low rate of profit, on the definition given, there is no goodwill. When there is a high rate of return goodwill is in existence. Clearly, if consistency is to be achieved—and this is essential—it is better to exclude the value of goodwill from all capital employed computations. A similar argument can be used to exclude other intangible assets.

Exclusion from capital employed appears particularly appropriate when assets are taken at current replacement costs—normally the values of tangible assets will represent the true value of the business. On the other hand, when historical costs are used and goodwill has been purchased, the amount paid for goodwill will tend to represent the difference between the historical costs and the replacement costs of tangible assets. In this case, inclusion of goodwill may be appropriate to reflect the actual capital employed.

## CASH IN HAND AND AT BANK

There is no general agreement on the question of whether or not cash should be included in the capital employed figure. Certain subsidiary questions have to be satisfactorily answered before reaching any conclusion; viz.:

1. Can the cash be regarded as being part of the capital for *normal* purposes?

If there has been an abnormal inflow of cash such as when there has been a new issue of shares or a sale of plant then clearly the *total* cash on hand should not be regarded as being capital employed.

On the other hand, it may be felt that a normal amount of cash should be included in the capital employed figure. Here a policy decision should be made on what is a normal amount of cash. Some accountants have suggested using the amount required for a specified period; *e.g.* to cover four weeks. If this method is adopted it should be realised that each four-weekly period may not require exactly the same figure for cash. If production or selling are subject to fluctuations then clearly the cash requirements will tend to vary from one period to another. A way to overcome this difficulty would be to use the *average* cash requirements.

No matter what decision is reached regarding cash, whether to include or exclude from capital employed, an important matter should not be overlooked. Cash by itself is an "idle asset"; if there appears to be an excessive amount of cash being employed then clearly the Management Accountant has a duty to perform—he is probably in the best position to inform management of the surplus and also to suggest profitable ways of investing (*see* Chapter 6). Accordingly he should report on the cash position at regular intervals.

2. For what purpose is the percentage return on capital employed being computed?

If a company is being regarded as a total entity then cash could logically be shown as part of the capital employed.

On the other hand, if a company is divided into a number of units and the purpose is to measure the profitability of each unit then cash may be excluded on the grounds that the management of each unit would have no control over the cash policy. It could even be argued that finance and its control is outside the jurisdiction of all but the board of directors and financial controller.

There is no doubt whatsoever that cash is a vital asset. Accordingly, there appears to be a strong case for including normal cash requirements for each business unit. Clearly, although local management may have no *direct* control over cash, indirectly their actions must affect the position.

3. Is a bank overdraft to be regarded as part of the capital employed?

Much of what has been stated under the previous heading (question (2)) applies here. The remarks on "net capital" and "gross capital" are also appropriate.

Those accountants who prefer the net capital employed approach will tend to exclude overdrafts and other short-term liabilities from the capital. The danger of this method is that by excluding short-term liabilities the percentage return will tend to be overstated. This very fact may promote the view that short-term funds should be employed as much as possible and the disadvantages of this policy would then have to be suffered (Chapter 9 deals with this matter).

If the gross capital is regarded as the capital employed then a bank overdraft would be included in the figure. Clearly, if this is the case, then in the interests of consistency, cash should also be included as part of the capital.

## DEBTORS

Normal trade debtors are usually included as part of capital employed. Any bad debts or bad debts provisions are generally excluded, the debtors thus being shown at net value.

## STOCKS

All stocks, whether raw materials, work-in-progress or finished goods should be included in the capital employed figure. When valuing stocks a proper basis of valuation should be used (*see* Chapter 25).

Consistency is essential. One basis of valuation should be used and should not be varied without very good reason.

When comparing the results of different companies or units in the same company the bases used should be fully understood. There is likely to be a different valuation of the same quantities of stocks for two companies if one company uses, say, first in, first out, whereas the other uses, say, last in, first out. Moreover, the latter will tend to show a valuation, in times of rising prices, which is below the actual amount invested. When a company adopts marginal costing techniques, the fixed overhead costs will not appear in finished or part-finished stocks and, therefore, the valuation is affected.

## INVESTMENTS

Investments vary to a considerable extent in their nature and in their objectives. By the latter is meant the prime reason for the investment, which may be to employ surplus funds, to obtain a trade interest in another company or for some other purpose.

If the purpose of computing the return on capital employed is to measure the profitability and, therefore, efficiency of management then any investment which does not affect the efficiency of that management may well be excluded from capital employed. From this it follows that money invested *outside* the business may well be disregarded when ascertaining total capital employed.

Trade investments which are part of a company's normal earning potential may well be included in capital employed. This should present no difficulty when considering a company as a whole. However, there may be difficulty in investments employed for separate units within a group of companies, especially if investments are made by head office.

Sometimes the real purpose of the investment may not always be very clear. Is the purchase of shares in a company which uses your products to be regarded as an "internal" or "external" investment? If investments outside the business are quite substantial there may be justification for computing at least two figures of capital employed—one with investments and one without—and also the relevant rates of return.

Investments in tax reserve certificates deserve mention. These are generally regarded as external investments and as such are excluded from capital employed.

## FICTITIOUS ASSETS

Fictitious assets such as preliminary expenses, advertising suspense account or discounts on Debentures should be excluded from capital employed.

## LIABILITIES AND CAPITAL

Even though the "assets approach" is used to compute capital employed, this does not mean that liabilities can be ignored. Adjustments of assets may be necessary and this could involve deducting some of the items appearing amongst the liabilities and capital.

Share capital and Debentures present no problems. Bank overdrafts and creditors were dealt with earlier. Reserves expected to be retained in the business for an indefinite period of time are generally regarded as being part of capital employed. Future income tax reserves may also be treated as part of capital. Often the amount varies from one year to another and when considering a particular balance sheet the specific amount does not become due until well after the date of the balance sheet.

Items which may be deducted from total assets are all those which represent (a) a payment to be made within a very short time or (b) a permanent balance which does not represent funds retained within the business. An example of (a) is a provision for taxation whereas (b) can be illustrated by reference to a staff pension fund when the amount transferred to the fund is invested outside the business and does not increase the effectiveness of the business.

These remarks can only serve as a guide. Much depends upon which definition of capital employed is being adopted. Accountants who use the gross capital definition may prefer to use *all* assets without any deductions. On the other hand, those who advocate the net capital approach may prefer to deduct all current liabilities.

In some cases a compromise may be thought necessary. Having regard to the definition of current liabilities—those to be paid off within a year—some accountants would prefer to analyse these into (a) permanent and (b) current. Thus, for example, a bank overdraft of £10,000 may be regarded as being a permanent part of capital employed and any figure in excess of this would be regarded as a temporary debt which would be excluded from capital employed by deducting from total assets.

These remarks have applied chiefly to the gross capital and net capital concepts: proprietors' net capital is discussed below.

## PROPRIETORS' NET CAPITAL (CAPITAL CONTRIBUTED)

The definition of the proprietors' net capital was given earlier. The shareholders of a company should be paid a reasonable rate of return. Whether they actually are being paid this return can only be seen by computing the capital contributed by each major class of shareholder.

Management theorists have long since recognised that management has a social obligation to perform in connection with shareholders; *i.e.* there should be a return which is adequate having regard to the risk involved. Accordingly, calculation of the return on proprietors' capital, it can be argued, should be the concern of the Management Accountant as well as the gross or net capital previously described.

## CURRENT REPLACEMENT COSTS

The broad question of replacement costs is covered in Chapter 27. However, for convenience the bases used for converting the main types of assets to current replacement costs are summarised below:

1. Fixed Assets.

These may be converted to replacement costs by using index numbers, by referring to current prices for similar machines or by having a physical appraisal and then valuing, having due regard to current prices.

2. Debtors and Creditors.

The figures for debtors and creditors may not require adjustment. However, much depends on the extent of the revaluation principles being applied.

3. Investments.

When investments are quoted on a Stock Exchange that valuation can be taken. If there have been fluctuations throughout the year an average value may be preferred.

Trade investments in companies whose shares are not quoted may be valued on the basis of the current replacement costs of the assets owned. If a controlling interest is held in a company there should be no difficulty in obtaining sufficient information to value the assets at current replacement costs. In other cases the basis of the yield being obtained should be used.

## PROFIT

There are many possible definitions of "profit." The revenue or income taken for a period may be varied in size with the items included; similar variations are possible with the expenditure or costs. Accounts may be prepared for different purposes and in each case the profit shown may be different. Examples of these accounts are those to comply with the Companies Acts, those to meet the requirements of the Commissioners of Inland Revenue and those for computing estate duty.

For management planning and control an entirely different type of accounts should be employed.* The profit shown by these accounts should be such that as far as possible the true economic facts relating to the business are reflected. For the purpose of computing profit for management purposes the following rules have been developed:

1. There must be a correct matching of capital employed and revenue—any revenue from assets not included in the capital employed figure should not form part of the profit for management purposes.

2. Abnormal, exceptional, or non-recurring gains or losses should be excluded from the calculation of profit.

Gains or losses from the sale of fixed assets or from foreign exchange transactions are typical examples. An award made as a result of a legal action such as the infringement of a patent may also come under this heading.

3. Depreciation charged in the accounts should be based on replacement costs.

Only by using replacement costs will the economic loss in effective asset-power be recognised. Capital is maintained intact in real terms.

4. There must be a clear distinction between capital and revenue expenditure.

Care should be taken to ensure that only the correct proportion of capital expenditure is written off. This rule should be applied whether referring to fixed assets, research and development expenditure capitalised, or to advertising costs "suspended."

5. The convention that stipulates that all possible losses should be covered in the accounts, whereas possible gains should be disregarded, applies when computing management profit.

6. The revenue for the period being considered and for no other time should be included in the profit computation. This is similar to (1) above. Here the matching is concerned with capital employed in a period with revenue received in a period. The revenues from sales

---

* Management accounts will not necessarily *replace* the other types of accounts; they all serve a particular purpose.

made in previous periods should be excluded from this period's revenue.

Ideally there should be no arbitrary "cut-off" periods. However, this dividing cannot be avoided. For all practical and legal purposes a company has perpetual existence, so there is no alternative except to divide this life into yearly divisions.

It is very important to note that the profit should be computed in respect of the definition adopted for "capital employed." If gross capital is taken then the profit should relate to gross capital; on the other hand if net capital is appropriate then the profit should be what is earned by that capital.

## EXAMPLE OF PRINCIPLES

In this section the principles explained earlier are put into practice. This is accomplished by working through a problem and by giving notes, where appropriate, on difficult points of procedure.

### QUESTION

The balance sheet given on pages 394 and 395 is based on historical costs. In the progressive company whose position and resources are summarised in the balance sheet, the board of directors are very concerned with obtaining the true return on capital after current replacement costs are used to convert assets and when due recognition has been given to maintaining capital intact. You are required to show (a) capital employed—"gross" and "net" (b) computation of profit for management planning and control and (c) an expression of such profit as a percentage of capital employed.

The suggested solution is given on pages 396, 397, and 398.

*Notes on Computation of Capital Employed*

1. The goodwill, being of no value, is excluded from the computation.
2. Quoted investments are also excluded from the capital employed. The object is to show only the capital which is within the control of the management of the company. Naturally the decision on whether to continue investing in that particular source rests with top management, but "control" referred to in this paragraph means two things: (a) the transactions are part of the normal business carried on; e.g. manufacturing and selling products, and (b) the success or failure is within the responsibilities of the management. This is a loose definition, but it should be adequate to show why the quoted investments are not included.
3. Preliminary and other capital expenses are excluded on the grounds that these are a fictitious asset.
4. Current replacement values are taken and any adjustments in current assets (*i.e.* stocks in this case) are brought in when calculating the capital employed.
5. Provided the earlier text in this chapter has been read and understood there should be no difficulty in following the computation.

[*Continued on page 396.*

| | £ Authorised | £ Issued |
|---|---|---|
| *Share Capital* | | |
| 150,000 4½% Redeemable Cumulative Preference Shares of £1 each fully paid (Redeemable 19..) ... ... ... | 150,000 | 150,000 |
| 200,000 5½% Redeemable Cumulative 2nd Preference Shares of £1 each fully paid (Redeemable 19..) ... ... | 200,000 | 200,000 |
| 5,000,000 Ordinary Shares of £0·05 each ... ... ... | 250,000 | 250,000 |
| | 600,000 | 600,000 |
| *Capital Reserve* | | |
| Premium on Shares ... ... ... ... ... ... | | 48,000 |
| *Revenue Reserve* | | |
| Profit and Loss Balance ... ... ... ... ... | | 262,000 |
| | | 910,000 |
| *Taxation Equalisation* ... ... ... ... ... | | 140,000 |
| *Amounts Owing to Subsidiaries* ... ... ... ... | | 28,000 |
| *Current Liabilities* | | |
| Creditors and Accrued Charges ... ... ... ... | 382,000 | |
| Bank Loan ... ... ... ... ... ... ... | 10,000 | |
| | | 392,000 |
| *Dividends—Accrued, Proposed and Unclaimed* | | |
| Preference Share Dividends Accrued ... ... ... | 1,000 | |
| Ordinary Share Dividends Proposed ... ... ... | 33,000 | |
| Dividends Unclaimed ... ... ... ... ... | 500 | |
| | | 34,500 |
| *Provisions* | | |
| Taxation (on Current Year's Profits) ... ... ... | | 54,000 |
| | | £1,558,500 |

*Notes on Balance Sheet*

1. Additions to the balances of the original costs of assets necessary to convert to replacement costs:

(a) Freehold Property £100,000 ⎱
(b) Leasehold Property £4,000 ⎰ NET, *i.e.*, less depreciation.
(c) Plant, etc. £30,000

2. Shares held in subsidiary companies are currently valued at £100,000.

3. Trade investments are valued at £48,000 and unquoted investments at £30,000. The quoted investments are not connected with the normal operations of the company.

4. Stocks.

Adjustments required are as follows:

(a) Increase in value of raw materials contained in stocks figure is £40,000.

(b) Obsolete components included in stocks £1000 to be written off.

5. Goodwill represents the "extra amount" paid for a company which has now gone into liquidation. The patents and trade marks have a market value of £30,000 which is a conservative estimate of the price which could be obtained if they were sold.

AS AT 31ST MARCH

|  | £ | £ |
|---|---|---|
| *Intangible Assets* | | |
| Goodwill at cost ... ... ... ... ... ... | 8,000 | |
| Patents and Trade marks at cost less amounts written off ... ... ... ... ... ... ... ... | 100 | |
| | | 8,100 |

| *Fixed Assets* | £ Original Cost | £ Aggregate Depreciation | £ Book Value |
|---|---|---|---|
| Freehold Property ... ... ... ... | 180,000 | 25,000 | 155,000 |
| Leasehold Property ... ... ... ... | 5,000 | 500 | 4,500 |
| Plant, Machinery, Motor Vehicles, Furniture, Fixtures and Fittings ... ... | 62,000 | 30,000 | 32,000 |
| | | | 191,500 |

|  | £ | £ |
|---|---|---|
| *Subsidiary Companies* | | |
| Shares held ... ... ... ... ... ... ... | 80,000 | |
| Amounts owing ... ... ... ... ... ... | 400,000 | |
| | | 480,000 |
| *Investments* | | |
| Quoted (market value at this date £50,000) ... ... ... | 10,000 | |
| Trade Investments ... ... ... ... ... ... | 40,000 | |
| Unquoted Investments ... ... ... ... ... | 20,000 | |
| | | 70,000 |
| *Current Assets* | | |
| Stocks ... ... ... ... ... ... ... ... | 192,000 | |
| Debtors, Bills Receivable and Payments in Advance ... | 600,000 | |
| Cash in Hand and at Bank ... ... ... ... ... | 20,000 | |
| | | 812,000 |
| Preliminary and other Capital Expenses ... ... ... | | 5,000 |
| | | £1,558,500 |

## Notes on Transactions Affecting Profit

1. The profit for the year as per the accounts is £300,000.

2. Additional depreciation based on the new replacement costs is as follows:

Freehold Property £5000; Leasehold Property £400, Plant, etc. £3000 and Patents and Trade marks £3000.

3. Legal costs of an exceptional nature, deducted in arriving at the profit for the year, £3000. Interest on Bank Loan, £500.

4. Surplus obtained from the favourable movement of foreign exchange, included in the profit for the year, £4000.

5. Sales made in previous year amount to £100,000 on which the estimated profit is £11,000. This figure has been included in the current year's profit. On the other hand, profit on completed contracts, not yet brought into the accounts, amounts to £6000.

6. Goodwill written off in the current year's accounts is £2000.

7. A machine formerly used on the production line of the company's factory was sold during the year to which the accounts refer. The loss incurred on the sales was £500 which has been treated as a cost in arriving at profit.

8. Income from quoted investments included in the profit for the year amounts to £5000.

SUGGESTED SOLUTION

(a) *Capital Employed as at 31st March* ......

### Current Replacement Costs Used

| Fixed Assets* | £ | £ |
|---|---|---|
| Freehold Property ... ... ... ... ... | | 255,000 |
| Leasehold Property ... ... ... ... ... | | 8,500 |
| Plant, Machinery, etc. ... ... ... ... ... | | 62,000 |
| | | 325,500 |
| Patents and Trade marks ... ... ... ... | | 30,000 |
| *Subsidiary Companies* | £ | |
| Shares held ... ... ... ... ... ... | 100,000 | |
| Amounts owing ... ... ... ... ... ... | 400,000 | |
| | | 500,000 |
| *Investments* | £ | |
| Trade Investments ... ... ... ... ... | 48,000 | |
| Unquoted Investments ... ... ... ... ... | 30,000 | |
| | | 78,000 |

| Current Assets | | | |
|---|---|---|---|
| Stocks ... ... ... ... ... | 192,000 | | |
| | + 40,000 | | |
| | 232,000 | | |
| | − 1,000 | | |
| | | 231,000 | |
| Debtors, Bills Receivable and Payments in Advance ... | | 600,000 | |
| Cash in Hand ... ... ... ... ... ... | | 20,000 | |
| | | | 851,000 |
| GROSS CAPITAL EMPLOYED ... | | | £1,784,500 |

| *Less* Adjustments: | £ | £ |
|---|---|---|
| Amounts owing to subsidiaries ... ... | 28,000 | |
| Creditors ... ... ... ... ... | 382,000 | |
| Bank Loan ... ... ... ... ... | 10,000 | |
| Dividends: Preference ... ... ... | 1,000 | |
| Ordinary ... ... ... ... | 33,000 | |
| Unclaimed ... ... ... | 500 | |
| Provision for Taxation ... ... ... ... | 54,000 | |
| | | 508,500 |
| NET CAPITAL EMPLOYED | | £1,276,000 |

\* It is assumed that the extra depreciation has already been deducted.

*(b) Profit Computation for Management Planning and Control*

| | | £ | £ |
|---|---|---:|---:|
| Profit on Gross Capital Employed | | | |
| Profit for Year  ...  ...  ...  ...  ... | | | 300,000 |
| *Add* Unusual or Exceptional Items | | | |
| Loss from Sale of Machine ...  ...  ... | | 500 | |
| Legal Costs  ...  ...  ...  ...  ... | | 3,000 | |
| Estimated Profit on Completed Contracts  ... | | 6,000 | |
| Amount written off goodwill ...  ...  ... | | 2,000 | |
| Interest on Bank Loan  ...  ...  ... | | 500 | |
| | | | 12,000 |
| | | | 312,000 |
| *Less* Unusual or Exceptional Items | | | |
| Depreciation: additional charges based on replacement costs: | | | |
| Freehold Property ...  ...  ...  ... | | 5,000 | |
| Leasehold Property...  ...  ...  ... | | 400 | |
| Plant, etc.  ...  ...  ...  ...  ... | | 3,000 | |
| | | 8,400 | |
| Depreciation: Patents, etc.  ...  ...  ... | | 3,000 | |
| Income from Quoted Investments  ...  ... | | 5,000 | |
| Profit: Sales made in the previous year  ... | | 11,000 | |
| Profit on foreign exchange  ...  ...  ... | | 4,000 | |
| | | | 31,400 |
| | | | £280,600 |

*Notes on Profit Computation*

1. An argument could be put forward for calculating profit for (*a*) gross capital employed and (*b*) net capital employed. However, this view has not been taken in the example given. The only possible variation between the two definitions of profit, based on (*a*) and (*b*), is the £500 for interest on bank loan which is slight in relation to the total profit.

2. The items added or deducted are not all those likely to be met in practice. Indeed, it would be difficult to cover every possible adjustment. However with the earlier text, and the example, the reader should be able to tackle most profit computations of this nature.

3. It has been assumed that the stock adjustments brought in to arrive at capital should not be included in the profit computation. However, this assumption should not be regarded as formulating an inflexible rule. The windfall profit on stocks may have crystallised over a number of years. Accordingly, it could be argued that a *proportion* of the profit should be included in this year's profit.

(c) *Percentage Return on Capital Employed*

| | |
|---|---|
| Gross Capital Employed ... ... ... | £1,784,500 |
| Net Capital Employed ... ... ... | £1,276,000 |
| Profit for Management Planning ... | £280,600 |

Percentage: Profit on Capital Employed:
    (a) Gross Capital = 15·7%
    (b) Net Capital  = 22%

## SIGNIFICANCE OF THE RETURN ON CAPITAL EMPLOYED

The fact that profit is the principal motivating force of businessmen is noted at the beginning of this chapter. This cannot be denied. Here the analysis is taken a step further and the significance of the return on capital employed is considered. In order to accomplish this end, examination of a number of definitions of profit is necessary. These are considered in the next few paragraphs.

A starting point in budgeting and management planning should be the determination of a minimum rate of profit. This is the lowest return expected on capital employed. In order to continue attracting capital to a particular business a fair return should be paid. This is not the only reason for laying down a minimum return. All business activity involves choice; the correct choice should result in at least a reasonable (minimum) return. If this minimum return is not forthcoming then management should look elsewhere for alternative investments—new products or services. The determination of what is a minimum return is far from easy. Different suggestions have been put forward as a basis. The Bank Rate, the rate of interest charged by the Bank of England for discounting first class bills of exchange, may be used as a guide. However, an argument against using the equivalent of the Bank Rate is the fact that it is essentially a short-term rate and since companies are a permanent form of investment, a long-term rate would be more appropriate. Accordingly, the rate paid on gilt-edged securities may be regarded as a much better criterion. If this rate is taken then it seems logical to take the return on the actual market price prevailing at the time and not on the *nominal* value of the securities.* In effect, the minimum profit is the rate expected from an investment which carries very little risk.

All business ventures involve some degree of risk and, therefore, it is necessary to allow for this in arriving at a figure which may be regarded as "normal profit." Attempts have been made to classify businesses on the basis of risk involved. One possible classification is as follows:

    (a) Businesses producing staple products or services whose demand does not fluctuate to a great extent. Food manufacturers and

---

* Limitation of space does not permit a full examination of long and short-term rates of interests or the changes in the value of money which affect these rates and security values.

businesses which make certain types of household commodities such as soap, polishes, and matches may come into this category. There is a regular demand which is not affected by changes in fashions so the risk involved is not very great. A rate of return between 2 and 4% may be appropriate, this being in addition to the return expected as minimum profit.

(b) Businesses which produce household commodities, foodstuffs, clothing, and other goods which fluctuate in demand, but which can, with sound management planning and control, keep in touch with current problems and forecast likely changes, thereby maintaining progress.

The risk for this second class of business is clearly greater than for the first type ((a) above). An additional rate of return, over and above the minimum return, may be over 4% and up to 10%.

(c) Businesses which are of a speculative nature such as property development, gold mining, oil prospecting, and other ventures whose outcome is very uncertain.

A return of over 10% could be expected for a business coming within this category. Again, this rate is in addition to the minimum return.

This classification and the rates of return are only suggestions. There may be others which would be more suitable. The division of businesses into three classes may in fact be too narrow and some difficulty may be experienced in fitting some types of business into the categories as defined. The rates of return may vary from one period to another with changes in business confidence and the structure of interest rates. Nevertheless, these should serve as a guide when establishing the normal profit for the specific business.

After the minimum profit and normal profit have been defined it should be possible to establish a "final profit" figure. In fixing this final profit a number of factors should be considered. There is the need to maintain real capital intact (considered in Chapter 27). In addition, possible fluctuations in trade have to be covered. The profit target should be high enough to cover trade recessions and meet any other difficulties. There is also the provision of finance for future growth. If profit is large enough adequate reserves can be built to meet all these essential requirements: maintenance of real capital, trade setbacks and normal growth, adequate dividends to shareholders. If there are any fixed charges, such as interest on debentures or rental for leasing of premises, the fact that these have to be covered each year before it can be said that a profit has been earned, should not be overlooked.

The burden of taxation also affects the return expected. If taxation absorbs, say, 50% then this must have an important effect on the determination of the final profit. The tax laws may favour one course of action rather than another; e.g. profit distributed may be taxed

O

at a heavier rate than retained profit. The *current* law should be considered.

If an adequate dividend to shareholders (on actual value of capital contributed) is 5% this could be taken as a starting point for setting a final profit figure. For the type of business concerned a normal cover of the yield by earnings to allow for the factors outlined previously may be, say, five times. If so, then 25% may be the final profit. The cover of five times is, of course, quite high and in some businesses a two or three times cover is more usual. However, the principle is not affected by this fact. The figure obtained by this method could be compared with the figure obtained by working via minimum and normal profits.

Once the final profit has been determined this becomes the criterion for establishing future plans. Budgets for each division should show that the profit target is expected to be achieved. Otherwise management should consider alternative and more profitable uses of capital.

## VARIATIONS IN DEFINITION

Besides having the different definitions of gross capital, net capital and proprietors' capital, defined earlier, it may be possible to have different concepts of "capital employed" on the basis of responsibility. This is in line with modern practice which attempts to locate responsibilities by function or department—a process which may be termed "responsibility accounting." Some idea of these different concepts may be obtained from the following:

| *Executive* | *Capital Employed* | |
|---|---|---|
| Managing Director | Gross Capital<br>Net Capital<br>Proprietors' Capital | for the company<br>as a whole and<br>its divisions. |
| Divisional Manager | Gross Capital and/or Net Capital *for the division.* | |
| Production Manager | Gross and/or Net Capital for the production division. | |
| Sales Manager | Gross and/or Net Capital for the assets of the sales division. | |
| Ordinary Shareholders | Proprietors' Capital excluding preference shares and loans. | |

This summary should give some idea of the capital employed figure which could be used for indicating the profitability for that part of the business which is important to the manager named. Naturally there may be some difficulty in dividing the capital employed and the profit into these different categories. However, for some businesses the process may be quite feasible and worthwhile.

## ADVANTAGES OF CONCEPT—"RETURN ON CAPITAL EMPLOYED"

The return on capital employed concept has many advantages over other methods of measuring efficiency. It is the only measure which can be said to show satisfactorily the benefits being obtained for the sacrifice involved, the latter being represented by capital invested. Some of the benefits and advantages of calculating the return on capital employed are summarised below:

1. It allows external comparisons to be made. The progress of one company or companies generally may be compared with the progress being made by the accountant's own company.

Information on other companies may be obtained from newspapers, professional journals and published accounts. Earnings for different industries are published from time to time in *The Economist*. In addition, information may be obtained from The Centre for Interfirm Comparison, an organisation which was set up by The British Institute of Management in association with The British Productivity Council (the work of the Centre is covered in Chapter 17). The ratio of operating profits to assets employed is taken by the Centre to reflect the earning power of a "primary ratio," which may be analysed into its constituent subsidiary ratios.

2. Internal comparisons can be made in respect of different divisions or departments of a business.

3. The relative profitability of different products may be illustrated by reference to the capital employed to produce and sell each product.

This advantage may not always be available to a business, for the simple reason that the assets employed produce and sell a large variety of products and there is no way of showing in accurate terms what value of the capital or what figure of profit, relates to specific products. In such circumstances *estimated* figures of capital employed and profit for each product may be used to give a guide to the relative profitability.

4. The relative profitability of future courses of action may be obtained. Expansion of plant, introduction of a new product or other development, may be assessed in terms of profit through the estimated return on estimated capital to be employed.

5. When the return on capital employed is calculated any changes in circumstances, since the previous return was calculated, may be taken into consideration without difficulty. Increases in assets employed and even changes in the value of money can be reflected in the calculations. How this is done is shown earlier in the chapter, in the example in question-and-answer form.

6. The return on capital employed can become an integral part of the Budgetary Control System. Significant percentages and ratios may be

shown in the Master Budget. Subsequently any profit variances may be calculated so that management is able to follow progress being made and, if necessary, to take corrective action, such as changing the use to which capital is to be put.

7. If management ensures that an adequate return on capital is earned then many indirect benefits should accrue to the business concerned. Some of these are listed below:

(a) Regular and satisfactory dividends to shareholders.

(b) Adequate reserves allowing progress to be made, the company being able to grow at a rate which may be regarded as healthy.

(c) Because of (a) and (b) there may be no need to seek outside funds. If the latter have to be sought then, because of the financial standing of the company, there should be no difficulty in obtaining them.

(d) The business should be able to ward off any unexpected competition or other adversities without great difficulty.

(e) Because of the confidence and security which must inevitably arise from earning adequate profits the business will tend to have a good credit rating and to attract the best type of workers and management.

## SIGNIFICANCE OF TAXATION AND INTEREST PAID

The earlier sections explained the significance of the return on capital concept and how it was calculated. An important question is how is the return calculated in practice?

Generally, the return is calculated *before* interest and tax have been deducted. In terms of a formula this means:

$$\frac{\text{Profit before interest and tax}}{\text{Total assets employed}} \times 100 = \text{Return on capital employed}$$

The reason for exclusion of tax in the calculation of company profits for management control is because the Corporation Tax figure is based on the Finance Acts and these are obviously quite outside the control of management. There is the added advantage that where the return is calculated for different divisions within a Group, comparison between the figures is much more meaningful.

An earlier chapter deals with the different types of capital structure. When calculating the return on capital employed the exclusion of interest has the effect of removing the consequences of having debentures or other loans in the capital employed figure.

It is general practice to show interest on debentures as a deduction in arriving at the profit for the period. On the other hand, dividends are shown as an *appropriation* of profit. A company with no debentures will tend to show a larger profit than would an identical company with, say, 50% of its capital in debentures. To eliminate this effect the interest due to the debenture holders should be added back to the *conventional* profit to arrive at the profit for *management planning and control.*

Like all other ratios, the return on capital employed should not be taken in isolation. Indeed, trends are more important than single figures. Comparison with companies in unrelated industries may also be misleading. However, comparison with the ratios of leaders in the same industry can be a very useful exercise. If budgetary control is employed the target profit will have been planned in advance, so a comparison with this will also be possible.

Although comparison with each other would serve no useful purpose each of the following figures may serve as a guide for companies in the same industries:

*Return on Capital Employed*
%

| | |
|---|---|
| Philips Electrical Co. Ltd. | 10·5 |
| Fisons Ltd. | 11·0 |
| Imperial Tobacco Group Ltd. | 17·1 |
| British Oxygen Co. Ltd. | 12·1 |

These figures are for 1968 and in each case are calculated on profit before taxation and interest charges.

A further refinement which may be carried out is to take the *average* of the capital employed by considering the beginning and end of the financial year.

### PRACTICAL EXAMPLES

A summary of the financial results covering ten years is shown as a Statistical Record in Fig. 66. This is reproduced by kind permission of Fisons Limited and represents how progressive companies are presenting the most important facts over a ten-year period.

An alternative arrangement is given from The British Oxygen Company Limited (Fig. 67). Again, this is taken from the 1968 reports and accounts. The period taken in this case is also ten years.

A very useful addition to annual reports are the block diagrams which show (*a*) Group Profits (Fig. 68), and (*b*) Group Sales and Capital Employed (Fig. 69).

There are many important facts highlighted in the two statements and the diagrams. Comparison should also be made with the statistics of the Philips Electrical Company (pages 434 and 435). Some of the more important statistics are as follows:

### 1. *Sales*

Besides noticing the size of the sales it is also important to study the figure in relation to other figures. Thus, for example, the Sales to

## Fisons Limited—Statistical Record 1959–1968

| | 1959 (£000) | 1960 (£000) | 1961 (£000) | 1962 (£000) | 1963 (£000) | 1964 (£000) | 1965 (£000) | 1966 (£000) | 1967 (£000) | 1968 (£000) |
|---|---|---|---|---|---|---|---|---|---|---|
| **ASSETS** | | | | | | | | | | |
| Land, buildings, plant and equipment (including development expenditure) | 22,113 | 21,423 | 22,328 | 23,990 | 24,076 | 27,254 | 29,321 | 34,498 | 41,240 | 44,316 † |
| Interests in Associated Companies | 2,800 | 1,998 | 2,553 | 2,927 | 3,617 | 3,550 | 3,915 | 5,007 | 6,443 | 5,969 |
| Trade investment | — | — | 1,125 | 1,125 | 1,125 | — | — | — | — | — |
| | 24,913 | 23,421 | 26,006 | 28,042 | 28,818 | 30,804 | 33,236 | 39,505 | 47,683 | 50,285 |
| Net current assets | 12,634 | 15,606 | 12,975 | 10,888 | 11,494 | 12,593 | 14,679 | 17,555 | 11,592 | 18,319 |
| Goodwill | — | 120 | 289 | 427 | 610 | 3,085 | 4,192 | 4,998 | 5,147 | — |
| | 37,547 | 39,147 | 39,270 | 39,357 | 40,922 | 46,482 | 52,107 | 62,058 | 64,422 | 68,604 |
| **FUNDS EMPLOYED** | | | | | | | | | | |
| Ordinary stock | 11,610 | 15,480 | 15,480 | 15,480 | 15,480 | 15,480 | 15,480 | 20,640 | 20,640 | 20,640 |
| Reserves | 10,622 | 7,585 | 8,284 | 8,722 | 8,957 | 10,115 | 11,937 | 7,259 | 7,413 | 8,094 |
| Ordinary stockholders interests | 22,232 | 23,065 | 23,764 | 24,202 | 24,437 | 25,595 | 27,417 | 27,899 | 28,053 | 28,734 |
| 4½% cumulative preference stock | 4,259 | 4,259 | 4,259 | 4,259 | 4,259 | 4,259 | 4,259 | 4,259 | 4,259 | 4,259 |
| Minority interests | 366 | 349 | 359 | 721 | 825 | 802 | 382 | 421 | 431 | 491 |
| Loans | 8,089 | 7,978 | 7,846 | 7,723 | 8,486 | 12,901 | 16,941 | 26,745 | 27,893 | 28,827 |
| Investment Grants account | 2,601 | 3,496 | 3,042 | 2,452 | 2,915 | 2,925 | 3,108 | 333 | 1,055 | 1,433 |
| Taxation accounts | | | | | | | | 2,401 | 2,731 | 4,860 |
| | 37,547 | 39,147 | 39,270 | 39,357 | 40,922 | 46,482 | 52,107 | 62,058 | 64,422 | 68,604 |
| **Sales (excluding Associated Companies):** | | | | | | | | | | |
| Home | 37,262 | 41,317 | 43,105 | 41,444 | 42,964 | 48,587 | 54,758 | 59,939 | 63,896 | 68,953 |
| Overseas | 3,098 | 3,692 | 4,463 | 5,872 | 6,041 | 7,830 | 13,002 | 13,308 | 14,537 | 17,470 |
| | 40,360 | 45,009 | 47,568 | 47,316 | 49,005 | 56,417 | 67,760 | 73,247 | 78,433 | 86,423 |
| Trading profit | 3,554 | 4,314 | 3,292 | 2,424 | 2,763 | 3,698 | 4,651 | 3,985 | 4,129 | 7,011 |
| RATIO TO SALES | 8·8% | 9·6% | 6·9% | 5·1% | 5·6% | 6·6% | 6·9% | 5·4% | 5·3% | 8·1% |
| Investment income | 519 | 623 | 739 | 703 | 782 | 788 | 770 | 779 | 477 | 504 |
| Profit before taxation and interest charges | 4,073 | 4,937 | 4,031 | 3,127 | 3,545 | 4,486 | 5,421 | 4,764 | 4,606 | 7,515 |
| RATIO TO FUNDS EMPLOYED | 10·8% | 12·6% | 10·3% | 7·9% | 8·7% | 9·7% | 10·4% | 7·7% | 7·1% | 11·0% |
| Taxation on profits for the year | 1,942 | 2,524 | 1,853 | 1,277 | 1,738 | 1,861 | 1,846 | 1,038 | 1,049 | 2,440 |
| Loan interest | 432 | 428 | 425 | 417 | 467 | 538 | 885 | 1,189 | 1,648 | 1,774 |
| Profits of minorities | 4 | 4 | 7 | 81 | 37 | 14 | 70 | 60 | 26 | 44 |
| Profit available for appropriation | 1,695 | 1,981 | 1,746 | 1,352 | 1,303 | 2,073 | 2,620 | 2,477 | 1,883 | 3,257 |
| Cost of dividends—Preference | 112 | 117 | 117 | 117 | 117 | 117 | 116 | 132 | 192 * | 192 * |
|     Ordinary | 854 | 1,043 | 1,043 | 948 | 948 | 1,138 | 1,273 | 1,614 | 2,167 * | 2,167 * |
| Profit retained | 729 | 821 | 586 | 287 | 238 | 818 | 1,231 | 731 | 476 | 898 |
| ORDINARY DIVIDEND EARNINGS TIMES COVERED | 1·9 | 1·8 | 1·6 | 1·3 | 1·2 | 1·7 | 2·0 | 1·5 | 0·8 | 1·4 |

\* Gross.     † After revaluation.

FIG. 66.—Statistical Record for the Years 1959-68 (Fisons Limited)

## The British Oxygen Company Limited and Subsidiary Companies—Comparison of Results 1959–1968

|  | 1959 (£000) | 1960 (£000) | 1961 (£000) | 1962 (£000) | 1963 (£000) | 1964 (£000) | 1965 (£000) | 1966 (Note 1) (£000) | 1967 (£000) | 1968 (£000) |
|---|---|---|---|---|---|---|---|---|---|---|
|  | ← Income tax/Profits tax system applicable → | | | | | ← Corporation tax system applicable → | | | | |
| **Group sales and profits** | | | | | | | | | | |
| Sales | 54,882 | 59,778 | 62,510 | 67,987 | 73,363 | 84,437 | 92,026 | 95,297 | 99,986 | 134,363 |
| Profit before interest and taxation | 9,302 | 10,274 | 9,352 | 9,302 | 10,275 | 12,647 | 13,281 | 12,019 | 13,036 | 17,216 |
| *Less* interest | 715 | 758 | 742 | 840 | 1,158 | 1,197 | 1,406 | 1,969 | 2,876 | 3,944 |
| Profit before taxation | 8,587 | 9,516 | 8,610 | 8,462 | 9,117 | 11,450 | 11,875 | 10,050 | 10,160 | 13,272 |
| Profit after taxation attributable to ordinary shareholders (Investment allowances excluded for 1965 and 1966) | 3,861 | 4,352 | 4,642 | 4,311 | 5,144 | 5,409 | 5,341 | 4,229 | 4,349 | 5,514 |
| Exceptional profits *less* losses | — | | | | | | | | 1,556 | 287 |
| Earnings per ordinary share (Note 2) (excluding exceptional items) | ← Applicable to corporation tax periodically → | | | | | | 7·8d. | 6·2d. | 6·3d. | 7·7d. |
| **Capital employed** | | | | | | | | | | |
| Ordinary shareholders' capital and reserves | 34,630 | 37,317 | 52,216 | 54,902 | 57,887 | 61,082 | 64,920 | 63,227 | 65,797 | 78,113 |
| Deferred taxation | 4,084 | 4,459 | 3,519 | 3,987 | 4,862 | 6,081 | 4,724 | 4,482 | 6,121 | 7,157 |
| Preference stockholders' capital | 2,500 | 2,500 | 2,500 | 2,500 | 2,500 | 2,500 | 2,500 | 2,500 | 2,500 | 2,500 |
| Interests of minority shareholders | 3,774 | 4,168 | 4,867 | 5,252 | 6,028 | 8,458 | 9,969 | 10,239 | 10,819 | 13,580 |
| Loan capital (including bank overdrafts) | 12,813 | 12,817 | 12,763 | 19,814 | 24,121 | 20,624 | 27,122 | 36,133 | 53,365 | 52,749 |
|  | 57,801 | 61,261 | 75,865 | 86,455 | 95,398 | 98,745 | 109,235 | 116,581 | 138,602 | 154,099 |
| Return on average capital employed (Note 3) (Based on trading profit before interest and taxation) | 16·6% | 17·3% | 13·6% | 11·5% | 11·3% | 13·0% | 12·8% | 10·6% | 10·6% | 12·1% |
| Issued ordinary share capital (Note 2) | (£000) 17,047 | (£000) 17,047 | (£000) 30,683 | (£000) 30,683 | (£000) 30,783 | (£000) 41,044 | (£000) 41,044 | (£000) 41,044 | (£000) 41,044 | (£000) 42,771 |
| Ordinary dividend rates (adjusted for scrip and rights issues) | 6·5% | 7·5% | 8% | 8% | 9% | 10% | 11% | 10% | 10% | 10·4% |
| **Number of employees** | | | | | | | | | | |
| United Kingdom | 14,000 | 15,100 | 16,100 | 15,400 | 14,700 | 14,500 | 15,400 | 15,500 | 13,200 * | 16,500 † |
| Overseas | 9,900 | 10,600 | 10,900 | 11,500 | 12,600 | 13,500 | 14,100 | 14,500 | 14,800 | 15,100 |

\* Excludes BOC-Airco Cryogenic Plant Ltd.  † Includes Murex and Edwards High Vacuum.

NOTES

1. In 1966 £2,500,000 was written off small capacity plants against which a similar amount was released from reserves.
2. Excluding initial instalment of rights issue made in 1968.
3. Capital employed adjusted for subsidiary company not consolidated in 1967, £8,127,000.

FIG. 67.—*Comparison of Results for the Years 1959-68*
*(Reproduced by courtesy of The British Oxygen Co., Ltd.)*

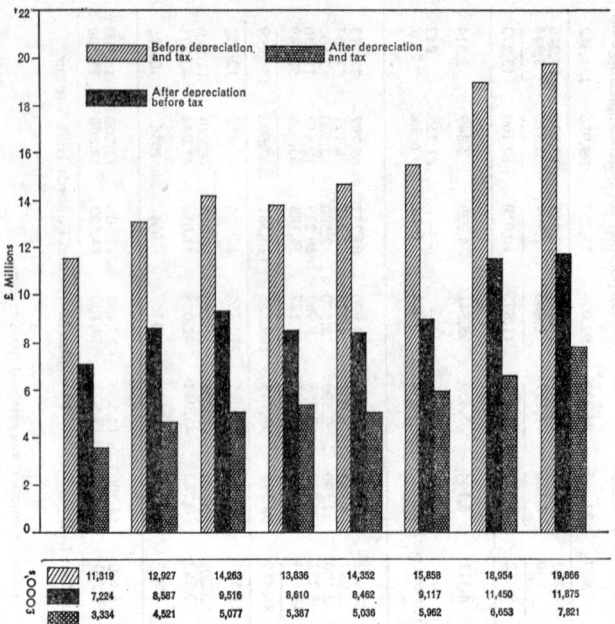

FIG. 68.—*Diagram to show Group profits in successive years*

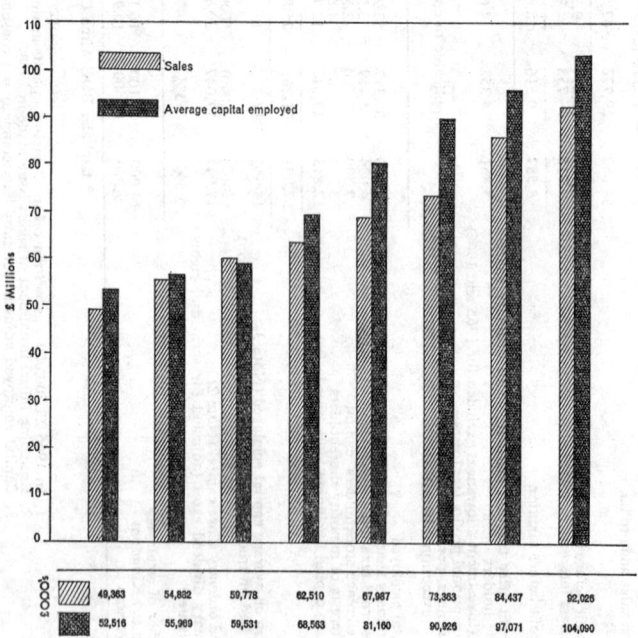

FIG. 69.—*Diagram to show Group sales and capital employed in successive years*

Profit is an indication of how the company's resources are being *managed*. The formula for calculating this ratio is:

$$\frac{\text{Profit}}{\text{Sales}} \times \frac{100}{1}$$

This may be trading profit as in the case of Fisons Limited. Alternatively, the net profit may be taken.

A further example is Sales to Total Assets. This ratio is a guide to the *intensity* with which the total assets are being employed.

## 2. *Assets employed*

The breakdown of assets into various classes over the number of years covered can be seen at a glance. This is the basis of the capital employed figure. Alternatively, the total of share capital, debentures, and reserves may be taken.

## 3. *Utilisation of funds*

How the funds have been employed can be seen and the likely growth prospects will be indicated.

## 4. *Appropriation of profit*

The division of the return among shareholders is detailed. Dividends paid, profits retained, and the dividend cover are all shown.

### REVALUATION IN PRACTICE

Reference to revaluation of fixed assets is made earlier in this chapter. How far is this notion being carried out by leading companies?

Unfortunately, it cannot be said to be the general practice of companies to revalue fixed assets by appraisal, index numbers, or other method. There are difficulties associated with this process, but the likely benefits are immense (*see* Chapter 27).

Examples of companies which have revalued are: Fisons Limited; Tube Investments Limited; Philips Electrical Limited; Imperial Chemical Industries Limited; Laporte Industries Limited; Marks and Spencer Limited.

This list does *not* cover all companies; its purpose is to show that many leading companies are now recognising that revaluation is necessary to allow for the tendency for costs to increase.

### DIVISIONAL BREAKDOWN

Capital employed, and the return therefrom, are the main indicators of managerial efficiency. How far the analysis should be taken depends upon the circumstances. A number of simple rules have been formulated:

1. Both capital employed and return must be capable of calculation for each division.

2. Each manager should understand the size of the investment under his control.

3. Dividing a business into very small units may not serve any useful purpose.

4. Capital employed may be calculated on:

(a) assets basis; or

(b) share capital basis.

However, when considering divisions it is likely that the assets basis is more acceptable. Allocation of responsibility according to assets employed is much more realistic than attempting to apportion share capital.

5. Capital employed figures should represent, as far as possible, the economic and technical value of the assets being used.

Strictly speaking, the economic and technical value of an asset is the price it would fetch while being used within a business for the purpose of earning profit. There can be no question of a piece-meal sale; rather it is the value of the asset *within* the business which is operating as a going concern. There is no way of assessing this value unless the business is sold and, therefore, a compromise is necessary. As stated earlier, replacement costs are likely to be the best solution in obtaining a realistic value for capital employed.

6. Whenever possible allocate the assets to the divisions in which they are actually being employed.

This is generally possible when divisions are self-contained, but when a further breakdown is necessary some kind of apportionment will be necessary for some of the costs. Reference to Chapter 2 on how overhead costs are apportioned will show how the problem may be tackled.

## PRACTICAL ILLUSTRATION

An example of how sales, capital employed and profit are analysed is reproduced below:

| £ millions | Sales | | Capital Employed* | | Trading Profit | |
|---|---|---|---|---|---|---|
| | 1968 | 1967 | 1968 | 1967 | 1968 | 1967 |
| Tobacco | 928·3 | 887·0 | 227·8 | 216·6 | 41·0 | 37·4 |
| Paper and board | 18·9 | 17·0 | 15·9 | 15·4 | 1·5 | 1·3 |
| Distributive trade | 74·3 | 61·6 | 7·0 | 5·4 | 1·4 | 0·9 |
| Food | 35·2 | 15·3 | 22·8 | 16·5 | 3·2 | 0·8 |
| General trade | 4·3 | 4·3 | 4·4 | 4·8 | 0·4 | (0·3) |
| Totals | 1,061·0 | 985·2 | 277·9 | 258·7 | 47·5 | 40·1 |
| Less inter-company sales | 48.2 | 40·0 | | | | |
| Total external sales | 1,012·8 | 945·2 | | | | |

* Operating capital at book value, at 31st October in each year.

This diagram is taken from the Report and Accounts of the Imperial Tobacco Company Limited for 1968 (reproduced by kind permission). The comparative figures for 1967 are also given.

## INTER-COMPANY PRICING

A policy decision which should be made in connection with the measurement of management efficiency is the selection of a method of pricing between divisions. Any price selected should be fair and equitable to the division supplying, and the division receiving, the products.

What should be remembered is that managers have to make decisions. If prices charged are too high, then the receiving division may think that it would be better off purchasing from external sources. There would be little justification for charging another division a price which is above the market price. On the other hand, from the point of view of evaluating the performance of managers, market prices are likely to be the most realistic. The chief difficulty is that many products are really special "raw materials," so that no market prices are known.

The other methods of pricing are based on costs. Examples are:

1. Prime cost.
2. Total factory cost.
3. Total factory cost *plus* a percentage for profit.
4. Variable costs only.
5. Variable costs *plus* a percentage for profit.

There are many other variations which may also be employed. If marginal costing is employed, then variable costs are likely to be the most acceptable. However, like all other prices which are based purely on costs without additions, the effect is to penalise the division making the products for transfer. Moreover, with marginal costing there is the question of non-recovery of fixed costs.

There is little doubt that some addition of profit is very desirable. This provides an incentive for the divisional managers. However, there are two main problems.

1. How is the profit to be assessed?

A standard percentage may be added to costs, but if this is the case there should be a clear definition of how the costs are to be calculated. Alternatively, divisional managers may be encouraged to compete with each other to the extent of fixing their own prices.

2. Inter-company profits have to be eliminated when calculating the profit for the Group as a whole.

This problem is not insurmountable. If measurement of management efficiency is the aim, then it seems inevitable that it will have to be faced. The profit motive is the driving force which is understood by all types of managers and, therefore, it is very logical for prices to include some margin of profit.

There is no doubt that a keen watchfulness, to ensure that all divisions of a business earn an adequate return, is likely to be of great value to any business. Efficiency will also be watched; every function which affects profit-earning will be under constant scrutiny. Accordingly, assets are used in the most effective way possible. Management thereby serves the community and the shareholders in the best possible manner and fulfils what are now regarded as essential social functions. (There are three major social groups (i) the community, (ii) shareholders, (iii) employees. Management has a social obligation to each. For (i) supply of the best goods and services at reasonable prices and the most effective use of assets; for (ii) adequate dividends and for (iii) good conditions of employment, rates of pay, and promotion prospects.)

### EXAMINATION QUESTIONS

1. Explain what is meant by "capital employed."
2. What is the most significant measure for indicating efficiency?
3. What are the two basic causes of under-absorption of works overhead? Mention two examples, which may be met in practice, of each cause.

Where such under-absorption at the end of a particular month applies to production delivered, work-in-progress, and finished products awaiting despatch, show a composite journal entry indicating the general ledger accounts affected. (*I.C.W.A.*)

4. (*a*) In many manufacturing processes waste products and by-products are produced. What problems do these present in costing the main product and how are they overcome?

(*b*) The XY Chemical Company manufactures one basic product which passes through several processes during manufacture. You are given the following information which relates to Process No. 2 for the month of May, 1961, and you are required to prepare the process account for the period and to write a brief report on the variances disclosed and their meaning.

The company uses the direct cost method, *i.e.* overheads are not allocated to processes. Output is transferred to the next process and finished stock is valued at direct standard cost.

The standard cost sheet for Process 2 is as follows:

| | | | £ |
|---|---|---|---|
| *Direct Standard Cost per gallon* | | | |
| *Material:* 1 gallon of A from Process 1 | | | 2·38 |
| *Labour:* Grade I, 2 hours × £0·45 hour | £0·90 | | |
| Grade II, 1 hour × £0·40 hour | £0·40 | | |
| | | | 1·30 |
| | | | £3·68 |
| Normal loss during process no scrap value: | | | |
| 2 gallons per 100 = 2% | | | 0·07 |
| ∴ Direct Standard Cost per gallon = | | | £3·61 |

During the period 500 gallons were received from Process 1; 90 gallons completely processed were in stock at the beginning of the period and 80 gallons at the end; 470 gallons were transferred to Process 3 and there was no work in progress at the beginning or end of the period. Actual labour charges were: Grade I, 1100 hours at a total cost of £495; and Grade II, 550 hours at a total cost of £233·75. (*A.C.C.A.*)

5. The AB Company Ltd. budget to sell in the month of January 2500 lbs. of product A at £3 per lb., 1200 lbs. of product B at £2 per lb. and 2000 lbs. of product C at £2·50 per lb. During the month, actual sales were 2000 lbs. of product A for £5500, 1800 lbs. of product B for £4050, and 2200 lbs. of product C for £4950. Budgeted costs of A—£2 per unit, B—£1·50 per unit, and C—£2 per unit were in line with actual. You are required to calculate the effect of sales variances (price, quantity, and mix) on budgeted profit and to prepare a statement showing how each product has contributed to the increase or decrease in budgeted profit. (*A.C.C.A.*)

6. The Beta Company Limited has established a monthly profit target of £15,825. In the month of October this was to be achieved by selling 20,000 of product A, 25,000 of product B, and 22,000 of product C. The standards for these products can be got from the standard cost and price lists which are reproduced below. During October, the actual profit achieved was £12,215. From the following information you are required to prepare a statement analysing this difference between target and actual profit. The statement should be such that the portion of the difference which is the responsibility of the sales departments and the portion which is the responsibility of the factory departments should be clearly distinguished. This statement should be accompanied by a report explaining, in non-accounting language, the significance of the profit differences.

|  | Standard Cost per Unit | Standard Selling Price per Unit |
|---|---|---|
|  | £ | £ |
| Product A | 1·25 | 1·50 |
| B | 0·90 | 1·02 |
| C | 1·90 | 2·25 |
| D | 1·38 | 1·50 |
| E | 2·50 | 22·50 |

*October—Actual Results*

|  |  | £ |
|---|---|---|
| Sales Turnover | A | 29,000 |
|  | B | 24,150 |
|  | C | 4,500 |
|  | E | 49,500 |
| Sales Quantities | A | 20,000 units |
|  | B | 23,000 units |
|  | C | 2,000 units |
|  | E | 22,000 units |

|  | £ |
|---|---|
| Material Price Variance | 550 debit |
| Material Usage Variance | 375 credit |
| Labour Idle Time Variance | 125 debit |
| Labour Mix Variance | 150 credit |
| Labour Efficiency Variance | 130 debit |
| Factory Overheads Capacity Variance | 210 debit |
| Factory Overheads Expenditure Variance | 450 credit |
| Sales Overheads Expenditure Variance | 550 credit |
| Advertising Expenditure Variance | 845 debit |

(*A.C.C.A.*)

7. There are many large groups of companies where the top management is anxious to:

(i) maintain reasonable autonomy for individual companies within the group;
 (ii) preserve the idea of profit centres; and
(iii) retain internal profit measurement.

This is often made difficult by the fact that goods and services are transferred from one company to another within the group, and it is difficult to devise a sound scheme for pricing the intra-group transactions.

(a) What are the objectives which must be kept in mind when deciding upon pricing methods?
(b) How do the ideas of:

(i) marginal costing as opposed to absorption costing; and
(ii) standard costing as opposed to actual costing

apply to this problem? (I.C.W.A.)

# CHAPTER 16

## ACCOUNTING RATIOS

THE term "accounting ratios" is used to describe significant relationships which exist between figures shown on a Balance Sheet, in a Profit and Loss Account, in a Budgetary Control system or in any other part of the accounting organisation.

These ratios may serve many purposes; they can assist management in its basic functions—forecasting, planning, co-ordination, control, and communication. Properly used they can improve efficiency and, therefore, profits. In the wrong hands they may mislead and result in the wrong conclusions being reached. Generally single ratios are of limited value; this is so because *trends* are of great importance. In addition, a change in one ratio may be of significance only when viewed in relation to other ratios. Some of the possible uses of accounting ratios are summarised below:

1. Past ratios indicate trends in costs, sales, profit, and other relevant facts. Accordingly, they may be very useful for forecasting likely events in the future.

2. The plans made can be "signposted" by accounting ratios. These ratios thereby become an integral part of the accounting or Budgetary Control system.

This matter is dealt with more fully in Chapter 3, dealing with the master budget.

3. Ideal ratios can be established and the relationships between primary ratios may be used to establish the desirable co-ordination or balance. Again, this is normally linked with Budgetary Control.

4. Control may be materially assisted by the use of ratios. This includes control of performances (*e.g.* sales quotas) as well as control of costs.

5. "Communication" is the term used to describe the processes used to impart knowledge within the business or to outside shareholders or other interested parties. Ratios can play a vital role in informing what has happened from one period to another.

6. Ratios may be used as measures of efficiency. This may be so for a single company when comparing changes through time *or* for a number of businesses whether related or not (inter-firm comparisons). There is no doubt that accounting ratios aid uniformity and, therefore, can make comparisons much more valid. This is a question which is discussed later, in the chapter which deals with inter-firm comparisons.

This is a very brief outline of possible uses of accounting ratios. Additional purposes will become apparent from the descriptions of the ratios given later.

## VALUE OF RATIOS

There is no doubt that ratios can be an invaluable aid to management and others who are interested in analysing the operations and the state of affairs of a business. Absolute figures may be misleading unless compared one with another: ratios provide the means of showing the inter-relationships which exist. In addition, ratios enable masses of data to be summarised and simplified. Perhaps one of the most important by-products is the systematic analysis which comes through developing a system of ratios.

## COMPILING AND USING RATIOS

Ratio analysis used properly can be a great boon to assessing important characteristics such as solvency, overtrading, and profitability. However, great care has to be taken to ensure that the person using the ratios understands the figures which were employed for compiling them. This is particularly important when attempting to compare the efficiency of one business with that of another. Even within the same organisation any lack of consistency in method or definition can invalidate any comparisons being made from one period to another. In other words the ratios to be compared should be *capable* of being validly compared.

Speedy compiling of ratios is generally essential. They should be determined and submitted to interested parties in time for constructive action to be taken. This does not necessarily mean *immediately* after the event; much depends upon the nature of the ratio and the purpose for which it is intended. Immediate preparation may be too costly to achieve: *cost* and *benefits* to be obtained from the ratios should be compared and the former should be kept within reasonable dimensions. This applies to the preparation of all accounting information including reports and statements.

Presentation of ratios in the appropriate manner is essential. The problem being considered and the responsibilities of the recipients must obviously affect the form of presentation. A sales manager will normally be interested in ratios on sales, selling costs and related aspects. On the other hand, the production manager will be interested primarily in the operating ratios relating to the production function. When setting out the ratios a plan usually followed is to show the major ratios first and then finish up with the less important ones.

A question which is bound to arise is whether or not the framework of ratios developed for the particular business can be used permanently without alteration. Obviously much depends upon the types and number of ratios developed in the first place. A business generally starts with using a few ratios and then builds up a complete framework after the management have been "educated" as to their use.

A complete record of the ratios employed is advisable; an explanation of each, and actual ratios year by year, should be included. This record may be part of the Accounts Manual or alternatively a special Ratio Register may be maintained.

## CLASSIFICATION OF RATIOS

Ratios may be classified in a variety of ways. Some of the possible methods are shown below.

### STATEMENT CLASSIFICATION

This classification is based on the nature of the accounting statement on which the ratios appear, viz.:

    (a) Balance Sheet Ratios. (Also known as *Financial Ratios*.)
      (i) Quick or Liquid Ratio.
      (ii) Current or 2 to 1 Ratio.
      (iii) Stock Ratios.
      (iv) Capital or Earnings Ratios.

    (b) Profit and Loss Ratios. (Also known as *Operating Ratios*.)
      (i) Turnover or Sales Ratios.
      (ii) Capital or Earnings Ratios.
      (iii) Cost or Expense Ratios.

Some ratios may draw information from *both* the balance sheet and the profit and loss account. Thus, for example, capital ratios are shown for both (a) and (b) above.

### NATURE OF RATIO CLASSIFICATION

Here the concern is with classifying according to the nature of the ratios. One possibility is as follows:

    (a) Liquidity, Solvency or Working Capital Ratios.
    (b) Stock or Inventory Ratios.
    (c) Debtors and Creditors Ratios.
    (d) Sales Ratios.
    (e) Earning and Dividend Ratios.
    (f) Cost Ratios.

An alternative method, coming under this heading, is the one used by the British Institute of Management for inter-firm comparisons. This is as follows:

    (a) Primary Ratio (operating profit to capital employed).
    (b) Secondary Ratios.

The secondary ratios are further subdivided to meet the needs of the particular business. (*See* Chapter 17.)

Generally this classification is linked with that given above—financial ratios and operating ratios.

## DESCRIPTION OF PRINCIPAL RATIOS

A full description of *all* possible ratios is outside the scope of a book of this nature which covers a very wide range of related topics. Nevertheless, most of the important ratios are explained. It is essential to remember that a *single* ratio may tend to mislead. Another possible weakness is the danger of the uninitiated assuming that standard ratios can be established (*e.g.* 2 to 1 ratio) for all types of business.

### RETURN ON CAPITAL EMPLOYED (PRIMARY RATIO)

This ratio compares the earnings with assets employed. It is a reflection of the overall efficiency of the business. This is considered more fully below. Chapter 15 deals with this subject in detail.

### QUICK OR LIQUID RATIO

The quick or liquid ratio shows the ability of a business to meet its immediate commitments. This ratio is also known as the "acid-test ratio."

With this ratio the concern is with liquid assets and liquid liabilities. The former are also referred to as "quick assets" or "near money."

The formula for calculating this ratio is as follows:

$$\text{Quick or Liquid Ratio} = \frac{\text{Liquid Assets}}{\text{Current Liabilities}}$$

The liquid assets would include cash, debtors (excluding bad debts), and securities which can be realised without difficulty. Current liabilities would include creditors and any amounts due but unpaid. Generally the ratio should be at least 1 to 1. If not, and liquid assets do not cover current liabilities, then steps should be taken to obtain additional cash.

If the quick ratio is to be of some value then the nature of the assets and liabilities included should be appreciated. Thus, for example, if some of the debtors are slow payers this fact should be allowed for in the calculation of the ratio. In addition, when there is the *possibility* of bad debts, a provision should be created, the debtors being reduced by the amount involved.

There is no doubt that this ratio can be a very realistic guide to solvency. However, any ratio (other than a planning ratio) is based on figures available after the events they portray. For this reason they may be out-of-date at the time the ratios are first computed. A sudden increase in credit purchases due to overtrading would not be apparent from the historical ratios.

The standard ratio of 1 to 1 should not be regarded as showing precisely the same state of solvency. One business will not have the same problems as another. This was noticed earlier in connection with debtors. A similar remark may apply to creditors; some suppliers insist on payment within a fairly short period whereas others are quite happy to wait for 4 weeks, 6 weeks, or even longer. A 1 to 1 ratio may be perfectly all right for one business, but a 2 to 1 ratio (liquid assets *twice* current liabilities) may be essential for another.

This ratio is linked with the current ratio discussed in the next section.

## CURRENT OR 2 TO 1 RATIO

The current or 2 to 1 ratio shows the relationship between total current assets and total current liabilities; *i.e.*, cash, or those expected to be converted into cash within a year (current assets) and those to be paid off within the same period (current liabilities). The "year" in each case is naturally the maximum period; many of the current assets and liabilities being considered at any one time may change their form over and over again during the course of a single period.

Expressed as a formula the current ratio is as follows:

$$\text{Current Ratio} = \frac{\text{Current Assets}}{\text{Current Liabilities}}$$

Because of its link with working capital the current ratio is not unnaturally sometimes referred to as the "working capital ratio." Indeed the ratio is a vital measure of working capital available at a particular time. (Calculation of working capital needs is covered on pages 126 and 140.) This assumes that working capital is defined as the excess of current assets *over* current liabilities. However, not all users of the term "working capital" have this definition in mind. Sometimes, the *total* money invested in current assets is regarded as working capital.

The rule of thumb implied by the term "2 to 1 ratio" can be very misleading because conditions vary so much from one business to another. At times a much higher ratio than 2 to 1 may be very desirable whereas at other times a ratio of less than 2 to 1 may be regarded as quite satisfactory. The major questions to ask, in addition to the size of the ratio, depend upon the type of business and the circumstances existing at the time. However some idea of the pattern these may follow may be gleaned from the questions given below:

1. What type of business is involved and, in particular, whether of a speculative nature?
2. Is the trade seasonal? If so what period is being considered—the peak *or* low-sales period?

In a peak period when sales are at a high figure there should be a tendency for the ratio to be quite high; *i.e.* current assets greatly in excess of current liabilities.

3. Does the ratio represent the true position and take into consideration major plans to be carried out within the immediate future?

Information on major contracts or purchase of fixed assets may be vital in showing the true current ratio. The existence of overtrading will also be of great significance.

4. What are the facts regarding the constituent items forming the background to the ratio? Thus, for example, subsidiary questions which may arise are:

(a) What is the period of credit allowed by creditors and permitted to debtors?

(b) What does the figure of stock represent?

If there is a large proportion of raw materials not yet converted then clearly these cannot become cash until they have been worked on. The length of the production cycle, the state of the production programme and the extent of the orders on hand, may all be very pertinent to this problem of deciding how quickly will funds be made available from the stocks.

When there is a considerable sum invested in work-in-progress this *may* be a sign that production planning is inefficient. On the other hand, an excessive stock of finished goods may indicate that the sales division is not obtaining adequate orders. These, and similar questions, are vital in determining the worth of the current ratio as a measure of solvency.

5. Are there any long-term liabilities? If in one business there is a loan covered by mortgage or other security a higher ratio is generally desirable than in a similar business where there is no long-term borrowing.

This question also affects the ability of a business to meet its commitments in adverse conditions. If a company has a large amount of fixed charges to meet each year then the outlook for the shareholder as regards dividends may be quite dismal when there is a trade recession.

6. Is there evidence of overtrading or undertrading?

When working capital fails to grow in relation to the volume of production and/or sales a business is said to be "overtrading." Put another way, overtrading involves rapid expansion of business without sufficient working capital. This important topic is discussed later in this section.

Undertrading generally means that there is an inadequate volume of business. Trade falls off and activity is reduced to the extent that assets are not being fully employed. If this state of affairs continues a business will have to cover its fixed overhead costs and its reduced variable costs from internal resources (current assets). Finally, when sales fall to a very low level a company unable to meet its commitments may be forced into liquidation. Undertrading is, therefore, the opposite situation from that experienced with overtrading. There is, however, a grave factor common to both—the danger that financial distress may bring about serious consequences and possibly the end of the business concerned.

From the observations made earlier the reader will appreciate that it is not the ratio itself, but rather the *content* of the totals of the current assets and current liabilities which is the more important.

The idea of having current assets twice that of current liabilities (the 2 to 1 ratio) is to allow for any possible loss which may be incurred in the realisation of the assets. In addition, the excess can cover any contingency which may arise and a certain amount of expansion. That a ratio of larger or smaller dimensions than 2 to 1 may be reasonable was noted earlier. In connection with a larger ratio it is important to observe that an *excessive* ratio is a sign of inefficiency. Whether a ratio is excessive should be determined by the circumstances prevailing and care must be taken to distinguish between a temporary or short-term surplus and a permanent surplus of working capital. If a temporary increase in stocks is due to *normal* circumstances such as seasonal sales then there may be no need to regard the change with disfavour. On the other hand, a permanent increase in stocks may be the first signs of undertrading. When there is an unduly large figure of cash the possibility of investment should be considered (*see* page 132).

The assets and liabilities to be included in the calculation of the current ratio are stated at the beginning of this section. Items which are usually included in current assets* are:

> stock-in-trade
> work-in-progress
> debtors
> readily realisable investments
> tax reserve certificates
> bills receivable
> prepayments
> cash at bank and in hand.

Current liabilities generally include creditors, bills payable and any other short-term debts. Whether a bank overdraft should be regarded as a current liability is a question which must be settled. Often an arrangement with a bank may be regarded as "permanent" and, therefore, an argument may be advanced for regarding the overdraft as a long-term liability. However, although this form of argument may have a substantial amount of truth in it, the fact remains that a bank overdraft facility may be cancelled. Accordingly, because of this reason, and the need for conservatism in interpreting a situation, the inclusion of the bank overdraft in current liabilities seems advisable.

In the interest of clarity a decision must be reached on the matter

* As recommended by the Institute of Chartered Accountants in England and Wales.

of which current assets are liquid and which are not. A suggested division is given in the section on the quick or liquid ratio. An extension of this principle is to divide current assets and current liabilities as follows:*

    1. Current Assets divided into:

        (a) Liquid Assets.

        (b) Deferred Assets.

    2. Current Liabilities divided into:

        (a) Liquid Liabilities.

        (b) Deferred Liabilities.

All current assets are classified into 1 (a) or 1 (b) according to a simple rule. This rule is that all current assets expected to be paid within a month are grouped under (a) whereas those of a longer duration would be included under (b). A similar principle is applied to group the current liabilities under 2 (a) or 2 (b).

Clearly the criterion on how the assets or liabilities should be classified depends upon the purpose for which the current ratio is to be used. If the power of a business to pay off its immediate debts is in question, then a division of assets and liabilities into the categories given will be advantageous.

When considering the current ratio a *change* from previous periods may be more important than the ratio itself. In other words, the trend in the size of the ratio is of vital consequence.

An example of how the current ratio is calculated can be seen from analysis given on pages 437 and 438.

## MINIMUM AND MAXIMUM CASH

The ratios described earlier in this section deal with the question of an adequate holding of cash. They are guide-posts to the cash which should be kept by a business.

When considering the cash position it is clearly very important to establish an optimum level: this may be regarded as the "financial capacity." Its size is determined by two main factors:

    (1) Working capital required; and

    (2) Cash being received from sales.

The *financial capacity* should be set between the *minimum* amount dictated by working capital requirements and the *maximum* amount as indicated by the volume of sales. There should be a buffer stock of cash to meet any contingencies which may arise; at the same time there should be a limit set beyond which the amount of cash should not be

---

\* A. H. TAYLOR, A.A.C.C.A., in an article entitled "Liquidity and The Balance Sheet" in *The Accountant* dated 31st January, 1959, suggests a division into Deferred Variable Assets (or liabilities) and liquid assets (or liabilities).

permitted to go. The simple diagram given in Fig. 70 illustrates the concept of the financial capacity.

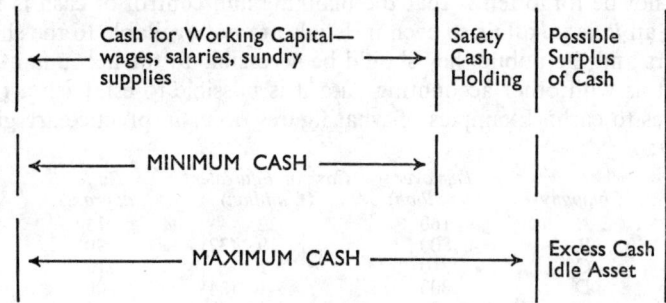

FIG. 70.—*Financial capacity for cash*

## MINIMUM CASH

The absolute minimum of cash will tend to be that which will just permit a company to meet its current obligations such as wages. Any debts payable within seven days should be available in the minimum cash balance.

From past experience it should be possible to determine whether an allowance should be made to cover contingencies. An appropriate percentage can be added.

If the total payments expected to be made in cash is obtained and is divided by 52, this will give the basis for the minimum cash holding at any time. An example should suffice to explain the principles:

| | |
|---|---|
| Wages for Year | £20,000 |
| Sundry Supplies | 4,500 |
| Miscellaneous | 1,500 |
| | £26,000 |

From this it may be assumed that the basic minimum is £500. Adding, say, 10% to this figure for contingencies will give a minimum of £550.

## MAXIMUM CASH

The revenue being received from sales has a considerable influence on the amount of cash available at any time. It follows, therefore, that there should be a definite relationship between the cash held and the sales being achieved.

In Great Britain there has been a tendency for some companies to avoid revealing the total sales for the year, and, for this reason, the fullest possible information has not been made available. Furthermore, the *annual* published accounts have their limitations in that they deal with cash only as at a particular point, at the end of a financial year.

The number of companies now revealing turnover is undoubtedly increasing and the publication of information more regularly in the form of interim accounts is a very encouraging sign. Moreover, what must not be forgotten is that the planning and control of cash is very much an *internal* affair so even if details are not available to the shareholders and the public they should be accessible to the accountants.

Just as with other accounting data it is possible to establish a ratio of sales to cash. Examples of what figures occur in practice are given below:

| Company | Turnover (£ million) | Cash or Equivalent (£ million) | | Ratio (approx.) |
|---|---|---|---|---|
| A | 160 | 12 | | 13 |
| B | 800 | 9 | (32) | 90 |
| C | 210 | 1 | | 210 |
| D | 800 | 1 | (34) | 800 |
| E | 80 | 1 | (2) | 80 |

In theory, the ideal ratio is around 20 to 1. From the figures shown above, taken at random for five large companies, it will be seen that the ideal is not achieved. Indeed, since the figures in brackets represent overdrafts or other short-term borrowing, there are indications that overtrading is taking place. The figures have been rounded off for ease of reference.

What should be appreciated is that, although a company can earn substantial profits, and at the same time have an overdraft, this is not the ideal state. Many thousands of pounds will have to be paid in interest when a very large overdraft is carried. Accordingly, if this can be eliminated, profits should increase by at least the same amount. Indeed, if adequate cash is available, full advantage can be taken of any new opportunities which arise. This could lead to larger profits still. All this is sound common sense—*it is better to use your own money rather than borrow*. Unfortunately, this important principle is often ignored which is all right provided profits are earned; once losses are incurred then the borrowing strength will be greatly reduced.

The 20 to 1 ratio is only a guide and not a rigid standard. Management should fix a maximum level which is around this figure, but a higher or lower ratio may be acceptable in appropriate circumstances. If the cash balance is too large, steps should be taken to invest the proceeds as described on pages 132 to 137. Students should realise that a very high ratio (*e.g.* 200 to 1) represents a relatively small balance of cash whereas a small ratio (*e.g.* 5 to 1) can be an extremely large figure.

## OVERTRADING

Overtrading is a malady brought about by extending turnover at a too rapid rate. The ultimate result is a serious shortage of cash when wages, trade creditors and tax due to the Commissioners of Inland Revenue cannot be met.

A typical pattern of events may commence by taking on additional orders; this would then be followed by engaging additional workers or working overtime. At the same time, extra materials would be purchased on credit. If the production cycle is fairly long this means that, although extra cash has to be paid out more or less immediately, additional revenue may not materialise for a considerable period. This assumes that the additional production will be sold without delay; in some circumstances the process may take the form of a build-up of stock. If this is the case then the shortage of cash may necessitate an emergency sale at greatly reduced prices—an action which is unlikely to improve the profit situation.

When analysing the situation shown on a balance sheet it is very important to look for signs of overtrading. Some of the most important of those signs which show the financial position are summarised below:

1. A business is taking a much longer time to pay off its creditors. This fact may not always be easy to determine. An increase in the *total* creditors or an increase of creditors in relation to debtors may be an indication. Comparing the period of credit being taken with what is normal for the particular trade may also be a useful guide to solvency.

2. Stocks increase and yet there is no increase in turnover. A more positive sign is an increase in stock and a *reduction* in turnover.

3. There is a growth in the rate of borrowing so that the proportion of borrowing in relation to the assets owned by shareholders is quite excessive.

4. Total profit—gross and/or net—begins to diminish.

5. Any sudden upward or downward swing in any figures or the appearance of new items such as bills payable should be investigated.

Some of the other indications of possible financial instability or weakness may be revealed by the other ratios covered below. At this stage, the fact that a single ratio is of limited value should be remembered. If at all possible three or more successive years should be compared for only then will a *trend* be discernible.

## STOCK RATIOS

Ratios relating to different types of stocks may be an important indication of efficiency in the control of stocks of raw materials, work-in-progress and finished goods. Carrying excessive stocks has to be avoided for these involve unnecessary storage, insurance, and related costs.

Problems relating to stocks vary from one business to another. When production is carried out in accordance with customers' specifications (job production) there should be no stocks of finished goods. However, there will be a problem in controlling work-in-progress and raw material stocks.

When products are produced for stock there may be little or no work-in-progress. Controlling stocks of raw materials and finished goods so that they are kept to a minimum may be far from easy.

Bearing these differences in mind an attempt has to be made to determine what is a *reasonable* level for each main type of stock.

The effect of stock levels on the current ratio is covered earlier in this chapter. If very large stocks are carried the current assets are swollen, but this fact may not be an advantage when liquidity is being considered.

There is no *easy method* of controlling stocks. Ratios may serve as a guide, but they are a poor substitute for efficient storekeeping, stores records, perpetual inventory system, continuous stock-taking and related techniques.

Many ratios exist which include stock; these may be summarised as follows:

1. *Raw material stock to total turnover* (total turnover in this sense means total sales).
2. *Work-in-progress stock to total turnover.*
3. *Raw material stock to purchases.*

These ratios may reflect efficiency in production. The first shows stock-holding in relation to the total amount produced and sold. When sales vary from one period to another the production figure may be better than sales. Many companies have a policy of keeping a definite number of months' stock on hand; the ratio shows whether this objective is being realised.

What should be appreciated is that conditions and circumstances change and, therefore, any upward or downward swing in the ratio may not be a sign of a deviation in efficiency, but rather a countermeasure *necessary* to the problems being encountered. This reasoning naturally applies to other ratios. However, in some companies there is often a marked vulnerability brought about by the possibility of price fluctuations in raw materials. Wide variations in prices have been experienced in recent times in wool, various types of metals, and in many other materials and commodities. If a business is carrying large stocks of these materials and there is a price fall, serious consequences may result.

The third ratio shows the average stock turnover for the year. The average stock figure for the month, divided into total purchases for the year shows how many times the stocks are turned over each year.

4. *Finished stock to total turnover.*

The finished stock ratio is an important indication of how long goods are kept before being sold. Clearly, the quicker stock can be sold the better—profit is then likely to be maximised.

Different interpretations exist on the way this ratio should be calculated; viz.:

(a) $$\frac{\text{Turnover at selling prices}}{\text{Stock at cost}}$$

(b) $$\frac{\text{Turnover at cost}}{\text{Stock at cost}}$$

(c) $$\frac{\text{Turnover at selling prices}}{\text{Stock at selling prices}}$$

Quite often objections are raised against (a) because the stock at *cost* is being divided into turnover at selling prices. A more realistic turnover is given when the denominator and numerator are *both* at cost (or selling prices). Quite often (a) is used because inadequate information is available for converting the turnover to cost *or* the stock to sales values.

When calculating the ratio it is usual to take the *annual* turnover and divide by the *monthly* stock calculated as an average on the stock figures at the end of each month and not simply the opening and closing stocks for the year. The latter action takes into account any seasonal changes in stock holdings.

Irrespective of the calculation used the more rapid the turnover, the more efficient the business. This remark applies to a specific business. Obviously different ratios will apply from one company to another, so a company with a higher ratio than a different company may not necessarily be more efficient.

Any reduction in the ratio indicating that the stock turnover is slower may call for action to increase sales. Alternatively, if there is over-production there may have to be curtailment of output—in short, sales and production will have to be co-ordinated. If turnover of stock increases too much there may be a danger that customers' needs cannot be met promptly—this fact may prevent maximum profit being earned.

### SALES OR TURNOVER RATIOS

Many ratios exist which include sales as a major element. This is not surprising; in many companies a large volume of sales is essential to earn a reasonable profit. When computing the ratios it is usual to take *net* sales. Some of the principal turnover ratios are as follows:

1. *Sales to Stock.*

This is covered in the previous section—finished stock to turnover.

2. *Sales to Debtors.*

A formula for calculating this ratio is as follows:

$$\frac{\text{Sales}}{\text{Debtors}}$$

This ratio shows the rate at which money is being received from credit sales. There should be a definite relationship between the terms of credit and the ratio. If terms of payment are thirty days, then the normal ratio is 12 to 1 (365 divided by 30). Accordingly, if annual turnover is £12,000 the debtors figure should be in the region of £1000. There may be variations from month to month to allow for seasonal sales.

If money is not being collected fast enough steps may have to be taken to remedy this fact. This is discussed in detail in Chapter 24 which deals with credit control.

### 3. *Sales to Fixed Assets.**

This ratio shows the efficiency achieved in the use of the fixed assets. The sales per £1 of investment are calculated. Generally speaking, the higher the sales per £1 of fixed assets the greater tends to be the efficiency.

If the fixed assets do not earn sufficient this may be a sign that they are not being employed *fully* (excess capacity) or that they are not being used in the best possible manner.

The sales to fixed assets ratio may indicate an important relationship for a business which supplies services. This is especially so when there is a large investment in fixed assets.

### 4. *Sales to Share Capital or total Net Worth.*

Often the share capital considered is the equity capital; *i.e.* the ordinary share capital. Strictly, the reserves attaching to the equity share capital should also be included and this accounts for the use of the term "net worth."

If preference share capital is in existence then some accountants would advocate its inclusion in the capital so that *total* capital and not simply equity capital is compared with sales.

This ratio shows the "rate of turnover" of the capital employed in the business. The more times capital is covered the better tends to be the profit. However, this generalisation has to be used with caution. If sales are too large in relation to capital then the business is said to be overtrading, a condition described earlier in this chapter.

On the other hand, if the sales volume is relatively small undertrading is present, indicating that management is not obtaining an adequate volume of production and sales from the facilities employed.

When considering this ratio the observation made earlier—that a ratio should not be dealt with in isolation—is very appropriate. Other facts such as stocks, debtors, creditors and long-term liabilities should also be studied before reaching any decision.

### 5. *Sales to Working Capital.*

A *normal* ratio between sales and working capital should be established which is neither too high nor too low. Sales should not increase to too high a figure, otherwise there may be a deterioration in the current ratio (*see* description of overtrading on page 422).

---

* Method of valuing Fixed Assets affects this ratio. *See* Chapter 27 on Revaluation.

The ratio shows the efficiency with which the working capital is being employed. At the same time, care has to be taken to ensure that over-trading does not occur.

## CAPITAL AND RELATED RATIOS

Many different capital ratios may be computed, each one serving a particular purpose. Some of the most usual of these are given below:

1. *Net Worth* (*i.e.* Capital Employed)* *to Total Indebtedness.*

The net worth is total share capital (proprietors' capital) and reserves of all types which may be said to belong to the shareholders.

A view generally expressed is that indebtedness should not exceed the total investment of the shareholders in the business. Accordingly, there arises another 1 to 1 ratio (the liquid ratio described earlier is the other), but just as with the other ratio caution should be exercised in establishing a rigid rule for much depends upon the nature of the business and upon the general economic situation. In times of prosperity there is a tendency for a larger volume of borrowing to be undertaken and for this to be regarded as being quite normal. On the other hand, in a trade recession total indebtedness would be expected to be much lower than the net worth.

When considering this ratio it is advisable to classify the debts into (*a*) current liabilities and (*b*) long-term liabilities. In this way the analyst is able to see the nature of the liabilities and when they have to be met.

2. *Capital Employed* *to Fixed Assets.*

The owners of the business should have a substantial stake in the fixed assets. In fact, ideally they should own the fixed assets and part of the current assets. If the value of fixed assets is greatly in excess of the share capital this usually means that part of the fixed assets is owned by Debenture holders or other creditors. Excessive reliance upon creditors is almost bound to be a weakness in the financial structure. The presence of fixed charges, such as Debenture interest, inevitably cuts down the chance of earning sufficient profit to pay shareholders a reasonable rate of dividend.

3. *Total Investment to Long-term Liabilities.*

This makes a different approach to the problem of how the business is financed. The ratio is computed by comparing share capital and loan capital *with* total loan capital.

There should not be too high a proportion of long-term liabilities. However, it should be noted that convertible loan stock is a feature of modern times. This is no doubt due to the taxation laws allowing debenture interest to be charged before calculation of profit and also the

* For this purpose there appears to be a preference for taking equity capital only; *i.e.* ordinary shares plus reserves. However, this is not an inflexible rule. What is important to notice is that there are different meanings given to the term "Capital Employed." (*See also* Chapter 15.)

high level of interest rates which has prevailed as part of the Government's plan to control the granting of credit and loans; *i.e.* the "credit squeeze."

4. *Preference Capital and Loan Capital to Ordinary Capital.*

This ratio is also known as the "capital structure" or "capital gearing" ratio. Capital gearing is discussed on pages 174 and 178 inclusive to which reference should be made.

5. *Earning Ratios.**

Earnings ratios may give very useful information to actual or would-be shareholders. They are generally expressed as percentages, examples being as follows:

(*a*) Equity Capital Earnings.

This shows the net profit belonging to the shareholders. Expressed as a formula the ratio is calculated:

$$\frac{\text{Net Profit (excluding preference dividends)}}{\text{Equity Capital}}$$

There are several different interpretations of "equity capital." Thus:

(i) total nominal value (*e.g.* 10,000 £1 ordinary shares).
(ii) total equity capital employed; *i.e.* nominal value plus reserves.
(iii) real value of capital employed; i.e. the current value of assets *less* Preference share capital and any liabilities.

In a period of rising prices the last definition will tend to give the most realistic and conservative rate of earnings.

(*b*) Retained Earnings Percentage.

The retained earnings calculated as a percentage of total earnings indicate the dividend policy of the directors and also the growth prospects of the shares. A proportion of earnings *should* be retained in order to cover a reasonable rate of expansion. If too much is retained, a take-over bid may be a serious danger (*see* Chapter 22).

(*c*) Dividend Cover.

This is obviously linked with the other ratios. The strong company generally covers dividends a number of times. There is no *standard* number of times for dividends to be covered. However, two or three times is a common ratio to be found in practice at the time of writing.

(*d*) Earnings per Ordinary Share.

The earnings available for the Ordinary shareholders, as computed in (*a*) above, are divided by the number of Ordinary shares to give the earnings per Ordinary share.

(*e*) Preference Dividend Cover.

The number of times the preference dividend is covered by earnings

---

* Earnings may be considered before *and/or* after taxation.

will clearly be a very important guide to the extent of the risk involved for the Preference shareholder.

(*f*) Gross Profit to Sales.

Gross profit is calculated by deducting the factory cost of sales from the net sales figure. Expressed as a percentage of sales the gross profit margin serves as a guide to the efficiency of the production unit. However, by itself it may be misleading. One product may be quite costly to produce and yet have little or no selling expenses, whereas another may have very small costs of production and extremely large selling costs. Accordingly, consideration of all costs is advisable; only then will it be possible to see the true position. Some of these costs ratios are given below.

## COST OR EXPENSE RATIOS

Many cost or expense ratios exist. Here a number of the most important are indicated. The trend of the costs and the relative size of each principal type of cost in relation to some important factor such as sales will be seen from a study of the ratios.

A list of these ratios is given below:

1. Factory Costs to Sales.
2. Administration Costs to Sales.
3. Research and Development Costs to Sales.
4. Capital Expenditure to Sales.
5. Selling Costs to Sales.
6. Distribution Costs to Sales.

These would all be analysed according to the principal types of cost. Thus for example a minimum breakdown of factory costs into direct labour, direct material and factory overhead would be essential.

Changes in costs may or may not be of any real significance. If figures are being considered by the internal analyst—one who has full knowledge of the *nature* of any changes—then he should be able to distinguish between those changes which are of a controllable nature and those which are uncontrollable (*e.g.* due to a general price increase). On the other hand, the external analyst would not be aware of the reason for the change and, therefore, would be working in the dark.

A most important fact to remember—and this was stressed earlier—is that ratios can be no better than the figures from which they are compiled. Accordingly, if historical costs are employed the ratios must necessarily be historical. The most significant disadvantage arising from this is that there is no realistic yardstick against which to measure progress. When actual costs are used as units of measurement for comparing results there is no way of telling whether the actual costs represent efficient performances and achievements. Only by using carefully compiled budgeted costs or standard costs can any useful criterion of efficiency be established.

## OTHER RATIOS

Many ratios other than those given above may be computed. Moreover they may be regarded in different ways. Thus for example, a ratio may be expressed as "stock to turnover" *or* "sales to stock." Neither is there any standard terminology for the titles given to the ratios: one

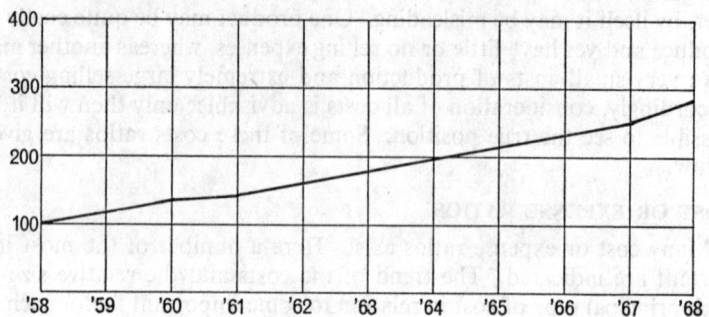

FIG. 71.—*Sales Chart*
Philips' world sales in index figures.

writer may use one name, whereas another writer may prefer an entirely different designation to describe the same ratio.

When standard costing or budgetary control is employed, special ratios for internal use may be compiled based either on current *or* on basic standards. Current standards are those which are generally

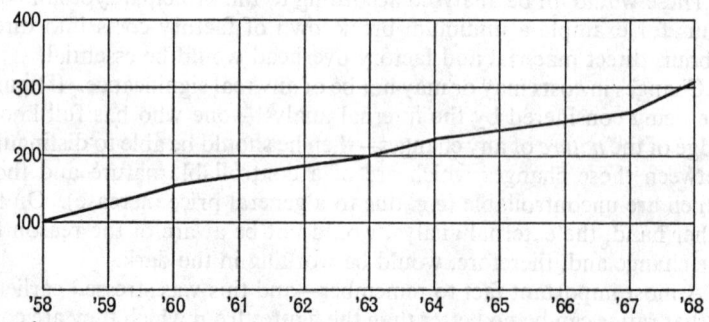

FIG. 72.—*Production Chart*
Production in Philips' Netherlands factories, in index figures.

amended each year whereas basic standards are those which remain in force for a number of years. In the case of basic standards the ratios are "index numbers" portraying the relationships between standard costs and actual costs. The trends which have occurred from the base year to the present time can be seen from a study of the ratios.

This method of presenting ratios in the form of index numbers is not limited to standard costing. Some companies show significant results in the same way. An example of how this is done can be seen from the charts* given above in respect of sales (Fig. 71) and production (Fig. 72).

The base year is 1958, this representing 100; changes since then are shown through to the year 1968.

Ratios need not be limited to *financial* figures. Physical quantities may also be as a basis for calculating them. Such ratios are generally confined to *internal* control, but this is not an invariable rule. If they improve the meaning of published accounts then they could be an integral part of these. Examples of these ratios are as follows:

1. Activity Ratio calculated as follows:

$$\frac{\text{Standard Hours for Actual Output}}{\text{Standard Hours for Budgeted Output}} \times \frac{100}{1}$$

This shows what part of the budgeted production has been completed.

2. Efficiency Ratio calculated as follows:

$$\frac{\text{Standard Hours for Actual Output}}{\text{Actual Hours for Actual Output}} \times \frac{100}{1}$$

This ratio indicates the efficiency realised in producing a stated output. If the actual hours are 1200 and the standard hours for the actual output are 1000 then the efficiency attained is:

$$\frac{1000 \times 100}{1200} = 83 \cdot 33\%$$

Sometimes the ratio is calculated by showing actual hours *over* standard hours. However, this method can be misleading and a true indication of efficiency is obtained only by the method indicated.

3. Volume or Capacity Ratio which may be calculated as shown below:

$$\frac{\text{Actual Hours Worked}}{\text{Budgeted Hours}} \times \frac{100}{1}$$

The object is to show whether or not the available hours are being fully utilised. The hours may be the direct labour hours or the machine hours. If actual hours worked are 1200 and budgeted hours are 1400 then the volume or capacity ratio is:

$$\frac{1200}{1400} \times \frac{100}{1} = 85 \cdot 71\%$$

This indicates that the available capacity has not been fully employed.

* From the Annual Report for 1968 of Philips Electrical Company of the Netherlands.

P

## RATIOS IN PUBLISHED ACCOUNTS

There is a tendency for many progressive companies to show the most significant ratios in the annual report. These illustrate the most important facts and trends and show shareholders and other interested parties how the company is progressing.

An illustration of these ratios is shown on pages 434 and 435 (Fig. 73). These refer to Philips Electrical Company of the Netherlands. Careful study of these ratios should be very rewarding. In fact there are some ratios included in this example which have not been covered earlier.

From the illustration the ten-year trend is clearly discernible. In addition, the method of calculating the ratios can be seen.

The method of presenting the ratios is especially worthy of note. If a business is being valued or its position is being analysed, compiling the figures in this fashion can help to simplify the process. Figures for ten years may not be available and, in any case, in some companies the number of years may with advantage be limited. A period of five years may be quite adequate for assessing the trend from the past to the present and for estimating the future.

### ANALYSIS OF FINANCIAL ACCOUNTS

When analysing financial results the remark made earlier on ascertaining the *trend* by studying a number of years' results is extremely important. For this purpose a period of five years is generally regarded as quite satisfactory. If fewer years' figures are available then the best use has to be of these.

A clear understanding of the *purpose* of the financial analysis is imperative before any attempt is made to carry out the work. In addition, the extent and reliability of the information possessed for the analysis should be fully appreciated.

By "purpose" is meant the main reason for undertaking the financial analysis. This will tend to differ according to the analyst concerned, whether a creditor, a would-be lender, a prospective shareholder or a potential take-over bidder. Each will be concerned with his own particular problem. Thus, for example, if a bank or other institution is to lend money then it will wish to know that the borrower is likely to be in a position to pay back and, possibly, that there is adequate collateral security.

When faced with a problem it is very important when compiling ratios that these are selected with great care. There is nothing to gain by producing every possible ratio. Instead of enlightening, too many ratios may confuse. An example of the most important ratios likely to be required by top management is given in the next chapter which deals with uniform costing and inter-firm comparisons. The pyramid method of showing ratios (page 447) may be studied with advantage for this emphasises all the important ratios likely to be needed by general management for assessing the overall efficiency of a business.

A simple example of the *method of approach* should serve as a guide in assessing the profitability and degree of risk involved in a particular concern. A number of steps can be followed and these are as outlined below:

### 1. *Is profit adequate?*

This can be seen by considering the profit earned in relation to assets employed. The risks involved in the particular business should also be considered: these indicate what is a *reasonable* return on the capital employed (*see* page 398).

### 2. *Is profit increasing or decreasing and at what rate?*

This can be seen from comparing the profits for a number of consecutive years.

If there has been a change for the worse then investigation into volume of turnover, prices, and costs may be necessary. This assumes that such information is available to the analyst; it is very desirable that this should be, but often it is not and, therefore, the analyst has to glean the reason for the change from some other source (*e.g.* current assets may show that stocks carried are much larger).

### 3. *What is the position regarding solvency?*

Here it will be necessary to study the quick and current ratios. In particular the danger of overtrading or undertrading should be looked into. This matter was described earlier in the Chapter.

Analysis of the current ratio into its main parts, relating one to the other, may also be advisable. Thus, for example, the size of stocks in relation to debtors should be studied.

### 4. *The sales or turnover ratios should be computed.*

The purpose here is to indicate whether the volume of sales is adequate in relation to other key factors. The ratio of sales to total assets employed may be an important criterion, especially when the trend over three or four years is observed.

### 5. *Ascertain if the capital structure is appropriate for the business concerned.*

The profit being earned should be adequate to cover the payment of dividends to all classes of shareholder. This matter is very much linked with capital gearing (discussed on page 174).

## QUESTION ON FINANCIAL ANALYSIS

In order to illustrate the principles involved in financial analysis a question is given on page 436 and this is followed by a suggested solution and, where necessary, notes to explain the method of approach.

*General*

| | 1968 | 1967 | 1966 | 1965 | 1964 | 1963 | 1962 | 1961 | 1960 | 1959 |
|---|---|---|---|---|---|---|---|---|---|---|
| Sales | 9,721 | 8,695 | 8,069 | 7,545 | 7,002 | 6,224 | 5,535 | 4,936 | 4,762 | 4,182 |
| Increase on preceding year | 1,026 | 626 | 524 | 543 | 778 | 689 | 599 | 174 | 580 | 587 |
| Percentage increase on preceding year | 12 | 8 | 7 | 8 | 12 | 12 | 12 | 4 | 14 | 16 |
| Net profit | 439 | 355 | 347 | 399 | 405 | 366 | 343 | 326 | 397 | 351 |
| Percentage increase on preceding year | 24 | 2 | −13 | −2 | 11 | 7 | 5 | −18 | 13 | 44 |
| Rate of total capital turnover | 0·91 | 0·85 | 0·82 | 0·85 | 8·88 | 0·86 | 0·83 | 0·86 | 0·96 | 0·96 |
| Employees (in thousands) at end of year | 265 | 241 | 244 | 252 | 252 | 234 | 233 | 226 | 211 | 189 |
| Wages, salaries and social costs | 3,621 | 3,234 | 3,076 | 2,833 | 2,509 | 2,146 | 1,978 | 1,745 | 1,523 | 1,285 |

*Profit*

| | 1968 | 1967 | 1966 | 1965 | 1964 | 1963 | 1962 | 1961 | 1960 | 1959 |
|---|---|---|---|---|---|---|---|---|---|---|
| Trading profit | 1,121 | 901 | 862 | 908 | 935 | 826 | 767 | 731 | 862 | 740 |
| As a percentage of sales | 11·5 | 10·4 | 10·7 | 12·0 | 13·4 | 13·3 | 13·9 | 14·8 | 18·1 | 17·7 |
| As a percentage of total capital employed | 10·5 | 8·8 | 8·8 | 10·2 | 11·7 | 11·4 | 11·5 | 12·8 | 17·4 | 17·0 |
| Net profit | 439 | 355 | 347 | 399 | 405 | 366 | 343 | 326 | 397 | 351 |
| As a percentage of sales | 4·5 | 4·1 | 4·3 | 5·3 | 5·8 | 5·9 | 6·2 | 6·6 | 8·3 | 8·4 |
| As a percentage of net worth | 8·8 | 7·5 | 7·5 | 9·2 | 10·1 | 9·8 | 10·9 | 12·5 | 16·6 | 16·7 |
| Per ordinary share of f25 (in guilders) | 9·65 | 7·59 | 7·53 | 8·68 | 9·31 | 8·75 | 8·59 | 10·56 | 13·86 | 12·77 |
| Tax of profits | 431 | 329 | 315 | 347 | 389 | 337 | 306 | 313 | 407 | 367 |
| As a percentage of profit | 50 | 49 | 48 | 46 | 49 | 47 | 47 | 48 | 50 | 51 |
| Retained profit | 210 | 126 | 125 | 170 | 206 | 175 | 161 | 180 | 257 | 217 |
| As a percentage of net profit | 48 | 36 | 36 | 43 | 51 | 48 | 47 | 55 | 65 | 62 |
| Dividend Per ordinary share of f25 (in guilders) | 4·50 | 4·50 | 4 | 4·50 | 4 | 4 | 4 | 4 | 4 | 4 |
| Per preference share of f25 (in guilders) | 2·10 | 2·10 | 2 | 2·10 | 2 | 2 | 2 | 2 | 2 | 2 |

    1. In calculating the ratios the averages are taken of the total capital employed and of the net worth at the beginning and end of the year.
    2. In the years from 1959 up to and including 1965 an annual distribution of ordinary shares was made, charged to the Share Premium Account, amounting to 5% to holders of ordinary shares and 1% to holders of preference shares.
    3. At the same time as the distribution of the dividend for 1966, the U.S. Philips Trust made a distribution of U.S.$ 0·125 per ordinary share of f25 and U.S.$ 0· 025 per preference share of f25.
    4. For calculating the net profit per ordinary share of f25 the amounts distributed to others entitled to a share in the profit are deducted from the net profit figure.

*Amounts in millions of guilders.*

FIG. 73.—*Analysis o*

*Financial position*

|  | 1968 | 1967 | 1966 | 1965 | 1964 | 1963 | 1962 | 1961 | 1960 | 1959 |
|---|---|---|---|---|---|---|---|---|---|---|
| Ordinary share capital | 1,017 | 1,017 | 1,017 | 1,017 | 968 | 920 | 875 | 685 | 651 | 619 |
| Preference share capital | 144 | 144 | 144 | 144 | 144 | 144 | 144 | 144 | 144 | 144 |
| Share premium account | 456 | 456 | 456 | 456 | 506 | 553 | 598 | 88 | 122 | 154 |
| Retained profit | 2,585 | 2,375 | 2,249 | 2,124 | 1,954 | 1,748 | 1,573 | 1,412 | 1,232 | 975 |
| Revaluation | 925 | 795 | 864 | 742 | 621 | 480 | 298 | 360 | 377 | 374 |
| Net worth | 5,127 | 4,787 | 4,730 | 4,483 | 4,193 | 3,845 | 3,588 | 2,689 | 2,526 | 2,266 |
| Minority shareholders' interests | 237 | 171 | 166 | 151 | 145 | 124 | 112 | 91 | 74 | 58 |
| Long-term liabilities and provisions | 3,070 | 2,505 | 2,347 | 1,996 | 1,770 | 1,560 | 1,595 | 1,391 | 1,079 | 875 |
| Short-term liabilities and provisions * | 3,899 | 3,627 | 3,537 | 3,247 | 2,697 | 2,265 | 2,055 | 2,080 | 1,816 | 1,497 |
| Total liabilities | 6,969 | 6,132 | 5,884 | 5,243 | 4,467 | 3,825 | 3,650 | 3,471 | 2,895 | 2,372 |
| Total capital employed | 12,333 | 11,090 | 10,780 | 9,877 | 8,805 | 7,794 | 7,350 | 6,251 | 5,495 | 4,696 |
| Total liabilities as a percentage of total capital employed | 57 | 55 | 55 | 53 | 51 | 49 | 50 | 56 | 53 | 51 |

* This heading includes profit for distribution

*Assets employed*

|  | 1968 | 1967 | 1966 | 1965 | 1964 | 1963 | 1962 | 1961 | 1960 | 1959 |
|---|---|---|---|---|---|---|---|---|---|---|
| Property, plant and equipment (book value) | 3,855 | 3,615 | 3,546 | 3,215 | 2,900 | 2,251 | 2,387 | 2,035 | 1,735 | 1,430 |
| Other fixed assets | 1,523 | 1,121 | 799 | 646 | 548 | 422 | 315 | 244 | 215 | 159 |
| Total fixed assets | 5,378 | 4,736 | 4,345 | 3,861 | 3,448 | 2,943 | 2,702 | 2,279 | 1,950 | 1,589 |
| Stocks | 2,935 | 2,775 | 3,046 | 2,849 | 2,481 | 2,050 | 2,062 | 1,880 | 1,481 | 1,181 |
| Debtors | 3,286 | 2,836 | 2,648 | 2,383 | 2,147 | 1,989 | 1,723 | 1,548 | 1,420 | 1,268 |
| Liquid assets | 734 | 743 | 741 | 784 | 729 | 812 | 863 | 544 | 644 | 658 |
| Total current assets | 6,955 | 6,354 | 6,435 | 6,016 | 5,357 | 4,851 | 4,648 | 3,972 | 3,545 | 3,107 |
| Total assets | 12,333 | 11,090 | 10,780 | 9,877 | 8,805 | 7,794 | 7,350 | 6,251 | 5,495 | 4,696 |
| Property, plant and equipment Book value as a percentage of replacement value | 54 | 55 | 56 | 57 | 58 | 58 | 60 | 60 | 59 | 57 |
| Net acquisition for year | 481 | 503 | 563 | 535 | 506 | 442 | 496 | 472 | 425 | 279 |
| Depreciation for year | 461 | 420 | 388 | 351 | 305 | 277 | 245 | 209 | 179 | 158 |
| Ratio of net acquisitions to depreciation | 1·0 | 1·2 | 1·5 | 1·5 | 1·7 | 1·6 | 2·0 | 2·3 | 2·4 | 1·8 |
| Stocks As a percentage of sales | 30 | 32 | 38 | 38 | 35 | 33 | 37 | 38 | 31 | 28 |
| Trade debtors Average credit term (in months) | 2·8 | 2·8 | 2·9 | 2·7 | 2·7 | 2·7 | 2·6 | 2·7 | 2·7 | 2·5 |
| Ratio of current assets to short-term liabilities and provisions | 1·8 | 1·8 | 1·8 | 1·9 | 2·0 | 2·1 | 2·3 | 1·9 | 2·0 | 2·1 |

*Financial Accounts*

QUESTION

Parlow Ltd. has been operating for two years. The most important facts from its published accounts are given below.

*Balance Sheets—Parlow Ltd., at year end*

| | Year 1 £ | Year 2 £ | | Year 1 £ | Year 2 £ |
|---|---|---|---|---|---|
| Ordinary Shares of £1 each... ... | 10,000 | 10,000 | Goodwill purchased from G. Parlow | 6,000 | 6,000 |
| Capital Reserves | 2,000 | 3,000 | Fixed Assets (at cost) ... ... | 14,000 | 16,000 |
| Profit and Loss Balance ... | 3,000 | 2,000 | Stocks ... ... | 3,000 | 6,000 |
| Loan on Mortgage | 8,000 | 8,000 | Debtors ... ... | 3,000 | 6,000 |
| Trade Creditors ... | 5,000 | 7,000 | Tax Reserve | | |
| Bank Overdraft ... | — | 2,000 | Certificates ... | 1,000 | — |
| Taxation: Current | 1,000 | 1,000 | Cash in Hand ... | 3,000 | — |
| Future | 1,000 | 1,000 | | | |
| | £30,000 | £34,000 | | £30,000 | £34,000 |

*Profit and Loss Accounts of Parlow Ltd. for the two years*

| | £ | £ | | £ | £ |
|---|---|---|---|---|---|
| | | | Balance b/d | | 3,000 |
| Transfer to Reserve | 2,000 | 1,000 | Profit for the year after taxation, interest on loan and normal running costs (except depreciation) | 7,000 | 5,000 |
| Directors' Remuneration | 1,000 | 3,000 | | | |
| Dividends ... | 1,000 | 2,000 | | | |
| Balance c/f ... | 3,000 | 2,000 | | | |
| | £7,000 | £8,000 | | £7,000 | £8,000 |

You are told that total sales amounted to £60,000 in the first year and £50,000 in the second year.

Examine the details and analyse them in a manner which indicates the overall efficiency of the business and its financial position; *i.e.* its likely ability to meet present and future commitments.

SUGGESTED SOLUTION

Since only two years' figures are available the best use has to be made of these. A step-by-step analysis reveals the following facts:

1. *Profit Earned*

This has declined from £7000 the first year to £5000 the second year. Since it is usual to regard directors remuneration as a normal cost the figures for profit become £6000 and £2000 respectively.

Apparently nothing has been charged in the accounts for depreciation. This is a matter which calls for further investigation. If the fixed assets consist of plant and machinery then a charge of 10% may be quite appropriate. A much smaller rate would apply for freehold property.

Ignoring the depreciation and directors' remuneration the rate of return on capital is as follows:

$$\text{Year 1.} \qquad \frac{7000}{30,000} \times \frac{100}{1} = 23 \cdot 3\%$$

$$\text{Year 2.} \qquad \frac{5000}{34,000} \times \frac{100}{1} = 14 \cdot 7\%$$

This employs the formula:

$$\frac{\text{Net Profit}}{\text{Total Assets}} \times \frac{100}{1}$$

Many variations of this formula are in existence. The profit may be taken *before* taxation and many authorities on this matter prefer to adopt this procedure.* There are many definitions of capital employed,* but the total of all assets gives the most conservative result and is, therefore, adopted for this purpose. Strictly speaking the loan interest should be added back to profit, because the loan is included in the gross capital figures of £30,000 and £34,000.

From the percentages given it is apparent that there has been a marked decline in the rate of profit-earning, a matter which calls for further investigation. The falling off in the volume of sales may be the reason, but in the absence of further information it is difficult to be positive on this fact.

There is a large loan on mortgage and this is bound to affect the size of the profit. The fixed interest charge imposes a burden which must be met before profit is earned.

Whether the *rate* of earning is adequate depends upon the nature of the business and the risks involved. No information is given on this point. The fall in profit cannot be regarded as satisfactory, but, on the other hand, the percentage of 14·7 may not be unreasonable for the risks involved provided that this can be *maintained* in the future. However, as indicated, what is a reasonable rate must be determined by the circumstances.

### 2. The Solvency Position

Whether or not Parlow Ltd. is in a reasonably sound financial position can be seen from the following:

(*a*) Current Ratio; *i.e.* $\dfrac{\text{Current Assets}}{\text{Current Liabilities}}$

(*b*) Quick Ratio; *i.e.* $\dfrac{\text{Liquid Assets}}{\text{Current Liabilities}}$

Calculation of the *current ratio* is straightforward and involves bringing together the current assets and liabilities. This is done as follows:

* *See* Chapters 15 and 17 on Capital Employed; and Uniform Costing and Inter-firm Comparisons; also earlier in this Chapter, page 427.

|  | Year 1 | | Year 2 | |
|---|---|---|---|---|
|  | Assets | Liabilities | Assets | Liabilities |
|  | £ | £ | £ | £ |
| Stocks ... ... | 3,000 | | 6,000 | |
| Debtors ... ... | 3,000 | | 6,000 | |
| Tax Reserve Certificates ... | 1,000 | | | |
| Cash in Hand ... | 3,000 | | | |
| Trade Creditors ... | | 5,000 | | 7,000 |
| Bank Overdraft ... | | — | | 2,000 |
| Taxation: Current... | | 1,000 | | 1,000 |
|  | 10,000 | 6,000 | 12,000 | 10,000 |

**Year 1 Current Ratio**

| | £ |
|---|---|
| Current Assets | 10,000 |
| Current Liabilities | 6,000 |
| Working Capital | £4,000 |

The ratio is, therefore, 1·666 to 1 which, although not substantial, may be adequate.

**Year 2 Current Ratio**

| | £ |
|---|---|
| Current Assets | 12,000 |
| Current Liabilities | 10,000 |
| Working Capital | £2,000 |

The ratio in this case is 1·2 to 1, a positive weakening in the solvency position. Analysis of the current assets and liabilities is clearly needed. It does not require calculation of any more ratios to see the following salient facts:

*Stocks* appear to have increased out of proportion to other items. The next question is to determine the nature of the stock, but this is not clear from the Question. If further information is available on stocks they would be broken down into:

　　(i) raw materials;　(ii) work-in-progress;　(iii) finished goods.

The question to be asked is, what class of stock ((i) to (iii)) has increased? If the increase has been in the raw materials this may be due to over-purchasing. An increase in the work-in-progress probably indicates that there is something wrong with the routing of work through the factory; *i.e.* production control. When stocks of finished goods are slow-moving the blame may be put at the door of the sales department. These are indications of what avenues to look at to determine the nature of a weakness.

*Debtors* have increased to the extent of £3000; this again is clearly a weakness. Sales divided by the debtors' figure shows:

Year 1　$\dfrac{£60,000}{£3,000} = 20$ to 1　　Year 2　$\dfrac{£50,000}{£6,000} = 8·33$ to 1

If all goods are sold on credit for payment within one month (30 days) the ratio should be in the region of 12 to 1 so the second year balance cannot be said to be satisfactory.

The lack of cash and the creation of a bank overdraft shows a definite deterioration in the financial position. Tax reserve certificates present in the first year have disappeared in the second year, once more a sign of a cash shortage.

The *quick ratio*, which shows liquid assets over current liabilities, is as shown below:

$$\text{Year 1} \quad \frac{£7,000}{£6,000} = 1\cdot2 \text{ to } 1 \qquad \text{Year 2} \quad \frac{£6,000}{£10,000} = 0\cdot6 \text{ to } 1.$$

In the case of the first year the liquid assets are taken to be cash plus debtors and tax reserve certificates. Current liabilities are trade creditors and the current liability for taxation.

The ratio is shown as 0·6 to 1 for the second year. The liquid assets are smaller than current liabilities showing that £4000 has to be found from somewhere.

### 3. Sales

As indicated there has been a falling off in sales. The sales to total assets employed are as follows:

$$\text{Year 1} \quad \frac{£60,000}{£30,000} = 2 \text{ to } 1 \ (\textit{i.e. each £1 invested produces £2 in sales})$$

$$\text{Year 2} \quad \frac{£50,000}{£34,000} = 1\cdot47 \text{ to } 1 \ (\textit{i.e. each £1 invested produces £1·47 in sales})$$

There has been an increase in fixed assets (capital employed) and yet the volume of sales has reduced by one-sixth.

### 4. Capital Structure

The capital gearing is not very sound. There is too much reliance on borrowing. From the balance sheets the following facts emerge:

|  | | Year 1 £ | Year 2 £ |
|---|---|---|---|
| Proprietors' Proportion of Assets | ... | 16,000 | 16,000 |
| Outsiders' Proportion of Assets | ... | 14,000 | 18,000 |
|  | | £30,000 | £34,000 |

The "outsiders' liability" includes loan on mortgage, trade creditors, bank overdraft, and *current* taxation: the balance belongs to the proprietors.

From the Question can be seen that the fixed assets are covered in both years by the proprietors' investment. In the first year there is £2000 towards Goodwill. At the best of times Goodwill is a doubtful asset which is very difficult to value. No attempt has been made to write off the cost of this intangible asset and yet there is general agreement amongst accountants that Goodwill should be eliminated as quickly as possible.

CONCLUSION. The analysis shown above has, as its main purpose, the illustration of the principles of financial analysis. Many more ratios could have been covered. In the interest of simplicity this has not been done. Even so, from what *has* been covered it will be apparent that Parlow Ltd., is in need of reorganisation. Particular attention should be paid to the volume of sales; possibly the profit margin (this is not clear from the information given), the turnover of stock and the collection of debts. Above all, steps should be taken to improve the financial position. Naturally some improvement can be expected from increasing sales and reducing stocks and debtors. However, a much more radical reorganisation may be essential; in particular it may be desirable to change the capital and pay off the whole or part of the loan covered by mortgage.

In a problem of this type only general suggestions can be made. When full details of the industry and company are available the analyst will probably be able to establish *normal relationships* and these can be shown in the form of ratios. There is then a set of guides or signposts against which progress can be measured.

## EXAMINATION QUESTIONS

1. A company manufacturing high-grade metal alloys has its head office and factory in the outskirts of London. The following are brief particulars of the last three balance sheets as at 31st December in each year:

| | 19.. £'000 | | | 19.. £'000 | | | 19.. £'000 | | |
|---|---|---|---|---|---|---|---|---|---|
| Share capital—issued and fully paid (all of one class) | | | 750 | | | 750 | | | 50 |
| Revenue reserves | | | 282 | | | 460 | | | 687 |
| Reserve for future taxation | | | 270 | | | 280 | | | 300 |
| | | | 1,302 | | | 1,490 | | | 1,737 |
| Fixed assets—at cost | | 700 | | | 770 | | | 800 | |
| Less Depreciation | | 300 | 400 | | 360 | 410 | | 430 | 370 |
| Current assets: | | | | | | | | | |
| Stocks and work in progress | | 500 | | | 480 | | | 670 | |
| Debtors | | 402 | | | 475 | | | 565 | |
| Cash, Government securities | | 520 | | | 675 | | | 666 | |
| | | 1,422 | | | 1,630 | | | 1,901 | |
| Less Current liabilities: | | | | | | | | | |
| Trade creditors | 210 | | | 220 | | | 180 | | |
| Dividends (net) | 60 | | | 60 | | | 74 | | |
| Income tax and Profits tax | 250 | 520 | 902 | 270 | 550 | 1,080 | 280 | 534 | 1,367 |
| | | | 1,302 | | | 1,490 | | | 1,737 |
| Other information available is: | | | | | | | | | |
| Sales turnover (£'000) | | | 4,000 | | | 4,600 | | | 5,200 |
| Net profit before tax (£'000) | | | 480 | | | 540 | | | 620 |
| Dividends paid or proposed | | | 20% | | | 20% | | | 22½% |

The Board has decided to set up its own research department and has recently appointed a Research Manager, who has now submitted three alternative proposals, viz.:

| | Capital Expenditure £ | Annual Expenses (excl. Depreciation) £ | Time to complete |
|---|---|---|---|
| A. Limited scheme on same site as factory | 80,000 | 30,000 | 18 months |
| B. Same as A but on a new site, with space for further development | 95,000 | 35,000 | 21 months |
| C. Wider scheme on new site | 200,000 | 75,000 | 36 months |

You are asked to give your views on the financial implications of these proposals in a report to the Board.                (*I.C.W.A.*)

2. State four accounting ratios likely to be of assistance in the formation of an opinion on the efficiency of the management of a manufacturing business.
(*S.C.A.*)

3. A person is considering the purchase of a large retail hardware store and has called upon you to carry out an investigation. In particular, he is concerned about the considerable variation in the ratio of gross profit to turnover disclosed by the accounts of the business for the last five years.

Outline the procedure you would follow and suggest possible reasons for the variation in profit ratios.                (*S.C.A.*)

4. State fully to what points you would devote attention when examining the published accounts and directors' report of a limited company if you were acting on behalf of:

(*a*) a creditor;
(*b*) a debenture-holder; and
(*c*) a prospective shareholder.                (*S.C.A.*)

5. Draft the Balance Sheet, as at 31st March, 19.., from the following summary of the balances at that date. Make a brief report on the position revealed, for the benefit of a holder of Ordinary Stock.

|  | £ |
|---|---|
| Amounts set aside for Provisions ... ... ... ... ... | 110,000 |
| Provision for Bad Debts ... ... ... ... ... ... | 17,000 |
| Bank Overdraft ... ... ... ... ... ... ... | 2,353,334 |
| Bonuses to Employees ... ... ... ... ... ... | 104,000 |
| Balance at Bank ... ... ... ... ... ... | 199,143 |
| Cost of issuing 4 per cent. First Mortgage Debenture Stock ... | 144,684 |
| Current Liability for Taxation ... ... ... ... ... | 1,831,432 |
| Contingencies Reserve ... ... ... ... ... ... | 2,800,000 |
| 4 per cent. First Mortgage Debenture Stock, 1967–82 ... ... | 3,000,000 |
| Future Taxation, Reserve for Income Tax, 1961–62 ... ... | 1,180,000 |
| General Revenue Reserve ... ... ... ... ... ... | 2,000,000 |
| Land and Buildings ... ... ... ... ... ... | 5,674,796 |
| Plant and Machinery ... ... ... ... ... ... | 2,417,361 |
| Profit and Loss Account ... ... ... ... ... ... | 459,120 |
| Proposed Ordinary Final Dividend and Bonuses ... ... ... | 207,808 |
| Premium on Shares ... ... ... ... ... ... | 2,627,560 |
| Share Capital: Authorised and Issued | |
|     6½ per cent. Cumulative Preference Stock ... ... ... | 1,359,447 |
|     4 per cent. Cumulative Redeemable Preference Stock ... | 3,000,000 |
|     Ordinary Stock ... ... ... ... ... ... | 2,638,829 |
| Debtors and Bills Receivable ... ... ... ... ... | 2,484,277 |
| Creditors ... ... ... ... ... ... ... ... | 831,271 |
| Stock-in-Trade, as certified by Managing Director ... ... | 13,391,677 |
| Trade Investments ... ... ... ... ... ... | 207,863 |
|  | (*S.C.A.*) |

6. The managing director has been presented with the following statement:

## Comparative Profit Statement

| | | April 1967 | | April 1968 | |
|---|---|---|---|---|---|
| Number of working days ... | | 20 | | 22 | |
| | £ | £ | | £ | £ |
| Sales ... ... ... ... | | 42,500 | | | 45,800 |
| Stock increase at prime cost ... | | 1,000 | | | 160 |
| | | 43,500 | | | 45,960 |
| Cost of production: | | | | | |
| Materials ... ... ... | 12,600 | | | 14,200 | |
| Direct labour ... ... ... | 10,000 | | | 10,950 | |
| Variable overhead ... ... | 2,500 | | | 2,920 | |
| Fixed overhead ... ... | 6,000 | | | 6,710 | |
| | | 31,100 | | | 34,780 |
| Fixed cost of administration ... | | 3,000 | | | 3,400 |
| Cost of selling and distribution: | | | | | |
| Variable ... ... ... | 1,260 | | | 1,380 | |
| Fixed ... ... ... ... | 3,000 | | | 3,400 | |
| | | 4,260 | | | 4,780 |
| | | 38,360 | | | 42,960 |
| Profit ... ... ... ... | | £5,140 | | | £3,000 |

Data concerning the three products: A, B and C made by the company is as follows:

| Product | A | B | C |
|---|---|---|---|
| April 1967: | | | |
| Product variable costs, per unit: | | | |
| Direct material, quantity in lb ... | 50 | 30 | 10 |
| (Price per lb averaged £0·90) | | | |
| Direct labour, operating hours ... | 50 | 30 | 30 |
| (Rate per hour £0·50) | | | |
| Production variable overhead | | | |
| (Rate per hour £0·0125) | | | |
| Selling and distribution, variable cost | | | |
| per unit ... ... ... ... | £3 | £2 | £2 |
| Sales price per unit ... ... ... | £100 | £80 | £60 |
| Production, in units ... ... ... | 100 | 200 | 300 |
| Sales, in units ... ... ... | 90 | 190 | 305 |
| April 1968: | | | |
| Production, in units ... ... ... | 110 | 220 | 310 |
| Sales, in units ... ... ... ... | 130 | 240 | 210 |

You are required to compile, for presentation to the managing director, a statement giving an analysis into causes of the decrease in the profit in April 1968 as against the profit in April 1967. (*I.C.W.A.*)

# CHAPTER 17

# UNIFORM COSTING AND INTERFIRM COMPARISONS

## UNIFORM COSTING

UNIFORM cost accounting is not a new concept; since Cost Accounting was first introduced in its modern form different attempts have been made to establish standardised principles in the United States of America, in Great Britain, in Australia, and in many European countries.

There is no generally accepted definition of uniform costing. Usually though the essential feature is that *standardised* principles and methods of Cost Accounting are employed by a number of different companies and firms. This *standardisation* may, and often does, extend to the following:

1. Method of Cost Accounting, *e.g.* job costing, process costing, or a variation of one or both of these.
2. Accounting classification including codes.
3. Content of each account.
4. Methods of defining costs—

    (*a*) direct material;
    (*b*) direct labour;
    (*c*) direct expense;
    (*d*) overhead costs:

        (i) factory,
        (ii) selling,
        (iii) distribution,
        (iv) administration,
        (v) research and development.

5. Methods of recovering depreciation.
6. Methods of allocating and/or apportioning overhead costs to cost centres and jobs or products.
7. Material control including the pricing of issues and valuation of stocks.
8. Methods of recording accounting data; *e.g.* integrated accounting system.
9. Reports and statements for planning and control.
10. Systems of remunerating labour; *e.g.* time rates or piece-rates.
11. A central body, such as a trade association, is established for carrying out the work (1 to 10 above).

In brief, *all* aspects must receive attention, thus making comparisons of results possible between different businesses. The latter may be in the same trade—most uniform costing systems have been designed for this purpose. However, many accountants take the view that a uniform Cost Accounting system should be capable of being used in any business irrespective of the trade or industry. Whether the degree of flexibility necessary to make a system *generally* applicable is likely to reduce its usefulness is a debatable issue. Certainly there are bound to be problems many of which will be extremely difficult to overcome.

There is no doubt that the task of making the results of different concerns capable of being validly compared is simplified by having a small number of businesses each having similar characteristics and operating under similar conditions. The principal advantages which may accrue from uniform Cost Accounting are summarised below.

### ADVANTAGES OF UNIFORM COST ACCOUNTING

Advantages which may accrue to the participating concerns from the use of uniform Cost Accounting are as follows:

1. Greater operating efficiency arising from:

    (*a*) a more extensive and thorough understanding of all costs;
    (*b*) a competitive spirit introduced by comparison of costs with the costs of other businesses or averages for the industry.

2. Facilitates the establishment of realistic pricing policies.

3. Establishment of the best methods and principles of costing.

4. Through the central organisation (*e.g.* trade organisation) the provision of information which assists in formulating policy, carrying out plans, controlling internally, and facilitating the making of plans to meet competition.

5. The additional advantages discussed below under *Interfirm Comparisons*.

### DISADVANTAGES OF UNIFORM COST ACCOUNTING

Establishing and operating any form of uniform costing system is bound to be attended with many problems and difficulties. Some of the objections which have been raised are summarised below:

1. Standardisation of definitions and methods is difficult to accomplish.

2. Even when (1) is achieved there is bound to be great difficulty in fitting the methods advocated by the system into the framework of each individual business.

Many differences exist such as age of plant, geographical location, availability of labour, cash and other vital ingredients of successful production, and the degree of mechanisation. How can a factory producing mainly by manual labour be compared with a factory which is highly mechanised, possibly automated? Fortunately when comparing firms within an industry there tends to be a definite pattern of production methods. Leading firms within a specific industry tend to use modern methods and, therefore, are capable of being compared.

3. Many companies will not disclose the figures to the trade association in the belief—normally mistaken—that confidential information will be disclosed to competitors.

The general practice with trade associations and similar bodies is that details relating to an individual firm are not disclosed or published. Instead, average results and trends are disclosed. These are likely to be beneficial to a business, and yet there is no danger of operating results falling into the wrong hands. Naturally, additional clerical work will be involved in completing any returns required by the trade association. However, the extra effort should be more than off-set by the benefit received.

A natural outcome of uniform costing systems is inter-firm comparisons. These depend very much upon the acceptance of standard terms, definitions, and methods of Cost Accounting, which form the foundation-stone of any system of interfirm comparison. A scheme for many industries which is run along national—and to some extent international—lines is that organised by the Centre for Interfirm Comparison. In addition there are schemes run by trade associations: typical of these is that established by the British Federation of Master Printers. These schemes are outlined below.

## INTERFIRM COMPARISONS

### CENTRE FOR INTERFIRM COMPARISON*

Interfirm comparisons may take a variety of different forms. In Great Britain, the best example of how interfirm comparisons can be made may be seen from a study of the operations of the Centre for Interfirm Comparison, a body which was established by The British Institute of Management and The British Productivity Council in 1959.

A good idea of what is meant by the term "interfirm comparison" may be obtained by considering the main objects of the exercise. In other words, an interfirm comparison consists of the following procedure:

1. Data are collected from participating organisations by the Centre for Interfirm Comparison.

2. The Management of an organisation are provided with information which will allow them to determine the efficiency being achieved, measured by comparing the performances of other businesses.

3. An attempt is made to show why results vary from one business to another; i.e. any weaknesses are highlighted.

Extensive use is made of financial or cost ratios. These are selected with great care bearing in mind the problems which are being faced.

* The author gratefully acknowledges the assistance given by H. Ingham, the Director of the Centre for Interfirm Comparison Ltd.

## PURPOSE OF INTERFIRM COMPARISONS

The main purpose of interfirm comparisons is as indicated in the previous section; namely, the improvement of efficiency by showing management the present achievements and possible weaknesses.

Firms contribute figures to the Centre which is a "neutral" body. Great care is taken to ensure that confidences are never betrayed, and only *participants* are given a report on any comparison which is made.

Many problems may be overcome through the assistance of inter-firm comparisons. More usually attention is focussed on any weaknesses which may exist. Some of these special problems may be the following:

1. Is profit adequate?
2. How efficient is selling?
3. How efficient is production?

These and similar questions are always present in any business, so obviously any system, method or device which assists in providing solutions is to be welcomed. More details of these problems are now considered.

### ADEQUACY OF PROFIT

The principal motivating force in any commercial enterprise is profit. Success is measured by the size of the profit in relation to the capital employed (covered in detail in Chapter 15).

The Centre for Interfirm Comparison recognises the importance of this measure and calls it the "primary ratio."

If the earning power of a business does not at least equal that of other similar concerns then there is probably some factor or a combination of factors which is not operating efficiently. These may then be isolated by means of other types of ratios. There are (a) supporting ratios, (b) general explanatory ratios, and (c) specific explanatory ratios. All the ratios may be taken together to form a pyramid diagram of ratios as illustrated in Figs. 74 and 75.

The advantages to be gained from using the measure of return on capital employed are discussed in Chapter 15. Here it is important to note that the profit taken is the normal net profit as defined by accountants, but before charging taxation; *i.e.* taxation is treated as an appropriation of profit.

The assets employed are taken at current replacement values so that the *real* capital, and not simply the total historical costs or nominal value, is represented.

### EFFICIENCY IN SELLING

Unless goods are sold there can be no profit. The size of the total sales to operating profit and to assets employed are key ratios in

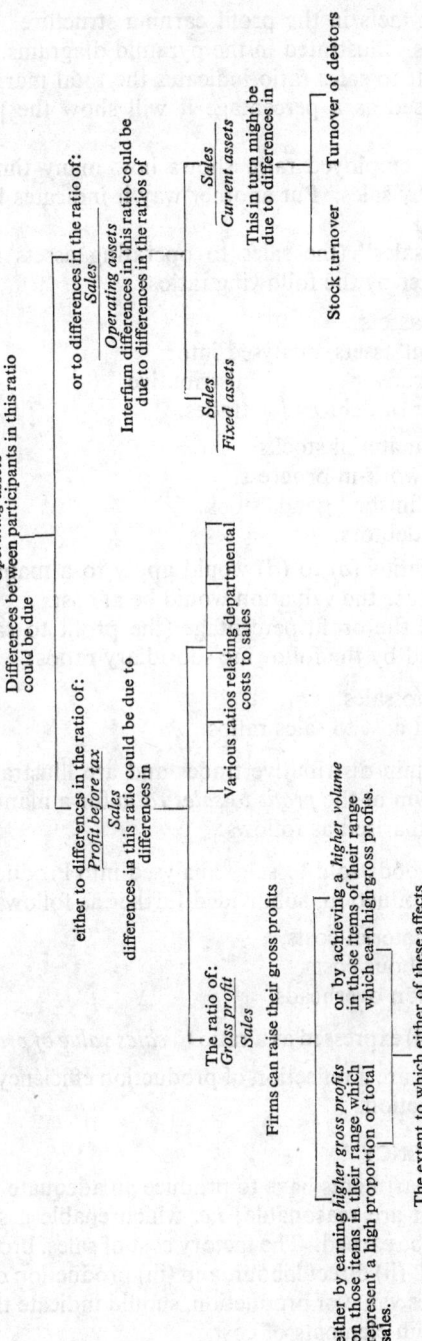

Fig. 74.—*Pyramid diagram of ratios—certain distributive trades*

The "pyramid" method of selecting ratios was first devised by H. Ingham and J. L. Taylor Harrington. This method has the advantage of showing the ratios in order of importance, the most important (return on capital) being at the apex of the pyramid.

illustrating important facts in the profit earning structure. These are the "supporting ratios" illustrated in the pyramid diagrams.

The operating profit to sales ratio indicates the total margin earned by the sales. Expressed as a percentage it will show the percentage earned on sales.

The sales to assets employed ratio shows how many times capital employed is covered by sales. Put another way it indicates how much is sold per £1 invested.

The "size of the sales" (the sales to operating assets ratio) can be analysed still further by the following ratios:

1. Sales to fixed assets.
2. Sales to current assets, analysed into:
   (a) Stock turnover ⎫ distributive
   (b) Turnover of debtors ⎰ trades.

or  (a) Sales to material stocks.
    (b) Sales to work-in-progress.
    (c) Sales to finished goods stock.
    (d) Sales to debtors.

The last batch of ratios (a) to (d) would apply to a manufacturing industry and in each case the valuation would be at cost.

On the other hand, the profit percentage (the profit to sales ratio) will tend to be affected by the following subsidiary ratios:

(a) Gross profit to sales.
(b) Departmental cost to sales ratios.

These apply to certain distributive trades and are illustrated above (Fig. 68). A subdivision of the *profit to sales ratio* for a manufacturing industry may be summarised as follows:

Factory cost of goods sold to sales analysed into Production costs to Sales value of production, subdivided further as follows:

(i) Direct material costs,
(ii) Direct labour costs,
(iii) Production overheads,

in each case (i) to (iii) expressed as a ratio to *sales value of production*.

The last three ratios are a reflection of production efficiency, a matter covered in the next section.

## PRODUCTION EFFICIENCY

The production departments have to produce an adequate volume of output at costs which are reasonable; *i.e.* which enable a sufficiently large gross margin to be earned. The factory cost of sales, broken down into (i) direct material, (ii) direct labour, and (iii) production overheads, and related to the sales value of production, should indicate the relative size of these three main elements of cost.

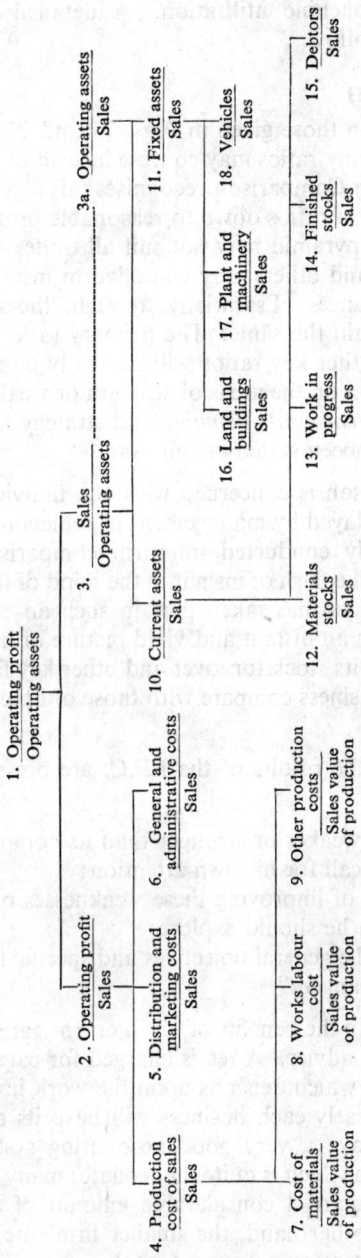

FIG. 75.—*Pyramid diagram of ratios—manufacturing industries*

Copyright © Centre for Interfirm Comparison Ltd. 1969

Comparisons with other firms' figures or with its own preceding periods' figures may point out a possible source of inefficiency; *e.g.* labour utilisation or machine utilisation. A detailed analysis and investigation can then follow.

## METHOD OF APPROACH

Many more ratios than those given in Figs. 74 and 75 can be computed. However, too many ratios may confuse instead of enlightening. The Centre for Interfirm Comparison recognises this fact and, accordingly, keeps the number of ratios down to reasonable proportions. All the ratios shown in the pyramid may not suit all trades or industries: some may be removed and others may be added to meet the needs of the particular circumstances. Essentially, though, the basic pattern illustrated tends to remain the same. The primary ratio is always the starting point and the other key ratios will normally be present.

I.F.C. focuses attention on the areas of strength or weakness—which it is essential to know if *corporate planning* and strategy are to be successful. This aspect has been stated as follows:

> "Interfirm comparison is concerned with the individual firm, its success and the part played by management in achieving it. The end product of a properly conducted interfirm comparison is not a statistical survey, but the flash of insight in the mind of the Managing Director of a firm which has taken part in such an exercise. The results of this give him an instant and vivid picture of how his firm's profitability, its costs, its stock turnover and other key factors affecting the success of a business compare with those of other firms in his industry.

> The way in which the results of the I.F.C. are presented to him makes him see clearly:

> where his firm is weaker or stronger than its competitors;
> what weaknesses call for his own attention;
> what possibilities of improving these weaknesses or reinforcing the firms strength he should explore;
> in what respects the general objectives and specific targets of the firm should be changed."

Firms wishing to obtain the benefits of an interfirm comparison may approach the Centre for advice. A fee is charged for carrying out the comparisons, the size of which depends upon the work involved. This is to be expected for clearly each business will have its own peculiar problems; some may have a very good accounting system whereas others may have a system which is quite inadequate: many concerns are quite large and may require a considerable amount of analysis and interpretation. On the other hand, the smaller firm's needs may not involve anything like the same volume of work.

The precise method of approach adopted by the Centre will be governed by the type of industry or trade and the problems and circumstances present. However, a guide may be obtained from the following summary of possible procedures:

1. Firms which are to participate in an interfirm comparison exercise submit figures to the Centre.

These figures are compiled on the basis of uniform definitions of terms, procedures, methods, and accounting periods.

2. After all necessary steps have been taken to ensure that the firms participating can benefit from the comparison a number of ratios are compiled.

These are shown in summary form distinguishing:

(a) Ratios for the *group* of firms participating in the interfirm comparison.

(b) Ratios for a single firm.

Each firm is given a report compiled along these lines. Naturally the figures relating to the single firm will be those of the firm to which a specific report is issued.

3. The ratios for the group and the ratios for the single firms are compared one by one.

An example of how these comparisons are made can be seen by studying the illustration (Fig. 76).

4. Once any significant deviation from the *norm* (average return on capital employed) is established, the possible reason for this deviation may be located by examining the remaining ratios.

## CONTENTS OF REPORT

Each company receives a confidential report which explains in detail the comparative table (Fig. 76). Extracts from a typical report for business "F" are shown below:

"You have stated that whilst in your year 1 sales of stock produced standard products represented 15% of your total sales, you had estimated that with more intensive marketing of these lines their sales might represent 20% of total sales in year 2. You expected that this would make it necessary to spend more on selling, but that the additional selling expenditure would be offset by production economies achieved through longer production runs. These longer runs would reduce idle hours (due to changes in machine set up) and thereby result in lower works labour costs, less work-in-progress and better machine utilisation. Furthermore, greater concentration on certain stock items would enable you to purchase some materials in larger quantities and therefore at lower prices. In fact, you found at the end of the year that sales of these stock lines had not represented 20% but only 18% of your total sales.

These developments would seem to explain the rises in your finished stock (ratio 14) and your distribution and marketing cost (ratio 5), as well as the falls in your production cost ratios (ratios 4, 8 and 9), your materials stock (ratio 12), your work in progress

| Ratios | Firm | | | | | | |
|---|---|---|---|---|---|---|---|
| | A | B | C | D | E | F | G |
| *Return on assets* | | | | | | | |
| 1. Operating profit/Operating assets (%) | 22·9 | 20·7 | 16·6 | 13·1 | 10·3 | 9·8 | 4·2 |
| *Profit margin on sales and turnover of assets* | | | | | | | |
| 2. Operating profit/Sales (%) | 18·9 | 18·0 | 14·4 | 12·4 | 9·9 | 9·0 | 4·7 |
| 3. Sales/Operating assets (times per year) | 1·21 | 1·15 | 1·15 | 1·06 | 1·04 | 1·09 | 0·89 |
| *Departmental costs (as a percentage of sales)* | | | | | | | |
| 4. Production of sales | 66·0 | 67·5 | 71·0 | 74·0 | 76·2 | 77·1 | 81·7 |
| 5. Distribution and marketing costs | 8·2 | 7·9 | 7·4 | 5·9 | 6·0 | 6·5 | 5·6 |
| 6. General and administrative costs | 6·9 | 6·6 | 7·2 | 7·7 | 7·9 | 7·4 | 8·0 |
| *Production costs (as a percentage of sales value of production)* | | | | | | | |
| 7. Materials cost | 33·1 | 32·7 | 32·9 | 33·7 | 33·9 | 33·7 | 35·8 |
| 8. Works labour cost | 18·8 | 21·1 | 24·2 | 25·1 | 26·8 | 27·9 | 29·4 |
| 9. Other production costs | 14·1 | 13·7 | 13·9 | 15·2 | 15·5 | 15·5 | 16·5 |
| *General asset utilisation (£s per £1000 of sales)* | | | | | | | |
| 3a. Operating assets | 827 | 872 | 866 | 942 | 958 | 913 | 1127 |
| 10. Current assets | 448 | 469 | 477 | 529 | 534 | 479 | 654 |
| 11. Fixed assets | 379 | 403 | 389 | 413 | 424 | 434 | 473 |
| *Current asset utilisation (£s per £1000 of sales)* | | | | | | | |
| 12. Materials stock | 80 | 95 | 105 | 97 | 107 | 100 | 110 |
| 13. Work in progress | 71 | 76 | 87 | 105 | 147 | 130 | 205 |
| 14. Finished goods stock | 87 | 85 | 77 | 108 | 58 | 40 | 115 |
| 15. Debtors | 210 | 213 | 208 | 219 | 222 | 209 | 224 |
| *Fixed asset utilisation (£s per £1000 of sales)* | | | | | | | |
| 16. Land and buildings | 188 | 207 | 190 | 197 | 200 | 200 | 214 |
| 17. Plant and machinery | 185 | 191 | 194 | 213 | 221 | 230 | 256 |
| 18. Vehicles | 6 | 5 | 5 | 3 | 3 | 4 | 3 |

The firms whose ratios are shown in this table have used the same definitions of accounting terms and the same valuation principles, so that their ratios are comparable. They will, for instance, all have expressed the values of their plant and machinery in terms of current replacement values, not in terms of historical cost. This is important, because the figures which appear in balance sheets do not necessarily indicate the true relative value of the fixed assets employed as between one company and another, and can therefore not be taken for interfirm comparison purposes. Depreciated book values cannot be used because they do not take into account the effects of inflation, and because depreciation policies and practices will differ between companies. Income tax written down values are not suitable because they are also based on original cost, and cost allowances have varied from year to year.

Fig. 76.—*Interfirm Taxation comparison (7 companies in light engineering)*

(ratio 13) and your plant investment (ratio 17). Furthermore, you seem to have taken action to improve your debtors ratio (ratio 15).

As you will see from the comparative table, your stock investment (ratio 14), though higher than last year, is the lowest of the seven firms; furthermore, your marketing cost (ratio 5) is lower than those of the more successful firms (A to C). In fact, the apparently less favourable ratios of these firms reflect their policy of reducing production planning problems, through production in economic runs for stock of both finished products and certain components which are common to a fairly large number of their end products—and making a greater marketing effort in order to sell these stock products. Whilst, as you have stated, your company also manufactures certain components for stock, the percentage of finished stock sales achieved by you (*i.e.* 18% of your total sales) is considerable lower than the corresponding percentages of firms A to C. Thus, whilst as the background information provided by you indicates, your sales of products which are neither made for stock nor can be assembled from standard components represent 57% of total sales, the corresponding percentages of firms A to C are 21, 33 and 41 respectively.

These figures largely explain why your works labour cost, other production costs, work-in-progress and plant investment (ratios 8, 9, 13 and 17) compare unfavourably with those of firms A to C.

If you would work towards the policies of these firms you would be able to improve your capacity utilisation and could raise your level of sales with your existing production facilities. You will see from the pattern of ratios of firms A to C that the adverse impact on the primary ratio of higher finished stock investment and marketing ratios can be offset by the lower ratios related to production, which could be achieved with the policy adopted by these firms."

The report would also suggest ratio targets towards which firm F could work in the short term by changing either its finished stock policy, or its policy with regard to the standardisation of components, or both.

From the details given it should be apparent that the exercise is concerned with *major causes* of inefficiency presented in a manner suitable for top management.

This explanation is a very simplified version of what is involved in an interfirm comparison. Nevertheless, it should serve as a guide to the basic principles.

The work of the Centre extends beyond the purely interfirm comparison. It provides a consultancy service for trade associations, undertakes research, organises and runs seminars, and provides lecturers for conferences.

## DEALING WITH SPECIAL PROBLEMS

Interfirm comparisons are not limited to comprehensive assessments which cover all operations. Special problems may also be dealt with: there may be difficulties being experienced in, say, machine utilisation or in obtaining orders. A sub-pyramid of ratios may be prepared along the lines shown in Fig. 77. This is in two parts, one covering the use made of works employees and the other plant and machinery utilisation.

*"Instant Assessment" Service for*
*Light Engineering Manufacturers*

SUB-PYRAMID I

*Possible reasons for interfirm differences*
*in the use made of works employees*

\* Ratio 8b.  Sales value of production per works employee
Ratio 8c.  Value added as a percentage of sales value of production
Ratio 8d.  Value added per works employee

| Ratio 21f.  Plant and machinery (at new replacement value) per works employee (showing interfirm differences in the degree of mechanisation of participants). | Order In-flow factors (Information on the impact of different kinds of orders on the production efficiency; capacity utilisation, stock levels, marketing effort, etc., of different firms.) |
|---|---|

SUB-PYRAMID II

*Possible reasons for interfirm differences*
*in the use made of the investment in plant and machinery*

Ratio 21.  Investment in plant and machinery (depreciated current value) per £1000 of sales

| \* Ratio 21a.  Depreciated current value of plant and machinery as a percentage of its new replacement value (showing interfirm differences in the age of plant and machinery). | \* Ratio 21b.  Plant and machinery at new replacement value per £1000 of sales Ratio 21c.  Value added as a percentage of sales Ratio 21d.  Plant and machinery at new replacement value per £1000 of value added Ratio 21e.  Value added per £1000 invested in plant and machinery at new replacement value |
|---|---|

| Ratio 21f.  Plant and machinery (at new replacement value) per works employee (showing interfirm differences in the degree of mechanisation of participants). | Order In-flow factors (Information on the impact of different kinds of orders on the production efficiency; capacity utilisation, stock levels, marketing effort, etc., of different firms.) |
|---|---|

\* NOTE 1.  Ratios 8b and 21b would differ between firms because of differences in the material cost content of their sales value of production and their sales respectively.  To eliminate this influence ratios 8b and 21b are converted into ratios 8d, 21d and 21e, which show the value added (sales or sales value of production minus material costs) per works employee and per £1000 invested in plant and machinery.  The two items shown below ratios 8d and 21e refer to major factors likely to cause interfirm differences in these ratios.  The impact of these factors will be fully discussed in the reports on this I.F.C.
2.  Reasons for the selection of ratio 21a as an indication of comparative plant age will be given in the report on this I.F.C.

FIG. 77.—*Sub-pyramid of Ratios*

## EXTENT OF USE OF I.F.C.

The idea of interfirm comparisons through the Centre appears to be extending to a considerable number of industries in Great Britain.  In July, 1969, the centre had carried out comparisons in the following industries and trades:

Bedding manufacture
Biscuit manufacture
Blanket manufacture
Building and civil engineering
Cable trunking manufacture
Carpet manufacture
Central heating equipment manufacture
Chemical manufacture*
"C" Licence vehicle operating
Clothing manufacture
Cold rolled sections manufacture
Cotton spinning
Colour makers
Confectionery manufacture
Corn and agricultural merchants
Crane manufacture
Drop forgers
Electrical contractors
English woollen and worsted industry
Flexible packaging manufacture
Food manufacture
Forgemasters
Footwear manufacture
Fork lift manufacture
Furniture warehousing and removing
Gauge and tool manufacture
Glass container manufacture
Hand tool manufacture
Insurance brokers
Joinery manufacture
Leather dressing
Light engineering*
Machine tools manufacture
Mains cable manufacture
Malsters
Medium/heavy engineering*
Narrow fabric manufacture
Nylon hose dyeing
Painting and decorating contractors
Paper manufacture
Pharmaceutical manufacture

Pipework contractors
Plastics moulding
Publishing:
 (a) books
 (b) periodicals
Pump manufacture
Radio and electronic component manufacture
Rayon weaving
Road-haulage:
 (a) bulk haulage contractors
 (b) express carriers
Road haulage:
 RHA "Cost and Productivity Scheme" for general haulage; long-distance haulage; agricultural haulage and tipping vehicle operators
Rubber manufacture:
 (a) adhesives and solutions
 (b) conveyor belting
 (c) general rubber goods
 (d) hose
 (e) seals and "O" rings
 (f) mill-room productivity
 (g) extrusion productivity
Scientific instrument manufacture
Scottish woollen industry
Shirt manufacture
Soft drinks manufacture
Steel stockholders
Stockbrokers
Structural steelwork (fabrication and erection)
Synthetic resin manufacture
Tank and industrial plant contractors
Throwsters
Timber engineers
Timber importers
Timber merchants
Tufted carpet manufacture
Valve manufacture (industrial)
Warp knitting

## POSSIBLE ADVANTAGES OF I.F.C.

The advantages which accrue from using ratios are discussed in the previous chapter. At this point it is appropriate to outline the advantages of using the type of interfirm comparison outlined in this section.

* Covering various types and size groups.

One of the most important benefits is the fact that any weaknesses are revealed. Management is put on its guard and this can lead to remedial action. A corollary of this benefit is the indication of the *trend* of sales, profit, or costs of an industry or trade as shown by the ratios. If all firms are suffering from a falling off in sales then this malady will show itself in the sales *to* assets employed ratio. Accordingly, the single firm, comparing its own ratios with the ratios for the group will see that there is a general reduction in sales.

Ratios are carefully selected by the Centre so that the management concerned is given the most significant facts. All that is left for this management is the study of the ratios and the necessary action. There is no question of having to spend time on deciding—in many cases a very unreliable fashion—whether or not the firm is doing better in or worse than other firms. This fact is made known through the ratios; uncertainty can be replaced by positive steps to improve efficiency.

The experience of the Centre for Interfirm Comparison is at the disposal of those participating in the comparisons. This knowledge can be invaluable. A variation between two ratios is of use only when its significance is understood. Statistics and experience possessed by the centre are used to interpret results. Thus, for example, the Centre has found that there is a wide range of results as between different firms even in the same industry.

A further advantage comes from the voluntary basis on which the comparisons are made. The businesses give information willingly, knowing that this remains confidential. There is no question of having to rely on published profit and loss accounts and balance sheets. Instead, questionnaires are drafted in such a manner that data accumulated is of a standardised nature with a clear understanding of definitions. From this combination of mutual trust and clearness of definition should come greater accuracy in results and these results should be capable of being compared. As every student of statistical method knows, like must be compared with like; and this is an essential requirement for inter-firm comparisons.

Recognition by the Centre that capital employed should be in terms of current replacement costs brings home to management the necessity of thinking in terms of maintaining capital intact in real terms. This principle is vital to the long-term earning power of a business; if assets are not replaced with those of equivalent earning capacity then eventually profit must suffer.*

The Centre stresses the need to involve senior managers. Starting at the top ensures that there is the necessary backing from those who are concerned with the broad issues of planning and control. The reasons for this approach are as follows:

---

* Replacement Value Accounting is covered in Chapter 27.

"(a) I.F.C. provides a stimulus to self-criticism which, if it starts at the top, will have the strongest impact on the development of the firm concerned;

(b) top management can take a bird's eye view of the firm; it is therefore in the best position to decide on remedial action and to see to its implementation;

(c) top management is in the best position to decide whether the firm concerned should take part in an I.F.C."

The possible benefits arising from interfirm comparisons are outlined above. These can be negated by misuse of the ratios. As indicated, facts compared must be so similar in nature that their comparison can be said to be of significance. Thus, for example, very misleading results may be obtained by comparing the ratios relating to bedding manufacture with those of building and civil engineering. Only by understanding what the ratios represent and using them in a proper manner can any significance be attached to comparisons. The discussion of ratios in the previous chapter is very pertinent to this section.

## INTERFIRM COMPARISONS IN THE PRINTING INDUSTRY *

The printing industry has played a leading part in the establishment of uniform costing in Great Britain by being the first to adopt a uniform costing system. This was introduced in 1913 and has been generally accepted in that industry for many years. Naturally, improvements and modifications have been made since its first appearance.

In 1957 a scheme of interfirm comparisons was introduced, with the title of "Ratios for Management." This scheme also adopts the pyramid structure of ratios developed by the Centre for Interfirm Comparisons, with the return on capital employed ratio as the principal ratio. Due recognition is given to the fact that firms have different characteristics by dividing the industry into groups each having its own ratios. The division is based upon the following:

(1) activity carried on, e.g. general printers, book printers, newspaper houses; and

(2) size determined by number of employees.

The second is a subdivision of the first. By dividing into groups in this way the results become much more realistic and meaningful. The firms know that the ratios being compared are *capable* of being compared.

Actual figures of profit or other details are not issued to members, so there is no betraying of confidences. At all times the emphasis is on showing the average results so that a single firm can make a comparison

* Due acknowledgment is made to the assistance given by H. KENDALL, Head of Economics Division, British Federation of Master Printers, from whom full details are available.

to see whether or not its own ratios are equal, better, or worse than the average for its own particular group. For each ratio the median and upper and lower quartiles are computed, this method having the advantage of eliminating any extreme items which would invalidate a result when the normal arithmetical average is used.

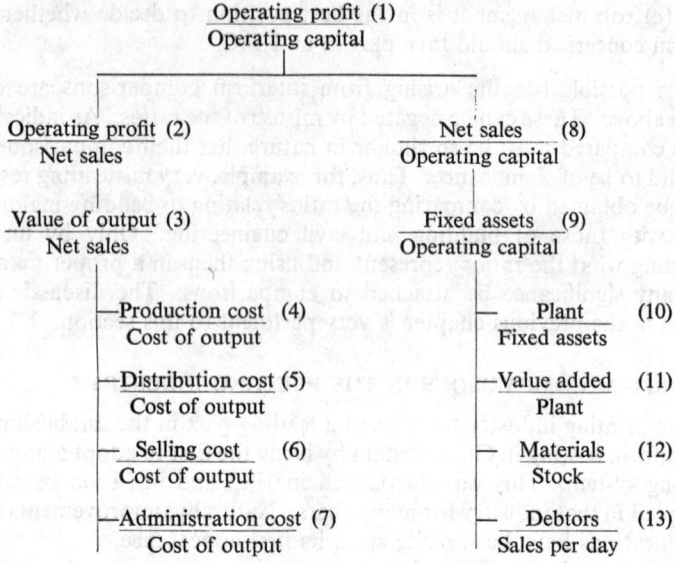

$$\frac{\text{Operating profit}}{\text{Operating capital}} \quad (1)$$

$$\frac{\text{Operating profit}}{\text{Net sales}} \quad (2) \qquad\qquad \frac{\text{Net sales}}{\text{Operating capital}} \quad (8)$$

$$\frac{\text{Value of output}}{\text{Net sales}} \quad (3) \qquad\qquad \frac{\text{Fixed assets}}{\text{Operating capital}} \quad (9)$$

$$\frac{\text{Production cost}}{\text{Cost of output}} \quad (4) \qquad\qquad \frac{\text{Plant}}{\text{Fixed assets}} \quad (10)$$

$$\frac{\text{Distribution cost}}{\text{Cost of output}} \quad (5) \qquad\qquad \frac{\text{Value added}}{\text{Plant}} \quad (11)$$

$$\frac{\text{Selling cost}}{\text{Cost of output}} \quad (6) \qquad\qquad \frac{\text{Materials}}{\text{Stock}} \quad (12)$$

$$\frac{\text{Administration cost}}{\text{Cost of output}} \quad (7) \qquad\qquad \frac{\text{Debtors}}{\text{Sales per day}} \quad (13)$$

FIG. 78.—*Principal ratios used*

## The Ratios Used

The ratios used in the scheme are divided into:

1. Primary Ratios (illustrated in Fig. 78).
2. Secondary Ratios.

Both these are listed below:

| RATIOS | UNIT EMPLOYED | RATIOS | UNIT EMPLOYED |
|---|---|---|---|
| 1. $\dfrac{\text{Operating profit}}{\text{Operating capital}}$ | per cent. | 4. $\dfrac{\text{Production cost (gross)}}{\text{Cost of output}}$ | per cent. |
| *Operating Costs* | | 5. $\dfrac{\text{Distribution cost}}{\text{Cost of output}}$ | per cent. |
| 2. $\dfrac{\text{Operating profit}}{\text{Net sales}}$ | per cent. | 6. $\dfrac{\text{Selling cost}}{\text{Cost of output}}$ | per cent. |
| 3. $\dfrac{\text{Value of output}}{\text{Net sales}}$ | per cent. | 7. $\dfrac{\text{Administration cost}}{\text{Cost of output}}$ | per cent. |

| RATIOS | UNIT EMPLOYED |
|---|---|
| *Use of Capital* | |
| 8. $\dfrac{\text{Net sales}}{\text{Operating capital}}$ | per cent. |
| 9. $\dfrac{\text{Fixed assets}}{\text{Operating capital}}$ | per cent. |
| 10. $\dfrac{\text{Plant}}{\text{Fixed assets}}$ | per cent. |
| 11. $\dfrac{\text{Value added}}{\text{Plant}}$ | per cent. |
| 12. $\dfrac{\text{Materials}}{\text{Stock}}$ | Times per year |
| 13. $\dfrac{\text{Debtors}}{\text{Sales per day}}$ | Days credit |
| *Secondary Ratios* | |
| 14. $\dfrac{\text{Value added}}{\text{Factory employees}}$ | £ per employee |
| 15. $\dfrac{\text{Value added}}{\text{Factory wages}}$ | per £ |
| 16. $\dfrac{\text{Production cost (net)}}{\text{Cost of output}}$ | per cent. |
| 17. $\dfrac{\text{Factory wages}}{\text{Production cost (net)}}$ | per cent. |
| 18. $\dfrac{\text{Factory management salaries}}{\text{Production cost (net)}}$ | per cent. |
| 19. $\dfrac{\text{Depreciation}}{\text{Production cost (net)}}$ | per cent. |
| 20. $\dfrac{\text{Other factory expenses}}{\text{Production cost (net)}}$ | per cent. |

| | RATIOS | UNIT EMPLOYED |
|---|---|---|
| 21. | $\dfrac{\text{Factory wages}}{\text{Factory employees}}$ | £ per capita |
| 22. | $\dfrac{\text{Male factory employees}}{\text{Factory employees}}$ | per cent. |
| 23. | $\dfrac{\text{Factory management salaries}}{\text{Factory management staff}}$ | £ per capita |
| 24. | $\dfrac{\text{Plant}}{\text{Factory employees}}$ | £ per employee |
| 25. | $\dfrac{\text{Sales staff remuneration}}{\text{Sales staff}}$ | £ per capita |
| 26. | $\dfrac{\text{Administration expenses}}{\text{Administration cost}}$ | per cent. |
| 27. | $\dfrac{\text{General management salaries}}{\text{Administration cost}}$ | per cent. |
| 28. | $\dfrac{\text{Administrative staff salaries}}{\text{Administration cost}}$ | per cent. |
| 29. | $\dfrac{\text{Administration cost}}{\text{Printing jobs}}$ | £ per job |
| 30. | $\dfrac{\text{General management salaries}}{\text{General management staff}}$ | £ per capita |
| 31. | $\dfrac{\text{Administrative staff salaries}}{\text{Administrative staff}}$ | £ per capita |
| 32. | $\dfrac{\text{Male administrative staff}}{\text{Administrative staff}}$ | per cent. |

A very brief explanation of some of the ratios is given below:

*Return on Capital*

Ratio 1—the return on capital employed—is the ratio which will quickly give a reliable indication of the overall success of a business. It is the main ratio for general management.

Since this ratio is a comparison of profit earned with the value of capital used whilst trading, it follows that it will be governed by two factors:

(a) *The level of operating costs* shown by ratios 2, 3, 4, 5, 6 and 7, and

(b) *The use of capital* shown by ratios 8, 9, 10, 11, 12, and 13.

There is, of course, a certain degree of inter-relation between these two aspects, since (because of depreciation charges, etc.) a relatively poor use of the capital invested in plant and machinery will certainly have an adverse effect on operating costs in relation to the sales volume achieved.

### The Use of Capital

The relationship of sales to capital employed will reveal how effectively is the use made of capital. Ratio 8 shows how many times capital has been turned into sales.

*Fixed Assets.* Capital may be broken down into two broad categories—fixed assets and current assets—and different considerations will apply to their use. Ratio 9 will indicate whether there is a greater proportion of capital invested in fixed assets than the average firm.

*Current Assets.* Ratios 12 and 13 are designed to show whether there is more capital invested in current assets than may be necessary.

### Operating Costs

Ratio 2 expresses profit as a percentage of sales. The result of this ratio can be misleading if there is a substantial difference in the opening and closing work-in-progress values, therefore an indication of this is given at ratio 3.

If ratio 2 is lower than average it can be an indication that operating costs are unduly high. At ratios 4 to 7 operating costs are broken down into four broad headings and each part is expressed as a percentage of total cost. Materials and other direct charges are included at this stage. The four headings are: Production Cost (ratio 4); Distribution Cost (ratio 5); Selling Cost (ratio 6); Administration Cost (ratio 7).

*Production Costs.* A broad indication of the part played by production costs is to be found at ratio 4 and some supporting figures are given at ratios 14 to 24.

*Distribution Cost.* A broad indication only of this aspect of cost is given at ratio 5, since more detailed reliable ratios related to distribution cost would necessitate some analysis and a more complicated questionnaire.

*Selling Cost* is shown broadly at ratio 6 with an indication of earnings per head of sales staff at ratio 25. Lower than average figures for ratio 6 are seldom indicated in the results of the more successful firms, as a poor selling effort may easily lead to under-utilisation of facilities.

*Administration Cost.* Administration costs are broadly indicated at ratio 7 and supporting figures can be found at ratios 26 to 32. Once again when interpreting these figures it should be remembered that the results of the more successful firms seldom indicate lower than average administration costs. The administration cost per job is indicated at ratio 29.

At ratios 26 to 28 administration cost is broken down into three broad parts: Administration Expenses (ratio 26); General Management Salaries (ratio 27); Administrative Staff Salaries (ratio 28).

At ratio 30 General Management salaries are shown per head of General Management Staff and similarly Administrative Staff Salaries are shown per head of Administrative Staff at ratio 31. The proportion of male staff to the total is indicated at ratio 32.

*General.* One aspect that may be the cause of unsatisfactory trading results, but which cannot be indicated clearly in ratios of this nature, except by elimination, is that of unrealistic selling prices for particular sections of turnover. However, a sound costing system, incorporating an analysis of sales, will clearly reveal such a state of affairs.

## EXAMINATION QUESTIONS

1. A company with a number of works in different parts of the country each making similar products finds that orders are falling off to a serious extent. It appears to be inevitable that one of the works will have to close down. Budgetary control and standard costing are in use at each works. The standard cost of any one product is different at each of the works.

Set out the points you would consider in making your recommendation as to which works should be closed. *(I.C.W.A.)*

2. You have undertaken an investigation on behalf of a trade association in order to establish the possibility of recommending uniform costing methods for the trade, and you are satisfied that such methods are practicable. You are next called upon to write a uniform costing manual for circulation to members of the association.

Draft a schedule of main and sub-headings for the manual, and indicate briefly the points to be covered under each heading. *(I.C.W.A.)*

3. Explain the objectives of uniform costing and outline the main causes of differences in costs between undertakings within the same industry.

*(I.C.W.A.)*

4. State the essential principles of a uniform costing system and the advantages which may be derived therefrom, applied:

   (*a*) to a large undertaking controlling subsidiaries;
   (*b*) to a whole industry.

*(I.C.W.A.)*

5. What matters would you expect to find dealt with in a manual issued to members of an association of manufacturers in connection with a system of uniform costing to be adopted by its members? *(I.C.A.)*

6. "Some progressive businesses would like to have the advantages of uniform cost accounting, and are prepared to exchange costs with other businesses with the object of ascertaining the best production and commercial methods." (*Uniform Cost Accounting, etc., I.C.W.A.*, paragraph 8.)

What are "the advantages of uniform cost accounting"?

What type of cost information could be exchanged, and how could this best be done without the disclosure of confidential information? *(I.C.W.A.)*

7. The following figures were taken from the annual accounts of two electricity supply boards working on uniform costing methods:

Meter reading, billing and collection costs:

| Salaries and wages of: | Board A (£000s) | Board B (£000s) |
|---|---|---|
| Meter readers ... ... ... | 150 | 240 |
| Billing and collection staff ... | 300 | 480 |
| Transport and travelling ... ... | 30 | 40 |
| Collection agency charges ... ... | — | 20 |
| Bad debts ... ... ... ... | 10 | 10 |
| General charges ... ... ... | 100 | 200 |
| Miscellaneous ... ... ... ... | 10 | 10 |
| | 600 | 1,000 |
| Units sold (millions) ... ... ... | 2,880 | 9,600 |
| Number of consumers (thousands) ... | 800 | 1,600 |
| Sales of electricity (millions) ... ... | £18 | £50 |
| Size of area (square miles) ... ... | 4,000 | 4,000 |

Prepare a comparative cost statement using suitable units of cost. Brief notes should be added, commenting on likely causes for major differences in unit costs so disclosed.

(I.C.W.A.)

8. L. Engineering Co. Ltd. keep their financial accounts separate from their cost accounts. In the cost ledger on 1st July, 1966, the balances were as follows:

| | £ |
|---|---|
| Stores ledger control ... ... ... ... ... ... | 10,000 |
| Work-in-progress control ... ... ... ... ... | 15,500 |
| Finished stock control ... ... ... ... ... | 3,500 |
| Cost ledger control ... ... ... ... ... ... | 29,000 |

Transactions for the year ended 30th June, 1967 were:

| | £ | £ |
|---|---|---|
| Purchase of raw materials ... ... ... ... ... | | 55,000 |
| Wages—direct ... ... ... ... ... | 79,000 | |
| indirect ... ... ... ... ... | 21,000 | |
| | | 100,000 |
| Factory overhead expenses: incurred ... ... ... | | 36,000 |
| absorbed ... ... ... | | 55,000 |
| Administration overhead expenses: incurred ... ... | | 12,500 |
| absorbed ... ... | | 12,400 |
| Selling overhead expenses: incurred ... ... ... | | 7,500 |
| absorbed ... ... ... | | 7,600 |
| Materials issued to production ... ... ... ... | | 57,500 |
| Sales ... ... ... ... ... ... ... | | 265,000 |
| Work-in-progress: value at 30th June, 1967 ... ... | | 13,500 |
| Finished stock: value at 30th June, 1967 ... ... ... | | 4,000 |

It is established that the following items have been recorded in the financial accounts only:

|  | £ |
|---|---|
| Debenture interest paid ... ... ... | 8,000 |
| Loss on sale of investment ... ... | 2,500 |
| Dividends received ... ... ... | 3,000 |

The value of stocks and work-in-progress in the company's balance sheets were as follows:

|  | £ |
|---|---|
| As at 30th June: 1966 ... ... ... | 31,000 |
| 1967 ... ... ... | 24,500 |

You are required to:

(a) show the accounts in the cost ledger for the year ended 30th June, 1967;

(b) prepare a statement reconciling the profit disclosed by the cost accounts with the profit prior to taxation shown in the financial accounts.

(*I.C.W.A.*)

Q

# Chapter 18

# CAPITAL EXPENDITURE

## *INTRODUCTION*

The forecasting and budgeting of capital expenditure is a vital part of policy making, management, and Budgetary Control. Fixed assets have to be purchased in advance of production. The longer the serviceable life of assets the greater the risk involved.

Capital expenditure forecasting is not an intermittent or sporadic function which is dealt with from time to time and then forgotten until a problem recurs. It is essentially a long-term function. A keen watchfulness and a positive awareness of capital expenditure needs is essential at all times. The progressive business grows; it expands its fixed assets and other means of increasing the volume and improving the quality of the products made. Innovation is often the means of continuing to make maximum profits. Investment in fixed assets, both for replacements and new projects, goes hand-in-hand with progress.

With the advent of automation the problem becomes more urgent. The capital investment involved is very large. Unless the plant and machinery can be utilised fully the investment is a doubtful proposition. Only by careful analysis of each project in terms of possible annual profit will a sound decision be possible. Some of the principal methods used for assessing the profitability of each project are explained below.

## *IMPORTANCE OF CAPITAL EXPENDITURE FORECAST*

Some of the reasons for the capital expenditure forecast are summarised below. These may not be present at all times; nor is the list exhaustive. However, they should indicate the importance of the forecast:

1. Shows the possibility of expanding the production facilities to cover additional sales shown in the sales forecast.

2. Allows alternative forms of assets to be considered as replacements for assets which are wearing out or are in danger of becoming obsolete.

The criterion generally taken is the estimated profitability of each project.* This will involve consideration of capital and running costs, a matter which is covered later.

3. Facilitates the making of long-term plans and assists in the formulation of general policy.

* There are exceptions, *e.g.* welfare projects or pure research projects.

The cost of fixed assets, including running and maintenance costs, has to be compared with expected revenues. An adequate return on capital employed will normally be expected on all projects undertaken.

4. Enables the cash forecast to be completed.

Obviously there will be other cash commitments and these too will have to be known to be able to complete the cash forecast.

5. Assists in formulating a sound depreciation and asset replacement policy.

6. May be useful when considering methods of reducing costs. A cost reduction campaign may necessitate the consideration of purchasing more up-to-date equipment.

7. The feasibility of replacing manual work by machinery may be seen from the capital forecast.

8. The capital cost of improving working conditions or safety can be obtained through capital expenditure forecasting.

These purposes are not fulfilled by *all* capital expenditure forecasts. An appreciation of the two basic types of forecast is essential to understand why this is the case. The long-term forecast is one which covers a number of years up to five years, or even longer. The longer the period involved the more uncertain is the likelihood that the forecast will be put into operation in the precise form envisaged at the present time. Nevertheless, long-term forecasts are essential. A business should progress in a systematic manner. The capital expenditure forecast is a reflection of these long-term plans. Possible developments in new products or services require a definite policy to be followed.

The short-term forecast interprets that part of the long-term policy which is being considered for inclusion in the overall budget plan for the next budget period. Projects included in this forecast are influenced by urgency and financial resources. If the former is very pressing then it will usually mean that the finance will have to be found. Clearly though, if the long-term forecast had been kept under constant review some provision would have been made to make sure that the necessary cash could be made available without great difficulty. In some circumstances, of course, the availability of surplus cash may *require* that management considers investing in some profitable venture rather than letting it remain idle.

The urgency of the need for certain fixed assets may arise from one or a combination of a number of factors. The development of new products, the expansion of the output of existing products, the need to reduce costs, or fight competition, or a requirement on safety are possible examples.

When considering the cash forecast, the possibility of cost reduction or asset replacement or business expansion, within the next budget period, the short-term capital expenditure forecast will be the appropriate forecast. Factors which affect long-term planning should be considered with the long-term forecast in mind.

## CAPITAL EXPENDITURE DECISIONS

The methods used for assessing the profitability of capital projects have received a good deal of attention in recent years both in textbooks and in accountancy journals. Unfortunately there appears to be no very strong evidence in this country that the most suitable methods are used. Indeed, the intuitive approach to problems seems to be very common. Since a man's judgment and opinions can be influenced to a great extent by the information in his possession it follows that the more facts that are available on a particular project the more accurate is likely to be the decision made, provided that there are not so many facts that there is confusion. Put another way, a manager's decision is likely to be only as good as the information he has available for comparing alternative courses of action. Intuition and judgment cannot be replaced by the collection of facts, but there is no doubt that the decision-making mechanism is likely to be strengthened materially by the systematic collection and analysis of relevant data.

Below are listed the principal methods used for assessing the profitability of each capital expenditure project. Clearly, not all projects may be capable of being assessed in terms of profitability; as noticed earlier, pure research and welfare projects may not have to be justified in this way. The planning and laying out of beautiful gardens or playing fields in the grounds of a factory or works may also be difficult to justify in terms of profit. Many of these general, "unessential" projects may, of course, lead to better labour relations and, therefore, to an improvement in profit earning. However, actually showing that such projects *are* profitable would be extremely difficult and probably impossible.

Even on the capital expenditure projects which are expected to improve the volume of output or result in some other tangible benefit, not one of the methods explained below can give absolute accuracy. Each has its own peculiar advantages and disadvantages. The one likely to give the best results should be the one selected. Study of the theoretical principles will assist in selecting the best method. Practical experience will show what modifications or adjustments are necessary in order to employ the method to meet the needs of the particular business.

**METHODS EMPLOYED**

The principal methods employed for ascertaining the profitability of each project are as follows:

1. Pay-back Method.
2. Return on Investment Method.
3. Present-value Return on Investment Method.
4. Return on Total Capital Employed.

This method approaches the problem by ensuring that the total capital employed earns an adequate return. Additional assets purchased should increase, or at least keep constant, the percentage rate of return on total capital employed. Chapter 15 deals with this matter.

5. Minimum Total Cost or Unit Cost.

All these methods can be used for comparing alternative investments. For all methods, but especially those using present-value techniques, it is better to use the expected cash flow (*i.e.* cash to be received or paid) rather than profit or gain computed by conventional accounting.

## Pay-back Method

The "pay-back method" is concerned with equating the revenue and costs relating to a capital expenditure project over a period of time. Put another way the method attempts to determine the number of years in which the investment is expected to pay for itself. If a machine is to cost £5000 and extra revenue is expected to amount to £1000 the first year, £2000 the second year, and £2000 in the third year then the pay-back period is three years.

If a machine can be treated in isolation from other machines then the yearly sales value of the products from the machine *less* any running and maintenance costs shows the annual profit. A number of years are taken to calculate the pay-back period.

In practice a fixed asset cannot usually be treated as a separate entity. The introduction of a new machine often introduces problems. It may displace an older machine. There may have to be a rearrangement of duties between workers. Quite likely some costs may be reduced. Therefore, both the costs incurred and the costs saved will have to be taken into account.

When comparing alternative investments the one which pays for itself first is the one selected.

*Advantages and Limitations.* The pay-back method is simple to understand and operate. Furthermore, it shows how quickly the investment will be recovered. This can be very important for a company short of cash. Normally, only investments with a short pay-back period are considered. No doubt the convention which lays down this rule arises from the fact that there is great difficulty in forecasting the sales, costs, and serviceable life of a fixed asset for any period in excess of, say, five years. In an industry which is experiencing rapid technological development the limited pay-back period offers some protection from the danger of obsolescence. There is a quick recovery of the cash invested.

Although the method has many followers it also has many critics. Some accountants have rightly pointed out that the true profitability of investments cannot be determined merely by considering the pay-back period. Indeed, in that period only the recovery of costs is considered. The profit comes after all costs have been recovered and not before. Therefore, much better results would be obtained by considering the full serviceable life of each asset: only then can the total, expected profit be ascertained. A further possible disadvantage is the fact that limiting the investments to those with a short pay-back period (*e.g.* up to five years) may mean overlooking many profitable investments. A machine may have a serviceable life of twenty years and, over that life, may be quite profitable. However, if the pay-back period extends beyond that laid down by policy this means automatic exclusion from being considered. A serious limitation is the ignoring of the time factor. Sums of money received at different times in the *future* have to be discounted to *present* value. Otherwise no true comparison of different investments can be made. The "present value return method", discussed below, overcomes this obvious weakness of the pay-back method. A further criticism sometimes advanced against the pay-back method is that too much importance is attached to the quick recovery of cash. Investment in fixed assets must necessarily be a lengthy process. The artificial attempt to "shorten the period" may be useful when forecasting cash flows, but it should be remembered that the chief concern is with profitability. Accordingly, this should be the factor to determine the most suitable method.

A practical illustration of the method is shown later in this chapter.

### Return on Investment Method

This method considers the rate of return likely to be obtained from the investment. When comparing alternative courses of action the investment which shows the highest return is the one normally selected.

The rate of return may be expressed as a *percentage* of the average amount of the investment. A simple method of obtaining the "average amount" is to divide the total investment by two. Thus if the proposed investment is £10,000 then the average investment over the entire life, considering depreciation, is taken to be £5000. This assumes that the amount recovered in the form of depreciation will be used to purchase materials or other supplies or alternatively will be invested internally or externally; outside the business. Not all accountants agree with the view that half the investment should be taken for measuring the expected rate of return. When the investment is made the total amount has to be spent; this is the total sacrifice to be made. Accordingly, it can be argued that the total investment involved should be the amount taken.

Care has to be taken when considering "rate of return," to make sure that the precise rate being calculated is understood. The term may refer to total return obtained; *e.g.* in the illustration given below Machine X is shown to result in a £1 return for each £1 invested. Alternatively, "rate of return" may refer to "net return"; *i.e.* the net *profit* actually obtained. For Machine X in the example given there is no net return: each £1 results in £1 with no surplus for the purpose of comparison. Which definition is used does not really matter. However, it is very important to understand which definition *is* being used. Otherwise *actual* profitability will not be understood.

Other measures are the amount obtained per pound sterling invested and the *average* amount obtained each year per pound sterling invested. The former method involves dividing the total profit expected by the total investment. The latter—the average yearly calculation—involves finding the average annual profit and then dividing that by the total investment. A simple illustration is shown below.

ILLUSTRATION

A company is considering the purchase of a new machine. There are two machines which will do the work, the details of which are as follows:

|  | Year | Machine X | Machine Y |
|---|---|---|---|
| Capital Cost | | £20,000 | £24,000 |
| Earnings | 1 | £10,000 | £8,000 |
| (or net cash flow) | 2 | £10,000 | £8,000 |
| | 3 | Nil | £20,000 |

Calculate the rate of return (*a*) per £1 invested and (*b*) per £1 invested on an average annual basis.

SUGGESTED APPROACH

(*a*) *Per £1 Invested*

|  | Machine X | Machine Y |
|---|---|---|
| Earnings | £20,000 | £36,000 |
| Investment | £20,000 | £24,000 |
| Rate of Return per £1 Invested | £1 | £1·5 |

(*b*) *Per £1 on Annual Basis*

|  | Machine X | Machine Y |
|---|---|---|
| Earnings | £20,000 | £36,000 |
| Average Annual Profit | £10,000 | £12,000 |
| Investment | £20,000 | £24,000 |
| Rate of Return | £0·5 | £0·5 |

From the examples given it will be evident that there are many weaknesses in both methods of expressing the rate of return per pound sterling. The straightforward rate per pound invested shows the clear superiority of Machine Y and this result would have been shown even if the full £36,000 had been forthcoming in the third or even later years. In other words, the timing of the receipts is ignored—money to be received earlier is more valuable, yet the method ignores this fact completely. The second rate of return (the average method) ranks both machines as being equal, yet it is quite clear they are not equal. A much better result would have been obtained if the earning periods had been the same; *i.e.* both three years. This could be overcome to some extent by dividing the £20,000 for Machine X by 3 instead of 2. This would then give an average annual profit of £6666⅔ and a rate of return of £0·33 per annum. Even when this modified procedure is followed the timing of the receipts is not taken into account and for this reason the method is not to be recommended.

The percentage rate of return is probably the most satisfactory method, but even this has the definite weakness of ignoring the fact that receipts occur at different time intervals. If the earnings from the different investments do accrue at the same time then obviously this method can be used. If the timings are different then the present-value return method is much better. This is covered in the next section.

A further problem which may arise is connected with calculating a reasonable rate of return on investments. Some companies stipulate a minimum rate. Investments which do not show this rate are automatically excluded from consideration. The general procedures and pertinent considerations relating to determination of a reasonable rate of interest are most relevant to the profitable employment of capital, a topic which is considered in Chapter 15.

*Present-value Return on Investment Method\**

A person faced with the choice of having £100 now or in one year's time would normally elect to have it now. If he was offered £100 now, but £110 in a year then he may be tempted to wait for the £110, for quite clearly, unless the risk involved in waiting is very great, the £100 he is foregoing is going to earn him 10% which is quite a reasonable return.

This simple example should illustrate the present value concept of money. The £100 due in one year is not worth as much as £100 *now*. In fact if 10% is taken to be a normal rate of return for a particular type of investment the £100 due in one year is at present worth only £90·91. If it is necessary to wait two years for the £100, then taking compound interest at 10% the present value is £82·64.

When considering different investments, with earning patterns which are not the same, it should be clear that only by discounting the earnings to present values can any valid comparisons be made. The timing of the receipts is thus taken into consideration. Similarly, when costs are incurred at different intervals they too can be converted into present values.

The object of all the methods being described is to arrive at the most profitable investment. The present-value return method is no exception. When this method is used there are two ways of tackling the problem of calculating profitability. These may be summarised as follows:

1. Trial and Error Yield Method.     2. Net Gain Method.

\* Terminology differs! The Trial and Error Method is often referred to as the "Discounted Cash Flow Method," "Yield Method," or "Internal Rate of Return Method." The Net Gain Method is also known as the "Present Value Method." Sometimes *all* methods are simply termed "DCF methods," this being a collective description.

In both cases the cost of the investment and the expected receipts have to be considered. As already mentioned earlier in the chapter, the expected *cash* payments and receipts, not the costs incurred and sales values as shown by the accounts, should be the figures taken. Clearly if a sale is expected to be made in one year, but is not expected to be paid for until the next, then it cannot be said that cash is to be received in the first year. The same applies to materials and services purchased. Fortunately in many businesses the regularity in each year of sales, stocks, and costs is such that costs and receipts tend to approximate to cash flows. When wide variations do occur so that the cash flows are different then adjustments of sales and costs will be necessary.

A problem which must inevitably arise is what points of time are to be used for assessing the present values. Cash from sales flows throughout a year. Similarly the costs incurred are paid for throughout a particular year. Therefore the question which must be answered is which date (or dates) can be taken for calculating present values. If six-monthly intervals are taken then a different result would be obtained from when yearly intervals were taken. Again, fortunately, a simplified approach can be taken, the cash being assumed to be received at the end of each year. The net cash flow is, therefore, sales *minus* costs bearing in mind the fact that the sales and costs should relate to cash to be received and to be paid. Adjustments may also have to be made to cover the effects of corporation tax, interest, and any special working capital changes brought about by the investment.

The functioning of the two different ways is described below.

*Trial and Error Yield Method.* As the name suggests the object is to find the expected yield from the investment. This procedure involves a number of stages which may be summarised as follows:

1. List the annual sales and costs other than depreciation and, deducting the latter from the former, obtain the net cash flow.

2. Obtain the capital cost. Often this will already be at present value because the cash is spent *now*.

3. Calculate the present value of the net cash flow by using an appropriate rate of interest. This rate is found by trial and error from present-value tables. The object is to make the cash flow equal to the capital cost.

4. Carry out this procedure for each project being considered and then rank the projects in order of preference.

A simplified example now follows.

EXAMPLE: TRIAL AND ERROR YIELD METHOD

A company is considering the purchase of a machine. The following data are available for two suitable machines.

|  | Machine X | Machine Y |
|---|---|---|
| Capital Cost | £20,000 | £24,000 |
| Net Cash Flow: Year 1 | £10,000 | £8,000 |
| 2 | £10,000 | £8,000 |
| 3 | Nil | £20,000 |

You are required to calculate the yield for each machine.

*Suggested Approach*

| | Machine X | | | Machine Y | | |
|---|---|---|---|---|---|---|
| | Cash Flow | Conversion Factor | Present Value of Cash | Cash Flow | Conversion Factor | Present Value |
| | £ | £ | £ | £ | £ | £ |
| Net Cash Flow Year 1 | 10,000 | | | 8,000 | 0·8333 | 6,666 |
| 2 | 10,000 | No differ- | | 8,000 | 0·6944 | 5,555 |
| 3 | — | ence between cash flow and capital cost | | 20,000 | 0·5787 | 11,574 |
| Capital Cost | 20,000 | | | 24,000 | | 23,795 |

| Rate of Return = 0% (There is actually a net loss) | Rate of Return = Approximately 20% |
|---|---|

This method shows quite clearly that Machine Y is a much better investment than X. The rate of return method (the second method discussed)
purported to show that Machine X investment would result in a definite
return. In actual fact the investment cost is only just covered and when the
receipts are discounted to present values (using *any* reasonable rate of
interest) a loss is incurred.

For Machine X there is no need to convert the cash flow to present value
because it is quite obvious that the former is smaller than the latter.

The rate of interest of 20% for Machine Y is found by referring to interest
tables. At this stage the trial and error procedure has to be adopted. A good
plan is to use the conversion factor for each year at stages of 10%. The
approximate point on the scale of interest rates can be located quickly and
then the actual rate can be found. The reader is advised to experiment with
the tables shown on pages 474–476 (Figs. 79–81).

When a number of alternatives are available the same procedure is followed.
This will allow a table showing the relative profitability of all projects.
Generally speaking the investment with the highest return is the one selected.

*Net Gain Method.* The net gain method attempts to arrive at the
difference between the present value of receipts and payments. As with
the previous method the *cash* flows should be taken.

One of the difficulties of this method is the selection of an appropriate rate of interest. One rate will give different results from another. The principal object should be to assess a return which reflects what can be expected from putting the money in alternative investments. This is a matter which is discussed later.

EXAMPLE: NET GAIN METHOD

Taking the problem shown in the previous section the suggested approach is as shown below.

*Net Gain Schedule*

|  | Machine X £ | Machine Y £ |
|---|---|---|
| Capital Cost (present value equals original cost) | 20,000 | 24,000 |
| Cash Flow (present value converted by using 10% discount) | 17,355 | 28,910 |
|  | £2,645 (loss) | £4,910 (gain) |

Machine Y is clearly the more profitable investment. In fact, Machine X incurs a loss.

*Expressing the Return as a Percentage*

The return on the investment may be expressed as a percentage of the amount invested by the following formula:

$$\frac{\text{Average Annual Net Profit}^* \times 100}{\text{Average Investment}^\dagger}$$

This may be used with the present value methods or the ordinary rate on investment methods which do not convert cash flow (receipts) to present values. Obviously the concern is with an average percentage which though suffering from the limitations of all averages should give a very good guide to profitability.

The fact that the average investment is obtained by dividing the total investment by two has already been noted.

ILLUSTRATION OF THE PRINCIPLE

Taking the figures for Machine Y used in the previous example the percentage rate of return (net profit) is as follows:

Unadjusted Figures: $\dfrac{£4,000}{£12,000} \times \dfrac{100}{1} = 33\%$ (approx.)

Figure adjusted to Present Values: (10% discount) $\dfrac{£3,005}{£12,000} \times \dfrac{100}{1} = 25\%$ (approx.)

* Or Net Cash Flow.
† Or Total investment. (See page 468.)

| n | 1% | 2% | 3% | 4% | 5% | 6% | 7% | 8% |
|---|---|---|---|---|---|---|---|---|
| 1 | 0·9901 | 0·9804 | 0·9709 | 0·9615 | 0·9524 | 0·9434 | 0·9346 | 0·9259 |
| 2 | 0·9803 | 0·9612 | 0·9426 | 0·9246 | 0·9070 | 0·8900 | 0·8734 | 0·8573 |
| 3 | 0·9706 | 0·9423 | 0·9151 | 0·8890 | 0·8638 | 0·8396 | 0·8163 | 0·7938 |
| 4 | 0·9610 | 0·9238 | 0·8885 | 0·8548 | 0·8227 | 0·7921 | 0·7629 | 0·7350 |
| 5 | 0·9515 | 0·9057 | 0·8626 | 0·8219 | 0·7835 | 0·7473 | 0·7130 | 0·6806 |
| 6 | 0·9420 | 0·8880 | 0·8375 | 0·7903 | 0·7462 | 0·7050 | 0·6663 | 0·6302 |
| 7 | 0·9327 | 0·8706 | 0·8131 | 0·7599 | 0·7107 | 0·6651 | 0·6227 | 0·5835 |
| 8 | 0·9235 | 0·8535 | 0·7894 | 0·7307 | 0·6768 | 0·6274 | 0·5820 | 0·5403 |
| 9 | 0·9143 | 0·8386 | 0·7664 | 0·7026 | 0·6446 | 0·5919 | 0·5439 | 0·5002 |
| 10 | 0·9053 | 0·8203 | 0·7441 | 0·6756 | 0·6139 | 0·5584 | 0·5083 | 0·4632 |
| 11 | 0·8963 | 0·8043 | 0·7224 | 0·6496 | 0·5847 | 0·5268 | 0·4751 | 0·4289 |
| 12 | 0·8874 | 0·7885 | 0·7014 | 0·6246 | 0·5568 | 0·4970 | 0·4440 | 0·3971 |
| 13 | 0·8787 | 0·7730 | 0·6810 | 0·6006 | 0·5303 | 0·4688 | 0·4150 | 0·3677 |
| 14 | 0·8700 | 0·7579 | 0·6611 | 0·5775 | 0·5051 | 0·4423 | 0·3878 | 0·3405 |
| 15 | 0·8613 | 0·7430 | 0·6419 | 0·5553 | 0·4810 | 0·4173 | 0·3624 | 0·3152 |
| 16 | 0·8528 | 0·7284 | 0·6232 | 0·5339 | 0·4581 | 0·3936 | 0·3387 | 0·2919 |
| 17 | 0·8444 | 0·7142 | 0·6050 | 0·5134 | 0·4363 | 0·3714 | 0·3166 | 0·2703 |
| 18 | 0·8360 | 0·7002 | 0·5874 | 0·4936 | 0·4155 | 0·3503 | 0·2959 | 0·2502 |
| 19 | 0·8277 | 0·6864 | 0·5703 | 0·4746 | 0·3957 | 0·3305 | 0·2765 | 0·2317 |
| 20 | 0·8195 | 0·6730 | 0·5537 | 0·4564 | 0·3769 | 0·3118 | 0·2584 | 0·2145 |
| 21 | 0·8114 | 0·6598 | 0·5375 | 0·4388 | 0·3589 | 0·2942 | 0·2415 | 0·1987 |
| 22 | 0·8034 | 0·6468 | 0·5219 | 0·4220 | 0·3418 | 0·2775 | 0·2257 | 0·1839 |
| 23 | 0·7954 | 0·6342 | 0·5067 | 0·4057 | 0·3256 | 0·2618 | 0·2109 | 0·1703 |
| 24 | 0·7876 | 0·6217 | 0·4919 | 0·3901 | 0·3101 | 0·2470 | 0·1971 | 0·1577 |
| 25 | 0·7798 | 0·6095 | 0·4776 | 0·3751 | 0·2953 | 0·2330 | 0·1842 | 0·1460 |
| 26 | 0·7720 | 0·5976 | 0·4637 | 0·3607 | 0·2812 | 0·2198 | 0·1722 | 0·1352 |
| 27 | 0·7644 | 0·5859 | 0·4502 | 0·3468 | 0·2678 | 0·2074 | 0·1609 | 0·1252 |
| 28 | 0·7568 | 0·5744 | 0·4371 | 0·3335 | 0·2551 | 0·1956 | 0·1504 | 0·1159 |
| 29 | 0·7493 | 0·5631 | 0·4243 | 0·3207 | 0·2429 | 0·1846 | 0·1406 | 0·1073 |
| 30 | 0·7419 | 0·5521 | 0·4120 | 0·3083 | 0·2314 | 0·1741 | 0·1314 | 0·0994 |
| 35 | 0·7059 | 0·5000 | 0·3554 | 0·2534 | 0·1813 | 0·1301 | 0·0937 | 0·0676 |
| 40 | 0·6717 | 0·4529 | 0·3066 | 0·2083 | 0·1420 | 0·0972 | 0·0668 | 0·0460 |
| 45 | 0·6391 | 0·4102 | 0·2644 | 0·1712 | 0·1113 | 0·0727 | 0·0476 | 0·0313 |
| 50 | 0·6080 | 0·3715 | 0·2281 | 0·1407 | 0·0872 | 0·0543 | 0·0339 | 0·0213 |

FIG. 79.—*Interest Table: present value of £1 (1 to 8%)*

$$(1 + r)^{-n}$$

The average investment is the original cost of £24,000 divided by two, a principle already explained. The average net profit is found by dividing total net profit by three (the life of the machine). The simplest way is to take the £4000 and convert to the present value assuming that the amount accrues at the end of the third year.

*Pros and Cons of Present Value.* There is no doubt that the present-value concept has much to offer when attempting to assess profitability. Due recognition is given to risk and uncertainty and their corollary, the fact that money due in the future is not worth its face value in the present. In other words the timing of the expected receipts is given due recognition in the calculations Moreover, the full period involved (the

| n | 9% | 10% | 11% | 12% | 13% | 14% | 15% | 16% |
|---|---|---|---|---|---|---|---|---|
| 1 | 0·9174 | 0·9091 | 0·9009 | 0·8929 | 0·8850 | 0·8772 | 0·8696 | 0·8621 |
| 2 | 0·8417 | 0·8264 | 0·8116 | 0·7972 | 0·7831 | 0·7695 | 0·7561 | 0·7432 |
| 3 | 0·7722 | 0·7513 | 0·7312 | 0·7118 | 0·6931 | 0·6750 | 0·6575 | 0·6407 |
| 4 | 0·7084 | 0·6830 | 0·6587 | 0·6355 | 0·6133 | 0·5921 | 0·5718 | 0·5523 |
| 5 | 0·6499 | 0·6209 | 0·5935 | 0·5674 | 0·5428 | 0·5194 | 0·4972 | 0·4761 |
| 6 | 0·5936 | 0·5645 | 0·5346 | 0·5066 | 0·4803 | 0·4556 | 0·4323 | 0·4104 |
| 7 | 0·5470 | 0·5132 | 0·4817 | 0·4523 | 0·4251 | 0·3996 | 0·3759 | 0·3538 |
| 8 | 0·5019 | 0·4665 | 0·4339 | 0·4039 | 0·3762 | 0·3506 | 0·3269 | 0·3050 |
| 9 | 0·4604 | 0·4241 | 0·3909 | 0·3606 | 0·3329 | 0·3075 | 0·2843 | 0·2630 |
| 10 | 0·4224 | 0·3855 | 0·3522 | 0·3220 | 0·2946 | 0·2697 | 0·2472 | 0·2267 |
| 11 | 0·3875 | 0·3505 | 0·3173 | 0·2875 | 0·2607 | 0·2366 | 0·2149 | 0·1954 |
| 12 | 0·3555 | 0·3186 | 0·2858 | 0·2567 | 0·2307 | 0·2076 | 0·1869 | 0·1685 |
| 13 | 0·3262 | 0·2897 | 0·2575 | 0·2292 | 0·2042 | 0·1821 | 0·1625 | 0·1452 |
| 14 | 0·2992 | 0·2633 | 0·2320 | 0·2046 | 0·1807 | 0·1597 | 0·1413 | 0·1252 |
| 15 | 0·2745 | 0·2394 | 0·2090 | 0·1827 | 0·1599 | 0·1401 | 0·1229 | 0·1079 |
| 16 | 0·2519 | 0·2176 | 0·1883 | 0·1631 | 0·1415 | 0·1229 | 0·1069 | 0·0930 |
| 17 | 0·2311 | 0·1978 | 0·1696 | 0·1456 | 0·1252 | 0·1078 | 0·0929 | 0·0802 |
| 18 | 0·2120 | 0·1799 | 0·1528 | 0·1300 | 0·1108 | 0·0946 | 0·0808 | 0·0691 |
| 19 | 0·1945 | 0·1635 | 0·1377 | 0·1161 | 0·0981 | 0·0829 | 0·0703 | 0·0596 |
| 20 | 0·1784 | 0·1486 | 0·1240 | 0·1037 | 0·0868 | 0·0728 | 0·0611 | 0·0514 |
| 21 | 0·1637 | 0·1351 | 0·1117 | 0·0926 | 0·0768 | 0·0638 | 0·0531 | 0·0443 |
| 22 | 0·1502 | 0·1228 | 0·1007 | 0·0826 | 0·0680 | 0·0560 | 0·0462 | 0·0382 |
| 23 | 0·1378 | 0·1117 | 0·0907 | 0·0738 | 0·0601 | 0·0491 | 0·0402 | 0·0329 |
| 24 | 0·1264 | 0·1015 | 0·0817 | 0·0659 | 0·0532 | 0·0431 | 0·0349 | 0·0284 |
| 25 | 0·1160 | 0·0923 | 0·0736 | 0·0588 | 0·0471 | 0·0378 | 0·0304 | 0·0245 |
| 26 | 0·1064 | 0·0839 | 0·0663 | 0·0535 | 0·0417 | 0·0331 | 0·0264 | 0·0211 |
| 27 | 0·0976 | 0·0763 | 0·0597 | 0·0469 | 0·0369 | 0·0291 | 0·0230 | 0·0182 |
| 28 | 0·0895 | 0·0693 | 0·0538 | 0·0419 | 0·0326 | 0·0255 | 0·0200 | 0·0157 |
| 29 | 0·0822 | 0·0630 | 0·0485 | 0·0374 | 0·0289 | 0·0224 | 0·0174 | 0·0135 |
| 30 | 0·0754 | 0·0573 | 0·0437 | 0·0334 | 0·0256 | 0·0196 | 0·0151 | 0·0116 |
| 35 | 0·0490 | 0·0356 | 0·0259 | 0·0189 | 0·0139 | 0·0102 | 0·0075 | 0·0055 |
| 40 | 0·0318 | 0·0221 | 0·0154 | 0·0107 | 0·0075 | 0·0053 | 0·0037 | 0·0026 |
| 45 | 0·0207 | 0·0137 | 0·0091 | 0·0061 | 0·0041 | 0·0027 | 0·0019 | 0·0013 |
| 50 | 0·0134 | 0·0085 | 0·0054 | 0·0035 | 0·0022 | 0·0014 | 0·0009 | 0·0006 |

FIG. 80.—*Interest Table: present value of* £1 (9 *to* 16%)

$$(1 + r)^{-n}$$

life of the asset) is considered without affecting the validity of any conclusions reached. It will be recalled that the pay-back method takes into consideration only a *limited* period and this tends to be a weakness. A very strong point in favour of using present values is the fact that the true relative profitability will be shown.

Possible weaknesses of the system are few. One of the major criticisms from a practical point-of-view is that fact that too many refinements are introduced into what must necessarily be an exercise which includes numerous uncertainties. The most accurate figure will probably be the capital cost which could change before the asset was purchased. The sales and costs figures have to be forecast; they are

| $n$ | 17% | 18% | 19% | 20% | 21% | 22% | 23% | 24% |
|---|---|---|---|---|---|---|---|---|
| 1 | 0·8547 | 0·8475 | 0·8403 | 0·8333 | 0·8264 | 0·8197 | 0·8130 | 0·8065 |
| 2 | 0·7305 | 0·7182 | 0·7062 | 0·6944 | 0·6830 | 0·6719 | 0·6610 | 0·6504 |
| 3 | 0·6244 | 0·6086 | 0·5934 | 0·5787 | 0·5645 | 0·5507 | 0·5374 | 0·5245 |
| 4 | 0·5337 | 0·5158 | 0·4987 | 0·4823 | 0·4665 | 0·4514 | 0·4369 | 0·4230 |
| 5 | 0·4561 | 0·4371 | 0·4190 | 0·4019 | 0·3855 | 0·3700 | 0·3552 | 0·3411 |
| 6 | 0·3898 | 0·3704 | 0·3521 | 0·3349 | 0·3186 | 0·3033 | 0·2888 | 0·2751 |
| 7 | 0·3332 | 0·3139 | 0·2959 | 0·2791 | 0·2633 | 0·2488 | 0·2348 | 0·2218 |
| 8 | 0·2848 | 0·2660 | 0·2487 | 0·2326 | 0·2176 | 0·2038 | 0·1909 | 0·1789 |
| 9 | 0·2434 | 0·2255 | 0·2090 | 0·1938 | 0·1799 | 0·1670 | 0·1552 | 0·1443 |
| 10 | 0·2080 | 0·1911 | 0·1756 | 0·1615 | 0·1486 | 0·1369 | 0·1262 | 0·1164 |
| 11 | 0·1778 | 0·1619 | 0·1746 | 0·1346 | 0·1228 | 0·1122 | 0·1026 | 0·0938 |
| 12 | 0·1520 | 0·1372 | 0·1240 | 0·1122 | 0·1015 | 0·0920 | 0·0834 | 0·0757 |
| 13 | 0·1299 | 0·1163 | 0·1042 | 0·0935 | 0·0839 | 0·0754 | 0·0678 | 0·0610 |
| 14 | 0·1110 | 0·0985 | 0·0876 | 0·0779 | 0·0693 | 0·0618 | 0·0551 | 0·0492 |
| 15 | 0·0949 | 0·0835 | 0·0736 | 0·0649 | 0·0573 | 0·0507 | 0·0448 | 0·0397 |
| 16 | 0·0811 | 0·0708 | 0·0618 | 0·0541 | 0·0474 | 0·0415 | 0·0364 | 0·0320 |
| 17 | 0·0693 | 0·0600 | 0·0520 | 0·0451 | 0·0391 | 0·0340 | 0·0296 | 0·0258 |
| 18 | 0·0592 | 0·0508 | 0·0437 | 0·0376 | 0·0323 | 0·0279 | 0·0241 | 0·0208 |
| 19 | 0·0506 | 0·0431 | 0·0367 | 0·0313 | 0·0267 | 0·0229 | 0·0196 | 0·0168 |
| 20 | 0·0433 | 0·0365 | 0·0308 | 0·0261 | 0·0221 | 0·0187 | 0·0159 | 0·0135 |
| 21 | 0·0370 | 0·0309 | 0·0259 | 0·0217 | 0·0183 | 0·0154 | 0·0129 | 0·0109 |
| 22 | 0·0316 | 0·0262 | 0·0218 | 0·0181 | 0·0151 | 0·0126 | 0·0105 | 0·0088 |
| 23 | 0·0270 | 0·0222 | 0·0183 | 0·0151 | 0·0125 | 0·0103 | 0·0086 | 0·0071 |
| 24 | 0·0231 | 0·0188 | 0·0154 | 0·0126 | 0·0103 | 0·0085 | 0·0070 | 0·0057 |
| 25 | 0·0197 | 0·0160 | 0·0129 | 0·0105 | 0·0085 | 0·0069 | 0·0057 | 0·0046 |
| 26 | 0·0169 | 0·0135 | 0·0109 | 0·0087 | 0·0070 | 0·0057 | 0·0046 | 0·0037 |
| 27 | 0·0144 | 0·0115 | 0·0091 | 0·0073 | 0·0058 | 0·0047 | 0·0037 | 0·0030 |
| 28 | 0·0123 | 0·0097 | 0·0077 | 0·0061 | 0·0048 | 0·0038 | 0·0030 | 0·0024 |
| 29 | 0·0105 | 0·0082 | 0·0064 | 0·0051 | 0·0040 | 0·0031 | 0·0025 | 0·0020 |
| 30 | 0·0090 | 0·0070 | 0·0054 | 0·0042 | 0·0033 | 0·0026 | 0·0020 | 0·0016 |
| 35 | 0·0041 | 0·0030 | 0·0023 | 0·0017 | 0·0013 | 0·0009 | 0·0007 | 0·0005 |
| 40 | 0·0019 | 0·0013 | 0·0010 | 0·0007 | 0·0005 | 0·0004 | 0·0002 | 0·0002 |
| 45 | 0·0009 | 0·0006 | 0·0004 | 0·0003 | 0·0002 | 0·0001 | 0·0001 | 0·0001 |
| 50 | 0·0004 | 0·0003 | 0·0002 | 0·0001 | 0·0001 | 0·0000 | 0·0000 | 0·0000 |

FIG. 81.—*Interest Table: present value of £1 (17 to 24%)*

$$(1 + r)^{-n}$$

estimates which depend upon many variable factors. Accordingly, it is argued, why bother to go to the trouble of discounting to show present values. There may be some merit in this line of thought. Nevertheless, it should be remembered that if the principle of forecasting is to be accepted as being an essential part of business management—and the author believes that it must be—then risks and uncertainties are inevitable. Indeed, if there were no risks or uncertainties then profit would be non-existent. Management is expected to overcome the risks through decision-making. The more information available the greater the possibility that the decision will be correct. Present values show a truer position, so they should be used.

A further difficulty is the calculation of the rate of interest or discount which should be used to convert to present values. This is never an easy matter. Economic conditions change frequently and, therefore, so does the structure of interest rates which in Great Britain is linked with Bank Rate. This problem is not confined to discounting of present values. The question of what is a reasonable return on capital employed should be in the foreground of all progressive policy-making. In fact this is such an important matter that Chapter 15 is devoted to discussing some of its implications.

Allowing for these possible defects there is still a very strong case for using the present-value concept. Values and costs should be shown at their true worth; only then can the management accountant say that he is truly presenting facts which represent economic realities and not simply a list of unrelated figures—some accruing this year, some next and possibly some in five years' time. The process of discounting brings them all into present-day terms, allowing valid comparisons to be made.

### Minimum Total Cost or Unit Cost

These do not show profitability. Nevertheless, they may be useful for comparing alternative machines or methods. If, for example two machines produce at the same rate then the minimum cost would indicate the better proposition. An example is given on pp. 487–9.

## PRINCIPLES OF CAPITAL EXPENDITURE DECISION-MAKING

Some of the main principles involved in selecting the most profitable project should be apparent from what has already been said. As will be appreciated the most appropriate method should be selected from those described above. A table of comparative returns can be produced and from this the order of preference can be seen. Only by considering alternative courses of action can management exercise the initiative and judgment so essential for maximising profit.

Matters which require further explanation are covered below.

### DEPRECIATION

For making decisions on whether or not to purchase a fixed asset a problem arises in connection with depreciation. Should the annual depreciation charge be included in the costs and, therefore, be deducted from the value of the sales to arrive at the net cash flow?

When comparing different propositions—whether to purchase machine A, B or C—the fact that the total capital cost is being taken into the calculation for assessing the profitability of each machine means that a depreciation charge is quite *unnecessary*.

When comparing the costs on a single-year basis, such as when considering the substitution of a new machine for an old one, then the inclusion of depreciation will be necessary.

The figure to be taken for depreciation purposes for an old asset is not always understood. There appears to be no justification for taking depreciation based on the written down book value. Clearly when a machine is nearing the end of its useful life the cost balance may not show the true present value. The question to ask is what is the value (*a*) if disposed of now and (*b*) at the end of the serviceable life (*i.e.* the residual value). The difference between (*a*) and (*b*) should be the basis of the annual depreciation charge. Some accountants state this principle in a different manner, but the result should be the same. They suggest that the estimated sales value *now* should be compared with the estimated sales value at the end of the year taken for comparative purposes. The difference in the beginning and end figures should be the depreciation charge. It is a real cost—the cost of an opportunity foregone. If management decides to dispose of the old machine now then the business gains from the sale. Alternatively, if the asset is retained there is a loss equivalent to the difference between the value now and the value at the end of the year. This opportunity cost should be taken to represent the true depreciation for decision-making purposes.

The effect of depreciation on the amount of tax payable may have to be taken into account. However, the observations made in this section under the heading "Taxation" are very relevant to this point.

## OBSOLESCENCE

The danger of a machine or other fixed asset becoming outdated before the end of its useful life should be considered when dealing with capital expenditure decisions. Clearly, any premature shortening of the life of an asset will have the effect of reducing the total cash flow.

If there is a real danger of obsolescence then a deliberate limit can be placed on the number of years taken into the calculation of earnings and costs. Unfortunately, by doing this the true position is not being shown and as a result a possible, profitable investment may be rejected.

A better plan would be to draft a *supplementary* report on the probable effects of obsolescence. Management can then take these into consideration before reaching any decision.

## INTEREST

An appropriate rate of interest has to be used to convert to present values when these are to be used in assessing profitability. This is an accepted fact.

There is no general agreement on the use of a notional rate of interest to reflect the different capital costs of alternative projects. If machine A is expected to cost £10,000 and machine B is expected to cost £30,000 then the use of a percentage interest charge would reflect the fact that the capital cost of B is three times that of A. Those in favour of including interest argue that the money could be earning interest if invested elsewhere: therefore, the argument continues, interest should be shown to indicate the true cost of the decision to be made. In these circumstances interest is not being treated as a cost of production—cost accountants have long since agreed that this should not be so—but rather is a reflection of the sacrifice involved, which is more in the nature of an opportunity cost.

Certainly there appears to be justification in including interest in appropriate circumstances. However, much depends upon the views of the accountant concerned. The question to be settled is whether or not the inclusion of a notional interest rate will help management to reach a logical decision.

If interest is included then the net receipts (the net cash flow) will be reduced by the total interest involved.

Some accountants advocate the charging of interest on the cost outlays; *i.e.* all costs to be incurred with the exception of depreciation and, of course, of the notional interest charge on the investment.

## TAXATION

A question which is bound to arise is the effect of taxation. Will the present (or future) taxation laws make a proposition more desirable or less desirable? From this emerges a second question—should the estimated effects in terms of financial gains or losses be shown in the schedules compiled for the purpose of showing expected profitability?

There is no definite answer to the second question. Some accountants would argue that profitability is determined before tax is charged and, therefore, any decision made should ignore taxation. Moreover, who knows what the incidence of tax will be over the life of an asset—possibly over ten years?

The best solution may be in adopting a compromise. A decision on the most profitable investment could be made without taking into account the effects of taxation. Before reaching a *final* decision the likely effects could be summarised on a supplementary schedule. It should be remembered that the income tax payable reduces the net cash flow and, therefore, makes an investment less attractive. If taxes are paid at the same *rate* on all possible investments then there would be the same position of relative profitability even when taxes have been considered. On the other hand, if different allowances for different investments are in operation then their effects should be considered.

No attempt is made here to show the rates of Corporation Tax. These vary so much from one year to another that the reader is advised to study the regulations in force at the present time. Once the rates have been obtained the following rules can be applied in respect of possible investments:

1. When allowances vary with the value of the asset, then the asset receiving the highest rate is at an advantage.
This would apply to any form of initial allowance, investment allowance or to wear and tear allowances.

2. If the receipts and payments are converted to present values the taxes payable and tax allowances should also be converted. However, not all the sums involved need to be discounted. The net amount after deduction of tax can be taken. This can be done quite simply by deducting the investment allowance from the capital cost of the asset and then subtracting the total tax payable at the appropriate percentage rate from the net revenues (*i.e.* net cash flow). For each investment there is thus one net figure to be discounted.

This procedure does not follow the suggestion made above that taxes should be dealt with on a supplementary schedule. However, as will be appreciated, there can be no hard-and-fast rule on this matter. If the tax burden is very heavy then inclusion in the computation becomes essential. If taxes continue to rise a point may be reached when investment in gilt-edged securities may be much more profitable than further expansion of the business.

### SIGNIFICANCE OF RATE OF RETURN

The general rule followed with investments is to select the project expected to give the largest return. Management will wish to know the answers to the following questions:

1. How much significance can be attached to the rate of return shown for each project?
2. Can all investments be measured by the rate of return?

The answer to the first question cannot take a very positive form. Much depends upon the care and attention paid in collecting and using the data. This is something which can be watched by management. What cannot be watched is the uncertainty of the future. The serviceable life of the asset has to be estimated. Here many factors are involved: among other things the quality of the asset, the way it is handled and, of course, the rate of production must all be considered. Forecasting sales figures is fraught with uncertainties; many of the economic factors are discussed in the chapter on sales forecasting. The forecasting of costs is influenced to a very large extent by the conditions expected in the future. If these are not as expected then the cost estimate will be inaccurate. Put in a nutshell it can be stated that the rate of return estimated to accrue from a proposed investment should be taken only as a *guide* to profitability.

Recognising that uncertainty could invalidate any of the facts many accountants suggest that not one forecast, but a number of forecasts should be made to cover each project. Thus, for example, data could be shown for periods of three, five, and ten years, three separate schedules being compiled. Another variation is the rate of interest for discounting to present values or the rate of return regarded as being "reasonable." Again separate schedules could be prepared for each possible rate.

There should be no jumping to the conclusion that the whole process of using facts and figures to reach capital investment decisions is a waste of time. Provided the limitations which may exist are recognised nothing but good can come from these very practical exercises. Without them management has no guide at all and the result could be—and most likely will be—catastrophe. Of course, it is not simply a matter of compiling one set of schedules and making one decision. A number of decisions have to be made each year. If a logical, well-conceived and efficiently organised decision-making system deals with each problem as it arises then inevitably some lessons will be learnt. Management, including the management accountant, should find that practice does *not* make perfect, but at least it leads towards improvement and to better decision-making.

On the second question—can all investments be measured by the rate of return—the answer must be "no." If only the rate of return is considered many desirable projects would be excluded from the capital expenditure forecast. Examples of possible projects of this nature are summarised below:

1. Pure research or applied research of a nature which does not permit the results to be stated in terms of profit or loss. Often the benefits are realised many years ahead, but there is no certainty that this will be so, or even that there will be any benefits.

2. Welfare projects intended to improve working conditions. Clearly such projects will tend to be of a beneficial nature, but it will be extremely difficult to measure them in terms of profitability.

3. Educational and training projects.

4. Prestige-value projects such as having an exhibition which portrays the history and growth of the product being made.

5. Office blocks, showrooms, store rooms, and other service buildings the use of which cannot easily be stated in profit-earning terms.

6. Replacement projects which cannot be avoided, such as when a machine in a linked process has to be replaced by a new machine. The replacement may have to be purchased even though the rate of return is quite low for the single machine.

7. Projects to comply with statutory or safety requirements; *e.g.* Factories Acts.

These are but a few examples. There are many others. The existence of such projects does not change the procedures already outlined for those projects which can be measured in terms of profit or cost savings. However, it should be noted that some accountants advocate that the minimum rate of return set for a project should be high enough to cover the existence of non-profit making projects. This principle can be extended to all capital expenditure projects and in respect of *all* costs which cannot be attributed to a particular project.

However, this is not an easy matter. Many fixed costs would be incurred whether or not a certain project is developed. A company may have fixed costs of £100,000. A decision on whether or not to purchase a machine for £10,000 is now being taken. Should the decision be affected by the fixed costs *already* being incurred—obviously the fixed cost *per unit* produced will tend to reduce with an increase in output. This fact may be apparent, but in the complex organisation the determination of the effect on unit costs may be very difficult to determine. The accountant can assist by estimating the probable effect.

Not only present fixed costs have to be considered. The proposed project may result in further fixed costs being incurred. In addition, a fact often overlooked, there is the possibility that one project will spark off the need for further capital expenditure. The introduction of a new machine will increase the volume of output. It may also bring problems. If the increase in output is quite large the internal transport system may have to be improved or extended; the Stores department may need extending; there may even be a need to purchase a new lorry for distributing the additional units. Supplementary estimates should be prepared to show the possible changes in annual costs and, of course, the capital expenditure costs. Single projects should not be viewed in isolation; all factors should be made known so that the decision is reached with a full knowledge of all facts. Obviously the capital expenditure forecast is not to be considered as a list of unrelated projects. In some measure they are all related and this fact should not be overlooked.

How are the projects which do not result in "a rate of return" to be classified into "desirable" and "undesirable" categories? In all decision-making personal opinions must enter into the choice. With special projects, of the type listed above, personal opinions must play a more important part in any decisions made. There is no standard measure (the rate of return) for comparing different investments. Accordingly, the benefits—whether tangible or intangible—are often largely a matter of what one executive or another believes will be the result of the proposed investment.

The management accountant can still assist by providing data on capital expenditure and annual running costs. If welfare, educational, or similar matter which affects employees is being considered, a report from the Personnel Manager may be very helpful.

Armed with all facts that can be gathered management has to consider (*a*) can we afford to spend money on a project which does not directly increase profit and (*b*) how desirable is the proposed project? The first answer can be obtained by referring to the cash forecast. The second question can be dealt with by the capital expenditure committee (often the same as the budget committee). Consideration of all facts by each member of the committee can lead to a decision on the desirability of a proposed project. All decisions should be made after considering all alternatives. The projects likely to result in a rate of return should be compared with the other projects. If a project shows a possible return of 6% and another project, costing the same in capital expenditure and annual running costs, is in the form of a proposed medical block for employees, which is the more desirable? Management has to decide whether it can afford to forgo the 6%. In other words, is the stated return less desirable than the medical block? In some types of business the medical block may be most essential; e.g. in the case of a foundry the accident rate from burns or small metal particles from fettling may be serious enough to warrant very urgent consideration of the project. Where the need is not so obvious management has still to reach a decision by selecting the more desirable project.

## CONSIDERING ALTERNATIVE INVESTMENTS

The methods used for ranking investments on a rate of return or similar basis were outlined earlier in the chapter. This section is concerned with applying the principles explained. It is very important to note that the procedures shown relate to comparing a new asset with one or more alternative new assets. Whether to replace an *old* asset with a new one is covered in the next section.

A question is shown below. This is followed by a suggested solution. Where necessary, notes are added. Before attempting to work through the problem the reader is advised to study the text dealing with the methods of arriving at the most profitable investments.

QUESTION

Rapid Techniques Ltd., a specialised engineering company, is considering the purchase of a machine. There are two possible machines which will produce the additional output. Details of these are shown below with the estimated costs and sales values.

|  | Machine X £ | Machine Y £ |
|---|---|---|
| Capital Cost | 30,000 | 30,000 |
| Sales (Production at standard prices) | 50,000 | 40,000 |
| Costs: |  |  |
| Direct Labour | 5,000 | 3,000 |
| Direct Material | 4,000 | 5,000 |
| Factory Overhead | 6,000 | 5,000 |
| (this is the net figure, *savings* have been deducted) |  |  |
| Administration Costs | 2,000 | 1,000 |
| Selling and Distribution Costs | 1,000 | 1,000 |

X is expected to have a serviceable life of two years and Y three years. Sales are expected to continue at the rates shown for each year for the full period of each machine. The costs shown relate to annual expenditure resulting from each machine.

The total tax to be paid is estimated at 50% of net earnings. It may be assumed that the cash for sales and costs is received or paid out in the years shown. For the purpose of the calculation these cash receipts and payments may be taken to be settled on the last day of each year. Interest on capital is to be ignored. The appropriate rate of interest for converting to present values may be taken as 10%.

Show the most profitable investment on the facts given by the following methods:

    1. Pay-back Method.
    2. Return on Investment Method.
    3. Present-value Return on Investment Method.

SUGGESTED SOLUTION

1. *Pay-back Method*

|  | Machine X | | Machine Y | | |
|---|---|---|---|---|---|
|  | Year 1 | Year 2 | Year 1 | Year 2 | Year 3 |
|  | £ | £ | £ | £ | £ |
| Sales ... ... ... | 50,000 | 50,000 | 40,000 | 40,000 | 40,000 |
| COSTS: | £ | £ | £ | £ | £ |
|   Direct Labour ... | 5,000 | 5,000 | 3,000 | 3,000 | 3,000 |
|   Direct Material ... | 4,000 | 4,000 | 5,000 | 5,000 | 5,000 |
|   Factory Overhead ... | 6,000 | 6,000 | 5,000 | 5,000 | 5,000 |
|   Administration Costs | 2,000 | 2,000 | 1,000 | 1,000 | 1,000 |
|   Selling and Distribution | | | | | |
|     Costs ... ... | 1,000 | 1,000 | 1,000 | 1,000 | 1,000 |
|  | 18,000 | 18,000 | 15,000 | 15,000 | 15,000 |
| Net Earnings (Net Cash Flow) ... ... ... | 32,000 | 32,000 | 25,000 | 25,000 | 25,000 |
| Taxation at 50% ... | 16,000 | 16,000 | 12,500 | 12,500 | 12,500 |
| NET CASH FLOW after Tax | £16,000 | £16,000 | £12,500 | £12,500 | £12,500 |

$$\text{Capital Costs:} \quad \frac{X}{£30,000} \quad \frac{Y}{£30,000}$$

*Ranking of Investments*

Machine X    Pay-back period $1\frac{7}{8}$ Years.
Machine Y    Pay-back period $2\frac{2}{5}$ Years.

On the basis of the earlier pay-back period Machine X is given the first place in the ranking.

*Note*. In actual fact the total *net* return on Machine Y is £37,500, which means that this machine *may* be a better proposal than Machine X. However, the fact that the timing of receipts is ignored invalidates even this conclusion.

Some accountants have suggested modifying the pay-back method by applying a formula which considers the profit earned *after* the pay-back period has expired. Thus:

$$\text{Total Net Cash Flow} - \text{Capital Cost} = \text{Profit}$$

Deduction of the capital cost from the total net cash flow shows the net profit expected. However, this is not strictly the pay-back method. It is more correctly a stage of the rate of return method shown below.

### 2. *Return on Investment Method*

(a) *Per £1 Invested*

|  | Machine X | Machine Y |
|---|---|---|
| Net Cash Flow | £32,000 | £37,500 |
| Investment | £30,000 | £30,000 |
| Rate of Return per £1 Invested | £1·067 | £1·250 |

(b) *Per £1 Invested on an Annual Basis*

|  | Machine X | Machine Y |
|---|---|---|
| Net Cash Flow | £32,000 | £37,500 |
| Average Annual Cash Flow | £16,000 | £12,500 |
| Investment | £30,000 | £30,000 |
| Rate of Return | £0·533 | £0·417 |

(c) *Percentage Rate of Return*

The percentage rate of return is calculated as follows:

$$\frac{\text{Average Annual Net Cash Flow} \times 100}{\text{Average Investment}}$$

$$\text{Machine X} \quad \frac{£16,000}{£15,000} \times \frac{100}{1} = 107\%$$

$$\text{Machine Y} \quad \frac{£12,500}{£15,000} \times \frac{100}{1} = 83\%$$

As already shown, the percentage return can be based on annual net profit after deduction of the cost of the investment. The figures involved in this case would be as follows:

$$\text{Machine X} \quad \frac{£1,000}{£15,000} \times \frac{100}{1} = 6\frac{1}{2}\%$$

$$\text{Machine Y} \quad \frac{£2,500}{£15,000} \times \frac{100}{1} = 17\%$$

It will be seen, that, taken on an annual basis, Y is more profitable than X. Clearly when the periods involved are of different lengths this version is better than the earlier version. If the periods are equal the second version may produce more realistic results.

The percentages are taken to the nearest whole number and the average investment is obtained by the procedure previously explained.

### Ranking of Investments

(a) Per £1 Invested.   Machine Y superior.
(b) Per £1 Invested on an Annual Basis.   Machine X superior.
(c) Percentage Rate of Return.   Machine X superior.
       Percentage Rate of Return (net profit).   Machine Y superior.

3. *Present-value Return on Investment Method*
    (a) *Trial and Error Method*

| | Machine X | | | Machine Y | | |
|---|---|---|---|---|---|---|
| Net Cash Flow (after tax) | Cash Flow | Conversion Factor | Present Value | Cash Flow | Conversion Factor | Present Value |
| | £ | £ | £ | £ | £ | £ |
| Year 1 | 16,000 | 0·9615 | 15,384 | 12,500 | 0·8929 | 11,161 |
| „ 2 | 16,000 | 0·9246 | 14,794 | 12,500 | 0·7972 | 9,965 |
| „ 3 | — | | | 12,500 | 0·7118 | 8,898 |
| | | | 30,178 | | | 30,024 |
| Capital Cost | | | £30,000 | | | £30,000 |
| | Rate of Return = 4% (approx.) | | | Rate of Return = 12% (approx.) | | |

*Note.* As explained previously the appropriate conversion factors, found by reference to present-value interest, are taken until the one is found which makes cash flow (present value) and capital cost approximately equal. Obviously a 4% return is unlikely to be acceptable. It will not even cover the minimum discount for converting to present values.

    (b) *Net Gain Method*

| | | Machine X £ | | Machine Y £ |
|---|---|---|---|---|
| Capital Cost | | 30,000 | | 30,000 |
| | £ | | £ | |
| Cash Flow   Year 1   16,000 | | 14,546 | 12,500 | 11,364 |
| (present value)   „ 2   16,000 | | 13,222 | 12,500 | 10,330 |
| (Rate taken 10%) | | | 12,500 | 9,391 |
| | | 27,768 | | 31,085 |
| | | £2,232 (loss) | | £1,085 (gain) |

Machine Y is clearly superior. There is a definite gain even though the fairly high rate of 10% is taken to convert to present values. If a lower rate of interest is taken different results will be shown.

#### Summary of Rankings

| Method | First Preference |
| --- | --- |
| 1. Pay-back Method | Machine X |
| 2. Return on Investment: | |
|   (*a*) Per £1 Invested | Machine Y |
|   (*b*) Per £1 Invested on Annual Basis | Machine X |
|   (*c*) i. Percentage Rate of Return | Machine X |
|      ii. Percentage Rate of Return on Net Profit | Machine Y |
| 3. Present-value Return on Investment: | |
|   (*a*) Trial and Error Method | Machine Y |
|   (*b*) Net Gain Method | Machine Y |

From the summary it will be seen that three methods rank X as first preference whereas the other four rank Y. With this kind of conflict how is management to select the more profitable investment? In the simple example given, the selection is fairly straightforward. However, when there are longer periods and more alternatives the investment to choose will be a much more difficult proposition.

The answer is to select carefully the method used. Clearly the pay-back method and the return on investment per £1 invested on an annual basis and on a percentage return basis are unlikely to be satisfactory unless the serviceable life is the same for each asset being considered. Even if the lives are equal the fact that the timing of the receipts is being ignored makes these methods undesirable.

### Special Note on Method of Approach

In the Question shown expected sales values are given. It may not always be possible to show the direct sales contribution made by a particular machine. In this case the expected cost savings may be taken.

## CONSIDERING REPLACEMENT INVESTMENTS

The previous section is concerned with ranking *alternative* investments—whether to purchase one fixed asset or another. In this section the analysis is taken a step further: the possibility of improving profit earning by substituting one machine for another (new) machine or replacing hand labour by a new machine. Methods explained earlier can still be used for selecting the best machine for the work to be done. There is then the problem of ascertaining which is more profitable— buying the new asset or carrying on with the old asset or method.

Earlier in the chapter, some of the most important principles affecting replacement decisions are covered. These should be understood before going on to the question and suggested answer given below. Additional matters not previously mentioned, but introduced into the Question, are explained in the Solution.

##### QUESTION

Innovation Ltd. has been using machine number 358 for five complete years. Quite recently a new machine, which renders machine number 358 obsolete, has been introduced. The board of directors wishes to know whether to purchase the new machine or continue to work the old machine. The following data are available:

|  | New Machine £ | Machine 358 £ |
|---|---|---|
| Power and Lighting | 3,000 | 2,000 |
| Direct Labour | 10,000 | 24,000 |
| Supplies | 1,000 | 500 |
| Indirect Labour | 2,000 | 1,800 |
| Building Expense | 1,000 | 1,000 |
| Depreciation (Machines) | 5,000 | 5,000 |
| Capital Cost | 55,000 | 55,000 |

The costs shown relate to one year. The capital cost shown for Machine 358 is the original cost. The present saleable value of the old machine is £5200 and £4200 at the end of the year, but if it is retained until the end of its life—in another five years—the residual value will be £200.

The volume of output for both machines may be taken as 10,000 units of product "R." However, if the new machine is worked to full capacity it is capable of producing an *additional* 2000 units; all these units are expected to continue to sell at £4 each. Interest is to be allowed on the cost of capital and the annual outlays at a rate of 10%. Taxation may be ignored.

You are required to show the figures in such a way that they reflect the investment which should be selected. The methods to be employed should show the following:

1. Minimum Total Cost
2. Minimum Unit Cost          } on an annual basis.
3. Percentage Rate of Return

Show the relevant figures for both possible volumes of output relating to the new machine; *i.e.* 10,000 units and 12,000 units. It may be assumed that building expense and depreciation are fixed costs whereas the others are variable costs. The latter, shown in the schedule above, relate to 10,000 units.

SUGGESTED SOLUTION

### Comparative Cost Schedule

|  | NEW Machine | | Machine 358 (OLD) |
|---|---|---|---|
| Sales at £4 each ... ... ... | £40,000 | £48,000 | £40,000 |
|  | 10,000 *units* | 12,000 *units* | 10,000 *units* |
| Annual Costs: | £ | £ | £ |
| Power and Lighting ... ... | 3,000 | 3,600 | 2,000 |
| Direct Labour ... ... ... | 10,000 | 12,000 | 24,000 |
| Supplies ... ... ... ... | 1,000 | 1,200 | 500 |
| Indirect Labour ... ... ... | 2,000 | 2,400 | 1,800 |
| Building Expense ... ... | 1,000 | 1,000 | 1,000 |
| Depreciation (Machines) ... | 5,000 | 5,000 | 1,000 |
| Interest on Capital Cost ... | 5,500 | 5,500 | 520 |
| Interest on Cost Outlay ... ... | 1,700 | 2,020 | 2,930 |
|  | £29,200 | £32,720 | £33,750 |

*Notes.*

1. The depreciation for the old machine is calculated on the expected saleable value. For the purpose of comparing costs the book value has no significance. This principle is explained earlier in the chapter.

2. The costs for the 12,000 units are obtained by adding one-fifth to the costs of 10,000 units. Fixed costs remain the same irrespective of volume.

3. Cost outlay does not include depreciation or interest on capital although some accountants suggest the latter could rightly be regarded as an outlay.

4. Interest on capital is taken on the full capital cost for the new asset and on the saleable value for the old asset. An alternative method, sometimes advocated, is to take the average investment; *i.e.* half the original capital cost.

### Ranking of Alternatives

1. *Minimum Total Cost*

For 10,000 units the minimum cost relates to the new machine.
This is also the case for 12,000 units.

2. *Minimum Unit Cost*

$$\text{New machine 10,000 units} \quad \frac{£29,200}{10,000} = £2 \cdot 920$$

$$\text{New machine 12,000 units} \quad \frac{£32,720}{12,000} = £2 \cdot 727$$

$$\text{Old machine 10,000 units} \quad \frac{£33,750}{10,000} = £3 \cdot 375$$

3. *Percentage Rate of Return*

|  | New Machine | | Old Machine |
|---|---|---|---|
|  | 10,000 units | 12,000 units | 10,000 units |
|  | £ | £ | £ |
| Sales | 40,000 | 48,000 | 40,000 |
| *less* Costs | 29,200 | 32,720 | 33,750 |
| NET PROFIT | £10,800 | £15,280 | £6,250 |

The percentage rate of return could be calculated for both the new and old machine. The difficulty is deciding what figure to take as capital invested. Should it be £55,000, £30,000 (book value) or £5200? If the old machine is sold immediately the sum obtainable is £5200. Not selling the machine involves forgoing the £5200. This has the same effect as spending the same sum. Accordingly, there appears to be a strong case for using £5200 as the capital invested.

Unfortunately, taking half of £5200 does not produce a realistic percentage return. With a net profit of £6250 the return approaches 240%. Clearly this is quite unrealistic and is unlikely to show whether or not the new machine is a worthwhile proposition.

An alternative approach is to deduct the present market value of the old machine from the total capital to be invested on the new machine: this gives the additional investment. Next the profit resulting from the *additional* investment is ascertained by deducting the profit from the old machine from the profit from the new machine. The return is then calculated.

In the problem the relevant figures are as follows:

| | |
|---|---|
| Total Investment | £55,000 |
| *less* Market Value (Old Machine) | 5,200 |
| | £49,800 |

Additional Profit:

| | |
|---|---|
| New Machine   10,000 units | £10,800 |
| *less* Profit from Old Machine | 6,250 |
| | £4,550 |

| | |
|---|---|
| New Machine   12,000 units | £15,280 |
| *less* Profit from Old Machine | 6,250 |
| | £9,030 |

Formula for Calculation:

$$\frac{\text{Additional Net Profit}}{\text{Average Investment}} \times \frac{100}{1}$$

New Machine (10,000 units): $\dfrac{£4550}{\frac{1}{2} \text{ of } £49,800} \times \dfrac{100}{1} = 18\%$ (approx.)

New Machine (12,000 units): $\dfrac{£9030}{\frac{1}{2} \text{ of } £49,800} \times \dfrac{100}{1} = 36\%$ (approx.)

Both returns are quite good; in fact 36% may be excellent for some types of business. Accordingly, the additional investment may be worthwhile.

The investment on the new machine is taken as the total of £55,000. Some accountants may prefer to take the net figure of £50,000; *i.e.* after deducting the residual value.

| *Summary of Findings* | *First Preference* |
|---|---|
| 1. *Minimum Total Cost* | New Machine (10,000 units) |
| 2. *Minimum Unit Cost* | New Machine (12,000 units) |
| 3. *Percentage Rate of Return* | New Machine (12,000 units) |

In the case of the minimum total cost method it will be appreciated that an attempt is being made to compare incomparable items; *i.e.* the cost of 10,000 units with the cost of 12,000 units. For this reason the ranking given by the minimum cost method can be disregarded. Clearly, therefore, on the information given, the new machine with an output of 12,000 units is an attractive investment.

## CONCLUSION

As stated earlier, the most appropriate method for calculating the profitability of each project has to be selected. Once the best method has been found it will be advisable to use it consistently.

From the explanation of the methods already given, the reader will appreciate that any method which uses actual costs without discounting is likely to give realistic results only when the alternative investments have the same life span with returns accruing at approximately the same intervals of time. In other circumstances one of the present-value methods is likely to be of the greatest use.

### EXAMINATION QUESTIONS

1. State and give your reasons for what you think would be a reasonable basis of valuation for balance sheet purposes of the following:

(a) Secondhand books acquired in substantial quantities from various sources and held as stock by a book-seller.

(b) A block of flats is in course of construction. The builder has contracted to sell them for £100,000 and has estimated that at the end of his financial year they were half completed. At that time his costs, including overheads, amounted to £55,000 whereas he originally estimated that his total costs for erection would be £80,000.

(c) Small tools owned by an engineering company. (A.C.C.A.)

2. Your directors are considering introducing additional capital into a business to:

(a) replace old machinery with modern equipment;

(b) build and equip a new department to manufacture a part of the final product which has hitherto been bought from outside.

Discuss the various factors you would consider to ascertain the additional profits which will result from this new capital expenditure. (I.C.W.A.)

3. Your company is considering investing in a project for which the investment data are as follows:

Capital outlay £200,000.

Depreciation charge 20 per cent p.a.

Forecasted annual income, before charging depreciation, but after all other charges.

| Year | £ |
|---|---|
| 1 | 100,000 |
| 2 | 100,000 |
| 3 | 80,000 |
| 4 | 80,000 |
| 5 | 40,000 |
| | 400,000 |

In connection with the foregoing you are asked to employ methods of measuring the return on the capital employed with a view to ascertaining the value to the company of the proposed investment.

On the basis of the figures given above set out calculations illustrating and comparing the following methods of evaluating the return on capital employed:

(a) Payback period.
(b) Rate of return on original investment.
(c) Rate of return on average investment.
(d) Discounted cash flow.

State clearly any assumptions you make.
Taxation to be ignored.
Calculations may be approximate. (A.C.C.A.)

4. A tool room in a general engineering factory:

(a) makes tools for sale;
(b) makes new tools for use in the factory;
(c) repairs tools for use in the factory.

What problems of cost ascertainment, allocation and apportionment arise, and how are these problems dealt with? (I.C.W.A.)

5. Discuss the significance of Cash Flow in Management Accounting:

(a) The AB Company Limited is proposing to make a capital investment of £200,000 which it is estimated will produce the following profit figures after allowing for depreciation over five years on a straight basis:

| Year 1 | £30,000 | Profit |
|---|---|---|
| 2 | £30,000 | Profit |
| 3 | £20,000 | Profit |
| 4 | £10,000 | Profit |
| 5 | £15,000 | Loss |

To undertake this, the company will require to issue loan stock at 6% per annum. Over the past few years the company's profits have been of the order of 20% on the equity interest. You are required to prepare a statement for management indicating the apparent profitability or otherwise, of this proposal and to state, giving reasons, whether you think that management are acting in the best interests of the shareholders in undertaking this.

*Note:* The present value of £1:

| | | | | | | |
|---|---|---|---|---|---|---|
| one | year hence at 6% is | £0·943 | at 20% | £0·833 |
| two | ,, ,, ,, | 0·890 | ,, | 0·694 |
| three | ,, ,, ,, | 0·890 | ,, | 0·579 |
| four | ,, ,, ,, | 0·792 | ,, | 0·482 |
| five | ,, ,, ,, | 0·741 | ,, | 0·402 |

*Note:* Taxation can be ignored.

(b) In present-day circumstances do you think that taxation can be ignored when investment opportunities are being considered? Give reasons for your answer. (A.C.C.A.)

6. A garage has recently installed a special machine for washing cars which has cost £7500. Its annual operating costs will total £5000 excluding depreciation, and these costs are base on an annual volume of 100,000 cars washed. At this volume "other costs" are expected to total £40,000 per

annum, and the average price of a car-wash will be £0·50. The machine has a four-year life with no residual value.

A machine salesman is now offering a different machine which promises to do the same job at an annual operating cost of £3000 exclusive of depreciation, and will give the same capacity, the same "other costs" and a four-year life with no residual value. This different machine will cost £9000 installed and the makers would offer £3750 for the present machine which would cost £750 to remove.

(a) Prepare on a yearly basis for the four years:

(i) comparative net income statements; and
(ii) comparative net cash flow statements;

for the installed machine and the proposed machine.

(b) Explain what further calculations would be necessary before deciding which alternative to recommend. (I.C.W.A.)

7. Your company plan to operate department D at normal capacity next year producing 100,000 units of product P. Assuming no defective work, these units can be manufactured in 250,000 labour hours at a cost of £0·50 per hour. Factory overhead would amount to £150,000 of which £50,000 would be fixed. Five units of material M will be used in each unit of product P. Materials can be purchased in two qualities; a high quality at £1·05 per unit or a lower quality at £0·80 per unit.

Under expected conditions, using high quality materials, 10% of the work will be defective requiring complete replacement of the materials, additional labour costs and variable overhead. Scrap materials recovered from defective production could be sold at £0·30 per unit of high quality material used.

As an alternative to this arrangement, the use of the lower quality material is being considered, but this would require an extra operation to be performed on it. An additional machine and tooling would be needed at a cost of £3000 per annum. The additional operation would take half an hour for each unit of product P produced, not taking defective work into account. It is estimated that 20 per cent of the work would be defective all of which would require complete replacement. Scrap materials from the lower quality material could be sold for £5000.

Present information to management indicating the more profitable course of action. (I.C.W.A.)

8. The management of a factory propose to replace existing road vehicles used for transporting liquid products by installing a pipeline. It is desirable because of operating difficulties to use large diameter pipes, but the cost of installation and maintenance increases more than proportionately to the increase in the size of the pipe installed.

The following details apply:

| Pipeline size: | 3 in. | 4 in. | 5 in. | 6 in. | 7 in. |
|---|---|---|---|---|---|
| Investment required (£000) ... ... | 16 | 24 | 36 | 64 | 150 |
| Gross annual savings in operating costs before deduction for depreciation and tax (£000) ... ... | 20 | 25 | 30 | 35 | 32 |

The installation is to be depreciated over 10 years on the straight-line method.

You are to assume that taxation in all its aspects is 50 per cent of savings made.

(*a*) Calculate the net annual savings, after deduction of tax, obtainable from each size of pipe; and

(*b*) recommend to management the largest size pipeline that should be installed to optimise investment if 15 per cent net after tax is the minimum acceptable return on initial investment.      (*A.C.C.A.*)

# Chapter 19

# CONTROL OF CAPITAL EXPENDITURE

The total capital expenditure to be incurred in a budget period is shown in the Capital Expenditure Budget. This budget is compiled from the annual forecast submitted by each division of the business. The forecasts are sent to the Capital Expenditure Committee on a stated date: if the budget period commences on 1st January the date for submission may be around the previous mid-November. Obviously, the precise date will have to be established by the Budget Controller.

Authorisation of the original forecast means that this becomes the budget. Alternatively, amendments may be suggested and these are then incorporated before the budget is compiled. The budget may be authorised along broad lines. Some projects will be covered by Capital Expenditure Sanctions; others will be shown in outline for later authorisation on Sanction forms; miscellaneous items can be covered in a block allowance. Items not individually sanctioned should be covered by a formal application before any expenditure is incurred.

Selection of the most important projects from the long-term forecast should be justifiable to the committee. In some circumstances a preliminary meeting of each divisional or functional manager with the Capital Expenditure Committee may be a good plan. Proposals for inclusion in the annual forecast can be discussed and general agreement on the lines to follow can be explained by the committee. Subsequent authorisation of the Capital Expenditure Forecast is likely to be greatly simplified by this preliminary meeting. When the long-term forecast has been reduced by one year's projects another year's can be added. If the forecast covers five years then any transfers should later be "replaced," thus maintaining the same period.

An example of an annual forecast is shown in Fig. 82. The same ruling can also be used for the Capital Expenditure Budget. Each division's budget can be merged into the budget for the business as a whole. Again a similar ruling can be used. An overall return on capital expenditure may be shown on each divisional budget and on the summary budget.

Any system for controlling capital expenditure should cover the following functions quite adequately:

1. Authorisation.
2. Recording and Control of Expenditure.

These matters are considered in this chapter.

ANNUAL CAPITAL EXPENDITURE FORECAST

Division................                    Period................

| Project No. | Description of Fixed Asset | External Costs (£) | | | Internal Costs (£) | | | | Grand Total | Estimated Life of Asset (Years) | Benefits Expected i.e. Rate of Return or Cost Savings | Asset to be Replaced | | Remarks |
|---|---|---|---|---|---|---|---|---|---|---|---|---|---|---|
| | | Asset | Delivery | Total | Labour | Material | O/head | Total | | | | Description | Cost | |
| | | | | | | | | | | | | | | |
| | | | | | | | | | | | | | | |

FIG. 82.—Example of an Annual Capital Expenditure Forecast

## AUTHORISATION

When a new project is suggested, whether from the need to develop new products, to replace obsolete or worn-out assets, to reduce costs, to increase plant capacity or to comply with statutory requirements, it is absolutely essential that a close watch be maintained on all expenditure.

The asset requirements for long-term plans can be worked out and shown on the Capital Expenditure Forecast. There is no doubt that top management must take a very active interest in stimulating thought from which new ideas emerge. Creation should not be left entirely to development engineers. Supervisors, foremen, and workers should understand the importance of suggesting improvements. Salesmen should be asked to report on demands for new products. An efficient system of communication, backed by some form of suggestion scheme, is essential to the development of new ideas.

Once an idea has been received it should be channelled to all executives likely to be involved and finally should reach the Capital Expenditure Committee.* For this purpose a standardised form should be used, setting out estimated costs, receipts, and serviceable life. Examples of two such forms are given in Figs. 83 and 84. Naturally these are not intended as specimens suitable for *all* business organisations. They should be modified to suit the particular needs of the business.

If the completion of the form to show costs and receipts is felt to involve too much work for an idea which may be rejected as being impracticable without reference to costs or benefits, a slightly modified procedure may be followed. All ideas could be stated in *general* terms with an outline of expected benefits and issued to the capital expenditure committee for approval. If the idea appears to have possibilities the committee would then forward the proposal to the accountant responsible for capital expenditure who would then take the necessary action to complete the formal application for approval, showing, of course, all details of costs and benefits. Needless to say, the project may still be rejected on the grounds of an inadequate return on investment. Some companies require authorisation at a level beyond the capital expenditure committee; *i.e.* at Board level. Often this is a formality. Nevertheless, it does keep the Board informed of what is going on.

Some accountants have suggested that a number of estimates should be made on the probable outcome of each project, thus giving the capital expenditure committee more facts to work on. Thus, for example, estimates could cover: (*a*) most likely results, (*b*) best possible results and (*c*) worst possible results. This gives a range of possibilities which may be very useful in arriving at the decision on whether or not to go ahead.

Projects which involve a relatively small amount of expenditure may be approved by a senior manager without reference to the committee.

* Would generally be the Budget Committee explained earlier.

Proposal No. .......................
Date of Proposal ..............

# CAPITAL EXPENDITURE SANCTION
### (REPLACEMENT/NEW* PROJECTS)

To: Capital Expenditure Committee*/General Manager*
From: Capital Budget Department

---

Application is submitted for authority to incur the following capital expenditure:

---

Project:                                          Estimated Life ...................
(Full details to be inserted)

---

| Expenditure | | £ | | | £ |
|---|---|---|---|---|---|
| | Cost of Asset | .............. | Own Labour | | .............. |
| | Delivery Charges | .............. | Own Material | | .............. |
| | | | Own Overhead | | .............. |
| Total £ ................ (A + B) | | A £ ———— | | B | £ ———— |

---

Reasons for Expenditure:

---

Expected Receipts:
(Give details of products to be sold summarised from Sales Forecast attached)

| | | | Sales Values £ | Present Value of Future Sales Values £ |
|---|---|---|---|---|
| Products: | | | | |
| YEAR 1 | ...................... at Standard Price | ........ | | |
| ,, 2 | ...................... ,, ,, ,, | ........ | | |
| ,, 3 | ...................... ,, ,, ,, | ........ | | |
| ,, 4 | ...................... ,, ,, ,, | ........ | | |
| | | | £ | |

Expected Running Costs:
(Per Detailed Statement Attached)

| | | Costs £ | Present Values of Costs £ |
|---|---|---|---|
| YEAR 1 | | | |
| ,, 2 | | | |
| ,, 3 | | | |
| ,, 4 | | | |
| | | £ | |
| | Net Cash Flow (or Net Profit) £ | | |

Expected Return on Investment =

---

Capital Expenditure Committee                    APPROVAL/REJECTION*
                                    Date ...........................

Reason for Rejection (if applicable) .................................................
Recommendations (if applicable including recommended accounting year for purchase)
.......................................................................................

Signed ....................................        Signed ....................................
          (Budget Controller)                              (Chairman)

---

Board of Directors' Approval ...................................
Date ...................................                    Secretary
(Note: All figures to be supported by detailed schedules)
* Delete where appropriate

FIG. 83.—*Example of a Capital Expenditure Sanction*
*(Net Cash Flow or Net Profit)*

This has the advantage of not overburdening the committee with insignificant items. However, it does have the disadvantage, so far as control is concerned, that a large capital expenditure project may be "slipped through" by local management in the guise of a number of small, unrelated projects. This kind of thing has to be guarded against. For these expenditures there should be a total allowance for each department, which should not be exceeded in the period in question.

---

Proposal No. .....................
Date of Proposal ...............

## CAPITAL EXPENDITURE SANCTION
### (REPLACEMENT/NEW* PROJECT)

To:   Capital Expenditure Committee*/General Manager*
From:  Capital Budget Department

Application is submitted for authority to incur the following capital expenditure:

(1)  Project:
     (Full details)

(2)  Capital Expenditure:

| | £ | | £ |
|---|---|---|---|
| Cost of Asset ............ | | Own Labour ............ | |
| Delivery Charges ............ | | Own Material ............ | |
| | | Own Overhead ............ | |

Total £......... (A + B)              A £              B £

(3)  Expected Cost Savings per Annum:

(4)  Rate of Return:

(Note:  All figures to be supported by detailed schedules)

Capital Expenditure Committee     APPROVAL/REJECTION*
                                  Date ...............................

Reason for Rejection (if applicable)    ...............................................
Recommendations:
* Delete where appropriate

---

FIG. 84.—Sample Capital Expenditure Sanction
(Cost Savings)

When the Capital Expenditure Forecast is compiled it will be necessary to decide the order of priority for individual projects. Having regard to the urgency or profitability of each project and the cash expected to be available in the future budget period the annual budget can be compiled. As is shown earlier the most acceptable criterion for evaluating investments is rate of return. The most profitable investments should be included in the annual budget bearing in mind, of course, that provision should be made to include essential projects such as replacement of a key machine and also very desirable welfare or other non-profit producing projects.

The costs included in the schedules submitted to the Capital Expenditure Committee for authorisation should be all those which are likely to result from purchasing the fixed asset: the purchase price of the asset, delivery costs, and the company's own internal costs connected with installation and related work. Some accountants advocate the exclusion of fixed overhead costs from the total capital cost of the asset. Since these are "period costs" there is probably some merit in this suggestion. In some cases, special costs, such as legal or development charges may be capitalised as part of the project.

The Capital Expenditure Sanction forms illustrated (Figs. 83 and 84) show that a project may be judged on the net cash flow, net profit, or cost savings. Clearly, although these measures are of prime importance they may not be the only consideration. The management accountant may be required to submit details on such important matters as the cash position for the period in question and other projects which have already been sanctioned for the same period. One of the major problems in authorising expenditure is the best allocation of available cash.

It may be a relatively simple matter to say "yes" or "no," but it is not so easy to fit each project into a co-ordinated pattern of acceptances bearing in mind, of course, the limited cash resources in any one year. Nevertheless, this is what should be done. Only then can the necessary degree of harmony (co-ordination) be achieved and profits maximised.

On the question of keeping a running account of current expenditures to be met, the Purchasing Department may perform a valuable service by compiling a schedule of capital expenditure orders placed and delivered in the budget period. Obviously, this can only be done after the event has taken place so this does limit its value. Nevertheless, it can be very useful for showing stages of progress and cash commitments.

## RECORDING AND CONTROL OF EXPENDITURE

Once each project has been sanctioned, the capital expenditure sanction form is returned to the accountant in charge of the accounting for capital expenditure. The routine followed from this point will vary from one business to another. However, the following procedures may serve as a guide:

1. A Capital Project Sheet is given a serial number and is entered up with full details of the authorised project.

One sheet, suitably cross-referenced to the Sanction, should be maintained for each project. A loose-leaf system is likely to give the flexibility desired.

An example of a Capital Project Sheet is given opposite (Fig. 85). The number given to each project should indicate the division and department as well as the numerical sequence of the project. Letters are often used as prefixes to denote the division and department.

2. All expenditure incurred on capital projects is picked up at regular intervals and entered on the appropriate project sheet.

## CAPITAL PROJECT SHEET

Department ..........................................     Project No. ...............................
    Sanction No. ...............................
Description  ..........................................     Date commenced  ........................
    Date Finished ...............................

Costs Authorised:

|  | £ |
|---|---|
| Purchase Price | .............. |
| Transport Charges | .............. |
| Own Labour | .............. |
| Own Material | .............. |
| Own Overhead | .............. |
| £ | |

| External Costs | | | | Internal Costs | | | | | |
|---|---|---|---|---|---|---|---|---|---|
| Date | Ref. | Supplier and Details | £ | Date | Ref. | Mat. £ | Lab. £ | O/head £ | Total £ |
|  |  |  |  |  |  |  |  |  |  |
|  |  |  |  |  |  |  |  |  |  |

FIG. 85.—*Example of a Capital Project Sheet*

NOTES

1. The external charges would be extracted from invoices sent by suppliers.

2. In the Supplier and Detail column would appear the name of the supplier, and then immediately below a full description of the asset. Care should be taken when compiling this description because the information will be used later to write up the Plant and Machinery Register described below.

3. Internal charges will be extracted from material requisitions and time sheets.

4. The form illustrated has been kept as simple as possible. In practice much more information may be included.

5. A decision should be made on whether to capitalise projects or to write them off wholly or partially to revenue.

The "rules" for differentiating between capital and revenue expenditure tend to be the same in principle for all types of business. However, there are different applications of rules and whilst assets which have an estimated life of more than one year are normally treated as capital expenditure, this is not a rigid formula. Often the cost involved determines whether an item is capital or revenue; *e.g.* assets costing less than £25 may be treated as revenue even though the estimated life is two, three or more years.

6. Transfers should be made to a Plant and Machinery register. This may be done once a year.

The costs may come from many sources. Invoices will be used for asset costs and delivery charges. Material requisitions will show material costs, and time sheets from service departments, such as the maintenance department, will give labour costs. The overhead absorption can be made on the basis of machine or labour times.

Obviously the system should cover notification of project details and project numbers to responsible managers such as the maintenance engineer or to departmental clerks. Correct tracing of costs then becomes possible and the project number(s) can be shown on invoices and other forms.

3. Careful control over expenditure has to be maintained and progress reported upon to management.

Sometimes a special return may be used for this purpose. A ruling for such a statement is shown in Figure 86. This is called a Capital Expenditure Progress Statement. As with all the examples, the rulings and headings may be varied to suit the particular needs.

4. Supplementary Sanctions should be obtained for projects likely to exceed the original figure.

An example of a Capital Expenditure Sanction form has already been given. The same type of form could be used to apply for authority to incur additional expenditure.

5. An account should be maintained in the financial or integrated ledger to show total capital expenditure for the year to date.

The total of the figures from all Capital Project Sheets should be reconciled with the Capital Expenditure Account at regular intervals.

A ruling for a page of a Plant and Machinery Register is shown in Fig. 87. The register may be in the form of a loose leaf binder or a card system. The postings may be performed by hand or by accounting machine, including a punched card accounting machine.

In the illustration given it will be seen that full particulars of the asset are shown. Each year the depreciation is calculated and entered in the appropriate column and then the balance of the asset cost is shown in the column headed "Book Value." At any time the total depreciation and net book value are immediately obtainable. The maintenance record indicates the reliability of the particular asset. This may be useful when considering the asset's replacement. The importance of maintaining capital intact is discussed in Chapter 27. Provision on the record for replacement cost assessments recognises the problem of finding sufficient funds to meet replacements in a period of rising prices. Some accountants may prefer to keep the historical cost record and the replacement problem quite distinct from each other. This is a matter of opinion. There seems nothing wrong in incorporating replacement figures in the Plant and Machinery Register. Indeed it can be argued

## CAPITAL EXPENDITURE PROGRESS STATEMENT

Period Covered to................

| Department | Project No. | Project Description | Authorised (£) | | Expenditure Last Year (£) | | Balance Available (£) | | Expenditure This Year (£) | | Balance to date* | | Remarks |
|---|---|---|---|---|---|---|---|---|---|---|---|---|---|
| | | | External | Internal | External | Internal | External | Internal | External | Internal | External | Internal | |

Fig. 86.—*Ruling for Capital Expenditure Progress Statement*

\* Overspending in red.

that the replacement costs are likely to be of greater interest to management than are the historical costs.

There is no doubt that the Plant and Machinery Register is an essential record for all types of business. The adequacy of depreciation charges will be revealed and the experience obtained can be used in the future. Another advantage is the fact that a formal record is kept which

*Page No. ......*

*Project Sheet No.........*

**PLANT & MACHINERY REGISTER**

**Fixed Asset Description** ............................ **Department** ........

**Maker's Number** ............................... **Departmental Number** .....

**Supplier** ......................... **Depreciation Plan** .........................

**Residual Value** £............................

**Purpose** ...................... **Horse-Power** ...............................

**Floor Space Occupied** ................square feet **Insurance Cover** £.............

| | £ | Year | Depreciation | Book Value | Year | Depreciation | Book Value |
|---|---|---|---|---|---|---|---|
| *Costs*<br>Purchase Price<br>Installation<br>Modifications | | | | | | | |

| Maintenance Record | Year | Details | Cost | Year | Details | Cost |
|---|---|---|---|---|---|---|
| | | | | | | |

| Replacement Cost Assessments | Year | Method | Estimated Replacement Cost | Year | Method | Estimated Replacement Cost |
|---|---|---|---|---|---|---|
| | | | | | | |

FIG. 87.—*Ruling for Plant and Machinery Register*

shows all the fixed asset information required in the Profit and Loss Account (depreciation) and on the Balance Sheet (original cost, aggregate depreciation and book value). The needs of insurance companies, the Commissioners of Inland Revenue* and management, so far as fixed assets are concerned, should all be covered in the register. Often the value of fixed assets owned by a company runs into millions of pounds; this fact in itself should testify how very important it is for adequate records to be maintained.

* Capital allowances could be shown on the record, thereby having all the information together.

## EXAMINATION QUESTIONS

1. The Board of your company has decided upon a major scheme of capital expenditure on additional buildings and plant for the purpose of extending its activities. Explain how this expenditure could be controlled. (*I.C.W.A.*)

2. Your board complains that it is presented with requests for the sanction of capital expenditure which may be sponsored by any one of a number of company officials and supported by information varying widely in content, presentation and degree of detail.

You are asked to advise on a uniform procedure for the sponsoring and mode of presentation of such requests. (*I.C.W.A.*)

3. Expenditure on the purchase of consumable tools by an engineering company is found to have increased considerably in the past twelve months without any corresponding increase in the level of activity in the factory. Investigation shows that the increased expenditure is due partly to higher prices paid, partly to increased quantities purchased. The higher prices have been mainly due to the use of tools of higher quality, which have been purchased without sufficient attention being given to securing compensating benefits in the form of lower factory operating costs or improved quality of product. It is also feared that there may have been some extravagance in consumption. What steps would you take to ensure economy both in regard to the quality of tools purchased and in their use? (*I.C.W.A.*)

4. It is the practice of a large manufacturing organisation to put all its capital expenditure work, with the exception of general-purpose machine-tool purchase, through its civil and plant engineering sections. These sections also undertake the maintenance and repairs of the company's assets.

Describe the system you would use to ensure accurate cost ascertainment and adequate cost control of capital expenditure in this circumstance.

(*I.C.W.A.*)

5. What method do you recommend, and why, for the absorption into cost of capital expenditure on machinery for productive processes? Justify the difference, if any, between your method and the present Inland Revenue Taxation allowances relating to such expenditure. (*I.C.W.A.*)

# CHAPTER 20

## INTERNAL CONTROL AND INTERNAL AUDIT

CONTROL has to be exercised over all aspects of a business. Methods of control should be incorporated into all accounting systems; without them a system is likely to be ineffective and too costly to operate in relation to benefits received.

The need to install control methods grows with the increase in size and complexity of the business organisation. With the tendency for different businesses to amalgamate, or for the stronger to absorb the weaker, there is inevitably more emphasis placed upon the control aspect.

A question which must arise is what aspects are to be controlled and how are these aspects to be broken down into lines of responsibility. Because of the different types of organisation that exist, and also the attitude of top management towards the control function, no standard pattern can be laid down. However, some idea of the aspects to be covered and the persons who may be responsible, giving emphasis to the work of the internal auditor, are summarised below:

1. *Control of Costs.*

Through the design of appropriate systems to cover labour, material and overheads, and the reporting on variances to all levels of management, cost control is exercised. The cost accountant is, therefore, the prime mover in the cost-control function.

However, this is not to say that the cost accountant *actually controls* the costs. Without the co-operation of personnel, including all levels of management and operatives and other workers, there can be no effective control. Furthermore, the control should be exercised at the point at which the costs are incurred—once more emphasising the importance of cost consciousness stretching beyond the accounting department.

Accounting reports, cost variances, and other techniques are discussed in other chapters. (*See* especially Chapter 14.)

2. *Detection of Errors.*

The detection of errors is the responsibility of all levels of management. Each departmental head has a duty to ensure that work produced is of high quality. In the producing departments the Inspection Department takes over the function of checking. When clerical procedures are involved the head of each administration department should arrange that the work of one clerk is automatically checked by another—this procedure is known as *internal check.*

Besides internal check, there is *internal audit* which also detects errors. Unless management can rely on the facts being recorded, analysed and presented there can be no faith in the accounting system. The internal auditor has, therefore, a very important role to play; ensuring that a high standard of accuracy is achieved. Because of the complexity of modern business the external auditor cannot possibly cover every transaction as part of the statutory audit.

### 3. Detection and Prevention of Fraud.

This function is closely linked with the detection of errors. Both involve checking the work carried out by clerks, accountants, and other personnel. Detecting any misappropriation of funds or the misuse of any of a company's assets should be a prime function of the internal auditor. Generally he pays particular attention to transactions which involve cash, but other transactions are not excluded. How successful internal control can be depends just as much on the initial design of the accounting system.

### 4. Detecting Errors of Principle.

Accounting systems are based on written procedures, on legal requirements and on accounting conventions which represent generally accepted accounting practice. Reporting on deviations from the written or unwritten standard procedures should be an important part of the internal auditor's work.

The organisation and methods staff will also be concerned with detecting errors of principle. Indeed, it may be to the Organisation and Methods Department that the internal auditor will turn for guidance on how the errors of principle are to be eliminated. Close co-operation between the two staffs—internal audit and O and M—will be vital in obtaining the fullest benefit from the two departments. What shape the co-operation will take will depend upon the stated responsibilities of each department. The internal audit department may detect the error and report upon it, whereupon the O and M Department then conducts an investigation with a view to carrying out corrective action.

### 5. Scrutiny and Verification of Assets and Liabilities.

This important function is usually covered by the internal audit department. Attention should be paid to the valuation and depreciation of fixed assets and the control of current assets and current liabilities. Whether or not real capital is being maintained intact should possibly also be the subject of the auditor's report. However, this is a matter on which there is no general agreement: it centres around the argument whether historical cost or replacement cost should be used for recording fixed assets and, in addition, what significance should be attached to keeping intact the net current assets.

### 6. Focusing Attention on Weaknesses of System.

Normally the internal auditor should observe and report to the Organisation and Methods Department (usually shortened to O and M).

If there is no O and M department the internal audit department may report to management with a view to obtaining sanction to eliminate the weaknesses. They may make general observations on their nature, but, after that, the installation of new procedures, methods and systems should be left to the O and M specialists. Only when the latter are not employed should the internal auditor carry out the O and M function.*

When appraising systems, the internal auditor should consider how *effective* these are. In particular, attention should be paid to ascertaining what functions the management accounting records are supposed to serve and whether or not they actually meet with these requirements. The internal auditor is in a very favourable position for comparing different systems and for selecting the most efficient methods.

Reports and statements have to be kept to a minimum. Unnecessary forms add to clerical costs and yet serve no useful purpose. The internal auditor should make a study of all forms used and determine whether any should be eliminated.

Material control should also receive attention. The procedures for purchasing, receiving, inward inspection, storing, issuing and valuation of stocks all come within the area for appraisal.

In the field of labour costs the internal auditor scrutinizes the procedures relating to timekeeping, calculation and payment of wages and the analysis and recovery of wages in the costs of the products.

Factory and other overhead costs have to be absorbed by the methods which result in tracing benefits received or responsibilities incurred. If the most appropriate methods are not being used the internal auditor may detect this fact and report to the chief management accountant.

### 7. *Special Investigations.*

Whether or not special investigations should come within the jurisdiction of the internal audit department is a matter for debate. Some accountants take the view that internal audit should be a continuous and systematic process and, therefore, if special assignments are to be covered by the internal auditor they may reach such proportions that the *normal* work is neglected.

On the other hand, there are other accountants who take the view that the internal auditor should be in a position to carry out special investigations.†

If special investigations *are* to be carried out by the internal auditor there seems to be merit in limiting these to the enquiries which are directly connected with the internal auditor's work and which do not interfere unduly with the normal checking and appraisal.

* This follows closely the recommendation of the Association of Certified and Corporate Accountants. See *The Modern Approach to Internal Auditing* (A.C.C.A.), page 12.

† See *The Modern Approach to Internal Auditing* (A.C.C.A.), page 10. However this is not put forward as an invariable rule.

Cost reduction programmes and system analysis are both in the nature of special investigations. The internal auditor may bring to light the *need* for these investigations, but it is probably better to reduce costs by means of cost investigators on the staff of the chief cost accountant and to introduce a new system through an organisations and methods department. By their nature such investigations call for the fullest possible attention and expert knowledge and, therefore, when the business is large enough they should be dealt with by experts in the particular field.

### 8. *Collaboration with the Statutory Auditors.*

The internal auditor is in a position to simplify the work of the external auditor. Accordingly, the two functions, although different in nature, should be viewed together. In this way a clear division of the work can be obtained. The advantages* of close collaboration may be as follows:

(*a*) The statutory auditor can draw on the experience of the internal auditor on technicalities of the business and the accounting system.

(*b*) The volume of work to be done by the statutory auditor can be reduced to a minimum. This is achieved by cutting out detailed checking already covered by the internal auditor.

The internal audit reports can be scrutinised by the external auditors thereby ensuring that a high standard of work is being achieved by the internal audit department.

(*c*) An understanding of what work is being performed by the internal auditor will indicate whether or not the internal control system is operating satisfactorily.

In effect, therefore, the external auditor delegates much of the detailed work to the internal auditor. The Association of Certified and Corporate Accountants recommend that an agreement on how the work should be divided between the external auditor and internal auditor should be in writing. Such delegation does not relieve the statutory auditor of his obligations as laid down by the Companies Act, 1948.†

### INTERNAL CHECK AND INTERNAL AUDIT

There are different interpretations placed on what is meant by "internal check." Sometimes "internal check" is confused with "internal audit." Yet the distinction is quite clear.

*Internal check* covers the detection of fraud, of errors, and of inferior

---

* See *Notes on the Relation of the Internal Audit to the Statutory Audit* published by The Institute of Chartered Accountants in England and Wales.

† See *The Modern Approach to Internal Auditing* (A.C.C.A.).

quality work. It involves following a number of principles, the main ones being as follows:

1. Work is divided so that no single person has sole control over a complete cycle of work. Thus, for example, the cashier should not post the ledgers. Instead, this function should be carried out by an independent person responsible to the accountant.

2. The work flows from one person to another and in the process each stage is subjected to an independent check. This is done with the minimum amount of duplication. An illustration of this principle can be taken from the Wages Department. Here it is usual for the work to be divided so that one clerk calculates the amount of wages, another enters the details on the pay roll, and so on.

3. When the checks are not automatically carried out as part of the system, special checks should be carried out by a senior clerk. In an accountant's department a senior assistant may check the ledger postings made by other assistants.

These are the main features of internal checking. In addition attention should be paid to the following:

4. At regular and irregular intervals physical and book figures should be reconciled. This applies particularly to cash and stocks of raw materials and finished goods.

5. Proper lines of authority should be established for dealing with the passing of invoices, authorising expenditure, signing of cheques, handling money, issuing of materials, and other functions which are of such a nature that carelessness could lead to fraud.

*Internal Audit* covers all those functions outlined earlier in this chapter. As will be apparent even from the outline, the scope of the work of the internal auditor is now very wide. Where there is an internal auditing department which is fully accepted as part of the management control system, the work is not simply that of checking and detecting fraud and errors. These must still be part of the responsibility of that department, but by no means the most important part. Neither is the checking, reporting, and advising limited to the purely financial accounting. All administrative functions, procedures, and systems may be examined by the internal auditor. Indeed, because of the existence of the statutory auditor the internal auditor fulfils his role to the best advantage by broadening his net and taking in the work of all administrative departments. That there is no general agreement on how far the internal audit work should go especially when it impinges on organisation and methods work has already been noticed.

The distinction between internal check and internal audit should now be clear. The former is much narrower than the latter being limited to purely routine checking. Moreover, internal check is carried out by personnel as part of their normal, everyday work. On the other hand, internal audit is in the hands of specialist auditors whose function is to carry out this work and no other.

Two principal questions arise in connection with internal audit. The first is what qualifications and qualities should be possessed by an internal auditor and the second queries how internal audit should be organised. These are dealt with below.

## QUALITIES OF THE INTERNAL AUDITOR

There is general agreement that an internal auditor should be qualified both by examinations and experience to carry out the work with which he is entrusted. Unless he is a member of a recognized accountancy body the internal auditor is unlikely to receive the support and respect of qualified members who are responsible for the work being audited.

The experience required should ideally be of a wide and varied nature. He should have a working knowledge of Cost Accounting, Budgetary Control and other management accountancy techniques, preferably gained from practical experience. Accordingly, there is much to be gained from using men who have had a number of years' experience in different firms and on all aspects of industrial accounting. Furthermore, the internal auditor should be thorough and painstaking with a tenacious inquiring mind. The ability to deal with other people in a tactful manner is, of course, essential. If the internal auditor is to remain a useful member of the administrative team he should be able to co-operate with all members of the staff.

The internal auditor is primarily an adviser to management. He is not a manager,* but he can contribute to greater efficiency. Indeed the internal audit work is likely to keep each departmental manager on his toes and this should result in continuous improvement.

Differences of opinion exist on the ideal relationship of the auditor within the organisation. The main question is: to whom should the internal auditor report and to whom should he be responsible?

A suggestion sometimes put forward is that, because the internal auditor investigates and reports on the accounting function, he should *not* be responsible to the chief accountant. However, this is not a view to be taken too seriously. The chief accountant has normally sufficient integrity and status to disarm any criticism that he should be "watched" by internal auditors. In fact, in the interest of efficiency it is very desirable that the chief accountant should formulate policy on what role the internal audit department is to play within the organisation. Normally, therefore, the chief internal auditor should report to the chief accountant and look to this executive for instructions and guidance.

* This is used in the wide sense of managing one of the basic functions such as production and selling. Obviously the chief internal auditor is a line manager because he is responsible for the work of the staff in his department.

When a business is divided into divisions the internal auditor may report to the divisional accountant as well as the chief internal auditor. In these circumstances a common practice is to centralise the internal audit department. This centralisation may be "complete" in the sense that the internal audit staff report to headquarters for duty and are then assigned to a particular division. The principal advantage of this procedure is that an auditor can be assigned to one division for a limited period and then to another, the changes taking place at fairly frequent intervals. This changing around of personnel tends to avoid the possibility of divisional staff and audit staff becoming *too* friendly and, therefore, avoids the possibility of collusion. On the other hand, if the changes occur very frequently an auditor will have difficulty in familiarising himself fully with a division's organisation and systems and, therefore, he may not be able to carry out his work as efficiently as when he has a more extensive knowledge. Another possible disadvantage is the expense involved in travelling and staying in hotels; in addition, there is the corollary of wasted time due to travelling from one division to another.

Irrespective of the disadvantages of complete centralisation there is no doubt that properly organised this system can be more efficient than complete decentralisation. In the latter case there is a danger that the internal auditors will be dominated by the local management with a resultant deterioration in the effectiveness of the audit work.

When a company's divisions extend over a large geographical area a compromise may be advisable. The internal audit department may be centralised with a number of auditors attached to it and, in addition, a number of auditors would be located permanently in each division, but would report to, and be supervised by, the chief internal auditor. Regular visits to divisions by the chief internal auditor or his deputy could maintain the essential contact with headquarters.

## *METHOD OF OPERATION*

How the internal audit department will be organised and the way it will be operated depend upon the extent of its activities and the views of the chief accountant and the chief internal auditor. The opinion of these executives will be influenced by the nature of the acceptance of the internal audit service by top management. In some companies, where the internal audit is restricted to the checking of figures to detect errors and fraud, the method of operation will be relatively straightforward and should not be difficult to plan.

If the internal audit service is to be utilised to the fullest possible extent the planning and carrying out of the work tends to be more complex. In addition to normal checking there will be the appraisal of management accounting records and systems, and special investigations into problems which arise and on which management requires further information. However, even in these circumstances the routine work can be scheduled and a timetable compiled. Extra staff—over and above those required for the routine auditing—will provide the necessary flexibility needed to cover the special assignments.

Irrespective of the method of operation adopted it is essential to plan the audit in a manner which interferes with the work in each department to the minimum extent. Some interference will be inevitable, but care should be taken to ensure that this does not become excessive.

The chief internal auditor should ensure that each auditor understands the principles being followed, and the purpose of each audit. An audit manual can cover all procedures and give examples of forms to be employed including standard questionnaires to be used to check the systems of control. An example of an internal control check list is given below (Fig. 88).

Prompt reporting on each completed audit programme is essential. Generally an audit report is compiled immediately after an audit is completed. It should be concerned with the most important findings and should make suggestions to overcome the major difficulties. The reports should be concise yet informative and above all they should be designed for management; that is to say, they should provoke thought and, when necessary, action. Normally the report will be presented via the chief accountant, since this enables the latter executive to study the contents and call for any further details he considers will be required by management to supplement the report. A special investigation may emerge from the needs of management.

As indicated, much of the work of the internal auditor may be of a routine nature. Accordingly, there is a need to establish standard procedures for checking the accuracy of work. Generally the following matters will be incorporated into the routine system:

1. Checking that all documents and vouchers from which action is taken, including posting to ledgers and payment or receipt of cash, are correctly authorised and represent a legitimate transaction.

This process is known as "vouching." It means tracing a transaction to its source and being satisfied that everything is proper and legal. If necessary, explanations should be sought from staff responsible for the work being audited.

2. All transactions relating to a particular control area should be checked in the same audit. Thus, for example, if cash receipts are being checked then *all* aspects of receiving cash should be covered in one exercise.

3. Ticks or codes should be used to show what work has been checked. These are generally known only by the audit staff and are written or stamped with a distinctive coloured ink.

4. Notes and working papers should be compiled on all vital facts relating to an audit.

| | **INTERNAL CONTROL CHECK LIST**<br>**CASH CONTROL** | | |
|---|---|---|---|
| **Date** ........................... | | **Prepared By** ........................ | |
| Question<br>No. | Question | Answer<br>Yes or<br>*No* | Remarks |
| 1. | Are all cash receipts banked each day? | | |
| 2. | Are official receipts issued for all payments? | | |
| 3. | Does the cashier ever issue temporary receipts? | | |
| 4. | Is the total cash banked and total on receipts reconciled? | | |
| 5. | Are paying-in slips completed by the cashier when he pays in the cash at the bank? | | |
| 6. | Does the bank stamp or duplicate of the paying-in slip indicate that the money has been banked? | | |
| 7. | Is a bank reconciliation statement prepared at least each month? | | |
| 8. | Does the cashier make the entries in the ledger? | | |
| 9. | Are cheques used for paying out all significant amounts? | | |
| 10. | Is the imprest system employed for controlling petty cash? | | |
| 11. | Are cheques signed only by authorised personnel? | | |
| 12. | Are petty cash vouchers authorised? | | |
| 13. | Is a frequent but irregular check made on the balance of cash kept by the cashier? | | |
| 14. | Are adequate safeguards present for ensuring that all remittances received by post reach the cashier without delay? | | |

FIG. 88.—*Internal Control Check List*

NOTES

1. The check list provides a method of checking through the most important facts relating to a particular control system. A summary of the overall effectiveness of the system is obtained.

2. In the example given a number of questions have been framed to illustrate the principles involved in checking a control system. Each *section* of the system may be covered by separate check lists. There may be one for cash payments, another for cash receipts and a further one for petty cash.

The list of questions should not be regarded as exhaustive. Many more can be added to give a more detailed analysis.

3. Any weaknesses in a system are revealed by the check list. They can be investigated and remedied.

The notes can become a sort of vade-mecum on audit procedures. The working papers are a collection of check lists, queries that have arisen during an audit, explanations obtained, and other relevant details appertaining to the audit.

5. Audit Reports—these may be divided into (a) routine reports and (b) special reports. The general rules relating to reports and statements, discussed in Chapter 14, also apply to Audit Reports.

## SYSTEM DESIGN

System design is an integral part of efficient business organisation. Each system used should be appropriate to the purpose and should result in accurate recording, and be relatively inexpensive to operate. A carefully planned system can help to keep down the work of the internal auditor to a minimum and it is for this reason that some accountants believe that the internal auditor should play a major part in the introduction of a system. Other authorities on management accounting prefer to see all system design carried out by members of the organisation and methods department. Irrespective of the department responsible the following matters will require attention:

### 1. *Organisation and Lines of Responsibility.*

A sound plan is to use organisation charts both for the business as a whole and the breakdown into divisions and departments. This practice can save a lot of trouble and prevent overlapping of duties.

Particular attention should be paid to the principles followed to ensure that there is an adequate system of internal check (*see* page 482).

### 2. *Operating Routines.*

The work to be done for the purposes to be accomplished should be determined. Following this the most suitable operating routines can be selected. This will involve a study of *possible* methods and by the means of flow charts and other aids, the most effective procedures should emerge.

When the most suitable procedures are being selected it is important to maintain contact with the executives who are to be directly concerned with the new proposals. A good plan is to draft procedures along broad lines and then have a discussion with the departmental heads affected before drafting the final proposals. Probably the simplest way is to call a meeting of all affected so that suggestions can be received, and problems arising from the proposals can be overcome.

Also at this stage the forms to be used, including the number of copies, can be discussed. The principal object should be to keep the number of forms to a minimum, avoiding duplication.

### 3. *Written Procedures and Installation.*

When agreement has been reached on procedures, the latter can be put into the form of written instructions. A date for the introduction of the system has to be fixed and the installation completed. Copies of the instructions should be routed to all interested personnel in good time—this allows a study to be made and queries to be raised before the date for the introduction of the new system.

After a system has been installed and has been operating for a few months a follow-up audit is usually made and any amendments are incorporated into the standard procedures. Again these should be put into written form and issued. Being in writing means that there is less danger of procedures changing their form without due authorisation. In addition, written procedures are a valuable aid to the training of new personnel.

### AREAS OF CONTROL

The internal auditor has many areas to watch over. In a book of this nature which is concerned with the wide field of management accountancy it is impossible to cover details of all items to be checked. So far as systems and management records are concerned guidance can be obtained on the basic principles of particular aspects from the appropriate chapters. Some of the most important areas over which control has to be exercised are as follows:

### 1. *Cash Control.*

Care has to be taken to prevent fraudulent conversion or larceny. Many of the points to watch on cash control are shown on page 514 being listed in the Internal Control Check List (Fig. 88).

### 2. *Stores (Material) Control.*

Attention should be paid to the following:

(*a*) Incoming materials—whether checked promptly and proper records are prepared.

(*b*) Storage of materials—bins and shelves should be appropriate for the materials being stored. They should be indexed and each bin or shelf should have a printed label showing its contents.

(*c*) No stores should be issued without a properly authorised Material Requisition.

(*d*) Returns to Stores should be covered by a Material Return Note.

(*e*) The forms—Goods Inwards Notes, Material Requisitions, Material Return Notes—should be routed to the Costing Department without delay.

(*f*) Perpetual inventory and continuous stock-taking.

At all times the balances on hand both in quantities and values should be available. These are obtained by suitably designed bin cards, Stores Ledgers and Factory Ledgers. Each addition or issue is "automatically" brought into, or deducted from the net balance.

Continuous stock-taking means that a number of items of stock are checked each day so that during the course of a year each type of material is checked at least twice. This ensures accuracy between physical quantities and book quantities and allows management to control more effectively. There is less danger of loss in production, and pilfering and carelessness tends to be kept to a minimum.

(g) Annual stock-taking—is this carried out in the most efficient manner and are slow-moving and obsolete stocks noted?

(h) Stock valuation—are the principles of valuation being adopted the most appropriate for the business concerned and are they being applied consistently?

These indicate the most important features of Stores control. The internal auditor will be concerned with detecting fraud and errors as well as flaws in the system.

### 3. *Labour Controls.*

Some of the most important matters which should receive attention are given below:

(a) Procedures for recording attendance times—are these as foolproof as possible?

(b) Are job or process times recorded in an efficient manner? There should be reconciliation of attendance and *effective* time; *i.e.* on jobs or processes.

(c) Division of work in the wages department. This should be arranged so that one clerk checks the work of another. Duties should be changed around from time to time so that the danger of collusion is reduced to a minimum.

(d) Overtime—should be authorised.

(e) Physical numbers and payroll numbers. Checks should be made to ensure that the payroll is not padded by fictitious personnel.

(f) The paying out of wages should be supervised and the clerks involved in giving out the wages should be changed from time to time.

(g) The absorption of labour costs in the cost of the products: are the procedures accurate and appropriate?

Careful checking of total wages, deductions, and net wages will be essential, preferably by referring back to basic documents such as clock cards and rate books. The total wages paid and the cheques drawn should be compared for each week. Any defects in the system will call for prompt attention for it is in the field of wages procedures that a considerable amount of fraud has been committed.

### 4. Overhead Costs.

The methods of authorising overhead expenditure; its recording; the apportionment to cost centres and the absorption of overheads in product costs should all be subjected to scrutiny.

### 5. Miscellaneous Matters.

Other matters which have to be covered are creditors, debtors, purchasing procedures, canteen procedures, capital expenditure classification and control, and personnel policy. Whether the latter should be part of the normal internal auditor's duties is a doubtful point. Preferably personnel matters should be audited by someone who is well versed in what are reasonable rates of pay, working conditions, promotion prospects, and related matters. Even though this may not be regarded as a usual internal audit assignment it is, nevertheless, extremely important and should receive attention; otherwise a high labour turnover and dissatisfied staff may result.

### EXAMINATION QUESTIONS

1. As the Chief Accountant of a manufacturing company with some 5,000 employees which has no system of Internal Audit, you propose to report to your Managing Director on the desirability of such an audit and your suggestions for its organisation.

Enumerate briefly the main points of your report, covering:

(a) the advantages of an Internal Audit;

(b) to whom it should be responsible (with reasons);

(c) its relationship to the statutory audit;

(d) the main scope of its duties beyond those usually performed by the statutory audit. (I.C.W.A.)

2. Define internal control, internal check and internal auditing and give your views on the field of relationship and co-operation between the statutory and the internal auditor. (A.C.C.A.)

3. State the functions of an internal auditor and indicate his relationship to management. (A.C.C.A.)

4. As cost auditor to a group of factories, describe the procedure you would adopt with regard to labour and material costs. (I.C.W.A.)

5. Draft an audit programme for the systems of material control, purchasing and stores procedures of a large organisation in which the production is largely jobbing and small batch, and where the costing is of the order type, that is, the system of comparing part-order costs with planned costs which are drawn up upon receipt of order. (I.C.W.A.)

CHAPTER 21

## COMPANY ACCOUNTS

THIS chapter gives an outline of the principles normally followed when compiling company accounts. Although the remarks and explanations given apply to *company* accounts, many of them will also have relevance to other types of accounts.

In Chapters 1 and 10 the different forms which accounts may take were noticed.* Here the concern is with the conventional accounts which are normally prepared during the course of, and at the end of, each year. For convenience these may be classified as (*a*) interim accounts and (*b*) final accounts.

### *INTERIM ACCOUNTS*

Interim Accounts may be prepared monthly, quarterly, or at other convenient divisions of a year. They are very much a part of management accounting because usually they aim at showing management what progress has been made, and indicate—if properly compiled—what control action is necessary. Many reports and operating statements could come into this category, although strictly, they are not in account form. For convenience, these reports and statements are dealt with in Chapter 14.

The Interim Profit and Loss Account can be a very valuable guide to progress being made month by month throughout the year. This will be particularly so when this account is linked with budgetary control. The plans made and actual progress, both in financial terms, can be compared for each control period. Whether to adopt the marginal *or* orthodox† form of Profit and Loss Account is a matter to be decided by the accountant concerned. The marginal form avoids the problem of including stocks in the computations, but this may not be a desirable feature when, for example, stocks of raw materials tend to fluctuate and management wishes to watch these variations. Furthermore, it should be remembered that the marginal accounts may give undue emphasis to the sales aspect with consequent neglect of reporting on the state of production.‡

An example of an orthodox Profit and Loss Statement is shown below (Fig. 89).§ This can be varied to meet particular needs. *Monthly*

* Accounts may vary according to the *purpose* for which they are intended; *e.g.* for calculation of tax payable; to compute estate duty.
† "Orthodox" refers to the "total cost" or "absorption cost" approach where *all* costs are included in the Profit and Loss Account.
‡ Marginal Costing is dealt with in detail in Chapter 10.
§ This Statement is used in connection with Budgetary Control.

## INTERIM PROFIT AND LOSS STATEMENT (Quarterly)
### X. Y. Co. Ltd.

Factory: ...........................  |  No. of Weeks: ....................  |  Period Ending: .................

| Nature of Income or Cost | Month: ............... | | | | Month: ............... | | | | Month: ............... | | | | Totals to date | | | |
|---|---|---|---|---|---|---|---|---|---|---|---|---|---|---|---|---|
| | Actual | Budget | Variance | % | Actual | Budget | Variance | % | Actual | Budget | Variance | % | Actual | Budget | Variance | % |
| **OUTPUT** | | | | | | | | | | | | | | | | |
| **SALES VALUE OF PRODUCTION** Controllable  Labour  Materials  Expenses  **Direct Cost of Manufacture** | | | | | | | | | | | | | | | | |
| Uncontrollable  Fixed expenses  **Total Mfg. Services** | | | | | | | | | | | | | | | | |
| **Cost of Manufacture** | | | | | | | | | | | | | | | | |
| **PRODUCTION SERVICES & ADMINISTRATION**  Cost Centre  A  B  C  **Total Production Services** | | | | | | | | | | | | | | | | |
| **Total Administration** | | | | | | | | | | | | | | | | |
| **COST OF PRODUCTION** | | | | | | | | | | | | | | | | |
| **WORK-IN-PROGRESS**  Opening  Closing | | | | | | | | | | | | | | | | |
| **COST OF PRODUCTION ACTUAL—**  Passed to Finished Stock | | | | | | | | | | | | | | | | |
| **OPERATING MARGIN ON PRODUCTION  SALES INVOICED GROSS** | | | | | | | | | | | | | | | | |
| **FINISHED GOODS STOCKS AT COST**  Opening  Closing | | | | | | | | | | | | | | | | |
| **PRODUCTION COST OF SALES** | | | | | | | | | | | | | | | | |
| **OPERATING MARGIN ON SALES** | | | | | | | | | | | | | | | | |
| **SALES AND DISTRIBUTION**  Carriage and Warehousing  Selling Costs | | | | | | | | | | | | | | | | |
| **NET PROFIT ON COMMERCIAL ACTIVITY** | | | | | | | | | | | | | | | | |

FIG. 89.—*Orthodox Interim Profit and Loss Statement* (*Quarterly*)

Note: This statement may be summarised or extended to meet particular requirements.

profit and loss statements could be prepared along the same lines. The assumption made in the example is that the output consists of identical units; *e.g.* sacks of flour or cwts of cement. If many products are produced and volume is to be shown then a different layout will be necessary.

From time to time suggestions have been made that interim profit and loss accounts should be issued to shareholders. These may take the form of quarterly or half-yearly statements. Many arguments have been used *for* and *against* the preparation of these interim accounts, but there seems to be a stronger case for their preparation, particularly if the business concerned is subjected to seasonal or other fluctuations in trade.

In favour of producing interim statements the following arguments are often used:

1. Safeguards the present or potential shareholders. The fortunes of a company can fluctuate tremendously during the course of a year: at the beginning it may be at the height of a boom whereas at the end there may be trade recession. Interim statements would tend to warn the investor of what is taking place and he would then purchase shares (or sell them) with a fuller knowledge of the facts.

The danger of investors being misled tends to be aggravated when most companies are enjoying good fortune. A sudden downward swing in profits may be quite unexpected and investors will continue to buy shares which they would not have considered buying had they known the truth; *i.e.* if an interim statement had been issued by the company concerned.

2. Employees are kept informed of the state of the company's affairs.

With the emphasis on increased wages for increased productivity the issue of interim reports can be very valuable. This is very much the case when productivity is *not* rising, but demands for wages are very persistent. Trade unions tend to be more satisfied when the true facts are made known to them. Obviously, any *increase* in productivity and profits will have the opposite effect and may result in giving the unions a stronger case for being awarded an increase. However, presumably the company is then in a position to consider a wage award so no real harm is done.

Arguments *against* issuing interim reports are more numerous than those in favour. However, most of these criticisms cannot be taken too seriously or if they are a definite disadvantage they can be overcome. A summary of the objections is given below:

1. Preparation and circulation of the reports throws a greater burden on the accounting staff with a consequent increase in costs. This objection cannot be taken too seriously because if the manage-

ment accountant is providing essential control information the preparation of interim statements should not involve much extra work, especially if the accounting is mechanised. The printing and circulation must increase costs, but the value given by the reports is likely to be much greater than the cost.

2. When trade is seasonal, interim reports can be very misleading, particularly to the uninitiated, such as the small investor. This objection implies that the seasonal variations are not apparent from the statement. If this is the case then the statement is at fault. Clearly, comparative figures for previous periods and explanatory notes can offset this alleged disadvantage.

3. Valuation of stocks creates difficulties.

There are two main problems in stock valuation: ascertaining quantities and calculating costs. In some types of business there is no denying that difficulties can arise. However, most of these can generally be overcome by efficient system design. In most companies there is a system of perpetual inventory, which includes continuous stock-taking, so that at any time the physical quantities and monetary values on hand are always available. Therefore, there should be no great difficulty in ascertaining the value of the stocks of raw materials or, for that matter, finished goods. The continuous stock-taking normally takes the form of a routine checking of each type of material kept in the Stores at least twice a year. The necessity to have a complete stock-taking for each interim statement is thus avoided.

The valuation of the stock of Work-in-progress is not always straightforward. This may be particularly so when non-standard products are made to customers' specifications; *i.e.* job production. However, again an efficient system can overcome the problem. The costing records can be used to supply the necessary information. When the records are inadequate careful estimates may fill in the gaps.

Other objections are sometimes raised, such as the danger of competitors being given too much information. The rate of expansion may become apparent from the Interim Accounts. This, it is argued, may spur competitors to greater effort. On the other hand, if the publication of the results is delayed until the end of the year then competitors will not be able to see trends so easily or be able to take quick retaliatory action.

### PREPARATION OF INTERIM REPORTS

The Interim Reports should be compiled with the same care as the Final Accounts discussed later. They should be accompanied by explanatory notes which enable the reader to follow the results without difficulty or danger of misunderstanding.

In recent times many companies have decided to issue Interim Reports. A standard pattern is tending to emerge and many suggestions have been put forward by the accountancy profession and the City on the timing and content of these statements. There appears to be a strong body of opinion which favours Quarterly Accounts which include comparative figures for the previous quarter. In addition, it is suggested that four-quarter moving totals with comparative figures for the previous four-quarterly period should be given.*

The Council of the Stock Exchange requires that interim reports should be issued to shareholders on an half-yearly basis. This requirement is covered in detail in Appendix IV of this book under the heading: PART AA, SUPPLEMENTAL UNDERTAKING (COMPANIES). The report should be issued not later than six months from the date of the notice calling the Annual General Meeting of the Company.

A typical interim report is illustrated in Fig. 90 (CARRERAS LIMITED), pages 524. This covers a six-monthly period and goes into some detail on the past and future position. The principal reason for the issue of interim reports has been stated as follows:

"The interval which elapses between the issue of companies annual reports is in many cases too long a period for shareholders and the investing public to be without information, particularly when developments are taking place or trading conditions are changing." (From a document issued by the Stock Exchange.)

It is interesting to notice that some companies are now issuing reports at *quarterly* intervals. Although this practice may throw a strain on a company's accounting resources there is strong evidence to suggest that the task is not too formidable.

The Council of the Stock Exchange have agreed to dispense with the obligation to *circularise* the interim report to shareholders provided the necessary details are included as paid advertisements in at least two leading London daily newspapers.

## FINAL ACCOUNTS

The "Final Accounts" of a company are the annual Profit and Loss and the Balance Sheet at the end of the year. Basically there are two sorts of final accounts.

There are those intended for *internal* circulation only; they are used by directors and top management. Obviously these should be in a form which informs management of what has happened. Remember, though, management is being supplied with information throughout the year; moreover, they are on the spot and can request further details to clarify or expand on any aspect contained in the accounts which is ambiguous.

The second type of Final Accounts, the *published accounts*, are those

* See, for example, *Compiling and Presenting Company Reports* by The Society of Investments Analysts; page 27, 1962 edition. Prepared in co-operation with Daniel Greenaway & Sons Ltd.

# CARRERAS LIMITED

To All Share and Loan Stockholders

Dear Sir (or Madam)

## Interim Report
### for the Six Months ended 31st December 1968

1. The Directors announce the following unaudited results of the Carreras Group for the six months ended 31st December 1968 compared with those for the corresponding period in 1967 and the audited results for the year ended 30th June 1968:

|  | Six months to 31st December, 1968 | Six months to 31st December, 1967 | Year to 30th June, 1968 |
|---|---|---|---|
|  | (£000s) | (£000s) | (£000s) |
| (a) Group Profit before taxation | 3,954 | 2,914 | 6,693 |
| (b) Estimated Taxation thereon | 1,880 | 1,338 | 2,981 |
| (c) Group Profit after Taxation | 2,074 | 1,576 | 3,712 |
| (d) Amount of (c) attributable to the members of Carreras Limited | 1,894 | 1,402 | 3,392 |

The estimated taxation charge for the six months to 31st December 1968 is based on Corporation Tax at 45%.

2. All the principal divisions of the Company and its Subsidiaries have contributed to the higher earnings for the period. The continued growth of the Company's export and overseas business has been particularly encouraging.

3. An interim dividend of 5½% will be paid on 16th May 1969 on the Ordinary and "B" Ordinary Shares of the Company to the holders of such Shares appearing on the Register on 25th April 1969. The cost of the dividend will be £680,000. This compares with an interim dividend of 4% paid last year, the cost of which was £494,000.

4. The increase in the interim dividend is attributable both to the higher earnings for the period under review and to the desire of the Board to reduce the disparity in the rates of the interim and final dividends on the Ordinary and "B" Ordinary Shares of the Company.

5. The Directors intend, in the absence of unforeseen circumstances, to recommend a final dividend on the Ordinary and "B" Ordinary Shares for the current year of 12%, making a total of 17½%, compared with 16% for the preceding year.

**17th April 1969**            **On behalf of the Board**
*L. A. H. SARL*
SECRETARY

FIG. 90.—*Interim Report*
(*Courtesy: Carreras Limited*)

which are intended for circulation to actual and potential shareholders. Often the latter are unskilled and uninitiated in the complexities of company accounts and finance. It is hardly surprising that the law stipulates the *minimum* information which must be shown in the Final Accounts. However, enlightened companies go further than the requirements of the Companies Acts. Many benefits can accrue from well-conceived, and carefully drafted, Final Accounts. These benefits are summarised below:

1. Would-be investors are able to see the nature of the company's activities in a favourable manner.

2. Company accounts receive free publicity in the financial columns of newspapers and in accountancy and economic journals.

3. Suppliers of raw materials, fixed assets, and services often assess creditworthiness from a company's accounts. Accordingly, the more attractive the layout and presentation of information the greater will tend to be the confidence of the would-be creditor.

4. Banks and other financial institutions use the Final Accounts to assess the financial standing and present worth of the business. Well drafted accounts are likely to be viewed with greater favour than those that are ambiguous and/or fail to disclose vital information.

### LEGAL REQUIREMENTS FOR PUBLISHED ACCOUNTS

The legal requirements relating to company accounts are contained in various sections of the *Companies Acts, 1948* and *1967*, and in the Eighth and Second Schedule respectively to the same Acts. These are summarised below under the headings (1) Profit and Loss Account and (2) Balance Sheet.

### Profit and Loss Account

The Profit and Loss Account must give a *true and fair view* of the profit or loss for the financial year.\* This account must be produced before the company in general meeting not later than eighteen months after incorporation of the company and subsequently at least once in each calendar year. It should be made up to a date not earlier than the date of the general meeting by more than nine months (twelve months for a company carrying on business or having interests abroad).†

In brief terms the requirements of the Acts as to the *contents* of the Profit and Loss Account are as follows:‡

1. Provisions for depreciation of fixed assets, stating method used (if no provision is made this should be stated).

2. Interest on Debentures or other fixed loans.

3. Details of taxation—amount and basis of charge for U.K. income tax and corporation tax.

4. Amounts provided for redemption of share capital and loan capital.

5. Transfers to and from reserves.

6. Transfers to and from provisions other than depreciation of fixed assets, (1) above.

---

\* Section 149, Companies Act, 1948.      † Section 148, Companies Act, 1948.

‡ This is not intended to be a *precise* statement of the law. Full details may be obtained from the Companies Acts.

7. Investment income showing separately that from (*a*) quoted investments and (*b*) unquoted investments.

8. Aggregate amount of dividends paid and proposed (gross).

9. Rent (net) from land, if substantial.

10. Charges for the hire of plant and machinery.

11. Any charges or credits which have arisen from transactions in a preceding year should be shown separately.

12. Remuneration of auditors, including expenses.

13. Turnover—this need not be disclosed if the business is concerned with banking or discounting, or the company is not part of a Group and its turnover does not exceed £50,000.

14. Transactions which are of an exceptional or non-recurring nature; *e.g.* capital profit on sale of fixed assets.

15. Items shown in *statements to be included* on page 528.

All these have to be shown separately together with the corresponding amounts for the immediately preceding financial year.

NOTE: The outline example (Fig. 91) should be studied along with the explanatory Notes.

## Balance Sheet

The balance sheet must be drafted as at the date of the period-end for the Profit and Loss Account. It should also give a *true and fair view* of the state of affairs at that date.

The Acts require disclosure of the following information:

1. Summaries of share capital (authorised and issued), reserves, provisions, liabilities and assets (all to be separately identified).

2. Special details of share capital and Debentures:

(*a*) Redeemable Preference shares and dates of redemption.

(*b*) Share capital on which interest is paid and the rate of such interest.

(*c*) Share Premium Account.

(*d*) Redeemed Debentures which the company has power to reissue.

3. Under separate headings:

(*a*) Preliminary expenses.

(*b*) Issue expenses—shares or Debentures.

(*c*) Commission—shares or Debentures.

(*d*) Discount on Debentures.

(*e*) Discount on shares.

(*f*) Reserves.

(*g*) Provisions (other than depreciation).

(*h*) Liabilities.

(*i*) Fixed assets (at cost or valuation).

(*j*) Current assets (showing valuation of stock and work-in-progress).

(*k*) Investments distinguishing between:

(i) trade investments and (ii) other investments showing "quoted" and "unquoted."

(*l*) Goodwill, patents and trade marks.

(*m*) Loans made by the company for the purchase of its shares under special provisions.

(*n*) Bank loans, overdrafts and other loans, distinguishing those which are repayable by instalments.

(*o*) Dividends (*gross*) for distribution.

4. *Aggregate* depreciation to date.

5. Details of any liability secured on any assets.

6. Company's Debentures (nominal and book values) held by a nominee or trustee for the company.

7. Shares on which there is an option to subscribe for, including details of the option period and price.

8. Arrears of dividends on Cumulative shares.

9. Charges on the assets of the company to secure the liabilities of any other person.

10. Contingent liabilities including estimated amounts: *e.g.* law suits commenced, bills of exchange discounted, guarantees of bank overdrafts of associated companies.

11. Contracts for capital expenditure (actual or authorised by directors) including aggregate amounts involved.

12. Probable loss in value of *current* assets as estimated by the directors.

13. Market value of quoted investments other than trade investments.

14. Conversion rates for foreign currencies.

15. How taxation has been computed, including tax equalisation amounts, *i.e.* adjustments to prevent fluctuations in payments.

Again the comparative figures for the previous year-end must be shown.

Special provisions apply to holding companies and these are covered later in this chapter.

## Directors' Report

Attached to the Balance Sheet should be a Directors' Report containing the following:

1. Principal *activities* of the company and its subsidiaries, including any significant changes during the year.

2. Significant changes in *fixed assets* and in the *value of land* as shown on the balance sheet.

S

3. *Issues* of shares, stocks or debentures during the year.

4. *Directors' interests* in contracts.

5. Where *turnover* has to be disclosed, how this is divided between different activities where these are substantially different. Also the amount exported unless disclosure is against the national interest.

6. Amounts in excess of £50 given for *political or charitable purposes.*

7. Transfers to *reserves* and *recommended dividends.*

9. *Directors'* names, their interest in the company and arrangements with them to acquire shares or debentures.

9. Number of *employees* each week and annual aggregate remuneration where more than 100 employed.

10. Statement on the company's affairs including any material facts.

Corresponding figures are not required for these items. Readers will find more detailed information on some of these aspects in the section headed Design of Annual Reports.

### Statements to be included

Statements should be included in the accounts to cover the following matters:

1. *Subsidiary companies*—names, country of incorporation, nominal value of shares held.

2. Directors' emoluments:

    (*a*) Chairman.

    (*b*) Highest paid director.

    (*c*) Numbers of directors with emoluments classified in "bands" of £2500, £5000, £7500 and so on (*see* example).

    (*d*) Numbers who waived their emoluments, including aggregate amount.

*Example of requirements (note attached to Balance Sheet)*

|  | This year | Last year |
|---|---|---|
| Directors' emoluments: | | |
| Chairman    ...    ...    ...    ... | £15,800 | £14,900 |
| Highest paid director ...    ...    ... | £17,000 | — |
|  | Number | Number |
| Up to  £2,500    ...    ...    ... | 5 | 5 |
| £5,001 to  £7,500    ...    ...    ... | — | 1 |
| £7,501 to £10,000    ...    ...    ... | 1 | — |
| £12,501 to £15,000    ...    ...    ... | — | 3 |
| £15,001 to £17,500    ...    ...    ... | 3 | — |
| Emoluments waived (nine directors)    ... | £12,800 | £12,800 |

3. Senior employees' emoluments classified:
  (*a*) £10,001–£12,500
  (*b*) £12,501–£15,000

and so on in bands of £2500 showing the number for each.

*Example of requirements*

|  | This year | Last year |
| --- | --- | --- |
| Senior employees' emoluments: | Number | Number |
| £10,001 to £12,500 ... ... ... | I | — |

Corresponding amounts for the previous financial years have to be given for these items.

## EXAMPLE AND NOTES

An example of a typical Profit and Loss Account prepared for publication is shown in Fig. 91. This complies with the requirements of the Companies Acts, 1948 and 1967. This example does not cover all possible items, but is typical of a Consolidated Profit and Loss Account found in practice. For the purpose of illustration Notes are referred to in the *pro forma* example and are explained below:

1. *Turnover*

The basis of the turnover should be given; *e.g.*

Sales are based on invoiced value excluding inter-company sales.

The total amount exported would also be shown separately.

2. *Trading Profit*

Many companies show the profit before depreciation *or* before interest, and then indicate by way of a Note the deductions for such items as depreciation and interest.

EXAMPLE

| | £ This year | £ Last year |
| --- | --- | --- |
| **Group trading profit before interest** | | |
| The Group trading profit (which does not include the exceptional items taken direct, after adjustments for taxation, to revenue reserves—see note X) is arrived at after deducting: | | |
| Depreciation of fixed assets ... ... ... ... | × × × | × × × |
| Auditors' fees and expenses ... ... ... ... | × × | × × |
| Emoluments of Directors of the parent company: | × × × | × × × |
| Fees ... ... ... ... ... ... ... ... | × | × |
| Remuneration as managers (including contributions to pension schemes) ... ... ... ... ... | × × × | × × × |
| Pensions and retirement gratuities in respect of past Directors' services as managers ... ... ... ... | × × | × × |

## PRO-FORMA PROFIT AND LOSS ACCOUNT

*X Co. Ltd., and Subsidiary Companies for the year ended.............*

|  |  | This year | Last year |
|---|---|---|---|
|  | £ | £ | £ |
| Sales (Note 1) ... ... ... ... |  |  |  |
| Trading Profit before bringing into account the following (Note 2): |  |  |  |
| *Add:* |  |  |  |
| Income from Investments (Note 3) ... |  |  |  |
| *Deduct:* |  |  |  |
| Depreciation (Note 5) ... ... ... |  |  |  |
| Auditors' Remuneration and Expenses |  |  |  |
| Pensions Contributions (Directors) ... |  |  |  |
| Additional Provision for Liabilities not yet ascertained (to be detailed) |  |  |  |
| Hire of plant and equipment (Note 6) |  |  |  |
| Debenture and Loan Interest (Note 4) |  |  |  |
| Bank Interest Paid (Note 4) ... ... |  |  |  |
| *Deduct:* |  |  |  |
| Taxation (Note 7) ... ... ... |  |  |  |
| *Deduct:* |  |  |  |
| Proportion of Profit of a Subsidiary Company attributable to shareholders outside the Group ... ... ... |  |  |  |
| CONSOLIDATED NET PROFIT FOR THE YEAR |  |  |  |
| *Deduct:* |  |  |  |
| Preference Dividends for the year (gross) |  |  |  |
| 5% Preference Stock (gross) ... ... |  |  |  |
| 7% Preference Stock (gross) ... ... |  |  |  |
| Proposed Ordinary Dividend for the year (gross) |  |  |  |
| PROFIT FOR THE YEAR RETAINED |  |  |  |
| *Add:* |  |  |  |
| Unappropriated Profits brought fwd. |  |  |  |
| *Transfer to:* |  |  |  |
| General Reserve ... ... ... |  |  |  |
| Unappropriated Profits carried forward |  | £ | £ |

FIG. 91.—*Minimum requirements for Profit and Loss Account*

### 3. *Income from Investments*

Quoted and unquoted investments have to be distinguished.

EXAMPLE

| Investment income | £ This year | £ Last year |
|---|---|---|
| Quoted investments ... ... ... ... ... ... | X X | X X |
| Unquoted investments ... ... ... ... ... ... | X X | X X |

### 4. *Bank and other Interest*

This has to be classified as follows:

    (*a*) Bank.
    (*b*) Loans repayable within 5 years by instalments.
    (*c*) Loans repayable within 5 years other than by instalments.
    (*d*) Other loans.

EXAMPLE

| Interest charges | £ This year | £ Last Year |
|---|---|---|
| Interest on Unsecured Loan Stock | | |
|   Repayable—within five years ... ... ... ... ... | X X X | X X X |
|   —after more than five years ... ... ... | X X | X X |
| | X X X | X X X |
| Bank and other short-term loan interest ... ... ... | X X | X X |
| | X X X | X X X |

### 5. *Depreciation*

The method employed to arrive at the amount of the fixed assets should be stated. If depreciation is not provided, this fact should be declared. For details, *see* Chapter 26.

### 6. *Hire of Plant and Equipment*

A simple statement of the amounts will suffice. This also applies to Rents from land.

### 7. *Taxation*

There has to be shown separately:
    (*a*) U.K. income tax and corporation tax.
    (*b*) Details of relief from double taxation.
    (*c*) Other taxation.
    (*d*) Special circumstances affecting taxation.

EXAMPLE

| Taxation | £ This year | £ Last year |
|---|---|---|
| Estimated to be payable on the Group profit for the year: | | |
| Corporation tax at ......% ... ... ... ... ... | × × × | × × × |
| Less: Double taxation relief ... ... ... ... ... | × × × | × × × |
| | × × × × | × × × × |
| Add: Overseas tax... ... ... ... ... ... ... | × × | × × |
| | × × × × | × × × × |

## ADDITIONAL INFORMATION

Although possibly the body of opinion which favours the conversion of fixed assets to current replacement costs (see Chapter 27) is nothing near what may be regarded as a majority there is, nevertheless, a strong feeling that such conversion has many advantages. Many of these are discussed in the chapters which deal with take-over bids and the measurement of capital employed.

The calculation of the profit figure is another aspect which has received attention. Showing "trading profit before depreciation" has been criticised, and quite rightly, for depreciation is very much a legitimate cost and there can be no profit until this has been charged in the accounts.

Many accountants and investment analysts would prefer to see more than the comparative figures for the *previous year* in the published accounts. The disclosure of five, ten, and even fifteen, yearly interval figures, they feel, would be worthwhile. On this matter the author feels that much depends upon circumstances. When a business has changed its form in a very substantial manner so that it is, in effect, a different company and, furthermore, circumstances and conditions have also changed radically, then the figures of fifteen years ago may be meaningless or even misleading. Clearly, how far back the figures should go must depend upon the history of the company concerned.

## DESIGN OF ANNUAL REPORTS

The Society of Investment Analysts* have recommended, *inter alia*, that the following information should be shown in the Annual Reports including company accounts:

1. Sequence of information:

(*a*) Chairman's address.

(*b*) Statutory Report of the Directors together with summarised accountancy information or highlights; also a list of the Directors and the executive position (if any) held by each.

(*c*) Profit and Loss Accounts ⎫ with supporting Notes
(*d*) Balance Sheets          ⎭ and the Auditors' Report.

(*e*) Miscellaneous Statistics.

* *Compiling and Presenting Company Reports* prepared in co-operation with Daniel Greenaway & Sons Ltd.

2. Contents of the Chairman's Address. The subjects and order in which they could be presented are as shown below:

(*a*) Succinct description of the *important features*, good and bad, *of the company's performance during the financial year under review.* This should aim at providing an interesting verbal alternative to the accounts for the benefit of those who cannot cope with figures. If the company's achievement can be described in real terms (physical output, man hours worked, etc.) as well as in financial terms, so much the better.

(*b*) Description of the *environment* in which the firm found itself *during that year;* that is, of the economic and political circumstances, favourable or adverse.

(*c*) *Reconciliation* (so far as the past financial year is concerned) *between performance and environment,* by describing how problems were confronted or opportunities exploited, and with what success.

(*d*) Brief but similar three-part analysis (performance, environment, and reconciliation) of the *current financial year,* if some significant period of that year has passed at the time of the review.

(*e*) *Prospects* for the rest of the *current financial year:* expected performance in the light of the anticipated environment; and the Board's plans (so far as security allows them to be announced) for combating difficulties or exploiting advantages.

(*f*) Discussion which puts *past and current years into perspective.* This might include: (i) a description of trends, both physical and financial, over several past years as applied to the company itself, (ii) relevant trends in the industry of which the company forms part, (iii) longer-term expectations for the industry and the company, and (iv) national and international facts and trends affecting the company.

There are two further topics which are most suitably dealt with in the Chairman's review as an addition to statistics, charts or illustrations supplied in the report:

(*g*) Account of the company's *main activities*, given in some detail, indicating their relative importance. Some shareholders may be only hazily aware of the exact nature of the company's main activities and many of the general public not at all. These activities should be reviewed regularly in broad and simple terms, with news of developments in the use of the company's products or services.

(*h*) Comment on *employee relations.* Often employee relations are not referred to at all, or only briefly as an afterthought. In view of their importance to most businesses, employee relations and their development in the past year should be described in nearly every Chairman's review. The human interest can be stimulated by references to long or commendable service to the company. As it is equally important that the staff be kept acquainted with the progress of the company as a whole, the report and accounts and the Chairman's review should be made available to all employees.

3. Summary of Company Accounts—Profit and Loss Account and Balance Sheet.

The object is to present the salient features in a manner easily understandable by the non-professional reader. The example given (Figs. 92 and 93) may be varied to suit the circumstances.

4. Directors' Report.

No recommendations are made in respect of this statutory report as this will tend to vary from one company to another.

5. Profit and Loss Account and Balance Sheet.

The Society suggests that the information required by the Companies Acts should be regarded as the minimum needs. Additional accounts recommended are as follows:

(a) Trading Account showing
    (i) turnover; *i.e.* sales of goods or services.
    (ii) total costs under a few main headings.

(b) Profit and Loss Account of the *parent* company when a holding company itself engages in trade.

(This is not required by the Companies Act, 1948.)

(c) Accounts in summarised form of any *important company* (not being a subsidiary) whose shares are held as a trade investment.

For this purpose a 25 to 50% interest may be used as a guide in determining what is an "important company."

6. Miscellaneous Statistics.

In this section the following represent some of the recommendations made by the Society:

(a) *Analysis* of turnover.

(b) Changes in physical output and value of sales and trend of average selling prices.

(c) *Backlog of orders* when manufacturing to customers' specification and not for stock.

(d) Volume and value of sales in direct and indirect exports.

(e) *Contribution*, to turnover or profits or both, of the various branches of the group's activities.

(f) Number of employees and shareholders, and the amount of capital invested per employee.

(g) Details of:
    (i) factories;
    (ii) products;
    (iii) chief subsidiaries and sub-subsidiaries;

(iv) capital expenditure including arrangements for financing;
(v) research and development expenditure.

(*h*) A "Source and disposition of funds" or a "cash flow" statement should be included.

An example is given below:

|  | £ |
|---|---|
| Profit retained per accounts: | × × × × |
| *Add* Items such as depreciation, charged before arriving at such profits and not requiring the payment of money. | × × × |
| Taxation similarly charged and not immediately payable | × × |
| Proceeds of the sale of fixed assets | × × |
| Proceeds of issues of share or loan capital | × × |
| | |
| *Deduct* | |
| Expenditure on fixed assets | × × |
| Taxation paid | × × |
| Funded liabilities redeemed | × × |
| | |
| Increase/Decrease in working capital | × × |

In addition to the foregoing the Society feels that there is a need for an up-to-date valuation of the fixed assets at not more than five-yearly intervals and suggests that this matter should be made the subject of special study.

Undoubtedly these recommendations would be given the unqualified approval of a large number of accountants. They would standardise as far as possible the methods of presentation and allow inter-firm comparisons to be made more easily. Above all they would *inform* the shareholders, Debenture holders and other interested parties of the state of affairs of a company in no uncertain manner.

Many progressive companies have already recognised the need for the fullest possible information and attractive design and layout. This is reflected in many of the company accounts now being issued. However, there is still room for improvement and, unfortunately, some companies appear very reluctant to make any attempt to give more details than they are already giving unless compelled to do so by law.

### THE FORM OF PUBLISHED ACCOUNTS

One of the strongest criticisms on the form of published accounts is that they tend to be complex and drafted in a way that is only understood by the financial expert. The question which must inevitably arise from this criticism is: for whom are published accounts intended?

Clearly, the most important recipients are the shareholders and the public at large. Management theory recognises that sound management

[*Continued on page 540.*

## PROFIT AND LOSS ACCOUNT
X Co. Ltd.; and Subsidiary Companies for Year Ended ......

|  | This year (date to be given) £ | Last year (date to be given) £ |
|---|---|---|
| 1. SALES FOR PERIOD ... ... ... ... |  |  |
| *Less* Expenditure of Trading and Manufacture:<br>Materials Consumed ... ...<br>Wages and Salaries ... ... ...<br>Overhead Costs (suitably detailed)... |  |  |
| 2. TOTAL EXPENDITURE ... ... ... ... | £ | £ |
| 3. GROSS PROFIT (1 above less item 2) ... |  |  |
| 4. *Less* Depreciation on *cost* ... ... ... |  |  |
| 5. TRADING PROFIT (3 above less item 4) ... | £ | £ |
| 6. *Add* Gross Income from Investments: (distinguishing between income from quoted and unquoted investments) ... |  |  |
| 7. TOTAL GROSS PROFIT ... ... ... | £ | £ |
| *Less* Finance and Tax Charges:<br>Interest on Debentures (other types also to be given in detail) ... ...<br>Taxation (on present year's profits):<br>(*a*) United Kingdom ...<br>(*b*) Overseas taxes on profits ...<br>*Less* Proportion attributable to outside shareholders in subsidiaries distinguishing between paid and retained) |  |  |
| 8. TOTAL CHARGES: Finance, Taxation and Minority Interests ... ... ... | £ | £ |
| 9. NET PROFIT FOR YEAR (7 above less item 8) ... | £ | £ |
| APPROPRIATION ACCOUNT showing how profit is appropriated to Shareholders and retained in company ... ... ... |  |  |

[Continued

10. BALANCE OF NET PROFIT (9 above) ... ... | £ | £

*Less* Appropriations:
    (a) Transfer to Fixed Assets Replace-
        ments Reserve ... ... ...
    (b) Transfer to Debenture Redemption
        Reserve ... ... ... ...
    (c) Transfer to Preference Share Re-
        demption Fund ... ... ...
    (d) Dividends (gross) ... ... ...

| | £ | £ |
|---|---|---|
| Preference dividends... | | |
| Ordinary dividends ... | | |

(Distinguish between dividends paid and
 proposed.)
    (e) Other transfers to reserves (detailed)

11. TOTAL APPROPRIATIONS ... ... ... | £ | £

12. PROFIT AND LOSS BALANCE (10 above less
    item 11) ... ... ... ... ...
*Add* Profit and Loss Balance from *Previous*
    Year ... ... ... ... ...

BALANCE OF PROFIT CARRIED FORWARD ... | £ | £

FIG. 92.—*Pro-forma example of Profit and Loss Account*

NOTES

1. Details of physical output and analysis into classes of products could be shown in the account. However, many accountants will prefer to show these by way of Notes.

2. Depreciation on *cost* is shown as a *charge against* profits whereas additional depreciation to cover replacement is treated as an *appropriation* of profit. This is now a generally accepted practice. However, some authorities would prefer to see the transfer to the Fixed Assets Replacements Reserve as a charge against profits, thereby recognising the importance and, indeed, necessity of maintaining real capital intact in terms of assets employed. There is great merit in this alternative procedure.

3. The proportion attributable to outside shareholders (the minority interest) will apply only when dealing with a Consolidated Profit and Loss Account.

4. No provision has been made for non-recurring items, such as profit or loss on the sale of fixed assets. These could be added or deducted in the Profit and Loss Account, or perhaps better still in the Appropriation Account. The latter method does not distort the net profit arising from *normal* operations, and, therefore, is to be recommended.

5. Irrespective of the classification of overhead costs it will be essential to show:

    (a) Directors' emoluments.
    (b) Auditors' fees and expenses.

These are explained in the previous section which details the requirements of the Companies Acts.

## BALANCE SHEET AS AT...

*CAPITAL EMPLOYED* (Sources of Funds)

| Ordinary Share Capital: | Authorised | | This year Issued | Last year Issued |
|---|---|---|---|---|
| Full details to be shown of authorised and issued capital including numbers of shares and nominal values, whether fully paid or not, to be stated including amount | *This year* | *Last year* | £ | £ |
| | £ | £ | | |

*Capital Reserves:*
Share Premium Account    ...    ...    ...
Capital Redemption Reserve Fund    ...    ...
Debenture Redemption Reserve    ...    ...
Fixed Assets Replacements Reserve ...    ...
Preference Share Redemption Fund ...    ...

*Revenue Reserves*
Profit and Loss Balance    ...    ...    ...
General Reserve    ...    ...    ...    ...

| | This year Issued | Last year Issued |
|---|---|---|
| 1. TOTAL EQUITY CAPITAL   ...   ...   ... | £ | £ |
|     Asset value of each Ordinary Share   ... | £ | £ |

*Preference Share Capital:*

| Full details to be shown of different classes of authorised and issued capital including numbers of shares and nominal values, whether fully paid or not, to be stated including amount | Authorised | |
|---|---|---|
| | *This year* | *Last year* |
| | £ | £ |
| | £ | £ |

| | This year Issued | Last year Issued |
|---|---|---|
| 2. PREFERENCE CAPITAL   ...   ...   ... | £ | £ |
| *Interest of Minority Shareholders* (Details to be given)   ...   ...   ... | | |
| 3. MINORITY INTEREST ...   ...   ...   ... | £ | £ |
| 4. LONG-TERM LIABILITIES   ...   ...   ... Debentures and other long-term liabilities would be detailed. | | |
| TOTAL CAPITAL EMPLOYED $(1 + 2 + 3 + 4)$ | £ | £ |

*CURRENT ASSETS*
Stocks    ...    ...    ...    ...    ...
Debtors    ...    ...    ...    ...    ...
Marketable Securities (short-term investments)    ...    ...    ...    ...
Cash    ...    ...    ...    ...    ...
Prepayments    ...    ...    ...    ...

| | This year | Last year |
|---|---|---|
| 1. TOTAL CURRENT ASSETS   ...   ...   ... | £ | £ |

[Continued

*EMPLOYMENT OF CAPITAL* (How the funds are employed)

| | This year £ | Last year £ |
|---|---|---|
| **CURRENT LIABILITIES** | | |
| Creditors ... ... ... ... ... | | |
| Overdraft at Bank... ... ... ... | | |
| Taxation (detailed) ... ... ... | | |
| Final Dividends (gross) (detailed) ... | | |
| 2. TOTAL CURRENT LIABILITIES ... ... | £ | £ |
| 3. NET CURRENT ASSETS (Working Capital) ... (1 above less item 2) | £ | £ |

| FIXED ASSETS | Cost | Aggregate Depreciation | Net (This year) | Net (Last year) |
|---|---|---|---|---|
| Land and Buildings ... | | | | |
| Plant and Machinery ... | | | | |
| (Other details to be given when necessary) | | | | |
| 4. TOTAL FIXED ASSETS | | | £ | £ |
| **INVESTMENTS** | | | | |
| Details of investments to be given showing | | | | |
| (i) trade investments ... ... ... ... | | | | |
| (ii) other investments ... ... ... ... | | | | |
| (a) quoted including market values ... | | | | |
| (b) unquoted ... ... ... | | | | |
| 5. TOTAL INVESTMENTS ... ... ... ... | | | £ | £ |
| TOTAL CAPITAL EMPLOYED (3 + 4 + 5) ... | | | | £ |

FIG. 93.—*Pro-Forma Balance Sheet*

NOTES

1. This balance sheet is usually called the "vertical type" balance sheet. The principal advantage claimed for its use is that it presents the facts clearly without having the capital and liabilities on the left-hand side and the assets on the right-hand side with the consequent confusion to the layman.

2. Current assets (or liabilities) are those expected to be owned (or paid off) for less than (or within) twelve months. If assets are to be held for longer than twelve months they should strictly be included under the "fixed assets" heading. Generally there are few problems in determining which are current assets and which are fixed assets. Current liabilities are not always easy to classify. Loans for longer than twelve months are clearly long-term liabilities. However, the position is not always clear when the company borrows money on overdraft on what is virtually a permanent arrangement. Some companies have been known to have an overdraft of a few million pounds for a number of years. In these circumstances there is probably no hope of ever paying off the overdraft without issuing further shares; the only logical way to deal with the overdraft is to include it under long-term liabilities.

3. The item relating to minority shareholders will apply only when dealing with a consolidated balance sheet.

4. There is no need to segregate capital reserves and revenue reserves, but movements should be shown (Companies Act, 1967).

ensures that shareholders receive adequate dividends and that the community is served best by making the most efficient use of the productive resources. Unless information from companies is complete and generally understood by the person of average intelligence, who is to judge whether or not a company is fulfilling its economic and social obligations? Perhaps the expert can reach some conclusion on this matter; but even he would have a difficult task in interpreting some accounts! In any case the obligation is to shareholders and society—they should be able to judge for themselves. If the management accountant is to play his part in the management team he must surely endeavour to compile accounts which are in the simplest possible form.

Some of the more obvious points to watch *besides* those covered in the previous section are listed below:

1. Use the statement form of accounts and balance sheet as much as possible thus avoiding the confusion of debit and credit entries.

2. Layout of company accounts and in particular:

(*a*) Headings and sub-headings should be so arranged that they show the details in the simplest and clearest manner.

(*b*) Good quality paper and different sizes of type should be employed.

(*c*) Use should be made of modern techniques of design. "Colour, illustrations, graphs, diagrams, and layout must all combine to enlighten, not confuse."*

3. Technical and financial jargon should be avoided.

4. The booklet containing the accounts should be attractively designed and of a convenient size.

5. Notes and other additional matter should be arranged in a manner which allows the reader to refer to them with minimum inconvenience.

In the desire to disclose all relevant information there is always a danger that *too much* information will be packed into the report with a consequent "overwhelming" of the reader and possibly confusion.

All these requirements must inevitably raise the question, should a specialist (in addition to the accountant) be employed? There is no doubt that the specialist company-report printer has much to offer and the fullest use should be made of his services. He will give advice on design and, moreover, can provide a speedy printing and distribution service so essential if shareholders and others are to receive the report as quickly as possible and, thereby, obtain maximum benefit.

If the many recommendations for improvement are incorporated into the Final Accounts the Profit and Loss Account may take the form shown in Figure 92 and the Balance Sheet as shown in Figure 93. These are very simplified versions and will naturally have to be modified to cover

* From *Compiling and Presenting Company Reports* prepared by The Society of Investment Analysts and Daniel Greenaway & Sons Ltd.

the requirements of the company concerned. The examples are given not to cover all possible details, but rather to illustrate the basic principles.

A PRACTICAL ILLUSTRATION

Examples of published accounts which illustrate the use of full re-valuation accounting are given at the end of Chapter 27—these refer to the Philips Electrical Company. As a further illustration of a vertical balance sheet readers are referred to the Consolidated Balance Sheet of Fisons Limited and Subsidiaries (Fig. 94).

This example shows how effectively all the salient facts may be sum-marised, thus allowing shareholders to see the essential details without being overwhelmed by figures. The extra information required by the Companies Acts is then explained by Notes which are appended to the Balance Sheet (these are not included in this book).

Items which merit special mention are:

1. *Tax Equalisation Account.*

This account is used to avoid having considerable fluctuations in the tax payable from year to year. In the illustration the account "mainly represents estimated taxation deferred by reason of capital allowances."

2. *Movement of Reserves.*

This is an important requirement stipulated by the Companies Act, 1967. Any *material* changes must be explained in the Balance Sheet or by way of notes or a supplementary statement. An example from Fisons Limited is given in Fig. 95, (Movements on Reserve Accounts Statement). Readers should note that there is a cross reference to the Balance Sheet (Fig. 94). This supplementary statement gives very useful information on how the company is building up its reserves and the sources of the significant amounts.

GRAPHS, DIAGRAMS, AND SUPPLEMENTARY STATEMENTS

Many companies now incorporate graphs, charts, diagrams, supple-mentary statements, and other devices into the annual report as an aid to simplifying the results so that a person with little knowledge of accounting principles can appreciate their significance.

The most important and significant facts can be summarised in the statistical graph or other aids being employed. *Many* figures can be put into a form which enables their nature to be understood quickly and easily. This is a real advantage, but it should not be forgotten that the use of a chart or graph may result in some loss of accuracy.

Trends and comparisons are often more discernible from charts and graphs than from a mass of figures. The shareholder, attempting to judge whether his investment is growing in value, will be very much concerned with the general trends in the activities of the company. He will want to know whether profits and dividends are increasing or reducing.

Employees and trade unions will be interested to see what share of the company's income is being paid in wages and salaries. The breakdown of each £1 of sales into costs, dividends, and profit appropriations will serve this purpose.

CONSOLIDATED BALANCE SHEET 30th June, 1968

Figures in *italics* represent deductions

| | 1968 £000 | 1967 £000 |
|---|---|---|
| 1. *Preference Capital* ... ... ... ... ... | 4,259 | 4,259 |
| 2. *Ordinary Stockholders' Interests:* | | |
| Ordinary Stock of Fisons Limited ... ... ... | 20,640 | 20,640 |
| Reserves (Statement 3) ... ... ... ... | 8,094 | 7 413 |
| | 28,734 | 28,053 |
| 3. *Minority Interests in Subsidiaries* ... ... ... | 491 | 431 |
| 4. *Loan Capital* ... ... ... ... ... ... | 23,146 | 23,295 |
| 5. *Loans* ... ... ... ... ... ... ... | 5,681 | 4,598 |
| 6. *Investment Grants Account* ... ... ... ... | 1,433 | 1,055 |
| 7. *Tax Equalisation Account* ... ... ... ... | 3,347 | 2,685 |
| 8. *Corporation Tax payable 1st January, 1970* ... ... | 1,513 | 46 |
| FUNDS EMPLOYED | 68,604 | 64,422 |
| 9. *Land, Buildings, Plant and Equipment* (Statement 4) ... | 42,963 | 40,787 |
| 10. *Development Expenditure less amounts written off* ... | 1,353 | 453 |
| 11. *Goodwill, Patents and Trade Marks at Cost* ... ... | — | 5,147 |
| 12. *Interests in Associated Companies* ... ... ... | 5,969 | 6,443 |
| FIXED ASSETS | 50,285 | 52,830 |
| 13. *Current Assets:* | | |
| Stocks ... ... ... ... ... ... ... | 14,747 | 13,022 |
| Debtors ... ... ... ... ... ... | 18,067 | 15,537 |
| Short term loan ... ... ... ... ... | 3,250 | — |
| Bank balances and cash ... ... ... ... | 1,237 | 712 |
| | 37,301 | 29,271 |
| 14. *Current Liabilities and Provisions:* | | |
| Creditors ... ... ... ... ... ... | 13,306 | 11,113 |
| Bank overdrafts (secured £1,441,000) ... ... | 3,648 | 4,727 |
| Provision for Past Service Pension Fund contributions ... ... ... ... ... ... | 78 | 123 |
| Provision for supplementary pensions ... ... | 240 | — |
| Current taxation (including Corporation Tax payable 1st January, 1969) ... ... ... ... | 368 | 374 |
| Ordinary dividend proposed ... ... ... | 1,342 | 1,342 |
| | 18,982 | 17,679 |
| NET CURRENT ASSETS | 18,319 | 11,592 |
| TOTAL ASSETS | £68,604 | £64,422 |

FIG. 94.—*Vertical Balance Sheet*
(*Courtesy: Fisons Limited*)

Figures in *italics* represent deductions

| | Fisons Limited £000 | Group £000 |
|---|---|---|
| *Share Premium Account:* | | |
| As at 1st July, 1967 ... ... ... ... ... | 33 | 66 |
| *Capital Reserve:* | | |
| As at 1st July, 1967 ... ... ... ... ... | 1,328 | 1,328 |
| Profit on sale of Investments ... ... ... | 2,207 | 2,207 |
| Net surplus on revaluation of Fixed Assets ... ... | 2,753 | 2,753 |
| Net surplus on revaluation of Investments in and loans from overseas associated and subsidiary companies | 427 | 427 |
| Goodwill, Patent and Trade Marks, relating to subsidiaries, written off ... ... ... ... ... | (*5,147*) | (*5,147*) |
| Provision for supplementary pensions *less* estimated future tax relief ... ... ... ... ... ... | (*240*) | (*240*) |
| | 1,328 | 1,328 |
| TOTAL CAPITAL RESERVES | 1,361 | 1,394 |
| *General Reserve:* | | |
| As at 1st July, 1967 ... ... ... ... ... | 5,700 | 5,700 |
| Amount transferred at 30th June, 1968 (Note 12, Statement 1) ... ... ... ... ... ... | 800 | 800 |
| | 6,500 | 6,500 |
| *Profit and Loss Account:* | | |
| As at 1st July 1967 after adjustment as regards the Group (£*154,000*) arising from sterling devaluation | 294 | 165 |
| Taxation adjustments in respect of prior years ... | (*219*) | (*63*) |
| Amount transferred at 30th June, 1968 (Note 12, Statement 1) ... ... ... ... ... ... | 84 | 98 |
| | 159 | 200 |
| TOTAL PROFITS RETAINED | 6,659 | 6,700 |
| TOTAL RESERVES | 8,020 | 8,094 |

FIG. 95.—*Movements on Reserve Accounts Statement*
(*Courtesy: Fisons Limited*)

Care has to be taken to ensure that the report does not become over-crowded with graphs and other "aids" to the extent that confusion results. The normal Profit and Loss Accounts and Balance Sheet will still be included so, obviously, if these are designed in a manner which makes them intelligible there will be less need for supplementary graphs and statements. If the latter are used they should be along simple lines and as concise as possible. (The principles followed for report writing are covered in Chapter 14.)

Some of the types of information which may be summarised are as follows:

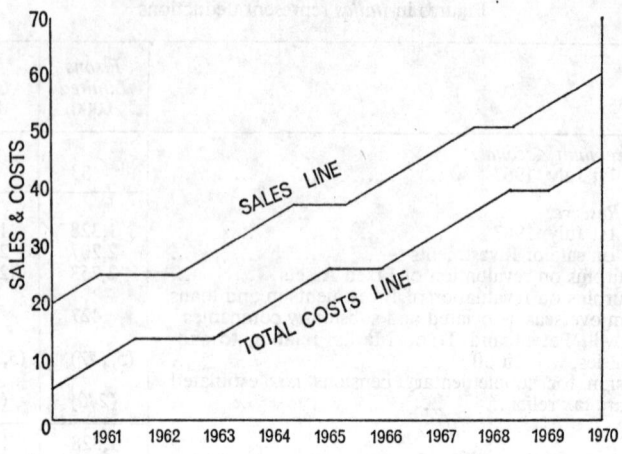

FIG. 96.—*Profit Trend Chart*

1. Profit trends plotted on, say, a ten-year chart (Fig. 96).
2. Analysis of turnover.
3. How earnings are shared.
4. Source and application (or disposition) of funds (*see* pages 151 and 535.
5. Capital Employed Statement.
6. Those listed under "Miscellaneous Statistics" earlier in this Chapter (page 534).

*Examples of Supplementary Material*

Examples of some of the supplementary charts and statements which have been employed are given below:

*Profit Trend Chart*

This chart shows the *general trend* of profits over the ten years. In addition the value of sales and total costs can be seen.

---

*Analysis of Turnover Statement*

How the Income from Sales went in ...... (year)

*Every £100 received by the Group for sales went as follows:*

|  | £ |
|---|---|
| Cost of materials and supplies, etc., was ...      ...      ...      ... | 38·20 |
| Wages and cost of pensions, etc., amounted to ...      ...      ... | 46·35 |
| Taxation, including P.A.Y.E. amounted to      ...      ...      ... | 8·00 |
| Dividends amounted to      ...      ...      ...      ...      ... | 2·00 |
| Attributable to minority shareholders in subsidiary companies  ... | 0·20 |
| Amount retained in the business for development ...      ...      ... | 5·25 |
|  | £100·00 |

---

A better description of this statement is "Analysis of Sales Income." The term "analysis of turnover" is sometimes used to describe the breakdown of turnover into product classes.

---

## How Earnings are Shared Statement

How the Profit went ...... (year)

The Group's profit was £500,000

| | £ | £ |
|---|---|---|
| This was used as follows: | | |
| Dividends to shareholders ... ... ... | | 100,000 |
| In payment of taxation ... ... ... ... | 200,000 | |
| Retained in the business for development ... | 175,000 | |
| | | 375,000 |
| Attributable to minority shareholders in subsidiary companies ... ... ... ... | | 25,000 |
| | | £500,000 |

---

The figures have been simplified. In practice they would be taken to the nearest £1.

---

## Capital Employed Statement

How we stood financially at the end of ...... (year)

| | | £ | £ |
|---|---|---|---|
| We had | Cash ... ... ... ... ... | 200,000 | |
| | Tax Reserve Certificates ... ... | 400,000 | |
| | Investments ... ... ... ... | 100,000 | |
| | Materials ... ... ... ... ... | 900,000 | |
| | Owing to us ... ... ... ... | 800,000 | |
| | Buildings, Land and Plant ... ... | 1,500,000 | |
| | | | 3,900,000 |
| We owed | For Taxation ... ... ... ... | 900,000 | |
| | And otherwise ... ... ... ... | 1,000,000 | |
| | | | 1,900,000 |
| We had left as Capital employed in the business ... | | | £2,000,000 |

---

On this capital of £2,000,000 the Group earned a profit of £500,000; i.e. 25%.

---

Another useful addition to this Capital Employed Statement is the value of each ordinary share. The capital employed is taken as "net", but this is not a generally accepted definition (see Chapter 15, "Return on Capital Employed").

## Make Use of Published Accounts

Here it has been possible to show only a few examples of supplementary graphs, charts, and statements. The reader is advised to study published accounts and extracts from them which are published regularly in accountancy journals.

## HOLDING COMPANY ACCOUNTS

A holding company is one which controls one or more other companies (subsidiaries), either through the composition of the board of directors or by virtue of holding more than 50% of the nominal value of the equity share capital; *i.e.* generally the Ordinary shares carrying voting rights.

The possible motives and benefits of holding companies are discussed in Chapter 22 which deals with amalgamations and take-over bids.

Special provisions relating to holding company Accounts are contained in the Companies Acts, 1948 and 1967. These are summarised below. However, it is important to notice that the requirements of the Act relating to the accounts of companies generally outlined earlier, also apply to holding companies. Important exceptions are the need to show the total of directors' emoluments or other payments and loans to officers—these are shown in the accounts of the separate companies.

A holding company must publish Group Accounts in the form of:

1. A Consolidated Balance Sheet.
2. A Consolidated Profit and Loss Account.

There are exceptions to this general rule, such as when the holding company is a wholly owned subsidiary of another British company, *or* where the directors are of the opinion that group accounts would be misleading or impracticable *or* where the Board of Trade gives special dispensation.

The principal legal and practical requirements relating to consolidated accounts are as follows:

1. The financial year of each of the subsidiaries must coincide with that of the holding company unless the directors have good reasons for not obtaining this uniformity (1948 Act, Section 153).
2. The *Consolidated* Profit and Loss Account may be published as the Profit and Loss Account of the holding company; *i.e.* no separate profit and loss account need be prepared if a consolidated account is published.
3. Separate balance sheets must be prepared for (*a*) the holding company and (*b*) the group.
4. The contents of the Consolidated Balance Sheet should include or deal with, *inter alia*, the following:

(*a*) Inter-company transactions must be considered so that there is no "double-counting." Examples of these are:

(i) Debts owing to subsidiaries by the holding company or *vice versa.*

(ii) Bills of exchange drawn and accepted within the company. This does not apply to bills which have been discounted by the company receiving them; these appear as Bills Payable in the Consolidated Balance Sheet.

(iii) Profit on goods sold within the group must be eliminated in respect of goods unsold. This is done by reducing (*a*) the stock of the buying company and (*b*) the profit of the selling company.

(*b*) If the shares of a subsidiary are purchased at a premium, the difference between the net tangible assets purchased and the cost of control should be debited to a Goodwill Account. Conversely, if the shares are purchased at a discount a Capital Reserve will be credited.

(*c*) Minority shareholders' interest should be shown as a *separate item* on the liabilities side of the Consolidated Balance Sheet.

This is done for Ordinary shareholders by adding together the nominal value of shares and the appropriate proportion of reserves and undistributed profits.

(*d*) Pre-acquisition profits on the balance sheet of a subsidiary company at the date of purchase should be divided into those belonging to: (i) the holding company and (ii) the minority shareholders.

The amount under (i) should be used to reduce the Goodwill Account or should be added to Capital Reserve Account. If there is a pre-acquisition *loss* the proportion belonging to the holding company will be added to Goodwill or deducted from Capital Reserve.

5. The Consolidated Profit and Loss Account deals with the summarised results of a year's activities for the holding company and its subsidiaries.

Obviously the account should show a true and fair view for the Group as a whole. In order to accomplish this end the following rules should be observed:

(*a*) Each class of expense is dealt with in turn. The separate totals of each class of expense are transferred to the Consolidated Profit and Loss Account.

(*b*) Pre-acquisition profits of subsidiaries are transferred to General Reserve or used to reduce Goodwill (4(*d*) above). This means that these profits will *not* appear in the Consolidated Profit and Loss Account.

(*c*) The Minority Interest in current profits is deducted from the total profits relating to the Group.

(*d*) Transfers to Reserve consist of the total for the holding company and the holding company's *proportion* of the subsidiary company's transfer. This total is included in the Consolidated Profit and Loss Account.

(*e*) Inter-company purchases, sales, and dividends are eliminated so that the profit taken into the Consolidated Profit and Loss Account refers only to the holding company's interests (*i.e.* its *own* profits plus the appropriate proportion of the post-acquisition profits of subsidiaries).

## Example of Consolidated Accounts

To illustrate the principles involved in preparing consolidated accounts a Question and Suggested Solution are given below. In practice, problems will tend to be much more complicated. Readers wishing to study this topic in greater detail are advised to consult a book which specialises in Group Accounts.

QUESTION

Take-over Limited acquired on 1st April, 1968, 8000 £1 ordinary shares in Suppressed Limited at a cost of £14,000. At this date the Profit and Loss Balance and General Reserve of Suppressed Limited amounted to £3000 and £5000 respectively.

At the 31st March 1969 the skeleton balance sheets are as follows:

| | T. Ltd. £ | S. Ltd. £ | | T. Ltd. £ | S. Ltd. £ |
|---|---|---|---|---|---|
| Paid-up Ordinary shares of £1 each ... ... | 40,000 | 10,000 | Fixed Assets at cost ... | 60,000 | 18,000 |
| Paid-up 5% Preference | | | *Less* Depreciation ... | 11,000 | 2,000 |
| shares of £1 each ... | 20,000 | Nil | | 49,000 | 16,000 |
| Profit and Loss Account | 8,000 | 4,000 | Investment in S. Ltd.... | 14,000 | — |
| General Reserve ... | 6,000 | 7,000 | Stock ... ... ... | 5,400 | 6,000 |
| Creditors ... ... | 1,600 | 500 | Debtors... ... ... | 12,000 | 5,500 |
| Bills Payable to T. Ltd. | | 3,000 | Cash ... ... ... | 6,600 | 1,000 |
| Proposed Dividend ... | 5,000 | | Bills Receivable from | | |
| Corporation Tax ... | 8,400 | 4,000 | S. Ltd. ... ... | 2,000 | |
| | £89,000 | £28,500 | | £89,000 | £28,500 |

*Notes.*

1. Part of the stock of Suppressed Ltd. was transferred from Take-over Ltd., and included an inter-company profit of £1000. The cost of the stock was £4000.

2. A number of bills drawn by Take-over Ltd. on Suppressed Ltd., had matured at 31st March, 1969.

The skeleton profit and loss accounts for the year ended 31st March, 1969, are as follows:

| | T. Ltd. £ | S. Ltd. £ | | | T. Ltd. £ | S. Ltd. £ |
|---|---|---|---|---|---|---|
| Administration Expenses | 21,600 | 7,000 | | | | |
| Depreciation ... | 6,000 | 1,000 | Balance b/d ... ... | | 6,000 | 3,000 |
| Corporation Tax ... | 8,400 | 4,000 | Trading Profit ... ... | | 45,000 | 15,000 |
| Proposed Dividend ... | 5,000 | — | | | | |
| General Reserve ... | 2,000 | 2,000 | | | | |
| Balance c/f ... ... | 8,000 | 4,000 | | | | |
| | £51,000 | £18,000 | | | £51,000 | £18,000 |

You are required to prepare:

(*a*) A Consolidated Profit and Loss Account for year ended 31st March, 1969.

(*b*) A Consolidated Balance Sheet as at 31st March, 1969.

SUGGESTED SOLUTION

## Consolidated Accounts

(*a*) *Consolidated Profit and Loss Account of Take-over Ltd., and its subsidiary Suppressed Ltd., for Year Ended 31st March, 1969.*

| | £ | | £ |
|---|---|---|---|
| To Administration Expenses... ... | 28,600 | By Trading Profit for Year ... ... | 60,000 |
| „ Depreciation ... ... ... | 7,000 | *Less* Profit on Stock ... ... ... | 800 |
| „ Taxation ... ... ... ... | 12,400 | | |
| „ Proportion of Profit to Minority | | | 59,200 |
| Interest ½ × £3000 ... ... | 600 | | |
| Group Profit for Year c/d ... | 10,600 | | |
| | £59,200 | | £59,200 |
| To Transfer to Reserve ... ... | 3,600 | By Gross Profit b/d ... ... ... | 10,600 |
| „ Proposed Dividends ... ... | 5,000 | „ Balance b/f ... ... ... | 6,000 |
| „ Balance c/f ... ... ... | 8,000 | | |
| | £16,600 | | £16,600 |

## Notes on Consolidated Profit and Loss Account

1. The two trading profits are added together and then the *holding company's* share of the profit on stock transferred within the Group is deducted.

2. The administration costs for the subsidiary and holding company are added together. Depreciation is dealt with in a similar manner.

3. The total general reserve figure is made up of £2000 plus ⅘ of £2000, the latter representing the holding company's share of the general reserve transfer.

4. The minority interest in the profit is found by deducting from trading profit any taxation or expenses; *i.e.* £7000 administration costs, £1000 depreciation and £4000 Corporation Tax is deducted from £15,000 trading profit.

5. The reader should have studied pages 546–548 very carefully before working through the solution.

*Special Note.* The example is given to illustrate the general principles. For compliance with the Companies Acts on *layout* the whole of this Chapter should be studied.

### (b) Balance Sheet of Take-over Ltd., and its subsidiary Suppressed Ltd., as at 31st March, 1969

| | £ | £ | | £ | £ |
|---|---|---|---|---|---|
| *Capital* | | | *Fixed Assets* | | |
| Authorised and Issued (Fully Paid): | | | At cost ... ... ... 78,000 | | |
| Ordinary Shares of £1 each... | 40,000 | | Less Depreciation ... ... 13,000 | | |
| 5% Preference Shares of £1 each... ... ... ... | 20,000 | | | | 65,000 |
| | | 60,000 | *Current Assets* | | |
| *Capital Reserves* ... ... | | 400 | Stock ... ... ... 11,400 | | |
| *Revenue Reserves* | | | Less Inter-Company Profit ... 800 | | |
| General Reserve: Take-over Ltd. ... ... ... ... | 6,000 | | | 10,600 | |
| Share of Increase in General Reserve in Suppressed Ltd. (Take-over Ltd. ⅘) ... ... | 1,600 | | Debtors... ... ... ... 17,500 | | |
| | | | Cash ... ... ... ... 7,600 | | |
| | 7,600 | | | | 35,700 |
| Profit and Loss Balance ... | 8,000 | | | | |
| | | 15,600 | | | |
| *Minority Interests* ... ... | | | | | |
| Suppressed Ltd. Share Capital | 2,000 | | | | |
| General Reserve (⅕) ... ... | 1,000 | | | | |
| Profit and Loss Balance (⅕)... | 600 | | | | |
| Proportion of Profit for Year | 600 | | | | |
| | | 4,200 | | | |
| *Current Liabilities* | | | | | |
| Creditors ... ... ... | 2,100 | | | | |
| Corporation Tax ... ... | 12,400 | | | | |
| | | 14,500 | | | |
| Bills Payable (discounted by T. Ltd.) ... ... ... | 1,000 | | | | |
| Proposed Dividend ... ... | 5,000 | | | | |
| | | 6,000 | | | |
| | | £100,700 | | | £100,700 |

## Notes on Consolidated Balance Sheet

1. Compare price paid with value received so as to determine Goodwill *or* Capital Reserve figure.

Price paid for 8000 shares (*i.e.* ⅘ of value of business) is £14,000.

*Received* the following

| | £ |
|---|---|
| Shares nominal value | 8,000 |
| ⅘ × £3000 (P/L Balance) | 2,400 |
| ⅘ × £5000 (General Reserve) | 4,000 |
| | £14,400 |

The profit and loss balance and general reserve figure are those at the date of *acquisition*.

There is a difference of £400 which goes to Capital Reserve. If a company pays *more* than the value received then the excess goes to Goodwill.

2. Fixed assets—the two figures on the separate balance sheets are added together.

3. The value of the stock is reduced by the holding company's share of the inter-company profit.

4. Debtors and cash are found from the separate balance sheets. No adjustments are necessary.

5. The shares of the holding company are shown on the Consolidated Balance Sheet.

6. The capital reserve figure is found as explained in (1).

7. Preference shares in the holding company are entered.

8. The general reserve total is made up of the holding company's reserve plus four-fifths of the Increase in the General Reserve of Suppressed Ltd., *i.e.* the proportion belonging to the holding company.

9. The profit and loss balance is transferred from the Profit and Loss Appropriation Account. It is the total for Take-over Ltd., £8000 *plus* four-fifths of the increase of profit in Suppressed Ltd. ($\frac{4}{5}$ × £1000 = £800), *less* the profit on the unrealised stock (*i.e.* £800).

10. The minority interests figures are those belonging to the outside shareholders in Suppressed Ltd., who own one-fifth of the nominal value of the shares (total £10,000: $\frac{1}{5}$ = £2000). To the latter is added the same proportion of General Reserve, the Profit and Loss Balance at the date of acquisition and the profit for the current year.

11. The bills discounted by Take-over Ltd. are a liability and, therefore, have been included.

*Special Note.* For ease of reference calculations have been shown on the Balance Sheet. In practice such detail would be given in the Notes.

## EXAMINATION QUESTIONS

1. From the following list of balances in the books of A. Ltd. and its subsidiary company, B. Ltd., as at 31st March, 19.., prepare a consolidated balance sheet showing thereon, or by notes, the details of the various adjustments made.

|  | A. Ltd. | | B. Ltd. | |
|---|---|---|---|---|
|  | *Dr.* | *Cr.* | *Dr.* | *Cr.* |
|  | £ | £ | £ | £ |
| Goodwill ... ... ... ... | 55,000 | | | |
| Land and buildings ... ... | 330,000 | | 120,000 | |
| Fittings and fixtures ... ... | 35,000 | | 15,000 | |
| Stock in trade ... ... ... | 85,000 | | 55,000 | |
| Investments: | | | | |
|   125,000 shares in B. Ltd. ... | 155,000 | | | |
|   40,000 debentures B. Ltd. ... | 40,000 | | | |
|   5,000 shares in A. Ltd. ... | | | 5,000 | |
| Trade debtors ... ... ... | 80,000 | | 45,000 | |
| Bank and cash balances ... | 20,000 | | | |
| Share capital: | | | | |
|   Ordinary shares of £1 each ... | | 700,000 | | 150,000 |
| General reserve ... ... ... | | | | 10,000 |
| Profit and loss account ... ... | | 55,000 | | 8,000 |
| Debentures ... ... ... | | | | 50,000 |
| Bank overdraft ... ... ... | | | | 8,000 |
| Trade creditors ... ... ... | | 45,000 | | 14,000 |
|  | £800,000 | £800,000 | £240,000 | £240,000 |

Included in the trade debtors of A. Ltd. is £8,000 for goods supplied to B. Ltd., of which £4,000 remained in stock at 31st March, 19.., on which A. Ltd. had a profit of 10%. *(I.C.W.A.)*

2. The Board of Directors require a monthly statement detailing the factors which contribute to the net profit or loss for each month.

Give a pro-forma of the statement you would present. *(I.C.W.A.)*

3. The Mastermind Manufacturing Co. Ltd. approaches you as a consult-ant to advise them on the form of their end-of-period financial management statements. The company is engaged in manufacturing and selling.

You are to submit for consideration revenue statements and a vertical type balance sheet for internal management control purposes.

(*a*) Draft these revenue statements and balance sheet. Figures are *not* required, but you must include sufficient items to demonstrate your proposals fully.

(*b*) Give a very brief explanation of *three* management control ratios which could be obtained from your proposed statements. *(A.C.C.A.)*

4. The managing director of a manufacturing company and his chief departmental executives hold regular monthly meetings at which the trading and financial position of the company is reviewed. As the chief accountant, draft in outline a one-page monthly report suitable to be laid before the meeting. *(I.C.W.A.)*

5. Draft the Balance Sheet, as at 31st March, 19.., from the following summary of the balances at that date. Make a brief report on the position revealed, for the benefit of a holder of Ordinary Stock.

|  | £ |
|---|---|
| Amounts set aside for Provisions ... ... ... ... ... | 110,000 |
| Provision for Bad Debts ... ... ... ... ... ... | 17,000 |
| Bank Overdraft ... ... ... ... ... ... ... | 2,353,334 |
| Bonuses to Employees ... ... ... ... ... ... | 104,000 |
| Balance at Bank ... ... ... ... ... ... | 199,143 |
| Cost of issuing 4 per cent. First Mortgage Debenture Stock ... | 144,684 |
| Current Liability for Taxation ... ... ... ... ... | 1,831,432 |
| Contingencies Reserve ... ... ... ... ... ... | 2,800,000 |
| 4 per cent. First Mortgage Debenture Stock, 1967–82 ... ... | 3,000,000 |
| Future Taxation, Reserve for Income Tax, 1961–62 ... ... | 1,180,000 |
| General Revenue Reserve ... ... ... ... ... ... | 2,000,000 |
| Land and Buildings ... ... ... ... ... ... ... | 5,674,796 |
| Plant and Machinery ... ... ... ... ... ... | 2,417,361 |
| Profit and Loss Account ... ... ... ... ... ... | 459,120 |
| Proposed Ordinary Final Dividend and Bonuses ... ... ... | 207,808 |
| Premium on Shares ... ... ... ... ... ... ... | 2,627,560 |
| Share Capital: Authorised and Issued— |  |
|   6½ per cent. Cumulative Preference Stock ... ... | 1,359,447 |
|   4 per cent. Cumulative Redeemable Preference Stock ... | 3,000,000 |
|   Ordinary Stock ... ... ... ... ... ... ... | 2,638,829 |
| Debtors and Bills Receivable ... ... ... ... ... | 2,484,277 |
| Creditors ... ... ... ... ... ... ... ... | 831,271 |
| Stock-in-Trade, as certified by Managing Director ... ... | 13,391,677 |
| Trade Investments ... ... ... ... ... ... ... | 207,863 |

*(S.C.A.)*

6. Discuss the arguments for and against the publication of turnover figures by a large public company. *(S.C.A.)*

7. State concisely under suitable headings the main rules which you consider should be applied when drafting financial statements for presentation to management. *(S.C.A.)*

8. Explain the methods by which information may be presented to management graphically or pictorially. Illustrate your answer by suitable examples. *(S.C.A.)*

# CHAPTER 22

## AMALGAMATIONS AND RELATED TECHNIQUES

LEGAL and financial experts have attempted to define the multitude of terms used to describe changes in (*a*) *ownership* of companies and (*b*) *the form* taken by a company or group of companies. Unfortunately even now there is no straightforward, precise, generally acceptable group of definitions. For this reason those definitions given below should not be regarded as the only possibilities.

### *DEFINITIONS*

**AMALGAMATION**

The term "amalgamation" describes the process whereby two or more companies merge together. Alternatively, one company may be absorbed by another.

Quite often the amalgamation takes place after consultations and negotiations have gone on between the directors of the companies concerned. This fact distinguishes between normal amalgamations and take-over bids described below.

Other terms used to describe an amalgamation are: merger, integration, absorption and combination.

**TAKE-OVER BID**

A "take-over bid" is an offer to purchase shares with the object of absorbing one company with another. The company taken over may continue to operate in substantially the same manner as before or may lose its old identity altogether.

In the early days of take-over bids there was often no pre-consultation with the directors. Instead, a direct approach was made to the shareholders with an offer for the Ordinary shares, thereby obtaining control of the company.

Today the recommended approach is via the Board of directors of the offeree company so the distinction between "amalgamation" and "take-over" is to some extent academic. Where two companies merge and retain equal status this could be regarded as an amalgamation, but the difference between the two approaches is not always clear. In practice, an amalgamation may become a take-over simply as a result of the strength of the chairman and/or managing director.

## RECONSTRUCTION

A "reconstruction" is a *drastic* rearranging of a company's structure, generally involving the transfer of the assets of one company to another, yet both companies remain under the same ownership.

## CAPITAL REORGANISATION

The term "capital reorganisation" embraces a great variety of methods which may be used to change the capital structure or the rights of shareholders within a *single* company.

These definitions have been kept as brief as possible. For this reason they may be criticised; however, it is hoped that the omission of complex details will emphasise the essential differences.

## AMALGAMATION

As indicated by the definition of "amalgamation," this act generally takes place after pre-consultation with the boards of the companies who are to amalgamate. It is true to say, therefore, that any amalgamation normally takes place when there is a good chance of one or both companies obtaining benefit. The advantages of amalgamations are covered later in this chapter.

One indirect advantage, not specifically mentioned in the economic factors discussed, is the fact that amalgamations may have an important effect on the liquidity position of a group. On the one hand, an amalgamation may be a very profitable form of investment. Accordingly, a company with surplus funds may find itself in the position of being able to grow from strength to strength by the proper use of the funds available. In some circumstances, a converse situation arises. One company may find it beneficial to amalgamate with another company which has a very good liquid position. The surplus funds can be used by the group and thereby increase the earning capacity.

There is no *essential difference* between the normal amalgamation and the take-over amalgamation. Both are the merging together of two companies by means of a holding company or by complete integration (absorption). The difference lies in the way the merging is accomplished and the possible motives behind the amalgamation. Because of pre-consultation the normal amalgamation may take place in a friendly and cordial manner. This is often quite different to the take-over bid atmosphere where a board may fight to the end to prevent the proposed amalgamation taking place.

A recent development has been the urge for companies to expand by amalgamating with companies which have *unrelated* activities. This is known as *conglomerate diversification* and may be classified into:

1. *Concentric Growth*—developing in a very broad area, but with clearly defined policy and strategy.

2. *Profit Motivated Growth*—absorbing any company which appears to be a profitable investment.

Management problems may be very large in the conglomerate type of organisation. Accordingly, the need for effective planning and control will be very real. Management accountancy can play a large-part in ensuring that the necessary systems are available, and that figure show the areas for development indicating quite clearly the strengths and weaknesses of the Group.*

## TAKE-OVER BIDS

Take-over bids are a feature of the 1939–45 post-war era. This refers to take-over bids in their modern form. "Take-over bids" in a wide sense have been present for generations. In an article "An Accountant Looks at Take-over Bids," by Douglas A. Clarke, LL.B., F.C.A. the author quotes a take-over bid of property from Chapter 21 of the First Book of Kings where King Ahab made an offer for the vineyard of Naboth the Jezreelite! This article appeared in *The Accountant* dated 7th November, 1959.

The principal reasons for their emergence are summarised below:

1. The practice of valuing fixed assets at historical costs has resulted in undervaluation with the result that the take-over companies can often purchase assets at figures which are much less than their true current values. (Replacement values are covered in Chapter 27.)

2. Limitation of dividend payments by directors tended to keep down the prices of shares, which in turn meant that control could be obtained at relatively low cost. Needless to say, this limitation or restraint may be due to low profits, possibly indicating inefficient management.

The past tense is used because at the time of writing there has been a considerable increase in share prices compared with, say, ten years ago. The index of ordinary shares compiled by *The Financial Times* is around 400, a rise of approximately 300 points in less than 20 years. Clearly, the higher the index the less chance there is of a take-over bid. The take-over experts looks for gains; these do not exist if share prices reflect current values based on asset and earning-power values.

3. All the possible advantages and motives outlined below, in connection with amalgamations.

The take-over bid carries with it an opportunity to purchase effective control, quite often at a figure which is much below the total value of assets taken over. The capital gearing affects the position. If there is

* For a fuller discussion, see J. Batty, *Corporate Planning and Budgetary Control*, Macdonald & Evans.

a small number of Ordinary (voting) shares reasonably priced then the task of obtaining more than 50% may be relatively easy.

## ETHICS OF TAKE-OVER BIDS

The rights or wrongs of take-over bids form a controversial topic. Is it feasible, fair, and just that directors who may have spent many years building up a business are suddenly removed from office by the technique of the take-over bid?* Answering this question is very difficult for much depends upon the circumstances. Also an argument can be put forward that the most important factor is not the assured employment of directors, but the most effective use of the productive resources. The latter may be forthcoming from new management.

Some criticism may be levelled against the method of approaching shareholders without consulting the directors. That this has been possible arises from the fact that management and ownership are separated. Ownership lies in the shareholders who may have no interest in the company beyond the receiving of dividends and capital profits. The latter becomes a very real issue when a take-over bid is made. Provided the terms are attractive enough, obtaining sufficient shares to give more than half the votes and, thereby control, should be possible.

On this matter the recommendations, of *The City Code on Take-overs and Mergers*,† are most relevant. In brief this recommends that the following code of behaviour should be observed in spirit as well as obeying the rules:

1. The approach should be made by making an offer to the Board of the offeree company by or on behalf of a disclosed principal.

2. A Board receiving an offer should inform shareholders without delay by press notice.

3. Before there is a firm offer absolute secrecy is essential.

4. Directors should act in the interests of shareholders. Full details should be issued.

5. High standards are essential for preparing the document or advertisement which gives the shareholders the facts and advice on the offer (or its rejection). Any forecasts or estimates should have the backing of independent accountants and advisers.

6. Offers should generally be made for 100% of the equity shares, with at least 21 days being allowed for the initial response.

7. A Panel on Take-over and Mergers is available to answer any questions which may arise.

---

* Authority for removal is given by Section 184 of the Companies Act, 1948.

† Obtainable from The Secretary, Issuing Houses Association, 19, Fenchurch Street, London, E.C.3. (*See* Appendix VI.)

This is a very brief summary of the provisions of *The City Code*; it is *not* put forward as a precise statement of the rules. Accordingly, those who are concerned with take-over bids or mergers should obtain a copy of the booklet (*see also* Appendix VI). What should be stressed is that the rules do not have direct legal backing but are based on the belief that voluntary action is better than depending upon a statute. However, a serious breach of the rules could lead to the Board of Trade taking appropriate measures such as revoking the licence of a Licensed Dealer. Power for taking action is given under the Prevention of Fraud (Investments) Act, 1958.

Reference has already been made to obtaining control of a company. This involves the purchase of 51% of the equity shares. A company may decide to make an offer for sufficient shares to give this control and to take no more even if more are offered. This is a partial offer, a technique that *The City Code* regards as undesirable. In these circumstances the shareholders who fail to sell their shares may find themselves in an unfavourable, minority position which is not of their own making. Clearly, the total bid for ownership is to be preferred. Here an offer is made for all the equity shares, the offer being conditional upon receiving at least 90% of possible acceptances. Once 90% is purchased then the balance can be made the subject of a compulsory purchase under Section 209 of the Companies Act, 1948. This section applies in two ways: the company is entitled to purchase from minority shareholders; the latter can compel the company to purchase the shares at the same terms as given to the majority shareholders. There are many conditions to be satisfied before Section 209 can be operated. The decisions of the courts must also be considered. Generally the take-over companies have been able to exercise their rights to purchase without difficulty; any cases which have been tried have tended to be in their favour. One notable exception was the decision in Re Bugle Press Ltd.*

Some people have tended to regard the take-over technique as oppressive to the minority shareholders who cannot take advantage of Section 209. This may be so in some cases. However, it is not always a disadvantage. A partial offer from a company of substance and of national importance may result in the minority being placed in a more favourable position than they would have been under the old regime. New management in control could mean more effective use of resources and, therefore, much larger profits. Clearly, though, it is difficult to generalise. Some take-over bids may have as their main object the earning of capital profits or other gain and not the well-being of the industry.

Protection of the shareholders of a company being taken over is

---

\* (1960) 1. All E.R. 768. Quoted in an article—"Compulsory Purchase of Minority shareholdings," *The Accountant*, 8th October, 1960.

further dealt with by The Prevention of Fraud (Investments) Act, 1958, and The Licensed Dealers (Conduct of Business) Rules S.I. 1960, No. 1216 issued by the Board of Trade. The relevant sections of the Companies Acts, also provide further safeguards.

These then are the principal considerations; some may have a direct bearing on the rights and wrongs of take-over bids, others affect the issue in an indirect manner. One of the great problems for the accountant who is likely to be on the wrong end of a bid is how can take-over bids be avoided. Some of the possible measures are summarised below:

1. Increase the rate of dividend being paid and thereby cause prices of shares to increase to current market values as reflected by the full earning power.

The contents of Chapter 15 on return on capital employed are very relevant here. If a fair return is paid to shareholders, based on capital employed at current values, then there is less danger of a take-over bid. If on the other hand a 20% return is being paid, based on historical costs, and there has been a fourfold increase in the price of assets, the effective return is merely 5% which may be quite inadequate having regard to the risk involved.

Clearly, the increase in the rate of dividend may be possible only after profits have been increased. Alternatively, instead of retaining profits in the business a company could seek fresh capital. Possibly the answer lies in the management itself: improve that and the danger of a take-over bid will disappear.

2. Streamline the organisation by disposing of unprofitable assets and investments. Make full use of cash resources and look into the possibilities of diversification or simplification.

3. Revalue fixed assets so that they reflect current values. This may prevent the bid being successful for a short time only. The fact that assets are shown at higher figures may spur the take-over bidder to greater efforts with an offer of an increased price for the shares.

4. Bring share capital into line with current share values by capitalising reserves. Again this may merely be a temporary measure. If earnings are not increased and there is no increase in dividends then capitalisation can make no difference in the long run.

Essentially action should be taken before any take-over bid is made. In other words, prevention is better than cure. Avoiding a weak position can also avoid the take-over bid. However, if the bid does come because no action on the lines suggested has been taken then the directors may be able to retaliate by promising that measures are to be taken which will improve the situation.

A statement should be made which reveals (*a*) the position of the company as regards the future, including present values of asset and (*b*) the directors' views of the take-over bid. If the directors do not feel

T

disposed to recommend acceptance they are probably in the strongest position if they give the reasons—a critical analysis of the terms of the take-over bid may serve this purpose. Any figures given on statements should be up-to-date, clearly explained and authenticated by an auditor's certificate.

How far a director can go in resisting a take-over bid is not altogether clear. Certainly directors should be expected to behave in a reasonable manner, respecting the interests of all parties—employees, customers, and shareholders. On occasions directors have attempted to dispose of the assets and then lease them back to the company with a limitation on their use. A now classical illustration is the sale and lease-back of The Berkeley Hotel by the board of Savoy Hotel Ltd., when they were faced with a take-over bid. The Board of Trade Inspector reporting on the action came to the conclusion that, although the directors had acted in good faith, he thought they had exceeded their powers. Apparently any actions taken should be capable of being justified on economic or business grounds and not simply on the basis of taking the control of a company's assets away from shareholders. This "decision" does not have legal backing, but many accountants believe that a similar view would be taken with an appropriate case brought before the Courts. Another point on which directors should be careful is the spending of money to resist a take-over bid. According to the report of a law case on this matter the directors would be acting *ultra vires* by spending money on resisting a normal commercial take-over bid, though not if resisting nationalisation.*

## PROFIT FORECASTS†

*The City Code* recommends that statements issued by Boards to justify or disprove of merger proposals should be substantiated by "profit forecasts." Quite rightly the Institute of Chartered Accountants in England and Wales have stressed that these profit forecasts are *probabilities* relating to the future. They have the following characteristics:

1. They are based on subjective judgments and opinions of the directors.
2. They deal with the future, and many of the estimates assume conditions which may change.
3. Trade and other conditions may change.

The further into the future a forecast is made the more uncertain it becomes. Accordingly, great care should be observed by an accountant

---

* Morgan *v.* Tate and Lyle Ltd., (1955) AC 21.

† Accountants are advised to study the *Statement* issued by the Institute of Chartered Accountants in England and Wales in April 1969. This should be read in conjunction with *The City Code*. This section draws heavily on the recommendations contained in that Statement.

when he reports on the profit forecast. He can verify that the forecast has been prepared in accordance with accepted principles which are consistently employed. However, there should be no question of accepting responsibility for a profit forecast—this should rest with the directors who have the necessary facts on policy, strategy and commercial possibilities. The accountant should advise on the proper form of the profit forecast and, therefore, would be responsible for any matter which is affected by his technical competence; *e.g.* accuracy, accounting principles, and presentation of the information in the most suitable manner.

The period to be covered by the profit forecast should be the remainder of the current accounting year, and possibly the following accounting year. No specific period is recommended in the Statement, but there is a clear indication that the forecasting should not extend much beyond one year from the date of the forecast.

Matters to be considered by the reporting accountant when carrying out a review are as follows:

1. *Principal activities of the business.*

2. *Accounting principles and procedures adopted; e.g.* stock situation, calculating profit on long-term contracts, depreciation methods, research and development accounting, taxation, unusual or exceptional transactions.

3. *Commercial assumptions.* The accountant should report whether the forecast appears logical and consistent with the assumptions stated by the directors.

4. *Preparation of forecasts.* Such matters as accuracy, reasons for their preparation, whether the standards set are realistic and the degree of consistency achieved in the past, should all be considered. Attention should be paid to accepting accounting principles for dealing with losses, depreciation, exceptional items and other transactions which can affect the validity of a forecast. The financial arrangements for the short-term should be examined to ensure the adequacy of working capital.

Once this review has been made the accountants' report can be made. This should be addressed to the directors and would include statements on the accounting bases, calculations, sources of information (*e.g.* subsidiary forecasts) and whether the forecast appears to be properly compiled. If the accountant has not been able to audit the figures, this fact should be stated, as should any material reservations on any of the matters on which he is reporting; *e.g.* lack of accounting information or incorrect valuation of fixed assets.

From the observations made above it will be apparent that the accountant can only be held responsible for the work which comes within his professional competence. Merchant bankers and other financial advisers, and the directors have a duty to ensure that assumptions made are realistic. Profit forecasts and asset valuations should be based on accepted principles and methods, thus ensuring that very high standards are maintained.

## ECONOMIC ADVANTAGES OF AMALGAMATIONS

The possible advantages and/or motives which bring about amalgamations, whether of the normal type or take-over bid type, are given below. In the previous section on take-over bids the principal reasons why these bids take place are discussed: they should be kept in mind when considering the advantages listed.

In summary form the advantages may be as shown. Many of these are economies of large scale production which have been discussed and considered by economists over a long period. Many textbooks exist which cover these advantages in great detail. These include technical, financial, and managerial economies which are as follows:

### 1. *Pooling of Research and Development*

In many industries such as chemical manufacturing and electronics many millions of pounds are spent on research each year. Where research and development is a major factor in an industry's progress then great economies may be possible through amalgamation of companies engaged in related fields. The most able scientists and research workers may be brought together and used to the best advantage. Laboratories, test equipment and machinery and other research and development assets hitherto duplicated may be centralised.

### 2. *Saving in Capital Expenditure*

This may arise from making fullest use of special purpose machinery, from better planning and control of the purchase of fixed assets and from avoiding duplication.

### 3. *Economy in Selling and Distribution Costs*

If the companies amalgamating are engaged in related fields of activity then one product may help to sell another. There is the goodwill of each company. In addition, salesmen can carry a wider range of products or, alternatively, if the volume of separate products grows to a large enough extent, then salesmen may be permitted to specialise. Irrespective of the method used there should be a more effective coverage of a sales area with a resultant lowering of costs per unit sold.

Similarly, delivery and other distribution costs may be reduced in total by centralising the hitherto separate entities. There would be no need to duplicate showrooms and stores depots. Better planning of delivery loads may also be possible.

Advertising costs may be reduced substantially especially if before the amalgamation the products involved were in direct competition with each other.

If amalgamation moves in a forward direction—towards the market —then the profits of intermediaries such as wholesalers may be eliminated. Thus, for example, a manufacturing chemist may amalgamate with a company which owns a chain of chemists' shops. In this way a channel of distribution comes under the control of the parent company.

### 4. Increased Financial Standing

The larger company is generally able to command greater financial resources. For one thing there are more fixed assets and, therefore, greater security. This in itself should improve a company's credit-standing. In addition, there will be a larger body of shareholders who may be approached with "rights issues." There are also the economies of large scale production which should bring increased profits, which in turn will also increase credit-standing.

### 5. Elimination of a Possible Price War

Instead of competing with each other the companies come together and, therefore, intensive competition is avoided.

### 6. Diversification

Diversification is the process of extending and increasing the range, variety and desirable features of products. Used in connection with amalgamations it means merging with companies which manufacture products in industries where there is a wide range of products. Any difficulties involved with some products may be offset by the profits earned by other products. Further possible advantages are the creation of a means for disposing of by-products and the acquisition of valuable patents and commercial goodwill.

### 7. Improved Management

The large organisation can afford to employ experts in every important function. A central advisory service is possible and this can be backed by a central library and related facilities. Organisation and methods, operational research, work study and computer services may all be made available when a company expands until it is large enough to make economical use of these facilities.

Generally the greater bargaining power of the large company will tend to mean that they can employ the most efficient managers. This greater bargaining power comes from being able to pay higher salaries. Unfortunately, amalgamation brings its managerial problems. These are discussed below under disadvantages.

### 8. *Greater Commercial Bargaining Power*

With growth comes greater commercial bargaining power. Quantity discounts may be obtained. Long-term contracts or contracts for larger quantities can be entered into; these can be at prices which are lower than those paid by smaller companies. If backward integration takes place—towards the source of raw materials—a company may strengthen its standing as a purchaser. If the merging is with a company that supplies the material then the need to bargain is eliminated by a much stronger force.

### 9. *Amalgamations may Provide New Markets*

This advantage is of particular importance for companies who wish to expand in home or foreign countries.

Examples of industries which have expanded the home market in this way are flour milling and brewing. Interest in the Common Market has resulted in amalgamations in many European countries.

These are possible advantages: there are others which may also accrue. However, there are disadvantages which outweigh to some extent the possible gains.

## ECONOMIC DISADVANTAGES OF AMALGAMATIONS

Amalgamation increases the complexity of an organisation and, therefore, brings in its wake many problems. Some may be overcome, or at least the effects may be reduced, by efficient management. These disadvantages are summarised below:

### 1. *Loss of Trade Name and Goodwill*

The amalgamation which results in one company losing its identity may mean the loss of a valuable asset—the trade name and the commercial goodwill. The latter may have been built up by many years of costly advertising and sales publicity.

One way of preventing this loss is for each company to operate under its own name as before the amalgamation. Another way is to merge the names as well as the companies; *e.g.* the two specialist flour millers Hovis and MacDougall combined together and became Hovis and MacDougall.* Clearly, though, this joining together of names cannot go on indefinitely. The title, even with only two names, may tend to be lengthy and cumbersome.

### 2. *Remoteness in Personnel Relations*

There is a tendency for the large organisation to be very impersonal. The individual may feel that he is a very small and insignificant figure

* Later amalgamated with Ranks the flour millers.

in a vast and complex organisation. This disadvantage may be overcome to some extent by a well-conceived and executed personnel policy including effective communication.

### 3. Problems of Integration

Many problems may arise in connection with the integration of the hitherto separate companies.

There is the difficulty of reallocating duties between directors. Naturally, if there is a take-over bid this problem may not arise. However, with the normal amalgamation there are sure to be some problems. In some circumstances directors and managers may feel that they have been demoted and will resent that fact.

Another problem will be to determine what is the best form of control; *i.e.* which type of amalgamation will be the most effective. There are two principal types of amalgamation:

(*a*) Holding Company.

This is a technique whereby the control of subsidiary companies is vested in the parent company through the holding of at least sufficient share capital to give a controlling interest. The subsidiary companies often operate as separate entities, only the major policy decisions being made by the directors of the holding company.

(*b*) Complete Integration (Absorption).

The companies amalgamating would go into liquidation and their assets and liabilities would be taken over by a new company formed for that purpose. Alternatively, the major company involved would take over the assets and liabilities, the rest of the companies going into liquidation. Because of formation and liquidation expenses this method may be more costly than (*a*) above.

In addition, there is the form of amalgamation which may be of a temporary nature and for this reason is probably better excluded from the definition of an amalgamation. There may be technical collaboration between companies attempting to solve a problem in which they are both interested. Alternatively they may join together for a particular purpose, such as the development of a natural product. An example is the consortium of merchant bankers and other companies set up to bring methane gas from the Sahara.

Other forms of association which may also be regarded as amalgamations are pools, cartels, interlocking directorates (boards having common directors) and associated companies (shares exchanged but neither company controls the other).

The holding company method may be preferred when a company is amalgamating willingly; *i.e.* after consultations on all sides. There may be little or no prestige lost by a company when this method is employed. However, much depends upon the circumstances. If a complete re-organisation is felt to be necessary in order, for example, to be able to enjoy fully the economies of large scale production by bringing all production under one management, then the complete integration may be the better method. If the amalgamation follows a take-over bid there may be no feelings or prestige to consider; the fact that a take-over bid has been made often means that the directors being "taken over" have little or no say in the future policy of the business. In these circumstances the better method should be selected by considering the economic benefits likely to accrue from the two types of amalgamation.

A summary of the possible economic benefits and disadvantages is given below. There is inevitably a certain amount of overlapping with the benefits or disadvantages covered earlier in this section.

### In Favour of Holding Companies

(i) The amalgamation is fairly easy to accomplish and generally cheaper than the complete integration.

Because no attempt is made to integrate harmoniously each company coming into the group into the existing framework, the holding company type of amalgamation is cheaper, but this may only be a short-term tendency.

(ii) There is less likelihood of redundancy of workers and management. This is normally the case because the subsidiary companies operate in very much the same way as they did before the amalgamation took place.

(iii) All the benefits of decentralisation are obtained.

With complete integration excessive centralisation may result.

(iv) Problems are kept to a minimum, so profits from the new company become part of group profits immediately.

### Against Holding Companies

(i) The *fullest* economies of large scale production and marketing may not be realised.

Obtaining the full advantages may require *concentration* of production. Furthermore, concerted effort in the field of selling may be very difficult to achieve unless there is complete integration of all the sales divisions.

(ii) *Effective* control may be difficult to achieve.

One of the ways of trying to achieve the control is to have directors from the central board on each of the subsidiary boards. Clearly though, this is often *nominal* control only. There will need to be more than representation on boards for real control. In particular, there should be utilisation of the best possible methods. Yet if each company is virtually autonomous the introduction of the best methods may be extremely difficult. Uniform costing and accounting are also very desirable, but the introduction and integration of the necessary systems is far from easy.

(iii) Although the holding company type of amalgamation may appear to offer an easy way out so far as personnel problems are concerned, this may not always be the case.

In the long run there may be more jealousies and friction simply because there are no clear lines of authority. The complete integration can enable authority and responsibilities to be defined positively and clearly so that there is no misunderstanding.

The disadvantages of the holding company are obviously the advantages of complete integration. In practice, the fully centralised type of complete integration may be feasible, but it should be appreciated that this is the exact opposite of the holding company with autonomous subsidiary companies. Each extreme will tend to bring out its own peculiar advantages and disadvantages to the maximum extent. For example, centralised integration may result in an inflexible and bureaucratic system. Accordingly, whether the holding company form or complete integration is selected, there may be a need for a compromise which will avoid the principal evils of either extreme.

Naturally the nature of the business will play an important part in determining which method is appropriate. If the companies amalgamated are in a related field then the necessary concentration of development, production and selling may best be accomplished through complete integration. On the other hand, if the companies in the group are producing and selling a wide variety of unrelated products then the holding company type of amalgamation may be better. Clearly, in this case, benefits which may result from complete integration would not be available to the group simply because each company would be dealing with problems which arise in that company and in no other. Thus, for example, if one company made clothing whereas another manufactured industrial instruments then co-ordination between the two would be extremely difficult, even if any useful purpose would be served by such action.

## 4. *Accounting Problems*

The larger and more diverse a company becomes the more difficult becomes the accounting, both in the financial and costing spheres.

On the financial accounting side there must be compliance with the Companies Acts. In addition, there should be an attempt to put the accounts of each company within the group on a basis which allows valid comparisons to be made. If the fullest possible information is to be given to shareholders then profit from each company should be calculated in the same way; the same rules applied for differentiating between capital and revenue expenditure; stocks should be valued on the same basis. Analysis of profits to show the effect of each new company added to the group is also desirable. There is the need to formulate a policy on inter-company transactions—the prices to be charged by one subsidiary when selling to another.

In the costing of products some form of uniform costing may be very desirable. This in itself creates many problems. How are materials to be priced? *e.g.* average price or FIFO. What method is to be used for absorbing overhead costs? *e.g.* machine hour rate or direct-labour hour or both. If Standard Costing or Budgetary Control are to be employed how are the differences in age of plant, different wage-rates in different plants and the fact that some plants are highly mechanised, whereas others employ hand labour methods, to be reconciled? Moreover, what adjustments are to be made so that costs of different plants can be compared with an assurance that any differences indicate the degree of efficiency being achieved? These are only a few of the problems which may be encountered. If there is to be *effective* control then these problems have to be resolved.

### 5. *Excessive Cost of Control*

There is a danger, particularly in the field of take-over bids, that too much will be paid for the cost of control of the company being taken over. This tendency may be aggravated when a number of competing companies are interested in taking over a particular company. Bids and counter-bids inevitably raise the price of the shares. Caution may be thrown to the winds and a company may be taken over at a price far in excess of its true value as measured by earning power and the current value of assets. This state of affairs may be avoided if accountants give the full benefit of their special knowledge and training by preparing realistic valuations and management reports.

## STATUTORY IMPLICATIONS

The statutory implications of an amalgamation are not straightforward. The statutory and related common law provisions are contained in many acts and law cases. Only a very brief summary of the main provisions is covered here. These are as follows:

1. Relief from companies' capital duty and *ad valorem* conveyance duty.

This may apply to both amalgamations and reconstructions and is contained in Section 55 of the Finance Act, 1927.* Conditions are laid down which must be complied with before the relief can be

---

* As amended by Section 31 of the Finance Act, 1928, and Section 41 of the Finance Act, 1930.

obtained. Section 42 of the Finance Act, 1930, deals with relief from *ad valorem* conveyance duty on property transfers between companies associated with each other. Section 50 of the Finance Act, 1938, also deals with this matter.

## 2. Taxation Gains.

Tax savings may be an important factor in determining which amalgamation method to use. Accordingly, the legislation in force for the time being should be studied very carefully before selecting the most appropriate method.

# RECONSTRUCTIONS

There are two main types of reconstruction, distinguished by reference to the sections of the Companies Act, 1948, which cover the relevant provisions. These are as follows:

1. Provisions of Section 287.
2. Provisions of Sections 206–208.

Details of these are given below.

## PROVISIONS OF SECTION 287

In this case one company takes over the assets of another company, yet the same persons retain control.

The provisions of section 287 must be followed. Very briefly these involve a members' voluntary winding up and the appointment of a liquidator to carry out the sale. The latter appointment must be covered by *special* resolution.

There is, therefore, a liquidation followed by a reflotation. The usual object is to adjust the capital so that it is brought into line with assets owned and, therefore, earning capacity.

Shareholders are issued with shares in the new company. The entitlements are settled strictly by reference to the class rights attaching to the shares on a winding up. Any shareholders who do not agree with the terms of the reconstruction will have to be paid off by the liquidator. This may create difficulties and is, therefore, a disadvantage. On the other hand, there is no need to apply to the Court for approval of the scheme.

The creditors' rights, including Debenture holders', cannot be varied. Moreover, they are given certain protection under section 287.

## PROVISIONS OF SECTIONS 206–208

These sections deal with a compromise or arrangement. These terms may include variations in the rights held by the following:

1. Debenture holders.
2. Creditors.
3. Shareholders.

The approval of three-fourths in value of each class, whether Debenture holders, creditors or shareholders, must be obtained before the scheme can be put to the Court for sanction. The latter is essential. Once sanctioned, the scheme is binding provided an office copy of the order from the Court has been delivered to the Registrar of Companies.

A scheme of arrangement under these sections may be carried out because a company is in financial difficulties. There may be difficulty experienced in obtaining funds for working capital. Accordingly, a new company may be formed to take over the assets of the old company. The purchase consideration in these circumstances may be partly-paid shares in the new company which are exchanged for the shares in the old company. The shareholders may then be asked for the unpaid call on the new shares.

However, liquidation is not an essential condition for being able to take advantage of sections 206–208. Any compromise or arrangement may be submitted to the Court for approval.

A scheme coming under sections 206–208 may be part of a general amalgamation. In fact there may, in some circumstances, be no financial problems, but simply an amalgamation of two or more companies.

## CAPITAL REORGANISATION

In some circumstances a scheme of capital reorganisation varying the rights of shareholders may be very desirable for the following reasons:

1. Accumulated past losses have to be written off so that current profits can be used to pay dividends.

The scheme may be referred to as a "reduction of capital scheme" and is covered by sections 66 to 71 of the Companies Act, 1948.* The shareholders must approve the reduction by passing a special resolution which subsequently has to be given Court sanction before the reduction scheme can be put into effect.

2. A complicated capital structure which requires to be simplified, thus complying with modern ideas and practice. If there is a large variety of types of shares these may be reduced to, say, two types only.

3. The nominal value of shares needs changing so that they are attractive to future investors; e.g. if a new issue is to be made.

4. The capital gearing is not appropriate to the business concerned so a change is considered essential. The subject of capital gearing is covered in Chapter 7.

* Sometimes a capital reduction scheme is referred to as an "internal *reconstruction*." This illustrates how terminology varies.

There may be other reasons or a combination of those given above. The important point to remember is that with the reorganisation there is *no liquidation* involved.

## GUIDANCE IN DRAFTING SCHEMES

As indicated earlier in this chapter there are very many possible types of reconstructions and reorganisations (these terms are defined on page 554). Sometimes reorganisations may precede or follow a reconstruction so that in effect there is a combining of the two principal types of scheme. Some of the difficulties which have to be resolved when drafting suitable schemes are outlined below. These are kept as brief as possible: there are books devoted entirely to reconstructions and related matters and the reader is advised to study one of these if he wishes to obtain more detail than is given here.

The points to consider and watch are:

1. Define clearly the *objects* of the proposed reconstruction or reorganisation.

The main object may be to eliminate losses so that dividend payments can be resumed; to bring share capital into line with assets owned, or to make the company a better-risk proposition when new finance is being sought. Whatever the reason this should be clearly understood and remembered *throughout* the drafting of the scheme.

2. Consideration must be given to the rights of shareholders as laid down in the Memorandum and Articles of Association or any other document which deals with the rights of members. There may be special provisions regarding the rights on liquidation.

3. Legal requirements must be complied with at all times. In particular, attention should be paid to the requirements of the Companies Act, 1948. Some of the sections of this Act (287, 206–208 and 66–71) have already been noted earlier in this chapter. The sections which are appropriate to the particular scheme should, of course, be determined and followed.

4. As far as possible the rights of shareholders, creditors and Debenture holders should be varied in a manner which is fair and equitable to *all* parties concerned.

Attention should be paid to the rights of members as regards income, voting rights and on liquidation. Taking each of the main parties in turn possible action is discussed:

### (a) Ordinary shareholders

Some accountants suggest that if losses are brought about because the venture is based on an unsound idea then the Ordinary capital may rightly be eliminated altogether. However, if the idea is *really* that unsound then clearly there is need for more than a variation of share-holders' rights. The author believes that the circumstances which call for complete elimination of Ordinary shares would be very exceptional and unusual. In any scheme there may be a drastic reduction in the Ordinary share capital, but reduction of each share to *less* than one penny should not be necessary. As will be appreciated, provided the Ordinary shares are not eliminated altogether the Ordinary share-holders will be no worse off than before the capital reduction. They will still have the same voting rights and be entitled to the same proportion of profits. Thus, for example, if normally the Ordinary shareholders take 50% of profit, they can still take the 50% even though the nominal value of each share has been reduced.

### (b) Preference shareholders

The Preference shareholders cannot be expected to assume the same burden of risk as Ordinary shareholders. Accordingly, they should be treated more lightly than the owners of the equity capital.

How lightly they should be treated depends upon the rights attach-ing to the Preference shares and the rights they are called upon to give up if the reconstruction or reorganisation takes place. There may be arrears of dividends on the cumulative Preference shares. If the Preference shareholders agree to forgo the arrears of dividends then they should be given some compensation; *e.g.* a number of Ordinary shares. If the Preference shareholders have the first right to repay-ment of capital then the loss to be borne by them should be kept to a minimum. If the cumulative Preference shares do have to be partially written off then they again may be given compensation either by increasing the rate of dividend (*e.g.* from 5% to 7%) or by giving them Ordinary shares. When *participating* Preference shares are involved they may properly be expected to bear a sizeable proportion of the loss.

### (c) Creditors and Debenture holders

A meeting of each class of creditors will be necessary. Clearly each class will try to obtain as much as possible from the scheme; in other words, they will oppose any reduction in rights as energetically as they are able.

It will probably be necessary to convince the creditors and De-benture holders that reductions in rights *are essential*. The strongest argument may be a statement of the likely position if the reductions are not affected. Clearly, *all* possible capital reductions should be made or proposed before asking creditors to forgo any rights.

If Debenture holders or other creditors have a charge against assets then they may have to be paid off or otherwise satisfied before any scheme can be drawn up. They may insist upon being represented on the board of directors until they receive payment in full.

5. There should be a realistic valuation of *all* assets. Fixed assets should be revalued having regard to current and future earning capacity. Any fictitious assets such as preliminary expenses or a debit Profit and Loss Balance should be written off. Intangible assets—goodwill, patents and trade marks—may be retained *if* of value. However, since these intangibles, in the circumstances, are likely to be of little value a clean sweep, by complete elimination, would be a better plan. Current assets should also be given attention: stocks have to be valued realistically allowing for obsolescence; in addition, any possible bad debts should be written off bringing debtors down to represent a figure which can actually be recovered.

6. Attention should be paid to obtaining finance needed for the future development which is necessary to put the company back in a stable position and also to a state where profit earning can recommence.

This may involve trying to obtain more capital from existing shareholders. Clearly in these circumstances there must be good faith on all sides. The shareholders should be given the fullest possible information on present and future prospects.

Outside funds from other than existing shareholders may be difficult to obtain. A possible source of loan capital is secured Debentures. Whether this would be possible depends upon the state of confidence existing in the money market and the value of fixed assets which are free to be used as securities. If secured Debentures *already* exist there may be great difficulty in attracting a new loan.

The first scheme drafted may be far from suitable. There may be disagreement amongst shareholders or no co-operation from creditors. For these reasons a sound plan is to draft a number of different schemes and compare the relative merits of each. The likely position if *no* reconstruction or reorganisation is carried out should also be forecast. In practice the employment of an independent adviser, such as an issuing house, may be a distinct advantage. Shareholders may place more reliance upon the information given and may be more willing to put additional capital into the company. The issuing house can give guidance on the best method of obtaining funds in the form of loans or new share capital.

The precise approach made to deciding how the losses should be apportioned between members and possibly creditors may vary according to the circumstances. However, a possible plan is one which considers the total loss involved and then, commencing with Ordinary shares, what is considered an equitable share of the loss is written off each class of shares. A simple example will illustrate the procedure.

The following summarised balance sheet, which shows tangible assets at realistic valuations, indicates the position at 31st December:

*Balance Sheet*
*as at 31st December . . .*

| | £ | | £ |
|---|---|---|---|
| Ordinary Shares of £1 each | 60,000 | Sundry Assets | 80,000 |
| 6% Preference Shares of £1 each | 100,000 | Profit and Loss Balance | 80,000 |
| | £160,000 | | £160,000 |

The action to be taken would depend upon the rights of the members, but a possible approach may be as follows:

(*a*) Reduce Ordinary shares to (£0·01) each. This reduces them as far as practicable without complete elimination. This assumes that the Ordinary shareholders control the business and bear the largest burden of risk.

(*b*) Write down the Preference shares by the amount of loss still left; *i.e.* £20,600 (£80,000−£59,400 written off Ordinary shares).

(*c*) Compensate the Preference shareholders for the loss incurred or any rights which they agree to forgo.

The amount of compensation depends upon what type of Preference shares are involved. As far as possible their rights should be the same as those enjoyed before the scheme was proposed.

If, because the shares are participating, the Preference shareholders are to stand the total loss of £20,600 then it will be necessary to reduce the value of each share by the appropriate sum (£20,600 divided by 100,000; *i.e.* £0·206 per share).

When dividends are in arrears for a number of years and the cumulative Preference shareholders agree to give up their right to receive payment the compensation may take the form of an increased rate of dividend or a number of Ordinary shares.

These remarks should serve to illustrate the line to follow when drafting a scheme of reconstruction or reorganisation. To show all possible schemes would need a complete volume. Here only a brief outline of the general procedures has been possible. In the next section the accounting entries are shown.

## *ACCOUNTING FOR AMALGAMATION*

The possible reasons for amalgamation are covered earlier in this chapter. Once the decision to amalgamate has been taken the accounting entries will have to be dealt with. The procedure followed depends upon the type of amalgamation, viz.:

1. Holding Company Type.
2. Complete Integration (Absorption).

These are discussed and illustrated in turn.

## HOLDING COMPANY TYPE

In the holding company type of amalgamation the companies continue to operate as separate entities. The holding company becomes a major shareholder in the subsidiary company. Accordingly, the entries in the holding company books must reflect this fact. These may be summarised as follows:

### Journal of Holding Company

|  | Dr. | Cr. |
|---|---|---|
| Shares in Subsidiary Company Account | £000 | |
| To Cash Account* | | £000 |

Alternatively, a Debenture Account or Share Capital Account may be credited. Which account to take obviously depends upon the terms of the purchase.

The requirements of the Companies Acts regarding holding companies also have relevance; these are covered in Chapter 21.

## COMPLETE INTEGRATION (ABSORPTION)

Accounting for complete integration involves debiting asset accounts in the books of the purchasing company.

If the amount paid for the company being taken over exceeds the value of the tangible assets then the difference should be debited to a Goodwill (or Cost of Control) Account. When the value of assets exceeds the purchase consideration then a Capital Reserve Account should be credited with the difference.

On amalgamation the assets acquired may be revalued (e.g. at current prices) and, if so, these new values should be entered into the purchasing company's books.

An example in question and answer form is shown below. This is extremely simple, but nevertheless should serve the main object—that of explaining the principles involved. It will be seen that journal entries are necessary to integrate the assets and liabilities in the purchasing company's books.

The liquidation of the company being taken over is not dealt with.

QUESTION

The balance sheets of Integrations Limited and Underlings Limited are as follows:

* Given for the purpose of illustration. Usually cash transactions are not journalised.

## Balance Sheet of Integrations Ltd.,
### as at 31st December 19...

| | £ | | | £ | £ |
|---|---|---|---|---|---|
| *Issued Share Capital* | | *Intangible Assets* | | | |
| 63,000 Ordinary of £1 each ... ... | 63,000 | Goodwill ... ... ... | 10,000 | | |
| Capital Reserves ... ... ... | 30,000 | Patents ... ... ... | 5,000 | | |
| Revenue Reserves ... ... ... | 30,000 | | | | 15,000 |
| *Current Liabilities* | | *Fixed Assets* | | | |
| Sundry Creditors ... ... ... | 2,000 | Property ... ... ... | | 25,000 | |
| | | Machinery ... | 40,000 | | |
| | | *Less* Depreciation | 5,000 | | |
| | | | | 35,000 | |
| | | | | | 60,000 |
| | | *Current Assets* | | | |
| | | Stock ... ... | 10,000 | | |
| | | Debtors ... | 10,000 | | |
| | | Cash at Bank... | 30,000 | | |
| | | | | 50,000 | |
| | £125,000 | | | | £125,000 |

## Balance Sheet of Underlings Ltd.,
### as at 31st December, 19...

| | £ | £ | | £ | £ |
|---|---|---|---|---|---|
| *Issued Share Capital* | | | *Intangible Assets* | | |
| 10,000 5% Preference Shares | | | Goodwill ... ... ... | | 10,000 |
| of £1 each ... ... ... | 10,000 | | *Fixed Assets* | | |
| 20,000 Ordinary Shares of £1 | | | Property ... ... ... | 20,000 | |
| each ... ... ... ... | 20,000 | | *Less* Depreciation ... ... | 5,000 | |
| | 30,000 | | | | 15,000 |
| *Less* Profit and Loss Balance | 10,000 | | *Current Assets* | | |
| | | 20,000 | Stock ... ... ... ... | 5,000 | |
| | | | Debtors ... ... ... | 10,000 | |
| *Current Liabilities* | | | | | 15,000 |
| Sundry Creditors ... ... | 10,000 | | | | |
| Bank Overdraft ... ... | 10,000 | | | | |
| | | 20,000 | | | |
| | | £40,000 | | | £40,000 |

Underlings Limited is to be amalgamated with Integrations Limited, being completely absorbed by the latter. The terms of the sale were agreed as follows:

1. Integrations Limited to take over both assets and liabilities.

2. Ordinary shareholders in Underlings Limited to receive £1 Ordinary shares in Integrations Limited; one *new* share for each ten old shares.

3. Preference shareholders in Underlings Limited to receive 5% Preference shares of £1 each in Integrations Limited; one *new* share for each two shares previously held.

4. Costs of liquidating Underlings Limited amounted to £500. These are to be met by Integrations Limited.

5. Integrations Limited have had the property of Underlings Limited revalued. A conservative valuation has given a figure of £40,000. This figure is to be brought into the books of Integrations Limited. A provision of £1000 has to be made for expected bad debts in Underlings Limited.

You are required to show the journal entries in the books of Integrations Limited and a balance sheet after the absorption has taken place. Assume that the additional capital to be issued is already authorised.

## Journal of Integrations Ltd.

| 19...<br>Dec. 31 | | | Dr.<br>£ | Cr.<br>£ |
|---|---|---|---|---|
| | Property | Dr. | 40,000 | |
| | Stock | ,, | 5,000 | |
| | Debtors | ,, | 10,000 | |
| | To Sundry Creditors | | | 10,000 |
| | ,, Bank Overdraft | | | 10,000 |
| | ,, Bad Debts Provision | | | 1,000 |
| | ,, Underlings Ltd. | | | 7,000 |
| | ,, Capital Reserve | | | 27,000 |
| | Being assets and liabilities taken over from Underlings Limited as per the agreement dated............................ | | | |
| Dec. 31 | | | | |
| | Underlings Limited | Dr. | 7,000 | |
| | To Ordinary Share Capital | | | 2,000 |
| | ,, Preference Share Capital | | | 5,000 |
| | Being purchase consideration for assets and liabilities of Underlings Limited. Agreement and resolution dated.............. refers. | | | |

*Notes on Journal Entries*

1. Most of the items in the first journal entry should need no explanation. They are simply the transfers from the balance sheet of Underlings Limited, together with the adjustment for Property and the Provision for Bad Debts.

2. The credit entry to Underlings Limited in the first journal entry has to be computed by reference to the purchase consideration (shown in the second journal entry).

3. The credit to Capital Reserve is simply the difference between assets acquired and liabilities plus payments to be made in shares; *i.e.* £55,000–£28,000.

4. Shares issued are at par. Had they been at a premium (due to market price exceeding nominal value) then a Share Premium Account would have to be credited with the value of the premium.

### Balance Sheet of Integrations Limited
### as at 31st December ...

#### (After amalgamation of Underlings)

| | £ | £ | | £ | £ |
|---|---|---|---|---|---|
| *Share Capital* | | | *Intangible Assets* | | |
| 65,000 Ordinary Shares of £1 each ... ... ... ... | 65,000 | | Goodwill ... ... ... | 10,000 | |
| 5000 5% Preference Shares of £1 each ... ... ... | 5,000 | | Patents ... ... ... | 5,000 | |
| | | 70,000 | | | 15,000 |
| | | | *Fixed Assets* | | |
| Capital Reserves ... ... | | 57,000 | Property ... ... ... | 65,000 | |
| Revenue Reserves ... ... | | 30,000 | Machinery ... 40,000 | | |
| *Current Liabilities* | | | *Less* Depreciation 5,000 | | |
| Sundry Creditors ... ... | 12,000 | | | 35,000 | |
| Bank Overdraft ... ... | 10,000 | | | | 100,000 |
| | | 22,000 | *Current Assets* | | |
| | | | Stock ... ... 15,000 | | |
| | | | Debtors ... 19,000 | | |
| | | | Cash at Bank... 29,500 | | |
| | | | | | 63,500 |
| | | | Capital and Issue Expenses of Underlings Ltd. ... ... | | 500 |
| | | £179,000 | | | £179,000 |

*Notes on Balance Sheet*

1. The items from the balance sheets of both Integrations Ltd., and Underlings Ltd. (now liquidated) are added together. Care must be taken to ensure that only assets and liabilities taken over are included on the new balance sheet. Accordingly it will be safer to obtain the amounts to add to the balances of Integrations Ltd., from the journal entries.

2. There are no instructions in the Question on: (a) Goodwill and Capital Reserve, and (b) Cash at Bank and Bank Overdraft.

In both these cases one item could be used to cancel the other. For example, part of Capital Reserve could be used to eliminate Goodwill; at the same time it seems rather ludicrous to have a large bank balance and yet have a bank overdraft.

3. The fictitious asset—Capital and Issue Expenses—should be eliminated as soon as possible by writing it off to profit and loss appropriation account.

## REORGANISATION

An example of a reorganisation is given below in question and answer form.

QUESTION

XY & Co. Ltd. have been having a difficult trading period and at 31s December, 19... their balance sheet was as set out below:

| Capital | £ | £ | Buildings | £ | £ |
|---|---|---|---|---|---|
| 30,000 6% cum. pref. shares | | | At cost less depreciation | | 25,000 |
| of £1 | 30,000 | | Plant and Machinery | | |
| 70,000 ord. shares of £1 | 70,000 | | At cost less depreciation | | 38,000 |
| | | | *Current Assets* | | |
| | 100,000 | | Stock and work-in-progress | 50,000 | |
| *Less* Profit and Loss Account | 25,438 | | Debtors | 68,000 | |
| | | 74,562 | | | 118,000 |
| Debentures | | | Goodwill | | 20,000 |
| £50,000 at 5% | | 50,000 | | | |
| *Current Liabilities* | | | | | |
| Debenture interest for 1 year | | | | | |
| (net) | 1,438 | | | | |
| Trade creditors | 40,000 | | | | |
| Bank | 35,000 | | | | |
| | | 76,438 | | | |
| | | £201,000 | | | £201,000 |

## Notes

(*a*) The dividend on the Preference shares is two years in arrears.

(*b*) The Debenture holder has agreed to waive his arrears of interest and to exchange his Debenture for 55,000 6% cumulative participating Preference shares of £1 each entitled to a non-cumulative participation of 3% with the Ordinary shares after the latter have received 10%.

(*c*) The capital loss is to be written off against the existing capital in the following proportions:

Preference share capital $\frac{1}{3}$

Ordinary share capital $\frac{2}{3}$

(*d*) The existing Preference shareholders as reduced in note (*c*) to receive a premium of 20% in shares from the Ordinary shareholders on agreeing to accept Ordinary shares in exchange and to waive their arrears of dividend.

(*e*) The existing Ordinary shareholders to provide £45,000 of additional capital.

(*f*) The reduction in capital to be used to write off goodwill entirely, stocks and work in progress by £10,000 and debtors by £8000 and to eliminate the debit balance in the profit and loss account.

You are required to write up the share capital accounts and the capital reconstruction account and show the balance sheet after the above transactions have been completed.                     (*I.C.W.A. Final*)

SUGGESTED SOLUTION

*Preliminary Notes*

1. The first step is to enter the balances in the appropriate accounts.

2. A Capital Reconstruction Account* (or capital *reduction* account) is opened and any assets or debit balances being written off are debited; the corresponding credit entries are posted to the asset or other accounts affected by the reduction. The question being solved does not ask for asset accounts to be given and for this reason they are omitted.

The capital reductions for each class of share are credited to the reconstruction account and the share capital accounts are debited.

3. The adjustments should be carried out in the order in which they are given in the question. This allows a question to be answered in a logical

---

* In view of title of this section it would be better to have a *Reorganisation* Account. The Question asks for a Reconstruction A/c.

sequence and, at the same time, may assist in the interpretation of the instructions which have to be followed.

4. Care must be taken to distinguish between transactions which require ledger entries and those which do not have to appear in the ledger. An example of the latter is the transfer of Ordinary shares to Preference shareholders. This would require transfer entries in the Share Register, but the share capital accounts remain the same.

If the reader checks each double entry he should have no difficulty in following the principles involved in answering similar questions.

## LEDGER OF XY & CO., LTD.

### 6% Cumulative Preference Share Capital

| Dr. | | | | | | Cr. |
|---|---|---|---|---|---|---|
| | | £ | | | | £ |
| Dec. 31 | To Reconstruction Account ¼ | 6,000 | Dec. 31 | By Balance | | 30,000 |
| | Ordinary Share Capital | 24,000 | | | | |
| | | £30,000 | | | | £30,000 |

### Ordinary Share Capital

| | | £ | | | £ |
|---|---|---|---|---|---|
| Dec. 31 | To Reconstruction Account ⅘ | 56,000 | Dec. 31 | By Balance | 70,000 |
| | | | | 6% Cum. Pref. Shares | 24,000 |
| | Balance c/d | 83,000 | | Ordinary Shareholders | 45,000 |
| | | £139,000 | | | £139,000 |
| | | | Jan. 1 | By Balance b/d | £83,000 |

### Capital Reconstruction Account

| | | £ | | | £ |
|---|---|---|---|---|---|
| Dec. 31 | To Profit and Loss A/c | 25,438 | Dec. 31 | By 6% Cum. Pref. Shares | 6,000 |
| | Stock and WIP | 10,000 | | Ord. Share Capital | 56,000 |
| | Debtors | 8,000 | | Deb. Interest | 1,438 |
| | Goodwill | 20,000 | | | |
| | | £63,438 | | | £63,438 |

### Debenture Account

| | | £ | | | £ |
|---|---|---|---|---|---|
| Dec. 31 | To Debenture Holders | 50,000 | Dec. 31 | By Balance | 50,000 |

### Debenture Holder's Account

| | | £ | | | £ |
|---|---|---|---|---|---|
| Dec. 31 | To 6% Cum. Part Pref. | | Dec. 31 | By Debenture Account | 50,000 |
| | Share Capital | 50,000 | | | |

### 6% Cumulative Participating Preference Share Capital

| | | | | | £ |
|---|---|---|---|---|---|
| | | | Dec. 31 | By Debenture Holders | 50,000 |
| | | | | Discount Account | 5,000 |
| | | | | | £55,000 |

*Discount on Preference Shares*

| | | £ |
|---|---|---|
| Dec. 31 | To 6% Cumulative Pref. Share Capital | 5,000 |

*Profit and Loss Account Balance*

| | | £ | | | £ |
|---|---|---|---|---|---|
| Dec. 31 | To Balance | 25,438 | Dec. 31 | By Reconstruction Account | 25,438 |

*Ordinary Shareholders*

| | | £ | | | £ |
|---|---|---|---|---|---|
| Dec. 31 | To Ordinary Share Capital | 45,000 | Dec. 31 | By Bank | 45,000 |

*Bank Account*

| | | £ | | | £ |
|---|---|---|---|---|---|
| Dec. 31 | To Ordinary Shareholders | 45,000 | Dec. 31 | By Balance | 35,000 |
| | | | | Balance c/d | 10,000 |
| | | £45,000 | | | £45,000 |
| Jan. 1 | To Balance b/d | £10,000 | | | |

### After reconstruction
### Balance Sheet of XY & Co. Ltd.,
### as at 31st December, 19...

| | £ | £ | | £ | £ |
|---|---|---|---|---|---|
| **Capital Accounts** | | | **Fixed Assets** | | |
| Ordinary Shares ... ... | 59,000 | | Buildings (*net*) ... ... | 25,000 | |
| Transferred from 6% Cumulative Pref. Shares ... ... | 24,000 | | Plant and Machinery... ... | 38,000 | |
| | | 83,000 * | | | 63,000 |
| | | | **Current Assets** | | |
| **6% Cumulative Pref. Participating Shares** ... ... | 55,000 | | Stock ... ... ... | 40,000 | |
| *Less* Discount ... ... | 5,000 | | Debtors ... ... ... | 60,000 | |
| | | 50,000 | Bank ... ... ... | 10,000 | |
| | | | | | 110,000 |
| **Current Liabilities** | | | | | |
| Sundry Creditors ... ... | | 40,000 | | | |
| | | £173,000 | | | £173,000 |

## VALUATION OF SHARES

The directors of one company contemplating taking over another company will want to know what is a fair valuation of the Ordinary shares. There are three principal methods:

* Entry of balance of £83,000 is all that is necessary. Transfer of the £24,000 is shown to make the illustration clearer.

1. Yield on Shares Method.
2. Assets Valuation Method.
3. An average of 1 and 2.

These are considered below.

## 1. YIELD ON SHARES METHOD

The profit available to Ordinary shareholders is ascertained and then this is capitalised by use of a reasonable rate of return for the type of business concerned.

### EXAMPLE

Page Ltd. is an old established company with an issued *Ordinary* share capital of £100,000: *i.e.* 100,000 Ordinary shares of £1 each. The average profits *after* paying Preference shareholders are £40,000 per annum and this is expected to continue for a number of years.

Under existing conditions and taking into account the existing interest rate structure a reasonable return on capital employed may be taken as 20%.

Calculate the value of each Ordinary share.

### SOLUTION

$$\frac{£40,000}{1} \times \frac{100}{20} = £200,000$$

$$\text{Each share is worth } \frac{£200,000}{100,000} = £2 \text{ each}$$

This method may give a reasonable valuation when a business is well-established and there are no wide fluctuations in profit from one year to another. However, when the future is very uncertain it will be difficult to estimate what significance can be attached to past profit figures. The past is no certain guide to the future and, for this reason, what a company has accomplished in previous years should be used with caution and not construed as indicating that the trend will continue. A change in management, in products made, or any other significant factor can alter the profit prospects of a company.

When *past* profits are to be used as a basis for estimating future profits it will be necessary to make adjustments for any expenses which are considered excessive or have been omitted. Thus, for example, directors' remuneration may be reasonable at £5000 per annum. If £8000 has been charged in the accounts each year then past profits should be increased by £3000. Similarly if *inadequate* depreciation has been charged then the amount undercharged should be deducted from the profit for each year.

## 2. ASSETS VALUATION METHOD

The *assets valuation method* considers what part of the total assets can be said to "belong" to the ordinary shareholders. From total assets are deducted creditors, Debentures and Preference shares. The balance left can be regarded as the capital, reserves and profit attributable to the Ordinary shareholders.

EXAMPLE

| | | |
|---|---:|---:|
| Total Assets including Goodwill | | £320,000 |
| *Less* Creditors | £10,000 | |
| Debentures | £40,000 | |
| Preference Shares | £50,000 | |
| | | £100,000 |
| Net Assets attributable to | | |
| Ordinary Shareholders | | £220,000 |

There are 100,000 Ordinary shares of £1·00 each.

$$\text{Value of Ordinary Shares} = \frac{£220,000}{100,000} = £2·20 \text{ each}$$

If this method is to be employed the assets should be valued on a realistic basis; *i.e.* at current replacement values. In addition, the way in which the assets are being used will be important. There would be no justification in placing current values on assets if these are not used effectively.

## 3. AVERAGE METHOD

An average valuation may be obtained by adding together the figures obtained by methods (1) and (2) and then dividing by two; viz.:

$$\frac{£2 + £2·20}{2} = £2·10 \text{ each}$$

## SPECIAL FACTORS

The methods of valuation described do not enjoy general acceptance by the accountancy profession. However, they do provide logical bases which may be adapted to suit particular circumstances. Generally the problem of valuing shares will arise when dealing with a private company.

If the concern is with a *public* company the Stock Exchange quotation will be a guide and the mean price may be taken. However, as the number of take-over bids which have taken place for public companies shows, the Stock Exchange quotation is not necessarily a true indication of the value of the Ordinary shares. Dividend restrictions, valuation of assets at historical costs and inefficient management all contribute to relatively low prices being quoted. Quite often the price directors are willing to pay will be influenced by the urgency of obtaining control of a company. In certain circumstances, the Articles of Association may stipulate how shares should be valued.

## EXAMINATION QUESTIONS

1. XY Ltd., a manufacturing company with issued capital of £650,000, finds itself short of liquid capital after a period of expansion. The Board do not think the time opportune for raising funds by borrowing or by an issue of shares for cash, and propose instead to obtain a controlling interest on an exchange of shares basis in AB & Sons Ltd., a private company which carries on business in the same industry and in the same neighbourhood, and which has substantial cash funds. There are 100,000 unissued £1 ordinary shares of XY Ltd. The undernoted figures have been extracted from the accounts of AB & Sons Ltd. You are asked to report to the Board of XY Ltd., commenting on their proposal and indicating what further information should be obtained before a final decision is taken.

*Balance sheets*

|  | 1967 £'000 | | 1968 £'000 | | 1969 £'000 | |
|---|---|---|---|---|---|---|
| Share capital authorised and issued: | | | | | | |
| 2,000 founders shares of £10 each ... ... | | 20 | | 20 | | 20 |
| 180,000 Ordinary shares of £1 each ... ... | | 180 | | 180 | | 180 |
| | | 200 | | 200 | | 200 |
| Capital reserve ... ... | | 180 | | 180 | | 180 |
| Revenue reserves: | | | | | | |
| Future taxation ... | 6 | | 7 | | 6 | |
| General ... ... ... | 150 | | 150 | | 150 | |
| Profit and loss account... | 27 | 183 | 29 | 186 | 27 | 183 |
| | | 563 | | 566 | | 563 |
| Fixed assets: | | | | | | |
| Goodwill, at cost ... | | 60 | | 60 | | 60 |
| Plant, machinery and equipment, at cost ... | 140 | | 142 | | 145 | |
| *Less:* Depreciation ... | 94 | 46 | 102 | 40 | 110 | 35 |
| | | 106 | | 100 | | 95 |
| Current assets: | | | | | | |
| Stocks and Work-in-progress | 72 | | 65 | | 67 | |
| Trade debtors ... ... | 68 | | 65 | | 73 | |
| British Gov't securities... (market value 31/12/69, £167,000) | 180 | | 180 | | 180 | |
| Cash ... ... ... | 206 | | 223 | | 215 | |
| | 526 | | 533 | | 535 | |
| *Less:* current liabilities: | | | | | | |
| Trade creditors ... | 58 | | 55 | | 54 | |
| Dividends (net) ... | 5 | | 6 | | 6 | |
| Income tax & profits tax | 6 | 69 | 457 | 6 | 67 | 466 | 7 | 67 | 468 |
| | | 563 | | 566 | | 563 |

*Profit and Loss Accounts*

| | 1967 £'000 | | 1968 £'000 | | 1969 £'000 | |
|---|---|---|---|---|---|---|
| Trading profit ... ... | | 6 | | 10 | | 5 |
| After charging the following: | | | | | | |
| Depreciation ... ... | 8 | | 8 | | 8 | |
| Audit fees ... ... | 1 | | 1 | | 1 | |
| Directors' emoluments for management services ... ... | 25 | | 30 | | 20 | |
| Interest on Gov't securities | | 5 | | 5 | | 5 |
| | | 11 | | 15 | | 10 |
| *Deduct:* Income Tax and profits tax ... ... | | 6 | | 7 | | 6 |
| | | 5 | | 8 | | 4 |
| Add: Balance of profit brought forward from previous year ... | | 27 | | 27 | | 29 |
| | | 32 | | 35 | | 33 |
| *Deduct:* Dividends proposed (net) ... ... | | 5 | | 6 | | 6 |
| Balance of profit carried forward, as shown on balance sheet ... ... | | 27 | | 29 | | 27 |

(*I.C.W.A.*)

2. Your board of directors have had conversations with a firm which has recently developed a new patented product which your directors consider would be a very suitable component in one of your company's products. The negotiations have included the possible provision by your company of finance for the firm. Your chairman hands you the last balance sheet of the firm which is shown overleaf.

You obtain the following additional information:

(*a*) A friend of Harry Robinson is prepared to provide capital sufficient to pay off the bank overdraft provided he is given the best security available and provision for ultimate repayment.

(*b*) The possibility of winding up the firm had been considered before the negotiations had commenced, when a valuation of the fixed assets had been obtained showing the following figures:

| | | | | | |
|---|---|---|---|---|---|
| Buildings | ... | ... | ... | ... | ... £40,000 |
| Fixed plant | ... | ... | ... | ... | 8,000 |
| Loose plant | ... | ... | ... | ... | 12,000 |

It has also been found that the raw materials were over-valued by £1,000, and that the trade debtors included an account of £800 expected to realise £0·125 per £1.

(*c*) The firm had been carried on up to 31st December, 1966, by three brothers, Tom, Dick and Harry Robinson, sharing profits and losses in the ratio of 2/5, 2/5 and 1/5 respectively, no account being taken of interest on capital.

Tom died on 1st January, 1967, and Dick on 30th June, 1968. Their capital was left in the business as loans with interest at 6%. On Tom's death, Dick and Harry shared profit and losses in the ratios, 2/3 and 1/3.

## A. ROBINSON & CO.
### Balance Sheet
#### As at 31st December, 1969

| Liabilities | | £ | Assets | | | £ |
|---|---|---|---|---|---|---|
| Trade creditors ... ... | | 5,000 | Buildings ... ... | | | 44,000 |
| Bank overdraft secured over | | | Fixed plant ... ... | | | 10,000 |
| the works property ... | | 25,000 | Loose plant ... ... | | | 15,100 |
| Loans: | | | Stocks on hand: | | | |
| Representatives | | | Raw materials | £4,000 | | |
| of T. Robinson | £33,295 | | Finished goods | 5,000 | | |
| Representatives | | | | | | 9,000 |
| of D. Robinson | 23,675 | | Work in progress | ... | | 2,500 |
| | | 56,970 | Trade debtors ... | ... | | 4,270 |
| | | | Cash on hand ... | ... | | 200 |
| | | | Deficiency of capital— | | | |
| | | | H. Robinson ... | ... | | 1,900 |
| | | £86,970 | | | | £86,970 |

The results of the past three years are as follows:

| | | | Interest on Loans | | Losses after charging |
|---|---|---|---|---|---|
| | | | T.R. | D.R. | interest on loans |
| | | | £ | £ | £ |
| Year to 31st December, 1967 | ... | ... | 1,035 | | 10,500 |
| Half year to 30th June, 1968 | ... | ... | 535 | | 5,500 |
| Half year to 31st December, 1968 | | ... | 545 | 387 | 5,000 |
| Year to 31st December, 1969 | ... | ... | 1,180 | 838 | 8,000 |
| | | | | | £28,000 |

In view of the losses incurred, the representatives of the deceased partners, with the consent of the beneficiaries, have agreed to restrict their loans to the amounts of capital Tom and Dick would have had in the business at 31st December, 1969, had they remained alive as partners at that date on the original basis of sharing profits and losses. The losses on the revaluation of assets are to be shared on the same basis.

(d) Harry has to be credited with a premium of £5,000 for the new patent which is his invention.

(e) Harry provided £3,000 of additional capital, which he paid in on 1st January, 1968, and which has to be granted priority as regards interest and repayment of capital over the existing capital.

(f) The trade creditors have agreed to accept a composition of £0·75 per £1·00 in settlement of their claims.

(g) The development of the new product will require the alteration of existing plant and facilities and the provision of new plant estimated to cost £10,000, and additional working capital required is estimated at a further £10,000. The future annual profits are expected to amount to £7,500 per annum after providing for corporation tax at 42·5%.

You are requested to draft a scheme for consideration by all the parties interested showing:

(i) The re-allocation of the capital accounts in terms of the arrangement with the representatives of the deceased partners.

(ii) Your proposals regarding the capital structure, showing how the expected future earnings might be distributed.

(iii) A balance sheet as at 31st December, 1969, giving effect to your proposals. (*I.C.W.A. adapted*)

3. Charles Jaques contemplates making a bid to take over the business of Momba Ltd. The financial position of the company at the date of the last balance sheet was as under:

BALANCE SHEET, *31st December, 1969*

| 1968 | | £ | £ | £ |
|---|---|--:|--:|--:|
| | Assets, *less* Current Liabilities: | | | |
| | Fixed Assets— | | | |
| | Freehold Premises ... ... | 225,000 | | |
| | *Less* Depreciation ... ... | 65,000 | | |
| 182,000 | | | 160,000 | |
| | Plant and Machinery ... ... | 197,500 | | |
| | *Less* Depreciation ... ... | 62,500 | | |
| 146,000 | | | 135,000 | |
| | Transport Vehicles ... ... | 72,960 | | |
| | *Less* Depreciation ... ... | 30,460 | | |
| 28,750 | | | 42,500 | |
| 356,750 | | | | 337,500 |
| | Current Assets: | | | |
| 76,410 | Work in Progress ... ... | | 167,400 | |
| 40,246 | Stock at cost ... ... ... | | 46,829 | |
| 46,757 | Sundry Debtors ... ... ... | | 58,444 | |
| 6,844 | Cash at Bank ... ... ... | | 24,246 | |
| 484 | Cash in hand ... ... ... | | 814 | |
| 170,731 | | | 297,733 | |
| | *Less* Current Liabilities: | | | |
| 33,666 | Creditors ... ... ... ... | 37,839 | | |
| | Provisions for Taxation and | | | |
| 18,312 | other liabilities... ... ... | 18,641 | | |
| 153 | Preference Share Dividend | 153 | | |
| | Final Dividend on Ordinary | | | |
| 2,450 | Shares ... ... ... ... | 2,450 | | |
| 54,581 | | | 59,083 | |
| 116,150 | Net Current Assets ... ... | | | 238,650 |
| £472,900 | | | | £576,150 |

1968 Financed as follows:

| | | Authorised in Shares of £1 each | | Issued and fully paid up |
|---|---|---|---|---|
| | Capital and Reserves: | £ | £ | £ |
| | Capital— | | | |
| | 6% Preference .. ... | 25,000 | | 25,000 |
| | Ordinary ... ... ... | 150,000 | | 100,000 |
| 125,000 | | 175,000 | | 125,000 |
| | Reserves employed in the business: | | | |
| 50,000 | Share Premium Account ... | | 50,000 | |
| 75,000 | Capital ... ... ... ... | | 90,000 | |
| 120,000 | Revenue ... ... ... | | 175,000 | |
| 41,700 | Profit and Loss Account ... | | 63,550 | |
| | | | | 378,550 |
| 411,700 | | | | 503,550 |
| 61,200 | Taxation ... ... ... ... | | | 72,600 |
| £472,900 | | | | £576,150 |

A dividend of 7% (including a final dividend at 4%) has been paid in each of the five years since 1st January, 1965, on which date the equity of the company was as follows:

| | | £ |
|---|---|---|
| Issued Share Capital ... ... ... | | 125,000 |
| Share Premium Account ... ... ... | | 50,000 |
| Capital Reserve ... ... ... ... | | 15,000 |
| Revenue Reserve ... ... ... ... | | 40,000 |
| Profit and Loss Account ... ... ... | | 16,800 |
| | | £246,800 |

Freehold premises were valued in 1967 at £325,000 and plant and machinery is currently insured for £220,000. The market price of the company's ordinary shares fluctuated between £1·93 and £2·06 during the period January–May, 1970.

The preference shares carry the right to a non-cumulative dividend of 6% and to priority in the repayment of capital in a winding-up, but are not entitled to any further participation in the profits or assets of the company.

You are required to:

(a) Advise Jaques as to the approximate intrinsic value of the undertaking of Momba Ltd.

(b) State how much of the share capital you would recommend him to acquire, and

(c) Outline the terms of the offer you would advocate should be made to the shareholders of Momba Ltd.

Give reasons for your conclusions and recommendations.

(A.C.C.A. adapted.)

4. The capital of a company consists of:

2,000,000 Ordinary Shares of £1 each.

500,000 Non-cumulative 5% Preference Shares of £1 each.

For many years the company have been making losses which have more than accounted for the reserves and left it with an accumulated loss. The company's trading position has now begun to improve and it expects to make a profit in the current year of £20,000.

Suggest a scheme for the reconstruction of the capital of the company which will write off the accumulated loss, bring the capital into line with the company's reduced earning power and enable dividends to be resumed if possible to all shareholders.

Illustrate your answer by means of a simple tabulation comparing shareholders' existing and proposed rights at different profit levels. (*A.C.C.A.*)

5. An industrial group bids for and acquires 100% shareholding of a previously independent competitor. Review the arguments for and against retaining the subsidiary company's separate legal existence, particularly from the viewpoint of business management.          (*A.C.C.A.*)

6. Outline the advantages and disadvantages of large scale organisation and indicate the type of business most likely to grow large.          (*A.C.C.A.*)

7. A client intending to purchase a controlling interest in a limited company, instructs you to investigate the position with a view to ascertaining a fair price. The company is old-established and the present management will be discontinued. There are three subsidiaries, each manufacturing a specific type of product, and it is contemplated developing further the possibilities of diversification within the group.

Outline the steps you would take in order to carry out your instructions, and indicate the likely points with which your report would deal.          (*A.C.C.A.*)

8. Discuss the factor which may influence the making of a "take-over bid" at a price which exceeds the current quotation.          (*S.C.A.*)

9. A manufacturing company in the United Kingdom is considering a proposal to establish a factory overseas. List the points on which you, as chief accountant, would seek information in order to advise your Board on the project.          (*I.C.W.A.*)

10. You are consulted by a client, A. Brown, concerning a capital reconstruction scheme for Hopeful Ventures Ltd., a company in which Brown owns 10,000 Preference Shares of £1 each. For several years, this company has suffered severe losses which have now resulted in there being a debit balance on the Profit and Loss Account and all other revenue reserves have been exhausted. However, the company now expects to produce a profit of £50,000 in the current year and future prospects are much improved.

The scheme now being considered provides, inter alia, that the 5% Non-cumulative Preference shares of £1 each should be written down to 10*s*. whilst the Ordinary shares of £1 each be reduced to £0·05 each. Advise your client whether he should accept the scheme. If you consider that the scheme is not suitable, suggest an alternative. Support your answer by appropriate calculations.

N.B.—The issued capital of Hopeful Ventures Ltd. is:

3,000,000 Ordinary shares of £1 each.

1,500,000 Non-cumulative 5% Preference shares of £1 each.

(*A.C.C.A.*)

11. A company whose issued capital consists of 2,400,000 Ordinary shares of £1 each wishes to raise £500,000 additional capital by an issue of shares.
Suggest:— (i) the way in which the company should raise the capital.
(ii) the terms of the new issue.
The shares are quoted currently at £2·25. (*A.C.C.A.*)

12. You are auditor of a private limited company. In terms of the articles if a member wishes to sell his shares they must first be offered to the directors at a value fixed by the auditor. Mr. A. B., the major shareholder in the company, died recently and his representatives wish to sell his holding of 12,000 ordinary shares.

You are required to draft a letter to the representatives giving your valuation of the shares, together with your working papers showing the basis of valuation.

The last balance sheet which has been prepared is in respect of the year to 31st March, 1969, and is as follows:

| | Cost £ | Depreciation £ | Book Value £ |
|---|---|---|---|
| *Fixed Assets:* | | | |
| Buildings ... ... ... ... | 20,000 | | 20,000 |
| Plant and Machinery ... ... | 14,000 | 5,000 | 9,000 |
| Other fixed assets ... ... | 1,200 | 400 | 800 |
| | £35,200 | £5,400 | £29,800 |

| | | | |
|---|---|---|---|
| *Current Assets:* | | | |
| Stock ... ... ... ... | | 7,500 | |
| Work-in-progress ... ... ... | | 9,500 | |
| Trade debtors ... ... ... | | 6,300 | |
| Cash-in-hand ... ... ... | | 200 | 23,500 |
| | | | £53,300 |
| *Current Liabilities:* | | | |
| Creditors and accrued charges ... | | | 22,000 |
| | | | £31,300 |

| | | |
|---|---|---|
| Represented by: | | |
| 20,000 shares of £1 each, fully paid ... ... ... ... | 20,000 | |
| General reserves ... ... | 11,300 | |
| | | £31,300 |

The summary of the Profit & Loss Account for the last three years is as follows:

| | 1967 £ | 1968 £ | 1969 £ |
|---|---|---|---|
| Gross Profit ... ... ... | 14,000 | 16,000 | 17,000 |
| *Less:* Overheads ... ... | 6,000 | 6,500 | 7,000 |
| Directors' remuneration ... | 5,000 | 6,000 | 7,000 |
| | (11,000) | (12,500) | (14,000) |
| Net Profit before taxation ... ... | 3,000 | 3,500 | 3,000 |

The directors hold all the shares in the company with the exception of those held by the representatives of Mr. A. B., who was a director. It is estimated that a reasonable remuneration of the directors for services rendered would be £4,000.

The property has been valued by an independent valuer at £25,000.

The rate of return on capital employed in similar businesses is $12\frac{1}{2}\%$.

13. The following is the summarised Balance Sheet of Progress Ltd., as at 31st December, 19...

| | £ | £ | | £ | £ |
|---|---|---|---|---|---|
| *Authorised Capital:* | | | *Fixed Assets:* | | |
| 100,000 Ordinary Shrs. of £1 each ... ... | 100,000 | | Freehold Properties ... | | 190,000 |
| *Issued Capital:* | | | Furniture & Fittings ... | | 5,000 |
| 65,000 Ordinary Shares of | | | Motor Vehicles ... ... | | 10,000 |
| £1 each, fully paid ... | | 65,000 | Plant & Machinery ... | | 50,000 |
| | | | | | 255,000 |
| *Capital Reserves:* | | | *Current Assets:* | | |
| Loan Redemption Reserve | 14,000 | | Stock and Work-in- | | |
| Share Premium Account | 20,000 | | Progress ... ... | 14,000 | |
| | | 34,000 | Tax Reserve Certificates | 27,000 | |
| *Revenue Reserves:* | | | Debtors ... ... ... | 49,000 | |
| General Reserve ... ... | 62,000 | | Bank ... ... ... | 8,000 | |
| Future Taxation ... ... | 35,000 | | | | 98,000 |
| Profit & Loss Account ... | 17,000 | | | | |
| | | 114,000 | | | |
| Secured Long Term Loan | | 40,000 | | | |
| *Current Liabilities:* | | | | | |
| Trade ... ... ... | 60,000 | | | | |
| Current Taxation ... | 40,000 | | | | |
| | | 100,000 | | | |
| | | £353,000 | | | £353,000 |

The profits, after providing for depreciation and directors' fees, have for each of the past five years approximated to £30,000 and dividends of 25% have been paid.

The present-day value of the freehold properties is considerably in excess of the book value.

The directors are considering the reorganisation of the capital structure of the company to counteract a potential take-over bid.

You are required to make suggestions for the consideration of the directors.

*(A.C.C.A.)*

14. (*a*) "The current trend of amalgamations, with a parent body controlling subsidiary units each having a large measure of autonomy, creates problems of integration of a management accounting system."

Discuss the management policy involved in the integration of a management accounting system in relation to the above statement.

(*b*) Your company is considering whether to discontinue making or whether to buy-in a particular article with a sales value of £1,000,000 p.a.

Manufacturing costs are £700,000, while buying-in purchase costs would amount to £750,000. Selling costs are £100,000, administrative expenses are £40,000 and would be £10,000 less if the article were bought-in.

Capital requirements are:

To make ... ... £1,600,000
To buy ... ... £960,000

The manufacturing plant has a life of four years, and before renewal a decision on making or buying has to be made.

U

You are required to examine the above data critically and to state

    (i) Your initial findings.

    (ii) How your recommendations would be influenced by each of the following circumstances:

        (1) That the company has surplus funds for investment.

        (2) That the company would have to raise additional capital to renew the plant.

        (3) That the labour involved is highly specialised.

        (4) That there is only one outside source of supply for the bought-in article.

(c) Your company manufactures products A and B from the same basic raw material. There is a small proportion of waste and residue and each ton of input produces 14 cwt. of product A and 5 cwt. of product B. Of the production costs 90% are common to both joint products and the other 10% relates to the cost of containers and the filling thereof.

State how you would deal with the apportionment of costs to the two products. Make any assumptions you wish.         (A.C.C.A.)

15. The following is the Balance Sheet of the Ballyfermot Manufacturing Co. Ltd. at 31st March, 19...

| | £ | | | | £ |
|---|---|---|---|---|---|
| Ordinary Stock (£1 Units) | 100,000 | Premises... | ... | ... | 50,000 |
| Trade Creditors ... | ... 30,000 | Plant ... | ... | ... | 180,000 |
| General Reserve ... | ... 250,000 | Stock ... | ... | ... | 70,000 |
| Profit and Loss Account ... | 150,000 | Debtors ... | ... | ... | 60,000 |
| | | Cash at Bank ... | | ... | 170,000 |
| | 530,000 | | | | 530,000 |

The profits for the last three years have been averaging £90,000 per annum and the dividends have for many years been 10% p.a. The £1 units are quoted on the Dublin Stock Exchange at £2·50 and the stock is widely held by some 500 shareholders.

Competitors who are clients of yours—Bagsnatch Ltd.—consult you regarding the possibility of a takeover offer and ask you to report fully under the following headings:

    (i) As to whether it is considered that the Ballyfermot Company might be taken over by Bagsnatch Ltd.

    (ii) As to what prices should be offered for the shares of Ballyfermot either in,

        (a) Cash,

        (b) Cash and shares in Bagsnatch Ltd., or

        (c) Shares in Bagsnatch Ltd., (whose capital is £300,000 in units of £0·25 each, quoted at £1·50).

    (iii) To outline the general procedure of the takeover:

        (a) To whom the offer should be made by Bagsnatch Ltd. in the first instance, i.e., to either the directors or the shareholders.

        (b) whether, if the offer was first made to the directors, it would be advisable to proceed if the directors were not prepared to recommend the offer.

(c) As to the requisite information which should be made available to the Ballyfermot shareholders.

(d) As to how secrecy might be maintained.

(e) As to whether the offer should be for the whole capital or merely for a controlling interest.

(f) As to whether it might be an advantage to attempt to buy, say, 10% of the stock on the Stock Exchange before making the approach.

(iv) To indicate what procedure should be adopted with the Stock Exchange authorities. Draft your report.                                   (A.C.C.A.)

16. The company of which you are Chief Accountant is considering acquiring a private company, XY Ltd., in the same line of business in an industry which is flourishing and for which the future prospects are bright.

The last audited Balance Sheet of XY Ltd. and details of its profits for the past six years are shown below. To enable the Board to consider the matter before calling for a complete investigation, prepare a preliminary report giving the approximate price you would advise them to pay based solely on the figures available to you, accompanied by an appendix setting out the further enquiries you would like to make before preparing a final report.

### XY LTD.
#### Balance Sheet at 31st December, 19..

| | £ | | | £ | £ |
|---|---|---|---|---|---|
| Share Capital— | | | Goodwill at cost | | 40,000 |
| 75,000 Ord. Shares of £1 | | | Freehold Prop- | | |
| each fully paid | ... | 75,000 | erty at cost ... | | 71,000 |
| | | | Plant & Mach- | | |
| Capital Reserve ... | ... | 40,000 | inery at cost | 38,000 | |
| General Reserve ... | ... | 150,000 | Less: Deprecia- | | |
| Profit and Loss Account | | | tion ... ... | 15,000 | |
| balance ... ... | ... | 115,000 | | | 23,000 |
| | | ——— | Furniture & | | |
| | | 380,000 | Fixtures ... | | 14,000 |
| Future Taxation ... | ... | 60,000 | Motor Cars at | | |
| | | | cost ... ... | 6,500 | |
| | | | Less: Deprecia- | | |
| | | | tion ... ... | 3,500 | |
| | | | | | 3,000 |
| Current Liabilities— | £ | | Current Assets— | | |
| Sundry Creditors | 47,000 | | Stock in Trade | 229,000 | |
| Taxation ... | 70,000 | | Debtors ... | 130,000 | |
| Proposed Dividend | | | Cash at Bank ... | 58,000 | |
| | 11,000 | | | | 417,000 |
| | ——— | 128,000 | | | |
| | | £568,000 | | | £568,000 |

Profits for the last 6 years after providing for Depreciation and Directors' Fees, but before taxation:

£
75,000
87,000
132,000
49,000
93,000
122,000 (current year)

(*I.C.W.A.*)

17. You are appointed to a manufacturing business where monthly trading statements are prepared from costing records, while financial accounts are compiled six-monthly, in June and December. The monthly trading statements are prepared in four-weekly and five-weekly periods, and emphasise departmental performances and spending against prepared budgets, whereas the financial accounts follow the traditional pattern of shareholders' accounts.

You are required to advise top management of the advantages to be secured from integration of the two functions, quoting in your report:

(*a*) the main difficulties of this integration;

(*b*) how you propose to overcome such difficulties. (*I.C.W.A.*)

18. A company which has surplus production capacity has acquired the whole of the share capital of a smaller company in the same industry which also has spare capacity. As cost accountant to the larger company, make a report to management indicating how *production* economies may be made.

(*I.C.W.A.*)

19. Explain the methods by which information may be presented to management graphically or pictorially. Illustrate your answer by suitable examples. (*S.C.A.*)

20. Alpha Ltd. and Beta Ltd. propose to sell their businesses for shares in a new company and you are given the following Balance Sheets as at 31st March, 1969, and particulars of profits:

| | Alpha Ltd. £ | Beta Ltd. £ | | Alpha Ltd. £ | Beta Ltd. £ |
|---|---|---|---|---|---|
| Ordinary Shares of £1 each | 10,000 | 3,750 | Fixed Assets at cost less depreciation | 8,475 | 2,500 |
| Revenue Reserves— | | | Investment in Government | | |
| General | 5,000 | 500 | Stock at 4% (nominal | | |
| Profit and Loss Account | 1,000 | 450 | value £2,000) | 1,800 | |
| Creditors | 2,612 | 612 | Stocks | 4,000 | 1,062 |
| | | | Debtors | 2,337 | 1,250 |
| | | | Bank | 2,000 | 500 |
| | £18,612 | £5,312 | | £18,612 | £5,312 |

Adjusted Net Earnings—

| | Alpha Ltd. £ | Beta Ltd. £ |
|---|---|---|
| Year ended 31st March, 1969 | 3,050 | 1,025 |
| 1968 | 2,662 | 800 |
| 1967 | 2,525 | 675 |

Draft a concise report setting out the basis upon which you consider the sale of shares should take place and indicate your views as to the capitalisation of the new company. (*S.C.A.*)

21. Discuss the modern trends in accounting principles with particular reference to the lay-out of published accounts.

22. Household Products, Ltd., was formed on 1st January, 1959, to operate various patents in connection with kitchen utensils. On 1st January, 1968, the Balance Sheet of the Company was as follows:

| | £ | £ | | £ | £ |
|---|---|---|---|---|---|
| **Share Capital—** | | | | | |
| Authorised: | | | | | |
| Ordinary Shares of £1 each | 20,000 | | Freehold Buildings at cost ... | | 15,559 |
| 7% Cumulative Preference | | | Plant and Machinery at cost... | | 36,947 |
| Shares of £1 each ... | 20,000 | | Patents and Development | | |
| | | 40,000 | Expenses at cost ... ... | | 5,319 |
| | | | | | 57,825 |
| Issued: | | | Bank Balance... ... ... | | 3,210 |
| 11,000 Ordinary Shares of | | | Profit and Loss Account: | | |
| £1 each ... ... | 11,000 | | Balance at 1st January, 1967 | 12,210 | |
| 13,000 7% Preference | | | Profit for Year to 1st January, | | |
| Shares of £1 each ... | 13,000 | | 1968... ... ... ... | 475 | |
| | | 24,000 | | | 11,735 |
| 6% Debentures (Secured on | | | | | |
| Freehold Buildings, Plant | | | | | |
| and Machinery) ... ... | | 46,000 | | | |
| Trade Creditors ... ... | | 2,770 | | | |
| Contingent Liability— | | | | | |
| Arrears of Preference Divi- | | | | | |
| dend for four years, £3,640 | | | | | |
| | | £72,770 | | | £72,770 |

It is estimated that in future the annual profits available for dividends will amount to at least £2,500, and, in order that dividends may be paid, the directors accordingly recommend the following Reconstruction Scheme:

(i) A new Company (Household Products, 1969, Ltd.) is to be formed with an Authorised Capital of 5,000 Ordinary Shares of £1 each, and 10,000 6 per cent. Non-cumulative Preference Shares of £1 each.

(ii) Shares of the new Company are to be allotted as follows:

1 Ordinary Share for every 10 Ordinary Shares of the old Company.
3 Ordinary Shares for every 10 Preference Shares of the old Company.
The Arrears of Preference Dividend will be cancelled.

(iii) The new Company will take over the whole of the Assets and Liabilities of the old Company, subject to the following amounts being written off:

|  | £ |
|---|---|
| Plant and Machinery ... ... ... | 1,947 |
| Patents and Development Expenses ... | 5,319 |
| Profit and Loss Account ... ... ... | 11,735 |

(iv) 6% Debentures of the new Company will be issued in place of the existing Debentures.

(v) The whole of the new Preference Shares will be allotted at par for cash.

(vi) The expenses (amounting to £700) will be paid by the new Company.

You are required:

(a) To prepare the opening Balance Sheet of Household Products, 1969, Ltd., showing the effect of these transactions; and

(b) To prepare a short report as to whether in your opinion the suggested scheme is reasonable, having regard to the facts that the shares of both Companies will carry one vote and that the Preference Shares of the old Company were preferential as to capital and dividends unpaid. (S.C.A.)

# CHAPTER 23

## ACCOUNTING RECORDS

### INTRODUCTION

A NUMBER of questions must inevitably arise regarding the appropriate accounting system to employ for recording management information. Some of the most important of these are:

1. Should the costs and financial transactions be treated quite separately so far as the accounting records are concerned?

2. How should the accounts be classified and coded?

3. To what extent should control information be recorded in the books of account? Thus, for example, should cost variances be incorporated into the double-entry system?

4. Should the accounting be mechanised or computerised?

All these and related matters should receive attention. The objects are to select the system of accounting which provides all the necessary information in a suitable form; which is based on sound organisational principles and, in particular, sets out the different fields of responsibility; and does these things at minimum cost.

The elementary principles of accounting are well known. Records are kept on a double-entry basis, each transaction being represented by a debit and a credit. The assumption made throughout this chapter is that the reader is already familiar with the double-entry system. If he is not then reference should be made to a suitable book.*

The first question—on whether or not the financial and costing transactions should be recorded separately—is dealt with in the next section. This is followed by a brief description of classification and coding and then the recording of control information. Mechanisation is dealt with in the latter part of the chapter.

### RECORDING OF COST AND FINANCIAL TRANSACTIONS

Broadly speaking there are two principal systems of accounting. These are:

1. Where separate ledgers are maintained for

    (a) cost accounting;
    (b) financial accounting.

This separation usually also implies the division of responsibilities, a cost accountant being responsible for the recording of the costing

* For example, *Practical Book-keeping* (Part I) W. H. H. LANE (Macdonald and Evans).

transactions, whereas the financial accountant is in charge of the financial records. Normally a chief accountant co-ordinates the two.

2. Integral (or Integrated) Accounting when both the costing and financial aspects are covered in the *one* ledger and system.

Integral accounting can offer many advantages the principal of which may be summarised as follows:

(*a*) No necessity to reconcile the costing and financial records. When the two aspects are recorded separately each will give a different profit and these have to be reconciled.

(*b*) There is no duplication of recording and effort. If the cost ledger is kept quite separate from the financial ledger there is inevitably some overlapping and duplication which will generally mean higher clerical and accountancy costs.

(*c*) Co-ordination of all aspects of accounting is greatly facilitated. This aspect is particularly important for only by maintaining a high degree of co-ordination will it be possible for management accounting to reach the level of maximum efficiency.

(*d*) Centralisation of the accounting function is likely to be simplified. If a computer is to be employed complete centralisation and integration will be essential.

## SEPARATE COST AND FINANCIAL LEDGERS

When a *separate* Cost Ledger is maintained the following accounts are generally present:

1. *Cost Ledger Control Account* (also known as General Ledger Control Account)

This account is necessary to make the Cost Ledger "self-balancing." All transactions which originate in the financial accounts must be credited in the Cost Ledger Control Account. Usually these are payments which have been made or credit obtained in respect of material, labour and overhead costs.

If a transaction is of an *internal* nature, affecting the cost accounts only; *e.g.* a transfer from Stores Control Account to Work-in-progress Account; then *no entry is necessary* in the Cost Ledger Control Account because a double-entry is possible without recourse to this balancing account.

The sales for the period are transferred to the debit side of the Cost Ledger Control Account from the Cost of Sales Account.

2. *Stores Control Account*

All purchases of materials for the Stores are debited and issues are credited. Adjustments will also be necessary for any discrepancies which arise from stock-taking; losses will be credited and gains debited.

Issues are taken to Work-in-progress Account or Factory Overhead Control Account.

### 3. *Direct Labour Control Account*

Some systems use a Wages Control Account and debit *total* wages to this account, subsequently transferring the direct wages to the Direct Labour Control Account and indirect wages to Factory Overhead Control.

When only the Direct Labour Control Account is employed this account contains the direct labour cost which is transferred to Work-in-progress Account.

### 4. *Factory Overhead Control Account*

Indirect costs are debited to this Account, the opposite entry being in the Cost Ledger Control Account.

The internal transaction is the transfer to Work-in-progress. The latter account is debited and the Factory Overhead Control Account is credited.

If predetermined overhead costs are used, as in job costing, it will be necessary to deal with under- or over-absorption of overhead costs, possibly by transfer to Costing Profit and Loss Account.

### 5. *Selling and Distribution Costs Account*

Selling and distribution costs incurred are credited to the Cost Ledger Control Account and debited to the Selling and Distribution Costs Account.

Later a transfer is made to Cost of Sales Account, the latter account being debited. Particular notice should be taken of this transfer. An error of principle would occur if a transfer is made to Work-in-progress Account. Selling and distribution costs are incurred to sell and distribute a specific quantity within an accounting period: accordingly, it is logical to write off these costs against the sales obtained.

### 6. *Administration Costs Account*

The costs incurred are debited, the corresponding credit being in the Cost Ledger Control Account.

When the administration costs are transferred the debit may be to *one* of the following:

(*a*) Costing Profit and Loss Account.

(*b*) Work-in-progress (treated as a production cost).

(*c*) Work-in-progress Account *and* Cost of Sales Account (costs are apportioned between production and sales on some equitable basis).

Differences of opinion exist on which method to employ. In the flow chart (Fig. 97) method (*a*) is used, but one of the other two could quite easily have been taken.

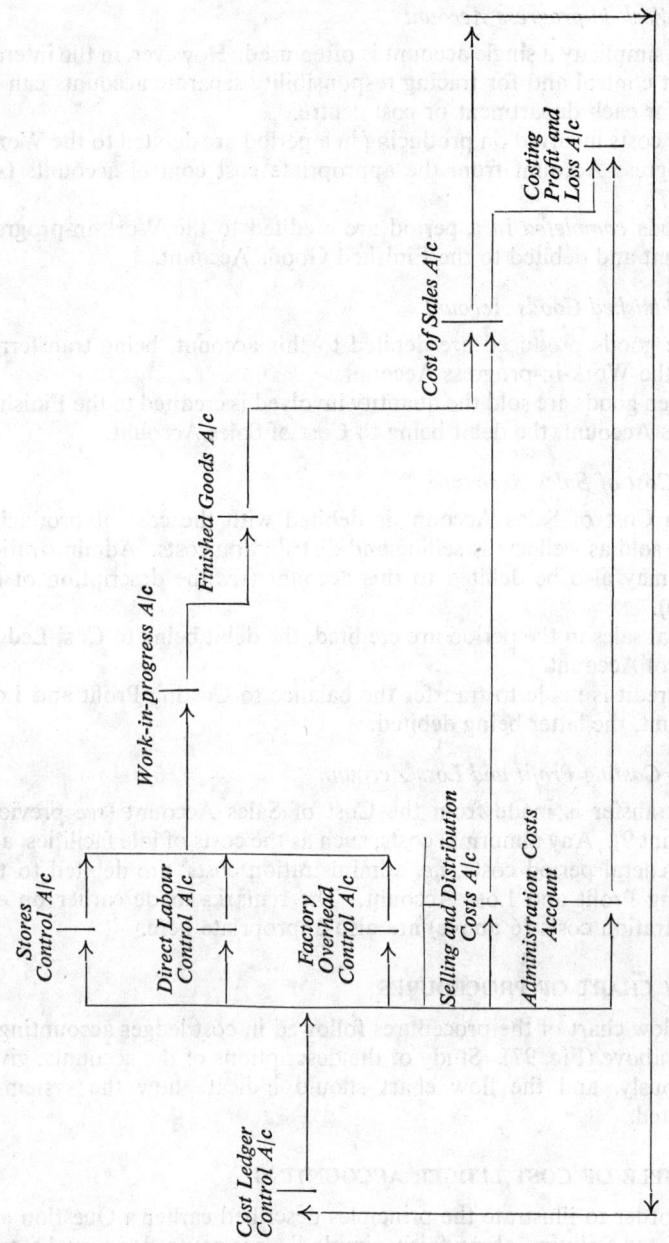

FIG. 97.—*Flow Chart: Cost Ledger Accounting*

### 7. *Work-in-progress Account*

For simplicity a single account is often used. However, in the interest of cost control and for tracing responsibility separate accounts can be used for each department or cost centre.

The costs incurred on producing in a period are debited to the Work-in-progress Account from the appropriate cost control accounts (*see* Fig. 97).

Goods *completed* in a period are credited to the Work-in-progress Account and debited to the Finished Goods Account.

### 8. *Finished Goods Account*

The goods produced are debited to this account, being transferred from the Work-in-progress Account.

When goods are sold the quantity involved is credited to the Finished Goods Account, the debit being to Cost of Sales Account.

### 9. *Cost of Sales Account*

The Cost of Sales Account is debited with the cost of producing goods sold as well as the selling and distribution costs. Administration costs may also be debited to this account (*see* the description of (6) above).

Total sales in the period are credited, the debit being to Cost Ledger Control Account.

A credit is made to transfer the balance to Costing Profit and Loss Account, the latter being debited.

### 10. *Costing Profit and Loss Account*

A transfer is made from the Cost of Sales Account (*see* previous Account 9). Any abnormal costs, such as the costs of idle facilities, and any general period costs, *i.e.* administration costs, are debited to the Costing Profit and Loss Account. The remarks made earlier on administration costs (6 above) are also appropriate here.

#### FLOW CHART OF PROCEDURES

A flow chart of the procedures followed in cost ledger accounting is given above (Fig. 97). Study of the descriptions of the accounts, given previously, and the flow chart should indicate how the system is operated.

#### EXAMPLE OF COST LEDGER ACCOUNTING

In order to illustrate the principles described earlier a Question and Suggested Solution along fairly simple lines is covered; journal entries are not given although in practice they would be necessary.

QUESTION

The Auto Co., Ltd. has the following balances in its Cost Ledger on 1st January:

|  | £ | £ |
|---|---|---|
| Stores Control Account ... ... ... ... ... | 18,000 | |
| Work-in-progress Account ... ... ... ... ... | 17,000 | |
| Finished Goods Account ... ... ... ... ... | 13,000 | |
| | | 48,000 |

Transactions for the six months ended 30th June, were:

|  | £ |
|---|---|
| Wages—indirect ... ... ... ... ... ... | 5,000 |
| Wages—direct ... ... ... ... ... ... | 87,000 |
| Stores purchased ... ... ... ... ... ... | 100,000 |
| Stores issued to repair orders ... ... ... ... | 2,000 |
| Stores issued to production ... ... ... ... ... | 110,000 |
| Goods finished in the period at cost ... ... ... | 215,000 |
| Goods sold in the period: | |
| at sales value ... ... ... ... ... ... | 300,000 |
| at costs ... ... ... ... ... ... ... | 220,000 |
| Works Overhead Costs recovered ... ... ... ... | 45,000 |
| Administration Costs ... ... ... ... ... | 12,000 |
| Works Overhead Costs ... ... ... ... ... | 40,000 |
| Selling and Distribution Costs ... ... ... ... | 14,000 |

Write up the accounts in the Cost Ledger and take out a Trial Balance. Administration Costs are to be written off direct to Profit and Loss Account.

SUGGESTED SOLUTION with explanatory notes

The first step is to open up all the necessary accounts in the ledger and enter the opening balances. After that the transactions for the period can be posted. The notes given earlier in this chapter should be used as a guide to the procedure followed.

From the figures given it will be seen that there is under-absorption of factory overhead costs to the extent of £2000. This is transferred to Costing Profit and Loss Account. However, it should be noted that this is not the only method of dealing with any discrepancy in the overhead absorption. Some accountants may prefer to adjust the work-in-progress, finished goods and cost of sales accounts. Much depends upon the size of the error in the absorption and the significance attached to the figures by management.

The balance on Costing Profit and Loss Account—the profit for the period —is transferred to the debit of Cost Ledger Control Account.

## COST LEDGER OF THE AUTO CO., LTD.

*Stores Control Account*

| Dr. | | £ | | | Cr £ |
|---|---|---|---|---|---|
| Jan. 1 | To Balance b/d | 18,000 | June 30 | By Work-in-Progress Account | 110,000 |
| June 30 | „ Cost Ledger Control Account | 100,000 | „ | „ By Works Overhead Control Account | 2,000 |
| | | | | „ Balance c/d | 6,000 |
| | | £118,000 | | | £118,000 |
| | „ Balance b/d | 6,000 | | | |

*Work-in-progress Account*

| | | £ | | | £ |
|---|---|---|---|---|---|
| Jan. 1 | To Balance b/d | 17,000 | June 30 | By Finished Goods Account | 215,000 |
| June 30 | „ Wages Control Account | 87,000 | | „ Balance c/d | 44,000 |
| | „ Stores Control | 110,000 | | | |
| | Works Overhead Control | | | | |
| | Account | 45,000 | | | |
| | | £259,000 | | | £259,000 |
| July 1 | „ Balance b/d | 44,000 | | | |

*Finished Goods Account*

| | | £ | | | £ |
|---|---|---|---|---|---|
| Jan. 1 | To Balance b/d | 13,000 | June 30 | By Cost of Sales Account | 220,000 |
| June 30 | „ Work-in-progress | 215,000 | | „ Balance c/d | 8,000 |
| | | £228,000 | | | £228,000 |
| July 1 | „ Balance b/d | 8,000 | | | |

*Wages Control Account*

| Dr. | | | | | Cr |
|---|---|---|---|---|---|
| | | £ | | | £ |
| June 30 | To Cost Ledger Control | | June 30 | To Work-in-progress | |
| | Account | 92,000 | | Account | 87,000 |
| | | | | „ Works Overhead Control | |
| | | | | Account | 5,000 |
| | | £92,000 | | | £92,000 |

*Works Overhead Control Account*

| | | £ | | | £ |
|---|---|---|---|---|---|
| June 30 | To Cost Ledger Control | | June 30 | By Work-in-progress | |
| | Account | 40,000 | | Account | 45,000 |
| | „ Wages Control Account | 5,000 | | „ Overhead Adjustment | |
| | | | | Account | 2,000 |
| | „ Stores Control Account | 2,000 | | | |
| | | £47,000 | | | £47,000 |

*Cost of Sales Account*

| | | £ | | | £ |
|---|---|---|---|---|---|
| June 30 | To Finished Goods Account | 220,000 | June 30 | By Cost Ledger Control | |
| | „ Selling and Distribution | | | Account | 300,000 |
| | Costs Account | 14,000 | | | |
| | „ Costing Profit and Loss | | | | |
| | Account | 66,000 | | | |
| | | £300,000 | | | £300,000 |

*Selling and Distribution Costs Account*

| | | £ | | | £ |
|---|---|---|---|---|---|
| June 30 | To Cost Ledger Control | | June 30 | By Cost of Sales Account | |
| | Account | 14,000 | | | 14,000 |

*Administration Costs Account*

| | £ | | £ |
|---|---|---|---|
| June 30 To Cost Ledger Control Account | 12,000 | June 30 By Costing Profit and Loss Account | 12,000 |

*Cost Ledger Control Account*

| | £ | | | £ |
|---|---|---|---|---|
| June 30 To Cost of Sales Account | 300,000 | Jan. 1 | By Balance b/d | 48,000 |
| ,, Balance c/d | 58,000 | June 30 | ,, Wages Control Account | 92,000 |
| | | | ,, Stores Control Account | 100,000 |
| | | | ,, Administration Costs Account | 12,000 |
| | | | ,, Selling & Distribution Costs Account | 14,000 |
| | | | ,, Works Overhead Control Account | 40,000 |
| | | | ,, Profit and Loss Account | 52,000 |
| | £358,000 | | | £358,000 |
| | | July 1 | ,, Balance b/d | 58,000 |

*Costing Profit and Loss Account*

| | £ | | £ |
|---|---|---|---|
| June 30 To Administration Costs Account | 12,000 | June 30 By Cost of Sales Account | 66,000 |
| ,, Overhead Adjustment Account | 2,000 | | |
| ,, Cost Ledger Control Account | 52,000 | | |
| | £66,000 | | £66,000 |

*Overhead Adjustment Account*

| | £ | | £ |
|---|---|---|---|
| June 30 To Works Overhead Control Account | 2,000 | June 30 By Costing Profit and Loss Account | 2,000 |

*Trial Balance—The Auto Co., Ltd.*

30th June, 1962

| | | | | | | | Dr. £ | Cr. £ |
|---|---|---|---|---|---|---|---|---|
| Cost Ledger Control Account | ... | ... | ... | ... | ... | ... | | 58,000 |
| Work-in-progress Account | ... | ... | ... | ... | ... | ... | 44,000 | |
| Finished Goods Account | ... | ... | ... | ... | ... | ... | 8,000 | |
| Stores Control Account | ... | ... | ... | ... | ... | ... | 6,000 | |
| | | | | | | | £58,000 | £58,000 |

## INTEGRAL ACCOUNTING

As noted earlier, integral or integrated accounting means keeping the records in one ledger instead of having separate systems—one for financial accounts and one for cost accounting. In effect, it means more than simply having one *ledger*; it should result in an accounting system which is complete and co-ordinated. Moreover, there should be a better service for a lower cost.

The purpose of a Cost Ledger Control Account is to make a *Cost Ledger* self-balancing. Because an integrated ledger contains both the financial and costing transactions it follows that there is no need to have this control account.

In order to be able to control costs and advise management on their behaviour the same classification as used in the Cost Ledger is employed in an integrated ledger. In addition, all matters which are normally *excluded* from a Cost Ledger are *included* in an integrated ledger. Thus, for example, additional accounts which are necessary are:

Creditors Control Account.
Debtors Control Account.
Bank Account.
Fixed Assets Account—this is divided to suit particular require-
  ments; *e.g.* Machinery Account; Motor Vehicles Account, etc.
Share Capital Account.
Profit and Loss Account.
Cost Control Account.

The Creditors and Debtors Control Accounts record in total the dealings with these parties. Purchases from suppliers and payments to them are shown in a Creditors Control Account. On the other hand, sales are debited to a Debtors Control Account and credited to a Cost of Sales Account.

The Bank Account shows all receipts of cash or cheques and any payments made. Accounts for fixed assets, share capital and profit and loss serve the same purpose as under a normal system of financial accounting.

A very important part of the procedures is the posting to a *Cost Control Account*. This account should not be confused with the Cost Ledger Control Account explained earlier. Its purpose is not to make the ledger self-balancing, but rather to act as a central Control Account in which costs are accumulated for a period and then transferred to Work-in-progress Account. The total for the transfer is obtained from cost analysis sheets and the process of accumulation, classification and analysis of the costs outside the double-entry system is known as *making third entries*.

There is more to cost control than simply entering figures in a ledger. Suitable analysis is essential for correct interpretation of the figures. Accordingly, making third entries is a simple description of what may be a complex and important part of the management accountancy system.

Payments in advance are debited to a Prepayment Account and credited to the Cost Control Account. It should be noted that only the *actual amount prepaid* is treated in this way. If rates of £100 have been paid in a period and £80 related to future periods, then it is the £80 which is transferred to a Prepayments Account, not the full £100.

Amounts due, but not yet paid (accruals) are dealt with by debiting the Cost Control Account and crediting an Accruals Account with the amount unpaid which related to the particular period. Income tax on the PAYE system is an accrual and, therefore, is dealt with in this way.

In the type of problem presented in examinations, the third entries will generally take the form of a single analysis sheet, divided so as to show the functional breakdown of costs into production, selling, administration and so on. In the example given below this procedure has been followed. However, as indicated earlier, in practice making third entries will probably involve a good deal of analysis and other detailed work.

## FLOW CHART OF PROCEDURES

A flow chart of the procedures followed when an integral accounting system is employed is given in Fig. 98. Careful study of this is advised before going on to the example of integral accounting shown below.

## EXAMPLE OF INTEGRAL ACCOUNTING

A Question and Suggested Solution on integral accounting are now given. This is restricted to ledger entries, but in practice, and for examination purposes, journal entries may also be required.

### QUESTION

The Auto Co. Ltd. has the following balances in its integrated Ledger on 1st January.

|  | Dr. | Cr. |
|---|---|---|
| Stores Control Account ... ... ... ... ... | 18,000 | |
| Work-in-progress Account ... ... ... ... ... | 17,000 | |
| Finished Goods Account ... ... ... ... ... | 13,000 | |
| Cash in Bank ... ... ... ... ... ... ... | 10,000 | |
| Creditors Control Account ... ... ... ... ... | | 8,000 |
| Fixed Assets Account ... ... ... ... ... | 55,000 | |
| Debtors Control Account ... ... ... ... ... | 12,000 | |
| Share Capital Account ... ... ... ... ... | | 80,000 |
| Depreciation Provision Account ... ... ... ... | | 5,000 |
| Profit and Loss Account ... ... ... ... ... | | 32,000 |
|  | £125,000 | £125,000 |

Transactions for the six months ended 30th June were:

|  | £ |
|---|---|
| Wages—indirect ... ... ... ... ... ... | 5,000 |
| Wages—direct ... ... ... ... ... ... | 87,000 |
| Stores purchased on credit ... ... ... ... ... | 100,000 |
| Stores issued to repair orders ... ... ... ... | 2,000 |
| Stores issued to production ... ... ... ... ... | 110,000 |

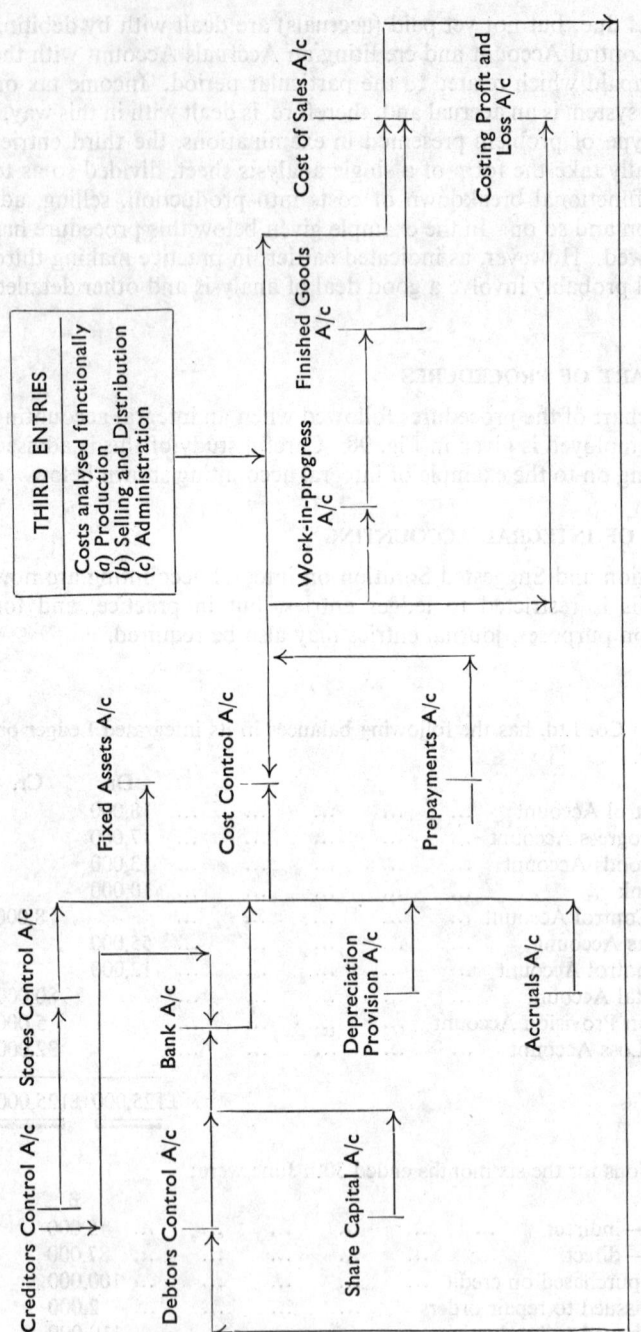

FIG. 98.—*Flow Chart: Integral Accounting*

*Notes.* 1. All transactions relating to both financial and cost accounting are recorded in the one self-contained ledger.
2. In the fixed assets and share capital accounts, balances would be entered as well as any new transactions affecting these.
3. Accounts relating to selling, distribution and administration have been omitted, although these may be shown separately.

|  | £ |
|---|---|
| Goods finished in the period at cost ... ... ... | 215,000 |
| Goods sold in the period at sales value (on credit)... ... | 300,000 |
| Goods sold in the period at cost ... ... ... ... | 220,000 |
| Works Overhead Costs recovered ... ... ... ... | 48,000 |
| Administration Costs ... ... ... ... ... | 12,000 } paid |
| Works Overhead Costs ... ... ... ... ... | 40,000 } for by |
| Selling and Distribution Costs ... ... ... ... | 14,000 } cheque |
| Depreciation for period (Works) ... ... ... ... | 1,300 |
| Payments to suppliers ... ... ... ... ... | 101,000 |
| Payments from customers ... ... ... ... ... | 290,000 |
| Rates prepaid included in Works Overheads paid ... ... | 300 |

You are required to write up the accounts in the Integral Ledger and take out a Trial Balance. The administration costs are to be written off to Profit and Loss Account.

SUGGESTED SOLUTION

## INTEGRAL LEDGER OF THE AUTO CO., LTD.

*Stores Control Account*

| Dr. | | £ | | | | Cr.<br>£ |
|---|---|---|---|---|---|---|
| Jan. 1 | To Balance b/d | 18,000 | June 30 | By Cost Control A/c<br>(issues to production) | | 110,000 |
| June 30 | ,, Creditors Control A/c | 100,000 | | ,, Cost Control A/c<br>(issues to repair orders)<br>,, Balance c/d | | 2,000<br>6,000 |
| | | £118,000 | | | | £118,000 |
| July 1 | ,, Balance b/d | 6,000 | | | | |

*Work-in-Progress Account*

| | | £ | | | £ |
|---|---|---|---|---|---|
| Jan. 1 | To Balance b/d | 17,000 | June 30 | By Finished Goods A/c | 215,000 |
| June 30 | ,, Cost Control Account:<br>direct costs<br>indirect costs | 197,000<br>48,000 | | ,, Balance c/d | 47,000 |
| | | £262,000 | | | £262,000 |
| July 1 | ,, Balance b/d | 47,000 | | | |

*Finished Goods Account*

| | | £ | | | £ |
|---|---|---|---|---|---|
| Jan. 1 | To Balance b/d | 13,000 | June 30 | By Cost of Sales Account | 220,000 |
| June 30 | ,, Work-in-progress Account | 215,000 | | ,, Balance c/d | 8,000 |
| | | £228,000 | | | £228,000 |
| July 1 | ,, Balance b/d | 8,000 | | | |

### Bank Account

| | | £ | | | £ |
|---|---|---|---|---|---|
| Jan. 1 | To Balance b/d | 10,000 | June 30 | By Cost Control Account: | |
| June 30 | „ Debtors Control Account | 290,000 | | „ Wages—direct | 87,000 |
| | | | | „ Wages—indirect | 5,000 |
| | | | | „ Works Overhead Costs | 40,000 |
| | | | | „ Administration Costs | |
| | | | | „ Account | 12,000 |
| | | | | „ Selling and Distribution | |
| | | | | Costs Account | 14,000 |
| | | | | „ Creditors Control Account | 101,000 |
| | | | | „ Balance c/d | 41,000 |
| | | £300,000 | | | £300,000 |
| July 1 | „ Balance b/d | 41,000 | | | |

### Creditors Control Account

| | | £ | | | £ |
|---|---|---|---|---|---|
| June 30 | To Bank Account | 101,000 | Jan. 1 | By Balance b/d | 8,000 |
| | „ Balance c/d | 7,000 | June 30 | „ Stores Control Account | 100,000 |
| | | £108,000 | | | £108,000 |
| | | | July 1 | „ Balance b/d | 7,000 |

### Debtors Control Account

| | | £ | | | £ |
|---|---|---|---|---|---|
| Jan. 1 | To Balance b/d | 12,000 | June 30 | By Bank Account | 290,000 |
| June 30 | „ Cost of Sales Account | 300,000 | | „ Balance c/d | 22,000 |
| | | £312,000 | | | £312,000 |
| July 1 | „ Balance b/d | 22,000 | | | |

### Cost of Sales Account

| | | £ | | | £ |
|---|---|---|---|---|---|
| June 30 | To Finished Goods Account | 220,000 | June 30 | By Debtors Control Account | 300,000 |
| | „ Selling and Distribution | | | | |
| | Costs Account | 14,000 | | | |
| | „ Costing Profit and Loss | | | | |
| | Account | 66,000 | | | |
| | | £300,000 | | | £300,000 |

### Administration Costs Account

| | | £ | | | £ |
|---|---|---|---|---|---|
| June 30 | To Bank Account | 12,000 | June 30 | By Costing Profit and Loss | |
| | | | | Account | 12,000 |

### Selling and Distribution Costs Account

| | | £ | | | £ |
|---|---|---|---|---|---|
| June 30 | To Bank Account | 14,000 | June 30 | By Cost of Sales Account | 14,000 |

### Prepayments Account

| | | £ | | | £ |
|---|---|---|---|---|---|
| June 30 | To Cost Control Account | 300 | June 30 | By Balance c/d | 300 |
| July 1 | „ Balance b/d | 300 | | | |

*Costing Profit and Loss Account*

| | | £ | | | £ |
|---|---|---|---|---|---|
| June 30 | To Administration Costs Account | 12,000 | June 30 | By Cost of Sales Account | 66,000 |
| „ „ | „ Balance c/d | 54,000 | | | |
| | | £66,000 | | | £66,000 |
| | | | July 1 | „ Balance b/d | 54,000 |

*Fixed Assets Account*

| | | £ | | | £ |
|---|---|---|---|---|---|
| Jan. 1 | To Balance b/d | 55,000 | June 30 | By Balance c/d | 55,000 |
| July 1 | „ Balance b/d | 55,000 | | | |

*Share Capital Account*

| | | £ | | | £ |
|---|---|---|---|---|---|
| June 30 | To Balance c/d | £80,000 | Jan. 1 | By Balance b/d | £80,000 |
| | | | July 1 | „ Balance b/d | 80,000 |

*Profit and Loss Account*

| | | £ | | | £ |
|---|---|---|---|---|---|
| June 30 | To Balance c/d | £32,000 | Jan. 1 | By Balance b/d | £32,000 |
| | | | July 1 | „ Balance b/d | 32,000 |

*Depreciation Provision Account*

| | | £ | | | £ |
|---|---|---|---|---|---|
| June 30 | To Balance c/d | 6,300 | Jan. 1 | By Balance b/d | 5,000 |
| | | | June 30 | „ Cost Control Account | 1,300 |
| | | 6,300 | | | 6,300 |
| | | | July 1 | „ Balance b/d | 6,300 |

*Cost Control Account*

| | | £ | | | £ |
|---|---|---|---|---|---|
| June 30 | To Bank Account | 92,000 | June 30 | By prepayments Account | 300 |
| „ „ | „ Bank Account | 40,000 | | „ Work-in-progress Account: | |
| „ „ | „ Stores Control Account | 110,000 | | direct costs | 197,000 |
| „ „ | „ Stores Control Account | 2,000 | | indirect costs | 48,000 |
| „ „ | „ Depreciation Provision A/c | 1,300 | | | |
| | | £245,300 | | | £245,300 |

*Notes.* The overhead and labour control accounts used in the example for cost ledger accounting are merged in the Cost Control Account.

The credits transferring the costs to work-in-progress are obtained from the third entry analysis sheet shown below.

*Third Entries for 6 months
to 30th June*

| | Production | | | Selling and |
| | Direct | Indirect | Administration | Distribution |
|---|---|---|---|---|
| | £ | £ | £ | £ |
| Wages | 87,000 | 5,000 | | |
| Materials | 110,000 | 2,000 | | |
| Overheads | | 40,000 | 12,000 | 14,000 |
| Depreciation | | 1,300 | | |
| | 197,000 | 48,300 | 12,000 | 14,000 |
| Less Rates Prepaid | | 300 | | |
| | 197,000 | 48,000 | 12,000 | 14,000 |

*Note.* The above is an analysis of the costs incurred. In practice, much more detail would be encountered. Actual and absorbed works overhead costs coincide.

### The Auto Co. Ltd.

| | | Dr. | Cr. |
| Trial Balance for 6 months ended 30th June | | £ | £ |
|---|---|---|---|
| Work-in-progress Account ... ... ... ... | | 47,000 | |
| Finished Goods Account ... ... ... ... | | 8,000 | |
| Stores Control Account ... ... ... ... | | 6,000 | |
| Bank Account ... ... ... ... ... ... | | 41,000 | |
| Creditors Control Account ... ... ... ... | | | 7,000 |
| Debtors Control Account ... ... ... ... | | 22,000 | |
| Fixed Assets Account ... ... ... ... ... | | 55,000 | |
| Share Capital Account ... ... ... ... ... | | | 80,000 |
| Profit and Loss Account ... ... ... ... | | | 32,000 |
| Depreciation Provision Account ... ... ... | | | 6,300 |
| Prepayments Account ... ... ... ... ... | | 300 | |
| Costing Profit and Loss Account ... ... ... | | | 54,000 |
| | | £179,300 | £179,300 |

## NUMBER OF ACCOUNTS

The number of accounts shown in the examples given above has been limited, the emphasis being on "control accounts." In practice much more detail may be required and an account may be kept for each department or cost centre. However, as noticed earlier, the so-called third entries may be used to provide all the *details* required for control and managerial purposes. Many accountants prefer to limit the number of accounts shown in the ledger proper. Which method to use is largely a matter of opinion on which best serves the business.

It will be appreciated, of course, that the debtors control account and creditors control account shown in the integral system will be represented in detail in the sales and purchase ledgers respectively.

## CLASSIFICATION AND CODING

Classification and coding are taken together because they are very much related to each other. The former term relates to the way the accounts are grouped, whereas the latter covers the process of assigning codes or symbols to main- and subdivisions of the accounting classifications and to individual accounts.

Many forms of classification and coding exist. There is no standardised system for the simple reason that accounting systems vary from one business to another. This is natural because any accounting system should suit the requirements of the particular business. The principal methods of classification and coding are covered below.

### METHODS OF CLASSIFYING ACCOUNTS

The method selected for a particular business will tend to be influenced by the *main purpose* to be served by the accounting system. Examples of methods of classification are as follows:

1. According to the nature of transaction.

This may be influenced by financial and legal considerations. Thus, for example, accounts are often classified into "real," "nominal," "personal," and "private." In addition, the classification may be affected by the legal requirements specified by the Companies Acts; these are outlined in Chapter 20.

2. According to the nature of the cost incurred.

Cost accounting adopts this type of classification. Costs are grouped on the basis of material, labour and expense; these are then further divided according to whether they are direct or indirect.

3. According to the functional divisions of the business.

Again cost accounting uses this classification which is generally incorporated with (2) above. The conventional division is into: production; selling and distribution; research and development, and administration.

As is shown below, a costing classification may be varied according to whether historical or standard costs are being employed.

4. On the basis of information required for showing accounting ratios.

Thus, for example, if inter-firm comparisons are to be carried out the classification may be influenced by this fact.

5. On the basis of what is owned and what is owed; *i.e.* assets and liabilities.

This method gives emphasis to the preparation of the balance sheet.

These are not the only possible classifications. In addition, those given may be varied and may be combined one with another. Here the concern must be with a suitable management accountancy classification.

Because of the nature of management accountancy, with its emphasis upon the *future*, the classification should try to reflect the dynamic state of the business concerned. Some of the purposes which the classification should serve may be summarised as follows:

(*a*) Responsibilities should be shown by the accounts. This aspect is generally described as "responsibility accounting."
The division to show responsibility may be as follows:

(i) Production.
(ii) Selling and Distribution.
(iii) Administration.
(iv) Research and Development.

These are then further divided into cost centres.

(*b*) Plans in financial terms should be clear from the information recorded.

Budgetary Control and Standard Costing systems both rely on predetermination of performances and costs.

(*c*) Deviations from the plans (variances) should be obtainable from the system.

Whether the variances should appear in the ledger accounts themselves is a matter on which there are differences of opinions. It may be argued that inclusion makes them an essential part of the accountancy system and, accordingly, they are not simply "adjustments" which are of such minor importance that they do not even appear in the books of account.

As noticed earlier many possible variations of account classifications are available. In addition, the *detail* shown in the classification, *i.e.* the number of accounts, will tend to differ from one business to another. In some, extensive use may be made of "Control Accounts" in the ledger proper, the detail being shown in third entries. Thus, for example, all the factory overhead costs may be analysed and then summarised in a loose-leaf book, the posting to the overhead control account being made once a month or at another suitable interval. On the other hand, a detailed analysis may be shown via the accounts in the ledger proper.

A pro-forma chart of accounts is shown (Fig. 99). This is given to illustrate the principles involved in compiling a chart and *should not* be taken as a complete and ideal system for each and every business. It is not complete because many accounts are not included. There can be no question of its being an ideal system because there is no such thing when dealing generally with the very many types of business organisation that are to be found in practice. Obviously each business should design a system which suits its own needs. What the chart does show is that some form of logical division of activities is essential. A suitable coding system has to be selected. The principal codes used are discussed later.

1. *Fixed Assets*

11 Land
12 Buildings
13 Plant
14 Machinery

2. *Current Assets*

211 Stores Control Account (Raw Materials)
212 Work-in-progress Account
213 Finished Goods Account
214 Debtors Control Account
215 Cash at Bank
216 Cash in Hand

3. *Capital and Loans*

311 Share Capital—Ordinary
313 Share Capital—Preference
313 Share Premium
314 General Reserve
315 Profit and Loss Balance

4. *Current Liabilities*

411 Sundry Creditors
412 Bank Overdraft

5. *Production Costs and Variances*

511 Labour Control Account
512 Material Control Account*

*\* Often omitted, the transfer being made direct to Work-in-progress Account.*

513 Factory Overhead Control Account
514 Labour Efficiency Variance
515 Labour Rate Variance
516 Material Usage Variance
517 Material Price Variance
518 Overhead Budget Variance
519 Overhead Efficiency Variance
520 Overhead Volume or Capacity Variance
521 Overhead Calendar Variance

6. *Selling and Distribution Costs and Variances*

611 Selling and Distribution Costs
612 Sales Value Variance
613 Sales Volume Variance
614 Sales Price Variance
615 Selling Costs Variance
616 Distribution Costs Variance

7. *Administration Costs and Variances*

711 Administration Costs
712 Administration Costs Variance

8. *Research and Development*

811 Research and Development Costs
812 Research and Development Costs Variance

Fig. 99.—*Pro-forma Chart of Accounts*

Consideration should be given to what extent the fixed and variable costs should be distinguished in the accounts. If the distinction is not made in the ledger proper there is certainly a strong case for making it in the subsidiary records, thereby allowing full use to be made of Marginal Costing techniques.

## CODES AND SYMBOLS

Codes and symbols are an essential part of any accounts classification. Often written descriptions are capable of being misinterpreted; the use of a number or other code avoids ambiguity, introducing a standardisation of terms. Moreover, long descriptions can often be replaced by short codes, thus economising in report writing, and in the preparation of forms such as material requisitions. Because of the shortening of descriptions there should be a reduction in the time required for recording the accounting information. A very real benefit is the simplifying of information so that it can be recorded by means of accounting machines and computers. Finally, if secrecy is essential the use of symbols may achieve this end.

The principal codes or symbols are as follows:

### 1. *Alphabetical Codes*

As the name implies, these involve the use of letters to show the different classes of accounts. Thus, for example, "A" may be used to signify fixed assets. This can then be divided on an alphabetical basis.

*Example:*

A   Assets (fixed)
Aa   Land
Ab   Buildings
Ac   Plant
Ad   Machinery

Other assets and liabilities can be covered by different letters, B, C, D, etc., the division in each case being made by the small letters a, b, c, d and so on.

A variation of the alphabetical method is the mnemonic code. This means using the letters in a logical manner in a way that signifies a definite meaning. In the example given earlier "A" is used to indicate "Assets." This form of designation would be followed throughout a mnemonic method.

*Example:*

A   Assets (fixed)
Al   Land
Ab   Building
Ap   Plant
Am   Machinery

*or,*

AC   Assets (current)
ACs   Stores Control
ACwp   Work-in-progress
ACfg   Finished Goods
ACd   Debtors
ACcb   Cash at Bank
ACc   Cash in Hand

It will be seen that the first letter shows the general class to which the individual account belongs. The second, third and subsequent letters describe the particular account.

The use of the small letters, as shown above, to indicate a certain account, is not the only way of devising a mnemonic classification. Many variations are possible. It is important to select the letters with care making sure that there is no possibility of confusing one account with another. Certain letters, I, O and Q, are often omitted from the classification because it has been found that these may lead to confusion.

Many novel and ingenious systems have been devised. Unfortunately, letters do not lend themselves to the same ease of manipulation as figures, particularly when dealing with machine accounting. Moreover, if too many letters are used the system becomes cumbersome and, therefore, is not very flexible. Accordingly, there is a preference for numerical codes.

## 2. Numerical Codes

Numerical codes are more popular than those employing letters. There are so many possible variations of numerical codes and this introduces considerable flexibility. If necessary, decimal points can be introduced to widen the scope of each division within the classification. An example of a numerical classification is given below.

A well-known method is that which assigns a series of numbers to each general class. This is known as the "block number system." One block covers all the accounts within the division. An example is given below.

| Example: | | |
|---|---|---|
| | Fixed Assets | 100–199 |
| | Current Assets | 200–299 |
| | Capital and Loans | 300–399 |
| | Current Liabilities | 400–499 |
| | Production Costs and Variances | 500–599 |

In effect this method is similar to that shown on page 613, the exception being fixed assets. The large range of numbers within each block gives all the flexibility required and additional accounts can be introduced without any difficulty.

Subdivisions within each broad division are sometimes necessary. Thus, for example, taking an account from Fig. 99 the subdivision may be as follows:

12 Buildings
121 Factory Buildings
122 Office Buildings
123 Warehouse Buildings,
and so on.

## 3. Combination Codes

A combination of letters and figures may be quite feasible.

| Example: | A | Assets (fixed) |
|---|---|---|
| | A11 | Land |
| | A12 | Buildings |
| | A13 | Plant |
| | A14 | Machinery |

If an account is to be kept for each cost centre then letters may be used to distinguish each.

*Example:* A Preparation Department
B Mixing Department
C Cooking Department
D Packing Department

Amounts relating to each of these would be indicated by the appropriate letter and then accounts would be designated by figures.

*Example:* A14 Machinery in Preparation Department
B14 Machinery in Mixing Department
C14 Machinery in Cooking Department
D14 Machinery in Packing Department

This envisages an entirely different system to the one suggested by the immediately preceding example. It is very important to use one code or symbol to describe only one account. On no account should the same letter or number be used for different purposes. If a classification is to be of maximum value then there should be no danger of misunderstanding.

The examples given to illustrate the principles have been kept to a minimum. It is not essential for an accountant to memorise all possible classifications. What is important is to understand the principles involved and procedures followed.

### ADVANTAGES OF CLASSIFICATION

Many advantages can accrue to a business from the use of an appropriately designed accounts classification. These are summarised below:

1. The accounts classification forms the framework of the management accounting system. Furthermore, because the framework is put into a written form, consistency in definition and purpose is achieved.

2. There are clearly defined areas of responsibility, and within each division the necessary degree of analysis can be achieved.

Reference to Fig 99 which portrays a possible accounts classification will indicate how this aim may be achieved.

3. All transactions are recorded in a systematic and orderly manner. This should mean that trends are apparent from the accounts and valid comparisons, made from one period to another, will be possible.

4. The preparation and presentation of information to management is made much easier. Information can be accumulated in a desired manner so that no time is lost in presenting reports and statements to all levels of management.

5. Instructions are provided to all staff concerned with the management accounting system. The training of new staff tends to be simplified by the use of an accounts classification.

6. Flexibility, which is essential in any accounting system, can be achieved without difficulty. All that is necessary is to have a sufficiently large range of codes for each general class and each subdivision of that class. This is referred to in connection with the "block number system" outlined earlier.

7. Management is provided with a blue-print of how the business operates. Accounting is the language of business and commerce, and the accounts classification traces the functioning of the organisation from the development of the product to its sale and distribution.

8. Any accounting legal requirements, such as those laid down by the Companies Acts, can be easily covered by the appropriately designed accounts classification.

9. The introduction of mechanical aids, whether these are the relatively simple accounting machines or the more advanced punched-card machines or computers, is made much simpler by the existence of an accounts classification.

10. The recording and tracing of costs throughout an organisation is greatly facilitated. The appropriate code numbers can be used on material requisitions, invoices, job clock cards and other forms, thus enabling responsibility to be traced without error.

In short, therefore, the accounts classification provides an orderly and systematic method of dealing with all business transactions. Without this there is likely to be chaos and muddle.

Once a suitable accounts classification has been designed it should become part of the Accounts Manual or Budget Manual; the latter is discussed in Chapter 3.

## ACCOUNTING FOR STANDARD COSTS

When Standard Costing is employed it is usual to show the variances in the ledger. The same system can be employed in principle with Budgetary Control.

Either Cost Ledger Accounting or Integral Accounting described earlier in this chapter can be employed to record the standard costs. The systems employed are normally distinguished by reference to the *type* of standard cost; *i.e.* whether current *or* basic standards (defined in Chapter 2) are being used. The two systems are explained below.

### ACCOUNTING FOR CURRENT STANDARDS

The principles explained earlier in connection with recording historical costs also apply to standard costs. However, the recording of actual costs, standard costs, and variances obviously makes the procedures more complex.

Within the category that deals with current standard costs it is usual to distinguish two accounting systems:

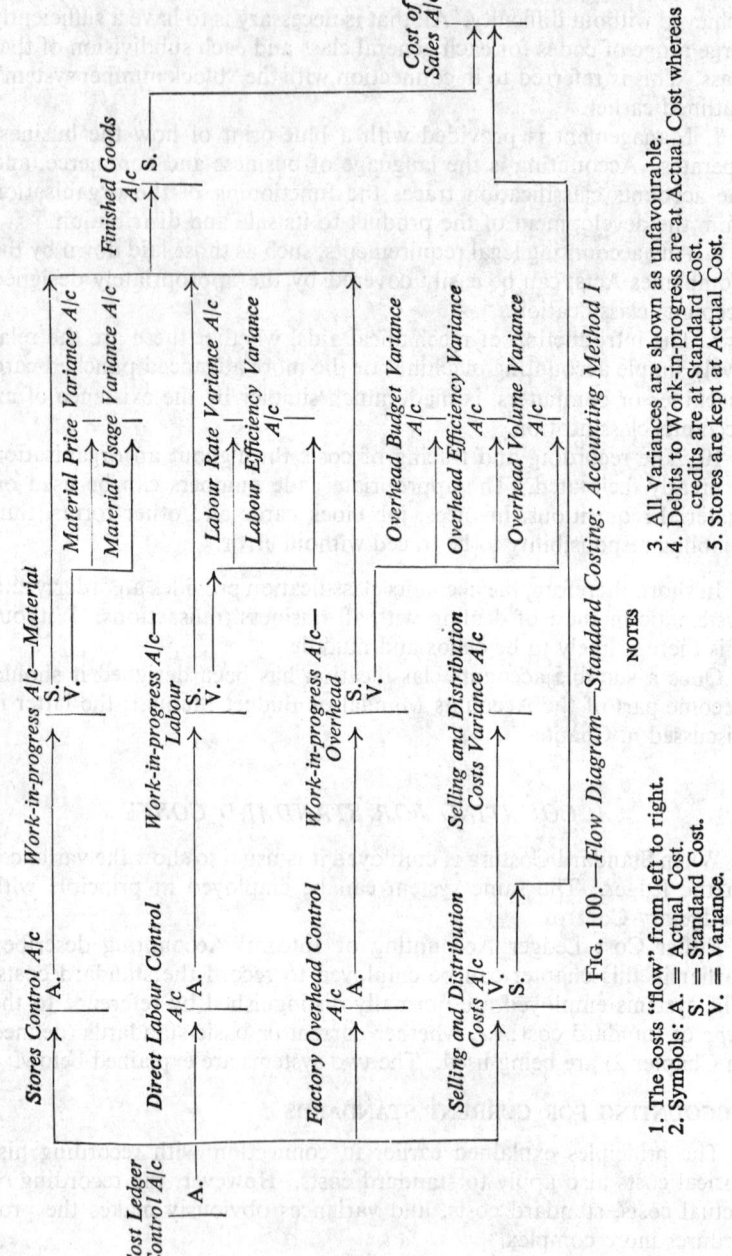

FIG. 100.—*Flow Diagram—Standard Costing: Accounting Method I*

NOTES

1. The costs "flow" from left to right.
2. Symbols: A. = Actual Cost.
   S. = Standard Cost.
   V. = Variance.
3. All Variances are shown as unfavourable.
4. Debits to Work-in-progress are at Actual Cost whereas credits are at Standard Cost.
5. Stores are kept at Actual Cost.

1. Accounting Method I, when the work-in-progress accounts are debited with actual costs and credited with standard costs, the variances being debited or credited depending upon their nature; *i.e.* whether unfavourable or favourable.

2. Accounting Method II, when the work-in-progress accounts are debited and credited with standard costs and the variances do not appear in these accounts.

## CONTROL VIA THE ACCOUNTS

There is no doubt that a useful purpose is served by designing the accounting system so that control information is brought to light automatically. The principal question is to what extent should the "exceptions to the rule" be shown within the double entry system? When drafting a scheme the two points given below should be considered:

1. Should a distinction be made between fixed and variable costs? This is a matter which is discussed in Chapter 10 which deals with Marginal Costing.

Fixed costs are a matter of policy and are, therefore, to a large extent uncontrollable from one period to another. For this reason many accountants would prefer to record the two types of cost quite separately. There is no doubt that recognition of the two classes—fixed and variable—is essential even if they do not form part of the formal accounts classification.

2. What variances should be included in the books of account? As a minimum the principal variances should be included in the accounts. Some accountants would also show sub-variances—major parts of the main variances—in separate accounts. Thus, for example, the material usage variance may be separated into a material mixture sub-variance, and a material yield sub-variance. The way variances may be incorporated into the double-entry system is shown in Figs. 100 and 101.

It will be noted that a Work-in-progress (or Work-in-process) Account is suggested for each element of cost—material, labour and factory overhead. This practice facilitates the separation of the variances. The principal accounts are shown and within each is indicated whether the costs are kept at "actual" or "standard."

## ACCOUNTING FOR BASIC STANDARDS

When basic standard costs are employed a columnar form of ledger is kept, both actual and standard costs being recorded on the debit and credit sides. In addition, it is usual to have a column to show the relationship between the actual and standard costs, this being given as a ratio.

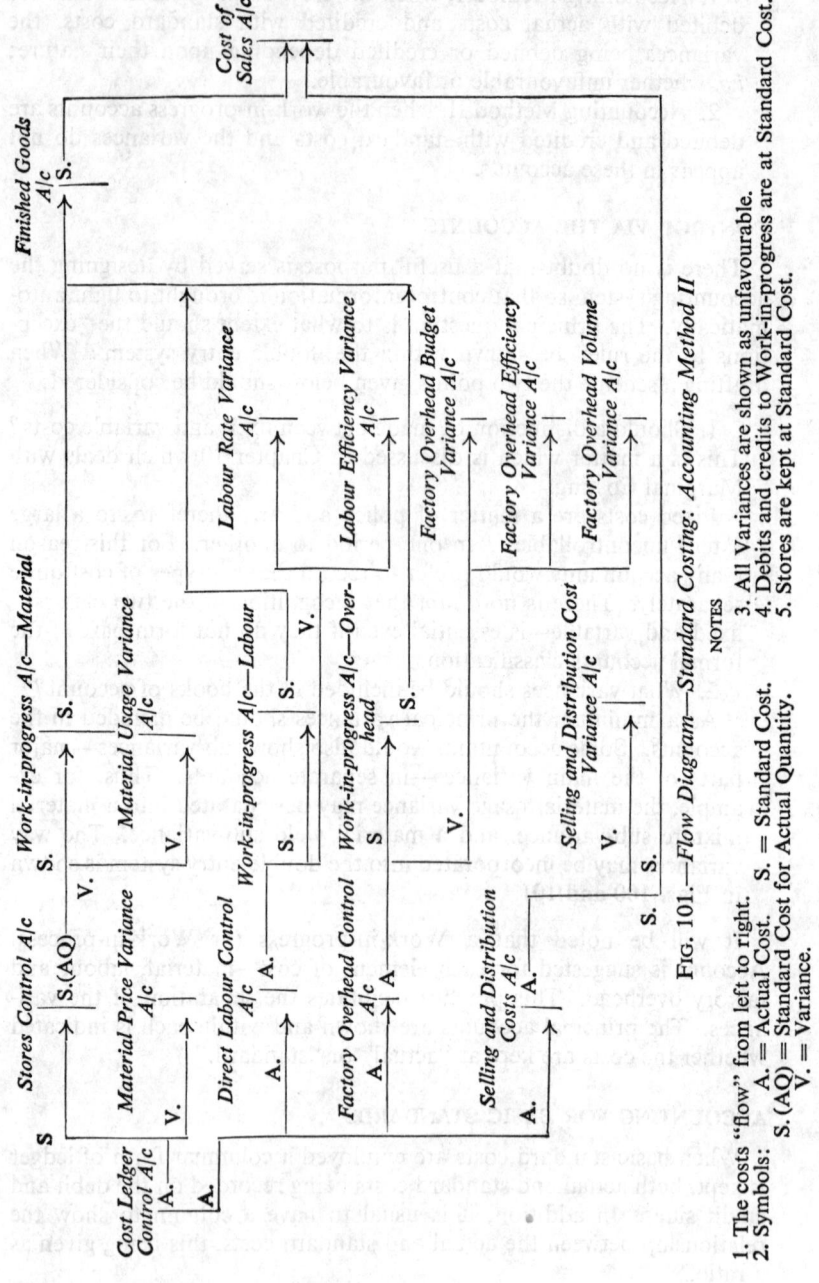

FIG. 101.—*Flow Diagram—Standard Costing: Accounting Method II*

NOTES

1. The costs "flow" from left to right.
2. Symbols:
   A. = Actual Cost.   S. = Standard Cost.
   S.(AQ) = Standard Cost for Actual Quantity.
   V. = Variance.

3. All Variances are shown as unfavourable.
4. Debits and credits to Work-in-progress are at Standard Cost.
5. Stores are kept at Standard Cost.

*Example*

An example of a work-in-progress account is given below to illustrate the procedure followed:

Dr.                 *Work-in-progress Account—Materials*           Cr.

| | £<br>*Actual* | £<br>*Standard* | *Ratio* | | £<br>*Actual* | £<br>*Standard* | *Ratio* |
|---|---|---|---|---|---|---|---|
| Stores Control and Cost Ledger Control | 565·987 | 550·000 | 1·0291 | Finished Goods<br>Balances c/d | 520·708<br>45·279 | 506·000<br>44·000 | 1·0291<br>1·0291 |
| | 565·987 | 550·000 | 1·0291 | | £565·987 | £550·000 | 1·0291 |
| Balances b/d | £45·279 | £44·000 | 1·0291 | | | | |

This method can be very useful for showing statistical trends and changes in rates and prices over a number of years. Accordingly, it provides management with important facts which may be useful for formulating policy and planning activities.

## MECHANISATION AND COMPUTERS

There is no doubt that, except in the smallest business, some form of mechanised accounting system will be essential. Legibility of entries, speed of recording and the ease with which a large volume of work can be handled by a small number of machine operators are a few of the factors which make mechanisation essential. Many books exist on the different types of accounting machine which may be purchased. If the reader wishes to obtain details of particular machines he should consult a specialist work on the subject.

The purpose of this section is to show how to go about deciding the extent of the mechanisation necessary for the business concerned. In particular, the use of a computer is discussed.

What should be made clear is that the mechanical device selected should be appropriate for the size of the business and the volume of work involved. Management accountancy is feasible in any size of organisation, but the employment of a computer is clearly out of the question for the majority of small and medium-sized concerns. The relatively simple adding, calculating, and accounting machines are generally adequate for all their needs. Accordingly, a choice should be made of the machine or machines most appropriate.

In the medium-sized concern which has a large volume of information to record, a punched-card accounting installation may serve quite efficiently. It may also be feasible to rent time on a computer to deal with any seasonal excess of work or particularly large problem.

When a business is large and complex a computer may be a practical proposition. However, it should be appreciated that a computer is capable of carrying out a fantastic volume of work and, therefore, great care should be exercised before deciding to go ahead and purchase one.

The methods employed for assessing the feasibility of capital expenditure projects discussed in Chapter 18 apply to any type of accounting machine from the simplest to the most advanced. The expected cost–savings may be the most important consideration. However, there are others. The importance of the volume of work has already been noted. This applied to *actual* volume. In addition, there is in a business a *potential* volume—additional information produced faster to help management to become more efficient. This may be equally (if not more) important than cost savings. If management can make decisions more efficiently then higher profits can be earned; this is the true criterion to be used, but, unfortunately, it is very difficult to estimate the effect of purchasing a machine on the profitability of a business.

### ELECTRONIC DATA-PROCESSING

"Electronic data-processing," often abbreviated to "E.D.P." is the term given to the employment of an electronic digital computer in the field of management accountancy for recording, storing, analysing and otherwise dealing with information. (E.D.P. may also be used to describe work carried out by punched-card machines.) A computer is fitted with a number of basic units (Fig. 102); it can carry out instructions automatically and follow a predetermined programme; it can store a vast amount of data and can operate at very fast speeds.

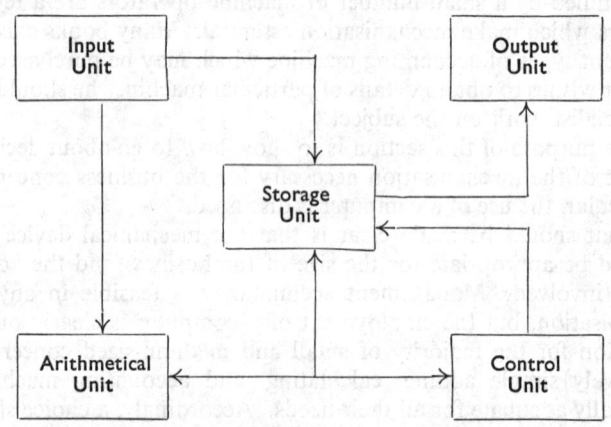

This diagram is a very simplified version of the processes involved.

FIG. 102.—*Principal units of a computer*

Information and instructions are fed into an input unit by means of punched cards or tape. This is then fed into the storage unit and any calculations are carried out in the arithmetical unit. Output emerges from the output unit and the entire process is "watched over" by the control unit. Before being fed into a computer any information has to be stated in terms of binary notation. This is a system of numbering which deals only with two digits—one and zero. Comparison of the normal numbering (denary notation) with the binary system is carried out below:

| Denary | Binary |
| --- | --- |
| 1 | 1 |
| 2 | 10 |
| 3 | 11 |
| 4 | 100 |
| 5 | 101 |
| 6 | 110 |
| 7 | 111 |
| 8 | 1000 |
| 9 | 1001 |
| 10 | 1010 |
| 11 | 1011 |
| 12 | 1100 |
| 20 | 10100 |
| 21 | 10101 |
| 50 | 110010 |

Conversion tables can be employed to convert to and from binary notation.

## EMPLOYING A COMPUTER

Whether or not to employ a computer is a decision which should not be taken lightly. The use of computers in industry is a new development which offers tremendous prospects provided the full implications are understood and the installation is planned carefully over a sufficiently long period. Some of the most important factors to consider and the way to approach the entire problem are discussed stage-by-stage below.

### 1. *The Steering Committee*

The usefulness of a computer and the feasibility of acquiring one may be recognised as *possibilities* by the board of directors or the management accountant. Alternatively, the idea of using a computer may come from some other field such as production control or operational research. Irrespective of the source of the idea it is clear that the board of directors will have to give its sanction before steps should be taken to consider whether or not a computer should be acquired.

There should be a clear understanding of the principal factors which the board of directors consider to be relevant to the question of whether a computer is a worthwhile proposition. Are these the reduction of clerical operations, the availability of more information at increased speeds or some other purpose? It may simply be that the board feel that they should be in fashion and, therefore, would like all avenues explored to see if a computer is likely to improve efficiency before going ahead.

The task of investigating the feasibility of employing a computer is

X

generally assigned to a special committee referred to here as a "steering committee."

This chapter deals with accounting records. However, when considering the feasibility of employing a computer the fields should *not* be limited to accounting records. Except in a very large company, and not always then, a computer would not be employed *only* on the accounting. All fields should be considered and, in fact, should be worked into any plan which recommends the use of a computer. Production control, stores and stock movement, market research, operational research and the provision of information to management should all be within the terms of reference given to the committee. A very large sum of money is involved in purchasing a computer and, therefore, the possibility of employing it fully calls for a thorough investigation.

The steering committee should be formed of senior managers, including experts in organisation and methods, mathematics, and office machinery. Investigating the problem should not be regarded as a purely accounting function. In view of the need to integrate all information so that it can be worked upon by a computer there must be co-operation of technologists, production engineers and other specialists. A representative from the company who may supply the computer would be a definite asset. However, this does not avoid the necessity of having staff trained in computer techniques before a computer is purchased.

A great deal of investigation work will call for detailed analysis of the functions being carried out. This may be assigned to particular specialists on the steering committee. Alternatively, sub-committees may be formed to produce information on particular aspects, the leader of the sub-committee reporting back to the main committee.

The management accountant may act as chairman of the steering committee. This procedure is followed in the chart shown in Fig. 103. Alternatively, he may be the secretary of the committee convening the meetings and ensuring that the necessary co-ordination of all aspects of the work is obtained. Later he may be responsible for ensuring that a special report is compiled along the lines suggested in Chapter 14, "Control and Communication." A very thorough investigation is essential before a special report is prepared. The report should include, *inter alia*, the following matters:

(a) Investigations carried out.

(b) Fields in which a computer could be employed.

(c) An assessment of the volume of work to be performed by a computer.

(d) The size of computer recommended and details of estimated costs of purchase, installation, housing, running, staffing and launching. Possible cost *savings* could also be included—in effect comparing the old system with the proposed new system.

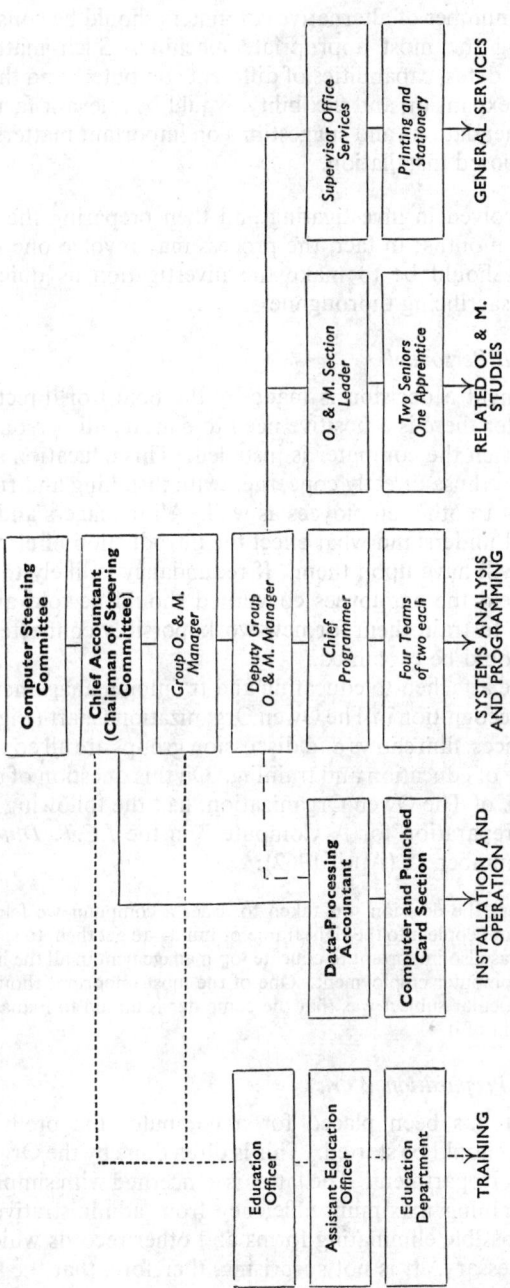

FIG. 103.—*Procedure for introduction of Electronic Data-processing*

The chart shows the organisation behind the planning for and introduction of electronic data-processing at the Owen Organization. Bold wording, steering committee and operation; italic wording, group O. & M. department; roman wording, education. Unbroken lines show direct responsibility; broken lines, liaison; dotted lines, associate responsibilities.

Obviously a number of alternative computers should be considered before selecting the most appropriate machine. Such matters as prices, delivery dates, capabilities of different computers and the need to provide for expansion and flexibility, would be relevant factors.

(e) Recommendations and suggestions on important matters relating to the proposed installation.

The period involved in investigating and then preparing the report may cover many months; in fact, the process may involve one or two years. The aim should be to make the investigation as quickly as possible without sacrificing thoroughness.

## 2. *Educating all Personnel*

From the moment a decision is made by the board of directors to acquire a computer there is a positive need to educate all personnel on what to expect when the computer is installed. This education should extend not only to those directly concerned with installing and running the computer, but to other employees as well. All managers and other employees should understand what effect the introduction of electronic data-processing will have upon them. If redundancy is likely to occur in a particular field the employees concerned should be told and the steps to be taken to train them for new work, possibly connected with the computer, should be explained.

The importance attached to educating and training management and workers is given recognition in The Owen Organization Chart (Fig. 103). Courses, conferences, film shows and discussion groups are all contained in the programme of education and training. On this question of education Mr. J. Antill, of The Owen Organization, had the following to say in an article: "Preparation for A Computer" in the *I.C.T. Data Processing Journal*, number 11 (April 1962):

"From the moment the decision was taken to order a computer we felt it was most important to put people into the right frame of mind—to get them to speak the same language. It was also important to educate top management in all the implications arising from computer employment. One of the most important thoughts to get over on this particular subject was that the computer is an aid to management and not a replacement of it."

## 3. *Preliminary Preparation Work*

Once an order has been placed for a computer the preliminary preparation work should be started. This is often done by the Organisation and Methods Department. The latter is concerned with simplifying routines and obtaining maximum efficiency from administrative procedures, where possible eliminating forms and other records which are considered unnecessary. It is not surprising, therefore, that the O and M staff play an important part in paving the way for the computer.

Study of existing procedures and then possible improvements should be the first consideration. This should be followed by the preparation of programmes* and flow charts for the functions which are to be the subject of electronic data-processing. Although complete integration of all recording is essential, this may have to be accomplished gradually. The computer may be employed on a relatively straightforward problem such as the payroll and then, after experience has been gained, may graduate on to more advanced problems such as stores and stock control, production control, and the provision of information for management decisions.

It has been assumed that experienced programmers are employed in the O and M Department. If they are not, then at least one programmer who has the experience and skill to supervise the work of a group should be engaged. Naturally, full use should be made of the guidance which may be obtained from the manufacturer of the computer.

At this stage attention should be paid to the building in which the computer is to be installed. There should be no need to add that the physical conditions should be suitable for the purpose—the installation and operation of the computer.

An equally important problem is the classification and coding of data. Linked with this is the selection of the medium to employ for recording data. Quite often punched cards are used in the early stages and then a conversion is made to paper tape or magnetic tape.

Standardisation of the layout and content of the programmes, in such a way that the staff who are to code them and carry out the programming can do their work in the quickest and most effective manner, is essential. A data-processing manual should be compiled as soon as possible to put into written form all instructions and procedures. Full details, including working papers, should be collected and incorporated into the manual.

A number of trial runs on a computer is very desirable at this stage. The supplier of the computer will be able to help with this matter.

### 4. Install the Computer

The preparation period will cover many months. Study of examples to be found in practice show that two or even more years is a normal period required for dealing with the initial work.

Once the computer has been installed there will be a need to prepare further programmes and to make adjustments to those in existence. Complete merging of the old system into the new system should take place as soon as possible.

The training of staff should have continued throughout the preparation period so that there should be sufficient personnel to carry out all the work involved in the new system.

Particular attention should be paid to ensuring that *Integrated* Data-Processing is practised. This involves recording all information in such

* The modern spelling *program*s may be preferred.

a manner that no matter what the problem is the answer can be found from the data recorded. Separate departments or functions are not regarded as distinct entities for recording purposes; instead they are all co-ordinated and linked through the data processing. This theme should be present throughout management accountancy; there should be complete integration of all functions through the records.

## POSSIBLE ADVANTAGES OF E.D.P.

Advantages claimed for electronic data-processing used in appropriate circumstances are as follows:

1. All administrative functions are examined and made efficient as a natural consequence of introducing data-processing.

This is true, but it is also true of the work of the O and M Department.

2. Clerical drudgery and costs may be reduced.

This is often true, although not necessarily so; what is possibly more true is the fact that management is served much better with less clerical drudgery and effort. The information becoming available is likely to be of greater volume and value than with any other system.

3. Complicated exercises can be carried out on the computer and large and complex problems can be solved.

4. Information can be *stored* until required and then used to compare results or to answer questions.

5. Facts and figures can be made available to management within a very short space of time. This allows management to act promptly.

6. Analysis of the results of market research or economic surveys can be carried out swiftly, again allowing management to take prompt action. Possible *future* trends can be assessed by the computer.

7. If a computer is centralised a large degree of standardisation can be achieved which could assist in establishing realistic uniform cost accounting and inter-firm comparisons.

8. Integration of all management functions becomes possible through the use of a computer.

9. It should greatly facilitate the preparation of forecasts and budgets.

10. Alternative courses of action, and the likely effect of each on profit, may be obtained without delay. This is the field of operational research—a fertile one for the employment of computers.

These are only a few examples of possible benefits. It should not be forgotten that a computer will cost many thousands of pounds and, therefore, the expected benefits should obviously be very real before a computer is purchased. Furthermore, top management should be prepared to wait a number of years before seeing the full results of deciding to employ electronic data-processing.

## MANAGEMENT INFORMATION SYSTEMS

The developments in the systems approach to management information have been accelerated by the improvements made in computer technology. It is now possible to centralise the data-processing systems, thus allowing a more comprehensive approach to be adopted for the collection and dissemination of information. There is no intention of implying that a computer is *essential* for all M.I.S. installations; however, similar principles and methods can be employed in designing a suitable system even though this is not computer-oriented.

There are many possible approaches to M.I.S., but there are two basic methods:

1. The *total* system when all information is centralised and fully integrated.
2. The *piece-meal* or *problem oriented* system which introduces the means of providing answers in the form of information or control methods when difficulties arise.

In practice both methods will tend to be used, but there should be integration so that a fully co-ordinated system is achieved. The *total* system is largely a theoretical concept; conditions change so rapidly that the ideal system envisaged by the supporters of a fully centralised system is unlikely to be a practical reality. However, there is a strong possibility that a high degree of centralisation could be achieved within an integrated system.

### ESTABLISHING THE OBJECTIVES

The company *objectives*—products to be made and methods for achieving the desired results—should be established before any attempt is made to install M.I.S. Once these have been defined plans can be made and the appropriate organisation can be developed.

### PARTIES TO M.I.S.

The parties giving or receiving information within M.I.S. make up an "information net-work." There should be recognition of all the internal and external uses made of facts and figures—this is an aspect which is often neglected under some of the more conventional approaches. In summary form the principal parties are as follows:

1. General public.
2. Shareholders.
3. Board of directors.
4. Divisional managers.
5. Functional managers.
6. Line managers.
7. Supervisors.
8. Trade associations.

    9. Banks and financial institutions.
   10. Government departments.

There should be collection of information from all these sources and then carefully selected facts should be fed back, so that planning, co-ordination and control are exercised as effectively as possible. Chapter 14 deals with control and communication.

### APPLICATIONS

The possible applications for M.I.S. are very wide. They can cover all aspects of production, marketing, administration, and research and development.

An advanced system is available from Honeywell's Micro Switch Division,* and this gives a fully integrated system of planning and control. This consists of a number of *sub-systems*, one for each of the following:

    1. *Design and Manufacturing Engineering.*

    This covers all aspects of design—production specifications, bills of materials and drawings; and manufacturing engineering—methods of producing, tools and equipment, operations to be performed and labour standards.

    2. *Sales Order Processing.*

    This includes all the procedures for "screening" the order and preparing for despatch and invoicing. Statistics are also prepared.

    3. *Materials Planning and Control.*

    The material requirements are forecast, and minimum, maximum and re-order levels are established. Requisitioning of stocks is also covered.

    4. *Production Scheduling and Dispatching.*

    All the necessary information relating to production requirements is collected and processed. Instructions can then be issued for materials, labour and machine utilisation. Production schedules can be finalised and put into operation.

    5. *Financial Control.*

    Standard costs are developed for planning and control. All aspects of cost and financial accounting are included in the sub-system.

    6. *Management Planning.*

    The company objectives are incorporated into a *master plan* which covers long-range goals and short-term courses of action. Sales and production forecasts are broken down so that detailed manufacturing and marketing procedures can be worked out and executed.

* The kind assistance given by Honeywell Ltd. is gratefully acknowledged.

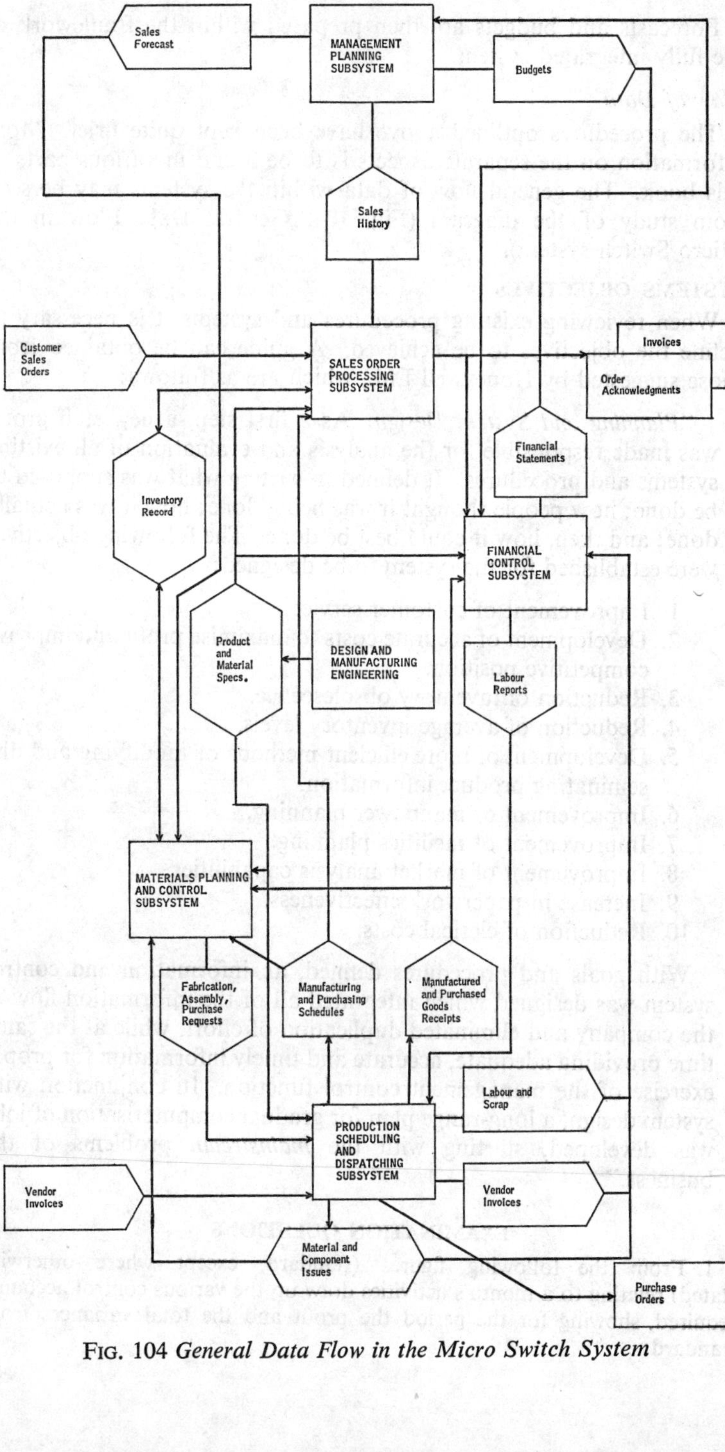

FIG. 104 *General Data Flow in the Micro Switch System*

Forecasts and budgets are then prepared within the framework of the fully integrated system.

## Flow of Data

The procedures outlined above have been kept quite brief. More information on the separate aspects is to be found in various parts of this book. The general flow of data within the systems may be seen from study of the diagram (Fig. 104, General Data Flow in the Micro Switch system).

## SYSTEMS OBJECTIVES

When reviewing existing procedures and systems it is necessary to define the objectives to be achieved. A guide can be obtained from those suggested by Honeywell Ltd., which are as follows:

"*Planning and System Design.* As a first step, a new staff group was made responsible for the analysis and evaluation of all existing systems and procedures. It defined in writing what was supposed to be done; how people thought it was being done; how it was actually done; and then, how it could best be done. The following objectives were established for the system to be designed:

1. Improvement of customer service.
2. Development of accurate costs to maximise profit and improve competitive position.
3. Reduction of inventory obsolescence.
4. Reduction of average inventory levels.
5. Development of more efficient methods of modifying and disseminating product information.
6. Improvement of manpower planning.
7. Improvement of facilities planning.
8. Improvement of market analysis capabilities.
9. Increase in paperwork effectiveness.
10. Reduction of clerical costs.

With goals and procedures defined, an information and control system was designed which integrated all of the information flow in the company and eliminated duplication of effort, while at the same time providing adequate, accurate and timely information for proper exercise of the management control function. In conjunction with system design, a long-range plan for gradual computerisation of jobs was developed, starting with the *mainstream* problems of the business."

## EXAMINATION QUESTIONS

1. From the following figures (standard, except where otherwise stated) relating to a month's activities draw up the various control accounts required, showing for the period the profit and the total variances from standard:

| | | | £ | £ |
|---|---|---|---:|---:|
| Stock brought forward— | steel bars | ... | 7,000 | |
| | pressings | ... | 5,000 | |
| | tools | ... | 1,000 | |
| | consumable stores | | 2,000 | |
| | | | | 15,000 |
| Work-in-progress brought forward ... ... ... | | | | 11,000 |
| Direct wages— | machine shop | ... | 3,000 | |
| | assembly shop | ... | 7,000 | |
| | tool room | ... | 2,000 | |
| | | | | 12,000 |
| Overheads— | machine shop | ... | 6,000 | |
| | assembly shop | ... | 3,500 | |
| | tool room | ... | 3,000 | |
| | | | | 12,500 |
| Sales (actual) ... ... ... ... ... ... | | | | 42,000 |

| Purchases— | | | | | actual £ | standard £ | |
|---|---|---|---|---|---:|---:|---:|
| steel bars | ... | ... | ... | ... | 6,140 | 6,000 | |
| pressings | ... | ... | ... | ... | 6,090 | 6,000 | |
| tools ... | ... | ... | ... | ... | 1,050 | 1,000 | |
| consumable stores | ... | ... | ... | 1,020 | 1,000 | |
| | | | | | 14,300 | | 14,000 |

| | | | | | | £ | £ |
|---|---|---|---|---|---|---:|---:|
| Issues from stores— | | | | | | | |
| steel bars to machine shop ... | ... | ... | ... | | 6,500 | |
| pressings to assembly shop ... | ... | ... | ... | | 5,500 | |
| tools ... ... ... ... ... | ... | | | | 500 | |
| Consumable stores— | | | | | £ | | |
| Machine shop | ... | ... | ... | | 750 | | |
| Tool room ... | ... | ... | ... | | 250 | | |
| | | | | | | 1,000 | |
| | | | | | | | 13,500 |
| Production— | | | | | | | |
| Machine shop ... | ... | ... | ... | ... | | | 20,500 |
| Assembly shop ... | ... | ... | ... | ... | | | 16,750 |
| Scrapped work-in-progress— | | | | | | | |
| Machine shop ... | ... | ... | ... | ... | | 750 | |
| Assembly shop ... | ... | ... | ... | ... | | 250 | |
| | | | | | | | 1,000 |
| Work-in-progress carried forward ... | ... | ... | | | | | 12,000 |
| Cost of Sales ... ... ... | ... | ... | ... | | | | 35,250 |
| Allocation of tool room costs— | | | | | | | |
| Machine shop ... | ... | ... | ... | ... | | 5,000 | |
| Assembly shop ... | ... | ... | ... | ... | | 750 | |
| | | | | | | | 5,750 |

NOTE.—Total variance only is required and no attempt should be made to analyse by causes.                                   *(I.C.W.A.)*

2. The following balances are shown in a Cost Ledger as at April 1, 19..:

|  | Dr. £ | Cr. £ |
|---|---|---|
| Work-in-progress Account ... ... ... ... ... | 3,920 | |
| Finished Stock Account ... ... ... ... ... ... | 2,930 | |
| Works Overheads Suspense Account ... ... ... | 200 | |
| Office and Administration Overheads Suspense Account ... | 100 | |
| Stores Ledger Control Account ... ... ... ... ... | 5,250 | |
| Cost Ledger Control Account ... ... ... ... ... | | 12,400 |

Transactions for the year ended March 31, 19.., were:

|  | £ |
|---|---|
| Wages—Direct Labour ... ... ... ... ... ... ... | 30,600 |
| Wages Indirect Labour ... ... ... ... ... ... ... | 1,400 |
| Works Overheads allocated to Production ... ... ... | 9,350 |
| Office and Administration Overheads allocated to Production ... | 3,100 |
| Stores issued to Production ... ... ... ... ... | 19,650 |
| Goods finished during year ... ... ... ... ... | 60,000 |
| Finished goods sold ... ... ... ... ... ... ... | 66,000 |
| Stores purchased ... ... ... ... ... ... ... | 18,000 |
| Stores issued to Factory Repair Orders ... ... ... ... | 750 |
| Carriage inwards on stores issued for Production ... ... ... | 300 |
| Works expenses ... ... ... ... ... ... ... | 7,000 |
| Office and administration expenses ... ... ... ... | 3,000 |

Write up Accounts in the Cost Ledger to record the above transactions, make the necessary transfers to Control Accounts, and prepare a Trial Balance as at March 31, 19... Compute the profit or loss for the year.

(S.C.A.)

3. Describe a method of collecting together variances from standard material costs in order to balance standard and actual costs. (S.C.A.)

4. Draw a diagram showing how the Cost Accountant justifies in his books every disbursement recorded in the financial books. (S.C.A.)

5. State, in brief numbered paragraphs, the *general principles* to be followed in preparing a code of accounts. Give illustrative examples appropriate to a company which manufactures and sells its own products. (I.C.W.A.)

6. (a) State briefly two fundamental rules, in the classification of accounts, governing the division into classes.

(b) In classifying and coding accounts relating to wages paid, illustrate with a simple tabulation how you would subdivide and code the following two of the main divisions: (i) payments for lost time; (ii) extra payments.

(I.C.W.A.)

7. Design a simple flow diagram to illustrate standard costing procedure when production department accounts are debited at actual, and credited at standard, cost. Show two service, and two production, departments. Costs should be confined to material, wages, and overhead without additional detail. The main variances for direct costs, and for indirect, should be shown. (I.C.W.A.)

8. It is proposed to integrate the cost and financial accounts in a company in which they have previously been separate. State the advantages to be derived from this process and the main adjustments to procedure which will be needed. Also show how the process might affect the organisation of the cost department and its relation to other departments. (I.C.W.A.)

9. If cost information is limited to an analysis of actual costs, state how this would affect cost control. (I.C.W.A.)

10. You are the accountant of a medium-sized engineering factory which has employed a detailed system of management accounts for many years. A computer feasibility study has recently been completed and although this indicates that a computer could be utilised effectively, no decision has yet been made as to the size, type, and make which should be employed. You feel that it would be advantageous to gain experience by using a computer service bureau before coming to a final decision.

Prepare a memorandum statement for the board of management outlining your reasons for this and also the necessary steps which would have to be taken before such a scheme could be implemented. *(A.C.C.A.)*

11. The following details apply to a manufactured product:

|  |  | £ |
|---|---|---|
| Standard cost each: | | |
| Direct material: A—2 units ... ... ... ... ... | | 0·600 |
| B—6 units ... ... ... ... ... | | 5·400 |
| C—4 units ... ... ... ... ... | | 1·000 |
| | | 7·000 |
| Direct labour, £0·325 per hour ... ... ... ... | | 1·500 |
| Variable overheads, 25% of direct labour ... ... ... | | 0·375 |
| Fixed overheads (based on budgeted production of 1080 units per month) ... ... ... ... ... ... | | 0·625 |
| | | £9·500 |

The budgeted selling price is £12·50 each.
The transaction for a month were as follows:

Direct material:

| | Purchased | | Issued to Production |
|---|---|---|---|
| | Units | Price per unit | Units |
| A | 2080 | £0·325 | 2010 |
| B | 6400 | £0·875 | 6080 |
| C | 4260 | £0·300 | 4040 |

| | Hours | Rate per Hour |
|---|---|---|
| Direct wages | 3600 | £0·375 |
| | 240 | £0·400 |
| Overheads: Variable | £380 | |
| Fixed | £650 | |
| Production (units) | 1000 | |

| | Units | Each |
|---|---|---|
| Sales: Home | 700 | £12·50 |
| Export | 200 | £12·25 |

There was no opening stock of material and no opening or closing stock of work in progress.

An integrated system of accounting is in operation and the raw material stock account is kept at standard.

Journalise the above transactions for the month, reflecting all sales and production variances. *(I.C.W.A.)*

12. At the beginning of the current financial year the following list of balances were extracted from the integrated accounts of a manufacturing company:

|  | £ |
|---|---|
| Debtors ... ... ... ... ... ... | 180,000 |
| Creditors ... ... ... ... ... ... | 115,000 |
| Cash ... ... ... ... ... ... | 54,000 |
| Fixed assets at cost ... ... ... ... | 350,000 |
| Raw materials at standard ... ... ... | 85,000 |
| Finished goods at standard ... ... ... | 50,000 |
| Work-in-progress at standard ... ... ... | 90,000 |
| Depreciation, fixed assets ... ... ... ... | 95,000 |
| Investments ... ... ... ... ... ... | 20,000 |
| Ordinary share capital ... ... ... ... | 500,000 |
| Profit and loss, credit balance ... ... ... | 119,000 |

The following information is provided of transactions in the first quarter of the current financial year:

|  | Actual £ | Standard £ |
|---|---|---|
| Direct wages ... ... ... ... ... ... | 22,000 | 21,000 |
| Materials issued to production at standard prices... | 36,500 | 35,000 |
| Purchase of raw materials, on credit ... ... | 41,500 | 40,000 |
| Factory overhead, including indirect wages and £4000 depreciation... ... ... ... ... | 20,100 | |
| Factory overhead absorbed, at 95% normal capacity ... ... ... ... ... ... | | 19,000 |
| Administration, selling, and distribution expenses | 13,000 | |

|  | | Budget |
|---|---|---|
| Sales, on credit ... ... ... ... ... | 97,600 | £100,000 |

The cash transactions are as follows:

|  | | £ | |
|---|---|---|---|
| Payments: | Net wages | 26,500 | (after subtracting deductions £3,500) |
| | Creditors | 70,000 | |
| Receipts: | Debtors | 100,000 | |

Overhead expenses (except wages) should be regarded as credit transactions.

At the end of the quarter the following balances have been calculated on a basis of standard costs:

|  | £ |
|---|---|
| Work-in-progress ... ... ... | 95,000 |
| Finished goods ... ... ... | 48,000 |

Wages earned during the quarter have all been paid.

The following adverse variances have been calculated and with the other variances to be ascertained are to be charged against profit:

| | | | | £ |
|---|---|---|---|---|
| Overhead expenditure | ... | ... | | 100 |
| Sales price ... | ... | ... | ... | 1400 |
| Labour rate... | ... | ... | ... | 1200 |

You are required to:

(*a*) record the above information in integral form in the books of the company;

(*b*) prepare for presentation to management the interim:

    (i) profit and loss account for the quarter;

    (ii) balance sheet at end of the quarter. (*I.C.W.A.*)

# Chapter 24

# CREDIT CONTROL

The need for "credit" is now generally accepted. It involves granting the use of values in the present against the promise to repay in the future. Selling goods on credit means permitting the buyer to have immediate use of them on the understanding that payment is made according to the terms laid down; *e.g.* within a month. This process of dealing with goods on a credit basis is known as "trade credit" and it is with this aspect that the present chapter concerns itself. However, many of the remarks on creditworthiness could apply equally to the acceptance of any form of credit by a lender or seller.

There is no doubt that the existence of credit facilities can increase sales. A business wanting to purchase goods will go where the best terms are offered—and these will include the terms of payment which may be especially important to an expanding concern. Accordingly, it may be said that selling goods on credit terms can be an advantage to the seller as well as the buyer. There is the important proviso that the seller should be able to collect the money due from the buyer; otherwise a bad debt is incurred which will reduce profit. Furthermore, the money should be collected as quickly as possible or additional capital may have to be obtained.

## CHECKING CREDITWORTHINESS

The *methods* used for checking creditworthiness are discussed in the next paragraph. For the moment it is important to notice the *general factors* which influence credit rating. These are concerned with assessing the likelihood of a buyer being in a position to pay his accounts on the due dates. They may be summarised as follows:

1. Ability to pay. } For both of these there should be
2. Intention to pay. } sound management.
3. General trade conditions—affects the ability to pay.
4. Any special risks associated with the business concerned.

These factors may be assessed by one or more of the following methods:

1. Past records relating to customers.
2. Credit controller's personal knowledge and judgment.
3. Salesman's opinions and knowledge obtained by interviewing the potential customer and/or by survey of his (the customer's) property.
4. Professional valuation and survey of the potential customer's factory and other fixed assets.

5. Analysis of final accounts (covered in Chapter 16).

6. Information volunteered by the potential customer in the form of a letter or on a form designed for the purpose or at an interview with a member of the credit controller's staff.

7. Sample orders gradually increasing the volume of business when intention to pay is shown.

All these are referred to as *direct* methods. Each has its use in appropriate circumstances.

Past records and experience may be a good *guide* to creditworthiness, but they may not show the entire picture. For one thing conditions may have changed; the records accumulated and experience gained when trade is good may not indicate what is likely to happen when trade is unfavourable. Similarly, a salesman's estimate should not be taken at its apparent full value. Any salesman worthy of that name is intent on selling and sometimes signs of credit weakness may be overlooked in the effort to sell. The professional valuation will show the assets owned and indicate *possible* earning power. However, it will not show *actual* earning power; the products manufactured and sold and the effectiveness of the employment of the assets will determine the rate of earning. When analysing final accounts it is important to remember that they may be quite out-of-date, the "current" accounts being anything up to a year old. Information volunteered by the potential customer should be treated with some reserve for clearly no prospective buyer of goods on credit is likely to give information which is detrimental to his credit-standing. Because of these possible weaknesses of the direct methods it is usual and wise to obtain additional facts via one or more of the indirect methods explained below.

The *indirect* methods of establishing creditworthiness may be summarised as follows:

1. Bank reports.
2. Trade references.
3. Trade Protection Associations and General Mercantile Enquiry Agents.
4. Newspapers and journals including the *Board of Trade Gazette*.
5. Official records such as those kept at the Companies' Registration Department.

The first three are considered below.

### BANK REPORTS

Approaching a bank for information on a potential customer is a very favoured method of checking creditworthiness. The enquirer's bank then contacts the prospective customer's bank who will give the information required. There is no doubt that a banker is in a very favourable position for assessing financial strength. However, a bank reference alone should not be regarded as positive evidence of creditworthiness for two main reasons. A bank manager will give as much information as possible, but he will naturally wish to be as fair as possible to his own customer and this attitude may not always result in a report which is very informative on *credit* standing. Another related factor is that the bank may not be in possession of many important facts which are important to credit-standing. Any hire purchase commitments or heavy indebtedness may be incurred without the bank being aware of their existence.

A further possible failing is the relative slowness of the method compared with other possibilities. Approaching one bank who must in turn seek information from the potential customer's bank inevitably leads to some delay. Yet delay could cause annoyance on the part of the would-be purchaser, a condition which should be avoided if at all possible.

There is no doubt that the bank reference can play an important part in establishing credit rating, but the credit controller may be unwise to rely entirely on this information. If the bank report states that the potential customer is financially very sound then obviously a credit limit may be assessed on this alone. However, if there is any hint of financial instability in the report further enquiries will be essential.

## TRADE REFERENCES

Upon receipt of an order from a would-be customer an enquiry is sent to his referees; other firms with whom he has done business on a credit basis. The most usual questions asked are: does he pay promptly; what is the limit of credit allowed; how much business has been transacted; how long has he dealt with the particular concern and is he likely to be a good risk for a specific amount of credit?

Again, this source of information may not be altogether reliable. The buyer may have friends who will act as referees or he may have special accounts which he always pays promptly to ensure that he has good references. Nevertheless, when these possible weaknesses are kept in mind the method can be quite useful, especially if a status report is required very quickly. The credit controller may be in a position to obtain the information from the referees by use of the telephone, speaking to his counterparts whom he may know quite well. However, it is not suggested that the telephone should be used as a regular form of enquiry. A written report carefully compiled may be much more reliable.

## PROTECTION ASSOCIATIONS AND ENQUIRY AGENTS

There are many organisations which collect and disseminate information relating to credit standing. Some are local firms, others operate on a regional or national basis. Many, such as the trade protection societies, specialise to a large degree in giving a service to wholesalers, retailers, and those businesses who are connected in some way with retailing. Often the nature of the field in which the organisation works is apparent from its name. The following list, though by no means complete, gives some indication of the sources of credit information:

1. London Association for the Protection of Trade (LAPT).
2. Hire Purchase Trade Association.
3. National Check Trader's Federation.
4. National Federation of Credit Traders.
5. British Furniture Manufacturers Credit Bureau.
6. Dun and Bradstreet.
7. Seyde and Co.
8. Stubbs.
9. Kemps.

Those listed at the end (6 to 9) are commercial credit houses. The others are trade protection societies who deal with the members who form them.

All offer a service which aims to minimise bad debts. Unfortunately, although they may co-operate with each other and exchange information, there is no one organisation which can supply every requirement needed for credit control. For this reason care should be taken to select the source which can supply information which is relevant and up-to-date.

*Work of the London Trade Protection Association (LAPT)*

In a way the prefix "London" is a misnomer. In actual fact, it does have branch offices in Newcastle, Hull, Exeter and Plymouth. In addition, there are affiliated organisations in different towns and cities throughout Britain and many other countries.

The services offered by the LAPT are as follows:

1. *Status reports.*
A status report may cover an individual, a firm or a company. Information will be given on reputation, financial resources, credit dealings, likely intention to pay and similar facts. Some idea of the extent of the organisation may be obtained from a study of the main sources of information; viz.:

(*a*) Credit records.
All relevant facts relating to credit-standing are filed in the records of the LAPT. Balance sheets of public companies, company registrations and liquidations, county court judgments, mortgages of companies, bankruptcies, bills of sale, and overdue and unpaid accounts are all used in writing up a status report.

(*b*) Local correspondents.
In addition to making use of the credit records, extensive use is made of the services of correspondents in the area in which

the would-be buyer has his business. The correspondent checks with local tradesmen and possibly views the buyer's premises and, if necessary, interviews the buyer.

(c) Information is obtained from members of the LAPT and also from affiliated bodies and organisations.

The status report may be compiled in *full* after all possible enquiries have been made. Alternatively, a report based entirely on register searches may be compiled. This can be prepared much more quickly than the full report and is, therefore, much cheaper: moreover it will be quite adequate for establishing creditworthiness in a large number of cases.

Enquiries can be made by post or by telephone; in the latter case a written report will still be sent by the LAPT.

2. *Collection of debts.*

Instead of putting the matter of unpaid debts into the hands of a solicitor it may be desirable, in the interest of maintaining goodwill, to let an organisation which specialises in debt collection take over the task. The LAPT will undertake such an assignment.

### The Hire Purchase Trade Association

The Hire Purchase Trade Association is closely associated with the London Association for Protection of Trade; in fact, they both operate from the same address. The similarity extends into the methods of operating. A register is maintained and members of the association can obtain information on prospective clients; *e.g.* dealers and retailers who wish to be financed by a finance house.

An obvious difference is the nature of the work undertaken by the members. The LAPT members are manufacturers, wholesalers, retailers, mail order houses and others who sell on credit. Members of the HPTA are traders, finance houses and others who sell by means of hire purchase or supply the financial backing for hire purchase transactions.

### Commercial Credit Houses

The commercial credit houses maintain registers and on request supply information on the credit-standing of a firm or company. In addition, various publications are made available by these houses. The most important of these are credit rating books which show the financial and credit standing of each major business by means of a "credit rating." These books are normally supplemented by news letters which report any important changes. Obviously, since the credit rating books are published annually some method of keeping them up-to-date is absolutely essential.

The use of credit rating books can be recommended, especially when a large volume of credit business is transacted. There is a very wide coverage of all medium and large businesses. A sound guide is given when planning a selling campaign of an expensive product which is likely to interest only those companies with a high credit-standing. Perhaps one of the most valuable benefits is the speed with which creditworthiness can be checked: the credit rating can be turned up within minutes.

If a business deals with small retailers, wholesalers or other types of concern whose total purchases are relatively small, credit rating books will not be of any value. Instead, one of the other sources will have to be used.

## ORGANISATION FOR CREDIT CONTROL

The organisation of the Credit Control Department tends to vary from one business to another. Because of differences in the products sold, the volume of trade, the customers dealt with, and the ratio of cash to credit transactions, it is not surprising that organisations do not follow a standard pattern. Obviously the aim should be to build an organisation which is appropriate to the particular business concerned.

One of the first requirements is to appoint an executive to the post of Credit Controller. In a large company the position will be a full-time responsibility; in other cases it can be combined with work of a related nature such as sales ledger accounting. Irrespective of the precise responsibilities the Credit Controller should have a thorough knowledge of the particular trade, be fully conversant with all sources of credit information, be firm yet tactful and, at the same time, be able to analyse all relevant facts relating to a prospective buyer and reach a decision without undue delay.

The purpose of credit control is not to avoid *all* possible bad debts, but rather to *minimise* them as far as possible. If all bad debts were avoided then the business would probably be selling a much smaller volume than could normally be expected. In other words, credit control should consider two aspects: the need to sell and the minimising of bad debts. Both have to be considered so that some form of compromise is reached. A business cannot afford to lose orders which carry with them reasonable risk; nor can the Credit Controller indulge in the fancy that the bad payer is suddenly going to reform for new orders supplied to him. A realistic approach to the problem of accepting credit trade is, therefore, essential.

Because of the conflicting interests of maximum sales and minimum bad debts the Credit Control Department within the organisation is probably best dealt with by being quite separate from either the Sales Department or the Accounts Department proper. There are different views held on this matter. Theoretically the Credit Control Department which is quite separate has much to recommend it. However, from the point of view of practical convenience, many companies find that combining Credit Control with Sales Ledgers is the best plan. When this is done all the necessary records for customers can be entered up in the one department. Moreover, there is available on the one record (*e.g.* the Sales Ledger Card) the credit limit and the actual amount of indebtedness. If there is any unauthorised increase in the balance due then this can be questioned promptly before the matter proceeds to the point where there is a danger of not being able to recover the amount due. In any case the importance of credit control to the liquidity position usually means that the management accountant must be very much concerned with the function.

Irrespective of the place of the Credit Control Department within the organisation, it will be essential to establish a routine for dealing with orders. The object should be to deal with orders as quickly as possible, passing them through the system so that delivery can be made without undue delay. How this is to be accomplished depends very much upon the type of business and whether the orders are sent by post or are collected by salesmen. A typical system may take the form outlined below:

1. Orders are taken by salesmen, by telephone or through the post. In all these cases the information is immediately written, or is transferred, on to the official order.

A number of copies are made at the same time by means of carbon paper. A convenient method is to have the orders in pad form. The precise number of copies will depend upon the system adopted; there may be one for despatch, one for the customer and one for the salesman.

2. When an order is received it should be examined and classified according to the method of payment.

If for cash, then the order should be given immediate attention. If on credit terms, the order should be given a prompt clearance if at all possible.

For an established customer the checking of the credit limit should not involve great difficulty. This may be done in the Credit Control Department, or in the Despatch Department on information received from the Credit Control Department or Sales Ledgers Department.

With the entirely new customer there will be the need to check credit-worthiness. This would be accomplished by one of the methods outlined earlier.

3. Credit limits are established.

The limits to which customers can obtain goods on credit should be fixed very carefully. If there is any doubt as to the amount of credit to be allowed it would appear to be wise to err on the side of permitting a smaller sum—this can be increased later when satisfactory dealings have been established.

Credit limits do not generally remain static. Some businesses expand, others shrink. A vital part of credit control is keeping the credit information up-to-date. The index cards which summarise the financial standing of each customer should be checked and, if necessary, amended. Similarly, Balance Sheets, or even Credit Rating Books, should not be taken at face value: they may be out-of-date and, therefore, of limited value for checking creditworthiness. If the credit limits are placed on the Sales Ledger Cards then any change in status should be noted immediately on these cards.

Examination of news letters from trade protection associations, salesmen's reports, overdue accounts statements and the *Board of Trade Gazette* and other journals for details of liquidations, deeds of arrangement, bankruptcies and similar occurrences will also be essential. Any relevant facts can then be noted on the credit control files.

Some of the methods which may be used for establishing credit limits are:

(*a*) A "sample order" is accepted on credit terms for a small amount. If the customer meets his commitments he may be allowed a larger credit limit. This procedure can be followed until a maximum limit, based on one of the other factors outlined below, is reached.

(*b*) The limits permitted by other businesses for the particular customer are ascertained by the use of trade references. A credit limit is then based on the experience of other traders.

(*c*) Balance sheet ratios may be ascertained and then limits set.

(*d*) Credit-agency ratings obtained from credit rating books may be used as the basis for the limits.

These methods cannot replace the systematic collection of information and the exercise of discretion and judgment. Nonetheless, used with caution they may serve as a guide to what are reasonable credit limits. Authorities on credit control suggest referring to a number of key factors when establishing credit limits; these are as follows:

(i) Size of the debtor's business; *i.e.* the capital employed and the sales turnover.

(ii) Efficiency of the management. Sound management is essential. Adequate resources backed by efficiency are the major factors in profit earning.

(iii) Stability of debtor's business. If this is of a highly speculative nature then the credit limit should be kept quite low.

The number of products being made by the debtor is also important. The larger the range of profitable lines the better is the risk spread. Dependence upon a single product may indicate a weak business, although, naturally, much depends upon the *type* of product. Some businesses have gone from strength to strength relying on a single product only.

(iv) Total credit which is reasonable for both creditor and debtor. The Credit Controller must keep the total debts owing to his business at any one time within reasonable limits. A regular inflow of cash to balance the outflow is essential. Working capital must be adequate at all times.

When fixing the amount of credit which is reasonable for the debtor the Credit Controller should try to visualise what rate of turnover the debtor is likely to get in the goods he is purchasing. In this way the "self-liquidating principle" is followed; the goods, all being well, should provide for their own payment within a reasonable time.

(v) Trade custom. If competitors offer very generous credit terms then there may be a tendency to emulate them. However, this is not a wise policy and may result in "burnt fingers."

There may be other factors. However, from what has been said it should be clear that businesses can be classified according to credit risk. The well-established company with large share capital and sales turnover and no loan capital or other large amount of indebtedness may be classified as "class A" which can be granted credit up to, say, £5000 a month or even more with special sanction from the Board of Directors. Other businesses could be graded into B, C, D, and E or, if necessary, even further subdivisions. Those who do not manage to scrape into "class E" may have orders accepted on C.O.D. terms or possibly on a sample basis as described earlier in this section.

4. When orders have been despatched, invoices should be forwarded to customers without delay and then postings should be made with equal speed in the sales ledgers.

Speed of posting is essential, otherwise there may be a danger that additional orders could be accepted which are in excess of a stated credit limit.

5. Debts should be collected as quickly as possible.

How quickly debts can normally be gathered in depends upon the terms of sale. The latter will generally be determined by the customs which exist in the particular trade and the liquidity position at the particular time. If there is a shortage of cash the payment of a cash discount may be advisable. On the other hand, if a business has more ready cash than it can use, there may be little justification for awarding cash discounts.

Cash discount recognises that there are two types of customers; those who pay cash within a reasonable time (*e.g.* 7 days) and those who expect to be financed for as long as possible. The latter are charged an extra amount, whereas those who pay cash are given a cash discount, this representing the charge made for financing the customer.

A method frequently used for reminding customers that payment is overdue is the issue of monthly statements. There is no doubt that some debtors expect monthly statements and will not pay until they are received. On the other hand, preparation of statements can involve a good deal of work. Furthermore, if they are to be of value in debt collection, the statements should be sent promptly at the end of each month and not some time after. Some companies adopt a compromise and send out statements to debtors who have owed money for a month. Obviously, if a large number of statements is to be prepared then some form of accounting machine will generally be essential.

An alternative method is to spread out the preparation of statements, different customers having different settlement days. The division may be based on the alphabet, the "As" being prepared one day, the "Bs" the next, and so on. Another variation is to prepare statements up to the end of the first week for one ledger; the second ledger would then be dealt with the second week and, in this way, assuming there are four ledgers, all would be covered in the month. This procedure of "staggering" the preparation of statements is known as "cycle billing."

When accounts are overdue, prompt action should be taken, but the exercise of tact will be essential. The credit controller should know from experience which debtors are slow payers. He should also be aware of what attitude to adopt when attempting to collect the overdue account. If the debtor is a good customer then care has to be taken not to lose his trade. On the other hand, in some circumstances failure to take prompt action may result in a bad debt.

The methods used for reminding customers that payment is overdue are many and varied. Printed tags in a distinctive colour may be affixed to the statement, or a rubber stamp may be employed, to show that payment is expected immediately. A more direct and personal approach is obtained by issuing overdue account statements to salesmen who are then expected to call on the customers concerned and collect the accounts due. A similar collection could be carried out by a credit control clerk. A further alternative is to send a politely worded letter asking for the account which has apparently been overlooked to be settled as soon as possible. When these normal methods fail, resort to a debt collector or a trade protection association so that the amount can be collected by a specialist may be necessary. In the last resort, the matter may be put into the hands of a solicitor. This is a serious step to take for it is often a sure sign that a customer has been lost. Rather than do this some companies have been known to permit the defaulting customer to have further orders for cash only and at the same time he is expected to pay off his outstanding account by instalments. In this way, the custom is retained and, provided the instalments are paid, a bad debt is avoided. This practice may be used when there is a genuine case of hardship such as may be experienced by the small retailer, due to illness or similar reason. However, this action is not to be recommended as a *regular* feature of credit control.

If all action to recover the debts has failed, they should be written off and the sales ledger and credit files should be noted so that there is no danger of credit being allowed to defaulters in the future. In any case, there is the necessity to show debtors at a realistic figure on the balance sheet. Naturally this can be done by creating a bad debts provision, the latter being based on a percentage of the sundry debtors at the end of the year. However, this is a convention which does not excuse careful watchfulness on credit at all times. A method of keeping management informed on the position is to prepare a Debtors Analysis Schedule, an example of which is shown below (Fig. 105).

## DEBTOR'S ANALYSIS SCHEDULE
### as at 30th June, 19...

| | Current Balances | Overdue Accounts | | | | Bad Debts | Remarks |
|---|---|---|---|---|---|---|---|
| | | 1 month | 2–3 months | 4–6 months | Over 6 months | | |
| | £ | £ | £ | £ | £ | £ | |
| Sundry Debtors Ayres, L. | 30,000 | 40 | | | | | Cheque promised. |
| Barnes & Co. | | | 30 | | | | Orders for C.O.D. only. |
| Body, M. | | 30 | | | | | |
| Crowther, C. | | 20 | | | | | |
| Dove, G. Ltd. | | | | 50 | | | Trade Protection Assoc. collecting |
| Dover, R. | | | 40 | | | | Cheque promised. |
| Evans Drills Ltd. | | | | | 2,000 | | Court Action pending. |
| Fox, L. | | | | | 50 | 50 | Irrecoverable. |
| Gardner Ropes Ltd. | | 500 | | | | | Query on Invoice now settled. |
| Smith & Co. | | 30 | | | | | |
| Thomas, S. | | | 50 | | | | Cheque promised. |
| Wade & Co. | | 30 | | | | | Investigating. |
| | £30,000 | 1,000 | 200 | 100 | 2,100 | 150 | |

| Significant Ratios | £ | Ratio |
|---|---|---|
| Total Sales: | | — |
| Credit Sales: | | — |
| Credit Sales to date: | | |
| Debtors: | | — |
| Creditors: | | — |
| Debtors: | | — |

FIG. 105.—*Example of a Debtors Analysis Schedule*

The analysis shown on the Schedule may be varied to meet particular needs. Ratios may be shown at the foot of the schedule: some of these are indicated. The relationships expressed by the ratios may vary according to the nature of the business concerned. If one month's credit is allowed the ratio of credit sales to debtors should be in the region of six to one at the end of June, seven to one at the end of July and so on, assuming that the financial year runs from 1st January to 31st December. Seasonal trade may affect the ratios.

## CONTROL OF CASH DISCOUNTS

If cash discounts are included in the terms of sales then care should be taken to ensure that they are only allowed when justified. Sometimes the easiest way out is taken. If a debtor deducts a cash discount—say, 2½ per cent for 7 days when he pays on the ninth day—then the simplest way for the credit controller is to allow the discount and say nothing to the debtor. However, this is not "control"; certainly not by the credit controller. Indeed, if the debtors are allowed to do as they please, they are controlling.

A firm, yet fair policy is essential. Once the debtor understands this policy, he is likely to act within its framework and only deduct the cash discounts to which he is entitled. Moreover, contrary to what some salesmen appear to believe, there should be no loss of goodwill.

When cash is collected by salesmen they should follow the rules laid down for allowing cash discounts. Bank paying-in statements should be checked to ensure that there is no relaxation.

If remittances from debtors are received by post a normal practice is to keep the envelope for proof of the date of posting, this being the date taken for determining the rate of cash discount, if any, which may be deducted from the amount due. The remittance may be taken by the cashier, the envelope being attached to the account returned by the debtor, or if the account is not returned details of the debtor and account paid may be entered on the envelope by the postal room supervisor or cashier. Subsequently the returned account and/or envelope may be used as the medium for posting in the sales ledgers.

## BUDGETING FOR CREDIT CONTROL

Just as with any other function, budgeting for credit control—debtors, cash discounts and bad debts—is essential. Ideal ratios are normally established and these form an integral part of the Budgetary Control System. The cash budget is affected vitally by the credit control policy; any slowness in collecting debts may mean that budgeted plans will not be realised and profit may be reduced. A simple calculation of the debtors' and related figures is shown below.

|  |  | £ |
|---|---|---|
| Debtors at the beginning of the Year |  | 6,000 |
| Sales for the Year (forecast) NET |  | 80,000 |
|  |  | 86,000 |
|  | £ |  |
| Estimated Cash Discount | 1,200 |  |
| Estimated Cash Receivable | 80,000 | 81,200 |
| Estimated Debtors at end of Year |  | £4,800 |

The sales for the year are shown at "net"; *i.e.* after deducting bad debts. This sales figure will be the one used in the sales forecast and subsequently in the sales budget. A further breakdown in the figures will be essential. The estimated figure for debtors at the end of the year may not be the same from one month to another. This will clearly be so when sales are of a seasonal nature. The ideal ratio between sales and debtors for each period should be part of the budgetary control system. Any sharp deviation from this norm will call for management action.

## CREDIT INSURANCE

An essential part of credit control is to determine what insurance cover should be obtained for possible bad debts. Accountants are not altogether in accord on this matter. Some argue that, provided full use is made of credit information, there should be very few bad debts and, therefore, the insurance premiums would exceed any likely claims. When general trade conditions are good this argument may be reasonably sound. However, this reasoning can be used to exclude the use of all insurance. There is no doubt that if a prudent policy is to be followed then credit insurance is just as essential as any other insurance.

When considering overseas trade the risks of incurring bad debts may be multiplied. There is not only the creditworthiness of the overseas debtor to consider—and this is difficult enough to determine—but there are also political risks. There may be change of government or import restrictions imposed or some restriction placed upon the transfer of currency; these and other risks all increase the possibility of incurring bad debts.

The facilities available for insuring against bad debts are considered under the headings: (1) Home Credit Insurance and (2) Overseas Credit Insurance.

### HOME CREDIT INSURANCE*

Like any other insurance the main object of credit insurance is to cover risk. In this case the risk is the possibility of not being able to recover debts due to insolvency of the debtor or other reason which prevents him from paying his account.

Avoiding bad debts can result in many advantages to the flourishing business. These are as follows:

1. Backed by credit information, credit insurance *completes* the credit control system.

2. Plans made can be carried out with more confidence because there is no danger that bad debts will deplete working capital to an extent that would cause financial difficulties.

Any bad debts are normally indemnified to an extent of 75 to 85% of the full amount due.

* Much of this section is based on information kindly given by the Credit Insurance Association Limited.

3. Banks, acceptance houses and others, who are concerned with providing short-term finance, may prefer the debts to be covered by credit insurance.

4. Attempts can be made to expand sales even in periods when, due to adverse trade conditions, risks are quite great. If credit insurance is not employed, the fear of incurring debts may be the prime consideration with the result that goods will not be sold.

There may be other, subsidiary advantages. The most important is possibly the increased confidence that the insurance can give to the management of a business.

Many types of policy exist to meet particular circumstances. However, two principal types may be distinguished.

There is the Whole Turnover policy which covers total turnover for the period of twelve months, the latter being the normal policy period, though if desired a three-year policy can be arranged. Premiums on this policy are expressed as a rate of so many shillings per £100 of turnover and are payable on total turnover with the exception of the turnover of associated companies and that of government departments, nationalised industries and local authorities—these are deemed to be free of risk. The premium rate varies from one business to another. This is to be expected because of varying circumstances. Much depends upon the nature of the product being sold, the spread of business, the credit control system, the credit-standing of the buyers and the past record of the business. On average the rates are in the region of £0·125 to £0·50. %. However, these are approximate figures only and higher or lower rates may operate dependent upon the insurance company and the insured.

The second principal type of policy is the Specific Account Policy whereby a trader can cover any account which involves a large amount of indebtedness. Again the premium will be determined by circumstances.

Which type of policy—Whole Turnover or Specific Account—should be used depends upon the nature of the business concerned. Apparently there is a tendency to prefer the Whole Turnover and there is no doubt that this gives the maximum possible cover and, accordingly, is very suitable for a business which has a small to medium number of accounts each representing a fairly substantial sum of money. In these circumstances the failure to recover one of the outstanding accounts could be quite serious; hence the need to cover the total turnover. However, if a business deals with thousands of customers, each account representing a relatively small sum, as would be the case when distributing through small retailers, then the Whole Turnover policy in its normal form may not give the most appropriate cover at the lowest cost. In such circumstances, a few failures may be absorbed, the bad debts involving only small losses. If the business agrees to meet these "normal" losses, the insurance company only being required to indemnify when a stated sum has been lost, then a much lower premium would be payable. Having the insured bear the first loss to a stated amount is a feature of many types of insurance. In the case of credit insurance there is provided, with the modified policy, a definite protection against heavy losses which may be brought about by a trade recession or, oddly enough, even at the peak of a boom for it is then that many businesses are launched on inadequate capital with the danger of them incurring bad debts.

When a business has a large number of small accounts and a few large ones, then the Specific Account Policy will probably be appropriate. The large sums can be covered against loss, whereas the small accounts, if lost, can be borne by the business itself.

In addition to the cover described, additional risks may also be insured against; e.g. the risk of a seller failing to deliver goods for which he has already been paid or the possible loss on work-in-progress.

### OVERSEAS CREDIT INSURANCE

Credit insurance is a vital part of overseas trading. Any exporter generally faces far more risks than does the seller in the home market. In addition to the possible insolvency of the buyer there are many political risks, covered below, which increase the danger of incurring bad debts.

The facilities for insuring overseas trade fall into two categories:

1. The Export Credits Guarantee Department, which is a Government Department established solely to assist British exporters.

2. Private Insurance Companies.

The cover given by private companies is similar to that described in the previous section which deals with Home Credit Insurance.

#### Export Credits Guarantee Department (ECGD)*

The Export Credits Guarantee Department does not exist to subsidise exports; its object is to assist exporters by offering export credit insurance at rates which enable the Department to operate on a sound commercial basis. The principles are:

1. Sound insurance principles are followed, thus making ECGD self-supporting.

2. The business supported is of the kind which has a fair prospect of being settled within a reasonable period—bad debts are not encouraged.

3. The exporter should be assisted as far as possible to make him competitive with suppliers overseas.

*The Risks Covered.* The precise risks covered depend upon the type of policy which is taken out by the exporter to meet his particular needs. However, the following may be taken as a general guide:

* This general description of ECGD should not be regarded as an exhaustive account of its work. Exporters wishing to make use of the facilities are advised to write to ECGD for full details of the policy required or to raise specific queries.

"Insolvency of the buyer.

Buyer's failure to pay within six months of due date for goods which he has accepted.

Buyer's default on contract after shipment (where not caused or excused by exporter's actions), and, where the buyer is a government, such default before shipment.

Government action which blocks or delays transfer of payment in sterling to the exporter.

Imposition of new import licensing restrictions in the buyer's country, or cancellation of a valid import licence.

War between the buyer's country and the U.K.

War, revolution, or civil disturbance in the buyer's country.

Cancellation or non-renewal of a U.K. export licence, or imposition of new export licensing restrictions.

Additional handling, transport, or insurance charges arising from interruption or diversion of voyage which cannot be recovered from the buyer.

Any other cause of loss occurring outside the U.K. and not within the control of the exporter or the buyer, and not normally insurable with commercial insurers."*

Any possible loss due to fluctuations in exchange rates is *not* covered.

*Types of Policy.* The types of export credit insurance policy which are available are:

1. Comprehensive Guarantee.

2. Comprehensive Guarantee (Shipments).

Both these policies ((1) and (2)) are intended to cover exports sold on short-term credit; *i.e.* for payment within a period not exceeding six months. The first policy covers the risks from the date of contract until payment is actually received. On the other hand, the second type of policy takes effect from the time of shipment so that any pre-shipment risks are *not* covered (these *are* covered with the normal Comprehensive Guarantee policy). The second type of policy (2) is slightly cheaper than the first (1).

Certain engineering goods can obtain cover for sales which are expected to be paid for within a period not exceeding 5 years through an Extended Terms Endorsement to these policies. Examples of these engineering goods are commercial vehicles, medium range machine tools and agricultural tractors.

3. Specific Policies.

Specific policies are for individual transactions involving capital goods which are sold on credit of three years or more after shipment. Large units of plant and machinery are typical examples of the kind of business covered by these policies. Where there is evidence that a

* Source: Booklet entitled *Payment Secured* issued by ECGD.

foreign competitor has official support in offering credit in excess of five years, ECGD will generally match these terms.

In addition, for contracts to the value of £2 million or more (£1 million in the case of ships) *Financial Guarantees* have been introduced. ECGD will guarantee the full amount of the repayment by instalments of any loan advanced to an *overseas* buyer by a U.K. financial institution such as a bank. The buyer is expected to find an initial down-payment and normally a final payment out of his own funds. The balance may be borrowed from the U.K. institution and covered by ECGD. These guarantees are only available when the Government is of the opinion that there is need for long-term finance and that the transaction involved is likely to be beneficial to the U.K. economic position. The goods to be covered are high-value capital goods (including ships) and major construction projects. In very exceptional circumstances an important project may be financed from Government funds.

A further service is the *Buyer Credit* facility which is in some respects an extension of the *Financial Guarantees* facility. The aim is to guarantee a loan made by a British bank or financial institution direct to an overseas buyer, to enable him to pay cash for goods and services performed. Contracts coming under this heading would be for capital goods in excess of £1 million.

4. Services Policies.

These cover the risks incurred by a business providing services abroad as distinct from physical goods. For example, insurance premiums, shipping freights, royalty and copyright payments and also payments for British consultants service on the building of bridges, dams and similar projects are service earnings and, therefore, may be covered by these policies.

5. Guarantees to Banks.

In conjunction with his normal policy, an exporter can for a small extra charge obtain finance in credit transactions. Where a contract involves credit of 30 days to two years ECGD will give a 100% unconditional guarantee to the financing bank against loss from non-payment by the overseas buyer of a bill of exchange or promissory note or by failure of the exporter to meet the bank's interest charges (Bank Rate with a minimum of $4\frac{1}{2}\%$). For those contracts involving credit of two years or more ECGD will also give a guarantee to the bank, facilitating at a fixed rate of $5\frac{1}{2}\%$.

A further facility under this heading is the *Comprehensive (Open Account) Bank Guarantee*. Finance is guaranteed for short-term export transaction on "open account." The banker advances money to the exporter (90% of the net invoice) for which a promissory note is given. If the exporter fails to honour his obligation ECGD will pay the bank and in turn have recourse to the exporter.

6. External Trade Policies.

There are two types of External Trade Policy: one which gives cover from date of contract and the other from the date of shipment only. There is some similarity between these, and the Comprehensive Guarantee and Comprehensive Guarantee (Shipments) policies. The difference lies in the nature of the business covered, and the cause of loss under external trade policies is severely restricted.

The policies cater "for U.K. merchants trading in raw materials, consumer or durable goods of *overseas origin* (provided their sale does not prejudice that of similar U.K. products) sold on terms of payment not normally exceeding 180 days credit."*

7. The Small Exporter Policy.

A small exporter is a firm with an *export* turnover of less than £10,000 per annum. The Small Exporter Policy is designed to encourage the small business to sell overseas. All normal risks are covered, but the procedures have been designed so that the small exporter can insure a *single* buyer. This is fundamentally different from cover under a Comprehensive policy where an exporter is required to insure either all his export trade or at least a spread of markets agreed with ECGD.

8. Other Policies.

In addition to the policies listed above there are special forms of cover including those designed for the sale of ships and aircraft, for sales from overseas subsidiary companies and stockholding abroad.

*Premium Payable.* The premium charged on a policy (with the exception of the Small Exporter policy and Bankers Guarantee or shorter credit which have a flat rate of premium) will vary according to the market and credit period involved. Over the years most premium rates have been substantially reduced. Today, the average cost of insuring all business on up to six months credit is around £0·25 to £0·30 per £100.

In accordance with normal insurance practice an exporter has to retain an interest in the transaction and for this reason ECGD provides up to a maximum of 95% cover.

*All* policies except Guarantees to banks cover 90% of loss due to the buyer becoming insolvent or if, for any other reason, he fails to pay within six months of the due date.

When loss is incurred for a reason other than insolvency or default of the buyer then the cover under a Comprehensive Guarantee is 90% when the loss occurs before export and 95% if after export. An exception to this is where the buyer wilfully does not take delivery of the goods: the exporter must bear a first loss of 20% of the contract price and ECGD bears 90% of the *balance*.

In the case of specific Policies all losses are covered to the extent of 90%.

* Quoted from leaflet issued by ECGD on External Trade Policies.

Y

The Small Exporter Policy gives 90% cover whether the loss is due to the buyer's insolvency or default or other reasons which are outside the control of the buyer or seller. A full list of the risks generally covered is given on pages 652–3.

*Business to be Covered.* As a general rule, the Comprehensive policies are designed to cover the whole of an exporter's overseas business. However, there are exceptions to this. Insurance to cover a limited range of markets may be possible if ECGD is satisfied that there is a reasonable spread of risks. A second exception is The Small Exporter Policy which may cover a single buyer.

*Settlement of Claims.* When claims are settled by ECGD depends upon the *reason* for the claim being made.

A claim because of insolvency of the buyer is settled immediately insolvency is established. When delay in payment is the cause of the claim, payment will be made by ECGD six months after the due date of the account.

If there is default before delivery, the buyer refusing to accept the goods, then the claim will be settled one month after resale of the goods.

When a claim arises from some cause other than those given immediately above, settlement is normally effected four months after due date of payment or date of event causing loss.

For guarantees to banks ECGD will pay unconditionally three months after due date if the buyer fails to pay an accepted bill or note.

*Finance and Export Credit Insurance.* Although the ECGD does not provide the finance for overseas trade it can be instrumental in enabling an exporter to obtain finance from banks or similar sources. The clearing banks are covering up to five years at a fixed rate of $5\frac{1}{2}\%$ irrespective of the changes in the Bank Rate, whereas insurance companies are lending for periods exceeding five years at a constant rate of $6\frac{1}{2}\%$. This is a major step both for banks and insurance companies, especially since the interest rates are fixed and the finance is being provided for fairly long periods to cover the export of capital goods.

## EXAMINATION QUESTIONS

1. A company manufacturing branded food products sells to a large number of wholesalers and retailers of varying size both at home and overseas. Describe the credit control policy which you would recommend the company to follow and outline the methods by which it would be operated.
(*I.C.W.A.*)

2. What organisations exist to help the exporter of capital goods who must grant medium term or long term credit to his customers? Explain the special contribution of each. (*A.C.C.A.*)

3. Assuming your own data, prepare for submission to the managing director a brief report on the efficiency of the Credit Department of the business for the year to the 31st March, 19... Details of monthly sales, debtors and cash collections are available for your use. (*S.C.A.*)

# CHAPTER 25

# STOCK VALUATION

## *INTRODUCTION*

THIS chapter is concerned with the valuation of stock-in-trade and work-in-progress. The topic is of great importance for a number of reasons:

1. The desire to show a true and fair view of the operations for a particular year in terms of profit earned.

Changing the basis of valuing stocks of raw materials or work-in-progress can affect the figure shown for profit. Accordingly, there is general agreement that, once the most suitable method of valuing has been determined, this should be used consistently.

Arising from (1) above, there are other factors which may be affected:

2. Profit earned affects the tax payments due in respect of a particular year.

3. The capital of a business, expressed in *real terms* (*see* Chapter 27), is affected by the method of pricing issues from the Stores. Some methods use actual costs and, therefore, tend to overstate profit in a period of rising prices. Others attempt to employ current material prices and, therefore, to charge replacement costs, thus more truly stating the profit earned in a particular period.

4. The price of shares of a company tends to be affected by the cyclical movements of profits.

5. Optimism or pessimism may be induced by the profit earned in a particular year. This can have far-reaching effects on the attitude of directors and lending institutions such as banks, leading, in turn, to expansion or reduction of production capacity. In short, there tends to be a close link between trade recessions and profit-earning.

These are only a few of the factors which may be affected by the profit earned and, therefore, stock valuation. Obviously, the latter is not the only matter which affects profit, but it is sufficiently important to warrant very serious consideration.

## *ESSENTIALS OF THE PROBLEM*

In dealing with the question of stock valuation it is possible to cover the essential aspects in a logical sequence. A suggested approach is outlined below:

1. Select the appropriate method of computing cost for each type of material held in the Stores; *i.e.* select the pricing method for issues.

This deals with the direct material cost plus any other direct expenditure such as transport costs or storekeeping costs.

2. Determine what overhead costs, if any, should be included in the valuation of stocks.

In considering these two questions regard must be had to the best current practice as formulated by the accountancy profession and the views of the Commissioners of Inland Revenue.

## COMPUTING COST

The computation of cost refers to the determination of the most appropriate method of pricing the material requisitions. The prices charged on material requisitions are reflected in the material costs charged to production. Any stocks remaining are generally valued at the cost remaining in the stores ledger at the end of the period. There are exceptions to the latter statement; thus, for example, when Standard Costing is employed the charges to production and the basis for stock valuation should be the same.

In selecting a method of pricing material issues attention should be paid to the following points:

1. Ease of pricing and operation of stores ledger.
2. Effect of using the method on the profit figure calculated.
3. Acceptance by the Commissioners of Inland Revenue.

It should be appreciated that the faster the turnover of the stocks of raw material the less important will tend to be the choice of method. If materials are purchased today and used tomorrow then it will be of little importance whether average price, last in first out, first in first out, or another method is employed. On the other hand, if material is in stock six months before being used, then the choice of method becomes of great significance.

The matter of indicating how profits will be affected by the method of pricing is far from easy. How costs and selling prices are related to each other will affect the position. The position of the trade cycle, whether on the upward or downward swing, is also of significance. This is a complex subject and here it is only possible to indicate tendencies in a general sort of way.

The diagram given (Fig. 106) summarises the principal methods available for pricing and relates each one to the points (1) to (3) listed in this section. Generally speaking the method of pricing adopted in this country will be selected from: the weighted average price; first in first out; or standard price. The remarks made on whether a method is acceptable for taxation purposes are only intended as a guide. There is no definite code of practice which applies to *every* business; from time to time exceptions will arise and any new cases may affect the position.

Once the most suitable method of pricing has been selected it should be employed in a proper fashion and consistently.

## INCLUSION OF OVERHEADS IN STOCKS

A question which arises in connection with valuation of stocks of work-in-progress and finished goods is whether or not overhead costs should be part of the valuation. It has been decided in the Duple Motor Bodies Case* that any method which is based on facts which can be established may be acceptable for valuation purposes. This case dealt with the valuation of work-in-progress. It was held that the latter could be valued on a direct cost basis, thus following the practice carried on for many years.

In effect, therefore, there are three principal methods which may be adopted for valuation:

1. Prime cost; *i.e.* direct labour, direct material and direct expense.

All overhead costs whether fixed or variable would be *excluded* from the valuation and so should be written off within the period in which they are incurred.

2. Prime cost and variable overhead costs.

This would be the costs in (1) together with all overheads which tend to vary with changes in output. An alternative description would be the "marginal costs valuation." Reference should be made to Chapter 10, "Marginal Costing," when the effect on profit of using this method or (3) below can be seen.

3. Total Cost; *i.e.* prime cost plus an appropriate amount for fixed and variable overhead costs.

This is the "total cost" basis. Alternative terms are "full cost" or "absorption cost" method.

Many writers have taken the decision in the Duple Motor Bodies Case as indicating a victory for the supporters of Marginal Costing. In actual fact, it is a victory to no one body of opinion, unless to sound common sense. What is now clear is that, provided the method adopted gives a true and fair view of the profit or loss for the year, this is acceptable. Recommendation No. 22† of the Institute of Chartered Accountants reaffirms this view by stating:

"Circumstances vary so widely that no one basis of arriving at the amount is suitable for all types of business nor even for all undertakings within a particular trade or industry. Unless the basis adopted is appropriate to the circumstances of the particular undertaking and used consistently from period to period, the accounts will not give

---

* Ostime *v.* Duple Motor Bodies Ltd. ((1961) 2 All E.R. 167).
† Recommendation on Accounting Principles, No. 22. Treatment of Stock-in-Trade and Work-in-Progress in Financial Accounts.

| Method of Pricing | Brief Definition | Ease of Pricing and Stores Ledger | Likely Effect on Profit | Acceptance by Inland Revenue* | Remarks |
|---|---|---|---|---|---|
| Average Cost (normally weighted average price) | Purchases of each type of material in stock are taken together and an average price computed. | If prices fluctuate considerably many calculations will be involved. It is usual to calculate a new average after each delivery. The pricing book, if used, and the stores ledger will require frequent amendment. | Average prices are charged and, therefore, whether the charges to production represent current replacement costs depends on the turnover of the stocks. In a period of rising prices slow turnover will tend to mean that costs which are lower than present day costs will be charged. In these circumstances there is an overstatement of profit.* | Average cost may be regarded as actual cost and is, therefore, acceptable as a basis for stock valuation. | In appropriate circumstances the use of the average cost will have a stabilising effect on prices used for issues and, therefore, profit. |
| Base Stock Method | Issues are priced at actual cost. There is, however, a minimum quantity of stock maintained, which is always regarded as a fixed asset. This minimum stock is carried forward at the end of each year at the original price paid when the business commenced to operate, which may have been many years ago. | This method may operate in roughly the same way as FIFO, but excluding the base stock. | As for FIFO; however, base stock valued at original price so, therefore, in this respect it is similar to LIFO. | Not acceptable (Patrick v. Broadstone Mills Ltd., (35 T.C. 44; 32 ATC 332)). | |

| | | | | |
|---|---|---|---|---|
| *First In, First Out* FIFO | Items received first are assumed to be used first and, therefore, the prices charged are those paid for the early purchases. | Prices charged are actual prices and, therefore, there is no question of having to re-calculate a new price each time a new purchase is received. Care has to be taken to ensure that each quantity is issued at the correct price. | If prices are rising costs of products will be understated and, therefore, profit will tend to be overstated. On the other hand, stock valuations should approximate current replacement values. | Acceptable. | The need to maintain capital intact in real terms in a period of inflation has tended to make accountants stress the value of LIFO. |
| *Last In, First Out* LIFO | Items received last are assumed to be issued first, and, therefore, the latest prices paid are used. | As for FIFO. | When prices are rising profit is not overstated. If turnover is rapid the charges to production should be near enough to current replacement prices. | Apparently not acceptable (Minister of National Revenue v. Anaconda American Brass Ltd., 1955). It is not clear what would be decided by the Courts if the stock held had been recently acquired, The Courts take the view that the method employed should "as nearly as possible accord with the facts".* | |
| *Standard Cost* | Material prices are predetermined with the object of showing what they *should be* at the expected level of efficiency. (See Chapter 2, section on Standard Costing.) | The pricing of Material Requisitions can be avoided and stores ledgers can be kept in terms of quantities. This can result in considerable savings in clerical labour. | The same prices will be charged to production and for valuing stocks of raw materials. Profit figures should be more realistic than when other methods are used. | Acceptable *provided* the standard costs are reasonably accurate and are not out-of-date. The view taken is that the standard costs approximate actual costs.* | The use of standard costs has much to offer and, therefore, when standard costing is employed this method of computing material cost is strongly recommended. |

* See *The Accountant* dated February 17th, 1962, an article entitled: "Stock Valuation—The Revenue's View," by H. G. THOMAS.

FIG. 106.—*Computation of Cost: the pricing of Material Issues*

a true and fair view either of the state of affairs of the undertaking as on the balance sheet date or of the trend of its trading results from period to period. The need to give a true and fair view is the over-riding consideration applicable in all circumstances."

There is no doubt that direct expenditure on the purchase and acquiring of stocks should be included in a valuation. What the accountant has to decide is what proportion, if any, of overhead costs can be "deferred" by inclusion in stock valuation.

## CLASSIFICATION OF OVERHEAD COSTS

Recommendation No. 22 classifies overhead expenditure into the following groups:

1. Production Expenses.
2. Administration Expenses.
3. Selling Expenses.
4. Finance Charges.

These are then subdivided into (a) fixed overheads and (b) variable overheads.

Which of these overhead costs should be included in the value of stock depends upon the type of business and the circumstances and conditions which exist. Apparently there is general agreement that selling and finance costs should not be included. This rule should logically also apply to distribution costs.

Production overhead costs and, possibly, administration overhead costs may be recovered in the cost of the products. This remark may apply to total overheads or only to variable overheads. In deciding which approach should be made, Recommendation No. 22 suggests that all relevant matters should be considered in reaching a decision. Once decided upon the method should be used consistently.

Examples of matters which may be considered are: the nature of the business; the levels of production and sales; exceptional disruption of production; risks of realisation at a loss; maturing stocks; long-term contracts and the extent of the variation in fixed costs.

If levels of production and sales are subject to wide fluctuations this means that one year may have very large stocks whereas another has small stocks. Accordingly, it is probably better to exclude the overhead costs from the valuation of stock.

When there has been an exceptional curtailment of output due to a strike, a fire, or a trade recession, overhead costs recovered, it is felt, should not exceed those which would be recovered on a basis of normal capacity (see Chapter 2, regarding what is meant by "normal capacity"). In other words, any abnormal events should not bring about the valuation of stock at an unrealistically high figure. This follows the normal rule that abnormal costs, such as under-absorption of overhead costs due to the existence of idle facilities, should be written off to the profit and loss account in the period in which they are incurred.

In a business which is in a very competitive industry, where there is a danger that the full costs may not be recovered in the price, *exclusion* of overhead costs would be the safest procedure. Recommendation No. 22 quotes businesses dealing in "fashion" goods as an example.

When stocks are held for a long period so that they may mature it is a common practice to exclude fixed overhead costs. This is on the grounds that the recovery of the latter in the selling price may be uncertain. Examples of stocks which mature are whisky, wine and timber.

On the question of long-term contracts the Institute points out in the Recommendation that a consistent and regular application of overheads is essential to avoid wide fluctuations in profit from one year to another. Provided, therefore, that overheads are recoverable in the price they can be included in the value of stocks. Part of the relevant section is reproduced below:

> *"Long-term contracts*
>
> In businesses which undertake contracts extending over a period of years the normal tendency is to include overhead expenditure in work in progress except where it is considered to be irrecoverable. If overheads are not included in work in progress on such contracts the accounts for the early years may indicate losses, followed by unduly large profits in the years when the contracts are completed. This would be a wholly unrealistic presentation in relation to a contract showing a normal profit. . . ."

The final point—the extent of the variation in fixed costs—is of significance to the subject of Marginal Costing. If the fixed costs are definitely *fixed*, not varying at all with changes in output and, therefore, being incurred on a time basis, they are probably better excluded from the valuation. Put another way the fixed costs should be written off to Profit and Loss Account in the period in which they are incurred. In effect, therefore, in the circumstances envisaged—constant fixed costs— it would seem that the Institute advocates a Marginal Costing approach to stock valuation.

However, this is not as straightforward as at first sight it appears. Over a long period—a number of years—*all* costs are variable costs. Even fixed costs vary; as policy changes it is inevitable that these costs change. Expansion of production facilities; a change in the organisation; the acquisition of a computer and any other radical change will bring about a variation in fixed costs. Accordingly, before coming to any conclusion on whether or not the Institute favours Marginal Costing, the period the Council had in mind when drafting Recommendation

No. 22 would have to be known. The relevant section of the Recommendation is as follows:

"(*g*) *The extent of the variation in fixed or standing charges*
The less the fixed or standing charges vary in amount with variations in the volume of output, and the more they accrue on a purely time basis, the greater is the justification for their exclusion."

As pointed out, over a long period all costs vary, so no final conclusion can be reached from the section as it stands.

## DESCRIPTION OF STOCKS

The normal rule for stock valuation has been for many years "cost or market value whichever is lower." This generally means that, in a period of rising prices, stocks would be shown at cost less any deductions for obsolete or unusable stocks.

Recommendation No. 22 recognises that the term "cost or market value" covers a multitude of possible meanings without being definite on any particular one. A number of alternative descriptions are given and these are summarised below:

### NORMAL BASES

1. "at cost."
2. "at the lower of cost and net realisable value."
3. "at the lowest of cost, net realisable value and replacement price."
4. "at cost less provision to reduce to net realisable value" (or "to the lower of net realisable value and replacement price").

### SPECIAL BASES

5. At selling prices; *i.e.* prices realised subsequent to the balance sheet date less only selling costs. This is a basis customary in some tea, rubber, and mining companies.
6. Long-term contracts including a reasonable proportion of earned profit (provided this is certain).
7. Base stock valuation (defined earlier in this Chapter).
8. Last in, first out (LIFO) (defined earlier).

The appropriate description should be used in the final accounts produced annually. If the word "cost" is used to describe the valuation it is recommended that a clear explanation of what is included in the term should be shown; *i.e.* whether: prime cost only, prime cost plus variable overheads *or* prime cost plus production and administration overhead costs.

In most businesses the Recommendation suggests that descriptions (2) and (3) would be appropriate. In connection with "cost" and these two descriptions the Recommendation contains the following explanations:

The following are the meanings attributed to "cost," "net realisable value" and "replacement price" in this Recommendation:

(*a*) "cost" means all expenditure incurred directly in the purchase or manufacture of the stock and the bringing of it to its existing condition and location, together with such part, if any, of the overhead expenditure as is appropriately carried forward in the circumstances of the business instead of being charged against the revenue of the period in which it was incurred.

(*b*) "net realisable value" means the amount which it is estimated, as on the Balance Sheet date, will be realised from disposal of the stock in the ordinary course of business, either in its existing condition or as incorporated in the product normally sold, after allowing for all expenditure to be incurred on or before disposal.

(*c*) "replacement price" means an estimate of the amount for which in the ordinary course of business the stock could have been acquired or produced either at the Balance Sheet date or in the latest period up to and including that date. In a manufacturing business this estimate would be based on the replacement price of the raw material content plus other costs of the undertaking which are relevant to the condition of the stock on the Balance Sheet date.

The comparison between cost and net realisable value or replacement price may be made by considering each article separately, or by grouping articles in categories having regard to their similarity or interchangeability, or by considering the aggregate cost of the total stock in relation to its aggregate net realisable value or, as the case may be, aggregate replacement price. The aggregate method involves setting foreseeable losses against unrealised profits on stock and may not be suitable for businesses which carry stocks which are large in relation to turnover.

The Institute recommend that the most appropriate method, once selected, should be employed consistently. Stock should not be omitted* or included at a false figure. There should be no anticipation of profit unless justified by a special basis; in all cases there should be provision made for losses. The method selected should be such that the accounts show a true and fair view of the trading results and the financial position. Finally, if a change in the basis or method of valuing stocks is necessary because of changed circumstances, then, if material, the fact that a change has been made should be shown by way of note in the Profit and Loss Account.

* This does not apply to stocks which are of no value due to obsolescence or other reasons.

## EXAMINATION QUESTIONS

1. In valuing inventories should Standard cost be used instead of Actual cost, or market price, if the Standard cost be lower than either of these? State your reasons. *(I.C.W.A.)*

2. Write brief notes on stock valuation, dealing in particular with the inclusion or exclusion of certain items and different types of overhead. *(I.C.W.A.)*

3. State in tabular form the effects upon production costs and stock values of using each of the three methods of pricing issues from stocks known as:

(*a*) First in first out; (*b*) Average cost; (*c*) Last in first out. *(S.C.A.)*

4. As Cost Accountant in a large factory, draw up a memorandum on stock valuation of raw materials, work-in-progress, and finished goods.

Assume:

(*a*) that market prices of some materials have changed since purchases were made;

(*b*) that departmental rates of overhead absorption include:

  (i) percentage on labour;
  (ii) labour hour rate;
  (iii) machine hour rate;

(*c*) that administration, selling and distribution expenses are usually absorbed as a percentage of production cost. *(I.C.W.A.)*

5. Although stock levels may remain practically the same year by year, circumstances affecting stocks may vary, *e.g.*:

| *Present costs* | *Future possibilities* |
| --- | --- |
| (*a*) prices low | prices likely to rise |
| (*b*) prices high | prices likely to fall |

Draw up a tabulation, providing for the circumstances mentioned, to show four methods of pricing issues, with the effect each method has on current production costs and on year-end valuation of stock. *(I.C.W.A.)*

CHAPTER 26

## DEPRECIATION AND OBSOLESCENCE

### INTRODUCTION

BECAUSE of the necessity of having fiscal years there is the problem of
dividing total costs of fixed assets over their useful lives. A machine
purchased today may have an expected life of 10 years and, therefore,
the original cost should be apportioned over the period, each accounting
year being charged with the appropriate amount. This is the historical
cost approach—ensuring that what has been paid is recovered as a
normal operating expense.

When depreciation is viewed in this sense—the charging of the *actual*
costs—the definition considers only the matter of ensuring that costs
are spread equitably over the life of the assets. Depreciation *accounting*
strictly construed is concerned with the *recording aspect* and valuation
is considered only in an indirect fashion. Put another way the problem
is one of allocation and apportionment, not of asset valuation.

Each year a proportion of the total expense of a fixed asset is written
off, the balance representing the unexpended cost. If possible the *method*
of depreciation selected should result in the correct matching of the
reduction in cost and the amount of the asset "consumed." In practice,
there are many factors which affect the useful life of a fixed asset and,
therefore, the depreciation charge is at best a reasonable estimate.

Changes in the value of money also affect the problem. Fixed assets
purchased, say, 5 years ago and now to be replaced, may cost considerably more than the original purchase. There are two related problems.
The first is the correct calculation of profit—ensuring that capital is
maintained intact. This aspect is covered in the next chapter. Forecasting capital expenditure and cash represents the second factor—
there should be adequate finance to ensure that fixed assets can be
replaced when necessary. A number of earlier chapters discuss this
matter.

This chapter is concerned with the nature of depreciation and the
methods used to ensure its recovery in the accounts. There are a
number of aspects to consider. There is the responsibility of the Board
of directors to ensure that the full cost is recovered over the useful life
of each fixed asset; linked with this is the maintenance of capital, considered from the point of view of equivalent money's worth. A further
aspect is the absorption of the depreciation in the costs of the products
or services, and realistic pricing so that *all* costs are recovered. Disclosure in the published accounts of limited companies is also of great
importance—this has to comply with the legal requirements of the
Companies Acts. Related to this aspect is the reconciliation with the

667

laws relating to taxation—capital allowances and depreciation charges often do not agree and, therefore, adjustments have to be made before the profit can be accepted by the Inspector of Taxes.

These matters are considered below under the following headings:

1. Factors Affecting Depreciation.
2. Methods of Depreciation.
3. Depreciation and Management Decisions.
4. Depreciation in Published Accounts.
5. Depreciation and Taxation Allowances.
6. Depreciation in Practice.

These are considered in the order shown. References to depreciation are also made in other chapters, and a detailed examination of revaluation accounting—the accounting for changes in the value of money as affecting assets—is made in Chapter 27.

## FACTORS AFFECTING DEPRECIATION

As indicated earlier in this chapter there are two problems associated with depreciation accounting.

1. Charging the *original* cost of a fixed asset to specific accounting years and to the products or services.

Often the *total* amounts charged in the cost accounts and financial accounts do agree, but this is not necessarily the case. For managerial decisions economic realities have to be faced and, therefore, a true indication of the usage of a fixed asset may call for inclusion of "costs" which are additional to those based purely on historical figures. The process of charging original cost implies a static situation which is very unlikely to exist in practice.

2. Allowing for changes in the value of money as discussed in Chapter 27.

Dealing with the first problem it should be observed that the accountant has to consider a number of related factors in his estimates. There is the question of the physical properties of the fixed asset. If it is used for a period, by how much has its usefulness been reduced? Similarly, can the assumption be made that the length of time is the determining factor in assessing the useful life of an asset? Intensity of use as well as the time factor should be considered in the selection of a suitable method.

From these observations it should be apparent that there are many aspects to consider, and these are summarised in the tabulation (Fig. 107). The main features are discussed in turn.

### NORMAL PHYSICAL WEAR AND TEAR

The physical usage of an asset tends to be the most important single factor in decreasing its useful life. Parts are worn down by the interaction of friction, vibration, heating and chemical change. While modern lubricants can do a considerable amount to delay wear and tear, the inevitable wearing out process continues with all fixed assets. The rate at which assets *depreciate* will vary with the type of asset, the operating conditions and the intensity at which they are employed. Different rates are generally used to allow for what is the normal expected life of an asset. The repairs and maintenance programme affects the position.

Within reason the life of an asset can be prolonged for a considerable period. Repairs, replacements and periodic maintenance can influence the rate at which an asset will be expected to wear out. Many managers stress the importance of *preventive maintenance*, whereby there is a systematic approach made to routine work on fixed assets so as to keep them in satisfactory condition.

| *Asset* | *Depreciation* | *Possible Reasons* |
|---|---|---|
| *Fixed Asset* | Reduction in | 1. Normal physical wear and tear. |
| Plant | usefulness and, | 2. Custom or usage. |
| Machinery | therefore, in | 3. Abnormal occurrences such as |
| Buildings | value. | accidents, defects in materials or |
| Equipment | | other contingency. |
| | | 4. Technological change and development. |

FIG. 107 *Reasons for Depreciation*

Generally, as a fixed asset becomes older more costs have to be incurred on repairs, replacements and maintenance. In selecting the basis for calculating depreciation a number of observations are relevant:

1. The decline in value of an asset tends to be greater in the earlier years. An asset costing £2000 may be regarded as being worth, say, 25% less after the first year's operations. Later years will not generally show such a rapid rate of depreciation.

2. Costs on repairs increase at a time when the asset is declining in value. The pertinent question is what is the best time to dispose of an asset. Linked with this question is whether a smaller charge for depreciation should be made when repairs are increasing, thus having a reasonably constant charge in each year. This aspect affects the method of depreciation.

3. The useful life of an asset should be defined when the purchase is made. This is a vital question which affects the depreciation and replacement policy as well as estimation of the likely disposable value. A "useful life" is a relative term which is influenced by many factors. Theoretically a fixed asset should be employed so long as it continues to operate efficiently: it should come to an end when an alternative asset is more profitable to operate. Costs, obsolescence, production policy and other considerations will affect the decision.

## CUSTOM OR USAGE

With some types of fixed assets there are customs which have been established on the rate of wear and tear normally expected each year. The best example is to be found with cars and other vehicles, where second-hand prices are published each month. Whilst these prices may not strictly reflect the rate of depreciation which is occurring, they do indicate the extent of the likely occurrence.

The opinions of professional bodies can affect the outlook on depreciation. For example, the Institute of Chartered Accountants in England and Wales have issued a Recommendation (Ref. N9) on the *Depreciation of Fixed Assets*. For general application the Institute favours the straight line method, at the same time recognising that other methods may be appropriate for some classes of assets.

## ABNORMAL OCCURRENCES

Much of the theory and practice relating to depreciation is based on the assumption that it is possible to forecast future events with reasonable certainty. Linked with this notion is the idea that a *normal* rate can be established, thus implying conditions which are not likely to change very much. In fact, of course, in many industries unforeseen circumstances do occur with alarming regularity.

The technological aspects of change are dealt with later in this section. At this stage it is important to notice some of the factors which can shorten the expected life of an asset. Possibilities are as follows:

1. Accidental damage—tools, nuts, bolts or other articles falling into a machine; physical impact caused by dropping or impact with a vehicle; use of wrong materials causing damage; or reckless handling by an inexperienced operator.

2. Excessive wear and tear—climatic conditions such as dampness or the presence of acid or another foreign body which causes damage. In addition, there may be metal fatigue or a similar occurrence brought about by usage in unexpected conditions.

3. Contingent occurrences which accelerate the depreciation process; *e.g.* hairline cracks appearing in boilers which have been adequately tested.

All these factors can affect the amount of depreciation which should be charged if a realistic cost is to be covered in the accounts of the business for each period. This is the case even when dealing with the limited definition which is concerned with the absorption of the *historical* costs. If replacement problems are also considered the issues become extremely complex.

## TECHNOLOGICAL CHANGE AND DEVELOPMENT

The startling progress which has been made in many industries in the last decade can be regarded as significant for the country and the world at large. In plastics, photographic equipment and processes, computers and many other industries the progress has been phenomenal. While the benefits can be recognised there are also many dangers, one of which is *obsolescence* of fixed assets. A machine purchased in anticipation of a useful life of 10 years may suddenly become an uneconomic proposition after being used, say, for 5 years. The accountant has to consider this danger both for the annual accounts and for its influence on management decisions.

There are many influences which should be borne in mind; some of the possibilities are as follows:

1. New products which supersede those already being made.
2. Change in production methods which require different types of fixed asset, such as machine tools.
3. Improved machines which render existing machines quite uneconomical.
4. Inadequacy of a fixed asset to carry out the necessary function.

Some accountants would prefer to see *inadequacy* treated as a separate and distinct cause of depreciation. For example, if an office or factory becomes much too small for the activities being covered, then the asset is said to be inadequate. On the other hand, if it becomes much too costly to maintain and offers conditions which do not comply with modern standards, then the asset has reached the point where it is *obsolete*. The two concepts are very much related: the intensity of use can affect both. For example, if the demand for a product necessitates overtime or double shift operations, then, if likely to be of a permanent nature, consideration should be given to the *adequacy* problem. At the same time, provided overtime working is kept within reasonable limits, the obsolescence factor should be reduced—the shorter life of the fixed asset owing to overtime should ensure that this is the case.

Each industry has its own problems associated with technical obsolescence. For this reason no attempt can be made to formulate *general* rules. The fact remains that the cost of this contingency has to be met and, therefore, the financial policy of the individual business should be quite explicit on the procedure to follow. Possible courses of action are:

1. Inflate the depreciation rate to cover obsolescence.
2. Have a separate rate to cover obsolescence.
3. Carry the "loss" in the books of account and charge future periods with depreciation of this capitalised figure.
4. Transfer to a reserve each year a figure which covers obsolescence and the increasing cost of replacements.

Other variations could be found, but enough has been stated to show the possible approach. If obsolescence is a regular feature of a particular industry, then there should be no problem in anticipating the expected life of an asset or group of assets. The latter may provide a more realistic approach—*group depreciation* discussed later in this chapter is a method of charging depreciation on a totals basis rather than for individual assets. It allows changes in the composition of the group of assets without necessarily amending the overall rate being charged.

Methods 3 and 4 may not be as acceptable as the first two. Obsolescence is certainly a *cost* and not an appropriation of profit, and for this reason the transfer to a reserve would not be a true representation of the facts.* Similarly, the idea of carrying a figure in the books representing an asset which no longer exists does tend to distort the facts. If a special account is opened against which depreciation is charged each year to cover obsolescence, this method may be more acceptable. An example will show what is meant:

Obsolete Assets Account†

| | £ | | | | £ |
|---|---|---|---|---|---|
| Year 2 To Machinery | | Year 1 By Profit and Loss | | | |
| Account | 800 | Account (Deprecia- | | | |
| | | tion) | | | 500 |
| | | 2 | ,, | ,, ,, | 500 |
| | | 3 | ,, | ,, ,, | 500 |

The expectation would be for this account to balance itself over a period of years. Any obsolete machinery would be debited at the book value (less sales from disposal) and credited with a predetermined amount for obsolescence. In this way there would be equalisation of the depreciation charge for obsolescence.

## METHODS OF DEPRECIATION

A number of methods of depreciation are employed, some of which are used regularly whereas others are relatively uncommon. The majority are concerned with the charging of the original cost in the accounts over the useful life of the asset, usually after deducting the estimated value of the asset concerned. Others introduce refinements such as allowing for interest received on amounts invested (*e.g.* sinking fund method), or changes in the intensity of use (*e.g.* production unit method).

Irrespective of the method selected it is necessary to follow certain principles:

1. The method selected should be employed consistently and not varied to suit particular financial years or changed circumstances.

* Some accountants would prefer to treat the cost of obsolescence as an appropriation of profit. This viewpoint carries weight when the obsolescence is unusual or irregular.

† In practice the account would be "balanced" each year.

The principle applies to all bases of accounting. If there is a change, this fact should be made known to managers and shareholders (in the published accounts) or comparisons are made difficult.

2. As far as possible the method used should be administratively convenient.

Refinements to calculations may not be justified, nor may the use of complicated formulae. The method selected should be relatively easy to understand and employ.

3. Depreciation should be regarded as a legitimate cost, not simply an adjustment of profit.

Some businesses adopt the idea of charging what the "traffic will bear" so when profits are high the depreciation charge is also high; the converse applies when trade is depressed. However, accounting should present a true and fair view of the operations irrespective of the fortunes of the particular business.

4. There should be an understanding of the nature of depreciation as a cost.

Different versions have been put forward as to how the depreciation *process occurs*. Some accountants view it as a *period cost* being exhausted as a result of the passing of time. If this view is accepted then, looked at from a management accountancy point of view, depreciation is a *fixed cost*—one which remains constant irrespective of the volume of output. As an easy solution to the charging of depreciation in the annual financial accounts this approach may be satisfactory. Moreover, there is no doubt that a proportion of depreciation does arise from the passing of time.

An alternative approach is to regard depreciation as a purely variable cost which is influenced by the volume of output. For certain assets such as mines and quarries there will be a definite reduction in value with each ton or other measure which is extracted. With some assets such as, say, the Forth Road Bridge in Scotland, there should be an increase in *revenue* from the increased flow of traffic, thus offsetting the depreciation charge. However, this type of situation could be regarded as constituting a special category. More usually, with many assets, the depreciation charge will tend to consist of both a fixed and a variable element so, as far as possible, the method selected should recognise this fact.

5. Legal requirements should be observed (*e.g.* Companies Acts, Income Tax Acts and Finance Acts), but attention should also be paid to the requirements of management.

For management decisions the charges for depreciation may not necessarily be identical with those allowed by law. While quite often the commercial and legal requirements do coincide, it should not be assumed that they are always in step. The method which shows managers how best they can operate the business should be the one to use, especially in the accounts prepared for *internal* use. Subsequently, adjustments would be made to satisfy the law.

6. Strictly speaking the depreciation method and the basis of the calculation should be determined *before* an asset is purchased.

If *cash flows* from each year are to be considered, as with the discounted cash flow techniques, then the net profit for each year cannot be calculated until the depreciation charge is known. The selection of one method rather than another could affect the outcome when alternative investments are being compared (*see* Chapter 18).

### METHODS IN USE

The methods of depreciation which may be employed are summarised below:

1. Straight Line Method.
2. Production Based Methods:
    - (*a*) per unit, or
    - (*b*) per hour.
3. Retirement Accounting Method.
4. Reducing Balance Method.
5. Repair Provision Method.
6. Annuity Method.
7. Sinking Fund Method.
8. Endowment Policy Method.
9. Sum of the Digits Method.
10. Revaluation Method.

Some companies use more than one method; for example, it may be feasible to adopt the straight line method for buildings and the reducing balance method for machinery. Each method is now considered in the order shown.

### Straight Line Method

This method is sometimes called the "proportional method" or "equal instalment method"—the latter probably sums up the approach better than the term now in vogue. There is an assumption made that the fixed asset in question will wear out at precisely the same rate over its useful life. Writers in the United States of America have linked this concept with the legendary "one-horse shay" which went on operating without repair until one day it disintegrated and crumbled to dust. They have argued that for some assets this approach is logical because the one-horse shay with a determinable life should be written off at the same rate over its useful life.*

---

* See, for example, Myron J. Gordon and Gordon Shillinglaw, *Accounting—A Management Approach*, Richard D. Irvin, Homewood, Illinois, 1964, p. 342.

The straight line method requires a forecast to be made of the following:

    (*a*) Serviceable life in years.

    (*b*) Residual value at the end of its useful life.

EXAMPLE

    Asset to be purchased—cost £10,000; residual value, £400; the balance of £9600 to be written off over the service life. If the latter is 10 years then the annual charge is £960. This amount would be debited to a Depreciation Account each year or debited to Profit and Loss Account and credited to a provision account.

    *Advantages.* A number of advantages can be claimed for the straight line method:

    1. Simple to understand and operate.

    2. Recommended by the Institute of Chartered Accountants in England and Wales.

    3. Frequently used in practice.

    4. Recognises that the passing of time is a major factor in depreciation. The obsolescence factor can be taken into consideration simply by assuming a shorter life for the asset when the depreciation calculation is carried out.

    5. The depreciation is in the nature of a fixed cost, and since the acquisition of fixed assets reflect the policy being followed, this could be regarded as a logical classification.

    *Special Note.* Some accountants would argue very strongly that depreciation of plant and machinery would more logically be regarded as a *variable* cost. At the same time, buildings may depreciate more in accordance with the straight line approach. The position emerges where a cost can be a variable cost or fixed cost depending upon the views of the accountant concerned—this is certainly an illogical state of affairs, which should be resolved by a clear understanding on whether specific assets depreciate *primarily* by the passing of time or by use through wear and tear.

    *Disadvantages.* The weaknesses of the straight line method are as follows:

    1. The idea that a fixed asset wears out at exactly the same rate during its life is unlikely to apply in many cases. This artificial assumption makes the system too rigid, certainly from a cost accountant's point of view when he is attempting to calculate unit costs of products (*see* 2 below).

    2. Accounting for decisions requires a full knowledge of the effect on costs of the changing volume of output. The marginal costing supporters would possibly argue that there is no need for unit costs. However, there is more to the problem than arriving at product costs.

Even those who advocate marginal costing would not wish to define a variable cost as a fixed cost—the separation of these two costs into distinct categories is fundamental to the marginal costing approach.

3. The cost of capital (*i.e.* money used to finance the capital expenditure) is not taken into account except in a negative fashion, the assumption being that there is no cost involved.

Since finance has to be covered by the payment of an appropriate rate of interest it seems illogical to some accountants to ignore this fact. However, when the finance comes from internal sources it may seem artificial to consider the interest factor. Even when the capital comes from external sources the fact remains that the fixed asset does not earn interest as such, but produces goods or services which are sold at a profit. The latter may, therefore, be more relevant to management decisions than a notional figure for interest.

4. Repairs and maintenance tend to be higher in the later years of the life of a fixed asset. For this reason it may be better to charge a higher rate of depreciation in the earlier years. Since there is no certainty that high repair costs will be incurred towards the end of an asset's life this argument may not be a sound criticism.

5. If costs and revenues are to be matched, then logically the depreciation charge should reflect the *cash flow of earnings* coming into the business. This does not happen with the straight line method unless the fixed asset produces a constant stream of revenues of equal annual amounts.

6. When a *rate* of return on capital employed is calculated, there will be a tendency for this to increase in later years owing to the fact that the *net* balance on the asset account will be taken.

EXAMPLE

Machine purchased—cost £10,000; estimated life, 10 years (no residual value). Net revenue (excluding all costs except depreciation), £2000.
Earnings for the first 3 years would be as follows:

|  | Year 1 £ | Year 2 £ | Year 3 £ |
|---|---|---|---|
| Revenues | 2,000 | 2,000 | 2,000 |
| Depreciation | 1,000 | 1,000 | 1,000 |
| Profit | 1,000 | 1,000 | 1,000 |
| Capital employed: |  |  |  |
| Capital | £10,000 | £9,000 | £8,000 |
| Return | 10% | 11·1% | 12·5% |

If the income from the fixed asset is *invested* each year, then there would be *additional* revenue which would increase progressively over the life of the asset. At the end of year 2 there would be interest on £1000, at the end of the next year £2000 and so on. This would also augment the rate of return on the capital employed. If this measure is taken (quite erroneously in many cases) as an indication of efficiency, misleading conclusions may be reached.

Many accountants would argue that a notional rate of interest (also known as *imputed* interest) is unrealistic, especially as in most cases the profit would be appropriated as dividends and/or retained in the business. There is no denying this argument. On the other hand, if the money spent on the fixed asset was invested outside the business, interest would be earned. Therefore the charging of the notional rate is in the nature of an opportunity cost. Even so, except when comparing the relative merits of different investments, it is probably better to exclude interest from the calculations.

*Conclusion.* Because of the simplicity of this method it continues to be employed quite extensively. A number of the defects outlined under the disadvantages are also present with the alternative methods covered later in this chapter. When obsolescence is a strong possibility, then the time factor is of the utmost importance; accordingly, the straight line method, with the possibility of introducing a two-tier or accelerated rate at some stage when obsolescence becomes apparent, may be the correct approach. In other circumstances, when depreciation is largely caused by wear and tear, the straight line method is likely to give results which are not representative of the rate of usage of the fixed assets, especially when there are variations in the output of a business.

### Production Based Methods

The production based methods may give results which are similar to those given by the straight line method. If the basis of calculation—units or hours—are to accrue at the same rate for each year, then equal instalments will be charged each year.

Alternatively, if output per annum varies from one year to another and the charge is based on the actual hours, the total annual depreciation will not be the same as under the straight line method.

Formulae for calculating the rate of depreciation are as follows:

#### 1. Production Unit Method

$$\frac{\text{Value of Asset}}{\substack{\text{Number of Units} \\ \text{of Production}}} \qquad \textit{Example:} \qquad \frac{£9,600}{100,000 \text{ units}} = £0 \cdot 096 \text{ per unit}$$

#### 2. Production Hour Method

$$\frac{\text{Value of Asset}}{\substack{\text{Number of} \\ \text{Production Hours}}} \qquad \textit{Example:} \qquad \frac{£9,600}{200,000 \text{ hours}} = £0 \cdot 048 \text{ per hour}$$

The units or hours to be produced or worked have to be estimated for a future period which may be as long as a year. In some cases a quarterly estimate will be feasible. For some industries the forecasting of the number of production units or hours is a major problem which deters accountants from using the production based methods. Yet if budgetary control and related techniques are to be used the necessary forecasts must of necessity include the expected volume of output.

*Advantages.* The advantages claimed for this method will depend to a large extent upon the facilities available for forecasting the production units or hours. Unless a high degree of accuracy can be obtained, the charges made for depreciation in a particular period are unlikely to be a better reflection of the use of a fixed asset than under any other method. In summary form the possible advantages are given below:

1. An attempt is made to equate service and depreciation. Instead of assuming that depreciation is the same each year, the hours or units in each year would be estimated.

2. The method is more realistic where the depreciation is determined primarily by reference to the work done. If a machine is expected to operate for 40,000 hours, then this can become the basis of the calculation.

3. Linked with the Machine Hour Rate method of absorbing overhead costs the results obtained can be very satisfactory.

*Disadvantages.* There are some weaknesses of production-based methods which are as follows:

1. If the danger of obsolescence is high the straight line method may be more satisfactory. This aspect is explained earlier in connection with the straight line approach. However, this should not be overstated; if obsolescence can be foreseen then the reduction in serviceable life can be covered by increasing the rate.

2. There may be considerable difficulty experienced in forecasting:

    (a) the *total* production units or hours, and

    (b) the *annual* units or hours.

When the production units are not of a uniform or standardised pattern there may be difficulty in assessing the possible output in meaningful terms. The "standard hour"—the amount of work normally done in one hour—may be the alternative approach, but this is not a complete answer, because the use of work study, admirable though it may be in expert hands, does rely on subjective assessments for fatigue and other allowances. Accordingly, the assessment of hours may be made to vary according to the views of those calculating the output of each fixed asset.

3. Usually a fixed rate per unit is calculated, and yet a fixed asset may depreciate slower or quicker depending upon the conditions under which operations are carried out.

4. Repairs and maintenance costs tend to increase with the age of the fixed asset, yet this fact is not recognised by the production based methods.

5. If the efficiency of plant is being reduced—with the reduction in "service units"—then it is likely that revenues are also being diminished. A matching of costs and revenues requires this fact to be recognised by charging a lower amount for depreciation.

*Special Note.* Some accountants advocate that depreciation could be charged on the basis of the revenue earned by fixed assets. This then takes care of any falling off in sales. Unfortunately there are problems: one of these is the fact that many products involve multiple operations carried out over a considerable period of time. A further factor is the lack of positive relationship between depreciation and the earning of revenue.

*Conclusion.* Because of their strong links with cost accounting it seems surprising that production based methods are not employed more frequently. If production control, budgetary control and other modern techniques are employed, the information on the production capacity of the fixed assets will be essential. With electronic data processing and advanced quantitative techniques the estimating of service units—products or standard hours—should be a relatively straightforward task.

With the growth of management accountancy it seems likely that the choice of depreciation method will be influenced more by the requirements of planning and control. In the past the arguments used to favour particular methods have been based on such matters as the calculation of profit for a period or financial and taxation considerations. For the future the adoption of an overall (blanket) depreciation rate seems unlikely to be acceptable. Companies spend millions of pounds annually and how the expenditure is absorbed each year is a vital requirement, and the detail and analysis needed will be greater than is occurring in many companies.

## Depletion Unit Method

A special form of the production based methods is the depletion unit method employed for quarries, mines and other wasting assets. An estimate is made of the total tonnage or other unit, and this is divided into the total cost to give a unit rate. If the rate is £0·10 per ton this is charged for every ton extracted from the mine.

## Retirement Accounting Method

There are different points of view on what is meant by the "retirement accounting method." The most usual is to wait until a fixed asset is worn out and then to charge the full cost less any residual value as depreciation.

An alternative approach is to leave the amount of depreciation to the views of senior managers. In a prosperous trading year a large amount of depreciation would be charged; conversely, a small charge or none at all would be made in the lean years. Although this method is arbitrary it *may* consider output and, therefore, there is a matching of costs and revenue. What can lead to misleading results is when the depreciation charge is not based on some specific factor, *e.g.* sales values, and the method selected is not used consistently.

The more usual definition is the charging of total cost of the fixed asset once the latter has worn out. While this method cannot be advocated for general use—because most fixed assets have a life of a number of years—there are cases where this is the only practicable method of dealing with the cost.

In the building and construction industry, mechanical plant may be charged to a job when it is taken on the site. A further variation is to credit the job with the estimated value of the plant when the contract is completed. However, this is in effect a version of the revaluation method discussed below. Repairs and replacements are also usually charged to the contract account, and when the job is relatively small this so called "on and off" method may place a heavy burden on a specific contract.*

One of the claims sometimes made for this method is that it is the most *objective*—there can be no doubt as to the accuracy of the amount because the total is charged. However, this statement, while true, cannot really be taken seriously. The basic idea of depreciation is that the deferred expenditure is apportioned over the serviceable life of the fixed asset. Charging the total amount without regard to the length of period constitutes a breach of a principle of accounting—the importance of distinguishing between capital and revenue expenditure. This in itself is bound to lead to inaccurate accounting and misleading profit and cost figures.

### Reducing Balance Method

The reducing balance method is operated by taking a percentage or proportion of the balance remaining in the asset account. This procedure results in a diminishing amount being charged each year. Where there is a residual value this can be taken into consideration when the percentage is circulated.

EXAMPLE

Plant purchased at a cost of £10,000 (no residual value). Depreciation rate calculated at 20 per cent.

The calculations would be as follows:

Year 1  20% of £10,000 = £2,000
2  20% of  £8,000 = £1,600
3  20% of  £6,400 = £1,280
and so on.

The Commissioners of Inland Revenue stipulate *writing down*

* See Brandwood, F., *Builders' Cost Control, Bonusing and Accounts*, Gee & Co., London, where the possible methods of charging contracts are explained.

*allowances* which are based on the reducing balance method. This method, therefore, appears to be favoured for taxation purposes. However, where preferred, the alternative basis may be the straight line method at a reduced percentage.

On the matter of comparing the straight line and reducing balance methods it should be noted that an approximate percentage for the reducing balance is twice that for the straight line; *i.e.* if the percentage for the latter is 20%, then for the reducing balance method it should be around 40%. The precise percentage will be affected by the serviceable life of the asset.

*Advantages.* A number of advantages can be claimed for the reducing balance method:

1. Simple to understand and calculate. A mathematical formula can be employed to arrive at the appropriate percentage. The writing down allowances for taxation purposes may be used as a guide; these are given later.

2. The largest annual amount is charged in the first year and the smallest in the last year of the serviceable life of an asset. For many assets this follows the actual rate of depreciation which takes place. Accordingly, the method is logical.

3. Repairs and maintenance costs tend to be heavy in the later years when the rate of depreciation is smaller. This fact means that the total fixed asset charge (repairs plus depreciation) tends to remain at approximately the same level over the useful life. There is a considerable element of truth in this assertion, although in some cases the "balancing" may not always work out as expected. Some repairs can be anticipated, but others may have to be carried out quite unexpectedly.

4. If the original cost is construed to represent the discounted (present) value of future cash flows, then it is logical to have a larger charge in the earlier years. The reader can see how this applies by considering the present value tables on p. 474. For example, if receipts are expected over 5 years at £1000 per annum and the interest rate is 5%, each £1 will be worth £0·9524, £0·9070, £0·8638, £0·8227, £0·7835 at the end of each of the 5 years in that sequence. For the correct matching of costs and revenues it is logical to charge depreciation at a decreasing rate.*

*Disadvantages.* There are some weaknesses of the reducing balance method and these are as follows:

1. The percentage used will affect the accuracy of the method and, therefore, this should be fixed only after all factors have been considered. A standard percentage for all conditions may produce misleading results.

---

* The question of replacing fixed assets will also affect this matter, possibly resulting in increased charges (*see* Chapter 27).

2. Under the reducing balance method there would be no hope of ever writing off an amount completely. However, this is not really a serious weakness of the method; an adjustment at the end of the serviceable life can ensure that any small balance is written off with the final instalment. Where there is a residual value the problem does not arise, because the entries for the sale of the asset will take care of any small discrepancies.

3. If interest is earned or assumed to be earned on the amount of the fixed asset which is depreciated (*i.e.* total depreciation), then there should be an increase in revenue in the later years. This argument could be used to indicate that the method was illogical. In practice, many companies do not invest the "funds" which become available as a result of charging depreciation; indeed, as shown in Chapter 27, these funds may be in the form of current assets which are not easily realisable. For this reason many accountants would prefer to ignore the interest factor altogether.

*Conclusion.* The reducing balance method is a logical attempt to depreciate fixed assets along the lines which occur in practice. Revenue often does tail off at the end of the life of an asset: there may be a decline in usefulness (*e.g.* a machine tool) or in popularity (a hotel or place of entertainment). In addition, applying discounted cash flow concepts, money in the future is worth less than that expected quite soon. There is also the added advantage of recognising the growing cost of repairs and maintenance. Where a fixed asset does depreciate more rapidly in the earlier stages, then the reducing balance method has many factors in its favour.

### Repair Provision Method

The repair provision method attempts to carry out in a more positive fashion what the reducing balance method is alleged to achieve; *i.e.* the equalisation of the combined charges of depreciation *and* repairs and maintenance costs over the life of the asset, and this figure is added to the original cost to give a total capital outlay which is apportioned over the life of the asset.

EXAMPLE

Plant purchased at £10,000 (no residual value); expected life 10 years; repairs and maintenance estimated at £2000.

The total of £12,000 would be capitalised and written off over the ten year period.

This method, as indicated, could be construed as the reducing balance method with the added refinement of estimating in advance the cost of repairs and maintenance. However, it seems more likely that the method is treated as the straight line method because a *constant proportion* of the grand total should be taken.*

* See *Terminology of Cost Accountancy* published by the Institute of Cost and Works Accountants.

From what has been stated it will be seen that this method is not strictly a separate method, but rather a technique for dealing with depreciation, repairs and maintenance in a comprehensive fashion.

*Annuity Method*

With the annuity method, consideration is given to the original cost *and* interest on the written down value of the fixed asset. In effect, the assumption made is that the purchase of a fixed asset is an investment on which interest is earned. The "investment" for the purpose of the method is the written down value plus interest earned to date. A fixed rate of interest is determined beforehand and this is charged throughout the life of the asset.

EXAMPLE

Entries for a lease should illustrate the principle involved. The assumption made is that the life of the lease is 3 years:

*Lease Account*

| Dr. Year | | £ | Cr· Year | | £ |
|---|---|---|---|---|---|
| 1 | To Bank | 10,000·000 | 1 | By Depreciation | 3,672·086 |
| | „ Interest 5% | 500·000 | | „ Balance c/d | 6,827·914 |
| | | 10,500·000 | | | 10,500·000 |
| 2 | To Balance b/d | 6,827·914 | 2 | By Depreciation | 3,672·086 |
| | „ Interest | 341·396 | | „ Balance c/d | 3,497·224 |
| | | 7,169·310 | | | 7,169·310 |
| 3 | To Balance b/d | 3,497·224 | 3 | By Depreciation | 3,672·086 |
| | „ Interest | 174·862 | | | |
| | | £3,672·086 | | | £3,672·086 |

*Note.* 0·3672086 is the figure obtainable from annuity tables. This is multiplied by the cost of the lease.

The amount of depreciation to be charged each year is computed by reference to depreciation tables which are based on varying rates of interest. It should be observed that the amount of interest charged each year does reduce, whereas the depreciation increases—this follows quite automatically because the *total* charge is composed of depreciation and interest.

*Advantages.* The advantages claimed for the annuity method of dealing with depreciation are largely theoretical, being based on the fact that money should not be idle, but rather should earn a certain minimum rate of interest. More specifically, the arguments used in support are as follows:

1. If a fixed asset is regarded as the purchase of a future flow of cash (an annuity) this method gives full recognition to this fact.

2. At any time the balance on hand represents the present value of the services to be provided by the fixed asset.

3. Due recognition is given to the earning power of the fixed asset. It also gives emphasis to the decline in the number of "service units" contained in the original investment.

*Disadvantages.* In opposition to these views is the argument that the annuity method is based on artificial assumptions relating to the earning of interest. In most cases the interest *as such* never materialises. A further problem is how to deal with the accounting entries necessary for recording the interest. Assuming that interest will be earned is tantamount to anticipating a profit—this is contrary to accounting conventions. In cost accounting the controversy on whether to charge interest has raged over many years, but it now appears settled that for most purposes its exclusion from costs is to be preferred. For *ad hoc* reports on which to base decisions, to include interest may be helpful, but not as a permanent arrangement.

When the method is employed its application seems to have been limited to the *amortisation* of leaseholds, where there is a specific term of years. With plant, machinery and similar fixed assets the changes which take place such as sales, renewals and additions tend to make the annuity method difficult to apply.

## Sinking Fund Method

The sinking fund method combines depreciation and investment into a comprehensive approach to covering the original cost and possibly providing for replacement. For replacement, as shown in Chapter 27, covering historical costs is not the same as maintaining capital intact.

Basically, the method provides for an identical sum to be charged each year as depreciation. This is invested outside the business, so that from the end of the second year and each subsequent year interest is added. At the end of the serviceable life the total amount in depreciation plus compound interest should equal the original cost of the fixed asset.

This method has similar features to the annuity method. However, the sinking fund method has the distinction of investing in fixed interest securities so that the funds do become available at the end of the period. Like the sinking fund method, it is also suitable where there is a definite term of years such as a leasehold.

## Endowment Policy Method

The endowment policy method combines charging depreciation and investment in the form of an endowment policy. Each year the sum

charged is paid as a premium to an insurance company. At the end of
the life of the asset the sum payable should be equal to the original cost.

Again, this method has limited application for those circumstances
where this kind of investment would be appropriate. In most manufacturing companies it may be found that the more profitable course of
action would be to employ the funds within the business.

## Sum of the Digits Method

The sum of the digits method is a technique for varying the percentage
charged each year, but leaving the basis of the calculation as the total
original cost. By taking the digits which make up the number of years
and then dividing this into the number of the last year the percentage
for the first year is found. This procedure is followed for each year.

EXAMPLE

| Year | Original Cost | Rate | | Depreciation |
| | | Fraction | % | |
|---|---|---|---|---|
| | £ | | | £ |
| 1 | 10,000 | $\frac{4}{10}$ | 40 | 4,000 |
| 2 | 10,000 | $\frac{3}{10}$ | 30 | 3,000 |
| 3 | 10,000 | $\frac{2}{10}$ | 20 | 2,000 |
| 4 | 10,000 | $\frac{1}{10}$ | 10 | 1,000 |
| 10 | | | 100 | 10,000 |

The effect of this method is to charge depreciation at a decreasing
rate each year. If there is any residual value this would be deducted
from the original cost before the calculations are carried out.

Although the precise results will not be the same as under the
reducing balance methods, the application is so similar that the
advantages and disadvantages of the latter can be taken as referring to
the sum of the digits method. However, the reducing balance method
is better known and this fact alone is likely to make it a more obvious
choice.

## Revaluation Method

This method is an attempt to charge to a particular year the amount
of an asset which has been "used up." If the valuation at the beginning
of the period is £10,000 and at the end £9000, then the depreciation is
said to be the difference consisting of £1000. There is generally no
*direct* connection between this method and revaluation accounting
which is employed to deal with changes in the purchasing power of
money. Usually the revaluation method is concerned with the recovery
of original cost and not the replacement problem. However, if current

prices are being employed for valuation there is a strong possibility that the replacement aspect is being covered; nevertheless, this does not appear to be the intention of the method.

Rather it has grown from the difficulty of calculating the depreciation of certain fixed assets. There is acknowledgment that depreciation does take place, but the rate is not known until the assets are examined at the end of the year. Examples usually quoted are farmers' livestock, loose tools, plant used on contract work and similar items. Sometimes wheelbarrows, hammers and power tools are "lost" completely so that a total valuation would take care of the depreciation.

If there is an increase in the valuation of fixed assets such gain should be treated as a capital reserve. Strictly speaking, if the rise in value almost offsets the depreciation, then consideration should be given as to whether an amount should not be treated as a capital reserve; *i.e.* an appropriation of profit rather than a charge against profit. In this way a more accurate calculation of profit is possible.

## CALCULATION OF DEPRECIATION

Although discussions and books imply that each fixed asset will be treated separately for depreciation calculations, this is not usually the case. Instead, for administrative convenience, it is usual to classify the fixed assets into convenient groups so that those depreciating at the same rate can be dealt with in total. A columnar register in summary form can be maintained to show the original cost, depreciation and other details. Quite often this is in addition to the Plant and Machinery Register which gives full details of each individual fixed asset.

Terms used in connection with charging depreciation are:

1. *Group Depreciation or Composite Rate of Depreciation.* These terms apply when a number of assets are taken together for the purpose of calculating the rate of depreciation. The composite rate is acceptable provided the assets in a group are similar. If dissimilar machines are taken together very misleading results may be produced. However, it should be remembered that depreciation is based on *estimates* and, therefore, excessive refinements will not necessarily produce very accurate figures.

2. *Single Rate of Depreciation (for an individual fixed asset).* There may be changes in conditions or in the intensity of use of a fixed asset. If these result in a higher rate of depreciation an *accelerated rate* may be employed. This should be fixed after considering all relevant factors; working a double shift will not necessarily result in twice the rate used for a single shift. All the aspects outlined at the beginning of this chapter should be considered.

## DEPRECIATION AND MANAGEMENT DECISIONS

At regular intervals management decisions have to be made, some of considerable magnitude, others relatively unimportant. The purpose of this section is to outline some facets of decision making which may be influenced by capital expenditure and depreciation. Further details are contained in Chapters 12 and 18.

Earlier in this chapter the charging of depreciation is described as the recovery of original costs: this is the accepted approach. A fixed asset is regarded as a machine, building or piece of equipment for which capital expenditure is incurred. Subsequently, this expenditure is charged against the appropriate accounting period in the form of depreciation.

An alternative and more recent concept has been the development of the idea that the capital expenditure represents *the purchase of a cash flow in the future* over the life of the fixed asset concerned. If this view is accepted, then depreciation is the cost of cash receipts within a particular accounting period. Whether or not interest is also charged on the money invested, any management decision should consider the total cost and the total revenue: for this reason, although over the life of an asset a profit may appear to be indicated, because of the timing of the cash receipts there is a need to match each year's depreciation. The methods of depreciation outlined earlier may give quite different results and so the choice should be made with care.

## CHOICE OF METHOD

For the purpose of showing how depreciation may be charged a possible classification is as follows:

1. Constant Charge; *e.g.* straight line.
2. Reducing Charge; *e.g.* reducing balance.
3. Accelerating Charge; *e.g.* annuity method.
4. Variable Charge; *e.g.* production unit method.

If a decision is to be made on the profitability of a fixed asset, the *method* of depreciation selected should indicate characteristics which are similar to the *cash flow*. For example, if equal sums are expected each year the straight line method may be appropriate. However, the matter is not as simple as all that. Even if each year produces identical sums, when these have been discounted to present values the more remote the revenue the smaller it becomes. For this reason some accountants would prefer to use a reducing rate of depreciation, thus allowing for the discounting process.

The rate of return on investment is also affected. As shown in connection with the straight line method, the return on the *net* capital employed (after depreciation) tends to increase. This result is, of course, an artificial impression. For the purpose of computing the return on capital employed, the net balance of a single asset is misleading. What is happening to the depreciation? This is probably in the form of some other asset which is equally part of the capital employed.

z

Those accountants who advocate the charging of interest by using the annuity method, sinking fund method or simply charging on the investment in a fixed asset, state that this approach is recognising the time factor. The argument can be advanced further—if discounted cash flow techniques are to be employed, then it is logical to include interest as part of the depreciation method. While there is some logic in this reasoning, this does not mean that the interest should be brought into the accounts. Rather, such refinements should be incorporated into the special *ad hoc* computations which are carried out before a decision is made.

## CONTROL OF COSTS

Once a fixed asset has been purchased the cost has been expended; it is past history and nothing can be done to alter this fact. When considering *control*—the adherence to plans—how can this be effected, if at all?

The accepted view for cost control is that *fixed costs* are regarded as being uncontrollable. If this approach is taken to its logical conclusion it could be argued that depreciation is not capable of being controlled. However, this is an over-simplification. Senior managers and directors who make decisions to purchase fixed assets act on the assumption that the operations will produce revenue over a specified number of years. If the plans made are not realised, attention should be focused on the areas of weakness. There should be regular "capital expenditure audits" to ensure that results do come up to expectations and the depreciation policy is realistic.

At a lower level of management—those who are responsible for operating specific fixed assets—the production methods, maintenance, intensity of use and other factors will affect the actual rate of depreciation. There is, therefore, a case for considering depreciation as a *variable cost*. Unfortunately, there is difficulty in knowing the correct *rate* of depreciation until the fixed asset is replaced. Nevertheless, a study of all the technical factors affecting depreciation may enable a rate to be compiled on the basis of a production unit or standard hour. Once this is done it should be possible to calculate variances for the number of "units" and the over- or under-absorption of the depreciation; the normal capacity would be taken as the basis for calculating the total amount of depreciation in a particular period. There is need for experiments in the best methods to employ in the business concerned; certainly the negative approach of ignoring the problem by stating that depreciation is a policy cost is unlikely to assist in cost control.

When a machine hour rate is used to recover the costs of a single machine or a group having similar characteristics, the problem of variations in output has to be recognised. The depreciation would have to be charged on a suitable basis so that an overall rate could be applied to work being completed in the cost centre.

*Management Decisions*

Details of typical problems and suggested solutions are contained in Chapter 12. Because depreciation is a cost which has already been incurred (a *sunk* cost) it follows that for many decisions it may be of limited significance. Examples of the types of decisions are as follows:

1. Temporary Closing Down.
2. Permanent Closing Down.
3. Make or Buy Decisions.
4. Expand or Buy.
5. Comparing Machines and Hand Labour.
6. Substituting Machines for Hand Labour.
7. Profit Planning.
8. Pricing Products.

No hard-and-fast rule can be laid down on how to deal with depreciation for reaching management decisions. However, the following guidelines should indicate the method of approach:

1. Once a fixed asset is purchased depreciation occurs until the serviceable life is ended.

Suspending operations may slow down the rate of depreciation but will not generally eliminate the cost altogether.

2. If depreciation is regarded as the cost of producing revenue, then, if there is no use for a fixed asset, depreciation is of no relevance except to show the loss being incurred.

3. The effect on depreciation of carrying out one course of action rather than another should be considered when making a decision. If two methods are being compared the depreciation cost under each method should be computed.

4. Depreciation already written off may be of no significance for *future* decisions.

The question of whether depreciation is a fixed or variable cost is essential to the understanding of the problem. If purely fixed, then the expended cost may be irrelevant, but any future cost is still of considerable significance. The recognition of when depreciation is of importance is vital to the presentation of information to management.

## DEPRECIATION IN PUBLISHED ACCOUNTS

The Companies Acts 1948 and 1967 lay down rules for disclosure of depreciation in the Profit and Loss Account. In summary form, these are as follows:*

* For a precise statement of the law readers are advised to consult a book on Company Law. In this chapter the emphasis is on the practical aspects of depreciation accounting.

1. The amount charged by way of provision for depreciation, renewals or diminution in value of fixed assets must be shown.

2. Any amount charged for *renewals* should be shown as a separate item.

3. If the depreciation method considers factors other than the amount of the fixed assets shown on the balance sheet, this fact should be stated.

There has to be disclosure of the method of arriving at the amount of the fixed asset. Unfortunately, this requirement appears to relate to whether the figure is based on cost or some other basis. It does not stipulate that the *depreciation method* should be stated; *e.g.* whether "straight line" or "reducing balance". This vagueness in the legal requirements has resulted in different descriptions being employed in the published accounts. Examples are as follows:

1. Depreciation is provided annually on a straight line basis at rates estimated to write off the cost, less investment grants and building grants, over the effective useful lives of the assets concerned. . . .

2. The amount for depreciation is calculated by reference to the cost of the asset and its estimated useful life, *less* the proportion of investment grants attributable thereto.

3. Except for properties owned by the XYZ Co. Ltd., no amounts have been written off Freehold and Leasehold Properties.

*Author's Note.* This description covers the legal requirement that where no provision is made for depreciation this fact should be stated.

4. Land, buildings and plant are stated at cost. Depreciation is charged mainly on the basis of fixed percentages of cost at rates appropriate to each country.

5. Depreciation as recorded in the accounts is calculated at straight line rates based on the estimated useful lives of the respective assets.

6. Depreciation of the fleet has been based on an expected life of 20 years . . . (from the annual report of a shipping company).

7. On buildings, depreciation is based on the *original* cost, whereas for all other assets it is based on the written down value at the beginning of the final year.

*Note.* It will be seen that this particular company employs the straight line method for buildings and the reducing balance method for other fixed assets.

These descriptions are typical of those being employed in published accounts. Some could be more explicit on the precise depreciation method(s) being employed. Amounts in excess of normal depreciation: *i.e.* to write off the original cost of fixed assets, are treated as depreciation reserves. A typical entry in an annual report is as follows:

"The total depreciation charged against profits takes into account the reduced purchasing power of money. The amount provided in excess of that required to write off the original cost of fixed assets over their estimated life is transferred to the depreciation reserve."

This aspect is covered further in Chapters 21 and 27.

Further requirements for the Balance Sheet are as follows:

1. Any amount for depreciation in excess of normal requirements (as defined by the directors) should be treated as a reserve.

2. If assets are stated at valuation the years of valuation and amounts are to be given; if valued in the current year the names of the valuers or their qualification and the bases of valuation are to be given.

3. Additions and disposals are to be shown at an aggregate figure.

4. Freehold and leasehold to be subdivided between long leases (50 years or more unexpired) and short leases.

## DEPRECIATION AND TAXATION ALLOWANCES

Reference is made earlier in this chapter to the use of *writing down allowances*, these being the appropriate charges which are recognised when computing the profit accepted for taxation purposes. As noted, there appears to be a preference for using the reducing balance method, although the straight line method would also be acceptable.

The allowances and/or the rates at which they are computed tend to vary from one year to another and, therefore, readers are advised to obtain the latest information before making decisions or attempting to assess the profit for a particular year. At the time of writing the following apply:

1. *Initial Allowance.* This is payable once only and is taken into account when the various allowances are computed.

2. *Writing Down Allowances.* These are allowed each year at the rates stipulated by the Acts in force (*see* below).

3. *Balancing Allowance and Balancing Charge.* These are allowances or charges which are necessary when the fixed asset is sold or the business is discontinued. Adjustments can be carried out so that, within prescribed limits, the allowances are accurate.

### Rates of Writing Down Allowances

Percentage rates for plant and machinery are stipulated by the Commissioners of Inland Revenue. The minimum rate is 15% (on the reducing balance method)* and a schedule which sets out the rates is given below:

1. The rates are for all conditions of working except where otherwise appears.

| Industry | Description of Plant | Rate of Writing-down allowance Reducing balance method % |
|---|---|---|
| Farming | Sprayers and flaxpulling machines, fertiliser and lime spreaders, combine drills | $31\frac{1}{4}$ |
| | Tractors | $28\frac{1}{8}$ |
| | Sugar beet and potato harvesters and diggers. Manure spreaders | 25 |
| | Binders, reapers and combine harvesters | 20 |
| Building and public works contracting | Bulldozers | $28\frac{1}{8}$ |
| | Site plant, where used intensively | 25 |
| | Site plant, single shift working | 20 |
| Engraving | Klischograph engraving machine | 25 |
| Film producing | Cameras | 25 |
| Bowling alleys | Electrical alley equipment | 25 |
| Engineering | Precision machine tools (up to and including double shift working) | 20 |
| Coke manufacture | Ovens and ancillary plant | 20 |
| Plastics | Fabrication machines—(double shift working or over) | 20 |
| Hosiery | Process machinery | 20 |
| Clay and brick industry | Sandfacing brick and tile machines (single shift working) | 20 |
| Cotton | Process machinery and automatic looms (treble shift working or over) | 20 |
| | Rewinding machinery (double shift working or over) | 20 |
| Television and radio | Recording apparatus | 20 |
| | Land lines and outside cables | 20 |
| Glass bottle manufacture | Bottle making machines | 20 |
| Cinemas | Projectors and screens | 20 |
| Carpet manufacture | Tufting looms (up to and including double shift working) | 20 |

* Introduced by the *Finance Act*, 1963, Section 35, and operating at the time of writing.

| Industry | Description of Plant | Rate of Writing-down allowance Reducing balance method % |
|---|---|---|
| Launderettes | Washing machines and plant | 20 |
| Milk bars | Milk and ice cream refrigerating and delivery units | 20 |
| Creameries, dairies and ice cream factories | Refrigerators | 20 |
| Chemical | Superphosphate, synthetic dyestuffs and sulphuric acid plant | 20 |
| | Plastics materials manufacture (continuous operation) | 20 |

2. The following rates apply to particular classes of machinery or plant not peculiar to any one industry for all conditions of working:

Vans, lorries and motors 25%
Fork lift trucks 25%
Television sets 25%
Vending machines (drinks) 25%
Road rollers, diesel and petrol 25%
Electronic computers and data processing machines 25%
Vending machines (dry goods) 20%
Electronic trucks and trolleys 20%
Parking meters 20%
Electronic furnaces 20%
Diesel electric generating plant 20%

3. Rates may be subject to adjustment for any year in relation to any item of machinery or plant, if it appears that the wear and tear is greater or less than that which might be expected to be caused by normal use, e.g. where there is extra shift working or where machinery or plant is temporarily out of ordinary use. But such adjustment cannot result in a rate of writing-down allowance greater than 25% or less than 15%.

4. Representative bodies (or particular taxpayers concerned) may apply to the Commissioners of Inland Revenue for the increase, as respects any year of assessment, of any percentage rate of writing-down allowance, and may appeal to the Board of Referees if dissatisfied with the result (S. 287).

These rates can be used as a guide to the approximate rate of depreciation for specific plant and machinery. Some companies may find that higher or lower rates will be necessary, although those shown above must be used for taxation purposes.

## DEPRECIATION IN PRACTICE*

Very little information is available on the methods of depreciation used in practice. In the United States of America the tendency appears to be for the more popular methods to be used, such as the straight line and reducing balance methods—the latter has grown in popularity since it was recognised for taxation purposes.† Because of the dislike of using notional interest rates the annuity method is very rarely found in practice.‡

The Research and Publications Committee of The Institute of Chartered Accountants of Scotland through its members conducted two surveys: (1) a pilot scheme and (2) a more comprehensive survey. Summaries of the results are given below:

### 1. Pilot Scheme

"The tentative conclusions drawn from initial stages of the research (insofar as the United Kingdom is concerned) may be summarised briefly as follows:

(a) Most companies' depreciation policies base the amount to be written off fixed assets on their estimated working life.

(b) Most companies use historical cost as the basis upon which depreciation is calculated.

(c) Most companies favour the 'straight-line' method of write-off.

(d) Revaluation of fixed assets at regular intervals is not prevalent, but a fair proportion of companies revalue occasionally.

(e) Technical obsolescence of assets is borne in mind by a number of companies in fixing depreciation rates.

(f) A number of companies make provision, either through the depreciation account or separately, for replacement of fixed assets at costs higher than those at which they were bought."

### 2. Comprehensive Survey

"It was decided that it would be useful to know whether the tentative conclusions mentioned above and certain other information which also emerged from the preliminary survey would be confirmed by a larger sample. Accordingly members of the Institute in public practice were asked to provide—absolutely anonymously—certain information in respect of their industrial and commercial clients' depreciation policies, the clients

---

* For full details of the research findings in the U.K. mentioned in this section, readers are advised to see "Depreciation: Its Meaning, Purpose and Accounting Treatment" by P. N. McMonnies, C.A., in *The Accountants' Magazine* for February, 1969. Due acknowledgement is given to the editor and the author for kind permission to quote from the article.

† See Eldon S. Hendriksen, *Accounting Theory*, Richard D. Irwin, Homewood, Illinois, 1965, p. 325.

‡ See Eric L. Kohler, *A Dictionary for Accountants*, Prentice-Hall, Englewood Cliffs, 1963, p. 178.

being closen by them at random within certain size brackets. The following table summarises the information thus elicited:

(*a*) Number of companies basing the amount to be written off on the estimated life of the assets ... 79
(*b*) Companies using historical costs as basis for write-off—
for buildings ... 46
for plant and machinery ... 58
(*c*) Companies using straight-line method of write-off—
for buildings ... 58
for plant and machinery ... 57
(*d*) Number of companies revaluing their assets—
regularly ... 2
occasionally ... 34
(*c*) Number of the above companies taking cognisance of the revaluations in fixing the depreciation charge ... 14
(*f*) Number of companies taking account of technical obsolescence when fixing rates ... 23
(*g*) Number of companies making provision for replacement ... 22
(*h*) Total number of companies reported upon ... 89

It will thus be seen that the conclusions reached as a result of the pilot survey were largely confirmed. The only real variation that appeared was the use of the reducing balance method of write-off in a number of companies which, for the purpose of this particular exercise, are designated as 'small.' In fact 13 out of 40 used that method for buildings and 27 out of 47 for all or some part of their plant and machinery. The use of the straight-line method within the group showed 26 and 24 companies respectively. (It will be noted that some companies used both methods in certain cases.)"

These results give valuable insight into the methods employed. The author of the article does not claim that the samples taken are large enough to draw indisputable conclusions, but there is certainly sufficient evidence to be able to use the figures with reasonable confidence.

## ADEQUACY OF DEPRECIATION

The management accountant should ensure that adequate provision is made to cover depreciation. Very briefly this may be watched by paying attention to the following:

1. A realistic depreciation policy.
2. Regular appraisal of the methods and rates to ensure that they are producing consistent and satisfactory results.
3. Establishing ratios which indicate the acceptable size of depreciation charge. Examples are:

(*a*) Ratio of total depreciation to profit earned.
(*b*) Ratio of total depreciation to total fixed assets.

These ratios will vary from one business to another, but once established in accordance with sound principles they can be used on a regular basis.

## REVALUATION ACCOUNTING

The problems connected with rising prices and fixed asset replacement are considered in the next chapter. Methods of dealing with depreciation provisions and reserves are also covered.

## EXAMINATION QUESTIONS

(These cover work in previous chapters.)

1. The following figures were extracted from the trial balance of GH Limited before closing the books on 31st May, 1967:

|  | £ | £ |
|---|---|---|
| Materials stock, opening balance at 1st May ... | 43,670 | |
| Finished goods, opening balance at 1st May ... | 8,500 | |
| Sales during the month ... ... ... ... | | 29,000 |
| Selling cost ... ... ... ... ... ... | 1,200 | |
| Administration cost ... ... ... ... | 1,000 | |
| Direct material cost ... ... ... ... | 17,000 | |
| Direct labour cost ... ... ... ... | 6,500 | |
| Works overhead ... ... ... ... ... | 4,400 | |

The overhead apportioned to output during the month amounted to £3,950. Inaccuracy in the absorption rates used accounted for the variance, comprised as follows:

|  | £ |
|---|---|
| Work-in-progress ... ... | 15 |
| Finished goods ... ... | 150 |
| Cost of goods sold... ... | 285 |

At 31st May the following stock valuations were determined:

|  | £ |
|---|---|
| Materials ... ... ... | 43,670 |
| Work-in-progress ... ... | 530 |
| Finished goods ... ... | 11,800 |

Prepare statements as follows for the month of May:

    (a) cost of output of finished goods;
    (b) cost of sales;
    (c) profit or loss.                (I.C.W.A.)

2. The operations of a small factory, which makes two products Q and R, are summarised below for the month of May:

|  | Product Q | Product R |
|---|---|---|
| Production units | 2,400 | 2,700 |
| Sales units | 3,300 | 1,900 |
| Direct materials used | 17,000 units at £0·26 each | 47,000 units at £2·10 each |
| Direct wages | 12,500 hours at £0·46 per hour | 22,000 hours at £0·45 per hour |
| Actual overhead | £3,250 | £5,400 |

Standard costs are as follows:

|  | Product Q | Product R |
|---|---|---|
| Direct material | 7 units at £0·25 each | 18 units at £0·22 each |
| Direct wages | 5 hours at £0·45 per hour | 8 hours at £0·47 per hour |
| Overhead | 5 hours at £0·30 per hour | 8 hours at £0·25 per hour |

Budgeted figures for the month of May are as follows:

|  | Product Q | Product R |
|---|---|---|
| Production units | 2,000 | 2,500 |
| Direct wages | 10,000 hours | 20,000 hours |
| Overhead cost | £3,000 | £5,000 |

Budget overhead allowances based on standard hours for the month of May are:

Product Q: £3300    Product R: £5200

The accounting arrangements provide, for each product, a work-in-progress account, a finished goods account, and a variance account. The debit entries to work-in-progress accounts are at actual cost, and the credit entries are at standard cost.

At the beginning of May there were no stocks of work-in-progress, but finished goods, valued at standard, were as follows:

Product Q: 2000 units    Product R: 900 units

At the end of May there were no stocks of work-in-progress. Selling prices are £6·30 for product Q, and £10·75 for product R.

You are required to:

(a) journalise May transactions for the above;
(b) set out in detail for each product:

  (i) quantity and rate variances for materials and wages;
  (ii) volume and expenditure variances for overheads;

(c) prepare a profit and loss account for products Q and R and total, using standard costs and variances calculated above.    (*I.C.W.A.*)

3. An engineering company has three manufacturing departments and three service departments. The floor area occupied by each and the departmental expenses in 19.. were:

| Department | | | | Floor Area (Sq. ft) | Expense (£000) |
|---|---|---|---|---|---|
| Manufacturing: | | | | | |
| Foundry | ... | ... | ... | 2500 | 100 |
| Machining | ... | ... | ... | 4000 | 120 |
| Assembling | ... | ... | ... | 2000 | 50 |
| Service: | | | | | |
| Utilities | ... | ... | ... | 1500 | 11 |
| Maintenance | ... | ... | ... | 1500 | 8 |
| Stores | ... | ... | ... | 1000 | 3 |

The Utilities department expense is allocated to the other five departments on a floor area basis. The other two service departments' expense is apportioned as follows:

| To: | | | | Maintenance Department % | Stores Department % |
|---|---|---|---|---|---|
| Foundry ... | ... | ... | | 30 | 30 |
| Machining | ... | ... | | 25 | 10 |
| Assembly ... | ... | ... | | 20 | 40 |
| Maintenance | ... | ... | | — | 20 |
| Stores | ... | ... | ... | 25 | — |

Show the departmental accounts after the expense apportionments have been made.

Calculations should be to the nearest £1.

(*I.C.W.A.*)

4. In a factory the lighting requirement is 800,000 lumens. This is at present supplied by 1000 watt electric lamps with a light output of 16,000 hours and cost £0·626 each. They take half an hour of labour for each replacement.

It is proposed to replace these lamps by a more modern type of 500 watts giving a light output of 20,000 lumens and costing £1 each. They have a life of 1500 hours but need a conversion lamp holder adaptor costing £5 each and requiring one hour of labour to replace.

Labour cost is £0·625 per hour plus 40% overhead expense and electricity is £0·008 per unit (kilowatt).

There are 300 working days in a year with an average of 10 hours lighting each day.

For management purposes summarise these details in a comparative cost statement showing the financial position for one year in existing arrangements and for one year when the proposals have been implemented.

Calculations should be to the nearest £1.

(*I.C.W.A.*)

5. A plastic floor covering is produced in rolls 6 feet wide and 20 yards long. Production is in batches and materials are fed into a continuous processing machine. The standard mixture, which should produce 100 rolls of floor covering, is as follows:

Material X    1000 lb at £0·15 per lb
       „    Y     500 lb at £0·25     „
       „    Z     100 gallons at £1·25 per gallon of 10 lb

During a period in which 2009 rolls of floor covering were produced from 20 batches of material, the actual usage was:

Material X    20,160 lb at £0·154 per lb
       „    Y     9,984 lb at £0·270     „
       „    Z     2,020 gallons at £1·200 per gallon of 10 lb

Present to management a statement for the period showing the actual and standard costs of production with an analysis of the direct materials cost variance. (*I.C.W.A.*)

6. Demand for the output of a certain company is very elastic, and modern plant recently installed is capable of greatly increased production. Output at present is 80,000 units per year, and half a million units annually are estimated to be within the capacity of the new plant.

The present selling price per unit is £15.

The need for flexible budgeting is recognised and six alternative levels of output in addition to the present level are contemplated. Six equal increments in annual output level, up to a maximum of 500,000 units, would involve corresponding reductions of £1 each in unit price to £9 per unit at the maximum output.

The present variable costs amount to £400,000. Fixed costs which at present amount to £200,000 are not expected to increase for any of the six alternative output levels contemplated. Semi-fixed costs are expected to vary from the present annual figure of £230,000 to £320,000, the upward steps being to £260,000 at 220,000 units, £280,000 at 360,000 units, and £320,000 at 500,000 units. The costs classified as variable at the six projected levels of output are calculated to be as follows:

£750,000; £1,100,000; £1,500,000; £1,750,000; £2,050,000; £2,500,000.

(a) Tabulate the above data and show total costs, incremental costs, total and incremental sales income at the various output levels.

(b) Which volume should be set for budgeted output?

(c) What is the selling price at that volume? *(I.C.W.A.)*

7. A company manufacturing special-purpose equipment has a toolroom which undertakes the following activities:

makes loose tools in large batch quantities for the manufacturing departments;

makes special jigs and tools to facilitate the execution of individual production orders for special-purpose equipment;

manufactures jigs and tools for other engineering concerns;

machines components required by the company's maintenance department for maintenance, exceptional revenue and capital expenditure work.

Design the cost ascertainment and cost control procedures for this toolroom. *(I.C.W.A.)*

8. The monthly budgeted trading statement, based upon 20 working days, is as follows:

|  | Units | £ | £ |
|---|---|---|---|
| Sales ... ... ... ... | 240 |  | 120,000 |
| Cost of sales: |  |  |  |
| Direct materials... ... ... |  | 48,000 |  |
| Direct labour ... ... ... |  | 12,000 |  |
| Direct expenses ... ... ... |  | 2,400 |  |
| Variable works overhead ... |  | 9,600 |  |
| Fixed works overhead ... ... |  | 20,000 |  |
| Variable selling costs ... ... |  | 6,000 |  |
| Fixed selling costs ... ... |  | 2,000 |  |
|  |  |  | 100,000 |
| Net profit ... ... ... ... |  |  | £20,000 |

The actual trading statement for November, 22 working days, is as follows:

| | Units | £ | £ |
|---|---|---|---|
| Sales ... ... ... ... | 250 | | 123,500 |
| Cost of production: | | | |
| Direct materials... ... ... | | 54,300 | |
| Direct labour ... ... ... | | 13,200 | |
| Direct expenses ... ... ... | | 2,750 | |
| Variable works overhead ... | | 10,920 | |
| Fixed works overhead ... ... | | 22,000 | |
| Variable selling costs ... ... | | 6,500 | |
| Fixed selling costs ... ... | | 2,200 | |
| | | 111,870 | |
| Stock increase ... ... ... | 20 | 6,000 | |
| Cost of sales ... ... ... | | | 105,870 |
| Net profit ... ... ... ... | | | £17,630 |

Redraft both budget and actual trading statements to enable the calculation of the detailed variances in profit which have arisen.   (*I.C.W.A.*)

CHAPTER 27

## REVALUATION ACCOUNTING*

THE term "revaluation accounting" is used to denote the methods employed for overcoming the problems connected with fixed asset replacement in a period of rising prices. Basically there are two main problems, the first related to the second: these are as follows:

1. Maintaining intact the capital invested in *real terms*. The latter is normally regarded as meaning the equivalent producing or earning power. It is also taken to mean that the values of the assets in terms of *purchasing power* remain the same when the beginning and end of a year are compared. If a fixed asset is capable of producing 1000 units of X in a period and the problem of replacement arises then the new asset should be capable of producing 1000 units of X. Reference is made to fixed assets, but the same problem arises, although to a lesser extent, in the case of stocks of raw materials.

2. Calculating profit so that it really does indicate a *true and fair* view of a year's trading. As indicated, this is very much related to (1). A very important cost to be charged before calculation of profit is depreciation of fixed assets. In effect, depreciation represents the current cost of using a fixed asset. If historical costs are used as a basis for calculating the depreciation and prices have risen so that replacement costs are much higher than when the asset was purchased it means that the depreciation charge does *not* represent the true cost of using a fixed asset.

In addition, because the depreciation charge is less than it should be there is an *overstatement* of profit which, if distributed, results in capital erosion. Put another way, capital is not being maintained intact. Yet the management accountant has a duty to perform on this important matter; that is, to ensure that the capacity to earn is not depleted. If fixed assets are not maintained intact *future* profits may deteriorate.

There is nothing very new in the idea of attempting to charge realistic costs in accounts: cost accountants have done this for many years even to the extent of charging a rent or depreciation when no rent is actually payable or when a fixed asset has been fully depreciated. Often, of course, such notional charges appear in memorandum form and not as part of the double-entry system. They are of particular significance when management is comparing the efficiency of different factories or is fixing prices by reference to costs.

---

* Also known as "the replacement value theory," "stabilised accounting," "accounting for inflation," and "common dollar accounting."

Following the end of the 1939–45 War the chronic inflation and rising prices, up to the present day have made recognition of the revaluation problem essential. The way the problem has been tackled varies from one company to another. A few companies revalue all assets each year. Others make an assessment of current replacement costs periodically; *e.g.* every five years.

The form revaluation accounting will take must be influenced by the views of the accountant and directors who are faced with the problem of deciding whether or not a realistic profit is being computed. An outline of arguments used for and against revaluation accounting is, therefore, essential.

## ADVANTAGES OF REVALUATION ACCOUNTING

The advantages claimed for revaluation accounting are summarised below:

1. Full recognition is given to changes in the value of money associated with maintaining capital intact and showing an accounting profit which is also an "economic profit."

2. Showing costs at *current* figures with sales at *current* values is the only logical method of calculating the results of a year's operations. Management is shown clearly and precisely what has happened and is able to formulate policy and make plans with no misunderstanding regarding the results shown in the accounts.

3. Revaluation of assets shows the true value of the investment in a business. This in turn leads to the calculation of a return on capital employed which is a positive indication of efficiency. Capital employed calculated by reference to historical costs is full of unknowns and can have different meanings from one company to another.

4. In times of rising prices the profit calculated will tend to be lower than when historical costs are employed for calculating depreciation. This means that trade unions, employees, shareholders and the public at large are not misled by being given an exaggerated profit figure. The profit earned is taken as a guide to prosperity by actual and potential investors and, quite often, trade unions base their wage claims on the assumption that a company can afford to pay higher wages because profits are higher. If fixed assets are valued at current replacement costs there can be no misconceptions as to the size of the profit earned and if claims for wages are put forward then they can be dealt with on realistic grounds.

5. Historical costs—the actual costs in monetary terms—are of significance only when the assets are actually purchased. After the date of purchase they lose their significance and do not represent the true economic value of the fixed assets in use. The more remote in time is the date of purchase the less reliable is the historical cost for showing the worth of the asset.

6. If assets are purchased in the year being dealt with the depreciation charge will reflect current economic values. Therefore, it is argued, charging depreciation at historical costs for assets purchased previously is quite illogical: if this is done there is a mixture of *old* costs and *new* costs.

7. When assets are worn-out or obsolete they should be replaced with assets of equivalent production or earning capacity; *i.e.* representing equal purchasing power. (There are many difficulties associated with equating purchasing power with earning or production capacity. The assumption made is that they are equal.)

8. Depreciation results in cash being retained in the business and, therefore, in this sense maintains capital intact. How this is done may be seen from a simple example shown below.

*Company A*

*Balance Sheet* Year 1

| | £ | | £ |
|---|---|---|---|
| Share Capital | 2500 | Fixed Assets | 2000 |
| | | Cash | 500 |
| | £2500 | | £2500 |

*Profit and Loss Account*
End of Year 1

| | £ | | £ |
|---|---|---|---|
| Costs (excluding Depreciation) | 4000 | Sales | 5000 |
| Profit | 1000 | | |
| | £5000 | | £5000 |

If the company follows a policy of distributing all the profits to shareholders, the Balance Sheet at the beginning of the second year will be precisely the same as at the commencement of business. It will be noticed that no depreciation has been charged in the Profit and Loss Account. If depreciation is charged the position would be as follows:

*Profit and Loss Account*
End of Year 1

| | £ | | £ |
|---|---|---|---|
| Costs | 4000 | Sales | 5000 |
| Depreciation (say) | 200 | | |
| Profit | 800 | | |
| | £5000 | | £5000 |

The Balance Sheet at the beginning of the second year will now show a changed position.

*Balance Sheet*

| | £ | | £ | £ |
|---|---|---|---|---|
| Share Capital | 2500 | Fixed Assets | 2000 | |
| | | *less* Depreciation | 200 | |
| | | | —— | 1800 |
| | | Cash | | 700 |
| | £2500 | | | £2500 |

In practice, such simplified conditions will not operate. Nevertheless, the principle will still apply even in the most complex organisation. Naturally the "cash released" does not usually stay in the form of cash. There will be stocks and debtors which will be converted into cash, then again back into stocks and debtors. So long as a business is in existence this process continues.

9. Showing the current values of fixed assets in the published accounts helps to establish a realistic price for a company's equity capital and thereby tends to reduce the danger of take-over bids (*see* Chapter 22).

10. Revaluation accounting recognises that business operations are *dynamic* in nature, constantly subjected to change either through the quantities of the factors of production employed varying or through variations in price levels.

## DISADVANTAGES OF REVALUATION ACCOUNTING

Those accountants who do not agree with revaluation accounting put forward the following arguments:

1. The meaning of "depreciation" is the natural reduction in the *cost* of fixed assets. The "depreciation charge" represents the recovery of the original cost.

Actual cost represents the sacrifice involved in purchasing the assets. The only logical way of recovering actual cost is by charging actual cost.

There is no doubt that some confusion exists as to the true meaning of depreciation. There has been a great deal of discussion on the need to recover replacement costs *as depreciation*. This has led to the assertion—quite rightly—that charging depreciation is the recovery of original cost and, therefore, those that advocate recovering replacement costs are guilty of distortion of a fundamental principle.

While admitting that there is some confusion on the meaning of depreciation this does not mean that the replacement problem can be ignored. Capital should still be maintained intact and profit should be calculated as far as possible by matching present revenues with present costs. The additional depreciation can be treated as an *appropriation* of profit.

2. When fixed assets are to be replaced it is all very well to say that they should be replaced with equivalent assets, but it should not be forgotten that technological development often decrees that new, more advanced types of assets should be used. Sometimes there is a change in the products being made and this may involve the purchase of entirely different machinery or other fixed assets. These observations are quite true, but they do not invalidate the argument that capital should be maintained intact. The reference to maintaining capital intact can refer to the *total* purchasing power tied up in assets and not to individual assets. The fact that the individual parts, which go to make up the whole, change does not affect the position so far as maintaining total purchasing (and earning) power is concerned.

3. Calculation or estimation of replacement costs is fraught with difficulties. There is no generally acceptable method of ascertaining what replacement costs should be. There is even confusion on which year should be taken as a basis for calculating replacement costs. Should it be the current year being dealt with or should it be the actual year when the asset is to be replaced? The latter is really the more significant yet there is never any certainty when a fixed asset will be ready for replacement. If the current year's replacement cost is taken for *total* depreciation (original cost plus additional for replacement) there is a real danger that the amount charged will be smaller or larger than the final replacement cost.

There is no denying that difficulties do exist. However, these are not as insurmountable as some people appear to think. The methods available for estimating costs are covered below.

4. When revaluation accounting is employed the profit, the depreciation charge, and the value of the assets are not accepted by the taxation authorities for the purpose of computing tax liabilities. Because of this fact the argument is advanced that revaluation is "unacceptable."

A leading question which must inevitably arise here is: for what purpose are accounts prepared? If the purpose *is* to calculate the tax liability then clearly the accounts should be drafted so as to comply with this requirement to the exclusion of all others. However, very few, if any, directors or higher level management will take this view. The main purposes of accounting are to assist with planning, co-ordinating, controlling, and communicating. The computation of the tax to be paid is a subsidiary exercise. If the main purposes are ignored there may be no tax to pay because there may be no profit!

If the concern is with management accounting then the *complete* revaluation of assets or at least the recognition of the problem in the accounts is very desirable.

5. If revaluation principles were allowed for the purpose of calculating costs, in a period of rising prices the profit would be lower and this would tend to mean that lower taxes would be payable. This in turn would lead to a company's possessing more purchasing power and, therefore, the inflationary trend would be aggravated still further.

There may be some truth in this assertion. However, it should mean that companies are being treated more fairly because they would *all* be paying taxes on profit which has been calculated by considering current costs. If companies are being taxed on profits computed by reference to historical costs then they are paying a levy on something they have not really got; in effect, on part of the capital.

6. If revaluation accounting is taken to extremes and all assets and liabilities are converted into common monetary units then the work involved becomes tremendous. Furthermore, many complexities are introduced into an already complicated subject. Management accounting should elucidate, not complicate.

There is certainly a good deal of truth in these criticisms. The actual accounting becomes more complicated and presentation of information to management in a simple manner becomes quite a problem. However, the first criticism can be overcome by paying attention to formulating principles and incorporating these into the accounting system as well as by using modern accounting machines.*

The second objection may be overcome by making management conscious of the need to appreciate modern accounting methods. That this is possible may be evidenced by the fact that Budgetary Control, Marginal Costing, Standard Costing and other techniques have all been introduced into companies and are used fully by management with a full appreciation of what is being achieved. In actual fact, dealing with current replacement costs is not far removed from running a Budgetary Control or Standard Costing system.

*Conclusion:* there are many problems and difficulties associated with revaluation accounting; this cannot be denied. However, until some means can be found of stabilising the value of money there is clearly a duty for the management accountant to show the effects of changing values on the profit and the capital invested. Failure to do this means that the true economic significance of transactions is not being shown and management, shareholders, employees, and others, are all presented with a picture which is inaccurate and misleading. How the problem of revaluation should be tackled is discussed in the next section.

* See "An Application of Replacement Value Theory," by A. GOUDEKET in *The Manager* for January 1961, page 41.

## TWO METHODS OF APPROACH

There are two principal schools of thought on revaluation accounting. On the one hand, there is the body of accountants who advocate that the problem of maintaining capital intact should be recognised by making a special appropriation in the final accounts to cover the *additional* cost of replacement; *i.e.* the difference between the historical cost of the old asset and the price of the new asset. In this category there are some accountants who would show the present values of assets owned, but there are others who would prefer not to change the values; that is to say, they would prefer the old assets to remain at historical costs. Whichever variation of this method is taken there is an attempt made to provide for future replacement of assets and also to calculate profit in a manner which recognises that monetary values do change.

The second school of thought advocates revaluation accounting to the fullest possible extent.

For convenience these two methods may be classified as follows:

1. Partial Revaluation Accounting.
2. Complete Revaluation Accounting.

In both cases the stocks of raw materials can be issued on the basis of last-in, first-out or at standard prices, both of which can approximate current replacement prices.

Some idea of how these methods may be applied can be obtained later in this chapter. First though, the methods of converting assets to current values are covered.

## MEASURING CHANGES IN THE VALUE OF MONEY

A suitable basis has to be found for measuring changes in the value of the purchasing power represented by the assets and liabilities held by the particular business. It is not just a matter of measuring changes in *general* purchasing power. Each business is *individualistic* in that it uses its own methods of production, specific assets, raw materials suitable for its own particular needs and so on. Changes in purchasing power locked up in the assets of a particular company are not necessarily the same as changes in general purchasing power.

The principal methods which may be employed for measuring the changes are as follows:

1. *Cost of Living Index (Index of Retail Prices).*
   This is published monthly in the *Ministry of Labour Gazette* and the *Monthly Digest of Statistics*. Changes are also reported in the

national newspapers. At the time of writing the base is 1962, this representing 100.

Criticisms have been levelled against the index on the grounds that it is not representative of an "average household budget" and, therefore, it does not truly show the cost of living. Nevertheless, it is a good guide to what changes have taken place. However, because it deals with retail prices it may *not* be suitable for converting assets to current replacement values.

2. *Wholesale Price Index Numbers.*

   (*a*) Board of Trade.

   (*b*) *The Statist.*

3. *The Financial Times* Commodity Price Index.

4. *The Economist* Index of Commodity Prices.

Again, like the Index of Retail Prices, there is provided with (2) to (4) a measure of *general* changes, although these do apply to specific groups of commodities which are more likely to be of interest to companies than are retail prices.

Of course, it should be appreciated that even if an index does not refer to a specific asset it can still show the extent of general price changes which may be a reflection of the changes taking place in the prices of these particular assets. The problem is to determine whether or not this is the case.

5. *Index Numbers compiled by the company concerned.*

There is no doubt that this method is likely to give very good results. However, there is the necessity to create an organisation and system which can deal with the recording of the changes in prices of the assets concerned. It seems advisable to divide the assets into definite groups each having similar characteristics. An index can then be compiled for each main group.\*

6. *Professional Valuation.*

This method is favoured when a periodic valuation is carried out; *e.g.* every five years.

7. *Insurance Values.*

Insurance Values may be used as a guide to current values. Thus, for example, for plant and machinery, the value assessed for fire insurance may be used.

8. *The Net Annual Value (N.A.V.).*

The net annual values of land and buildings as assessed by the Land Valuation Office may be used as a guide to current values provided they are up-to-date.

9. *Market prices* of similar assets. These may be obtained from the suppliers of the assets.

Which method or combination of methods to employ must be determined by the accountant concerned. The one that gives the most

---

\* This is the method used by Philips Electrical Company of the Netherlands.

realistic results should be the aim. Experience should bring to light whether or not the method being employed is producing the most accurate figures.

One of the main problems encountered is to convert the costs of fixed assets purchased at different dates over a long period of time. Using index numbers of a suitable type is generally much more objective than a valuation. However, there is the problem that each asset's cost has to be converted separately using a different index number for each year. Furthermore, if the index number has changed its form several times, then different base years emerge to make the calculations and understanding even more difficult. Thus, for example, the Cost of Living Index in Great Britain commenced in 1914 and was revised in 1947 to become the Index of Retail Prices. This was then amended in 1952, 1953, 1956, and 1962. These changes are inevitable because of changes in the pattern of spending. However, they do not inspire confidence in the use of this index for revaluation accounting purposes.

Possibly the best solution for any business which is tackling the problem of revaluation accounting for the first time is to have an appraisal made of all assets by an expert valuer. Once this has been done index numbers can be compiled and used to take into account future changes in the purchasing power and, therefore, the value of fixed assets. Generally the latter are the items involved in a first revaluation. In times of rising prices fixed assets may appreciate in value to a considerable extent, particularly if these are freehold land and buildings. Stocks may be affected but to a lesser extent.

However, if a valuation is carried out it should be remembered that this depends to a high degree on the opinions of the valuers. These may vary from time to time even with the same valuers. Furthermore, the value may be higher or lower depending upon the general economic situation. If industry is facing even a minor recession there may be a tendency for property values to be depressed, whereas if trade is booming the sky is the limit. A suitably compiled index number can iron out any erratic fluctuations in values. It can be used regularly and not be a spasmodic tool of adjustment as is often the appraisal method. Furthermore, there tends to be less trouble in valuing by means of index numbers and as a result the operation can be much cheaper.

If Standard Costing is employed in a business the problem of compiling an index may be simplified. Information on price changes of materials used, labour employed and services and fixed assets purchased should be kept. From this information an index number can be compiled. If *Basic* Standard Costing is employed, changes are recorded automatically. A base year is fixed by the date when the Standards are set and then any changes can be seen through the ratios compiled as part of the system.*

---

* See J. Batty, *Standard Costing*, Macdonald and Evans.

## PARTIAL REVALUATION ACCOUNTING

As noted earlier, partial revaluation accounting may consist of the following features:

1. In addition to depreciation at original cost a special charge is made, akin to depreciation, to cover the additional cost of replacing the fixed assets.

This extra charge represents the increase in prices; *i.e.* the fall in the value of money.

2. Raw materials are issued at prices which reflect as nearly as possible current replacement prices.

This usually means using the last-in, first-out method or standard prices. However, a fact sometimes overlooked is that last-in, first-out will not result in current replacement charges if prices are rising at a rapid rate and turnover of raw materials is at a relatively slow rate.

3. Fixed assets are revalued by one of the methods described earlier; *e.g.* by index numbers or by expert valuation.

This revaluation is not always present in a partial scheme. Instead (1) and (2) only are carried out.

How features (1) and (3) may be incorporated into the accounting system is discussed below. Stock valuation is covered in Chapter 25 and is also dealt with under Complete Revaluation Accounting later in this chapter.

It seems fair to say that partial revaluation accounting is now widely accepted by the accountancy profession in most European countries and in the U.S.A. As yet *complete* revaluation does not have the same support.

### DEALING WITH DEPRECIATION AND REPLACEMENT COST

There are two possible methods of dealing with the *additional amount*, over and above normal depreciation at historical cost, required to finance replacement of fixed assets at current prices. These are:

1. Charge the amount to Profit and Loss Appropriation Account and then create a special capital reserve with a suitable title; *e.g.* Asset Replacement Reserve Account.

This is the method widely adopted.

2. Charge to the Profit and Loss Account proper thus treating this additional amount as a normal cost of operating. A replacement reserve would be created and shown on the Balance Sheet just as in (1).

Method (2) does not as yet appear to be employed very much. The majority of accountants seem to favour an *appropriation* of profit rather

than a *charge against profit* on the grounds that the additional charge
to cover price changes is an *unusual* or *exceptional* item of expenditure.
Nevertheless, support for inclusion in the Profit and Loss Account
proper does appear to be growing. The Society of Investment Analysts,
a body which carries weight in the City of London, has suggested that
the item should be included in the Profit and Loss Account and not the
Appropriation Account.*

In both these cases the normal depreciation based on historical costs
would be debited to the Profit and Loss Account.

The adjustments suggested can be carried out without affecting the
values of the fixed assets. Fundamentally, all that is involved is a
transfer from profit available for distribution to a capital reserve. In
this way there is no danger that real capital (*i.e.* assets invested) will be
depleted by a distribution which is imprudent. The Profit and Loss
Balance which appears as a revenue reserve will be reduced by the
extent of the transfer to the capital reserve.

## REVALUATION OF ASSETS

The many different methods available for revaluation are covered in
an earlier section (pages 707–709). The problem is to find the one which
is objective, is easy to use, is generally available through regular publication or other means and is not too costly to operate. One of the
major problems of revaluation accounting is to find a method which
is not affected by personal prejudice or bias.† When this has been
done there will be a more general acceptance of the revaluation
principles.

A simple example will illustrate the principles involved.

QUESTION

B.T. Co. Ltd. has a number of freehold properties, the dates of purchase
being as follows:

| Year of purchase | Cost £ | Serviceable life | Depreciation charge (on original cost balance) | Hypothetical Price Index |
|---|---|---|---|---|
| 1947 | 5,000 | 50 years | 1% per annum | 100 |
| 1957 | 10,000 | 40 „ | 2% „ „ | 150 |
| 1969 | 12,000 | 40 „ | 2% „ „ | 300 |

* See *Compiling and Presenting Company Reports* prepared by the Society in
co-operation with Daniel Greenaway & Sons Ltd., page 17–2 (*a*) and (*b*) refer.

† Noted in Recommendation XV of the Institute of Chartered Accountants in
England and Wales. Paragraph 289 states the principles should be "capable of
practical application to all kinds of businesses in a manner which would be independent of personal opinion to a degree comparable with the existing principles based
on historical cost."

At the end of the 1969 year the company carried out an appraisal of the properties and found the values to be as follows:

| Year of purchase | Value as per appraisal | Serviceable life |
|---|---|---|
| | £ | |
| 1947 | 13,000 | Unchanged |
| 1957 | 17,000 | ,, |
| 1969 | 11,700 | ,, |
| | £41,700 | |

Taking into account these facts, you are required to show the entries necessary for recording the changes in the ledger: (a) using the Index numbers, and (b) using the appraisal values.

The company has a balance of £50,000 on Profit and Loss Account and is going to use this in the adjustments. Depreciation has been charged at historical costs up to and including the year 1969.

SUGGESTED SOLUTION (with notes)

(a) Using index numbers

Preliminary Calculations. The calculations involved to convert to current values are as follows:

| Year | Cost £ | Index changes | New values £ |
|---|---|---|---|
| 1947 | 5,000 | $\frac{300}{100}$; i.e. 3 | 15,000 |
| 1957 | 10,000 | $\frac{300}{150}$; i.e. 2 | 20,000 |
| 1969 | 12,000 | $\frac{300}{300}$; i.e. 1 | 12,000 |
| | £27,000 | | £47,000 |

Note. The "index change" is compiled from the index for the year of purchase over the index of the current year. In other words, each asset is calculated to present values by use of the formula:

$$\frac{\text{Current year index}}{\text{Year of purchase index}} \times \text{Original cost}$$

When index numbers are used there is a necessity to adjust the depreciation also to present values; that is, to calculate total depreciation on the new values. There is no change in the estimated serviceable life of the asset; had there been, then further adjustments in depreciation would be essential.

## LEDGER ACCOUNTS

*Property Account*

| | | £ | | |
|---|---|---|---|---|
| 1947 | Balance | 5,000 | | |
| 1957 | " | 10,000 | | |
| 1969 | " | 12,000 | | |
| 1969 | Asset Replacement Reserve A/c (1) | 20,000 | | |
| | | £47,000 | | |

*Depreciation Provision Account*

| | | | Balance | 3,990 |
|---|---|---|---|---|
| | | 1969 | Profit and Loss Balance (2) | 4,900 |
| | | | | £8,890 |

*Revaluation Reserve Account*

| | | Property Account (1) | £20,000 |
|---|---|---|---|

*Profit and Loss Balance*

| 1969 | Depreciation Provision (2) | £4,900 | Balance | £50,000 |
|---|---|---|---|---|

*Notes on Adjustments:*

|  | £ |
|---|---|
| 1. New value of properties | 47,000 |
| *Less* Old value | 27,000 |
| Increase in value | £20,000 |

Entry:
Property Account   Dr. £20,000.
    To Asset Replacement Reserve Account £20,000.

2. The additional amount required to charge depreciation at current prices is £4900 calculated as shown below.

Assuming that the year of purchase and 1969 have to be brought into the calculation the depreciation charges would be as follows:

| *Historical Costs* | | £ |
|---|---|---|
| 1947 | 1% per annum for 23 years | 1150 |
| 1957 | 2% per annum for 13 years | 2600 |
| 1969 | 2% per annum for 1 year | 240 |
| | | £3990 |

| *Replacement Costs* | | |
|---|---|---|
| 1947 | 1% per annum for 23 years on £15,000 | 3450 |
| 1957 | 2% per annum for 13 years on £20,000 | 5200 |
| 1969 | 2% per annum for 1 year on £12,000 | 240 |
| | | £8890 |

The adjustment to cover depreciation on the extra value is, therefore, £4900.

*(b) Using Appraisal Values*

## LEDGER ACCOUNTS

### Property Account

| | | £ | | |
|---|---|---|---|---|
| 1969 | Balances | 27,000 | | |
| | Asset Replacement Reserve | 14,700 | | |
| | | 41,700 | | |

### Revaluation Reserve Account

| | | | £ |
|---|---|---|---|
| | | Property Account | 14,700 |

### Depreciation Provision Account

| | | | £ |
|---|---|---|---|
| | | Balance | 3,990 |

*Notes on Adjustments*

1. The difference between the present value and the historical cost is put through the books.

2. Since the appraisal relates to the position after depreciation there is no need to adjust the figure for depreciation.

3. In future the total amount of depreciation on the new values will be charged in the Profit and Loss Account and possibly also the Profit and Loss Appropriation Account.

## COMPLETE REVALUATION ACCOUNTING

Complete revaluation accounting adjusts all fixed assets to current values and, in addition, attempts to ensure that capital is maintained intact through consideration of the loss (or gain) in purchasing power of current assets. Reduced to the essentials the processes involved are as follows:

1. Convert fixed assets to current replacement costs. This will mean debiting the fixed asset accounts with the additional amounts required to bring up to current replacement costs.

The credit entry may be to a Revaluation Account or other appropriately named capital reserve. Alternatively, the index number may be applied to the share capital, thereby converting that figure to present values.

2. The change in purchasing power on the net current assets, *i.e.* the loss from holding current assets, must be taken into account when calculating the profit for the year.

This rule applies to the net current assets held at the *beginning* of the year. Only if these are maintained *intact* in terms of equivalent purchasing power can it be said that a profit has been earned.

3. Depreciation should be charged on the basis of current replacement costs.

Only fixed assets which do increase in value should be converted into current replacement costs. Accordingly, there should be consideration of the *economic* value of each asset. The revaluation accounting should not be regarded simply as an exercise in figures. If an asset is revalued; the new valuation should reflect its approximate economic worth to the business.

When intangible assets are being considered caution has to be exercised. Often the realisable value of patents, trade marks and commercial goodwill is very difficult to estimate and, therefore, following the normal practice of conservatism many accountants would prefer to exclude intangible assets from a revaluation.

The *year-end* current assets and liabilities will normally be in terms of current values. Often these change in form fairly quickly so they represent current purchasing power. This will generally be the case with debtors and cash. When dealing with stocks of raw materials there is the problem of ensuring that current replacement costs are charged in the costs of products. This may be accomplished by "last-in, first-out" if turnover of stocks is rapid; alternatively, standard prices or current replacement prices may be employed. The stocks at year-end are usually valued by one of the recommended methods discussed in Chapter 25. In this connection there is probably some merit in showing the closing stock value at a lower, rather than a higher figure. For example, in a period of rising prices actual cost for closing stock will show a lower profit than when replacement cost is used for valuation, and this follows the accounting convention that profit should not be anticipated.

## METHODS OF COMPLETE REVALUATION ACCOUNTING

There is no one *generally accepted* system for complete revaluation accounting. Some accountants advocate the revaluation of all assets, sales and costs. Others prefer a more conservative approach to the problem taking into consideration only items which represent significant changes. Since the index numbers used must of necessity be in the nature of approximations it is felt that extra refinements cannot be justified.

Neither do the mechanics of conversion enjoy the privilege of being "standardised." Some accountants revalue fixed assets, debiting the appropriate accounts, and show the increase in shareholders' equity in a capital reserve account. Others prefer to convert the value of the share capital into terms of current purchasing power. These differences in approach are reflected in the example given below, where a question is tackled in two different ways.

The first solution takes the form of memorandum adjustments, whereas the second shows journal entries, the intention being to incorporate the changes in the books of the business.

## EXAMPLE OF COMPLETE REVALUATION ACCOUNTING

In order to illustrate the principles involved a Question and suggested Solution are given below. These are along simple lines, the purpose being to illustrate the principles.

QUESTION

*Balance Sheets of R.M. Co. Ltd.*

|  | 1968 £ | 1969 £ |  | 1968 £ | 1969 £ |
|---|---|---|---|---|---|
| Ordinary Share Capital (fully paid-up 1957) ... | 10,000 | 10,000 | *Fixed Assets:* Land and Buildings Purchased 1957 Cost £6000 | 6,000 | 6,000 |
| Profit and Loss Balance ... | 1,000 | 1,300 | Machinery Purchased 1957 Cost £5200 | 3,000 | 2,800 |
| *Current Liabilities:* Creditors ... | 1,000 | 1,400 | *Current Assets:* Stocks ... | 1,200 | 1,400 |
|  |  |  | Debtors (net) | 1,000 | 1,500 |
|  |  |  | Cash ... | 800 | 1,000 |
|  | £12,000 | £12,700 |  | £12,000 | £12,700 |

The fixed assets are shown at the present net figure; *i.e.* after charging depreciation.

The index numbers are as follows:

|  | *Index of General Price* |
|---|---|
| *Accounting Year-End* | *Level (hypothetical)* |
| 1957 | 100 |
| 1968 | 200 |
| 1969 | 300 |

No dividends have been paid for the year which ended in 1969.

SUGGESTED SOLUTION

The following work sheet is not an essential part of the solution. However, it does set out the method of converting the fixed assets to current replacement costs and also the way of calculating the present value of the beginning-of-the-year current assets and liabilities.

## Conversion of Assets and Liabilities to 1969 Accounting Year-End Values

| | Historical Costs 1968 | Historical Costs 1969 | Conversion Factor | 1968 converted to 1969 values | 1969 in 1969 values |
|---|---|---|---|---|---|
| | £ | £ | £ | £ | £ |
| Land and Buildings ... | 6,000 | 6,000 | $\frac{300}{100}$ | 18,000 | 18,000 |
| Machinery ... | 3,000 | 2,800 | $\frac{300}{100}$ | 9,000 | 8,400 |
| Stocks ... ... | 1,200 | 1,400 | $\frac{300}{200}$* | 1,800 | 1,400 |
| Debtors ... ... | 1,000 | 1,500 | $\frac{300}{200}$* | 1,500 | 1,500 |
| Cash ... ... | 800 | 1,000 | $\frac{300}{200}$* | 1,200 | 1,000 |
| | £12,000 | £12,700 | | £31,500 | £30,300 |
| Creditors | 1,000 | 1,400 | $\frac{300}{200}$* | 1,500 | 1,400 |
| Balances: Proprietors' Net Worth | 11,000 | 11,300 | | 30,000 | 28,900 |
| | £12,000 | £12,700 | | £31,500 | £30,300 |

The balances—the proprietors' net worth for each year—are found by deducting creditors from *total* assets. There is a reduction of £1100 between the end of 1968 and 1969. This indicates a loss of that amount, subsequently to be adjusted through the Profit and Loss adjustment.

### Profit and Loss Account (1969)

| | £ | | £ |
|---|---|---|---|
| Depreciation (Machinery) (additional amount required to bring the total to that required on replacement costs; *i.e.* £600-£200) † ... | 400 | Balance (£1300−£1000) | 300 |
| | | Balance Loss for Year ... | 1,100 |
| Loss on net current assets (Note 2) ... ... ... | 1,000 | | |
| | £1,400 | | £1,400 |

* Relevant only for converting 1968 to 1969 values. 1969 current assets and liabilities already at 1969 values.
† Depreciation of £600 is based on valuation of £9000.

*Notes.*

1. No information is given on sales and costs other than depreciation. If these had been included in the Question then some accountants would advocate converting to present values by means of an *average* index number. Thus, for example, if sales occur evenly throughout the year, then the mid-value would be taken (in the question the average would be 250—half-way between 200 and 300).

2. The loss from holding *net* current assets is £1000. This is found as follows:

|  | Beginning of Year (Current Values) | Historical Costs |
|---|---|---|
|  | £ | £ |
| Stocks | 1,800 | 1,200 |
| Debtors | 1,500 | 1,000 |
| Cash | 1,200 | 800 |
|  | 4,500 | 3,000 |
| *Less* Creditors | 1,500 | 1,000 |
|  | £3,000 | £2,000 |

There has been an increase of £1000 and this is treated as a loss. This is the amount which has to be recovered from profit in order to maintain capital intact.

*Balance Sheet of R.M. Co. Ltd.,*
*as at 1969 Year-End (Current Values)*

| | £ | | | £ |
|---|---|---|---|---|
| Ordinary Share Capital fully | | *Fixed Assets:* | | |
| paid up ...  ...  ... 10,000 | | Land and Buildings at | | |
| Revaluation   £ | | 1969 valuation  ... | | 18,000 |
| Account   20,000 | | Machinery at 1969  £ | | |
| *Less* Loss for Year ... 1,100 | | valuation  ... 9,000 | | |
| ——— 18,900 | | *Less* Depreciation  600 | | |
| | | ——— | | 8,400 |
| *Current Liabilities:* | | | | 26,400 |
| Creditors  ...  ...  ... 1,400 | | | | |
| | | *Current Assets:* | | |
| | | Stocks ...  ... 1,400 | | |
| | | Debtors  ... 1,500 | | |
| | | Cash  ...  ... 1,000 | | |
| | | ——— | | 3,900 |
| | £30,300 | | | £30,300 |

*Notes.*

1. The Share Capital is shown at the *nominal* value. An alternative procedure is to show the *real* value of the Ordinary shares by multiplying by the index number; *i.e.* 300. This would result in a figure of £30,000 and would mean that the Revaluation and Profit and Loss Accounts would have to be adjusted. This alternative procedure is given below.

2. The Revaluation Account is the addition to *Capital* arising from the revaluation; *i.e.* $\left(£10,000 \times \dfrac{300}{100}\right) - £10,000 = £20,000.$

3. Current assets and liabilities are not converted. They are already at current values.

SUGGESTED SOLUTION (Alternative Approach)

*Journal Entries (Adjustments)*

|  |  |  | Dr.<br>£ | Cr.<br>£ |
|---|---|---|---|---|
| **1968**<br>End of<br>Year | Purchasing Power Adjustment Account<br>  To Paid-up Capital<br>    Being conversion of Paid-up Capital to 1968 values<br>    $£10,000 \times \dfrac{200}{100} = £20,000$<br>    *Less* Old Value      10,000<br>                  £10,000 | Dr. | 10,000 | 10,000 |
| | Land and Buildings<br>Machinery Account<br>  To Purchasing Power Adjustment Account<br>    Being conversion of fixed assets to 1968 values.<br>    Land and Buildings   £6000 $\times \dfrac{200}{100}$<br>    Machinery           £3000 $\times \dfrac{200}{100}$<br><br>    Land and Buildings:<br>      New Value     £12,000<br>    *Less*  Old Value    6,000<br>                £6,000<br><br>    Plant and Machinery:<br>      New Values    £6,000<br>    *Less*  Old Value    3,000<br>                £3,000 | Dr.<br>Dr. | 6,000<br>3,000 | 9,000 |
| | Profit and Loss Balance<br>  To Purchasing Power Adjustment Account.<br>    Being transfer of balance on Purchasing Power Adjustment<br>    Account, thereby correcting profit up to end of 1968. | Dr. | 1,000 | 1,000 |
|  |  |  | Dr.<br>£ | Cr.<br>£ |
| **1969**<br>End of<br>Year | Purchasing Power Adjustment Account<br>  To Paid-up Capital<br>    Being conversion from 1968 to 1969 values.<br>    $£20,000 \times \dfrac{300}{200} = £30,000$<br>    *Less* 1968 Value    20,000<br>                  £10,000 |  | 10,000 | 10,000 |
| | Land and Buildings<br>Plant and Machinery<br>  To Purchasing Power Adjustment Account<br>    Being conversion of fixed assets from 1968 to 1969 values.<br>    Land and Buildings<br>    $£12,000 \times \dfrac{300}{200} = £18,000$<br>    *Less* 1968 Value    £12,000<br>                 £6,000<br>    Plant and Machinery<br>    $£6000 \times \dfrac{300}{200} = £9,000$<br>    *Less* 1968 Value    £6,000<br>                £3,000 | Dr. | 6,000<br>3,000 | 9,000 |

AA

| | | | Dr. £ | Cr. £ |
|---|---|---|---|---|
| 1969 End of Year | Profit and Loss Balance To Purchasing Power Adjustment Account. Being loss in value of net current assets between end of 1968 and end of 1969, viz.: | | 1,000 | 1,000 |

$$
\begin{array}{llll}
 & & £ & \\
\text{Stocks} & 1800 & (\text{i.e. } \tfrac{300}{200} \times £1200) \\
\text{Debtors} & 1500 & (\text{i.e. } \tfrac{300}{200} \times £1000) \\
\text{Cash} & 1200 & (\text{i.e. } \tfrac{300}{200} \times £800) \\
 & \overline{4500} \\
\text{Less Creditors} & 1500 \\
 & \overline{\phantom{0}} & £3000 \ (£3000-£2000 \text{ historical costs})
\end{array}
$$

| | | Dr. | | |
|---|---|---|---|---|
| Depreciation Account To Plant and Machinery | | | 400 | 400 |

$$£200 \times \frac{300}{100} = £600$$

Less Charge already made   £200
                  ——    £400

### Balance Sheet of R.M. Co. Ltd., as at 1969 Year-End (Current Values)

| | £ | | £ | £ |
|---|---|---|---|---|
| Ordinary Share Capital fully paid-up | 30,000 | *Fixed Assets* | | |
| *Less* Loss to date | 1,100 | Land and Buildings at 1969 valuation | | 18,000 |
| | 28,900 | Machinery at 1969 valuation | 9,000 | |
| *Current Liabilities* | | *Less* Depreciation | 600 | |
| Creditors | 1,400 | | —— | 8,400 |
| | | | | 26,400 |
| | | *Current Assets* | | |
| | | Stocks | 1,400 | |
| | | Debtors | 1,500 | |
| | | Cash | 1,000 | |
| | | | | 3,900 |
| | £30,300 | | | £30,300 |

The total loss to date is found as shown in the Profit and Loss Adjustment Account shown below. How the entries in the account arise can be seen from the journal entries given earlier.

### Profit and Loss Adjustment Account

| | £ | | £ |
|---|---|---|---|
| Fixed Assets Adjustment to 1968 values | 1,000 | Balance | 1,300 |
| Current Assets Adjustment to 1969 values | 1,000 | Loss to date when capital is maintained | |
| Depreciation for 1969 (additional amount) | 400 | intact at present values | 1,100 |
| | £2,400 | | £2,400 |

## A PRACTICAL ILLUSTRATION—PHILIPS*

Many accountants appear to regard complete revaluation accounting as a *theoretical* exercise which has little or no practical value. However,

---

* Philips Electrical Company of the Netherlands (N. V. Philips' Gloeilampen-fabrieken) who kindly gave permission for details to be reproduced from the Annual Report for 1968.

this is far from true and many writers have attempted to show that the theory can be put into practice. A few companies have incorporated the principles into their accounting systems. One very notable example is the revaluation accounting system operated by the Philips Electrical Company of the Netherlands. Some of the main features of the system are given below.

## Philips' Published Accounts

The published accounts of the Philips Company for the year 1968 are given below. Throughout the accounting system the revaluation principles outlined in the previous section are followed.

The Company has a highly organised system for recording changes in the value of money. Index numbers based on specific prices are used for converting fixed assets to replacement values. These assets are divided into major groups each representing those of a similar nature; e.g. machine tools go into one group and buildings into another. A separate index number is compiled for each group. Information on prices is collected by a special department and is recorded in a suitable manner by the accounting department.

Stocks are kept at standard prices and are revalued, when necessary, to replacement value. This is explained in the "principles" in the next section.

The Revaluation Account is the central adjustment account through which increases or reductions in value are credited or debited. This account is debited with the liability for future taxation.

As will be apparent, the replacement value principles are incorporated fully into the double-entry accounting system.

### PRINCIPLES OF VALUATION

#### Property, plant and equipment

These assets and their depreciation are valued on the basis of replacement value. Changes in the replacement value are either credited or charged to the Revaluation Account.

#### Intangible assets

Expenditure on research, development and patents, and amounts paid for goodwill, are shown at no value.

#### Interests in non-consolidated subsidiaries and associated companies

Non-consolidated investments are included at an amount not exceeding their intrinsic value.

#### Sundry non-current assets

These assets are shown below or equal to the amount at which they are expected to be realised.

[Continued at foot of page 725.

## CONSOLIDATED STATEMENT OF

| | 1968 | | 1967 | |
|---|---|---|---|---|
| **Property, plant and equipment** | | | | |
| Replacement value | 7,177,872,000 | | 6,556,415,000 | |
| Depreciation | −3,323,428,000 | 3,854,444,000 | −2,941,787,000 | 3,614,628,000 |
| **Intangible assets** | | — | | — |
| **Interests in non-consolidated subsidiaries and associated companies** | | 1,250,199,000 | | 893,456,000 |
| **Sundry non-current assets** | | 272,977,000 | | 227,813,000 |
| **Stocks** | | | | |
| Factory stocks | 1,576,048,000 | | 1,473,877,000 | |
| Advance payments by customers | −171,120,000 | | −181,180,000 | |
| | 1,404,928,000 | | 1,292,697,000 | |
| Commercial stocks | 1,529,859,000 | 2,934,787,000 | 1,482,006,000 | 2,774,703,000 |
| **Debtors** | | | | |
| Trade debtors | 2,951,627,000 | | 2,591,103,000 | |
| Discounted bills | −247,527,000 | | −229,083,000 | |
| | 2,704,100,000 | | 2,362,020,000 | |
| Other debtors | 366,979,000 | | 286,915,000 | |
| Prepaid expenses | 215,020,000 | 3,286,099,000 | 187,604,000 | 2,836,539,000 |
| **Liquid assets** | | | | |
| Marketable securities | 104,264,000 | | 80,099,000 | |
| Cash at bank and in hand | 629,937,000 | 734,201,000 | 663,164,000 | 743,263,000 |
| Amounts in guilders. | | 12,332,707,000 | | 11,090,402,000 |

## CONSOLIDATED STATEMENT OF RESULTS

| | 1968 | | 1967 | |
|---|---|---|---|---|
| **Sales** | | 9,720,701,000 | | 8,694,636,000 |
| **Costs:** | | | | |
| Cost of sales | 6,416,224,000 | | 5,787,027,000 | |
| Selling and general expenses | 2,182,993,000 | 8,599,217,000 | 2,006,490,000 | 7,793,517,000 |
| **Trading profit** | | 1,121,484,000 | | 901,119,000 |
| Other income and charges: | | | | |
| Interest paid | 240,598,000 | | 235,744,000 | |
| Miscellaneous | 83,802,000 | | 45,334,000 | |
| | 324,400,000 | | 281,078,000 | |
| Interest received | 58,385,000 | 266,015,000 | 49,679,000 | 231,399,000 |
| **Profit before taxation** | | 855,469,000 | | 669,720,000 |
| Tax on profits | | 431,054,000 | | 329,325,000 |
| **Profit after taxation** | | 424,415,000 | | 340,395,000 |
| Share in net profit of non-consolidated companies | | 36,154,000 | | 25,096,000 |
| | | 460,569,000 | | 365,491,000 |
| Minority shareholder's interests | | 22,042,000 | | 10,731,000 |
| **Net profit** | | 438,527,000 | | 354,760,000 |
| Amounts in guilders. | | | | |

## FINANCIAL POSITION

|  | 1968 |  | 1967 |  |
|---|---|---|---|---|
| **Share capital and reserve** |  |  |  |  |
| Ordinary share capital | 1,017,428,000 |  | 1,017,428,000 |  |
| 6% cum. part. pref. share capital | 144,000,000 |  | 144,000,000 |  |
| Share premium account | 456,160,000 |  | 456,160,000 |  |
| Retained profit | 2,584,403,000 |  | 2,374,872,000 |  |
| Revaluation | 924,893,000 | 5,126,884,000 | 795,209,000 | 4,787,669,000 |
| **Minority shareholders' interests** |  | 236,585,000 |  | 170,510,000 |
| **Sundry provisions** |  |  |  |  |
| Long-term provisions | 1,021,829,000 |  | 891,005,000 |  |
| Short-term provisions | 284,794,000 | 1,306,623,000 | 229,574,000 | 1,120,579,000 |
| **Long-term liabilities** |  |  |  |  |
| 4¾% convertible debentures (unsecured) | 360,000,000 |  | — |  |
| Other debentures (unsecured) | 435,960,000 |  | 439,702,000 |  |
| Other long-term liabilities | 1,252,553,000 | 2,048,513,000 | 1,174,498,000 | 1,614,200,000 |
| **Current liabilities** |  |  |  |  |
| Banks | 1,056,550,000 |  | 1,045,726,000 |  |
| Creditors | 1,507,286,000 |  | 1,378,318,000 |  |
| Provisions for tax on profits | 364,925,000 |  | 305,520,000 |  |
| Accrued expenses | 456,345,000 | 3,385,106,000 | 439,062,000 | 3,168,626,000 |
| **Profit for distribution** |  | 228,996,000 |  | 228,818,000 |
|  |  | 12,332,707,000 |  | 11,090,402,000 |

Amounts in guilders.

## EXPLANATORY NOTES

EXPLANATORY NOTES TO ASSETS AND LIABILITIES

**Property, plant and equipment**

| | | |
|---|---|---|
| Book value as at 1st January, 1968 | | 3,614,628,000 |
| *Changes:* | | |
| Investments in land, buildings and houses | 109,816,000 | |
| Investments in plant and equipment | 376,158,000 | |
| Net decrease due to assets withdrawn from use, improvements and overhauls | −5,096,000 | |
| Net acquisitions | | 480,878,000 |
| Depreciation on buildings and houses | −104,092,000 | |
| Depreciation on plant and equipment | −356,502,000 | |
| | | −460,594,000 |
| Revaluation | | 113,122,000 |
| Increase due to new consolidations | | 106,410,000 |
| Book value as at 31st December, 1968 | | 3,854,444,000 |

|  | replacement value | depreciation | book value |
|---|---|---|---|
| Vacant sites | 86,248,000 | — | 86,248,000 |
| Land and buildings | 3,503,304,000 | 1,016,846,000 | 2,486,458,000 |
| Houses and land | 83,357,000 | 29,882,000 | 53,475,000 |
| Plant and equipment | 3,504,963,000 | 2,276,700,000 | 1,228,263,000 |
| Balance as at 31st December, 1968 | 7,177,872,000 | 3,323,428,000 | 3,854,444,000 |

**Interests in non-consolidated subsidiaries and associated companies**
      This item includes loans and other long-term debts receivable totalling ƒ634,500,000; in the Consolidated Statement of Results the interest received on this amount is comprised under "Other income and charges." Short-term amounts due from these companies are included under "Trade debtors."
      The investment in Pye Holdings Ltd., also included under this heading, has been valued in the same way as at 31st December, 1967. This means that the part of this investment in respect of which holders of option certificates can exercise options in the years 1970 up to and including 1973 (47½%) is taken up at the amount of 14 shillings per share which will be received upon exercise of these options, and the remaining holding (53½%) has been valued at intrinsic value. As mentioned on page 16, the investment in Chappell & Co. Inc., New York, and in Chappell & Co. Ltd., London, has provisionally been included under this heading at cost, less the applicable portion of the results since acquisition date.

**Sundry non-current assets**

| | |
|---|---:|
| Loans | 203,166,000 |
| Securities not officially quoted | 39,313,000 |
| Sundry assets not immediately realisable | 28,243,000 |
| Deposit for personnel certificates | 2,255,000 |
| | 272,977,000 |

**Stocks**
      Stocks were decreased in 1968 by ƒ9,910,000 to the debt of the Revaluation Account.

**Debtors**
*Trade debtors*
      This item includes amounts due under hire-purchase and instalment agreements totalling ƒ264,228,000, and short-term amounts due from non-consolidated subsidiaries and associated companies totalling ƒ123,914,000.

**Liquid assets**
*Marketable securities*
      In this item ƒ2,899,750 in ordinary shares and ƒ22,800 in 6% cum. part. preference shares of N.V. Gemeenschappelijk Bezit van Aandeelen Philips' Gloeilampenfabrieken are included at par. The market value of the total holding of securities is ƒ128,733,000.

**Share capital and reserves**
*Ordinary share capital (authorised ƒ2,750 million)*

| | | | |
|---|---:|---:|---:|
| Issued as at 31st December, 1968, unchanged at | | | 1,017,428,000 |

*6% cum. part. pref. share capital (authorised ƒ250 million)*

| | | | |
|---|---:|---:|---:|
| Issued as at 31st December, 1968, unchanged at | | | 144,000,000 |

*Share premium account*

| | | | |
|---|---:|---:|---:|
| Balance as at 31st December, 1968, unchanged at | | | 456,160,000 |

*Retained profit*
Balance as at 1st January, 1968:

| | | | |
|---|---:|---:|---:|
| Retained profit N.V. Philips | 2,092,391,000 | | |
| Net worth United States Philips Trust | 282,481,000 | 2,374,872,000 | |

*Added in* 1968:

| | | | |
|---|---:|---:|---:|
| Retained profit N.V. Philips | 172,466,000 | | |
| Increase in net worth of United States Philips Trust | 37,065,000 | 209,531,000 | |

Balance as at 31st December, 1968:

| | | | |
|---|---:|---:|---:|
| Retained profit N.V. Philips | 2,264,857,000 | | |
| Net worth United States Philips Trust | 319,546,000 | | 2,584,403,000 |

| | |
|---|---:|
| *Revaluation* | 924,893,000 |
| Total | 5,126,884,000 |

**Sundry provisions**
      The provision for latent tax liabilities is included under this heading.

**Long-term liabilities**
*Unsecured debenture loans*

| | | |
|---|---:|---:|
| 4¾% convertible debentures | 360,000,000 | |
| Other debentures | 435,960,000 | 795,960,000 |

*Private loans*

| | | |
|---|---:|---:|
| Bank loans | 286,467,000 | |
| Other loans | 629,217,000 | 915,684,000 |

*Personnel debentures*

| | | |
|---|---:|---:|
| 5% convertible debentures | 7,470,000 | |
| Participating debentures | 203,488,000 | 210,958,000 |

| | | |
|---|---:|---:|
| Mortgages | | 54,416,000 |
| Miscellaneous | | 71,495,000 |
| Balance as at 31st December, 1968 | | 2,048,513,000 |

In the next five years an amount of ƒ794,734,000 will become payable. That part which falls due in 1969 is included under "Current liabilities."

At the end of 1968 the average interest rate on debenture loans was 5¼% and on private loans 6%. The personnel debentures, though redeemable on demand, are in fact in the nature of long-term loans.

### Current liabilities

*Banks*

This item includes the part of long-term bank loans falling due in 1969.

### Creditors

This item includes short-term loans, and amounts totalling ƒ82,468,000 due to non-consolidated subsidiaries and associated companies.

### Contingent liabilities in respect of guarantees

Contingent liabilities in respect of guarantees on behalf of third parties and non-consolidated subsidiaries and associated companies amount to ƒ658,865,000.

### Information for American shareholders

The accounting principles customarily followed by N.V. Philips' Gloeilampenfabrieken for the calculation of profits differ in several respects from those generally accepted in the United States. For the convenience of American readers an attempt is therefore made below to estimate what adjustment to net profit would be required if the principles generally accepted in the United States were employed. The replacement value method has been compared with historical cost for fixed assets and with historical cost on a first-in first-out basis for stocks.

| | thousands of Neth. guilders | thousands of U.S. dollars |
|---|---|---|
| Net profit 1968 shown in the Consolidated Statement of Results | 438,527 | 121,813 |
| Adjustment of net profit on the basis of accounting principles generally accepted in the United States | 50,332 | 13,981 |
| Adjusted net profit | 488,859 | 135,794 |
| Net profit per ordinary share on the basis of the American principles is arrived at as follows: | | |
| Adjusted net profit | 488,859 | 135,794 |
| Deduct: | | |
| Profit-sharing with Supervisory Board, Board of Management and senior executives, and personnel | 33,763 | 9,379 |
| Cash dividends on participating preference shares | 12,096 | 3,360 |
| Adjusted net profit accuring to ordinary shares | 443,000 | 123,055 |
| Number of ordinary shares (par value ƒ25) of N.V. Philips' Gloeilampenfabrieken issued at the end of 1968 | 40,697,120 | |
| Per ordinary share of N.V. Philips' Gloeilampenfabriken (par value ƒ25): | | |
| Adjusted net profit | ƒ10·89 | $ 3·02 |
| Cash dividend | ƒ 4·50 | $ 1·25 |

Assuming conversion of all outstanding convertible debentures into ordinary shares, the adjusted net profit per ordinary share would be ƒ10·40 ($ 2·89).

If the method of historical cost had been applied in the past, it is estimated that the revaluation surplus, as shown in the Consolidated Statement of Financial Position as at 31st December, 1968, would have appeared as follows:

| | thousands of Neth. guilders | thousands of U.S. dollars |
|---|---|---|
| Addition to retained profit | 697,244 | 193,679 |
| Deduction from property, plant and equipment and stocks | 227,649 | 63,236 |
| | 924,893 | 256,915 |

*Continued from page 721.*]

## Stocks

Stocks are valued at replacement value. Changes in this value are either credited or charged to the Revaluation Account; reductions in value resulting from technological improvements in our production processes are charged to the Profit and Loss Account. The provision for the risk of obsolescence is deducted from the total figure for stocks. Profits arising from transactions within the Philips organisation are eliminated.

### Debtors

Debtors are shown at nominal value, after deduction of the provision for the risk of bad debts.

### Liquid assets

Securities are valued at purchase price or at their Stock Exchange quotation at the end of the year, whichever is the lower.

### Minority shareholders' interests

Minority interests in consolidated subsidiaries are valued on the basis of their intrinsic value.

### Foreign currencies

Amounts in foreign currency are converted into guilders at the official rates of exchange, unless the circumstances, as, for instance, the purchasing power of the currency concerned, call for the adoption of a lower rate.

### Replacement value

The replacement value is determined on the basis of the price trends of the various assets, making use of indices.

#### PRINCIPLES OF CALCULATING PROFIT

1. The sales figure represents the proceeds from goods and services supplied to third parties.

2. Depreciation of property, plant and equipment, consumption of raw materials and the other elements in the cost of sales are calculated on the basis of replacement value.

3. To maintain the purchasing power of the share capital and reserves invested in other than physical assets, amounts are added where necessary to the Revaluation Account, and charged to the Profit and Loss Account.

4. Provisions for risks inherent in the course of business are built up in proportion to the volume of business.

5. Intangible assets are charged to the Profit and Loss Account.

6. Provisions for tax on profits are made on the basis of the profit determined in accordance with our principles of valuation, which implies that latent tax liabilities and claims are taken into account.

## EXAMINATION QUESTIONS

1. State, with reasons, whether or not in your opinion—

    (a) depreciation on plant should be based on actual cost or on a replacement basis;

    (b) fixed overheads should be included in the valuation of manufactured stock and work in progress. (I.C.W.A.)

2. In considering the accountancy of changing price levels, what are the main principles to be observed concerning the maintenance of *real* capital? (I.C.W.A.)

3. "The charge against profits for depreciation of fixed assets provides the funds for their replacement."

Do you agree with the above statement? Is there any method of safe-guarding provisions for replacement? When considering the extent of the provision to be made for the depreciation of an asset, do you consider it necessary from an accounting viewpoint to base your calculations on the estimated replacement cost and, if so, how would you deal with the amount written off in the accounts? (*S.C.A.*)

4. What are the arguments for and against the calculation of depreciation on the estimated replacement cost of fixed assets? How could such a method be employed in practice? (*S.C.A.*)

CHAPTER 28

## CASE STUDIES IN MANAGEMENT ACCOUNTANCY

CASE studies have been employed for many years in the teaching of Management. Indeed, what has now become known as the "Harvard Approach" is the teaching of management principles and practice via the employment of case studies.

There is a danger that case studies, which are the written procedures followed or problems being encountered within a business, will be employed to the exclusion of all other types of teaching. This is quite wrong and is, in fact, a dangerous practice. Participants who are to obtain value from the use of cases should understand the basic principles of the particular subject before they are asked to solve problems.

The perfect type of case study or the correct approach to the case study method has not yet been invented. It is true to say that the flexibility of the method is one of its greatest assets and, therefore, any attempt to standardise would be dangerous. Case studies may be long or very short. If long they become difficult to follow and because of the time factor should be given to students in advance of the actual discussion period. A better plan is to use shorter case studies which can be read and discussed in the same session. In this way the discussion can be more natural and simultaneous.

### USES OF CASE STUDIES

The main purpose of case studies is to teach through the medium of *student participation*. Members of the group set the discussion in motion. The main idea is for the students to recognise and discuss the problems and, finally, to reach a conclusion.

One of the principal dangers is for the leader of the group to dictate the discussion. He should regard himself as an arbitrator or passive chairman who enters into the discussion only to offer advice and ensure that progress is being made.

The uses to which case studies may be put, have been summarised as follows:

The approach to solving business problems is very important and case studies provide valuable experience in:

(1) defining the problems to be solved;
(2) appreciating the inter-dependence of data;
(3) realizing the complexities of most business problems;
(4) recognizing the limits on efficient decision-making where all the necessary information is unobtainable;
(5) recognizing what additional information can be obtained to improve the quality of decisions reached;

(6) identifying irrelevant matter;

(7) developing a logical and analytical approach to the solution of problems;

(8) reaching a solution with the co-operation of others;

(9) broadening the view of students who generally regard problems from their own limited experience;

(10) improving the communication ability of students.

Business facts are selected to describe a business situation, and one or more problems may require solution. Some case studies also describe the action taken to solve the problem(s) and the trainee may then be asked such questions as:

(1) Do you think a satisfactory solution has been found?

(2) Could the problem be solved in any other way?

Cases are usually drawn from life but they can be fictitious, providing they are realistic. Students are given time to review the facts of the case and they may be able to obtain further background knowledge. If, for example, the case study is presented in advance of the time designated for its consideration, students may study the textbooks or visit the library in an effort to review material which may help in solving the problem(s). Various possible lines of action can then be discussed and at this stage each alternative will be evaluated. A decision will then be reached and this should be supported with pertinent arguments and evidence. Written reports may be requested from students to give practice in this form of communication.

In leading case study sessions, the lecturer may often require to do nothing more than keep the discussion on the subject, but he may also ask pertinent questions that will lead the discussion to an acceptable conclusion. Sometimes it may be necessary for him to offer an opinion.*

## CASE STUDIES PROVIDED

The case studies provided below have been collected from various sources. Those given towards the end of the chapter are not strictly case studies, but are past examination questions. However, they have been selected carefully to serve the same purpose as case studies.

Questions given at the end of each case study are not essential. They may be varied by the lecturer to suit his own requirements. The main purpose in including them is to show the line of approach which may be followed.

Where the case studies are based on material collected by the author, fictitious names have been inserted. In addition, facts have been varied so that the actual company cannot be recognised.

\*          \*          \*

\* From "Case Studies in Teaching Management Accounting" by Norman Thornton, F.C.W.A., A.M.B.I.M., M.I.O.M.; an article which appeared in *The Accountant* for 19th March 1966. Quotation by kind permission of the Editor.

## CASE STUDY 1—COSTING SYSTEM

The Arcway Co. Ltd. was incorporated as a limited company in 1938. It has two factories, one in London and the other in Newcastle upon Tyne. The former also serves as the Head Office and has a Company Secretary, Financial Accountant and Cost Accountant.

In Newcastle upon Tyne the factory is concerned with producing on instructions received from the Head Office. There is no regular "call off," because a wide variety of components are manufactured and assembled into approximately thirty different machines. A Sales Forecast is compiled for a year ahead, and this is broken down into thirteen equal periods of four weeks' duration.

The material requirements and machine hours required for the annual production are worked out in detail. Production of components and assembly is based on one month's demand plus one month's surplus. Stocks of components are maintained in the Assembly Stores and the machines are then assembled on the basis of the "call off" requests from Head Office.

The Profit and Loss Account for the year just ended shows that the Newcastle upon Tyne factory has incurred a loss of £25,000, yet the plant has been operating overtime for most of the period. A team of four experts is sent from Head Office to look into the procedures being followed. In summary form the findings relating to the cost accounting are as follows:

### MATERIALS

Materials are obtained by Production Order Material Issue Slip or Material Requisition. These are not priced or summarised.

The materials used are obtained from the Master Cards held in Planning; the quantities taken are thus what should be used and not what are actually used. Any extra materials used on a job are not costed, nor is any account taken of returns into Stores.

The price used is the latest price shown on the price card held in the Costing Department, *i.e.* the price that was last calculated—the calculation is done whenever possible, but in any case there is approximately, at least, a three to four months' lapse since the work of calculating through the cards takes three to four months to do. Thus no definite price, *e.g.* average or F.I.F.O., can be said to be used consistently throughout the costing system.

Material is transferred from Production to Maintenance both for maintenance and for capital jobs, but no record is kept.

### LABOUR

Direct labour only is charged to costs. This includes the Machine Shop and all Assembly Departments and Inspection. It also includes supervision, *e.g.* foremen. It does not include the Paint Shop.

The general wage rate (at present £0·4) is calculated with reference to the above departments, the hours, both ordinary and overtime for a *certain week* (no particular week, just the week when the wages rate changes) being taken, and the totals calculated and then an average general (or standard) rate being obtained.

The definition of direct and indirect labour is not very clear, *e.g.* Stores and Despatch are shown as "Direct" on the Wages Analysis Sheet, yet are not included in the general rate for Direct labour. Stores and Despatch personnel are not in any case "Direct" labour. No reconciliation between the pay-roll and cost accounts total is ever made.

## BOOKING OF TIMES IN MACHINE SHOP

A batch of Production Orders is issued to the charge-hand on the Section. He detaches the Material issue slips and takes them to the Stores for the material to be issued.

*Booking on to jobs.* A Production Order is given to the machine operator who then books on the job. In some cases the setting is done by a setter; in other cases the operator does the setting. In both instances the time is booked by the operator from the time when the work is put into operation.

*Booking off jobs.* When the job is completed the operator goes to the Machine Shop Office Window and states the number of hours worked on the job or, alternatively, the time he would like to be booked on the job. He does *not* book off the moment he has completed the job so that the Machine Shop Clerk can enter the time from an official clock, but books off at his leisure. In a few cases two jobs may be booked off together.

When the operator does book off the job he should book on to another: he does not always do this but books on to another job at his convenience. He is able to do this for no account is taken of idle time, nor are the total hours worked on a Section in a given period reconciled with the times booked on the jobs within the same period.

## ASSEMBLY DEPARTMENTS

The Assembly Departments do *not* keep any regular record of times taken on Assembly.

### Required

1. Discuss whether you consider the cost accounting methods employed are adequate. If not, pinpoint the main weaknesses.
2. What are the most likely causes for the loss incurred by the Newcastle factory?
3. Outline the changes, if any, which should be made. What additional staff or machinery are considered necessary?

\*       \*       \*

## FOSSEWAY MANUFACTURING LTD.
### Operating Cost Summary: Year to 30th April 1968

| | Cheltenham Works | | | Coventry Works | | |
|---|---|---|---|---|---|---|
| | Adjusted Budget | Actual | Variances (F) = Favourable (A) = Adverse | Adjusted Budget | Actual | Variances (F) = Favourable (A) = Adverse |
| | £ | £ | | £ | £ | |
| Direct Materials | 77,000 | 76,000 | Price: 2,500 (A) Usage: 3,500 (F) = 1,000 (F) | 70,000 | 71,500 | Price: 1,800 (F) Usage: 3,300 (A) = 1,500 (A) |
| Direct Labour | 82,500 | 80,625 | Rate: 1,875 (A) Effic.: 3,750 (F) = 1,875 (F) | 60,000 | 70,000 | Rate: 4,375 (A) Effic.: 5,625 (A) = 10,000 (A) |
| **Variable Overheads:** | | | | | | |
| Indirect Material and Power | 16,500 | 16,000 | 500 (F) | 12,000 | 12,700 | 700 (A) |
| Maintenance and Repairs | 4,400 | 5,400 | 1,000 (A) | 6,000 | 11,500 | 5,500 (A) |
| Lost Time | 550 | 225 | 325 (F) | 400 | 1,700 | 1,300 (A) |
| Overtime Cost | 3,850 | 3,050 | 800 (F) | 2,400 | 4,500 | 2,100 (A) |
| Total | 25,300 | 24,675 | 625 (F) | 20,800 | 30,400 | 9,600 (A) |
| **Fixed Overheads:** | | | | | | |
| Production Planning | 12,000 | 12,250 | 250 (A) | 12,000 | 8,500 | 3,500 (F) |
| Inspection | 15,000 | 14,500 | 500 (F) | 14,000 | 11,000 | 3,000 (F) |
| Storekeeping | 8,000 | 8,100 | 100 (A) | 7,500 | 7,900 | 400 (A) |
| Supervision | 10,000 | 10,500 | 500 (A) | 11,000 | 11,500 | 500 (A) |
| General Administration | 20,000 | 18,500 | 1,500 (F) | 21,000 | 20,500 | 500 (F) |
| Depreciation | 10,000 | 10,000 | — | 8,500 | 8,500 | — |
| Total | 75,000 | 73,850 | 1,150 (F) | 74,000 | 67,900 | 6,100 (F) |
| Total Works Cost | 259,800 | 255,150 | 4,650 (F) | 224,800 | 239,800 | 15,000 (A) |
| Sales Value | 307,300 | 307,300 | | 235,000 | 235,000 | |
| Operating Profit | 47,500 | 52,150 | 4,650 (F) | 10,200 | 4,800 * | 15,000 (A) |
| | Budget | Actual | | Budget | Actual | |
| Number of Direct Workers | 100 | 100 (average) | | 100 | 90 (average) | |
| Direct Labour Hours | 200,000 | 210,000 | | 200,000 | 175,000 | |
| Standard Hours Produced | 200,000 | 220,000 | | 200,000 | 160,000 | |

EXHIBIT 1

* Indicates loss.

## CASE STUDY 2—BUDGETARY CONTROL*

**FOSSEWAY MANUFACTURING LTD.**

Fosseway Manufacturing operates two factories, one in Cheltenham, the other in Coventry, producing accessories for the car industry. The two factories are of similar size and have comparable production facilities, but recruitment of labour is more difficult in Coventry because of higher rates paid in the nearby car factories. The Company offers a standard rate of £0·375 per hour at both factories, but the

|  | **FOSSEWAY MANUFACTURING LTD.** Works Budgets, Year to 30th April 1969 | |
|---|---|---|
|  | Cheltenham | Coventry |
|  | £ | £ |
| **Direct Materials** | 84,000 | 78,000 |
| **Direct Labour** | 90,000 | 72,000 |
| **Variable Overheads:** | | |
| Indirect Material and Power | 17,850 | 14,500 |
| Maintenance and Repairs | 5,400 | 13,500 |
| Lost Time ⎱ Direct | 250 | 2,000 |
| Overtime Cost ⎰ Labour | 4,500 | — |
|  | 28,000 | 30,000 |
| **Fixed Overheads:** | | |
| Production Planning | 13,500 | 10,000 |
| Inspection | 16,500 | 11,500 |
| Storekeeping | 8,500 | 8,400 |
| Supervision | 10,500 | 12,500 |
| General Administration | 21,000 | 21,000 |
| Depreciation | 10,000 | 8,600 |
|  | 80,000 | 72,000 |
| Total Budgeted Works Cost | 282,000 | 252,000 |
| Budgeted Sales Value | 330,000 | 270,000 |
| Budgeted Operating Profit | 48,000 | 18,000 |
| Number of Direct Workers | 108 | 90 |
| Direct Labour Hours | 240,000 | 180,000 |
| Standard hours to be produced | 240,000 | 180,000 |

EXHIBIT 2

* This case study was compiled by A. S. Johnson, B.A., A.C.W.A., of the Ashridge Management College, Berkhamsted, Herts. It is reproduced by kind permission.

Employment Officer in Coventry has to resort to local allowances in order to attract men to the factory. Direct workers are given 50% of efficiency gains as a bonus payment added to the standard rate.

Your syndicate represents the Board of Directors of Fosseway Manufacturing and you have before you the operating summaries for the two factories, covering the year to 30th April, 1968 (Exhibit 1). You also have the works budgets for the year to April 1969 (Exhibit 2). These budgets were accepted when they were first submitted three months ago, but in the light of the final operating summary, the Coventry budget now seems rather optimistic.

### Required

1. What action is needed by (a) the Works Manager at Coventry, and (b) the Board, to improve the operating results at Coventry?
2. What financial information should the Works Manager at Coventry and the Board receive (form, content and frequency of reports) to assure those concerned that the programme of action is getting the required results?

\*      \*      \*

## CASE STUDY 3—INSTALLATION OF BUDGETARY CONTROL

The Fitwell Shoe Co. Ltd., a medium-size Company specialising in the production of high-quality boots and shoes for men and women, has been operating for a number of years. Annual profit and loss accounts are prepared and time recorders are in use, as well as suitable forms for controlling the issue of materials.

Competition in the industry has become intense and the Directors are concerned with the reduced profit margins. They feel that the accounting and other office staff could provide much more information to aid management.

The Production Division is divided into the following departments:

1. Skin Room and Store.
2. Clicking Room.
    This department is concerned with the cutting of the uppers from the skins. Certain other operations are also carried out in this department.
3. Machine Room.
    All the various parts of the uppers are machined together.
4. Lasting Room.
    In this department the soles and uppers are joined together by sewing or riveting.
5. Finishing Room.

The sole and heel of each shoe is ground down to give a smooth finish. They are also coloured, dried and polished.
6. Press Room.
This department is concerned with cutting up the sole leather and bottoms. Once the operations are carried out the appropriate numbers of each size are transferred to the Lasting Room.

One of the main difficulties being encountered by the Company is that sales fluctuate considerably between winter and summer. Spring and summer sales represent 100% of normal capacity, but the winter sales are only around 70% capacity. There are no immediate plans for a large expansion, but the Directors would like to eliminate the idle capacity. Due to the changes in fashion the keeping of stocks of finished shoes is impracticable.

### Required

1. Discuss the methods you would employ for ascertaining the share of the market which may be expected by the business.
2. Suggest ways of overcoming the problem of idle capacity.
3. Give a detailed, yet concise, explanation of a budgetary control system which would be suitable for the Fitwell Shoe Co. Ltd.
4. Explain how the budgetary control system will operate.
5. Discuss the benefits the Directors can hope to achieve from the installation of the system.

\*      \*      \*

## CASE STUDY 4—FINANCIAL ORGANISATION

R. Perry and M. Cooper, Electronic Engineers, rented a factory for the purpose of producing and marketing industrial instruments which measure the flow of liquids and assist in obtaining automatic control of certain processes. Initially the capital required is provided by the two partners. Five years later a private limited company, the Excel Instrument Co. Ltd., is formed, and J. Turner and R. Ford are brought in; they become responsible for Sales and Office Administration respectively. The additional capital they introduce, together with accumulated funds, enable a large new factory to be acquired.

Ten years later the Company has five factories and has a turnover of £6 million. The four Directors, Perry, Cooper, Ford and Turner are still with the business. Perry is the Managing Director, Turner is the Sales Director and Ford is the Director responsible for dealing with special problems which arise as well as coping with the office administration. There has been a tendency for more and more time to be taken up by Ford dealing with personnel problems and negotiating with trade unions.

On the technical side the Company is at the forefront of its industry. There is a market for the Company's products, but in the past year a great deal of sales resistance is being felt. Competitive products are being offered at prices which are lower by as much as 25%.

Each of the five factories in the Group has its own Office Manager and staff who deal with all accounting and related matters. Monthly profit and loss accounts are submitted to the Managing Director after being approved by the appropriate Factory Manager. No detailed costs are available for the different lines produced, but each Factory Manager has submitted estimates, and it is on these that prices are based. There is a considerable difference in the estimates supplied by the factories for the same instruments. Yet each Factory Manager is convinced that his own estimates are correct. Since the geographical distance between factories is up to 300 miles there is difficulty in checking which estimates are correct.

The Managing Director has asked Ford to look into the possibility of getting more information from each factory. Six months have passed and the position has not improved. Meetings with the Office Managers have revealed that each Factory Manager would be reluctant to take steps which would "interfere with production."

### Required

1. Discuss the management structure of the Excel Instrument Co. Ltd.
2. Draft an organisation chart to show the *present* structure.
3. Suggest the principal problems being faced by the Company.
4. Formulate a plan for modifying the existing structure and draft organisation charts to show (*a*) the general structure, and (*b*) the management accounting structure recommended for the *future*.

\* \* \*

### CASE STUDY 5—PRICING POLICY

The Smith General Engineering Co. Ltd. is a family business which was established in 1900 by James and George Smith. The Managing Director is now Clive Smith a son of James. He is assisted by two nephews, John and William. The Company has one large factory which is managed as follows:

General Manager—William Smith
Sales Manager—A. Bourne
Production Manager—M. Clarke
Accountant—J. Gray

The General Manager co-ordinates the work of the three functional managers and ensures that the policy is put into practice. Regular meetings are held to discuss particular problems.

At a meeting held recently the Sales Manager complained that the Accountant's systems were not providing the necessary information for pricing products. Although products are made to customer's specifications the majority of parts are common to each main line manufactured. Yet the following costs have been produced for identical products made during the year.

| | Direct Labour | Direct Material | Factory Overhead |
|---|---|---|---|
| January | £1·00 | £1·30 | £3·45 |
| February | £1·10 | £1·40 | £3·75 |
| March | £1·50 | £1·25 | £4·12 |
| April | £1·40 | £1·40 | £4·20 |
| May | £1·15 | £1·15 | £3·45 |

Prices are determined by adding 20% to total factory cost. Estimates for enquiries from customers are based on past costs.

The procedures followed are summarised below:

## 1. *Direct Labour*

Time cards are used throughout the factory. When a job is completed the employee enters the time taken on to his card.

## 2. *Direct Material*

Material requisitions are completed by employees and signed by a foreman. In the past six months there have been considerable variations in the prices paid. For this reason a new average unit price is calculated each time a purchase is received.

## 3. *Factory Overhead*

A predetermined overhead rate is calculated which is stated as a percentage on prime cost. Previous experience has indicated that the rate employed does not result in too wide an error over the full year. However, there is under- or over-absorption from one month to another.

## 4. *Cost Sheets*

Cost sheets are kept for the products made. When the forms for labour and material are received in the Cost Office they are priced and the total is entered on the appropriate cost sheets.

A profit or loss is then calculated for each customer's order.

### CUSTOMER REACTION

One customer has complained that he was charged £4·15 in January and £5·05 in April for identical products. He has quite recently been quoted a different figure. Since he is a sub-contractor he is having difficulty with estimating for his jobs.

**Required**

1. What are your views on the general organisation of the Company?
2. Discuss the costing system.
3. Is the system functioning as it should for the pricing of products?
4. What alternative arrangements could be made to ensure greater stability in pricing?

\*    \*    \*

## CASE STUDY 6—THE DEVELOPMENT OF MANAGEMENT CONTROLS\*

### INTRODUCTION

*1.* It is with considerable diffidence that we approach this paper, particularly on a subject so broad as this one, but we make no apologies for its length. The subject is an important one and demands full treatment. Perhaps a few words about the title would help to show what we are trying to achieve.

*2. Development.* The word development in our title was chosen to convey the essentially individual nature of control schemes. Each is a process of evolution in itself and in every case much trial and error will be needed before the ideal is reached. There is no set scheme, only certain principles which have to be applied and moulded differently in each business. Every business will pose its own peculiar problems and special techniques will have to be evolved to meet them.

*3. Management controls.* Why have we used "control" instead of "accountancy"? The term accountancy is usually exclusively concerned with one only of the important factors in business economics— namely expense. A modern industrial accountant is concerned with all facets of the Company's business and sometimes is in fact called the Controller.

*4. Case study.* We have chosen the approach of using a hypothetical case in order to emphasise the practical nature of the paper. It is the practice of installation rather than the theory of management accounting that we are discussing. We have therefore assumed that the reader already has some knowledge of budgetary control and standard costs. The case Company is a hypothetical one, composite of the authors' experience, because this gives us the freedom to highlight certain features which we think important but which would not be all present in the same actual Company.

\* This case study was compiled by D. H. Hill, F.C.A., F.C.W.A., and J. A. Chudley, A.C.W.A. It appeared in *The Cost Accountant* (now *Management Accounting*) for March 1956. It is reproduced by kind permission of the authors and the Editor.

**THE CASE COMPANY**

5. Our hypothetical Company, which we shall call "H. & C. Limited," employs about 500 people and produces a synthetic material from which a variety of articles is made by both machines and craftsmen. Both processing and fabricating techniques are used.

6. During the war H. & C. Limited expanded enormously on one particular product for which the demand has since dropped. The capacity is now being used by a variety of different products selling in several different competitive industries.

7. The management structure, like Topsy, "just growed" and in many cases the jobs were made to fit the man rather than the right man found for each job. The quality of the staff was the usual mixture of good, bad and indifferent found in every firm.

8. The cost accounting organisation hummed quietly in the background producing so-called actual cost after each job was complete but with no direct link with the financial accounts. Waste statistics were available for certain operations only. No attempt was made to decide the correct level of expense, efficiency of production or volume of waste and in all cases the only comparison was with the past. At infrequent intervals approximate profit and loss accounts were prepared.

9. In recent years H. & C. Limited had fallen upon lean times and the Directors were faced with the fact that the information supplied to them was hopelessly inadequate. The far-reaching decisions which were being forced upon them by adverse conditions could not be made on the basis of that information alone. A specialist was called in to review the control procedures and to ascertain facts upon which the directors could base decisions.

10. It is now quite apparent, looking back on this period, that the Directors were not really clear what they wanted. They were feeling uncertainly for guidance but the data they required were not available, or else it was lost in a welter of figures presented with only one objective —total profit or loss! The Managing Director was not sure whether the unfortunate position of the Company was due to internal or external forces. If the former, was it methods of manufacture, working efficiency, excessive material waste, excessive overheads, direction of sales policy, basis of fixing selling prices or one or more of many other possible factors?

11. The scientific and logical approach of the specialist to the problems of the Company was enlightening. Although his ultimate objectives were not immediately apparent to the onlooker, it will probably be of assistance in the understanding of this paper to mention some of them at this stage:

(a) Profitability of each main product group.

(b) Influence of turnover on profits—i.e. the effect of fixed expenses as may be shown on a break-even chart.

(c) The efficiency of the various centres of production and the possible effect of the introduction of incentives to increase efficiency.

(d) The present costs of certain processes and operations with particular reference to the savings possible on new methods.

(e) The pattern of expenditure—where were the sources of possible savings and where could expenditure be increased to give a greater return? In particular were there any possible savings in material expenditure?

12. In this paper we are attempting to show how these and other objectives were achieved, not merely for the purpose of a special investigation but with the aim of permanently establishing a smooth-running machine, which would supply not only the bases for decisions but also a continual check on the effects of the decisions taken.

## THE PROCESS OF DEVELOPMENT

13. There were three main phases in the development of the controls in H. & C. Ltd., planning, installing and consolidating. These phases are self-evident and would be present in any considered attempt at the introduction of controls. But certain of the steps within each phase which we record below are not necessarily in the best order for every set of circumstances and, of course, some steps will be taken simultaneously.

### PHASE I—PLANNING

14. The first step taken in H. & C. Ltd. was to draw up an organisation chart for the whole Company from charge-hand to Managing Director showing clearly the scope and responsibility of each person in authority. This is an absolutely vital step because none of the information which will be produced finally will be of full use unless it is suitably departmentalised so that there is someone specifically responsible for taking action on it. It is also a most difficult step to take. Our friend the specialist ran slap into the old, old story of the Managing Director with thirty-nine people reporting direct to him, of Charlie Bloggs who was damned if he'd let himself be put on a lower line than Bert Higgins and of old Dick, who had been absolutely indispensable for forty-two years, going home in disgust when he saw himself as third planning clerk on the left! These anomalies and many others had to be ironed out before clear lines of responsibility were established.

15. Next the specialist spent two or three weeks getting under the skin of the business. He first met the senior executives, the Sales Manager, the Works Manager and the Accountant, and then interviewed each foreman and followed the manufacturing process through, first on the shop floor and then in the production control office. It was not until he felt thoroughly conversant with the organisation of the factory that he ventured inside the accounting offices and examined

their existing methods. This is a wise approach in any circumstances as the reasons for the various features are only apparent when the background is known. Furthermore, it is always best, initially at any rate, to use as much of the existing system as possible.

16. For the next week or two the "outside help" disappeared completely. Rumour had it that Harry Smith, who never did like Nosey Parkers anyway, had stuffed him in the boiler to improve his fuel efficiency but a few fleeting visits to check facts reassured the management. In fact, the specialist was deciding what scheme of management controls he would apply.

17. In any scheme control by budgets is inevitable but complete standard costing does not necessarily follow, and in fact in H. & C. Ltd. two different approaches were used. The repetitive products enabled an approach through the process and the full application of standard costing. The craftsman-produced, non-repetitive products required a different approach, in that each job had to be specially estimated beforehand using standard costing rates but individually estimated times. These were used for standard product costs and were the basis of the controls to be exercised on the materials and processes.

18. A complete plan of the scheme was prepared. A decision was also made on budget centres and cost centres to be used for control purposes, but this is relatively easy in most firms once an organisation chart has been agreed. Discretion must, however, be used to avoid having too many centres. There are many cases where the whole of the output of one process goes through another and one of these processes controls the speed of output of both. In such a case it is sometimes only necessary to control the master process while the ancillary one may be treated as an overhead of the master. Similarly, where a service labourer assists the operator of a machine it may not be necessary to treat him as a direct operative. In H. & C. Ltd. there was one particular machine where the number of service labourers varied with the product being processed. It was therefore found necessary to set up a separate service cost centre in addition to the process cost centre, so that the efficiency in use of service labour could be measured and the appropriate standard charge made to each product.

19. A demonstration board was constructed as part of the planning work. This was a large board on which was pinned a sample of each type of form to be used in recording, calculating and publishing data. On each form were dummy figures relating to one particular section of the business and lines were drawn from form to form following through the figures to the final results. A board of this type consolidates one's thoughts, and ensures that the broad plan is complete before a start is made on the actual installation. It was also used to "sell" the scheme to all those likely to be affected by it. It was of inestimable value in the following months in explaining the objectives to all levels of management, showing them the information that would be required of them as

well as given to them, and in training management and staff in the construction and use of the controls.

*20.* With the plan complete, a member of the existing accounts staff was selected who would ultimately take charge of the day-to-day running of the scheme. He was to take an active part in the installation from the commencement and thereby become thoroughly conversant with the reasons for all the features of the particular scheme. The early choice of an assistant for the work of installation is an important point and great care should be taken in his selection—preferably from among the present employees. To be successful he will, apart from his accounting abilities, require an interest in technical matters and an understanding of the manufacturing techniques of the business. He should also be a good mixer and be able to get on with, and have the confidence of, all levels of management especially foremen; from his point of view each foreman is as important to the success of the scheme as the managing director. A service has to be given to each and the full co-operation of both is essential to success.

## PHASE II—INSTALLATION

*21.* The scheme as planned fell under four main headings and rather than try to show the strict chronological order of the steps, which in any case is liable to alter with every firm, we have broken down the installation under these headings: (*a*) control of output; (*b*) control of expense; (*c*) control of materials; and (*d*) correlation of output and costs.

### Control of Output

*22. Measurement.* The accurate measurement of output is, of course, the first necessity of its control and it is here that the Controller steps out of the bounds of orthodox accounting and spreads his wings as an active executive instead of a "trouser-polisher." Except in the most elementary of single-product industries there is only one possible unit of measurement, namely, the "standard hour."

*23.* The fixing of the standard hour value of each process or operation for each product is a task that must be started as early as possible and calls for the wholehearted co-operation of the time-study staff. In H. & C. Ltd. care was taken to "woo" the time-study engineers from the start. They gave their enthusiastic support, but even so the lack of standard times was the main cause of delay in the full running of the scheme.

*24.* The ideal standard time is that obtained through the process or operation (and not through the job) by reference to machine speeds, etc., but in trying to take account of all the types of jobs or operations done on a machine this method sometimes becomes too elaborate. The purpose of control must not be lost sight of in the study of the means. Very often, in the early stages, rate-fixed times for each job are preferable to complicated formulae or charts. Elaborate shop floor records or cost office calculations should be avoided. It is very often difficult to impress on trained time-study personnel that absolute accuracy is not as vital to budgetary control as to, say, a detailed investigation into the relative advantages of different methods.

*25. Deciding the Budgeted Level of Output.* What is the best level of output on which to budget? Does one please the sales department or the works? It is very seldom that their capacities are balanced. In fact in H. & C. Ltd. two different techniques were used in successive years and each had its failings.

*26.* In the first year, a twelve months' sales budget was "extracted" from the Sales Manager and agreed with the Managing Director. This is always a difficult operation especially when there is no market research data to go on. The vacillation of the Sales Manager between his instinctive optimism and the fear of making a rod for his own back is not unnatural, but the pull of these conflicting forces usually gives a reasonable answer. This twelve months' budget must be broken down into sufficient detail to give a broad idea of the quantities of different products involved so that it may be converted into the terms of output of the various cost centres. Considerable difficulty was experienced in this conversion in the first year in H. & C. Ltd. as there were no previous records to help, but in subsequent years with more data available it became a relatively easy task.

*27.* This first converted sales budget proved extremely revealing of the lack of balance between the various centres of production involved and it was apparent that many adjustments would have to be made even allowing for stock policy. The subsequent discussion between the sales and works sides to balance the budget was a very healthy exercise in itself. Even so, the final budget still left much to be desired in the use of certain key plant.

*28.* In the second year of operations the output budgeting procedure was reversed. The management decided to base the sales budget on a definite volume of output from certain very costly plant, representing a reasonably economical level of production having in mind the capacity of the plant. This output was then turned into a quantity budget of the basic material on which the Sales Manager was asked to base a complete budget of finished products.

*29.* There was considerable criticism of this method, in that it gave the sales staff an impossible target, but at least it had the probable advantage of showing a true volume variance in the accounts. The standard costs, based on this budget, reflected the economical cost of the products and showed clearly to management why on some products it was difficult to sell at competitive prices. The management decided at a later date to run parallel with the master budget, described above, another sales budget within the representatives' reach which was termed the "realistic" budget. One wonders which was the more "realistic" in terms of the hard facts of competition.

*30.* Whatever method is used for preparing the output budget, it must be done at an early stage in the proceedings. Little headway is possible on expense budgeting until the output budget is fixed.

*31. Allowing for non-productive time.* Up to now we have been talking entirely in terms of productive output, its measurement and expected level. Every productive worker and machine spends some time which is non-productive and the control of this is an important part of the control of output. Rest periods, etc., were included in the standard times allowed, but there are many other stoppages in production, both unavoidable and otherwise, which occur and must be brought to light, such as machine breakdown, normal maintenance, change-over of production, meetings, setting time (where not treated as productive and therefore included in the standard time), waiting instructions, waiting materials.

*32.* The unavoidable items must be carefully budgeted. If this is not done any attempt to control the efficiency of actual production is meaningless since "unavoidable" lost time is a wonderful hiding-place for excess time on the job. It was surprising how many foremen thought they could get away with "fiddling" the booking until it was brought home to them that budgetary control is like a balloon—if you push it in at one place it pops out somewhere else.

*33. Weekly control statistics.* So far the control of output had been all "take" and no "give," but the regular and prompt issue of weekly control statistics quickly righted the balance and handsomely repaid the Company for the begrudged "non-productive" time spent in supplying the basic data. This document is probably the most important one produced and to save lengthy explanations we include as Exhibit 1 a sample form of weekly control statistics. This form is self-explanatory if studied in conjunction with the calculation key in column five. From the control point of view the three most important figures on this form are: *Activity*—the comparison of actual output with that budgeted. *Efficiency* expressed as a percentage of that expected— the comparison of actual time taken with the standard time as used in product costs, after allowing for unusual circumstances outside the foreman's control (extra allowances) and budgeted efficiency which need not necessarily be 100%, and *capacity usage* expressed as a percentage of that expected—the comparison of actual lost time with that budgeted.

*34.* In H. & C. Ltd. the weekly control statistics were the first concrete results that were produced by the budgetary control scheme. In their production we learned, sometimes from bitter experience, four most important principles, which incidentally apply to any new accounting information issued.

1. Accuracy in preparation is at first more important than speed— if any data is to be effectively used the recipient must have confidence in it from the start and mistakes cannot be afforded.

CONTROL STATISTICS

BUDGET CENTRE: Finishing
COST CENTRE: Assembly

DISTRIBUTION: Works manager
Finishing dept. manager
Assembly foreman

| | DETAILS | BUDGET FOR 44HR. WEEK | LINE NO. | CALCULATIONS | PERIOD NO. 1 — WEEK ENDING 9/4 | 16/4 | PERIOD NO. 4 — /7 | 15/7 | 22/7 |
|---|---|---|---|---|---|---|---|---|---|
| | | | | | 1 | 2 | 4 | 15 | 16 |
| | NORMAL SHIFT HOURS | 308 | 1 | | 308 | | 308 | | |
| | OVERTIME | 77½ | 2 | | 61 | | 43¾ | | |
| | TOTAL AVAILABLE HOURS | 385½ | 3 | 1 & 2 | 369 | | 351¾ | | |
| | LESS | | | | | | | | |
| | Unused available hours: | | | | | | | | |
| | Shortage of orders | | | | | | | | |
| | Shortage of personnel | | | | 44 | | | | |
| CLOCK HOURS | Machine breakdown | | | | | | | | |
| | | | 4 | | 44 | | | | |
| | OCCUPIED HOURS | 385½ | 5 | 3 - 4 | 325 | | 351¾ | | |
| MAN ~~MACHINE~~ | LOST TIME: | | | | | | | | |
| | Supervision | 6 | | | 1½ | | 3 | | |
| | Shop labour | 9 | | | 6 | | 7¾ | | |
| | Machine maintenance | 3½ | | | ¼ | | ½ | | |
| | Setting | 43 | | | 37¾ | | 48½ | | |
| | Training | 5 | | | - | | - | | |
| | Sundry | 3 | | | 3½ | | 5½ | | |
| | TOTAL LOST TIME | 69½ | 6 | | 49 | | 65¼ | | |
| | PRODUCTIVE HOURS | 316 | 7 | 5 - 6 | 276 | | 286½ | | |
| PROCESS STANDARD HOURS | NORMAL | 284¼ | 8 | | 284¼ | | 284¼ | | |
| | PRODUCED | | 9 | | 288½ | | 261¼ | | |
| | ALLOWED | | 10 | | 288½ | | 271¾ | | |
| PERCENTAGES | ACTIVITY | 100 | 11 | 9/8 | 101 | | 92 | | |
| | EFFICIENCY | | | | | | | | |
| | Produced | - | 12 | 9/7 | 105 | | 91 | | |
| | Allowed | 90 | 13 | 10/7 | 105 | | 95 | | |
| | Of expected | 100 | 14 | 13/B | 117 | | 106 | | |
| | CAPACITY USAGE | | | | | | | | |
| | Actual | 82 | 15 | 7/5 | 85 | | 81 | | |
| | Of expected | 100 | 16 | 15/B | 104 | | 99 | | |
| WAGES PAID FOR PRODUCTIVE WORK | TOTAL AMOUNT | £54·800 | 17 | | £54·200 | | £57·300 | | |
| | PER PRODUCED STANDARD HOUR | £ 0·192 | 18 | 17/9 | £ 0·187 | | £ 0·219 | | |
| | PER PRODUCTIVE CLOCK HOUR | £ 0·172 | 19 | 17/7 | £ 0·167 | | £ 0·200 | | |
| MEMORANDA | Weekly production of front assemblies | | | | 73 | | 75 | | |
| KEY TO GRAPH | ACTIVITY | ———— | 11 | % 120 | | | | | |
| | EFFICIENCY Of expected | ········ | 14 | 110 | | | | | |
| | CAPACITY USAGE Of expected | – – – – | 16 | 100 | | | | | |
| | Week 14 - Extra allowances - 10½ hrs. Compressed air not available part of the week | | | 90 | | | | | |
| | | | | 80 | | | | | |
| | | | | 70 | | | | | |
| | | | | 60 | | | | | |

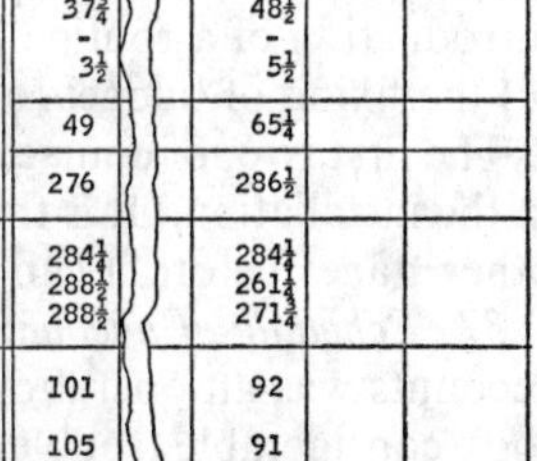

EXHIBIT 1

2. No data should be issued to anybody who has not been thoroughly briefed on the construction and meaning of it. Follow-up with regular briefings.

3. Senior management must follow-up with regular discussions on the results with foremen—nothing is so frustrating to the accounting staff, nor so open to ridicule on the shop floor, as unused control data.

4. Preparation work must be according to a routine from the beginning. You cannot afford to be behind with any job at a time when so many other new routines will be coming along.

### Control of Expense

*35.* The fact that we have placed this stage of the installation second to control of output does not mean that we consider it any less (or for that matter—more) important than the latter. Nor does it mean that work on control of expense must wait until the control of output is fully operative. But to be truly effective any control of expense must be related to output and basic data collected for the control of output will also be used at this stage.

*36.* There were three clearly-defined steps taken in this stage of the installation: (*a*) the preparation of a schedule of accounts; (*b*) the introduction of a routine for actual expense coding and collection; and (*c*) the fixing of budgets against which to control expenditure.

The first two, of course, can and should be started as soon as possible in the installation. It is the third that is dependent on the completion of other stages before it can be commenced.

*37. Schedule of accounts.* The preparation of a detailed schedule of accounts was an operation on which our "outside help," quite rightly, took considerable trouble. He defined, with great care, the items which should be included under each account heading (amounts budgeted under one account and charged to another all too frequently make control statements ridiculous) and also the classification of each account for control purposes.

*38.* This classification for control purposes will vary in detail with every Company, depending on the scope of authority of each person in the chain of command. Broadly speaking accounts are grouped as in Exhibit 2.

*39.* As in any scheme of control, the expense analysis envisaged in

| | |
|---|---|
| Direct labour—analysed to cost centre<br>Direct expense—analysed to budget centre | Expenses over which the foreman can have some control |
| General works expenses—separate budget centre for each factory | Controlled by works manager |
| Administration expenses | Controlled by chief executive |
| Selling expense | Controlled by sales manager |
| Distribution expense | Controlled by distribution manager |

EXHIBIT 2

the schedule of accounts was objective rather than subjective. It is more important to know the cause of the expense rather than the source; thus materials used on the repair of a machine is analysed under maintenance of machinery and not under indirect materials. One useful technique employed in H. & C. Ltd. was the setting up of composite expense accounts within a budget centre for a function which was too small to warrant a separate budget centre. For instance, the boiler house was allocated a single account to which all expenses incurred in its running were charged (*e.g.* fuel, wages, water, maintenance) and control was exercised on the total expenditure. If desired, this total figure could, of course, be analysed to source and compared in detail with the budget.

*40. Coding and collection of actual expense.* Why had a routine to be introduced for the coding and collection of actual expense? Surely H. & C. Ltd. were not so backward that they had no such routine before the outside help moved in? Of course they had a routine, and like most of its kind it lacked three essentials of control—consistency, speed and accuracy.

*41.* Real consistency can only be achieved by thorough briefing of the person or persons (preferably person) who will do the actual coding of the expense documents. This is *not* a junior job.

*42.* It cannot be emphasised too often that speed is vital to control. It is usually found necessary for example, to analyse wages before payment if any control data is to be produced in time to be useful. The routine for the collection of actual expense for control statements must be carefully planned in advance so that the minimum time elapses between the end of the period and the issue of the control statements.

*43.* By accuracy we do not mean the ability to balance the books, or the publication of results to the nearest penny. Both were present in the old scheme at H. & C. Ltd., the latter without adding one jot to the value of the results. What is so often lacking is the routine for the inclusion of the correct amount of expense in periodical accounts in respect of items paid at infrequent intervals. At H. & C. Ltd. a whole series of accrual or reserve accounts were set up, from which an appropriate amount was transferred to the expense accounts each period and to which the actual payments, when made, were charged. The charge to expense accounts is calculated either on the basis of consumption (metered or otherwise) as in the case of electricity, or on the basis of time as in the case of rent, rates, etc. When the actual charges come through, adjustments are made for any difference from the amount accrued or reserved.

*44.* A problem common to any scheme of regular periodical accounts is the fluctuations of profit between one period and another, due to the effect of holidays on the available working hours in each period. The recovery of expense (or the "earning power" of the factory) will tend to move in proportion to the working hours while certain expenses, such as rent, theoretically remain unchanged. To overcome this problem at H. & C. Ltd., fixed expenses were artificially charged into the accounts pro rata to the working days by means of accrual or reserve accounts. To do this, a calendar factor, expressing the working hours in each period as a proportion of the average period, was developed and used for calculating the correct charge.

45. *Fixing of budgets.* The third step of expense control involves the co-operation of all levels of management from shop floor to board in an operation about which the average technician knows little.

46. The method used at H. & C. Ltd. was to form a committee of the chief executive, the accountant, and the person responsible for the installation of the scheme, and to co-opt the departmental head and foreman for the meetings at which the budgets which concerned them were discussed. On such a committee it is essential that, firstly, the chief executive should be chairman; the lead must come from him, not from the accountant! The budgets should be management's budgets, not the accountant's. Secondly, any person whose activities are to be controlled by the scheme should be represented—no taxation without representation applies just as much to budgetary control as to politics.

47. The committee considered two things:

(*a*) The correct amount of each expense to achieve the budgeted level of output.

(*b*) The way in which each expense would react to changes in conditions, *i.e.* the control basis and allowance curves. This is, of course, necessary to enable the application of flexible budgetary control. For practical purposes seven different control bases were used at H. & C. Ltd. Firstly, three categories of expenses—fixed (F), curved (or semi-variable) (C), and variable (V), and, secondly, for both curved and variable expenses, three different causes for variations:

Occupied hours—the total hours spent (*i.e.* productive hours plus lost time) (O)

Productive hours—the total direct hours (P)

Standard hours produced—the quantity of output (Q).

48. Thus an expense would be classified as one of the following:

|  | Code |
|---|---|
| Fixed | F |
| Curved: | |
| The variable part moving with occupied hours | CO |
| The variable part moving with productive hours | CP |
| The variable part moving with standard hours | CQ |
| Variable: | |
| Moving with occupied hours | VO |
| Moving with productive hours | VP |
| Moving with standard hours | VQ |

Other bases can be used as well as the above. The intention is to find a fair basis upon which to give expense allowances for the circumstances prevailing in the period. The above bases are usually sufficient for most circumstances, but other bases will have to be found in certain cases. In H. & C. it was found more accurate to base allowances for certain expenses on the hours of a specific cost centre, although, in fact, expenses were controlled by Budget Centre. Another exception was car-running expenses, for which allowances were based on mileage.

*49.* In considering the budgeted amount of expense great care and attention to detail is well worth while, especially when it is being done for the first time. A large amount of research into past costs should be undertaken before the committee starts its work. We do not intend to suggest that budgets should be fixed solely on past experience, but it is really surprising how little most managements know about the detailed make-up of their costs, even in physical terms. With no facts to guide them, managements frequently put forward the wildest guesses at the amount of some expenses. The result of bad budgeting can only be control statements that make mockery of the principle of control by exception. A useful check on the budgeting is to make sure that every person on a current payroll is either accounted for or deliberately left out. We have known many cases of workmen left out because everybody thought they were responsible to someone else. Some of the direct expense budgets can and must be calculated quite precisely by reference to the productive and non-productive hours already fixed in compiling the output or normal standard hour budget.

*50. Operating statement.* This is the ultimate document of expense control. In fact, it is a combination of both output and expense and this of course is essential as the correct level of expense (or allowance) can only be gauged in relation to the actual output and the actual conditions of production. It shows the sterling values of the variances shown weekly in the production statistics as well as the pure under- or over-spending on each item of expense. An operating statement is issued, for each budget centre every four weeks, to the person in charge of the budget centre and to his immediate superiors in the chain of command. It is important that it should show only those variances over which the recipient can have some measure of control.

*51.* These statements can and should be issued before the final stages of the installation are reached, and formal meetings to discuss them and decide action should be promoted as soon as the first ones are out. The attitude that "these meetings are a good idea but production must come first" is one that must be resisted from the start.

## Control of Material

*52.* We have discussed so far the control of output and the control of expense. Control of Material is the third dimension of the Control scheme and is in theory simpler to understand and operate than the other two. The main difficulty in practice is to obtain sufficiently accurate and detailed basic records. In H. & C. Ltd. materials amounted to well over one-third of the selling price of the product and yet prior to the installation of the control scheme not one-tenth of the clerical effort was expended in recording its movements and consumption. There are three objectives in material control: (1) price control; (2) physical control; and (3) waste control.

*53. Price control.* This is probably the most neglected feature in management today. For ten years during the war and after, buying was a case of "get what you want and pay what you have to." The habit dies hard. Now, as competitive conditions creep into one industry after another, the amount that can be gained or lost by good or bad buying soars and the need for up-to-date information on the success of the function soars with it.

*54.* The basis of price control is, of course, the standard price for each commodity. Standard prices must be fixed for all direct materials. It is also desirable to fix standard prices of indirect materials and stores, but in practice this often entails considerable clerical work which is not justified by results. In fact, in H. & C. Ltd. indirect materials are charged to the appropriate expense account at average buying price of current stock. This means, of course, that there is an element of price variance included in the expense variances, but it is not usually significant.

*55.* A price variance can be thrown up at the time of purchase or on consumption. It gives a closer control on the purchasing function, and it is much simpler, to throw it up at the time of purchase and initially this was done throughout on all direct materials in H. & C. Ltd. However, it was later decided in the case of the *most important* raw material to throw up the price variance at the time the material is issued to the shop floor. This particular material represents about 25% of the selling price of most products. This change had the following advantages:

1. Stock records were maintained at FIFO which is the basis upon which stock is evaluated for annual accounts purposes. The interim profit and loss accounts will not, therefore, as far as this item is concerned, be on a different basis from the audited accounts.

2. Price variance bears a relation to the volume of production for the period and the price variance is not influenced by fluctuation of the volume of raw material stocks.

3. Where batches of inferior material are purchased at a lower price the "black" price variance is thrown up in the same period as the "red" usage variance.

*56. Physical control.* The methods of instituting physical and clerical control of materials are too well known to require elaboration, but the following practical points which arose at H. & C. are worth mentioning.

*57.* The traditional method of keeping, in the stores, bin cards showing physical quantities only and, in the cost office, a comprehensive stores control ledger showing physical quantities and values, has been discarded to save clerical labour. The stores ledger was transferred to the stores office and replaced the bin cards. Control accounts for groups of items, in value only, were opened in the general ledger. The stores ledger is written up by a clerk functionally responsible to the cost accountant and a continual check of physical stock is made by a cost office clerk. The stores ledger is also balanced regularly to the general ledger control accounts.

*58.* Clerical control was attempted on finished stock without physical control and the results of the clerical control proved only that physical control was necessary, without signalling the cause of differences. There were no proper storage facilities for finished stock and as it was not a readily saleable article management thought it was unnecessary. The finished stock was therefore left lying about the factory and for accounting purposes had to be treated as work-in-progress.

*59.* On the completion of the first year's operation of standard costing there was a serious difference between physical value of work-in-progress (including finished stock) and the balance disclosed on the work-in-progress account. After considerable investigation most of the difference was attributed to finished stock and it transpired that:

(*a*) scrapped work was not all being recorded;

(*b*) basic output records were incorrect.

If finished stock had been handed into the control of a stock-keeper, maintaining the normal stock records, immediately on completion of the manufacture of the article, these hidden losses would have been brought to light much sooner. This experience throws into relief the interdependence of all sections of an effective control scheme.

*60. Waste control.* The techniques of waste control will differ in each industry. The two main approaches are either through the process or through the job. Both are used at H. & C. Ltd. on different types of materials. The approach through the job is relatively easy, being based on the accurate recording of issues and returns offset against a standard for each job. However, the control of waste of materials issued in bulk to continuous processes is usually more difficult and frequently presents special problems. At H. & C. Ltd. the control of the waste of the principal raw material was through the process and posed several problems. The manner in which the specialist dealt with them may be interesting to those faced with similar difficulties.

*61.* Being a natural material there was considerable variation in quality which had an important, but not exclusive, effect on the waste at the first process. To separate the quality waste from the process waste, a sample of each batch issued from store is tested and a batch

BB

standard set. This standard is interposed between the actual waste and the master standard as used in the product cost, thus analysing the variance.

*62.* In one particular chain of processes there are no facilities for measuring the throughput of the individual processes. The needs of output control are satisfied by a record of one or two dimensions or the number of pieces, but the continuous recording of the final dimensions would be impracticable. Large inter-process stocks are carried. For material usage control purposes the chain had to be considered as one process and a periodical stocktaking of the partly processed stocks was instituted so that the total throughput could be measured and compared with the known output of the final process. In order that this calculated throughput should not be affected by the change in distribution of the volume of stock among the processes, between the beginning and end of each period, the physical stock at each stage is converted back to original issue quantity or size by adding a percentage for each process it has passed through. This percentage is based on samples of the waste occurring at each process.

*63.* When large stocks have to be taken into account in the calculation of waste statistics the time cycle on which the statistics are based is important. The longer the period involved, the more accurate the statistics, as errors in interim stocktakings have less influence, but statistics based on a shorter period result in quicker corrective action. It is usually helpful to show cumulative or moving annual total statistics to underline trends.

*64.* In controlling waste it is preferable not only to know the total waste but also if possible the process at which it occurs and its causes only some of which may be under the control of the shop floor.

Causes could be as shown in Exhibit 3.

| | |
|---|---|
| 1. Variation in original quality | Indicates effectiveness of buying and inspection |
| 2. Material deliberately cut to waste as a result of correct issue size not being available or time expired material | Indicates ineffectiveness of planning and buying |
| 3. Handling ⎱ ? <br> 4. Processing ⎰ | Indicates effectiveness of works management |

EXHIBIT 3

*Correlation of Output and Costs*

*65.* The combination of the three "dimensions" of output, expense and materials is the finishing touch to the "3-D" picture of management controls. The metaphor is apt, for it is this feature more than any other that brings life to the picture presented to management and raises the comprehensive control scheme above the flat two-dimensional level of older methods.

*66.* This correlation is needed firstly, to complete the budget picture; to show the effect of the plan behind the budgets on the finances of the company and the cost of its products. Secondly, to provide the data for reflecting variations from plan for day-to-day control of the operations of the Company. Thirdly, to provide the basis of the pricing policy of the company.

## 1. *Correlation of Budgeted Output and Costs*

*67.* To complete the budget picture the following final calculations are required per paragraphs 68 to 73.

*68. Budgeted annual profit and loss account.* In the authors' experience no individual budget can be considered fixed until this has been produced and approved. Frequently managements are surprised and shocked when they see the final effect of their deliberations in many unrelated budget committee meetings, and hasty revisions are sometimes necessary. From the practical point of view the main difficulty is encountered in forecasting the direct materials consumption. A fairly detailed break down of the sales budget is necessary combined with past records of actual consumption under varying sales mixes. Useful extensions of this correlation are a cash forecast and a budgeted balance sheet for twelve months hence, each of which also require capital and stock budgets.

*69. Standard costing rates.* An essential feature of the control scheme is, of course, to calculate a labour and overhead costing rate for each cost centre. The budgeted expenses (including general overheads) where not forecast by cost centre, must be allocated, each on an equitable basis, and the resultant total divided by output to give a rate per unit of output (usually standard hour). It is important that the allocation is done carefully and in detail if the costing rates are to reflect the true incidence of costs.

*70.* The fixed overheads should be totalled and shown separately as well as included in the total cost, so that the fixed element of the costing rate can be calculated. This fixed element should be traced through to the standard product costs and shown separately in calculating the actual recovered or cleared in cost.

*71.* In many companies it is quite equitable to include selling expenses in general overheads and allocate them through processes to the product. However, in H. & C. Ltd. these expenses varied considerably between product groups using the same processes. They were therefore allocated individually to product groups and selling expense costing rates were expressed as a percentage of the budgeted works cost for each group.

*72. Standard product costs.* A standard cost for each product manufactured must be built up. The calculations are relatively simple, but considerable clerical labour is required if the range of products is large and it is advisable to plan the operation well in advance. Once calculated, however, they remain fixed until a complete rebudgeting is undertaken. The basic data required are as follows:

1. A manufacturing layout for each product giving materials required and operations performed.
2. Material standard prices as fixed for material control.
3. Operation or process times as fixed for output control.
4. Standard costing rates for each cost centre.

*73.* The importance of accurate and carefully prepared standard product costs cannot be overstressed. The standard cost is the summary yardstick of cost of production; it should not be idealistic but should be a cost that can be reasonably achieved, as indeed should be the individual standards or yardsticks which have been used to build up the standard costs. It is often difficult to persuade management that a standard product cost based on a carefully planned and documented set of conditions is far truer than so called actual costs based on a completely random and largely unknown set of conditions which occurred some time in the past.

### 2. *Correlation of Actual Output and Cost with Budget*

*74.* The second stage of correlation, the comparison of actual results with budget, is the ultimate instrument of control. Where the budget is the "chart," this is the sextant and compass. The calculations required are discussed in the following paragraphs 75 to 78.

*75. Standard profit on actual sales.* The standard profit is sales less standard cost of sales. The standard cost is recorded on the office copy of each sales invoice and the standard profit margin calculated on each invoice. The sales and standard cost are analysed to product group at the same time. Scrutiny of standard profit margins gives an invaluable control on accuracy of sales invoicing and quotations to customers; it also shows the relative profit margins of different products. At H. & C. Ltd. a sales return analysed to main product groups, showing sales and standard profit expressed in value and as a percentage of sales, was circulated to Directors at four-weekly intervals. This is now done weekly and it has been found possible to complete the return by Wednesday evening for the previous week.

*76. Variances from standard.* The technique of calculating variances is beyond the scope of this paper. Each Company will have variances peculiar to its own operations. The variances from standard which could arise and were measured at H. & C. Ltd. were as in Exhibit 4.

*77. Profit and loss account.* This is no more than a summary of the control statements already discussed, plus adjustments for non-trading receipts and payments, special development expenditure and, in H. & C. Ltd., distribution income and expenditure which is not within the budgetary control and standard cost scheme. Net profit is thus standard profit (paragraph 75 above) plus or minus variances (paragraph 76 above) plus or minus the adjustments referred to in the previous sentence. This, of course, is the same profit as would be arrived at under traditional methods.

| Material | Price | |
|---|---|---|
| | Usage | |
| Recovery of | Efficiency | Comparison of actual times with standard |
| expense | Extra allow- | |
| | ances | Abortive operations, etc. |
| | Capacity | |
| | usage | Comparison of actual lost time with budgeted |
| | Volume | Cost of output gained or lost from causes other than above. Usually due to sales volume but could be effect of planning, etc. |
| Amount of | Budget | Temporary revisions of budget which have |
| expense | revision | not, for the sake of simplicity, been absorbed in costing rates |
| | Expense | This is the variance remaining between actual |
| | variance | and standard cost after efficiency, extra allowances, capacity usage, volume, and budget revision variances have been extracted. It indicates whether expenses were excessive or otherwise for the output produced in the period |
| Manufacturing | Alternate | Cost gained or lost by different routing of |
| method | machine | particular jobs |
| | Average | Where certain average conditions have to be |
| | conditions | assumed in the cost of a product this variance measures the extent to which actual conditions vary from the standard average conditions |

EXHIBIT 4

*78. Presentation of documents.* The pyramid method of presentation of documents is employed. A summary of results is supplied to the Board of Directors and supporting documents are available to be called for as necessary. These supporting documents are presented to Departmental Managers, foremen, etc. All documents are prepared four-weekly except the weekly production statistics. In the case Company, presentation is as in Exhibit 5 on page 682.

## 3. Determination of Selling Prices

*79.* The third stage of correlation is the determination of selling prices, and this is discussed in the following paragraphs 80 to 83.

*80.* Although in the long run selling prices must leave a reasonable margin over costs, the determination of selling prices is a policy decision. It is not often that selling prices of a Company can be fixed by ascertaining cost and adding to it a fixed profit margin thought to be reasonable by the Company. Some product groups will carry greater profit margins than others. It is often possible, however, to fix profit margins for each product group and instruct the estimator accordingly. But there will always be instances where the sales department requires the fixing of a selling price to be given special consideration and it is in these cases where the analysis of total cost of a product between fixed and variable expenses is useful. The sales department may be "after a sprat to catch a mackerel," or there *may* be justification for selling abroad or to a special customer at a low price if otherwise no sale would be made, and as long as it covers variables and contributes to fixed overheads.

| | Board of Directors | General Manager | Sales Manager | Works Manager | Production Dept. Managers | Foremen |
|---|---|---|---|---|---|---|
| Balance sheet | × | × | | | | |
| Profit and loss account | × | × | | | | |
| Sales and standard profit analysed to product groups | × | × | × | | | |
| Summary operating statement (see note below) | × | × | | | | |
| Admin. expense operating statement | | × | | | | |
| Sales expense operating statement | | × | × | | | |
| General works expense operating statement | | × | | × | | |
| Departmental operating statements | | × | | × | × | |
| Material control sheets | | × | | × | × | × |
| Weekly production statistics | | | | × | × | × |

*Note:* The summary operating statement summarises all operating statements (by budget centre) and the material control sheets. It shows for each budget centre the period activity (output), efficiency (speed of operation), standard cost, actual cost and the analysis of the total variance to cause.

EXHIBIT 5

*81.* Should the profit margin sought be expressed as a percentage of standard cost or adjusted cost (standard cost adjusted for variances)? The purist will probably contend the former and that variances will supplement, or be recovered from, profit margin. This approach was considered by H. & C. Ltd. and it is no doubt correct where all the "red" variances can be put right in reasonable time; it can be argued that some of the variances are temporary and have arisen fortuitously, or that they are lower down in the queue for attention and it is unfair that they should be passed to the customer.

*82.* One has to remember however the only object in calculating the adjusted cost; it is an intermediary stage in the making of a *policy* decision on selling price. In H. & C. Ltd. those variances which are likely to be long standing are added back to standard cost. These are mainly material price (raw material costs are steadily rising), budget revisions and volume variance. The variances that it is decided to add back are analysed to cost centre and a correction factor is calculated for each costing rate. Similarly, a correction factor is calculated on standard buying price of raw material in respect of the material price variance. A typical cost sheet showing standard cost, adjusted cost and calculation of selling price is shown in Exhibit 6.

*83.* When management has before it the standard cost, adjusted cost and the fixed overhead recovery of a job it is in a much better position to make a reasoned decision on a selling price.

## PRODUCT COST SHEET

| Cost Sheet No. 535 | Prepared by | DB/ | Checked IM | Product Cost Quantity | 1 |
|---|---|---|---|---|---|
| Date 15/6/55 | Calculated by | SHC/ | TB | Batch Quantity | 100 |
| Product | Connecting Rods | | | Code 73/163/X | |

Description and Drawing

Connecting Rods for Heath-Robinson Pea Splitter to drawing 59/73/5123 Cr.

### LABOUR AND OVERHEADS (PER DETAIL ON OPERATION LAYOUT)

| Cost Centre | | Product Standard Hours | Rate per Hour | | Standard Cost | | Correction Factor | | Adjusted Cost | |
|---|---|---|---|---|---|---|---|---|---|---|
| Name | No. | | Total £ | Fixed £ | Total £ | Fixed £ | Total % | Fixed % | Total £ | Fixed £ |
| Cutting | A2 | 0·05 | 0·625 | 0·412 | 0·031 | 0·021 | 105 | 110 | 0·033 | 0·023 |
| Turning | A3 | 1·33 | 1·180 | 0·667 | 1·573 | 0·889 | 90 | 90 | 1·416 | 0·800 |
| Drilling | A4 | 0·50 | 0·836 | 0·518 | 0·418 | 0·259 | 110 | 100 | 0·460 | 0·259 |
| Assembly | B2 | 0·75 | 0·484 | 0·216 | 0·363 | 0·162 | 80 | 75 | 0·290 | 0·122 |
| Total Labour and Overheads C/D | | | | | 2·385 | 1·331 | | | 2·199 | 1·204 |

### MATERIAL

| Description | | | | | Standard Price per Unit £ | Standard Cost £ | Correction Factor % | Adjusted Cost £ |
|---|---|---|---|---|---|---|---|---|
| Type | Dimensions | Waste % | Quantity | Unit | | | | |
| Match-wood | 24″ × 3″ × 3″ | 25 | 0·156 | cu. ft. | 10·000 | 1·560 | — | 1·560 |
| String | 50 ft. | 10 | 55 | ft. | 0·006 | 0·330 | 110 | 0·363 |
| Glue | 1 lb. | 15 | 1·15 | lb. | 0·015 | 0·017 | — | 0·017 |
| Total Material C/D | | | | | | 1·907 | | 1·940 |

| | Standard | | Adjusted | |
|---|---|---|---|---|
| | Total £ | Fixed £ | Total £ | Fixed £ |
| Total Labour and Overheads | 2·385 | 1·331 | 2·199 | 1·204 |
| Total Material | 1·907 | — | 1·940 | — |
| Works Cost | 4·292 | 1·331 | 4·139 | 1·204 |
| Selling Expenses—Std | Total 5·0% | Fixed 4·5% of Total | 0·215 | 0·194 | — | — |
| —Adj | 5·5% | 4·95% of Total | — | — | 0·237 | 0·213 |
| Total Cost ex Works | | | 4·507 | 1·525 | 4·476 | 1·417 |

**Pricing:**

| | £ |
|---|---|
| Ex Works Cost  Standard / Adjusted  (delete as applicable) | 4·477 |
| Profit, Royalty etc.  25% on Cost | 1·119 |
| **Selling Price ex Works—Per Each........** | 5·596 |

**Carriage etc.:**

Selling Price Delivered .............. per ...............

EXHIBIT 6

## PHASE III—CONSOLIDATION

*84.* On completion of the first full set of control data for the board there is a temptation to sit back under the delusion that the objective has been achieved. If a consultant has been employed to assist in the installation it is at this stage that he usually leaves, and this is what happened in H. & C. Ltd. In fact, at this stage, there is still a lot to be done and the following paragraphs 85 to 92 are based on our experience at H. & C. Ltd.

*85.* The first set of control data was produced five or six weeks after the period end; much too late to be of full value. It was necessary over the following months gradually to speed up presentation of results. This not only requires training of accounts department staff but also the co-operation of all departments from whence basic data is obtained. The aim must be to get all departments on to a four-weekly routine as soon as possible and when this is achieved the flow of control data will be automatic and positive.

*86.* A typical routine four-weekly period of the cost accountant is: *First two weeks:* preparing control data for previous four weeks. *Third week:* investigating variances and interpreting results to all levels of management at cost reduction committee meetings, etc. *Fourth week:* special investigations, reviewing clerical methods, etc.

*87.* There should be constant education of employees outside the accounts office, not only those to whom control data is supplied but also those who have to supply essential basic data. A person who is able to appreciate the significance of the data he supplies, and the use to which it is put, is more likely to take care to see that it is accurate and produced expeditiously.

*88.* Constant training and education of cost office staff must not be overlooked, the apparently obvious is often passed over by a person close to the job. One advantage of the type of control scheme already described is that it can be conveniently sectionalised and, apart from the cost accountant who must be able to understand the full picture and be able to lock each section together, it does not need highly skilled staff. Because of this sectionalisation, it is important that each section knows how the data it produces is used and its benefit to the company.

*89.* During this consolidation stage one should always be seeking to improve clerical methods and the form of presentation of the data. But in the excitement of developing new ideas it is necessary to ensure that prior stages do not lag and follow up is not overlooked.

*90.* Presentation of first data, no matter to which level of management it may be, should always be effected by the senior person in charge of the installation. First impressions are important and care should be taken to ensure that no control data is issued that is not understood by the recipient. This is sometimes more difficult than would be expected, especially with top management who are often not prepared to attend lectures or explanatory meetings. The greatest difficulty arises with the type of person who insists that he understands immediately all that is put before him. It is often all too apparent that the opposite is the truth, and that he does not even begin to appreciate the wealth of information given. The solution in these cases is often the oblique approach tempered by patience. An interest in the data and intelligent action thereon can often be awakened by careful selection of a part which indicates urgent corrective action and making it the subject of a special report, not forgetting to mention in the report from whence the information was gleaned.

91. Initial briefings on control documents must be followed up regularly. The cost accountant must ensure constantly that the data he produces is understood by those who have the authority to take corrective action.

92. It is unfortunate that sometimes the cost accountant's job does not finish with the presentation of control data and ensuring that it is understood. It is often necessary to exert pressure on management to take action to improve the efficiency and profitability of the Company. There is nothing more frustrating and injurious to morale than to produce control data period by period upon which little or no action is taken when it is obviously necessary. Remember the ultimate objective. Management controls are instituted as a tool of management to give them information upon which to take action to improve the running efficiency and profitability of the Company.

*Refinement*

93. After the consolidation phase an opportunity should be found to consider refinements. This is not a phase but a continuing process. The details of the structure of management controls should be constantly changed to keep pace with the changes in the business. Many necessary improvements and refinements will come to light in running the scheme.

94. An excellent opportunity to introduce refinements will occur on the first rebudgeting which will normally be immediately prior to the commencement of the next financial year. It is opportune then to re-arrange cost centres and budget centres, improve the accuracy of standard times, and probably, in the light of experience, alter the schedule of accounts. An effort should also be made to streamline the scheme. It may be decided that the presentation of some data can be discarded or, on the other hand, presentation of additional data may be desirable.

95. Other uses for the data being produced can be considered. For example, it can be used for bonus schemes or to assist in production planning, but it may be desirable before putting it to this sort of use to await the completion of rebudgeting and the results based on the new budgets. Accurate budgeting, especially of expense, is a technique that can only be learned by experience, and accuracy can only be achieved

by a person with a thorough knowledge of the business. It is a skill which develops each year.

96. Various types of bonus schemes can be worked out on control data. For example, a group incentive scheme for foremen and operators at H. & C. Ltd. has been based on the efficiency disclosed on weekly production statistics, and it is expected that the next rebudgeting will be sufficiently accurate to enable the operating statement results to become the basis of a bonus scheme for departmental managers.

97. It will have become apparent in reading the paper so far that the control scheme described is far-reaching and the cost office is perforce dependent for basic information on a variety of departments, and especially the time-study and planning sections of the production control department. The cost office can in turn give valuable assistance to the production control office including the following:

(a) Supplying detailed information of actual times on jobs or operations compared with standard times.

(b) Details of extra allowances claimed and reasons for them.

(c) Comparative cost of different methods of production.

(d) Machine loading and delivery dates. The weekly production statistics show data which is extremely useful in machine loading. To be accurate machine loading cannot rely alone on standard time which is not always achieved. If however the standard times are factored by current efficiency and allowance is made for lost time as disclosed by the production statistics, then machine loading becomes more accurate.

*Miscellany*

98. The great advantage of a control procedure such as described in this paper is its comprehensiveness. All angles of a business are encompassed and it is a principle of the scheme that all sections are interlocked. The work-in-progress account ties the final knot and is a valuable barometer in indicating the efficiency of the scheme. The reconciliation, at the financial year-end, of the calculated work-in-progress balance with the value of work-in-progress disclosed by a physical stocktaking, is the real test of the efficiency, comprehensiveness and arithmetical accuracy of the scheme.

99. The speed with which a new scheme of controls is installed is worthy of a special note. Every business has its own peculiar problems and the correct speed of installation will depend on the individual circumstances. But there is a correct speed for each business and it should be given special consideration.

100. If a scheme is pushed in too quickly it will only result in the first figures produced being incorrect and possibly misleading. This may undermine the confidence of management in the results at a time when management will be most critical. This lost ground will take a

long time to recover. It must not be forgotten that a complete installation of management controls results in considerable retraining of staff, not only those in the cost office. Too great an urgency only results in poor briefing and ineffective training, which leads to bad basic records and budget guesses instead of reasoned estimates based on all obtainable facts.

*101.* On the other hand, too slow an installation can be just as disastrous. It is a period of upheaval and from this point of view alone the sooner it is over the better. There may also be a period when it is necessary to run some old and new records in parallel.

*102.* The most significant disadvantage of too slow an installation is its effect on management, which will soon lose patience if no results are forthcoming after a long period wherein it was supplying information for standard times, expense budgets, etc. The installation should therefore be planned so that there is a steady stream of new results from successive sections. This will keep the attention of management and also enable it to absorb new data gradually without suffering mental indigestion. In these circumstances management is more likely to be patient until the completion of the final link in the chain to give a complete set of accounts.

*103.* There are certain foibles of management which seem common throughout industry, some of which are discussed in the remaining paragraphs of this miscellaneous section. The aspiring controller, for example, must expect to meet resistance in the early stages of development. It is the manifestation of the human element in all levels of management and it must not be overriden. If gentle and tactful persistence is used this resistance will melt as management gradually realise the value of what is put before them.

*104.* There is a natural resistance from those uncertain of their ability or position to the showing up of inefficiencies. This sort of resistance is sometimes difficult to combat. It is tragic if it is allowed to upset an installation, especially as the inefficiencies are often not the fault of the person concerned. It is more likely that the fault is due to information, which the new control data aims to supply, not being available to all levels of management, and the person concerned not getting support from his superiors.

*105.* In the small and medium firm, especially, there is usually an unwillingness to tackle a problem scientifically. It is extraordinary how often one meets the executive who will rely quite unnecessarily on some undefined mystery called "business acumen" when the facts upon which to make a decision are available if only the trouble were taken to get them. In fact, when the first results are produced it is not long before one meets the executive who says they are all nonsense, just because they are not as expected. "Expected" being his mental arithmetic based on unchecked formulae, some of which were passed on to him by the previous generation!

*106.* The introduction of a control scheme forces on management the scientific approach to problems. For example, in preparing standard and adjusted product costs on the lines previously explained, all facets of a job are considered before a selling price is fixed. It is surprising how often one finds selling prices being fixed on incomplete information, especially for non-standard products. A common fault seems to be the failure to decide in detail the method of manufacture before proceeding with an estimate. In these circumstances the estimator seems satisfied to cover himself for contingencies by adding a fixed percentage; but then fails to understand why his price is not competitive and the company fails to get the order.

*107.* We once heard a peculiar argument employed against integrated cost and financial accounts in general, and budgetary control and standard costing in particular. This was to the effect that they were impracticable because the auditors would not approve. What nonsense! In fact, in our experience auditors are most co-operative, and in particular the auditors of H. & C. Ltd. showed patience, willingness to learn, and appreciation of what was being done. There are, of course, difficulties in preparing an orthodox profit and loss account from books keyed in to standard costing, but, if standard cost entries are marked distinctively in the books when made, it is a relatively simple task to reverse them in the final adjustments.

*108.* The authors look forward to finding, one day, a management bold enough to supply shareholders with a budget at the beginning of the year and a variance statement at the end!

## Conclusion

*109.* There is no denying that the introduction of a comprehensive scheme of management controls, such as that already described, is a complicated procedure which should not be haphazardly undertaken. It should be pre-planned with the same thoroughness as a military offensive. It requires the co-operation of all departments with the cost accountant at the hub, but, unlike the military commander the cost accountant can only ask for, not demand, help from outside his department. It is for this reason that the cost accountant is entitled to expect and must obtain the continuous support of top management. The techniques to be employed in a complete overhaul of a company's control and costing procedures are relatively easy to describe but not so easy to apply. The human element is substantially involved and a pleasing but yet forceful personality is no doubt an essential characteristic of the successful modern cost accountant.

*110.* There are other essentials for success. The person in charge of the exercise should have had previous experience. He should also have nothing else to think about; he is doomed to failure if at the same time he is trying to perform routine duties. The installation of a scheme of management controls is not a precise science but an art, and one must be always calling on past experience and using one's judgment to decide how far to go.

*111.* There was a time not so many years ago when it was generally thought that this type of control procedure could only be applied successfully in the more simple repetitive type of business. This belief has lingered and even today one meets the occasional person who strongly holds this view. In the authors' opinion there is no type of business where the principles employed in this case study cannot be put to good use. In fact, the more complicated the business the more necessary it is to introduce a comprehensive control procedure.

*112.* One final word: the time to install a control procedure is when the Company is thriving, not, as is so often done, when a Company is in difficulties. Prevention is better than cure. Management decisions are relatively easy if facts are available and a comprehensive control procedure should supply many of the necessary facts.

### Required

1. What lessons can be learned from the experiences of H. & C. Ltd. in the realm of management organisation?
2. Discuss the main phases in the development of the managerial controls. What alternative approaches could have been made?
3. Draft a flow chart to illustrate the procedures followed in the development of the management controls.

\* \* \*

## CASE STUDY 7—REORGANISATION OF COSTING ARRANGEMENTS\*

### INTRODUCTORY

This paper describes a reorganisation of costing arrangements and presentation introduced by the writer some years ago, in a Company engaged in a process industry. Although the products of this Company were of a homogeneous nature (cellulose film) there were a number of types (involving different chemical treatment, coatings, etc.), and these were supplied in different gauges and forms (*e.g.* reels or sheets), with the result that a three-figure range of product costs was involved.

The primary objective of the reorganisation was to provide more effective control of profits, but it had also a secondary objective—a substantial reduction in the amount of clerical work necessary to compute and present product cost and profit information in the light of continually changing circumstances. After the acid test of several years' operation it can now be said that both objectives were achieved.

\* This case study was compiled by A. W. H. Lamond, B.L., C.A., F.I.O.M., M.B.I.M., J.Dip.M.A. It appeared in *Office Management* for June 1960, and is reproduced by kind permission of the Author and the Secretary of the Institute of Office Management.

The reorganisation can best be described in four parts as follows:

A brief indication of the costing arrangements available before reorganisation.

An outline of the general considerations of principle to meet which changes were made.

Development of the methods chosen to meet the requirements thus established.

An illustration of the resultant new arrangements and presentation.

In showing how the methods chosen were developed and in illustrating the resultant new arrangements and presentation all figures used are, of course, purely imaginary ones adopted for illustrative purposes only.

## COSTING ARRANGEMENTS AVAILABLE BEFORE REORGANISATION

Before the reorganisation there had been already developed a fully comprehensive system of standard costing and budgetary control. At the beginning of each half-year a sales forecast was made in considerable detail and this was reconciled with production plans to give a sales/production forecast of activity on the basis of which a budget and profit forecast was prepared for the half-year. As the months went by actual results were compared in considerable detail with this budget to throw up excess costs or savings against the budget. This comparison took the form of monthly accounts involving a score or so pages of tabulated typescript which were circulated to top management. These accounts were rather typical of the conventional accounting presentation. They included a wealth of information, but much of it was of no great significance to top management and considerable study was involved if the grain was to be extracted from the chaff. Changes in circumstances could, moreover, invalidate the budget, but because of the large amount of clerical work involved rebudgeting took time and would tend not to be undertaken except if circumstances were such as to render this unavoidable.

As regards product costs a comprehensive schedule setting out the standard cost of each of the product variations was prepared on the basis of each budget and this constituted the main guide to the cost aspect of product pricing. Apart from the home market, however, products were being sold in a large number of markets throughout the world and adjustment had to be made in respect of costs peculiar to these markets. This approach was thus, again, a rather conventional accounting approach. It suffered from the defect that while conditions (*e.g.* total volume) could change rapidly the clerical work involved in rebudgeting and recosting products in the light of such changes was so considerable as to make the approach an unwieldy one—to say the least.

## GENERAL CONSIDERATIONS OF PRINCIPLE

In planning the reorganisation the starting-point was certain general considerations of principle which may be said to apply to any attempt to "control" profits through accounting and costing aids. As will be seen, certain logical requirements arise from these general considerations.

The profits of business ventures obviously depend very largely on external factors and to this extent cannot be controlled in an absolute sense. Within the limits imposed by those external conditions, however, a measure of control can be exercised, and it was considered that control in this sense should embody three features:

1. A profit target, which should be the final expression of a feasible plan of activity prepared in advance;

2. Day-to-day controls or means of assessing action taken or contemplated in terms of its effect in relation to the target; and

3. A periodic summary, or analysis of the reasons for deviations which emerge on comparison of actual results with the target.

### Profit Targets

In common with many other companies, the Company had felt the pinch of the 1952 recession. As already explained, we had well-developed standard costing and budgetary control techniques, based on detailed forecasts of sales by product lines and by markets, and these techniques had worked admirably under seller's market conditions. New plant did not fall unheralded from the sky, nor was existing plant suddenly withdrawn without notice. Production capacity could therefore be readily assessed. A satisfactory mix of products could be established and their allocation rather than sale, could be predetermined with the knowledge that most customers could be relied upon to take what they were offered.

In 1952, however, the market had changed. It became very difficult to make reliable forecasts of sales. This did not mean, of course, that such forecasts were not made; on the contrary, forward sales planning became more imperative. It did mean, however, that under the competitive conditions we had to face, forecasts had to be much more frequently adjusted to meet changing external conditions. Moreover, forecasts which were continually changing were, to say the least, an inconvenient foundation on which to build a pyramid of cost detail. Indeed, if a detailed method were used, the result could well be that the basic forecast was already out of date by the time a complete cost budget could be worked out. There was a need, therefore, for a simple and flexible method of assessing and applying profit targets. The selling organisation had to be free, within the overall target, to modify its detailed plans as might be necessary even from day to day without sacrificing the benefit of control on the one hand, or occasioning disproportionate clerical effort in recalculation of cost data on the other.

## Day-to-day Controls

The Company was fortunate in having adequate techniques for the control of costs. Such techniques are, of course, essentials in all businesses and many varieties are available. For the purpose of this paper, therefore, adequate cost control will be assumed to exist. The changing pattern of markets in 1952, however, had emphasised the need to pay more attention to the strictly trading aspect. In purely trading concerns it is clearly evident that success depends on two simple achievements: the sale of goods for more than they cost or getting a margin, and the sale of a sufficient quantity of them, or volume. The compound of those two determines the profit or overall measure of success.

In businesses which manufacture what they sell, the volume factor remains clear, since it is easy to measure orders booked in terms of value, weight or some other convenient yardstick. The margin of profit earned is influenced, however, by numerous manufacturing factors, including volume, and is therefore more obscure, at least until the effects of these have been computed. Even so, it remains true that the level of trading profit is broadly established at the time when orders are booked, since it depends primarily on the margin accorded by the price coupled with the volume of orders obtained and acceptable. Given satisfactory estimating and cost control, the factory should not often dissipate profit possibilities thus created. Conversely, it cannot be expected to pull chestnuts out of the fire! We found a need, therefore, for a day-to-day control of profit at the order stage, so that at the time of booking orders, or considering them, they could be assessed, not only in terms of the volume they contributed but also in terms of the margin they afforded, the two together indicating their effect in relation to the profit target.

## Periodic Summaries

The third feature of profit control as we had defined it was the periodic summary of results which must follow the close of each accounting period. Here we again found there were many available techniques of accounting analysis and presentation. Inasmuch as corrective action should take place from day to day, it was to the day-to-day controls of costs and trading that we considered we should look for action. The periodic summary was of the nature of a post-mortem telling top management broadly what, if anything went wrong. There was a need, therefore, to put it into its right perspective, as the final stage of profit control. If the day-to-day job had been done effectively the periodic analysis would serve only to summarise the overall effect of the many deviations from target which had already been the subject of day-to-day study and action by those responsible. The final analysis could be relatively simple, as indeed any final analysis must be if it is to convey a clear picture.

*Requirements*

Once these general principles had been accepted it became clear that in selecting methods to apply profit control under more competitive conditions, we had to meet the following requirements:

1. The profit target had to be established and applied in a simple and flexible way, so that sales plans could be revised as often as need be with a minimum of rebudgeting and recalculation of costing data.

2. Day-to-day control of costs had to be effectively applied. (This is a subject in itself and is not covered in this paper.)

3. Day-to-day control of profit margins had to be exercisable at the time when orders were booked or considered.

4. The periodic overall analysis did not need to be complex but had to be simple, to convey a clear picture.

**DEVELOPMENT OF METHODS TO MEET THESE REQUIREMENTS***

Under the conditions envisaged, a simple approach to the problem was provided by the familiar profit graph. Such graphs are commonly drafted in the form of a Break-even Chart, such as Exhibit 1. This

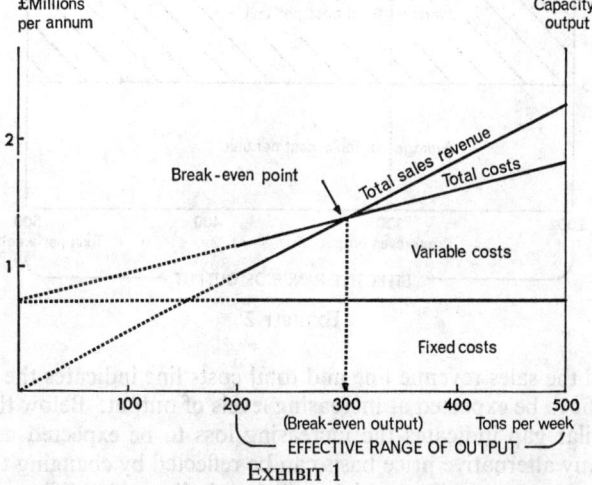

EXHIBIT 1

indicates total costs and total sales revenue over a range of output levels. Total costs include (strictly) three types of costs:

Fixed costs, such as rent, depreciation, salaries, etc., which may be expected to remain constant in amount throughout the range of output levels under consideration. (Very low levels are usually omitted.)

Semi-fixed costs, such as indirect labour, maintenance, etc., which may be expected to vary or fluctuate, but not necessarily directly in relation to the volume of output.

* Not surprisingly, being a case study, this section is historical. Converting the £sd to £p (decimal) system would have made the example meaningless.

Variable costs, such as materials, direct wages and other items which may be expected to vary directly with the volume of output.

For practical purposes, semi-fixed costs can often be allocated as between fixed and variable components in such a way as to simplify the picture (as in the example) without causing significant error.

The sales revenue, on any given price basis, is obviously a straight line from the point of origin. This line crosses the total costs line at the level of output at which neither profit nor loss would be expected—known as the break-even point. Above this level, the widening gap

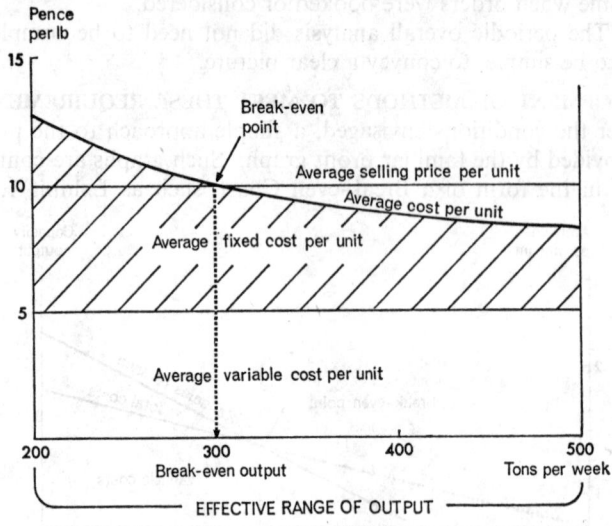

**EXHIBIT 2**

between the sales revenue line and total costs line indicates the increasing profit to be expected at increasing levels of output. Below this level, the similar gap indicates the increasing loss to be expected as output falls. Any alternative price basis can be reflected by changing the slope of the sales revenue line, which will then indicate the different break-even and profit possibilities resulting.

The profit graph can also be drafted to show the average profit (or loss) per unit of output throughout the range of output levels selected—as in Exhibit 2. In terms of cost per unit, the variable costs become the constant and are expressed, on this type of graph, by a horizontal straight line, while the fixed costs and, therefore, total costs have to be expressed by a curve. The average selling price per unit is also expressed by a straight horizontal line. The break-even point will, of course, occur at the same level of output as on the first graph but the widening gaps above (or below) it will indicate, for each level of output, the average profit (or loss) to be expected per unit instead of the total profit (or loss). Such a graph has interesting possibilities both as an aid in establishing a target profit under given conditions and as a method of presenting cost information.

The graph shown in Exhibit 2, is, of course, an overall picture for the whole business. The unit figures for selling price, cost and profit are, therefore, averages for all products in all markets. If information is to be given for specific products and markets, deviations from these

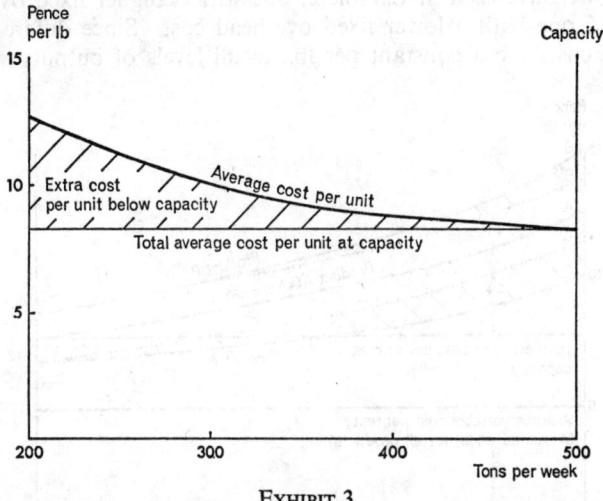

EXHIBIT 3

averages must be known. Exhibit 3 shows the same total cost per unit as was used in Exhibit 2, but splits this total cost into two components:

1. The average cost per unit when the factory is operating at capacity output (which is a constant).

2. The average extra cost per unit when the factory is operating below capacity output (which is represented by the shaded area and increases rapidly as the level of output falls).

If we adopt the historical cost concept, then, whenever output is below capacity, both these components enter into the so-called actual cost of any product. If we adopt the capacity cost concept, the extra cost per unit incurred when output is below capacity (*i.e.* the shaded area on the graph) is no part of the cost of the units actually produced but is rather a part of the cost of the units not produced. If the latter concept is accepted, it is clear that it would be improper to allocate this extra cost of idle capacity to products as a matter of costing. It is true, nevertheless, that, if a profit is to be ensured, this expenditure must be recovered, but how this should be done becomes rather a matter of policy than of cost allocation. One rational method is to "levy" the extra expenditure equally over all units of product—as is automatically done in Exhibit 2 which shows overall average figures.

Whichever concept is adopted, differences in variable costs as between products will obviously remain constant at all levels of output and can be expressed as a simple deviation of (say) $\pm x$ pence per lb., from the average. The treatment of fixed costs, however, will depend on the concept adopted and, to present this simply, it is assumed in Exhibit 4 that there are only three products—one coinciding with the average we have seen in Exhibit 2, one with a higher fixed overhead cost, and one with a lower fixed overhead cost. Since differences in variable costs are a constant per lb., at all levels of output, we shall

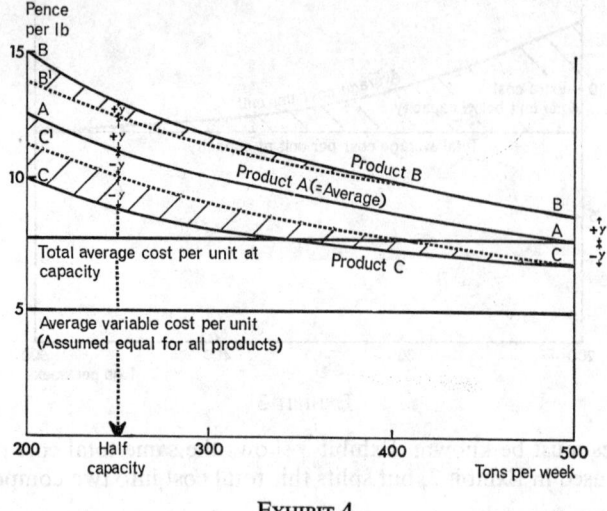

EXHIBIT 4

simplify the picture further by assuming at this stage that these are the same for all three products.

If we adopt the historical cost concept, the costs of products B and C are given by the lines B–B and C–C respectively while the cost of product A remains the overall average given by A–A. The differences $+y$ and $-y$ represent more and less than average fixed overheads attracted by products B and C respectively at capacity output. When output is at half capacity, however, product B attracts fixed overheads in excess of the average to the extent of $2y$. This is difficult to justify, inasmuch as the extra fixed overheads which are being manipulated in this way may have little connection with the products, the costs of which are fluctuating because of them. The reduction to half-capacity might be due, for example, to a falling off in the volume of product A. This concept of cost is, therefore, dangerous, since the cost of products with high fixed overhead content tends to be exaggerated through having to carry an undue proportion of idle capacity cost at low levels of output. If pricing policy has regard to such costs, these products can be "costed off the market." Products with low fixed overhead content, on the other hand, tend to escape their fair share of idle capacity costs.

If we adopt the capacity cost concept, all product costs are established at capacity level and we apply a "levy" to cover idle capacity costs on some fair basis. The basis to be adopted is a policy decision which must be taken in the light of the particular circumstances of the business. Once the basis has been established as a policy matter, however, the levy can for practical purposes be included in the quoted cost figure (really true cost + levy), which is used to determine sales policy. To continue to handle the levy as a separate factor would be a needless complication, although it may be useful to know its extent at any level of output for purposes of marginal cost pricing.

If we assume that, in our example, the basis chosen is (say) weight of product, the effect on our graph (Exhibit 4) is that the shaded areas can be ignored, and will, of course, cancel each other. The costs of products B and C (including the levy) are shown by $B^1$–B and $C^1$–C. At all levels of output, deviations from average fixed costs then become a constant per unit, based on their amount at capacity output. Deviations in variable costs are also a constant per unit, and the two can therefore be added together for each product to give a total deviation: $\pm x \pm y =$ (say) $\pm z$. The appropriate overall average read from the graph, together with the resultant deviation of $\pm z$ pence per lb., will then give the cost of any product at any level of output. In this cost is, of course, included a "fair share" of idle capacity cost if any.

A unit cost graph, on the lines of the shaded part of Exhibit 5, showing the average unit cost for the whole business (or for some suitable division of it) will thus provide a simple means of conveying overall cost information to those responsible for determining sales policy. By supplementing it with a simple schedule of deviations in cost per lb. ($= \pm z$ above), along the lines of Exhibit 6, it can obviate recalculation and issue of cost data for different levels of output each time changes are made in sales plans. Such information can be easily kept up to date as regards other variables by the issuance of a new graph whenever significant changes take place in the overall picture and by amendments to the deviation schedule as and when necessary.

Before going into the uses of Exhibits 5 and 6, however, let us consider briefly the construction of the cost graph constituting the shaded part of Exhibit 5. Standard cost methods of cost finding, using capacity standards, will most readily provide the data required, and, if the costs used are based on reliable estimates of future variances—rather than past experience—the best possible guidance will be given to those responsible for establishing sales policy. Exhibits 7 and 8 give details of the construction of such a unit cost graph by scheduling fixed

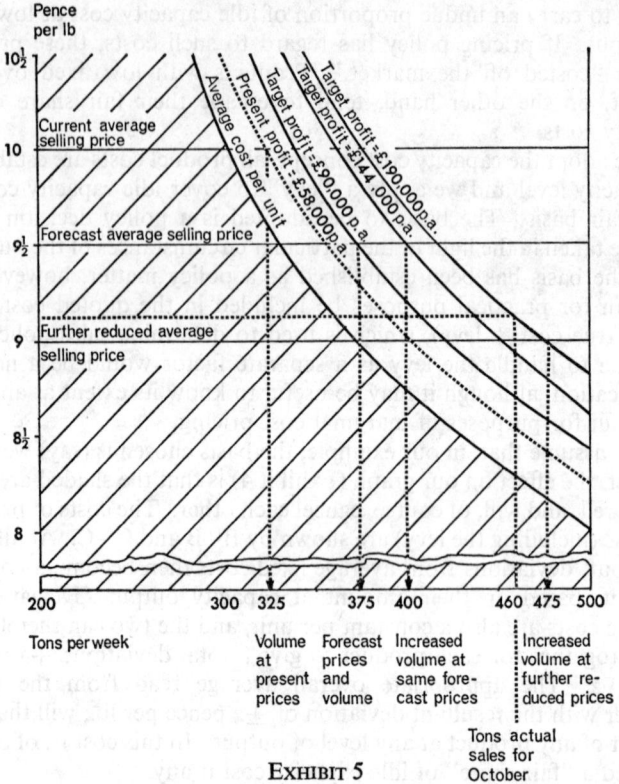

EXHIBIT 5

overheads, together with the estimated cost of semi-fixed items at selected points throughout the range of output levels covered. It may be convenient to include on this schedule (as indicated by Exhibit 8) all administration and selling expenses, even those which are wholly variable, such as commission. It may also be convenient to deal with

| Product | Deviations in pence per lb. | | |
| --- | --- | --- | --- |
| | Home Market | S. American Market | N. American Market |
| A | Nil | +2 | +1 |
| B | +1 | +3 | +2 |
| C | −1 | +1 | Nil |
| D | −5 | −3 | −4 |
| E | +2 | +4 | +3 |

EXHIBIT 6

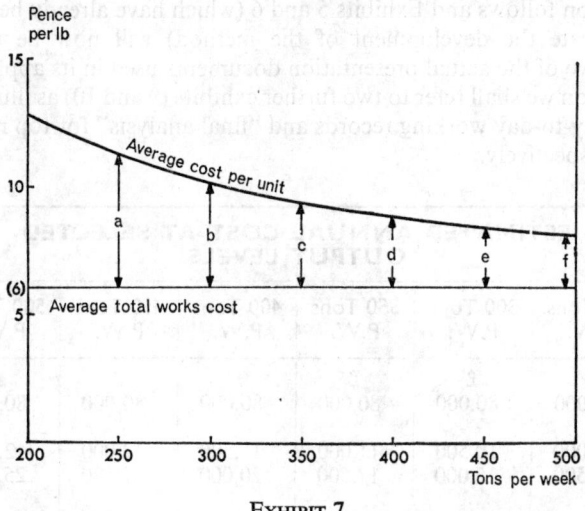

EXHIBIT 7

"Average total works cost" includes Fixed and Semi-fixed Overheads on "Capacity basis" estimated for the next period of (say) 3 months.

*Note:* The average is calculated on the current mix of products adjusted broadly for any significant changes which can be anticipated in the next 3 months.

all works costs as a constant per lb. of product on a capacity basis (as shown in Exhibit 7) and to include in the administration and selling costs schedule (Exhibit 8) the estimated under-recovery of fixed or semi-fixed works costs at each selected output level below capacity. The total cost curve can thus be established without great difficulty and with adequate accuracy.

Having seen something of the construction of the unit cost graph, we can now revert to Exhibit 5 on which it appears as the shaded portion. This becomes a profit graph when we superimpose on it the current average selling price to show the average margin available per unit at each level of output. Lines can also be drawn to indicate the combinations of average price per unit and volume which would result in any given overall profit rate per annum for the whole business. Three such lines are shown in Exhibit 5. If the overall average selling price does not fluctuate violently month by month, this type of graph can be used to establish profit targets on a broad basis. By reference to current volume forecasts and selling price trends, a feasible profit target can be readily selected for the next period of (say) six months.

## ILLUSTRATION OF NEW ARRANGEMENTS AND PRESENTATION

In order to demonstrate fully the new arrangements and presentation adopted as a result of the reorganisation a complete (but simplified) illustration follows and Exhibits 5 and 6 (which have already been used to illustrate the development of the method) will now be used as illustrative of the actual presentation documents used in its application. In addition we shall refer to two further exhibits (9 and 10) as illustrative of the day-to-day working records and "final analysis" for top management, respectively.

| ESTIMATED ANNUAL COST AT SELECTED OUTPUT LEVELS | | | | | |
|---|---|---|---|---|---|
| 250 Tons P.W. | 300 Tons P.W. | 350 Tons P.W. | 400 Tons P.W. | 450 Tons P.W. | 500 Tons P.W. |
| £ 80,000 | £ 80,000 | £ 80,000 | £ 80,000 | £ 80,000 | £ 80,000 |
| 10,000 12,500 | 10,500 15,000 | 11,000 17,500 | 11,500 20,000 | 12,000 22,500 | 12,500 25,000 |
| 60,000 | 60,000 | 60,000 | 60,000 | 60,000 | 60,000 |
| 20,000 25,000 | 21,000 30,000 | 22,000 35,000 | 23,000 40,000 | 24,000 45,000 | 25,000 50,000 |
| 116,700 5,000 | 93,700 3,000 * | 70,300 3,000 | 47,000 2,000 | 23,300 2,000 | Nil Nil |
| £583,000 | £560,000 | £530,000 | £513,300 | £490,000 | £466,700 |
| 5·00d. | 4·00d. | 3·25d. | 2·75d. | 2·33d. | 2·00d. |
| (a) | (b) | (c) | (d) | (e) | (f) |

EXHIBIT 8

## Setting of Profit Target

Having established a Profit Graph in the form of Exhibit 5, we have seen that this enables us by reference to current volume forecasts and selling price trends to select a feasible profit target for the next period of (say) six months.

For example, let us assume that it is planned to reduce certain selling prices and that the estimated effect of these reductions on the overall average will be to reduce it by $\frac{1}{2}d$. to $9\frac{1}{2}d$. per lb. Let us assume also that sales forecasts—taking into account the effect of the new prices—indicate an output level of (say) 375 tons per week for the next six months. Such anticipations will, of course, be calculated in as much detail as the significance of the anticipated changes may justify. Having assessed future conditions in this way, an overall target profit rate of

£90,000 per annum is indicated by the graph and may reasonably be adopted for the next six months.

Such a target can be readily changed without extensive rebudgeting, whenever sales volume forecasts or price changes require this. Moreover, sales forecasts can be varied within limits, both as to volume and margin, without significantly altering the approximate level of profit aimed at. In fact, the selling organisation should always try to compensate in other directions for any adverse factors as they arise, so that, once a profit target has been set, they can maintain this target as long as practicable. We shall see later that the nature of the day-to-day control adopted encouraged this attitude.

Profit targets set by the method thus developed may not have so precise an appearance as targets based on detailed forecasts of sales by products and markets for which costs and invoice values have been computed and budgeted in corresponding detail. It is doubtful, however, if the apparent precision of such forecasts is real. In many businesses today, forward forecasts, although made (quite properly) in great detail, cannot be claimed to be, in fact, so realistic that it is worth while to make the calculations of cost and profit follow the full detail of the forecasts. Their extension in this way may well be equivalent to working to several insignificant places in an arithmetical calculation! As an alternative, therefore, the kind of result which can be much more easily achieved by the overall methods described may give as high a degree of accuracy as was possessed by the forecasts themselves. When one considers also that, under competitive conditions, frequent changes in the forecasts may be necessary, the clerical effort of trying to make detailed cost calculations follow these changes, becomes even more prohibitive.

## Applying Day-to-day Control

Once the profit target has been set the next problem is to develop a simple way of applying it in the course of day-to-day control. For this purpose we introduce the concept of target selling prices which are the purely hypothetical prices at which each product would have to be sold in order to contribute its fair share of the overall profit target on some rational basis. It is important to emphasise that there is no suggestion that actual selling prices should be adjusted to coincide with these target selling prices. Actual prices can rarely be rational (in relation to costs) since, under normal competition, they must always be determined by market conditions. Inevitably, some products in some markets, will contribute more than their fair share of the total profit targeted. Other product/market combinations will, correspondingly, produce less than their fair share.

The purpose of the target selling prices, therefore, is merely to enable assessment to be made of the satisfactoriness, or otherwise, of any given selling price at any time, from the standpoint of the current target rate of profit for the business as a whole. In this assessment lies the key to control of profits at the time when orders are booked or considered. It is insufficient that this assessment be made only periodically or haphazardly. It should be applied, as a matter of routine, to all incoming orders, so that their attractiveness, or otherwise, from the point of view of profit rate, is known and the cumulative result, as regards orders taken for any period, is continuously available.

This continuous assessment can be provided by the operation of a simple order record maintained for each period's orders, in the form illustrated by Exhibit 9. This record is planned to show (by reference to the target rate of profit for the business as a whole) the deviation in profit arising from each order booked and the cumulative deviation for all orders to date. The target profit rate is, of course, confidential and need not be known to the clerical staff. Once the target has been set for a period, the staff is advised only of the average target selling price corresponding to the target profit at the anticipated level of output. This figure can be read from the confidential graph. For example, having set the target profit rate of £90,000 per annum at an output level of 375 tons per week, the average target selling price (as shown by Exhibit 5) is $9\frac{1}{2}d.$ per lb. Deviations from this average target selling price for individual products can then be taken to be the same in amount as the deviations from average cost. Thus the deviation schedule, in conjunction with the given average target selling price of $9\frac{1}{2}d.$ per lb., enables the staff to make entry of the target price for any order.

For example, for the first order recorded on Exhibit 9, we get a target selling price of $11\frac{1}{2}d.$ per lb. made up:

| | |
|---|---|
| Average target selling price for period | $9\frac{1}{2}d.$ |
| Deviation for product E in the home market, per deviation schedule (see Exhibit 6) | $+2d.$ |
| Total target selling price for this product market combination | $11\frac{1}{2}d.$ |

It is then simple arithmetic to extend the profit deviation per lb., as compared with the actual selling price, and to calculate the total profit deviation for the whole order. The profit deviations on all orders are then cumulated in the end column. Orders which are yielding more than their share of the target rate of profit are thus recorded with a correspondingly favourable deviation, while orders that are yielding less, will show an unfavourable deviation. In this way, orders can be judged good or bad from the margin or profit angle, apart from the mere volume or weight of production they contribute.

The cumulative profit deviation (plus or minus) on all orders in any given period is the measure of the extent to which the selling organisation has been successful in balancing the mix of orders from the standpoint of maintaining the target profit rate for the business as a whole.

Thus, when Exhibit 9 has been completed up to point (*a*) the executive concerned knows that his target is a profit rate of £90,000 per annum and that this should give a profit of £7200 for October on the basis of the number of production days in that month. The deviation of +£1540 on the control sheet tells him that, so far, the orders booked should give a profit of £8740 provided that he reaches the target volume of 375 tons per week.

It is true, of course, that the target rate of profit may need to be revised. The forecast volume of sales for any period may change and/or selling prices may be raised or lowered. Changes in either of these two factors can be easily dealt with.

To illustrate how this can be done Exhibit 5 shows a number of such changes—many more, in fact, than would be likely, in practice, to arise in a single month. If, for example, there is a major change in market conditions and the forecast volume increases from 375 tons per week to (say) 400 tons per week with no change in forecast selling price levels, then the new profit target (as shown by Exhibit 5) becomes £144,000 per annum. As the forecast average selling price has not changed, this new profit target does not alter the day-to-day profit control figures, but the cumulative deviation they record now relates to the new profit level of £144,000 per annum. At point (*b*) therefore, the control (Exhibit 9) tells the executive concerned that the October profit should be £500 above this new limit—giving about £12,000 profit for the month— provided that he reaches the new target volume of 400 tons per week.

If, on the other hand, it is decided to reduce selling prices by (say) a further $\frac{1}{2}d$. per lb. (from the beginning of the month for which orders are now being booked) and it is anticipated that the effect of this will be to increase volume still further to (say) 475 tons per week, then the new profit target (as shown by Exhibit 5) becomes £190,000 per annum. (We may note here that the graph can be helpful in considering the desirability of such decisions—and this is a good example of "desirability"!) Under the new conditions the average target selling price now becomes 9*d*. per lb. and the profit control figures shown on Exhibit 9 can be simply adjusted. On being advised of the new figure of 9*d*. per lb. the record clerk notes that this represents a decrease of $\frac{1}{2}d$. per lb. on the old figure of $9\frac{1}{2}d$. per lb. The total weight of orders booked to date is, therefore, added (giving £480,000 as shown on Exhibit 9) and this total is multiplied by $\frac{1}{2}d$. per lb. to give a total money adjustment of +£1000. The cumulative deviation is now therefore £1500—and this, of course, applies to the new profit rate of £190,000 per annum. At point (*c*), therefore, the control indicates a profit for October of £16,700, provided the new target volume of 475 tons per week is reached.

At the end of each period, the order control will be finally adjusted to the level of sales volume in fact achieved. For example, let us assume that, on closing the order record for October, the orders actually booked total 4,121,600 lb. and this is equal to an average of (say) 460 tons per week, whereas the target selling price of 9d. was based on a forecast of 475 tons per week. Reference to the profit graph then tells us that the target selling price corresponding to a corrected forecast of

| Order Refer-ence | Product | Market | Weight (lbs.) | Selling Price per lb. | | Profit Dev. per lb. | | Profit Deviation | | | |
|---|---|---|---|---|---|---|---|---|---|---|---|
| | | | | Actual (pence) | Target (pence) | + (pence) | − (pence) | Total per Order | | Cumulative Total | |
| | | | | | | | | + £ | − £ | + − | £ |
| 1234 | E | Home | 48,000 | 12 | 11½ | ½ | | 100 | | + | 100 |
| 1235 | A | N. America | 14,400 | 9½ | 10½ | | 1 | | 60 | + | 40 |
| 1236 | D | S. America | 120,000 | 9½ | 6½ | 3 | | 1,500 | | + | 1,540 (a) |
| 1351 | C | Home | 24,000 | 7½ | 8½ | 1 | | 100 | | + | 500 (b) |
| On revising Target Adjustment of Target Selling Price from 9½d. to 9d. on total to date | | | 480,000 | | | | | 1,000 | | + | 1,500 (c) |
| On closing from period Total Order booked for Period | | | 4,121,600 | | | | | | | + | 817 |
| Equal to | | | 460 tons p.w. | Final Adjustment of Target Selling Price from 9d. to 9·1d. per lb. | | 0·1 | | 1,717 | | − | £900 (d) |

SIGNIFICANCE (to Executive knowing confidential Profit Target):

| | Profit Target | |
|---|---|---|
| | P.A. for October | |
| At point (a) | £90,000 | £7,200 |
| At point (b) | £144,000 | £11,520 |
| At point (c) | £190,000 | £15,200 |
| At point (d) | £190,000 | £15,200 |

£1540 above target means a profit of £8740 for October—if orders reach target of 375 tons p.w.
£500 above target means a profit of £12,020 for October—if orders reach new target of 400 tons p.w.
£1500 above target means a profit of £16,700 for October—if orders reach new target of 475 tons p.w.
£900 below target means a profit of £14,300 for October—orders having been closed at only 460 tons p.w.

On preparation of Accounts—actual profit per Exhibit 10 £14,200 for October—due to other deviations as analysed on Exhibit 10.

(Note: In practice one would not expect targets to change so frequently but an abnormal number of changes have been illustrated in order to demonstrate the flexibility of the method.)

EXHIBIT 9

460 tons per week would have been (say) 9·1d. per lb. We, therefore, calculate, as a negative deviation, the 0·1d. per lb. on the total orders actually booked of 4,121,600 lb. to arrive at a final adjustment of £1717, making the cumulative deviation from the target profits £900. In other words, the control indicates, at point (d), that the actual profit for the month should be £900 short of the target rate of £190,000 per annum, and may, therefore, be estimated at £14,300.

*Final Analysis*

If profits and costs have been effectively controlled from day to day, the final analysis at the end of each accounting period need not be complex. A statement on the lines of Exhibit 10 will tell top management simply and clearly:

1. The target profit as agreed in advance.
2. The actual profit as shown by the financial accounts.
3. The overall deviation from the target.

This overall deviation may be analysed as far as it is worthwhile to take it. The extent will depend on what aspects are most significant in the particular business at the particular time with which we are concerned. As an example, the "Analysis of deviations" given in Exhibit 10 includes the following columns:

**Sales volume and margin.** If all orders booked for delivery in each month are in fact dispatched in the month, the figure appearing

### PERIODIC SUMMARY AND ANALYSIS OF DEVIATIONS FROM TARGET

| Month | No. of Days | Current Target Profit = £190,000 p.a. per Graph | Actual Profit | Overall Deviation + − | | Analysis of Deviations | | | |
|---|---|---|---|---|---|---|---|---|---|
| | | | | | Amount | Sales Volume and Margin | Con-trollable Selling Expenses | Con-trollable Pro-duction Costs | Adminis-trations and Other Costs |
| | | £ | £ | | £ | £ | £ | £ | £ |
| October | 28 | 15,200 | 14,200 | − | 1,000 | −900 | −150 | −100 | +150 |
| November | 28 | 15,200 | 14,600 | − | 600 | −400 | −100 | −150 | + 50 |
| December | 30 | 16,286 | 15,986 | − | 300 | −100 | − 50 | −200 | + 50 |
| January | 28 | 15,200 | | | | | | | |
| February | 28 | 15,200 | | | | | | | |
| March | 30 | 16,286 | | | | | | | |

### CUMULATIVE FIGURES

Months to

| | | | | | | | | | |
|---|---|---|---|---|---|---|---|---|---|
| 2nd November | 56 | 30,400 | 28,800 | − | 1,600 | −1,300 | −250 | −250 | +200 |
| 3rd December | 86 | 46,686 | 44,786 | − | 1,900 | −1,400 | −300 | −450 | +250 |
| 4th January | 114 | 61,886 | | | | | | | |
| 5th February | 142 | 77,086 | | | | | | | |
| 6th March | 172 | 93,372 | | | | | | | |

EXHIBIT 10

here will agree with the total deviation built up from day to day as the orders were booked. To the extent to which dispatches are not as programmed, a reconciliation can be made if the difference is material. The figure shown can, of course, be further broken down into its volume and margin components and, beyond this, any necessary explanations can be obtained by reference to the profit control on orders booked, which reveals the effect even of individual orders booked.

**Controllable selling expenses/Controllable production costs.** Here will be shown the total excess cost or saving against budget or standard for such selling expenses and production costs as can be controlled on a day-to-day or week-to-week basis. Again, this will be merely the summary of figures already known through their control in this way. Any further explanations required can thus be readily supplied by reference to the appropriate expense or cost control statement.

**Administration and other costs.** Under this heading will be reflected the deviation from forecast for all other costs, most of which are not controllable from day-to-day, but only by periodic (perhaps annual) review. If costs have been intelligently anticipated in the chart used for target purposes, there should be little adjustment necessary here.

The analysis could give more detail, if significant. The effect of sales volume and sales margin might be shown separately. Reductions below list price could be shown as a further subdivision of the sales margin deviation, if important. Special allowances to customers could also be spotlighted, if material. Controllable administration costs could be shown separately, if the fluctuations in items which were controllable on a day-to-day or week-to-week basis, were material in amount.

Stock valuation basis would be a legitimate analysis heading if the stock valuation basis used for financial accounts purposes were so conservative as to give materially increased profits in periods during which stocks are being liquidated, and, correspondingly, reduced profits in periods during which they are being built up. This would be significant, however, only to the extent to which there were fluctuations in the level of stocks. If the financial basis, approximated to capacity works cost, there would, again, be no deviation in this respect, even if stocks did fluctuate, since the method of forecasting assumes that all administration, selling and unrecovered fixed works costs (as indicated by Exhibit 8) are being recovered against current sales. A comparison of stock values on the basis of capacity works cost with the financial valuation would, however, give the deviation in this respect, if any.

Many other useful analysis headings will no doubt suggest themselves, but the criterion should be whether or not the deviations due to any given cause are sufficiently material to justify segregation. This must obviously depend on the nature of the business and the aspects which are currently vital.

*General Application*

Although developed with reference to the particular nature of the business for which it was designed the simplified illustration given can be assumed to apply to any business selling a range of (say) 100 products by weight. Although broadly homogeneous, the products vary significantly in cost, selling price and margin—not only as between different products but also in different countries. The mix of products sold and the mix of markets in which they are sold, are therefore both significant factors in determining the profit earned over any long period. On the other hand, the spread of products is sufficient to ensure that overall average costs do not fluctuate violently from month to month. This is a normal condition whenever changes in mix of products entail changes in manufacturing arrangements which limit the rate of change.

Although the example given is admittedly a relatively simple one, the methods it serves to illustrate are capable of adaptation to most businesses, provided that a satisfactory common measure of volume can be introduced and used also as a cost denominator. In some cases, actual weight, length, area or bulk will serve. In others, it may be necessary to introduce the concept of an equivalent standard weight, length, area or bulk, which reflects the relative absorption of factory capacity. Even where production is of a heterogeneous nature (as in general engineering), estimated or standard hours or cost, can be adapted to the same end. Where there are violent fluctuations from month to month in overall average costs per unit, it may be necessary to deal separately with groups of products within which this condition does not arise.

### A Road Out of the Woods

The many aspects of the profit situation of a company, and the changes in and changing importance of these parts of the total picture, sometimes render the most painstaking accounting analysis useless to management. Detail in schedules and recomputation for altered situations may result only in confusion, inaccuracy or—at best—delay. A compact and primarily graphic tool, on the other hand, has greater promise. It is with this thought that the approach here described has been offered.

### Required

1. Discuss the problems facing the Company before the reorganisation took place.
2. What alternative steps could have been taken?
3. Study the new system and discuss the likely effectiveness of the techniques described.
4. Could the techniques be employed in your business?

\*      \*      \*

## CASE STUDY 8—FINANCIAL PLANNING

The Balance Sheet of Excelsior Ltd. is shown below. In the last financial year the profit for the year was £500,000, this representing a low rate on capital employed. The Directors are rather concerned with the decline in profits and have decided to diversify by producing a new line at a completely new plant which is to be built on a site at Liverpool.

The cost of the new plant is estimated to be in the region of £500,000. Annual running expenses, when operating at full capacity, will be around £100,000 variable costs and £50,000 fixed costs. Break-even point—when sales revenue and costs agree—is expected to be reached after six months' operations. Before that time the short-fall in working capital is expected to be £30,000.

No decision has been made on how the additional finance should be raised. The Directors are not too happy about the falling off in profits and the consequent deterioration which has taken place in the cash

EXCELSIOR

Balance Sheet

|  | This Year | | Last Year | |
|---|---|---|---|---|
|  | £ | £ | £ | £ |
| **Share Capital:** | | | | |
| Authorised, issued and fully paid— | | | | |
| 6% cumulative preference shares of £1 each | | 300,000 | | 300,000 |
| 6% "A" cumulative preference shares of £1 each | | 50,000 | | 50,000 |
| 7% "B" cumulative preference shares of £1 each | | 30,000 | | 30,000 |
| Ordinary shares of £0·125 each | | 8,000,000 | | 8,000,000 |
| | | 8,380,000 | | 8,380,000 |
| **Capital Reserve** | | | | |
| General reserve | | 5,400,000 | | 5,400,000 |
| **Revenue Reserves** | | | | |
| General reserve | 500,000 | | 500,000 | |
| Contingencies reserve | 200,000 | | 180,000 | |
| Unappropriated profits | 10,000 | | 8,000 | |
| | | 710,000 | | 688,000 |
| Total Capital and Reserves | | 14,490,000 | | 14,468,000 |
| Amounts Set Aside for Future Taxation | | 400,000 | | 700,000 |
| **Current Liabilities and Provisions** | | | | |
| Creditors and Accrued charges | 2,000,000 | | 1,800,000 | |
| Bank overdrafts | 6,000,000 | | 3,500,000 | |
| Current taxation | 1,200,000 | | 600,000 | |
| Proposed final ordinary dividend | 800,000 | | 500,000 | |
| | | 10,000,000 | | 6,400,000 |
| | | £24,890,000 | | £21,568,000 |

resources. The general economic climate is rather uncertain, although the prospects for the new line appear quite good.

## Required

1. Discuss the importance of the correct "economic climate" and suggest ways of ascertaining the likely results in the next five years.
2. Analyse the financial situation as revealed by the Balance Sheet. Do you regard the position as potentially safe or potentially dangerous?
3. Prepare a summary of the cash requirements clearly stating any assumptions made.
4. There are many ways of raising finance (*see* Chapters 7 and 8). Isolate the most important factors bearing on this Company's position and ascertain the most advantageous method(s) of raising the finance required.

## LIMITED

*30th June 19*

| | This Year £ | This Year £ | Last Year £ | Last Year £ |
|---|---|---|---|---|
| | | Cost *less* Depreciation | | |
| **Fixed Assets:** | | | | |
| Land and Buildings— | | | | |
| Freehold | | 80,000 | | 35,300 |
| Leasehold | | 1,000,000 | | 800,000 |
| Machinery, equipment and motor vehicles | | 3,000,000 | | 2,800,000 |
| | | 4,080,000 | | 3,635,300 |
| **Subsidiary Companies** | | | | |
| Shares at cost *less* amounts written off | | 4,000,000 | | 4,000,000 |
| **Trade Investments** | | | | |
| Quoted at cost (market value £1,500,000) | 1,300,000 | | 800,000 | |
| Unquoted at cost | 3,000,000 | | 3,000,000 | |
| | | 4,300,000 | | 3,800,000 |
| **Current Assets** | | | | |
| Stock | 10,500,000 | | 8,000,000 | |
| Debtors | 2,000,000 | | 1,132,700 | |
| Bank balances and cash | 10,000 | | 1,000,000 | |
| | | 12,510,000 | | 10,132,700 |
| | | £24,890,000 | | £21,568,000 |

CC

## CASE STUDY 9—ORGANISATION AND CORPORATE PLANNING*

### POLYCOAT LIMITED

Leonard Sutton completed his chemical studies at a Technical College in 1952. In his final year he had taken a special interest in the application of plastics to metal surfaces and had developed a process which provided a durable finish. This was obtained by pre-heating the article to be coated, immersing it in a bath of liquid plastic and the subsequent curing in a curing oven. At each stage of the process temperatures were critical, and careful control of conditions was needed. He realised that he had discovered a process that could be exploited commercially. The finish was attractive in appearance and capable of being produced in various shades. It was resilient, protected against corrosion and provided insulation—properties which could make it in many ways superior to other finishes, such as galvanising, plating or painting. Moreover, in contrast to paint finishes, a single application provided a much higher degree of long-term protection.

Having managed to persuade a manufacturer of household articles to use the process for a kitchen dish drainer, he formed a Company and set up a small coating plant in early 1953 in rented premises in North London with the help of a bank loan of £5000. Two years of intensive sales effort enabled capacity to be quadrupled and Sutton felt now sure that plastic coating as an industrial finish had arrived. Demand continued to increase, and in early 1956 the company moved to new premises obtained on lease some 20 miles distant in Surrey. Its complement then was 25 people—20 process workers, one foreman, one storekeeper, two office staff and one accountant.

During the next few years Sutton's time was divided between selling, the development of the process and of plant to widen the range of articles that could be dealt with, as well as the general supervision of production.

The company's success continued, the factory was expanded and by the end of 1958 employees had risen to 60, sales to £121,000 and profits to £17,000. Sutton felt that he himself must now concentrate more on development. In 1960 he engaged Charles Groves, A.M.I.Mech.E., aged 38, as production manager and in the following year Reginald Carter, M.A., aged 29, as sales manager. James Hall, B.A., aged 35, joined the company in 1961 as manager designate for a new plant which was opened in the Cheshire development district in 1962. Financial aid had been obtained from the Industrial and Commercial Finance Corporation for equipping the new factory which was to include facilities

* Compiled by J. S. Adler, B.Com., of The Robert Gordon's Institute of Technology, Aberdeen. The facts and figures have been altered to avoid recognition of the company involved.

for coating heavy articles and also for additional working capital. An engineering section had been added to the Surrey factory which dealt with the construction of the company's plant requirements, and laboratory facilities had been extended to develop coating compounds with special physical and chemical properties in order to widen the application of coating to industrial products.

In 1963 Carter made an extended tour of European countries and the U.S.A. and managed to interest foreign manufacturers in the process. Orders for plant and coating materials followed which led to the extension of the company's engineering activities and raw materials compounding operations. The latter were concentrated during 1964 in new premises located in Sussex at a distance of some ten miles from head office.

In searching for new applications Sutton had experimented with the coating process as a basis for the manufacture of flexible plastic products, and 1965 saw the commencement of production of tool grips, handle-bar grips, followed by road markers used for the temporary diversion of traffic, and plastic bellows in the new Sussex premises.

In 1965 a coating plant was erected in the Birmingham area to serve the needs for coating facilities of the industrial Midlands. James Maitland, B.Sc., A.R.I.C., Ph.D., aged 35, a leading plastics chemist, joined the company in 1965 to take over development work and also the raw materials compounding operations, which now left Sutton free to act solely in the capacity of chairman and managing director. The company has since started producing plastic coating materials in aerosols for application by spray.

To meet further demand in the greater London area a new plant was opened in 1968 in Hertfordshire with capacity adequate to meet expected increasing local demand up to the end of 1971.

By 1968 the company had 750 employees. It was the largest firm of its kind in Europe, the leader in plastic coating technology; it had over 5000 customers; 85% of its activities were concerned with coating; exports of plant and materials amounted to 4% of total sales. Since it had started its export operations the company had delivered to over 45 countries and its plant now was frequently installed in foreign locations by its own engineers. Plant and materials sales to home manufacturers were on the increase and sales of plastics were showing promise.

The company's organisation had developed piecemeal with its rapid growth. As each factory was established, it was put in charge of a factory manager who was made responsible for day-to-day local selling operations. The Cheshire factory operated as an independent unit under Hall who was responsible for all contracts and employed an accountant and a production superintendent. Hall was directly responsible to Sutton; the other factory managers answered to Groves the production co-ordinator at head office where all other functions were centralised. Carter, in charge of sales and marketing, negotiated new contracts with important customers and was in charge of exports. Two salesmen dealt with flexible plastics and aerosols, four technical salesmen followed up enquiries concerning coating and plant installations. Maitland, apart from his development responsibilities, looked after technical and quality aspects of all company products. The Engineering operations at Head Office were headed by a chief designer who answered to Groves. Ronald Clark, A.C.W.A., now chief accountant, had been with the company from its early beginnings. He was responsible for the detailed accounting operations including costing for all factories, with the exception of the Cheshire factory which looked after its own costing and whose accounts were completed locally and consolidated at head office.

Reviewing the situation in 1968 Sutton came to the conclusion that in order to safeguard the company's future it would have to go public, and this operation was carried through in early 1969. It had now become clear that it would be essential to define company objectives in the light of a thorough assessment of market prospects and to effect organisational changes to provide a structure which would deal effectively with current work and prove adaptable to future requirements.

These problems formed the agenda for the first board meeting with his executive directors who held the following responsibilities:

| | |
|---|---|
| Charles Groves, A.M.I.Mech.E. | Production co-ordinator |
| Reginald Carter, M.A. | Sales and Marketing |
| James Hall, B.A. | In charge of Cheshire works |
| James Maitland, B.Sc., A.R.I.C., Ph.D. | Development and Materials operations |

## Appendix I

### PRODUCTION OF THE COMPANY

*Light Coating*
Domestic wirework
Hardware
Washing-up machine backets
Refrigerator trays
Electronic components
Motor-vehicle components

*Heavy Coating*
Lighting and road sign columns
Balustrading
Machine-tool parts
Chemical pipework and tanks
Rollers for paper-making machinery
Window frames
Metal furniture

*Flexible Plastic Products*
Handle-bar grips
Tool grips
Road markers
Bellows

*Plant*
Installations for light and heavy coating

*Materials*
Plastic coating compounds with different properties

*Other*
Aerosols

## Appendix II

### *FACTORIES*

| Head Office and Factory | Location | Employment | Production |
|---|---|---|---|
| I | Surrey | 290 | Coating light<br>Plant production<br>Laboratories |
| II | Cheshire | 180 | Coating heavy<br>Coating light |
| III | Sussex | 140 | Material compounding<br>Flexible mouldings<br>Aerosols |
| IV | Birmingham | 80 | Coating light |
| V | Hertfordshire | 60 | Coating light<br>Coating heavy |

Coating materials were supplied to all factories from factory III by own transport in the London area and by carrier to Birmingham and Cheshire.


## Appendix III

### *SALES AND PROFITS (BEFORE TAX)*

| Year | Sales (£000) | Profits (£000) | % |
|---|---|---|---|
| 1955 | 50 | 3 | 6 |
| 1956 | 73 | 8 | 11 |
| 1957 | 90 | 12 | 13 |
| 1958 | 121 | 17 | 14 |
| 1959 | 186 | 24 | 13 |
| 1960 | 307 | 41 | 13 |
| 1961 | 419 | 53 | 13 |
| 1962 | 486 | 46 | 9 |
| 1963 | 677 | 80 | 12 |
| 1964 | 971 | 122 | 12 |
| 1965 | 1163 | 133 | 11 |
| 1966 | 1532 | 177 | 12 |
| 1967 | 1644 | 161 | 10 |
| 1968 | 2100 | 190 | 9 |

## Appendix IV

### SALES AND PROFITS BY PRODUCT 1965–1968

(£000s)

| | Total | Coating | | | Machinery | | | Materials | | | Plastics | Aerosols |
|---|---|---|---|---|---|---|---|---|---|---|---|---|
| | | Total | Light | Heavy | Total | Home | Export | Total | Home | Export | | |
| **1965** | | | | | | | | | | | | |
| Sales | 1,163 | 1,060 | 900 | 160 | 53 | 28 | 25 | 40 | 25 | 15 | 10 | 8 |
| Per cent. | 100 | 91·2 | 77·4 | 13·8 | 4·5 | 2·4 | 2·1 | 3·4 | 2·1 | 1·3 | 0·9 | 0·5 |
| Profits before tax | 133 | 121 | 97 | 24 | 7 | 4 | 3 | 5 | 2·5 | 2·5 | — | — |
| Per cent. (detail to nearest whole %) | 11·4 | 11 | 11 | 15 | 13 | 14 | 12 | 12 | 10 | 17 | — | — |
| **1966** | | | | | | | | | | | | |
| Sales | 1,532 | 1,363 | 1,140 | 223 | 84 | 40 | 44 | 48 | 30 | 18 | 37 | — |
| Per cent | 100 | 89 | 74·4 | 14·6 | 5·5 | 2·6 | 2·9 | 3·1 | 1·9 | 1·2 | 2·4 | — |
| Profits before tax | 177 | 156 | 125 | 31 | 12·5 | 6·5 | 6 | 5 | 2·5 | 2·5 | 3·5 | -4 |
| Per cent. (detail to nearest whole %) | 11·5 | 11 | 11 | 14 | 15 | 16 | 14 | 10 | 8 | 14 | 9 | — |
| **1967** | | | | | | | | | | | | |
| Sales | 1,644 | 1,430 | 1,180 | 250 | 99 | 44 | 55 | 57 | 34 | 23 | 50 | — |
| Per cent. | 100 | 87 | 71·8 | 15·2 | 6 | 2·7 | 3·3 | 3·5 | 2·1 | 1·4 | 3 | — |
| Profits before tax | 161 | 140·5 | 110·5 | 30 | 13 | 6 | 7 | 5·5 | 2·5 | 3 | 6 | -50 |
| Per cent. (detail to nearest whole %) | 9·8 | 10 | 9 | 12 | 13 | 14 | 13 | 10 | 7 | 13 | 12 | — |
| **1968** | | | | | | | | | | | | |
| Sales | 2,100 | 1,785 | 1,435 | 350 | 129 | 71 | 58 | 76 | 46 | 30 | 98 | 12 |
| Per cent. | 100 | 85 | 68·3 | 16·7 | 6·1 | 3·4 | 2·7 | 3·6 | 2·2 | 1·4 | 4·7 | 0·6 |
| Profits before tax | 190 | 150 | 115 | 35 | 18 | 10·5 | 7·5 | 8 | 3 | 5 | 13 | 1 |
| Per cent. (detail to nearest whole %) | 9·1 | 8 | 8 | 10 | 14 | 15 | 13 | 11 | 7 | 17 | 13 | 8 |

## Required

1. What do you consider the chief factors in the success of the company to date?
2. (a) Consider the company's present position in the light of recent trends and suggest possible courses of future development.
   (b) What information would you require in order to forecast company sales for a period of five years ahead, and how would you set about obtaining the necessary data?
3. (a) What changes would you introduce in the current organisation structure of the company?
   (b) How would you plan for this company's future expansion?

\* \* \*

## CASE STUDY 10—CASH PLANNING\*

The Alpha Company Ltd. are about to negotiate with the bank the short-term financing of a new venture until it has concluded arrangements for more permanent finance. However, before doing so it wishes to know if its present arrangements, *i.e.* overdraft facilities up to £17,000 will be sufficient to cover its existing operations. Although the funds flow statement prepared at the beginning of the period indicated a satisfactory cash position at the end of the year the Directors now wish to know the monthly position, and the reasons for it, at the end of June, July, August and September 19.. by which time the arrangements mentioned above should have been concluded. From the information given below you are required to prepare the monthly cash forecast as requested by the Directors. Unless stated otherwise all items can be treated on a cash basis. On the assumption that the actual results for April and May were below budget, append to your statement a brief note qualifying the figures accordingly.

### Summary Profit/Loss Account

| | April 19.. (Actual) | | May 19.. (Actual) | | June 19.. (Budget) | | July 19.. (Budget) | | August 19.. (Budget) | | Sept. 19.. (Budget) | |
|---|---|---|---|---|---|---|---|---|---|---|---|---|
| Sales (Equivalent Units) | 40,000 *units* | | 50,000 *units* | | 55,000 *units* | | 60,000 *units* | | 40,000 *units* | | 60,000 *units* | |
| | £ | £ | £ | £ | £ | £ | £ | £ | £ | £ | £ | £ |
| Sales | | 45,000 | | 56,000 | | 60,000 | | 65,000 | | 42,000 | | 66,000 |
| Cost: | | | | | | | | | | | | |
| Material | 15,000 | | 18,000 | | 20,000 | | 21,000 | | 14,000 | | 23,000 | |
| Labour | 9,000 | | 11,000 | | 12,000 | | 12,000 | | 8,000 | | 13,000 | |
| Direct Expenses | 300 | | 400 | | 500 | | 600 | | 250 | | 600 | |
| Factory Overhead | 3,500 | | 3,750 | | 3,875 | | 4,000 | | 3,500 | | 4,000 | |
| Selling Overhead | 2,500 | | 2,700 | | 2,800 | | 2,900 | | 2,500 | | 2,900 | |
| Administration Overhead | 1,500 | | 1,500 | | 1,500 | | 1,500 | | 1,500 | | 1,500 | |
| | | 31,800 | | 37,350 | | 40,675 | | 42,000 | | 29,750 | | 45,000 |
| Profit | | £13,200 | | £18,650 | | £19,325 | | £23,000 | | £12,250 | | £21,000 |

\* Case Studies from this point are selected examination questions from past papers.

*Note:* 1. Production and sales quantities coincide.
2. The material cost has been arrived at as follows:

| | April £ | May £ | June £ | July £ | August £ | September £ |
|---|---|---|---|---|---|---|
| Opening Stock | 3,000 | 5,000 | 6,000 | 6,000 | 1,000 | 3,000 |
| Purchases | 17,000 | 19,000 | 20,000 | 16,000 | 16,000 | 24,000 |
| | 20,000 | 24,000 | 26,000 | 22,000 | 17,000 | 27,000 |
| Closing Stock | 5,000 | 6,000 | 6,000 | 1,000 | 3,000 | 4,000 |
| Cost of Usage | 15,000 | 18,000 | 20,000 | 21,000 | 14,000 | 23,000 |

3. The sum owing for wages at any point of time is equal to one-eighth of the labour cost.
4. The terms of credit for both debtors and creditors are one month after the end of the month in which the goods are delivered.
5. Depreciation is based on £0·025 per equivalent unit and is included in factory overheads.
6. The overhead costs include the following items which have been allocated on an equal monthly charge but which are payable as follows:

| Overhead | Item | Monthly Charge £ | Date of Payment |
|---|---|---|---|
| Factory | Rent | 50 | 1st April |
| Selling | Sales Rebate | 150 | 31st December |
| Administration | Debenture Interest | 51 (net) | 30th June |

7. An assessment for Tax of £2500 is due by 30th June 19...
8. The company pays its preference dividend on the 100,000 6% £1 Preference Shares twice yearly on 31st August and 28th February.
9. The capital budget indicates that capital payments will be as follows:

| | £ |
|---|---|
| May | 1,000 |
| June | 4,000 |
| July | 10,000 |
| August | 10,000 |
| September | 14,000 |

10. The bank overdraft at 1st June 19.. stood at £15,042.

*(A.C.C.A.)*

\*   \*   \*

## CASE STUDY 11—SALES BUDGETING

(*a*) What essential principles must be inherent in a sales budget before it can be accepted as an integral part of overall Company policy?

(*b*) Table I shows the preliminary sales budget figures for the year 1970 which have been submitted to the budget committee for consideration. The Company manufactures and sells only the three products mentioned, each of which requires highly skilled labour which cannot easily be replaced. In addition to the 1970 budget figures, the

## TABLE I

### Sales Budget Provisional Figures for 1970

(1969 Budget shown for comparison purposes)

|  | Product A Units | | Product B Units | | Product C Units | | Total Units | |
|---|---|---|---|---|---|---|---|---|
|  | 1969 | 1970 | 1969 | 1970 | 1969 | 1970 | 1969 | 1970 |
| 1st Quarter | 4,125 | 3,250 | 5,500 | 6,250 | 9,000 | 10,250 | 18,625 | 19,750 |
| 2nd Quarter | 4,125 | 3,250 | 5,500 | 6,250 | 9,000 | 10,250 | 18,625 | 19,750 |
| 3rd Quarter | 4,125 | 3,250 | 5,500 | 6,250 | 9,000 | 10,250 | 18,625 | 19,750 |
| 4th Quarter | 4,125 | 3,250 | 5,500 | 6,250 | 9,000 | 10,250 | 18,625 | 19,750 |
| Total | 16,500 | 13,000 | 22,000 | 25,000 | 36,000 | 41,000 | 74,500 | 79,000 |
| Selling Price (per unit) | £1·05 | £1·05 | £1·275 | £1·15 | £0·40 | £0·40 | — | — |
| Turnover | £17,325 | £13,325 | £28,050 | £28,750 | £14,400 | £16,400 | £59,775 | £58,475 |

actual results for 1969 are given in Table II. Applying the principles mentioned in Question 1 (*a*) what comments would you, as management accountant, make on the sales estimates for 1970? On the assumption that these figures are the best possible in the circumstances, what action would you recommend to the budget committee?

## TABLE II

### Actual Trading Results for 1969

| Sales | Product A Units | | Product B Units | | Product C Units | | Total Units | |
|---|---|---|---|---|---|---|---|---|
| 1st Quarter |  | 4,260 |  | 5,200 |  | 8,900 |  | 18,360 |
| 2nd Quarter |  | 3,600 |  | 5,075 |  | 8,850 |  | 17,525 |
| 3rd Quarter |  | 3,450 |  | 5,000 |  | 13,300 |  | 21,750 |
| 4th Quarter |  | 3,690 |  | 4,725 |  | 8,950 |  | 17,365 |
|  |  | 15,000 |  | 20,000 |  | 40,000 |  | 75,000 |
| Turnover |  | £15,000 |  | £25,000 |  | £15,000 |  | £55,000 |
| *Less:* Costs |  |  |  |  |  |  |  |  |
| Material | £8,250 |  | £14,750 |  | £9,950 |  | £32,950 |  |
| Labour | 3,000 |  | 5,050 |  | 1,550 |  | 9,600 |  |
| Direct Expenses | 1,350 |  | 1,800 |  | 1,200 |  | 4,350 |  |
| Fixed Expenses | 2,493 |  | 3,172 |  | 1,597 |  | 7,262 |  |
|  |  | 15,093 |  | 24,772 |  | 14,297 |  | 54,162 |
| Profit/Loss |  | £93 |  | £228 |  | £703 |  | £838 |

(A.C.C.A.)

\*     \*     \*

## CASE STUDY 12—VALUATION OF COMPANY

The Major Company Ltd., a wholly owned subsidiary of Billings Ltd., a holding Company, is unable to meet all of the demands for its products, in particular for the chemical compound SK 567, for which there were unfulfilled orders for the last twelve months of 245,000 cwts. and this is expected to increase to between 250,000–260,000 cwts. It is felt that the time taken to build new premises and install new plant is such that it would enable the Company's main competitors from overseas to satisfy this excess demand and to put them in a stronger position to compete for the Company's other major customers. The Major Company have always managed to retain all of the big customers in this market and the overseas companies have been restricted to users whose combined demand is quite substantial but individual demand small. It has been decided, therefore, that existing facilities will have to be taken over. In particular, the management feel that the A.B. Company Ltd. is ideal for this purpose. This is a privately owned company which only manufactures SK 567 for sale to many small users, and which has an annual capacity of 260,000 cwts. From the following information relating to the A.B. Company Ltd. and the additional notes, prepare a report for management commenting: (a) on the current performance of the A.B. Company; (b) on the price to be offered for the company; (c) the apparent profitability which would accrue to the Major Company, and, (d) whether or not proposals to extend facilities by Major Ltd. are reasonable.

*Summary Profit/Loss Account of the A.B. Company*
*for Year ended 31st May 19..*

|  |  | £ |
|---|---:|---:|
| **Sales** |  | 482,500 |
|  |  |  |
| Trading Profit |  | 58,000 |
| *Less*: Debenture Interest | 250 |  |
| Depreciation | 12,500 |  |
| Directors' Emoluments |  |  |
| Fees | 150 |  |
| Others | 2,350 |  |
|  |  | 15,250 |
|  |  |  |
| Profit before Taxation |  | 42,750 |
|  |  |  |
| **U.K. Taxation Based on Profits to Date** |  |  |
| Corporation Tax |  | 21,140 |
|  |  |  |
| Profit after Taxation |  | 21,610 |
| Balance of Profit Brought Forward |  | 15,856 |
|  |  |  |
|  |  | 37,466 |
|  |  |  |
| **Appropriations** |  |  |
| Dividends 400% on Ordinary Shares | 9,792 |  |
| Transfer to Reserve | 7,882 |  |
|  |  | 17,674 |
|  |  |  |
|  |  | £19,792 |

## Summary Balance Sheet of the A.B. Company
### as at 31st May 19..

| | £ | £ | | Cost £ | Depr. to date £ | £ |
|---|---|---|---|---|---|---|
| **Capital** | | | | | | |
| Authorised and Issued | | | | | | |
| 4,000 Ordinary Shares | | | **Fixed Assets** | | | |
| of £1 | | 4,000 | Land and Buildings | 15,000 | — | 15,000 |
| **Reserves** | 20,500 | | Plant and Machinery | 102,500 | 48,950 | 53,550 |
| Revenue Reserve | 153,761 | | Motor Vehicles | 3,490 | 2,490 | 1,000 |
| Profit and Loss Account | 19,792 | | | | | |
| | | 194,053 | | £120,990 | £51,440 | 69,550 |
| **Taxation Equalisation** | | 15,000 | | | | |
| Debentures—5% 19../.. | | 5,000 | Goodwill | | | 750 |
| **Current Liabilities** | | | Trade Investments | | | 2,500 |
| Creditors | 19,860 | | **Current Assets** | | | |
| Taxation | 21,200 | | Cash in Bank and on | | | |
| Proposed Dividends | 9,792 | | Hand | 3,495 | | |
| | | 50,852 | Sundry Debtors | 124,206 | | |
| | | | Stocks | 68,404 | | |
| | | | | | | 196,105 |
| | | £268,905 | | | | £268,905 |

*Additional Notes*

1. The only other information, all of which has been estimated, about the A.B. Company is as follows:

   (*a*) Sales were 240,500 cwts. and this probably coincided with production.
   (*b*) Fixed expenses are in the region of £124,000 per annum.
   (*c*) Because of its smaller usage material prices will probably be 10% higher than those of the Major Company.
   (*d*) There is no reason to believe that there will be a significant variation between the other variable expenses and those of the Major Company.
   (*e*) It is thought that the owners of the A.B. Company regard 12½% as a fair capitalisation rate for the pre-tax profits which the Company earns.

2. For the Major Company the standard selling price and cost for SK 567, based on an annual output of 1,000,000 cwts. is as follows:

|  | £ |
|---|---|
| Standard Selling Price | 2·000 per cwt. |
| | |
| Standard Cost: | |
| Material | ·825 per cwt. |
| Labour | ·350 |
| Variable Expenses | ·050 |
| Fixed Expenses | ·475 |
| | £1·700 |

The Major Company have been set a profit target of 20% on capital employed by their holding Company.　　　　　(*A.C.C.A.*)

\*　　　\*　　　\*

## CASE STUDY 13—REORGANISATION OF CAPITAL STRUCTURE

The undermentioned details relate to the consolidated balance sheet of "A" Company Limited.

|  | (£000's) |
|---|---|
| Loans | (DR.) 500 |
| Bank acceptances | 200 |
| Creditors | 5,700 |
| Debtors and trade bills | 8,600 |
| Short term loans | 735 |
| Bank balances and cash | 650 |
| Current taxation | 1,200 |
| Dividends due to members of parent company | 240 |
| Stocks at cost or net realisable value if lower | 3,864 |
| Tax reserve certificates | 430 |
| Staff retirement benefits | 450 |
| Miscellaneous provisions | 200 |
| Treasury bills | 650 |
| Trade investments at cost *less* amounts written off | 2,000 |
| Future taxation | 200 |
| Freehold and leasehold property (cost £1,800,000) | 1,200 |
| Plant and machinery (cost £850,000) | 500 |
| Furniture and fixtures (cost £500,000) | 350 |
| Bank overdraft | 2,000 |
| General reserve | 4,000 |
| Capital reserve | 300 |
| Profit and loss account | 1,064 |
| Minority interest in subsidiary companies | 100 |

|  | Authorised (£000's) | Issued and fully paid (£000's) |
|---|---|---|
| **Share capital** | | |
| 6% Cumulative preference shares of £1 each | 1,000 | 700 |
| 10% Preferred ordinary shares of £1 each | 1,000 | 1,000 |
| Deferred ordinary shares of £1 each | 2,500 | 2,500 |
| Founders shares of £0·05 each | 25 | 25 |

In general terms the rights of shareholders are as under:

| | |
|---|---|
| 6½% cumulative preference shares of £1 each | First priority on profits for dividend payment and entitled to one vote per share at any meeting if dividends are six months in arrear. |
| 10% preferred ordinary shares of £1 each | Second priority on profits after 6½% cumulative preference shares. Entitled to one vote per share. |

Founders shares of £0·05 each — Rank for gross dividend of £2500 after cumulative preference shares and preferred ordinary shares. Entitled to one vote per share.

Deferred ordinary shares of £1 each — Rank for balance of profits after satisfying capital above. Entitled to one vote per £5 deferred ordinary shares.

The net profit of the group, after taxation and minority interests, is estimated to be £700,000 per annum, the ordinary shareholders receiving a dividend of 18% gross. The Directors are desirous of raising additional funds and expanding the Company's interests in order to acquire further subsidiary companies, but find the capital structure cumbersome. You are required to suggest a revised capital structure with an authorised capital of £10,000,000 detailing a revised balance sheet and the procedure necessary to implement your recommendations.

(*A.C.C.A.*)

\*     \*     \*

## CASE STUDY 14—SALES PROMOTION

The trading position of the Gamma Company Ltd. for Year 2 is as follows:

*Summary Profit/Loss Account for Year 2*

|  | £ | £ |
|---|---|---|
| **Sales** 200,000 units |  | 600,000 |
| **Factory Cost** |  |  |
| Material | 200,000 |  |
| Labour | 75,000 |  |
| Variable Expenses | 25,000 |  |
| Fixed Expenses | 200,000 |  |
|  |  | 500,000 |
| **Manufacturing Profit** |  | 100,000 |
| **Selling Expenses** |  | 60,000 |
| Selling Profit |  | 40,000 |
| **Administration Expenses** |  | 60,000 |
| Net Loss |  | £20,000 |

*Note*: No opening or closing stocks. Plant capacity 400,000 units.

In an attempt to overcome this unsatisfactory position the Managing Director decides to increase sales promotion expenditure by £100,000 in Year 3 and in anticipation of increased sales production is increased to 400,000 units. During Year 3 actual sales increased to 260,000 units, and the trading position is as follows:

*Summary Profit/Loss Account for Year 3*

|  | £ | £ |
|---|---|---|
| **Sales 260,000 units** |  | 780,000 |
| **Factory Cost** |  |  |
| Material | 400,000 |  |
| Labour | 150,000 |  |
| Variable Expenses | 50,000 |  |
| Fixed Expenses | 200,000 |  |
|  | 800,000 |  |
| *Less* Closing Stock | 280,000 |  |
|  |  | 520,000 |
| Manufacturing Profit |  | 260,000 |
| **Selling Expenses** |  | 160,000 |
| Selling Profit |  | 100,000 |
| **Administration Expenses** |  | 60,000 |
| Net Profit |  | £40,000 |

The Managing Director is delighted with the results of his policy which he maintains must be pursued even more vigorously in the future.

Do you agree with the Managing Director? What qualification would you put on the interpretation of the results of Year 3 and what information would you require about future years in order to make this qualification? What alternative costing method for the valuation of closing stock could be adopted and what arguments are there in favour of this?                    (*A.C.C.A.*)

# APPENDIX I

## *MEMBERS OF THE ACCEPTING HOUSES COMMITTEE*

Arbuthnot Latham & Co. Ltd. — 37, Queen Street, E.C.4.
Baring Brothers & Co. Ltd. — 8, Bishopsgate, E.C.2.
Wm. Brandt's Sons & Co. Ltd. — 36, Fenchurch Street, E.C.3.
Brown, Shipley & Co. Ltd. — Founders Court, Lothbury, E.C.2.
Charterhouse Japhet & Thomasson Ltd. — 30, St. Swithin's Lane, E.C.4.
Antony Gibbs & Sons Ltd. — 22, Bishopsgate, E.C.2.
Guinness Mahon & Co. Ltd. — 53, Cornhill, E.C.3.
Hambros Bank Ltd. — 41, Bishopsgate, E.C.2.
Hill, Samuel & Co. Ltd. — 100, Wood Street, E.C.2.
Kleinwort, Benson Ltd. — St. Albans House, Goldsmith Street, E.C.2.

Lazard Brothers & Co. Ltd. — 11, Old Broad Street, E.C.2.
Samuel Montagu & Co. Ltd. — 114, Old Broad Street, E.C.2.
Morgan Grenfell & Co. Ltd. — 23, Gt. Winchester Street, E.C.2.
N. M. Rothschild & Sons — New Court, St. Swithin's Lane, E.C.4.

J. Henry Schroder Wagg & Co. Ltd. — 120, Cheapside, E.C.2.
S. G. Warburg & Co. Ltd. (incorporating Seligman Brothers) — 30, Gresham Street, E.C.2.

# APPENDIX II

## MEMBERS OF THE ISSUING HOUSES ASSOCIATION

Anglo-Scottish Amalgamated Corporation Ltd. — 68, Bishopsgate, E.C.2.

Henry Ansbacher & Co. — 1, Noble Street, Gresham Street, E.C.2.

Arbuthnot Latham & Co. Ltd. — 37, Queen Street, E.C.4.

Baring Brothers & Co. Ltd. — 8, Bishopsgate, E.C.2.

Bentworth Trust Ltd. — 41, Bishopsgate, E.C.2.

Birmingham Industrial Trust Ltd. — Edmund House, 12–22, Newhall Street, Birmingham, 3.

Wm. Brandt's Sons & Co. Ltd. — 36, Fenchurch Street, E.C.3.

The British Empire Trust Co. Ltd. — Garrard House, 31–45, Gresham Street, E.C.2.

British Trusts Association Ltd. — 39, King Street, E.C.2.

Brown, Shipley & Co. Ltd. — Founders Court, Lothbury, E.C.2.

Charterhouse Japhet & Thomasson Ltd. — 30, St. Swithin's Lane, E.C.4.

Close Brothers Ltd. — Gillett House, 55, Basinghall Street, E.C.2.

Dawnay, Day & Co. Ltd. — 82, King William Street, E.C.4.

Electric and General Industrial Trusts Ltd. — 8, Cleveland Row, St. James's, S.W.1.

English Transcontinental Ltd. — 2, London Wall Buildings, E.C.2.

The Federated Trust & Finance Corporation Ltd. — 20, Copthall Avenue, E.C.2.

Robert Fraser & Partners Ltd. — Clements House, Gresham Street, E.C.2.

Antony Gibbs & Sons, Ltd. — 22, Bishopsgate, E.C.2.

Gresham Trust Ltd. — Barrington House, Gresham Street, E.C.2.

Guinness Mahon & Co. Ltd. — 3, Gracechurch Street, E.C.3.

Gwent and West of England Enterprises Ltd. — 31, Windsor Place, Cardiff.

Hambros Bank Ltd. — 41, Bishopsgate, E.C.2.

Hart Son & Co. Ltd. — Augustine House, Austin Friars, E.C.2.

Hill, Samuel & Co. Ltd. — 100, Wood Street, E.C.2.

Industrial and Commercial Finance Corporation Ltd. — 7, Copthall Avenue, E.C.2.

The Industrial Finance & Investment Corporation Ltd. — 82, King William Street, E.C.4.

Ionian Bank Ltd. — 64, Coleman Street, E.C.2.

Leopold Joseph & Sons Ltd. — 31–45, Gresham Street, E.C.2.

Keyser, Ullmann Securities — 85, Gracechurch Street, E.C.3.

Kleinwort, Benson Ltd. — St. Albans House, Goldsmith Street, E.C.2.

| | |
|---|---|
| Lazard Brothers & Co. Ltd. | 11, Old Broad Street, E.C.2. |
| Leadenhall Investments & Finance Ltd. | 40/42, Cannon Street, E.C.4. |
| Leadenhall Securities Corporation Ltd. | 120, Cheapside, E.C.2. |
| London and Yorkshire Trust Ltd. | 63, Brook Street, W.1. |
| Lothbury Assets Ltd. | 52/54, Gracechurch Street, E.C.3. |
| Manchester and Liverpool Industrial Securities Ltd. | 63, Brook Street, W.1. |
| Matheson & Co., Ltd. | 3, Lombard Street, E.C.3. |
| Minster Trust Ltd. | Minster House, Arthur Street, E.C.4. |
| Samuel Montagu & Co. Ltd. | 114, Old Broad Street, E.C.2. |
| Morgan Grenfell & Co. Ltd. | 23, Gt. Winchester Street, E.C.2. |
| Neville Industrial Securities Ltd. | Neville House, 42/46, Hagley Road, Birmingham, 16. |
| Northern Ireland Industrial Development and Finance Corporation Ltd. | 63, Brook Street, W.1. |
| Ocean Trust Company Ltd. | 99a, Park Lane, W.1. |
| Old Broad Street Securities Ltd. | 39, King Street, E.C.2. |
| Power Securities Corporation Ltd. | Bow Bells House, Bread Street, (Cheapside), E.C.4. |
| Rea Brothers Ltd. | 36–37, King Street, E.C.2. |
| N. M. Rothschild & Sons | New Court, St. Swithin's Lane, E.C.4. |
| St. Michaels Securities Ltd. | Billiter Buildings, 22, Billiter Street, E.C.3. |
| J. Henry Schroder Wagg & Co. Ltd. | 120, Cheapside, E.C.2. |
| Scottish Industrial Finance Ltd. | Grosvenor Guildings, 68, Gordon Street, Glasgow, C.1. |
| Seton Trust Ltd. | 3, London Wall Buildings, E.C.2. |
| Singer & Friedlander Ltd. | 20, Cannon Street, E.C.4. |
| Standard Industrial Trust Ltd. | Shelley House, Noble Street, E.C.2. |
| S. G. Warburg & Co. Ltd. (incorporating Seligman Brothers) | 30, Gresham Street, E.C.2. |

# APPENDIX III

## SPECIMEN OFFER FOR SALE (Abridged)

A copy of this Offer for Sale, having attached thereto the documents specified below, has been delivered to the Registrar of Companies in Edinburgh for registration.

Application has been made to the Council of The Stock Exchange, London and to the Committee of the Glasgow Stock Exchange for permission to deal in and for quotation for the whole of the issued share capital of the Company.

*The application lists for the Ordinary Shares now offered will open at 10 a.m. on Thursday, 24th November, 1960, and will close on the same day.*

### ANDERSON, BOYES & COMPANY, LIMITED

*(Incorporated in Scotland under the Companies Acts, 1862 to 1900)*

*Electrical, mining and mechanical engineers and manufacturers of underground coalcutters and power loading machines*

SHARE CAPITAL

| *Authorised* | *Issued and Fully Paid* |
|---|---|
| **£3,375,000 in Ordinary Shares of £1 each**     ...     ... | **£3,343,392** |

Neither the Company nor its subsidiary has any mortgages, debentures or other loan capital or any bank overdraft outstanding.

### J. HENRY SCHRODER & CO. LIMITED
and
### HELBERT, WAGG & COMPANY, LIMITED

#### Offer for Sale

*910,000 Ordinary Shares of £1 each at 29s. (£1·45) per Share payable in full on application*

The shares now offered rank in full for all dividends hereafter declared on the ordinary share capital of the Company.

---

[*Note.* Method of applying for shares stated in this section—omitted for brevity.]

Acceptance of applications (including underwriting applications) will be conditional upon the Council of The Stock Exchange, London, and the Committee of the Glasgow Stock Exchange granting permission to deal in and quotation for the whole of the issued share capital of the Company not later than 30th November, 1960. Moneys paid in respect of such applications will be returned if such permissions and quotations are not granted by that date, and in the meantime will be retained in a separate account.

---

[*Note*. Details of directors, etc. have been omitted, but would be shown
under separate headings.]

The following is a copy of a letter received from Mr. James Anderson,
Chairman of the Company:—

*The Directors*

> J. HENRY SCHRODER & CO. LIMITED,
> HELBERT, WAGG & COMPANY, LIMITED.

Flemington Electrical Works,
Motherwell.
*18th November, 1960*

Gentlemen,

In connection with your Offer for Sale of Ordinary Shares of £1 each in
Anderson, Boyes & Company, Limited ("the Company") I have much
pleasure in supplying you with the following information:—

HISTORY AND BUSINESS.—The Company was incorporated in Scotland on
5th April, 1904, to acquire the business founded in 1899 by my father,
Alexander Anderson, and his two partners, Thomas Boyes and Daniel Burns.
From small beginnings the Company has grown into a business of international standing. Its expansion has been financed entirely out of retained
profits and, of its present issued share capital, £5,358 was issued in connection
with the acquisition of the business in 1904 and the balance of £3,338,034 has
arisen from the capitalisation of undistributed profits and reserves. The
Company was today converted into a public company.

The Company carries on business as Electrical, Mining and Mechanical
Engineers, and manufacturers of underground coalcutters, power loading
machines and mining type switchgear. The Company has played a leading
part in the design, development and application of mining machinery and has
supplied a large proportion of the coalcutting and power loading machinery
now in use in British mines. A continuous programme of research is pursued
and the Company manufactures to its own designs a wide range of mining
machinery which includes machines suitable for work under the most varied
conditions. The Company's latest trepanning machine has been a great
success due to its ability to cut large coal at small labour cost.

The Company's most important customer is the National Coal Board
which at present takes the major part of the Company's output. The Company exports to many of the principal coal producing countries including
India, France, Poland, Czechoslovakia, South Africa and Australia. The
Company's machines are also extensively used in the potash mines of Alsace
and Lorraine. The treatment received by underground mining machinery is
necessarily harsh and the supply of spares and replacements for the Company's products accounts for more than half of its total sales.

Those of the Company's machines which are most in demand in the French
market are manufactured under licence by a leading French engineering
company. A sales and servicing organisation for these machines is operated
by Anderson, Boyes & Company (France) S. a r. l., a wholly-owned subsidiary of the Company, which was incorporated in France on 21st January,
1954, and has an issued share capital of 200 units of Frs. 50 each. This
French connection, although not of major importance, is a valuable one and
should benefit the Company in the new trading pattern which is emerging as
a result of the Common Market.

From 1951 to 1957 the Company successfully manufactured machine tools on a sub-contracting basis for one of the largest British manufacturers. Because of the heavy demand for the Company's traditional products machine tool manufacture was stopped in 1957. However, the Company has the equipment and organisation necessary for the manufacture of complete machine tools and is now having discussions with manufacturers with a view to expanding in this field on a licence basis. It is proposed that manufacture should take place in the Company's new factory at Glenrothes.

PREMISES AND PLANT.—The Company owns its main factory and offices at Motherwell. The floor area of the factory is approximately 320,000 square feet and there are a further six acres of land available for expansion. The Company also has a modern factory and offices at Glenrothes, Fife, with a floor area of approximately 60,000 square feet; these premises, which were built to the Company's specification, were completed in 1959 and are held on a lease (having 39 years unexpired) from the Glenrothes Development Corporation.

In addition to its factories and offices at Motherwell and Glenrothes the Company has service branches at Gateshead and Rotherham and is at present negotiating the building of two further service branches, one at Stafford and one near Cardiff; the latter will replace a building now occupied by the Company on a short-term lease.

The Company's factories are equipped with modern machinery and the buildings and plant are maintained at a high standard. The Directors' policy of continuous replacement ensures that the plant is kept up to date; capital expenditure on extensions and additions to plant and buildings during the last five years has exceeded £1,125,000.

MANAGEMENT AND STAFF.—All the Directors are full-time executives and, with the exception of Mr. Boyes, have entered into service agreements with the Company for periods ranging from four to ten years.

I am 51 years of age and have been employed by the Company for 32 years, for the last 5 years of which I have been Chairman and Managing Director. My cousin, Mr. Forrest Anderson, who is in charge of mining development, is aged 59 and has been with the Company for 40 years. Mr. Mowat (aged 59), who is responsible for electrical design, has been with the Company for 41 years. Mr. Boyes (aged 68) is technical representative for Scotland and has been 52 years with the Company. Mr. Dykes (aged 61), who is in charge of mechanical design, has been 45 years with the Company. Mr. Deas (aged 52) has been Secretary since 1931.

It is intended that, after completion of the present sale of part of the share capital of the Company to the public, the management of the business shall continue as heretofore. Nearly 50 per cent. of the share capital will still be beneficially owned by descendants of the original founders of the business, and it is the desire of my colleagues and myself to remain in the service of the Company for whose development and expansion in the future we feel the same responsibility as we have felt in the past.

The Company has given great attention to the training of junior executives and technicians to ensure that skilled management is available at all levels.

The total works and staff personnel numbers about 1,650 of whom some 300 have been employed by the Company for over twenty years. The Company operates superannuation schemes for staff and works employees. The management takes a great interest in welfare facilities for the employees, and relations between management and employees are excellent.

WORKING CAPITAL.—Taking into account the existing liquid resources and the sums expected to be retained in the business from profits and depreciation provisions, the Directors are of the opinion that the Company will have adequate working capital for its foreseeable requirements and sufficient funds for the replacement of plant and machinery as this becomes necessary.

PROSPECTS, PROFITS AND DIVIDENDS.—The British coal industry has been going through a difficult phase; and the fall in demand for coal with the consequent re-assessment of requirements by the National Coal Board led to a reduced overall demand for new machinery. The Directors believe, however, that the coal industry can only maintain its competitive position by continuing the pursuit of more efficient methods of mining through greater mechanisation and that the level of orders will build up again. Indications have recently been received from the National Coal Board that its orders for capital equipment from the Company's production are likely to be higher in 1961 than in 1960. The demand for spares and replacements for the Company's machines continues to be maintained at a satisfactory level.

As will be seen from the Accountants' Report set out in your Offer for Sale profits before taxation increased from £514,186 in the year ended 28th February, 1951, to £1,170,038 in the year ended 28th February, 1959. As a result of the reduction in demand for new machinery, profits for the year ended 29th February, 1960, were somewhat lower than those for the previous year. This trend continued during the early months of the current financial year, but demand has since improved and the present rate of sales is more satisfactory. The Directors are of the opinion that profits for the current year will, in the absence of unforeseen circumstances, be not less than £900,000, before taxation, in which event they would recommend the payment of a dividend for the year of 9 per cent. (less income tax) on the issued ordinary share capital of £3,343,392. It is expected that this dividend will be paid in July, 1961.

If, from a profit of £900,000, there were deducted income tax and profits tax at current rates, there would remain £438,750. A dividend of 9 per cent. (£300,905 gross), less income tax at 7s. 9d. (£0·387) in the £, would require £184,304 net and would be covered nearly 2.4 times. On the basis of an annual dividend of 9 per cent. the Ordinary Shares would show a return of 6.2 per cent. on the price of 29s. at which they are being offered for sale.

Yours faithfully,

JAMES ANDERSON, *Chairman*

ACCOUNTANTS' REPORT.—The following is a copy of the report received from Paterson & Steel and Cooper Brothers & Co., Chartered Accountants:—

*The Directors*
ANDERSON, BOYES & COMPANY, LIMITED,
J. HENRY SCHRODER & CO. LIMITED,
HELBERT, WAGG & COMPANY, LIMITED.

*18th November, 1960.*
Gentlemen,

1. We have examined the audited accounts of Anderson, Boyes & Company, Limited for the ten years ended 29th February, 1960.

2. The results of the subsidiary in France, the accounts of which are made up to 31st December, have been excluded for the purpose of this report except to the extent of dividends received, because the amounts involved are not significant.

PROFITS

2. The profits of the company for the ten years ended 29th February, 1960, arrived at on the basis described in paragraphs 4 and 5 below were as follows:

| Year ended 28th or 29th February | | | | Profits before Taxation £ |
|---|---|---|---|---|
| 1951 | ... | ... | ... | 514,186 |
| 1952 | ... | ... | ... | 455,232 |
| 1953 | ... | ... | ... | 591,729 |

| 1954 | ... | ... | ... | 685,063 |
|------|-----|-----|-----|---------|
| 1955 | ... | ... | ... | 886,731 |
| 1956 | ... | ... | ... | 817,829 |
| 1957 | ... | ... | ... | 946,568 |
| 1958 | ... | ... | ... | 1,025,076 |
| 1959 | ... | ... | ... | 1,170,038 |
| 1960 | ... | ... | ... | 1,014,938 |

4. Detailed stock and work in progress records for the years 1950 to 1956 inclusive were not available and during the period covered by this report changes were made in the basis of valuing stock and work in progress. In arriving at the profits set out in paragraph 3 we have endeavoured, as far as practicable, to adjust the valuations of stock and work in progress in each year so as to place them on a consistent basis.

5. The profits set out in paragraph 3 have been arrived at after making the adjustments referred to in paragraph 4, such other adjustments as appeared to us to be appropriate, and

(a) after charging all expenses of working and management including depreciation and directors' emoluments,

(b) before all taxation including profits tax.

6. The aggregate emoluments, including pension contributions, of the directors of the company for the year ended 29th February, 1960, amounted to £32,779. Under the arrangements now in force the corresponding annual charge will be approximately £42,000.

NET ASSETS

7. The net assets of the company at 29th February, 1960, based on the audited balance sheet at that date were as follows:—

| | Cost | Accumulated Depreciation | |
|---|---|---|---|
| *Fixed Assets* | £ | £ | £ |
| Land ... ... ... ... ... | 9,409 | 4,195 | 5,214 |
| Buildings ... ... ... ... | 548,143 | 205,092 | 343,051 |
| Plant ... ... ... ... ... | 1,448,404 | 760,177 | 688,227 |
| Motor vehicles ... ... ... | 22,928 | 10,915 | 12,013 |
| | £2,028,884 | £980,379 | 1,048,505 |

| | |
|---|---|
| *Subsidiary Company* | |
| Shares at cost ... ... ... ... | 1,023 |
| *Current Assets* | |
| Stock and work in progress at the lower of cost or market value ... | 2,327,699 |
| House loans to employees ... ... | 42,137 |
| Trade debtors ... ... ... ... | 771,805 |
| Other debtors and prepayments ... | 81,693 |
| Unquoted investments (local authority mortgages) ... ... ... | 290,000 |
| Quoted investments (market value £37,812) ... ... ... ... | 40,689 |
| Tax reserve certificates ... ... | 500,000 |
| Cash and bank balances ... ... | 485,945 |
| | 4,539,968 |

*Current Liabilities*
| | | | | |
|---|---|---|---|---|
| Trade creditors | ... | ... | ... | 170,836 |
| Accrued liabilities | ... | ... | ... | 37,448 |
| Current taxation | ... | ... | ... | 115,000 |
| Proposed dividend (net) (since paid)... | | | | 184,304 |
| | | | | 507,588 |

| | | | | |
|---|---|---|---|---|
| *Net Current Assets* | ... | ... | ... | 4,032,380 |
| *Less:* | | | | 5,081,908 |
| *Future taxation*—income tax, 1960/61 ... | | | | 460,000 |
| *Net Assets*, exclusive of goodwill | | ... | | £4,621,908 |

8. At 29th February, 1960, the outstanding commitments for capital expenditure amounted to approximately £80,000.

9. The net assets of the subsidiary in France at 31st December, 1959, as shown in its audited accounts at that date, amounted to £5,846 (current assets £6,285 less current liabilities £439) at the rate of exchange then current.

DIVIDENDS AND ACCOUNTS

10. Dividends at the following rates, less income tax, were paid on the issued capital of the company for the ten years ended 29th February, 1960.

| Year ended 28th or 29th February | | | Issued Capital £ | | | Rate of Dividend % |
|---|---|---|---|---|---|---|
| 1951 | ... | ... | ... 278,616 | ... | ... | ... $8\frac{1}{3}$ |
| 1952 | ... | ... | ... 278,616 | ... | ... | ... $8\frac{1}{3}$ |
| 1953 | ... | ... | ... 278,616 | ... | ... | ... $8\frac{3}{4}$ |
| 1954 | ... | ... | ... 278,616 | ... | ... | ... $8\frac{3}{4}$ |
| 1955 | ... | ... | ... 1,114,464 | ... | ... | ... 5 |
| 1956 | ... | ... | ... 1,114,464 | ... | ... | ... 6 |
| 1957 | ... | ... | ... 1,114,464 | ... | ... | ... $7\frac{1}{2}$ |
| 1958 | ... | ... | ... 1,114,464 | ... | ... | ... 25 |
| 1959 | ... | ... | ... 2,228,928 | ... | ... | ... $12\frac{1}{2}$ |
| 1960 | ... | ... | ... 2,228,928 | ... | ... | ... $13\frac{1}{2}$ |

11. Audited accounts have not been made up since 29th February, 1960.

We are, Gentlemen, Yours truly,

PATERSON & STEEL, COOPER BROTHERS & CO.

GENERAL INFORMATION.—On 18th November, 1960, the authorised share capital of the Company was increased from £2,250,000 to £3,375,000 by the creation of 1,125,000 additional Ordinary Shares of £1 each and the sum of £1,114,464 was capitalised and applied in paying up in full 1,114,464 Ordinary Shares of £1 each which were issued credited as fully paid to the holders of the then existing 2,228,928 issued Ordinary Shares of £1 each in the proportion of one new share for every two shares held on that date. On the same date, the Company converted itself into a public company and adopted new Articles of Association. Under Contract No. (2) below J. Henry Schroder & Co. Limited and Helbert, Wagg & Company, Limited have agreed to purchase 910,000 Ordinary Shares of £1 each at the price of 28s. 4d. (£1·416) per share, conditional upon permission to deal in and quotation for the whole of the issued share capital of the Company being granted by the Council of The Stock Exchange, London, and the Committee of the Glasgow Stock Exchange not later than 30th November, 1960. The purchase price is payable within ten days after the granting of such permissions and quotations.

Under the above contract J. Henry Schroder & Co. Limited and Helbert, Wagg & Company, Limited will pay the expenses of printing, advertising, and circulating this Offer for Sale, an underwriting commission of 4½d. per share and an overriding commission of 1½d. per share, brokerage, their own legal expenses, a fee to Cooper Brothers & Co. and the fees payable to The Stock Exchange, London, and the Glasgow Stock Exchange, the whole of which expenses are estimated to amount to £43,400. The Company will pay its own legal and accountancy expenses and the expenses of or incidental to the increase of capital (including £5,625 capital duty on such increase), the capitalisation of reserves and the adoption of new Articles of Association, the whole of which expenses are estimated to amount to £7,800; the Company will also pay J. Henry Schroder & Co. Limited and Helbert, Wagg & Company, Limited a fee of £31,000 for their services in connection with the conversion of the Company into a public company and the obtaining of permission to deal in and quotation for its share capital.

The following contracts, not being contracts entered into in the ordinary course of business, have been entered into during the two years preceding the date of this Offer for Sale and are or may be material:—

(1) Dated 18th, 18th, 7th, 27th and 18th July, 1960, being five service agreements between the Company (i) and Mr. James Anderson, Mr. F. S. Anderson, Mr. J. M. Mowat, Mr. A. S. Dykes and Mr. G. S. Deas respectively (ii) for periods, from 1st July, 1960, of 10 years in the cases of Mr. James Anderson and Mr. Deas and of approximately 6, 6 and 4 years respectively in the cases of Mr. F. S. Anderson, Mr. Mowat and Mr. Dykes, at salaries (including Directors' fees) aggregating £35,500 per annum.

(2) Dated 18th November, 1960, between the Directors of the Company on behalf of themselves and the other vendors (i), the Directors (ii), the Company (iii), and J. Henry Schroder & Co. Limited and Helbert, Wagg & Company, Limited (iv) being the contract of purchase referred to above.

Surtax clearances under the Income Tax Act, 1952, have been obtained in respect of the profits of the Company for the six years up to and including the financial year ended 29th February, 1960. Under Contract No. (2) above indemnities have been given against any claims for estate duty under the provisions of the Finance Act, 1940, as amended.

After the sale of the shares pursuant to Contract No. (2) above, the Directors, together with their wives and children, will own rather less than one quarter of the Company's issued share capital.

The Articles of Association of the Company contain *inter alia* provisions to the following effect:—

(a) The remuneration of the Directors shall be such a sum as shall from time to time be determined by ordinary resolution of the Company. The Directors shall also be entitled to be paid their reasonable travelling, hotel and incidental expenses of attending and returning from meetings of the Board or committees of the Board or general meetings or otherwise incurred while engaged on the business of the Company. Any Director who, by request, performs special services or goes or resides abroad for any purposes of the Company may be paid such extra remuneration by way of salary, percentage of profits or otherwise as the Board may determine.

(b) A Director, notwithstanding his interest, may be counted in the quorum present for the purpose of considering the appointment of himself or of any other Director to hold any office or place of profit under the Company or of arranging the terms of any such appointment, and he may vote on any such appointment or arrangement other than his own appointment or the arrangement of the terms thereof.

(c) The Board may pay pensions or other retirement, superannuation, death or disability benefits or allowances to or to any person in respect of any Director or former Director who may hold or may have held any executive office or employment under the Company or any subsidiary company and may contribute to any scheme or fund and may make payments towards insurances or trusts in respect of such persons.

(d) The Board may exercise all the powers of the Company to borrow money and to mortgage or charge its undertaking, property and uncalled capital or any part thereof and to issue debentures and other securities whether outright or as collateral security for any debt, liability or obligation of the Company or of any third party. The Board shall restrict the borrowings of the Company and exercise all voting and other rights or powers of control exercisable by the Company in relation to its subsidiary companies (if any) with a view to securing that the aggregate amount for the time being remaining outstanding of moneys so borrowed or secured and of moneys borrowed or secured by any subsidiary of the Company (exclusive of moneys outstanding in respect of borrowings by the Company from any such subsidiary or by any such subsidiary from another such subsidiary or from the Company) shall not at any time without the previous sanction of an ordinary resolution of the Company exceed the aggregate of the nominal amount of the issued and paid up share capital and the amount for the time being standing to the credit of any share premium account of the Company.

Save as herein mentioned (i) no capital of the Company or of its subsidiary is under option or agreed conditionally or unconditionally to be put under option; (ii) no capital of the Company or of its subsidiary has within the two years preceding the publication of this Offer for Sale been issued, nor is any proposed to be issued, either for cash or as fully or partly paid up otherwise than for cash; (iii) no commissions, discounts, brokerages or other special terms have been granted within the said two years in connection with the issue or sale of any share or loan capital of the Company or of its subsidiary. The Company has no litigation or claims of material importance pending or threatened against it.

Paterson & Steel and Cooper Brothers & Co. have given and have not withdrawn their written consent to the issue of this Offer for Sale with their report included therein in the form and context in which it is included.

The documents attached to the copy of this Offer for Sale which was delivered to the Registrar of Companies in Edinburgh for registration are the written consent above referred to, a written statement of adjustments made by Paterson & Steel and Cooper Brothers & Co. in arriving at the figures set out in their report and copies of the contracts mentioned above.

Copies of the Memorandum and Articles of Association of the Company, the above-mentioned written consent and statement of adjustments, the contracts mentioned above, the report of Paterson & Steel and Cooper Brothers & Co. and the audited accounts of the Company for the two financial years ended 29th February, 1960, may be inspected at the offices of Slaughter and May, 18, Austin Friars, London, E.C.2, and of Parsons & Co., 49, Bath Street, Glasgow, C.2, during usual business hours on any week-day (except Saturdays) within fourteen days after the publication of this Offer for Sale.

Copies of this Offer for Sale and Application Forms may be obtained from J. Henry Schroder & Co. Limited, 145, Leadenhall Street, London, E.C.3, National Commercial Bank of Scotland Limited, 113, Buchanan Street, Glasgow, C.1, and branches in Scotland, and from the Brokers.

Dated: *18th November, 1960.*

# APPENDIX IV

## STOCK EXCHANGE REQUIREMENTS
### (The Federation of Stock Exchanges)

APPENDIX, April, 1969

REQUIREMENTS FOR QUOTATION

### *Introduction*

These requirements are not exhaustive and the Committee may add thereto or subtract therefrom in any particular case, as a variety of conditions may exist which require *ad hoc* decisions by the Committee.

In connection with certain of these requirements, memoranda of guidance have been issued; those currently in issue are:

(a) Admission of Securities to Quotation.

(b) Reports by Accountants with respect to Profits, Assets and Liabilities for Purposes of Prospectuses, Offers for Sale, Advertised Statements and Circulars.

(c) Acquisitions and Realisation of Subsidiary Companies Businesses or Fixed Assets by Quoted Companies and Bids and Offers for Securities of a Company.

(d) Information required in Prospectuses and Circulars issued by Property Companies.

(e) Requirements for Quotation for the Securities of Foreign Companies and Organisations and the presentation of their Annual Accounts.

(f) Communication of Announcements.

The serial numbers in the right-hand margin are for convenience of reference to the various paragraphs.

*Definitions.* In this Appendix the following expressions shall, save where the context otherwise requires, have the following meanings:

"Capital" includes Share and Loan capital.

"The Committee" means the Committee on Quotations or other Committee, through which the Council exercises its powers.

"Company" includes corporation.

"The Council" means the Council or Committee or other governing body of a Federated Stock Exchange.

"The Department" means the Quotations Department of The Stock Exchange, London, or administrative department of a Federated Stock Exchange.

"Federated Stock Exchange" includes The Stock Exchange, London, The Midlands and Western Stock Exchange, The Northern Stock Exchange, The Scottish Stock Exchange, the Belfast, Cork, and Dublin Stock Exchanges and the Provincial Brokers Stock Exchange.

"Loan Capital" includes Debenture Stock, Debentures and Loan Stock, whether secured or unsecured.

"Prospectus" includes Offer for Sale, Advertisement, Circular, Scheme of Arrangement, or other equivalent document, published or circulated or proposed to be published or circulated relating to the securities for which quotation is sought.

"Quoted" means, except where the context otherwise requires, in relation to any securities, quoted on the Stock Exchange on which application for quotation is being sought.

"Securities" includes Shares.

"Share" includes Stock.

"Temporary Document of Title" includes Allotment Letters, Letters of Acceptance, Letters of Right, Scrip Certificates and any other temporary documents of title, including Renounceable Share Certificates.

"Trust Deed" includes Supplemental Trust Deed.

### *Arrangement of Appendix*

SECTION A. COMPANIES AND STATUTORY BODIES TO WHICH THE PROVISIONS OF THE COMPANIES ACTS RELATING TO PROSPECTUSES APPLY.

SECTION A. COMPANIES AND STATUTORY BODIES TO WHICH THE PROVISIONS OF THE COMPANIES ACTS RELATING TO PROSPECTUSES APPLY.

### *Part I*

*Quotations for Securities of Companies no part of whose Capital is already quoted*

I. Application, which should be made at the earliest possible date (1) in the form set out in Schedule I, can only be made in respect of a Company if that Company has a minimum market value of £250,000, and in respect of any security only if that security has a minimum market value of £100,000. If a Placing or Introduction is intended the application must be accompanied or preceded by a request to use such method, together with a statement as to whether or not any application or approach of any kind has been made to any other Stock Exchange and any result thereof, supported by such other information as the Committee may from time to time require.

II. (A) Applicants must submit for initial approval, at least four-  (2)
teen days prior to publication or posting:

(i) four proof prints of the Prospectus which, in the case of a
Placing or Introduction and, in such other cases as the Committee
may require, must, unless the Committee otherwise agree, take the
form of an Advertisement for circulation by the Exchange Telegraph
Company Limited and Moodies Services Limited in their statistical
services, which must be published in two leading London* daily
newspapers, save that

(a) in the case of Placings or Introductions of United Kingdom
securities it shall be sufficient for the Prospectus to be published in
one leading London* daily newspaper only provided abridged
particulars appear in a second leading London* daily newspaper;
(b) in the case of Placings or Introductions of fixed income
securities (other than those having equity conversion rights)
denominated solely in a foreign currency, it shall be sufficient for
abridged particulars to be published in one leading London*
daily newspaper only provided that the advertisement indicates
that further particulars are contained in the new issue cards circulated by the Exchange Telegraph Company Limited and
Moodies Services Limited;

four proof prints of such abridged particulars must also be submitted.
(ii) four proof prints of the Temporary Document of Title proposed to be issued, which must comply with Schedule III;
(iii) two proof prints of the Definitive Certificate or other
definitive documents of title proposed to be issued, which must
comply with Schedule IV; as indicated in that Schedule, it is advisable for proofs to be submitted as early as possible.
(iv) two proof prints or copies of the Memorandum and Articles
of Association or other corresponding document, which must
comply with Part A of Schecule VII.
(v) in the case of Loan Capital two proof prints or copies of the
Trust Deed or other document securing or constituting the Loan
Capital. These must comply with Part B of Schedule VII.

(B) The Prospectus must comply with Part A of Schedule II.
(C) Where it is desired to advertise abridged particulars or a Preliminary Announcement of a Public Offer in the Press, Applicants
must submit four copies of the drafts of such documents (which must
not contain any material information not included in the Prospectus),
for approval at least four days prior to insertion in the Press.
(D) Where, following submission pursuant to this paragraph II, any
amendment is made in any document, a like number of further copies
must be submitted for approval. Such copies must be marked in red to
indicate amendments made to conform with points raised by the
Department and in blue or black to indicate other amendments.

III. The following documents must be lodged at least two days  (3)
prior to the hearing of the Application by the Committee:

---

* Where no application is made to The Stock Exchange, London, but application
is being made to another Federated Stock Exchange, the newspapers may be those
circulating in such centres as the Committee may determine.

(A) A formal application in the form issued by the Department, signed by the Broker appointed by the Company and supported, in the case of The Stock Exchange, London, by at least two firms of Jobbers in the Market concerned who are prepared to deal, together with payment of the appropriate charge for quotation.

(B) (i) Four copies of the Prospectus one of which must be dated and signed by every person who is named therein as a Director or proposed Director of the Company or by his agent authorised in writing.

(ii) Where any document referred to in (i) is signed by an Agent a certified copy of the authorisation for such signature.

(c) A copy of the Exchange Telegraph and Moodies Services cards (if any) and of each newspaper (if any) in which the Prospectus or any Abridged Particulars of Preliminary Announcement appeared.

(D) A certified or photostat copy of the Certificate of Incorporation.

(E) A certified or photostat copy of the Certificate (if any) entitling the Company ro commence business.

*(F) A specimen of the Memorandum and Articles of Association or other corresponding document.

*(G) A specimen of the Trust Deed or other document securing or constituting the Loan Capital.

(H) (i) The general undertaking in the form set out in Part A of Schedule VIII.

(ii) Where required by the Committee, a certified copy of a resolution of the Board of Directors in the following terms:

"In compliance with the requirements of the Council of The Stock Exchange, London [or, as the case may be, other Federated Stock Exchanges] it was resolved that the Company shall not act as Stock or Share Brokers or Dealers in Securities and shall exercise all voting and other rights or powers of control exercisable by the Company in relation to its subsidiary companies for the time being so as to secure (so far as by such exercise the Company can secure) that no such subsidiary shall act in manner aforesaid."

(I) A certified copy of—

(i) the Resolution(s) of the Board authorising the issue of all securities for which quotation is sought and subsequently allotting the same; and

(ii) the Resolution(s) of the Board approving and authorising the issue of the Prospectus.

(J) In the case of a Placing, a copy of the Placing Letter and a Marketing Statement by the Broker in the form set out in Schedule IX or as near thereto as circumstances admit.

* In the event of any of these documents not complying with the requirements of the Committee and if it is impracticable for the Company to alter them before making the application for quotation, the Committee may accept an undertaking to amend these documents at the earliest possible opportunity. Where Loan Capital is to be secured by a Trust Deed and such Trust Deed will not have been entered into by the time of the hearing, a copy of the latest draft should be lodged for approval by the Department and in that event a copy of the Trust must be lodged with the Department as soon as possible after execution together with a letter from the Trustees' solicitors certifying that it complies in all respects with the draft as finally approved by the Department except (if such be the case) as otherwise subsequently agreed with the Department, particulars of the agreed variation(s) being given in the letter.

(κ) A certified copy of every Letter, Report, Balance Sheet, Valuation, Contract, Resolution or other document any part of which is extracted or referred to in the Prospectus.

(ʟ) A certified copy of the written consent by any expert to the inclusion in the Prospectus of—

(i) a statement purporting to be a copy of or extract from or summary of or reference to a Report or Valuation or other statement by such expert;

(ii) any recommendation by such expert in relation to acceptance or rejection of an offer or proposal.

(ᴍ) Three specimens of the Notice(s) of Meeting referred to in the Prospectus and Temporary Document of Title.

(ɴ) A specimen of the Definitive Certificate or other definitive document of title.

(ᴏ) A statement in the form set out in Schedule V, which includes an undertaking to submit the Declaration set out in Schedule VI.

(ᴘ) Where any scrip is to be issued by any person other than the Company whose scrip it is, a certified copy of the Resolution or other document, evidencing the authority to issue the scrip.

(ǫ) Where the vendor of a security offered for sale has not paid in full for that security at the date of the offer:

(i) a certified copy of an irrevocable authority given by the vendor to the Bankers to the offer authorising the Bankers to earmark the proceeds of the offer to discharge the obligation of the vendor to make payment for the security on the date or dates for payment as laid down in the Contract for the acquisition of the security by the Vendor, and

(ii) a certified copy of the Bankers' acknowledgment of this authority and an agreement to act on it.

(ʀ) A letter from the issuing house, or, in the absence of an issuing house, from the sponsoring brokers, stating that they have satisfied themselves that the statement in the Prospectus as to the sufficiency of working capital has been made by the Directors after due and careful enquiry. Such letter will normally be required to state that there is written confirmation from persons or institutions on whom reliance is placed for the provision of finance that such facilities exist.

IV. The following documents may be required:                          (4)

(ᴀ) Where the promoter or other interested party is a limited company or a firm a Statutory Declaration as to the identity of those who control it or are interested in its profits or assets.

(ʙ) A declaration by each Director in conformity with the Rules and Regulations of the Stock Exchange.

*Part II*

*Quotations for Securities of Companies part of whose Capital is already quoted*

I. Application, which should be made at the earliest possible date      (5)
in the form set out in Schedule I, can only be made in respect of a security which has a minimum market value of £100,000. If a Placing

or Introduction is intended the application must be accompanied or preceded by a request to use such method, together with a statement as to whether or not any application or approach of any kind has been made to any other Stock Exchange and any result thereof, supported by such other information as the Committee may from time to time require.

II. (A) Applicants must submit for initial approval at least four-teen days prior to publication or posting: (6)

(i) four proof prints of the Prospectus which, in the case of a Placing or Introduction and, in such other cases as the Committee may require, must, unless the Committee otherwise agree, take the form of an Advertisement* for circulation by the Exchange Tele-graph Company Limited and Moodies Services Limited in their statistical services which must be published in two leading London† daily newspapers, save that in the case of Placings or Introductions of fixed income securities (other than those having equity con-version rights), it shall be sufficient for abridged particulars to be published in two leading London† daily newspapers (one leading London daily newspaper only in the case of securities denominated solely in a foreign currency), provided that the advertisement indicates that further particulars are contained in the new issue cards circulated by the Exchange Telegraph Company Limited and Moodies Services Limited; four proof prints of such abridged particulars must be submitted;

(ii) four proof prints of the Temporary Document of Title pro-posed to be issued, which must comply with Schedule III;

(iii) two proof prints of the Definitive Certificate or other defini-tive document of title proposed to be issued, unless previously supplied, which must comply with Schedule IV; as indicated in that Schedule, it is advisable for proofs to be submitted as early as possible;

(iv) two proof prints or copies of the Memorandum and Articles of Association or other corresponding document, unless previously supplied, which must comply with Part A of Schedule VII, together with two proof prints or copies of all Special Resolutions or Resolu-tions increasing the share capital or capitalising reserves;

(v) in the case of Loan Capital two proof prints or copies of the Trust Deed or other document securing or constituting the Loan Capital. These must comply with Part B of Schedule VII.

(B) The Prospectus must comply with Part B of Schedule II, except that where the securities for which quotation is sought are being issued by way of capitalisation paragraphs 1, 3 and 9 and, if applicable, 5, 6 and 7 only of Part B of Schedule II need be complied with.

(C) Where it is desired to advertise abridged particulars or a Pre-liminary Announcement of a Public Offer in the Press applicants must submit four copies of the drafts of such documents (which must not contain any information not included in the Prospectus) for approval at least four days prior to insertion in the Press.

---

* No Advertisement will be required in cases where securities are offered or issued primarily to existing holders or employees.

† Where no application is made to The Stock Exchange, London, but application is being made to another Federated Stock Exchange, the newspapers may be those circulating in such centres as the Committee may determine.

(D) Where, following submission pursuant to this paragraph II, any amendment is made in any document, a like number of further copies shall be submitted to the Department for approval. Such copies must be marked in red to indicate amendments made to conform with points raised by the Department and in blue or black to indicate other amendments.

III. The following documents must be lodged at least two days (one day in the case of placings of fixed income securities) prior to the hearing of the Application by the Committee: (7)

(A) A formal application in the form issued by the Department, signed by the Broker appointed by the Company and, except in the case of issues by way of right or capitalisation, supported in the case of The Stock Exchange, London, by at least two firms of Jobbers in the Market concerned who are prepared to deal, together with payment of the appropriate charge for quotation.

(B) (i) Four copies of the Prospectus one of which, in the case of a Prospectus officially advertised, must be dated and signed by every Director or proposed Director of the Company or by his agent authorised in writing.

(ii) Where any document referred to in (i) is signed by an Agent a certified copy of the authorisation for such signature.

(C) A copy of the Exchange Telegraph and Moodies Services cards (if any) and of each newspaper (if any) in which the Prospectus Abridged Particulars or Preliminary Announcement of a Public Offer appeared.

(D) A certified copy of—

(i) the resolution(s) of the Board authorising the issue of all securities for which quotation is sought and subsequently allotting the same;

(ii) the Resolution(s) of the Board approving and authorising the issue of the Prospectus; and

(iii) the Resolution(s) of the Company in General Meeting (if any) authorising the issue of all securities for which quotation is sought.

(E) In the case of a Placing, a copy of the Placing Letter and a Marketing Statement by the Broker in the form set out in Schedule IX or as near thereto as circumstances admit.

(F) A certified copy of every Letter, Report, Balance Sheet, Valuation, Contract, Resolution or other document any part of which is extracted or referred to in the Prospectus.

(G) A certified copy of the written consent by any expert to the inclusion in the Prospectus of—

(i) a statement purporting to be a copy of or extract from or summary of or reference to a Report or Valuation or other statement by such expert;

(ii) any recommendation by such expert in relation to acceptance or rejection of an offer or proposal.

(H) Three specimens of the Notice(s) of Meeting referred to in the Prospectus and Temporary Document of Title.

(I) Unless the securities are or are to be identical with some already quoted a specimen of the Definitive Certificate or other definitive document of title.

DD

(J) A statement in the form set out in Schedule V, which includes an undertaking to submit the Declaration set out in Schedule VI.

(K) Where any scrip is to be issued by any person other than the Company whose scrip it is, a certified copy of the Resolution or other document, evidencing the authority to issue the scrip.

(L) Where the vendor of a security offered for sale has not paid in full for that security at the date of the offer:

(i) a certified copy of an irrevocable authority given by the vendor to the Bankers to the offer authorising the Bankers to earmark the proceeds of the offer to discharge the obligation of the vendor to make payment for the security on the date or dates for payment as laid down in the Contract for the acquisition of the security by the Vendor, and

(ii) a certified copy of the Bankers' acknowledgment of this authority and an agreement to act on it.

(M) A letter from the issuing house, or, in the absence of an issuing house, from the sponsoring brokers, stating that they have satisfied themselves that the statement in the Prospectus as to the sufficiency of working capital has been made by the Directors after due and careful enquiry. Such letter will normally be required to state that there is written confirmation from persons or institutions on whom reliance is placed for the provision of finance that such facilities exist.

IV. The following documents may be required: (8)

*(A) A specimen of the Memorandum and Articles of Association or other corresponding document and copies of all subsequent Special Resolutions or Resolutions increasing the share capital or capitalising reserves.

*(B) In the case of Loan Capital a specimen of the Trust Deed or other document securing or constituting the Loan Capital.

(C) The general undertaking in the form set out in Part A of Schedule VIII.

### Part III

*Quotations for Securities already quoted on another Federated Stock Exchange where no further issue is being made*

I. Application should be made at the earliest possible date in the (9) form set out in Schedule I, together with a letter giving the number of shareholders and, in so far as it is reasonable to ascertain the same,

---

* In the event of any of these documents not complying with the requirements of the Committee and if it is impracticable for the Company to alter them before making the application for quotation, the Committee may accept an undertaking to amend these documents at the earliest possible opportunity. Where Loan Capital is to be secured by a Trust Deed and such Trust Deed will not have been entered into by the time of the hearing, a copy of the latest draft should be lodged for approval by the Department and in that event a copy of the Trust Deed must be lodged with the Department as soon as possible after execution together with a letter from the Trustees' solicitors certifying that it complies in all respects with the draft as finally approved by the Department except (if such be the case) as otherwise subsequently agreed with the Department, particulars of the agreed variation(s) being given in the letter.

particulars of the ten largest holdings assessed according to beneficial ownership.

II. Applicants must submit for initial approval, at least fourteen     (10)
days prior to the hearing of the Application by the Committee:

(A) a certified copy of any Prospectus formerly published or statement compiled by the Company to comply with the requirements of the Stock Exchange on which the security is already quoted;

(B) a copy of the audited accounts for the last three years together with a statement giving particulars of any material changes in the assets and liabilities or earnings position of the Company or in the nature of its business since the last audited accounts or, if there are no such changes, a statement to that effect;

(C) two proof prints or copies of the Definitive Certificate, which must comply with Schedule IV;

(D) two proof prints or copies of the Memorandum and Articles of Association or other corresponding document which must comply with Part A of Schedule VII.

(E) In the case of Loan Capital two proof prints or copies of the Trust Deed or other document securing or constituting the Loan Capital. These must comply with Part B of Schedule VII.

III. The following documents must be lodged at least two days     (11)
prior to the hearing of the Application by the Committee:

(A) A formal application in the form issued by the Department, signed by the Broker appointed by the Company and supported, in the case of The Stock Exchange, London, by at least two firms of Jobbers in the Market concerned who are prepared to deal, together with payment of the appropriate charge for quotation.

(B) A letter from the Secretary of the relevant Stock Exchange giving particulars of the securities quoted at the date of the application.

*(C) A specimen of the Memorandum and Articles of Association or other corresponding document.

*(D) A specimen of the Trust Deed or other document securing or constituting any Loan Capital.

(E) The general undertaking in the form set out in Part A of Schedule VIII.

(F) A specimen of the Definitive Certificate.

(G) A statement in the form set out in Schedule V, which includes an undertaking to submit the Declaration set out in Schedule VI.

IV. A declaration by each Director in conformity with the Rules     (11a)
and Regulations of the Stock Exchange may be required.

* In the event of any of these documents not complying with the requirements of the Committee and if it is impracticable for the Company to alter them before making the application for quotation, the Committee may accept an undertaking to amend these documents at the earliest possible opportunity. Where Loan Capital is to be secured by a Trust Deed and such Trust Deed will not have been entered into by the time of the hearing, a copy of the latest draft should be lodged for approval by the Department and in that event a copy of the Trust Deed must be lodged with the Department as soon as possible after execution together with a letter from the Trustees' solicitors certifying that it complies in all respects with the draft as finally approved by the Department except (if such be the case) as otherwise subsequently agreed with the Department, particulars of the agreed variation(s) being given in the letter.

SECTION B. GOVERNMENTS, MUNICIPALITIES, LOCAL AUTHORITIES
AND STATUTORY BODIES NOT FALLING WITHIN SECTION A.

[The relevant sections have been omitted from this book. Obtainable from the Share and Loan Department of the Stock Exchange.]

## SCHEDULE I

### Letter of Application (16)

To the Secretary,
　　The Quotations Department.

..........................19........

DEAR SIR,

　　We are instructed by.....................................................................

................................................................... (Name of Co.)

to make application for permission to deal in and for quotation for:

*(1) ...................................................................................

.........................................................................................

†(2) ...................................................................................

.........................................................................................

We shall be glad to receive in due course a note of the requirements of the Department.

Application is being made simultaneously to the...........................

...............Stock Exchange.

We are,
Yours faithfully,

....................................Brokers.

* 1. Set out securities for which Application is made.
† State how it is proposed to issue the securities, i.e. whether by Prospectus, Offer for Sale, Circular (Conversion, Exchange, Rights, Open Offer, Capitalisation of Reserves), Vendor Consideration, Placing or Introduction.

## SCHEDULE II

### PART A

#### Contents of Prospectus

*In the case where quotation is sought for securities of a Company no part of whose capital is already quoted*

1. The full name of the Company. (17)

2. In the case of an Advertisement required to be circulated by the (18) Exchange Telegraph Company Limited and Moodies Services Limited in their statistical services, a Statement as follows:

"This Advertisement is issued in compliance with the Regulations of the Council of The Stock Exchange, London [or, as the case may be, other Federated Stock Exchange] for the purpose of giving information to the Public with regard to the Company. The Directors collectively and individually accept full responsibility for the information given and confirm, having made all reasonable enquiries, that to the best of their knowledge and belief there are no other facts the omission of which would make any statement in the Advertisement misleading."

3. A statement that application has been made to the Council of The Stock Exchange, London [or, as the case may be, other Federated Stock Exchange] for permission to deal in and for quotation for the securities.     (19)

4. The authorised share capital, the amount issued or agreed to be issued, the amount paid up and the description and nominal value of the shares. In cases where 25% or more of the voting capital (unclassified shares being counted as voting capital) is unissued, a statement that no issue will knowingly be made which could effectively alter the control of the Company without prior approval of the shareholders in general meeting.     (20)

5. (i) The authorised loan capital of the Company and any of its subsidiaries, the amount issued and outstanding or agreed to be issued, or, if no loan capital is outstanding, a statement to that effect.     (21)

(ii) Particulars of any bank overdrafts or other similar indebtedness of the Company and any of its subsidiaries as at the latest convenient date or, if there are no bank overdrafts or other similar indebtedness, a statement to that effect.

(iii) Particulars of any mortages, charges, hire purchase commitments or guarantees or other material contingent liabilities of the Company and any of its subsidiaries, or, if there are no such liabilities, a statement to that effect.

6. The full name, address and description of every Director and, if required by the Committee, particulars of (A) any former Christian names and surname, (B) his nationality, if not British, and (C) his nationality of origin if his present nationality is not the nationality of origin.     (22)

7. The full name and professional qualification of the Secretary and situation of Registered Office and Transfer Office (if different).     (23)

8. The names and addresses of the Bankers, Brokers, Solicitors, Registrars and Trustees (if any).     (24)

9. The name, address and professional qualification of the Auditors.     (25)

10. The date and country of incorporation and the authority under which the Company was incorporated.     (26)

In the case of a Company not incorporated in the United Kingdom, the address of the head office and of the principal place of business (if any) in the United Kingdom

11. If the application is in respect of shares:     (27)

(i) The voting rights of shareholders.

(ii) If there is more than one class of share, the rights of each
class of share as regards dividend, capital, redemption, and the
creation or issue of further shares ranking in priority to or *pari
passu* with each class other than the lowest ranking equity.

(iii) A summary of the consents necessary for the variation of
such rights.

12. The provisions or a sufficient summary of the provisions of the        (28)
Articles of Association, By-Laws or other corresponding document
with regard to:

(i) Any power enabling the Directors, in the absence of an independent quorum, to vote remuneration (including pension or other
benefits) to themselves or any members of their body.

(ii) Borrowing powers exercisable by the Directors and how
such borrowing powers can be varied.

(iii) Retirement or non-retirement of Directors under an age
limit.

13. Where quotation is sought for loan capital, the rights conferred        (29)
upon the holders thereof, and particulars of the security (if any)
therefor.

14. A statement of:        (30)

(i) any alterations in the share capital of the Company within the
two years preceding the publication of the Prospectus; and

(ii) the persons holding or beneficially interested in any substantial part of the share capital of the Company and the amounts
of the holdings in question together with particulars of the interests
of each director (and also, so far as he is aware of or can by reasonable inquiry ascertain the same, of his family interests) in the share
capital of the company and, otherwise than through the company,
any of its subsidiaries, distinguishing between beneficial and other
interests; the expression "family interests" includes, in relation to a
director, spouse, children under 21 years of age, trusts of which the
director or spouse is a settler or trustee and in which the director or
spouse or any of such children are beneficiaries or discretionary
objects and companies known to him to be controlled by him and/or
spouse and/or such children and/or the trustees of any such trusts as
aforesaid in their capacity as such trustees.

Subject to the necessity to distinguish between beneficial and
other interests, between the Company and each subsidiary and
between each class of capital each director's interests may be aggregated with those of his family interests.

15. The general nature of the business of the Company or Group        (31)
and, in cases where the Company or Group carries on two or more
activities which are material, having regard to profits or losses, assets
employed or any other factor, information as to the relative importance
of each such activity. If the Company or Group trades outside the
United Kingdom a statement showing a geographical analysis of its
trading operations.

16. (i) In regard to every company the whole of, or a substantial        (32)
proportion of whose capital (either directly or indirectly) is held or is
about to be held, or whose profits or assets make or will make a

material contribution to the figures in the Auditors' Report or next published accounts, particulars of: The name, date, country of incorporation, whether public or private, general nature of business, issued capital and the proportion thereof held or about to be held.

(ii) In regard to the company and every subsidiary or company about to become a subsidiary, particulars of: The situation, area and tenure (including in the case of leaseholds the rent and unexpired term) of the factories and main buildings, the principal products and approximate number of employees.

17. Wherever possible, a statement showing the sales turnover (33) figures or gross trading income during the preceding three financial years which should contain a reasonable breakdown between the more important trading activities. In the cases of a group, internal sales should be excluded.

18. (i) A statement as to the financial and trading prospects of the (34) Company or Group, together with any material information which may be relevant thereto, including, where known to the directors, special trade factors or risks (if any) which are not mentioned elsewhere in the prospectus and which are unlikely to be known or anticipated by the general public, which could materially affect the profits, and details of any waiver of future dividends.

(ii) Where quotation is sought for fixed income securities, particulars of the profits cover for dividend/interest and of the net tangible assets available for capital cover.

19. A statement by the Directors that in their opinion the working (35) capital available is sufficient, or, if not, how it is proposed to provide the additional working capital thought by the Directors to be necessary.

20. Where the securities for which quotation is sought were issued (36) for cash within the two years preceding the publication of the Prospectus, or will be issued for cash, a statement or an estimate of the net proceeds of the issue and a statement as to how such proceeds were or are to be applied.

21. A report by the Auditors of the Company: (37)

(i) with respect to the profits or losses of the Company in respect of each of the ten completed financial years immediately preceding the publication of the Prospectus, or in respect of each of the years since the incorporation of the Company, if this occurred less than ten years prior to such publication; and, if in respect of a period ending on a date earlier than three months before such publication no accounts have been made up, a statement of that fact;

(ii) in the case of an issue by a holding company, in lieu of the report in (i), a like report with respect to the profits or losses of the Company and of its subsidiary companies, so far as such profits or losses can properly be regarded as attributable to the interests of the holding company;

(iii) as to the rate of dividend for each class of shares during each of the five financial years preceding the issue of the prospectus with details of any waiver of dividends in such years;

(iv) with respect to the assets and liabilities of the Company and in the case of an issue by a holding company, a like report with respect to the assets and liabilities of the Company and of its subsidiary companies so far as such assets can properly be regarded as attributable to the interests of the Company, including an explanation of the bases used for the valuations of fixed assets and a reasonably detailed indication of the nature of the tangible assets;

(v) with respect to the aggregate emoluments paid to the Directors by the Company during the last period for which the accounts have been made up and the amount (if any) by which such emoluments would differ from the amounts payable under the arrangements in force at the date of the Prospectus;

(vi) with respect to any other matters which appear to the auditors to be relevant having regard to the purpose of the report.

In making such report the auditors shall make such adjustments (if any) as are in their opinion appropriate for the purposes of the Prospectus.

22. If after the latest date to which the accounts of the Company (38) have been made up and audited the Company or any of its subsidiaries has acquired or agreed to acquire or is proposing to acquire a business or shares in a company which will by reason of such acquisition become a subsidiary of the Company or any of its subsidiaries and no part of the securities of that subsidiary is already quoted, a report made by qualified accountants who shall be named in the Prospectus:

(i) with respect to the profits or losses of the business or to the profits or losses attributable to the interests acquired or being acquired in respect of each of the ten completed financial years immediately preceding the publication of the Prospectus, or in respect of each of the years since the commencement of the business or the incorporation of such subsidiary company if this occurred less than ten years prior to such publication; and if in respect of a period ending on a date earlier than three months before such publication no accounts have been made up, a statement of that fact:

Provided that where any such subsidiary is itself a holding company the report shall be extended to the profits or losses of that company and its subsidiary companies which shall be ascertained in the manner laid down in sub-paragraph (ii) of paragraph 21;

(ii) with respect to the assets and liabilities of the business or of the subsidiary and where such subsidiary is itself a holding company, the report shall be extended to the assets and liabilities of that company and of its subsidiary companies in the manner laid down in sub-paragraph (iv) of paragraph 21;

(iii) with respect to any other matters which appear to the accountants to be relevant having regard to the purpose of the report.

In making such report the accountants shall make such adjustments (if any) as are in their opinion appropriate for the purposes of the Prospectus.

23. Particulars of any capital of the Company or of any of its sub- (39) sidiaries which has within two years immediately preceding the publication of the Prospectus been issued or is proposed to be issued fully or partly paid up otherwise than in cash and the consideration for which the same has been or is to be issued.

24. Particulars of any capital of the Company or of any of its    (40)
subsidiaries, which has within two years immediately preceding the
publication of the Prospectus been issued or is proposed to be issued
for cash, the price and terms upon which the same has been or is to be
issued and (if not already fully paid) the dates when any instalments are
payable with the amount of all calls or instalments in arrear.

25. Particulars of any capital of the Company or of any of its    (41)
subsidiaries which is under option, or agreed conditionally or unconditionally to be put under option, with the price and duration of the
option and consideration for which the option was or will be granted,
and the name and address of the grantee.

Provided that where an option has been granted or agreed to be
granted to all the members or debenture holders or to any class thereof,
it shall be sufficient, so far as the names are concerned, to record that
fact without giving the names and addresses of the grantees.

26. (i) Particulars of any preliminary expenses incurred or pro-    (42)
posed to be incurred and by whom the same are payable.

(ii) The amount or estimated amount of the expenses of the issue
and of the application for quotation so far as the same are not
included in the statement of preliminary expenses and by whom
the same are payable.

27. Particulars of any commissions, discounts, brokerages or other    (43)
special terms granted within two years immediately preceding the
publication of the Prospectus in connection with the issue or sale of
any capital of the Company or of any of its subsidiaries.

28. Details of Directors' existing or proposed service contracts    (44)
including those (if any) with any subsidiary.

29. Full particulars of the nature and extent of the interest direct    (45)
or indirect, if any, of every Director in the promotion of, or in any
assets which have been, within the two years preceding the publication
of the Prospectus, acquired or disposed of by or leased to, the Company
or any of its subsidiaries, or are proposed to be acquired, disposed of
by or leased to the Company or any of its subsidiaries, including

(A) the consideration passing to or from the Company or any of
its subsidiaries; and

(B) short particulars of all transactions relating to any such assets
which have taken place within two years immediately preceding the
publication of the Prospectus.

30. A statement that the Company has or has not (as the case may    (46)
be) any litigation of claims of material importance pending or
threatened against it.

31. (i) The name of any promoter; and (if a company) the Com-    (47)
mittee may require a statement of the issued share capital; the
amount paid up thereon; the date of its incorporation; the names of
its Directors, Bankers and Auditors; and such other particulars as
the Committee think necessary in connection therewith.

(ii) The amount of any cash or securities paid or benefit given
within the two years immediately preceding the publication of the
Prospectus, or proposed to be paid or given to any promoter and
the consideration for such payment or benefit.

32. Where the Prospectus includes a statement purporting to be (48) made by an expert, a statement that the expert has given and has not withdrawn his written consent to the issue of the Prospectus with the statement included in the form and context in which it is included.

33. When relevant, in the absence of a statement that income tax (49) and sur-tax clearances have been obtained, a statement that appropriate indemnities have been given. (The Committee may require such indemnities to be supported by continuing guarantees.)

34. When relevant, in the absence of a statement that estate duty (50) indemnities have been given, a statement that the Directors had been advised that no material liability for estate duty would be likely to fall upon the Company or any subsidiary. (The Committee may require any indemnities to be supported by continuing guarantees.)

35. The dates of and parties to all material contracts (not being (51) contracts entered into in the ordinary course of business) entered into within two years immediately preceding the publication of the Prospectus, together with a description of the general nature of such contracts, and particulars of any consideration passing to or from the Company.

36. A reasonable time (being not less than fourteen days) during (52) which and a place in the City of London [or such other centre as the Committee of a Federated Stock Exchange, other than London, may determine] at which the following documents (or copies thereof) where applicable may be inspected: The Memorandum and Articles of Association; Trust Deed; each contract disclosed pursuant to paragraph 35 or, in the case of a contract not reduced into writing, a memorandum giving full particulars thereof; all reports, letters, or other documents, balance sheets, valuations and statements by any expert any part of which is extracted or referred to in the Prospectus; a written statement signed by the auditors or accountants setting out the adjustments made by them in arriving at the figures shown in their report and giving the reasons therefor; and the audited accounts of the Company and its subsidiaries for each of the two financial years preceding the publication of the Prospectus together with all notes, certificates or information required by the Companies Act.

*Note 1.*—In the case of a Company which has carried on the same business for more than the two years immediately prior to the publication of the Prospectus, application may be made to the Committee to dispense with the requirements of paragraphs 26 (1), 29, in so far as it relates to interests in the promotion, and 31 (1).

*Note 2.*—In the case of foreign companies, the documents to be offered for inspection will be the documents corresponding to those above mentioned in the case of British companies, and where such documents are not in the English language notarially certified translations thereof must be available for inspection.

*Note 3.*—In cases where it is contended that contracts cannot be offered for inspection without disclosing to trade competitors important information the disclosure of which might be detrimental to the Company's interests, application may be made to the Committee to dispense with the offering of such documents for inspection.

*Note 4.*—In any case where information is not given under any of paragraphs 23, 24 and 25, the Prospectus must include the appropriate statements. In the absence of information under paragraphs 27 and 28, an appropriate negative statement must be supplied in the form of a letter addressed to the Department.

# APPENDIX IV

825

*Note 5.*—Under paragraphs 5, 14 (ii), 23, 24, 25, 27 and 28, reference to subsidiaries is to be construed as including any company which will become a subsidiary by reason of an acquisition falling within paragraph 22.

*Note 6.*—The requirements stated above are in general applicable to an industrial company. The Committee will require additional or alternative information for companies engaged in other enterprises, *e.g.*, mining.

## SCHEDULE II

### PART B

#### Contents of Prospectus

*In the case where quotation is sought for securities of a Company some part of whose capital is already quoted*

1. The full name of the Company. (53)

2. In the case of an Advertisement required to be circulated by the (54) Exchange Telegraph Company Limited and Moodies Services Limited in their statistical services, a statement as follows:

"This Advertisement is issued in compliance with the Regulations of the Council of The Stock Exchange, London [or, as the case may be, other Federated Stock Exchange], for the purpose of giving information to the Public with regard to the Company. The Directors collectively and individually accept full responsibility for the accuracy of the information given and confirm, having made all reasonable enquiries, that to the best of their knowledge and belief there are no other facts the omission of which would make any statement in the Advertisement misleading."

3. A statement that application has been made to the Council of (55) The Stock Exchange, London [or, as the case may be, other Federated Stock Exchange], for permission to deal in and for quotation for the securities.

4. In the case of a prospectus advertised in the Press and accompanied by a form of application:

(i) The full name, address and description of every Director and, if required by the Committee, particulars of (A) any former Christian names and surname, (B) his nationality, if not British, and (C) his nationality of origin if his present nationality is not the nationality of origin.

(ii) The full name and professional qualification of the Secretary and situation of Registered Office and Transfer Office (if different)

(iii) The names and addresses of the Bankers, Brokers, Solicitors, Registrars and Trustees (if any).

(iv) The name, address and professional qualification of the Auditors.

5. Where quotation is sought for shares which will not be identical (56) with shares already quoted:

(A) a statement of the rights as regards dividend, capital, redemption and voting attached to such shares and (except as regards the lowest ranking equity) as to the right of the Company to create or issue further shares ranking in priority to or *pari passu* therewith;

(B) a summary of the consents necessary for the variation of such rights.

6. In the case of an increase in the authorised capital where 25% (57) or more of the voting capital (unclassified shares being counted as voting capital) will remain unissued, a statement that no issue will be made which would effectively alter the control of the Company without prior approval of the shareholders in General Meeting.

7. Where quotation is sought for loan capital which will not be (58) identical with loan capital already quoted, the rights conferred upon the holders thereof, and short particulars of the security (if any) therefor.

Where Debentures or Stock are or is issued by way of conversion or replacement of Debentures or Debenture Stock previously issued a statement of all material differences between the security for the old Debentures or Debenture Stock and the security for the new Debenture Stock or, if there be none, a statement that the security for the new Debentures or Debenture Stock is identical with the security for the Debenture or Debenture Stock.

8. Where the securities for which quotation is sought are offered by (59) way of right to the holders of an existing quoted security, the Provisional Allotment Letter, Letter of Rights or other document of offer must show:

(i) as a heading, the date the offer expires and that the document is of value and negotiable and that a stockbroker, banker, solicitor or other professional adviser should be consulted immediately in all cases of doubt; and

(ii) how shares not taken up will be dealt with and a time, being not less than 21 days, in which the offer may be accepted; and

(iii) the *pro rata* entitlement, the last date on which transfers were accepted for registration for participation in the issue, how the shares rank for dividend, the nature of the document of title and proposed date of issue, and how the fractions are to be treated.

9. Where the securities for which quotation is sought are allotted by (60) way of capitalisation of reserves or undivided profits to the holders of an existing quoted security the document of offer or circular giving information must show:

the *pro rata* entitlement, the last date on which transfers were or will be accepted for registration for participation in the issue, how the shares rank for dividend, the nature of the document of title and proposed data of issue, and how fractions are to be treated.

10. Particulars of any bank overdrafts or other similar indebtedness, (61) mortgages, charges, hire purchase commitments, or guarantees or other material contingent liabilities of the Company and any of its subsidiaries, or, if there are no such liabilities, a statement to that effect.

11. (i) A statement as to the financial and trading prospects of the (62) Company or Group, together with any material information which may be relevant thereto, including all special trade factors or risks (if any) which are not mentioned elsewhere in the prospectus and

which are unlikely to be known or anticipated by the general public, which could materially affect the profits, and details of any waiver of future dividends.

(ii) Where quotation is sought for fixed income securities particulars of the profits cover for dividend/interest and of the net tangible assets available for capital cover.

12. A statement by the Directors that in their opinion, the working (63) capital available is sufficient, or, if not, how it is proposed to provide the additional working capital thought by the Directors to be necessary.

13. Where the securities for which quotation is sought were issued (64) for cash since the date to which the last published audited accounts of the Company were made up or will be issued for cash, a statement or an estimate of the net proceeds of the issue and a statement as to how such proceeds were or are intended to be applied.

14. If after the latest date to which the accounts of the company (65) have been made up and audited the company or any of its subsidiaries has acquired or agreed to acquire or is proposing to acquire a business or other assets or shares in a company which will by reason of such acquisition become a subsidiary of the company or any of its subsidiaries:

(1) a report made by qualified accountants who shall be named in the Prospectus:

(a) with respect to the profits or losses of the business or to the profits or losses attributable to the interests acquired or being acquired in respect of each of the ten completed financial years immediately preceding the publication of the Prospectus or in respect of each of the years since the commencement of the business or the incorporation of such subsidiary company if this occurred less than ten years prior to such publication; and, if in respect of a period ending on a date earlier than three months before such publication no accounts have been made up, a statement of that fact;

provided that where any such subsidiary is itself a holding company the report shall be extended to the profits or losses of that company and its subsidiary companies which shall be ascertained in the manner laid down in sub-paragraph (ii) of paragraph 21 of Part A of Schedule II;

(b) with respect to the assets and liabilities of the business or of the subsidiary and where such subsidiary is a holding company, the report shall be extended to the assets and liabilities of that company and of its subsidiary companies in the manner laid down in sub-paragraph (iv) of paragraph 21 of Part A of Schedule II;

(c) with respect to any other matters which appear to the accountants to be relevant having regard to the purpose of the report;

in making such report the accountants shall make such adjustment (if any) as are in their opinion appropriate for the purposes of the Prospectus;

(2) a statement as to any change in the financial and trading position since the date to which the last accounts which are the subject of the above report were made up;

(3) a statement of the general nature of the business acquired or proposed to be acquired together with particulars of the situation, area and tenure (including in the case of leaseholds, the rent and unexpired term) of the factories and buildings and the principal products;

(4) a statement of the consideration for the acquisition and how it was or is to be satisfied;

(5) a statement of the total emoluments received by the directors of the Company in the past financial year together with an indication of what emoluments will be payable after the acquisition to the directors of the Company.

The requirements of this paragraph will be relaxed in the case of non-material acquisitions and may be relaxed on application to the Committee to the extent that:

(i) the information about the acquisition has already been circulated to shareholders; or

(ii) the company acquired or to be acquired being a company part of whose securities are already quoted, the information is available in the Statistical Services and other publications.

15. A statement of the persons holding or beneficially interested in   (66) any substantial part of the share capital of the Company and the amounts of the holdings in question together with particulars of the interests of each director (and also, so far as he is aware of or can by reasonable enquiry ascertain the same, of his family interests) in the share capital of the Company and, otherwise than through the Company, any of its subsidiaries, distinguishing between beneficial and other interests; the expression "family interests" includes, in relation to a director, spouse, children under 21 years of age, trusts in which the director or spouse is a settler or trustee and in which the director or spouse or any of such children are beneficiaries or discretionary objects and Companies known to him to be controlled by him and/or spouse and/or such children and/or the trustees of any such trusts as aforesaid in their capacity as such trustees. (The Committee may dispense with this statement in the case of a Prospectus where there is no invitation to subscribe capital.)

Subject to the necessity to distinguish between beneficial and other interests, between the company and each subsidiary and between each class of capital each director's interests may be aggregated with those of his family interests.

16. Particulars of any capital of the Company or of any of its   (67) subsidiaries which has, since the date to which the last published audited accounts of the Company were made up, been issued or is proposed to be issued fully or partly paid up otherwise than in cash and the consideration for which the same has been issued or is proposed to be issued.

17. Particulars of any capital of the Company or of any of its   (68) subsidiaries which has, since the date to which the last published audited accounts of the Company were made up, been issued or is proposed to be issued for cash, the price and terms upon which the same has been or is to be issued and (if not already fully paid) the dates when any instalments are payable with the amount of all calls or instalments in arrear.

18. Particulars of any capital of the Company or of any of its sub-    (69)
sidiaries which is under option, or agreed conditionally or unconditionally to be put under option, with the price and duration of the
option and consideration for which the option was or will be granted,
and the name and address of the grantee.

Provided that where an option has been granted or agreed to be
granted to all the members or debenture holders or to any class
thereof, it shall be sufficient, so far as the names are concerned, to
record that fact without giving the names and addresses of the grantees.

19. The amount or estimated amount of the expenses of the issue    (70)
and of the application for quotation and by whom the same are
payable.

20. Particulars of any commissions, discounts, brokerages or other    (71)
special terms granted, since the date to which the last published audited
accounts of the Company were made up, in connection with the issue
or sale of any capital of the Company or of any of its subsidiaries.

21. Details of all contracts of service (unless expiring, or determin-    (72)
able by the employing company without payment of compensation,
within one year) of any Director with the company or any of its subsidiaries; or where applicable, a statement to the effect that (i) there
are no such contracts or (ii) all such contracts are available for
inspection in like manner as required under paragraph 27 and none of
such contracts was entered into or varied after the date of the notice
convening the last annual general meeting.

22. Full particulars of the nature and extent of the interest direct or    (73)
indirect, if any, of every Director in any assets which, since the date to
which the last published audited accounts of the Company were made
up, have been acquired, disposed of by or leased to the Company or
any of its subsidiaries or are proposed to be acquired, disposed of by
or leased to the Company or any of its subsidiaries, including

(A) the consideration passing to or from the Company or any of
its subsidiaries; and
(B) short particulars of all transactions relating to any such assets
which have taken place since such date.

23. When relevant, in the absence of a statement that income tax    (74)
and sur-tax clearances have been obtained, a statement that appropriate indemnities have been given. The Committee may require such
indemnities to be supported by continuing guarantees.

24. When relevant, in the absence of a statement that estate duty    (75)
indemnities have been given, a statement that the Directors had been
advised that no material liability for estate duty would be likely to fall
upon the Company or any subsidiary. The Committee may require
such indemnities to be supported by continuing guarantees.

25. Where the Prospectus includes a statement purporting to be    (76)
made by an expert, a statement that the expert has given and has not
withdrawn his written consent to the issue of the Prospectus with the
statement included in the form and context in which it is included.

26. The dates of and parties to all material contracts (not being (77) contracts entered into in the ordinary course of business) entered into within two years immediately preceding the publication of the Prospectus together with a description of the general nature of such contracts, and particulars of any consideration passing to or from the Company.

27. A reasonable time (being not less than fourteen days) during (78) which and a place in the City of London [or such other centre as the Committee of a Federated Stock Exchange, other than London, may determine] at which the following documents (or copies thereof) where applicable may be inspected: The Memorandum and Articles of Association; Trust Deed; each contract disclosed pursuant to paragraph 26 or, in the case of a contract not reduced into writing, a memorandum giving full particulars thereof; all reports, letters or other documents, balance sheets, valuations and statements by any expert any part of which is extracted or referred to in the Prospectus; a written statement signed by the auditors or accountants setting out the adjustments made by them in arriving at the figures shown in their report and giving the reasons therefor; and the audited accounts of the Company and its subsidiaries for each of the two financial years immediately preceding the publication of the Prospectus together with all notes, certificates or information required by the Companies Act.

*Note 1.*—In the case of foreign companies, the documents to be offered for inspection will be the documents corresponding to those above mentioned in the case of British companies, and where such documents are not in the English language notarially certified translations thereof must be available for inspection.

*Note 2.*—In cases where it is contended that contracts cannot be offered for inspection without disclosing to trade competitors important information the disclosure of which might be detrimental to the Company's interests, application may be made to the Committee to dispense with the offering of such documents for inspection.

*Note 3.*—In any case where information is not given under any of paragraphs 16, 17 and 18, the Prospectus must include the appropriate negative statements. Where information is not given under paragraph 20 a letter in regard to the absence of commissions, etc., must be lodged with the Department.

*Note 4.*—Under paragraphs 15, 16, 17, 18, 20 and 22, reference to subsidiaries is to be construed as including any company which will become a subsidiary by reason of an acquisition falling within paragraph 14.

*Note 5.*—The requirements stated above are in general applicable to an industrial company. The Committee will require additional or alternative information for companies engaged in other enterprises, *e.g.*, mining.

## SCHEDULE II

### PART C

#### Contents of Prospectus

*In the case where quotation is sought for securities of a Government, Municipality, Local Authority or Statutory Body not falling within Section A*

[The relevant sections have been omitted from this book. Obtainable from the Share and Loan Department of The Stock Exchange.]

## SCHEDULE III

### Temporary Documents of Title

1. Documents must be serially numbered, printed on good quality (93)
paper and must be examined and autographically signed or initialled
by a responsible official of the company or authorised agent. The
name and address of the first holder and names of joint holders (if
any) should be stated and, in the case of fixed income securities, a
statement as to the amount of the next payment of interest or dividend
must be included.

2. Where the right of renunciation is given: (94)

(i) The form of renunciation and the registration instructions must
be printed on the back of, or attached to, the document.

(ii) There must be provision for splitting (without fee) and split
documents must be certified by an official of the company or
authorised agent. There must not be more than one clear business
day between the last day for splitting and the last day for renunciation.

(iii) When, at the same time as an allotment is made of shares
issued for cash, shares of the same class are also allotted, credited as
fully-paid, to vendors or others, the period for renunciation may
be the same as, but not longer than that provided for in the case of
shares issued for cash.

3. When a security is offered in conversion of another security and (95)
is also offered for subscription in cash, the Allotment Letters must be
marked "Conversion" and "Cash" respectively.

4. Letters of Allotment or Right must be issued simultaneously and (96)
in the event of its being impossible to issue letters of regret at the same
time a notice to that effect must be inserted in the Press and appear on
the morning after the Allotment Letters have been posted.

5. In the absence of contrary instructions from the shareholder all (97)
Letters of Right to shareholders with addresses outside the United
Kingdom and the Irish Republic must be dispatched by air mail.

## SCHEDULE IV

### Definitive Documents of Title

#### A. Registered Securities (98)

1. The overall size of the certificate should if possible be no larger
than 9 inches × 8 inches (22·5 cm. × 20 cm.).

2. The following matters must appear on the face of the certificate: (99)

(a) The authority under which the Company or Organisation is
constituted.

(b) Preferably at the top right-hand corner, the number of shares
or amount of stock the certificate represents and if applicable the
number and denomination of units.

(c) A footnote stating that no transfer of the security or any portion thereof represented by the certificate can be registered without production of the certificate.

(d) If applicable, the minimum amount and multiples thereof in which the security is transferable.

3. Certificates must be dated and (in the absence of statutory authority for issue under signature of appropriate officials) be issued under seal.

4. If relating to securities other than share capital, state on the face (100) the rate of interest payable and the interest payment dates and include on the back (preferably with reference shown on the face) a statement or summary of the conditions as to redemption or repayment and (where applicable) conversion.

5. If relating to share capital there being more than one class in issue, the certificates of the preferential classes must also bear (preferably on the face) a statement of the conditions conferred thereon as to capital and dividends.

### B. Bearer Securities                                              (101)

1. Proofs of securities and coupons must be submitted to the Department for approval at as early a stage as possible preferably in "sketch" form.*

2. The Printing of bearer securities must be entrusted to recognised security printers; it is preferable that one and the same printer should be employed on behalf of a particular Company or Borrowing Organisation.

3. The paper for securities and coupons must be first class Bond or (102) Banknote Paper containing a watermark of the Printer, Borrowing Organisation or Issuer. Accurate records must be kept regarding manufacture and consumption of security paper. The watermark should be repeated at staggered intervals of not more than 8 inches.

4. The overall size of the security (excluding sheets of coupons) should, if possible, be 9 inches × 8 inches (22·5 cm. × 20 cm.), but no more than $11\frac{3}{4}$ inches × $8\frac{1}{4}$ inches (29·7 cm. × 21 cm.). (Some modification of the size of the security may be necessary if the arrangements referred to in the Note under paragraph 6 are followed. There are no specific limitations on the size of coupons but regard will be given to this matter when proofs are submitted for approval.)

5. The serial number of the security must appear in the top right- (103) hand corner of each security, on the talon and on each coupon and should be printed from a unique type-face and by indestructible ink.

6. The Coupon sheets must be attached to the right-hand side or foot of the security and each coupon must bear the serial number of the security and be numbered consecutively. If a talon or renewal coupon is used it must be so placed as to be the last coupon to be removed. The margin between the coupons must be sufficiently wide to

* It is advisable for proofs to be submitted at least three to four weeks prior to the application for quotation being considered by the Committee.

ensure that the text of any coupon is not damaged when coupons are detached.

*Note.*—Having regard to the possibility of coupons being cleared with cheques, the Issuing Authorities may wish to consider the issue of a large-sized coupon on a paper of a standard suitable to meet the requirements for mechanisation as set out in the Committee on London Clearing Bankers' Requirements for Automatic Cheque Processing.

This may also determine the standard of paper to be used for the security.

Sheets of coupons of this type should cover a short period only in order to allow for any development in this process.

7. Securities must have at least one printing by Direct Engraved (104) Steel Place which must include the border. The plates must be produced by the security printer by mechanical or electrolytic means from original steel engravings and must remain in the responsible custody of the security printer. The impression must be perfect, giving uniform sharpness, no interrupted or broken lines and no choking or widening at points of intersection. Background colours must be chosen which cannot easily be distinguished by photographic means.

8. If the name of the security printer appears it must be placed outside the border at the foot of the security and of each coupon.

9. The following matter must appear on the face of the security:    (105)

(*a*) The authority under which the Company or Borrowing Organisation is constituted.

(*b*) The authority under which the security is issued.

(*c*) The dates when fixed interest or dividend is due.

If the Company is incorporated in the United Kingdom the security must be under seal and bear any requisite signatures.

10. The following matter must appear on the face or back of the security:

(*a*) In the case of a Loan, all conditions of issue as to redemption, conversion, meetings and voting rights.

(*b*) In the case of Shares with preferential rights, a statement of the conditions conferred thereon as to capital (including redemption), dividends, meetings and voting rights.

11. A declaration is required from the security printers that:    (106)

(*a*) The security is being produced in accordance with the Rules and Regulations of The Stock Exchange, London, or other appropriate Federated Stock Exchange.

(*b*) Records will be kept of the production and consumption of the security paper.

(*c*) The steel engraved plates have been produced by the security printers on their premises and since production they have remained and will remain under their control and will not be used on the securities of any other Company or Borrowing Organisation.

(*d*) At the request of the issuer all plates used in the preparation of the securities will be destroyed and satisfactory proof of destruction will be produced to the issuer.

### SCHEDULE V

*Particulars of Securities to be Quoted*

To: *The Secretary*,
    *Quotations Department.*

.........................19........

........................................Limited    (107)

*Share Capital*

| Authorised £ | | Issued and inclusive of present issue £ |
|---|---|---|
| in | Stock/Shares of | |
| in | Stock/Shares of | |
| in | Stock/Shares of | |
| in | Stock/Shares of | |
| £ | | £ |

1. Amounts and description of securities for which application is now made .................................................................

2. Distinctive numbers of shares (if any) ...............................

.........................................................................................

The securities for which quotation is sought

    (*a*) are/are not identical in all respects; and
    (*b*) are/are not identical in all respects with an existing class of security.

(Delete as appropriate. If they are not identical now, but will so become in the future, a statement as to when they will become identical must be added to (*a*) or (*b*) above and Definitive Certificates issued before that date must be enfaced with a note to this effect.)

Renounceable Certificates/Letters of Allotment/Acceptance/Rights

may not be renounced/may be renounced up to........................and

split up to..........................

The Definitive Certificates have already been issued in respect of

.........................or will be ready on ...........................in

respect of.........................................................................

I undertake to lodge with you the required Declaration in due course.

*Signed*......................................

Secretary or other
Authorised Officer.

*Note.*—"Identical" means in this context:

1. The shares or units are of the same nominal value with the same amount called up or paid up.

2. They are entitled to dividend/interest at the same rate and for the same period, so that at the next ensuing distribution, the dividend/interest payable per unit will amount to exactly the same sum (gross and net).

3. They carry the same rights as to unrestricted transfer, attendance and voting at meetings and are *pari passu* in all other respects.

## SCHEDULE VI

### Declaration

*(The following is a suggested form of declaration which will need amendment to meet individual cases.)*

We,                          and                          (108)
a Director and the Secretary respectively of
Limited (hereinafter called "the Company"), do declare as follows:

1. That all documents required by the Companies Acts to be filed with the Registrar of Companies in connection with the Issue/Offer/Placing/Introduction on...................................19.........of the following shares/securities of the Company namely
   *(insert particulars)* have been duly filed and that to the best of our knowledge information and belief compliance has been made with all other legal requirements in connection with such Issue/Offer/Placing/Introduction.

2. That          Shares of                    *(Number & Class)*
£          Debenture Stock          Debentures/Notes have been subscribed/purchased for cash and duly allotted/transferred to the Subscribers/Purchasers (and that the said Shares have been converted into £          Stock).

3. That all money due to the Company in respect of the issue/offer has been received by it.

4. That          Shares of
£          Debenture Stock          Debentures/Notes have been issued credited as fully paid by way of conversion/exchange/consideration for property acquired/other consideration not being cash and have been duly allotted/transferred to the persons entitled thereto (and that the said Shares have been converted into £          Stock).

5. That the definitive documents of title have been delivered/are ready to be delivered.

6. That completion has taken place of the purchase by the Company of all property shown in the Prospectus, Offer for Sale, Advertisement or Circular to Members dated                    , 19          to have been purchased or agreed to be purchased by it and the purchase consideration for all such property has been duly satisfied.

7. That the Trust Deed/Deed Poll relating to the said Debenture Stock or Notes has been completed and executed and a copy has been lodged with the Department and that particulars thereof, if so required by Statute, have been filed with the Registrar of Companies.

8. That all the Shares/Debenture Stock/Notes of each class for which quotation exists are in all respects identical.

9. That there are no other facts bearing on the Company's application for quotation which, in our opinion, should be disclosed to The Stock Exchange, London [of other appropriate Federated Stock Exchange].

And we make this declaration conscientiously believing the same to be true.

*Signed*

...........................................*Director.*

...........................................*Secretary.*

...........................................*Date*

*Note.*—"Identical" means in this context:

1. The shares or units are of the same nominal value with the same amount called up or paid up.

2. They are entitled to dividend/interest at the same rate and for the same period, so that at the next ensuing distribution, the dividend/interest payable per unit will amount to exactly the same sum (gross and net).

3. They carry the same rights as to unrestricted transfer, attendance and voting at meetings and are *pari passu* in all other respects.

## SCHEDULE VII

### PART A

#### Articles of Association

The articles of Association or other corresponding document must conform with the following provisions and, where necessary, a certified copy of a resolution of the Board of Directors undertaking to comply with the appropriate provisions must be lodged with the Department:

*A. as regards Transfer and Registration*                          (109)

1. That transfers and other documents relating to or affecting the title to any shares shall be registered without payment of any fee.

2. That full-paid shares shall be free from any restriction on the right of transfer and shall also be free from all lien.

3. That where power is taken to limit the number of shareholders in a joint account, such limit shall not prevent the registration of a maximum of four persons.

4. That the closing of the registers shall be discretionary.

*B. as regards Definitive Certificates*                          (110)

1. That all Certificates for Capital shall be under the Common Seal, which shall only be affixed with the authority of the Directors.

2. That the charge for a new Certificate issued to replace one that has been worn out, lost or destroyed shall not exceed one shilling and that where the holder has sold part of his holding, he shall be entitled to a certificate for the balance without charge.

3. Where power is taken to issue Share Warrants to Bearer, that no new Share Warrant shall be issued to replace one that has been lost, unless the Company is satisfied beyond reasonable doubt that the original has been destroyed.

## C. as regards Dividends (111)

1. That any amount paid up in advance of calls on any share may carry interest but shall not entitle the holder of the share to participate in respect thereof in a dividend subsequently declared.

2. Where power is taken to forfeit unclaimed dividends, that power shall not be exercised until twelve years or more after the date of declaration of the dividend.

## D. as regards Directors (112)

1. Borrowing Powers.—That the Directors shall be under an obligation to restrict the borrowings of the Company and exercise all voting and other rights or powers of control exercisable by the Company in relation to its subsidiary companies (if any) so as to secure (as regards subsidiary companies so far as by such exercise they can secure) that the aggregate amount for the time being remaining undischarged of all moneys borrowed by the Company and/or any of its subsidiaries (exclusive of inter-group borrowings) shall not, except with the consent of the Company in general meeting, exceed an ascertainable amount.

2. That a Director shall not, except as is provided by Table A, Part I, to the Companies Act, 1948, vote on any contract in which he is interested and if he do so vote, his vote shall not be counted.

3. That any person appointed by the Directors to fill a casual vacancy on or as an addition to the Board shall hold office only until the next following Annual General Meeting of the Company, and shall then be eligible for re-election.

4. That, where not otherwise provided by law, the Company in General Meeting shall have power by Ordinary Resolution to remove any Director (including a Managing Director, but without prejudice to any claim for damages under any contract) before the expiration of his period of office.

5. Notice to the Company of the intention to propose a person for election as a Director, and notice to the Company by such person of his willingness to be elected, may be given during a period of at least seven days ending not more than seven days before the date of the meeting appointed for such election.

## E. as regards Accounts (113)

That a printed copy of the Report, accompanied by the Balance Sheet (including every document required by law to be annexed thereto) and Profit and Loss Account or Income and Expenditure Account, shall, at least twenty-one days* previous to the General Meeting, be delivered or sent by post to the registered address of every member, and that four copies of each of these documents shall at the same time be forwarded to the Secretary of the Quotations Department, The Stock Exchange, London, [or, as the case may be, to the appropriate Federated Stock Exchange].

* In the case of a Company registered abroad, this period must be extended to such a time as will enable the members who have a registered address within the United Kingdom to be represented at the Meeting at which the accounts are considered.

*F. as regards Rights*          (114)

1. That adequare voting rights are in appropriate circumstances secured to Preference Shareholders.

2. That the quorum for a separate class meeting (other than an adjourned meeting) to consider a variation of the rights of any class of shares shall be the holders of at least one third of the issued shares of the class.

*G. as regards Investment Trusts*          (115)

Where it is desired that the securities of the Company be included in the "Investment Trusts" section of the Official List, that all moneys realised on the sale or other realisation of any capital assets in excess of book value and all other moneys in the nature of accretion to capital shall not be treated as profits available for dividend.

*H. as regards Notices*          (116)

1. That where power is taken to give notice by advertisement such advertisement shall be inserted in at least one leading London daily newspaper.

2. That a Company incorporated outside the United Kingdom shall give notice sufficient to enable members, whose registered addresses are within the United Kingdom, to exercise their rights or comply with the terms of the notice.

3. That where it is provided that notices will be given only to those members whose registered addresses are within the United Kingdom, any member, whose registered address is not within the United Kingdom, may name an address within the United Kingdom which, for the purposes of notice, shall be considered as his registered address.

*I. as regards Redeemable Shares*          (117)

That, where power is reserved to purchase for redemption a redeemable share:

(*a*) Purchases not made through the market or by tender shall be limited to a maximum price.
(*b*) If purchases are by tender, tenders shall be available to all shareholders alike.

*J. as regards Capital Structure*          (118)

That the structure of the share capital of the Company be stated and where the capital consists of more than one class of security it must also be stated how the various classes shall rank for any distribution by way of dividend or otherwise.

*K. as regards Non-Voting or Restricted Voting Shares*          (119)

1. That, where the capital of the Company includes shares which do not carry voting rights, the words "non-voting" must appear in the designation of such shares.

2. That, where the equity capital includes shares with different voting rights, the designation of each class of shares, other than those

with the most favourable voting rights, must include the words "restricted voting" or "limited voting."

*L. as regards Proxies*                                          (120)

1. That where provision is made in the Articles as to the form of proxy this must be so worded as not to preclude the use of the two-way form.

2. That a Corporation may execute a form of proxy under the hand of a duly authorised officer.

## SCHEDULE VII

### PART B

*Trust Deeds or other documents securing or constituting Loan Capital*

[The relevant sections have been omitted from this book. Obtainable from the Share and Loan Department of the Stock Exchange.]

## SCHEDULE VII

### PART C

*Preliminary Profits Announcements*

In the absence of any special circumstances the following minimum information should be included when preliminary announcements in respect of any year, half-year or other accounting period or part thereof are made in relation to:

1. *A Holding Company* (*within the meaning of the Companies Act*, 1948)   (128)

(*a*) Group profit (or loss) after all charges including taxation.

(*b*) United Kingdom and, where material, overseas taxation charged in arriving at (*a*).

(*c*) Amount of (*a*) attributable to members of Holding Company, *i.e.* after deduction of outside interests.

(*d*) If material, extent to which (*a*) has been affected by special credits (including transfers from reserves) and/or debits.

(*e*) Rates of dividend(s) of Holding Company paid and proposed and amount absorbed thereby.

(*f*) Comparative figures of (*a*) to (*e*) inclusive for the corresponding previous period.

(*g*) Any supplementary information which in the opinion of the Directors is necessary for a reasonable appreciation of the results or of other material changes in the aggregate of the balances on profit and loss account and other reserves of the Group.

2. *A Company which is not a Holding Company*                    (129)

(*a*) Profit (or loss) after all charges including taxation.

(*b*) United Kingdom and, where material, overseas taxation charged in arriving at (*a*).

(*c*) If material, extent to which (*a*) has been affected by special credits (including transfers from reserves) and/or debits.

(*d*) Rates of dividend(s) paid and proposed and amount absorbed thereby.

(*e*) Comparative figures of (*a*) to (*d*) inclusive for the corresponding previous period.

(*f*) Any supplementary information which in the opinion of the Directors is necessary for a reasonable appreciation of the results of the year or of other material changes in the aggregate of the balance on profit and loss account and other reserves.

*Note 1.*—Where in the opinion of the Directors of a Holding Company the amounts involved in respect of one or more subsidiary companies are insignificant, they need not be included in preliminary announcements, and where the Directors are of such an opinion in respect of each of the subsidiary companies, the information contained in preliminary announcements may be restricted to that requested in 2 above.

*Note 2.*—Figures which are provisional or subject to audit should be so qualified.

## SCHEDULE VIII

### PART A

#### General Undertaking (Companies)

1. To notify the Department without delay of the date of the board (130) meeting at which the declaration or recommendation of a dividend will be considered, or at which any announcement of the profits or losses in respect of any financial period or part thereof will be approved for publication.

2. To notify the Department by telex, telegram, telephone or letter (131) immediately after the relevant board meeting has been held:

(*a*) of all dividends and/or cash bonuses recommended or declared or the decision to pass any dividend or interest payment;

(*b*) of the preliminary profits announcements for the year and half year required by Schedule VII Part C;

(*c*) of short particulars of any proposed cash issue of shares or other securities or any proposed change in the capital structure. (Note: Announcement of a new issue may be delayed to avoid prejudicing underwriting.)

3. To notify the Department without delay: (132)

(*a*) of such particulars of any acquisitions or realisations of assets as are prescribed in the Acquisitions Memorandum issued in September, 1968;

(*b*) of any information required to be disclosed to the Stock Exchange under the provisions of The City Code on Take-overs and Mergers;

(*c*) of any changes in the directorate; (Note: In the case of the appointment of a director (other than a director of another company part of whose share or loan capital is already quoted) that director must submit a declaration in conformity with the Rules and Regulations of The Stock Exchange.)

(*d*) of any proposed change in the general character or nature of the business of the company or of the group or any change in voting control or in beneficial ownership of the securities carrying voting control;

(*e*) of any extension of time granted for the currency of temporary documents;

(*f*) of intention to make a drawing of any redeemable securities, intimating at the same time the amount and date of the drawing and, in the case of a registered security, the period of the closing of the transfer books (or the date of the striking of the balance) for the drawing;

(*g*) of the amount of the security outstanding after any purchase or drawing has been made;

(*h*) of any other information necessary to enable the shareholders to appraise the position of the company and to avoid the establishment of a false market in the securities.

4. To forward to the Department four copies of: (133)

(*a*) Proofs for approval (through the company's brokers), of all circulars to holders of securities, notices of meetings (other than those relating to routine business of the annual general meeting), forms of proxy and notices by advertisement to holders of bearer securities;

(*b*) all circulars, notices, reports or other documents at the same time as they are issued to holders of securities;

(*c*) all resolutions passed by the company other than resolutions passed at an annual general meeting for the purpose of adopting the report and accounts, declaring dividends and re-electing directors and Auditors.

5. To circularise to the holders of securities, not later than six (134) months from the date of the notice calling the annual general meeting of the company, a half-yearly interim report containing similar information to that required in Schedule VII, Part C (see Note (iv)).

6. To include in or circulate with each annual directors' report and (135) audited accounts or chairman's statement:

(*a*) (1) A description of the operations carried on by the company or, if the company has subsidiaries, the group.

(2) If the company or, as the case may be, the group carries on widely differing operations, a statement showing the contributions * of such respective differing operations to its trading results.

(3) If the company or, as the case may be, the group trades outside the United Kingdom, a statement showing a geographical analysis * of its trading operations.

(*b*) If the company has subsidiaries (See Notes (ii) and (iii)), a list giving for each:

(1) its name and country of operations;

(2) the percentage of its equity capital attributable to the company's interest (direct and/or indirect).

(*c*) If the company or, as the case may be, the group has interests in associated companies (see Notes (i) and (ii)), a list giving for each:

(1) its name and country of operation;

(2) particulars of its issued share and loan capital and the total amount of its reserves;

(3) the percentage of each class of share and loan capital attributable to the company's interest (direct and/or indirect).

* Figures or percentages.

(*d*) A statement of persons holding or beneficially interested in any substantial part of the share capital of the company and the amounts of the holdings in question together with particulars of the interests of each director (and also, so far as he is aware of or can by reasonable inquiry ascertain the same, of his family interests) in the share capital of the company and, otherwise than through the company, any of its subsidiaries, distinguishing between beneficial and other interests; the expression "family interests" includes, in relation to a directors, spouse, children under 21 years of age, trusts of which the director or spouse is a settler or trustee and in which the director or spouse or any of such children are beneficiaries or discretionary objects and companies known to him to be controlled by him and/or spouse and/or such children and/or the trustees of any such trusts as aforesaid in their capacity as such trustees. Subject to the necessity to distinguish between beneficial and other interests, between the company and each subsidiary and between each class of capital each director's interests may be aggregated with those of his family interests (see Note (vi)).

(*e*) Particulars of any arrangement whereunder any director has waived or agreed to waive any emoluments.

7. (*a*) To prepare and make available for inspection at the registered (136) office or transfer office during the usual business hours on any week-day (Saturdays and public holidays excluded) from the date of the notice convening the annual general meeting until the date of the meeting and to make available for inspection at the place of meeting for at least 15 minutes prior to the meeting and during the meeting:

(1) a statement, made up to a date not more than one month prior to the date on which it is made available for inspection, for the period from the end of that covered by the last previous state-ment (or, in the case of the first such statement, for not less than 12 months) of all transactions (including put or call options, whether or not exercised) of each director (and also, so far as he is aware of or can by reasonable inquiry ascertain the same, of his family interests) in each class of the equity share capital of the company and any of its subsidiaries since the end of the period covered by the last published statement of such transactions, or during the previous twelve months if no such published statement has been issued; the expression "family interests" includes, in relation to a director, spouse, children under 21 years of age, trusts of which the director or spouse is a settler or trustee and in which the director or spouse or any of such children are bene-ficiaries or discretionary objects and companies known to him to be controlled by him and/or spouse and/or such children and/or the trustees of any such trusts as aforesaid in their capacity as such trustees. The word "director" includes a person who was a director at any time during the relevant period but the information required shall not extend to transactions at a time when he was not a director (see Note (vii));

(2) copies of all contracts of service unless expiring, or deter-minable by the employing company without payment of com-pensation, within one year, of any director of the company with the company or any of its subsidiaries and, where any such con-tract is not reduced to writing, a memorandum of the terms thereof (see Note (viii)).

(*b*) To state in or by way of note to the notice convening the annual general meeting or any accompanying circular letter, that the said statement or summary of transactions and copies or, as the case may be, memoranda of the said contracts of service will be available for inspection as aforesaid and if there are no such contracts to state that fact.

8. To insert in the press a notice showing the basis of allotment in prospectus and other offers, and, if applicable, excess shares, such notice to appear not later than the morning after the allotment letters were posted. (137)

9. To certify transfers against definitive certificates or temporary documents and to return them on the day of receipt or (should that not be a business day) on the first business day following their receipt and to split and return renounceable documents within the same period (see Note (v)). (138)

10. To register transfers and other documents without payment of any fee (see Note (v)). (139)

11. To issue, without charge, definitive certificates within: (140)

(*a*) one month of the date of expiration of any right of renunciation;
(*b*) 14 days of the lodgment of transfers (see Note (v)).

12. If requested by holders of securities, to arrange for designated accounts (see Note (v)). (141)

13. Where power has been taken under the articles to issue share warrants to bearer: (i) to issue such warrants in exchange for registered shares within fourteen days of the deposit of the share certificates; and (ii) to certify transfers against the deposit of share warrants to bearer. (142)

14. To send out with the notice convening a meeting to all shareholders and debenture holders entitled to vote thereat proxy forms with provision for two-way voting on all resolutions intended to be proposed (other than resolutions relating to the procedure of the meeting or to the remuneration of the auditors). (142a)

15. In the absence of circumstances which have been agreed by the Committee to be exceptional to obtain the consent of equity shareholders in general meeting prior to issuing for cash to other than the equity shareholders of the company: (143)

(i) equity capital or capital having an equity element,
(ii) securities convertible into equity capital, and
(iii) warrants or options to subscribe for equity capital.

16. In the event of a circular being issued to the holders of any particular class of security, to issue a copy or summary of such circular to the holders of all other quoted securities unless the contents of such circular are irrelevant to such other holders. (144)

*NOTES*

(i) For the purpose of this Undertaking "associated company" means a company which is not a subsidiary but in which 25 per cent. or more of the equity is held by the company or, if the company has subsidiaries, by the group companies collectively (*i.e.* before excluding any proportion attributable to interests of outside shareholders in the subsidiaries).

(ii) The particulars required in paragraphs 6 (*b*) and 6 (*c*) in relation to subsidiaries and associated companies need not be given for any such company which is dormant or is not material. For this purpose a subsidiary or associated company should be considered material if

(*a*) the total investment in it normally represents more than 5 per cent. of the assets of the company or, as the case may be, of the group;

OR

(*b*) the interest in its profit or loss normally represents an amount which is more than 5 per cent. of the profit or loss shown by the accounts of the company or, as the case may be, of the group.

(iii) Under circumstances to be adjudicated by the Committee the particulars required in paragraph 6 (*b*) in relation to subsidiaries may be omitted for non-trading subsidiary holding companies.

(iv) As an alternative to circularisation interim reports may be inserted as paid advertisements in at least two leading daily newspapers.

(v) If the company does not maintain its own registration department, appropriate arrangements must be made with the registrars to ensure compliance with the provisions of paragraphs 9, 10, 11 and 12.

(vi) A relaxation of the requirement contained in paragraph 6 (*d*) will be allowed in those cases where the size of the interests of all the directors of a company and their family interests is, in the aggregate, very small. Accordingly, in those cases where the interests of all the directors of a company and their family interests do not, in the aggregate, exceed 5 per cent. in respect of either share capital or voting control or, in the case of a group, 5 per cent. of the parent company or of any one subsidiary, a statement to that effect will be acceptable in place of the particulars otherwise required.

(vii) If, in the case of a company to which the Companies Act 1967 applies, the directors are satisfied that there are no transactions required to be disclosed under paragraph 7 (*a*) (1) which are not required to be disclosed under the Act, it will be sufficient if reference is made in the annual report to the fact that the register kept under the Act is open for inspection at the annual general meeting.

(viii) In cases where the exhibition of contracts of service required by paragraph 7 (*a*) (2) presents difficulties, particularly where one contract covers both directors and executive officers, the Committee will be prepared to accept the exhibition of a memorandum of the terms of such contract as regards directors.

## SCHEDULE VIII

### PART B

*General Undertaking (Governments, etc.)*

[The relevant sections have been omitted from this book. Obtainable from the Share and Loan Department of The Stock Exchange.]

## SCHEDULE IX

### Marketing Statement (Placings)

1. Name of Company .............................................................

2. Description of Security.......................................................

3. Total amount involved in marketing operation ....................

at ...............................................................................................

4. State how allocated, whether subject to quotation or not, and at what price, e.g.,

Retained at issuing House (if any) .........................................

Placed with Issuing House's Clients .......................................

at ...............................................................................................

Retained by Broker .............................................................

Placed with Broker's Clients...................................................

at ...............................................................................................

Placed with Members of other Federated Exchanges ..................

at ...............................................................................................

Placed with Market*...............................................................

at ...............................................................................................

                                                    Total

5. State how allocated by Market and at what price to:

Broker applying for quotation................................................

at ...............................................................................................

Other Brokers.........................................................................

at ...............................................................................................

Retained by Market for free dealings at opening of the Market

.................................................................................................

6. Description of pooling arrangements, if any .......................

7. Expected "opening price" when free dealings commence (i.e.,

apart from all placing arrangements) ......................................

8. Details of proposed orders to repurchase at opening of Market

.................................................................................................

* If applicable, show separate figures for first and second tranches of fixed income securities.

9. Details of further selling limits and whether left firm with Market

...................................................................................................

10. General statement that these arrangements have been completed and no other arrangements at other prices have been made

...................................................................................................

11. Details of any other circumstances attending this placing which the Committee should know before giving their decision with regard to granting of quotation ...................................................

...................................................................................................

(See question 4)

Name of Jobber(s) .......................... Amount* ....................

            .........................            ....................

            .........................            ....................

                       .......................... Brokers.

                       Dated ........................ 19...

## CHARGES FOR QUOTATION ON THE STOCK EXCHANGE, LONDON

*Initial Charges*

(No fee is charged for applications for conversion into stock units, unnumbering, or applications arising out of change of name, denomination, dividend rights, or exercise of conversion or option rights.)

1. For securities to be quoted in the following sections of the Official List:

British Funds.
Corporation and County Stocks—Great Britain and Northern Ireland.
Public Boards, etc.—Great Britain and Northern Ireland.
Commonwealth Government and Provincial Securities.
Commonwealth Corporation Stocks.

(*a*) Having a life of five years or less     ...     ...    Nil
(*b*) Having a life of over five years:

| | | | | |
|---|---|---|---|---|
| Money value not exceeding | £1,000,000 | ... | 200 | guineas. |
| ,, | ,, | £10,000,000 | ... | 500 ,, |
| ,, | ,, | £50,000,000 | ... | 750 ,, |
| ,, | ,, | £100,000,000 | ... | 1,000 ,, |
| ,, | exceeding | £100,000,000 | ... | 1,500 ,, |

2. For securities to be quoted in sections of the Official List other than those referred to in paragraph 1 above involving a money value of not more than £100,000:

| | | | | |
|---|---|---|---|---|
| Up to £4,999 | ... | ... | ... | Nil |
| £5,000 to £19,999 ... | ... | ... | 10 guineas. |
| £20,000 to £49,999 | ... | ... | 25 ,, |
| £50,000 to £100,000 | ... | ... | 50 ,, |

3. For securities to be quoted in sections of the Official List other than those referred to in paragraph 1 above involving a money value in excess of £100,000:

* If applicable, show separate figures for first and second tranches fixed income securities.

(*a*) Category I. Prospectuses, Offers for Sale, Placings, Introductions, Rights, Open offers, Reconstructions and vendor consideration issues. Quotation Charges are in accordance with the following scale:

| Money value not exceeding | £200,000 | ... | 100 guineas. |
|---|---|---|---|
| ,, ,, | £400,000 | ... | 200 ,, |
| ,, ,, | £600,000 | ... | 300 ,, |
| ,, ,, | £800,000 | ... | 400 ,, |
| ,, ,, | £1,000,000 | ... | 500 ,, |
| ,, ,, | £2,500,000 | ... | 750 ,, |
| ,, ,, | £5,000,000 | ... | 1,000 ,, |
| ,, ,, | £10,000,000 | ... | 1,500 ,, |
| ,, ,, | £20,000,000 | ... | 2,000 ,, |
| ,, ,, | £30,000,000 | ... | 2,500 ,, |
| ,, ,, | £50,000,000 | ... | 3,500 ,, |
| ,, ,, | £75,000,000 | ... | 4,500 ,, |
| ,, exceeding | £75,000,000 | ... | 5,000 ,, |

(*b*) Category II. Capitalisations, Conversions and further issues of identical securities not included in Category I. Quotation charges are half the scale for Category I.

### Notes

*Note 1.*—In the case of a joint application for quotation in London and on one or more other Federated Exchanges, the initial London charge will be reduced by 12½ per cent or the total of the initial fees charged by the other Federated Exchanges whichever is the less.

*Note 2.*—Where the money value of an issue is in doubt it will be fixed by the Committee for the purposes of the Schedule.

### Annual Charges

Except in the case of a security quoted in the sections of the Official List referred to in paragraph 1, a quotation charge for each company, Corporation or Authority of 100 guineas per annum.

## CHARGES FOR QUOTATION ON THE BELFAST, MIDLANDS & WESTERN, NORTHERN AND SCOTTISH STOCK EXCHANGES

### (*Charges are in guineas*)

BRITISH FUNDS, CORPN. & COUNTY STOCKS, G.B. & N.I., PUBLIC BOARDS, ETC., G.B. & N.I., COMMONWEALTH GOVT. & PROVINCIAL SECS., COMMONWEALTH CORPN. STOCKS, HAVING A LIFE OF OVER FIVE YEARS

| Money Value | Total fee divided equally between whichever of the Belfast, Midlands, Northern and/or Scottish Exchanges are involved |
|---|---|
| Not exceeding £1,000,000 ... ... | 25 |
| Not exceeding £10,000,000 ... ... | 62½ |
| Not exceeding £50,000,000 ... ... | 93¾ |
| Not exceeding £100,000,000 ... ... | 125 |
| Exceeding £100,000,000 ... ... | 187½ |

EE

## ALL OTHER SECURITIES

|  |  |  | Where application is made simultaneously to The Stock Exchange, London, and | | | |
|---|---|---|---|---|---|---|
| Money Value | Belfast, Midlands, Northern or Scottish only | Two or more of these Exchanges (each) | either Belfast, Dublin, Midlands, Northern or Scottish | any two of these Exchanges (each) | any three of these Exchanges (each) | any four or all of these Exchanges (each) |
| Up to £4,999 ... ... | 5 | 5 | Nil | Nil | Nil | Nil |
| £5,000 to £19,999 ... | 5 | 5 | $2\frac{1}{2}$ | 2 | $1\frac{1}{2}$ | $1\frac{1}{2}$ |
| £20,000 to £49,999 ... | $12\frac{1}{2}$ | $7\frac{1}{2}$ | $6\frac{1}{2}$ | 5 | $3\frac{3}{4}$ | $3\frac{3}{4}$ |
| £50,000 to £100,000 ... | 25 | 15 | $12\frac{1}{2}$ | 10 | $7\frac{1}{2}$ | $7\frac{1}{2}$ |
| *Not exceeding £200,000 | 50 | 30 | 25 | 20 | 15 | 15 |
| *Not exceeding £400,000 | 100 | 60 | 50 | 40 | 30 | 30 |
| *Not exceeding £600,000 | 150 | 90 | 75 | 60 | 45 | 45 |
| *Not exceeding £800,000 | 200 | 120 | 100 | 80 | 60 | 60 |
| *Not exceeding £1,000,000 | 250 | 150 | 125 | 100 | 75 | 75 |
| *Not exceeding £2,500,000 | 375 | 225 | $187\frac{1}{2}$ | 150 | $112\frac{1}{2}$ | $112\frac{1}{2}$ |
| *Not exceeding £5,000,000 | 500 | 300 | 250 | 200 | 150 | 150 |
| *Not exceeding £10,000,000 | 750 | 450 | 375 | 300 | 225 | 225 |
| *Not exceeding £20,000,000 | 800 | 600 | 500 | 400 | 300 | 300 |
| *Not exceeding £30,000,000 | 800 | 750 | 625 | 500 | 375 | 375 |
| *Not exceeding £50,000,000 | 800 | 800 | 875 | 700 | 525 | 525 |
| *Not exceeding £75,000,000 | 800 | 800 | 1,125 | 900 | 675 | 675 |
| *Exceeding £75,000,000 | 800 | 800 | 1,250 | 1,000 | 750 | 770 |

\* Capitalisations and Conversions (money value in excess of £100,000) Charges are one-half of above scale.

## CHARGES FOR QUOTATION ON THE DUBLIN STOCK EXCHANGE

Issue up to £200,000 money value ... ... ... ... ... £100
Issues over £200,000 and up to £300,000 money value ... ... £150
   ,,     £300,000 and up to £400,000 money value ... ... £200
   ,,     £400,000 and up to £600,000 money value ... ... £250
   ,,     £600,000 and up to £800,000 money value ... ... £300
   ,,     £800,000 and up to £1,000,000 money value ... ... £350
   ,,     £1,000,000 money value ... ... ... ... ... £400

For  (a) Issues on behalf of a Corporation or Public Board, or of Securities guaranteed by the Government, and
     (b) further issues of identical securities and for issues by way of Capitalisation, Rights, Conversion or Reconstruction,

charges are one-half of the above scale.

No fee is charged for Securities quoted under "Government Funds."

In the case of applications for the Quotation of Securities, other than those to be quoted solely in Dublin, the scale of Fees shall be in accordance with the scale for "All Other Securities" above.

### Annual Charge

In addition to the above Fees, each Company obtaining a quotation shall pay an Annual Quotation Charge of 50 guineas, but such charge shall not apply when an Annual Charge is payable to another Federated Exchange. Such charge is payable on 1st July each year.

## *CHARGES FOR QUOTATION ON THE CORK STOCK EXCHANGE*

| | |
|---|---|
| Issues up to £100,000 money value ... ... ... ... | 25 guineas |
| Issues over £100,000 and up to £150,000 money value ... | 50 ,, |
| ,, £150,000 and up to £200,000 money value ... | 75 ,, |
| ,, £200,000 and up to £250,000 money value ... | 100 ,, |
| ,, £250,000 and up to £300,000 money value ... | 125 ,, |
| ,, £300,000 money value ... ... ... ... | 150 ,, |

For (a) issues on behalf of a Corporation or Public Board or of securities guaranteed by the Government, and
   (b) further issues of identical securities and for issues by way of Capitalisation, Rights, Conversion, Reconstruction or Acquisition,
charges are one-half of the above scale.

No fee is charged for Securities quoted under "Government Funds."

## *CHARGES FOR QUOTATION ON THE PROVINCIAL BROKERS STOCK EXCHANGE*

| | |
|---|---|
| New Issues ... ... ... | 10 guineas irrespective of size of issue. |
| Further Issues ... ... ... | At discretion. |

# APPENDIX V

## ACCOUNTANT'S MEMORANDUM:* REPORTS BY ACCOUNTANTS WITH RESPECT TO PROFITS, ASSETS AND LIABILITIES FOR PURPOSES OF PROSPECTUSES, OFFERS FOR SALE, ADVERTISED STATEMENTS AND CIRCULARS

### REQUIREMENTS

1. The Appendix requires *inter alia* that all prospectuses (the document) should include a report by the auditors of the company, with respect to:

(*a*) its profits or losses in respect of each of the ten completed financial years immediately preceding the issue of the document, or, if it has been incorporated less than ten years, in respect of each of the years since its incorporation, and stating the charge for depreciation for each year reported on (see paragraph 12);

(*b*) its assets and liabilities;

(*c*) the aggregate emolument of its directors during the last year and a comparison with the amount payable under the arrangements in force at the date of the document; and

(*d*) such other matters which appear to the auditors to be relevant. "Prospectus" is defined in the Introduction to the Appendix and includes circulars relating to material acquisitions by a company.

*(Appendix Serial 37.)*

Where any such report is made jointly by the auditors and another firm of qualified accountants, such accountants should be independent as described in paragraph 2 below.

A report which contained any significant qualification or reservation as to any of the profits or losses reported upon or as to the assets and liabilities would not be regarded by the Department as acceptable.

There should be included, where appropriate, an explanation of the trend of profits as shown in the accountants' report; dealing in particular with the effects of changes in the financing of the company, borrowings and the structure of the share capital, and of the acquisition of subsidiaries, etc.

2. A similar report by qualified accountants has to be furnished with respect to the profits, assets and liabilities, etc. (but not directors' emoluments) of a business being acquired or of a company being acquired which will then become a subsidiary and no part of whose securities are already quoted. If the business or new subsidiary has not been in existence for ten years the period is restricted accordingly. *(Appendix Serials 38 and 65.)*

The accountants should be independent both of the company and of any other company concerned to the same degree as is required of auditors under the Companies Acts (see, for example, paragraph 6 of the Fifth Schedule to the Companies Act 1948 (the Act)).

3. In the case of groups of companies, the requirements envisage a statement of the company's net assets and a statement, usually in consolidated form, of profits and losses and assets and liabilities of the group.

---

* References are to the regulations of the Federation of Stock Exchanges (*see* Appendix IV).

4. Where, in view of the materiality of such matters in relation to their report as a whole, the reporting accountants make reference to reports, confirmations or opinions of valuers or other accountants, the names, addresses and professional qualifications of such other persons or firms should be stated in the report.

5. It should be noted that the Council are not normally prepared to grant an initial quotation where the figures reported on are more than nine months old.

### COMPUTATION OF PROFITS

6. Neither the Appendix nor the Act lays down the basis on which profits or losses are to be computed. It is the practice, however, for the accountants to indicate in the report the basis which has been adopted. This normally states that the profits or losses have been arrived at after charging all expenses, after dealing with such items as depreciation, amortisation, directors' remuneration, interest, etc., on defined bases and after making such adjustments as are appropriate.

### STATEMENT OF ADJUSTMENTS

7. Provision is also made in the Appendix for a written statement (the statement of adjustments) signed by the accountants, setting out the adjustments made by them in arriving at the figures shown in their report and giving the reasons therefor, to be available for inspection by the public.

*(Appendix serials 52 and 78.)*

### METHOD OF SETTING OUT THE STATEMENT OF ADJUSTMENTS

8. In order that the Department can obtain what is required in sufficient detail and on a reasonably uniform basis, the statement of adjustments as regards profits and losses should be divided into two sections as follows:

SECTION "A"

This section should begin with the net increase or decrease in the balance at credit or debit of profit and loss account shown by comparison of the balance sheets at the beginning and end of each of the financial periods under review; the net increase or decrease in the balance on profit and loss account for each of the last two years should normally be capable of ascertainment from the accounts which are required to be made available for inspection under serials 52 and 78 of the Appendix. There should then be shown and added to or deducted from this amount:

(i) The items which are required by the Act to be stated separately in the profit and loss account, notes being included to disclose any further information required by the Act to be disclosed by way of note to the profit and loss account.

(ii) Interest charges, analysed under appropriate headings, in addition to those payable on debentures and other fixed loans (which are covered by item (i) above).

(iii) Material revenue items which have been dealt with otherwise than through the profit and loss accounts.

The sum finally arrived at in this section would normally be the profit or loss for the year before taking account of interest and of items which the Act requires in any event to be stated separately:

SECTION "B"

This section should commence with the final figure of profit or loss shown in Section "A" and should show in detail the adjustments made thereto in arriving at the profits or losses shown in the accountant's report and giving the reasons therefor.

9. As regards assets and liabilities, if the final total amount of the net assets in the report differs from the total amount of net assets dealt with in the latest audited balance sheet, and the relevant adjustments are not set out in the report, a statement should be submitted showing the adjustments made and reconciling these totals.

### STATEMENTS OF ADJUSTMENTS OF HOLDING COMPANIES

10. If the company is a holding company, the statements of adjustments may deal with the consolidated figures of the company and of its subsidiaries or with the figures of the separate companies or groups of companies comprising the holding company and its subsidiaries. In the latter case, a summary combining the figures so as to arrive at those shown in the accountants' report should be submitted.

### SUBMISSION OF STATEMENTS OF ADJUSTMENTS TO THE DEPARTMENT

11. The statement of adjustments, a draft of which must be submitted *at least ten days* prior to the date on which it is proposed to publish the document, should be accompanied by a letter from the accountants to the Department which should confirm that all adjustments which are appropriate for the purposes of the report have been made to the profits and losses (in respect of each year under review) and to the net assets and that no other adjustments have been made.

### DEPRECIATION

12. The report, and the statement of adjustments, should state the amount of the charge, in each period reported upon, for amortisation, depreciation and obsolescence. The Department will consider some adaptation of this requirement in cases which involve complex multi-column statements.

If the circumstances appear to warrant it, the Department may ask for information about the basis on which the charges for depreciation have been calculated and, in special cases, for the inclusion of an appropriate explanatory statement in the report.

### LETTER TO BE SUBMITTED TO THE DEPARTMENT CONCERNING CERTAIN ACCOUNTING MATTERS

13. There should be submitted to the Department by the accountants a letter confirming the following three matters:

(i) *Stocks and Work in Progress*

That, save as indicated in their report, they have obtained sufficient information about the stocktakings and have examined sufficient records and other evidence to enable them to form the opinion that throughout the period under review stocks and work in progress were properly ascertained and, in arriving at the reported profits and losses, were brought into account on bases in accordance with generally accepted accounting principles which were applied consistently.

(ii) *Depreciation and Amortisation*

That they have satisfied themselves that the provisions for depreciation and amortisation charged in arriving at the reported profits and losses, considered in conjunction with any qualifications or notes included in their report are in their opinion reasonable having regard, *inter alia*, to:

(*a*) assets in respect of which it has been or will be the company's practice to make no provisions for depreciation or amortisation (which policy would require to be referred to in their report) and

(*b*) any revaluation of fixed assets either already incorporated into the company's accounts or to be incorporated therein.

### (iii) *Equalisation of Taxation*

That the net book value of the fixed assets appearing in the report in respect of which depreciation and/or amortisation will require to be provided out of future profits does not exceed by a material amount the corresponding amounts on which capital allowances will be obtained for taxation purposes, or, in the event of there being a material difference, how this has been taken into account, unless it is apparent from the document (*e.g.* by setting up a tax equalisation account which is deducted in arriving at the net assets or by including a suitable explanation in the accountants' report or elsewhere in the prospectus and making an appropriate adjustment for the non-allowable proportion of depreciation in computing the tax payable on the profit figures included in any forecast future profits).

### PERIOD COVERED BY THE REPORT

14. Although the report is required to deal with the profits or losses of each of the preceding ten financial years, application may be made to cover a shorter period where it is considered that inclusion of the earlier years may be irrelevant or misleading.

### OVERSEAS INTERESTS

15. Where a material proportion of the profits arises overseas or a material proportion of the assets are situated overseas, the report or the document should give the best practicable indication of the amount and situation or source of such assets and profits. In the case of businesses with overseas interests, the basis on which overseas currencies and overseas taxation have been dealt with should, if the accounting treatment of these matters is material, be set out in the report.

The Department would also normally require the document to contain an adequate explanation with regard to any restrictions affecting the remittance of profits or repatriation of capital from the countries concerned.

### LONG-TERM HIRE OF PLANT

16. Where contracts exist for the hire of plant to the company for a period of over one year which are substantial in relation to the company's business, details should be supplied to the Department, who may require details to be disclosed in the document.

### DIRECTORS' EMOLUMENTS

17. The Appendix requires the accountants to deal in their report with the aggregate emoluments of the directors of the company for whose securities a quotation is sought. The exact comparison to be given must depend on the circumstances of each case and the comparison should normally deal with the emoluments of any person who is a director at the time of the report. The emoluments for this purpose should follow the definition contained in section 196 of the Act.

## ADDITIONAL INFORMATION

18. For certain types of company the Department may require information to be given in the document additional to that which is normally provided. Examples would be:

(*a*) Building contracting and similar companies engaged in carrying out contracts of a long term nature, where these form a substantial proportion of the business. In such cases the method of taking credit for profits and of arriving at the amounts at which stocks and work in progress were brought into account should be defined in the document.

In such cases the Department would require the letter from the accountants to state also that in their opinion the methods used are in accordance with generally accepted accounting principles which have been consistently applied.

(*b*) Hire purchase finance companies where the methods of valuing debts and taking credit for profits should be defined in the document. In such cases the Department would require the letter from the accountants also to confirm that the valuation of hire purchase debts and the method of taking credit for profits have been on bases which in their opinion are in accordance with generally accepted accounting principles which have been consistently applied.

## GENERAL

*It is emphasised that neither the Appendix nor this Memorandum are exhaustive and that further information may be required, or the required information varied by the Department where it is deemed to be relevant. In cases of doubt the accountants should consult the Department through the company's brokers, in consultation with the issuing house, where one is concerned.*

# APPENDIX VI

## THE CITY CODE ON TAKE-OVERS AND MERGERS
### (Abridged)*

### INTRODUCTION

The City Code on Take-overs and Mergers first appeared in its present form in March 1968. It was prepared and issued by the City Working Party, a body originally set up in 1959 and reconvened by the Governor of the Bank of England in 1967 for that purpose. On it are now represented the Issuing Houses Association, the Accepting Houses Committee, The Association of Investment Trust Companies, the British Insurance Association, The Committee of London Clearing Bankers, the Confederation of British Industry, the National Association of Pension Funds and The Stock Exchange, London. This new edition incorporates a limited number of revisions and additions made by the City Working Party in the light of experience gained in its operation since that date. Certain of these modifications are the result of suggestions made by the Panel on Take-overs and Mergers established in September 1967 on the proposal of the Governor to supervise the operation of the Code. The Code, nevertheless, both as to its principles and rules, remains substantially in the form in which it was originally issued.

### THE PANEL ON TAKE-OVERS AND MERGERS

The Panel referred to in the Introduction is now situated at the Bank of England Building, New Change, London, E.C.4, and communications intended for it should be addressed to The Secretary of the Panel on Take-overs and Mergers at that address.

### GENERAL PRINCIPLE

It is considered to be impracticable to devise rules in such detail as to cover all the various circumstances which arise in take-over or merger transactions. *Accordingly, persons engaged in such transactions should be aware that the spirit as well as the precise wording of these general principles and of the ensuing rules must be observed.*

### RULES

*The Approach*

1. The offer should be put forward in the first instance to the Board of the offeree company or to its advisers.

2. If the offer or an approach with a view to an offer being made is not made by a principal, the identity of the principal must be disclosed at the outset.

3. A Board so approached is entitled to be satisfied that the offeror company is or will be in a position to implement the offer in full.

4. Where an offer is being made by a parent company for minority shareholdings of a subsidiary, or in any other case where the offer is not completely at arm's length, it is essential that competent outside advice be obtained in order to ensure, and to satisfy the offerees, that their interests are fully protected.

---

* Readers wishing to have full details of the provisions may obtain copies of *The City Code* from The Secretary of the Issuing Houses Association.

*Early Stages*

5. When any firm intention to make an offer is notified to a Board from a serious source (irrespective of whether the Board views the offer favourably or otherwise), shareholders must be informed without delay by Press notice. The Press notice should normally be followed as soon as possible by a circular.

Where there have been approaches which may or may not lead to an offer, the duty of a Board in relation to shareholders is less clearly defined. There are obvious dangers in announcing prematurely an approach which may not lead to an offer. By way of guidance it can be said that an announcement of the facts should be made forthwith as soon as two companies are agreed on the basic terms of an offer and are reasonably confident of a successful outcome of the negotiations.

In any situation which might lead to an offer being made, whether welcome or not, a close watch should be kept on the share market; in the event of any untoward movement in share prices an immediate announcement, accompanied by such comment as may be appropriate, should be made.

6. Joint statements are desirable whenever possible, provided that agreement thereon does not lead to undue delay. The obligation to make announcements lies no less with the potential offeror company than with the offeree company.

7. The vital importance of absolute secrecy before an announcement must be emphasised.

8. When an offer is announced, the identity of the offeror company must be disclosed and that company must disclose any existing holding in the offeree company which it owns or over which it has control.

*Board Consideration of an Offer*

9. Directors must always have in mind that they should act in the interests of the shareholders taken as a whole. Shareholders in companies which are effectively controlled by their Directors have to accept that in respect of any offer the attitude of their Board is decisive. Exceptionally, there may be good reasons for such a Board preferring a lower offer or rejecting an offer. Nevertheless, where a Board recommends acceptance of the lower of two offers, or, being a controlling Board, accepts such lower offer or rejects an offer, thus in effect frequently forcing the minority shareholders to act similarly, it must very carefully examine its motive for so doing and be prepared to justify its good faith in the interests of the shareholders as a whole.

10. Directors whose shareholdings, together with those of their families and trusts, effectively control a company, or shareholders in that position who are represented on the Board of a company, and who contemplate transferring control, should not, other than in special circumstances, do so unless the buyer undertakes to extend within a reasonable period of time a comparable offer to the holders of the remaining equity share capital, whether such capital carries voting rights or not. In such special circumstances the Panel must be consulted in advance and its consent obtained.

11. Any information including particulars of shareholders given to a preferred suitor should on request be furnished equally and as promptly to a less welcome but *bona fide* potential offeror. In case of difficulty the Panel must be consulted and its consent obtained.

12. It is essential that after an offer has been announced the offer document and a letter setting out the views of the Board of the offeree company should be circulated as soon as practicable.

If any offeror who has announced his intention to make an offer does not proceed with the formal offer within a reasonable time, he must be prepared to justify the circumstances of the case to the Panel.

*Formal Offers, Documents supporting an Offer or recommending the Acceptance or Rejection of an Offer*

13. Any document or advertisement addressed to shareholders under these headings must be treated with the same standards of care with regard to the statements made therein as if it were a prospectus within the meaning of the Companies Act 1948. This applies whether the document or advertisement is issued by the company direct or by an adviser on its behalf. Each document sent to shareholders of the offeree company must state that the Board of the offeror company and/or, where appropriate, of the offeree company (or a Committe of the Board duly authorised by the Board so to act) have considered all statements of fact and opinion contained therein and accept, individually and collectively, responsibility therefor and consider that no material factors or considerations have been omitted.

A copy of the authority from the Board of the company (or the Committee, as the case may be) for the issue of such document must be lodged with the Panel Secretariat.

14. Shareholders must be put into possession of all the facts necessary for the formation of an informed judgement as to the merits or demerits of an offer. Such facts must be accurately and fairly presented and be available to the shareholder early enough to enable him to make a decision in good time. The obligation of the offeror company in these respects towards the shareholders of the offeree company is no less than its obligation towards its own shareholders.

15. Without in any way detracting from the imperative necessity of maintaining the highest standards of accuracy and fair presentation in all communications to shareholders in a take-over or merger transaction, attention is particularly drawn in this connection to profit forecasts and asset valuations.

Notwithstanding the obvious hazard attached to the forecasting of profits, profit forecasts must be compiled with the greatest possible care by the Directors whose sole responsibility they are.

When profit forecasts appear in any document addressed to shareholders in connection with an offer, the assumptions, including the commercial assumptions, upon which the Directors have based their profit forecasts, must be stated in the document.

The accounting bases and calculations for the forecasts must be examined and reported on by the auditors or consultant accountants. Any Merchant Bank or other adviser mentioned in the document must also report on the forecasts. The accountants' report and, if there is an adviser, his report, must be contained in such document and be accompanied by a statement that the accountants and, where relevant, the adviser, have given and not withdrawn their consent to publication.

Wherever profit forecasts appear in relation to a period in which trading has already commenced, the latest unaudited profit figures which are available in respect of the expired portion of that trading period together with comparable figures for the preceding year must be stated. Alternatively, if no figures are available, that fact must be stated.

When revaluations of assets are given in connection with an offer the Board should be supported by the opinion of independent professional experts and the basis of valuation clearly stated.

16. The offer document must state the shareholdings of the offeror company in the offeree company together with the total of the shareholdings in the offeree company in which Directors of the offeror company are interested. The document of the offeree company advising its shareholders on an offer (whether recommending acceptance or rejection of the offer) must (a) detail the shareholdings of (i) the Directors of the offeree company in the offeree company and the offeror company and (ii) the offeree company in the offeror company and (b) inform shareholders whether the Directors of the offeree company intend, in respect of their own beneficial shareholdings, to accept or reject the offer. If any such shareholdings referred to in this Rule have been purchased within six months of the date of the offer document, the details, including dates and costs, must be stated. If no such purchases have been made, this fact must be stated.

17. Where the offer is for cash or includes an element of cash, the offer document must include confirmation by the adviser or by another appropriate independent party that resources are available to the offeror company sufficient to satisfy full acceptance of the offer.

18. Documents sent to shareholders of the offeree company recommending or rejecting offers must contain particulars of all service contracts in force for Directors with the offeree company or any of its subsidiaries which have more than twelve months to run and, if entered into within six months of the date of the document, the dates of the contracts and particulars of any immediately preceding contracts. Offer documents on behalf of the offeror company should state whether its Directors' emoluments will be affected by the acquisition of the offeree company.

19. In order to facilitate the work of the Panel, copies of all public announcements made and all documents bearing on a take-over or merger transaction must be lodged with the Panel Secretariat at the same time as they are made or despatched.

*Mechanics of the Formal Offer*

20. No offer for the whole of the equity share capital of a company (or for a proportion of such equity capital which, if accepted in full, would result in the offeror company having voting control of the equity share capital of the offeree company) shall be made unless it is a condition of such offer that the offer will not become or be declared unconditional unless the offeror company has acquired or agreed to acquire (either pursuant to the offer or by shares acquired or agreed to be acquired before or during the offer) by the close of the offer shares carrying over 50 per cent. of the voting rights attributable to the equity share capital. Accordingly no such offer shall become or be declared unconditional unless the offeror company has acquired or agreed to acquire more than the said 50 per cent.

21. An offer must initially be open for at least twenty-one days after the posting of the offer and, if revised, it must be kept open for at least eight days from the date of posting written notification of the revision to shareholders: an acceptor shall be entitled to withdraw his acceptance in any case after the expiry of twenty-one days from the first closing date of the initial offer, if the

offer has not by such expiry become or been declared unconditional; such entitlement to withdraw shall be exercisable until such time as the offer becomes or is declared unconditional.

No offer (whether revised or not) shall be capable of becoming or being declared unconditional after the expiration of sixty days from the date the offer is initially posted, nor of being kept open after the expiry of such period unless it has previously become or been declared unconditional.

Other than in the circumstances that a competing offer has been declared or has become unconditional, a formal offer may not be withdrawn during its currency except with the permission of the Panel. An offer which is allowed to lapse because of the nonfulfilment of a condition is not to be treated as withdrawn for the purpose of this Rule.

22. After an offer has become or is declared unconditional, the offer must remain open for acceptance for not less than fourteen days, except in the event that the offer becomes or is declared unconditional on an expiry date and the offeror company has given at least ten days' notice in writing to the shareholders of the offeree company that the offer will not be open for acceptance beyond that date.

If in accordance with the provisions of Rule 24 an unconditional declaration becomes void and is subsequently reinstated, the period of fourteen days above referred to will run from the date of the second declaration.

23. An offeror company which has extended an offer must announce the fact not later than 9.30 a.m. on the working day next following the day on which the offer would otherwise have expired.

24. By 9.30 a.m. at the latest on the working day next following the expiry of the first offer, or of any extended or revised offer, whichever may be the later (the relevant day), the offeror company shall announce and simultaneously inform the Stock Exchange:

(a) either that the offer has become or is declared unconditional or that the offer has been allowed to lapse, and in the first event,

(b) the total number of shares (as nearly as practicable) (i) for which acceptances of the offer have been received, (ii) held before the offer period and (iii) acquired or agreed to be acquired during the offer period.

If the offeror company is unable within the above time limit to comply with any of these requirements, the Stock Exchange will consider the suspension of dealings in the offeree company's shares and, where appropriate, in the offeror company's shares until the relevant information is given. If the offeror company, having declared an offer unconditional, fails by 3.30 p.m. on the relevant day to comply with any of the requirements of sub-para (b) of this Rule, its unconditional declaration shall be void. Immediately thereafter and until the offer is again declared unconditional any acceptor shall be entitled to withdraw his acceptance. Subject to the provisions of the second paragraph of Rule 21, the offeror company may again declare the offer unconditional after it has satisfied the requirements of sub-para (b) of the Rule but not before the expiry of eight days after the relevant day.

25. The obligations of the offeror company and the rights of the offeree company shareholders under Rules 20–24 must be specifically incorporated in the offer document.

26. Generally speaking bids for less than 100 per cent. of the equity capital of an offeree company not already owned by the offeror company or any of

its subsidiaries are undesirable. If there are circumstances in which a general offer for less than 100 per cent. is in the opinion of the offeror company justified, it must be made to all shareholders of the class and arrangements must be made for those shareholders who wish to do so to accept in full for the relevant percentage of their holdings. Other than in special circumstances (in which case the consent of the Panel must be obtained) no partial bid may be made to which Rule 20 would not apply. A partial bid to which Rule 20 is not applicable may not be declared unconditional unless acceptances are received for the number of shares bid for.

It is recognised that there may be very exceptional circumstances where in the interests of all the shareholders a deal might be made with a significant minority without a similar offer being made to the other shareholders. In such circumstances the Panel must be consulted in advance and its consent obtained.

27. Where an offer is made for more than one class of share, separate offers must be made for each class and the offeror company should state that it will resort to compulsory acquisition powers under Section 209 of the Companies Act 1948, only in respect of each class separately.

28. Where an offer is made for equity capital and there are convertible securities outstanding, arrangements must be made to offer to the holders of such securities such amendment of the conversion terms or other appropriate arrangements as to ensure that their interests are not prejudiced. Where options or subscription rights are outstanding this Rule also applies *mutatis mutandis.*

*Dealings*

29. Save in so far as appears from this Code, it is considered undesirable to fetter the market. Accordingly, all parties to a take-over or merger transaction (other than to a partial bid) and their associates are free to deal at arm's length subject to daily disclosure to The Stock Exchange, the Panel and the Press (not later than 12 noon on the dealing day following the date of the relative transaction) of the total of all shares of any offeror company or the offeree company acquired or sold by them or their respective associates for their own account on any day during the offer period in the market or otherwise and at what average price.

In addition all purchases and sales of shares of any offeror or the offeree company made by associates for account of investment clients who are not themselves associates must be similarly reported to the Stock Exchange and to the Panel, but need not be disclosed to the Press.

In the case of a partial bid the offeror company and its associates may not deal in shares of the offeree company during the offer period for their own account, nor in the case of a partial bid to which Rule 20 does not apply may the offeror company or its associates, unless the Panel specifically so agrees, purchase shares of the offeree company for their own account during a period of twelve months beginning on the last day of the offer period.

30. No dealings of any kind (including option business) in the shares of the offeror and offeree companies by any person who is privy to the preliminary take-over or merger discussions or to an intention to make an offer may take place between the time (*a*) when the initial approach is made or intimated or (*b*) when there is reason to suppose that an approach or an offer will be made and the announcement of the approach or offer or of the termination of the discussions as the case may be.

31. If the offeror company alone or in association with others purchases shares in the market or otherwise during the offer period at above the offer price (being, in the event of the terms of an original offer being revised, the final bid price under the revised terms of an offer) then it shall offer an increased price to all acceptors, such price being not less than the weighted average price (excluding stamp duty and commission) of the shares so acquired during the offer period. If the offer involves a further issue of already quoted securities, the value of such securities shall normally be calculated for the purpose of ascertaining what increased price shall be paid (but not for the purpose of establishing whether any purchase was made at a price above the offer price) by reference to the average of the mean of the daily quotation (as stated in the Stock Exchange official list) of the securities during the offer period. If the offeror company considers that the terms of the previous sentence should not apply to an offer (if, for instance, it considers there has been a general change in market prices during the offer period or facts have been published causing a change in the market value of the securities of the offeror company) the offeror company should consult the Panel. If the offer involves the issue of securities which are not already quoted the value shall be based on a reasonable estimate of what the opening price might be.

32. Since arrangements to deal, purchases and sales with special conditions attached are not capable in every circumstance of being extended to all shareholders, such arrangements to deal, purchases and sales whether during, or in anticipation of, a bid must not be made.

33. Since dealings in the market or otherwise by an associate of an offeror or offeree company may result in a *bona fide* offer being frustrated or may affect the outcome of a bid, such associate is advised to consult the Panel in advance and where he has not done so must be prepared to satisfy the Panel that his action was not prejudicial to the interests of shareholders generally of the offeror or the offeree company as the case may be.

### Changes in the Situation of a Company During a Bid

34. During the course of an offer, or even before the date of the offer if the Board of the offeree company has reason to believe that a *bona fide* offer is imminent, the Board must not, except in pursuance of a contract entered into earlier, without the approval of the shareholders in general meeting, issue any authorised but unissued shares, or issue or grant options in respect of any unissued shares, create or issue or permit the creation or issue of any securities carrying rights of conversion into or subscription for shares of the company, or sell, dispose of or acquire or agree to sell, dispose of or acquire assets of material amount or enter into contracts otherwise than in the ordinary course of business. Where it is felt that an obligation or other special circumstance exists, although a formal contract has not been entered into, the Panel must be consulted and its consent obtained.

### Registration of Transfers

35. The Board and officials of an offeree company should take action to ensure during a take-over or merger transaction the prompt registration of transfers so that shareholders can freely exercise their voting and other rights. Provisions in Articles of Association which lay down a qualifying period after registration during which the registered holder cannot exercise his vote are highly undesirable.

*April,* 1969.

# APPENDIX VII

## BIBLIOGRAPHY

No book can possibly cover all aspects of management accountancy. For this reason, it seems very desirable that readers should have a bibliography. There are those who require an introduction to the subject and others who may wish to study particular topics in more detail. An attempt has been made to meet both requirements without making the list too long.

### Introductory Books

Hartley, W. C. F. *An Introduction to Business Accounting for Managers*, Pergamon Press, Oxford.

Taylor, A. H., and Shearing, H. *Financial and Cost Accounting for Management*, Macdonald and Evans, London.

### Specialist Books

Sutton, Owen. *Machine Accounting*, Macdonald and Evans, London.

Sorgdrager, A. J. E. *The Particularization of Indirect Cost in Modern Costing Administration*, Ajax, Potchefstroom, South Africa.

Baynes, Hamilton T. A. *Share Valuations*, Heinemann, London.

Moonitz, Maurice, and Littleton, A. C. *Significant Accounting Essays*, Prentice Hall, New Jersey.

Backer, Morton, and Jacobsen, Lyle E. *Cost Accounting—A Managerial Approach*, McGraw-Hill, New York.

Jones, Frank H. *Guide to Company Balance Sheets and Profit and Loss Accounts*, Heffer, Cambridge.

Batty, J. *Standard Costing*, Macdonald and Evans, London.

Batty, J. *Corporate Planning and Budgetary Control*, Macdonald and Evans.

Beattie, C. N. *Corporation Tax*, Butterworths, London.

Association of Certified and Corporate Accountants' *Corporation Tax* publication.

Institute of Cost and Works Accountants' *Management Information Systems and the Computer*.

Gower, L. C. B. *Principles of Modern Company Law*, Stevens, London.

# INDEX

## A

ABNORMAL costs, 10
Absorption costing, 226
Absorption Rates, 19, 34–43
Acceptance credits, 209, 212
Accepting Houses Committee Members, 797
Accountants' Report, 194
Accounting:
  administration costs, 44, 598
  Amalgamation, 574
  Basic Standard Costs, 619
  capital expenditure, *see* Capital Expenditure
  cost ledger, 596
  integrated (integral), 597, 603
  Method I (Current Standards), 618, 619
  Method II (Current Standards), 619, 620
  research and development, 43
  ratios, *see under* Ratios
  Records, 596
  selling and distribution, 44, 598
  Stock Exchange Requirements, 851
Accounts chart, 612
Accounts, classification of, 611
Accounts, company, 519
Accounts Department, 12–13
Accounts, final, 523
Accounts, interim, 519
Accounts, Management, 1–15
Accounts Manual, 617, *see* Budget Manual
Accounts, Published, 523
Accounts, supplementary statements, 541
Activity Ratio, 431
Actual Costs, 6, 45, 384
Adler, J. S., 784
Administration costs:
  accounting, 44, 598
  budget, 95, 103

Administration costs (*contd.*):
  definition of, 31
  disposition of (absorption), 44
Advertising costs:
  budget, 95, 100
  operating statement, 366
  statement, 366
Agricultural Mortgage Corporation Ltd., 214
Amalgamations, 554, 555
Amounts due, accounts for, 604
Analysis of accounts, 413, 432
Anderson, Boyes and Co., Ltd., 189, 801
Angle of Incidence (Break Even Analysis), 276
Antill, J., 626
Apportionment Bases:
  administration costs, 44
  capital expenditure, *see* Capital Expenditure
  manufacturing overhead costs, 12, 36, 226
  research and development costs, 43
  selling and distribution costs, 44
Assets—current, 419
Attendance Time Performance Ratio or Index, 367
Auditing, 506
Authorising capital expenditure, 495
Average Cost or price, 660

## B

Balance Sheet Forecast, 148
Balance sheets, 526, 542
Base Stock Method, 660
Basic Standard Costing, 45, 430
Batch Costing, 22
Bibliography, 865
Bill of Material (Material Specification), 46
Bin Card, 32

867